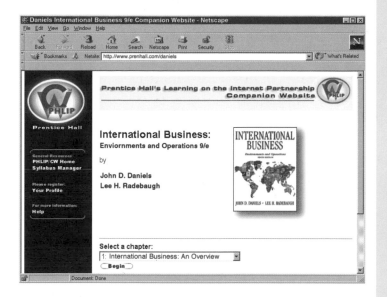

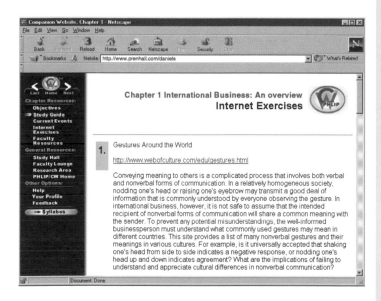

FOR THE PROFESSOR

◆ TEACHING RESOURCES include resources contributed by professors throughout the world, including teaching tips, techniques, academic papers, sample syllabi, and TALK TO THE TEAM, a moderated faculty chat room.

◆ ON-LINE FACULTY SUPPORT including downloadable supplements, additional cases, articles, links, and suggested answers to current events activities.

◆ WHAT'S NEW gives you one-click access to all newly posted PHLIP resources.

FOR THE STUDENT

◆ TALK TO THE TUTOR, virtual office hours that allow students to post questions from any supported discipline and receive responses from the dedicated PHLIP/CW faculty team.

◆ WRITING RESOURCE CENTER, an on-line writing center that provides links to on-line directories, thesauruses, writing tutors, style and grammar guides, and additional tools.

◆ CAREER CENTER, helps access career information, view sample résumés, even apply for jobs on-line.

◆ STUDY TIPS, an area for students to learn to develop better study skills.

INTERNATIONAL BUSINESS

Environments and Operations

NINTH EDITION

INTERNATIONAL BUSINESS

Environments and Operations

NINTH EDITION

JOHN D.
DANIELS

University of Miami

LEE H.
RADEBAUGH

Brigham Young University

Prentice
Hall

Upper Saddle River, New Jersey 07458

148818

Library of Congress Cataloging-in-Publication Data

Daniels, John D.
  International business : environments and operations / John D. Daniels, Lee H.
Radebaugh.--9th ed.
    p. cm.
  A multi-media instructional package, including a Web site, is available to supplement
the text.
  Includes bibliographical references.
  ISBN 0-13-030801-3
    1. International business enterprises. 2. International economic relations. 3.
Investments, Foreign. I. Radebaugh, Lee H. II. Title.

HD2755.5 .D35 1998
658.1′8--dc21   00-055085

Executive Editor: David Shafer
Managing Editor (Editorial): Jennifer Glennon
Assistant Editor: Michele Foresta
Editorial Assistant: Kim Marsden
Development Editor: Audrey Regan
Media Project Manager: Michele Faranda
Executive Marketing Manager: Michael Campbell
Managing Editor (Production): Judy Leale
Production Assistant: Keri Jean
Permissions Coordinator: Suzanne Grappi
Associate Director, Manufacturing: Vincent Scelta
Production Manager: Arnold Vila
Design Manager: Pat Smythe
Senior Designer: Cheryl Asherman
Interior Design: Brigid Kavanagh
Cover Design: Cheryl Asherman
Cover Art: Photoillustration by Blair Brown
        (Fabrics: Giraudon/Resource, N.Y.; SuperStock, Inc.; The Bridgeman Art Library International; The Bridgeman
        Art Library International; SuperStock, Inc.; Jennifer Steele/Art Resource, N.Y.; Art Resource, N.Y.)
Illustrator (Interior): Electragraphics
Associate Director, Multimedia Production: Karen Goldsmith
Manager, Print Production: Christina Mahon
Composition: Graphic World, Inc.
Full-Service Project Management: Carol O'Connell
Printer/Binder: Courier/Kendallville

Credits and acknowledgments from other sources and reproduced with permission in this textbook appear on the appropriate page within text. Photo credits appear on page 788.

10 9 8 7 6 5 4 3 2 1
ISBN 0-13-030801-3

BRIEF CONTENTS

Contents

Each part features a textile from one of the seven regions of international business—Africa, Asia, East Asian, European, Oceanic, North American, and South American. This textile is called "The Wine Harvest," sixteenth century, European region.

Part Two
Comparative Environmental Frameworks 44

CHAPTER 2
THE CULTURAL ENVIRONMENTS FACING BUSINESS 44

CHAPTER 3
THE POLITICAL AND LEGAL ENVIRONMENTS FACING BUSINESS 84

CHAPTER 4
THE ECONOMIC ENVIRONMENT 114

This textile is a Nigerian costume, African Region, twentieth century.

This textile is from India Asian Region, nineteenth century.

This textile is a silk robe of China's Qing Dynasty (1644–1911), East Asian Region.

Part Five
The Dynamics of International Business-Government Relationships 372

CHAPTER 11
GOVERNMENTAL ATTITUDES TOWARD
FOREIGN DIRECT INVESTMENT 372

CHAPTER 12
INTERNATIONAL BUSINESS NEGOTIATIONS AND DIPLOMACY 404

This textile is a Navajo blanket, North American Region, late nineteenth century.

Part Six
Operations: Overlaying Tactical Alternatives 440

CHAPTER 13
COUNTRY EVALUATION AND SELECTION 440

CHAPTER 14
COLLABORATIVE STRATEGIES 478

This textile is called "Sweet Potato Production," Oceania Region, twentieth century.

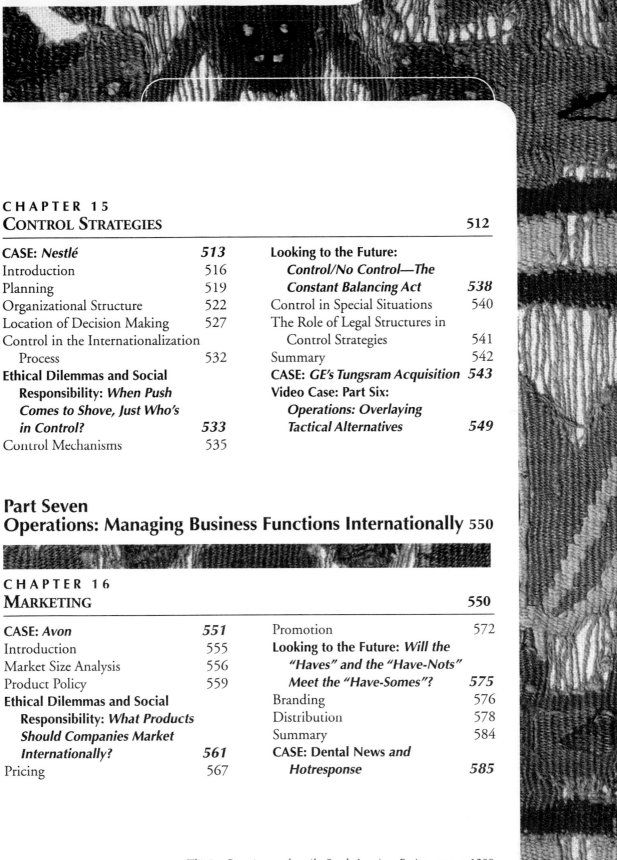

This is a Peruvian wool textile, South American Region, pre A.D. 1200.

Now accompanied by an unparalleled package of teaching and learning tools. See pages xxvi-xxviii of this preface!

Preface

Comprehensive and complete...
Authoritative yet accessible...

Daniels and Radebaugh's timeless classic is so current, so dynamic, so thorough, it will take your students right into the twenty-first century!

Consistent quality, based on a tradition of success and totally updated coverage, makes the ninth edition of **International Business: Environments and Operations** a cause for celebration! No other textbook has the exciting new cases and totally revised map program included here, and no other book for the course is as up-to-date and time-tested. Daniels and Radebaugh include comprehensive coverage of international business and international business management, designed with introductory students in mind. With authors this experienced, respected, and well-traveled, and coverage this complete, no wonder this book is the market leader.

Daniels and Radebaugh have connected the ninth edition to the Internet, allowing instructors and students access to the latest information. As events change the dynamics of international business, you have access to current data—via the fascinating book-specific Web site that accompanies this text at **www.prenhall.com/daniels**.

The new coverage, new cases, and new maps in the ninth edition make this the essential book for the course. This preface will show you why! ➤

Integrated cases, new new coverage of

Based on their own experience and that of other educators who teach international business, Daniels and Radebaugh's enhancements make the ninth edition the best teaching and learning tool for the course. In addition to its integrated cases and new visuals, the ninth edition has completely updated examples, new tables and figures, and greater use of maps. And, new content on today's technology and its use in international business shows how international managers operate in this information age.

CASE
THE *STAR WARS* QUARTET[1]

Lucasfilm released *Star Wars: Episode I: The Phantom Menace* in 1999, the first prequel to the original trilogy (*Star Wars, The Empire Strikes Back,* and *Return of the Jedi*). You have probably seen at least one of these—at least once—because the sequence is the most commercially successful ever produced. By late 1999, *Star Wars* ticket sales of $461 million were second only to those of *Titanic.* When ticket sales are adjusted for inflation, they are second only to those of *Gone with the Wind. The Phantom Menace's* ticket sales for 1999 were $417 million, which was more than double the ticket sales of any other movie released that year.

The intergalactic aspect of the quartet is obvious. Less obvious, though, are the international dimensions, right here on Planet Earth, that contributed to the films' success.

The deal to produce *Star Wars* was international from the start. George Lucas, the American producer, had written short summaries of two films he wished to make. He took the ideas to every studio in Hollywood, and each one turned him down. In desperation, he used his last $2,000 to buy a ticket to the Cannes (France) Film Festival, in the hope of gaining some backing. There he made an agreement with a Hollywood studio for production of *American Graffiti* and *Star Wars.* The studio, Twentieth Century Fox, thought that *Star Wars* was too high a risk to warrant giving Lucas its customary signing bonus of about a half million dollars. Instead, the studio gave him all sequence and merchandising rights, which it has regretted ever since.

George Lucas filmed only part of each movie in the *Star Wars* quartet in the United States.

Each chapter opens with a case on a specific international company. The case is carried through the chapter so readers can see its application.

Chapter-Opening photos from around the world introduce chapter material. And, each of the book's seven parts features a textile from one of the seven regions of international business—Africa, Asia, East Asia, Europe, North America, Oceania, and South America.

VIDEO CASE

PART ONE: BACKGROUND FOR INTERNATIONAL BUSINESS
LANDS' END AND YAHOO!

BACKGROUND

This video case shows how two very different companies, Lands' End and Yahoo!, approached the same goal—expansion into international markets. Lands' End is a retail business that sells its products through its print and on-line catalogs. Yahoo! is an Internet search engine that supplies its service to Web surfers worldwide.

A firm may decide to go international for any number of reasons, including the drive to increase sales volume and to access resources in other national markets. Lands' End wanted to increase its sales volume in markets such as Japan, Germany, and the United Kingdom. Yahoo! wanted to dominate the global Internet industry by penetrating markets such as China, Japan, Sweden, Norway, France, and others. This video illustrates how the two companies localized their products and services to meet the needs and preferences of consumers in new markets.

lion, making the company one of the largest apparel brands in the United States.

YAHOO! INC.

Yahoo! is an Internet search engine headquartered in Santa Clara, California, that helps people navigate the World Wide Web. The company's principal product is an ad-supported Internet directory that links users to millions of Web pages. The site leads the field in traffic (95 million pages viewed each day) and is second only to Netscape in on-line advertising revenues. Yahoo! has targeted guides for geographic audiences (Yahoo! Finance and Yahoo! News), demographic audiences (see Yahooligans!, a Web guide for children), special-interest audiences (Yahoo! Finance and Yahoo! News), and community services (Yahoo! Chat). The company is moving into the Internet access market through an alliance with AT&T and has agreed to acquire fellow Internet player, GeoCities. Japan's

New part-ending video cases link each part's material to some of today's most exciting international companies, such as Yahoo!, MTV, and Lands' End.

visual content, and communication and technology

- Its current product mix
- Its facilities and equipment
- Its marketing policies
- Its customer profile
- The principles it represents and the importance of the inquiring company to its overall business
- Its promotional strategies[14]

A company that has sufficient financial and managerial resources and decides to export directly rather than working through an intermediary must set up a solid organization. This organization may take any number of forms ranging from a separate international division, to a separate international company, to full integration of international and domestic activities. Whatever the form, there commonly is an international sales force separate from the domestic sales force because of the different types of expertise required in dealing in foreign markets.

Exporters can also sell directly to foreign retailers. Usually, these products are limited to consumer lines, but the growth of large retail chains around the world has facilitated the export of products to the large chains, which gives the exporter instant coverage to a wide area. Exporters can also sell directly to end users. This can be done through catalogs or at trade shows, or the sales can be in response to foreign buyers getting a hold of company brochures or responding to advertisements in trade publications.

DIRECT EXPORTING THROUGH THE INTERNET AND ELECTRONIC COMMERCE

Internet marketing allows all companies—both large and small—to engage in direct marketing quickly, easily, and cheaply.

Electronic commerce is an important way for companies to export their products to end users. It is especially important for SMEs (small and medium-size enterprises) that can't afford to establish an elaborate sales network internationally. E-commerce is easy to

You'll also find engaging discussions on the **Internet and electronic commerce**. In Chapter 1, students will learn how this technology has influenced recent international business growth, and in Chapter 13, they will learn how international business managers use the Internet to gather information and help make decisions. Then in Chapter 16, students will see how these technologies affect and enhance international marketing strategies. In Chapter 17, the authors discuss direct exporting through the Internet and electronic commerce, and Chapter 21 covers the increasing use of Net meetings in lieu of international travel. And, the book practices what it preaches. Each chapter ends with a "Web Connection" box that points students to the book's Web site for more international business learning.

Fascinating **new examples** are included throughout the book to illustrate key topics. For example, in Chapter 14, the authors' discussion of international collaborative arrangements is strengthened by examples of Mondavi and Rothchild in winemaking, and Duracell and Gillette in combining sales forces. And **margin notes** reinforce key concepts, summarize text passages, and highlight the managerial aspects to international business.

communications systems. From such an arrangement's inception, different companies (sometimes from different countries) agree to take on the high cost and high risk of developmental work for different components needed in the final product. Then a lead company buys the components from the companies that did parts of the developmental work.

Gain Market Knowledge Many companies pursue collaborative arrangements to learn about a partner's technology, operating methods, or home market so that their own competencies will broaden or deepen, making them more competitive in the future. Recall Chapter 11's case on FDI in China that Chinese governmental authorities allow foreign companies to tap the Chinese market in exchange for their transference of technology. Sometimes each partner can learn from the other, a motive driving joint ventures between U.S. and European wine makers, such as the Opus One Winery owned by Robert Mondavi from the United States and Baron Philippe de Rothschild from France.[10]

MOTIVES FOR COLLABORATIVE ARRANGEMENTS: INTERNATIONAL

In this section, we'll continue discussing the reasons why companies enter into collaborative arrangements, covering those reasons that apply only to international operations. Specifically, these reasons are to gain location-specific assets, overcome legal constraints, diversify geographically, and minimize exposure in risky environments.

Gain Location-Specific Assets Cultural, political, competitive, and economic differences among countries create barriers for companies that want to operate abroad. When

---

The authors also include new information on:

the Asian financial crisis • the economies of Russia and Eastern Europe • NAFTA • the debut and performance of the euro • China's transition to market economies • governmental incentives in where to locate production • the latest in regional integration • environmentally friendly technologies • how FDI is replacing foreign aid as a source of capital in emerging economies • protecting intellectual property rights • country-by-country best practices • global manufacturing and supply chain management • the use of cross-national teams • and much more!

Outstanding, contemporary cases define the ninth edition

In addition to the chapter-opening cases, Daniels and Radebaugh's closing cases pose questions that students must answer based on what they have learned in the chapter. These closing cases contain questions that are answered in the instructor's manual.

CASE

THE DAEWOO GROUP AND THE ASIAN FINANCIAL CRISIS[42]

In 1999, Daewoo Group (*www.daewoo.com*), Korea's second largest *chaebol*, or family-owned business conglomerate, was staggering under $50 billion in debt and considering whether or not to sell its flagship business, Daewoo Motor Company Ltd., to General Motors. The Asian financial crisis, which had hammered the Korean economy for two years, had finally taken its toll on the expansion-minded Daewoo and forced both Daewoo and the Korean government to decide what would be Daewoo's future.

Kim Woo-Choong started Daewoo in 1967 as a small textile company with only 5 employees and $10,000 in capital. In just 30 years, Mr. Kim had grown Daewoo into a diversified company with 250,000 employees worldwide, over 30 domestic companies and 300 overseas subsidiaries, generating sales of more than $100 billion annually. However, some estimated that Daewoo and its subcontractors employ 2.5 million people in Korea. Although Daewoo started in textiles, it quickly moved into other fields, first

- Electronics and Telecommunications
- Finance and Service

However, Daewoo was struggling. Its $50 billion debt was 40 percent greater than in 1998, equaling 13 percent of Korea's entire GDP. A good share of that, about $10 billion, was owed to overseas creditors. Its debt-to-equity ratio (total debt divided by shareholder's equity) in 1998 was 5 to 1, which is higher than the 4 to 1 average of other large *chaebol*, but significantly higher than the U.S. average, which usually is around 1 to 1 but rarely climbs above 2 to 1. Of course, there is no way of knowing the true picture of Daewoo's financial information because of the climate of secrecy in Korean companies. In addition, it is possible that its estimated debt might be greatly underestimated because no one knows whether or not the $50 billion includes debt of foreign subsidiaries.

How did Daewoo get into such a terrible position, and how much did the nature of the Korean economy and the Asian financial crisis affect Daewoo?

KOREAN ECONOMY

The impact of the Asian financial crisis on Korea was partly a result of the economic system of state intervention adopted by Korea since the mid-1950s. Modeled after the Japanese economic system, the Korean authoritarian government targeted export growth as the key for the country's future. Initially, the

---

CASE

DENTAL NEWS AND HOTRESPONSE*

In 1987, John Schwartz, an American living in Hong Kong, founded the family-owned *Dental News*, a quarterly magazine circulating to people interested in dental equipment, supplies, and technical developments. Medi Media Pacific, a Hong Kong–based company specializing in medical publications, bought *Dental News* from the Schwartz family in 1993. Havas, a French multimedia company, acquired Medi Media Pacific in 1999. Both Medi Media and Havas have contracted Logan Media International to handle all print activity from its headquarters in McMinnville, Oregon (USA). The Schwartz family owns Logan Media International, which is headed by Allen Logan Schwartz, the son of *Dental News*'s founder. Allen, collaborating closely with his brother, John Schwartz, also conceived and developed Hotresponse under another company, Dissemination Inc., which their father had recently established to exploit market synergies between print and the Internet. Hotresponse is an on-line service that connects magazine subscribers with magazine advertisers. The first client for Hotresponse was *Dental News* in 1998. Since then, Dissemination Inc. has obtained other Hotresponse clients, such as *Esquire Magazine, Maxim, Outside,* and Penton Publishers.

Initially, *Dental News* circulated only to Asia-Pacific countries until its founders envisioned expansion into other emerging markets. In the early 1990s, Charles Buckwalter, president of Corexion International in Miami, Florida (USA),

products. *Dental News* targets nontriad markets (those outside Western Europe, Japan, and English-speaking North America). The *Dental News* management is convinced and has persuaded advertisers that potential dental product customers (such as dentists, public health officials, lab technicians, dental hygienists, and dental school professors) are inundated with product information in the triad countries. But, potential customers elsewhere have too little access to information and would like more. Still, companies will advertise in *Dental News* only if *Dental News* has a subscription base large enough to reach enough potential dental product customers.

Dental News elicits subscriptions from exhibition booths it places at dental trade shows and dental conferences held all over the world. The largest of the conferences is the annual meeting of the Fédération Dentaire Internationale (FDI). *Dental News* arranges for its magazine to be placed in registration packets at these dental conferences. In exchange, *Dental News* provides advertisers for upcoming meetings and lists these meetings in the calendar that appears in each

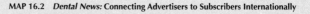

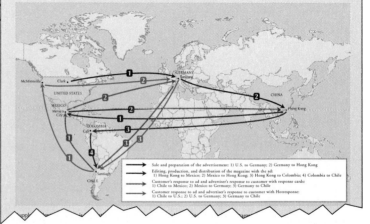

MAP 16.2 *Dental News:* Connecting Advertisers to Subscribers Internationally

List of chapter opening and closing cases

A new dynamic map program

Daniels and Radebaugh are known for their interesting and accurate maps, and the ninth edition carries on that tradition. All the maps for the ninth edition have been re-rendered, updated, and most have locator globes. Designed to help improve students' geographic literacy, the book's many maps (55 in all) add interest and illustrate facts and topics discussed in the text. Many case maps zero in on the case company's home country to give students a close-up look at foreign locales.

A complete atlas with index is available following Chapter 1.

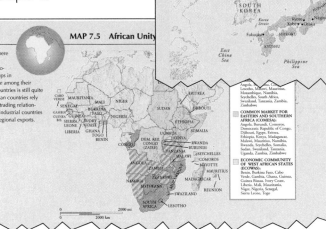

List of Maps

Teaching and Learning Resources

Instructor's Resource Manual
The Instructor's Resource Manual includes detailed chapter outlines with teaching tips, teaching notes for cases, discussion questions and answers, and additional international exercises.
0-13-018428-4

Test Item File
The Test Item File includes 25 true/false, 75 multiple-choice, and 10 essay questions per chapter. Together, the questions cover the content of each chapter in a variety of ways to give instructors flexibility in testing students' knowledge of the text.
0-13-018429-2

Windows/Prentice Hall Test Manager, Version 4.0.
Containing all of the questions in the printed Test Item File, Test Manager is a comprehensive suite of tools for testing and assessment. Test Manager allows educators to easily create and distribute tests for their courses, either by printing and distributing through traditional methods, or by on-line delivery via a Local Area Network (LAN) server.
0-13-031123-5

Instructor's Resource CD-ROM
This helpful CD-ROM includes the electronic Instructor's Manual, computerized Test Manager, and PowerPoint electronic transparencies.
0-13-018427-6

On Location! Video

Adopters of this text are entitled to part-ending video clips that correspond with the seven parts in the text. For more information, contact your local sales representative.
0-13-018433-0

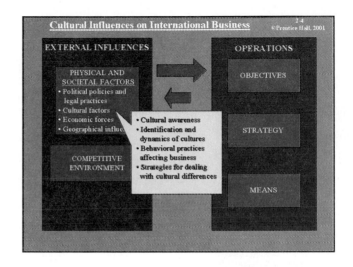

Overhead Color Transparencies

Approximately 100 of the most critical PowerPoint Electronic Transparencies are included in this package as full-color acetates and are provided on high quality mylar.
0-13-018420-9

GLOBE (Global Landscape of the Business Environment)

By Charles Stanfield and Jerry Westby, this electronic atlas offers political and physical maps to improve students' geography skills. In addition, regional overviews and statistics combine to offer student exercises that illustrate the impact of cultural and economic geography on business decisions. Available at a deep discount when purchased with the text.
0-13-016285-X

Study Guide

This print version of the on-line study guide questions is available as an alternative supplement for students. 0-13-018431-4

PHLIP/CW

Prentice Hall's Learning on the Internet Partnership (PHLIP) is a content-rich, multidisciplinary business education Web site created by professors for professors and their students. Developed by Professor Dan Cooper at Marist College, PHLIP provides academic support for faculty and students using Daniels and Radebaugh's text. PHLIP offers students a student study Hall, current events, an interactive study guide, and Internet resources. Instructors can choose from text-specific resources such as the Faculty Lounge, Teaching Archive, Help with Computers, and Internet Skills.

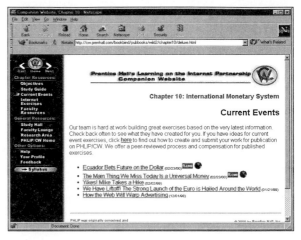

The Prentice Hall Companion Web site features an interactive and exciting on-line Student Study Guide. Students can access multiple-choice, true/false, and Internet-based essay questions that accompany each chapter in the text. Objective questions are scored on-line, and incorrect answers are keyed to the text for student review. For more information, contact your local sales representative.

WebCT/Blackboard Course Management Systems

Schools wishing to offer Distance Learning options, or simply enhance their course management, may use our preloaded content programs that are specific to this text. This product is free to adopters. With WebCT or Blackboard, you can create your own full-length, on-line courses, or simply produce on-line materials to supplement existing courses. With no technical experience or technical knowledge required, WebCT and Blackboard are both easy to use. A simple point-and-click system allows instructors to input the content of the course while WebCT or the Blackboard software systems integrates the interactivity, structure, educational tools, and administrative tools. **http://cms.prenhall.com**

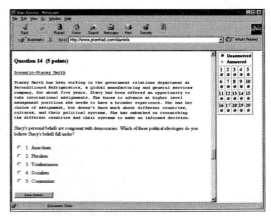

Two respected and renowned scholars show your students how dynamic, how real, how interesting the study of international business can be.

John D. Daniels, the Samuel N. Friedland Chair of Executive Management at the University of Miami, received his Ph.D. at the University of Michigan. His dissertation won first place in the award competition of the Academy of International Business. Since then he has been an active researcher. His articles have appeared in such leading journals as *Academy of Management Journal, California Management Review, Columbia Journal of World Business, Journal of Business Research, Journal of International Business Studies, Strategic Management Journal,* and *Weltwirtschaftliches Archiv.* On its thirtieth anniversary, *Management International Review* referred to him as "one of the most prolific American IB scholars." He has also served as president of the Academy of International Business and dean of its Fellows. He also served as chairperson of the international division of the Academy of Management. He has worked and lived a year or longer in seven different countries, worked shorter stints in about thirty other countries on six continents, and has traveled in many more. His foreign work has been a combination of private sector, governmental, teaching, and research assignments. He was formerly director of the Center for International Business Education and Research (CIBER) at Indiana University and holder of the E. Claiborne Robins Distinguished Chair at the University of Richmond.

Lee H. Radebaugh, is the KPMG Professor at Brigham Young University, the executive director of the BYU-University at Utah Center for International Business Education and Research, and the director of the School of Accountancy and Information Systems.

He received his MBA and doctorate from Indiana University. He taught at the Pennsylvania State University from 1972 to 1980. He also has been a visiting professor at Escuela de Administracion de Negocios para Graduados (ESAN), a graduate business school in Lima, Peru. In 1985, Professor Radebaugh was the James Cusator Wards visiting professor at Glasgow University, Scotland. His other books include *International Accounting and Multinational Enterprises* (John Wiley and Sons, 4th Edition) with S.J. Gray; *Introduction to Business: International Dimensions* (South-Western Publishing Company) with John D. Daniels; and seven books on Canada-U.S. trade and investment relations, with Earl Fry as co-editor. He has also published several other monographs and articles on international business and international accounting in journals such as the *Journal of Accounting Research, the Journal of International Financial Management and Accounting, the Journal of International Business Studies,* and the *International Journal of Accounting.* His primary teaching interests are international business and international accounting. He is an active member of the American Accounting Association, the European Accounting Association, and the Academy of International Business, having served on several committees as the president of the International Section of the AAA and as the secretary-treasurer of the AIB. He is a member of the Fellows of the Academy of International Business.

He is also active with the local business community as past president of the World Trade Association of Utah and member of the District Export Council. In 1998, he was named International Person of the Year in the State of Utah and Outstanding International Educator of the International Section of the American Accounting Association.

Acknowledgements

We have been fortunate since the first edition to have colleagues who have been willing to make the effort to critique draft materials, react to coverage already in print, advise on suggested changes, and send items to be corrected. Because this book is the culmination of several previous editions, we would like to acknowledge everyone's efforts. However, many more individuals than we can possibly list have helped. To those who must remain anonymous, we offer our sincere thanks.

Special thanks go to the faculty members who made detailed comments that contributed to the planning of this and previous editions:

CRAIG WOODRUFF, American Graduate School of International Management

ANN PERRY, American University

STAN FAWCETT, Brigham Young University

RON SCHILL, Brigham Young University

GEORGIA WHITE, Brigham Young University

MOONSONG DAVID OH, California State University at Los Angeles

RALPH GAEDEKE, California State University at Sacramento

ELDRIDGE T. FREEMAN, Jr, Chicago State University

JEAN J. BODDEWYN, City University of New York

LUCIE PFAFF, College of Mt. St. Vincent

URNESH C. GULATI, East Carolina College

GEORGE SUTIJA, Florida International University

ROBERT L. THORNTON, Miami University of Ohio

ROBERT BUZZELL, George Mason Univeristy

PHILLLIP D. GRUB, George Washington University

FERNANDO ROBLES, George Washington University

MICHAEL J. HAND, United States Department of Commerce

CHARLES MAHONE, Howard University

P. ROBERTO GARCIA, Indiana University, Kelley School of Business

ANDREW P. YAP, Florida International University

STANLEY E. FAWCETT, Brigham Young University

BIJOU YANG LESTER, Drexel University

SUMIT K. KUNDU, Saint Louis University

We would also like to thank the staff who have helped to research and prepare the manuscript for this edition: Michelle Walker, John Benson, Amber Benson, and Erik Reynolds all of Brigham Young University, and to Melanie Hunter for assisting in manuscript preparation.

INTERNATIONAL BUSINESS

Environments and Operations

NINTH EDITION

PART ONE

Background for International Business

CHAPTER 1

International Business: An Overview

The world is a chain, one link in another. —MALTESE PROVERB

OBJECTIVES

- To define international business and describe how it differs from domestic business
- To explain why companies engage in international business and why its growth has accelerated
- To introduce different modes a company can use to accomplish its global objectives
- To illustrate the role social science disciplines play in understanding the environment of international business
- To provide an overview of the primary patterns for companies' international expansion
- To describe the major countervailing forces that affect international business

Lucasfilm released *Star Wars: Episode I: The Phantom Menace* in 1999, the first prequel to the original trilogy (*Star Wars*, *The Empire Strikes Back*, and *Return of the Jedi*). You have probably seen at least one of these—at least once—because the sequence is the most commercially successful ever produced. By late 1999, *Star Wars* ticket sales of $461 million were second only to those of *Titanic*. When ticket sales are adjusted for inflation, they are second only to those of *Gone with the Wind*. *The Phantom Menace*'s ticket sales for 1999 were $417 million, which was more than double the ticket sales of any other movie released that year.

The intergalactic aspect of the quartet is obvious. Less obvious, though, are the international dimensions, right here on Planet Earth, that contributed to the films' success.

The deal to produce *Star Wars* was international from the start. George Lucas, the American producer, had written short summaries of two films he wished to make. He took the ideas to every studio in Hollywood, and each one turned him down. In desperation, he used his last $2,000 to buy a ticket to the Cannes (France) Film Festival, in the hope of gaining some backing. There he made an agreement with a Hollywood studio for production of *American Graffiti* and *Star Wars*. The studio, Twentieth Century Fox, thought that *Star Wars* was too high a risk to warrant giving Lucas its customary signing bonus of about a half million dollars. Instead, the studio gave him all sequence and merchandising rights, which it has regretted ever since.

George Lucas filmed only part of each movie in the *Star Wars* quartet in the United States. For example, he used studios outside London because the lower cost of British technicians more than offset the additional cost of transporting personnel from the United States to the United Kingdom. Lucas has already announced that the next two prequels will be filmed in Australian studios for the same reason. He filmed the desert planet Tatooine scenes from *Star Wars* and *The Phantom Menace* in the Sahara Desert of Tunisia. He filmed the ice planet Hoth scenes from *The Empire Strikes Back* above the Arctic Circle in Norway.

In addition to the logistics of filming real actors in different locations, Lucasfilm combined scenes with real actors with the miniature effects it made at a "monster factory" in California. As shots were completed, Lucasfilm transported videocassettes as much as 6,000 miles. Because of transportation and communications advances, global collaboration in filmmaking is commonplace. These advances enable us to see more realistic-looking scenes than were possible only a few years before Lucas began making the *Star Wars* quartet.

The actors have primarily been U.S. and U.K. nationals. Carrie Fisher, Harrison Ford, and Mark Hamill, who played Princess Leia Organa, Han Solo, and Luke Skywalker, respectively, are all from the United States. Alec Guinness and Ewan McGregor, who played Ben (Obi-Wan) Kenobi in different films, and Anthony Daniels, who played C-3PO, are from the United Kingdom. But Lucasfilm has used actors from elsewhere as well. Liam Neeson, who played Qui-Gon Jinn is from Ireland, and Natalie Portman, who played Queen Amidala, is from Israel.

The distribution of the films has been truly international. The expectation of receiving both domestic and foreign income is necessary to justify the risky investment in a high-cost film. About 40 percent of revenues have come from outside the United States; however, there have been some formidable obstacles. For example, some countries, such as Haiti and Mali, have such poor economies that few people can afford to see the films. Even if Lucasfilm could generate attendance, the moviegoers would pay in gourdes and francs, respectively. Because the governments are also poor, especially in ownership of other currencies, they would be hard pressed to convert the gourdes and francs to a currency that the producers can use. (The script of *The Phantom Menace* emulated this problem when the Tatooine merchant would not accept the heroes' galactic currency.) Lucasfilm has made separate agreements with each country that shows one of the *Star Wars* quartet so that it will receive revenues in U.S. dollars.

All the films have received high public acceptance almost everywhere they have been screened. For example, the debut of *The Phantom Menace* set attendance records in both Germany and Japan. This has been due at least in part to shrewd marketing and extraordinary special effects, yet many films that share these attributes still fail to become international hits. What these films did, which was probably the critical factor in their success, was to portray universal themes. The noted French anthropologist Claude Levi-Strauss has studied widespread cultures and observed common threads in their myths, tragedies, and fairy tales. He attributed this commonality to the fact that the mind classifies by opposing absolutes, such as good versus evil. Another explanation may be that there is a bit of the child in all of us, all over the world, and George Lucas says he makes movies for children and wants to teach them about goodness. Yet the success of the quartet has been more marked in some countries than in others. In Denmark, for example, revenues have been less than stellar, probably because the Danes simply aren't enthusiastic about science fiction.

In spite of the films' widespread acceptance, they have not been identical everywhere. The films must go through the costly process of dubbing or adding subtitles to appeal to the mass clientele who do not understand English. Censors in each country must review and approve them. In some cases they required Lucasfilm to remove scenes they considered too violent for children, such as one from *Return of the Jedi* in which a monster swallows its victims and lets them die slowly and painfully during a thousand-year dinner. Lucasfilm has made other alterations because of national technical differences. For instance, it must convert films to various home viewing systems because there is no worldwide standard for either televisions or tape players. Further, in some countries, people primarily watch movies at home on videocassettes, but in other countries they mainly use another medium such as CD-ROMs. The company has also encountered revenue loss from illegal copies of its movies where laws against the copying are not well enforced. For example, two days after Lucasfilm released *The Phantom Menace* in the United States, Malaysian stores were selling illegal copies.

One of the big revenue sources for the *Star Wars* quartet has been the sale of worldwide rights to companies to produce and sell products with characters and scenes from the movies. For example, Hasbro guaranteed Lucasfilm $500 million on sales of *Phantom Menace* toys using figures of Darth Maul, Jar Jar Binks, Mace Windu, and Princess Amidala. PepsiCo paid to put pictures of *Phantom Menace* characters on its soft drink cans, and Tricon Global Restaurants (Pizza Hut, KFC, and Taco Bell) paid to distribute *Phantom Menace* toys to its customers. Some companies that have gained rights from Lucasfilm have gone abroad to produce. The Lego Group from Denmark makes *Star Wars* construction toys called Mindstorms in Denmark, Switzerland, and the United States to use its existing construction capacity. Hasbro contracted companies in China to make its *Star Wars* toys because of low-cost Chinese labor. Figure 1.1 shows what might happen if the *Star Wars* intergalactic fantasy becomes reality.

The *Star Wars* quartet is typical of international business in that Lucasfilm produced and sold internationally. In doing so, it collaborated with other companies that did the same.

**FIGURE 1.1   Will Companies Keep Finding New Sources
of Cheap Labor?**

INTRODUCTION TO THE FIELD OF INTERNATIONAL BUSINESS

International business is all commercial transactions—private and governmental— between two or more countries. Private companies undertake such transactions for profit; governments may or may not do the same in their transactions. These transactions include sales, investments, and transportation.

Why should you study international business? A simple answer is that international business comprises a large and growing portion of the world's total business. Today, global events and competition affect almost all companies—large or small—because most sell output to and secure supplies from foreign countries. Many companies also compete against products and services that come from abroad.

A more complex answer is that a company operating in the international business field will engage in modes of business, such as exporting and importing, that differ from those it is accustomed to on a domestic level. To operate effectively, managers must understand these different *modes*, which we'll discuss shortly.

The conditions within a company's external environment (the conditions outside a company as opposed to its internal ones) affect the way business functions such as marketing are carried out. These conditions are physical, societal, and competitive. When a company operates internationally, it adds foreign conditions to its domestic ones, making its external environment more diverse. Figure 1.2 shows the relationship between

The goal of private business is to increase or to stabilize profits, which partly depends on

- **Foreign sales**
- **Foreign resources**

Government business may or may not be profit motivated.

Although companies operate in a world of many nations, business more and more overlaps the borders of any single nation. The photo of a three-dimensional computer graphic shows a communications satellite over Europe that hovers above the globe while providing commercial services to clients below. (The galactic fiction of the *Star Wars* film may be closer to reality than we think.) Countries cooperate in permitting the flyover of satellites, commercial airlines, and radio transmissions.

influences in the external environment—physical, societal, and competitive—and a firm's operations.

Even if you never have direct international business responsibilities, you may find it useful to understand some of its complexities. Companies' international operations and governmental regulation of international business affect company profits, employment security and wages, consumer prices, and national security. A better understanding of international business may help you to make more informed decisions, such as where you want to work and what governmental policies you want to support.

WHY COMPANIES ENGAGE IN INTERNATIONAL BUSINESS

When operating internationally, a company should consider its **mission** (what it will seek to do and become over the long term), its **objectives** (specific performance targets to fulfill its mission), and **strategy** (the means to fulfill its objectives). Figure 1.2 shows four major operating objectives that may influence companies to engage in international business. They are

- To expand sales
- To acquire resources
- To diversify sources of sales and supplies
- To minimize competitive risk

Expand Sales   Companies' sales are dependent on two factors: the consumers' interest in their products or services and the consumers' willingness and ability to buy them. The number of people and the amount of their purchasing power are higher for the world as a whole than for a single country, so companies may increase their sales by reaching international markets.

FIGURE 1.2 International Business: Operations and Influences

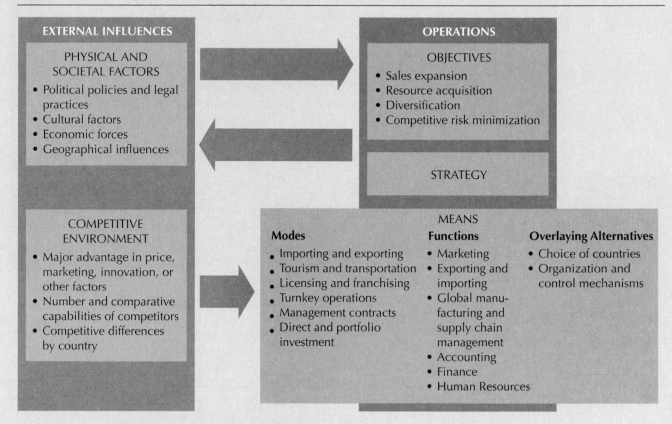

The conduct of international operations depends on companies' objectives and the means with which they carry them out. The operations affect, and are affected by, the physical and societal factors and competitive environment.

Ordinarily, higher sales mean higher profits, assuming each unit sold has the same markup. For example, the *Star Wars* films cost millions of dollars to produce, but as more people see the films, the average production cost per viewer decreases.

So increased sales are a major motive for a company's expansion into international business. Many of the world's largest companies derive over half their sales from outside their home country. You've heard of many of these companies (with their home country in parentheses)—BASF (Germany), Electrolux (Sweden), Gillette (the United States), Michelin (France), Nestlé (Switzerland), Philips (the Netherlands), and Sony (Japan). However, smaller companies also may depend on foreign sales. Pan Vera, a U.S. biotechnology research firm, makes about 25 percent of its $7-million-a-year sales abroad;[2] and the U.S. Small Business Administration estimates that small companies account for 31 percent of U.S. exports.[3] Many small companies also depend on sales of components to large companies, which in turn put them in finished products that they sell abroad.

Acquire Resources   Manufacturers and distributors seek out products, services, and components produced in foreign countries. They also look for foreign capital, technologies, and information they can use at home. Sometimes they do this to reduce their costs. For example, Hasbro relies on cheap manufacturing bases in China to make *Star Wars* figures. Sometimes a company operates abroad to acquire something not readily available in its home country, such as the Tunisian desert scenery Lucasfilm used in *Star Wars* movies. Acquiring resources may enable a company to improve its product quality and differentiate itself from competitors—in both cases, potentially increasing market share and profits. Although a company may initially use domestic resources to expand abroad, once the foreign operations are in place, the foreign earnings may then serve as resources for domestic operations. For example, McDonald's used the strong financial performance of its foreign operations to pour more resources into domestic expansion.[4]

Diversify Sources of Sales and Supplies   To minimize swings in sales and profits, companies may seek out foreign markets to take advantage of business cycle—recessions and expansions—differences among countries. Sales decrease in a country that is in a recession and increase in one that is expanding economically. By obtaining supplies of the same product or component from different countries, companies may be able to avoid the full impact of price swings or shortages in any one country.

Minimize Competitive Risk   Many companies enter into international business for defensive reasons. They want to counter advantages competitors might gain in foreign markets that, in turn, could hurt them domestically. For example, Company A and Company B compete in the same domestic market. Company A may fear that Company B will generate large profits from a foreign market if left alone to serve that market. Company B may then use those profits in various ways (such as additional advertising or development of improved products) to improve its competitive position in the domestic market. Companies harboring such a fear may enter foreign markets primarily to prevent a competitor from gaining advantages.

REASONS FOR RECENT INTERNATIONAL BUSINESS GROWTH—FROM CARRIER PIGEONS TO THE INTERNET

It's hard to determine just how much international business has occurred at different times in history. Shifting boundaries may cause what were domestic transactions to become international transactions, or vice versa. For example, when the former Soviet Union disbanded in 1991, business transactions between Russia and Ukraine changed from domestic to international.

Regardless, international business has been growing recently at a faster pace than global production. For example, global merchandise exports grew by 10 percent in 1997 and 3.5 percent in 1998 as compared with global production increases of 3 percent and 2 percent.[5] Further, the portion of world output accounted for by foreign-owned facilities has been growing substantially.[6]

It seems the reasons companies pursue international business—to expand sales, acquire resources, diversify sources of sales and supplies, and minimize competitive risk—would have applied in earlier periods as well. So what has happened in recent decades to bring about the increased growth in international business? The answer lies in the following four, sometimes interrelated, factors:

1. Rapid increase in and expansion of technology
2. Liberalization of governmental policies on cross-border movement of trade and resources
3. Development of institutions to support and facilitate international trade
4. Increased global competition

Expansion of Technology   It was only about a century ago that Jules Verne fantasized about people traveling around the world in *only* 80 days. Much of what we take for granted today results from technology that has been developed only within the last century. Before then, change occurred slowly. In recent years, however, the pace of technological advances has accelerated at a dizzying rate, while knowledge of products and services is available more widely and quickly because of tremendous strides in communications and transportation technology. As recently as 1970, there was no Internet as we know it today, no commercial transatlantic supersonic travel, no faxing or e-mailing, no teleconferencing or overseas direct-dial telephone service, and no sales over the Internet (e-commerce sales). Today, travelers commonly fly from New York to London in six-and-a-half hours (only three and a half if they go by Concorde), and communications are almost instantaneous. Moreover, the cost of the improved communications and transportation has risen more slowly than costs in general. A three-minute phone call from New York to London cost $10.80 in 1970 and $.30 in 2000.

By increasing the demand for new products and services, technology has tremendous impact on international business. As the demand increases, so do the number of international business transactions. But conducting business on an international level usually involves greater distances than does conducting domestic business, and greater distances increase operating costs and make control of a company's foreign operations more difficult. Improved communications and transportation speed up interactions and improve managers' ability to control foreign operations. Lucasfilm could control its far-flung production of the *Star Wars* films because it was able to move actors quickly from country to country and transport videos overnight from foreign shooting locations back to its production headquarters. When Lucasfilm completed production, transportation permitted it to distribute the films efficiently worldwide.

> **Business is becoming more global because**
> - **Transportation is quicker**
> - **Communications enable control from afar**
> - **Transportation and communications costs are more conducive for international operations**

Liberalization of Cross-Border Movements   Every country restricts the movement across its borders of goods and services and the resources, such as workers and capital, to produce both. Such restrictions make international business more expensive to undertake. Because the regulations may change at any time, international business is also risky.

Generally, governments today impose fewer restrictions on cross-border movements than they did a decade or two ago, but more than during the late nineteenth and early

> **Lower governmental barriers to the movement of goods, services, and resources enable companies to take better advantage of international opportunities.**

twentieth century until World War I.[7] With the enactment of the World Trade Organization (WTO) in 1995 (discussed in Chapter 6), the restrictions likely will continue to diminish. Although the past decrease in restrictions has been erratic, governments have lowered them for the following reasons:

1. Their citizens have expressed the desire for better access to a greater variety of goods and services at lower prices.
2. They reason that their domestic producers will become more efficient as a result of foreign competition.
3. They hope to induce other countries to reduce their barriers to international movements.

Fewer restrictions enable companies to take better advantage of international opportunities. However, with more competition, people have to work harder. Figure 1.3 shows this humorously.

The liberalization of cross-border movements isn't without controversy, however. The protests at the 1999 WTO meeting showed that many people favor trade restrictions because they fear they will be better off with more, rather than fewer, cross-border

---

FIGURE 1.3   A Downside of Competition Caused by Globalization

Although global competition brings more efficiency, it also requires companies and workers to expend more effort.

restrictions. These protests could influence governments to enact more, rather than fewer, restrictions.

Development of Supporting Services   Companies and governments have developed services that ease international business. For example, banks have developed efficient means for companies to receive payment for their foreign sales. As soon as a *Star Wars* film arrives in French customs, a bank in Paris can collect the distribution fee, in francs, from the French distributor and then make payment to Lucasfilm, in U.S. dollars, at a bank in the United States. In contrast, if business were still being conducted as in the era of early caravan traders, Lucasfilm probably would have to accept payment in the form of French merchandise, such as perfume or wine, which it would ship back to the United States and sell before receiving a usable income.

Although companies do barter internationally, it can be cumbersome, time-consuming, risky, and expensive.[8] Today, most producers can be paid relatively easily for goods and services sold abroad because of, for example, bank credit agreements, clearing arrangements that convert one country's currency into another's, and insurance that covers damage en route and nonpayment by the buyer.

Consider the transport of mail internationally. Until the sixteenth century, when the first international postal agreement was enacted (between France and part of what is now Germany), there was no postal system as we know it today (more along the lines of carrier pigeon). Citizens had to make separate arrangements for payment and shipment of each letter for each country through which it would pass. Today, because of postal agreements among countries, you can mail a letter to any place in the world using only stamps from the country where you mail it, regardless of how many countries the letter must pass through and regardless of the nationality of the company carrying it. For example, Lucasfilm can use U.S. postage stamps for a letter sent to its French distributors, even though the letter might be carried on an Indian airline that makes a stop en route in the United Kingdom. Or Lucasfilm can send its correspondence via any of the international package service companies, such as UPS or DHL, by simply paying them in U.S. dollars.

Increase in Global Competition   The pressures of increased foreign competition can persuade a company to expand its business into international markets. Today companies can respond rapidly to many foreign sales opportunities. They can shift production quickly among countries if they're experienced in foreign markets and because they can transport goods efficiently from most places.

Once a few companies respond to foreign market and production opportunities, other companies may see the foreign opportunities as well. For example, after Lucasfilm demonstrated the advantage of filming in Tunisia, other studios followed suit, shooting *Monty Python's Life of Brian* and *The English Patient* there.[9] Many other firms have to become more global to maintain competitiveness; failure to do so could be catastrophic for them.

MODES OF INTERNATIONAL BUSINESS
When pursuing international business, private enterprises and governments have to decide how to carry out their business, such as what mode of operation to use. Figure 1.4 shows that a company has a number of modes from which to choose.

Supporting services
- **Are made by business and government**
- **Ease flow of goods**
- **Reduce risk**

More companies operate internationally because
- **New products quickly become known globally**
- **Companies can produce in different countries**
- **Domestic companies' competitors, suppliers, and customers have become international**

FIGURE 1.4　Means of Carrying Out International Operations

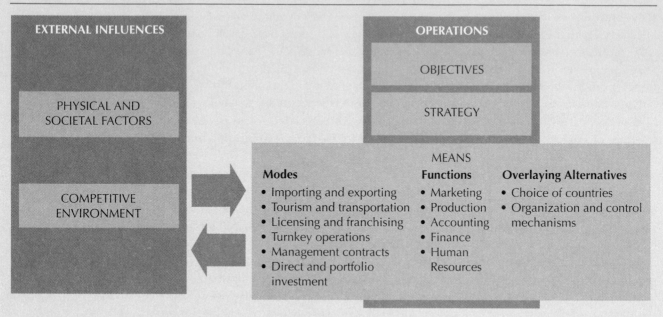

Companies may choose from a number of modes for conducting international business.

MERCHANDISE EXPORTS AND IMPORTS

Merchandise exports and imports usually are a country's most common international economic transaction.

Companies may export or import either goods or services. More companies are involved in exporting and importing than in any other international mode. This is especially true of smaller companies, even though they are less likely than large companies to engage in exporting. (Large companies are also more apt to engage in other forms of foreign operations in addition to exporting and importing.) **Merchandise exports** are tangible products—goods—sent out of a country; **merchandise imports** are goods brought in. Because these goods can be seen leaving and entering a country, they are sometimes called *visible exports* and *imports*. The terms *exports* and *imports* frequently apply to merchandise, not service. When a Chinese contractor sends *Phantom Menace* action figures from China to the United States, the contractor exports and Hasbro imports. The action figures are exports for China and imports for the United States. For most countries, exporting and importing of goods are the major sources of international revenue and expenditures.

SERVICE EXPORTS AND IMPORTS

Services are nonproduct auxiliary functions.

- Examples of services are travel and transportation fees
- They are very important for some countries
- They include many specialized international business operating modes

Service exports and imports are nonproduct international earnings. The company or individual receiving payment is making a **service export**. The company or individual paying is making a **service import**. Service exports and imports take many forms. In this section, we discuss the following sources of such earnings:

- Tourism and transportation
- Performance of services
- Use of assets

Tourism and Transportation   When Lucasfilm exports films from the United States, the films travel internationally, as do Lucasfilm employees when they go abroad to promote the films. Let's say that Lucasfilm sends its employees and films to Germany on Lufthansa, a German airline, and the employees stay in Germany for a few days. Their payments to Lufthansa and their expenses in Germany are service exports for Germany and service imports for the United States. International tourism and transportation are important sources of revenue for airlines, shipping companies, travel agencies, and hotels. Some countries' economies, too, depend heavily on revenue from these economic sectors. For example, in Greece and Norway, a significant amount of employment, profits, and foreign-exchange earnings comes from foreign cargo that is carried on ships owned by citizens of those countries. Earnings from foreign tourism are more important for the Bahamian economy than are earnings from the export of merchandise. Similarly, in recent years the United States has earned more from foreign tourism than from its exports of agricultural goods.

Performance of Services   Some services—banking, insurance, rentals (such as of *Star Wars* films), engineering, management services, and so on—net companies earnings in the form of **fees**, that is, payments for the performance of those services. On an international level, for example, companies pay fees for engineering services that are often handled through **turnkey operations**—construction, performed under contract, of facilities that are transferred to the owner when they are ready to begin operating. Companies also pay fees for **management contracts**—arrangements in which one company provides personnel to perform general or specialized management functions for another company. Disney receives management fees from managing theme parks in France and Japan.

Use of Assets   When companies allow others to use their assets, such as trademarks, patents, copyrights, or expertise under contracts, also known as **licensing agreements**, they receive earnings called **royalties**. On an international level, for example, Lucasfilm has licensed The Lego Group from Denmark to use its trademarked *Phantom Menace* figures in Mindstorm construction toys.[10] Royalties also come from franchise contracts. **Franchising** is a mode of business in which one party (the franchisor) allows another party (the franchisee) the use of a trademark that is an essential asset for the franchisee's business. The franchisor also assists on a continuing basis in the operation of the business, such as by providing components, management services, and technology.

Dividends and interest paid on foreign investments are also treated as service exports and imports because they represent the use of assets (capital). However, countries treat the investments themselves separately in the international economic statistics they report.

INVESTMENTS

Foreign investment means ownership of foreign property in exchange for financial return, such as interest and dividends. Foreign investment takes two forms: direct and portfolio.

Direct Investment   A **direct investment** is one that gives the investor a controlling interest in a foreign company. Such a direct investment is also a **foreign direct investment (FDI)**, a term common to this text. Control need not be a 100-percent or even a

Companies benefit from direct investment by
- **Control**
- **Access to foreign markets**
- **Access to foreign resources**
- **Higher foreign sales than exporting (often)**
- **Partial ownership (sometimes)**

50-percent interest. If a company holds a minority stake and the remaining ownership is widely dispersed, no other owner may be able to counter the company effectively. When two or more companies share ownership of an FDI, the operation is a **joint venture**. When a government joins a company in an FDI, the operation is called a **mixed venture**, which is a type of joint venture.

Companies may choose FDI as a mode to access certain resources or reach a market. Today, about 60,000 companies worldwide have FDIs that encompass every type of business function—extracting raw materials from the earth, growing crops, manufacturing products or components, selling output, providing various services, and so on.[11] FDI is not the domain of large companies only. For example, many small firms maintain sales offices abroad to complement their export efforts, which are FDI along with the real estate they own abroad. However, because large companies tend to have larger foreign facilities and operate in more countries, the value of their FDI is higher.

Key components of portfolio investment are

- **Noncontrol of foreign operation**
- **Financial benefit (for example, loans)**

Portfolio Investment   A **portfolio investment** is a noncontrolling interest in a company or ownership of a loan to another party. Usually a portfolio investment takes one of two forms: stock in a company or loans to a company or country in the form of bonds, bills, or notes that the investor purchases.

Foreign portfolio investments are important for most companies that have extensive international operations. Companies use them primarily for short-term financial gain, that is, as a means for a company to earn more money on its money with relative safety. Company treasurers routinely move funds among countries to get higher yields on short-term investments.

INTERNATIONAL COMPANIES AND TERMS TO DESCRIBE THEM

Many of the terms in international business are confusing because writers, both in the popular media and in governmental and academic reports, use them to define different things.

There are numerous ways that companies may work together in international operations, such as through joint ventures, licensing, management contracts, minority ownership in each other's company, or long-term contractual arrangements. An all-encompassing term to describe these operations is **collaborative arrangements**. Another term, **strategic alliance**, can sometimes mean the same thing, but more narrowly—to indicate an agreement that is of critical importance to the competitive viability of one or more partners. We shall use *strategic alliance* only in its narrower meaning.

The **multinational enterprise (MNE)** is a company that takes a global approach to foreign markets and production. It is willing to consider market and production locations anywhere in the world. The true MNE usually uses most of the modes discussed so far. However, it can be difficult to determine whether a company takes this global approach, so narrower definitions of the term *multinational enterprise* have emerged. For example, some say a company, to qualify as an MNE, must have production facilities in some minimum number of countries or be of a certain size (usually in terms of sales). Under this definition, an MNE usually would have to be a giant company. However, a small company also can take a global approach within its resource capabilities and might use most of the operating forms we have discussed; therefore, most writers today use the term to include any company that has operations in more than one country—the way that we use the term in this text.

The term **multinational corporation (MNC)** is also commonly used in the international business arena and often is a synonym for *MNE*. We prefer the MNE designation because there are many internationally involved companies, such as accounting partnerships, that are not organized as corporations. Another term sometimes used interchangeably with MNE, especially by the United Nations, is **transnational company (TNC)**. However, this term also has two other meanings. The first (and earliest) is a company owned and managed by nationals in different countries. For example, Royal Dutch Shell is a company whose owners and corporate management are split between the United Kingdom and the Netherlands. However, this type of company is uncommon, so we don't often use the term in this way. Today, the most common use of the term has come from writers on international business strategy. They use the term to mean an organization in which capabilities and contributions may differ by country but are developed and integrated into its worldwide operations. This type of organization learns from all its operating environments and uses that knowledge throughout its global operations.[12]

Companies with international operations can be global or multidomestic. A **global company**, sometimes called a **globally integrated company**, integrates its operations that are located in different countries. For example, it might design a product or service with a global market segment in mind. Or it might depend on its operations in different countries to produce the components used in its products and services. In this type of company, the development of capabilities and the decisions to diffuse them globally are essentially made in the company's home country. A **multidomestic company**, sometimes called a **locally responsive company** and sometimes a multinational company, allows each of its foreign-country operations to act fairly independently, such as by designing and producing a product or service in France for the French market and in Japan for the Japanese market. Thus a global company and a multidomestic company differ in the degree of integration among company operations in different countries. However, a company's operations may have elements of both. For example, its production may be global, while its marketing is multidomestic. The TNC is like the global company in that it leverages the capabilities of both the home country and the foreign countries where it operates, but its main location of power within the organization may be geographically dispersed.

EXTERNAL INFLUENCES ON INTERNATIONAL BUSINESS

A company should not form its strategies, or the means to implement them, without examining its external environment. Figure 1.5 shows that the external environment includes physical factors, such as a country's geography, and societal factors, such as a country's politics, law, culture, and economy. It also includes competitive factors, such as the number and strength of suppliers, customers, and rival firms. A company faces different external environments in each country where it operates.

A company that has a world-wide approach to markets and production is known as an MNE or TNC. It usually undertakes nearly every type of international business practice.

FIGURE 1.5 Physical and Societal Influences on International Business

Companies affect and are affected by their external environment.

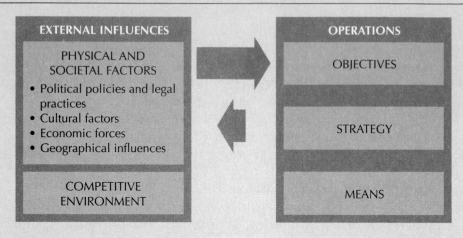

EXTERNAL INFLUENCES

PHYSICAL AND SOCIETAL FACTORS
- Political policies and legal practices
- Cultural factors
- Economic forces
- Geographical influences

COMPETITIVE ENVIRONMENT

OPERATIONS

OBJECTIVES

STRATEGY

MEANS

UNDERSTANDING A COMPANY'S PHYSICAL AND SOCIETAL ENVIRONMENTS

Managers in international business must understand
- **Social science disciplines**
- **All functional business fields**

To operate within a company's external environment, its managers should have, in addition to knowledge of business operations, a working knowledge of the basic social sciences: political science, law, anthropology, sociology, psychology, economics, and geography.

Politics helps shape business worldwide because the political leaders control whether and how international business takes place. For example, Lucasfilm cannot distribute *The Phantom Menace* in Cuba because political conflict between Cuba and the United States has led to trade restrictions. Political disputes, particularly those that result in military conflicts, can disrupt trade and investment. Even small conflicts can have far-reaching effects.

Each country has its own laws regulating business. Agreements among countries set international law.

Domestic and international *law* determines largely what the managers of a company operating internationally can do. Domestic law includes regulations in both the home and host countries on such matters as taxation, employment, and foreign-exchange transactions. For example, Japanese law determines how Lucasfilm revenues from Japanese screenings are taxed and how they can be exchanged from yen to U.S. dollars. U.S. law, in turn, determines how and when the losses or earnings from Japan are treated for tax purposes in the United States. International law in the form of legal agreements between two countries governs how the earnings are taxed by both. International law may also determine how and whether companies can operate in certain locales. For example, companies from most countries suspended sales to Iraq because of United Nations trade sanctions over Iraq's failure to allow access to weapons inspectors.[13] How laws are enforced also affects operations. For example, U.S. movie companies long avoided distribution in China because of fear that the Chinese authorities would not enforce their laws against the copying and sale of films.[14] Companies should understand the treaties among countries and the laws of each country in which they want to operate, as well as how laws are enforced, to operate profitably abroad.

The related sciences of *anthropology*, *sociology*, and *psychology* describe, in part, people's social and mental development, behavior, and interpersonal activities. By studying these sciences, managers can better understand societal values, attitudes, and beliefs concerning themselves and others. This understanding can help them function better in different countries. For example, Lucasfilm cut scenes of *Return of the Jedi* for Swedish distribution because of Swedish concerns about violence for youthful audiences.

Economics explains, among other concepts, why countries exchange goods and services with each other, why capital and people travel among countries in the course of business, and why one country's currency has a certain value compared to another's. By studying economics, managers can better understand why, where, and when one country can produce goods or services less expensively than another can. In addition, managers can obtain the analytical tools needed to determine the impact of an international company on the economies of the host and home countries and the effect of a country's economic policies and conditions on the company.

Managers who know *geography* can better determine the location, quantity, quality, and availability of the world's resources, as well as the best means to exploit them. The uneven distribution of resources results in different products and services being produced or offered in different parts of the world. Geographical barriers such as high mountains, vast deserts, and inhospitable jungles affect communications and distribution channels for companies in many countries. The probability of natural disasters and adverse climatic conditions such as hurricanes, floods, or freezing weather make it riskier to invest in some areas than in others. These factors also affect the availability of supplies and the prices of products. For example, the 1999 earthquake in Taiwan caused global shortages of vital computer components.[15] In addition, population distribution around the world and the impact of human activity on the environment exert a strong influence on international business. For example, concern about destroying the world's rain forests may lead to regulations or other pressures on companies to change the place or method of their business activities.

The political, legal, social, economic, and geographic environments affect how a company operates and the amount of adjustment it must make to its operations in a particular country, such as how it produces and markets its products, staffs its operations, and maintains its accounts. In fact, Figure 1.5 shows that the external environment may affect each functional area of the company. The amount of adjustment is influenced by how much the environments of home and host countries resemble each other.

THE COMPETITIVE ENVIRONMENT

In addition to its physical and societal environments, each company operates within its competitive environment. Figure 1.6 shows some of the most common competitive factors in international business. The competitive environment varies by industry, company, and country, and so, accordingly, do international strategies. For example, companies in industries with homogenous products, such as copper tubing, compete more on price than do companies in industries that compete more on differentiated and innovative products, such as branded toothpaste or state-of-the-art computer chips. Strategies for the former are usually more influenced than the latter by cost savings, such as developing better equipment and operating methods, producing on a large scale to spread fixed costs over more units, and locating to secure cheap labor and materials.

Companies within the same industry also differ in their competitive strategies. Volkswagen is more concerned with reducing automobile costs than is Rolls-Royce, explaining why the former has recently moved much of its automobile production to Brazil to take advantage of lower labor costs while the latter has not. Still another competitive factor is the size of the company and the resources it has compared to its competitors. For example, a market leader, such as Coca-Cola, has resources for many more international options than does a smaller competitor such as Royal Crown. But being a leader in one market does not guarantee leadership in all. For example, in most markets Coca-Cola is the leader, with Pepsi-Cola in a strong second position; however, Pepsi outsells Coke in India.

The competitive environment also varies in other ways among countries. For example, the domestic market in the United States is much larger than in Sweden. Swedish producers have had to become more highly dependent than U.S. producers are on foreign sales to spread fixed costs of product development and production. The Swedish company Electrolux, for instance, had to promote exports very early in its history and depends much more on foreign sales of household appliances than do its main U.S. competitors, GE and Whirlpool. Another result of the larger U.S. market is that foreign companies have to invest much more money to gain national distribution in the United States than they do in Sweden because there are more places to sell their products.

Still another competitive factor is whether companies face international or local competitors at home and in foreign markets. On the one hand, Boeing and Airbus compete with each other everywhere they try to sell commercial aircraft. So what they learn about each other in one country is useful in predicting the other's strategies and actions in other countries. On the other hand, Kmart faces different retailers as competitors in each of the foreign countries where it operates.

FIGURE 1.6   The Competitive Environment and International Business

Companies face different competitive environments depending on the products, strategies, and countries where they operate.

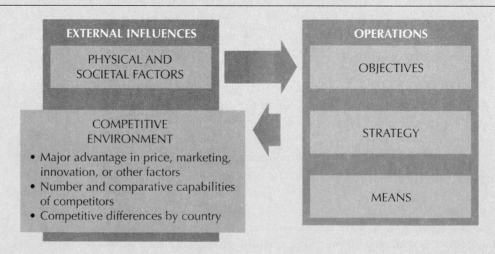

EVOLUTION OF STRATEGY IN THE INTERNATIONALIZATION PROCESS

When we think of multinational enterprises, we often think of giant companies like IBM or Nestlé, which have sales and production facilities in scores of countries. But companies do not start out as giants, and few think globally at their inception. As we discuss strategies, we shall note that companies are at different levels of internationalization and that their current status affects the strategic alternatives available to them. Although there are variations in how international operations evolve, some overall patterns do emerge, which Figure 1.7 shows. Most of these patterns are a product of risk minimization behavior—most companies view foreign operations as being riskier than domestic ones because they must operate in unfamiliar environments. Thus, they initially undertake international activities reluctantly and follow practices to minimize their risks. But as they learn more about foreign operations and experience success with them, they move to deeper foreign commitments that seem less risky.

PATTERNS OF EXPANSION

As you examine Figure 1.7, note that the farther a company moves from the center on any axis, the deeper its international commitment becomes. However, a company does not necessarily move at the same speed along each axis. A slow movement along one axis may free up resources that allow faster expansion along another. For example, a company may lack initial capacity to own facilities wholly in multiple foreign countries, so it may choose either to limit its foreign capital commitment by moving slowly along Axis C in order to move rapidly along Axis D (to multiple foreign countries), or vice versa.

Passive to Active Expansion   The impetus of strategic focus is shown on Axis A in Figure 1.7. Most new companies are established in response to domestic needs, and they frequently think only of domestic opportunities until a foreign opportunity presents itself to them. For example, companies commonly receive unsolicited export requests because someone has seen or heard of their products. Often these companies have no idea of how their products became known abroad, but at this juncture, they must make a decision to export or not. Many decide not to because they fear they will not be paid or they know too little about the mechanics of foreign trade. Those that do fulfill the unsolicited export orders and then see that opportunities are available to them abroad are later apt to seek out other markets to sell their goods. Even large companies may move from passive to active expansion with aspects of their business.

External to Internal Handling of Operations   A company commonly uses intermediaries to handle foreign operations during early stages of international expansion because it minimizes risk. It commits fewer of its resources to international endeavors and relies on intermediaries that already know how to operate in the foreign market. But if the business grows successfully, the company will usually want to handle the operations with its own staff. This is because it has learned more about foreign operations, considers them less risky than at the onset, and realizes that the volume of business may justify the development of internal capabilities such as hiring trained personnel to maintain a department for foreign sales or purchases. This evolution is shown on Axis B in Figure 1.7.

Strategies for heavy international commitments usually evolve gradually from

- Passive to active pursuit of opportunities
- External to internal handling of the business
- Limited to extensive modes of operations
- Few to many foreign locations
- Similar to dissimilar environments

FIGURE 1.7 The Usual Pattern of Internationalization

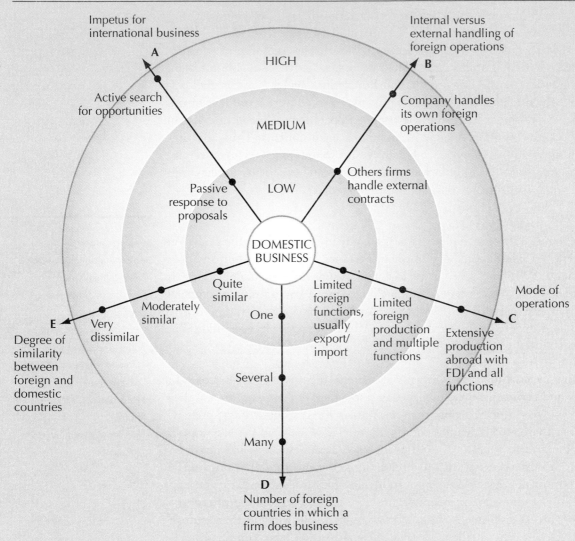

The farther out a company moves from the center of the diagram along any of the axes (A, B, C, D, or E), the deeper its commitment is internationally. The moves need not be at the same speed along each axis.

Deepening Mode of Commitment Axis C shows that importing or exporting is usually the first mode a company undertakes in becoming international. At an early stage of international involvement, importing and exporting require the least commitment and least risk to the company's resources, such as capital, personnel, equipment, and production facilities. A company could, say, use excess production capacity to produce more goods, which it would then export. By doing this, it would limit its need to invest more capital in such additional production facilities as plants and machinery and in such functions as managing a foreign workforce.

A company often moves into some type of foreign production after successfully building an export market. Initially this foreign production is apt to minimize the use of its resources by licensing a company to handle production abroad, sharing ownership in the foreign facility, or limiting the amount of manufacture, such as assembling output abroad. Nevertheless, this foreign production usually takes on greater international commitment of the company's resources than exporting or importing because the company has to send qualified technicians to the foreign country to establish and help run the new operation. Further, it must be responsible for multifunctional activities abroad, such as sales and production. Later, the company might make an even higher commitment through foreign direct investments to produce abroad. Its infusion of capital, personnel, and technology are highest for these operations.

A company typically does not abandon its early modes of operating abroad, such as importing and exporting, when it adopts other means of operating internationally. Rather, it usually either continues them by expanding its trade to new markets or complements them with new types of business activities.

Geographic Diversification   When companies first move internationally, they are most apt to do business in only one or very few foreign locations. Axis D in Figure 1.7 shows that over time, the number of countries in which they operate increases. The initial narrow geographic expansion parallels the low early commitment of resources abroad. The choice of countries in this geographic expansion also tends to follow certain patterns, as Axis E indicates. Initially, companies tend to go to those locations that are geographically close and similar. For example, when beginning foreign operations, most U.S. companies have gone first to Canada, and Canadian companies have gone first to the United States.[16] The closeness eases the process of control because of ease in moving personnel. There is also a perception of less risk because of greater familiarity with nearby areas and because of common languages and levels of economic development. However, this perception of similarity often masks subtle differences among countries, lulling companies into costly operating mistakes.[17] Later, companies move to more distant countries, including those that are perceived to have less similar environments to those found in the home country.

LEAPFROGGING OF EXPANSION

The patterns most companies have followed in their international expansion are not necessarily optimal for their long-range performance. The initial movement into a nearby country, such as a U.S. company moving into Canada, may delay entry into faster growing markets. There is, however, evidence that many new companies are starting out with a global focus because of the international experience and education of their founders. Further, because of technological advancements, especially in communications and the World Wide Web, these start-up companies have a better idea of where their markets are globally and how they may gain resources from different countries. II, a United Kingdom software designer, received initial financing from the United Kingdom, Germany, Austria, and Japan, and its first three customers were multinational companies in the United States and Japan.[18] In another case, the U.S. company Ecology Pure Air International sold its technology in Malaysia before selling in the United States because of U.S. federal and state requirements for extensive testing that slowed its domestic entry.[19]

COUNTERVAILING FORCES

In addition to the effect of external and competitive environmental factors, countervailing forces complicate decision making in international business. The strength of one force compared to that of another influences the choices available to companies that compete internationally. Some opposing choices that companies contend with are whether to institute global or national company practices, whether to focus on country or company competitiveness, and whether to develop sovereign or cross-national relationships.

GLOBALLY STANDARDIZED VERSUS NATIONALLY RESPONSIVE PRACTICES

Globally standardized practices tend to lower costs. Nationally responsive practices enable companies to adjust to unique local conditions.

Any company operating internationally must decide between the advantages of globally standardized practices and those practices that respond to different national preferences. These advantages may vary by product, function, and country of operation.[20]

The trends that have influenced the recent worldwide growth in international business—rapid expansion of technology, liberalization of governmental trade policies, development of the institutions and services needed to support and facilitate international trade, and increased global competition—also usually favor a global strategy. One advantage is that the company can reduce costs. For example, by designing a product or service to suit multiple countries, a company can avoid duplicating developmental expenses. It also may reduce manufacturing costs by serving multiple markets from a single production unit. In either case, the company gains from **economies of scale;** that is, when the cost per unit is lowered as output increases because fixed costs are allocated over more units of production.

However, when a company goes abroad, it faces conditions very different from those it encounters at home. The company may need to engage in national responsiveness, meaning it makes operating adjustments where it does business to reach a satisfactory level of performance. In such cases, a multidomestic approach often works better than a global one because the company managers abroad are best able to assess and deal with the environments of the foreign countries in which the company operates. As a result, they are given a great deal of independence in running facilities in those countries.

COUNTRY VERSUS COMPANY COMPETITIVENESS

Countries moderate companies' fulfillment of global efficiency objectives because of their rivalry with other countries.

So far we have addressed competition from the viewpoint of companies. Companies, at least those that are not government owned, may compete by seeking maximum production efficiency on a global scale. To accomplish this goal, the company's production would use the best inputs for the price, even if the production location moved abroad. The company would then sell the output wherever it would fetch the best price. Such practices should lead to maximum performance for the company.

But countries also compete with each other. They do so in terms of fulfilling economic, political, and social objectives. Countries are concerned not only with the absolute achievement of these objectives but also with how well they do compared to other countries. Keep in mind that competition among countries is the means to an end—the end being the well-being of a country's citizens. However, there is no consensus on how to measure well-being, and accepted indicators of current prosperity actually may foretell longer-term problems. For example, high current consumption may occur at the expense of investment for future production and consumption.[21]

At one time, the performance of a country and that of companies headquartered in that country were considered to be mutually dependent and beneficial; that is, they rose and fell together. For example, consider the once-popular expression "What's good for General Motors is good for the country." The idea was that if General Motors (GM) increased its global share of automobile production, the United States would benefit also—from more automobile sales, tax collections, and jobs, both production and managerial. This benefit was considered possible because almost all of the company's production and sales at the time were in the United States. But today, the relationship between country performance and company performance is not as clear-cut. GM could elect to improve its global or even its domestic market share by producing more cars in its foreign manufacturing units and fewer in the United States. What would this mean for the U.S. competitive performance?

In answering this question, some people would argue that the important indicator is the location of **high-value activities;** that is, activities that either produce high profits or are done by high-salaried employees such as managers. So GM's move to produce more cars abroad could improve the U.S. competitive position by increasing high-value activity at headquarters, in the form of more jobs for managers and executives, while reducing low-value activity in production, in the form of fewer jobs for U.S. assembly-line workers. In fact, there is evidence that the demand and income for higher-paid employees in the United States has increased as a result of U.S. companies' outsourcing to low-labor-cost countries.[22] However, other people would argue that U.S. competitiveness would deteriorate if there were a net loss in the number of U.S. jobs.[23]

Closely related to this debate is another regarding whether a government should be concerned if its production is foreign owned. For example, should it matter whether U.S. auto production is owned by Honda in Japan instead of GM in the United States? Some would argue that it would make no difference because the United States gains the jobs and production either way; others would argue that the high-value activity jobs would more likely be in Japan if Honda were the owner.[24] In actuality, there is little hard evidence to support any conclusion regarding the relationship between company and country performance.

Regardless of these unresolved debates, countries continue to entice companies to locate headquarters and production facilities within their borders. They do this through regulations and enticements. In the GM example, the U.S. government might enact regulations to prevent GM from expanding abroad, such as by limiting the capital it could send out of the country. Or the government could restrict imports of foreign-produced automobiles so that GM could sell more by producing in the United States. It might try to persuade GM by holding out the possibility of future defense contracts (for companies acting in the "national interest") or by appealing to nationalism. To improve the country's investment-worthiness, the U.S. government might improve the availability and quality of education, build roads and port facilities, or lower taxes. Any of these incentives could apply only to U.S.-based companies or to any company, regardless of nationality.

Business managers need to understand these complexities so they can argue logically and effectively regarding legislation that may affect their operations. At the same time, they must balance dual roles: In one, they are managers with global efficiency objectives;

in the second, they are members of a given society that has national rather than global objectives.

SOVEREIGN VERSUS CROSS-NATIONAL RELATIONSHIPS

Countries compete. They also cooperate. Countries sometimes cede sovereignty (freedom from external control) reluctantly because of coercion and international conflicts. However, they willingly cede sovereignty through treaties and agreements with other countries for the following reasons:

Countries reluctantly cede some sovereignty because of
- **Coercion**
- **International conflicts**

1. To gain reciprocal advantages
2. To attack problems that one country acting alone cannot solve
3. To deal with areas of concern that lie outside the territory of all countries

Countries willingly cede some sovereignty to
- **Gain reciprocity**
- **Attack problems jointly**
- **Deal with extraterritorial concerns**

Countries want to ensure that companies headquartered within their borders are not disadvantaged by foreign-country policies, so they enter into treaties and agreements with other countries on a variety of commercial activities, such as transportation and trade. Treaties and agreements may be bilateral (involving only two countries) or multilateral (involving a few or many). Countries commonly enter into treaties in which each allows the others' commercial ships and planes to use certain seaports and airports in exchange for reciprocal port use. They may enact treaties that cover commercial aircraft safety standards and flyover rights or treaties to protect property such as direct investments, patents, trademarks, and copyrights in each other's territory. They also may enact treaties for reciprocal reductions of import restrictions (and then retaliate when others raise barriers by, for example, raising barriers of their own or cutting diplomatic ties).

Countries also enact treaties or agreements to coordinate activities along their shared borders, such as building connecting highways and railroads or hydroelectric dams that serve all parties. They also enact treaties to solve problems they either cannot or will not solve alone because of one or both of two reasons:

1. The problem is too big or widespread
2. The problem results from conditions that spill over from another country

In the first case, the resources needed to solve the problem may be too large, or one country does not want to pay all the costs for a project that also will benefit another country. For example, countries may enact a treaty whereby they share the costs of joint technology development, such as Europe's Esprit program in electronics. In the second case, one country's economic and environmental policies may affect another country or countries. For example, high real interest rates in one country can attract funds from countries in which interest rates are lower, which can disrupt economic conditions in the latter countries because there will be a shortage of funds available for investment. This is why the seven largest industrialized countries (known as the G-7 countries)—Canada, France, Germany, Italy, Japan, the United Kingdom, and the United States—meet regularly to coordinate economic policies. In fact, with the ability of investors to sell on the Internet on the basis of up-to-the-minute information, an event in one country can have almost instantaneous effects in another.[25] In addition, most environmental experts agree that there must be cooperation among most countries to institute environmental policies. So far, countries have made agreements on such issues as restricting harmful emissions, keeping waterways unpolluted, preserving endangered species, and

Ethical Dilemmas and Social Responsibility
SORTING THROUGH THE WORLD OF RIGHT AND WRONG IN INTERNATIONAL BUSINESS

We all have beliefs about what is right and wrong based on family and religious teachings, the laws and social pressures of our societies, our observations and experiences, and our own economic circumstances. Our ethical beliefs tend to be deep-seated, so our debates with people of opposing views tend to be emotional. Even within a country, vastly opposing viewpoints frequently exist. This is demonstrated in the United States by the controversies on abortion, gay rights, capital punishment, gun control, euthanasia, organ transplants, marijuana use, and welfare payments. To further complicate matters, our own values on given issues may differ from our employers' policies, and any of these may differ from the prevalent societal norms or laws. As managers, we face domestic dilemmas on what we should do to be ethical and socially responsible. Internationally, the dilemmas are even greater.

An MNE can operate in foreign markets in which it has either narrower or greater latitude in making decisions than in its home country. Normal practices in a given foreign country will depend on that country's ethics, which may conflict with the company's domestic practices or with the beliefs of its domestic constituencies. For example, U.S. companies must contend with child labor laws at home that they probably wouldn't encounter in, say, Indonesia.

On the one hand, a company can face pressures to comply with a country's norms. These pressures may include laws that permit or even require certain practices, competitive advantages for rivals who adapt to local norms, or accusations of meddling if a company tries to impose its home-country practices in the foreign country. On the other hand, companies can face pressures not to comply. These pressures can come from a company's own ethical values, its home-country government, or constituencies that threaten to boycott its products or to spread adverse publicity about it or its products.

Many individuals and organizations have laid out minimum levels of business ethics that they say a company (domestic or foreign) must follow, regardless of the legal requirements or ethical norms prevalent where it operates.[26] They argue that legal permission for some action may be given by uneducated or corrupt leaders who either do not understand or do not care about the consequences, such as permission to import toxic wastes. They argue further that MNEs are obligated to set good examples that may become the standard for socially responsible behavior.

From a business standpoint, two possible objectives are to create competitive advantages through socially responsible behavior and to avoid being perceived as irresponsible. In terms of the former, it is argued that responsible acts create strategic and financial success because they lead to trust, which leads to commitment.[27] For example, the CEO of Levi-Strauss has argued that that company's practices (including the refusal to operate where there are substantial human rights violations or to buy from suppliers whose worker safety measures are poor) have enabled it to attract and maintain better employees and suppliers, gain more consumer loyalty, and maintain credibility during crises. In terms of the latter, the same CEO said, "In today's world, an exposé on '60 Minutes' can undo years of effort to build brand loyalty. Why squander an investment when, with foresight and commitment, reputational problems can be prevented?"[28]

In lower-income countries, both societies and companies often must choose between the lesser of two evils when it comes to criticism of their practices. For example, to protect the environment, higher-income countries banned the use of the pesticide DDT. Companies from those countries subsequently have been chided for selling DDT to lower-income countries, whose leaders say that without it they cannot produce enough food for their needs.[29]

Another ethical dilemma MNEs face is whether to abandon markets in which they are not allowed to operate according to their concept of social responsibility. In other words, some people argue that MNEs are so powerful and important that, if they cease operations in a troublesome market, the country will change its policies. Other people argue that MNEs are better able to bring about change by working within the system.[30] For example, Carlsberg, a Danish brewery, reluctantly gave in to pressure by Danish trade unions and consumers to drop out of a joint venture in Myanmar because of Myanmar's military dictatorship. Carlsberg said that it was not in business to pursue a foreign policy and the decision might weaken its future business possibilities in Myanmar compared to its competitors.[31] Anheuser-Busch, for example, continued its operations there.

Social responsibility requires human judgment, which makes it subjective and ambiguous. Many multilateral agreements exist that can help companies make ethical decisions. These agreements deal primarily with employment practices, consumer protection, environmental protection, political activity, and human rights in the workplace.[32] The U.S. government issued a voluntary code in 1995 for U.S. companies' operations abroad, including recognition of workers' rights to organize and the avoidance of using child or forced labor. Interestingly, this code calls for U.S. companies to publicize their positive accomplishments in the workplace abroad.[33] Despite this growing body of agreements and codes, no set of workable corporate guidelines is universally accepted and observed.

Clearly, many aspects of international business raise ethical questions. We'll discuss these ethical dilemmas and social responsibility issues in each chapter.

banning the use of certain pesticides. Despite these agreements, however, discussions among countries continue on these and other issues.

Three areas remain outside the territories of countries—the noncoastal areas of the oceans, outer space, and Antarctica. Until their commercial viability was demonstrated, these areas excited little interest in multinational cooperation. The oceans contain food and mineral resources. They also are the surface over which much international commerce passes. Today, treaties on ocean use set out the amounts and methods of fishing allowed, international discussion attempts to resolve who owns oceanic minerals,[34] and agreements detail how to deal with pirates (yes, pirates are still a problem).[35] Much disagreement exists on who should reap commercial benefits from space. For example, commercial satellites pass over countries that receive no direct benefit from them, but believe they should. Antarctica has minerals and abundant sea life along its coast and

Looking to the Future
SEIZING THAT WINDOW OF INTERNATIONAL BUSINESS OPPORTUNITY

A company wanting to capitalize on international opportunities can't wait too long to see what happens on political and economic fronts. Investments in research, equipment, plants, and personnel training can take many years to complete.

Forecasting foreign opportunities and risks correctly is not always possible. However, by envisioning different ways in which the future may evolve, a company's management may better avoid unpleasant surprises. Each chapter of this text contains a section that discusses foreseeable ways in which topics covered in the chapter may develop in the future.

attracts thousands of tourists each year. Consequently, a series of recent agreements limit its commercial exploitation.

In general, countries whose companies are technologically able to exploit ocean, space, and Antarctican resources believe that their companies should reap all the benefits from exploitation. However, other countries (generally the poorer ones) feel that commercial benefits from such exploitation should be shared by all countries. Until this debate is settled, companies will face uncertainty as to whether and how they can commercialize these new frontiers.

WEB CONNECTION

Check out our home page at www.prenhall.com/daniels for links to key resources for you in your study of international business.

SUMMARY

- Companies engage in international business to expand sales, acquire resources, diversify their sources of sales and supplies, and minimize competitive risk.

- International business has been growing rapidly in recent decades because of technological expansion, liberalization of governmental policies on trade and resource movements, development of institutions needed to support and facilitate international transactions, and increased global competition. Because of these factors, foreign countries increasingly are a source of both production and sales for domestic companies.

- When operating abroad, companies may have to adjust their usual methods of carrying on business. This is because foreign conditions often dictate a more appropriate method and because the operating modes used for international business differ somewhat from those used on a domestic level.

- A company can engage in international business through various modes, including exporting and importing merchandise and services, direct and portfolio investments, and strategic alliances with other companies.

- Multinational enterprises (MNEs) take a global approach to markets and production. They sometimes are referred to as multinational corporations (MNCs) or transnational corporations (TNCs).

- To operate within a company's external environment, its managers must have not only knowledge of business operations but also a working knowledge of the basic social sciences: political science, law, anthropology, sociology, psychology, economics, and geography.

- Few companies include a high commitment to international operations as part of their start-up strategy. However, the inclusion of this commitment within their growth and operating strategies evolves over time.

- Countervailing forces influence the conditions in which companies operate and their options for operating internationally. A company's quest for maximum global profits is inhibited by rivalry among countries, cross-national treaties and agreements, and ethical dilemmas.

CASE

DISNEY THEME PARKS[36]

The Walt Disney Company is the world's largest amusement park operator. It runs all its parks as theme parks, which are amusement parks that focus on a particular motif such as cartoon characters or animals, in addition to the traditional offerings of rides, food, and games. Map 1.1 shows that Disney operates seven of the world's ten most attended amusement parks.

In 2000, Disney's theme parks outside the United States included two in operation (Tokyo Disneyland and Disneyland Paris), one under construction (Tokyo DisneySea to be

MAP 1.1   The Ten Most Visited Amusement Parks

Seven of the ten most visited amusement parks in the world (those shown with mouse ears) are Disney or Disney-related parks. All ten parks are easily reached from highly populated areas. The six parks in the United States are more suitable, climate-wise, for yearlong outside activities than the other locations are.

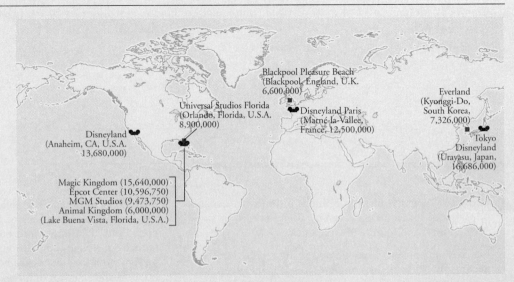

Source: Figures are 1999 estimates of attendance by *Amusement Business,* July 5, 1999, p. 15.

adjacent to Tokyo Disneyland and open in 2001), and two about ready to break ground (a not-yet-named movie theme park adjacent to Disneyland Paris to open in 2002 and Hong Kong Disneyland to open in 2005). When all of these are operating, Disney's theme park attendance outside the United States will about equal that inside the country.

Tokyo Disneyland opened in 1983 and is now the most attended amusement park in the world. The Oriental Land Company of Japan proposed the park to Disney, which accepted the concept but did not want to provide any financing. Therefore, the Oriental Land Company owns the park. Disney provided master planning, design, manufacturing and training services during construction, and consulting services after completion of the facility. Disney received fees for its efforts during the construction phase, and it now receives royalties from admissions and from merchandise and food sales. The Oriental Land Company will also own Tokyo DisneySea, and Disney will receive licensing royalties from the operation.

The Tokyo park is in some ways a paradox. Although such firms as Lenox China and Mister Donut had to adapt to Japanese sizes and tastes, Tokyo Disneyland is nearly a replica of Disneyland and the Magic Kingdom in the United States. Signs are in English, and most food is U.S.-style. The management of the Oriental Land Company demanded this because it wanted visitors to feel they were getting the real thing and because the company had noted the enormous success that such franchises as McDonald's have had in Japan as Japanese youth have embraced U.S.-style culture. Yet Disney made a few changes, such as the addition of a Japanese restaurant and a big-screen attraction showing Japanese history.

Because of Tokyo Disneyland's success and research showing that droves of Europeans were visiting Disney's U.S. parks, Disney announced in 1985 that it would open a theme park in either France or Spain. A location near Paris had advantages because its central location enabled a large population to easily drive there, Paris is the most visited European city, and the French are the largest European consumers of Disney products such as comic books. Nevertheless, because the park would employ thousands of people and attract large numbers of tourists, Disney acted like Scrooge McDuck as it played France against Spain to get incentives. Eventually, the French government offered to extend the Paris railway to the park (linking the park to the rest of Europe) at a cost of almost $350 million, to make available cheap land on which to build the park, and to lend Disney 22 percent of the funds needed to build it.

Disney invested only $140 million to take a 49-percent ownership in a $5 billion Euro Disney, the company that would own not only the park but also hotels, shopping centers, campgrounds, and other facilities. An international syndicate of banks and security dealers sold the remaining 51 percent to other investors, mainly in France and the United Kingdom. In addition, Disney contracted to receive a management fee and a royalty payment on admissions and food sales.

Even before Disney signed an agreement with the French government, it began to have problems in France. Critics referred to the park as a "cultural Chernobyl"; Disney's chairman was pelted by eggs in Paris; and *le Nouvel Observateur* magazine showed a giant Mickey Mouse stepping on the rooftops of Parisian buildings. Disney sought to head off criticism by agreeing to make French the first language in the park even though all employees had to speak another European language as well. (See Figure 1.8.) It also added some attractions to cater to French tastes, such as an exhibit based on the science-fiction stories of Jules Verne. Nevertheless, when Disneyland Paris opened in 1992, French farmers blocked transportation to and entry to the park because the French government had forced them to sell their land to Disney and because the United States was limiting importation of French agricultural products. Many potential customers instead visited the 1992 Olympics and World's Fair in Spain or other European amusement parks that sprang up or were refurbished as soon as Disney announced its plan to locate in France. At the time, the values of European currencies were fluctuating greatly, and many Europeans were wary that prices might be unexpectedly high once they got to the park. Although Disney put in fireplaces, protected waiting lines, and a glass dome over the teacup ride, the Parisian climate was too much colder than California's and Florida's to attract many winter visitors to the park. Finally, Disney put in a no-alcohol policy in the park to maintain its family image, but German and U.K. visitors balked, saying wine is part of the French experience.

The early problems almost bankrupted Euro Disney. But in 1994 a Saudi Arabian investor put up almost $400 million for about a 25 percent stake, while Disney's share went down to 39 percent, and that of the general public fell to 36 percent. In the meantime Disney lowered prices, eliminated its no-alcohol policy, and promoted the park more heavily while putting a moratorium on receipt of its royalty payments. Disneyland Paris now has more than twice as many visitors as the Louvre and is making small profits. In 1999, Disney

28

FIGURE 1.8

At Tokyo Disneyland, signs are in English. At Disneyland Paris, French is the first language.

Source: © The New Yorker Collection 1987 Frank Modell from cartoonbank. com. All Rights Reserved. Reprinted by permission.

agreed to put up 39 percent of the funds to build the movie theme park. The French government is loaning Euro Disney the remaining funds at an interest rate below the market rate.

Disney is interested in Asia because it accounts for about half the world's population and is becoming affluent enough so that more people can afford to take trips and pay for leisure activities. Further, China has had a one child per family policy, which has increased family disposable incomes and made parents reluctant to deny anything to their only child, such as a visit to a theme park.

Disney considered a number of Asian locations, mainly in China, before deciding on Hong Kong. Although Hong Kong has only 6.8 million people, it is Asia's largest tourist destination, getting about 10 million visitors per year. Further, Hong Kong has a better infrastructure (roads, airport, utilities) and higher family incomes than in mainland Chinese cities. Finally, since Hong Kong reverted from British to Chinese control, Asians have not found it as appealing a tourist destination, so the government of Hong Kong was eager to attract Disney to bolster its tourist industry. Disney expects that its park will attract another 1.4 million outside visitors in the first

year of operations and 2.9 million outside visitors within 15 years. Further, Hong Kong is presently not a family-oriented destination, and the Hong Kong government thinks that a Disney theme park can change that, thus bringing in a type of tourist that would not come otherwise. Finally, Disney expects that it will create 18,400 direct and indirect jobs in its first year of operation and 35,800 in later years.

Disney also saw a theme park in Hong Kong as a means of improving its relationship and business opportunities in mainland China. The Chinese government suspended distribution of Disney films after Disney released the movie, *Kundun*, in 1996 about the exiled Dalai Lama, whom the Chinese government considers to be a threat to its control over Tibet. Building a park in Hong Kong, which is a Chinese territory, shows Disney's willingness to cooperate with China. The Hong Kong park does not preclude Disney's later entry into mainland China.

Disney and the Hong Kong government negotiated for nearly a year. The final agreement is for a joint venture, Hong Kong International Theme Parks, owned 57 percent by the government of Hong Kong and 43 percent by Disney. The joint venture will own the theme park and other developments adjacent to it, such as hotels and restaurants. The Hong Kong government insisted that Disney invest money in addition to contributing know-how and the aura of its attractions and cartoon characters. In the end, the cost of the park and related projects—roads and a rail link to connect the park to the rest of Hong Kong—will probably exceed $4 billion.

The success of the park is far from assured. The cost of air transport and hotels may preclude visits from many Southeast Asian tourists. The only link by land to Hong Kong is China. Disney is obviously counting on Chinese visitors. Mainland Chinese must get exit visas from China and entry visas from Hong Kong to travel to Hong Kong. The Chinese government gives these visas sparingly, and the Hong Kong government issuance takes time. The Hong Kong government has indicated that it might eliminate the visa requirement for Chinese visitors coming for less than a week. Competition is another factor. Between 1994 and 1999, China built more than 2,000 amusement parks, ranging from lavish to shoddy. But most of these have not done well. Disney bets that the Chinese are not disinterested in amusement parks, only in the bad ones. Finally, there is the question of affordability. The joint venture is planning to build smaller, more affordable hotels to cater to Chinese visitors in an area almost as large as the park.

Given the financial problems of Euro Disney, Hong Kong Disneyland will be on a smaller scale than Disneyland Paris—needing 5 million annual visitors rather than the 10 million to break even. The park itself will incorporate an exhibit center modeled after Epcot along with the amusements. Disney does not expect that there will be a cultural backlash from the park like it encountered in France because people in Hong Kong are more interested in making money than in preserving culture. Disney says it plans to give the hotels and restaurants a strong Chinese flavor, but the Magic Kingdom portion will be "ruled by Mickey Mouse, not Chairman Mao."

QUESTIONS

1. What do you think motivated Disney to set up parks abroad, and what might be the pros and cons from the standpoint of the Walt Disney Company?

2. Why do you suppose Disney made no financial investment in Japan, one of $140 million in France, and then one of over $300 million in Hong Kong?

3. What factors in the external environment have contributed to Disney's success, failure, and adjustments in foreign theme park operations?

4. Might Disney set up theme parks elsewhere abroad? If so, where?

CHAPTER NOTES

1 We wish to acknowledge the cooperation of Robert M. Greber, chief executive officer, and Susan Trembly, publicity and advertising assistant, at Lucasfilm Ltd. for granting interview information. In addition, the case relied on data from Louise Sweeney, "Returns from 'Jedi': Marketing a Megahit," *Christian Science Monitor,* June 30, 1983, pp. B7–8; Gerald Clarke, "Great Galloping Galaxies!" *Time,* Vol. 121, May 23, 1983, pp. 62–65; Aljean Harmetz, "Showing of 'Star Wars' Trilogy Set," *New York Times,* February 28, 1985, p. 20; "Attendance Record as 'Star Wars' Prequel Hits Germany," *Deutsche Presse-Agentur,* August 20, 1999; "Darth Vader Backs Tunisia," *Middle East Economic Digest,* December 17, 1999, p. 22; "'Star Wars' Draws Estimated 500,000 on Opening Day," *Agence France Presse,* July 10, 1999; Judy Rumhold, "A Star Father," *Mail on Sunday,* July 18, 1999, p. 16; Andrew Pollack, "Hollywood Hits the Road," *International Herald Tribune,* May 12, 1999, pp. 11–12; Mark Landler, "In Hong Kong 'Star Wars: The Pirate Menace,'" *New York Times,* May 29, 1999,

p. B1; "Summer Movie Scoreboard," *Wall Street Journal,* August 27, 1999, p. W8; Stuart Eliot, "The Hype Is with Us," *New York Times,* May 14, 1999, pp. C1–2; and Lee Gomes and David P. Hamilton, ""The Phantom Plot Line," *Wall Street Journal,* May 21, 1999, p. B1.

2 Rick Romell, "Small Business Panel Praises Free Trade in Face of Protests," *Milwaukee Journal Sentinel,* December 2, 1999, Business Section p. 1.

3 Marla Dickerson and Lee Romney, "Small Business," *Los Angeles Times,* November 17, 1999, p. 10.

4 Richard Tomkins, "McDonald's Makes Skeptics Eat Their Words," *Financial Times,* March 11, 1996, p. 17.

5 "World Trade Growth Slower in 1998 After Unusually Strong Growth in 1997," World Trade Organization Press Release, April 16, 1999.

6 "Developed Countries Boost Foreign Direct Investment by 46 Percent to New Record," UNCTAD Press Release, TAD/INF/2826, September 23, 1999.

7 Paul Hirst and Grahame Thompson, *Globalization in Question* (London: Blackwell, 1996).

8 Nancy Dunne, "Barter Grows as Trade Deals Hit Problems," *Financial Times,* September 17, 1998, p. 7.

9 "Darth Vader Backs Tunisia."

10 Joseph Pereira, "Values Won't Be Stellar with a Galaxy of New Toys," *Wall Street Journal,* May 14, 1999, p. B6.

11 UNCTAD Press Release, TAD/INF/2820, September 23, 1999.

12 Christopher A. Bartlett and Sumantra Ghoshal, *Managing Across Borders* (Boston: Harvard Business School Press, 1989), pp. 63–64; and Christopher A. Bartlett and Sumantra Ghoshal, *Transnational Management* (Homewood, IL: Irwin, 1992), pp. 117–119.

13 Bert Sacks and Mira Tanna, "Sanctions Take Heavy Toll on Iraqi Civilians," *St. Louis Post Dispatch,* November 25, 1998, p. B7.

14 "Film Giants Scramble for China Screenings," *South China Morning Post* [Hong Kong], May 14, 1995, Money Section, p. 1.

15 Matt Forney, "Taiwan Chip Output to Start in 10 Days," *Wall Street Journal*, September 24, 1999, p. A12.

16 See, for example, Solange De Santis, "Many U.S. Companies Are Looking to Canada in Making Their Initial Foreign Expansions," *Wall Street Journal*, July 15, 1998, p. A10.

17 Shawna O'Grady and Henry W. Lane, "The Psychic Distance Paradox," *Journal of International Business Studies*, Vol. 27, No. 2, Second Quarter 1996, pp. 309–333.

18 Benjamin M. Oviatt and Patricia Phillips McDougall, "Global Start-Ups: Entrepreneurs on a Worldwide Stage," Academy of Management Executive, Vol. 9, No. 2, 1995, pp. 30–44.

19 "Enterprise," Wall Street Journal, July 16, 1996, p. B2.

20 For a coverage of the various countervailing forces affecting global versus multidomestic practices, see Bartlett and Ghoshal, *Transnational Management*, Chapter 2.

21 John D. Daniels, "The Elusive Concept of National Competitiveness," *Business Horizons*, November–December 1991, pp. 3–6.

22 Robert Feenstra and Gordon Hanson, *Foreign Investment, Outsourcing, and Relative Wages* (Cambridge, MA: National Bureau of Economic Research Working Paper No. 5121, 1995).

23 For examples of different views on the relationship of location of headquarters and production with national well-being, see Kenichi Ohmae, *Triad Power: The Coming Shape of Global Competition* (New York: Free Press, 1985); Michael E. Porter, *The Competitive Advantage of Nations* (New York: Free Press, 1990); and Robert B. Reich, *The Work of Nations: Preparing Ourselves*

for 21st Century Capitalism (New York: Alfred A. Knopf, 1991).

24 Paul Magnusson, "Why Corporate Nationality Matters," *Business Week*, July 12, 1993, pp. 142–143.

25 For a good coverage of this, see Thomas L. Friedman, *The Lexus and the Olive Tree* (New York: Farrar, Straus & Giroux, 1999).

26 See, for example, Thomas Donaldson, "Can Multinationals Stage a Universal Morality Play?" *Business & Society Review*, Spring 1992, pp. 51–55; and Richard T. De George, *Business Ethics* (New York: Macmillan, 1990), Chapters 19 and 20.

27 Larue Tone Hosmer, "Response to 'Do Good Ethics Always Make for Good Business?'" *Strategic Management Journal*, Vol. 17, 1996, p. 501.

28 Robert D. Haas, "Ethics in the Trenches," *Across the Board*, Vol. 31, No. 5, May 1994, pp. 12–13.

29 "Irradiated Food: People Have Little to Fear," *The Statesman* [India], April 1, 1998.

30 John Delaney and Donna Sockell, "Ethics in the Trenches," *Across the Board*, October 1990, pp. 15–21.

31 Hilary Barnes, "Carlsberg Drops Burma Project," *Financial Times*, July 7, 1996, p. 4.

32 The agreements are outlined in William C. Frederick, "Moral Authority of Transnational Corporate Codes," *Journal of Business Ethics*, March 1991, pp. 165–176; and David M. Schilling and Ruth Rosenbaum, "Principles for Global Corporate Responsibility," *Business and Society Review*, Vol. 94, Summer 1995, pp. 55–56.

33 Robert S. Greenberger, "Clinton to Unveil Voluntary Business Code," *Asia Wall Street Journal*, March 27, 1995, p. 12.

34 Canute James, "'Dead Sea Scroll' Shows Signs of Life," *Financial Times*, April 19, 1996, p. 23.

35 See, for example, Christopher Adams, "Action to Curb Rise in Piracy Urged," *Financial Times*, January 20, 1998, p. 8.

36 Rahul Jacob, "Disney Seals HK Park Deal," *Financial Times*, November 2, 1999, p. 4; Rahul Jacob, Christopher Parkes, and Ho Swee Lin, "Mickey Mouse to Fill Role Left Empty by Empire," *Financial Times*, November 3, 1999, p. 7; Mark Lander, "Mickey and Minnie Go to Hong Kong," *New York Times*, November 3, 1999, p. C1; Jon E. Hilsenrath and Zach Coleman, "Disney-Park Deal May Not Wave a Magic Wand Over Hong Kong," *Wall Street Journal*, November 4, 1999, p. A26; Mark Lander, "After Protracted Talks, a Disneyland Will Rise in Hong Kong," *New York Times*, November 1, 1999, p. C1; Mahon Meyer, "Mickey Goes to China," *Newsweek*, November 15, 1999, p. 42; "Fantasyland," *The Economist Newspaper*, November 6, 1999, n.p.; Christopher Parkes, "Disney's Sea Theme Park in Tokyo Gets Go-ahead," *Financial Times*, November 27, 1997, p. 1; Charles Fleming, "Euro Disney to Build Movie Theme Park Outside Paris," *Wall Street Journal*, September 30, 1999, p. A18; "Euro Disney to Open New Park," *Financial Times*, September 30, 1999, p. 26; Michael Dobbs, "Mickey Mouse Storms the Bastille," *Across the Board*, Vol. 23, No. 4, April 1986, pp. 9–11; "Trouble at Magic Kingdom," *Business Week*, September 26, 1992, p. 8; Peter Gumbel and David J. Jefferson, "Disney Continues Drive to Expand Worldwide," *Wall Street Journal*, November 20, 1992, p. B4; and Sharon Waxman, "Le Mouse That Roared Back," *Washington Post*, July 27, 1995, p. B9.

VIDEO CASE

PART ONE: BACKGROUND FOR INTERNATIONAL BUSINESS
LANDS' END AND YAHOO!

BACKGROUND

This video case shows how two very different companies, Lands' End and Yahoo!, approached the same goal—expansion into international markets. Lands' End is a retail business that sells its products through its print and on-line catalogs. Yahoo! is an Internet search engine that supplies its service to Web surfers worldwide.

A firm may decide to go international for any number of reasons, including the drive to increase sales volume and to access resources in other national markets. Lands' End wanted to increase its sales volume in markets such as Japan, Germany, and the United Kingdom. Yahoo! wanted to dominate the global Internet industry by penetrating markets such as China, Japan, Sweden, Norway, France, and others. This video illustrates how the two companies localized their products and services to meet the needs and preferences of consumers in new markets.

LANDS' END

In 1963, Gary C. Comer, a former advertising copywriter and an avid sailor, founded Lands' End, Inc., in Chicago, Illinois. The company began by selling sailboat hardware equipment by catalog. In 1978, Lands' End warehouse and phone operations moved to Dodgeville, Wisconsin, a rural community located 40 miles southwest of Madison, Wisconsin. In 1980, the company established a toll-free phone operation that ran 24 hours a day, and in 1985, the Lands' End catalog started coming out monthly. The company went public in 1986. In 1990, Lands' End launched three new specialty catalogs: "Coming Home" (bed and bath supplies, "Lands' End Kids," and "Beyond Buttonwoods" (men's tailored clothing). In 1991, it sent its catalog to customers in the United Kingdom for the first time, and in 1993 the company opened a warehouse and phone center there. In 1994, Lands' End opened operations in Japan and purchased the trademark of Willis & Geiger, a U.S.-based adventure outfitters company. In 1995, Lands' End launched its Web site on the Internet. Still building its overseas presence, Lands' End opened a phone center in Germany in 1996. By 1999, Lands' End net sales had reached $1.32 bil-

lion, making the company one of the largest apparel brands in the United States.

YAHOO! INC.

Yahoo! is an Internet search engine headquartered in Santa Clara, California, that helps people navigate the World Wide Web. The company's principal product is an ad-supported Internet directory that links users to millions of Web pages. The site leads the field in traffic (95 million pages viewed each day) and is second only to Netscape in on-line advertising revenues. Yahoo! has targeted guides for geographic audiences (Yahoo! Finance and Yahoo! News), demographic audiences (see Yahooligans!, a Web guide for children), special-interest audiences (Yahoo! Finance and Yahoo! News), and community services (Yahoo! Chat). The company is moving into the Internet access market through an alliance with AT&T and has agreed to acquire fellow Internet player, GeoCities. Japan's SOFTBANK, the largest shareholder in Yahoo!, has 15 international Web properties outside the United States. Yahoo! now has offices in Europe, the Asian Pacific, and Canada—and has a global network of 22 world properties. Net revenues for first quarter 2000 were over $228 million, which is a big increase over entire year 1998's $25.6 million.

QUESTIONS

As you watch the video, be prepared to answer the following questions:

1. Compare the different reasons why Lands' End and Yahoo! went international.
2. How did Lands' End succeed in establishing itself in the United Kingdom and Japan?
3. How did Yahoo! succeed in France and China?
4. What international issues have challenged the two companies?
5. How did Yahoo! customize its global products and services to local markets?
6. Break into groups of two or three people. Discuss the domestic and international environments for Lands' End and Yahoo!. Present your analysis to the rest of the class.

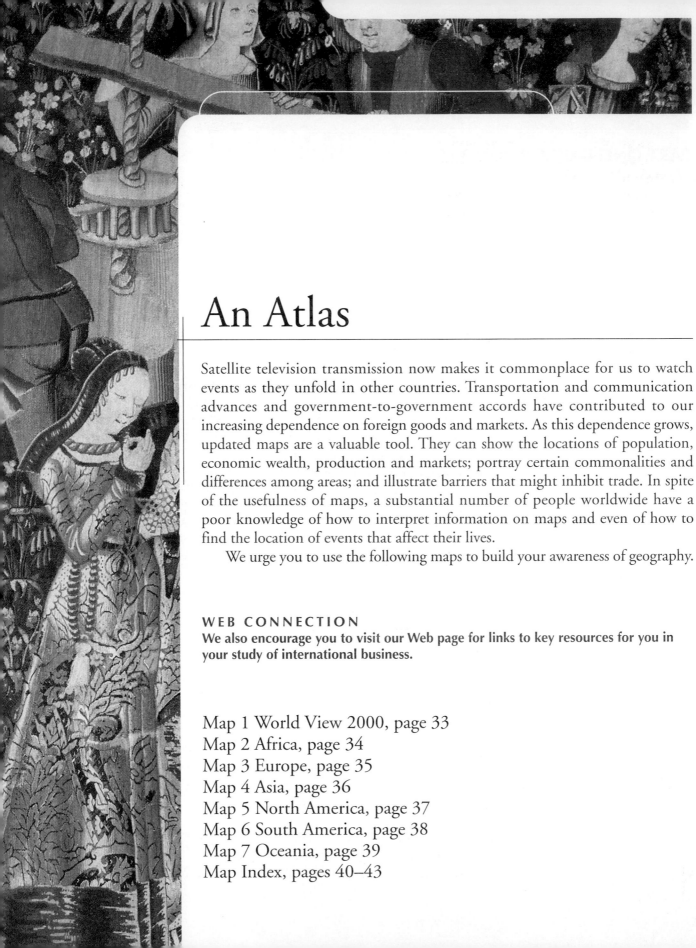

An Atlas

Satellite television transmission now makes it commonplace for us to watch events as they unfold in other countries. Transportation and communication advances and government-to-government accords have contributed to our increasing dependence on foreign goods and markets. As this dependence grows, updated maps are a valuable tool. They can show the locations of population, economic wealth, production and markets; portray certain commonalities and differences among areas; and illustrate barriers that might inhibit trade. In spite of the usefulness of maps, a substantial number of people worldwide have a poor knowledge of how to interpret information on maps and even of how to find the location of events that affect their lives.

We urge you to use the following maps to build your awareness of geography.

WEB CONNECTION
We also encourage you to visit our Web page for links to key resources for you in your study of international business.

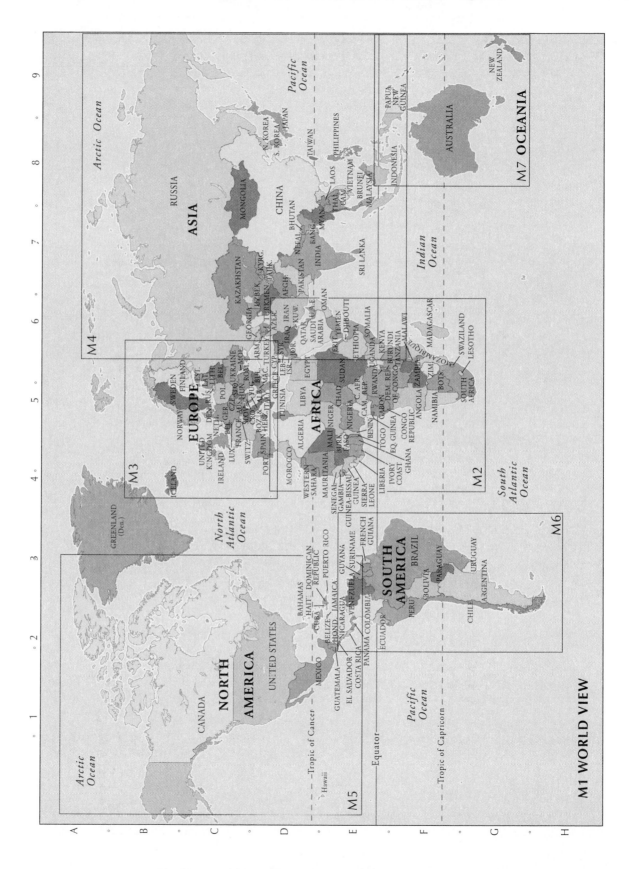

M1 WORLD VIEW

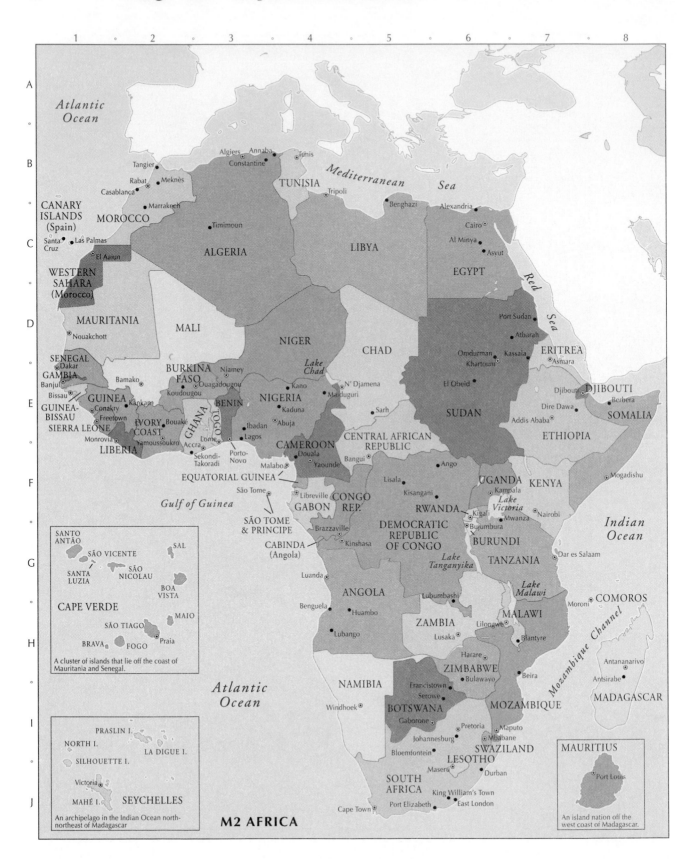

M2 AFRICA

A cluster of islands that lie off the coast of Mauritania and Senegal.

CAPE VERDE
SANTO ANTÃO
SÃO VICENTE
SAL
SANTA LUZIA
SÃO NICOLAU
BOA VISTA
SÃO TIAGO
MAIO
BRAVA FOGO
Praia

An archipelago in the Indian Ocean north-northeast of Madagascar.

SEYCHELLES
PRASLIN I.
NORTH I.
LA DIGUE I.
SILHOUETTE I.
Victoria
MAHÉ I.

An island nation off the west coast of Madagascar.

MAURITIUS
Port Louis

M3 EUROPE

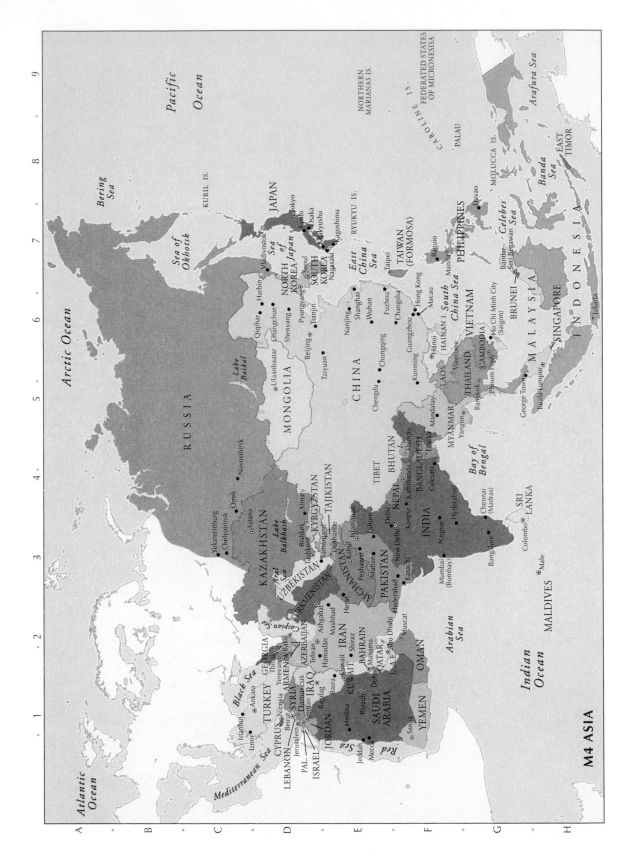

M4 ASIA

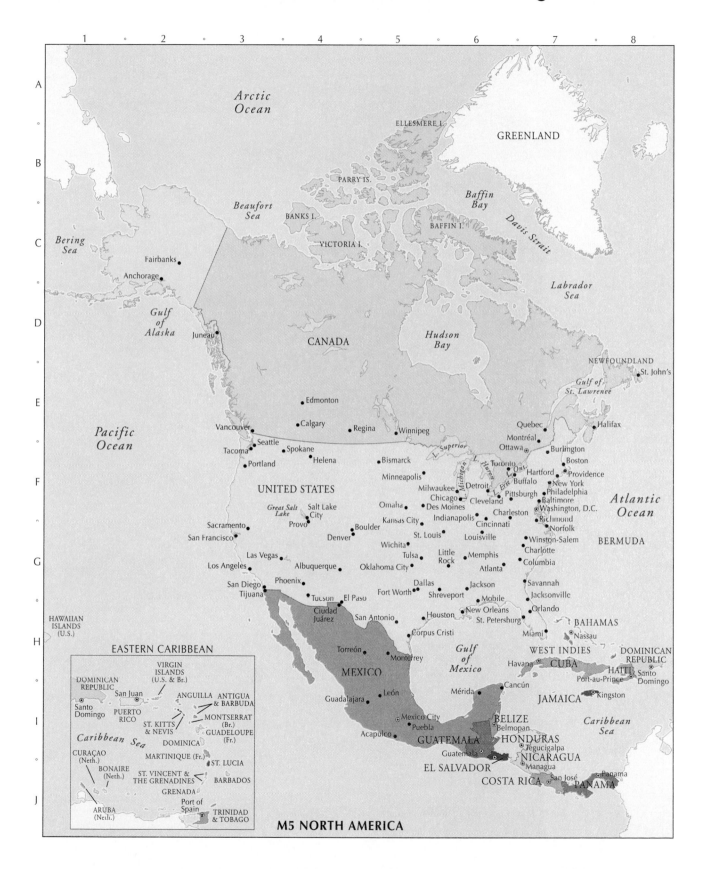

M5 NORTH AMERICA

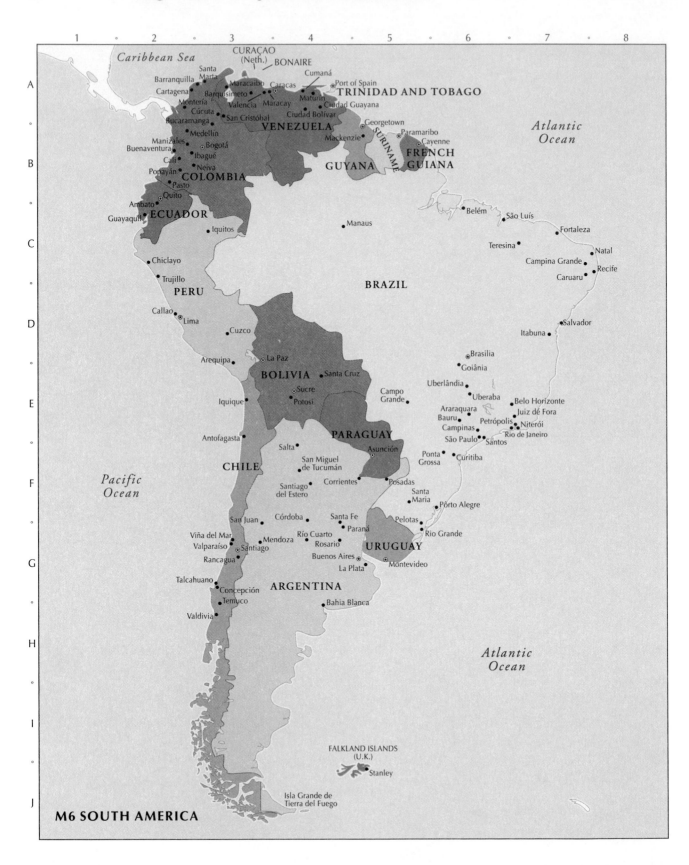

M6 SOUTH AMERICA

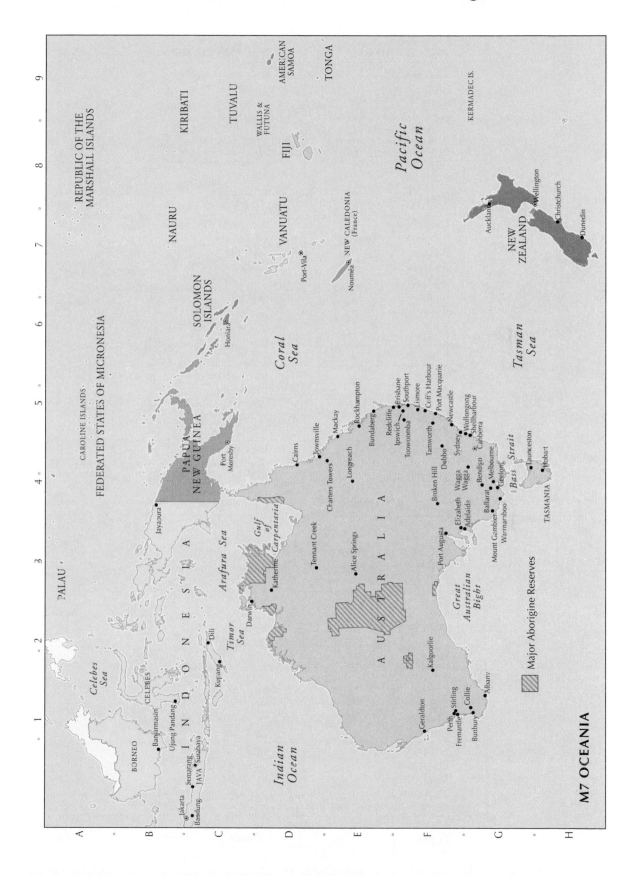

M7 OCEANIA

COUNTRY AND TERRITORY	PRONUNCIATION	MAP 1	MAPS 2-7
Afghanistan	af-'gan-ə-ˌstan	D7	Map 4, E3
Albania	al-'bā-nē-ə	C5	Map 3, I5
Algeria	al-'jir-ē-ə	D5	Map 2, C3
Andorra	an-'dȯr-ə	—	Map 3, H2
Angola	an-'gō-lə	E5	Map 2, G4
Antigua & Barbuda	an-'tē-g(w)ə / bär-'büd-ə	—	Map 5, I3
Argentina	ˌär-jen-'tē-nə	G3	Map 6, G3
Armenia	är-'mē-ne-ə	C6	Map 4, D2
Australia	ȯ-'strāl-yə	G8	Map 7, E4
Austria	'ȯs-trē-ə	C5	Map 3, G4
Azerbaijan	ˌaz-ər-ˌbī-'jän	D6	Map 4, D2
Bahamas	bə-hä'-məz	D3	Map 5, H7
Bahrain	bä-'rān	—	Map 4, E2
Bangladesh	ˌbäŋ-glə-'desh	D7	Map 4, F5
Barbados	bär-'bād-əs	—	Map 5, J3
Belarus	ˌbē-lə-'rüs	C5	Map 3, F6
Belgium	'bel-jəm	C5	Map 3, F3
Belize	bə-'lēz	D2	Map 5, I6
Benin	bə-'nin	E5	Map 2, E3
Bermuda	(ˌ)bər-'myüd-ə	—	Map 5, G8
Bhutan	bü-'tan	D7	Map 4, F5
Bolivia	bə-'liv-ē-ə	F3	Map 6, E4
Bosnia & Herzegovina	'bäz-nē-ə / ˌhert-sə-gō-'vē-nə	D5	Map 3, H5
Botswana	bät-'swän-ə	F5	Map 2, I5
Brazil	brə-'zil	F3	Map 6, D6
Brunei	broo-nī'	E8	Map 4, G7
Bulgaria	ˌbəl-'gar-ē-ə	D5	Map 3, H6
Burkina Faso	bȯr-'kē-nə-'fȧ-sō	E5	Map 2, E2
Burundi	bü-'rün-dē	E6	Map 2, G6
Cambodia	kam-'bd-ē-ə	E7	Map 4, G5
Cameroon	ˌkam-ə-'rün	E5	Map 2, F4
Canada	'kan-əd-ə	C2	Map 5, E5
Cape Verde Islands	'vard	—	Map 2, G1
Central African Rep.		E5	Map 2, E5
Chad	'chad	E5	Map 2, D5
Chile	'chil-ē	G3	Map 6, F3
China	'chī-nə	D8	Map 4, E5
Colombia	kə-'ləm-bē-ə	E3	Map 6, B3
Congo (Democratic Republic)	'käŋ(ˌ)gō	E5	Map 2, G5
Congo Republic	'käŋ(ˌ)gō	E5	Map 2, F4
Costa Rica	ˌkäs-tə-'rē-kə	E2	Map 5, J7
Croatia	krō-'ā-sh(ē)ə	D5	Map 3, H5
Cuba	'kyü-bə	E3	Map 5, H7
Curaçao	'k(y)ür-ə-'sō	—	Map 5, J1
Cyprus	'sī-prəs	D6	Map 4, D2
Czech Republic	ˌchek	C5	Map 3, G5
Denmark	'den-ˌmärk	C5	Map 3, E4
Djibouti	jə-'büt-ē	E6	Map 2, E7
Dominica	ˌdäm-ə-'nē-kə	—	Map 5, I3
Dominican Republic	də-ˌmin-i-kən	E3	Map 5, H8
Ecuador	'ek-wə-ˌdȯ(ə)r	E3	Map 6, C2
Egypt	'ē-jəpt	D5	Map 2, C6

COUNTRY AND TERRITORY	PRONUNCIATION	MAP 1	MAPS 2-7
Liechtenstein	lĭk'tən-stīn'	—	Map 3, G4
Lithuania	ˌlith-(y)ə-'wā-nē-ə	C5	Map 3, E6
Luxembourg	'lək-səm-ˌbərg	C5	Map 3, G3
Macedonia	ˌmas-ə-'dō-nyə	D6	Map 3, I6
Madagascar	ˌmad-ə-'gas-kər	F6	Map 2, I8
Malawi	mə-'lä-wē	F6	Map 2, H6
Malaysia	mə-'lā-zh(ē-)ə	E8	Map 4, G6
Maldives	môl'dīvz	—	Map 4, H3
Mali	'mäl-ē	D5	Map 2, D2
Malta	'mȯl-tə	—	Map 3, J5
Marshall Islands	mär'shəl	—	Map 7, A8
Mauritania	ˌmȯr-ə-'tā-nē-ə	D5	Map 2, D1
Mauritius	mô-'rĭsh'əs	—	Map 2, J8
Mexico	'mek-si-ˌkō	D2	Map 5, I5
Micronesia	mī'krō-nē'zhə	—	Map 7, A5
Moldova	mäl-'dō-və	D6	Map 3, G7
Mongolia	män-'gōl-yə	D8	Map 4, D5
Morocco	mə-'räk-(ˌ)ō	D5	Map 2, B2
Mozambique	ˌmō-zəm-'bēk	F6	Map 2, H6
Myanmar	'myän-ˌmär	E7	Map 4, F5
Namibia	nə-'mib-ē-ə	F5	Map 2, I4
Naura	nä'-ü-rü	—	Map 7, B7
Nepal	nə-'pȯl	D7	Map 4, E4
Netherlands	'neth-ər-lən(d)z	C5	Map 3, F3
New Caledonia	ˌkal-ə-'dō-nyə	—	Map 7, E7
New Zealand	'zē-lənd	G9	Map 7, H7
Nicaragua	ˌnik-ə-'räg-wə	E3	Map 5, I7
Niger	'nī-jər	E5	Map 2, D4
Nigeria	nī-'jir-ē-ə	E5	Map 2, E4
Norway	'nȯ(ə)r-ˌwā	C5	Map 3, D3
Oman	ō-'män	E6	Map 4, F2
Pakistan	ˌpak-i-'stan	D7	Map 4, E3
Palau	pä-lou'	—	Map 7, A3
Palestine	pa-lə-'stīn	—	Map 4, D1
Panama	'pan-ə-ˌmä	E3	Map 5, J8
Papua New Guinea	'pap-yə-wə	F9	Map 7, C5
Paraguay	'par-ə-ˌgwī	F3	Map 6, E4
Peru	pə-'rü	F3	Map 6, D2
Philippines	ˌfil-ə-'pēnz	E8	Map 4, F7
Poland	'pō-lənd	D5	Map 3, F5
Portugal	'pōr-chi-gəl	D5	Map 3, I1
Puerto Rico	ˌpōrt-ə-'rē(ˌ)kō	E3	Map 5, I2
Qatar	'kät-ər	D6	Map 4, E2
Romania	rō-'mā-nē-ə	D5	Map 3, H6
Russia	'rəsh-ə	C7	Map 3, D7; Map 4, C5
Rwanda	rü-'än-də	E6	Map 2, F6
St. Kitts & Nevis	'kits / 'nē-vəs	—	Map 5, I3
St. Lucia	sānt-'lü-shə	—	Map 5, I3
St. Vincent and the Grenadines	grĕn'ə-dēnz'	—	Map 5, J3
San Marino	săn mə-rē'nō	—	Map 3, H4

COUNTRY AND TERRITORY	PRONUNCIATION	MAP 1	MAPS 2-7
São Tomé and Príncipe	soun tōō -mĕ'prēn'-sēpə	—	Map 2, F3
Saudi Arabia	ˌsaüd-ē	E6	Map 4, E2
Senegal	ˌsen-i-'gȯl	E4	Map 2, D1
Seychelles	sā-shĕlz'	—	Map 2, J1
Sierra Leone	sē-ˌer-ə-lē-'ōn	E4	Map 2, E1
Singapore	'siŋ-(g)ə-ˌpō(ə)r	—	Map 4, H6
Slovakia	slō-'väk-ē-ə	C5	Map 3, G5
Slovenia	slō-'vēn-ē-ə	C5	Map 3, H5
Solomon Islands	'säl-ə-mən	—	Map 7, C6
Somalia	sō-'mäl-ē-ə	E6	Map 2, F8
South Africa	'a-fri-kə	F6	Map 2, J5
Spain	'spān	C5	Map 3, I1
Sri Lanka	(')srē-'läŋ-kə	E7	Map 4, G4
Sudan	sü-'dan	E6	Map 2, E6
Suriname	suṙ-ə-'näm-ə	E3	Map 6, B5
Swaziland	'swäz-ē-ˌland	F6	Map 2, I6
Sweden	'swēd-ᵊn	B5	Map 3, C5
Switzerland	'swit-sər-lənd	C5	Map 3, G4
Syria	'sir-ē-ə	D6	Map 4, D2
Taiwan	'tī-'wän	D8	Map 4, E7
Tajikistan	tä-ˌji-ki-'stan	D7	Map 4, E4
Tanzania	ˌtan-zə-'nē-ə	F6	Map 2, G6
Thailand	'tī-ˌland	E8	Map 4, F5
Togo	'tō(ˌ)gō	E5	Map 2, E3
Tonga	'tän-gə	—	Map 7, D9
Trinidad & Tobago	'trin-ə-ˌdad / tə-'bā-(ˌ)gō	—	Map 5, J3
Tunisia	t(y)ü-'nē-zh(ē-)ə	D5	Map 2, B4
Turkey	'tər-kē	D6	Map 4, D2
Turkmenistan	türk'-men-i-stăn'	D6	Map 4, D3
Tuvalu	tü'-vä-lü	—	Map 7, C9
Uganda	(y)ü-'gan-də	E6	Map 2, F6
Ukraine	yü-'krān	C6	Map 3, F7
United Arab Emirates	yoo-nī'tid ăr'əb i-mîr'its	D6	Map 4, E2
United Kingdom	king'dəm	C5	Map 3, F2
United States	yü-ˌnīt-əd-'stāts	D2	Map 5, F5
Uruguay	'(y)uṙ-ə-gwī	G3	Map 6, G5
Uzbekistan	(ˌ)uz-ˌbek-i-'stan	C6	Map 4, D3
Vanuatu	van-ə-'wät-(ˌ)ü	—	Map 7, D7
Vatican City	văt'ĭ-kən	—	Map 3, H4
Venezuela	ˌven-əz(-ə)-'wā-lə	E3	Map 6, A4
Vietnam	vē-'et-'näm	E8	Map 4, G6
Western Sahara	sə-hâr'ə	D4	Map 2, C1
Yemen	'yem-ən	E6	Map 4, F2
Yugoslavia	yōō'gō-slä'vē-ə	D5	Map 3, H2
Zambia	'zam-bē-ə	F5	Map 2, H5
Zimbabwe	zim-'bäb-wē	F6	Map 2, H6

* in thousands
+ in millions of U.S. dollars
** in U.S. dollars   [NA = Not Available]

Comparative Environmental Frameworks

CHAPTER 2

The Cultural Environments Facing Business

To change customs is a difficult thing. —LEBANESE PROVERB

OBJECTIVES

- To discuss the problems and methods of learning about cultural environments

- To explain the major causes of cultural difference and change

- To examine behavioral factors influencing countries' business practices

- To examine cultural guidelines for companies that operate internationally

Parris-Rogers International (PRI), a British publishing house, set up an operation in Bahrain to publish telephone and business directories for five Arab states, plus the seven autonomous divisions making up the United Arab Emirates (Map 2.1 shows the region). PRI discontinued this operation because of its inability to adjust efficiently to Middle Eastern customs. Because PRI could not find sufficient qualified people locally, it filled four key positions through advertisements in London newspapers. PRI hired Angela Clarke, an Englishwoman, as editor and researcher, and three young Englishmen as salespeople. The four new hires left immediately for Bahrain. None of the four had visited the Middle East before, and all expected to carry out business as usual.

The salesmen, hired on a commission basis, expected that by moving aggressively they could make the same number of calls as they could in the United Kingdom. They were used to working eight-hour days, to having the undivided attention of potential clients, and to restricting most conversation to the business transaction. To them, time was money.

The salesmen found the Middle East a different place in which to work. There was less time to sell than in Europe, first, because the Muslims prayed five times a day and, second, because the workday shrunk even further during the sacred ninth month, Ramadan, of the Muslim lunar year. The start of Ramadan depends on the sighting of a new moon, varies by a day or two among countries, and cannot be determined in advance—all of this meaning the salesmen had a hard time planning. The salesmen also felt that the Arabs placed less importance on appointments than they did. Appointments seldom began at the scheduled time and most often took place at cafés where the Arabs would engage in what the salesmen considered idle chitchat. Whether in a café or in the office, drinking coffee or tea and talking to acquaintances seemed to take precedence over business matters.

Angela Clarke, too, began to feel the cultural differences, and these differences added to operating costs. For example, PRI had based its budgets for preparing the directories on its English experience. In Bahrain, however, preparing such books turned out to be more time-consuming and costly. In most traditional Middle Eastern cities, there are no street names or building numbers. Clarke had to take a laborious census of Bahraini establishments, identifying the location of each as "below," "above," or "in front of" some meaningful landmark.

Clarke encountered still other problems, especially because she was a single woman. She was in charge of the research in all twelve states and had placed ads to hire freelance assistants in most of them. But her advertisements generated harassment and obscene telephone calls. In addition, Saudi authorities denied her entry to Saudi Arabia, and her visa for Oman took six weeks to process *each time she went there*. These experiences were particularly frustrating for her because both Saudi Arabia and Oman sometimes eased the entry of a single woman when her business was of high local priority or when she would be serving as a housemaid or nanny where her contact would be with women and children only. In the states she could enter, Clarke sometimes had to stay in only those hotels that government officials had approved for foreign women, and even there, she was prohibited from eating in the dining room unless accompanied by the hotel manager.

Clarke fared better as time went on, thanks to her compromises with Arab customs. She began wearing a wedding ring and registering at hotels as a married woman. When traveling, she ate meals in her room, conducted meetings in conference rooms, and had hotel operators

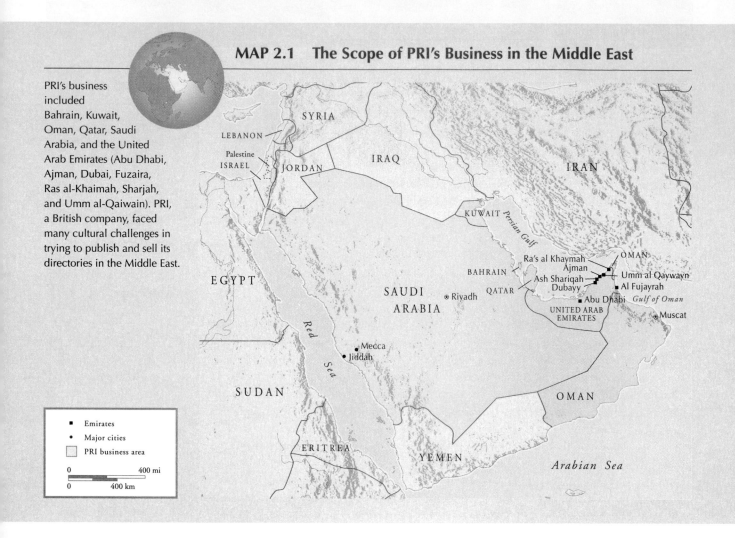

MAP 2.1   The Scope of PRI's Business in the Middle East

PRI's business included Bahrain, Kuwait, Oman, Qatar, Saudi Arabia, and the United Arab Emirates (Abu Dhabi, Ajman, Dubai, Fuzaira, Ras al-Khaimah, Sharjah, and Umm al-Qaiwain). PRI, a British company, faced many cultural challenges in trying to publish and sell its directories in the Middle East.

■ Emirates
• Major cities
☐ PRI business area

0 ———————— 400 mi
0 ———————— 400 km

screen all her incoming calls. To avoid arrest by decency patrols, she wore long-sleeved blouses and below-the-knee skirts in blue or beige. Still, in spite of her compromises, her difficulty in entering Saudi Arabia caused PRI to send in her place a salesman, whose performance was unsatisfactory because he was not trained to do directory research.

PRI's salesmen never adjusted to working in the Middle East. Instead of pushing PRI to review its commission scheme, they tried to change the Arab businessmen's behavior. For example, after a few months the salesmen refused to join their potential clients for refreshments and began showing their irritation at "irrelevant" conversations, delays, and interruptions from friends. The Arab businessmen responded negatively. PRI received so many complaints that it had to replace the salesmen. By then, however, PRI's sales had suffered irrevocable damage. PRI sold its Middle Eastern operation to a Japanese company, which also encountered problems of cultural adjustment. ∽

INTRODUCTION

The PRI case illustrates the major problems that occur when different cultures clash. By not recognizing differences in advance, PRI underestimated its cost of doing business in the Arab states. By not adjusting to the Arab way of doing business nor getting the Arabs to accommodate to its practices, PRI could not achieve its objectives. The English salesmen became so personally frustrated that PRI had to replace them. So, the major problems of cultural collision in international business are when

- A company implements practices that work less well than intended, and
- A company's employees encounter distress because of an inability to accept or adjust to foreign behaviors.

Business employs, sells to, buys from, is regulated by, and is owned by people. Because international business includes people from different cultures, every business function—managing a workforce, marketing output, purchasing supplies, dealing with regulators, securing funds—is subject to potential cultural problems. An international company must be sensitive to these cultural differences to predict and control its relationships and operations. Further, it should realize that its accustomed way of doing business may not be the only or best way. When doing business abroad, a company first should determine what business practices in a foreign country differ from those it's used to. Management then must decide what, if any, adjustments are necessary to operate efficiently in the foreign country.

In Chapter 1, you learned that companies need to understand external environments to operate efficiently abroad. Figure 2.1 illustrates that **culture**—the specific learned norms based on attitudes, values, and beliefs that exist in every nation—is an

Can there be a "global culture"? Look at these Buddhist monks breakfasting in Los Angeles. Although they were ordained in Thailand, they seem comfortable with some of the physical differences in another culture, such as the food that is foreign to them. However, they have maintained their traditional dress while abroad, and they have also undoubtedly maintained their values and attitudes—things that a photo cannot capture.

FIGURE 2.1 Cultural Influences on International Business

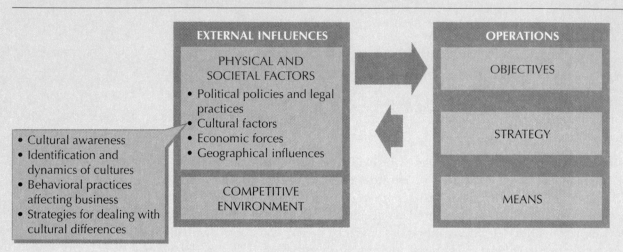

integral part of external environments. This chapter will first examine cultural awareness, especially the need for building it. Second, the chapter will discuss the causes of cultural differences, rigidities, and changes. Third, the chapter will describe behavioral factors that affect the conduct of business internationally. Finally, the chapter will explore why businesses and individuals adjust—or don't adjust—to another culture.

CULTURAL AWARENESS

Businesspeople agree that cultural differences exist but disagree on what they are.

Building cultural awareness is not an easy task, and no foolproof method exists for doing so. As we just said, culture consists of specific learned norms based on attitudes, values, and beliefs, all of which exist in every nation. Visitors remark on cultural differences, experts write about them, and international businesspeople find that they affect operations. Yet, controversy surrounds these differences because people disagree on what they are, whether they are widespread or exceptional differences, and whether the differences are deep-seated or superficial. Further, culture cannot easily be isolated from such factors as economic and political conditions. For example, an opinion survey of a country's citizens that measures, say, attitudes toward buying a new product may reflect a response to temporary economic conditions rather than basic values and beliefs that will have lasting effects on the product's acceptance.

Problem areas that can hinder managers' cultural awareness are
- **Subconscious reactions to circumstances**
- **Assuming all societal subgroups are similar**

Some differences, such as those regarding acceptable attire, are discerned easily; others may be more difficult to perceive. For example, all people have culturally ingrained responses to given situations and sometimes expect that people from other cultures will respond the same way as people in their own culture do. In business, people usually assume that others with similar titles will have comparable duties and privileges—an assumption that is often false. In the PRI case, the British salesmen budgeted their time and so regarded drinking coffee and chatting about nonbusiness activities in a café as "doing nothing," especially if there was "work to be done." In fact, their compensation system did not give them the privilege of spending much time on each business transaction. The Arab businessmen had no compulsion to finish at a given time, viewed time spent in a café as "doing something," and considered "small talk" an indication of whether they could get along with potential business partners. Because the Englishmen believed "you shouldn't mix business and pleasure," they became irritated when friends of the Arab businessmen joined their conversations. In contrast, the Arabs felt "people are more important than business" and saw nothing private about business transactions.

Some people seem to have an innate ability to do and say the right thing at the right time and others offend unintentionally or misrepresent what they want to convey. Nevertheless, there is general agreement that businesspeople can improve their awareness and sensitivity and that training about other cultures will enhance the likelihood of succeeding in those cultures.

Researching descriptions of a specific culture can be instructive. But managers must carefully assess the information they gather because it sometimes presents unwarranted stereotypes, offers an assessment of only a segment of the particular country, or reports outdated information. In a given society, managers can also observe the behavior of those people who have the respect they would like themselves. Of course, it helps to study the overseas market directly. Samsung, Korea's largest company, is experimenting with a cultural awareness program that sends employees abroad for a year. In the United States, for example, Samsung employees visit malls, watch people, and try to develop international tastes. The company is convinced this program will pay off in more astute judgments about what customers want.[2]

There are so many cultural variations that businesspeople cannot expect to memorize all of them for every country. Wide variations exist even in addressing people. For example, it may be difficult to know whether to use a given name or surname, which of several surnames to use, and whether a wife takes her husband's name.[3] Making a mistake may be construed by foreign businesspeople as ignorance or rudeness, which may jeopardize a business arrangement. Fortunately, there are guidebooks for particular geographical areas, based on the experiences of many successful international managers.[4] A manager also may consult with knowledgeable people at home and abroad, from governmental offices or in the private sector.

Not all companies need to have the same degree of cultural awareness. Nor must a particular company have a consistent degree of awareness during the course of its operations. As we discussed in Chapter 1, companies usually increase foreign operations over time. They may expand their cultural knowledge as they move from one to multiple foreign functions or locations, from similar to dissimilar foreign environments, and from external to internal handling of their international operations. A company that is new to international business may need only a minimal level of cultural awareness, but a highly entrenched company needs a high level of awareness because of its multifunctional operations in multiple countries.

When a company engages in few foreign functions—for example, just exporting its home-country production—it must be aware of only those cultural factors that may influence its marketing program. Consider advertising, which may be affected by the target market's perception of different words and images. A company undertaking a purely resource-seeking foreign activity by manufacturing abroad can ignore the effects of cultural variables on advertising but must consider factors that may influence management of a foreign workforce, such as management styles and operational practices

A company's need for cultural knowledge increases as

- **Its number of foreign functions increases**
- **The number of countries of operations increases**
- **It moves from external to internal handling of operations**

most likely to motivate its workforce. For multifunctional activities, such as producing and selling a product in a foreign country, a company must be concerned with a wide array of cultural relationships. The more countries in which a company does business, the more cultural nuances it must consider.

A company may handle foreign operations on its own or contract with another company to handle them. The risk of making operating mistakes because of cultural misunderstandings goes down if it turns foreign operations over to another company at home or abroad that is experienced in the foreign country. If the operations are contracted to a company abroad, then each company needs some cultural awareness to anticipate and understand the other company's reactions.

IDENTIFICATION AND DYNAMICS OF CULTURES

Cultures are elusive to study. There is no universally satisfactory definition of the domain of a culture. Cultures consist of people with shared attitudes, values, and beliefs; people simultaneously belong to national, ethnic, professional, and organizational cultures. At the same time, individual and group attitudes, values, and beliefs evolve. In the following discussion, we will first explain why nations are a useful, but not perfect, cultural reference for international business. Next, we'll discuss why cultures develop and change. Finally, we'll show the role of language and religion as stabilizing influences on culture.

THE NATION AS A POINT OF REFERENCE

The nation is a useful definition of society because

- **Similarity among people is a cause and an effect of national boundaries**
- **Laws apply primarily along national lines**

The nation provides a workable definition of a culture for international business because basic similarity among people is both a cause and an effect of national boundaries. The laws governing business operations also apply primarily along national lines. Within the bounds of a nation are people who share essential attributes, such as values, language, and race. There is a feeling of "we" whereas foreigners are "they." National identity is perpetuated through rites and symbols of the country—flags, parades, rallies—and a common perception of their history through the preservation of national sites, documents, monuments, and museums. These shared attributes do not mean that everyone in a country is alike. Nor do they suggest that each country is unique in all respects. In fact, nations usually include various subcultures, ethnic groups, races, and classes. However, the nation legitimizes itself by being the mediator of the different interests.[5] Failure to serve adequately in this mediating role may cause the nation to dissolve. Nevertheless, each nation possesses certain human, demographic, and behavioral characteristics that constitute its national identity and that may affect a company's methods of conducting business effectively in that country.

Managers find country-by-country analysis difficult because

- **Not everyone in a country is alike**
- **Variations within some countries are great**
- **Similarities link groups from different countries**

Similarities can link groups from different nations more closely than groups within a nation. For instance, regardless of the nation examined, people in urban areas differ in certain attitudes from people in rural areas, and managers have different work attitudes than production workers do.[6] Thus managers in countries A and B may hold more similar values with each other than either person holds with production workers in his or her own country. When international businesspeople compare nations, they must be careful to examine relevant groups, such as differentiating between people in rural and urban areas of a country when predicting what will be accepted.

CULTURAL FORMATION AND DYNAMICS

Culture is transmitted in various ways—from parent to child, teacher to pupil, social leader to follower, and one peer to another. The parent-to-child route is especially important in the transmission of religious and political affiliations.[7] Developmental psychologists believe that by age 10 most children have their basic value systems firmly in place, after which they do not make changes easily. These basic values include such concepts as evil versus good, dirty versus clean, ugly versus beautiful, unnatural versus natural, abnormal versus normal, paradoxical versus logical, and irrational versus rational.[8] The relative inflexibility of values helps explain the deeply rooted opinions of the Arab and British businessmen in the opening case in terms of the former's belief that "people are more important than business" and the latter's that "time is money."

However, individual and societal values and customs may evolve over time. Examining this evolution and its reasons is a useful indicator of the changing acceptance of practices that international companies might like to introduce. Change may come about through choice or imposition.[9] Change by choice may take place as a reaction to social and economic changes that present new alternatives. For example, when rural people choose to accept factory jobs, they change their customs by working regular hours that don't allow the social interaction with their families during work hours that farmwork allowed. Change by imposition, sometimes called **cultural imperialism**, has occurred, for example, when countries introduced their legal systems into their colonies by prohibiting established practices and defining them as criminal.[10] The introduction of some, but not all, elements of an outside culture often is called *creolization, indigenization*, or *cultural diffusion*. International business increases changes in cultures, and governments have often limited such business to protect their national cultures.

Cultural value systems are set early in life but may change through

- **Choice or imposition**
- **Contact with other cultures**

LANGUAGE AS A CULTURAL STABILIZER

In addition to national boundaries and geographical obstacles, language is a factor that greatly affects cultural stability. Map 2.2 shows the world's major language groups. When people from different areas speak the same language, culture spreads easily. That helps explain why more cultural similarity exists among English-speaking countries or among Spanish-speaking ones than between English-speaking and Spanish-speaking countries. Map 2.2 does not include most of the world's approximately 6,000 languages spoken in small areas by few people. When people speak only a language with few speakers, especially if those speakers are concentrated in a small geographic area, they tend to adhere to their culture because meaningful contact with others is difficult. For example, in Guatemala, the official language is Spanish. However, there are twenty-two ethnic groups, three main ethnic languages, and derivations of those three. Many parents do not permit their children to go to school because the public schools use Spanish. They fear that by learning Spanish, their children will lose their values and customs.[11] The ethnic differences in Guatemala (and in some other countries) have led to political strife that undermines the ability to conduct business. The language diversity has also created problems for companies in integrating their workforces and marketing products on a truly national level.

A common language within countries is a unifying force.

MAP 2.2
Major Languages
of the World

Thousands of languages are spoken globally, but a few dominate. This map shows the 11 major ones. Note that English, French, or Spanish is the primary language in over half of the world's countries. Some other languages, such as Mandarin and Hindi, are prevalent in only one country but are important to international business because of the number of speakers.

Source: From *The Economist Atlas, Second Edition* © 1989 and 1991 by The Economist Books Ltd. Reprinted by permission of Henry Holt and Company, LLC. The number of native speakers is taken from *The World Almanac and Book of Facts, 1999,* Funk & Wagnalls, p. 700.

The English, French, and Spanish languages have such widespread acceptance (they are spoken prevalently in 44, 27, and 20 countries, respectively) that native speakers of these languages don't generally try to learn other languages as much as do speakers of languages that are official in only one country, such as Finnish and Greek. Commerce can occur more easily with other nations that share the same language because expensive and time-consuming translation is unnecessary. When people study a second language they usually choose one that is useful in dealing with other countries, especially in commerce. Figure 2.2 shows the share of world output accounted for by major language groups. It is easy to see why English is the most important second language and why much of the world's business is conducted in English.

English, especially American English, words are making their way into languages worldwide, partly because the United States originates so much new technology, products, and services. When a new product or service enters another language area, it may

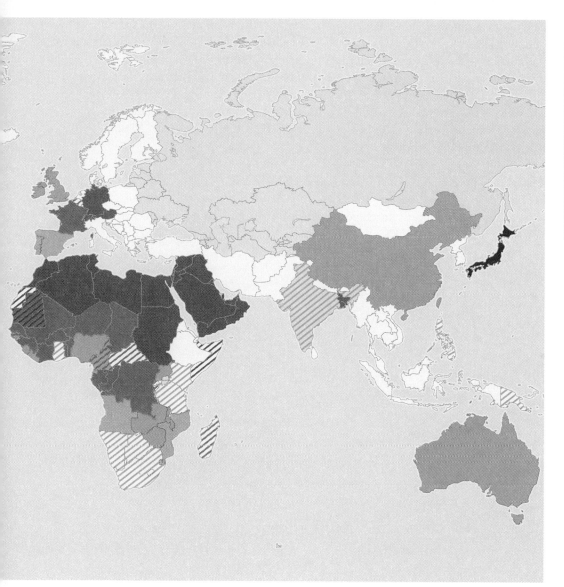

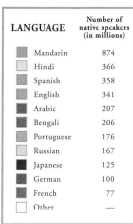

LANGUAGE	Number of native speakers (in millions)
Mandarin	874
Hindi	366
Spanish	358
English	341
Arabic	207
Bengali	206
Portuguese	176
Russian	167
Japanese	125
German	100
French	77
Other	—

FIGURE 2.2 Portion of World Output Accounted for by Major Language Groups

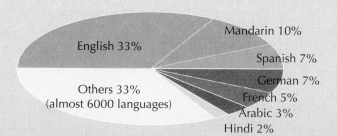

English 33%

Mandarin 10%

Spanish 7%

German 7%

French 5%

Arabic 3%

Hindi 2%

Others 33%
(almost 6000 languages)

The portion of world output (the value of goods and services produced) from language groups differs substantially from the portion of people in each language group that Map 2.2 shows. People tend to learn a second language because of their need to communicate where output takes place.

Source: Data were taken from estimates by Brian Reading, "Speaking in Tongues Won't Do at Work," *Financial Times,* January 17–18, 1998, p. xxi.

take on an Anglicized name. For example, Russians call tight denim pants *dzhinsi* (pronounced "jeansy") the French call a self-service restaurant *le self*, and Lithuanians go to the theater to see moving *pikceris*.[12] An estimated 20,000 English words have entered the Japanese language. However, some countries, such as Finland, have largely developed their own new words rather than using Anglicized versions. Because countries see language as an integral part of their cultures, they sometimes regulate their languages, such as by requiring that all business transactions be conducted and all "Made in _____" labels be printed in their language.

RELIGION AS A CULTURAL STABILIZER

Religion is a strong shaper of values. Map 2.3 shows the distribution of the world's major religions. Within these religions—Buddhism, Christianity, Hinduism, Islam, and

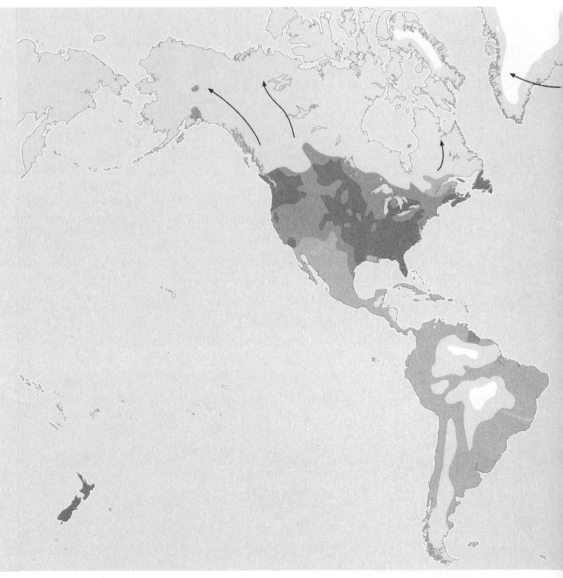

MAP 2.3
Major Religions of the World

Almost all regions have people of various religious beliefs, but a region's culture is most influenced by its dominant religion. Some religions' areas of dominance transcend national boundaries. The dominant religion usually influences legal and customary business practices, such as required days off for religious observance.

Source: Mapping © Bartholomews, 1990. Extract taken from Plate 5 of *The Times Comprehensive Atlas of the World*, 8th Edition, MM-0397-300. Numbers are taken from *The World Almanac and Book of Facts*, 1999, Funk & Wagnells, p. 731.

Judaism—are many factions whose specific beliefs may affect business, such as prohibiting the sale of certain products or work at certain times. For example, McDonald's agreed not to serve beef in India because of criticism from Hindus,[13] and El Al, the Israeli national airline, does not fly on Saturday, the holy day in Judaism. But not all nations that practice the same religion have the same constraints on business. For example, Friday is normally not a workday in predominantly Muslim countries because it is a day of worship; however, Turkey is a secular Muslim country that adheres to the Christian work calendar to be more productive in business dealings with Europe. In countries where rival religions vie for political control, the resulting strife can cause so much unrest that business is disrupted through property damage, difficulty in getting supplies, and the inability to reach customers. In recent years, violence among religious groups has erupted in India, Lebanon, Northern Ireland, and Yugoslavia.

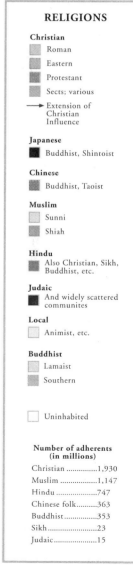

RELIGIONS

Christian
Roman
Eastern
Protestant
Sects; various
→ Extension of Christian Influence

Japanese
Buddhist, Shintoist

Chinese
Buddhist, Taoist

Muslim
Sunni
Shiah

Hindu
Also Christian, Sikh, Buddhist, etc.

Judaic
And widely scattered communites

Local
Animist, etc.

Buddhist
Lamaist
Southern

Uninhabited

Number of adherents (in millions)

Christian 1,930
Muslim 1,147
Hindu 747
Chinese folk..........363
Buddhist...............353
Sikh 23
Judaic....................15

BEHAVIORAL PRACTICES AFFECTING BUSINESS

Attitudes and values affect business behavior, from what products to sell to how to organize, finance, manage, and control operations. Researchers define cultural variables differently, attaching different names to slightly different and sometimes overlapping attitudes and values. Similarly, businesspeople define business functions differently. The result is that there are thousands of possible ways of relating culture to business—too many to discuss exhaustively in one chapter. The following discussion merely highlights those that international managers and academic researchers have most noted to influence business practices differently from one country to another. We shall further discuss the effect of these and other cultural variables in later chapters.

SOCIAL STRATIFICATION SYSTEMS

Group affiliations can be
- **Ascribed or acquired**
- **A reflection of resources and position**

Every culture values some people more highly than others, and this dictates a person's class or status within that culture. In business, this might mean valuing members of managerial groups more highly than members of production groups. However, what determines the ranking—or social stratification—varies substantially from country to country. A person's ranking is partly determined by individual factors and partly by the person's affiliation or membership in given groups. Affiliations determined by birth—known as **ascribed group memberships**—include those based on gender, family, age, caste, and ethnic, racial, or national origin. Affiliations not determined by birth are called **acquired group memberships** and include those based on religion, political affiliation, and professional and other associations. Social stratification affects such business functions as marketing. For example, companies choose to use people in their advertisements that their target market admires or associates. Further, stratification affects employment practices. A study comparing banks' hiring, promotion, compensation, and staff reduction showed that they differed by nationality on all four dimensions. For example, when the banks needed to make staff reductions, British banks were most prone to discharge on the basis of performance-to-salary (for example, a middle-age manager with high-salary and average performance) and German banks to discharge young managers (regardless of performance) who could find jobs more easily.[14]

Managers must consider local stratification systems when hiring personnel.

The following discussion centers on some of the characteristics and group membership that influence a person's ranking differently from country to country. In addition, two other factors are often very important—education (especially where it was received) and social connections (having friends in the highest places).[15]

Businesses reward competence highly in some societies.

Role of Competence Some nations, such as the United States, base a person's eligibility for jobs and promotions primarily on competence, creating a work environment driven more by competition than by cooperation. The United States values competence so highly that legislative and judicial actions aim to prevent discrimination on the basis of sex, race, age, and religion, even though such legislation is not fully effective. But in some other cultures, individual competence is of secondary importance. Whatever factor has primary importance—whether seniority, as in Japan (where the workplace is characterized more by cooperation than by competition), or some other quality—will largely influence a person's eligibility for certain positions and compensation.

Egalitarian societies place less importance on ascribed group memberships.

The more egalitarian, or open, a society, the less difference ascribed group membership makes for receiving rewards. However, in less open societies, laws sometimes enforce or are a means to overcome distinctions on the basis of ascribed group memberships. Laws requiring racial or ethnic quotas usually aim to counter discrimination. For example, Malaysia has long had employment quotas for three ethnic groups—Malays, Chinese, and Indians—to protect employment opportunities for Malays. South Africa has adopted quotas for blacks, women, and physically handicapped.[16] However, critics argue that quotas favor less competent over more competent people and are, therefore, discriminatory. In other cases, group memberships prevent large numbers of people from getting the preparation that would equally qualify them for jobs. For example, in the Middle Eastern and North African countries, the mean years of schooling for women is two to three years lower than for men. In Saudi Arabia, the difference is four years.[17] Companies face very different workforces from one country to another in terms of who is qualified and who among the qualified they can and do hire. In some places, such as Malaysia and South Africa, they must also maintain expensive record-keeping systems.

Even when individuals qualify for certain positions and there are no legal barriers to hiring them, social obstacles, such as public opinion in a company's home country against the use of child labor, may make companies wary of employing them abroad. Further, other workers, customers, local stockholders, or governmental officials may oppose certain groups, making it even more difficult for companies to hire them.

Gender-Based Groups   There are strong country-specific differences in attitudes toward males and females. In China and India there is an extreme degree of male preference. Because of their governmental and economic restrictions on family size and the desire to have a son to carry on the family name, the practices of aborting female fetuses and killing female babies are widespread despite governmental opposition. However, many Chinese and Indian females have been successful in business and government positions. In Afghanistan, the 1996 takeover by religious fundamentalists led to prohibiting women from attending school and working.[18]

Recall that in the PRI case Angela Clarke could not get permission to enter Saudi Arabia, a country with an extreme degree of behavioral rigidity toward gender. In Saudi Arabia, schools and most of social life separate the sexes, and women cannot drive cars. Few women work outside the home, and most of their work in professions entails little or no contact with males, such as teaching or providing medical treatment to other women. When women do work in integrated organizations, Saudis commonly place partitions between them and male employees. Pizza Hut adapted to Saudi customs by installing two dining rooms—one for single men and one for families. (Single women do not go out without their families.)

Even among countries in which women constitute a large portion of the working population, vast differences exist in the types of jobs regarded as "male" or "female." For example, in the United States, women fill 40 percent of administrative and managerial positions while in Japan, that figure is less than 10 percent.[19]

Culturally mandated male and female behaviors may carry over to other aspects of the work environment. For example, Molex, a U.S. manufacturing company in Japan, invited its Japanese workers and their spouses to a company dinner one evening. No Japanese females attended. To comply with Japanese standards, the company now has a "family day," which the women feel comfortable attending.[20]

Country-by-country attitudes vary toward
- **Male and female roles**
- **Respect for age**
- **Family ties**

Barriers to employment based on gender are easing substantially in many parts of the world. Statistical and attitudinal studies from even a few years ago may be considered unreliable. One change has been the growing numbers of women and men in the United States employed in occupations previously dominated by the other gender. Even in Saudi Arabia women now work at hotel reception desks.[21]

Age-Based Groups   Many cultures assume that age and wisdom are correlated. These cultures usually have a seniority-based system of advancement. But in the United States, retirement at age 60 or 65 was mandatory in most companies until the 1980s, revealing that youth has the professional advantage. For example, U.S. television scriptwriters complain of an inability of finding jobs after age 30. The emphasis on youth also explains the big U.S. market for products aimed to make people look younger. However, this esteem for youth has not carried over into the U.S. political realm where there is no mandatory retirement age. This difference in attitude toward age between business and government illustrates the issue's complexity. Clearly, companies need to examine reference groups when considering whom they may hire and how best to promote their products.

Family-Based Groups   In some societies, the family is the most important group membership. An individual's acceptance in society largely depends on the family's social status or respectability rather than on the individual's achievement. Because family ties are so strong, there also may be a compulsion to cooperate closely within the family unit while distrusting relationships with others. In societies where there is low trust outside the family, such as in China and southern Italy, small family-run companies are more successful than large business organizations. But the difficulty of sustaining family-run companies retards these countries' economic development because large-scale operations are often necessary for many products.[22]

The perception of what jobs are "best" varies somewhat among countries.

Occupation   In every society, people perceive certain occupations as having greater economic and social prestige than others. This perception usually determines the numbers and qualifications of people who will seek employment in a given occupation. Although some perceptions are universal (for example, professionals outrank street cleaners), there are some international differences. For instance, university professors are more influential as opinion leaders in Korea and Japan than in the United States and the United Kingdom.[23] The importance of business as a profession also is predictive of how difficult it may be for an international company to hire qualified managers. If, say, jobs in business are not as desirable as jobs in government, a company may have to spend more to attract and train local managers, or it may have to rely more on managers transferred from abroad.

Another international difference is citizens' desire to work as entrepreneurs rather than for an organization. For example, the Belgians and the French, more than most other nationalities, prefer, if possible, to go into business for themselves. Thus Belgium and France have more retail establishments per capita than most other countries. Owning a small or medium-size enterprise—rather than earning more income—is a means for Belgian and French people to move up socially from the working class. Further, psychological studies show that Belgian and French workers place a greater importance on personal independence from the organizations employing them than do workers in many other countries.[24] An implication is that foreign retailers operating in Belgium and France encounter competition much more from small local retailers than in most other countries.

Jobs with low prestige usually go to people whose skills are in low demand. In the United States occupations such as baby-sitting, delivering newspapers, and carrying groceries traditionally go to teenagers, who leave these jobs as they age and gain additional training. In most poor countries, these are not transient occupations but are filled by adults who have very little opportunity to move on to more rewarding positions.

MOTIVATION

Employees who are motivated to work long and hard are normally more productive than those who are not. On an aggregate basis, this influences economic development positively. For example, a study on why some areas of Latin America, such as Antioquia in Colombia, developed a higher economic level than others attributed differences to an early development of a strong work ethic.[25] International companies are concerned about economic development because markets for their products grow as economies grow. They are also interested in motivation because higher productivity normally reduces production costs. Studies show substantial country-to-country differences in how much people are motivated to work and why. The following discussion summarizes the major differences.

Materialism and Leisure   Max Weber, an early twentieth-century German sociologist, observed that the predominantly Protestant countries were the most economically developed. Weber attributed this fact to an attitude he labeled "the Protestant ethic." According to Weber, the Protestant ethic—an outgrowth of the Reformation—was when people viewed work as a means of salvation. Adhering to this view, people preferred to transform productivity into material gains rather than into leisure time. Historically, there is strong evidence that the desire for material wealth is a prime incentive for the work that leads to economic development.[26]

Some societies take less leisure time than others, which means they work longer hours, take fewer days for holidays and vacation, and spend less time and money on leisure. For example, on average, the Japanese take less leisure than do people in any other wealthy country. In the United States, another country where incomes probably allow for considerably more leisure time than most people use, there is still much disdain, on the one hand, for the millionaire socialite who contributes nothing to society and, on the other hand, for the person who receives unemployment benefits. People who are forced to give up work, such as retirees, complain of their inability to do anything "useful." This view contrasts with views in some other societies. In much of Europe, the aristocracy holds the highest rank in the social structure, a rank associated with leisure—but only leisure that is broadening. Leisure time is a sign of upward mobility.[27] In parts of some poor countries, such as in rural India, living a simple life with minimum material achievements is a desirable end in itself. When there are productivity gains, people are prone to work less rather than earn and buy more.

However, most people today consider personal economic achievement to be commendable regardless of whether they live in wealthy or poor countries. Most people believe they would be happy with just "a little bit more," until they have that "little bit

In the most economically developed countries, most people work to satisfy materialistic needs.

Good international managers know that the motives for working vary in different countries.

Employees' work attitudes may change as they achieve economic gains.

more," which then turns out to be "not quite enough." Nevertheless, countries differ in their degree of materialism. For example, some leaders in poor countries are rejecting the labels of "traditional" for themselves and "progressive" for the higher-income countries, as they stress the need for a culture that combines material comforts with spirituality.[28]

People are more eager to work if

- **Rewards for success are high**
- **There is some uncertainty of success**

Expectation of Success and Reward   One factor that motivates a person's behavior toward working is the perceived likelihood of success and reward. Generally, people have little enthusiasm for efforts that seem too easy or too difficult, where the probability of either success or failure seems almost certain. For instance, few of us would be eager to run a foot race against either a snail or a racehorse because the outcome in either case is too certain. Our highest enthusiasm occurs when the uncertainty is high—in this example, probably when racing another human of roughly equal ability. The reward for successfully completing an effort, such as winning a race, may be high or low as well. People usually will work harder at any task when the reward for success is high compared with that of failure.

The same tasks performed in different countries will have different probabilities of success. The same tasks in different countries will also have different rewards for success and different consequences for failure. In cultures where the probability of economic failure is almost certain and the perceived rewards of success are low, there is a tendency to view work as necessary but unsatisfying. This attitude may exist in harsh climates, in very poor areas, or in subcultures that are the objects of discrimination because people see little self-benefit from their efforts. In areas such as Scandinavia, where the tax structures and public policies redistribute income from higher earners to lower earners, enthusiasm for work is low. The greatest enthusiasm for work exists when high uncertainty of success is combined with the likelihood of a very positive reward for success and little or none for failure.[29]

Masculinity Index   The average interest in career success varies substantially among countries. For example, one study compared the attitudes of employees from 50 countries on a "masculinity index." Employees with a high masculinity score were those who admired the successful achiever, had little sympathy for the unfortunate, and preferred to be the best rather than on a par with others. They had a money-and-things orientation rather than a people orientation, a belief that it is better "to live to work" than "to work to live," and a preference for performance and growth over quality of life and the environment. Employees from countries with high scores on the masculinity index also believed that roles should be differentiated by gender and that men should dominate. The countries with the highest masculinity scores were Japan, Austria, Venezuela, and Switzerland. Those with the lowest scores were Sweden, Norway, the Netherlands, and Denmark.[30] These attitudinal differences help explain why local managers typically react differently from country to country, sometimes in ways that an international manager may neither expect nor wish. For instance, a typical purchasing manager from a low masculinity country has a high need for smooth social relationships that transforms into more concern with developing an amiable and continuing relationship with suppliers than with, say, reducing costs or speeding delivery. Or local managers in some countries may place such organizational goals as employee and social welfare ahead of the foreign company's priorities for growth and efficiency.

Need Hierarchy   The hierarchy of needs is a well-known motivation theory. According to the theory, people try to fulfill lower-order needs sufficiently before moving on to higher ones.[31] People will work to satisfy a need, but once it is fulfilled, it is no longer a motivator. The Calvin and Hobbes cartoon in Figure 2.3 ties the hierarchy of needs theory to materialism theory humorously. Because lower-order needs are more important than higher-order ones, they must be nearly fulfilled before any higher-order need becomes an effective motivator. For instance, the most basic needs are physiological, including the needs for food, water, and sex. One needs to satisfy or nearly satisfy (say, 85 percent satisfied) a physiological need before a security need becomes a powerful motivator. Then one must satisfy the security need, centering around a safe physical and emotional environment, before triggering the need for affiliation, or social belonging (peer acceptance). After filling the affiliation need, a person may seek an esteem need—the need to bolster one's self-image through receipt of recognition, attention, and appreciation. The highest-order need is that for self-actualization, which means self-fulfillment, or becoming all that it is possible for one to become.

The hierarchy of needs theory is helpful for differentiating the reward preferences of employees in different countries. In very poor countries, a company can motivate workers simply by providing enough compensation for food and shelter. Elsewhere, other needs will motivate workers. Researchers have noted that people from different countries attach different degrees of importance to needs and even rank some of the higher-order needs differently.

The ranking of needs differs among countries.

FIGURE 2.3

A fulfilled need is no longer a motivator. Materialism motivates work, which leads to productivity and economic growth.

RELATIONSHIP PREFERENCES

We have discussed two categories of behavioral practices affecting business—social stratification systems and motivation. Within social stratification systems, not everyone within a reference group is necessarily an equal. Further, there may be strong or weak pressures for conformity within one's group. In both cases, there are national differences in norms that influence management styles and marketing behavior. The following section discusses the values underlying these differences.

There are national variations in preference for autocratic or consultative management.

Power Distance   Employee preferences in how to interact with their bosses, subordinates, and peers varies substantially internationally. There is considerable anecdotal evidence that they perform better when their interactions fit their preferences. Therefore, companies may need to align their management styles to those preferences.

Power distance is a term describing the relationship between superiors and subordinates. Where power distance is high, people prefer little consultation between superiors and subordinates—usually wanting and having an autocratic or paternalistic management style in their organizations. Malaysia, Guatemala, Panama, and the Philippines are countries with high power distance. Austria, Israel, Denmark, and New Zealand are countries with low power distance, where people prefer and usually have consultative styles.[32]

If an international company transferred typical Austrian managers to Malaysia, these managers might consult with their subordinates in an attempt to improve their work. However, these efforts might make subordinates feel so uncomfortable that their performance deteriorates rather than improves.

Interestingly, those employees preferring an autocratic style of superior–subordinate relationship are also willing to accept decision making by a majority of subordinates. What they don't accept is the interaction between superiors and subordinates in decision making. Clearly, it may be easier for organizations to initiate certain types of worker-participation methods in some countries than in others.

"Safe" work environments motivate collectivists. Challenges motivate individualists.

Individualism versus Collectivism   Studies have compared employees' inclinations toward *individualism* or *collectivism*. Countries that rank individualism the highest are the United States, Australia, the United Kingdom, Canada, and the Netherlands. Attributes of individualism are low dependence on the organization and a desire for personal time, freedom, and challenge. Countries that rank high in collectivism (opposite of individualism) are Guatemala, Ecuador, Panama, Venezuela, and Colombia. Attributes of collectivism are dependence on the organization and a desire for training, good physical conditions, and benefits. In those countries with high individualism, self-actualization will be a prime motivator because employees want challenges. However, in countries with high collectivism, the provision of a safe physical and emotional environment (security need) will be a prime motivator.[33]

The degree of individualism and collectivism also influences how employees interact with their colleagues. Japan has a much more collectivist culture than the United States does, especially concerning the work group, and this causes contrasts at work.[34] For example, a U.S. scientist invited to work in a Japanese laboratory was treated as an outsider until he demonstrated his willingness to subordinate his personal interests to those of the group. He did so by mopping the lab floor for several weeks, after which he was invited to join the group.[35] In contrast, Levi's introduced team-based production for U.S. plants because its management had observed high productivity from that system in Asian plants. U.S. employees—especially the faster, more skilled ones—detested the system, productivity decreased, and Levi's abandoned the team-based production system.[36]

Although China and Mexico are also characterized as collectivist cultures, they differ from Japan in that the collectivism is based on kinship that does not carry over to the workplace.[37] Further, the concept of family in China and Mexico includes not only a nuclear family (a husband, wife, and minor children) but also a vertically extended family (several generations) and perhaps a horizontally extended one (aunts, uncles, and cousins). This difference affects business in several ways. First, material rewards from an individual's work may be less motivating because these rewards are divided among more people. Second, geographical mobility is reduced because relocation means other members of a family also have to find new jobs. Even where extended families do not live together, mobility may be reduced because people prefer to remain near relatives. Third, purchasing decisions may be more complicated because of the interrelated roles of family members. Fourth, security and social needs may be met more extensively at home than in the workplace.

Where collectivism is high, companies find their best marketing successes when emphasizing advertising themes that express group (rather than individual) values. For example, Marlboro cigarettes has had better success in Asian markets than Camel cigarettes, partially because of using group themes more.[38]

RISK-TAKING BEHAVIOR

Nationalities differ in how happy people are to accept things the way they are and how they feel about controlling their destinies. The following discussion examines three aspects of risk-taking behavior—uncertainty avoidance, trust, and fatalism—across nations.

Uncertainty Avoidance   Studies on uncertainty avoidance show that in Greece, Portugal, Guatemala, Uruguay, El Salvador, and Belgium—countries with the highest score on uncertainty avoidance—employees prefer set rules that are not to be broken even if breaking them is in the company's best interest. Further, these employees plan to work for the company a long time, preferring the certainty of their present positions over the uncertainty of better advancement opportunities elsewhere.[39] When uncertainty avoidance is high, superiors may need to be more precise and assured in the directions they give to subordinates because the subordinates are not prone to figure out and act in the company's best interests. At the low end of the uncertainty avoidance scale are Singapore, Jamaica, Denmark, Sweden, Hong Kong, the United Kingdom, and Ireland.

In countries characterized by high uncertainty avoidance, few consumers are prepared to take the social risk of trying a new product first. This is very important to firms choosing where to introduce new products. For example, 40 percent of Gillette's sales come from products it has introduced in the last five years. It may be advantageous for Gillette to enter markets such as Denmark and the United Kingdom before entering those in Belgium and Portugal.[40]

Trust   Surveys that measure trust among countries by having respondents evaluate such statements as "Most people can be trusted" and "You can't be too careful in dealing with people" indicate substantial international differences. For example, 61.2 percent of

---

Nationalities differ in
- **Ease of handling uncertainties**
- **Degree of trust among people**
- **Attitudes of self-determination and fatalism**

Norwegians think that most people are trustworthy, whereas only 6.7 percent of Brazilians feel that way. Where trust is high, there tends to be a lower cost of doing business because managers do not have to spend time foreseeing every possible contingency and then monitoring every action for compliance in business relationships. Instead, they can spend time investing and innovating.[41] Norwegians and Brazilians may actually be responding to the conditions existing in their respective countries. If a Norwegian businessperson goes to Brazil, he or she may act too naively, and when a Brazilian goes to Norway, he or she may act too cautiously.

Fatalism   If people believe strongly in self-determination, they may be willing to work hard to achieve goals and take responsibility for performance. But a belief in fatalism, that every event is inevitable, may prevent people from accepting this basic cause–effect relationship. The affect on business in countries with a high degree of fatalism is that people plan less for contingencies. For example, they may be reluctant to buy insurance. In this regard, religious differences play a part. Conservative or fundamentalist Christian, Buddhist, Hindu, and Muslim societies tend to view occurrences as "the will of God."

INFORMATION AND TASK PROCESSING

The nineteenth-century author Margaret Hungerford wrote, "Beauty is altogether in the eye of the beholder." People do perceive and reach conclusions differently. So do cultures. Further, once they have what they perceive as accurate information, they handle this information differently. The following discussion examines how people from different cultures perceive, obtain, and process information.

> All languages are complex and reflective of environment. Without knowing the language of the area, a manager may not perceive the subtleties of that environment.

Perception of Cues   We perceive cues selectively. We may identify what things are by means of any of our senses (sight, smell, touch, sound, or taste) and in various ways within each sense. For example, through vision we can sense color, depth, and shape. The cues people use to perceive things differ among societies. The reason is partly physiological. For example, genetic differences in eye pigmentation enable some groups to differentiate colors more finely than others. It also is partly cultural. For example, a richness of descriptive vocabulary can allow people to express very subtle differences in color.[42] Further, this difference in richness allows each culture to perceive some subjects more precisely than other cultures perceive them. For example, Arabic has more than 6,000 different words for camels, their body parts, and the equipment associated with them.[43] Arabic speakers can note things about camels that are likely concealed to other speakers.

> In information processing, it helps managers to know whether cultures favor
> - Focused or broad information
> - Sequential or simultaneous handling of situations
> - Handling principles or small issues first

Obtaining Information   In spite of vast differences within countries, some, such as the United States and those in northern Europe, are categorized as being **low-context cultures**—that is, most people consider relevant only firsthand information that bears directly on the decision they need to make. In business, they spend little time on "small talk" and say things directly. However, other countries, such as in southern Europe, are **high-context cultures**—that is, most people consider that peripheral information is valuable to decision making and infer meanings from things said indirectly. When managers from the two types of cultures deal with each other, the low-context individuals may believe the high-context ones are inefficient and time wasters. The high-context individuals may believe the low-context ones are too aggressive to be trusted.

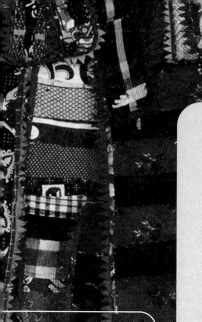

Ethical Dilemmas and Social Responsibility
TO INTERVENE OR NOT TO INTERVENE

In the international arena, companies, whether they know it or not, have two basic views about cultural practices that contradict their values. On the one hand, *relativism* affirms that ethical truths depend on the groups holding them, making intervention unethical. Adherence to other cultures is itself a Western cultural phenomenon that goes back at least as far as St. Ambrose's fourth-century advice: "When in Rome, do as the Romans do." On the other hand, *normativism* holds that there are universal standards of behavior (based on their own values) that all cultures should follow, making nonintervention unethical. Neither international companies nor their employees are expected always to adhere to a host society's norms. Exposure to certain practices may be traumatic to foreigners. For example, many practices that Western culture considers "wrong" are customary elsewhere, such as slavery, polygamy, concubinage, child marriage, and the burning of widows.[44] Some companies have avoided operating in locales in which such practices occur but others have pressured a host country to change the "wrong" behaviors. For example, complaints from international business leaders induced Papua New Guinea, which depends on foreign investment, to make payback killings a crime.[45]

Other behavioral differences may violate a manager's own ethical code to a lesser degree. For example, using gifts and flattery to gain business advantages may seem unethical to some people. But in many countries, particularly in Asia, failure to bring a small gift may not only be a breach of etiquette but also an indication of a lack of interest in doing business. The difference arises because most Westerners express gratitude verbally, and most Asians, particularly Chinese, express appreciation tangibly, such as with gifts.[46] Giving gifts to government officials may be particularly perplexing to Westerners. In many places such gifts or payments are customary in obtaining governmental services or contracts. Although this practice may be condemned officially, it is so embedded in local custom that it has nearly the prescribed enforcement of common law. In Mexico, for example, companies commonly give tips once a month to the mail carrier; otherwise, their mail simply gets lost.[47] The going rate of payment is rather easily ascertained and is usually graduated on the ability to pay. The practice of making payments to government officials is, in effect, a fairly efficient means of taxation in countries that pay civil servants poorly and do not have the means for collecting income taxes. Still, these payments are considered bribes by many multinational enterprises (MNEs), and the practice frequently is viewed by home-country constituents as so unethical that home-country laws against it are enforced in foreign operations.

In situations such as making payments to government officials, companies may operate inefficiently or lose business if they do not comply with local custom. This questions whether operational performance concerns should outweigh violating ethical standards. For example, many businesspeople feel it is more acceptable to give payments to government officials when a large, rather than a small, amount of business is at stake, and when they need to make small, rather than large, payments.

Another thorny ethical question concerns international businesses practices that do not clash with foreign values directly but that nevertheless may undermine the host country's long-term cultural identity. Consider the use of a company's home-country language or cultural artifacts and the introduction of products and work methods that cause changes in social relationships. Host countries have sometimes reacted negatively to such use. For example, Finns have criticized MNEs for introducing non-Finnish architecture,[48] and France fined Bodyshop for using English in its French stores.[49]

The Society for Applied Anthropology, which advises government and nongovernment agencies on instituting change in different cultures, has adopted a code of ethics to protect foreign cultures with which such agencies interact. The code considers whether a project or planned change actually will benefit the target population. Because the definition of what constitutes a benefit depends on cultural value systems, implementing this code is a challenge. Further, there may be balances to consider, such as a trade-off between economic gains for the target population and ending a way of life that gives that population great satisfaction. We often hear of "spiritual poverty in the midst of plenty" meaning aesthetic, philosophical, and human dimensions suffer in favor of economic prosperity. [50] Further, the concept of "quality of life" varies substantially among cultures.[51] The result is that an international company may be criticized as being socially irresponsible if it ignores the total spectrum of human needs for each place in which it operates.

Companies often lack complete information to guide them in advance of taking action abroad. For example, consider the area of human rights. In 1948, before most of today's nations were in existence, the United Nations adopted a Universal Declaration of Human Rights. Government and academic leaders from many countries have criticized the declaration for having too Western an orientation. Some provisions that lack universal acceptance include the right to individual ownership of property, the right to governance through universal secret elections, and the implicit statement that the nuclear family is the fundamental unit of society. In fact, not all countries have explicitly declared their concept of human rights. Without such declaration the accuracy of descriptions of the human rights sentiments of many countries is uncertain.[52]

Information Processing   Information processing is universal in that all cultures categorize, plan, and quantify. All cultures also have ordering and classifying systems. However, sometimes cultures do this differently from one another. In U.S. telephone directories, the entries appear in alphabetical order by last (family) name. In Iceland, entries are organized by first (given) names. Icelandic last names are derived from the father's first name: Jon, the son of Thor, is Jon Thorsson, and his sister's last name is Thorsdottir (daughter of Thor).[53] One needs to understand the different ordering and classifying systems to perform efficiently in a foreign environment. Further, the different ordering and classifying systems create challenges for companies to use global data effectively. Even the use of global personnel directories is problematic because of different alphabetizing systems. Information processing also includes ordering tasks. Cultures such as in northern Europe are called **monochronic,** preferring to work sequentially, such as finishing with one customer before dealing with another. Conversely, **polychronic** southern Europeans are more comfortable in working simultaneously with all the tasks they face. For example, they feel uncomfortable when not dealing immediately with all customers who need service.[54] Imagine the potential misconceptions that can occur. U.S. businesspeople might erroneously believe that their Italian counterparts are uninterested in doing business with them if they fail to give them their undivided attention.

Some cultures will determine principles before they try to resolve small issues (idealism), while other cultures will focus more on details rather than principles (pragmatism). From a business standpoint, the differences manifest information processing in a number of ways. For example, in a society of pragmatists such as the United States, labor disputes tend to focus on specific issues: Increase pay by a dollar per hour. In a society of idealists such as Argentina, labor disputes tend to make less precise demands and to depend instead on mass action, such as general strikes or support of a particular political party, to publicize their principles.

STRATEGIES FOR DEALING WITH CULTURAL DIFFERENCES

After a company identifies cultural differences in the foreign country where it intends to do business, must it alter its customary practices to succeed there? How can it avoid misrepresenting its intents? Can individuals overcome adjustment problems when working abroad? What strategies can companies follow to get host cultures to accept the innovations they would like to introduce? There are no easy answers.

MAKING LITTLE OR NO ADJUSTMENT

Although the PRI case illustrates the folly of not adjusting, such as the salesmens' alienation of Arab businessmen, international companies sometimes have succeeded in introducing new products, technologies, and operating procedures to foreign countries with little adjustment. That's because some of these introductions have not run counter to deep-seated attitudes or because the host society is willing to accept foreign customs as a trade-off for other advantages. Bahrain has permitted the sale of pork products (otherwise outlawed by religious law) as long as they are sold in separate rooms of grocery stores where Muslims can neither work nor shop. Thus, PRI's British employees who were based in Bahrain were not deprived of pork products because of cultural differences.

Often the local society looks on foreigners differently than on its own citizens. For example, Western female flight attendants are permitted to wear jeans and T-shirts when staying overnight in Jidda, Saudi Arabia—clothing local women cannot wear at all.[55] Members of the host society may even feel they are being stereotyped in an uncomplimentary way when foreigners adjust too much.[56] For example, Angela Clarke might have been even less effective for PRI if she had worn the traditional Arab dress and veil because local businessmen may have felt she was mocking their customs. Further, Western female managers in Hong Kong say local people see them primarily as foreigners, not as women, and are accepted as managers more readily than are the female citizens of Hong Kong. Foreign women are not subject to the same operating barriers that local females face as managers.[57]

Some countries are relatively similar to one another, usually because they share many attributes that help mold their cultures, such as language, religion, geographical location, ethnicity, and level of economic development. Map 2.4 groups countries by attitudes and

Host cultures do not always expect foreigners to adjust to them.

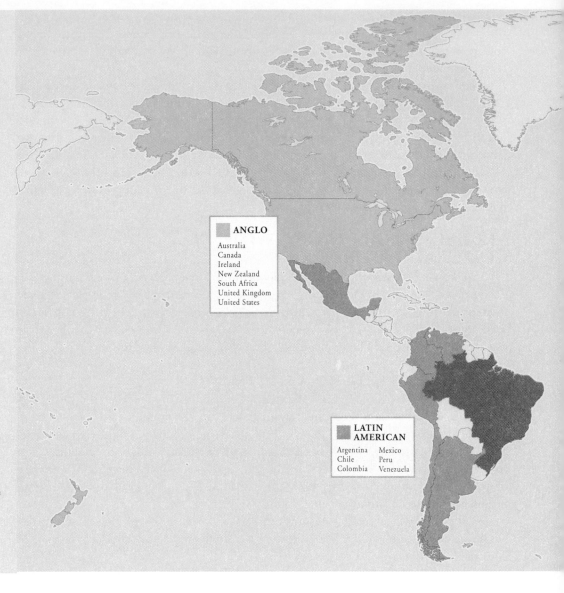

MAP 2.4
A Synthesis
of Country Clusters

This map shows that certain countries share similar cultural attitudes and values that may affect business practices. Not all countries have been studied sufficiently to determine how similar they are to other countries.

ANGLO

Australia
Canada
Ireland
New Zealand
South Africa
United Kingdom
United States

LATIN AMERICAN

Argentina   Mexico
Chile   Peru
Colombia   Venezuela

Source: Groupings taken from Simcha Ronen and Oded Shenkar, "Clustering Countries on Attitudinal Dimensions: A Review and Synthesis," *Academy of Management Review,* Vol. 10, No. 3, 1985, p. 449.

values based on data obtained from a large number of cross-cultural studies. A company should expect fewer differences (and have to consider fewer adjustments) when moving within a cluster (a Peruvian company doing business in Colombia) than when moving from one cluster to another (a Peruvian company doing business in Thailand). However, there still may be significant differences within similar countries that could affect business dealings. Managers may expect that seemingly similar countries (those within clusters) are more alike than they really are; a company may be lulled into a complacency that overlooks important subtleties. For example, in the PRI case the company expected the 12 Middle Eastern Arab countries to be more similar than they turned out to be. Bahrain allowed a foreign single woman, Angela Clarke, to establish residency there, to buy products prohibited by the Muslim religion, to drive a car, and to meet alone with businessmen. But Saudi Arabia prohibited her from even entering the country.

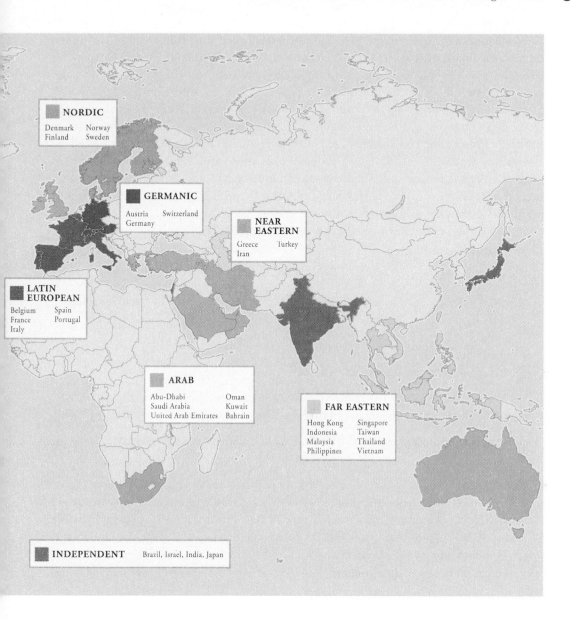

COMMUNICATIONS

So far we've seen how language affects culture—and international business. We now look at problems of communications—translating spoken and written language. These problems occur not only in moving from one language to another but also in communicating from one country to another that has the same official language. Second, we discuss communications outside the spoken and written language, the so-called "silent language."

Spoken and Written Language   Translating one language directly into another can be difficult, making international business communication difficult. First, some words do not have a direct translation. For example, in Spanish there is no one word for everyone who works in a business (employees). Instead, there is a word, *empleados*, which means "white-collar workers," and another, *obreros*, which means "laborers." This

Cross-border communications do not always translate as intended.

distinction shows the substantial class difference between the groups and affects international business because there may be miscommunication when managers in Spanish-speaking and English-speaking countries come together. Second, languages and the common meaning of words are constantly evolving. For example, Microsoft purchased a thesaurus code for its Spanish version of Word 6.0, but the meaning of many synonyms had changed and become insulting. The company corrected the software after newspapers and radio reports denounced the program, but by then Microsoft had alienated many potential customers.[58] Third, words mean different things in different contexts. For example, one company described itself as an "old friend" of China. However, it used the word for *old* that meant "former" instead of "long-term."[59] Finally, grammar is complex, and a slight misuse of vocabulary or word placement may change meanings substantially. Consider the following examples of signs in English observed in hotels around the world.

France: "Please leave your values at the desk."

Mexico (to assure guests about the safety of drinking water): "The manager has personally passed all the water served here."

Japan: "You are invited to take advantage of the chambermaid."

Norway: "Ladies are requested not to have children in the bar."

Switzerland: "Because of the impropriety of entertaining guests of the opposite sex in the bedroom, it is suggested that the lobby be used for this purpose."

Greece (at check-in line): "We will execute customers in strict rotation."

The above offers a humorous look at language barriers, and, in fact, the wrong choice of words usually is just a source of brief embarrassment. However, a poor translation may have tragic consequences. For example, inaccurate translations have caused structural collapses and airplane crashes, such as the collision between aircraft from Air Kazakhstan and Saudia Air over India.[60] In contracts, correspondence, negotiations, advertisements, and conversations, words must be chosen carefully. There is no foolproof way of handling translations. However, good international business managers use rules such as these.

- Get references on the people who will do translation for you.
- Make sure your translator knows the technical vocabulary of your business.
- Do a back translation for written work by having one person go, say, from English to French and a second person translate the French version back into English. If it comes back the same way it started, it is probably satisfactory.
- Use simple words whenever possible, such as *ban* instead of *interdiction*.
- Avoid slang. Such U.S. phrases as *blue chip stocks* and *ballpark figures* are likely to be meaningless to most businesspeople outside the United States.
- When you or your counterpart is dealing in a second language, clarify communications in several ways (such as by repeating in different words and asking questions) to assure all parties have the same interpretation.
- Realize and budget from the start for the extra time needed for translation and clarification.

When dealing with someone from another country that shares your official language, don't assume that communication will go smoothly. For example, between the United States and the United Kingdom, approximately 4,000 words have different meanings. Table 2.1 shows some common business terms that differ in the two countries.

Silent Language Of course, spoken and written language is not our only means of communicating. We all exchange messages by a host of nonverbal cues that form a silent language.[61] Colors, for example, conjure up meanings that come from cultural experience. In most Western countries, black is associated with death. White has the same connotation in parts of Asia and purple in Latin America. For products to succeed, their colors must match the consumers' frame of reference. For example, United Airlines promoted a new passenger service in Hong Kong by giving white carnations to its best customers there. The promotion backfired because people in Hong Kong give white carnations only in sympathy for a family death.

Another aspect of silent language is the distance between people during conversations. People's sense of appropriate distance is learned and differs among societies. In the United States, for example, the customary distance for a business discussion is five to eight feet. For personal business, it is eighteen inches to three feet.[62] When the distance is closer or farther than is customary, people tend to feel uneasy. For example, a U.S. manager conducting business discussions in Latin America may be constantly moving backward to avoid the closer conversational distance to which the Latin American official is accustomed. Consequently, at the end of the discussion, each party may distrust the other.

Perception of time and punctuality is another unspoken cue that differs by context and may differ across cultures and create confusion. In the United States, participants usually arrive early for a business appointment, a few minutes late for a dinner at someone's home, and a bit later for a cocktail party. In another country, the concept of punctuality in these situations may be different. For example, a U.S. businessperson in Latin

Silent language includes color associations, sense of appropriate distance, time and status cues, and body language.

Managers should know that perceptual cues—especially those concerning time and status—differ among societies.

TABLE 2.1	BUSINESS LANGUAGE DIFFERENCES

Below are a few of approximately 4,000 words whose common meaning differs between the United States and the United Kingdom. Although we usually expect problems of understanding when people from two different languages communicate, we may erroneously not expect miscommunication between people from two countries that share the same language.

UNITED STATES	UNITED KINGDOM
turnover	redundancy
sales	turnover
inventory	stock
stock	shares
president	managing director
paperback	limp cover

America may consider it discourteous if a Latin American manager does not keep to the appointed time. Latin Americans may find it equally discourteous if a U.S. businessperson arrives for dinner at the exact time given in the invitation. In one case, a U.S. company made a presentation in Mexico in competition with a French company. The U.S. company was confident that it would win the contract because of having the better technology. It scheduled a one-day meeting in Mexico City very tightly, allowing what it thought was plenty of time for the presentation and questions. However, the Mexican team arrived one hour late. One Mexican team member was called out of the room for an urgent phone call, and the whole Mexican team became upset when the U.S. team tried to proceed without the missing member. The French team allocated two weeks for discussions and won the contract even though its technology was widely known to be less sophisticated.[63]

Another silent language barrier concerns a person's position in a company. A U.S. businessperson who tends to place a great reliance on objects as prestige cues may underestimate the importance of foreign counterparts who do not have large, plush, private offices. A foreigner may underestimate U.S. counterparts who open their own doors and mix their own drinks.

Body language, or *kinesics* (the way in which people walk, touch, and move their bodies), also differs among countries. Few gestures are universal in meaning. For example, the "yes" of a Greek, Turk, or Bulgarian is indicated by a sideways movement of the head that resembles the negative head shake used in the United States and elsewhere in Europe. In some cases, one gesture may have several meanings, as Figure 2.4 shows.

CULTURE SHOCK

Some people get frustrated when entering a different culture.

A person who moves to another country frequently encounters culture shock—frustration from experiencing a new culture and having to learn and cope with a vast array of new cultural cues and expectations. People working in a very different culture may pass through stages. First, like tourists, they are elated with "quaint" differences. Later, they may feel depressed and confused—the culture shock phase—and their usefulness in a foreign assignment may be greatly impaired. Fortunately for most people, culture shock

FIGURE 2.4   Kinesics Are Not Universal

Few gestures are universal. This figure shows that a common and similar gesture has different connotations internationally. The meaning in Germany also prevails in most Latin American countries.

| **United States** | **Germany** | **Greece** | **France** | **Japan** |
| It's fine | You lunatic | An obscene symbol for a body orifice | Zero or worthless | Money, especially change |

Source: The meanings have been taken from descriptions in Roger E. Axtell, *Gestures* (New York: John Wiley, 1998).

begins to ebb after a month or two as optimism grows and satisfaction improves.[64] Interestingly, some people also encounter culture shock when they return to their home countries—a situation known as reverse culture shock—because they have learned to accept what they have encountered abroad. Dealing with transfers to a foreign country is a significant concern for companies and transferees, a concern covered in Chapter 21, "Human Resource Management."

COMPANY AND MANAGEMENT ORIENTATIONS

Whether and how much a company and its managers adapt to foreign cultures depends not only on the conditions within the foreign cultures but also on the attitudes of the companies and their managers. The following sections discuss three such attitudes or orientations—polycentrism, ethnocentrism, and geocentrism.

Polycentrism   In polycentric organizations, control is decentralized so that "our manager in Rio" is free to conduct business in what he thinks is "the Brazilian way." In other words, business units in different countries have a significant degree of autonomy from the home office and act very much like local companies. Because many discussions of international business focus on the unique problems that companies have experienced abroad, it is understandable that many companies develop a polycentric orientation. Polycentrism may be, however, an overly cautious response to cultural variety.

A company that is too polycentric may shy away from certain countries or may avoid transferring home-country practices or resources that may, in fact, work well abroad. When practices do not work abroad, management may point to the unique foreign environment. If the foreign environment is not the cause, the company might erroneously take a more polycentric orientation. For example, American Express assembled its worldwide personnel managers for an exchange of views on performance evaluation. The complaints from the overseas managers centered on certain corporate directives that they claimed did not fit "their" countries. These managers claimed that foreign operations were unique and that each overseas office should develop its own procedures. Further talks, however, revealed that the complaints really focused on one particular personnel evaluation form. If the company had delegated procedural control, as these overseas managers were suggesting, it would have risked not introducing abroad some of its other standard forms and procedures that would work reasonably well. Furthermore, it would have risked duplicating efforts by having each country's managers develop their own form, which might have been more costly than trying to administer the ill-suited form. Personnel managers in U.S. offices indicated, too, that they had just as many problems with the form as had their foreign counterparts. The problematic evaluation form, which managers originally attributed to cultural differences, was not a "cultural" problem at all.

To compete effectively with local companies, an international company usually must perform some functions in a distinct way, such as by introducing new products or ways to produce and sell them. Polycentrism, however, may lead to such extensive delegation of decision making or such extensive imitation of proven host-country practices that the company loses its innovative superiority. Furthermore, the company may lose overall control as managers within each country foster local rather than worldwide objectives.

> **Polycentrist management is so overwhelmed by national differences that it won't introduce workable changes.**

Ethnocentrism   Ethnocentrism is the belief that one's own culture is superior to others. In international business, it describes a company or individual so imbued with the belief that what worked at home should work abroad that it ignores environmental differences. Ethnocentrism takes three general forms.

> **Ethnocentrist management overlooks national differences and**
> - **Ignores important factors**
> - **Believes home-country objectives should prevail**
> - **Thinks change is easy**

1. Managers overlook important cultural factors abroad because they have become so accustomed to certain cause–effect relationships in the home country. To combat this type of ethnocentrism, managers can refer to checklists of cultural variables, such as those discussed in this chapter, to assure themselves that they are considering all the major factors.
2. Management recognizes the environmental differences but still focuses on achieving home-country rather than foreign or worldwide objectives. The result may be diminished long-term competitiveness because the company does not perform as well as its competitors and because opposition to its practices develops abroad.
3. Management recognizes differences but assumes that the introduction of its new products or ways to produce and sell them is both necessary and easy to achieve when it is really a complex process. Ethnocentrism is not entirely bad. Much of what works at home will work abroad. However, excessive ethnocentrism may cause costly business failures.

> **Geocentric management often uses business practices that are hybrids of home and foreign norms.**

Geocentrism   Between the extremes of polycentrism and ethnocentrism are business practices that are neither the home operation's nor the host-country company's but a hybrid of the two. When the host-country environment is substantially different from home, the international company must decide whether to persuade people in that country to accept something new (in which case, the company would be acting as a change agent) or to make changes in the company itself. Geocentrism is when a company bases its operations on an informed knowledge of home- and host-country needs, capabilities, and constraints. This is the preferred approach to business dealings with another culture because it increases introduction of innovations and decreases the likelihood of their failures.

STRATEGIES FOR INSTITUTING CHANGE

As we have indicated, companies may need to transfer new products or operating methods from one country to another if they are to have competitive advantages. How they make such introductions is important for assuring success. Fortunately, substantial change-agent literature deals with overcoming resistance in the international arena. Further, we can gain insights from the international experiences of businesses and not-for-profit organizations. We discuss these approaches and experiences in the following sections and conclude with a discussion on the importance for companies to treat learning as a two-way process, where they transfer knowledge from their home countries abroad and from abroad to their home countries.

> **The more a change upsets important values, the more resistance it will engender.**

Value System   It is much easier to adapt to things that do not challenge our value systems than to things that do. For example, Eritreans eat only 175 grams of fish per capita

Looking to the Future
THE GLOBALIZATION OF CULTURE

Contact across cultures is becoming more widespread than ever. This should lead to a leveling of cultures, which, on the surface, is occurring. People around the world wear similar clothes and listen to the same recording stars. Competitors from all over the world often buy the same production equipment, the use of which imposes more uniform operating methods on workers. This globalization of culture is illustrated by Japanese tourists listening to a Philippine group sing a U.S. song in an Indonesian hotel.

Cultures are becoming more similar in some respects but not in others.

However, below the surface people continue to hold fast to their national differences. In other words, although some tangibles have become more universal, how people cooperate, attempt to solve problems, and are motivated have tended to remain the same. Religious differences are as strong as ever. Language differences continue to bolster separate ethnic identities. These differences fragment the globe into regions and stymie global standardization of products and operating methods.

One factor that inhibits the leveling of cultures is nationalism. Without perceived cultural differences, people would not see themselves so apart from other nationalities; thus cultural identities are used to mobilize national identity and separateness. This is done by regulating and encouraging the so-called national culture.

International companies, therefore, are likely to continue to face diverse cultures in different parts of the world and for different parts of their operations. In some areas, diversity will decrease as small cultural groups are absorbed into more dominant national ones. For example, in recent years such absorption has led to the extinction of many languages. Only 5 percent of languages are "safe," meaning at least a million people speak them.[65] At the same time, there is evidence of more powerful subcultures within some countries because of immigration, the global rise in religious fundamentalism, and the growing belief among ethnic groups that they should be independent from dominant groups.

Two scenarios for future international cultures are
- **Smaller cultures will be absorbed by national and global ones**
- **Subcultures will transcend national boundaries**

All of these factors might lead to future problems in defining culture along national lines. Subcultures may transcend borders, and the distinct subcultures within a country may have less in common with each other than they do with subcultures in other countries. Examples of transnational subcultures are the Inuits that transcend country boundaries in Arctic lands and the Kurds that do the same in the Middle East. An interesting potential scenario is that cultural competition—the promotion of ideas, attitudes, norms, and values—among nations will become increasingly important as nations try to harness their distinctive human resource capabilities as a means of outperforming other countries economically.[66]

per year (compared with 20,000 times that in the United States and 70,000 times that in Japan) despite having a long coastline rich in seafood and enduring a recent famine. The Eritrean government and the United Nations World Food Program have faced formidable opposition in trying to persuade Eritrean adults to eat more seafood because their value system is too set. Many have religious taboos about eating insect-like sea creatures (such as shrimp and crayfish) and fish without scales, and most grew up believing that seafood tasted putrid. But there is little opposition to eating seafood among Eritrean schoolchildren. Simply, their value system and habits are not yet set.[67] The business lesson here is that the more a change disrupts basic values, the more the people affected will resist it. When changes do not interfere with deep-seated customs, accommodation is much more likely.

The cost of change may exceed its benefit.

Cost Benefit of Change   Some adjustments to foreign cultures are costly to undertake, while others are inexpensive. Some adjustments result in greatly improved performance, such as higher productivity or sales. Other changes may improve performance only marginally. A company must consider the expected cost-benefit relationship of any adjustments it makes abroad. For example, Cummins Engine shuts down its plant in Mexico each December twelfth so workers may honor the Virgin of Guadalupe. It throws a celebration in the company cafeteria for employees and their families that includes a priest who offers prayers to the Virgin at an altar.[68] The cost is worth the resultant employee commitment to the company.

Resistance to change may be lower if the number of changes is not too great.

Resistance to Too Much Change   When German company Gruner + Jahr bought the U.S. magazine *McCall's*, it quickly began to overhaul the format. Gruner + Jahr changed its editor, eliminated long stories and advice columns, increased coverage on celebrities, made the layouts more dense, started using sidebars and boxes in articles, and refused discounts for big advertisers. But employee turnover began to increase because of low morale, and revenues fell because the new format seemed too different to advertisers.[69] Employee and advertiser acceptance might have been easier to obtain had Gruner + Jahr made fewer demands at one time and phased in other policies more slowly.

Employees are more willing to implement change when they take part in the decision to change.

Participation   One way to avoid problems that could result from change is to discuss a proposed change with stakeholders in advance. By doing so, the company may learn how strong resistance to the change will be, stimulate in the stakeholders a recognition of the need for improvement, and ease their fears of adverse consequences resulting from the change. Managers sometimes think that stakeholder participation is unique to countries where people have educational backgrounds that enable them to make substantial contributions. Experience with government-to-government economic development and population-control programs, however, indicates that participation may be extremely important to companies even in countries where power distance and uncertainty avoidance are high. However, stakeholder participation is limited to the extent that proposed actions do not violate conditions in the prevailing value system and to the extent that participants are not so fatalistic that they believe they can have no control over the outcomes.

Employees are more apt to support change when they expect personal or group rewards.

Reward Sharing   Sometimes a proposed change may have no foreseeable benefit for the people who must support it. For example, production workers may have little incentive to shift to new work practices unless they see some benefits for themselves. A company's solution may be to develop a bonus system for productivity and quality based on using the new approach.

Opinion Leaders By discovering the local channels of influence, an international company may locate opinion leaders who can help speed up the acceptance of change. Opinion leaders may emerge in unexpected places. For example, in rural Ghana, government health workers frequently ask permission from and seek the help of village shamans before inoculating people or spraying huts to fight malaria. This achieves the desired result without destroying important social structures. Ford sends Mexican operatives, rather than supervisors, from its plants in Mexico to one in the United States to observe operating methods. Their Mexican peers are more prone to listen to them than to their supervisors.[70] Characteristics of opinion leaders may vary by country, such as generally being older people in India and Korea, but not in Australia.[71]

> Managers seeking to introduce change should first convince those who can influence others.

Timing Many good business changes fall flat because they are ill-timed. For example, a labor-saving production method might make employees fear losing their jobs, regardless of management's reassurances. However, less employee fear and resistance will occur if management introduces the labor-saving method when there is a labor shortage. A culture's attitudes and needs may change slowly or rapidly, so keeping abreast of these changes helps in determining timing. However, a crisis may stimulate acceptance of change. For example, family members dominate business organizations in Turkey. In some cases, poor company profits have stimulated a rapid change from "a family running the business" to a "family only on the board." But in other cases, family members continue to exert substantial influence on companies' practices even after they have no official responsibilities.[72]

> Companies should time change to occur when resistance is likely to be low.

Learning Abroad The discussion so far has centered on cultural differences among countries. As companies operate abroad, they affect the host society and are affected by it. The company may learn things that will be useful in its home country or in other operations. This last point is the essence for undertaking transnational practices in which the company seeks to capitalize on diverse capabilities among the countries in which it operates. Basically, companies believe natural intelligence exists in about the same proportion throughout the world and that innovations and good ideas may come from anywhere.

> International companies should learn things abroad that they can apply at home.

WEB CONNECTION

Check out our home page www.prenhall.com/daniels for links to key resources for you in your study of international business.

SUMMARY

- Culture includes norms of behavior based on learned attitudes, values, and beliefs. Businesspeople agree that there are cross-country differences but disagree as to what they are.

- International companies must evaluate their business practices to ensure they take into account national norms in behavioral characteristics.

- A given country may encompass very distinct societies. People also may have more in common with similar groups in foreign countries than with groups in their own country.

- Companies can build awareness about other cultures. The amount of effort needed to do this depends on the similarity between countries and the type of business operation undertaken.

- Cultural change may take place as a result of choice or imposition. Isolation from other groups, especially because of language, tends to stabilize cultures.

- People fall into social stratification systems according to their ascribed and acquired group memberships. These memberships determine a person's degree of access to economic resources, prestige, social relations, and power. An individual's affiliations may determine his or her qualifications and availability for given jobs.

- Some people work far more than is necessary to satisfy their basic needs for food, clothing, and shelter. People are motivated to work for various reasons, including their preference for material items over leisure, the belief that work will bring success and reward, and the desire for achievement.

- Nationalities differ as to whether they prefer an autocratic or a consultative working relationship, whether they want set rules, and how much they compete or cooperate with fellow workers.

- Nationalities differ in the degree to which people trust one another and believe in fate.

- Host cultures do not always expect companies and individuals to conform to their norms. They sometimes accommodate foreign companies and have different standards for foreigners.

- People communicate through spoken, written, and silent language, based on culturally determined cues.

- Information processing is greatly affected by cultural background. The failure to perceive subtle distinctions in behavior can result in misunderstandings in international dealings.

- People sometimes have a generalized frustration—culture shock—from experiencing a new and different culture.

- People working in a foreign environment should be sensitive to the dangers of excessive polycentrism and excessive ethnocentrism. They should try to become geocentric.

- In deciding whether to try to bring change to home- or host-country operations, an international company should consider how important the change is to each party, the cost and benefit to the company of each alternative, the use of opinion leaders, and the timing of change.

- Although increased contact among people is evoking more widespread cultural similarity among nations, people nevertheless tend to hold on to their basic values. These values are bolstered by efforts to protect cultural separateness and national identity.

CASE

JOHN HIGGINS[73]

Leonard Prescott, vice president and general manager of Weaver-Yamazaki Pharmaceutical of Japan, believed that John Higgins, his executive assistant, was losing effectiveness in representing the U.S. parent company because of an extraordinary identification with the Japanese culture. (Map 2.5 shows Japan and Table 2.2 on page 80 shows Japan's work customs.)

The parent company, Weaver Pharmaceutical, had extensive international operations and was one of the largest U.S. drug firms. Its competitive position depended heavily on research and development (R&D). Sales activity in Japan started in the early 1930s, when Yamazaki Pharmaceutical, a major producer of drugs and chemicals in Japan, began dis-

MAP 2.5 Japan

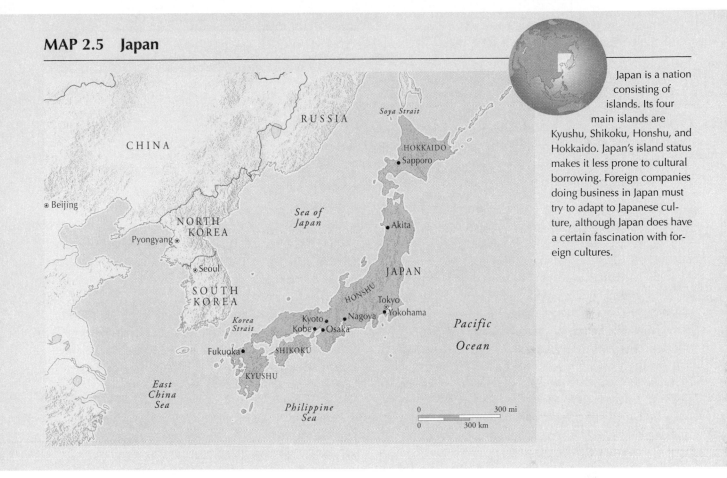

Japan is a nation consisting of islands. Its four main islands are Kyushu, Shikoku, Honshu, and Hokkaido. Japan's island status makes it less prone to cultural borrowing. Foreign companies doing business in Japan must try to adapt to Japanese culture, although Japan does have a certain fascination with foreign cultures.

tributing Weaver's products. World War II disrupted sales, but Weaver resumed exporting to Japan in 1948 and subsequently captured a substantial market share. To prepare for increasingly keen competition from Japanese producers, Weaver and Yamazaki established in 1954 a jointly owned and operated manufacturing subsidiary to produce part of Weaver's product line.

Through the combined effort of both parent companies, the subsidiary soon began manufacturing sufficiently broad lines of products to fill the general demands of the Japanese market. Imports from the United States were limited to highly specialized items. The subsidiary conducted substantial R&D on its own, coordinated through a joint committee representing both Weaver and Yamazaki to avoid unnecessary duplication of efforts. The subsidiary turned out many new products, some marketed successfully in the United States and elsewhere. Weaver's management considered the Japanese operation to be one of its most successful international ven-

tures and felt that the company's future prospects were promising, especially given the steady improvement in Japan's standard of living.

Shozo Suzuki headed the subsidiary, but, as executive vice president of Yamazaki and president of several other subsidiaries, limited his participation in Weaver-Yamazaki to determining basic policies. Prescott, assisted by Higgins and several Japanese directors, managed daily operations.

Weaver Pharmaceutical had a policy of moving U.S. personnel from one foreign post to another with occasional tours in the home-office international division. Each assignment generally lasted for three to five years. There were a limited number of expatriates, so company personnel policy was flexible enough to allow an employee to stay in a country for an indefinite time if desired. A few expatriates had stayed in one foreign post for over ten years. Prescott replaced the former general manager, who had been in Japan for six years. An experienced international businessman, who

TABLE 2.2	JAPANESE WORK CUSTOMS

Low employee turnover
Advancement based primarily on longevity with the company
Considerable after-work socializing among employees
Group work assignments and rewards
Bottom-up consensus building for decisions

had spent most of his twenty-five-year career at Weaver abroad, Prescott had served in India, the Philippines, and Mexico, with several years in the home-office international division. He was delighted to be challenged with expanding Japanese operations, and after two years he felt a sense of accomplishment in having developed a smoothly functioning organization. Born in a small midwestern town, Higgins entered his state university after high school. Midway through college, however, he joined the army. Because he had shown an interest in languages in college, he was able to attend the Army Language School for intensive training in Japanese. Fifteen months later, he was assigned as an interpreter and translator in Tokyo and took more courses in Japanese language, literature, and history. He made many Japanese friends, fell in love with Japan, and vowed to return there. After five years in the army, Higgins returned to college. Because he wanted to use Japanese as a means rather than an end in itself, he finished his college work in management, graduating with honors, and then joined Weaver. After a year in the company training program, Weaver assigned him to Japan, a year before Prescott's arrival.

Higgins was pleased to return to Japan, not only because of his love for the country but also because of the opportunity to improve the "ugly American" image held abroad. His language ability and interest in Japan enabled him to intermingle with broad segments of the Japanese population. He noted with disdain that U.S. managers tended to impose their value systems, ideals, and thinking patterns on the Japanese.

Under both Prescott and his predecessor, Higgins's responsibilities included troubleshooting with major Japanese customers, attending trade meetings, negotiating with government officials, conducting marketing research, and helping with day-to-day administration. Both general managers sought his advice on many difficult and complex administrative problems and found him capable. Prescott became concerned, however, with Higgins's attitude and thinking. He felt that Higgins had taken to the Japanese culture to such a degree that he had lost the U.S. point of view. He had "gone native," resulting in a substantial loss of administrative effectiveness.

Prescott mentally listed a few examples to describe what he meant by Higgins's "complete emotional involvement" with Japanese culture. The year before, Higgins had married a Japanese woman. At that time, Higgins had asked for and received permission to extend his stay in Japan indefinitely. According to Prescott, this marked a turning point in Higgins's behavior. Higgins moved to a strictly Japanese neighborhood, relaxed in a kimono at home, used the public bath, and was invited to weddings, neighborhood parties, and even Buddhist funerals. Although Weaver had a policy of granting two months' home leave every two years, with paid transportation for the employee and his family, Higgins declined to take trips, preferring instead to visit remote parts of Japan with his wife.

At work, Higgins also had taken on many characteristics of a typical Japanese executive. He spent considerable time listening to the personal problems of his subordinates, maintained close social ties with many men in the company, and had even arranged marriages for some of the young employees. Consequently, many employees sought out Higgins to register complaints and demands. These included requests for more liberal fringe benefits, such as recreational activities and the acquisition of rest houses for employees to use at resort areas. Many employees also complained to Higgins about a new personnel policy, which Prescott instituted, that moved away from basing promotions on seniority, considering instead superiors' evaluations of subordinates. The employees asked Higgins to intercede on their behalf. He did so, insisting their demands were justified.

Although Prescott believed it was helpful to learn the feelings of middle managers from Higgins, he disliked having to deal with Higgins as an adversary rather than an ally. Prescott became hesitant to ask his assistant's opinion because Higgins invariably raised objections to changes that were contrary to the Japanese norm. Prescott believed that there were dynamic changes occurring in traditional Japanese customs and culture, and he was confident that many Japanese were not tied to existing cultural patterns as rigidly as Higgins seemed to think. Indeed, Japanese subordinates were more willing than Higgins to try out new ideas. Prescott also thought that there was no point in a progressive U.S. company's merely copying the local customs. He felt that the company's real contribution to Japanese society was in introducing innovations.

There were more incidents that made Prescott doubt Higgins's judgment. One was the dismissal of a manager who, in Prescott's opinion, lacked initiative, leadership, and general competency. After two years of continued prodding by his superiors, including Prescott, the manager still showed little interest in improvement. Both Higgins and the personnel manager objected vigorously to the dismissal because the company had never fired anyone before. They also argued that the employee was loyal and honest and that the company was partially at fault for having kept him on for the last ten years without spotting the incompetency. A few weeks after the dismissal, Prescott learned that Higgins had interceded on behalf of the fired employee, so that Yamazaki

Pharmaceutical transferred him to its own operation. When confronted, Higgins said that he had done what was expected of a superior in any Japanese company by assuring a subordinate's continued employment.

Prescott believed these incidents suggested a serious problem. Higgins had been an effective and efficient manager whose knowledge of the language and the people had proved invaluable. Prescott knew that Higgins had received several outstanding offers to go with other companies in Japan. On numerous occasions, Prescott's friends in U.S. companies said they envied him for having a man of Higgins's qualifications as an assistant. However, Prescott felt Higgins would be far more effective if he had a detached attitude toward Japan. In Prescott's view, the best international executive was one who retained a belief in the fundamentals of the home point of view while also understanding foreign attitudes.

QUESTIONS

1. How would you describe Higgins's and Prescott's attitudes toward implementing U.S. personnel policies in the Japanese operations?
2. What are the major reasons for the differences in attitude?
3. If you were the Weaver corporate manager responsible for the Japanese operations and the conflict between Higgins and Prescott came to your attention, what would you do? Be sure to identify some alternatives first and then make your recommendations.

CHAPTER NOTES

1   Most data were taken from an interview with Angela Clarke, a protagonist in the case.

2   "Sensitivity Kick," *Wall Street Journal,* December 30, 1992, p. A1.

3   Frank L. Acuff, "Just Call Me Mr. Ishmael," *Export Today,* July 1995, p. 14.

4   A list of books appears in Katherine Glover, "Do's & Taboos," *Business America,* August 13, 1990, p. 5. See also Roger Axtell, *Do's and Taboos Around the World* (New York: John Wiley, 1992).

5   Robert J. Foster, "Making National Cultures in the National Ecumene," *Annual Review of Anthropology,* Vol. 20, 1991, pp. 235–260 discusses the concept and ingredients of a national culture.

6   Luis R. Gomez-Mejia, "Effect of Occupation on Task Related, Contextual, and Job Involve

ment Orientation: A Cross-Cultural Perspective," *Academy of Management Journal,* Vol. 27, No. 4, 1984, pp. 706–720.

7   L. L. Cavalli-Sforza, M. W. Feldman, K. H. Chen, and S. M. Dornbusch, "Theory and Observation on Cultural Transmission," *Science,* Vol. 218, 1982, pp. 19–27.

8   Harry C. Triandis, "Dimensions of Cultural Variation as Parameters of Organizational Theories," *International Studies of Management and Organization,* Winter 1982–1983, pp. 143–144.

9   William H. Durham, "Applications of Evolutionary Culture Theory," *Annual Review of Anthropology,* Vol. 21, 1992, pp. 331–355.

10 Sally Engle Merry, "Anthropology, Law, and Transnational Processes," *Annual Review of Anthropology,* Vol. 21, 1992, p. 364.

11 Rigoberta Menchú, *I, Rigoberta Menchú: An Indian Woman in Guatemala* (London: Verso,

1984); a 1999 referendum confirmed the use of Spanish in schools. See "Guatemalan Indians Lament Recognition Measure's Defeat," *New York Times,* May 18, 1999, p. A5.

12 Vivian Ducat, "American Spoken Here—and Everywhere," *Travel & Leisure,* Vol. 16, No. 10, October 1986, pp. 168–169; Bill Bryson, *The Mother Tongue: English and How It Got That Way* (New York: Morrow, 1990).

13 "Big Mac vs. Sacred Cows," *Business Week,* March 1, 1993, p. 58.

14 Michael Segalla, "National Cultures, International Business," *Financial Times,* March 6, 1998, mastering global business section, pp. 8–10.

15 Fons Trompenaars, *Riding the Waves of Culture* (Burr Ridge, IL: Richard D. Irwin, 1994), pp. 100–116.

16 Victor Mallet, "South Africa's 'Affirmative Action' Law Meets Some Negative Responses," *Financial Times,* September 11, 1998, p. 4.

17 Valentine M. Moghadam, "Responses to Jean Bonvin's Globalization and Linkages: Challenges for Development Policy," *Development,* Vol. 40, No. 3, 1997, pp. 62–69.

18 Barbara Crossette, "Afghans Draw U.N. Warning Over Sex Bias," *New York Times,* October 8, 1996, p. A1.

19 "Comparing Women Around the World," *Wall Street Journal,* July 26, 1995, p. B1.

20 Kenneth Dreyfack, "You Don't Have to Be a Giant to Score Big Overseas," *Business Week,* April 13, 1987, p. 63.

21 Steve Liesman, "Driven to Distration, Saudi Women May Soon Take the Wheel," *Wall Street Jounal,* March 1, 1999, p. A10.

22 Francis Fukuyama, *Trust: The Social Virtues and the Creation of Prosperity* (New York: Free Press, 1995).

23 Mary Jordan, "Respect Is Dwindling in the Hallowed-Halls," *Washington Post,* June 20, 1994, p. A3, citing data collected by the Carnegie Foundation for the Advancement of Teaching in a survey of 20,000 professors in 13 nations and Hong Kong.

24 Jean J. Boddewyn, "Fitting Socially in Fortress Europe: Understanding, Reaching, and Impressing Europeans," *Business Horizons,* November–December 1992, pp. 35–43; and Geert Hofstede, "National Cultures in Four Dimensions," *International Studies of Management and Organization,* Spring–Summer 1983, pp. 46–74.

25 Everett E. Hagen, *The Theory of Social Change: How Economic Growth Begins* (Homewood, IL: Richard D. Irwin, 1962), p. 378.

26 See, for example, David S. Landes, *The Wealth and Poverty of Nations* (New York: W.W. Norton, 1998).

27 Boddewyn, "Fitting Socially in Fortress Europe."

28 R. Inden, "Tradition Against Itself," *American Ethnologist,* Vol. 13, No. 4, 1986, pp. 762–775; and P. Chatterjee, *Nationalist Thoughts and the Colonial World: A Derivative Discourse* (London: Zed Books, 1986).

29 Triandis, "Dimensions of Cultural Variation as Parameters of Organizational Theories," pp. 159–160.

30 Geert Hofstede, *Cultures and Organizations: Software of the Mind* (New York: McGraw-Hill, 1997), pp. 79–108.

31 Abraham Maslow, *Motivation and Personality* (New York: Harper, 1954).

32 Hofstede, *Cultures and Organizations,* p. 26.

33 Ibid., pp. 49–78.

34 R. M. Kanter, "Transcending Business Boundaries: 12,000 World Managers View Change," *Harvard Business Review,* May–June 1991, pp. 151–164.

35 Book review of Patricia Gercik, *On the Track with the Japanese* (Kodansha, 1992), by James B. Treece, *Business Week,* December 28, 1992, p. 20.

36 Ralph T. King, "Jeans Therapy," *Wall Street Journal,* May 20, 1998, p. A1.

37 John J. Lawrence and Reh-song Yeh, "The Influence of Mexican Culture on the Use of Japanese Manufacturing Techniques in Mexico," *Management International Review,* Vol. 34, No. 1, 1994, pp. 49–66; P. Christopher Earley, "East Meets West Meets Mideast: Further Explorations of Collectivistic and Individualistic Work Groups," *Academy of Management Journal,* Vol. 36, No. 2, 1993, pp. 319–346.

38 Marieke De Mooij, *Global Marketing and Advertising* (Thousand Oaks, CA: Sage, 1998).

39 Hofstede, *Cultures and Organizations,* p. 113.

40 Jan-Benedict E. M. Steenkamp, Frenkel ter Hofstede, and Michel Wedel, "A Cross-National Investigation into the Individual and National Cultural Antecedents of Consumer Innovativeness," *Journal of Marketing,* Vol. 63, April 1999, pp. 55–69; and Hellmut Schütte, "Asian Culture and the Global Consumer," *Financial Times,* September 21, 1998, mastering marketing section, pp. 2–3.

41 Stephen Knack, "Low Trust, Slow Growth," *Financial Times,* June 26, 1996, p. 12; and Francis Fukuyama, *Trust: The Social Virtues and the Creation of Prosperity* (London: Hamish Hamilton, 1995).

42 For a survey of major research contributions, see Harry C. Triandis, "Reflections on Trends in Cross-Cultural Research," *Journal of Cross-Cultural Psychology,* March 1980, pp. 46–48.

43 Benjamin Lee Whorf, *Language, Thought and Reality* (New York: John Wiley, 1956), p. 13.

44 Bernard Lewis, "Western Culture Must Go," *Wall Street Journal,* May 2, 1988, p. 18.

45 Merry, "Anthropology, Law, and Transnational Processes," pp. 366–367.

46 Boye de Mente, *Chinese Etiquette and Ethics in Business* (Lincoln, IL: NTC, 1989).

47 Wiliam Stockton, "Bribes Are Called a Way of Life in Mexico," *New York Times,* October 25, 1986, p. 3.

48 Pirkko Lammi, "My Vision of Business in Europe," in *Business Ethics in a New Europe,* Jack Mahoney and Elizabeth Vallance, eds. (Dordrecht, the Netherlands: Kluwer Academic, 1992), pp. 11–12.

49 Andrew Jack, "French Prepare to Repel English Advance," *Financial Times,* January 7, 1997.

50 D. Paul Schafer, "Cultures and Economics," *Futures,* Vol. 26, No. 8, 1994, pp. 830–845.

51 William Kuyken, John Orley, Patricia Hudelson, and Norman Sartorius, "Quality of Life Assessment Across Cultures," *International Journal of Mental Health,* Vol. 23, No. 2, 1994, pp. 5–27.

52 Alison Dundes Renteln, "The Concept of Human Rights," *Anthropos,* Vol. 83, 1988, pp. 343–364; and Ingrid Mattson, "Law, Culture, and Human Rights: Islamic Perspectives in the Contemporary World," summary of a conference at Yale Law School (November 5–6, 1993) in *The American Journal of Islamic Social Sciences,* Vol. 11, No. 3, 1994, pp. 446–450.

53 Tony Horwitz, "Iceland Pushes Back English Invasion in War of the Words," *Wall Street Journal,* July 25, 1990, p. A8.

54 For an examination of subtle differences within northern Europe, see Malene Djursaa, "North Europe Business Culture: Britain vs. Denmark and Germany," *European Management Journal,* Vol. 12, No. 2, June 1994, pp. 138–146.

55 Daniel Pearl, "Tour Saudi Arabia: Enjoy Sand, Surf, His-and-Her Pools," *Wall Street Journal,* January 22, 1998, p. A1.

56 June N. P. Francis, "When in Rome? The Effects of Cultural Adaptation on Intercultural Business Negotiations," *Journal of International Business Studies,* Vol. 22, No. 3, 1991, pp. 421–422.

57 R. I. Westwood and S. M. Leung, "The Female Expatriate Manager Experience," *International Studies of Management and Organization,* Vol. 24, No. 3, 1994, pp. 64–85.

58 Don Clark, "Hey, #@*% Amigo, Can You Translate the Word 'Gaffte'?" *Wall Street Journal,* July 8, 1996, p. B6.

59 Rene White, "Beyond Berlitz: How to Penetrate Foreign Markets through Effective Communications," *Public Relations Quarterly,* Vol. 31, No. 2, Summer 1986, p. 15.

60 Mark Nicholson, "Language Error 'Was Cause of Indian Air Disaster,'" *Financial Times,* November 14, 1996, p. 1.

61 Much of the silent language discussion is from Edward T. Hall, "The Silent Language in Overseas Business," *Harvard Business Review,* May–June 1960. He included five variables (time, space, things, friendships, and agreements) and was the first to use the term *silent language.*

62 Ibid.

63 Trompenaars, *Riding the Wave of Culture,* pp. 130–131.

64 Adrian Furnham and Stephen Bochner, *Culture Shock* (London: Methuen, 1986), p. 234.

65 "Cultural Loss Seen as Languages Fade," *New York Times,* May 16, 1999, p. 12.

66 J. Ørstrøm Møller, "The Competitiveness of U.S. Industry: A View from the Outside," *Business Horizons,* November–December 1991, pp. 27–34; Richard Tomkins, "US Tops Poll on Cultural Exports," *Financial Times,* December 4, 1996, p. 9.

67 Geraldine Brooks, "Eritrea's Leaders Angle for Sea Change in Nation's Diet to Prove Fish Isn't Foul," *Wall Street Journal,* June 2, 1994, p. A10.

68 Marjorie Miller, "A Clash of Corporate Cultures," *Los Angeles Times,* August 15, 1992, p. A1.

69 Patrick M. Reilly, "Pitfalls of Exporting Magazine Formulas," *Wall Street Journal,* July 24, 1995, p. B1.

70 Roberto P. Garcia, "Learning and Competitiveness in Mexico's Automotive Industry: The Relationship Between Traditional and World-Class Plants in Multination Firm Subsidiaries," unpublished Ph. D. dissertation (Ann Arbor, MI: University of Michigan, 1996).

71 Roger Marshall and Indriyo Gitosudarmo, "Variation in the Characteristics of Opinion Leaders Across Cultural Borders," *Journal of International Consumer Marketing,* Vol. 8, No. 1, 1995, pp. 5–21.

72 "Business Must Come Before Family," *Euromoney,* Febuary 1999, pp. 92–96.

73 The case is a condensed version from *Case: John Higgins* by M. Y. Yoshino. Reprinted with permission of Stanford University Graduate School of Business, ©1963 by the Board of Trustees of the Leland Stanford Junior University.

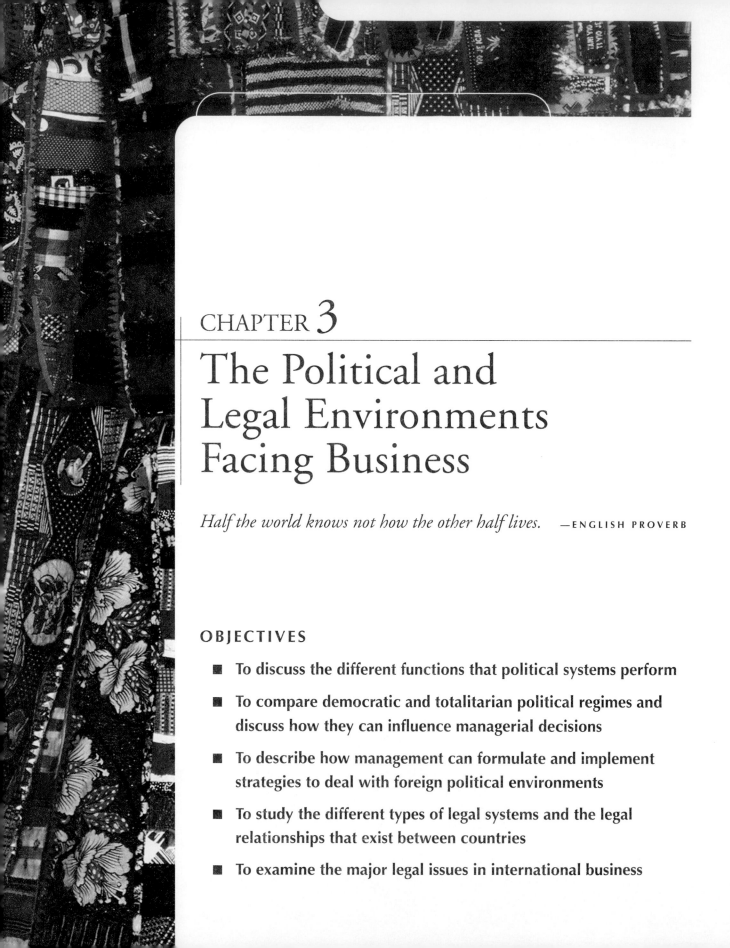

CHAPTER 3

The Political and Legal Environments Facing Business

Half the world knows not how the other half lives. —ENGLISH PROVERB

OBJECTIVES

- To discuss the different functions that political systems perform

- To compare democratic and totalitarian political regimes and discuss how they can influence managerial decisions

- To describe how management can formulate and implement strategies to deal with foreign political environments

- To study the different types of legal systems and the legal relationships that exist between countries

- To examine the major legal issues in international business

Peter Sutch is the chairman, or *taipan*, of Swire Pacific Ltd., one of the major *hongs*, or family-controlled trading houses prominent in Hong Kong business circles. Sutch must learn to operate successfully in Hong Kong now that it has reverted from British to Chinese rule. In addition, he must cope with the unstable economic environment brought on by the Asian financial crisis.

Swire Pacific Ltd. is a publicly quoted company (a company whose shares are listed on a stock exchange) with diversified interests under the control of six operating divisions: property, aviation, industries, trading, marine services, and insurance. Its two leading profit contributors, property and aviation, had a difficult year in 1998 in the wake of the Asian financial crisis as profits in the property division dropped 70 percent and aviation posted a loss of U.S. $14 million.

How could Hong Kong's new status be a problem to Swire? We'll need to learn some history. Until the mid-seventeenth century, China sought to minimize its contact with foreigners by restricting foreign trade to the port at Macao, which is 75 miles south of Canton, now known as Guangzhou. These restrictions resulted from a long history of mutual distrust and misunderstanding between the Chinese and foreigners. In the late eighteenth century, the Chinese opened more of their ports—a decision they soon regretted. By the middle of the nineteenth century, they again sought to restrict foreign trade, this time to Canton.

Despite the history of restrictions, trade between China and the West had been flourishing, especially with Britain. The British wanted Chinese tea; the Chinese wanted the opium that British traders shipped in from India. Although opium was illegal in China, its use was widespread so the Chinese government sought to halt its importation. Not surprisingly, the British protested. The results were three Opium Wars between the two countries within a period of 21 years (1839–1860). In all three, China emerged the loser. The first Opium War gave the British permanent ownership of the island of Hong Kong and its harbor (among other concessions). From the Third Opium War, they gained Kowloon. The New Territories, which comprise 90 percent of the land area of Hong Kong, came under British control in 1898 under the terms of a 99-year lease that expired June 30, 1997. Map 3.1 shows the region. Until the early 1980s, the issue of the 99-year lease's expiration was dormant. However, real estate in Hong Kong tends to be leased on a 15-year basis. So, in 1982 nervousness on the part of the Hong Kong business community led then–British Prime Minister Margaret Thatcher to initiate talks with the Chinese government about what would become of Hong Kong in 1997.

After prolonged negotiations, in 1984 the British and Chinese signed the Sino-British Joint Declaration. Under the agreement, China assumed control over Hong Kong on July 1, 1997, at which time Hong Kong became a Special Administrative Region of China, which allows Hong Kong to operate under a different legal, political, and economic system than the rest of China. The agreement called for "one country, two systems" meaning Hong Kong and China—together, "one country"—will have two governmental systems. China will continue its current economic structure, which means heavy governmental control. Hong Kong will retain its separate political and economic status for 50 years (until 2047) and continue to enjoy the free-wheeling, free-market economy that has flourished there. The Joint Declaration along with the Basic Law, the post-1997 Hong Kong constitution China developed, provides a sense of direction for economic and political change.

Democracy has never been a major part of the political landscape in Hong Kong. Only once in the first 140 years of British rule did Hong Kong consider representative rule, and that

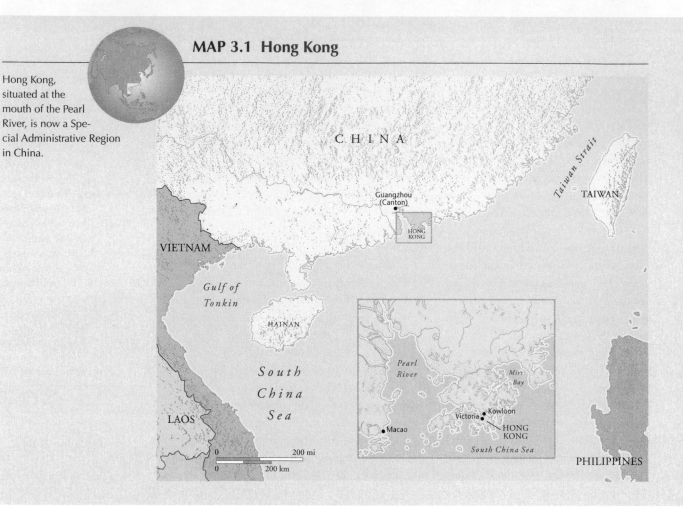

MAP 3.1 Hong Kong

Hong Kong, situated at the mouth of the Pearl River, is now a Special Administrative Region in China.

was quashed by the local business elite, who even today are more sympathetic to China's totalitarian point of view than to the democracy movement's point of view. They are more concerned about a stable economic climate than a democratic political climate, and they didn't really operate as a democracy under British rule. Until Hong Kong reverted back to China, it was considered a British colony, presided over by a governor appointed by the queen of England. Once the Joint Declaration of 1984 established a date for turnover of Hong Kong to China, the British began to push for democracy.

In 1990, political parties began to form, and in 1991 for the first time, the parties won the right to be represented in Hong Kong's Legislative Council (Legco). The people of Hong Kong directly elect only a small percentage of Legco's members. China appoints the rest, which represent probusiness, pro-Beijing forces. The Basic Law provides that 50 percent of the legislature may be directly elected by the people by 2004 and that full democratization should be discussed in 2007, but there is no way of knowing if this will ever happen.

However, on December 11, 1996, a 400-person committee appointed by the Chinese government voted for Hong Kong shipping magnate C. H. Tung as the first chief executive to run Hong Kong beginning July 1, 1997. Although Tung has pledged to continue with the best of the

West, he also hopes to reinforce traditional Chinese values. But despite Tung's desire to keep Hong Kong like it was, some changes are taking place. In mid-1999, Tung appealed to China to overturn a ruling made by Hong Kong's highest court, the Court of Final Appeal. Although China did not instigate the ruling, the action showed that the Tung was willing to set aside the rule of law outlined in the Basic Law and sacrifice Hong Kong's judiciary's independence. In addition, he has begun to tinker with Hong Kong's freedom from government intervention by propping up the stock and currency markets during the Asian financial crisis instead of letting the markets determine the prices of property and the Hong Kong dollar. Although Hong Kong's economy is ruled by market forces, the big business community rather than the political system has actually set the rules. There are some concerns voiced by the business community that the Hong Kong government is politicizing Hong Kong instead of taking a hands-off approach. However, many argue that it is about time that the business community cronyism, which was so much a part of the previous economic and political environment, be done away with and that the economic environment be opened up even more.

Swire is cooperating directly with China in a significant way. Swire even removed the Union Jack from its Cathay Pacific aircraft and repainted them an oriental jade color. The Swire family and its British-based parent company, John Swire & Sons, have some 90 percent of their assets in China and are involved in many Chinese joint ventures. Western investors who want to do business in China constantly approach Swire. However, Peter Sutch is still concerned about Swire's future in Hong Kong and China. Sutch is worried that China could seize its businesses, just as it did in Shanghai many years ago. More importantly, however, he worries that his Chinese partners will become more influential and sophisticated and will need to rely less on Swire's partnership. Will Sutch be able to negotiate the new political environment that is arising in Hong Kong? Will the trend toward democracy lessen his influence and control, or will he and the other business leaders in Hong Kong still have significant influence? Is he correct in pegging his future to the future of China, a country that is stable politically but searching for the best accommodation between a market economy and a totalitarian political regime?

INTRODUCTION

Multinational enterprises (MNEs) like Swire must operate in countries with different political and legal conditions. For the company to succeed, its management must carefully analyze whether its corporate policies will fit a desirable political and legal environment. Can it operate successfully in China doing the same things it does in Hong Kong, or must it adapt its operating strategies to fit the political and economic climate in China? This chapter discusses the political and legal systems that managers encounter and the factors they need to consider when operating in different countries.

THE POLITICAL ENVIRONMENT

Figure 3.1 shows how political and legal factors are part of the external environment that influences managerial decisions. A political system integrates the parts of a society into a viable, functioning unit. A major challenge of the political system is to bring together people of different ethnic or other backgrounds and allow them to work together to govern themselves. A country's political system influences how business is conducted domestically and internationally. In Hong Kong, for example, the political

The role of the political system is to integrate society.

Nongovernmental organizations (NGOs) represent people with many different political agendas. They seek support for their causes by maintaining Web sites, lobbying with governmental officials, introducing motions at companies' shareholder meetings, advertising their positions, and participating in high-visibility public protests. This photo shows some of the protestors at the 1999 World Trade Organization meetings in Seattle, Washington. At the forefront, protestors seek action to reduce world trade in forest products to maintain rainforests.

change from China taking control in 1997 worried many managers that China would change the relationship between government and business with the government exerting more influence and control in the business environment. In fact, several companies moved their head offices from Hong Kong to Singapore because of the insecurity. Jardine Matheson, one of the *hongs*, moved its domicile to Bermuda from Hong Kong because Bermuda offers freedom from Chinese control.

FIGURE 3.1 Political and Legal Influences on International Business

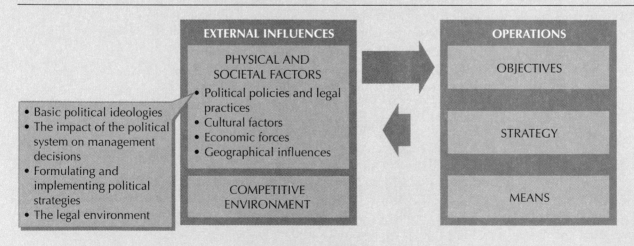

Figure 3.2 illustrates the development of political policies and their implementation. Political policies are established by aggregating, or bringing together, different points of view that are articulated by key constituencies, such as politicians, individuals, businesses, or other special-interest groups.[2] In the case of Hong Kong, business has always been the key constituency in establishing government policies. However, that is beginning to change; other interest groups are emerging to balance off the needs of business. Given the interests of different constituencies, governments identify policy alternatives and then decide on a specific policy to pursue. The policy is then implemented, and it may be altered depending on the reactions from political parties, government bureaucracies, legislatures, courts, and other constituencies. Normally, the chief executive officer (CEO) of an MNE watches policies as they develop and makes sure that the company voices its concerns in the interest articulation stage. Then, the CEO may want to work closely with a country's key decision makers in the

Political process functions
- **Interest articulation**
- **Interest aggregation**
- **Policy making**
- **Policy implementation and adjudication**

FIGURE 3.2 The Political System and Its Functions

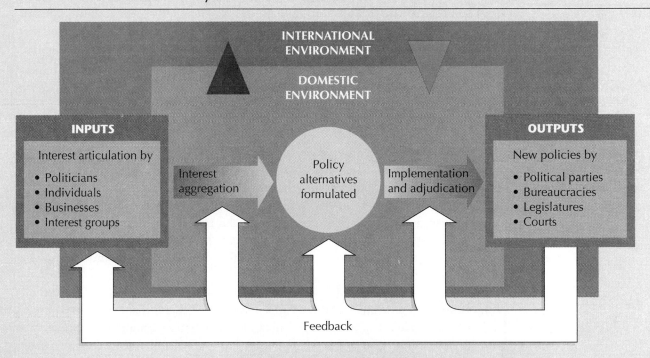

Governments formulate policy alternatives based on the inputs of different foreign and domestic entities, and then implement the policies. The marketplace then tests the outputs of these policies and revises them as necessary.

Source: From *Comparative Politics Today: A World View,* 3rd ed., by Gabriel A. Almond and G. Bingham Powell, Jr. Copyright ©1984 Gabriel A. Almond and G. Bingham Powell, Jr. Reprinted by permission Addison-Wesley Educational Publishers.

Interest aggregation is the collection of interests in the political system.

MNE management tries to influence governments on policies that affect it through lobbying.

policy formulation stage, which entails lobbying activities. Finally, the CEO may voice the company's stance on policies once they have been implemented. The key is to make sure that the company doesn't look like it's trying to influence laws inappropriately. Sometimes a CEO will try to influence the home-country government on policies that affect countries where the firm is operating. Prior to 2000 when the United States granted permanent normal trade relations to China, that decision had to be made annually. The United States–China Business Council, an organization of over 300 companies doing business in China, lobbies on behalf of its members for stable and expanded U.S.-China economic links.[3] The council includes companies such as Philip Morris, AT&T, Federal Express, BellSouth, and Lockheed Martin Company.

BASIC POLITICAL IDEOLOGIES

Political ideology—a body of constructs (complex ideas), theories, and aims that constitute a sociopolitical program.

Pluralism—the coexistence of different ideologies.

A **political ideology** is the body of constructs (complex ideas), theories, and aims that constitute a sociopolitical program. The liberal ideology of the Democratic Party and the conservative ideology of the Republican Party in the United States are examples of political ideologies. Most modern societies are **pluralistic** politically, meaning different ideologies coexist because there is no one ideology that everyone accepts. Pluralism arises because groups within countries often differ significantly from each other in language (e.g., India), ethnic background (e.g., South Africa), or religion (e.g., Northern Ireland). These and other cultural dimensions strongly influence the political system. Managers from the United States, where there are only two key political parties, might find it difficult to understand the political environment in a country where there are many different ideologies even within the political parties themselves. This makes it difficult for the manager to determine how to articulate the firm's interests and how to influence policy making.

The ultimate test of any political system is its ability to hold a society together despite pressures from different ideologies.

The ultimate test of any political system is its ability to hold a society together despite pressures from different ideologies tending to split it apart. The more different and strongly held the ideas are, the more difficult it is for a government to formulate policies that everyone can accept. Differing ideologies in countries such as Yugoslavia and the Soviet Union already broke those countries apart during the 1990s. The resulting political instability has made it difficult for them to attract foreign investment and for managers to feel comfortable operating in and committing resources to them.

However, ideologies also help bring countries together. One reason China wants Hong Kong back is because of ethnic Chinese ties. The belief is that a common Chinese heritage will enable Hong Kong and China to merge together faster than countries with very different ethnic ties. In fact, the U.S. government calls mainland China, Taiwan, Hong Kong, and Singapore the "Chinese Economic Area." Foreign companies that have had experience in Taiwan, Hong Kong, and Singapore can use that experience—and local management—to help them operate successfully in mainland China. Nike, for example, uses Taiwanese shoe manufacturers to invest in China and manufacture shoes using Chinese labor. Because of the strong ethnic Chinese ties between Taiwan and China, political disagreements notwithstanding, it is easier for Nike to use its Taiwanese partners than to manufacture shoes on its own.

THE IMPACT OF IDEOLOGICAL DIFFERENCES ON NATIONAL BOUNDARIES

Maps 3.2 to 3.5 illustrate how differences in history, culture, language, religion, and political ideology have affected boundaries in Europe. After World War I, the Austro-Hungarian Empire (see Map 3.2) broke up into Austria, Czechoslovakia, Hungary, Romania, and Yugoslavia (Map 3.3). With the advent of communist rule after World War II, countries often were formed from different ethnic groups held together by totalitarian rule. Yugoslavia, for example, comprised peoples that were ethnically and religiously very different from each other (Roman Catholic Croats, Greek Orthodox Serbs, Muslim Bosnians, and ethnic Albanians who lived in the southern Yugoslav province of Kosovo). The country's Croats and Serbs were on opposite sides during World War II, and Croats were accused of murdering thousands of Serbs. The Muslims in Bosnia and Kosovo were holdovers from the Ottoman Empire. As Map 3.5 shows, the breakup of the communist bloc in 1989 resulted in the disintegration of countries such as Czechoslovakia, the Soviet Union, and Yugoslavia due to the loss of totalitarian control and to

MAP 3.2 Europe on the Eve of World War I

The German, Russian, Ottoman, and Austro-Hungarian empires dominate the continent.

Source: Republished with permission of *The Boston Globe Magazine*, February 21, 1993. Permission conveyed through Copyright Clearance Center, Inc.

MAP 3.3 Europe After World War I

The empires have been broken up. Finland, Ukraine, and the Baltics (Estonia, Latvia, and Lithuania) are freed; Romania is enlarged; Poland, Czechoslovakia, Yugoslavia, and Turkey are created.

Source: Republished with permission of *The Boston Globe Magazine*, February 21, 1993. Permission conveyed through Copyright Clearance Center, Inc.

MAP 3.4 Europe After World War II

Germany is divided. Eastern European nations (including Albania) come under Soviet control. The red line separates the Soviet bloc and the Free West. Yugoslavia did become a communist nation not aligned with the bloc (dotted line).

Source: Republished with permission of *The Boston Globe Magazine*, February 21, 1993. Permission conveyed through Copyright Clearance Center, Inc.

MAP 3.5 Europe Today (After Communism)

Germany reunites, and the Soviet Union, Yugoslavia, and Czechoslovakia break up, creating 22 countries.

Source: Republished with permission of *The Boston Globe Magazine,* February 21, 1993. Permission conveyed through Copyright Clearance Center, Inc.

ethnic and other differences. When operating in a foreign country, it is important that managers understand its history and the present ethnic groups that could cause political tension and instability.

A POLITICAL SPECTRUM

Figure 3.3 presents a general schematic of the various forms of government. An example of a conservative democracy was the United States during the presidency of Ronald Reagan. An example of a liberal democracy was the United States during the presidency of Bill Clinton. China is an example of a communist totalitarian government, and Myanmar is an example of a fascist totalitarian government. The extremes for both democracy and totalitarianism are more theoretical than actual.

MNEs may be able to operate equally effectively in democratic and totalitarian regimes, but they prefer democracies because democracies usually have economic freedom and legal rules that safeguard individual (and corporate) rights. For example, the disbanding of the Soviet Union resulted in East Germany becoming a part of a new Germany, operating under political and economic freedom, which is very different than when it was part of the Soviet bloc. Companies that had previously avoided doing business in East Germany found it much different and much more attractive after reunification with West Germany. Let's now learn about the world's major political ideologies.

The two extremes on the political spectrum are democracy and totalitarianism.

FIGURE 3.3 The Political Spectrum

Although purely democratic and totalitarian governments are extremes, there are variations to each approach. For example, democratic governments range from radical on one side (advocates of political reform) to reactionary (advocates of a return to past conditions). The majority of democratic governments, however, lie somewhere in between.

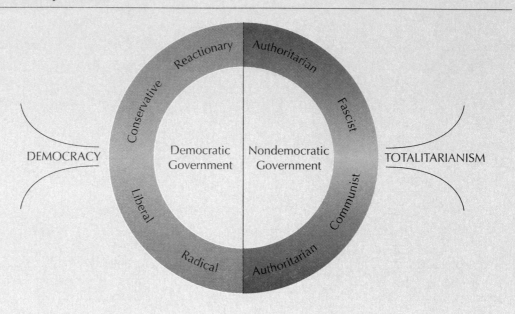

DEMOCRACY

Democratic systems involve wide participation by citizens in the decision-making process.

Winston Churchill (Great Britain's prime minister, 1940–1945, 1951–1955) once called democracy the worst form of government—except for all the others.[4] The ideology of pure democracy derives from the ancient Greeks, who believed all citizens should be equal politically and legally, should enjoy widespread freedoms, and should actively participate in the political process. In reality, society's complexity increases as the population increases, and so full participation by citizens in the decision-making process has become impossible in these modern times. Consequently, most democratic countries practice various forms of representative democracy, in which citizens elect representatives to make decisions rather than those citizens voting on every specific issue. Contemporary democratic political systems share the following

Representative democracy— majority rule is achieved through periodic elections.

1. Freedom of opinion, expression, press, and freedom to organize
2. Elections in which voters decide who is to represent them
3. Limited terms for elected officials
4. An independent and fair court system with high regard for individual rights and property
5. A nonpolitical bureaucracy and defense infrastructure
6. An accessibility to the decision-making process[5]

Factors for evaluating freedom
- **Political rights**
- **Civil liberties**

Political Rights and Civil Liberties   A key element of democracy is freedom in the areas of political rights and civil liberties. Each year since 1941, Freedom House, a New York nonprofit organization that monitors political rights and civil liberties around the world, has published a list of countries ranked according to the degree to which these freedoms exist. The major indicators for political rights are

- The degree to which fair and competitive elections occur
- The ability of voters to endow their elected representatives with real power
- The ability of people to organize into political parties or other competitive political groupings of their choice
- The existence of safeguards on the rights of minorities

The major indicators for civil liberties are

- The existence of freedom of the press
- Equality under the law for all individuals
- The extent of personal social freedoms
- The degree of freedom from extreme governmental indifference or corruption

Figure 3.4 illustrates that countries high in both political rights and civil liberties are "free," countries quite low in both political rights and civil liberties are "not free," and countries in between are "partly free." In 1998, 88 of the world's 191 countries were classified as free, while 53 countries were partly free, and 50 were not free. Partly free countries enjoy limited political rights and civil liberties, often in the context of corruption, weak rule of law, ethnic strife, or civil war. Not free countries deny their citizens basic rights and civil liberties.[6] The Freedom House survey identifies the number of countries in each category as well as the percentage of the world's population in each category. In 1998, it noted that there were 117 electoral democracies, more than double the number of countries that were called democracies in the early 1970s. The 117 electoral democracies represented 61 percent of the world's countries and nearly 55 percent of its population.[7] What some call the "third wave" of democratization started in the

FIGURE 3.4 Comparative Measures of Freedom

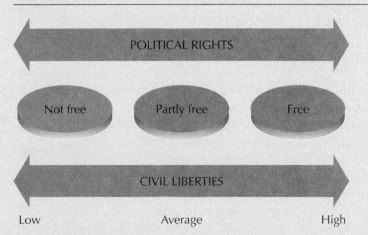

Countries classified as "free" in a political sense have a high degree of political rights and civil liberties. Those classified as "partly free" tend to be average to just below average in political rights and civil liberties. Those classified as "not free" tend to be quite low in both political rights and civil liberties. Examples of free countries include Australia, Bahamas, Belgium, Canada, Chile, Czech Republic, Estonia, Japan, South Africa, and South Korea. Partly free countries include Brazil, Burkino Faso, Cambodia, Malaysia, and Mexico. Not free countries include Algeria, China, Egypt, Ethiopia, Iraq, Kenya, Nigeria, North Korea, and Saudi Arabia.

Source: Original art based on Freedom House survey. Adrian Karatnycky, *Freedom in the World* (New York: Freedom House, 1995).

early 1970s and is still underway.[8] The following identifies the percentage of the total population living in free, partly free, and not free conditions in 1981, 1990, and 1998.[9]

	1981	1990	1998
Free	35.9%	21.6%	40.0%
Partly free	38.9	21.6	26.5
Not free	20.0	40.0	33.5

The trend toward democracy is increasing, but many new democracies are fragile and unstable.

The problem facing international business managers is the democracies that have emerged since the early 1970s, which are fragile and unstable. Indonesia and many of the former republics of the former Soviet Union are examples. Their instability stems from internal division, corruption, militaries and oligarchies (ruling power in the hands of a few), and destabilization from abroad. There is still concern over whether these democracies will continue on the path to freedom in political rights and civil liberties.

In a parliamentary system, the party with the most votes forms a government outright (if it has a majority) or through coalitions (if it has less than a majority).

In some democracies, such as the presidential form in the United States, people directly elect a president and a legislature. In other democracies, people vote for their representatives—or ruling party—and the ruling party selects the prime minister, who is the chief executive of the country. The parliamentary form of democracy in the United Kingdom is an example. There are also hybrids of each form. For example, Israel has a parliamentary government like that of the United Kingdom, but people vote directly for the prime minister as well.

Many democracies have only a few dominant parties, so it usually is not difficult for them to form a government. An exception to this is Israel, in which there are so many political parties that the government in power is usually a minority government (it has earned less than a majority of the votes) formed from a coalition of several minority parties. Minority governments tend to be unstable because the coalition can fall apart, forcing a new governing alliance to form. In the 1999 elections in Israel, Ehud Barak defeated the incumbent Prime Minister Binhyamin Netanyahu by 56 percent to 44 percent, but the parliamentary vote was much closer. Barak was forced to establish a coalition of at least seven different parties to form a majority ruling government.

Democracies differ not only in the amount of citizen participation in decision making but also in the degree of centralized control. Canada, for example, gives significant political power to the provinces at the expense of its federal government. A major difficulty in negotiating the Canada-U.S. Free Trade Agreement (FTA) was that many provinces had their own trade barriers. The United States also considers states' rights important as a counterweight to encroaching intervention and control by the central government, even though it has a stronger federal government than Canada does.

Companies may have difficulty determining how to act in decentralized democratic systems because they face many (sometimes conflicting) laws. For example, because of different state tax systems in the United States, foreign companies need to locate their U.S. headquarters carefully. In contrast, the political and legal systems of France and Japan are more highly centralized. Companies consequently find it easier to deal with those countries' systems because there is less variation from one part of the country to another.

The Internet is having a big effect on government, both democratic and totalitarian. The essence of politics is communication, and the Internet has made communicating that much easier and cheaper. Government documents that used to be available only through hard copy or CD-ROM are now available on the Internet, giving managers instant access to a lot of information that can help them in the decision-making process. Not only are companies using the Internet to get their message across to potential investors and customers, so are politicians and lobbyists. The United States–China Business Council has an Internet site with special services for its members. The Internet will not replace elected representatives, because democracy still needs specialists who can interpret and compromise, but the Internet makes it easier to find the information on which to base an informed decision, and it allows elected representatives to keep more in touch with constituents.

The Internet allows politicians and government to communicate more effectively with constituents and provide information to managers.

In addition, the Internet has an impact on totalitarian societies. Where people have access to the Internet, they can get a wealth of information about their own country, as well as the outside world—information the government may try to restrict. Access to more information could reduce the power of totalitarian regimes.

Stability in Democracies   Churchill's quote on democracy implies that democracies are not perfect. Just as new democracies have problems, so do mature democracies. In surveys on democracy in the United States, it is clear that confidence in politicians and government have continued to decline over the past quarter-century. People are concerned about whether or not politicians are trustworthy and care about voters. Confidence in the executive branch of government in the United States fell from 42 percent in 1966 to 12 percent in 1997 and trust in Congress fell from 42 percent to 11 percent.[10] In addition, the percentage of people voting is declining. The loss of faith in political institutions and the feeling that professional pressure groups and lobbying organizations are increasingly more influential than individuals are causes of concern in democracy. In spite of this, 75 percent of people in democracies strongly feel that democracy is the best form of government.[11]

Confidence in democracies is waning, but people in democratic countries still believe democracy is the best form of government.

TOTALITARIANISM

As Figure 3.3 showed, democracy is at one end of the political spectrum, and totalitarianism is at the other. Totalitarian governments are usually theocratic or secular. In theocratic totalitarianism, religious leaders are also the political leaders. This form is best exemplified in Middle Eastern Islamic countries such as Iran. In secular totalitarianism, the government often imposes order through military power. Examples of this form are found in Cambodia and Iraq. In a totalitarian state, a single party, individual, or group of individuals monopolizes political power and neither recognizes nor permits opposition. Only a few individuals participate in decision making. All countries considered not free and many considered partly free in Figure 3.4 are totalitarian.

Theocratic totalitarianism—religious leaders are the political leaders.

Secular totalitarianism—control is enforced through military power.

Totalitarianism takes several forms, including fascism, authoritarianism, and communism. Mussolini (Italy's dictator, 1924–1943) defined *fascism* as follows: "The Fascist conception of the state is all-embracing; outside of it no human or spiritual value may exist, much less have any value. Thus understood Fascism is totalitarian and the Fascist State, as a synthesis and a unit which includes all values, interprets, develops and lends additional power to the whole life of a people."[12] Examples of fascist totalitarianism in

In a totalitarian system, decision making is restricted to a few individuals.

the past include Germany under Hitler, Portugal under Salazar, and Spain under Franco. Examples of authoritarian totalitarianism include Chile under Pinochet, and South Africa prior to the end of apartheid and the initiation of black rule. Authoritarianism differs from fascism in that the former simply desires to rule people, while the latter desires to control people's minds and souls, to convert them to its own faith.[13]

Communism—a form of secular totalitarianism that combines political and economic systems into a sociopolitical agenda.

Communism is a form of secular totalitarianism in which political and economic systems (and philosophies) are virtually inseparable. Communists believe in the equal distribution of wealth, which entails total government ownership and control of resources. Communism has failed in most parts of the world. The Eastern European countries and the former Soviet Union have moved away from communism to various degrees of democracy. As communism moves toward democracy, the link between economics and politics in communist countries has been weakened, making countries such as Estonia, Latvia, and Lithuania free. China, North Korea, and Vietnam, however, are still communist countries with strong centralized authoritarian control over the political process.

As noted above, totalitarian regimes fit primarily in the not free category in Figure 3.4. Freedom House notes that 90 percent of the not free countries share one or more of the following characteristics

1. They have a majority Muslim population and frequently confront the pressures of fundamentalist Islam.
2. They are multi-ethnic societies in which power is not held by a dominant ethnic group (one that represents over two-thirds of the population).
3. They are neocommunist or postcommunist transitional societies.[14]

With few exceptions, most totalitarian governments have been opening up and liberalizing since 1989 when the Berlin Wall fell and the Soviet bloc broke apart. As these countries move from totalitarian to democratic states, the degree of instability increases. Accompanied by political changes are economic changes as these countries move more toward the market model. We'll discuss those economic issues in Chapter 4, but for now let's see how political systems affect international management.

THE IMPACT OF THE POLITICAL SYSTEM ON MANAGEMENT DECISIONS

As noted earlier, management at Swire Pacific, as is true of all Hong Kong companies, must cope with China's takeover of Hong Kong. Managers need to identify the new risks they face and determine how China is going to intervene in the economic affairs of Hong Kong.

POLITICAL RISK

Political risk—a risk that occurs because of political instability.

As managers evaluate countries as a potential place to do business and as they struggle to succeed once they have committed resources, they need to be aware of **political risk**. Political risk is when international companies fear that the political climate in a foreign country will change in such a way that their operating position will deteriorate. Although political risks can occur in democratic as well as totalitarian political regimes, they tend to be more prevalent in totalitarian regimes.

Types and Causes of Political Risk   Political actions that may affect company operations adversely are governmental takeovers of property, either with or without compensation; operational restrictions that impede the company's ability to take certain actions; and agitation that disrupts sales or causes damage to property or personnel. Although one usually thinks of political risk as not being able to operate in a specific country because of political instability in that country, there are other ways that political risk can affect a company. For example, during the period of apartheid in South Africa, many U.S. companies with investments in South Africa faced boycotts in the United States by groups that were morally opposed to apartheid. Similarly, groups opposed to doing business with China have put up Internet sites criticizing U.S. policy and U.S. companies doing business in China, hoping to exert the same kind of pressure that forced many companies out of South Africa.

Political risk may occur for the following reasons:

1. *Opinions of political leadership.* Political leaders' opinions may change over time, and the leaders could be replaced by force or election with politicians whose views toward business and foreign investment are much less positive. Changes may result in adverse operating regulations, such as limits on remittances or discriminatory taxes. They may breach existing contracts or take over the investors' property.

2. *Civil disorder.* Unrest may occur because of economic conditions, human rights violations, or group animosity within the society. A good example of this risk took place in Indonesia in 1998 during the height of the Asian financial crisis when people demonstrated against President Suharto, who had ruled Indonesia officially since 1968 and who was accused of widespread corruption, especially enriching his family and close friends, and failed economic policies.[15] Then demonstrators turned against ethnic Chinese, and conflicts arose between Christians and Muslims. Companies owned by ethnic Chinese or foreign companies using ethnic Chinese in management positions were the targets of demonstrators and incurred serious property damage.[16] Further, widespread crime, such as kidnapping of personnel, may result from inadequate police control. Conditions may result in procurement difficulties, work stoppages, shipment delays, and property damage. If carried to an extreme, the nation itself may break apart, leaving the investor to operate in a smaller market or be forced to leave the market.

3. *External relations.* Animosity between the host country and the foreign investor's home country may result in work-stoppage protests, forced divestment of operations, and loss of supplies and markets. Animosity, especially war, between the host country and any other country may result in property damage and inability to get supplies or deliver goods.

Causes of political risk
- **Changing opinions of political leadership**
- **Civil disorder**
- **External relations**

Micro and Macro Political Risks   If political actions are aimed only at specific foreign investments, they are known as **micro political risks**. For example, after NATO forces accidentally (as claimed by NATO) bombed the Chinese embassy in Belgrade, Yugoslavia, on May 7, 1999, demonstrators trashed KFC stores in China but did not touch Pizza Hut stores, even though both were owned by Tricon Global Restaurants, a U.S.-based company. The Chinese, who were demonstrating primarily against the

Micro political risk—political actions are aimed at specific foreign investments.

Looking to the Future
WILL DEMOCRACY SURVIVE?

What will the world's political makeup look like in the next decade? Will democracy continue to grow, or will totalitarianism creep back? Remember Churchill's quote? He said democracy is the worst form of government, except for all the others. The next decade will test whether his statement is true and whether the 40 or so countries that have become democratic in the past two decades will remain democratic or slip back into totalitarianism.

Some people argue that democracy has certain preconditions, such as economic development. Indeed, most high-income or upper-middle-income countries are democratic, while most nondemocracies are poor, non-Western, or both.[17] Others argue that democracy is the product of political leaders with the will and skill to see democratization occur.[18] These people say that the move toward democracy in Russia occurred because of two men: Mikhail Gorbachev and Boris Yeltsin. When Gorbachev went as far as he could, Yeltsin was there for the next steps. After Yeltsin, someone else will probably take Russia to the next democratic plateau, although there are no guarantees. The economic chaos that has gripped Russia in recent years may slow the move to democracy. Only time will tell.

Democracy does not necessarily mean stability. The newer democracies of the 1990s, especially those in the former Soviet bloc countries, are still unstable enough to possibly threaten war. A war between two democracies has not happened in this century, but it could happen as the new democracies try to establish themselves. Managers ought not to assume that because they are operating in a democratic country there is no political risk. They still need to monitor the political environment just as they might in a less free country.

Asia is testing an alternative to democracy. With the exception of Japan, and to a lesser extent India and South Korea, most Asian countries are not democracies, and their leaders do not appear to want democracy. Instead, they are attempting to link strong economic growth and totalitarian political systems. This is clearly the case with China, and to a slightly lesser extent Singapore. However, encouraging signs are appearing for those who favor democracy, such as the elections in Taiwan that nudged that island nation closer to democracy and farther away from China's autocratic policies. In some respects, the elimination of strong central controls with the advent of democracy has created problems in some countries—problems such as the removal of individual moral constraints, resulting in crime, corruption, and an atmosphere of amoralism.[19]

The threat to democracy could come from a return to communism, from electoral victories of antidemocratic forces (such as Islamic fundamentalism), or from the concentration of power in a leader, which seems to be happening in East Asia. The key, then, is to define democracy in different national contexts. It could be argued, as totalitarian governments do, that democracy is not appropriate for all countries. Who is to say that China would fare any better if it held elections or allowed free speech. However, there is a clear link between political and economic freedom and economic growth. So, as the emerging democracies liberalize politically, they may loosen up economically, setting the stage for solid economic growth.

United States, targeted KFC, a well-known U.S. company, but left Pizza Hut untouched because they thought it was Italian-owned.

Companies most likely to be affected by micro political risk are those that may have a considerable and visible impact on a given country because of their size, monopoly position, importance to their home country's national defense, and dependence of other industries on them. If agitation's cause is animosity between factions in the host country and the government of a foreign country, protesters may target only the most visible companies from that foreign country, like KFC or McDonald's. There is also evidence that firms are apt to face adverse political situations if they act in a socially irresponsible manner.

If political actions affect a broad spectrum of foreign investors, they are **macro political risks**. For example, after the communist revolution in Cuba, the takeover of property was aimed at all foreign investors regardless of industry, nationality, or whether or not the investors' past behavior had been socially responsive. This is not as much an issue now as it was in the 1960s, when a number of countries declared their independence from previous colonial powers. Today most countries realize that they need the stability of foreign direct investment in order to grow.

> Macro political risk—political actions affect a broad spectrum of foreign investors.

GOVERNMENT INTERVENTION IN THE ECONOMY

As companies move abroad, management must deal with governments that have different attitudes about their economic influence. There are two ideological paradigms on the role of governments: *individualistic* and *communitarian*.[20]

The **individualistic paradigm** believes in minimal intervention in the economy. Individualistic states believe in regulation, and they are likely to be democratic and economically free. They will handle market defects, such as entry barriers and insufficient consumer knowledge and power, but they will not intervene too much. They believe in a limited role of government, in checks and balances, and have a high distrust of central government power. Government is essentially separate from business.

> Individualistic—minimal government intervention in the economy.

In a **communitarian paradigm**, government tends to be prestigious, authoritative, and sometimes authoritarian. It is very hierarchical and may be either democratic, as in the case of Japan, or autocratic, as in the case of China. It thrives on a respected, centralized bureaucracy with a stable political party or coalition in power.

> Communitarian—the government defines needs and priorities and partners with business in a major way.

Individualistic countries bring business activity into line with the needs of the community through promoting marketplace competition and by regulating the marketplace in those instances where competition by itself is unreliable or unacceptable, such as when a company might be able to establish a monopoly position or degrade the environment. Communitarian countries may do the same, but they also establish a partnership with business. The communitarian concept has spread to other Asian countries more anxious to mirror the examples of Japan and China than the more individualistic example of the United States.

Japan is a good example of how the communitarian philosophy can affect business. After World War II, Japan had to rebuild its economy. It focused on recovery rather than reform of its basic system. Because there was no need to focus on military and defense, it could put its efforts into infrastructure and the economy. It had good political stability and a highly educated workforce. At the time, Japan decided to insulate its economy from outside competition, even though it was highly competitive inside. However, that decision made it difficult for foreign companies to establish a market position in Japan, which is still true today. The government told companies to focus on scale (large size, which permits large production runs and lower costs per unit) and concentration (few competitors in an industry or at least lots of cooperation among competitors) rather than small entrepreneurial activities. It also encouraged companies to focus on export to high-income countries. Government's role was to establish a broad vision of the future and then set incentives and sanctions to accomplish these objectives. Japan's key government institutions were the Ministry of International Trade and Industry (MITI), the Ministry of Finance, the Bank of Japan, and the Economic Planning Agency. These institutions funded preferred industries and controlled access to technology, foreign exchange, and imports. In response, the Keidanren, an organization of the top companies in Japan, helped establish a consensus within the business community. Its main objective was to influence the government on policies responsive to its wishes.[21]

> **Government action isn't always consistent—different agencies may have different attitudes toward business issues.**

In addition to understanding governmental functions, managers also must realize that governmental action is not always consistent. In the United States, for example, significant conflict exists within government regarding how and to what extent it should regulate international business activities for firms operating abroad from a U.S. base. No specific government agency deals with international issues, so conflicting policies can exist. For example, at least three different U.S. government agencies share responsibility for regulating nonagricultural exports: the State Department, the Department of Defense, and the Department of Commerce. State is responsible for the overall political relationships between the United States and other countries, Defense is responsible for national defense, and Commerce is responsible for facilitating commercial—including export—activities. These agencies often have different viewpoints on how to regulate exports. For example, it might seem perfectly logical from a commercial standpoint to sell satellite technology to China, but the Defense Department might veto such sales in the name of national security.

If a U.S. company moves from the United States to Germany, Japan, or South Korea, three very communitarian countries, it may have to develop new strategies for its relationships with government, suppliers, customers, and competitors. In the United States, relationships may be arms' length, competitive, and adversarial, while in Germany, Japan, and South Korea, they may be much more cooperative.

FORMULATING AND IMPLEMENTING POLITICAL STRATEGIES

> **Formulating political strategies is complicated by the wide range of participants in the decision-making process, differences in logic, and institutional power.**

Formulating political strategies often is more complicated for managers than formulating competitive marketplace strategies. When dealing in the political arena, managers need to know how decisions are made that could influence their ability to operate. Then they need to know what the rules are for trying to influence political decisions.

There are certain steps that a company must follow if it wants to establish an appropriate political strategy in its countries of operation.

> **Establishing a political strategy involves identifying and defining the political situation, important institutions, and key individuals.**

1. Identify the issue. What is the specific issue facing a firm—trade barriers, environmental standards, worker rights?
2. Define the political aspect of the issue. Does the government feel strongly about the specific issue, or is it of minimal concern? Is there a political dimension to the issue, or is it something that can be dealt with outside of politics?

3. Assess the potential political action of other companies and special-interest groups. Who are the parties that are affected and able to generate political pressure? What are their strategies likely to be?

4. Identify important institutions and key individuals—legislatures, regulatory agencies, courts, important personalities.

5. Formulate strategies. What are the key objectives, the major alternatives, and the likely effectiveness of alternative strategies?

6. Determine the impact of implementation. What will be the public relations fallout in the home and host countries if the action taken is unpopular?

7. Select the most appropriate strategy and implement.[22]

Implementing a strategy means marshaling whatever resources are necessary to accomplish the company's political objectives. For example, in the United States, companies—domestic or foreign—hire lobbyists to educate and persuade government decision makers about the merits of their position. In a representative democracy, lobbyists represent constituencies and perform the important role of aggregating ideas and communicating them to decision makers. Without the freedom of expression—such as lobbying—democracy could not exist. As the ethics of government–business relationships have become more important even in totalitarian countries, companies have greater reason to examine carefully their policy formulation and implementation strategies.

> **Lobbyists educate and persuade government decision makers.**

A company also can attempt to influence governmental action from consumers on up by using a grassroots campaign or by building coalitions of different groups that share the company's interests. As noted earlier in the chapter, the United States–China Business Council is a lobbying organization that represents the interests of its members to the appropriate people in the U.S. government. Because of its size and the importance of its members, the council is able to wield a degree of influence that would not be possible for a single company.

> **Foreign companies often enlist the support of consumers to combat government restrictions and sales.**

Part of the problem with establishing a global political strategy is that democracies deal with companies differently than do totalitarian regimes. In general, foreign companies can influence democracies through lobbying. However, companies sometimes abuse their power by engaging in bribery and other illicit activities. Sometimes, a totalitarian regime might seem more stable because it doesn't have to deal with the pressures of democracy. But when such a regime is overthrown, the changes for business tend to be larger and more rapid than change typically is within a democracy. For example, when the Soviet Union broke up, foreign companies that had entered into contracts with the former central government found that these contracts were not binding on the individual republics' governments. Companies had to renegotiate the contracts or pull out of the country. In another example, Mozambique was a colony of Portugal. When it declared its independence in 1988, it forced Portuguese investors out of the country, telling them to abandon their investments. Even though the colony might have seemed stable, a change in government caused significant change in investment strategies.

THE LEGAL ENVIRONMENT

Closely related to the political system, the legal system is another dimension of the external environment that influences business. Managers must be aware of the legal systems in the countries in which they operate, the nature of the legal profession, both domestic and international, and the legal relationships that exist between countries. Legal systems differ in terms of the nature of the system—common law, civil law, and theocratic law—and the degree of independence of the judiciary from the political process. As noted in the opening case, for example, there was some concern in 1999 that Hong Kong was moving away from the legal traditions established by the British toward the influence of Beijing.

Also, some of the totalitarian countries that are going through a transition to democracy and to a free-market economy don't have a legal system in place that deals with business transactions in a global market context. A good example is the problems facing foreign firms doing business in Russia. Russian commercial law is undeveloped and inconsistent. For instance, the Central Bank of Russia forbids cash payments over a nominal sum, but that fell apart in 1998 when the banking system in Russia collapsed. Companies had no choice but to make large payments in cash. Scott Antel, a partner with Arthur Andersen in Moscow, said that most firms disobeyed the law just to survive.[23] Few U.S. companies with offices in Russia will actually reveal how they navigate the changing business environment for fear of exposing themselves to illegal activity, but the instability in the economic environment and vagaries of the legal system make it difficult for them to operate strictly legally.

KINDS OF LEGAL SYSTEMS

Legal systems usually fall into one of three categories: common law, civil law, and theocratic law.

Common Law   The United States and the United Kingdom are examples of countries with a **common law system**. Common law is based on tradition, precedent, and custom and usage. The courts fulfill an important role in interpreting the law according to those characteristics. Because the United Kingdom originated common law in the modern setting, its former and current colonies, such as Hong Kong, also have common law systems.

Civil Law   The **civil law system**, also called a **codified legal system**, is based on a detailed set of laws that make up a code. Rules for conducting business transactions are a part of the code. Over 70 countries, including Germany, France, and Japan, operate on a civil law basis.

The two legal systems differ primarily in that common law is based on the courts' interpretations of events, while civil law is based on how the law is applied to the facts. An example of an area in which the two systems differ in practice is contracts. In a common law country, contracts tend to be detailed, with all contingencies spelled out. In a civil law country, contracts tend to be shorter and less specific because many of the issues that a common law contract would cover already are included in the civil code. So, when entering into contracts abroad, it is important for the manager to understand which type of legal system will establish the contract. Also civil law tends to be less adversarial than common law because judges rely on detailed legal codes rather than on precedent. This is one reason why British and U.S. law firms encounter so much resistance when they enter civil law countries. They are used to the competitive, adversarial approach that the common law system engenders.

Countries in transition struggle to develop a legal system consistent with the global market economy.

A common law system is based on tradition, precedent, custom and usage, and interpretation by the courts.

A civil law system is based on a detailed set of laws organized into a legal code.

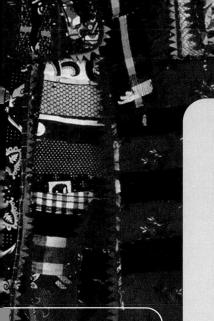

Ethical Dilemmas and Social Responsibility
IS "WHEN IN ROME, DO AS THE ROMANS DO" THE BEST APPROACH FOR GLOBAL ETHICS?

Ethical dilemmas entail balancing means and ends. Means are the actions one takes, which may be right or wrong; ends are the results of the actions, which may also be right or wrong. Ethics teaches that "people have a responsibility to do what is right and to avoid doing what is wrong."[24] Some people argue that cultural relativism, or the belief that behavior has meaning only in its specific cultural or ethical context, implies that no method exists for deciding whether behavior is appropriate. However, we contend that it is possible to measure whether behavior is appropriate. Individuals must seek justification for their behavior, and that justification is a function of cultural values (many of which are universal), legal principles, and economic practices.

Some people also argue that the legal justification for ethical behavior is the only important one. By this standard, a person or company can do anything that is not illegal. However, there are five reasons why the legal argument is insufficient.

1. The law is not appropriate for regulating all business activity because not everything that is unethical is illegal. This would be true of many dimensions of interpersonal behavior, for example.
2. The law is slow to develop in emerging areas of concern. Laws take time to be legislated and tested in courts. Further, they cannot anticipate all future ethical dilemmas; basically they are a reaction to issues that have already surfaced. Countries with civil law systems rely on specificity in the law, and there may not be enough laws passed that deal with ethical issues.
3. The law often is based on moral concepts that are not precisely defined and that cannot be separated from legal concepts. Moral concepts must be considered along with legal ones.
4. The law is often in need of testing by the courts. This is especially true of case law, in which the courts establish precedent.
5. The law is not very efficient. A reliance on legal rulings on every area of ethical behavior would not be in anyone's best interests.[25]

In spite of the pitfalls of using the law as the major basis for deciding ethical disputes, there also are good reasons for at least complying with it:

1. The law embodies many of a country's moral beliefs and is an adequate guide for proper conduct.
2. The law provides a clearly defined set of rules. Following those rules at least establishes a good precedent. Some people are afraid to go beyond the law because of the potential legal liability that could result if they did.
3. The law contains enforceable rules that all must follow. It puts everyone on an equal footing. For example, everyone working for a company established in the United States must comply with the Foreign Corrupt Practices Act, which prohibits bribery of foreign governmental officials for business benefit. As long as everyone complies with the law, no one will

have an edge due to bribery. However, laws are still subject to interpretation and often contain loopholes.

4. The law represents a consensus derived from significant experience and deliberation. It should reflect careful and wide-ranging discussions.[26]

The problem for companies that use a legal basis for ethical behavior is that laws vary among countries. For example, a major area of contention between industrial and developing countries is the protection of intellectual property, such as computer software. The industrial countries, which have strong laws concerning intellectual-property rights, argue that developing countries need to strengthen such laws and their enforcement. U.S. software manufacturers note that in some Asian countries it is possible to buy a heavily discounted pirated version of new software in one store and then go next-door and purchase a photocopy of the documentation for the legal version. Using a legal basis for ethical behavior would mean that such purchases are ethical because they occur in countries that either do not have laws on intellectual-property rights or do not enforce the laws. Although international trade agreements provide for better protection of intellectual property, it is up to the member countries to implement the provisions, and that is proceeding at a very slow pace. One could argue that the moral values that cross cultures will be embodied in legal systems, but as the software example demonstrates, that is too simplistic. Not all moral values are common to every culture. In addition, strong home-country governments may try to extend their legal and ethical practices to the foreign subsidiaries of domestically headquartered companies—an action known as extraterritoriality. For example, a subsidiary of a U.S. company operating in China might be forced to follow some U.S. laws, even though China has no comparable laws and other companies operating there are not subject to the U.S. laws. In some cases, such as with health and safety standards, extraterritoriality should not cause problems. In other cases, such as with restrictions on trade with enemies of the United States, extraterritoriality may cause tension between the foreign subsidiary and the host-country government.

As noted above, the law provides a clearly defined set of rules, which companies often follow strictly because of concerns about potential legal liability. However, a company may seek a loophole to accomplish an objective. Evaluating potential liability and legality of actions varies between countries with civil law systems and those with common law ones. Civil law countries tend to have a large body of laws that specify the legality of various behaviors. Common law countries tend to rely more on cases and precedents than on statutory regulations. A company must pay attention to laws to ensure the minimum level of compliance in each country in which it operates. When faced with conflicting laws, however, management must decide which applies.

A theocratic legal system is based on religious precepts, such as Islamic law.

Theocratic Law   The third type of legal system is the **theocratic law system**, which is based on religious precepts. The best example of this system is Islamic law, which is found in Muslim countries. Islamic law, or Shair'a, is based on the following sources

- The Koran, the sacred text
- The Sunnah, or decisions and sayings of the Prophet Muhammad

- The writings of Islamic scholars, who derive rules by analogy from the principles established in the Koran and the Sunnah
- The consensus of Muslim countries' legal communities[27]

Given that 25 percent of the world's population is Islamic, it is important to understand how Islam is translated into rules that govern economic transactions. This is true for Islamic countries—such as Iran, Sudan, and Pakistan, which have banned traditional commercial banking and adopted Islamic banking models—and for Muslims who live in non-Islamic countries.[28] Since the tenth century A.D., Islamic law has remained frozen—it cannot change, modify, or extend with changing times. Islamic law is a moral rather than a commercial law and was intended to govern all aspects of life. Many Muslim countries have legal systems that are a unique blend of the Islamic law system and a common or civil law system derived from previous colonial ties. Even though Islamic law is fixed, Islamic jurists and scholars are constantly debating its application in different modern settings. The key is to adhere to the constants of Islam while maintaining sufficient flexibility to operate in a modern economy.

An example of how Islamic law influences international business can be found in banking. According to Islamic law, banks cannot charge interest or benefit from interest.[29] Instead, banks have to structure fees into their loans to allow them to make a profit. For example, assume that a company needs to borrow money to purchase merchandise. It can approach a bank, which would buy the goods and sell them to the company, which will pay the bank at a future date at an agreed-upon markup.[30] Also, banks can structure loans so that they share in the profits of a venture rather than receive interest. The underlying principle is that money can earn a return by being employed productively, but not by being earned in financial markets.[31] There are approximately a 176 Islamic banks worldwide, with a total capital of more than $7.3 billion and total assets of about $148 billion.[32] Many western banks, such as Citi, J. P. Morgan, Deutsche Bank, and ABN AMRO Bank of the Netherlands, have Islamic units.[33]

> **Islamic law does not permit banks to pay or collect interest.**

CONSUMER SAFEGUARDS

A major challenge that companies face in the global environment is how to deal with product liability issues. Different legal systems provide different safeguards for consumers. For example, it appears that Japanese consumers have less access to and assistance from the legal community in Japan than American consumers do in the United States, given that they have fewer lawyers per capita than does the United States. Also, the Japanese legal system differs from the U.S. system in a variety of ways. The Japanese Federation of Bar Associations sets legal fees, foreign lawyers are prohibited from advising clients on Japanese law or from hiring local Japanese lawyers to do so, and advertising restrictions limit consumer information about legal services. In addition, the high cost of legal services and the long delays in the legal process discourage consumers from filing civil suits. A survey of 194 big Japanese manufacturers found that only 24 had ever faced a product liability suit at home and, of those, only 7 had lost. Further, one auto company had been hit with 250 product liability suits a year in the United States and only 2 in Japan.[34] It appears that in Japan consumers have less legal protection and corporations have fewer legal problems than is the case in the United States.

THE LEGAL PROFESSION

MNEs must use lawyers for a variety of services, such as negotiating contracts and protecting intellectual property. Lawyers and their firms vary among countries in terms of how they practice law and service clients.

Most legal firms are small.

Law firms that service international clients have changed over the years. In general, most law firms are quite small. In the United Kingdom and the United States, for example, 60 percent of lawyers are in firms of five persons or fewer.[35] There are still large firms servicing multinational clients, but many MNEs, concerned about upward-spiraling legal fees, have established in-house legal staffs. Smaller companies in international business still rely on outside legal counsel for help with a wide variety of issues, such as agent–distributor relationships and protecting intellectual property.

Large legal firms have surfaced, often through mergers, in response to the globalization of their large clients.

Just as MNEs have invested abroad to take advantage of expanding business opportunities, law firms have expanded abroad to service their clients. Laws vary from country to country, and legal staffs need to understand local practices. Also, law firms have had to overcome significant barriers as they have expanded. Those barriers include restrictions on foreign firms from hiring local lawyers, from forming partnerships with local law firms, or even from entering the country to practice law. However, there are countries that allow foreigners to practice law and to open offices within their borders. New York law firm Weil, Gotshal & Manges opened an office in London in 1996 to service its U.S.-based clients and to pick up business from British firms. The firm hired well-connected British lawyers to help it break into the British market and establish a client base. In addition, Weil, Gotshal's American lawyers cycle through London tending to the European needs of American clients.[36]

Some countries even allow law firms to merge—an aggressive move. In 1999, senior lawyers at Rogers & Wells in New York and Clifford Chance in London voted to join forces in what would be the first overseas merger of large law firms. The merger took place to service multinational clients better and to counter the competition of the global public accounting firms, such as Arthur Andersen, that had begun to move into the legal business. The firms will need to deal with cultural differences, but the new firm will give each of the two member firms access to the other's markets.[37]

A far less aggressive move overseas is for law firms to establish correspondent relationships with firms in other countries. For example, a law firm in the United States would refer clients looking to do work in France to a French law firm.

The manager doing business overseas has a number of ways to get legal work done in different countries. The key is to choose a law firm that has connections overseas, through the company's own offices, a merger, or correspondent relationships. The laws in each country differ so much that it is important to have some representation in the local environment.

LEGAL ISSUES IN INTERNATIONAL BUSINESS

Impact of laws on international business
- **National laws affect all local business activities**
- **National laws affect cross-border activities**
- **International treaties and conventions may govern some cross-border transactions**

National laws affect business within the country or business among countries. Some national laws on local business activity influence both domestic and foreign companies, especially in the areas of health and safety standards, employment practices, antitrust prohibitions, contractual relationships, environmental practices, and patents and trademarks. For example, the maximum workweek in Thailand is 84 hours, and that applies to domestic and foreign firms. Nike subcontracts its shoe manufacturing to a local Thai company. However, because of pressures from labor and consumer groups to follow better employment practices, Nike has established its own maximum of 60 hours, which the local contractor must follow. If Nike wanted to follow the Thai law, it could, but that would be in violation of its own code of conduct.

Laws also exist that govern cross-border activities, such as the investment of capital, the payment of dividends to foreign investors, and customs duties on imports. International laws, such as treaties governing the cross-border transfer of hazardous waste, can also determine how a firm operates in transporting shipments across borders.

Because laws affect so many aspects of international business, several subsequent chapters discuss legal issues in more depth. For example, we'll discuss laws governing the regulation of trade and investments, taxes, intellectual-property protection, regulation of financial flows and of ownership, reporting requirements, contractual relationships, extraterritoriality (the extension by a government of the application of its laws to foreign operations of companies), international treaties, and dispute resolution.

WEB CONNECTION

Check out our home page www.prenhall.com/daniels for links to key resources for you in your study of international business.

SUMMARY

- The political process involves inputs from various interest groups, articulation of issues that affect policy formulation, aggregation of those issues into key alternatives, development of policies, and implementation and adjudication of the policies.

- Most complex societies are pluralistic, which means they encompass a variety of ideologies.

- The ultimate test of any political system is its ability to hold a society together despite pressures from different ideologies.

- In democracies, there is wide participation in the decision-making process. In totalitarian regimes, only few citizens participate, although some regimes are beginning to allow greater participation in the decision-making process. Totalitarian regimes can be either theocratic or secular.

- Factors considered in measuring freedom include the degree to which fair and competitive elections occur, the extent to which individual and group freedoms are guaranteed, and the existence of freedom of the press.

- Political risk occurs because of changing opinions of political leadership, civil disorder, or external relations between the host country and the foreign investor's home country.

- Micro political risks occur when actions are taken against specific foreign investments; macro political risks occur when actions are taken against a broad spectrum of foreign investors.

- Managers of MNEs must learn to cope with varying degrees of governmental intervention in economic decisions, depending on the countries in which a company is doing business.

- Individualistic political regimes believe in minimal intervention in the economy by government; communitarian regimes believe that a government's role is to define a nation's needs and priorities and ensure that they are met through close cooperation between government and business.

- Companies try to educate government officials on specific actions that will benefit their ability to compete through lobbying efforts.

- In formulating political strategies, managers must consider the possible political actions that could affect the company, the different constituencies that might influence those political actions, the political strategies that would be in the best interests of the company, and the costs of implementing those strategies.

- Common law systems are based on tradition, precedent, and custom and usage. Civil law systems are based on a detailed set of laws organized into a code. Theocratic legal systems are based on religious precepts, as exemplified by Islamic law.

- Many law firms have increased their size through mergers to better service corporate clients in domestic and international mergers and acquisitions.

- There are national laws that govern local business activity of both domestic and foreign firms, national laws that govern cross-border activities, and international laws that govern cross-border activities.

- The legal environment can influence international companies in various ways; for example, by regulating trade and investment and protecting intellectual property.

- Although there is legal justification for some ethical behavior, the law is not an adequate guide for all such behavior. The legality of an action is one element that should be considered, but not the only one.

C A S E
THE BATA SHOE ORGANIZATION[38]

The Bata Shoe Organization, headquartered in Toronto, Canada, is the world's largest manufacturer and retailer of footwear. Its major challenge is to determine its future, both in defining its long-term strategy and in finding a top management team that will move the company into the twenty-first century. In doing so, it is being deeply affected by the dramatic political and economic changes taking place worldwide.

As war swept across Europe in 1939, Tom J. Bata was faced with a difficult situation. His father, Tomas, the ninth generation of a family of Czechoslovakian shoemakers, had built a worldwide shoe network in 28 countries, using machinery and the mass-production technology of the 1920s. On his father's death, Bata was left with the responsibility of expanding that empire during a period of great political uncertainty worldwide. Because of the Nazi invasion of Czechoslovakia and the uncertain future engendered by the resulting occupation, Bata sought to preserve his father's business by abandoning his Czechoslovakian operations and emigrating to Canada with a hundred of his managers and their families. His Czech operations were subsequently taken over by the communists after World War II.

Since that time, Bata's decision has been ratified through strong growth worldwide. As the company's home page (*www.bata.com*) says, "Activities are carried out in 60 coun-

tries on virtually every continent. More than 57,000 people around the world of many races and nationalities are employed. The Bata Shoe Organization operates 4,458 company-owned stores worldwide. In addition, it has over 100,000 independent retailers and franchisees. Operations span the globe with over 62 manufacturing units, which include shoe manufacturing plants, engineering plants producing moulds, quality control laboratories, hosiery factories, and tanneries. Active in world-wide markets since 1984, Bata now satisfies one million customers per day." These manufacturing units have shifted to developing countries, especially China and other countries in the Pacific Rim.

It might appear that Bata is a multidomestic company where local managers are free to adjust operating procedures to local environments, within certain parameters. However, Bata's core philosophies and strategies are tightly controlled by Bata himself and his son, Thomas G. Bata. In 1994, Thomas J. Bata hired the company's first nonfamily chief executive in an attempt to reinvigorate the paternalistic company, but disagreements over the company's future forced the resignation of the CEO and two of the top members of his management team in October 1995. In announcing his resignation, the CEO stated that he had tried to balance the strong values of the company with the need for change. But he appeared to have overestimated his ability to operate independently of the family shareholders. As one executive stated, "Tom J. Bata is a charismatic personality who exerts an awful lot of personal authority."

The problem is that the shoe business is changing, and Bata is being affected like any other company. The key to Bata's success has traditionally been a low-cost manufacturing base tied to an extensive distribution network. But Nike and Reebok turned the footwear industry into one that was market driven, not manufacturing driven. Bata had not yet made the transition from a manufacturing- to a market-driven strategy, but something needed to be done to help it survive. Several of Bata's retail outlets began losing money, and Bata was forced to close down 20 percent of its retail outlets in 1995 and 1996.

Although Bata has factories and operations of various forms in many countries, it does not own all of those facilities. Where possible, it owns 100 percent of them. The governments of some countries, however, require less-than-total control. In some cases, Bata provides licensing, consulting, and technical assistance to companies in which it has no equity interest.

The company's strategy for serving world markets is instructive. Some MNEs try to lower costs by achieving economies of scale in production, which means they produce as much as possible in the most optimally sized factory and then serve markets worldwide from that single production facility. Bata serves its different national markets by producing in a given country nearly everything it sells in that country. It does this in part because substantial sales volume in the countries in which it produces enables it to achieve economies of scale very quickly. It may seem difficult to believe that Bata can always achieve economies of scale, especially because the company has production facilities in some small African nations. However, Bata's management believes that the company can achieve scale economies very easily because its shoe production is a labor-intensive process and does not need the large production runs that a capital-intensive industry needs to be profitable. It also tries to buy all its raw materials locally, although this is not always possible, especially in some poorer countries.

Bata also prefers not to export production. When possible, it chooses local production to serve the local market rather than imports. However, some governments, in an attempt to preserve foreign exchange, will not allow companies to import raw materials unless the companies can earn foreign exchange through exports. In such cases, Bata must adjust to local laws and requirements for operation.

Bata avoids excessive reliance on exports partly to reduce its risks. For example, if an importing country were to restrict trade, Bata could possibly lose market opportunity and market share. In addition, Bata noted the benefit to a developing country:

> We know very well what kind of a social shock it is when a plant closes in Canada. Yet in Canada we have unemployment insurance and all kinds of welfare operations, and there are many alternative jobs that people can usually go to. In most of the developing countries, on the other hand, it's a question of life and death for these people. They have uprooted themselves from an agricultural society. They've come to a town to work in an industry. They've brought their relatives with them because working in industry, their earnings are so much higher. Thus a large group of their relatives have become dependent on them and have changed their lifestyle and standard of living. For these people it is a terrible thing to lose a job. And so we are very sensitive to that particular problem.

Bata operates in many different types of economies. It has extensive operations in both industrial democratic countries and developing countries. However, it was criticized for operating in South Africa, tacitly supporting the white minority political regime. It also has been censured for operating in totalitarian regimes, such as that in Chile. In the latter case, Bata countered by pointing out that the company had been operating in Chile for over 40 years, during which time various political regimes were in power.

Although Bata's local operations have never been nationalized (taken over by the government), the company has often had some fascinating experiences with such actions. For example, in Uganda, Bata's local operations were nationalized by Milton Obote, denationalized by Idi Amin, renationalized by Amin, and finally denationalized by Amin. During that time, the factory continued to operate as if nothing had happened. As Tom J. Bata, Sr., explained, "Shoes had to be bought and wages paid. Life went on. In most cases, the governments concluded it really wasn't in their interest to run businesses, so they canceled the nationalization arrangements."

Despite Bata's ability to operate in any type of political environment, Bata prefers a democratic system. He feels that both democratic and totalitarian regimes are bureaucratic, but a democracy offers the potential to discuss and change procedures, while under totalitarianism it sometimes is wisest to remain silent.

Bata has a multifaceted impact on a country. Its product is a necessity, not a luxury. The company's basic strategy is to provide footwear at affordable prices for the largest possible segment of the population. The production of shoes is labor intensive, so jobs are created, which increases consumers' purchasing power. Although top management may come from outside the country, local management is trained to assume responsibility as quickly as possible. Because the company tries to get most of its raw materials locally, it usually develops supply sources. Further, it likes to diversify its purchases, so it usually uses more than one supplier for a given product, which leads to competition and efficiencies.

Bata has faced problems trying to get back into Slovakia. As noted earlier, the Bata operations started in the former Czechoslovakia, and as Eastern Europe opened up, Bata immediately tried to recover lost investments in the Czech Republic and Slovakia. By 1999, both countries were considered free politically, but the Czech Republic was considered mostly free economically (and nearly in the free category), while Slovakia was considered mostly unfree. The problem was that the Czech and Slovak governments wanted compensation for the factories, but Bata felt the factories were still his. He eventually opened one factory in the Czech Republic and 48 retail outlets where the company sold 3 million pairs of shoes in the first year, capturing 11 percent of the Czech shoe market.

However, things were not so rosy in Slovakia. Bata said the problem is that "the company's former Slovak properties ended up in the hands of the Slovak government, which isn't interested in giving them up. Instead, we are expected to rebuild our Slovak business using our own resources." Bata says that he is still waiting for the government to keep the promise it made when his 45,000-employee factory in Slovakia was nationalized. Communists promised compensation but never paid. The official government position is that a new restitution law has been put into effect and that Bata has to raise his ownership claims with the new owner of the factory. If the two parties cannot resolve the problem, Bata can file a lawsuit against the new owner to be settled in Slovakian courts. Despite his success in the Czech Republic, Bata had not sold one pair of shoes in Slovakia.

QUESTIONS

1. Based on the economic freedom scales, what kind of differences do you think Bata might face in the Czech Republic and Slovakia?

2. What are the advantages and disadvantages to both Bata and the republic of Slovakia of having Bata take over his former operations? Why do you think the Czech Republic allowed Bata to reenter the market, but Slovakia did not?

3. Given the countries that Bata is operating in, what challenges does Tom Bata face in trying to establish an effective political strategy for the company?

4. Why do you think Tom J. Bata, Sr., has joined the list of entrepreneurs who cannot bear to loosen their grip on businesses they started? What is the risk to the Bata Shoe Organization if Thomas J. Bata cannot find a way to retire?

CHAPTER NOTES

1 The major sources for the case are as follows: "The Dragon's Embrace," *The Economist,* August 26, 1989, pp. 51–52; John Newhouse, "Tweaking the Dragon's Tail," *The New Yorker,* March 15, 1993, pp. 89–103; "Patten Sets t he Path," *The Economist,* October 10, 1992, pp. 35–36; Jonathan Karp, "Island Hopping: Jardine Matheson Flees Hong Kong for Bermuda," *Far Eastern Economic Review,* April 7, 1994, pp. 73–74; "The Noble Houses Look Forward," *The Economist,* October 1, 1994, pp. 77–78; "The Taipan and the Dragon," *The Economist,* April 8, 1995, p. 62; "Hong Kong," *The Economist,* September 23, 1995, pp. 29–32; "The Swire Group: Thin Ice?" *The Economist,* September 23, 1995, p. 58; "Boarding for Beijing," *The Economist,* May 4, 1996, p. 65; Mark Clifford and Joyce Barnathan,

"Beijing Is Buying Hong Kong—But at Its Own Price," *Business Week,* May 13, 1996, p. 64; Joyce Barnathan and David Lindorff, "Hong Kong's New Boss," *Business Week,* December 23, 1996, p. 50; Rahul Jacob and Louise Lucas, "Redefining the Territory: Businessmen Find That Hong Kong's Problem Since the Handover to China Is Not Too Little Political Freedom but Too Much," *Financial Times,* February 1, 1999, p. 12; Gregg Jones, "Democracy Still Questionable for Hong Kong Communists," *The Denver Post,* February 11, 1999, p. A38; "HK Swire Pacific Reports 74-Percent Fall in Profit," *Xinhua News Agency,* March 12, 1999 (news provided by COMTEX, *http://www.comtexnews.com*); Bretigne Shaffer, "Hong Kong Undermines Its Own Freedom," *Wall Street Journal,* July 2, 1999, p. A12; and

"Hong Kong Diminished," *The Economist,* July 3, 1999, p. 16.

2 Gabiel A. Almond and G. Bingham Powell, Jr., eds., *Comparative Politics Today: A World View,* 3rd ed. (Boston: Little, Brown, 1984), pp. 1–9.

3 "The United States–China Business Council," *http://www.uschina.org/benefits.html,* July 23, 1999.

4 "Politics Brief: Is There a Crisis?" *The Economist,* July 17, 1999, p. 49.

5 Robert Wesson, *Modern Government—Democracy and Authoritarianism,* 2nd ed. (Upper Saddle River, NJ: Prentice Hall, 1985), pp. 41–42.

6 Adrian Karatnycky, "Freedom's Gains," *San Diego Union-Tribune,* December 27, 1998, p. G1.

7 Ibid.

8 Samuel Huntington, "Democracy for the Long Haul," *The Strait Times,* September 10, 1995, p. 1, available: NEXIS Library: NEWS: CURNWS.

9 Adrian Karatnycky, *Freedom in the World* (New York: Freedom House, 1999), p. 4.

10 "Politics Brief: Is There a Crisis?"

11 Ibid.

12 Jaroslaw Piekalkiewicz and Alfred Wayne Penn, *Politics of Ideocracy* (Albany: State University of New York Press, 1995), p. 4.

13 Ibid., p. 17.

14 Karatnycky, *Freedom in the World,* pp. 6–7.

15 Michael Shari, "Up in Smoke," *Business Week,* June 1, 1998, p. 60.

16 "The Biggest Worry," *The World in 1999* (London: The Economist Publications, 1999), p. 35.

17 Huntington, "Democracy for the Long Haul."

18 Ibid.

19 Ibid.

20 George C. Lodge, "Roles and Relationships of Business and Government," Harvard Business School Case 9-388-159, pp. 1–48.

21 Audrey T. Sproat and Bruce R. Scott, "Japan D1: A Strategy for Economic Growth," Harvard Business School Case 9-378-106, pp. 1–35.

22 David P. Baron, *Business and Its Environment* (Upper Saddle River, NJ: Prentice Hall, 1993) pp. 177–179.

23 Mark Whitehouse, "For Business in Today's Dysfunctional Russia, Solutions Are Creative, but Not Necessarily Legal," *Wall Street Journal,* June 3, 1999, pp. A19, A21.

24 Alfred Marcus, *Business & Society: Ethics, Government, and the World Economy* (Homewood, IL: Richard D. Irwin, 1993), pp. 49–52.

25 John R. Boatright, *Ethics and the Conduct of Business* (Upper Saddle River, NJ: Prentice Hall, 1993), pp. 13–16.

26 Ibid., pp. 16–18.

27 Ray August, *International Business Law: Text, Cases, and Readings* (Upper Saddle River, NJ: Prentice Hall, 1993), p. 51.

28 Kirk Albrecht, "Turning the Prophet's Words into Profits," *Business Week,* March 16, 1998, p. 46.

29 Aline Sullivan, "Westerners Look at Risks and Rewards of Islamic Banking," *International Herald Tribune,* January 30, 1993, p. 1.

30 Albrecht, "Turning the Prophet's Words into Profits."

31 Shaun Harris, "Making Money the Muslim Way," *Africa News,* September 17, 1999, in LEXIS/NEXIS NEWS: CURNWS.

32 Ibid.

33 Albrecht, "Turning the Prophet's Words into Profits."

34 Ibid., p. 14.

35 Ibid., p. 5.

36 Paul M. Barrett, "Joining the Stampede to Europe, Law Firm Suffers a Few Bruises," *Wall Street Journal,* April 27, 1999, p. A1.

37 Melody Peterson, "2 Law Firms Plan to Bridge the Atlantic," *New York Times,* May 25, 1999, p. C1.

38 The material for the case was taken from the following sources: *www.bata.com;* Dean Walker, "Shoemaker to the World," *Executive,* January 1981, pp. 63–69; Gary Vineberg, "Bata Favors Free Trade but Tempers Asia Stance," *Footwear News,* Vol. 39, No. 24, June 13, 1983, p. 2; Ira Breskin and Gary Vinesbert, "Parent Bata Looks After Far Flung Footwear Family," *Footwear News,* Vol. 39, No. 23, June 6, 1983, p. 1; "After Sullivan," *The Economist,* June 13, 1987, p. 71; Robert Collison, "How Bata Rules Its World," *Canadian Business,* September 1990, pp. 28–34; Peter C. Newman, "The Return of the Native Capitalist," *Macleans,* March 12, 1990, p. 53; Tammi Gutner, "Bringing Back Bata," *International Management,* November 1990, pp. 41–43; "Faded Euphoria," Fortune, July 1, 1991; "Pulled Up by the Bootlaces," *Financial Times,* October 9, 1995, p. 23; James Anderson, "Bata Property Still Held by Slovak Government," *Prague Post,* July 26, 1995, p. 1, Available: NEXIS Library: NEWS: CURNWS; Bernard Simon, "Bata Executives Quit in Strategy Row . . . ," *Financial Times,* October 9, 1995, p. 25; and Bernard Simon, "Footwear Goes Out of Fashion," *Financial Times,* June 6, 1996, p. 18.

CHAPTER 4

The Economic
Environment

Poverty does not destroy virtue, nor does wealth bestow it.

—SPANISH PROVERB

OBJECTIVES

- **To learn the differences between the world's major economic systems**

- **To learn the criteria for dividing countries into different economic categories**

- **To discuss key economic issues that influence international business**

- **To assess the transition process certain countries are undertaking in changing to market economies—and how this transition affects international firms and managers.**

Some historians trace the origin of the hamburger to Russia. Supposedly, sailors took a dish made of raw ground beef and hot spices from Russia to the port of Hamburg, where the recipe was altered, popularized, and given its name. Hamburgers eventually showed up in England and then North America. If this historical account is accurate, then when McDonald's Corporation opened its first Moscow restaurant in 1990, the hamburger's round-trip journey was complete.

McDonald's entry into Russia capped a long and involved negotiation process. During the 1976 Olympics in Montreal, George A. Cohon, president of McDonald's Canadian subsidiary, made the first contact with Soviet officials. This contact began lengthy negotiations that culminated in the signing of a protocol agreement in 1987, shortly after the Soviets enacted legislation permitting joint ventures with Western companies. After that, the pace of negotiations quickened, until in 1988 a formal agreement was signed. In the meantime, McDonald's had opened restaurants in Hungary and Yugoslavia, thus providing the company with valuable experience in operating in communist countries. These moves were highly compatible with McDonald's growth strategy. By the mid-1980s, the company was expanding more rapidly outside the United States than inside, and company executives reasoned that if they were to meet the company's rapid growth objectives, that trend must continue.

The McDonald's–Russian joint venture is between McDonald's Canadian subsidiary and the Moscow City Council. Even with the Moscow City Council as a partner, the company repeatedly ran into negative responses, such as "Sorry, you're not in my five-year plan," when it attempted to obtain such materials as sand or gravel to build the restaurant. The company had to negotiate to ensure it would be allocated, in the Soviet central plan, sufficient sugar and flour, which were in chronically short supply. Even for some products in sufficient supply, such as mustard, government regulations prevented Soviet manufacturers from deviating from standard recipes in order to comply with McDonald's needs. In other cases, strict allocation regulations dictated that Soviet plants sell all output to existing Soviet companies, thus leaving them no chance to produce products for McDonald's. Yet another problem was that some supplies simply were not produced or consumed in the Soviet Union, including iceberg lettuce, pickling cucumbers, and the Russet Burbank potatoes that are the secret behind McDonald's french fries.

To handle these problems, McDonald's scoured the country for supplies, contracting for such items as milk, cheddar cheese, and beef. To help ensure ample supplies of the quality products it needed, it undertook to educate Soviet farmers and cattle ranchers on how to grow and raise those products. In addition, it built a $40 million food-processing center about 45 minutes from its first Moscow restaurant. Because distribution was as much a cause of shortages as production was, McDonald's carried supplies on its own trucks. The company had to import some other needed supplies.

The company placed one small help-wanted ad and received about 27,000 Russian applicants for its 605 positions. It sent 6 Russian managers to its Hamburger University outside Chicago, Illinois, in the United States for six months' training and another 30 managers for several months' training in Canada or Europe. The company translated training and operations manuals and videotapes into Russian so that trainees could learn everything from how to wash windows and mop floors to how to assemble a Big Mac. McDonald's employs about 5,000 people in Russia.

To establish a Western image, McDonald's used its name and familiar golden arches in Moscow. However, in 1993 a law was passed in that city requiring all stores to have Russian names, or at least names transliterated into the Cyrillic alphabet. Just as PepsiCo chose Cyrillic letters to convey the sound of "Pepsi" in Russian, McDonald's used the following Cyrillic letters that retain the sound of its name: **МАКДОНАЛДС**.

One problem McDonald's did not encounter was attracting customers. McDonald's did no advertising prior to its Moscow opening. However, Russian television covered the upcoming event extensively. When the restaurant's doors opened for the first time in January 1990, it was almost impossible to accommodate the crowd, even though it was the largest McDonald's in the world. An estimated 30,000 people were served the first day, eclipsing the previous daily record of 9,100 set in Budapest. The crowds continued to arrive, even though the price of a Big Mac, french fries, and soft drink equaled a Russian worker's average pay for 4 hours of work. In contrast, lunch at a state-run or private sector cafe cost 15 to 25 percent as much as a meal at McDonald's.

However, McDonald's was not satisfied with one restaurant in Moscow. It was obvious to McDonald's management that Moscow's 3 million commuters who were used to poor, slow service would warm to McDonald's immediately. For example, the first Moscow McDonald's in Pushkin Square serves an average of 20,000 customers per day, whereas the restaurant that formerly occupied the space served only 200 customers per day. To illustrate the potential, the United States has a population of 240 million people and 8,500 McDonald's restaurants, whereas Russia had 150 million people and only 45 restaurants, with the intent to open another 5 stores by early 2000.

But then in August 1998, the Russian ruble plunged by 70 percent, and the Russian economy collapsed, causing sales of most consumer products to fall. What will be the future of McDonald's in Moscow and the rest of Russia? Worldwide, McDonald's opened its 25,000th store in 1999. It sells food in 115 countries, with half of its restaurants outside of the United States. But in 1999, McDonald's decided to slow its expansion in Russian, even though it added 19 restaurants in Russia in 1998. Even Coca-Cola and its bottlers cut their Moscow workforce dramatically in 1999 due to a 60 percent drop in sales from August 1998 to August 1999. Which countries will be the ones where management will concentrate McDonald's growth in the future? Most of McDonald's future expansion is targeted for countries other than the United States. In particular, it is looking to the emerging economies, the source of most of the world's population and much of its growth. But as management commits resources to the politically and economically unstable emerging economies, does it place more of its assets at risk, resulting in greater volatility in revenues, profitability, and cash flows? Will the emerging economies themselves move more quickly along the path of economic transition to a more stable market environment? Will McDonald's management be able to choose the right countries, commit the right amount of resources, and provide a strategy for sound economic growth for the future? ගയ

Company managers need to understand economic environments to predict trends that might impact their performance.

INTRODUCTION

Understanding the economic environments of foreign countries and markets can help managers predict how trends and events in those environments might affect their companies' future performance there. In this chapter, we discuss the economic environments of the countries in which an MNE may want to operate. An MNE such as

The Caspian Sea may hold as much as 200 billion barrels of oil beneath it. However, the drilling and pollution have taken their toll: the sea's pike perch and sturgeon are becoming more scarce. With the transition from communism to a market economy, leaders hope that foreign investment will bring capital and technology to replace the antiquated drilling equipment— as much as 100 years old—that spills oil into the sea.

McDonald's knows how to operate in its home-country economic system. However, when such a company wants to do business in another country for the first time, it needs answers to questions such as these

1. Under what type of economic system does the country operate?
2. What are the size, growth potential, and stability of the market?
3. Is the company's industry in that country's public or private sector?
4. If it is in the public sector, does the government also allow private competition in that sector?
5. If the company's industry is in the private sector, is it moving toward public ownership?
6. Does the government view foreign capital as being *in competition* with or *in partnership* with public or local private enterprises?
7. In what ways does the government control the nature and extent of private enterprise?
8. How much of a contribution is the private sector expected to make in helping the government formulate overall economic objectives?

These questions appear simple to answer. However, because of the dynamic nature of political and economic events, the answers are complex—or yet to be seen. For example, foreign companies are still investing in Hong Kong even though the United Kingdom returned Hong Kong to China in 1997. China's economic system is different from Hong Kong's and so the business world is wondering whether China will stifle some of Hong Kong's economic freedoms. In addition, Hong Kong companies such as Swire are investing outside of that country because of the same uncertainty. Companies like McDonald's and Coca-Cola attempting to invest in Eastern Europe and the former Soviet Union are experiencing enormous difficulties because the economic environment in those countries is so different from any other in the world, and the changes taking place there are so rapid and unpredictable. The question is whether today's global companies can keep up with the world's changing economic landscape.

FIGURE 4.1   Physical and Societal Influences on International Business

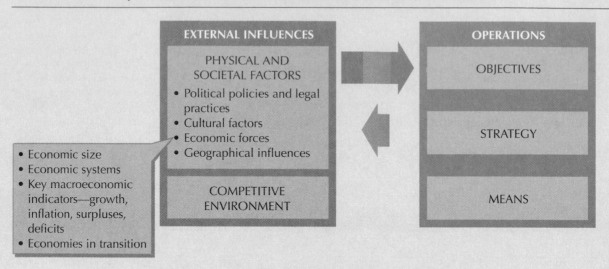

- Economic size
- Economic systems
- Key macroeconomic indicators—growth, inflation, surpluses, deficits
- Economies in transition

EXTERNAL INFLUENCES

PHYSICAL AND SOCIETAL FACTORS

- Political policies and legal practices
- Cultural factors
- Economic forces
- Geographical influences

COMPETITIVE ENVIRONMENT

OPERATIONS

OBJECTIVES

STRATEGY

MEANS

Key economic forces
- **The general economic framework of a country**
- **Economic stability**
- **The existence and influence of capital markets**
- **Factor endowments**
- **Market size**
- **Availability of economic infrastructure**

As Figure 4.1 notes, economic forces are an important part of the physical and societal factors that help comprise the external influences on company strategy. Economic forces include such issues as the general economic framework of a country, economic stability, the existence and influence of capital markets, factor endowments, the size of the market, and the availability of a good economic infrastructure, such as transportation and communications. Managers need to understand the nature of the world's economies if they are going to make wise investment decisions. To provide them with a frame of reference, we will first describe countries by income level and economic system. Then we will look at key economic indicators, such as economic growth, inflation, and surpluses and deficits, that impact the decision of management on where to commit MNE resources and efforts. Finally, we will examine the potential of the major geographic regions in the world, with special emphasis on countries in economic transition.

AN ECONOMIC DESCRIPTION OF COUNTRIES

There are 210 countries in the world with populations of more than 30,000.[2] Which of those countries are the ones where managers should commit resources? Although the answers vary by company, it is true that companies do business abroad for a variety of reasons, such as access to factors of production or demand conditions. **Factor conditions**, or production factors, include essential inputs to the production process such as human resources, physical resources, knowledge resources, capital resources, and infrastructure.[3] Physical resources include weather, the existence of waterways to get goods to and from market, and the availability of crucial minerals and agricultural products. Knowledge resources are best represented by research and development conducted by companies and governments. For example, the Silicon Valley in the United States is a hotbed of high-tech research, and the U.S. government has poured significant resources into the U.S.

Factor conditions—inputs to the production process, such as human, physical, knowledge, and capital resources and infrastructure.

aviation industry for the development of military aircraft, and this technology has been helpful in developing the civilian aircraft industry as well. Capital resources include the availability of debt and equity capital that firms can use to expand. Infrastructure includes roads, port facilities, energy, and communications.

Demand conditions, also known as market potential, include three dimensions: the composition of home demand (or the nature of buyer needs), the size and pattern of growth of home demand, and the internationalization of demand.[4] The composition of demand is known as the *quality of demand*, and size is known as the *quantity of demand*. Factor conditions are especially crucial for investments made for the production of goods, but demand conditions are crucial for market-seeking investments. The combination of factor and demand conditions, along with other qualities, make up the **location-specific advantage** that a country has to offer domestic and foreign investors.

Demand conditions
- **Composition of home demand (quality of demand)**
- **Size and growth of demand (quantity of demand)**
- **Internationalization of demand**

COUNTRIES CLASSIFIED BY INCOME

Although we can classify countries along any of the dimensions mentioned above, the key dimension we use to distinguish one country from another is the size of demand, or **gross national product** (GNP). In particular, we classify countries according to per capita GNP, or the size of GNP of a nation divided by its total population. Those countries with high populations and high per capita GNP are most desirable in terms of market potential. Those with low per capita GNP and low populations are least desirable, and the other countries fit somewhere in between.

What is GNP? It is the broadest measure of economic activity. It is the market value of final goods and services newly produced by domestically owned factors of production.[5] For example, the value of a Ford car manufactured in the United States and the portion of the value of a Ford manufactured in Mexico using U.S. capital and management counts in U.S. GNP. However, the portion of the value of a Japanese Toyota manufactured in the United States using Japanese capital and management would not be counted in U.S. GNP, but it would be counted in Japanese GNP. An alternative to GNP is **gross domestic product** (GDP), the value of production that takes place within a nation's borders, without regard to whether the production is done by domestic or foreign factors of production.[6] So both a Ford and a Toyota manufactured in the United States would be counted in U.S. GDP, but a Ford produced in Mexico would not.

Why do we use GNP to describe countries? The **World Bank** (*www.worldbank.org*), a multilateral lending agency, uses per capita GNP as a basis for its lending policies. The World Bank Group was founded in 1944 by the United Nations. It consists of five closely associated institutions: the International Bank for Reconstruction and Development (IBRD), the International Development Association (IDA), the International Finance Corporation (IFC), the Multilateral Guarantee Agency (MIGA), and the International Center for Settlement of Investment Disputes (ICSID). The World Bank is comprised of 181 countries, and its major objective is to provide development assistance to countries, especially the poorest of the poor. It uses per capita income to identify those countries that need help the most. In particular, its programs include

Gross national product
- **The market value of final goods and services newly produced by domestically owned factors of production**
- **Per capita GNP—GNP divided by total population**

Gross domestic product—the value of production that takes place within a nation's borders.

The World Bank—a multilateral lending institution that provides investment capital to countries.

- Investing in people, particularly through basic health and education
- Protecting the environment
- Supporting and encouraging private business development

- Strengthening the ability of the governments to deliver quality services, efficiently and transparently
- Promoting reforms to create a stable macroeconomic environment, conducive to investment and long-term planning
- Focusing on social development, inclusion, governance, and institution-building as key elements of poverty reduction[7]

The activities of the World Bank are important to MNEs, because they build infrastructure and promote economic growth and stability, improving the quality and quantity of demand. In particular, the World Bank is most interested in eliminating poverty and its demand-reducing influences. The World Bank classifies economies into one of the following categories according to per capita GNP.[8]

Per capita income classifications
- **Low income ($785 or less)**
- **Middle income ($786–$9,655)**
- **High income ($9,656 or more)**

Low income	$785 or less in 1997
Middle income	$786–$9,655
Lower middle income	$786–$3,125
Upper middle income	$3,126–$9,655
High income	$9,656 or more

Developing countries
- **Low- and middle-income countries**
- **Also called emerging economies**

The World Bank refers to the low- and middle-income countries as **developing countries**, even though it recognizes that not all "developing" countries are alike nor are they all "developing." Developing countries are also known as **emerging countries**, a term also used in describing the capital markets (debt and equity markets) in those countries as different from capital markets in the more advanced countries. In addition, the World Bank's terminology does not imply that the high-income countries have reached some preferred or final stage of development. High-income countries are also sometimes called **developed countries** or **industrial countries**. Initially this was because those countries had a relatively high percentage of their GNP and employment from industry rather than agriculture. Now, however, these countries have a larger percentage of their GNP and employment tied up in services rather than industry. But the term *industrial countries* is still popular. The developing countries include different types of countries—some with large populations, such as China (1.2 billion people) and India (962 million people), and others with small populations, such as Guyana (848,000 people). They also include countries in economic transition to a market economy, such as China, Poland, Russia, and Vietnam. Some developing countries, especially those in Asia and Latin America, are generally moving forward, while others, especially some in Africa, are not making much progress.

High-income countries—also known as developed or industrial countries.

Map 4.1 shows the geographic location of these countries (also see *www.worldbank.org/data/wdi* for individual country data). The high-income countries are clustered in just a few geographic areas, while the developing countries are found in all areas of the world. Table 4.1 illustrates the relative imbalance among the low-, middle-, and high-income countries in terms of number of countries, total GNP, and population. The high-income countries generate nearly 80 percent of the world's GNP, but they represent a relatively small number of countries and population. This illustrates the quandary that managers face. The high-income countries are a natural place to do business because of the quality and quantity of demand, but the developing countries exhibit

High-income countries generate 80 percent of the world's GNP. Developing countries comprise 74.3 percent of total countries and 84.1 percent of total population.

Ethical Dilemmas and Social Responsibility
HOW MUCH ECONOMIC ASSISTANCE IS TOO MUCH?

A major issue of economic social responsibility is the obligations of high-income countries to assist developing ones. Some of the areas in which the high-income countries might have an ethical obligation to provide support are access to markets for emerging economies' exports, foreign aid, and repayment of loans.

First, emerging economies must have access to markets in high-income countries to sell products. Many emerging economies have domestic markets of limited size, and their trade with each other is not significant. For example, Latin American countries on average export only about 10 percent of their products to other Latin American countries but almost 20 percent of them to the United States. However, politicians in high-income countries are sensitive to increased imports, which could lead to unemployment. That could lead to protectionist measures to limit imports from low-wage developing countries. If high-income countries discriminate against exports from emerging economies, they are hurting those countries' prospects for further development and the ability to develop into future markets.

As for foreign aid, there has been increasing pressure in the United States to cut down the amount of such aid and use the funds to improve the domestic economy. However, the United States and other high-income countries benefit from trade with emerging economies not only through gaining access to their markets but also through using their resources. Some high-income countries view foreign aid as a means of putting resources back into emerging economies. For example, high-income European countries, such as Germany and the Netherlands, provide funding to their developing neighbors Spain and Portugal to help them improve their infrastructure. In contrast, when the United States and Mexico were debating the North American Free Trade Agreement in 1993, much of the opposition to the agreement came from people who wondered how it was going to be funded rather than how the United States could help Mexico develop its economy.

A third ethical issue is the repayment of loans. Because of the overwhelming size of the external debt of many emerging economies, one possible solution is forgiveness of some or all of such debt. Another possibility is to restructure repayment so it is less burdensome to an emerging economy's economic growth. Forgiveness might be more appropriate for loans made by governments of high-income countries than for those made by private sector banks. But, in any case, some feel the high-income countries need to make an effort to be part of the solution to the debt crisis. Yet it is unlikely that banks are going to forgive loans to developing countries. When Russia defaulted on $40 billion of treasury debt in August 1998, it offered holders of the debt less than five cents on the dollar, and Deutsche Bank and Chase Manhattan Bank accepted their offer, much to the dismay of other foreign bankers.[9] However, will Deutsche Bank and Chase Manhattan Bank ever purchase Russian treasury debt again? That is unlikely. In fact, accusations of money laundering in Russia and misuse of IMF funds resulted in U.S. Treasury Secretary Larry Summers announcing that the United States would not support any more IMF credits for Russia until it had cleaned up its act.[10] Although that statement was later softened, it is clear that developing countries that default on their debts will have a more difficult time raising capital in the future. That will place more strain on the banks, both public and private, to determine how they will deal with heavily indebted countries in the future.

TABLE 4.1	RELATIVE SIZE AND WEALTH OF THE WORLD'S ECONOMIES IN PERCENT OF TOTAL		
	NUMBER OF COUNTRIES	GNP $MILLIONS, 1997	POPULATION MILLIONS, 1997
Low (61)	29.1	2.3	35.0
Middle (96)	45.2	18.0	49.1
High (54)	25.7	79.7	15.9
Total (211)	100.0	100.0	100.0

Source: From *The World Bank Atlas 1999,* p. 38. Reprinted by permission of The World Bank.

MAP 4.1
The World's Wealth Measured in Per Capita Income

High-income countries are clustered in a few geographic areas of the world, while the developing countries are scattered throughout. The low-income countries are located mostly in Africa and Asia. Per capita GNP is GNP divided by mid-year population.

Note: No data available for Western Sahara.

Source: From *The World Bank Atlas 1999,* p. 38. Reprinted by permission of The World Bank.

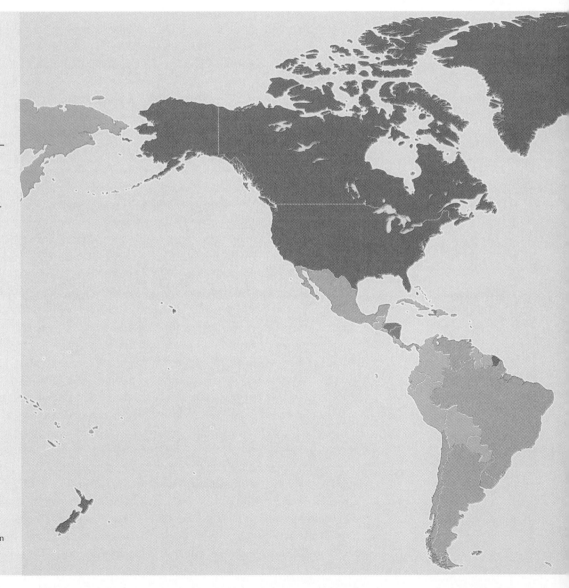

tremendous potential because of the sheer size of the population—74.3 percent of the total number of countries and 84.1 percent of the total population. It might be safer to focus on the high-income countries because of their relative political and economic stability, but the future is in the developing countries, and managers must establish a strategy for penetrating them in the short and long term.

Another measure of wealth, per capita GNP, is computed by taking the GNP of a country and converting it into dollars at market rates and then dividing the total by the population. However, the World Bank points out that nominal exchange rates (the actual market rates not adjusted for inflation) do not always reflect international differences in prices. For example, if you take the cost of a Big Mac in Russia and convert it into dollars at the market exchange rate, you don't come up with the same dollar price as a Big Mac in the United States. So the World Bank has come up with GNP per capita in international dollars converted at **purchasing power parity (PPP)** rates. PPP is the number of

Purchasing power parity per capita GNP

• **Another measure of wealth**

• **The number of units of a country's currency required to buy the same amount of goods and services in the domestic market as $1 would buy in the United States**

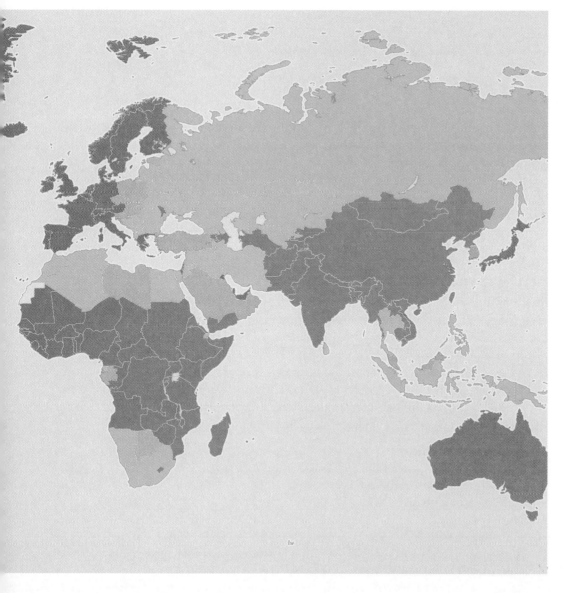

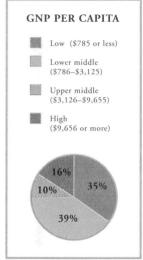

GNP PER CAPITA

Low ($785 or less)

Lower middle ($786–$3,125)

Upper middle ($3,126–$9,655)

High ($9,656 or more)

TABLE 4.2   **PER CAPITA INCOME MEASURED TWO WAYS**

COUNTRY	GNP PER CAPITA DOLLARS, 1997	PPP ESTIMATES OF GNP PER CAPITA CURRENT INTERNATIONAL DOLLARS, 1997
Brazil	4,720	6,240
China	860	3,570
Czech Republic	5,200	11,380
France	26,050	21,860
Japan	37,850	23,400
Mali	260	740
Mexico	3,680	8,120
Russian Federation	2,740	4,190
Thailand	2,800	6,590
U.S.	28,740	28,740

Source: The World Bank, *World Development Report 1999* (Washington, DC: The World Bank, 1999), pp. 190–191.

units of a country's currency required to buy the same amounts of goods and services in the domestic market that $1 would buy in the United States.[11] Table 4.2 provides some striking comparisons between GNP per capita and PPP GNP per capita for a small sample of countries. Note how much higher PPP income is for China and the Czech Republic than regular per capita GNP and how much lower Japan's PPP income is. In China's case, measuring its per capita income in PPP terms would raise it from a lower-middle-income country to an upper-middle-income country, which is more consistent with people's perceptions of economic improvements in China.

COUNTRIES CLASSIFIED BY REGION

Much of the World Bank data is provided by geographic region, and this will be especially important as we discuss economic growth in a future section of the chapter. However, the following groups listed include only the developing countries in their region. It is obvious from the map that Japan, Australia, and New Zealand are included in East Asia and Pacific geographically, although they are also high-income countries and therefore colored differently on the map. The same is true of Europe where Western Europe is colored differently from the developing countries of Europe and Central Asia. As noted in Map 4.2 on pages 126–127, the major regions are

- East Asia and Pacific
- Europe (East and Central Europe) and Central Asia
- Latin America and Caribbean
- Middle East and North Africa
- South Asia
- Sub-Saharan Africa
- High-income countries (which does not constitute a proximate geographic location as do the other regions)

These designations are important to MNEs, which tend to organize their operations along geographic lines. For example, IBM organizes its firm along the following lines: Africa, Americas, Asia Pacific, Europe, and Middle East. Siemens, the large German electronics company, discloses its sales by region according to Africa, Middle East, and CIS (Commonwealth of Independent States, the countries in the former Soviet Union); Asia-Pacific; the Americas; Europe; and Germany. Managers can use the data compiled and disclosed by the World Bank to spot trends in key markets. Investors can use the data to analyze where potential growth and risks exist in the regions where their companies operate.

Importance of regional groupings of countries
- **Similar economic conditions**
- **Mirrors the way companies organize their firms geographically**

COUNTRIES CLASSIFIED BY ECONOMIC SYSTEM

A final way of classifying countries is by their economic system. Every government struggles with the right mix of *ownership* and *control* of the economy, as illustrated in Figure 4.2. Ownership means those who own the resources engaged in economic activity—the public sector, the private sector, or both. Public sector ownership of economic activity refers to the existence of state-owned enterprises. A good example would be China prior to the reforms initiated in 1978 by Chinese leader Deng Xiaoping. At that time, all enterprises in the country were owned by the state. Private enterprise was not permitted nor encouraged. The same could be said of all countries under the control of the Soviet Union, such as Poland and Czechoslovakia (now the countries of the Czech Republic and Slovakia), where state-owned enterprises generated most of the economic activity of the country. However, state-owned enterprises are not just a phenomenon of the communist countries. Countries like Brazil in South America, India in South Asia, and France in Europe also have large state-owned enterprises that are an important part of the overall economy.

Ownership
- **Who owns the resources engaged in economic activity**
- **Can be public sector, private sector, or both**

FIGURE 4.2   Relationships Between Control of Economic Activity and Ownership of Production Factors

CONTROL OF ECONOMIC ACTIVITY	OWNERSHIP OF PRODUCTION		
	Private	**Mixed**	**Public**
Market	A	B	C
Mixed	D	E	F
Command	G	H	I

Control/Ownership	Control/Ownership	Control/Ownership
A. Market/Private	D. Mixed/Private	G. Command/Private
B. Market/Mixed	E. Mixed/Mixed	H. Command/Mixed
C. Market/Public	F. Mixed/Public	I. Command/Public

Although the most logical combinations of ownership and control are sectors A and I, most countries in the world have mixed economies with a variety of combinations of ownership and control.

MAP 4.2
The World by Region

Countries in different regions of the world, such as Argentina and Chile in Latin America, are often more similar to each other than they are to countries in other regions of the world, such as Thailand and Indonesia in East Asia. Because they are proximate geographically, they trade with each other, so it is interesting to examine factors such as growth in per capita income on a regional basis. However, there are differences within regions. For example, Japan and Malaysia are in East Asia (although Japan is classified as an OECD country), but they are very different from each other in terms of ethnic makeup, history, politics, and economics. OECD countries—those in the Organization for Economic Cooperation and Development—are considered high-income countries.

Source: From *The World Bank Atlas 1999,* pp. 2–3. Reprinted by permission of The World Bank.

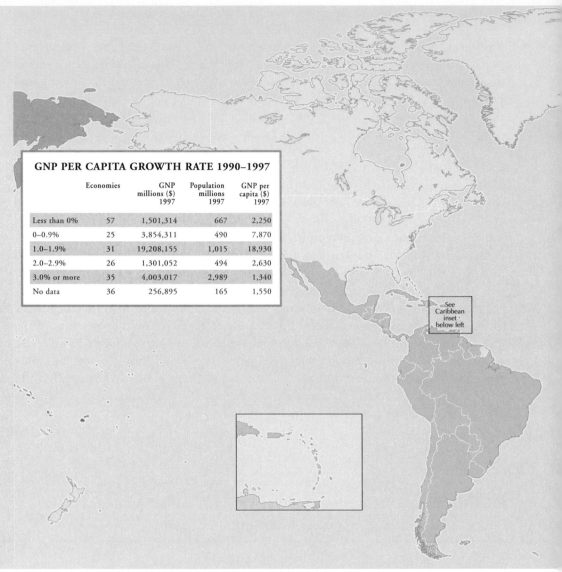

GNP PER CAPITA GROWTH RATE 1990–1997

	Economies	GNP millions ($) 1997	Population millions 1997	GNP per capita ($) 1997
Less than 0%	57	1,501,314	667	2,250
0–0.9%	25	3,854,311	490	7,870
1.0–1.9%	31	19,208,155	1,015	18,930
2.0–2.9%	26	1,301,052	494	2,630
3.0% or more	35	4,003,017	2,989	1,340
No data	36	256,895	165	1,550

See Caribbean inset below left

Control—whether resources are allocated and controlled by the public or the private sector.

Hong Kong and the United States are examples of the absence of state ownership in major economic activity. Although there are extremes, most countries are a mixture of public and private ownership of economic activity. The degree varies, but most countries with significant state-owned enterprises, such as those mentioned above, are moving toward less, not more, ownership of enterprises. This is known as the process of privatization, which we will discuss later in the chapter.

Control of economic activity means whether resources are allocated and controlled by the public or the private sector. Each year, the Heritage Foundation and the *Wall Street Journal* publish an index of economic freedom in which they rate countries according to 50 variables organized into 10 economic factors: trade policy, taxation, government intervention in the economy, monetary policy, capital flows and investment, banking, wage and price con-

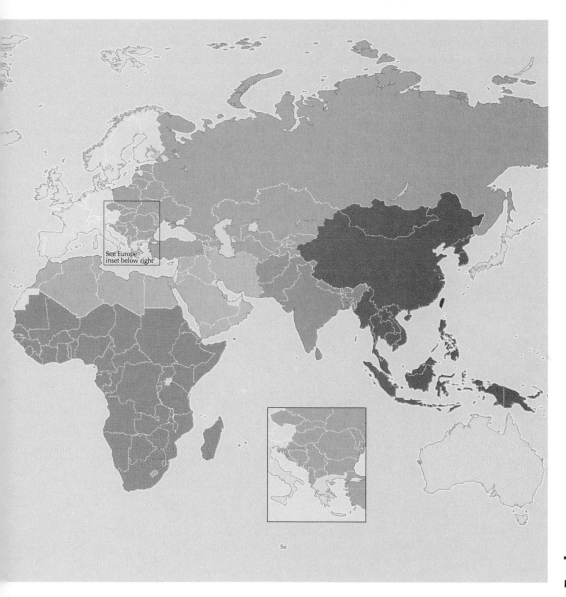

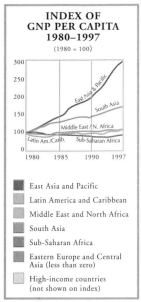

INDEX OF GNP PER CAPITA 1980–1997
(1980 = 100)

- East Asia and Pacific
- Latin America and Caribbean
- Middle East and North Africa
- South Asia
- Sub-Saharan Africa
- Eastern Europe and Central Asia (less than zero)
- High-income countries (not shown on index)

trols, property rights, regulation, and black markets. The study is helpful in that it identifies ways that governments control economic activity and the degree to which they do so.

Their 1999 index classified countries as follows:

CATEGORIES	NUMBER OF COUNTRIES	EXAMPLES OF COUNTRIES
Free	10	Hong Kong, Singapore, U.S.
Mostly free	61	Czech Republic, Japan, Canada
Mostly unfree	63	Zambia, Mexico, Brazil
Repressed	27	Iraq, Cuba, North Korea

Factors that determine economic freedom
- **Trade policy**
- **Taxation**
- **Government intervention in the economy**
- **Monetary policy**
- **Capital flows and investment**
- **Banking**
- **Wage and price controls**
- **Property rights**
- **Regulation**
- **Black market activity**

Countries with the freest economies have the highest annual growth in GNP.

Map 4.3 identifies the countries in the world as classified on page 127. In most cases, countries at the top of the index also have a high degree of political freedom; all of the countries at the bottom of the index have no political freedom. In addition, there is a high correlation between economic freedom and economic growth: the freer an economy, the better off the people—at all economic levels.[12] The study noted: "Countries with the freest economies had average annual growth rates of 2.9 percent from 1980 to 1993; countries with 'mostly free' ratings had average long-term growth rates of just under 1 percent. By contrast, 'mostly unfree' countries saw their economies contract over the same period by an average of 0.3% a year, and the economies of countries with repressive policies shrank by an average of 1.4% a year."[13] Countries that are high in economic freedom have more control in the private than the public sector.

MAP 4.3
Countries Ranked According to Economic Freedom

Economic freedom is measured according to 50 variables organized into 10 economic factors: trade policy, taxation, government intervention in the economy, monetary policy, capital flows and investment, banking, wage and price controls, property rights, regulation, and black markets. Countries are classified as free, mostly free, mostly unfree, and repressed, according to the degree to which governments intervene in these factors. There is a high correlation between economic freedom and economic growth: the freer an economy, the better off the people—at all economic levels.

Source: Bryan T. Johnson, Kim R. Holmes, and Melanie Kirkpatrick. *The 1999 Index of Economic Freedom* (The Heritage Foundation and *Wall Street Journal*, 1999). Reprinted by permission.

However, there are some advanced countries with significant government interference in the economy. Two examples are Japan and South Korea. After World War II, the Japanese government intervened in the economy in a significant way, even though it was not involved in the ownership of companies. For example, government agencies such as the Ministry of Finance, the Bank of Japan, and the Ministry of International Trade and Industry (MITI) helped establish a broad vision of Japan's future that rejected individualism and open markets. The government protected industry from outside competition, supported funding of preferred industries, told private banks which companies to lend to, and controlled access to technology, foreign exchange, and raw materials imports.[14] South Korea and much of Asia followed that same model by permitting government intervention in the operation of the economy. This led to spectacular growth during the decades of the 1970s, 1980s, and early 1990s. But as we'll see later in

LEVELS OF ECONOMIC FREEDOM

Free
Mostly free
Mostly unfree
Repressed
No data

State capitalism—a condition where some developed countries, such as Japan and Korea, have intervened in the economy to direct the allocation and control of resources.

the chapter, this strategy of heavy government intervention may have been one of the causes of the Asian financial crisis that erupted in July 1997 and has lead to a questioning of the government intervention model, also known as **state capitalism**, championed by Japan and Korea.

Market Economy   Now we need to take the concepts of ownership and control and put them into the context of two major economic systems: a market economy and a command economy. A **market economy** is one in which resources are primarily owned and controlled by the private sector, not the public sector. The key factors that make the market economy work are **consumer sovereignty**—that is, the right of consumers to decide what to buy—and freedom for companies to operate in the market. Prices are determined by supply and demand. In a market economy, for example, the price of gasoline rises during holidays because of the excess of demand over supply. Rising prices bring supply and demand into balance. At higher prices, consumers will eventually consume less, resulting in a drop in demand to match existing supply.

Market economy—resources are allocated and controlled by consumers.

Command economy—all dimensions of economic activity are determined by a central government plan.

Command Economy   In a **command economy**, also known as a **centrally planned economy**, all dimensions of economic activity, including pricing and production decisions, are determined by a central government plan. The government owns and controls all resources. The government sets goals for every business enterprise in the country—how much they produce and for whom. In this type of economy, the government considers itself a better judge of resource allocation than its businesses or citizens. To use the gasoline example described above in the market context, the price of gasoline always stays the same in a command economy, because the government determines its price. When supply becomes tight, people line up and buy gasoline until the supply is exhausted, so supply is allocated by the queue rather than by price. Before prices were freed in Russia, people used to say that if they ever saw a line, they just stood in it. When they got to the front of the line, they bought whatever was being sold. Even if they didn't need the item, they figured that someone in their extended family did, so they just bought it. When the supply ran out, there wouldn't be any more left, no matter what price you were willing to pay.

Mixed economy—different degrees of ownership and control best describe most countries.

Mixed Economy   In actuality, no economy is purely market or completely command. Most market economies have some degree of government ownership and control, while most command economies are moving toward a market economy and away from command concepts. If you think of economic systems as a spectrum with market on one end and command on the other, Hong Kong and the United States would represent two of the countries at the market end of the spectrum, and Vietnam and North Korea would represent two countries at the command end of the spectrum. In Hong Kong and the United States, the government plays a very small role in economic activity, desiring mainly to provide a stable environment in which economic activity can take place. In communist countries such as Vietnam and North Korea, the government still owns and controls most aspects of economic activity. China is an example of a communist country that is trying to move from command to market. Whereas state-owned enterprises conducted most economic activity prior to the Deng reforms, now the private sector is providing significant economic growth. The government is trying to privatize and loosen controls over economic activity. It is still closer to the command than the market end of the spectrum, but the direction is clearly toward the market, and the speed of change is faster than is the case in other communist countries like Cuba, Russia, Vietnam, and North Korea.

Another example of a mixed economy is **market socialism**, where the state owns significant resources, but allocation of the resources comes from the market price mechanism.[15] France, as mentioned above, is a good case in point. Although the government owns significant economic resources, it allows supply and demand, rather than government fiat, to set prices. Sweden is a country that owns few economic resources, but it levies heavy taxes to fund an aggressive social program. Although the market determines prices, a lot of economic activity is controlled by government fiscal policies.

As mentioned in the eight questions raised at the beginning of the chapter, managers need to be aware of the type of economic system in which they are doing business and what the role of their companies is and is likely to become. Many Western managers complain about the government bureaucracy in China and the degree of influence of the Chinese government in economic decision making. That should hardly be a surprise, given the history of China and its reliance on the ownership and control of resources by the state. China is going through a transition, so it is important for managers to understand the direction and speed of change and how their own industries will be affected by these changes. The same is true of any country, especially those going through transition, so managers need to understand the context of the ownership and control of resources of the countries where they wish to operate.

Market socialism—the state owns significant resources, but allocation comes from the market price mechanism.

KEY MACROECONOMIC ISSUES AFFECTING BUSINESS STRATEGY

In its 1998 Annual Report to Shareholders, top management of Intel stated

> We faced extraordinary business conditions in 1998. Competition in the value PC market segment, inventory corrections among some of our large customers in the first half of the year and an economic slowdown in some parts of the world all took their toll.

> In the year just ended, the Group suffered a major setback, interrupting our record of consistent and profitable progress over many previous years. . . . Overseas, economic turmoil and the consequent worsening trading conditions in the Far East coincided with the continued strength of the pound, which affected us particularly in Europe, and led to a severe fall in operating profits.

These are just two examples of the impact of the global economy on company profits and operating strategy. Management must learn to scan the environment to determine market conditions in the countries where it is doing business or contemplating entering the market. We will discuss three key issues in the following pages: economic growth, inflation, and surpluses and deficits. Then we will follow with a section discussing the unique challenges facing countries in transition from a command to a market economy. But to illustrate these key economic issues, we will first turn to the Asian financial crisis of 1997–1998.

The global economy can affect company profits and operating strategy.

ASIAN FINANCIAL CRISIS

In 1994 the World Bank predicted that annual real GDP growth would average 7.6 percent in East Asia and 5.3 percent in South Asia from 1994 to 2005. Further, it predicted that the top 10 economies in the world by 2020 would include China (1), Japan (3), India (4), Indonesia (5), South Korea (7), Thailand (8), and Taiwan (10). There were significant reasons for optimism. Annual average growth in per capita GNP from 1985 to 1995 was only 1.9 percent in the developed economies, but 7.2 percent in East Asia and the Pacific. Individually, Thailand was predicted to grow at 8.4 percent, China at 8.3 percent, Korea 7.7 percent, Indonesia 6 percent, and Malaysia 5.7 percent.[16] These countries were characterized by having a hard-working, well-educated, highly trained workforce. They exhibited relatively low inflation, very low government debt and budget deficits as a percentage of GNP, an entrepreneurial class, and relative economic freedom.

On July 2, 1997, however, the Thai baht, the currency of Thailand, was freed from government controls, and it fell 17 percent against the U.S. dollar. Then the currency weakness spread to South Korea, Malaysia, and Indonesia. By the end of 1997, the Thai baht had fallen by 42.7 percent, the South Korean won 46.2 percent, the Malaysian ringgit 33.4 percent, and the Indonesian rupiah 52.3 percent.

In addition to the currency crisis, the stock markets in Asia tumbled in 1997. This was largely as a result of the lack of confidence in their economies, the fall of their currencies, and the withdrawal of money by foreign investors. The stock market weakness spread to the United States on October 27, 1997, and then Europe.

The Asian crisis resulted in a liquidity crisis in both hard currency (such as the U.S. dollar) and soft currency (the local currency of each country, such as the Thai baht). A liquidity crisis is a shortage of money. Banks and investors had poured billions of dollars into the Asian markets. As soon as the currencies dropped, however, the money flowed back out. Countries had to raise interest rates in order to support their currencies, and that resulted in a slowdown in economic growth. As a result, companies went bankrupt, factories were closed, investment plans by foreign and local companies were suspended, unemployment increased and political instability resulted. In 1998, Indonesian President Suharto was forced to step down because of the economic crisis.

What were some of the major causes for the Asia crisis? Although there is disagreement as to the real causes, there were two theories circulating at the time of the crisis: too much government influence and control, and bad private sector decisions.[17] In reality, both factors were contributors. In terms of government influence and control, Asian countries relied very heavily on strategic trade policy. This policy was initiated by the Japanese and South Koreans and emulated by others. It resulted in governments targeting industries, controlling access to credit, foreign exchange, and imports. Japan and South Korea embarked on import substitution and export promotion policies. There was a close tie between the government, businesses, and banks. Governments would rather rescue the politically well-connected firms from insolvency instead of allowing them to go bankrupt.

However, bad private sector decisions, by both borrowers and lenders, were strong contributing factors. Risky projects were undertaken based on the hope of high upside profits and low downside risk. A large proportion of bank loans went to expensive building projects where there was already a glut in the market. Overcapacity caused rents and prices to fall sharply, so the lenders were not able to service their loans.

The devaluation of the Thai baht on July 2, 1997, started a downward spiral of economic growth, currency values, and capital markets in Asia.

The Asian banking crisis and flight of capital abroad resulted in a shortage of capital in Asia.

Possible causes of the crisis
- **Too much government influence and control**
- **Bad private sector decisions**

Because governments were so intertwined with business, banks assumed that projects that were blessed by the government would always be backed and that bankruptcy would never occur.

Another major contributor was the fact that a lot of countries linked their currencies to the U.S. dollar. This meant that they kept their currencies tied closely to the dollar, mainly by using their hard currency reserves (mostly U.S. dollars) to support their currencies. In the mid-1990s, the dollar was rising against most currencies in the world, so those countries that tied their currencies to the dollar also found their currencies rising. As a result, their exports became more expensive, and they found it more difficult to export products to the rest of the world.

In addition to dollar-linked exchange rates, a lot of the countries had incurred significant short-term debt. Even though the banks were borrowing the funds on a short-term basis in dollars, they were lending the funds in local currency for long-term projects. Much of this debt was coming due in 1998, and the countries were not generating enough hard currency (dollars) to pay off these debts. But because the exchange rates were fixed to the dollar, most banks assumed that there was no foreign-exchange risk. When their currencies fell against the dollar, they could not generate enough hard currency to pay off the debts.

Another major problem was the lack of financial transparency. It was very difficult for lenders to find out the creditworthiness of borrowers, because they could not rely on the financial statements. It was often said that the best way to make a loan was to take the borrower to lunch and a round of golf instead of analyzing the financial data. As a result, there was a tremendous amount of influence pedaling and corruption.

As the countries in Southeast Asia began to restructure in the mid-1990s, they shifted the production up to more capital-intensive processes. In order to do that, they had to import capital equipment from the west, which meant that they were also incurring hard currency debt. At the same time their imports were increasing, exports were dropping due to the strength of their currencies and competition from other parts of the world such as China. This combination of rising imports and falling exports resulted in a balance of trade deficit and a drop in reserve assets.

Although this general characterization of the Asian crisis shows the interrelationship of politics, economics, and business, the factors in each individual country varied. However, as the crisis developed, the **International Monetary Fund (IMF)** and Western countries stepped in to try to help minimize the crisis from moving to other parts of the world. As noted on its home page, "the IMF is an international organization of 182 member countries, established in 1946 to promote international monetary cooperation, exchange stability, and orderly exchange arrangements; to foster economic growth and high levels of employment; and to provide temporary financial assistance to countries under adequate safeguards to help ease balance of payments adjustment" (*www.imf.org*). Initially, the priorities of the IMF program in Asia were to stabilize the financial system and restore confidence in economic management. It encouraged countries to raise interest rates to strengthen their currencies, restrict imports, and revamp their financial systems. These policies resulted in slow growth in most East Asian countries. As noted in Table 4.3, real GDP growth slowed from 1996 to 1997, but the real drop occurred in 1998 with the crisis in full swing. As the crisis deepened in 1998, the IMF began to loosen its restraints, and most of the countries embarked on an expansionist policy

Countries tried to tie their currencies to the dollar, and they borrowed too much money from foreign banks.

Lack of financial transparency—financial statements that did not disclose the true picture of banks and other companies.

The International Monetary Fund—a multilateral organization that tried to help the Asian economies adjust by lending them money on the promise that they would control their economies and stabilize their currencies.

TABLE 4.3	ANNUAL REAL GDP GROWTH IN EAST ASIA				
	1995	**1996**	**1997**	**1998**	**1999 (EST.)**
Indonesia	8.2	8.0	4.6	−13.6	−3.9
Korea	8.9	7.1	5.5	−5.5	2.0
Malaysia	9.4	8.6	7.7	−7.5	−1.6
Thailand	8.8	5.5	−0.4	−8.0	1.0

Source: Tomás J. T. Baliño, Charles Enoch, Anne-Marie Gulde, Carl-Johan Lindgren, Marc Quintyn, and Leslie Teo, *Financial Sector Crisis and Restructuring: Lessons from Asia* (Washington, DC: IMF, September 1999), p. 13. Reprinted by permission.

where the governments stimulated the economy by increasing spending faster than they were collecting tax revenues. However, the policies seemed to work, and economic growth began to pick up in 1999.

In August 1998, Russia defaulted on some of its domestic and foreign debt, and it devalued its currency as well. The ensuing crisis in Russia continued well into 1999. In early 1999, the crisis moved to Brazil, which was also forced to devalue its currency and raise interest rates. However, Brazil had begun to recover by mid-1999.

ECONOMIC GROWTH

One of the major results of the Asian financial crisis was the slowdown in economic growth. This hurt companies who were exporting to Asian countries, because their markets basically dried up. It also hurt foreign companies that had invested in Asia to take advantage of its fast-growing markets, because the markets basically disappeared for almost two years. Companies would like every country in which they are investing or to which they are selling to have a high growth rate in GNP and per capita GNP. If this were the case, even if a company did not expand its share in each market, it would still be able to increase revenues at the same pace as the general growth in the economy. However, there are significant differences in growth rates worldwide, affecting the degree to which investments in or sales to a country can affect the bottom line of a company, as illustrated in the earlier Intel and Marks and Spencer examples.

Strong economic growth in Asia from 1990 to 1997 did not help forecast troubles that occurred in 1997 and beyond.

How can a manager determine which markets will exhibit solid growth in the future so that resources can be committed to that market? The best approach is to look at past history and try to forecast the future. But as the Asian financial crisis shows, it is difficult to forecast the future. Map 4.4 illustrates the average annual growth rate in real GNP per capita for each country in the world from 1990 to 1997. Strong growth of 3.0 percent or more can be found in most regions of the world except for North America and Central and Eastern Europe, but the really strong growth was found in East and South Asia.

But as noted by Marks and Spencer, worsening trading conditions in the Far East contributed to a sharp drop in countries' profits. The financial crisis in East Asia reduced GDP on average by an estimated 8 percent in the five countries most affected (Thailand, Malaysia, Indonesia, the Philippines, and South Korea).[18] In addition, Japan was going through a financial crisis of its own due to a banking crisis, and its GNP growth fell 2.9 percent in 1998.

While Asia was going through its crisis in economic growth, sub-Saharan Africa was quietly improving. Growth in real GDP actually rose by 5.8 percent in 1996, 4.9 percent in 1997, and an estimated 4.5 percent in 1998.[19] On average, growth averaged $4\frac{1}{4}$ percent a year during 1995–1998, up from less than $1\frac{1}{2}$ percent during 1990–1994.[20]

As illustrated by McDonald's in Moscow, a drop in economic growth can have detrimental effects on investment. New investors are hesitant to bring in their money, while existing investors are forced to cut back operations and maybe even pull out. Another example is Pizza Hut, which first entered Brazil in 1988 during a period of high inflation and economic instability through a franchisee who contacted the company. Over the next several years, Pizza Hut began to expand into different areas in Brazil. By 1993, Pizza Hut owned 35 units of its own, in addition to the franchises in existence. However, the Brazilian economy began to go through some adjustments as the government instituted a new currency to try to slow down inflation and bring the economy under control. When the Russian financial crisis hit in 1998, Brazil was affected as well. In early 1999, Brazil devalued its currency, the real, and raised interest rates to over 40 percent to try to slow down the economy and strengthen the currency. The economic climate in Brazil became so bad that Pizza Hut was forced to pull out completely. You see how changes in economic growth can affect company strategy.

INFLATION

Another economic factor that management needs to consider is inflation. **Inflation** means that prices are going up. The inflation rate is the percentage increase in the change in prices from one period to the next, usually a year. Economists use different types of indices to measure inflation, but the one they use the most is the **consumer price index (CPI)**. The CPI measures a fixed basket of goods and compares its price from one period to the next. A rise in the index results in inflation. Inflation occurs because aggregate demand is growing faster than aggregate supply. The demand can occur because of government spending where spending is rising faster than the tax revenues to fund the spending or because of increases in the money supply. Inflation affects interest rates, exchange rates, the cost of living, and the general confidence in a country's political and economic system.

High inflation often results in an increase in interest rates for two reasons. The first reason is that interest rates must be higher than inflation so that they can generate a real return on interest-bearing assets. Otherwise, no one would hold those assets. Second, monetary authorities such as the Federal Reserve Bank in the United States use high interest rates to bring down inflation. When interest rates rise, companies are more hesitant to borrow money, which tends to slow down economic growth. In addition, consumers are hesitant to incur consumer debt because of the higher cost of repayment. As demand falls, prices should stabilize or fall.

Inflation is also the most significant factor that influences exchange rates, as will be discussed in more detail in Chapter 10. Basically, the higher the inflation in a country, the more likely that country's currency will fall. Countries with low inflation should have stable or relatively strong currencies. Inflation also affects the cost of living. As prices rise, consumers find it more difficult to purchase goods and services unless their

---

Inflation—a condition where prices are going up.

Consumer price index—an index that measures a fixed basket of goods and compares its price from one period to the next.

High inflation results in higher interest rates for two reasons.
- **Banks need to offer high interest rates to attract money**
- **Governments raise interest rates to slow down economic growth**

MAP 4.4
GNP Per Capita Growth Rate

This map shows the average annual percentage change in a country's real GNP per capita. The growth rate excludes the effects of inflation. In spite of the economic problems in Asia that were manifest after the first half of 1997, the East and South Asian economies showed the fastest growth in the decade of the 1990s. The slowest growth was exhibited in the former Soviet Union and countries in Africa.

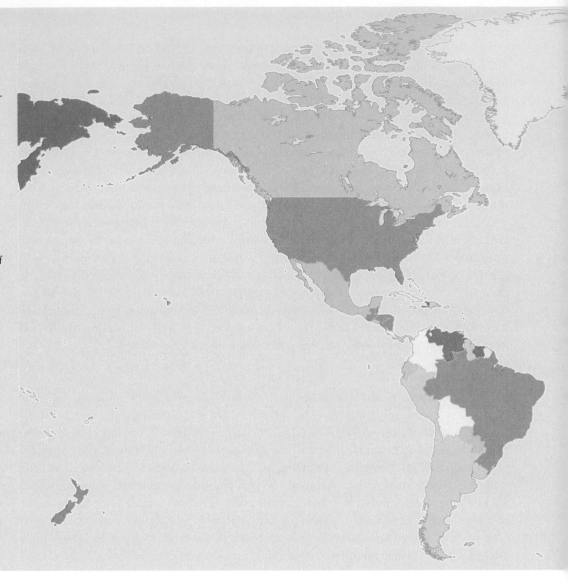

Source: From *The World Bank Atlas 1999,* p. 39. Reprinted by permission of The World Bank.

High inflation results in weaker currencies because increasingly expensive exports eventually drop and relatively cheaper imports rise.

income rises the same or faster than inflation. During periods of rapid inflation, such as Brazil in the early 1990s where inflation was rising at a rate of 1 percent per day, consumers have to spend their paychecks as soon as they get them, or they won't have enough money to buy goods and services later. Finally, inflation also affects confidence in the government. Because of the devastating effects of inflation on the consumer, governments are always under pressure to bring inflation back under control. If governments have to raise interest rates and slow down the economy to slow down inflation, social unrest could occur. This would also occur if governments control wages while other prices are spiraling out of control, leading to animosity among the population.

A good example of the impact of inflation on corporate strategy is Pizza Hut in Brazil. When inflation was running wild, no one really knew how to compare prices. Prices were changing daily, and salaries were going up as well, so people did not have a

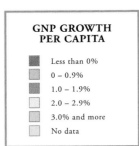

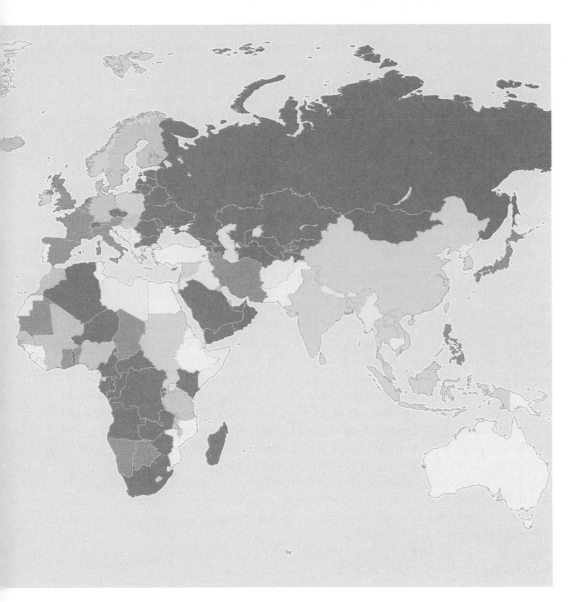

good reference point. After the new currency was implemented in 1994, people began to compare prices and make more informed decisions. At approximately $19 to $20 for a medium pizza, many consumers began to wonder if Pizza Hut was worth the price, given local alternatives. In the case of purchases, Pizza Hut used to collect sales immediately (the stores operated on a cash and carry basis) and delay the payment of supplies. Because Pizza Hut was constantly increasing prices, it was generating more than enough cash flow to pay for supplies once they came due. In effect, it was paying expenses in one period that were incurred in a prior period, and the money it was using was worth less than it was at the beginning of the period, even though it had more of it to spend. So it was paying for supplies with inflated sales revenues. However, this benefit disappeared once inflation slowed down. Mall leases were based on 6 percent of sales and were typically delayed 30 to 45 days, allowing Pizza Hut to use inflated revenues to pay for the leases. However, the drop in inflation after 1994 meant that Pizza Hut could not raise prices enough to cover its mall lease payments, so those expenses basically went up in real terms by 30 to 45 percent, the amount by which inflation had disappeared.

High inflation also creates problems for companies that deal in exports. If inflation is going up but the exchange rate is staying the same, the products will gradually become more expensive in export markets. For example, assume that a British exporter is trying to sell a product to a U.S. distributor for 100 pounds when the exchange rate is $1.59 per British pound. That means the product would cost the U.S. distributor $159.00. If, due to inflation in the United Kingdom, the price were to rise to 110 pounds, it would now cost $174.90 (110 x $1.59). At that new price, U.S. consumers might start looking for substitutes. However, one would expect the exchange rate to eventually change, causing the British pound to become weaker. If the rate falls to $1.47 per pound, the new dollar cost of the product would be $161.70 (110 × $1.47), which is only a slight rise over the previous price. If the demand by U.S. consumers is very sensitive to changes in prices, an increase in prices would result in a fall in demand. So, without a change in the exchange rate, inflation in Britain would take a toll on U.S. demand.

The decade of the 1990s was a decade of diminishing inflation. When the decade began, world inflation as measured by the CPI was 21.3 percent, with inflation in the high-income countries at 5.0 percent and in the developing countries at 103.7 percent. In addition, Argentina, Brazil, and Peru had inflation rates of 2,314 percent, 2,937.8 percent, and 7,481.7 percent, respectively. By the end of 1998, world inflation had fallen to 5.8 percent, high-income country inflation had fallen to 1.4 percent, and developing country inflation had fallen to 11.2 percent. Even Argentina, Brazil, and Peru had improved to inflation rates of only 0.9 percent, 3.2 percent, and 7.2 percent, respectively. The only countries with inflation rates above 100 percent in late 1998 and early 1999 were Belarus, Laos, and Russia.[21] Managers need to monitor trends in inflation to determine how inflation could affect their company's cost structure and competitiveness in world markets, and to anticipate possible changes in monetary policy in response to increases in inflation.

SURPLUSES AND DEFICITS

Other measures of a country's economic stability—and potential as a location for investment—are external and internal surpluses and deficits. Managers need to monitor these balances as indicators of economic strength or weakness. Surpluses rarely are a problem, but deficits are. An external deficit is when a country's cash outflows exceed its inflows. An internal deficit is when government expenditures exceed government revenues.

External Deficits   The **balance of payments** records a country's international transactions. These can be transactions between companies, governments, or individuals. The balance of payments is divided into the current account and the capital account. The **current account** is comprised of trade in goods and services and income from assets abroad. Part of the current account is **merchandise trade balance**, which measures the country's trade deficit or surplus. Merchandise includes goods such as automobiles and wheat. A country derives this balance by subtracting imports from exports. In the case of the

---

The latter part of the 1990s resulted in lower inflation worldwide, with the exception of a few countries.

Balance of payments—a record of a country's international transactions. Current account—trade in goods and services and income from assets abroad. Merchandise trade balance—the net balance of exports minus imports of merchandise. Deficit–imports exceed exports; surplus—exports exceed imports.

United States, this means subtracting the dollar value of its imports from its exports. If exports exceed imports, the country has a trade surplus, and if imports exceed exports, the country has a trade deficit. An export is considered positive because it results in a payment received from abroad—an inflow of cash. An import is considered negative because it results in a payment made to a seller abroad—an outflow of cash. For example, during the first half of 1999, the United States was headed for a record trade deficit. While weak world economies were keeping down the demand for U.S. exports, the strong U.S. economy was absorbing imports at a rapid pace. The U.S. trade deficit was rising to record levels, and the deficits with individual countries and regions, especially Japan, China, and Western Europe, were setting new records. As the deficit continued to climb, the U.S. dollar came under pressure in foreign-exchange markets, and the dollar began to fall. When the July 1999 numbers were released, showing the rise in the trade deficit, the U.S. stock market fell on worries that the Federal Reserve Bank might have to raise interest rates to support the dollar, and that could have a negative impact on company growth and earnings, which could drag down the stock market.

The second component of the current account is services, which includes transactions such as travel, passenger fares, and other transportation, and royalties and fees on licensing agreements with foreign customers. Although the popular definition of the trade balance usually refers just to merchandise trade, it is probably more accurate to measure the goods and services trade balance together. For some economies, like the United States, which generates a large percentage of its GNP from services, the balance on goods and services is a more accurate measure than just goods. In 1998, for example, the United States had a merchandise trade deficit of $246.932 billion, while it had a goods and services deficit of only $164.282 billion due to a services surplus of $82.650 billion.[22]

The third component of the current account is income receipts–payments on assets. This includes items such as receipts from foreign direct investments abroad. A final category, unilateral transfers, is typically not a significant component of the current account balance, but it includes government and private relief grants and income transferred abroad by guest workers, such as Turkish workers in Germany sending money back to their families in Turkey. The current account balance is an important long-run and comprehensive measure of a country's transactions with the rest of the world.

The **capital account** shows transactions in real or financial assets between countries. For example, when the Turtle Bay Hilton Hotel on the north shore of Oahu, Hawaii, was sold to Japanese investors, the transaction was recorded as an inflow of capital to the United States, which is a positive transaction in the capital account. Other examples of capital account transactions include foreign direct investments, such as the purchase of Chrysler (United States) by Daimler Benz (Germany); the purchase and sale of securities, such as the purchase of Brazilian stocks by an American investor; and the purchase of U.S. treasury bonds by a Japanese investor. Also measured in financial assets are changes in the official reserve assets of a country, such as gold, special drawing rights (which we'll discuss in Chapter 10), and foreign currencies.

What difference does it make to companies whether a country has a current account surplus or deficit? There probably is no direct effect. However, the events that comprise the balance-of-payments data influence exchange rates and government policy, which, in turn, influence corporate strategy. As a manager is monitoring the investment climate

Capital account—transactions in real or financial assets between countries, such as the sale of real estate to a foreign investor.

Companies monitor the balance of payments to watch for factors that could lead to currency instability or government actions to correct an imbalance.

of a country where the company has invested or is considering investing assets, it is important to watch for factors that might lead to currency instability. During the lead-up to the Asian financial crisis, many Asian countries were running current account deficits whereas they had always been running surpluses. As noted earlier, this was partly because they were importing capital goods as part of their transition to a more mature market economy. It was also partly because inflation was causing their goods to be less competitive in world markets, so exports were not rising very fast, and imports were growing more quickly. Eventually, the governments were forced to use their foreign currency reserves to purchase goods from abroad, and they eventually ran out of money. The only solution was to let the currency fall. When this happened, foreign managers became concerned over the stability of those countries and stopped investing. Ford had announced a huge investment in Thailand, but it was forced to delay its investment because of instability in the Thai market. To correct the trade imbalance, countries in East Asia were forced to slow down imports, devalue their currencies, and eventually raise interest rates to stop growth, stop inflation, and support their currencies. As the economies slowed down, they became less attractive as a place to manufacture and sell goods. By monitoring trends in the balance of payments, a manager can add one more piece of data in deciding whether or not to do business in a country.

External debt

- **The amount of money borrowed from foreign public or private sector banks**
- **Major debtor nations—Brazil, Mexico, Indonesia, China, and Russia**
- **African countries have the highest debt as a percentage of GNP in the world**

External Debt   As noted above, many of the Asian countries—both public and private sector—borrowed heavily abroad during the 1990s to fuel expansion. This external debt can be measured in two ways—the total amount of the debt and debt as a percentage of GDP. The larger these two numbers become, the more unstable the economies of those countries become. Foreign investors need to monitor debt to determine if the government will need to take corrective action to reduce its debt, normally by slowing down economic growth.

The most heavily indebted countries in the world in terms of total debt are Brazil ($179.0 billion), Mexico ($157.1 billion), Indonesia ($129.0 billion), China ($128.8 billion), and Russia ($124.8 billion). However, all of these countries are large in terms of GDP, so debt as a percentage of GDP was comparably small. In the case of Brazil, external debt is only 26 percent of GDP. However, 12 African countries have external debt in excess of 100 percent of GDP. The plight of the African countries is severe, because the only way to get access to foreign capital is to borrow it from international banks and institutions like the World Bank. They are not able to attract foreign investment because of small market conditions and political instability, so they must turn to foreign debt to expand. This is going to make it virtually impossible for them to pay off their debt. Most of the foreign exchange they earn from exports must be used to service the external debt (make principal and interest payments).

In the Asian financial crisis, most of the Asian countries had increased their external debt to fund growth. Local banks borrowed funds from foreign banks to fund growth in both the public and private sector. Once the Asian currencies began to slide in late 1997, the banks were not able to service their loans, so the foreign banks stopped lending money. That led to the liquidity crisis in hard currency.

Internal Debt and Privatization   External debt results from borrowing money abroad. Internal debt results from an excess of government expenditures over revenues.

The government budget deficits each year contribute to the overall debt. In the case of the European Union, the target is to have annual deficits no greater than 3 percent of GDP and total debt no greater than 60 percent of GDP.

Government internal deficits occur for one of several reasons: The tax system is so poorly run that the government cannot collect all the revenues it wants to, government programs such as defense and welfare are too big for revenues to cover, and state-owned enterprises run huge deficits. All governments, including those in transition from command to market, struggle with several issues, such as "rightsizing" government, setting spending priorities, working toward better expense control and budget management, as well as improving tax policy.[23]

As countries move to control expenditures and reduce their budget deficits, one important strategy to pursue is the **privatization** of state-owned enterprises. Privatization reduces debt by removing the need of the government to subsidize the state-owned enterprises. When the government owns enterprises, it often feels an obligation to keep the enterprises afloat to preserve jobs. Once it is free from ownership, the enterprises can succeed or fail on their own merits.

However, privatization is not easy. It is a political as well as an economic process, and political objectives do not always result in the best economic results. Many state-owned enterprises, such as Pemex, the state-owned oil company in Mexico, are considered to be the crown jewels of a country, and it is difficult to allow them to be sold off to private investors, especially foreign investors. In addition to political objectives are political impediments, such as the obstructive attitudes of existing managers and employees of state-owned enterprises.[24]

The key to successful privatization is the availability of capital. European companies had to raise more than $150 billion before the year 2000 to pay back their governments after they bought state-owned automakers, banks, oil companies, and telecommunications companies.[25] The existence of a large capital market in Europe will allow this to happen.

In most countries, the problem with privatization is selling the inefficient, unproductive enterprises—not those that have a chance to survive. Where permitted, the privatization process enables foreign companies to pick up assets and gain access to markets through acquisition. During the Asian financial crisis, some of the privatization was coming from foreign investors, because the local capital markets were insufficient to generate the funds needed to privatize state-owned enterprises. As long as those countries needed the foreign capital, foreign companies aided in the privatization process.

TRANSITION TO A MARKET ECONOMY

So far we've been learning about economic systems with the assumption that countries are in one economic system or another and that they were not in transition from one classification to another. However, for a great part of the world, that's not the case. Many countries are undergoing transition from command economies to market economies because of the failure of central planning to generate economic growth. The process of transition has made the world of international business very interesting indeed. Let's see why.

The breakup of the Berlin Wall and the overthrow of Eastern European communist dictatorships in 1989 renewed Western interest in doing business in countries that previ-

Internal deficits are the excess of government expenditures over tax receipts; debt is the accumulation of deficits over time

Privatization—the sale of state-owned enterprises to the domestic or foreign private sector; this process helps governments reduce internal debt.

The key to privatization is the availability of capital.

Most command economies are going through the process of transition to market economies; transition economies are in Asia, Europe, or Latin America (Cuba).

ously had been off limits. These countries were classified as command economies. Most of the command economies are in the process of transition to a market economy. Command economies in transition are typically grouped into East Asian (such as China and Vietnam) and European. The European countries in transition are identified in Map 4.5. Some have shown consistent economic growth since the transition process began, some have experienced growth reversals, and others have shown little or no growth.

What does transition mean? In general, transition implies

Transition includes liberalizing economic activity, reforming business activity, and establishing legal and institutional frameworks.

- Liberalizing economic activity, prices, and market operations, along with reallocating resources to their most efficient use
- Developing indirect, market-oriented instruments for macroeconomic stabilization
- Achieving effective enterprise management and economic efficiency, usually through privatization
- Imposing hard budget constraints, which provides incentives to improve efficiency

MAP 4.5   Eastern Europe and the Former Soviet Union Countries in Transition

COUNTRY GROUPINGS

- Central Europe
- Baltics
- Southeast Europe
- The Commonwealth of Independent States

ECONOMIC PERFORMANCE

- ✔ Consistent growth
- ☐ Little or no growth
- ■ Growth reversals

There has been basically four country "groups" in transition since 1989. The Central European and Baltic states have exhibited consistent growth since the transformation process began, but performance has been mixed for Southeast Europe and the Commonwealth of Independent States.

- Establishing an institutional and legal framework to secure property rights, the rule of law, and transparent market-entry regulations[26]

The process of transformation to a market economy differs from country to country—no single formula applies to all. In addition, the various economies in transition differ greatly in their commitment to and progress toward transformation into market economies. Figure 4.3 identifies some of the key policies that must be pursued for countries to have successful reform leading to economic progress. Figure 4.3 also points out the factors that retard reforms and economic progress. A study of the countries in transition have shown that a few key things must be done for successful transition:

- Sustained macroeconomic stabilization (inflation control) is essential.
- No pain, no gain. Delayed reforms may defer the pain, but they defer sustained recovery and increase the risk that growth will be reversed.
- There is no royal road to reform. There is no one key to growth; countries have to implement all the different components of reform.
- Developing an appropriate legal structure is indispensable.[27]

FIGURE 4.3 Reforms and Economic Progress

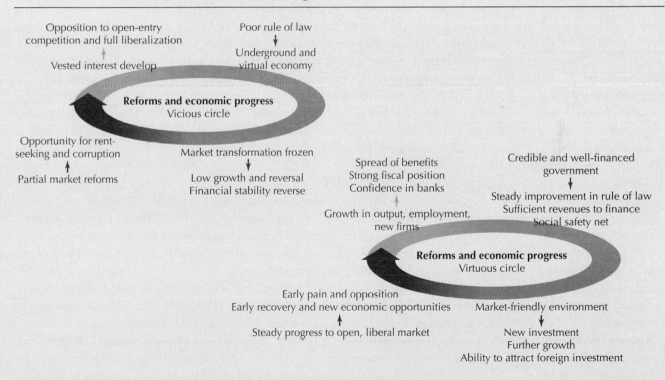

There are several reforms that are necessary to achieve economic progress, but there are also factors that retard economic progress.

Source: Oleh Havrylyshyn and Thomas Wolf, "Determinants of Growth in Transition Economies," *Finance and Development,* June 1999, p. 14. Reprinted by permission.

As countries continue the transition process, more opportunities for trade and investment should open up for MNEs.

Why do these changes bring renewed Western interest in doing business with economies in transition? The answer is partly political, partly economic. Most economies in transition experienced slow economic growth during the Cold War years of the 1970s and 1980s. Consequently, the outlook for foreign investors to do business in those countries seemed bleak. However, with the end of the Cold War came the hope that governments of these countries would eliminate their trade barriers, encouraging economic growth and increased business opportunities. However, there is still significant volatility in the midst of change. As the Russian economic crisis in 1998 showed, the transition is not smooth. Russia is one of the countries in transition showing little or no growth during transition, and it is the largest and most powerful economically of the European countries in transition.

THE PROCESS OF TRANSITION

The transition process has provided significant opportunities for MNEs. As the countries in transition have liberalized and opened the doors to the outside world, many foreign companies have increased their exports to them. In addition, the privatization process has provided many opportunities for foreign companies to acquire companies and enter the market through acquisition. In the Czech Republic, for example, so much foreign investment had come into the country by late 1999 to take advantage of the market and in expectation of the privatization of government assets in 2000 that the Czech currency, the koruna, had strengthened significantly. The Czech Central Bank was forced to lower interest rates nine times in 1999 to stimulate the economy and weaken the currency.[28] Lower interest rates will cause investors to sell their koruna for foreign currencies where interest rates are higher. The sale of koruna should lead to a fall in its value, allowing Czech exporters a better chance to sell their products abroad. The point is that the transition process was providing significant opportunities for foreign companies who wanted to do business in the Czech Republic. The transition process was attracting foreign capital and goods. To illustrate the transition process, let's look at three examples: Russia, Eastern Europe, and China.

RUSSIA'S TRANSITION

For Russia, the transition to a market economy has been difficult because the government has been trying simultaneously to change the country's economy and its political system. The resulting political turmoil is exacerbated by the battle between conservatives who are afraid of moving too fast and reformers who want to install capitalism quickly through privatization and price decontrol.

The Soviet economy was cumbersome, inefficient, and corrupt, but somehow it seemed to work. However, the breakup of the central Soviet government and the loss of the relationship Russia had with the other 14 Soviet republics and the former Eastern bloc countries resulted in a contraction of the economy every year since 1989. Although government statistics are not very reliable, it is estimated that the Russian economy by the end of 1996 was half the size of the economy in 1989, which is a steeper contraction than the Great Depression in the United States.[29]

The transition to a market in Russia has included massive privatization. In the early 1990s, 120,000 enterprises changed hands from the public to the private sector, and many Russians ended up holding shares in these companies. However, most of the

Russian transition

- Includes political and economic transition at the same time
- Initial transition steps resulted in steep economic declines
- The transition has involved massive, although not altogether effective, privatization
- Soft budgets—subsidies and other government-supporting activities—have continued
- Hard administrative constraints have disappeared, being replaced with connections and corruption
- Debts and deficits—both internal and external—are a real challenge

shares were sold off in the stock market, and an estimated 80 percent of the private companies are now majority owned by insiders, the former managers of the companies under communist rule.[30] It is also estimated that over 50 percent of the 100 largest companies in Russia have changed hands since the privatization effort began, with outsiders taking control. This should eventually lead to greater efficiency.

The economic crisis in Russia in August 1998 exposed a number of serious weaknesses. Under the socialist system that existed prior to 1989, the economy operated under soft budget constraints and hard administrative constraints. The focus was not on profits but on meeting the goals established by the state. Managers knew that they would receive subsidies, loans on easy terms, and a delay in tax payments to make up for a deficit in the bottom line.[31] However, Russian managers were under the control of the state and had to behave. They might have skimmed some profits for their private gain, but they had to meet the requirements of the central plan and take care of the workers. Any shortcomings in these areas were dealt with severely.[32]

Now Russia is trying to adjust to the market economy. Soft budgets have not been done away with entirely, but administrative constraints have disappeared. In their place is "old boy" cronyism and corruption.[33] The allegations of corruption, money laundering, and capital flight by key Russian businessmen, officials, and family members of high government officials illustrated this in 1999.[34]

The economy has also had a difficult time with fiscal and monetary reform. It has suffered large budget deficits for two major reasons. The first is that it was not collecting taxes. Managers never had to worry about taxes under the socialist system, so that attitude carried itself into transition. Taxes were paid according to negotiations with tax collectors, not law, which opened the door to corruption. In addition, the Yeltsin government was not able to get the Duma, the Russian parliament, to curtail spending, so the budget deficit was skyrocketing. By August 1998, the government was forced to default on domestic debt and some international debt and devalue the currency. Foreign banks, such as Deutsche Bank in Germany and Citibank in the United States, were forced to accept five cents for every dollar of debt.

Even though Russia is one of the richest countries in the world in terms of natural resources, has a well-educated and cheap workforce (labor costs are less than half of Poland's or Mexico's and under one-twentieth of Germany's), and a large consumer population, it is not able to attract significant foreign investment, especially in manufacturing.[35] As noted in the McDonald's case earlier in the chapter, even some foreign investors are pulling out of Russia because of the difficult economic climate. Until Russia can move faster along the transition process, it will have to generate its growth internally and will not be a location for foreign investment or market for exports by MNEs.

EASTERN EUROPE'S TRANSITION

In the three years following the overthrow of communism in 1989 and 1990, economic growth in Eastern Europe ground to a halt. From 1990 to 1992, GNP fell by 40 percent in Czechoslovakia, 32 percent in Hungary, and 32 percent in Poland. However, by 1992, the worst appeared to be over. The transition, especially in Poland, Hungary, and the Czech Republic, seemed to be moving much faster than in Russia because these countries want to join the European Union, and they know that they must transform to market economies for that to happen. Also, Western Europe became the major market for their exports, so the move to a market was much more important than for Russia.

However, the countries of Eastern Europe were different in terms of how they approached transition. Poland had a strong national identity, was strongly influenced by the Catholic Church, and had a strong agrarian tradition and strong labor movement. Like all centrally planned economies, Poland exhibited a dominance of the state sector in the economy, heavily distorted prices due to price subsidies and controls, an absence of market institutions, weak public administration, and a large socialist welfare state.[36] Poland's transition to a market economy can be best described as shock therapy. The government pursued immediate reform on three levels: macroeconomic stabilization, microeconomic liberalization, and institutional reform. Some of the reforms included tight monetary policy, liberalization of prices, trade liberalization, privatization of state-owned enterprises, the removal of barriers to foreign direct investment, tax reform, and the creation of a central bank. In the first year of reform, inflation shot up, industrial production declined by 20 percent, and unemployment shot up. After a few years of pain, however, the economy began to recover, and average annual GDP growth was 3.9 percent from 1990 to 1997, reaching 6.8 percent in 1996 to 1997, compared with an average annual decline over the same period of 9.0 percent in Russia, 0.4 percent in Hungary, and 0.1 percent in the Czech Republic.[37] The Czech Republic started the transition process in better financial shape than Poland, but it took a gradual approach to adjustment, and it has lagged behind in its progress. The Czech government delayed restructuring, allowing large state enterprises to continue to enjoy soft budget constraints during the first three years of transition. This delay has put it behind in the transition process.[38]

CHINA'S TRANSITION

In 1978, China's government launched reforms to transform the Chinese economy away from central planning, government ownership, and import substitution policies (the favoring of local production over imports) toward greater decentralization and opening up of the Chinese economy. Since then, the Chinese economy has grown dramatically. From 1990 to 1997, the economy grew at an average annual rate of 11.9 percent.[39]

The Chinese approach to transformation differs significantly from those of Russia and Central Europe. The Chinese leadership is not at all interested in democratic reform. It continues to hold tight to totalitarian political control. Initially, privatization was not an issue, but China has moved to liberalize its economy and allow private investment while not completely giving up control of the economy. However, every year, the Chinese government loosens the economy a little bit more. Chinese growth in GDP has exceeded that of the industrial countries, the world in general, and East Asia and the Pacific. However, China's growth is internal rather than being export-led as is the case of other East Asian countries like Korea, Japan, and Taiwan. But China struggles with its state-owned enterprises (SOEs). Although the SOEs are becoming less influential in the Chinese economy, they are still huge and a source of concern because of the large numbers of people they employ. Most of China's government subsidies have shifted from daily necessities to covering enterprise losses, which is the same as the soft budget constraints mentioned above. Although China has borrowed from abroad, it has financed over 75 percent of its growth from domestic sources, but it has among the largest foreign-exchange reserves in the world to back up current and future international borrowing.

The Asian financial crisis did not affect China as much as it did other countries in East Asia, but it still suffered. As markets contracted all over Asia, Chinese exports to those countries also fell. Although the Chinese currency was under pressure to devalue, the Chinese government resisted those pressures.

The challenge facing Chinese leadership is how to maintain economic growth as it continues to transition to a market economy while resisting the growing pressures to liberalize politically. The key is the reform of the SOEs. Although the Chinese government is supporting them so as not to have massive unemployment during transition, it is moving to privatize more of them each year so that it is not burdened with them in the future.

THE FUTURE OF TRANSITION

Earlier in this section, we identified some of the keys to a successful transition from a command to a market economy. Looking at just a few examples, it is obvious that the process is difficult and is compounded by the context in which the transition is occurring. Some countries, like those in Central and Eastern Europe and Russia, are attacking political and economic change at the same time. Others, such as Cuba, Vietnam, China, and North Korea, are not interested in political change. Some, such as Poland, Hungary, and the Czech Republic, are liberalizing their economies at a rapid rate. China is not liberalizing quite as fast, but it is certainly moving faster than Russia, Vietnam, Cuba, and North Korea. In the case of Cuba and North Korea, virtually no liberalization is taking place. Vietnam is the most recent of the command economies to initiate change, but it is moving very slowly. It is no coincidence that those countries that are moving the quickest to transform their economies are also dealing the most with MNEs in terms of trade and investment.

Each of these countries must establish market institutions, such as central banks and stock markets; stabilize the macroeconomic picture, especially controlling inflation and currency values; bring their internal debt into balance by establishing a good tax structure and collecting taxes as well as reducing government expenditures; privatize stateowned enterprises; and allow companies to operate in an atmosphere of greater freedom from control and soft budget constraints. In addition, the countries in transition must deal with other issues, such as environmental damage and the development of human capital.

The future of transition
- **Establish market institutions**
- **Stabilize the macroeconomic environment—especially inflation and exchange rates**
- **Improve tax collections and reduce government expenditures**
- **Privatize state-owned enterprises**
- **Allow private sector firms to grow**
- **Deal with environmental degradation and the development of human capital**

Environmental Damage   Environmental damage is a major concern for countries in transition. The two most important problems are air and water pollution. The former results from suspended metal dusts and particulate materials. The latter is exacerbated by careless disposal of toxic waste.[40] The major causes of environmental pollution are heavy coal use, old technology, and low energy prices, which serve as a disincentive to save energy and raw materials.

Some analysts argue that air pollution in the major towns and cities of Eastern Europe is no worse than in Western European cities of similar income levels and industrial structures. These analysts claim that environmental problems in Eastern Europe today are at the level they were in Western Europe and North America 20 to 30 years ago. But other analysts argue that water pollution and environmental damage from inadequate nuclear waste management are far more serious in Eastern Europe today than they were in the industrial countries 30 years ago. The cost of environmental

Looking to the Future
A GLOBAL ECONOMY IN THE NEW MILLENNIUM

As the twentieth century came to a close, the global economy was strengthening. Led by economic growth in the United States, accompanied by low inflation and low interest rates, economic growth was beginning to pick up in Asia, Latin America, Africa, and Europe. What will be the keys to the future? Will the global economy continue to expand, providing opportunities for MNEs?

Although the United States closed the millennium on a strong note, there was some concern about its ability to continue to demonstrate strong growth without igniting inflation. If the economy can grow in such as way as to prevent inflation, the Federal Reserve Board will be able to keep interest rates down. If inflation rears its ugly head, the Fed will be forced to raise interest rates, which will slow down economic growth, reduce corporate profits, and dampen the growth of the stock market. Most of the growth of the U.S. economy in the latter part of the 1990s was consumer-led, which itself was fueled by strong growth in the stock market. A contraction in the market will affect consumer confidence and, therefore, consumer spending. Because of strong economic growth in the United States compared to other economies, the United States closed the decade with a serious trade deficit. If the trade deficit continues to rise, it must be offset by an import of capital from abroad. If foreign investors lose confidence in the U.S. economy, they will move funds out of the United States until the U.S. government raises interest rates high enough to attract investment. However, that will result in a slowdown in economic growth, which could be damaging to global growth.

Asia, let by South Korea, will continue to recover from the devastating affects of the Asian financial crisis. However, its ability to sustain that growth will depend on a couple of things: the ability of Japan to solve its banking crisis and the desire of the Asian economies to reform. As the decade ended, Japan was still mired under a banking crisis approaching $500 billion. Banks in Japan had made bad loans to Japanese corporations as well as to Asian economies, and the economic crisis in Asia brought the debt crisis to a head. Japanese banks need to solve the debt crisis by writing off bad loans and allowing failing financial institutions to go bankrupt or merge with other institutions. If Japan cannot solve its banking crisis, there will not be enough liquidity in Japan to allow Japanese companies to restructure and expand. If the Japanese economy does not recover, the rest of Asia cannot recover. It relies on Japan as a market for raw materials as well as consumer and industrial products. Japan is certainly one of the keys. The other key is the restructuring of the Asian economy. In addition to solving macroeconomic problems, Asian governments need to restructure the interaction between government and business. Bankruptcy laws need to be put into place to allow bad companies to fail, the banking sector needs to be reformed so that bad loans are written off and new loans made on the basis of merit instead of connections, companies need to restructure to focus on their core competencies, and corruption needs to be rooted out. The concern is that the Asian economies are recovering too quickly to implement reforms and that many of the same mistakes will be made again. Asia is an extremely important region of the world because of its population base and growth potential.

Europe is beginning to recover and should provide a strong target for foreign investment and exports. Two things will help determine the future of Europe. The first is the success of the euro, the new currency of the European Union. A strong currency in Europe will be counterforce to the dollar in North America and the yen in Asia and provide a huge market for MNEs. As growth begins to pick up in Europe, the European countries should be able to reduce unemployment, which has hovered at close to 11 percent for most of the 1990s. However, Europe's inability to maintain economic growth in the face of market socialism is a real challenge. European countries refuse to adopt Anglo-American capitalism, which is much more market based and less reliant on a social welfare state, but they feel that their more humanitarian form of a market economy is superior.

Latin America should continue to grow, but the countries from Mexico on the north and Argentina on the south are still very fragile both politically and economically. Democracy in Latin America is alive and well, but it is also very new. Political instability can lead to economic instability, as Brazil found in early 1999 when the Brazilian state governors refused to rein in their budget deficits and created a crisis in the Brazilian currency, the real. To support their currencies and keep them locked onto the dollar, the Brazilians and the Argentines have been forced to raise interest rates to astronomical levels, but that has choked off economic growth, increased unemployment, and raised social instability. They need to figure out how to control internal deficits, maintain inflation-free growth, stabilize their exchange rates, and lower interest rates and unemployment.

Africa leads the world in debt as a percent of GDP and in the number of countries in the low-income category. However, sub-Saharan Africa has been growing at a relatively stable rate since the mid-1990s, and its growth should continue into the next decade. African countries are saddled with numerous problems, including small populations, and therefore markets, ethnic warfare, political instability, and huge debt burdens. However, an IMF official notes that "African countries have been implementing sound macroeconomic policies and structural reforms to raise real per capita incomes, reduce inflation, and narrow financial imbalances."[41] The problem is that Africa is far more reliant on external forces, such as commodity prices and global interest rates, than are most countries in the world, so there are major elements over which it has no control. In spite of that, African countries need to continue to reform internally if they are to have a chance to succeed.

cleanup is significant and reduces the amount of investment capital available to transform transition economies to market economies. China is also facing environmental crisis as it modernizes its economy. Major concerns are the pollution of air, water, and farmland. The problem is that these countries are more concerned about economic growth than environmental problems. Companies, which are the key polluters, have no incentive to clean up. It will take the passage of environmental laws and their enforcement for environmental damage to be reversed.

Human Capital   As a government eliminates central planning without also substituting knowledgeable owners to whom enterprise managers can report, there is little control over these managers' actions. Most managers have no experience in operating without a central plan that tells them what to produce and to whom to sell. Very few of these managers understand how to read or compile financial statements, how to respond to market signals (such as changes in demand), or how to market products when there is competition, especially in Western export markets. They also may lack a strong work ethic, being used to low pay and high job security. As noted in the McDonald's case, McDonald's sent its key managers abroad to train them in the McDonald's way of doing things. The key is the education of managers. Foreign investors can be part of this training process, but so far foreign investment has been spotty in some of the countries. This means a reorientation of the educational system through faculty exchanges with foreign universities, the establishment of management training programs, and sending high potential managers overseas to learn modern management techniques.

The process of transition is not easy, but it is obvious that most countries in the world are committed to the transition to a market, even though there will be differences from country to country in terms of how much they move to a market and how quickly they do it.

WEB CONNECTION

Check out our home page www.prenhall.com/daniels for links to key resources for you in your study of international business.

SUMMARY

- Understanding the economic environments of foreign companies and markets can help managers predict how trends and events in those environments might affect their company's future performance there.

- Companies enter foreign markets because of factor conditions—essential inputs to the production process—or demand conditions—the size and potential of the market.

- Gross national product is a broad measure of national income that is the market value of final goods and services produced by domestically owned factors of production. Per capita GNP is used to rank countries in terms of their individual wealth.

- Countries are classified by per capita GNP as follows: high income ($9,656 or more), middle income ($786–$9,655), and low income ($785 or less); high-income countries are also called developed or industrial countries, while low- and middle-income countries are developing countries, also known sometimes as emerging economies.

- Economic freedom is the degree to which governments intervene in economic activity. Free countries tend to have higher economic growth; people generally are better off than those in unfree or repressed countries.

- The economic system determines who owns and controls resources. In a market economy, private sector companies and individuals allocate and control resources, while in a command economy, the government owns and controls resources.

- The Asian financial crisis, which began with the devaluation of the Thai baht on July 2, 1997, spread to the rest of Asia and resulted in a dramatic slowdown in economic activity and crises in currency and equity markets.

- Economic growth is a good measure of the well-being of a country, and it refers to growth in GNP from one year to the next.

- Inflation, a condition where prices are going up, can be devastating to a country. It can result in high interest rates, which slow down economic growth and make a country less desirable as a place to do business. It can also result in a loss of confidence in the government.

- An excess of imports over exports causes external deficits. External deficits result in an outflow of capital.

- The trade balance measures exports less imports of goods. The current account measures exports less imports of goods and services, plus the net income earned from investments abroad and net unilateral transfers, such as the transfer abroad of money by foreign workers and public and private relief efforts.

• The capital account shows transactions in real or financial assets between countries.

• External debt occurs when countries borrow money from foreign public or private banks or other financial institutions. The biggest borrowers are Brazil, Mexico, Indonesia, China, and Russia, but many African countries have borrowed a larger amount as a percentage of GNP.

• Internal deficits occur because governments spend more than they collect in tax revenues. The accumulation of deficits over time results in internal debt.

• Privatization of state-owned enterprises is one way to reduce internal deficits.

• The transition to a market economy is where former command economies liberalize their economic policies and move from ownership and control of the economy by government to reliance on market forces to control economic activity.

• The process of transition differs from country to country—no one formula applies to all. Countries differ greatly in their commitment and progress to transformation to a market economy. Cuba, North Korea, and Vietnam have done rather poorly, while Poland, the Czech Republic, and Hungary have been more successful. China is somewhere in between but moving quickly toward a market economy.

• In addition to general economic issues, countries in transition need to deal with environmental damage and the development of human capital.

CASE

THE DAEWOO GROUP AND THE ASIAN FINANCIAL CRISIS[42]

In 1999, Daewoo Group (*www.daewoo.com*), Korea's second largest *chaebol*, or family-owned business conglomerate, was staggering under $50 billion in debt and considering whether or not to sell its flagship business, Daewoo Motor Company Ltd., to General Motors. The Asian financial crisis, which had hammered the Korean economy for two years, had finally taken its toll on the expansion-minded Daewoo and forced both Daewoo and the Korean government to decide what would be Daewoo's future.

Kim Woo-Choong started Daewoo in 1967 as a small textile company with only 5 employees and $10,000 in capital. In just 30 years, Mr. Kim had grown Daewoo into a diversified company with 250,000 employees worldwide, over 30 domestic companies and 300 overseas subsidiaries, generating sales of more than $100 billion annually. However, some estimated that Daewoo and its subcontractors employ 2.5 million people in Korea. Although Daewoo started in textiles, it quickly moved into other fields, first heavy and chemical industries in the 1970s, and then technology-intensive industries in the 1980s. By the end of 1999, Daewoo was organized into six major divisions:

• Trading Division
• Heavy Industry and Shipbuilding
• Construction and Hotels
• Motor Vehicle Division
• Electronics and Telecommunications
• Finance and Service

However, Daewoo was struggling. Its $50 billion debt was 40 percent greater than in 1998, equaling 13 percent of Korea's entire GDP. A good share of that, about $10 billion, was owed to overseas creditors. Its debt-to-equity ratio (total debt divided by shareholder's equity) in 1998 was 5 to 1, which is higher than the 4 to 1 average of other large *chaebol*, but significantly higher than the U.S. average, which usually is around 1 to 1 but rarely climbs above 2 to 1. Of course, there is no way of knowing the true picture of Daewoo's financial information because of the climate of secrecy in Korean companies. In addition, it is possible that its estimated debt might be greatly underestimated because no one knows whether or not the $50 billion includes debt of foreign subsidiaries.

How did Daewoo get into such a terrible position, and how much did the nature of the Korean economy and the Asian financial crisis affect Daewoo?

KOREAN ECONOMY

The impact of the Asian financial crisis on Korea was partly a result of the economic system of state intervention adopted by Korea since the mid-1950s. Modeled after the Japanese economic system, the Korean authoritarian government targeted export growth as the key for the country's future. Initially, the government adopted a strategy of import substitution, and that later gave way to a strategy of "export or die." Significant incentives were given to exporters, such as access to low-cost money (often borrowed abroad in dollars and loaned to companies at below-market interest rates in Korean won), lower corporate income taxes, tariff exemptions, tax holidays for domestic suppliers of export firms, reduced rates on public utilities, and monopoly rights for new export markets. Clearly, the government wanted Korean companies to export.

The *chaebol*, of which the four largest are Hyundai, Daewoo, Samsung, and the LG Group, became the dominant business institutions during the rise in the Korean economy. They were among the largest companies in the world and were very diversified, as can be seen by Daewoo's investment and business choices. They were held together by ownership, management, and family ties. In particular, family ties played a key role in controlling the *chaebol*. Until the 1980s, the banks in Korea provided most of the funding to the *chaebol*, and they were owned and controlled by the government. Because of the importance of exporting, the *chaebol* were all tied to general trading companies. The *chaebol* received lots of support from the government, and they were also very loyal to the government, giving rise to charges of corruption.

Most *chaebol* were initially involved in light industry, such as textile production, but the government realized that companies needed to shift first to heavy industry and then to technology industries. Daewoo transitioned to heavy industry in 1976 when the Korean government asked President Kim to acquire an ailing industrial firm rather than let the firm go out of business and create unemployment. That led to the creation of Daewoo Heavy Industries Ltd., which was followed up by another government-sponsored purchase of a shipyard, renamed Daewoo Shipbuilding & Heavy Machinery Ltd.

ASIAN FINANCIAL CRISIS AND ITS IMPACT ON KOREA

The country continued to liberalize, and democracy finally came into being in 1988 with the introduction of a new constitution and the election of Kim Young-Sam, the first democratic president in Korea. The economy also continued to grow at 5 to 8 percent annually during the early to mid-1990s, led primarily by exports, and the World Bank predicted that Korea would have the seventh largest economy in the world by 2020. However, the Asian financial crisis brought that growth to a halt. After the Thai baht was devalued on July 2, 1997, the Korean won soon followed, and the Korean stock market crashed as well. By the end of 1997, the

South Korean won was 46.2 percent lower than its predevaluation rate. At the time the crisis hit, Korea's external debt was estimated to be $110 billion to $150 billion, 60 percent of it maturing in less than one year. In addition, it had another $368 billion of domestic debt.

Korea's banks had been a tool of state industrial policy, with the government ordering banks to make loans to certain companies, even if they were not healthy. Banks borrowed money in dollars and lent them to firms in won, shifting the burden of the foreign exchange from the firms to the banks. Hanbo Steel and Kia Motors went bankrupt, leaving some banks with huge losses. The Korean won fell in the fall of 1997, causing the government to raise interest rates to support the won, resulting in more problem loans. Bad loans at the nine largest financial institutions in Korea ranged from 94 percent to 376 percent of the banks' capital, making them technically insolvent.

The *chaebol* were also very overextended. The top five *chaebol* were in an average of 140 different businesses, ranging from semiconductor manufacture to shipbuilding to auto manufacturing. This was happening during a time when most other companies in the industrial world were selling off unrelated businesses and focusing on their core competencies. Twenty-five of the top 30 *chaebol* had debt-to-equity ratios of 3 to 1, and 10 had ratios of over 5 to 1, as noted above. Compare this to Toyota Motor of Japan, which had a debt-to-equity ratio in 1998 of 0.7 to 1.

During this crisis, Korea began to negotiate with the IMF for help. The IMF agreed to help, but only if Korea raised interest rates to support its currency, reduced its budget deficits, reformed its banks, restructured the *chaebol*, improved financial disclosure, devalued the currency (to stimulate exports even more), promoted exports, and restricted imports. In return for a pledge to undergo the reforms, the IMF released funds to Korea to help pay off its foreign debt and keep its banks from going bankrupt. This in turn brought in more money from foreign banks who were encouraged that Korea had pledged to reform itself.

One of the IMF's key areas was banking reform. The IMF encouraged Korea to open up its banking sector to foreign investment, hoping that an infusion of foreign banking expertise might help the Korean banks make better loans. Of course, foreign banks had made a sizable amount of bad loans in Asia as well. In addition, the IMF encouraged the Korean government to pass good bankruptcy laws to allow bad companies, including banks, to fail. However, the IMF hoped that Korean banking institutions would merge, forming fewer but stronger banks. In addition, the IMF encouraged banking reform to cut the links between bankers and politics, tighten supervision and regulation of the banking industry, and improve accounting and disclosure.

IMPACT OF THE CRISIS ON DAEWOO

While the financial crisis was going on, Daewoo's President Kim ignored the warning signs and continued to expand. In 1998, a year when the Daewoo Group lost money, it added 14 new firms to its existing 275 subsidiaries. While Samsung and LG were cutting back, Daewoo added 40 percent more debt.

Finally, Korean President Kim Dae Jung had enough. He ordered the banks to stop lending to the *chaebol* until they came up with and began to execute a plan to sell off businesses and focus on their core competencies. But that didn't stop Daewoo. To get access to more money to feed its growth, Daewoo issued corporate bonds, which were purchased by Investment Trust Companies (ITCs), finance companies associated with the *chaebol*. The ITCs purchased nearly $20 billion in corporate bonds.

In early 1999, Daewoo announced a plan to sell off some of its businesses to comply with government restructuring requirements before the government took more drastic action, such as nationalization. However, the plans limped along until July 1999. At that point, Daewoo announced that it would go bankrupt unless its Korean creditors backed off. It basically could not even service its interest payments, let alone its principal. The government immediately stepped in and froze Daewoo's loans until November 1999. This shock rippled through Korea, because nobody thought a *chaebol* would ever be allowed to collapse. That had never happened before, and the close ties between government and business were such that it was never expected to happen. The shock of Daewoo's announcement negatively affected the corporate bond market, and the ITCs came under pressure because of their huge exposure to Daewoo. Negotiations in Korea involved 60 banks, some owned by the government, others in the private sector. On September 16, 1999, Daewoo asked its foreign creditors for a moratorium on interest payments until March 2000, so the instability spread to the international markets.

DAEWOO'S FUTURE

Will Daewoo survive? One possibility is to dismantle Daewoo and let it have only auto-related businesses. The plan would be to leave Daewoo with the following six businesses:
- Daewoo Motor
- Daewoo Motor Sales

- Daewoo Corporation, trading business only
- Daewoo Telecom, auto-parts business only
- Daewoo Capital
- Daewoo Heavy Industries, machinery business only

All of the other businesses would be sold off to domestic or foreign investors, and the name would be changed to something other than Daewoo. One way this could be accomplished would be for the government-owned banks that have large outstanding loans to Daewoo to convert the loans to equity. Technically, the government would then own Daewoo. The government could sell off the pieces to other companies or investors, both domestic and foreign.

Will President Kim Woo-Choong allow this to happen? Will he allow the company that he built from nothing to one of the most powerful in Korea be broken up by the government? As the Korean economy began to recover in 1999, some felt that the *chaebol* should weather the storm and not allow themselves to be broken up. However, President Kim Dae Jung had mandated that the *chaebol* get their debt-to-equity ratios from 5 to 1 to 2 to 1 by the end of 1999, and that looked impossible without a huge infusion of equity capital or a write-off of debt through debt restructuring with the banks or selling of debt-laden businesses to others. President Kim's political power began slipping in 1999, and it is unclear how much he can push the *chaebol*.

To raise more capital, should Daewoo sell off some of its auto assets to General Motors? Daewoo and GM had worked together before, but strategic differences forced GM to sell its 50 percent ownership in Daewoo's automotive unit back to Daewoo in 1992. Since then, Daewoo has expanded significantly into Central and Eastern Europe, as well as Korea and Southeast Asia, primarily Vietnam—all markets of interest to GM. However, GM didn't want to be burdened with Daewoo debt, and some estimated that Daewoo's auto unit had at least $8 billion of debt. Daewoo needs the cash, but should it get rid of the only major assets that the government wants it to retain?

QUESTIONS

1. How would you describe Korea's economic system? What are the key elements in that system? How would you describe the interaction between politics and economics in Korea?
2. Does Korea look like a good place to invest? Why or why not?
3. What should President Kim Woo-Choong do to rescue Daewoo?
4. What should General Motors do?

CHAPTER NOTES

1 Erich E. Toll, "Hasabburgonya, Tejturmix and Big Mac to Go," *Journal of Commerce,* August 24, 1988, p. 1A; Vincent J. Schodolski, "Moscovites Stand in Line for a 'Beeg Mek' Attack," *Chicago Tribune,* February 1, 1990, sec. 1, p. 1; Bill Keller, "Of Famous Arches, Beeg Meks, and Rubles," *New York Times,* January 28, 1990, p. A1; "McDonald's," *The Economist,* Vol. 313, No. 7629, November 18, 1989, p. 34; Peter Gumbel, "Muscovites Queue Up at American Icon," *Wall Street Journal,* February 1, 1990, p. A12; Ann Blackman, "Moscow's Big Mak Attack," *Time,* February 5, 1990, pp. 51, 80–91; Celestine Bohlen, "How Do You Spell Big Mac in Russian?" *New York Times,* May 25, 1993, p. B1; Oleg Vikhanski and Sheila Puffer, "Management Education and Employee Training at Moscow McDonald's," *European Management Journal,* March 1993, pp. 102–107; Richard Gibson, "Burger Bonanza: McDonald's to Open Its 25,000th Store, in South Chicago"; Aviva Freudmann, "Supplying Big Mac's: A Lesson in Logistics," *Journal of Commerce,* May 19, 1999, p. 1A; Bloomberg News, "McDonald's Is Slowing Its Expansion in Russia," *New York Times,* February 20, 1999, sec. C, p. 3; Natalia Olynec, "Big Mac Blues in Russia," *Chicago Sun Times,* February 28, 1999, p. 58.

2 The World Bank Group, *www.worldbank.org/data/databytopic/class.htm.*

3 Michael E. Porter, *The Competitive Advantage of Nations* (New York: Free Press, 1980), pp. 74–75.

4 Ibid., p. 86.

5 Andrew B. Abel and Ben S. Bernanke, *Macroeconomics* (Reading, MA: Addison-Wesley, 1992), p. 30.

6 Ibid, pp. 32–33.

7 The World Bank Group, *www.worldbank.org/html/extdr/about/role.htm.*

8 Data is from The World Bank, *The World Bank Atlas 1999* (Washington DC: The World Bank, 1999), p. 38.

9 Andrew Higgins, "Resilient Russia Dodges Calamities Predicted After Ruble's Collapse," *Wall Street Journal,* March 8, 1999, p. A1.

10 "Summers Says U.S. Should Pause Further IMF Loans to Russia," *New York Times,* September 1, 1999, *www.nytimes.com/99/09/01/late/russia-imf.html*

11 Ibid, p. 58.

12 Bryan T. Johnson, Kim R. Holmes, and Melanie Kirkpatrick, "Freedom Is the Surest Path to Prosperity," *Wall Street Journal,* December 1, 1998, p. A22; also see *www.heritage.org/index* for more details.

13 Ibid.

14 Bruce R. Scott and Audrey T. Sproat, "Japan D1: A Strategy for Economic Growth," Harvard Business School Case 9-378-106, rev. September 26, 1994, pp. 1–35.

15 Michael P. Todaro. *Economic Development,* 6th ed. (Reading, MA: Addison Wesley, 1996), p. 705.

16 "The Global Economy: A Survey," *The Economist,* October 1, 1994, p. r.

17 Charles Wolf, Jr., "Too Much Government Control," and Joseph Stiglitz, "Bad Private-Sector Decisions," *Wall Street Journal,* February 4, 1998, p. A22.

18 The World Bank, *World Bank Atlas 1999,* p. 12.

19 Alssane D. Ouattara, "Africa: An Agenda for the 21st Century," *Finance & Development,* March 1999, p. 3.

20 Ernesto Hernandez-Cata, "Sub-Saharan Africa Ecoomic Policy and Outlook for Growth," *Finance & Development,* March 1999, p. 10.

21 International Monetary Fund, *International Financial Statistics,* August 1999, pp. 57–61.

22 Bureau of Economic Analysis, "Survey of Current Business," October 1999, www.bea.doc.gov/bea/di/bopqtab.pdf.

23 The World Bank, *World Development Report 1996* (Washington, DC: 1996), pp. 113–120.

24 International Finance Corporation, *Privatization Principles and Practice* (Washington, DC: IFC, 1995), p. 1.

25 "The Perils of Privatization," *Business Week,* May 16, 1994, p. 48.

26 Oleh Havrylyshyn and Thomas Wolf, "Determinants of Growth in Transition Countries," *Finance & Development,* June 1999, p. 12.

27 Ibid, p. 15.

28 "Nothing to Do but Cut," *Business Week,* October 18, 1999, p. 32.

29 "Russia Survey: The Makings of a Molotov Cocktail," *The Economist,* July 12, 1997, p. 5.

30 Ibid., p. 12.

31 Yegor Gaidar, "Lessons of the Russian Crisis for Transition Economies," *Finance & Development,* June 1999, pp. 6–7.

32 Ibid., p. 7.

33 Ibid.

34 Timothy L. O'Brien, "Follow the Money, if You Can," *New York Times,* September 5, 1999, p. 1, money & business section.

35 "Russia Survey," p. 12.

36 Robert Kennedy and Amy Sandler, "Shock Therapy in Eastern Europe: The Polish and Czechoslovak Economic Reforms," Harvard Business School Case 9-797-068, rev. December 15, 1997.

37 The World Bank, *World Development Report 1998–1999,* (Washington, DC: World Bank, 1999), pp. 190–191, 210–211.

38 Giadar, "Lessons of the Russian Crisis for Transition Economies," p. 7.

39 The World Bank, *World Development Report 1998–1999,* p. 210.

40 Gordon Hughes, "Cleaning Up Eastern Europe," *Finance & Development,* September 1992, pp. 17–18.

41 Ouattara, "Africa," p. 2.

42 Benjamin Gomes-Casseres, "State and Markets in Korea," Harvard Business School Case 9-387-181, rev. August 16, 1995; *www.daewoo.com*; John Burton, "Daewoo to Cut Debts with Shipbuilding Sale," *Financial Times,* April 20, 1999, p. 22; John Burton, "Seoul Threatens Industry Giants," *Financial Times,* April 28, 1999, p. 4; John Burton, "Taming the Titans," *Financial Times,* April 28, 1999, p. 16; Jane L. Lee and Michael Schuman, "South Korea's Daewoo Gets Debt Reprieve from Creditors," *Asia Wall Street Journal,* July 19, 1999 (from *http://interactive.wsj.com*); Michael Shuman, "Daewoo's Woes Spark Jitters in South Korea," *Wall Street Journal,* August 3, 1999 (from *http://interactive.wsj.com*); David Roche, "The Daewoo Litmus Test," *Wall Street Journal,* August 3, 1999 (from *http://interactive.wsj.com*); Michael Shuman and Jane L. Lee, "Restructuring Likely to Disassemble Daewoo," *Wall Street Journal,* August 13, 1999, p. A8; Jennifer Veale, Larry Armstrong, and Joann Muller, "How Daewoo Ran Itself Off the Road," *Business Week,* August 30, 1999, p. 48; "The Sting of Death," *The Economist,* September 18, 1999, p. 82; "The Death of Daewoo," *The Economist,* August 21, 1999, pp. 55, 58–59; Robert L. Simison and Norihiko Shirouzu, "GM Intensifies Daewoo Talks and Courts Fuji's Subaru in Asian Acquisition Blitz," *Wall Street Journal,* October 21, 1999 (from *http://interactive.wsj.com*); "After the Shock: What the Markets Are Telling Us—And What We Need to Do," *Business Week,* November 10, 1997, pp. 39–59; "Rescuing Asia," *Business Week,* November 17, 1997, pp. 116–122; "What to Do About Asia," *Business Week,* January 26, 1998, pp. 27–33; Charles Wolf, Jr., and Joseph Stiglitz, "What Caused Asia's Crash," *Wall Street Journal,* February 4, 1998, p. A22; Jim Rohwer, "Asia's Meltdown: The Risks Are Rising," *Fortune,* February 16, 1998, pp. 84–90; "Asia: The Global Impact," *Business Week,* pp. 53–66.

PART TWO: COMPARATIVE ENVIRONMENTAL FRAMEWORKS
MTV EUROPE AND YAHOO!

BACKGROUND

This video case shows how MTV Europe and Yahoo! have taken into consideration sociocultural and political factors in penetrating markets abroad. In essence, the message from both companies is, " When in Rome, do as the Romans do." Both companies have been very sensitive to the various countries' cultures, social structures, and political climates, and have customized their products and services accordingly to satisfy local demands. These companies also looked at the long traditions and histories of the countries they wanted to do business in, such as China, France, Denmark, Sweden, and Mexico.

MTV EUROPE

Since it was launched in 1981, MTV has become an international player, especially in Europe, by "thinking globally and acting locally." Peter Einstein, president of MTV Europe, led the charge when he said, "Be there, giving them what they want, in whatever form." MTV Europe, which currently reaches 77 million homes, has adopted a European strategy—it offers local versions of its satellite/cable IV network programming to compete in individual European countries. These more-focused offerings have gradually been replacing MTV Europe's wider regional programming, and versions for the Netherlands, Spain, and Eastern European countries are

now being considered. When the network launched MTV Central Germany, it added 11.2 million homes to its customer base. Wider regional advertisers still make up the largest share of the network's ad revenues, but the number of advertisers has increased to 600 (local and regional) from 235 advertisers (most of which were regional) in 1995.

YAHOO! INC.

For information on this company, please refer to the Part I video case on page 31.

QUESTIONS

As you watch the video, be prepared to answer the following questions:

1. What do you think would have happened had MTV Europe not localized its content in each foreign market? How would that have helped MTV Europe? How would that have hurt MTV Europe?

2. How did MTV Europe approach penetrating the cultures of the various countries it had dealings with? Give details. What approach did Yahoo! take? Give details.

3. How might an Internet company such as Yahoo! undermine a country's authoritarian regime?

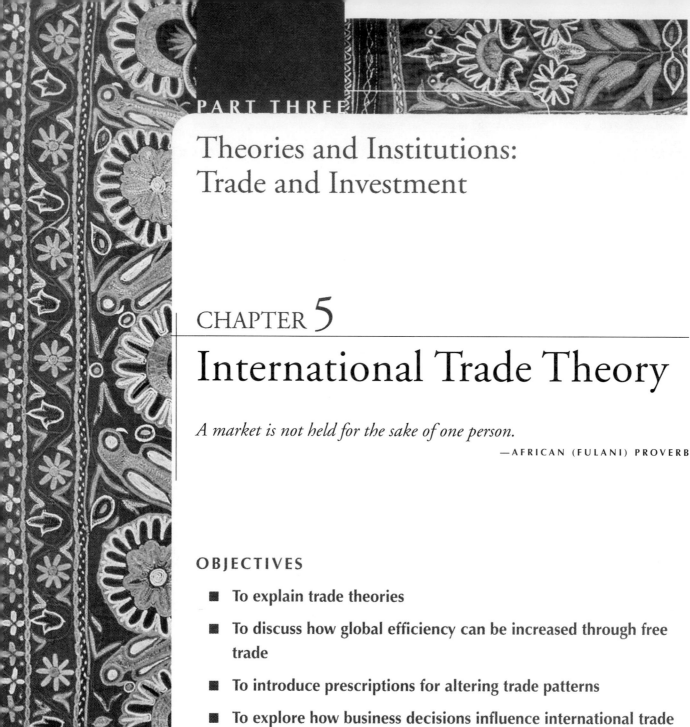

Theories and Institutions: Trade and Investment

CHAPTER **5**

International Trade Theory

A market is not held for the sake of one person.

—AFRICAN (FULANI) PROVERB

OBJECTIVES

- ■ To explain trade theories

- ■ To discuss how global efficiency can be increased through free trade

- ■ To introduce prescriptions for altering trade patterns

- ■ To explore how business decisions influence international trade

Sri Lanka, an island country of more than 16 million people off the southeast coast of India (see Map 5.1), received its independence from the United Kingdom in 1948. Known as Ceylon from the early sixteenth century until 1972, Sri Lanka is typical of most emerging economies. It has a low per capita income (about $900 per year), high dependence on a few minerals and agricultural products (known as primary products) for its foreign-exchange earnings, insufficient foreign-exchange earnings to purchase all desired consumer and industrial imports, and a high unemployment rate. In many other ways, however, Sri Lanka is atypical. On various measurements comparing the quality of life among countries, Sri Lanka ranks fairly high. Its literacy rate, standards of nutrition, health care, equality of income distribution, and life expectancy are some of the highest among emerging economies. Its recent population growth rate is one of the lowest.

Sri Lanka has a long history of international trade, such as with Ionian merchants in the middle of the third century B.C. and with King Solomon, who purchased Sri Lankan gems, elephants, and peacocks with which to woo the Queen of Sheba. One by one, European powers came to dominate the island to acquire products unavailable at home. The Portuguese, for example, sought such products as cinnamon, cloves, and cardamom. The English developed

MAP 5.1   Sri Lanka

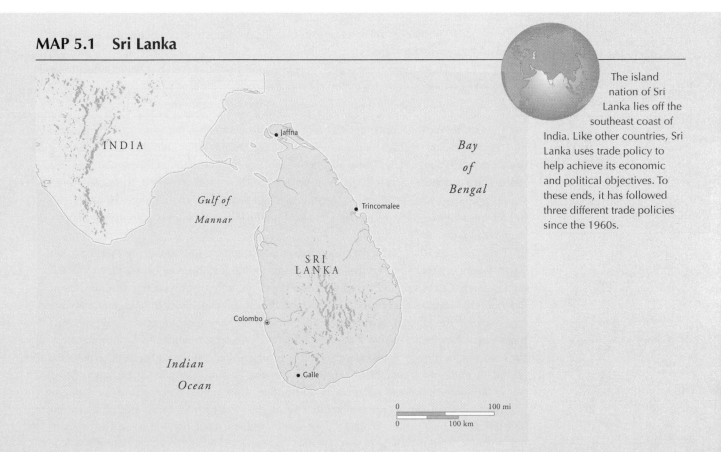

The island nation of Sri Lanka lies off the southeast coast of India. Like other countries, Sri Lanka uses trade policy to help achieve its economic and political objectives. To these ends, it has followed three different trade policies since the 1960s.

the island's economy with tea, rubber, and coconuts, all of which replaced rice as the major agricultural crops.

Since its independence, Sri Lanka has looked to international trade to help solve such problems as (1) shortage of foreign exchange, (2) overdependence on tea exports, (3) overdependence on the British market, and (4) insufficient growth of output and employment. First, foreign exchange is needed to buy imports, and Sri Lankan desires for foreign products or foreign machinery to produce them have grown more rapidly than the foreign-exchange earnings to buy them. Second, until 1975, more than half of the country's export earnings were from tea. Wholesale tea prices fluctuate by as much as 90 percent from one year to the next because of a bumper crop or natural disaster in any tea-exporting country. This fluctuation makes planning for long-term business or governmental projects difficult. Third, because Sri Lanka is a former British colony, many Sri Lankans also have been concerned that the country cannot be politically and economically independent as long as trade centers on the British market. At the time of independence, for example, one-third of Sri Lankan exports went to the United Kingdom. Fourth, world demand for Sri Lanka's traditional mining and agricultural products has not grown as rapidly as that for many other products, particularly manufactured ones. So, Sri Lanka has not met its economic objectives for growth and employment.

To help solve these interrelated problems, Sri Lanka has basically followed three different trade policies since 1960. These policies have reflected views of different political leaders and changes in Sri Lankan conditions. They are:

- 1960 to 1977, import substitution (seeking local production of goods and services that would otherwise be imported)
- 1977 to 1988, strategic trade policy (government actions to develop specific industries with export potential) along with import substitution
- 1988 to present, strategic trade policy along with openness to imports

Throughout the three trade periods, Sri Lanka has become less dependent on the tea market and on sales to any single market. However, the three periods differ in other respects. During the 1960 to 1977 period, Sri Lanka sought to export more of its traditional commodities—tea, rubber, and coconuts—and to diversify its production by restricting imports. Restricting imports would encourage local production, creating jobs and saving foreign exchange. However, this import substitution policy resulted in inefficient production that could survive only if imports were prohibited.

From 1977 to 1988, Sri Lanka continued to restrict imports substantially but shifted to the development of new industries that could export a part of their production, earning more foreign exchange. In this period, Sri Lanka's Ministry of Industries began taking an active role in determining what those products should be and how to get companies to produce them for foreign markets. The Ministry of Industries did this partly by identifying nontraditional products that were already being exported in small amounts, because such ability to export indicated the potential for growth. It also identified other products that could offer Sri Lanka a potential advantage in foreign competition by using inexpensive and abundant Sri Lankan resources—particularly semiskilled and skilled labor and certain raw materials for production and packaging. The Ministry further examined products for markets in which Sri Lanka was probably most able to sell because of special market concessions and low transportation costs. The products that emerged were ranked by export potential and expected benefits for the country. The leading items were processed tea (packaged tea bags and instant tea), ready-made garments (shirts, pajamas, and dresses), chemical derivatives of coconut oil, edible fats, bicycle tires and tubes, and other rubber products, such as automobile tires and tubes.

Identifying the most likely competitive industries encouraged some businesspeople to produce new products. In addition, the government established industrial development zones. Companies that produced in and exported production from these zones could qualify for lower taxes on their earnings. They also could defer taxes on imported goods and components until the resulting products were sold domestically. If the products were exported, there were no import taxes. The first producers to take advantage of the incentives were textile and footwear companies that had special access to the U.S. and European markets. Since then the company base has become more diverse and includes companies making PVC film, carpets, and companies entering information into computerized data banks.

Since 1988, the Sri Lankan government has continued to target industries that it deems to have export potential, such as by offering tax and investment incentives for ceramic and light engineering industries, companies doing software development, and companies using only locally derived raw materials. Sri Lanka also has encouraged the export of services, particularly earnings from its workers abroad and from foreign tourists visiting the country. For example, several hundred thousand Sri Lankans work in foreign countries and send remittances to their families. The government has promoted visits by foreign tourists, such as by legalizing gambling casinos and betting centers open only to foreigners. It also approved a British-Chinese consortium to develop the port at Galle so that it might become a major transshipment center like Colombo.

What has differentiated the period since 1988 from the earlier one is the use of more open markets (fewer import restrictions) to foster competition. Consequently, many companies and industries that started up when local production was protected have gone out of business. But the open economy has permitted Sri Lankan companies to more easily import materials, such as bulk rubber, so that they can process them for domestic and foreign sales.

In 1995 the World Trade Organization praised Sri Lanka for trade reforms that opened its markets. During the 1990s Sri Lanka's real GDP grew rapidly despite a civil war and heavy military expenditures. Recently, Sri Lanka has targeted information technology as a new growth industry.

The move to establish new export industries has accomplished many of Sri Lanka's objectives. Manufacturing has grown as a portion of total exports, and tea has fallen by more than half. Garments are now the largest export. Tea, though still a top export, is increasingly going out in value-added forms, such as instant tea and tea bags. The value-added forms create Sri Lankan jobs and do not fluctuate in price as much as bulk tea. In addition, Sri Lanka's export markets have become more dispersed, with such countries as the United States, Saudi Arabia, Germany, and India gaining in importance.

Sri Lankan trade policies have evolved in response to different objectives and conditions, both within and outside Sri Lanka. They will undoubtedly continue to evolve in the future.   ⟩ꟓ

INTRODUCTION

Why study trade theory? Figure 5.1 shows that trade in goods and services is one of the means by which countries are linked economically. Authorities in all countries wrestle with the questions of what, how much, and with whom their country should import and export. Once they make decisions, officials enact policies to achieve the desired results. These policies have an impact on business because they affect which countries

---

Trade theory helps managers and governmental policy makers focus on these questions:

- **What products should we import and export?**
- **How much should we trade?**
- **With whom should we trade?**

FIGURE 5.1 Companies' International Operations Link Countries Economically

To meet their international objectives, companies' strategies require them to trade and transfer means of production internationally, such as between countries A and B in the figure. This trading and transferring links countries economically. This chapter focuses on the trade linkages.

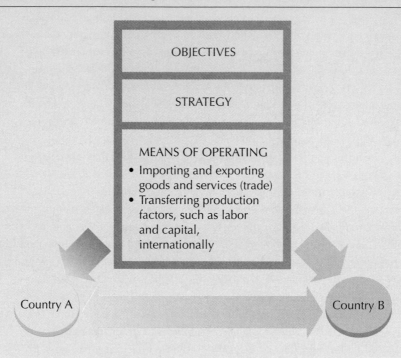

OBJECTIVES

STRATEGY

MEANS OF OPERATING
- Importing and exporting goods and services (trade)
- Transferring production factors, such as labor and capital, internationally

Country A

Country B

can produce given products more efficiently and whether countries will permit imports to compete against their domestically produced goods and services. In turn, a country's policies influence which products companies might export to given countries, as well as what and where companies can produce in order to sell in the given countries. This was demonstrated in the case of Sri Lanka, where officials have created policies to achieve trade objectives. Some countries take a more laissez-faire approach, allowing market forces to determine trading relations on the premise that governmental policies lead to less optimum results for economies. Whether taking activist or laissez-faire approaches, countries rely on trade theories.

Some theories explain trade patterns that exist in the absence of governmental interference.

Two general types of theories about trade pertain to international business: descriptive and prescriptive theories (see Table 5.1). Descriptive theories deal with the natural order of trade. They examine and explain trade patterns under laissez-faire conditions. Theories of this type pose questions of which products, how much, and with whom a country will trade in the absence of restrictions. For descriptive theories in Table 5.1, a check indicates the question pertains to the specific theory and a dash means the question does not pertain to the theory.

Some theories explain what governmental actions should strive for in trade.

The second type of theory prescribes whether governments should interfere with the free movement of goods and services among countries to alter the amount, composition, and direction of trade. Not all theories deal with whether governments should or should not interfere. Those that do not pertain have a dash under the question, "Should government control trade?" in the table. Those that do pertain have a "yes" or "no"

TABLE 5.1   **EMPHASES OF MAJOR THEORIES**

Trade theories have different emphases. Some theories are descriptive while others are prescriptive. A check mark indicates that a theory deals with the question for the column, and a dash indicates that it does not. In column 4, the "yes" or "no" answers the question at the head of the column, and a dash indicates that the theory does not address the question.

THEORY	DESCRIPTION OF NATURAL TRADE			PRESCRIPTIONS OF TRADE RELATIONSHIPS			
	HOW MUCH IS TRADED?	WHAT PRODUCTS ARE TRADED?	WITH WHOM DOES TRADE TAKE PLACE?	SHOULD GOVERNMENT CONTROL TRADE?	HOW MUCH SHOULD BE TRADED?	WHAT PRODUCTS SHOULD BE TRADED?	WITH WHOM SHOULD TRADE TAKE PLACE?
Mercantilism	—	—	—	yes	✔	✔	✔
Neomercantilism	—	—	—	yes	✔	—	—
Absolute advantage	—	✔	—	no	—	✔	—
Comparative advantage	—	✔	—	no	—	✔	—
Country size	✔	✔	—	—	—	—	—
Factor proportions	—	✔	✔	—	—	—	—
Product life cycle (PLC)	—	✔	✔	—	—	—	—
Country similarity	—	✔	✔	—	—	—	—
Dependence	—	—	—	yes	—	✔	✔
Strategic trade policy	—	✔	—	—	—	✔	—
Porter diamond	—	✔	—	—	—	—	—

under this question, which is followed by check marks to indicate whether the prescription covers how much, what products, or with whom to trade.

Both the descriptive and prescriptive types of theories influence international business. They provide insights about favorable market locales for exports as well as potentially successful export products. They also help companies determine where to locate their production facilities because, in the absence of governmental trade restrictions, exports of given products will move from lower-cost to higher-cost production locations. However, trade restrictions may diminish export capabilities and cause companies to locate some production in the restricting countries. The theories also increase understanding about governmental trade policies and predict how those policies might affect companies' competitiveness.

Because no single descriptive theory explains all trade patterns under laissez-faire conditions, and because all prescriptive theories influence government policies, this chapter examines specific trade theories while the next chapter covers governmental interference in trade.

MERCANTILISM

Why has Sri Lanka been so dependent on raw materials rather than manufactured products? Perhaps the answer lies in **mercantilism**, the trade theory that formed the foundation of economic thought from about 1500 to 1800.[2] Mercantilism held that a coun-

According to mercantilism, countries should export more than they import.

try's wealth was measured by its holdings of treasure, which usually meant its gold. According to the theory, countries should export more than they import and, if successful, receive gold from countries that run deficits. Nation-states were emerging during the period 1500 to 1800, and gold empowered central governments that invested it in armies and national institutions. These nation-states sought to solidify the people's primary allegiances to the new nation and lessen their bonds to such traditional units as city-states, religions, and guilds. You can see why mercantilism flourished.

To export more than they imported, governments imposed restrictions on most imports, and subsidized production of many products that could otherwise not compete in domestic or export markets. Some countries used their colonial possessions, such as Sri Lanka under British rule, to support this trade objective. Colonies supplied many commodities that the mother country might otherwise have had to purchase from a nonassociated country. Second, the colonial powers sought to run trade surpluses with their own colonies as a further means of obtaining revenue. They did this not only by monopolizing colonial trade but also by preventing the colonies from engaging in manufacturing. The colonies had to export less highly valued raw materials and import more highly valued manufactured products. Mercantilist theory was intended to benefit the colonial powers. The imposition of regulations based on this theory caused much discontent in the British colonies and was one cause of the American Revolution.

As the influence of the mercantilist philosophy weakened after 1800, the governments of colonial powers seldom aimed directly to limit the development of industrial capabilities within their colonies. However, their home-based companies had technological leadership, ownership of raw material production abroad, and usually some degree of protection from foreign competition. This combination continued to make colonies dependent on raw material production and to tie their trade to their industrialized mother countries. Some terminology of the mercantilist era has endured. A **favorable balance of trade**, for example, still indicates that a country is exporting more than it is importing. An **unfavorable balance of trade** indicates the opposite, which is known as a deficit. Many of these terms are misnomers: For example, the word *favorable* implies "benefit," and *unfavorable* suggests "disadvantage." In fact, it is not necessarily beneficial to run a trade surplus nor is it necessarily disadvantageous to run a trade deficit. A country that is running a surplus, or favorable balance of trade, is, for the time being, importing goods and services of less value than those it is exporting.[3] In the mercantilist period, the difference was made up by a transfer of gold, but today it is made up by holding the deficit country's currency or investments denominated in that currency. In effect, the surplus country is granting credit to the deficit country. If that credit cannot eventually buy sufficient goods and services, the so-called favorable trade balance actually may turn out to be disadvantageous for the country with the surplus.

Recently, the term **neomercantilism** has emerged to describe the approach of countries that try to run favorable balances of trade in an attempt to achieve some social or political objective. For instance, a country may try to achieve full employment by setting economic policies that encourage its companies to produce in excess of the demand at home and to send the surplus abroad. Or a country may attempt to maintain political influence in an area by sending more merchandise to the area than it receives from it, such as a government granting aid or loans to a foreign government to use for the purchase of the granting country's excess production.

Running a favorable balance of trade is not necessarily beneficial.

A country that practices neomercantilism attempts to run an export surplus to achieve a social or political objective.

Climatic conditions and inexpensive hand labor give Sri Lanka a comparative and competitive advantage in the production and sale of tea, which, along with textiles and rubber, is one of Sri Lanka's chief exports. Here we see tea pluckers working in Talawake, Sri Lanka.

ABSOLUTE ADVANTAGE

So far we have ignored the question of why countries need to trade at all. Why can't Sri Lanka (or any other country) be content with the goods and services produced within its territory? In fact, many countries, following mercantilist policy, did try to become as self-sufficient as possible through local production of goods and services.

In 1776, Adam Smith questioned the mercantilists' assumption that a country's wealth depends on its holdings of treasure.[4] Rather, he said, the real wealth of a country consists of the goods and services available to its citizens. Smith developed the theory of **absolute advantage**, which holds that different countries produce some goods more efficiently than other countries; thus, global efficiency can increase through free trade. Based on this theory, he questioned why the citizens of any country should have to buy domestically produced goods when they could buy those goods more cheaply from abroad.

Smith reasoned that if trade were unrestricted, each country would specialize in those products that gave it a competitive advantage. Each country's resources would shift to the efficient industries because the country could not compete in the inefficient ones. Through specialization, countries could increase their efficiency because of three reasons:

- Labor could become more skilled by repeating the same tasks.
- Labor would not lose time in switching from the production of one kind of product to another.
- Long production runs would provide incentives for the development of more effective working methods.

A country could then use its excess specialized production to buy more imports than it could have otherwise produced. But in what products should a country specialize? Although Smith believed the marketplace would make the determination, he thought that a country's advantage would be either *natural* or *acquired*.

According to Adam Smith, a country's wealth is based on its available goods and services rather than on gold.

NATURAL ADVANTAGE

A country may have a natural advantage in producing a product because of climatic conditions, access to certain natural resources, or availability of certain labor forces. The country's climate may dictate, for example, which agricultural products it can produce efficiently. Sri Lanka's climate supports production of tea, rubber, and coconuts. Climate also is a factor in Sri Lanka's export of services because foreign tourists visit its beaches. Sri Lanka imports wheat and dairy products. If it were to increase its production of wheat and dairy products, for which its climate is less suited, it would have to use land now devoted to the cultivation of tea, rubber, or coconuts, thus decreasing the output of those products. Conversely, the United States could produce tea (perhaps in climate-controlled buildings) but at the cost of diverting resources away from products such as wheat, for which its climate is naturally suited. These two countries can trade tea for wheat and vice versa more cheaply than each could become self-sufficient in the production of both. The more the two countries' climates differ, the more likely they will favor trade with one another.

Most countries must import ores, metals, and fuels from other countries. No one country is large enough or sufficiently rich in natural resources to be independent of the rest of the world except for short periods. Sri Lanka, for example, exports graphite but must import nitrates. Another natural resource is soil, which, when coupled with topography, is an important determinant of the types of products a country can produce most efficiently in different areas.

Variations among countries in natural advantages also help to explain in which countries certain manufactured or processed products might be best produced, particularly if processing an agricultural commodity or natural resource prior to exporting it can reduce transport costs. Recall that Sri Lankan authorities sought to identify industries that could use the country's primary commodities such as tea. Processing tea into instant tea decreases bulk and is likely to reduce transport costs on tea exports. Producing canned liquid tea could add weight, lessening its internationally competitive edge.

ACQUIRED ADVANTAGE

Most of the world's trade today is of manufactured goods and services rather than agricultural goods and natural resources. Countries that produce manufactured goods and services competitively have an **acquired advantage**, usually in either product or process technology. An advantage in product technology is a country's ability to produce a unique product or one that is easily distinguished from those of competitors. For example, Denmark exports silver tableware, not because there are rich Danish silver mines but because Danish companies have developed distinctive products. An advantage in process technology is a country's ability to produce a homogeneous product (one not easily distinguished from that of competitors) efficiently. For example, Japan has exported steel in spite of having to import iron and coal, the two main ingredients necessary for steel production. A primary reason for Japan's success is that its steel mills encompass new labor-saving and material-saving processes.

Rapid technological changes have created new products, displaced old ones, and altered trading partner relationships. The most obvious examples of change are new products, such as computers, which make up a large portion of international business. Products that existed in earlier periods have increased their share of world trade because of technological changes in the production process. For example, early hand-tooled automobiles reached only elite markets, but a succession of manufacturing innovations—from assembly lines to robotics—have enabled automobiles to reach an ever-widening mass market. In other cases, new uses have been found for old products, such as the use of aloe in sunscreen. Other products have been at least partially displaced by substitutes, such as cotton, wool, and silk by artificial fibers. Some products that were once major exports have been displaced by mechanically made products.[5] For example, U.S. companies used to export natural ice to Jamaica, but Jamaicans now buy mechanically made ice that is produced locally. However, new product and process technologies usually create trading advantages for the countries where they are developed. Because most technological advances have emanated from the most industrialized (richer) countries, companies from these countries control a greater share of the trade and investment in manufacturing, which has been the major growth sector. Consequently, many poorer countries have been accounting for a proportionately smaller share of the world's international trade.

RESOURCE EFFICIENCY EXAMPLE

We can demonstrate absolute advantage in trade by examining two countries (or regions within one country) and two commodities. In this example, the countries are Sri Lanka and the United States, and the commodities are tea and wheat. Because we are not yet considering the concepts of money and exchange rates, we shall define the cost of production in terms of the resources needed to produce either tea or wheat. This example is realistic in that real income depends on the output of goods compared to the resources used to produce them.

Start with the assumption that Sri Lanka and the United States are the only countries that exist and each has the same amount of resources (land, labor, and capital) to produce either tea or wheat. Using Figure 5.2, let's say that 100 units of resources are available in each country. In Sri Lanka, assume that it takes 4 units to produce a ton of tea and 10 units per ton of wheat. This is shown with the Sri Lankan production possibility line, whereby Sri Lanka can produce 25 tons of tea and no wheat, 10 tons of wheat and no tea, or some combination of the two. In the United States, it takes 20 units per ton of tea and 5 units per ton of wheat. This is shown in the U.S. production possibility line, whereby the United States can produce 5 tons of tea and no wheat, 20 tons of wheat and no tea, or some combination of the two. Sri Lanka is more efficient (that is, takes fewer resources to produce a ton) than the United States in tea production, and the United States is more efficient than Sri Lanka in wheat production.

To demonstrate how production can be increased through specialization and trade, we need first to consider a situation in which the two countries have no foreign trade. We could start from any place on each production possibility line; however, for convenience we assume that if Sri Lanka and the United States each devotes half of its resources to producing tea and half to producing wheat, Sri Lanka can produce $12\frac{1}{2}$ tons of tea (divide 4 into 50) and 5 tons of wheat (point A in Figure 5.2). The United States can produce $2\frac{1}{2}$ tons of tea and 10 tons of wheat (point B in Figure 5.2). Because each country has only 100 units of resources, neither can increase wheat production without decreasing tea production, or vice versa. Without trade between the two countries, the combined production is 15 tons of tea ($12\frac{1}{2}$ plus $2\frac{1}{2}$) and 15 tons of wheat (5 plus 10). If each country specialized in the commodity for which it had an absolute advantage, Sri Lanka then could produce 25 tons of tea and the United States 20 tons of

FIGURE 5.2   Production Possibilities with Absolute Advantage

Output will increase through specialization.

ASSUMPTIONS
for Sri Lanka

1. 100 units of resources available
2. 10 units to produce a ton of wheat
3. 4 units to produce a ton of tea
4. Uses half of total resources per product when there is no foreign trade

ASSUMPTIONS
for United States

1. 100 units of resources available
2. 5 units to produce a ton of wheat
3. 20 units to produce a ton of tea
4. Uses half of total resources per product when there is no foreign trade

PRODUCTION	Tea (tons)	Wheat (tons)
Without Trade:		
Sri Lanka (point A)	12½	5
United States (point B)	2½	10
Total	15	15
With Trade:		
Sri Lanka (point C)	25	0
United States (point D)	0	20
Total	25	20

wheat (points *C* and *D* in the figure). You can see that specialization increases the production of both products (from 15 to 25 tons of tea and from 15 to 20 tons of wheat). By trading, global efficiency is optimized, and the two countries can have more tea and more wheat than they would without trade.

COMPARATIVE ADVANTAGE

Gains from trade will occur even in a country that has absolute advantage in all products because the country must give up less efficient output to produce more efficient output.

What happens when one country can produce all products at an absolute advantage? In 1817, David Ricardo examined this question and expanded on Adam Smith's theory of absolute advantage to develop the theory of **comparative advantage**. Ricardo reasoned that there may still be global efficiency gains from trade if a country specializes in those products that it can produce more efficiently than other products—regardless of whether other countries can produce those same products even more efficiently.[6]

AN ANALOGOUS EXPLANATION OF COMPARATIVE ADVANTAGE

Although initially this theory may seem incongruous, an analogy should clarify its logic. Imagine that the best physician in town also happens to be the best medical secretary. Would it make economic sense for the physician to handle all the administrative duties of the office? Definitely not. The physician can earn more money by working as a physician, even though that means having to employ a less skillful medical secretary to manage the office. In the same manner, a country will gain if it concentrates its resources on producing the commodities it can produce most efficiently. It then will buy from countries with fewer natural or acquired resources those commodities it has relinquished. The following discussion clarifies why this theory is true.

PRODUCTION POSSIBILITY EXAMPLE

In this example, assume that the United States is more efficient in producing both tea and wheat than Sri Lanka is. The United States has an absolute advantage in the production of both products. As in the earlier example of absolute advantage, again assume that there are only two countries and each country has a total of 100 units of resources available. In this example, it takes Sri Lanka 10 units of resources to produce either a ton of tea or a ton of wheat, while it takes the United States only 5 units of resources to produce a ton of tea and 4 units to produce a ton of wheat (see Figure 5.3). Like our production possibility example for absolute advantage, we can start from any place on each production possibility line. However, once again for convenience, we assume that if each country uses half of its resources in the production of each product, Sri Lanka can produce 5 tons of tea and 5 tons of wheat (point A in the figure), and the United States can produce 10 tons of tea and $12\frac{1}{2}$ tons of wheat (point B in the figure). Without trade, neither country can increase its production of tea without sacrificing some production of wheat, or vice versa.

Although the United States has an absolute advantage in the production of both tea and wheat, it has a comparative advantage only in the production of wheat. This is because its advantage in wheat production is comparatively greater than its advantage in tea production. So, by using the same amounts of resources, the United States can produce $2\frac{1}{2}$ times as much wheat as Sri Lanka but only twice as much tea. Although Sri Lanka has an absolute disadvantage in the production of both products, it has a comparative advantage (or less of a comparative disadvantage) in the production of tea. This is because Sri Lanka is half as efficient as the United States in tea production and only 40 percent as efficient in wheat production.

Without trade, the combined production is 15 tons of tea (5 in Sri Lanka plus 10 in the United States) and $17\frac{1}{2}$ tons of wheat (5 in Sri Lanka plus $12\frac{1}{2}$ in the United States). By trading, the combined production of tea and wheat within the two countries can be increased. For example, if the combined production of wheat is unchanged from when there was no trade, the United States could produce all $17\frac{1}{2}$ tons of wheat by using 70 units of resources ($17\frac{1}{2}$ tons times 4 units per ton). The remaining 30 U.S. units could be used for producing 6 tons of tea (30 units divided by 5 units per ton). This production possibility is point D in Figure 5.3. Sri Lanka would use all its resources to produce 10 tons of tea (point C in the figure). The combined wheat production has stayed at $17\frac{1}{2}$ tons, but the tea production has increased from 15 tons to 16 tons.

If the combined tea production is unchanged from the time before trade, Sri Lanka could use all its resources on producing tea, yielding 10 tons (point C in Fig. 5.3). The United States could produce the remaining 5 tons of tea by using 25 units of resources. The remaining 75 U.S. units could be used to produce $18\frac{3}{4}$ tons of wheat (75 divided by 4). This production possibility is point E in the figure. Without sacrificing any of the tea available before trade, wheat production has increased from $17\frac{1}{2}$ tons to $18\frac{3}{4}$ tons.

FIGURE 5.3   Production Possibilities with Comparative Advantage

There are advantages to trade even though one country may have an absolute advantage in the production of all products.

ASSUMPTIONS
for Sri Lanka
1. 100 units of resources available
2. 10 units to produce a ton of wheat
3. 10 units to produce a ton of tea
4. Uses half of total resources per product when there is no foreign trade

ASSUMPTIONS
for United States
1. 100 units of resources available
2. 4 units to produce a ton of wheat
3. 5 units to produce a ton of tea
4. Uses half of total resources per product when there is no foreign trade

PRODUCTION	Tea (tons)	Wheat (tons)
Without Trade:		
Sri Lanka (point A)	5	5
United States (point B)	10	12½
Total	15	17½
With Trade (increasing tea production):		
Sri Lanka (point C)	10	0
United States (point D)	6	17½
Total	16	17½
With Trade (increasing wheat production):		
Sri Lanka (point C)	10	0
United States (point E)	5	18¾
Total	15	18¾

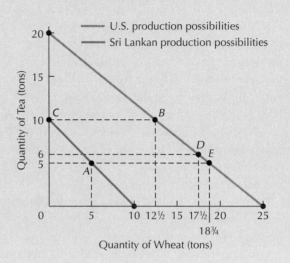

If the United States were to produce somewhere between points *D* and *E* in Figure 5.3, both tea and wheat production would increase over what was possible before trade took place. Whether the production target is an increase of tea or wheat or a combination of the two, both countries can gain by having Sri Lanka trade some of its tea production to the United States for some of that country's wheat output.

The comparative advantage theory is accepted by most economists and is influential in promoting policies for freer trade. Nevertheless, many governmental policy makers, journalists, managers, and workers confuse comparative advantage with absolute advantage and do not understand how a country can simultaneously have a comparative *advantage* and absolute *disadvantage* in the production of a given product. This misunderstanding helps to explain why managers face uncertain governmental trade policies that affect where they choose to locate their production.

SOME ASSUMPTIONS AND LIMITATIONS OF THE THEORIES OF SPECIALIZATION

Both absolute and comparative advantage theories are based on specialization. They hold that output will increase through specialization and that countries will be best off by trading the output from their own specialization for the output from other countries' specialization. However, these theories make some assumptions that are not always valid.

FULL EMPLOYMENT

The physician–secretary analogy we used earlier assumed that the physician could stay busy full time practicing medicine. If we relax this assumption, then the advantages of specialization are less compelling. The physician might, if unable to stay busy full time with medical duties, perform secretarial work without having to forgo a physician's higher income. The theories of absolute and comparative advantage both assume that resources are fully employed. When countries have many unemployed or unused resources, they may seek to restrict imports to employ or use idle resources.

> **Full employment is not a valid assumption of absolute and comparative advantage.**

ECONOMIC EFFICIENCY OBJECTIVE

The physician–secretary analogy also assumed that the physician who can do both medical and office work is interested primarily in maximization of profit, or maximum economic efficiency. Yet, there are a number of reasons why physicians might choose not to work full time at medical tasks. They might find administrative work relaxing and self-fulfilling. They might fear that a hired secretary would be unreliable. They might wish to maintain secretarial skills in the somewhat unlikely event that administration, rather than medicine, commands higher wages in the future. Countries also often pursue objectives other than output efficiency. They may avoid overspecialization because of the vulnerability created by changes in technology and by price fluctuations. Recall Sri Lankan concerns about price fluctuations of tea. Or they may have noneconomic objectives. For example, a Sri Lankan journalist said, "Our unique set of cultural values cannot fit into any sort of twisted, hybrid economic culture, haphazardly devised in the name of development and economic progress."[7]

> **Countries' goals may not be limited to economic efficiency.**

DIVISION OF GAINS

Although specialization brings potential benefits to all countries that trade, the earlier discussion did not indicate how countries will divide increased output. In the case of our wheat and tea example, if both the United States and Sri Lanka receive some share of the increased output, both will be better off economically through specialization and trade. However, many people, including governmental policy makers, are concerned with relative as well as absolute economic growth, relative meaning in comparison to trading partners. If they perceive a trading partner is gaining too large a share of benefits, they may forgo absolute gains for themselves so as to prevent relative losses.[8]

TWO COUNTRIES, TWO COMMODITIES

For simplicity's sake, Smith and Ricardo originally assumed a simple world composed of only two countries and two commodities. Our example made the same assumption. Although unrealistic, this assumption does not diminish the theories' usefulness. Economists have applied the same reasoning to demonstrate efficiency advantages in multi-product and multicountry trade relationships.

TRANSPORT COSTS

If it costs more to transport the goods than is saved through specialization, then the advantages of trade are negated. For example, if the countries can increase tea production by one ton while leaving wheat production unchanged, they will have to divert workers from tea production to ship tea and wheat between them. As long as the diversion reduces output by less than what they gain from specialization (in this case, one ton of tea), there are still gains from trade.

MOBILITY

Resources are neither as mobile nor as immobile as the theories of absolute and comparative advantage assume.

The theories of absolute and comparative advantage assume that resources can move domestically from the production of one good to another, and at no cost. But this assumption is not completely valid. For example, a steelworker in Indiana might not move easily into a software development job in California. That worker probably would have difficulty working in such a different industry and might have trouble moving to a new area. Nor is land currently producing wheat in Sri Lanka necessarily suitable to tea production. The theories also assume that resources cannot move internationally. However, increasingly they do. For example, thousands of Sri Lankans go to the Middle East to work. The movement of resources such as labor and capital is clearly an alternative to trade. However, it is safe to say that there is more domestic mobility of resources than there is international mobility.

SERVICES

The theories of absolute and comparative advantage deal with commodities rather than services. However, an increasing portion of world trade is in services. This fact does not render the theories obsolete because resources must go into producing services, too. For instance, some services that the United States sells extensively to foreign countries are education (many foreign students attend U.S. universities) and credit card systems and collections. However, the United States buys more foreign shipping services than foreigners buy U.S. shipping services. To become more self-sufficient in international shipping, the United States might have to divert resources from its more efficient use in higher education or the production of competitive products.

THEORY OF COUNTRY SIZE

Bigger countries differ in several ways from smaller countries. They

• Tend to export a smaller portion of output and import a smaller part of consumption

• Have higher transport costs for foreign trade

• Can handle large-scale production

The theories of absolute and comparative advantage do not deal with country-by-country differences in how much and what products will be traded through specialization. However, research based on country size helps explain these differences.

VARIETY OF RESOURCES

The theory of country size says that countries with large land areas are apt to have varied climates and an assortment of natural resources, making them more self-sufficient than smaller countries. Most large countries, such as Brazil, China, India, the United States, and Russia, import much less of their consumption and export much less of their production than do small countries, such as Uruguay, the Netherlands, and Iceland.

TRANSPORT COSTS

Although the theory of absolute advantage ignores transport costs in trade, these costs affect large and small countries differently. Normally, the farther the distance, the higher the transport costs. The average distance between production location and markets is higher for the international trade of large countries. Assume, for example, that the normal maximum distance for transporting a given product is 100 miles because,

Ethical Dilemmas and Social Responsibility
VALUES, FREE GLOBAL TRADE, AND PRODUCTION STANDARDS— A HARD TRIO TO MIX

There is usually heated debate over laissez-faire versus activist government trade policies and independence versus dependence of countries. Why? Because different country values underlie different positions.

For example, the argument for free-trade policy is based on the achievement of global economic efficiency. However, some countries may not be content only with global economic efficiency. In addition, some people argue that free trade, although leading to lower production costs, does not take into account differences in individual countries' standards—such as requirements for worker safety, disposal of wastes, and worker conditions. These standards reflect the social and environmental values of the countries' citizens. Because standards vary among countries, the costs producers incur vary as well, and producers who must adhere to more stringent standards argue against free trade. For example, environmental compliance costs are much lower in most countries than in the United States. Many U.S. companies have home-country cost disadvantages compared to production abroad. However, if other countries eventually establish and enforce standards similar to those in the United States, U.S. companies may have gained first mover advantages because of having developed technologies and gained experience with them.[9] In another case, the European Union has threatened to ban fur imports from Canada, Russia, and the United States because these countries use steel-jawed leghold traps, which reduce trapping costs but cause the animals great pain and a slow death.[10] Opponents of free trade in the United States have argued that imports should be disallowed from Malaysia because of its anti-union directives and from China when jailed workers produce their exports.

Ethical questions center on whether all countries should have similar production standards, whether countries should limit imports of competing products because of differences in standards, and whether companies should locate production to capitalize on less stringent standards that allow them to lower their costs.

A country also may be concerned about its overall trade dependence. In this context, relativists hold that it would be unethical for outsiders to interfere in a country's trade policy. In contrast, normativists argue that other countries have a duty to put pressure on a country when its trade policies cause hardship to its own citizens. For example, Bhutan pursues maximum independence in its trade policies and travel laws to preserve its culture. Further, all its citizens must wear traditional dress and buildings must conform to traditional architecture. Bhutan's foreign minister said that with more trade and contact, "within a year or two our value system would change."[11] But its isolation contributes to Bhutan's ranking as one of the poorest countries in the world.

beyond that distance, prices increase too much. Most U.S. production locations and markets are more than 100 miles from the Canadian or Mexican border. In the Netherlands, however, almost all foreign production locations and markets are within 100 miles of its borders. Transport costs make it more likely that small countries will trade internationally because their costs of getting products over their borders are worth the effort.

SIZE OF ECONOMY AND PRODUCTION SCALES

Although land area is the most obvious way of measuring a country's size, countries also can be compared on the basis of economic size. Countries with large economies and high per capita incomes are more likely to produce goods that use technologies requiring long production runs. This is because these countries develop industries to serve their large domestic markets, which in turn tend to be competitive in export markets.[12] In industries where long production runs are important for gaining competitive advantages, companies tend to locate their production in few countries, using these locations as sources of exports to other countries. Where long production runs are unimportant, companies are more apt to minimize exporting. Instead, they produce in most countries where they sell.[13] In addition, high expenditures on research and development create high fixed costs for companies. Therefore, the technologically intensive company from a small nation may have a more compelling need to sell abroad than would a company with a large domestic market. In turn, this pulls resources from other industries and companies within the company's domestic market, causing more national specialization than in a larger nation.[14]

FACTOR-PROPORTIONS THEORY

According to the factor-proportions theory, factors in relative abundance are cheaper than factors in relative scarcity.

Smith's and Ricardo's theories did not help to identify the types of products that would most likely give a country an advantage. Those theories assumed that the workings of the free market would lead producers to the goods they could produce more efficiently and away from those they could not produce efficiently. About a century and a quarter later, Eli Heckscher and Bertil Ohlin developed the **factor-proportions theory** based on countries' production factors—land, labor, and capital (funds for investment in plant and equipment). This theory said that differences in countries' endowments of labor compared to their endowments of land or capital explained differences in the cost of production factors. These economists proposed that if labor were abundant in comparison to land and capital, labor costs would be low relative to land and capital costs. If labor were scarce, labor costs would be high in relation to land and capital costs. These relative factor costs would lead countries to excel in the production and export of products that used their abundant, and therefore cheaper, production factors.[15]

LAND–LABOR RELATIONSHIP

On the basis of the factor-proportions theory, Sri Lankan authorities reasoned that their country had a competitive advantage in products that used large numbers of abundant semiskilled workers. The factor-proportions theory appears logical. In countries in which there are many people relative to the amount of land—for example, Hong Kong and the Netherlands—land price is very high because it's in demand. Regardless of climate and soil conditions, neither Hong Kong nor the Netherlands excels in the production of goods requiring large amounts of land, such as wool or wheat. Businesses in countries such as Australia and Canada produce these goods because land is abundant compared to the number of people.

Casual observation of manufacturing locations also seems to substantiate the theory. For example, in Hong Kong the most successful industries are those in which technology permits the use of a minimum amount of land relative to the number of people employed: Clothing production occurs in multistory factories where workers share minimal space. Hong Kong does not compete in the production of automobiles, however, which requires much more space per worker.

LABOR–CAPITAL RELATIONSHIP

In countries where there is little capital available for investment and where the amount of investment per worker is low, managers might expect cheap labor rates and export competitiveness in products requiring large amounts of labor relative to capital. They can anticipate the opposite when labor is scarce. For example, Iran (where labor is abundant in comparison to capital) excels in the production of handmade carpets that differ in appearance as well as in production method from the carpets produced in industrial countries by machines purchased with cheap capital.

Production factors are not homogeneous, especially labor.

However, the factor-proportions theory assumes production factors to be homogeneous. Labor skills, in fact, vary within and among countries because people have different training and education. Training and education require capital expenditures that do not show up in traditional capital measurements, which include only plant and equipment values. When the factor-proportions theory accounts for different labor groups and the capital invested to train these groups, it seems to hold. For example, because industrial country exports embody a higher proportion of professionals such as scientists and engineers than emerging economies' exports, those countries are using their abundant production factors. Exports of emerging economies, though, show a high intensity of less skilled labor.[16] This variation in labor skills among countries has led to more international specialization by task to produce a given product. For example, a company may locate its research activities and management functions primarily in countries with a highly educated population and its production work where less skilled, and less expensive, workers can be employed.

TECHNOLOGICAL COMPLEXITIES

The factor-proportions analysis becomes more complicated when the same product can be produced by different methods, such as with labor *or* capital. Canada produces wheat in a capital-intensive way (high expenditure on machinery per worker) because of its abundance of low-cost capital relative to labor. In contrast, India produces wheat by using a much smaller number of machines in comparison to its abundant and cheap labor. In the final analysis managers must compare the cost in each locale based on the type of production that will minimize costs there.

THE PRODUCT LIFE CYCLE THEORY OF TRADE

Raymond Vernon's international product life cycle (PLC) theory of trade states that certain kinds of products go through a continuum, or cycle, that consists of four stages—introduction, growth, maturity, and decline. The location of production to serve world

According to the PLC theory of trade, the production location for many products moves from one country to another depending on the stage in the product's life cycle.

markets will shift internationally depending on the stage of the cycle.[17] Table 5.2 highlights the stages.

STAGE 1: INTRODUCTION

The introduction stage is marked by
- Innovation in response to observed need
- Exporting by the innovative country
- Evolving product characteristics

Most new products are produced in and exported from the high-income industrial countries because of their combined demand conditions and labor skills. This combination is explained in the following sections.

Innovation, Production, and Sales in Same Country   Companies develop new products because there is a nearby observed need and market for them. This means that a U.S. company is most apt to develop a new product for the U.S. market, a French company for the French market, and so on. Once a company has created a new product, theoretically it can manufacture that product anywhere in the world. In practice, however, the early production generally occurs in a domestic location so the company can obtain rapid market feedback, as well as save transport costs.

TABLE 5.2

INTERNATIONAL CHANGES DURING A PRODUCT'S LIFE CYCLE

Overall, production and sales shift from industrial countries to emerging economies during a product's life cycle.

	LIFE CYCLE STAGE			
	1: INTRODUCTION	**2: GROWTH**	**3: MATURITY**	**4: DECLINE**
Production location	• In innovating (usually industrial) country	• In innovating and other industrial countries	• Multiple countries	• Mainly in emerging economies
Market location	• Mainly in innovating country, with some exports	• Mainly in industrial countries • Shift in export markets as foreign production replaces exports in some markets	• Growth in emerging economies • Some decrease in industrial countries	• Mainly in emerging economies • Some emerging economy exports
Competitive factors	• Near-monopoly position • Sales based on uniqueness rather than price • Evolving product characteristics	• Fast-growing demand • Number of competitors increases • Some competitors begin price-cutting • Product becoming more standardized	• Overall stabilized demand • Number of competitors decreases • Price is very important, especially in emerging economies	• Overall declining demand • Price is key weapon • Number of producers continues to decrease
Production technology	• Short production runs • Evolving methods to coincide with product evolution • High labor and labor skills relative to capital input	• Capital input increases • Methods more standardized	• Long production runs using high capital inputs • Highly standardized • Less labor skill needed	• Unskilled labor on mechanized long production runs

Location and Importance of Technology   Companies use technology to create new products and new ways to produce old products, both of which can give them competitive advantages. Their abilities to harvest technology differ substantially by country, so they locate production to take advantage of technological capabilities in order to serve world markets. Almost all new technology that results in new products and production methods originates in industrial countries. For example, the 50 companies worldwide that spend the most on R&D are all headquartered in industrial countries.[18] Many reasons account for the dominant position of industrial countries, including competition, demanding consumers, the availability of scientists and engineers, and high incomes.

Exports and Labor   At the introduction stage of a product's life cycle, companies may sell a small part of their production to customers in foreign markets who have heard about the new product and actively seek it. These foreign customers are mostly found in other industrial countries because they have incomes to spend on newer products.

The production process is apt to be more labor-intensive in this stage than in later stages. Because the product is not yet standardized, its production process must permit rapid changes in product characteristics, as market feedback dictates. This implies high labor input as opposed to automated production, which is more capital intensive. Furthermore, the capital machinery necessary to produce a product on a large scale usually develops later than product technology, only when sales begin to expand rapidly enough (Stage 2) to warrant the high development costs of the machines for the new process. The early production is most apt to occur in industrial countries, which have high labor rates. According to one view, the ability to produce with expensive labor stems from the monopoly position of original producers (because innovators have no competitors at first), which allows them to pass on costs to consumers who are unwilling to wait for possible price reductions later. Another explanation is education and skill levels of industrial country labor make it adept and efficient when production is not yet standardized. When production becomes highly automated, this labor becomes less competitive because unskilled labor may be quickly trained to perform highly repetitive tasks efficiently.

STAGE 2: GROWTH

As sales of the new product grow, competitors enter the market. At the same time, demand is likely to grow substantially in foreign markets, particularly in other industrial countries. In fact, demand may be sufficient to justify producing in some foreign markets to reduce or eliminate transport charges, but the output at this stage is likely to stay almost entirely in the foreign country with the additional manufacturing unit. Let's say, for example, that the innovator is in the United States and the additional manufacturing unit is in Japan. The producers in Japan will sell mainly in Japan for several reasons

Growth is characterized by
- **Increases in exports by the innovating country**
- **More competition**
- **Increased capital intensity**
- **Some foreign production**

1. There is increased demand in the Japanese market for the product.
2. Producers need to introduce unique product variations for Japanese consumers.
3. Japanese costs may still be high because of production start-up problems.

Because sales are growing rapidly at home and abroad, there are incentives for companies to develop process technology. However, *product* technology may not yet be well developed because of the number of product variations introduced by competitors also trying to gain market share. So, the production process may still be labor intensive during this stage, although it is becoming less so. The original producing country will increase its exports in this stage but lose certain key export markets in which competitors commence local production.

STAGE 3: MATURITY

Maturity is characterized by
- Decline in exports from the innovating country
- More product standardization
- More capital intensity
- Increased competitiveness of price
- Production start-ups in emerging economies

In Stage 3, maturity, worldwide demand begins to level off, although it may be growing in some countries and declining in others. There often is a shakeout of producers such that product models become highly standardized, making cost an important competitive weapon. Longer production runs become possible for foreign plants, which in turn reduce per unit cost for their output. The lower per unit cost creates demand in emerging markets.

Because markets and technologies are widespread, the innovating country no longer has a production advantage. There are incentives to begin moving plants to emerging markets where unskilled, inexpensive labor is efficient for standardized (capital-intensive) processes. Exports decrease from the innovating country as foreign production displaces it.

STAGE 4: DECLINE

Decline is characterized by
- Concentration of production in emerging economies
- Innovating country becoming net importer

As a product moves to the decline stage, those factors occurring during the mature stage continue to evolve. The markets in industrial countries decline more rapidly than those in emerging markets as affluent customers demand ever-newer products. By this time, market and cost factors have dictated that almost all production is in emerging markets, which export to the declining or small-niche markets in industrial countries. In other words, the country in which the innovation first emerged—and exported from—then becomes the importer.

VERIFICATION AND LIMITATIONS OF PLC THEORY

The PLC theory holds that the location of production to serve world markets shifts as products move through their life cycle. Such products as ballpoint pens and portable calculators have followed this pattern. They were first produced in a single industrial country and sold at a high price. Then production shifted to multiple industrial country locations to serve those local markets. Finally, most production is in emerging markets, and prices have declined. However, if transportation costs are very high, there is little opportunity for export sales, regardless of the stage in the life cycle. Additionally, there are many types of products for which shifts in production location do not usually take place.[19] In these cases, the innovating country maintains its export ability throughout the product's life cycle. These exceptions include

1. Products that, because of very rapid innovation, have extremely short life cycles, which make it impossible to achieve cost reductions by moving production from one country to another. For example, product obsolescence occurs so rapidly for many electronic products that there is little international diffusion of production.
2. Luxury products for which cost is of little concern to the consumer.
3. Products for which a company can use a differentiation strategy, perhaps through advertising, to maintain consumer demand without competing on the basis of price.

4. Products that require specialized technical labor to evolve into their next generation. This seems to explain the long-term U.S. dominance of medical equipment production and German dominance in rotary printing presses.[20]

In addition, changes in technology and demand might lead to all kinds of permutations. For example, microchip production began in the United States, at which time the United States was an exporter. But then production moved largely abroad, as would be predicted by PLC theory, and the United States became an importer. But then most production returned to the United States in response to further product innovations and changing market conditions, and the United States became an exporter again.

Regardless of the product type, there has been an increased tendency on the part of MNEs to introduce new products at home and abroad almost simultaneously as they move from multidomestic to global strategies. In other words, instead of merely observing needs within their domestic markets, companies develop products and services for observable market segments that transcend national borders. In so doing, they eliminate delays as a product is diffused from one country to another, and they choose a production location that will minimize costs for serving markets in multiple countries. Further, companies sometimes produce abroad simply to take advantage of production economies rather than in response to growing foreign markets. Singer, for example, produces certain sewing machine models in Brazil to sell in export markets, not to supply the Brazilian market.

COUNTRY SIMILARITY THEORY

So far in this chapter, the theories explaining why trade takes place have focused on the differences among countries. These theories tend to explain most of the trade among dissimilar countries, such as trade between an industrial country and an emerging economy or trade between a temperate country and a tropical one. On the basis of these theories, you would expect that the greater the dissimilarity among countries, the greater the potential for trade. For example, great differences in climatic conditions will lead to highly differentiated agricultural products. Countries that differ in labor or capital intensities will differ in the types of products they can produce efficiently. National differences in innovative abilities will affect how production of a product will move from one country to another during the product's life cycle.

> Most trade theories emphasize differences among countries in
> - Climate
> - Factor endowment
> - Innovative capability

ECONOMIC SIMILARITY OF INDUSTRIAL COUNTRIES

However, observations of trade patterns reveal that most of the world's trade occurs among countries that have similar characteristics, specifically among industrial, or developed, countries. For example, the United States is the world's largest trader, and 8 of its 10 largest trading partners are either industrialized or newly industrialized countries. Globally, 11 of the 12 largest traders are industrialized or newly industrialized countries.[21] Overall trade patterns seem to be at odds with the traditional theories that emphasize country-by-country differences.

The fact that so much trade takes place among industrial countries is due to the growing importance of acquired advantage (product technology) as opposed to natural advantage (agricultural products and raw materials) in world trade (see Figure 5.4). The

> Most trade today occurs among apparently similar countries.

country-similarity theory says that once a company has developed a new product in response to observed market conditions in the home market, it will turn to markets it sees as most similar to those at home.[22] In addition, markets in industrial countries can support products and their variations. Thus companies from different countries produce different product models, and each may gain some markets abroad. This theory helps explain why road vehicles (automobiles and small trucks) comprise both the largest category of U.S. imports and the second largest category of U.S. exports. In fact, about two-thirds of U.S. trade of manufactured goods with other industrial nations consists of intra-industry trade, such as passenger jet aircraft exports to Europe along with passenger jet imports from Europe.[23]

Although the markets within the industrial countries might have similar demands, countries also specialize to gain acquired advantages, such as by apportioning their research efforts more strongly to some sectors than to others. Germany is traditionally strong in machinery and equipment, Switzerland in pharmaceutical products, and Denmark in food products.[24]

The importance of industrial countries in world trade is due, in addition to specialization, to these countries' economic size. In other words, these countries produce so much, there is more to sell—both domestically and internationally. In addition, by producing so much, incomes are high and people buy more—from both domestic and foreign sources. At the same time, little of the trade of emerging economies is with other emerging economies. Instead, they mainly export primary products and labor-intensive

FIGURE 5.4   World Trade by Major Product Category as Percentage of Total World Trade for Selected Years

Manufactured products continue to be the largest product category traded (as a percentage of total world trade).

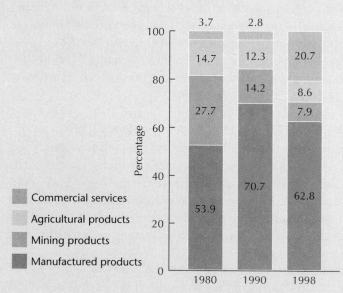

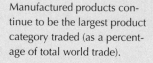

Source: From World Trade Organization, *Annual Report*, 1966, Vol. 1 (Geneva: World Trade Organization, 1996), p. 14. Reprinted by permission of World Trade Organization.

mature products to industrial countries in exchange for new and technologically advanced products.

SIMILARITY OF LOCATION

Although the theories regarding country differences and similarities help to explain broad world trade patterns, such as between industrial countries and emerging economies, they do little to explain specific pairs of trading relationships. Why, for example, will a particular industrial country buy more from one emerging economy than another? Why will it buy from one industrial country rather than another? Although there is no single answer to explain all product flows, the distance between two countries accounts for many of these world trade relationships. For example, Finland is a major exporter to Russia because transport costs are cheap and fast compared to transport to other countries. Acer, a Taiwanese computer maker, built a plant in Finland to serve Russia because of savings compared with shipments from Asia and because Finland provided more secure storage and ease of operations than if the plant were in Russia.[25]

But transport cost is not the only factor in trade partner choice. For example, New Zealand competes with Chile, Argentina, and South Africa for out-of-season sales of apples to the Northern Hemisphere, but with a disadvantage in freight costs. It has countered this disadvantage by increasing yields, developing new premium varieties, bypassing intermediaries to sell directly to supermarkets abroad, and consolidating efforts through a national marketing board. However, such methods to overcome distance disadvantages are difficult to maintain. For example, both Chinese and Chilean orchardists have smuggled new strains of apple tree cuttings out of New Zealand.[26]

CULTURAL SIMILARITY

Cultural similarity, as expressed through language and religion, also helps explain much of the direction of trade. Importers and exporters find it easier to do business in a country they perceive as being similar. Likewise, historic colonial relationships explain much of the trade between specific industrial countries and emerging economies. Likewise, much of the lack of trade among nations in the Southern Hemisphere is due to the absence of historic ties. Importers and exporters find it easier to continue business ties than to develop new distribution arrangements in countries in which they are less experienced.

SIMILARITY OF POLITICAL AND ECONOMIC INTERESTS

Political relationships and economic agreements among countries may discourage or encourage trade between them or their companies. An example of trade discouragement is the political animosity between the United States and Cuba that has caused mutual trade to be almost nonexistent for the last four decades. The United States replaced Cuban sugar imports with imports from such countries as Mexico and the Dominican Republic. An example of trade encouragement is the agreement among European Union (EU) countries to remove all trade barriers with each other. This agreement has caused a greater share of countries' total trade to be conducted within the group.

Military conflicts disrupt traditional international business trade patterns as participants divert their transportation systems and much of their productive capacity to the war effort. In addition, political animosity and transport difficulties may interfere with trading channels. For example, Iraq's international trade fell sharply after its

Trading partners are affected by
- **Distance**
- **Competitive capabilities**
- **Cultural similarity**
- **Relations between countries**

1990 invasion of Kuwait as other countries either severed trade relations or disrupted supply lines. The composition of trade changes from consumer goods to industrial goods, which the warring countries use to meet military objectives.

DEGREE OF DEPENDENCE

The theories of independence, interdependence, and dependence help to explain world trade patterns and countries' trade policies. They form a continuum, with independence at one extreme, dependence on the other, and interdependence somewhere in the middle. No countries are located at either extreme of this continuum but some tend to be closer to one extreme than the other.

INDEPENDENCE

In a situation of independence, a country would have no reliance on other countries for any goods, services, or technologies. However, because all countries need to trade, no country has complete economic independence from other countries. The most recent instances of economic near-independence have been the Liawep tribe, found in Papua New Guinea in 1993, and in present-day Bhutan.[27] Isolation from other societies brought certain advantages to the Liaweps and Bhutanese. They have not had to be concerned, for example, that another society might cut off their supply of essential foods or tools. Of course, for both societies the price of independence is having to do without goods they could not produce themselves. A further disadvantage of independence is that it hinders a country's ability to borrow and adapt technologies already in existence. Such borrowing and adaptation can add significantly to a country's economic growth.[28] In most countries, governmental policy has focused on achieving the advantages of independence without depriving its citizens. Governments try to forge trade patterns that are minimally vulnerable to foreign control of supply and demand. For example, the U.S. government maintains stocks of essential minerals so that its citizens will have access to them for a prolonged period if foreigners cut off supplies.

INTERDEPENDENCE

One way a country limits its vulnerability to foreign changes is through interdependence: the development of trade relationships on the basis of mutual need. France and Germany, for example, have highly interdependent economies. Each depends about equally on the other as a trading partner and so neither is likely to cut off supplies or markets for fear of retaliation. Such interdependence sometimes spurs international companies to pressure their governments to sustain trade relations. For example, about a third of world trade is intracompany trade—that is, companies export components and finished products between their foreign and home-country facilities. Any trade cessation would adversely affect these companies. For example, Ford buys and produces different components in different countries and would be severely affected if supplies from any one were to be suddenly disrupted.

DEPENDENCE

Many developing countries have decried their dependence because they rely so heavily on the sale of one primary commodity or on one country as a customer and supplier. Although most emerging economies depend on one commodity for over 25 percent of their export earnings, Iceland is the only industrialized country that depends on one product (fish) for over a quarter of its export earnings. While about one-quarter of emerging economies depend on one country (almost always an industrial one) for more than half of their export earnings, Canada is the only industrialized country with this high a dependence (on the United States). Because the emerging economies have low levels of production, they tend to be much more dependent on a given industrial country than the industrial country is dependent on them. Mexico, for example, depends on the United States for over 60 percent of its imports and exports, but the United States depends on Mexico for less than 10 percent of its imports and exports. U.S. policies can affect Mexico much more than Mexican policies can affect the United States. Furthermore, emerging economies primarily depend on production that competes on the basis of low-wage inputs.[29] This sort of dependence has led to concern among many economists that dependence will retard emerging economies' development.

Although theorists and policy makers wishing to lower dependency have proposed a number of different approaches, they all suggest that emerging economies intervene in foreign trade markets. As shown in the opening case, Sri Lanka has attempted to diversify its exports by developing nontraditional products that its policy makers believe can ultimately compete in world markets. But some emerging economies see that they have little opportunity to diversify production away from a basic commodity for which there is global oversupply. For them, the best economic assurance is continued dependence on an industrial country that preferentially imports their products.[30]

STRATEGIC TRADE POLICY

Given the importance of acquired advantage in world trade, it is understandable that governments have debated what their roles should be in affecting the acquired advantage of production within their borders. At the same time, governmental influence is seldom neutral, so even though governmental decisions and policies may not seek to affect world trade, they nevertheless have that effect. For example, U.S. governmental efforts to improve agricultural productivity and defense capabilities have undoubtedly helped the U.S. exports of farm and aerospace products. Further, a government's decision to help certain industries may hurt others. For example, European airlines have argued that their governments' support for high-speed rail traffic in Europe has hurt their ability to be competitive on international routes with U.S. air carriers, which profit from not having to compete much with railroads for passenger traffic in the United States.

From the standpoint of national competitiveness, the issue revolves around the development of successful industries. Of particular importance are emerging growth industries, because they offer the possibility of adding value (from high profits and wages) within the country in which most of the industry is headquartered. Further, by being first, there are marketing and production cost advantages that retard competition from other countries.[31] But to be internationally competitive, governments and companies must have the right resources that are needed for the targeted industry. Governments may try to alter their absolute and comparative advantages so that there is a fit, such as by importing and developing specific skills they need.

There are two basic approaches to government policy: (1) Alter conditions that will affect industry in general, (2) alter conditions that will affect a targeted industry.

Countries seek to improve their trade capabilities by
- Altering conditions for industries in general
- Targeting conditions for a specific industry

Regardless of whether a government takes a general or specific approach, it may alter the competitive positions of specific companies and production locations. The first approach means altering conditions that affect factor proportions, efficiency, and innovation. A country may upgrade production factors by improving human skills through education, providing infrastructure (transportation, communications, capital markets, utilities), promoting a highly competitive environment so that companies must make improvements, and inducing consumers to demand an ever higher quality of products and services.[32] This approach is general in that it creates conditions that may affect a variety of industries.

The second approach is to target specific industries. This approach has usually resulted in no more than small payoffs, largely because governments find it difficult to identify and target the right ones.[33] For example, a country may target an industry for which global demand never reaches expectations, such as France's support for supersonic passenger aircraft. Or the companies in the targeted industry do not become competitive, such as occurred with Thailand's support of the steel companies, which have had high costs because of poorly trained managers and rising labor costs in relation to other nearby countries.[34] Moreover, there has been a tendency for too many countries to identify the same industries, so excessive competition has led to inadequate returns.[35] Finally, relative conditions change, causing relative capabilities to change as well. For instance, Singapore successfully attracted companies in mature consumer electronics production and was able to compete globally because of its low wages in comparison to its productivity. However, in recent years, Singapore has been losing its competitive advantage because of its rising labor costs. It has also seen many companies move their production elsewhere, such as to Malaysia. Singapore is now trying to attract more research and development facilities for new products with higher profit margins.[36]

Nevertheless, there are some notable government successes. For example, the Indian Ocean country of Mauritius increased its adult literacy rate from 60 percent to 100 percent within three years. It successfully targeted textile manufacturing and a variety of service exports (such as tourism, banking, and phone betting) to transform its dependence on sugar production. The growth rate in the 1990s was one of the world's highest.[37]

WHY COMPANIES TRADE INTERNATIONALLY

Now that we know some *country* trade theories, let's see why *companies* trade. Regardless of the advantages a country may gain by trading, international trade ordinarily will not begin unless companies within that country have competitive advantages that enable them to be viable traders—and they must see profits in exporting and importing. Only if they perceive that the international opportunities might be greater than the domestic ones will they divert their resources to the foreign sector. To understand why trade takes place, it is useful to understand the competitive advantages and trade opportunities accruing to individual businesses.

THE PORTER DIAMOND

Why do specialized competitive advantages differ among countries—for example, why do Italian companies have an advantage in the ceramic tile industry and Swiss companies have one in the watch industry? Figure 5.5, the **Porter diamond**, shows that four conditions are important for competitive superiority: demand, factor endowment,

FIGURE 5.5 Determinants of Global Competitive Advantage

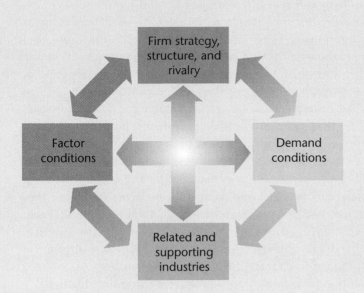

The Porter diamond shows the interaction of four conditions that usually need to be favorable if an industry in a country is to gain a global competitive advantage.

related and supporting industries, and firm strategy, structure, and rivalry. We have already discussed all four of these conditions in the context of other trade theories, but how they combine affects the development and continued existence of competitive advantages. The framework of the diamond is, therefore, useful for understanding how and where globally competitive companies develop. Usually, but not always, all four conditions need to be favorable for an industry within a country to attain global supremacy.

POINTS AND LIMITATIONS OF THE PORTER DIAMOND

Both PLC theory and country-similarity theory show that new products (or industries) usually arise from companies' observation of need or demand, which is usually in their home country. *Demand conditions* are the first point in the diamond. Companies then start up production near the observed market. This was the case for the Italian ceramic tile industry after World War II: There was a postwar housing boom, and consumers wanted cool floors because of the hot Italian climate. The second point of the Porter diamond—*factor conditions* (recall natural advantage within absolute advantage theory and the factor-proportions theory)—influenced both the choice of tile to meet consumer demand and the choice of Italy as the production location. Wood was less available and more expensive than tile, and most production factors (skilled labor, capital, technology, and equipment) were available within Italy on favorable terms. The third condition—the existence of nearby *related and supporting industries* (enamels and glazes)—was also favorable. (Recall discussions of the importance of transport costs in the theory of country size, assumptions of specialization, and limitations of PLC theory.)

The combination of three conditions—demand, factor endowment, and related and supporting industries—influenced companies' decisions to initiate production of

Countries' development of internationally competitive products depends on their
- **Demand conditions**
- **Factor conditions**
- **Related and supporting industries**
- **Firm strategy, structure, and rivalry**

ceramic tiles in postwar Italy. The ability of these companies to develop and sustain a competitive advantage required favorable circumstances for the fourth condition—*firm strategy*, *structure*, and *rivalry*. Barriers to market entry were low in the tile industry (some companies started up with as few as three employees), and hundreds of companies initiated production. Rivalry became intense as companies tried to serve increasingly sophisticated Italian consumers. These circumstances forced breakthroughs in both product and process technologies, which gave the Italian producers advantages over foreign producers and enabled them to gain the largest global share of tile exports.

The existence of the four favorable conditions does not guarantee that an industry will develop in a given locale. Entrepreneurs may face favorable conditions for many different lines of business. In fact, comparative advantage theory holds that resource limitations may cause companies in a country not to try to compete in some industries, even though an absolute advantage may exist. For example, conditions in Switzerland would seem to have favored success if companies in that country had become players in the personal computer industry. However, Swiss companies preferred to protect their global positions in such product lines as watches and scientific instruments, rather than downsizing those industries by moving their highly skilled people into a new industry.

A second limitation of the diamond concerns the increased ability of companies to gain market information, production factors, and supplies from abroad. At the same time, they face more competition from foreign production and foreign companies. The absence of any of the four conditions from the diamond domestically, therefore, may not inhibit companies and industries from becoming globally competitive. First, take the existence of demand conditions. We have already discussed how observations of foreign, rather than domestic, demand conditions have spurred much of the recent growth in Asian exports. In fact, such Japanese companies as Uniden and Fujitech target their sales almost entirely to foreign markets.[38] Second, domestic factor conditions can change. For example, capital and managers are now internationally mobile. Much of Singapore's recent global export growth of high-tech components has depended on the importation of these factors. Third, if related and supporting industries are not available locally, materials and components are now more easily brought in from abroad because of advancements in transportation and the relaxation of import restrictions. In fact, many MNEs now assemble products with parts supplied from a variety of countries. Finally, companies react not only to domestic rivals, but also to foreign-based rivals with which they compete at home and abroad.[39]

Most trade theories are based on a national perspective, but decisions to trade are usually made by companies.

COMPANIES' ROLE IN TRADE

Every trade transaction is an export for one party and an import for another. So, both the exporter and importer must see advantages of the transaction. The following discussion will describe these advantages.

Managers' incentives to export include

- **Use of excess capacity**
- **Reduced production costs per unit**
- **Increased markup**
- **Spread of risk**

STRATEGIC ADVANTAGES OF EXPORTS

Most companies would prefer to concentrate on domestic rather than foreign markets because of their greater familiarity with their own environments and of the desire to avoid trade regulations and converting currencies. However, there are compelling reasons that lead them to trade.

Looking to the Future
COMPANIES ADJUST TO CHANGING TRADE POLICIES AND CONDITIONS

When countries have few restrictions on foreign trade, companies have greater opportunities to gain economies of scale by servicing markets in more than one country from a single base of production. They also can pursue global, as opposed to multidomestic, strategies more easily. But governmental trade restrictions vary from one country to another, from one point in time to another, and from one product or service to others within the same economies. Nevertheless, it is probably safe to say that trade restrictions have been diminishing, primarily because of the economic gains that countries foresee through freer trade. For example, the fastest growing emerging markets have been those with the fewest import restrictions. This loosening of restrictions has allowed them to reduce costs of essential agricultural products and machinery and has given them advantages in developing exports.[40]

However, there are uncertainties as to whether the trend toward the freer movement of trade will continue. Groups worldwide question whether the economic benefits of more open economies outweigh some of the costs, both economic and noneconomic. Although the next chapter will discuss import restrictions (protectionism) in detail, it is useful at this point to understand the overall issues of evolving protectionist sentiment.

One key issue is the trade between industrial and developing countries. At the same time trade barriers are lessening, many emerging economies, where wage rates are very low, are increasing productivity more rapidly than are industrial countries. The result could mean certain shifts in production to emerging economies and the displacement of many jobs within industrial countries. There is uncertainty as to how fast new jobs will replace old ones in industrial countries and how much tolerance industrial countries will have for employment shifts that would be less likely to occur within protected markets.

A second key issue results from the concept of national sovereignty.[41] Separate nations exist because of differences in culture and in economic and political priorities. The more interdependent economies become because of trade, the more difficult it is for a country to maintain differences from its major trading partners. For example, two neighboring countries may differ in preferences for income equality, whether to place the major tax burden on companies or individuals, the level of employee safety provisions to require, and how much the environment should be protected. Such differences create production cost differences. With unrestricted trade, a country with more stringent (expensive) requirements may either have to relax those requirements or face production adjustments as products enter easily from abroad. At present there is evidence that many countries may invoke national sovereignty by preventing trade that may undermine their own priorities and objectives, even though such moves may have certain negative economic costs for them.

Companies must try to predict whether there will be freer or more restrictive trade in those industries in which they operate. Restrictive trade limits companies' options. Restrictions also may cause companies to make some decisions about where to locate and sell that are different than they would otherwise make. If present trends continue, relationships among factor endowments (land, labor, and capital) will continue to evolve. For example, the population growth rate is much higher in emerging economies, especially those of sub-Saharan Africa, than in developed countries. Two possible consequences of this growth are continued shifts of labor-intensive production to emerging economies and of agricultural production away from densely populated areas. At the same time, the finite supply of natural resources may lead to price increases for these resources, even though oversupplies have generally depressed prices for some time. The limited supply may work to the advantage of emerging economies because supplies in industrial countries have been more fully exploited.

Four factors are worth monitoring because they could cause product trade to become relatively less significant in the future.

1. There are some indications that protectionist sentiment is growing. This could prevent competitively produced goods from entering foreign countries. For example, major trading countries have recently squabbled over trade for a number of products, including genetically altered agricultural products, bananas, textiles, and passenger aircraft.

2. As economies grow, efficiencies of multiple production locations also grow, which may allow country-by-country production to replace trade in many cases. For example, most automobile producers have moved into Thailand or plan to do so as a result of Thailand's growing market size.

3. Flexible, small-scale production methods, especially those using robotics, may enable even small countries to produce many goods efficiently for their own consumption, eliminating the need to import those goods. For example, steel production used to take larger capital outlays that needed enormous markets before the development of efficient minimills that can produce on a small scale.

4. Services are growing more rapidly than products as a portion of production and consumption within industrial countries. Consequently, product trade may become a less important part of countries' total trade. Further, many of the rapid-growth service areas, such as home building and dining out, are not easily tradable so trade in goods plus services could become a smaller part of total output and consumption.

Use of Excess Capacity   Companies frequently have immediate or long-term output capabilities for which there is inadequate domestic demand. This excess capacity may be of known reserves of natural resources such as oil by Norway's Statoil or in the form of product-specific capabilities such as cosmetics by Estée Lauder. Moreover, the company may have a process technology that allows it to produce efficiently only on a larger scale than is possible for its domestic market, such as Caterpillar's production of earth-moving equipment. So, companies leverage their competencies by using them abroad.

Cost Reduction   A company can generally reduce its costs by 20 to 30 percent each time it doubles its output—a phenomenon known as the **experience curve**.[42] For instance, with a 20 percent cost reduction and an initial cost of $100 per unit, the second unit produced will cost $80, the fourth $64, and so on. The reduction may come about because of several factors: covering fixed costs over a larger output, increasing efficiency because of the experience gained through producing large quantities of units, and making quantity purchases of materials and transportation. Therefore, the market leader may garner cost advantages over its competitors that even discourage the entry of other companies in the industry. One way a company can increase output is by defining its market in global rather than domestic terms. In fact, many companies that are not the leaders in their domestic markets may be more active in seeking export sales in order to counter the leaders' volume advantage. For example, in Japan, Matsushita and Toyota are their industries' market leaders. However, Sony and Sanyo as followers of Matsushita and Nissan and Honda as followers of Toyota are more active in export markets.[43] However, the gains from the experience curve must be weighed against additional costs arising from exporting, such as those for product adaptation, management time, inventory increases, and more credit extension. These costs may outweigh the advantages of developing foreign markets.[44]

Greater Profitability   A producer might be able to sell the same product at a greater profit abroad than at home. This may happen because the competitive environment in the foreign market is different, possibly because there the product is in a different stage of its life cycle. A mature stage at home may force domestic price-cutting, while a growth stage abroad may make foreign price reductions unnecessary. Greater profitability also may come about because of different governmental actions at home and abroad that affect profitability—for example, differences in the taxation of earnings or the regulation of prices. If, however, companies must divert efforts from domestic sales to service foreign markets, they may lack the resources to sustain their overall growth objectives.[45]

Risk Spreading   By spreading sales over more than one foreign market, a producer might be able to minimize the effects of fluctuations in demand. Business cycles and product life vary among countries. In terms of the former, Donaldson Company, a U.S. manufacturer of filters, air cleaners, and mufflers, has countered U.S. recessions with its export sales.[46] In terms of the latter, Whirlpool, a U.S. manufacturer of major household appliances, has countered a maturing domestic market with a growth market in several Asian countries. Another factor in spreading risk through exportation is that a producer might be able to develop more customers, reducing its vulnerability to the loss of a single customer or a few.

STRATEGIC ADVANTAGES OF IMPORTS

The impetus for trade may come from either the importer or the exporter. Impetus may come from an importer because that company is seeking out cheaper or better-quality supplies, components, or products to use in its production facilities. Or a company may be seeking new foreign products that complement its existing lines, giving the importer more to sell.

If international procurement of supplies and components lowers costs or improves the quality of finished products, the procuring company may then be better able to combat import competition for the finished products. Or it may be able to compete more effectively in export markets. The automobile industry exemplifies global competition that depends on subcontractors, including foreign ones, to reduce production costs.[47]

An importer, like an exporter, might be able to spread its operating risks. By developing alternative suppliers, a company is less vulnerable to the dictates or fortunes of any single supplier. For example, many large U.S. steel customers, such as the automobile industry, have diversified their steel purchases to include European and Japanese

Managers' incentives to import include

- **Cheaper supplies**
- **Additions to product line**
- **Reduction of risk of no supply**

suppliers. This strategy has reduced the risk of supply shortages for the U.S. automobile industry in case of a strike among U.S. steelworkers. At the same time, however, it has contributed to the U.S. steel industry's problems. This is an industry with high fixed production costs; its loss of domestic market share increases its unit cost of steel. Its profits suffer because of fewer sales and lower per unit profits on remaining sales.

WEB CONNECTION

Check out our home page www.prenhall.com/daniels for links to key resources for you in your study of international business.

SUMMARY

- Trade theory is useful because it helps explain what might be produced competitively in a given locale, where a company might go to produce a given product efficiently, and whether governmental practices might interfere with the free flow of trade among countries.

- Some trade theories examine what will happen to international trade in the absence of governmental interference. Other theories prescribe how governments should interfere with trade flows to achieve certain national objectives.

- Mercantilist theory proposed that a country should try to achieve a favorable balance of trade (export more than it imports) to receive an influx of gold. Neomercantilist policy also seeks a favorable balance of trade, but its purpose is to achieve some social or political objective.

- Adam Smith developed the theory of absolute advantage, which says that consumers will be better off if they can buy foreign-made products that are priced more cheaply than domestic ones.

- According to the theory of absolute advantage, a country may produce goods more efficiently because of a natural advantage (e.g., raw materials or climate) or because of an acquired advantage (e.g., technology or skills).

- David Ricardo's comparative advantage theory says that total global output can increase through foreign trade,

even if one country has an absolute advantage in the production of all products.

- Policy makers have questioned some of the assumptions of the absolute and comparative advantage theories. These assumptions are that full employment exists, that output efficiency is always a country's major objective, that there are no transport costs among countries, that countries are satisfied with their relative gains, and that resources move freely within countries but are immobile internationally.

- The theory of country size holds that because countries with large land areas are apt to have varied climates and natural resources, they are generally more self-sufficient than smaller countries are. A second reason for this greater self-sufficiency is that large countries' production centers are more likely to be located at a greater distance from other countries, raising the transport costs of foreign trade.

- The factor-proportions theory holds that a country's relative endowments of land, labor, and capital will determine the relative costs of these factors. These factor costs, in turn, will determine which goods the country can produce most efficiently.

- The international product life cycle (PLC) theory states that companies will manufacture products first in the countries in which they were researched and developed.

These are almost always industrialized countries. Over the product's life cycle, production will shift to foreign locations, especially to emerging economies as the product reaches the stages of maturity and decline.

- According to the country-similarity theory, most trade today occurs among industrial countries because they share similar market segments and because they produce and consume so much more than emerging economies.

- Manufactured products comprise the bulk of trade among industrialized countries. This trade occurs because countries apportion their research and development differently among industrial sectors. It also occurs because industrial country consumers want and can afford to buy products with a greater variety of characteristics than are produced in their domestic markets.

- Some emerging economies are concerned that they are overly vulnerable to events in other countries because of their high dependence on one export product or one trad-

ing partner. As emerging economies try to become more independent of the external environment, however, they face the risk that their own consumers may have to pay higher prices or do without some goods.

- Countries seek to improve their national competitiveness by developing successful industries. They do this by altering conditions that affect industry in general or by targeting the development of specific industries (a strategic trade policy).

- Although most trade theories deal with cross-country benefits and costs, trading decisions usually are made at the company level, where both an exporter and importer see advantages from trade. Companies must have competitive advantages to be viable exporters. They may seek trading opportunities to use excess capacity, lower production costs, make greater profit, or spread risks. Importers seek cheaper or better-quality supplies and products that complement their existing lines.

CASE

THE CASHEW[48]

Even though the cashew tree grows fruit, it is best known for its nuts, which account for about 20 percent of the value of nuts produced worldwide—exceeded only by the value of almonds and walnuts. U.S. imports of cashew nuts in 1997 totaled about $310 million, about 60 percent of the world market and more than three times the imports into Europe, which is the next largest market.

The fruit of the tree (known as the cashew apple), however, drew the earliest attention. The Tupi Indians of Brazil first harvested the cashew apple in the wild. They later introduced it to early Portuguese traders, who in turn propagated the tree in other tropical countries. (See Map 5.2 for major production locations.) But attempts to grow the tree on plantations proved unsuccessful because it was vulnerable to insects in the close quarters of plantations. Instead, some of the abandoned plantation trees propagated new trees in the wild forests of India, East Africa, Indonesia, and Southeast Asia.

Two other factors inhibited early harvest of the cashew nut. First, cashew fruit matures before the nut, so the fruit spoils by the time the nut can be harvested usefully. Second, the processing of cashew nuts is tedious and time-consuming.

In the 1920s, however, India developed a cashew-processing industry in response to growing demand for cashew nuts among Indian consumers.

The processing required much manual dexterity and low wage rates because the nut is contained beneath layers of shell and thin skin. To remove the shell, workers must place the nut in an open fire for a few minutes and then tap it (while still hot) with a wooden hammer. If the nut breaks from the tapping, its value decreases considerably. Once workers remove the shell, they place the nut in an oven for up to 10 hours, after which they remove the skin by hand while the nut is still warm—without the use of fingernails or any sharp objects that can mark or break the surface. The workers then sort and grade the nuts into 24 size categories. The highest grade sells at about four times the price of the lowest grade, which is sold almost entirely to the confectionary industry.

India maintained a virtual monopoly on cashew processing until the mid-1970s. This monopoly was due to three factors.

1. India was the largest producer of cashews.
2. Early demand occurred largely in India, meaning that any other country would have to incur added transport charges to reach the Indian market.

MAP 5.2   Location of World's Cashew Nut and Export Supplies

The major cashew producing and exporting areas are all in the tropics. This map shows the locations of the three largest producing areas. The numbers show the percentage of world production of raw nuts in 1997.

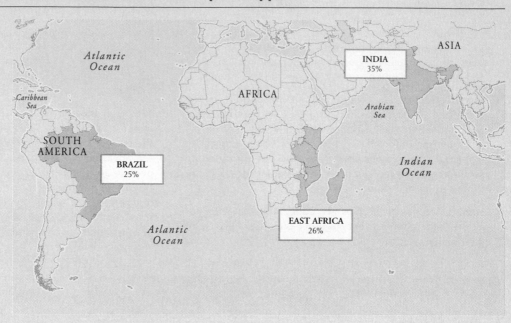

Source: Key Commercial Crops Development Program (KCCDP) on http://www.pworld.net.ph/user/nabcor/cashew.html

3. Most important, the Indian workers were particularly adept at the process technology.

Through the years, other factors threatened India's prominence as a cashew producer. First, a shortage developed when demand for the nuts grew in the United States and the United Kingdom. Second, because the nuts were ill-suited for plantation growth, India could not increase production and turned to East Africa, especially Mozambique, Tanzania, and Kenya, for supplies. Those countries were experiencing high unemployment and at first were eager to sell the raw nuts, which grew in their wilds. But by the 1950s, they began to realize they could bypass India by processing the raw nuts themselves. Cashew-processing methods were well known and did not require the East Africans to invest in expensive machinery, so there was no technological obstacle. However, because the Indian labor force worked on making handicrafts at home as children, by the time they were employed in cashew processing they could perform delicate hand operations efficiently. Without such training, the East Africans were at a fatal disadvantage.

Although the Africans' inability to compete granted a reprieve to the Indian industry, it put it on notice that it was vulnerable to supply cutoffs. The Indian Council for Agricultural Research, the International Society for Horticultural Sciences, and the Indian Society for Plantation Crops expanded their efforts to increase India's production of raw nuts. Concomitantly, three different companies developed mechanical equipment to replace hand processing. They sold equipment to East African countries and Brazil in the 1970s. These countries decreased their exports of raw nuts to India to maintain supplies for their own processing.

Three factors have kept India's hand-processing industry afloat. First, the machinery breaks many cashew nuts, so Indian processors still face little competition in the sale of higher-grade nuts. At any time, however, newer machinery might solve the breakage problem, again threatening the approximately 200 Indian processors and their 300,000 employees. Furthermore, there is increased competition for the lower-grade output. Second, Indian processors have been able to obtain increased supplies of raw nuts, partially as a result of Indian production increases. Pesticide technology now makes cashew tree plantations feasible, increasing the number of trees per acre. Indian experimentation in hybridization, vegetative propagation, and grafting and budding techniques promises to increase the output per tree to five times what it was in the wild. In addition, India has been increasing its imports of raw nuts substantially, primarily from Tanzania and Vietnam. Third, India uses fewer fertilizers than Brazil, the biggest export competitor, and the lack of fertilizer apparently gives Indian nuts a better flavor.

Because its exports consist of a higher portion of higher-grade nuts and because of flavor differences, Indian exports sell for a premium in comparison with those of competitors—for example, about 15 percent more than nuts from Brazil and about 25 percent more than those from Mozambique. However, yields are usually higher in Brazil, and Brazilian processors pay only between 30 and 36 percent of the price the Indian processors pay for raw nuts. Further, because of differences in domestic demand, India typically exports about 50 percent of the raw kernels that it processes, while Brazil exports about 85 percent. In the mid-1990s Brazil suffered crop problems, which enabled India to gain a temporary increase in global export share of processed cashew kernels.

The thawing of the Cold War hurt India's nut exports. Because India could no longer compete as well in its traditional North American and European markets for lower-grade nuts, it had begun to export more to the Soviet Union, which, during the 1980s, became India's largest cashew nut customer in terms of tonnage. The Soviets bought the nuts at a price above world market levels, a buying habit that was believed to have the political motive of influencing India's neutrality during the Cold War. But these sales decreased substantially at the end of the Cold War because the Soviets sought the cheapest prices.

There is potential for an excess supply of cashew nuts, which might result from plantation techniques and improved technology in India and elsewhere. To find outlets for a possible nut glut, the All-India Coordinated Spices and Cashew Nut Improvement Project has centered on finding new markets for products from the cashew tree. For example, experimentation is going on to harvest both the fruit and the nut. The fruit also is being studied for commercial use in candy, jams, chutney, juice, carbonated beverages, syrup, wine, and vinegar. Another area of research is in the use of cashew nutshell liquid (oil), which was once discarded as a waste product. It is now used extensively in industrial production of friction dusts for formulation in brake linings and clutch facings. So far, however, the extraction of cashew nutshell liquid has been too costly to make the product fully competitive with some other types of oils. There is also a potential for short-term cashew shortages, such as occurred in 1999 because of unfavorable climatic conditions. This has led India to try to increase its production and its foreign supplies.

QUESTIONS

1. What trade theories help to explain where cashew tree products have been produced historically?
2. What factors threaten India's future competitive position in cashew nut production?
3. If you were an Indian cashew processor, what alternatives might you consider to maintain future competitiveness?

CHAPTER NOTES

1 Mike Levin, "Sri Lanka: Getting the Numbers Right," *Asian Business*, April 1992, pp. 40–44; Ramesh Venkataraman, "Sri Lanka: Bad Old Politics and Great New Economics," *Wall Street Journal*, April 4, 1991, p. A14; "Sri Lanka Investment: Inside or Outside the Free Trade Zone?" *Business Asia*, April 24, 1981, pp. 134–135; P. Murugasu, "Selecting Products for Export Development," *International Trade Forum*, October–December 1979, pp. 4–7; Sarath Rajapatirana, "Foreign Trade and Economic Development: Sri Lanka's Experience," *World Development*, Vol. 16, No. 10,

October 1988, pp. 1143–1158; Vinita Piyaratna, "A Year of Living Optimistically," *Asian Business*, April 1993, pp. 37–38; "Foreign Investment and Trade," *BBC Summary of World Broadcasts*, July 3, 1996; Rohan Gunaskera, "Sri Lanka Seeks to Revive Port Fortunes," Reuter European Business Report, July 24, 1996; Rahul Sharma, "New Sri Lanka Government to Boost Local Industry," Reuters World Service, August 22, 1994; Rohan Gunaskera, "Sri Lankans Pore Over Instant Tea Exports," Reuter Asia-Pacific Business Report, March 24, 1996; John Zarocostas, "Sri Lanka

Receives Praise for Its Trade Reforms," *Journal of Commerce*, November 13, 1995, p. A3; Amal Jayasinghe, "Sri Lanka to Legalize Gambling," *Financial Times*, November 7, 1996, p. 6; A. G. (Sandy) Cuthbertson, "The Trade Policy Review of Sri Lanka," *The World Economy*, Vol. 20, No. 5, August 1999, pp. 633–648; "Sri Lanka," *Financial Times*, February 3, 1998, p. 21; Paul Taylor, "Sri Lanka," *Financial Times*, June 2, 1999, South Asian Software Services section, p. ii; and Amal Jayasinghe, "The Tea Industry," *Financial Times*, February 3, 1998, p. 23. For up-to-date information through the Internet on Sri Lanka, the address is *www.lanka.net/cgi-bin/index2.html.*

2 The mercantilist period is not associated with any single writer. A good coverage is in Lars Magnusson, *Mercantilism* (New York: Routledge, 1994).

3 For a review of literature, see Jordan Shan and Fiona Sun, "On the Export-Led Growth Hypothesis for the Little Dragons: An Empirical Reinvestigation," *Atlantic Economic Review*, Vol. 26, No. 4, December 1998, pp. 353–371.

4 Many publishers have subsequently printed his 1776 book. See, for example, Adam Smith, *An Inquiry into the Nature and Causes of the Wealth of Nations* (Washington: Regnery Publishing, 1998).

5 "The Ice Trade," *The Economist*, December 21, 1991–January 3, 1992, pp. 47–48.

6 David Ricardo, *On the Principles of Political Economy and Taxation*, originally published in London in 1817, has since been reprinted by a number of publishers. (See, for example, Amherst, NY: Prometheus Books, 1996.)

7 Gaston de Rosayro, "Sri Lanka in the Doldrums," *South China Morning Post*, June 1, 1995, p. 21.

8 For a good discussion of this paradoxical thinking, see Paul R. Krugman, "What Do Undergraduates Need to Know About Trade?" *American Economic Review Papers and Proceedings*, May 1993, pp. 23–26.

9 Chad Nehrt, "Maintainability of First Mover Advantages When Environmental Regulations Differ Between Countries," *Academy of Management Review*, Vol. 23, No. 1, 1998, pp. 77–97.

10 Caroline Southey, "EU and US Head for Fur Trade Showdown," *Financial Times*, December 10, 1996, p. 6.

11 John Ward Anderson and Molly Moore, "'Ethnic Cleansing Charges Echo in Himalayan Bhutan," *Washington Post*, April 8, 1994, p. A1.

12 Paul Krugman, "Scale Economies, Product Differentiation, and the Patterns of Trade," *American Economic Review*, Vol. 70, December 1980, pp. 950–959.

13 Gianmarco I. P. Ottaviano and Diego Puga, "Agglomeration in the Global Economy: A Survey of the 'New Economic Geography,'" *The World Economy*, Vol. 21, No. 6, August 1998, pp. 707–731.

14 For a discussion of scale efficiencies, see James R. Tybout, "Internal Returns to Scale as a Source of Comparative Advantage: The Evidence," *AEA Papers and Proceedings*, May 1993, pp. 440–444; for a discussion specific to R&D, see Rachel McCulloch, "The Optimality of Free Trade: Science or Religion?" *AEA Papers and Proceedings*, May 1993, pp. 367–371.

15 Eli J. Heckscher, *Heckscher-Ohlin Trade Theory* (Cambridge, MA: MIT Press, 1991).

16 See, for example, P. Krugman and A. J. Venables, "Globalization and the Inequality of Nations," *Quarterly Journal of Economics*, Vol. 110, 1995, pp. 857–880.

17 Raymond Vernon, "International Investment and International Trade in the Product Life Cycle," *Quarterly Journal of Economics*, May 1966, pp. 190–207; David Dollar, "Technological Innovation, Capital Mobility, and the Product Cycle in North–South Trade," *American Economic Review*, Vol. 76, No. 1, pp. 177–190.

18 "R&D Scoreboard," *Financial Times*, June 25, 1998, p. 14.

19 Ian H. Giddy, "The Demise of the Product Life Cycle in International Business Theory," *Columbia Journal of World Business*, Spring 1978, pp. 90–97.

20 David Dollar and Edward N. Wolff, *Competitiveness, Convergence, and International Specialization* (Cambridge, MA: MIT Press, 1993).

21 World Trade Organization Census Bureau data for 1998 as reported in Michael M. Weinstein, "Limits of Economic Diplomacy," *New York Times*, April 8, 1999, p. C1.

22 Stefan B. Linder, *An Essay on Trade Transformation* (New York: John Wiley, 1961).

23 Two recent discussions of intra-industry trade are Don P. Clark, "Determinants of Intraindustry Trade Between the United States and Industrial Nations," *The International Trade Journal*, Vol. XII, No. 3, Fall 1998, pp. 345–362; and H. Peter Gray, "Free International Economic Policy in a World of Schumpeter Goods," *The International Trade Journal*, Vol. XII, No. 3, Fall 1998, pp. 323–344.

24 Dirk Pilat, "The Economic Impact of Technology," *The OECD Observer*, No. 213, August–September 1998, pp. 5–8.

25 "That's Snow-biz," *The Economist*, April 13, 1996, p. 58.

26 Terry Hall, "NZ Finds Pirated Varieties in Chile," *Financial Times*, January 21, 1999, p. 24.

27 "New Tribe Found in New Guinea," *Herald-Times* (Bloomington, IN), June 28, 1993, p. 1.

28 David Dollar, "What Do We Know About the Long-Term Sources of Comparative Advantage?" *AEA Papers and Proceedings*, May 1993, pp. 431–435.

29 Refik Erzan and Alexander J. Yeats, "Implications of Current Factor Proportions Indices for the Competitive Position of the U.S. Manufacturing and Service Industries in the Year 2000," *Journal of Business*, Vol. 64, No. 2, 1991, pp. 229–253.

30 "Farm Trade: Gone Bananas," *The Economist*, March 28, 1992, pp. 76–77.

31 Peter Passell, "High-Tech Industry Is Hard to Help," *New York Times*, February 2, 1995, p. B5.

32 Michael E. Porter, "The Competitive Advantage of Nations," *Harvard Business Review*, Vol. 90, No. 2, March–April 1990, p. 78.

33 Paul Krugman and Alasdair M. Smith, eds., *Empirical Studies of Strategic Trade Policies* (Chicago: University of Chicago Press, 1993).

34 Paul M. Sherer, "Thailand Trips in Reach for New Exports," *Wall Street Journal*, August 27, 1996, p. A8.

35 Richard Brahm, "National Targeting Policies, High-Technology Industries, and Excessive Competition," *Strategic Management Journal*, Vol. 16, 1995, pp. 71–91.

36 James Kynge and Elisabeth Robinson, "Singapore to Revise Trade Priorities," *Financial Times*, January 21, 1997, p. 6.

37 Helene Cooper, "Trade Wins," *Wall Street Journal*, July 14, 1998, p. A1.

38 Kiyohiko Ito and Vladimir Pucik, "R&D Spending, Domestic Competition, and Export Performance of Japanese Manufacturing Firms," *Strategic Management Journal*, Vol. 14, 1993, pp. 61–75.

39 See, for example, Lawrence G. Franko, "Global Corporate Competition in the 1990s: The Japanese Juggernaut Rolls On," University of Massachusetts–Boston College of Management, working paper, June 1995.

40 Francis Ng and Alexander Yeats, *Did Africa's Protectionist Policies Cause Its Marginalization in World Trade?* (Washington, DC: World Bank research working paper No. 1636, 1996).

41 H. Peter Gray, "Free Trade, Economic Integration and Nationhood," *Journal of International Economic Integration*, Vol. 5, No. 1, 1990, pp. 1–12.

42 See, for example, Boston Consulting Group, *Perspective in Experience* (Boston: Boston Consulting Group, 1970); and Robert D. Buzzell, Bradley T. Buzzell, Gale Sultaw, and Ralph G. M. Sultaw, "Market Share: A Key to Profitability," *Harvard Business Review*, Vol. 58, No. 1, 1975.

43 Ito and Pucik, "R&D Spending, Domestic Competition, and Export Performance."

44 Jacques Liouville, "Under What Conditions Can Exports Exert a Positive Influence on Profitability?" *Management International Review*, Vol. 32, No. 1, 1992, pp. 41–54.

45 Will Mitchell, J. Myles Shaver, and Bernard Yeung, "Getting There in a Global Industry: Impacts on Performance of Changing International Presence," *Strategic Management Journal*, Vol. 13, 1992, pp. 419–432.

46 Richard C. Marais and Michael Schuman, "Hong Kong Is Just Around the Corner," *Forbes*, October 12, 1992, pp. 50–58.

47 Ulli Arnold, "Global Sourcing—An Indispensable Element in Worldwide Competition," *Management International Review*, Vol. 29, No. 4, 1989, p. 22.

48 Data for this case were taken from "L'Anac-arde ou Noix de Cajou," *Marches Tropicaux*, June 13, 1980, pp. 1403–1405; R. J. Wilson, *The Market for Cashew Nut Kernels and Cashew Nutshell Liquid* (London: Tropical Products Institute, 1975); J. H. P. Tyman, "Cultivation, Processing and Utilization of the Cashew," *Chemistry and Industry*, January 19, 1980, pp. 59–62; Jean-Pierre Jeannet, "Indian Cashew Processors, Ltd.," ICH Case 9-378-832 (Boston: Harvard Business School, 1977); Jean-Pierre Jeannet, "Note on the World Cashew Nut Industry," ICH Case 9-378-834 (Boston: Harvard Business School, 1977); "Meanwhile, Back in Mozambique," *Forbes*, Vol. 11, No. 16, November 16, 1987, p. 110; U.S. Department of Commerce, Bureau of the Census, U.S. Imports of Merchandise International Harmonized System Commodity Classification, 1992, on CD-ROM; Steven Jaffee, *Private Sector Response to Market Liberalization: The Experience of Tanzania's Cashew Nut Industry* (Washington, DC: World Bank, 1994); "Cashewnuts," *Handbook of Indian Agriculture* (New Delhi: Vikas Publishing House, 1995); and U.S. Department of Commerce, Bureau of the Census, "Merchandise Trade—U.S. Imports by Commodity, Cashew Nuts, document 0801300000, September 8, 1999.

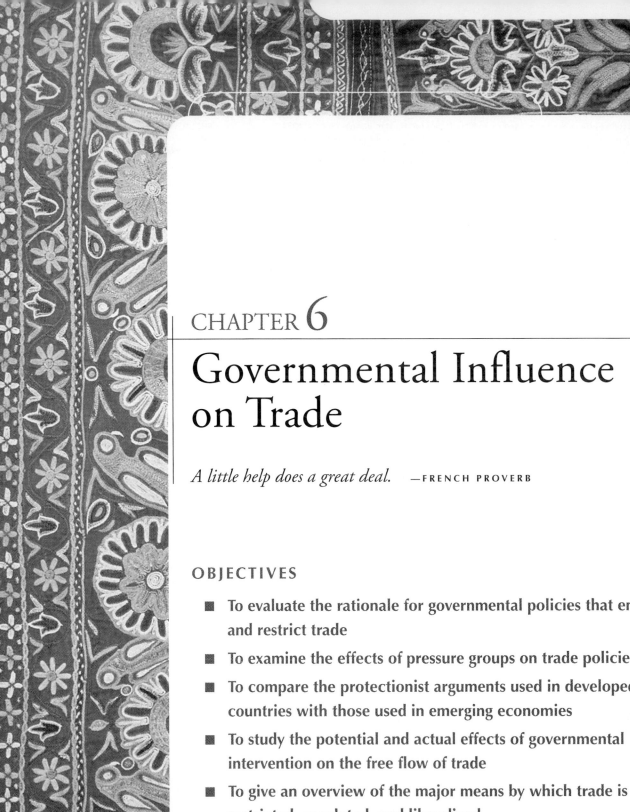

CHAPTER 6

Governmental Influence on Trade

A little help does a great deal. —FRENCH PROVERB

OBJECTIVES

- To evaluate the rationale for governmental policies that enhance and restrict trade
- To examine the effects of pressure groups on trade policies
- To compare the protectionist arguments used in developed countries with those used in emerging economies
- To study the potential and actual effects of governmental intervention on the free flow of trade
- To give an overview of the major means by which trade is restricted, regulated, and liberalized
- To examine the World Trade Organization
- To show that governmental trade policies create business uncertainties

The World Trade Organization (WTO), the institution that handles trade disputes among countries, ruled in 1999 that the United States could impose punitive tariffs (taxes) on $191.4 million of European Union (EU) products because of EU restrictions on banana imports. The tariffs of 100 percent of the value meant that EU exports to the United States of a variety of products would fall nearly to zero. That the EU would restrict banana imports seems ludicrous inasmuch as it has negligible banana production to protect. That the United States would take punitive measures to influence EU banana policy is equally incredulous inasmuch as U.S. banana production is inconsequential. Officially, the EU claims its restrictions are to help poor former colonies in the Caribbean, which otherwise would have almost nothing to export. Officially, the United States says that its actions are to force compliance with WTO agreements so that there will be a viable international trading order. It has argued that the United States, Canada, and Japan have adhered to WTO rulings against them, even though those rulings were very unpopular at home. Behind the positions of both the EU and the United States are a group of stakeholders who influence political decision makers.

The banana is grown almost entirely in tropical countries and was once a luxury in the United States and Europe because of high costs from plant diseases, attacks by insects, transportation, and spoilage in route. However, technology has overcome these problems so that the banana is now the world's most popular fruit. Billions of dollars and millions of jobs are at stake in the world banana trade, so companies, workers, producing countries, taxpayers, and consumers all try to influence both EU and U.S. policies on banana trade.

Before 1993, each EU country had its own banana import policy. For example, Germany, the largest EU banana consumer, bought bananas from the cheapest locations, while the United Kingdom, the second largest EU banana consumer, gave preference to higher-priced bananas from former colonies. Subsequently, each EU country established the same banana import policy, which is complex. Basically, there are three sales quotas, each of which has subquotas. Figure 6.1 shows EU supplies from the three major quota areas. The first is for bananas grown within the EU—in Greece and the off-continent areas of the Canary Islands (Spain), Martinique and Guadeloupe (France), and Madeira (Portugal). Producers lobbied hard for this protection. The second is for "traditional bananas" from certain African, Caribbean, and Pacific countries (mainly former colonies) to which the EU has pledged economic assistance. Such

FIGURE 6.1   Eu Banana Supplies, 1998, tons (m)

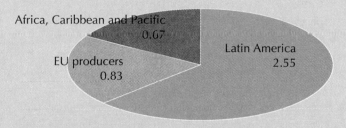

Africa, Caribbean and Pacific
0.67

EU producers
0.83

Latin America
2.55

The EU gives quotas for bananas produced in European Union countries and to some former EU colonies.

Source: European Commission as presented in *Financial Times*, April 8, 1999, p. 4. Reprinted by permission.

countries as St. Lucia lobbied with politicians of EU countries so that their share of the EU market increased. They argued that over 50 percent of their export earnings come from bananas and that their only potential market was in Europe. The third is for bananas from elsewhere, mainly Latin American countries. Although they have the bulk of the EU market, they lost market share in the quota allocation and turned to the United States for assistance in getting the EU to open its markets to them. For example, Ecuador, which lost market share, argued that bananas are also its largest foreign-exchange earner, that 10 percent of its population depends on banana sales, and that its per capita GNP is lower than that of St. Lucia.

The EU's quota system has affected competition and prices. First, because it allocates market share by country of production, there is no incentive for exporters to use price as a competitive weapon. Instead, prices are based on those of the high-cost producers in the eastern Caribbean—Dominica, Grenada, St. Lucia, and St. Vincent—which are three times those of some Latin American producers because of higher wages, lack of scale economies, and expensive shipping from having to make many port calls. To prevent low-cost producers from reaping a windfall gain from the higher prices, the EU has placed a tariff on their banana imports and forced them to pay for expensive import licenses. Second, very few companies handle banana exporting, which involves transportation, ripening, and distribution to retailers. In fact, three companies account for two-thirds of world trade. Because of the quota system that prevents them from increasing market share, they have little incentive to lower their prices. The result is that these middlemen's prices are much higher for European than for U.S. sales, raising prices even more for European consumers, which has infuriated German consumers. A World Bank economist estimated that European consumers pay about $2 billion a year in higher prices because of the quota system. Of this amount, only $150 million goes to the countries targeted to receive preferential EU treatment. The rest goes toward EU tariffs and added middlemen profits. In other words, EU consumers spend $13.25 for each $1 that goes to the producing countries they have targeted for help. Third, the higher cost for European consumers dampens demand for banana sales there. This falling demand causes excess supplies elsewhere and further depresses earnings of the banana countries that lost market share because of the EU quotas.

Two large U.S. companies, Chiquita and Dole, and a U.S.-based but Jordanian-controlled company, Del Monte, handle most of the Latin American banana trade. Chiquita, the successor to United Fruit, had the most to lose from EU restrictions and the most to gain through their removal. By far the largest banana distributor in Europe, Chiquita spent millions in plantations and ships in the early 1990s in anticipation that Europe would be more open to trade. Dole and Del Monte are more dependent on the U.S. market, so European actions affect them less.

Carl Lindner, the investor who controls Chiquita, was a major contributor to both the Democratic and Republican parties in the 1996 elections. He was an overnight guest of President Clinton in the Lincoln bedroom, and he allowed Senator Dole, the Republican candidate, to use his family's aircraft. He lined up support within both parties to bring WTO action against the EU and to pressure Latin American countries to act against the EU quotas. He was successful in the former and partially successful in the latter. This success led some critics to say that Lindner had turned the United States into another "banana republic," an analogy to the term describing Central American countries when United Fruit held high political clout within them. Ecuador, Guatemala, Honduras, Mexico, and Panama lodged complaints with the WTO along with the United States; however, Costa Rica, Colombia, Nicaragua, and Venezuela accepted a guaranteed share of the EU market instead. For example, the EU offered and Costa Rica accepted a 23.4 percent share of the Latin American quota. Once countries lodged their complaints, stakeholders who gained from the quota system began working hard to keep the status quo. For example, Neil McCann, the head of Europe's largest banana distributor, Fruit Importers of Ireland, lobbied hard within Europe. His supply sources are largely in the preferenced eastern Caribbean, where government leaders made references to the pittances paid by Chiquita to workers in Latin America and intimated they could no longer cooperate in drug control programs if the United States worked to take away their economic livelihood.

In 1997, the WTO ruled against the EU; however, during the next two years, the United States claimed the EU used delaying tactics and made only insignificant changes in its banana regime. The United States threatened to place punitive tariffs on $520 million of EU products to force EU action. This $520 million comprises less than one-quarter of 1 percent of U.S. imports from Europe; however, by targeting some specific products that depend heavily on the U.S. market, the United States hoped that those European producers would pressure their governments to reform the banana policy. The U.S. threat did not extend to products from Denmark and the Netherlands because they did not vote for the banana regime. Reactions were immediate but diverse. For example, the managing director of Arran Aromatics, the largest employer on a Scottish island, blamed the U.K. government publicly for his need to cut staff. The head of a U.K. packaging company, Beamglow, said it may have to relocate to the Netherlands. Some other companies sought exemptions in the U.S. position for their own products. For example, the Scottish cashmere industry estimated that 1,200 of its jobs were at stake, and its representative got cashmere removed from the list of punitive products after meeting with President Clinton and U.S. senators. However, this was not before the industry reduced imports of raw cashmere that caused unemployment in Mongolia's second biggest export segment. In the meantime, some U.S. companies complained of their losses because of rising costs of supplies. For example, Exide makes batteries and employs 18,000. Its CEO said the increase in the price of gel lead from Germany for its battery production "would cause a severe hardship." The EU sought another ruling on the punitive tariffs. The WTO ruled them permissible, but only for $191.4 million of EU imports.

INTRODUCTION

Why study governmental influence on trade? At some point, you may work for or own stock in a company whose performance, or even survival, may depend on governmental measures that limit foreign producers' ability to compete against you or that

Bananas are the world's most popular fruit; their cultivation, transportation, and sales are big business internationally. Many emerging economies, like Madagascar in the photo, depend on banana exports, which are sold mainly in industrial countries by industrial country distributors. The chapter's opening case illustrates the economic and political conditions that cause countries to disagree on banana trade policies.

create opportunities or reduce risks when you sell abroad. Likewise, governmental measures may limit your ability to sell abroad, such as by prohibiting the export of certain products or to certain countries. Collectively, these governmental measures are known as **protectionism**. In the opening case, EU protectionism helped the competitive position of some countries, such as Dominica, and some companies, such as Fruit Importers of Ireland. At the same time, it harmed the competitive position of some other countries, such as Panama, and some other companies, such as Chiquita. You also are affected as consumers and taxpayers in the amounts you pay for goods and taxes. For example, EU banana protectionism increased taxes on and prices of bananas in Europe. Similarly, governmental expenses rose in many countries because of actions to maintain or dismantle the EU banana import regulations.

In Chapter 5, we showed that trade is a major means of linking countries economically and that the linking improves global efficiency. However, the restrictions illustrated in the banana war case are not atypical. No country in the world permits an unregulated flow of goods and services across its borders. (Figure 6.2 illustrates the effect of governmental regulations on companies' competitive positions.) Governments place restrictions on imports and occasionally on exports. They frequently give direct or indirect subsidies to industries to enable them to compete with foreign production either at home or abroad. This chapter will first discuss the rationales—economic and noneconomic—for such trade protectionism, followed by an explanation of the major forms of trade controls and a summary of the purposes and activities of the World Trade Organization.

All countries seek to influence trade, and each has

- **Economic, social, and political objectives**
- **Conflicting objectives**
- **Interest groups**

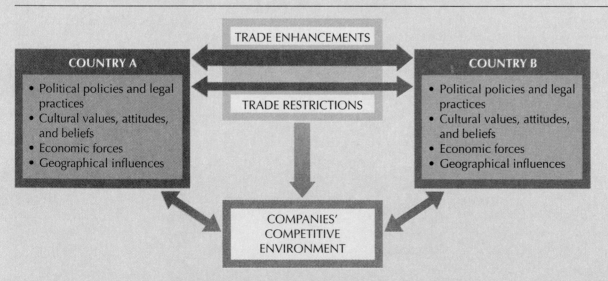

FIGURE 6.2 Physical and Societal Influences on Protectionism and Companies' Competitive Environment

In response to physical and societal influences, governments enact measures that enhance or restrict companies' international trade. These measures affect competition because of improving or retarding companies' abilities and needs to compete internationally. Companies likewise influence governments to adopt trade policies that benefit them.

CONFLICTING RESULTS OF TRADE POLICIES

In general, governments influence trade to satisfy economic, social, or political objectives. Often these objectives conflict (for example, the EU would like both to help poor former colonies economically and to keep its consumer prices low; however, its banana trade policy helped the former while hurting the latter). Governments would also like to help some of their companies and industries without harming others, but this is frequently impossible—especially if other countries retaliate against their protectionist actions. For example, the EU banana policy helped EU banana distributors but hurt a variety of other EU companies when the United States retaliated by restricting EU imports.

Not surprisingly, any proposal for trade regulation reform results in heated debate among pressure groups that believe they will be affected. Of course, those that are most directly affected (stakeholders) are most apt to speak up. For example, EU stakeholders whose livelihood depended on exports of cashmere wool to the United States (workers, owners, suppliers, and local politicians) perceived the losses from U.S. restrictions to be considerable. Workers saw themselves as being forced to take new jobs in new industries, perhaps in new locales. They feared prolonged periods of unemployment, reduced incomes, insecure work conditions, and unstable social surroundings. People threatened in this way are liable to constitute a very strong pressure group. In contrast, consumers usually do not understand how much prices rise because of import restrictions. Moreover, the economic costs are usually widely dispersed. The $2 billion a year in higher EU banana costs is certainly substantial; however, individual consumers have not been sufficiently affected to cause them to band together as an effective pressure group to persuade their governmental leaders to change banana import policies.

ECONOMIC RATIONALES FOR GOVERNMENTAL INTERVENTION

The reasons for governmental intervention in trade may be basically classified as either economic or noneconomic, as Table 6.1 shows.

UNEMPLOYMENT

Pressure groups pose a real challenge to government policy makers and businesspeople. Policy makers must decide which conflicting pressure groups to heed. Businesspeople must counter groups whose proposals will harm them by pressuring policy makers

The unemployed can form an effective pressure group for import restrictions.

TABLE 6.1	RATIONALES FOR GOVERNMENTAL INTERVENTION IN TRADE
ECONOMIC RATIONALES	**NONECONOMIC RATIONALES**
Prevent unemployment	Maintain essential industries
Protect infant industries	Deal with unfriendly countries
Promote industrialization	Maintain spheres of influence
Improve position compared to other countries	Preserve national identity

themselves. There is probably no more effective pressure group than the unemployed because no other group has the time and incentive to picket or write letters in volume to governmental representatives. For example, unemployed U.S. steelworkers have been very active in pressuring U.S. lawmakers to restrict steel imports.

One problem with restricting imports in order to create jobs is that other countries might retaliate with their own restrictions, such as U.S. restrictions on gel lead in response to EU banana import restrictions. New import restrictions by a major country have almost always brought quick retaliation, sometimes causing more job losses than gains in industries protected by the new restrictions.[2]

Two factors may mitigate the effects of retaliation. First, there may be a lower tendency to retaliate against a small country (in terms of economic power) that restricts imports. For example, Peruvian automobile import restrictions have caused no Japanese retaliation because the loss of sales by Japanese producers is too low. Second, if retaliation decreases employment in a capital-intensive industry but increases it in a labor-intensive industry, employment objectives may be achieved. For example, the United States limits imports of apparel, usually a labor-intensive good. Any resultant foreign retaliation against, say, U.S.-produced semiconductors of the same value as displaced apparel sales would probably threaten fewer U.S. jobs than would be gained from maintaining apparel production, because fewer people are needed to produce the same value of semiconductors. Even if no country retaliates, the restricting country will gain jobs one place and lose them somewhere else. That is because of losing import-handling jobs. When the United States threatened a 100 percent tax on luxury Japanese cars, Honda estimated that 100,000 Americans worked for Acura import operations and dealerships in the United States.[3]

Imports may also help create jobs in other industries, and these industries may form pressure groups against protectionism. Government policy makers must consider conflicting effects on different industries and companies. Consider the U.S. apparel industry. Such companies as Warnaco and Liz Claiborne joined retailers to protest textile import restrictions because they needed the variety and quality of foreign-made cloth to compete against global companies.[4] Imports also stimulate exports, although less directly, by increasing foreign income and foreign-exchange earnings, which are then spent on new imports by foreign consumers.

If import restrictions do increase domestic employment, there will still be costs to some people in the domestic society in the form of higher prices or higher taxes. Further, if managers believe protection to be permanent, they may not see a competitive need to invest enough in technological and product development, thus depriving consumers further.

Government officials should compare the costs of higher prices with the costs of unemployment and displaced production resulting from freer trade. In addition, they should consider the costs of policies to ease the plight of displaced employees, such as for unemployment benefits or retraining. These are challenging tasks. It is hard to put a price on the distress suffered by people who must be out of work, change jobs, or move. It is also difficult for working people to understand that they may be better off financially (because of lower prices) if part of their taxes go to help pay unemployment or welfare benefits for people whose positions were lost because of imports from freer trade.

Import restrictions to create domestic employment

- **May lead to retaliation by other countries**
- **Are less likely to be met with retaliation if implemented by small economies**
- **May decrease export jobs because of price increases for components**
- **May decrease export jobs because of lower incomes abroad**

Possible costs of import restrictions include

- **Higher prices**
- **Higher taxes**

Such costs should be compared with those of unemployment.

The employment issue complicates moving to freer trade because displaced workers are frequently the ones who are least able to find alternative work. In Canada's garment industry, for example, companies are transferring great numbers of sewing and cutting jobs to emerging economies. A high portion of the displaced sewers and cutters are immigrants who speak English poorly. Companies' and the Canadian government's record of retraining them has not been very successful because of language and their low education level in comparison to the needs of expanding industries.[5]

When displaced workers receive unemployment benefits, they often spend them on living expenses rather than on retraining in the hope that they will be recalled to their old jobs. When they do seek retraining, many workers, especially older ones, lack the educational background necessary to gain needed skills in a reasonable period of time.[6] Moreover, they often train for jobs that do not materialize.

INFANT-INDUSTRY ARGUMENT

In 1792, Alexander Hamilton presented what has come to be one of the oldest arguments for protectionism. The **infant-industry argument** holds that a government should guarantee an emerging industry a large share of the domestic market until it becomes efficient enough to compete against imports. Emerging economies still use this argument to support their protectionist policies. The infant-industry argument is based on the logic that although the initial output costs for an industry in a given country may be so high as to make it noncompetitive in world markets, over time the costs will decrease to a level sufficient to achieve efficient production. The cost reductions may occur for two reasons: As companies gain economies of scale and employees become more efficient through experience, total unit costs drop to competitive levels.

Although it is reasonable to expect costs to decrease over time, they may not go down enough, which poses two problems for protecting an industry. First, governments have difficulty identifying those industries that have a high probability of success. Some industries grow to be competitive because of governmental protection; automobile production in Brazil and South Korea are good examples. However, in many other cases—such as automobile production in Malaysia and Australia—the industries remain in an infant state even after many years of operation. If infant-industry protection goes to an industry that does not reduce costs enough to make it competitive against imports, chances are its owners, workers, and suppliers will constitute a formidable pressure group that may prevent the importation of a cheaper competitive product. The protection against import competition may be a disincentive for managers to adopt innovations needed to make their companies globally competitive.

Second, even if policy makers can ascertain which industries are likely to succeed, it does not necessarily follow that companies in those industries should receive governmental assistance. There are, of course, many examples of entrepreneurs who endured early losses to gain future benefits, and policy makers may argue that governments should assist new companies only if the entry barriers are very high. Some segment of the economy must absorb the higher cost of local production during infancy. Most likely, it will be the consumer who will pay higher prices for the protected companies' products. A government can subsidize companies so that consumer prices are not increased, but taxpayers pay for the subsidy. For the infant-industry argument to be fully viable, future benefits should exceed early costs.

The infant-industry argument says that production becomes more competitive over time because of

- Increased economies of scale
- Greater worker efficiency

INDUSTRIALIZATION ARGUMENT

Countries with a large manufacturing base generally have higher per capita incomes than do countries without such a base. Moreover, a number of countries, such as the United States and Japan, developed an industrial base while largely preventing competition from foreign-based production. Many emerging economies use protection to increase their level of industrialization because of industrial countries' economic success and experience. Specifically, they believe:

Countries seek protection to promote industrialization because that type of production
- **Brings faster growth than agriculture**
- **Brings in investment funds**
- **Diversifies the economy**
- **Brings more income than primary products do**

1. Surplus workers can more easily increase manufacturing output than they can increase agricultural output (faster growth).
2. Inflows of foreign investment in the industrial area will promote growth.
3. Prices and sales of traditional agricultural products and raw materials fluctuate too much.
4. Markets for industrial products will grow faster than markets for agricultural (primary) products.

Use of Surplus Workers   In many emerging economies, a large portion of the population lives in rural areas, and the agricultural output per person is low, particularly in countries that have little additional unused arable land, such as in India or Egypt. Consequently, many people can leave the agricultural sector without greatly affecting such a country's agricultural output. Like the infant-industry argument, this argument favoring industrialization says that importing cheaper products from abroad will prevent the establishment of domestic industry if free-market conditions prevail. However, this argument differs from the infant-industry argument in its assertion that output will increase even if domestic prices do not become globally competitive because the workers would otherwise produce so little.[7]

Shifting people out of agriculture is not without risk. Several problems can result:

When a country shifts from agriculture to industry
- **Demands on social and political services in cities may increase**
- **Output increases if the marginal productivity of agricultural workers is very low**
- **Development possibilities in the agricultural sector may be overlooked**

1. Workers may have high expectations from industrial jobs that are left unfulfilled, leading to excessive demands on social and political services. Indeed, a major problem facing emerging economies is the massive migration to urban areas of people who do not find suitable jobs, housing, and social services, and cannot be easily absorbed. There is no work for them either because the industrialization process has proceeded too slowly or because they lack the skills and work habits necessary for employment in manufacturing.
2. Agriculture may be a better means of effecting additional output than industry. Not all emerging economies use their land fully or efficiently, nor is industrial development the only means of economic growth. The United States, Canada, and Argentina grew rapidly during the nineteenth century, in large part through agricultural exports, and they continue to profit from such exports. Australia, New Zealand, and Denmark maintain high incomes along with substantial agricultural specialization.
3. If a government protects manufacturing companies, policy makers must decide on which type of industry to protect to minimize consumer price and tax increases.
4. Too much of a shift from rural to urban areas may reduce agricultural output in emerging economies, further endangering their self-sufficiency. Interestingly,

most of the world's agricultural production and exports come from industrial countries because they have highly efficient and capital-intensive agricultural sectors that permit resources to move into the manufacturing sector without decreasing agricultural output.

Promoting Investment Inflows   Import restrictions also may increase foreign direct investment. When countries restrict the purchase of foreign-made products, foreign companies may shift production to the restricting country to avoid the loss of a lucrative or established market. The influx of foreign companies may hasten a country's move from agriculture to industry. For example, Thailand's automobile import restrictions influenced foreign automakers to invest there. Investment inflows may also add to employment, which is especially attractive to policy makers.

> If import restrictions keep out foreign-made goods, foreign companies may invest to produce in the restricted area.

Diversification   Export prices of most primary products fluctuate widely. Price variations due to uncontrollable factors—such as weather affecting supply or business cycles abroad affecting demand—can wreak havoc on economies that depend on the export of primary products. This is especially true when an economy depends very heavily on a few commodities for employment and for export earnings. Because a large number of emerging economies depend on just one primary commodity, they frequently can afford foreign luxuries one year but are unable to afford replacement parts for essential equipment the next.[8]

However, a greater dependence on manufacturing does not guarantee diversification or stable export earnings. Most GDPs of emerging economies are small, so a change to manufacturing may simply shift dependence from one or two agricultural products to one or two manufactured ones.

Greater Growth for Manufactured Products   The **terms of trade** are the quantity of imports that a given quantity of a country's exports can buy. The prices of raw materials and agricultural commodities do not rise as fast as the prices of finished products, so over time it takes more primary products to buy the same amount of manufactured goods. Further, the quantity of primary products demanded does not rise as rapidly, so most emerging economies have become increasingly poorer compared to developed countries. Therefore, their governments help emerging manufacturing companies that use traditional raw materials and agricultural commodities to produce nontraditional products, such as Sri Lanka's help for companies making tea bags and instant tea from its tea leaves. The declining terms of trade for emerging economies have been explained in part by lagging demand for agricultural products and by changes in technology that have saved on the use of raw materials. A further explanation is that because of competitive conditions, industry savings due to technical changes that lower production costs of primary products go mainly to consumers, while cost savings for manufactured products go mainly to higher profits and wages.

> Terms of trade for emerging economies may deteriorate because
> - Demand for primary products grows more slowly
> - Production cost savings for primary products will be passed on to consumers

Import Substitution versus Export Promotion   So far we have discussed why emerging economies promote industrialization. They may do so by restricting imports in order to produce for local consumption goods they formerly imported. This is known as **import substitution**. In recent years, most countries have come to believe that import

> Industrialization emphasizes either
> - Products to sell domestically or
> - Products to export

substitution is not the best way to develop new industries. If the protected industries do not become efficient, consumers may have to support them by paying higher prices or higher taxes. In addition, because the industries must usually import capital equipment and other supplies, foreign-exchange savings are minimal. In contrast to import substitution, some countries, such as Taiwan and South Korea, have achieved rapid economic growth by promoting export industries, an approach known as **export-led development**. These countries try to develop industries for which export markets should logically exist. Such a change affects MNEs' operations in these countries because they may have to develop export markets for their foreign production. In reality, it is not easy to distinguish between the two types of industrialization, nor is it always possible to develop exports. Industrialization may result initially in import substitution, yet export development of the same products may be feasible later. China and India restrict the importation of vehicles and their parts so that local production can capture those sales in their rapidly growing markets. However, these countries might become future exporters.[9] The fact that a country concentrates its industrialization activities on products for which it would seem to have a comparative advantage does not guarantee that those products will become exports. There are various trade barriers, discussed later in this chapter, that are particularly problematic to the development of manufacturing exports from emerging economies.

ECONOMIC RELATIONSHIPS WITH OTHER COUNTRIES

Countries are interested not only in their absolute economic welfare, but also in how well they are performing compared to other countries. Governments will impose trade restrictions to improve their relative positions. They might buy no more from other countries than those countries buy from them. They might try to extract high export prices and keep import prices low—though not so low as to affect their domestic producers "unfairly."

Balance-of-Payments Adjustments   Because the trade account is a major part of the balance of payments for most countries, governments make many attempts to modify what would have been an import or export movement in a free market. For example, for many years the United States has imported more from Japan than it has exported there. Automobile trade comprises most of the difference. The U.S. government has at times tried to alter the imbalance by limiting the import of Japanese vehicles, persuading Japanese automotive companies to locate more production within the United States, and negotiating with the Japanese government to ease the entry of U.S.-made automobiles into Japan.

Comparable Access or "Fairness"   Many companies and industries argue that they should have the same access to foreign markets as foreign industries and companies have to their markets. From an economic standpoint, comparable access argues that in industries in which increased production will greatly decrease cost, either from scale economies or learning effects, producers that lack equal access to a competitor's market will have a disadvantage in gaining enough sales to be cost-competitive. This has been noted, for example, in the semiconductor, aircraft, and telecommunications industries.[10]

The argument for equal access also is presented as one of *fairness*. For example, the U.S. government permits foreign financial service companies to operate in the United

States, but only if their home governments allow U.S. financial service companies to operate there. The U.S. government also restricted France Telecom and Deutsche Telekom in the U.S. telephone market because of French and German restrictions on AT&T within their markets.[11] There are at least three arguments against this fairness doctrine. First, there are advantages of freer trade, even if imposed unilaterally. Restrictions may deny one's own consumers lower prices. Second, countries' imposition of additional import restrictions to coerce other countries to reduce their restrictions may escalate economic tensions rather than remove trade barriers. For example, France prohibited entry of U.S. hormone-treated beef. The United States countered by placing additional taxes on such French products as Roquefort cheese and foie gras in an effort to get France to rescind its restrictions. Not only did the French government not rescind the restrictions, French farmers protested at McDonald's restaurants by dumping manure at entryways and throwing potatoes at customers.[12] Third, governments would find it cumbersome and expensive to negotiate separate agreements for each of the many thousands of different products and services that might be traded.

Price-Control Objectives   Countries sometimes withhold supplies from international markets in order to raise prices abroad, an action that is most feasible when a few countries hold monopoly or near-monopoly control of certain resources. To maintain control and the resulting high prices, they strictly limit quantities sold so sales go only to those people who are willing to pay a higher price. However, this type of policy encourages smuggling and requires high prevention costs. For example, Colombia pays a high price to patrol its borders to try to prevent emeralds from flooding world markets. Further, export controls may be ineffective. Brazil lost its world monopoly in natural rubber after a contrabandist brought rubber plants into Malaysia. Also, if prices are kept too high or supplies too limited, substitutes may hit the market. Iranian controls on carpet exports have led to Iran's loss of market share because of cheaper carpets from China, India, and Pakistan.[13]

A country may also limit exports of a product that is in global short supply so that domestic consumers have more available to them. With a greater supply, their prices should be lower than the world market prices where shortages are greater. India has done this with rice.[14] The primary danger of these policies is that the lower prices at home will not entice producers to expand domestic output, whereas foreign output is expanded. This may lead to long-term market loss.

Countries also fear that foreign producers will price their exports so artificially low that they drive domestic producers out of business, resulting in a costly dislocation for workers and industries. If entry barriers are high, it is argued that the surviving foreign producers may charge exorbitant prices abroad or limit exports so that companies in their own countries gain better access to supplies. Hitachi, the only producer of a key computer chip, allegedly delayed deliveries to Cray Research, the leading U.S. supercomputer producer, to give Japanese computer companies an advantage.[15] However, if there is competition among foreign producers, they probably cannot charge exorbitant prices. Nor will they want to forgo selling abroad. For example, low import prices have eliminated most U.S. consumer electronics production, yet U.S. prices for consumer electronics are among the world's lowest. The ability to price artificially low abroad may result from high domestic prices due to a lack of competition at home or from home-country governmental subsidies.

Export restrictions may
- **Keep up world prices**
- **Require more controls to prevent smuggling**
- **Lead to substitution**
- **Keep domestic prices down by increasing domestic supply**
- **Give producers less incentive to increase output**
- **Shift foreign production and sales**

Import restrictions may
- **Prevent dumping from being used to put domestic producers out of business**
- **Get other countries to bargain away restrictions**
- **Get foreign producers to lower their prices**

Companies sometimes export below cost or below their home-country price, which is called **dumping**. Most countries prohibit imports of dumped products, but enforcement usually occurs only if the imported product disrupts domestic production. If there is no domestic production, then the only host-country effect is a low price to its consumers. Companies may dump because they cannot otherwise build a market abroad. They can afford to dump if the competitive landscape allows them to charge high domestic prices or if their home-country government subsidizes them. They may also incur short-term losses abroad if they believe they can recoup those losses after eliminating competitors in the market. Home-country consumers or taxpayers seldom realize that they are, in effect, paying so that foreign consumers have low prices. A company believing it is competing against dumped products may ask its government to restrict the imports. However, determining a foreign company's cost or domestic price is often difficult because of nonaccess to the foreign producers' accounting statements, fluctuations in exchange rates, and the passage of products through layers of distribution before reaching consumers. The result is that governments allegedly restrict imports arbitrarily through antidumping provisions of their trade legislation and are slow to dispose of the restrictions if pricing situations change. So, a company may quickly lose an export market it labored to build.[16] When U.S. avocado growers complained that they were competing against dumped New Zealand avocados, the U.S. government compared the prices of small New Zealand kiwis in the United States with those of large ones in New Zealand as the basis for limiting imports.[17]

A final price argument for governmental influence on trade that affects country relationships is the **optimum-tariff theory**, which holds that a foreign producer will lower its prices if the importing country places a tax on its products. If this occurs, benefits shift to the importing country because the foreign producer lowers its profits on the export sales. Assume that an exporter has costs of $500 per unit and is selling to a foreign market for $700 per unit. With the imposition of a 10 percent tax on the imported price, the exporter may choose to lower its price to $636.36 per unit, which, with a 10 percent tax of $63.64, would keep the price at $700 for the importer. The exporter may feel that a price higher than $700 would result in lost sales and that a profit of $136.36 per unit instead of the previous $200 per unit is better than no profit at all. An amount of $63.64 per unit has thus shifted to the importing country. As long as the foreign producer lowers its price by any amount, some shift in revenue goes to the importing country and the tariff is considered to be an optimum one. There are many examples of products whose prices did not rise as much as the amount of the imposed tariff; however, it is very difficult to predict whether exporters will in fact reduce their profit margins.

NONECONOMIC RATIONALES FOR GOVERNMENT INTERVENTION

We have discussed the economic rationales for government action on trade, but government rationales are often noneconomic, such as the following:

- Maintenance of essential industries (especially defense)
- Prevention of shipments to unfriendly countries
- Maintenance or extension of spheres of influence
- Conservation of activities that help preserve a national identity

Let's explore each of these reasons.

MAINTAINING ESSENTIAL INDUSTRIES

A major consideration behind governmental action on trade is the protection of essential domestic industries during peacetime so that a country is not dependent on foreign sources of supply during war. This is called the **essential-industry argument**. For example, the U.S. government subsidizes the domestic production of silicon so that domestic computer chip producers will not have to depend entirely on foreign suppliers. This argument for protection has much appeal in rallying support for import barriers. However, in times of real crisis or military emergency, almost any product could be essential. Because of the high cost of protecting an inefficient industry or a higher-cost domestic substitute, the essential-industry argument should not be (but frequently is) accepted without a careful evaluation of costs, real needs, and alternatives. Once an industry becomes protected, that protection is difficult to terminate because protected companies and their employees support politicians who will support their protection from imports. This is why the United States continued subsidies to mohair producers many years after mohair was no longer essential for military uniforms.[18]

> **In protecting essential industries, countries must**
> - **Determine which ones are essential**
> - **Consider costs and alternatives**
> - **Consider political consequences**

DEALING WITH "UNFRIENDLY" COUNTRIES

Groups concerned about security often use defense arguments to prevent exports, even to friendly countries, of strategic goods that might fall into the hands of potential enemies or that might be in short supply domestically. For example, the FBI and the U.S. Justice Department successfully prevented U.S. exports of data-encryption technology (data-scrambling hardware and software) until a group of U.S. high-tech companies allied themselves with privacy advocate groups to convince the executive and legislative branches of the U.S. government to eliminate the export curbs.[19] Export constraints may be valid if the exporting country assumes there will be no retaliation that prevents it from securing even more essential goods from the potential importing country. Even then, the importing country may simply find alternative supply sources or develop a production capability of its own. In this situation, the country limiting exports is the economic loser.[20]

Trade controls on nondefense goods also may be used as a weapon of foreign policy to try to prevent another country from easily meeting its economic and political objectives. For example, China tried to keep Taiwan from buying French fighter jets by announcing a ban on French companies' bidding on a Chinese subway contract if the sale went through.[21] But there is potential for trade gain as countries become friendlier. For example, the United States eliminated export restrictions on consumer goods to North Korea once North Korea agreed to halt its long-range missile testing.[22]

MAINTAINING SPHERES OF INFLUENCE

There are many examples of governmental actions on trade to support spheres of influence. Governments frequently give aid and credits to, and encourage imports from, countries that join a political alliance or vote a certain way within international bodies. For example, under the Caribbean Basin Initiative, the United States places low import restrictions on most products from Caribbean countries; in exchange, however, those countries must sign extradition treaties with the United States and cooperate in preventing controlled substances from entering the United States.[23] Another example is the EU's preferential treatment of bananas from certain former colonies, which was discussed in the opening case.

A country's trade restrictions may coerce governments to follow certain political actions, or punish companies whose governments do not follow the actions. For

FIGURE 6.3

The general public seldom understands how trade restrictions are carried out, or their ramifications.

"DO WE WANT TAKE-OUT CANTONESE, MANDARIN, OR SZECHUAN-- OR DO WE BOYCOTT UNTIL HUMAN RIGHTS QUESTIONS ARE SOLVED?"

Source: Pepper . . . and Salt © 1999 Harley Schwadron. Reprinted with permission of Harley Schwadron. All rights reserved.

example, China delayed permission for Allianz, a German insurance group, to operate in China after Germany gave a reception for the Dalai Lama, Tibetan spiritual leader in exile from China.[24] Many interest groups in the United States have favored trade restrictions on Chinese products because of China's human rights record, as Figure 6.3's cartoon points out.

PRESERVING CULTURES AND NATIONAL IDENTITY

Countries are held together partially through a common sense of identity that sets their citizens apart from other nationalities. To protect this separateness, countries limit foreign products and services in certain sectors. China limits rice imports partly because rice farming has been a historical and cohesive force in uniting Chinese families.[25] Canada limits foreign publishing, cable TV, and bookselling.[26] France protects its movie industry out of fear that the English language and Anglo-Saxon culture will weaken its cultural identity. Its government subsidizes the filmmaking and dubbing industries and limits the percentage of foreign films shown on French television.[27]

INSTRUMENTS OF TRADE CONTROL

We have focused on the end objectives governments seek when they attempt to influence exports or imports. Now we will see how they make these attempts. Because a country's trade policy will have repercussions abroad, retaliation from foreign governments looms as a potential obstacle to achieving the desired objectives. The choice of instruments for achieving trade objectives is therefore important, because each may elicit different responses from domestic and foreign groups. One way to understand the types of instruments is to distinguish between those that affect the amount traded indirectly by directly influencing the prices of exports or imports, and those that directly limit the amount that can be traded.

TARIFFS

Another common distinction is between tariff barriers and nontariff barriers. Tariff barriers affect prices; nontariff barriers may affect either price or quantity directly. A **tariff**, or **duty**, which is the most common type of trade control, is a tax governments levy on a good shipped internationally. If collected by the exporting country, it is known as an **export tariff**; if collected by a country through which the goods have passed, it is a **transit tariff**; if collected by the importing country, it is an **import tariff**. The import tariff is by far the most common.

Figure 6.4 illustrates how tariff and nontariff barriers affect both the price and the quantity sold, although in a different order and with a different impact on producers. Parts (a) and (b) both have downward-sloping demand curves (*D*) and upward-sloping supply curves (*S*). In other words, the lower the price, the higher the quantity consumers demand; the higher the price, the more suppliers make available for sale. The intersection of the *S* and *D* curves illustrates the price (P_1) and quantity sold (Q_1) without governmental interference. When a tax (tariff) raises the price from P_1 to P_2 in part (a), the amount consumers are willing to buy will fall from Q_1 to Q_2. Producers don't benefit because the price increase goes to taxes rather than to them. Part (b) shows a restriction in available supply; therefore a new supply curve (S_1) is imposed.

Tariffs may be levied
- **On goods entering, leaving, or passing through a country**
- **For protection or revenue**
- **On a per unit or a value basis**

FIGURE 6.4   Comparison of Trade Restrictions

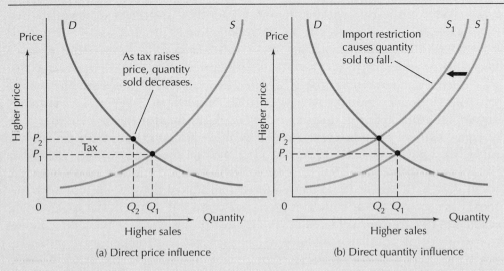

(a) Direct price influence

(b) Direct quantity influence

In (a), the tax on imports ($P_2 - P_1$) raises the price, which decreases the quantity demanded from Q_1 to Q_2. In (b), the quantity limit on imports ($Q_1 - Q_2$) decreases the supply available and raises prices from P_1 to P_2. The price rise in (b) is charged by producers.

The quantity sold now falls from Q_1 to Q_2. At the lower supply, sellers raise the price from P_1 to P_2, which is shown in the intersection of the D and S_1 curves. The major difference in the two forms of trade control is that sellers raise the price in (b), which helps compensate them for the decrease in quantity sold. In (a), producers sell less and are unable to raise their price because the tax has already done this.

Import tariffs primarily serve as a means of raising the price of imported goods so that domestically produced goods will gain a relative price advantage. A tariff may be protective even though there is no domestic production in direct competition. For example, a country that wants its residents to spend less on foreign goods and services may choose to raise the price of some foreign products, even though there are no close domestic substitutes, in order to curtail import consumption.

Tariffs also serve as a source of governmental revenue. Import tariffs are of little importance to large industrial countries (in fact, the EU now spends about the same to collect duties as the amount it collects[28]), but are a major source of revenue in many emerging economies. This is because government authorities in emerging economies may have more control over ascertaining the amounts and types of goods passing across their frontiers and collecting a tax on them than they do over determining and collecting individual and corporate income taxes. Although revenue tariffs are most commonly collected on imports, many countries that export raw materials use export tariffs extensively. New Caledonia, for example, has such a tariff on nickel. Transit tariffs were once a major source of revenue for countries, but they have been nearly abolished through governmental treaties.

A government may assess a tariff on a per unit basis, in which case it is a **specific duty**. It may assess a tariff as a percentage of the value of the item, in which case it is an **ad valorem duty**. If it assesses both a specific duty and an ad valorem duty on the same product, the combination is a **compound duty**. A specific duty is easy for customs officials who collect duties to assess because they do not need to determine a good's value on which to calculate a percentage tax. During periods of normal inflation, the specific duty will, unless changed, become a smaller percentage of a product's value and therefore be less restrictive to imports.

A tariff controversy concerns industrial countries' treatment of manufactured exports from emerging economies that are seeking to add manufactured value to their exports of raw materials (like making instant coffee from coffee beans). Raw materials frequently enter industrial countries free of duty; however, if processed, industrial countries assign an import tariff to them. Because an ad valorem tariff is based on the total value of the product, meaning the raw materials and the processing combined, nonindustrial countries argue that the *effective tariff* on the manufactured portion turns out to be higher than the published tariff rate. For example, a country may charge no duty on coffee beans but may assess a 10 percent ad valorem tariff on instant coffee. If $5 for a jar of instant coffee covers $2.50 in coffee beans and $2.50 in processing costs, the $0.50 duty is effectively 20 percent on the manufactured portion, because the beans could have entered free of duty. This situation has made it more difficult for emerging economies to find markets for their manufactured products. At the same time, industrial country governments cannot easily remove barriers to imports of emerging economies' manufactured products because such imports would largely affect unemployed workers who are least equipped to move to new jobs.

NONTARIFF BARRIERS: DIRECT PRICE INFLUENCES

We have shown how tariffs raise prices and limit trade. We will now explain other instruments governments use to limit trade by altering prices.

Subsidies　Countries sometimes make direct payments to domestic companies to compensate them for losses incurred from selling abroad, such as U.S. subsidies to cotton exporters.[29] However, they most commonly provide other types of assistance to make it cheaper or more profitable for them to sell overseas. For example, most countries offer their potential exporters an array of services, such as providing information, sponsoring trade expositions, and establishing foreign contacts. From an economic or market efficiency standpoint, service subsidies frequently are more justifiable than tariffs because they usually seek to overcome, rather than create, market imperfections, such as export and import promotion offices to help companies in emerging economies find foreign markets for their products.[30] There are also benefits to disseminating information widely because governments can spread the cost of collecting the information among many users. Other countries are not likely to complain about such types of assistance.

There is little agreement on what a subsidy is. Did Canada subsidize exports of fish because it gave grants to fishermen to buy trawlers? Did the United Kingdom subsidize steel when the government-owned steel company had severe losses? Did the United States block some automobile imports because states made numerous concessions to convince foreign automakers to locate plants there? Questions also surround various governments' support of R&D, as well as tax programs that directly or indirectly affect export profitability. One interesting subsidy case involves commercial aircraft. The United States subsidizes Boeing indirectly through payments for developments in military aircraft that have commercial applications. The EU subsidizes Airbus Industrie directly. The United States and the EU have set up a bilateral agreement to allow subsidies on commercial aircraft production but to limit the subsidy amounts.[31]

Aid and Loans　Governments also give aid and loans to other countries. If the recipient is required to spend the funds in the donor country, which is known as tied aid or tied loans, some products can compete abroad that might otherwise be noncompetitive. Tied aid is especially important in winning large contracts for infrastructure, such as telecommunications, railways, and electric-power projects. Most industrial countries also provide repayment insurance for their exporters, thus reducing the risk of nonpayment for overseas sales. Another scheme has been to combine aid with loans so that the interest rate on paper does not look as low to competitor countries as it really is.

Customs Valuation　What is to prevent exporters and importers from declaring an arbitrarily low price on invoices in order to pay a lower ad valorem tariff? Most countries have agreed on a procedure for assessing values when their customs agents levy tariffs. First, customs officials must use the invoice price. If there is none, or if its authenticity is doubtful, they must assess on the basis of the value of identical goods. If this isn't possible, they must assess on the basis of similar goods coming in at about the same time. For example, when goods enter for lease rather than purchase, there is no sales invoice, and customs officials base duty on the value of identical or similar goods.[32] If this basis cannot be used, officials may compute a value based on final sales value or on reasonable

Governmental subsidies may help companies be competitive.

- Subsidies to overcome market imperfections are least controversial.
- There is little agreement on what a subsidy is.
- There has been a recent increase in export-credit assistance.

Because it is difficult for customs officials to determine if invoice prices are honest

- They may arbitrarily increase value
- Valuation procedures have been developed

cost. For example, Argentine customs authorities revalued a shipment of 2,000 bicycles that the exporter invoiced for only $1.78 each.[33] In practice, however, discretionary power is sometimes used as an arbitrary means of preventing the importation of foreign-made products by assessing the value too high.

The fact that so many different products are traded creates valuation problems. It is easy (by accident or on purpose) to classify a product so that it will require a higher duty. With over 13,000 categories of products, a customs agent must use discretion to determine if silicon chips should be considered "integrated circuits for computers" or "a form of chemical silicon." A few examples should illustrate the possible problems. The U.S. Customs Service had to determine whether sport utility vehicles, such as the Suzuki Samurai and the Land Rover, were cars or trucks. It assessed the 25 percent duty on trucks instead of the 2.5 percent duty on cars. Later, a federal trade court ruled them to be cars. Procter & Gamble's Duncan Hines muffin mix operation had to suspend production for seven weeks while awaiting a favorable ruling that the topping brought in from its Canadian plant should not be classified as sugar. In Poland, automobile parts are assessed only about half the duty assessed on automobiles. But what is an automobile part? Thousands of Poles have discovered that they can go to Germany to buy cars, dismantle them just enough so that each section can be classified as a part, and bring the sections into Poland at the lower rate of duty.[34]

Other Direct Price Influences   Countries frequently use other means to affect prices, including special fees (such as for consular and customs clearance and documentation), requirements that customs deposits be placed in advance of shipment, and minimum price levels at which goods can be sold after they have customs clearance.

NONTARIFF BARRIERS: QUANTITY CONTROLS

We have described the instruments governments use to alter prices so that their domestic producers are more competitive internationally. But governments also limit import and export quantities directly.

A quota may
- Set the total amount to be traded
- Allocate amounts by country

Quotas   The most common type of import or export restriction based on quantity is the quota. From the standpoint of imports, a quota most frequently limits the quantity of a product allowed to be imported in a given year. The amount frequently reflects a guarantee that domestic producers will have access to a certain percentage of the domestic market in that year. For example, the EU's banana import quota gives its producers about 20 percent (and certain former colonies about 17 percent) of the EU market. This sort of restriction of supply usually will increase the consumer price because there is little incentive to use price as a means of increasing sales.

Problems arise when governments allocate quotas among countries because goods from one country might be transshipped to take advantage of another country's quota. This has been a problem with Chinese- and Vietnamese-made garments that are transshipped through various countries.[35] Similarly, the product may be transformed into one for which there is no quota. For example, Japan did not allow rice imports but did permit imports of processed food containing rice; thus Sushi Boy, a restaurant chain in Japan, imported frozen sushi (which was 80 percent rice) from the United States as a way of bypassing Japanese rice import prohibitions.[36]

Ethical Dilemmas and Social Responsibility
DO TRADE SANCTIONS WORK?

Many critics argue that countries should use trade policy to pressure other countries to change certain policies. For example, countries have limited trade with Iraq to weaken its repressive dictatorship, with India to protest its nuclear tests, with Malaysia so that it will prohibit the employment of child labor, with Taiwan so that it will curtail trade of endangered animals, and with Brazil so that it will restrict the cutting of Amazon forests. These pressures affect MNEs operating in those locales. Sanctions against a country's overall trade may prevent an MNE from exporting from that country even though the MNE may not be engaged in the so-called undesirable practices.

Although all of these causes have widespread public support, countries face dilemmas in whether to use trade policy to try to effect changes in other countries. Of course, one of these dilemmas concerns the argument of relativism versus normativism—whether or not to intervene. But there are other arguments as well. One argument is the practicality of making sanctions effective, especially if they intend to bring down repressive regimes. Often the targeted country manages to get what it wants from other countries. For example, the United States had a 20-year trade embargo with Vietnam, but Vietnamese consumers were able to buy U.S. consumer products, such as Coca-Cola, Kodak film, and IBM and Apple computers, through other countries that did not enforce the sanctions.[37] On the one hand, those governmental sanctions placed on South Africa and Haiti helped weaken regimes. On the other hand, Western trade embargoes against the former communist countries of Eastern Europe seemed to strengthen control by their leaders. Overall, trade sanctions aimed at changing policies in foreign countries seldom work and even cause job and economic losses in the sanctioning country.[38] In fact, it was after trade became more liberalized that leaders and systems in the former communist countries were overthrown. Some proponents of trade sanctions say it is irrelevant whether they bring about change or not. They argue that sanctions make an important statement.

Other arguments include

- The costs of sanctions on innocent people (This has occurred in Iraq, where there have been widespread reports of children's deaths because of inadequate supplies of food and medicine from the sanctions.[39])
- The unevenness with which policies are applied among countries (such as when the United States considered trade sanctions against Taiwan but not against China to curtail its trade in rhino horns and tiger bones used for traditional medicine)
- The need to look at a country's overall record rather than just its unpopular policy (Some critics have suggested that trade policies be used as a means of pressuring Brazil to restrict the cutting of Amazon forests, even though its overall environmental record, particularly its limiting of adverse exhaust emissions by converting automobile engines to use methanol instead of gasoline, is quite good.)
- The lack of agreement about the cause being protested (such as the argument that trade sanctions should be placed on countries permitting child labor, while others argue that the use of children on family farms is a means of binding family ties)

Import quotas are not necessarily intended to protect domestic producers. Japan maintains quotas on many agricultural products not produced in Japan. Imports are allocated as a means of bargaining for sales of Japanese exports as well as to avoid excess dependence on any one country for essential food needs, because supplies could be cut off by adverse climatic or political conditions.

A country may establish export quotas to assure domestic consumers of a sufficient supply of goods at a low price, to prevent depletion of natural resources, or to attempt to raise an export price by restricting supply in foreign markets. To restrict supply, some countries have banded together in various commodity agreements (Chapter 7) that have restricted and allocated exports from countries that produce such commodities as coffee and petroleum. The goal is to raise prices to importing countries.

A specific type of quota that prohibits all trade is an **embargo**. Like quotas, countries—or groups of countries—may place embargoes on either imports or exports, on whole categories of products regardless of destination, on specific products to specific countries, or on all products to given countries. Governments generally impose embargoes so that their economic effects will serve political purposes. For example, the United Nations voted an embargo on Haiti in 1993 because of political animosity toward the military dictatorship in power. But the effects on Haiti were economic: The country had difficulty getting supplies, particularly oil, and it could not easily sell its products abroad.

Through "buy local" laws
- **Government purchases give preference to domestically made goods**
- **Governments sometimes legislate preferences for domestically made goods**

"Buy Local" Legislation   Another form of quantitative trade control is "buy local" legislation. If government purchases are a large part of total expenditures within a country, they comprise an important part of the market. Most governments favor domestic producers in their purchases of goods. Sometimes they specify a content restriction—that a certain percentage of the product be of local origin. Sometimes they favor domestic producers through price mechanisms. For example, a government agency may buy a foreign-made product only if the price is at some predetermined margin below that of a domestic competitor. There is abundant legislation worldwide that simply prescribes a minimum percentage of domestic content that a given product must have for it to be sold legally within the country.

Other types of trade barriers include
- **Arbitrary standards**
- **Licensing arrangements**
- **Administrative delays**
- **Reciprocal requirements**
- **Service restrictions**

Standards   Countries commonly have set classification, labeling, and testing standards in a manner that allows the sale of domestic products but inhibits that of foreign-made ones. Take labels, for instance. The requirement that companies indicate on a product where it is made provides information to consumers who prefer buying products from certain locales. But this adds to a firm's production costs, particularly if the label must be translated for each country where the firm exports. Further, raw materials, components, design, and labor increasingly come from a variety of countries, so most products today are of mixed origin. This leads to labeling problems. For example, Infrared Research Labs, a small U.S. manufacturer of remote-control devices, cannot use a "Made in the U.S.A." label for U.S. sales because some components bought from U.S. suppliers originate in foreign countries; nevertheless, some governments require that label on Infrared's export sales to their markets.[40] The ostensible purpose of testing standards is to protect the safety or health of the domestic population. However, thwarted exporters have argued that such restrictions protect domestic producers instead. For example, the EU subjects many U.S. products it imports to some form of EU certification, such as costly retesting after the goods arrive in Europe.[41] In some cases, the EU standards keep U.S. products out of the market completely; this is the case with genetically engineered corn, even though the worldwide scientific community reports that the genetic engineering poses no human health risk, and even though France grows and sells a small amount of genetically engineered corn itself.[42]

Specific Permission Requirements   Some countries require that potential importers or exporters secure permission from governmental authorities before conducting trade transactions, a requirement known as an **import license**. To gain a license, a company may have to send samples abroad, which can restrict imports or exports directly by denying permission or indirectly because of the cost, time, and uncertainty involved in the process. Similar to an import license is a **foreign-exchange control**, which requires an importer of a given product to apply to a governmental agency to secure the foreign currency to pay for the product. As with an import license, failure to grant the exchange, not to mention the time and expense of completing forms and awaiting replies, constitutes an obstacle to foreign trade.

Administrative Delays   Closely akin to specific permission requirements are intentional administrative delays, which create uncertainty and raise the cost of carrying inventory. For example, South Korean customs routinely take 30 days or more to clear imported merchandise, adding to inventory costs and making some perishables unsalable. United Parcel Service suspended its ground service between the United States and Mexico because of burdensome Mexican customs delays.[43] But correcting delays may be difficult. For example, exporters to Japan have complained that stevedore practices at Japanese ports excessively delay and add costs to their shipments. However, Japanese authorities have claimed that they have no control over the practices because the stevedores work for privately run companies.[44]

Reciprocal Requirements   Governments sometimes require that exporters take merchandise in lieu of money or that they promise to buy merchandise or services in the country to which they export. This requirement is common in the aerospace and defense industries—sometimes because the importer is short of foreign currency to purchase what it wants. Russia's Aeroflot partly paid for Airbus aircraft with crude oil.[45] More frequently, however, reciprocal requirements are made between countries with ample access to foreign currency that want to secure jobs or technology as part of the transaction.[46] For example, McDonnell Douglas sold helicopters to the British government but had to equip them with Rolls-Royce engines (from the United Kingdom) and transfer much of the technology and production work to the United Kingdom.[47] These barter transactions are called **countertrade**, or **offsets**. They often require exporters to find markets for goods outside their lines of expertise or to engage in complicated organizational arrangements over which they lose desired control. Many companies avoid countertrade. However, some have developed competencies in these types of arrangements.

Restrictions on Services   In addition to depending on earnings from the sale of goods abroad, many countries depend substantially on revenue from the foreign sale of such services as transportation, insurance, consulting, and banking. These services account for nearly 20 percent of the value of all international trade. Nevertheless, countries restrict trade in services for three main reasons:

1. *Essentiality*. Countries consider certain service industries to be essential because they serve strategic purposes or because they provide social assistance to their citizens. They sometimes prohibit private companies, foreign or domestic, in some sectors because they feel the services should be not-for-profit. In other cases, they set price controls for private competitors or subsidize government-owned service organizations, giving disincentives for foreign private participation. Mail, education, and hospital health services are not-for-profit sectors in which few foreign firms compete. When a government permits private companies, foreign firms may not be able to compete because countries do not want to depend on foreign companies for a service they consider essential. For example, most countries, including the United States, restrict foreign companies from transporting cargo and passengers over their domestic routes. Other essential services in which foreign firms are sometimes excluded are communications, banking, and utilities. Service companies sometimes pressure their home governments to negotiate deregulation abroad when they believe they have competitive advantages. For example, the American International Group (AIG), the largest industrial insurer in the world, has pushed the U.S. government to help open the Japanese insurance market, where foreign companies have only about 2 percent of the sales.[48]

2. *Standards*. Governments limit foreign entry into many service professions to ensure the staffing of only qualified personnel. The licensing standards of these personnel varies by country and includes such professionals as accountants, actuaries, architects, electricians, engineers, gemologists, hairstylists, lawyers, physicians, real estate brokers, and teachers. At present, there is little reciprocal recognition in licensing from one country to another because requirements differ substantially. This means, for example, that an accounting or legal firm from one country cannot easily do business in another country, even to service its domestic client's needs. The company must usually hire professionals within each foreign country or else receive certification abroad. This may be very difficult because examinations will be in a foreign language and may emphasize materials different from those in the home country. Furthermore, there may be lengthy prerequisites for taking an examination, such as internships and courses within a local university.

3. *Immigration*. Clearing a foreign country's standards is no guarantee that it will permit foreign personnel to work there. Simply, countries want to protect the employment of their own citizens. But governmental regulations often require that an organization—domestic or foreign—search extensively for qualified personnel locally before it can even apply for work permits for personnel it would like to bring in from abroad. The delays favor local companies that can respond rapidly to unique market needs.

THE WORLD TRADE ORGANIZATION (WTO)

So far we have discussed reasons for and ways that governments restrict the free flow of trade. At the same time, governments work cooperatively to remove barriers to trade. The following discussion highlights the role of the World Trade Organization, along with the cooperative activity leading up to its formation.

The World Trade Organization is the major body for

- **Reciprocal trade negotiations**
- **Enforcement of trade agreements**

GATT: THE PREDECESSOR

In 1947, 23 countries formed an association called the General Agreement on Tariffs and Trade (GATT) to negotiate reductions in trade restrictions and work toward common procedures for handling imports and exports. By 1995, 117 countries were

Looking to the Future
THE PROSPECTS FOR FREER TRADE

Countries prefer to act independently; however, they cede authority on trade when they perceive cooperation to be in their overall best interest. For example, countries have ceded authority to the binding dispute-settlement provisions of the WTO, and they have banded together on other trade issues, such as multilateral treaties on ivory trade to save elephants. However, countries are free to withdraw from agreements. At some point, a country might withdraw from the WTO rather than follow its findings in a trade dispute. Such action could greatly hamper trade liberalization, particularly if the United States or the EU were to withdraw.

The issue of environmental standards for products and their production is far from settled. Countries with strict environmental regulations will undoubtedly consider imposing "green countervailing duties" to compensate for the cost advantages of operating where regulations are lax. Producers facing these import restrictions undoubtedly will claim that environmental standards are really a ruse to protect domestic producers. Further, governments of emerging economies fear that stricter standards on how to make products will place them at a disadvantage.[49]

Ultimately, trade policy depends heavily on public opinion, and groups that see themselves as adversely affected by imports are apt to be more vocal and persuasive at molding public opinion than people who benefit from trade. In this respect, a majority of people in the United States feel that foreign trade has been bad for the U.S. economy—even as the economy is booming economically.[50] This portends difficulty in bringing about much further trade liberalization.

Although the above examples seem to indicate possible difficulty in bringing about freer trade, there are other more optimistic indications regarding trade growth. Global trade has been growing rapidly and should continue to do so, in part because of the movement in many countries to privatize formerly government-owned companies and to open up import markets so that domestic companies will be forced to operate more efficiently by having to compete. These movements have been especially important in Eastern Europe, in the newly industrialized countries of Asia, and in Latin American countries.

participating. GATT's most important activity was sponsoring rounds, or sessions, named for the place in which each began, such as the Tokyo Round and the Uruguay Round. These led to a number of multilateral reductions in tariffs and nontariff barriers for its members. Reductions were across the board; that is, countries agreed to lower tariffs on all products from all countries by a given percentage over some specified time period. Not all countries reduced their tariffs by the same percentage though. One might reduce its tariffs by 25 percent, another by 30 percent. The amount of reduction depended on countries' different tariff levels before negotiations and their bargaining strengths. The across-the-board procedure simplified negotiations. Given the thousands of products traded, it would be nearly impossible for a country to negotiate each one separately, and even more difficult to negotiate each product separately with each country separately. Nevertheless, each country brought to the negotiations certain products and services and trade controls it considered exceptions to its own across-the-board reductions. These exceptions sometimes led to no reductions by the countries making them. For example, in the Uruguay Round that began in 1986 and took effect in 1995, France did not eliminate protection of its film industry and the United States kept its restrictions on shipping trade. Exceptions sometimes led to negotiated reductions in order to gain concessions from other countries. In the Uruguay Round, for example, the United States first said that it would not negotiate its antidumping laws. But because these laws were so unpopular in emerging economies, the United States finally agreed to cede antidumping disputes to an international tribunal in exchange for emerging economies' agreement to protect patents, trademarks, and copyrights. Such negotiations resulted in vast tariff reductions—an indication not only that countries are committed to work jointly toward freer trade but also that tariffs are the easiest trade barrier to tackle.

In addition to tariff concerns, negotiating rounds have grappled with the increasingly important and complex nontariff barriers, especially in five specific areas: industrial standards, government procurement, subsidies and countervailing duties (duties in response to another country's protectionist measures), licensing, and customs valuation. In each of these areas, conference members agreed on a code of conduct whereby they have the same product standards for imports as for domestically produced goods, treat bids by foreign companies on a nondiscriminatory basis for most large contracts, prohibit export subsidies except on agricultural products, simplify licensing procedures that permit foreign-produced goods to be imported, and use a uniform procedure to value imports when assessing duties on them.

In spite of its many accomplishments, GATT had inherent weaknesses. Because of having so many members negotiate simultaneously on so many products and issues, closure became more cumbersome. The last negotiations under the Uruguay Round took more than seven years and accomplished less than countries had originally envisioned. Next, GATT concessions applied to all countries (with a few exceptions) under a clause known as **most-favored nation**, which means that a country's most favorable trade concessions must apply to all trading partners. Thus, governments became concerned that nonmembers were "free riders," gaining freer foreign entry for their products without having to make concessions of their own. Finally, GATT provided no effective means of assuring compliance with negotiated agreements. Countries could take trade disputes to the membership, but GATT rules necessitated unanimity for trade penalties, and no country was apt to vote against itself when there were complaints against it. Instead, a GATT subgroup would investigate a complaint to determine whether allegations were valid. If so, GATT had to depend on a mutual commitment to cooperate in order to make countries alter their trade practices.

FUNCTIONS OF THE WTO

The WTO was formally established in 1995 to replace GATT and deal with its shortcomings. The WTO now has more than 130 members.

The Negotiating Process   GATT concentrated primarily on product tariffs, particularly those products that countries considered to be less sensitive to their national interests. By the time of the Uruguay Round, most of these tariffs had become negligible, but governments still saw a need to reduce barriers on more sensitive products, such as agricultural goods and textiles. Further, governments had more interest in restricting trade in services (such as financial services, domestic shipping, insurance, and telecommunications), nontariff barriers to trade, protection of intellectual-property rights (patents, copyrights, and trademarks), and investment policies that affect trade. It is simply not practical for representatives from over 130 countries to discuss all these issues simultaneously under one blanket agreement. As a result, WTO members are dealing with each of these areas separately and on a continual basis, such as with agreements to enter each other's telecommunications markets. Nevertheless, the WTO has not ruled out the possibility of future rounds of negotiations dealing with a broad spectrum of products and trade issues.

Granting of Normal Trade Relations   The WTO has replaced the most-favored-nation clause of GATT with the concept of normal trade relations, which applies only to WTO members. (Word usage changes slowly, and normal trade relations are still often called most-favored nation, or MFN.) The change effectively eliminates the free-rider complaint that existed during GATT. Countries sometimes make the following exceptions:

1. Emerging economies' manufactured products have been given preferential treatment over those from industrial countries. For example, most industrial countries grant tariff preferences to emerging economies under the Generalized System of Preferences (GSP), because emerging economies need to export more for their economic development.[51]
2. Concessions granted to members within a regional trading alliance, such as the EU or the North American Free Trade Association (NAFTA), have not been extended to countries outside the alliance. The rationale for regional trading arrangements is discussed in Chapter 7.
3. Exceptions are made in times of war or international tension. For example, the United States and Cuba do not grant normal trade relations to each other because of political tensions between them.

Settlement of Disputes   There are many ways in which countries might prevent imports even after they have negotiated their freer entry. They may set arbitrary health or safety standards that favor their home-country production. Under the WTO, there is a clearly defined dispute settlement mechanism. Countries may bring charges to a WTO panel, and countries accused of engaging in unfair trade practices may appeal. To ensure efficiency, there are time limits on all stages of deliberations. Ultimately the panel's rulings are binding. If an offending country fails to comply with panel recommendations, its trading partners are guaranteed the right to compensation. As a final resort, the trading partners are given the right to impose countervailing sanctions (such as the duties the United States placed on EU goods because of the EU's banana import restrictions) against the offending country. So far the WTO's dispute-settlement body has had a much heavier caseload than existed under the old GATT system, probably because of countries' confidence that there will be adherence to rulings. This confidence has caused small and emerging economies to complain more about trade practices in other countries. For example, India, Pakistan, Malaysia, and Thailand won their complaint against the United States over a shrimp import ban.[52] However, during the first five years of the WTO, the United States and the EU filed over half the complaints. By bringing cases to the panel, accused countries may agree to settle before a ruling is made. For example, South Korea agreed to extend the shelf life of meat products after the United States made a formal complaint that the short shelf life discriminated against imports.

When facing import competition, companies can
- **Move abroad**
- **Seek other market niches**
- **Make domestic output competitive**
- **Try to get protection**

DEALING WITH GOVERNMENTAL TRADE INFLUENCES

When companies have the potential of losing market share because of import competition, or when they are unable to compete effectively abroad, they have a number of options:

- Move production to a lower-cost country
- Concentrate on market niches in which there is less international competition
- Effect internal adjustments, such as cost efficiencies, product innovations, or improved marketing

Clearly, there are substantial costs, as well as considerable uncertainty as to outcome, associated with any one of these options. Nevertheless, companies follow all these options. For example, when faced with competition from Japanese imports, the U.S. automobile industry moved some production abroad, such as Ford sourcing in Mexico. The industry also arranged for foreign companies to supply their small cars, thus enabling them to concentrate more of their production efforts on larger cars, for which there is less foreign competition and where U.S. producers have demonstrated a competitive advantage. It also pursued cost-saving measures. However, these methods are not always feasible. For example, companies may lack the resources to shift production abroad. They may identify no apparent niches that are less competitive. Even if they manage to effect cost savings, these may be quickly copied by foreign competitors. In such a situation, companies may seek assistance from their governments to limit imports or open foreign markets for them. In the case of automobiles, the U.S. industry sought and received some protection from Japanese imports in the form of quotas. In the case of Chiquita and Dole's inability to increase their EU market share, they sought and received assistance from the U.S. government to pressure the EU through retaliatory tariffs.

However, governments do not take up the cause of every company with international competitive problems. Companies must convince governmental decision makers to take up their causes. To do so, they must identify who the key decision makers are. In the United States, they could be in the elected executive branch, in Congress, or among career civil servants. However, most policies are made by congressmen who are largely interested in what happens within their own districts.[53] In other countries, the key players may be somewhere else. To influence them requires presenting effective arguments and demonstrating that many voters and interest groups support the position. For example, managers may use any of the economic and noneconomic arguments presented in this chapter. It helps to get all companies from an industry allied. Otherwise, officials may feel problems are due to the company's inefficiencies rather than to import problems. It helps to get all stakeholders involved. When the U.S. auto industry sought relief from Japanese auto competition, for example, both company managers and union representatives worked together. Managers may also identify other groups that may have a common objective, even though for different reasons. For example, the International Brotherhood of Teamsters worried about U.S. job losses because of citrus imports from Brazil, and it allied with activist groups concerned about the use of child labor in Brazil in order to get support for citrus import restrictions.[54] Companies may also try to build public support by advertising their position. Finally companies need to lobby the decision makers and support the political candidates who can help their cause.

From the preceding discussion, it is clear that companies may take different approaches to counter changes in the international competitive environment. But they differ in their attitudes toward protectionism because of the investments they have already made to develop their international strategies.[55] Companies most apt to lose with increased protectionism are those that depend primarily on trade (whether market seekers or resource acquirers) and those that have integrated their production among different countries. Those companies most apt to gain have single or multidomestic production facilities, such as production in the United States to serve the U.S. market and production in Mexico to serve the Mexican market. Companies also differ in their perceived abilities to compete against imports. In nearly half the cases over the last 60 years in which U.S. firms have proposed protection for a U.S. industry, one or more companies in the industry have been against it. This is because they enjoy competitive advantages through such means as scale economies, relationships with suppliers, or differentiated products. They believe not only that they can compete but also that they will gain more power by having imports compete primarily against their weak domestic competitors, thus fragmenting that competition.[56] Moreover, governmental authorities may not help companies even when they present good cases.

The discussion in Chapter 5 showed that countries attempt to become more competitive by, say, upgrading production factors such as human skills. However, countries have objectives other than economic competitiveness that, when pursued, may harm their domestic production and economic efficiency. Governmental decision makers must respond to these objectives. We have alluded to several such situations in this chapter. For example, the cessation of trade for political reasons may hurt a country's exporters, sometimes abruptly, and may cause other domestic companies to encounter supply problems.

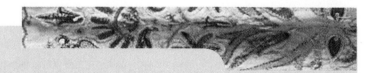

WEB CONNECTION

Check out our home page www.prenhall.com/daniels for links to key resources for you in your study of international business.

SUMMARY

- Despite the potential resource benefit of free trade, no country permits an unregulated flow of goods and services.

- Given the possibility of retaliation and the fact that imports as well as exports create jobs, it is difficult to determine the effect on employment of protecting an industry.

- Policy makers have not yet solved the problem of income redistribution due to changes in trade policy.

- The infant-industry argument for protection holds that without governmental prevention of import competition, certain industries would be unable to move from high-cost to low-cost production.

- Because industrial countries are generally more advanced economically than nonindustrial ones are, governmental interference is often argued to be beneficial if it promotes industrialization.

- Trade controls are used to regulate prices of goods traded internationally. Their objectives include protection of monopoly positions, prevention of foreign monopoly prices, greater assurance that domestic consumers get low prices, and lower profit margins for foreign producers.

- Much of the governmental interference in international trade is motivated by political rather than economic concerns, including maintaining domestic supplies of essen-

tial goods and preventing potential enemies from gaining goods that would help them achieve their objectives.

- Many nonindustrial countries are seeking export markets within the industrialized world for their manufactured products but argue that the effective tariffs on their products are too high.

- Trade controls that directly affect price and indirectly affect quantity include tariffs, subsidies, arbitrary customs-valuations methods, and special fees.

- Trade controls that directly affect quantity and indirectly affect price include quotas, buy local legislation, arbitrary standards, licensing arrangements, foreign-exchange controls, administrative delays, and requirements to take goods in exchange.

- The General Agreement on Tariffs and Trade (GATT) was the main negotiating body through which countries multilaterally reduced trade barriers and agreed on simplified mechanisms for the conduct of international trade. The World Trade Organization (WTO) replaced GATT and has a continual means of negotiating and a better means of enforcing agreements.

- A company's development of an international strategy will greatly determine whether it will benefit more from protectionism or from some other means for countering international competition.

C A S E

UNITED STATES–CUBAN TRADE[57]

In 1999, the Cuban National Assembly claimed the United States violated the 1948 United Nations convention against genocide through its 37-year trade embargo that brought hunger, sickness, suffering, and death on the Cuban people. Strangely, this pronouncement came shortly after the United States eased rules on U.S.-Cuban relations that included simplified permission for U.S. citizens to travel to Cuba, easier rules for sending pharmaceuticals to Cuba, and permission for U.S. households to send $1,200 per year via Western Union to people in Cuba. However, U.S.-Cuban relations have seen even stranger twists and turns during the 40 years since Fidel Castro came to power.

THE HELMS-BURTON LAW

In 1996, President Clinton signed the Helms-Burton bill. The legislation provides for legal action (to seize U.S. assets) against non-U.S. companies using expropriated property in Cuba that U.S. citizens (including Cuban exiles) had owned, and denies executives of these companies and their families the right to visit the United States. It also prohibits normal U.S. relations with any future Cuban government that includes Castro. Some proponents of the bill argued that its passage would lead to reduced business relations with non-U.S. companies in Cuba, a resultant weakening of the Cuban economy, and the downfall of the Castro government. Other proponents argued that its passage would send a strong message of disapproval about Cuban human rights, even if the above chain of actions did not transpire.

The impetus for the bill was the shooting down of two Miami-based civilian aircraft by Cuban jets. These and other aircraft flew frequently near Cuba to look for refugee boats. However, there was conflicting evidence on whether these particular aircraft had been in Cuban territory. Prior to this incident, there had been virtually no trade between the two countries since 1961.

BACKGROUND: THE EMBARGO

After Castro overthrew the Batista government in 1959, he made pronouncements about starting revolutions elsewhere in Latin America. The United States countered by canceling its agreements to buy Cuban sugar, and Cuba retaliated by seizing U.S. oil refineries. The oil companies then refused to supply Cuba with crude oil, and Cuba turned to the Soviet Union for supplies. Because this occurred at the height of the Cold War, when the United States and the Soviet Union had few business relations, the United States quickly severed diplomatic relations with Cuba. Figure 6.5 is a time line of major events in U.S.-Cuban relations.

The incidents that further strained relations during the next 35 years were too numerous to detail. Some were so serious that they threatened peace; others were almost ludicrous. They included the U.S. sponsorship of an invasion by Cuban exiles at the Bay of Pigs, the placement and removal of Soviet missiles in Cuba, the deployment of Cuban forces to overthrow regimes that the United States supported (such as in Nicaragua and Angola), and exposés that the CIA had tried to airlift someone to assassinate Castro and had spent thousands of dollars to develop a powder to make his beard fall out.

Initially, many countries supported the U.S. embargo on Cuba. All the members of the Organization of American States except Mexico agreed in 1964 to an embargo. But one by one, countries began trading with Cuba anyway. In 1995 the UN General Assembly voted 117 to 3 against the U.S. embargo. Only Israel and Uzbekistan voted with the United States, and both of these countries trade with Cuba.

OPPOSING VIEWPOINTS

Not all U.S. public opinion has favored U.S. economic sanctions against Cuba. Opponents of the Helms-Burton legislation believed that the reprisals on foreign companies would not weaken Castro's political power. Further, they argued that the legislation would lead to retaliation and a deepening of the U.S. immigration problem. In fact, many prominent people in the United States (including heads of major firms, senators from both parties, and labor leaders) favored normalization of U.S.-Cuban trade rather than tightening the economic noose on Cuba. They argued that the end of the Cold War had weakened Cuba's political and military threat, and that economic and political liberalization within Cuba is

FIGURE 6.5   Major Events in U.S.-Cuban Relations

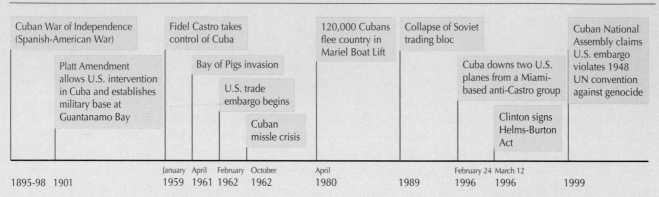

There have been many significant events affecting U.S.-Cuban relations during the last hundred years.

inevitable without massive Soviet assistance. Former U.S. Secretary of State Lawrence Eagleburger has indicated that U.S. trade actions have given Castro something, other than his inept policies, to blame for his economic policies. He said, "The worst thing that could happen would be for the U.S. to open the gates of trade and travel." Opponents further argued that increased trade with Spain and Hungary influenced their political changes, and that U.S. companies are losing business opportunities in Cuba to non-U.S. companies.

Will the Legislation Work?   Although the long trade embargo has not toppled Castro, proponents of Helms-Burton reason that the Cuban economy is so weak that a demoralized population will support a disgruntled military overthrow of the government if economic conditions deteriorate just a little more. They point to Cuba's poor economic conditions, electric outages, and a disintegrating infrastructure affecting roads, schools, and hospitals. They also cite examples of companies that have pulled out of discussions to do business in Cuba since the enactment of Helms-Burton, including Cemex from Mexico and ING from the Netherlands. Meanwhile, opponents point to signs of an improved Cuban economy since 1994 due to increases in tourism. This improvement, they reason, will strengthen Castro, who still enjoys considerable popularity (whether or not among a majority) in Cuba. They have also cited many examples of companies that are unconcerned about Helms-Burton. For example, executives of Spain's Sol Melía hotel chain said

they would continue expanding in Cuba even if it meant relinquishing their hotel properties in Florida.

Retaliation   Most major countries, such as Canada and Mexico—even the European Union—have condemned Helms-Burton, so much that the U.S. government has effectively waived the bill's enforcement.

Expropriation Issue   Expropriation of property that U.S. citizens owned in Cuba has been an issue in the normalization of U.S.-Cuban relations since the early 1960s. However, Cuba has settled with other countries by paying for the properties when they ended their embargoes. Cuba has also indicated a willingness to negotiate the expropriation issue with the United States. Helms-Burton makes this issue more complex because it addresses property that Cuba seized from Cuban citizens who subsequently became U.S. citizens. Concomitantly, by 1999 Cuba had signed bilateral investment accords with 36 countries.

Immigration Pressure   Proponents of Helms-Burton argue that the overthrow of Castro will eliminate pressure for the United States to accept political refugees from Cuba. However, opponents counter that most pressure to accept Cuban immigration has arisen because of economic conditions in Cuba, so any success at weakening the Cuban economy will increase immigration pressure

U.S. Business Losses   Before the Castro takeover in 1959, 80 percent of Cuba's imports were from the United States. Although this level of dependency is unlikely in the future, estimates say that the United States could sell $7 billion a year to Cuba if the embargo were lifted.

Human Rights   Both the supporters and opponents of U.S. economic sanctions against Cuba concur that Cuba's jails hold political prisoners under deplorable conditions. There is also agreement that Cuba violates most of the articles in the Universal Declaration of Human Rights. On the one hand, many critics of Castro argue that the situation is getting no better. On the other hand, many people acknowledge Cuba's record in education and social welfare. For example, Cuban life expectancy now exceeds that of the United States. Further, they argue that Cuba is changing. Since 1993, Cubans have been allowed to be self-employed in about 100 occupations. Since 1994, farmers can produce and sell as they see fit, even though they cannot own the land. Cubans can now sell produce, handicrafts, and light

manufactures. There is now freedom of religion and participation in municipal elections. Opponents of economic sanctions also argue that U.S. policy has never been consistent toward countries with human rights violations and that there are a number of countries with whom the United States trades whose records are as bad as Cuba's.

QUESTIONS

1. Should the United States seek to tighten the economic grip on Cuba? If so, why?

2. Should the United States liberalize business relations with Cuba? If so, what stipulations should be put on Cuba as a requirement for trade liberalization?

3. Assume you are Fidel Castro. What kind of trade relationship with the United States would be in your best interest? What type would you be willing to accept?

CHAPTER NOTES

1   Justine Newsome and James Wilson, "Latin American Banana Growers Hail WTO Ruling," *Financial Times*, April 9, 1999, p. 4; Holman W. Jenkins, Jr., "Business World," *Wall Street Journal*, February 10, 1999, p. A23; Quentin Peel, "Banana Republican," *Financial Times*, November 14–15, 1998, p.7; Martin Wolf, "Going Bananas," *Financial Times*, March 24, 1999, p. 14; Oswaldo Ramirez-Landazuri, "What Banana Trade Means to Ecuador," *Financial Times*, April 16, 1999, p. 16; Canute James and James Wilson, "The Big Place of the Banana in a Small Part of the World," *Financial Times*, March 19, 1999, p. 7; Mireya Navarro, "An Outpost in the Banana and Marijuana Wars," *New York Times*, March 4, 1999, p. A2; Canute James and George Parker, "US Faces Caribbean Threat to Quit Drugs Treaty," *Financial Times*, March 8, 1999, p. 1; Guy de Jonquières, "WTO Puts Skids Under Banana Regime," *Financial Times*, March 20, 1999, p. 7; Frances Williams, "WTO Ruling Could Ruin Poor Banana Economies," *Financial Times*, September 10, 1996, p. 4; David Rosenbaum, "U.S. Threatens Europe with 100% Tariffs," *New York Times*, November 11, 1998, p. C4; Andrew Harig, "Far More Is at Stake Than Bananas and Beef," *Journal of Commerce*, June 16, 1999, p. 8; Charles Ogletree and Randall Robinson, "The Banana War's Missing Link—Campaign Funding," *Christian Science Monitor*, March 31, 1999, p. 11; Daniel Dombey, "EU Finds Bananas a Slippery Case," *Financial Times*, January 16, 1998, p. 5; Rachel Simpson, "Banana War Victims Make Plea," *The Guardian* (London), June 19, 1999, p. 21;

Annette Mccann and Lucy Patton, "Split in Banana Dispute Tactics," *The Herald* (Glasgow), March 18, 1999, p. 2; Heidi Przybyla, "US Firms Slipping on EU Banana Tariff," *Journal of Commerce*, April 6, 1999, p. 1A; David Sanger, "Miffed at Europe, U.S. Raises Tariffs for Luxury Goods," *New York Times*, March 4, 1999, p. A1; Guy de Jonquières, "Trade Goes Bananas," *Financial Times*, January 26, 1999, p. 15; Teresa Poole, "Goatherds Hit Hard by Row over Bananas," *The Independent* (London), April 10, 1999, p. 16.

2   Nancy Dunne, "U.S. Shoots Itself in the Foot," *Financial Times*, August 22, 1995, p. 6, reporting on a 1995 study by the U.S. International Trade Commission, "The Economic Effects of Antidumping and Countervailing Duty (AD/CVD) Orders and Suspension Agreements."

3   "U.S. Turns Up Heat on Tokyo as List Is Due," *Asian Wall Street Journal*, May 16, 1995, p. 1.

4   Peter Truell, "Textile Makers Demanding More Protection Threaten Hopes for Seamless U.S. Trade Policy," *Wall Street Journal*, May 16, 1990, p. A20; and Eduardo Lachica, "Alliance of Textile and Apparel Makers Splits as Senate Mulls Import-Quota Bill," *Wall Street Journal*, July 13, 1990, p. A10.

5   Alexander Dagg, "Keeping the Jobs at Home," *Globe and Mail* (Toronto), July 3, 1990, p. 18. For experience of workers in the U.S. textile and apparel industries, see Ben S. Shipped, Jr., "Labor Market Effects of Import Competition: Theory and Evidence from the Textile and Apparel Industries," *Atlantic Economic Journal*, Vol. 27, No. 2, June 1999, pp. 193–200.

6   Ethan Kapstein, "Trade Liberalization and the Politics of Trade Adjustment Assistance," *International Labour Review*, Vol. 137, No. 4, 1998, pp. 501–516.

7   This argument is most associated with the writings of Raul Prebisch, Hans Singer, and Gunnar Myrdal in the 1950s and 1960s. For a recent discussion, see John Waterbury, "The Long Gestation and Brief Triumph of Import-Substituting Industrialization," *World Development*, Vol. 27, No. 2, February 1999, pp. 323–341.

8   Paul Cashin, Hong Liang, and C. John McDermott, "Do Commodity Price Stocks Last Too Long for Stabilization Schemes to Work?" *Finance & Development*, Vol. 36, No. 3, September 1999, pp. 40–43.

9   "Careering on to Asia's Highway," *Economist*, October 15, 1994, pp. 81–82.

10   Ravi Sarathy, "The Interplay of Industrial Policy and International Strategy: Japan's Machine Tool Industry," *California Management Review*, Vol. 31, No. 3, Spring 1989, pp. 132–160; David B. Yoffie and Helen V. Milner, "An Alternative to Free Trade or Protectionism: Why Corporations Seek Strategic Trade Policy," *California Management Review*, Vol. 31, No. 4, Summer 1989, pp. 111–131; and Laura D'Andrea Tyson, *Who's Bashing Whom?* (Washington, DC: Institute for International Economics, 1993).

11   Daniel Pearl and Helene Cooper, "FCC Adopts Rules That Will Toughen Foreign Entry into U.S. Phone Market," *Wall Street Journal*, November 29, 1995, p. A2.

12 Craig R. Whitney, "Protesters Just Say No to 'McDo'; Jospin Glad," *New York Times*, September 15, 1999, p. A17.

13 Harry Maurer and Afshin Molavi, "Carpet Merchants Need Some Magic," *Business Week*, No. 3638, June 7, 1999, p. 4.

14 Kunai Bose, "India Set to Abandon Rice Export Curbs," *Financial Times*, September 8, 1999, p. 22.

15 John Diebold, "Beyond Subsidies and Trade Quotas," *New York Times*, November 2, 1986, p. F3.

16 Paul Magnusson, "Bring Antidumping Laws Up to Date," *Business Week*, July 19, 1999, p. 45.

17 James Bovard, "Clinton's Dumping Could Sink GATT," *Wall Street Journal*, December 9, 1993, p. A14.

18 "Honey, Wool and Mohair Subsidies Are Cut," *New York Times*, October 3, 1993, p. A12.

19 Jeri Clausing, "In a Reversal, White House Will End Data-Encryption Export Curbs," *New York Times*, September 17, 1999, p. C1.

20 Michael Hirsh, "The Great Technology Giveaway?" *Foreign Affairs*, Vol. 77, No. 5, September–October 1998, pp. 2–9.

21 "France Confirms Sale of Fighter Jets to Taiwan," *Wall Street Journal*, January 8, 1993, p. A6.

22 David Sanger, "Trade Sanctions on North Korea Are Eased by U.S.," *New York Times*, September 18, 1999, p. A1.

23 William P. Corbett, Jr., "A Wasted Opportunity: Shortcomings of the Caribbean Basin Initiative Approach to Development in the West Indies and Central America," *Law and Policy in International Business*, Vol. 23, No. 4, 1992, p. 959.

24 Tony Walker, "China Warns Australia over Dalai Lama Visit," *Financial Times*, September 18, 1996, p. 1.

25 "GATT Turns Rice Trade Barriers into Tariffs,'" *Financial Times*, August 4, 1995, p. 27.

26 Bernard Simon, "US Accuses Canada of 'Unfair' Cultural Barriers," *Financial Times*, January 26, 1996, p. 5; Roger Ricklefs, "Canada Fights to Fend Off American Tastes and Tunes," *Wall Street Journal*, September 24, 1998, p. B1; and Julian Beltrame, "Pact Lets U.S. Publishers Wholly Own Canadian Magazines, Averting Battle," *Wall Street Journal*, May 27, 1999, p. B5.

27 Bill Grantham, "America the Menace," *World Policy Journal*, Vol. XV, No. 2, Summer 1998, pp. 58–65.

28 Guy de Jonquières, "Report Says EU's Tariffs No Longer Cost Effective," *Financial Times*, April 15, 1996, p. 3.

29 Ari M. Rubenstein, "Commodities Corner: Subsidize This," *Barron's*, August 23, 1999, p. MW12.

30 Gabriel R. G. Benito and Geir Gripsrud, "Promoting Efforts from Developing Countries: An Empirical Test of the Impact of Import Promotion Offices," *The International Trade Journal*, Vol. XIII, No. 2, Summer 1999, pp. 187–209.

31 "Subsidise, Apologise," *Economist*, April 4, 1992, pp. 80–82; and Asra Q. Nomani and Bushan Bahree, "Aircraft Firms Move to Delay Issue at GATT," *Wall Street Journal*, December 10, 1993, p. A3.

32 Donald L. Fischer, "Import ABCs," *Journal of Commerce*, June 30, 1999, p. 13.

33 David Pilling, "First, Bribe Your Customs Officer," *Financial Times*, October 31, 1996, p. 6.

34 Shoba Purushothaman, "Customs Classification Codes Confuse Importers, Who Cry 'Trivial Pursuit,'" *Wall Street Journal*, September 27, 1988, p. 38; Eduardo Lachica, "U.S. Designates Suzuki Samurai as Truck Import," *Wall Street Journal*, January 5, 1989, p. A3; Douglas Harbrecht and James B. Treece, "Tread Marks on Detroit," *Business Week*, May 31, 1993, p. 30; and Judy Dempsey, "Car Importers Take Apart Customs Regulations," *Financial Times*, June 29–30, 1996, p. 2.

35 Eduardo Lachica, "Evasion of Duties on Chinese Imports Costs U.S. Up to $300 Million a Year," *Wall Street Journal*, May 8, 1992, p. A3; Jonathan M. Moses, "Chinese Agency Indicted by U.S. in Customs Case," *Wall Street Journal*, October 10, 1992, p. A15; and John Ridding, "U.S. Clashes with Hong Kong over Textiles Exports," *Financial Times*, June 19, 1996, p. 4.

36 Andrew Pollack, "U.S. Sushi? Tokyo Frets. Sushi Boy Says Yes," *New York Times*, September 21, 1992, p. A5; Andrew Pollack, "Japan, Relenting, Plans to Allow Import of U.S.-Made Sushi," *New York Times*, October 4, 1992, p. 4; and "Sushi Boy Went Bankrupt, Japanese Sushi Importer Fails," *Wall Street Journal*, December 15, 1993, p. A10.

37 Philip Shenon, "In Hanoi, U.S. Goods Sold but Not by U.S.," *New York Times*, October 3, 1993, p. A1.

38 Kimberly Ann Elliott and Gary Clyde Hufbauer, "Same Song, Same Refrain? Economic Sanctions in the 1990s," *AEA Papers and Proceedings*, Vol. 89, No. 2, May 1999, pp. 405–420; and Richard N. Haass, "Sanctioning Madness," *Foreign Affairs*, Vol. 76, No. 6, November–December 1997, pp. 74–85.

39 See, for example, Michael Littlejohns, "Hunger Killing 4,500 Children a Month in Iraq," *Financial Times*, October 29, 1996, p. 7.

40 Robert Moore, "Mr. Clinton, Please Check the Label," *Wall Street Journal*, March 22, 1993, p. A14.

41 Erika Morphy, "Gauging Tomorrow's Standards," *Export Today*, August 1995, pp. 48–53.

42 James Carney, Dick Thompson, Bruce Crumley, and Maggie Sieger, "Food Fight," *Time*, September 13, 1999, pp. 43–44.

43 Steve Glain, "From Sausages to Autos, U.S. Products Still Face Trade Hurdles in South Korea," *Wall Street Journal*, May 31, 1994, p. A11; Julia Preston, "UPS Cancels Some Mexican Services in a Setback to Trade Pact," *New York Times*, July 13, 1995, p. C2.

44 Michiyo Nakamoto, "EU to Take Action on Japanese Port Practices," *Financial Times*, October 16, 1996, p. 7.

45 David Biederman, "Offsets and Countertrade," *Traffic World*, Vol. 259, No. 6, August 9, 1999, p. 18; and Jonathan Bell, "Plane Trading," *Airfinance Journal*, June 1998, pp. 34–36.

46 Jean-François Hennart and Erin Anderson, "Countertrade and the Minimization of Transaction Costs: An Empirical Examination," *Journal of Law, Economics, and Organization*, Vol. 9, No. 2, 1993, pp. 290–313.

47 "McDonnell and Partner Win $4 Billion British Copter Deal," *New York Times*, July 14, 1995, p. C5.

48 Robert Neff and Douglas Harbrecht, "U.S. Insurers Start Making Noise in Japan," *Business Week*, March 1, 1993, p. 56.

49 Diana Tussie, "The Environment and International Trade Negotiations: Open Loops in the Developing World," *The World Economy*, Vol. 22, No. 4, June 1999, pp. 535–545.

50 A poll by the *Wall Street Journal* and NBC indicated that 58 percent of people in the United States felt that trade is bad for the economy, 32 percent that it is good, and 10 percent had no opinion. Jackie Calmes, "Despite Bouyant Economic Times, Americans Don't Buy Free Trade," *Wall Street Journal*, December 10, 1998, p. A10. See also, Michael M. Knetter, "Free Trade: Why the Public Is Unconvinced," *Financial Times*, special section on mastering global business, April 3, 1998, pp. 12–14.

51 Frances Williams, "Rich Urged to Buy More from Poor," *Financial Times*, September 21, 1999, p. 10, referring to the annual trade and development report of the UN Conference on Trade and Development. See also Mark Suzman, "Fears Grow that U.S. Tariff Benefits for Poor Countries May Fall Foul of Congress Antagonism on Trade Issues," *Financial Times*, September 1, 1999, p. 8.

52 "World Trade Organization Rules Against U.S. Ban on Shrimp Imports," *New York Times*, October 16, 1998, in Bloomberg News Release (*http://www personal.umd.umich. edu/~mtwomey/newspapers/101698wt.html*).

53 Ralph G. Carter and Lorraine Eden, "Who Makes U.S. Trade Policy?" *The International Trade Journal*, Vol. XIII, No. 1, Spring 1999, pp. 53–100.

54 Matt Moffett, "Citrus Squeeze," *Wall Street Journal*, September 6, 1998, p. A1.

55 For a discussion of MNEs' lobbying efforts for protectionism, see Giles Merrill, "Coping with the 'New Protectionism': How Companies Are Learning to Love It," *International Management*, Vol. 41, No. 9, September 1986, pp. 20–26.

56 Eugene Salorio, "Trade Barriers and Corporate Strategies: Why Some Firms Oppose Import Protection for Their Own Industry," unpublished DBA dissertation, Harvard University, 1991.

57 Data for the case were taken from Alan Burchardt, "Containing Cuba" (graphic), *Indiana Daily Student* (Indiana University student newspaper, Bloomington, IN), August 1, 1996, p. 4; Mark Heinzl, "Canadian Will Take His Chances in Cuba," *Wall Street Journal*, July 29, 1996, p. A9; Julie Wolf and Brian Coleman, "U.S. Bid to Punish Foreign Companies Trading with Cuba Gets EU Challenge," *Wall Street Journal*, July 31, 1996, p. A11; Carla Anne Robbins and Jose de Cordoba, "Clinton Puts Cuba Lawsuits on Hold," *Wall Street Journal*, July 17, 1996, p. A10; Pascal Fletcher, "US Anti-Cuba Law Feeds Businessmen's Paranoia," *Financial Times*, July 2, 1996, p. 5; Pascal Fletcher, "Cuba Confident of Growth Despite US Legislation," *Financial Times*, June 18, 1996, p. 6; Lionel Barber, "Europe Vows to Act on US Anti Cuba Law," *Financial Times*, July 16, 1996, p. 1; "The Last Caudillo," Irving Louis Horowitz and Jaime Suchlicki, "Repression Forever?" and John Train, "The Demoralized Island," *Freedom Review*, Vol. 27, No. 2, March–April 1996, pp. 18–25; Wayne S. Smith, "Cuba's Long Reform," *Foreign Affairs*, March 1996, p. 99; Carla Anne Robbins, "Clinton to Ease Travel, Aid Limits on Cuba," *Wall Street Journal*, March 20, 1998, p. A3; David White, Robert Graham, and Stefan Wagstyl, "EU Groups Welcome Deal on US Sanctions," *Financial Times*, May 19, 1999, p. 11; William M. LeoGrande, "From Havana to Miami: U.S. Cuba Policy as a Two-Level Game," *Journal of Interamerican Studies and World Affairs*, Vol. 40, No. 1, Spring 1998, pp. 67–86; Albert R. Hunt, "End the Anachronistic Embargo Against Cuba," *Wall Street Journal*, April 22, 1999, p. A23; "Cuba Revisits Foreign Investment Policy," *New York Times*, May 16, 1999, p. 16; James C. McKinley, Jr., "In Cuba's New Dual Economy, Have-Nots Far Exceed Haves," *New York Times*, January 11, 1999, p. A1; Tim Golden, "U.S., Avoiding Castro, Relaxes Rules on Cuba," *New York Times*, July 7, 1999, p. A1; and Pascal Fletcher, "Cuba Brands US Sanctions 'Genocide,'" *Financial Times*, September 14, 1999, p. 6. For Internet information on the U.S. embargo on Cuba see *members.aol.com/USLAMAF/embargoinfo.html#anchor28266*. For Internet information on Cuban demographics and commerce, see *www.jmbco.com/cubafact.htm#SEC4*.

CHAPTER 7

Regional Economic Integration and Cooperative Agreements

Marrying is easy, but housekeeping is hard. —GERMAN PROVERB

OBJECTIVES

- To define different forms of economic integration and how it affects international business

- To describe the static and dynamic effects and the trade creation and diversion dimensions of economic integration

- To present different regional trading groups, such as the European Union (EU), the North American Free Trade Agreement (NAFTA), and Asia-Pacific Economic Cooperation (APEC)

- To describe the rationale for and success of commodity agreements

- To discuss the effects of economic integration on the environment

At the close of the 1990s, Ford Motor Company faced several key challenges in Europe. The introduction of the new European currency, the euro, meant that shoppers could compare prices across Europe easier than ever before and buy from the country with the cheapest prices. Asian auto manufacturers were also knocking at the door. The Europeans had successfully kept the Japanese and Koreans from mounting any serious market competition by restricting the amount of cars they could import into Europe. At the beginning of 2000, however, the European Union was poised to eliminate quotas on foreign imports, and the Japanese and Koreans were ready to enter Europe in a big way, putting pressure on the market share and profitability of Ford and other companies that had dominated the European market for so many years. Finally, Ford was in the midst of changing its European strategy to regain lost market share by becoming more country focused and less centralized, which was the opposite of what it had been doing.

FORD IN EUROPE—AN HISTORICAL OVERVIEW

Ford's first foray into Europe was in 1903, only six months after the company was founded, when it sold its first export to a customer in the United Kingdom. This was followed by Ford's first European sales branch in Paris in 1908 and a branch in the United Kingdom in 1909. Production began in a U.K. assembly plant in 1911, followed by a French assembly operation in 1913 and the establishment of a French company in 1916. Ford did not begin operations in Germany until 1925, and it established an assembly plant only a year later. During the next several decades, Ford's European operations ran as separate subsidiaries that reported to U.S. headquarters but did not coordinate their policies in any meaningful way. This occurred because individual countries had different environments, different consumer tastes and preferences, and unique tariff and nontariff barriers to trade.

Ford did come to consider Europe as one common market rather than a collection of individual markets. In 1967, Ford changed its management structure to include its European operations under one regional umbrella organization known as Ford Europe Incorporated. Its two large U.K. and German manufacturing centers remained an important dimension of the new strategy, but they were no longer considered separate, independently operating companies. Despite nationalistic tendencies on the part of host-country management, Ford decided that, from the company's perspective, it was best to obliterate national boundaries, allowing it to cut engineering costs and achieve economies of scale in purchasing and manufacturing.

Ford began designing and assembling similar automobiles throughout Europe, rather than engineering separate cars in each market, a strategy that resulted in such models as the Escort, the Capri, and the Fiesta. It also designed common components to be used in Ford automobiles. Acknowledging the importance of market size in developing this plan, one Ford executive commented, "Neither the British nor the German company could have come up with the Capri separately, tooled it separately. Only with the whole volume of Europe in prospect did the Capri become a viable product development program." As part of Ford's evolving European strategy, its management decided to design automobiles in Germany and the United Kingdom (Ford's largest European market) and manufacture them in Belgium, Germany, Spain, and the United Kingdom.

In 1994, Ford announced a new program called Ford 2000, which resulted a year later in Ford merging the North American Automotive Operations and European Automotive Operations into a single organization, Ford Automotive Operations. The major reason for the restructuring was to cut costs and be more competitive. As stated in the 1994 annual report, "We can't allow human and financial resources to be wasted duplicating vehicle platforms, powertrains and other basic components that serve nearly identical customer needs in different markets." In its 1995 annual report, Ford announced that it was reducing the number of engine and transmission combinations used worldwide and the number of basic vehicle platforms.

In addition, Ford replaced its regional profit centers with a product line focus. Five vehicle centers were established within Ford Automotive Operations, "each with responsibility for worldwide development of the cars or trucks assigned to them." Four of the centers were established in North America and one in Europe. Europe took responsibility for the development of small and midsize cars. As part of this reorganization, Ford transferred 500 managers between Europe and North America.

Ford also designed cars to operate in several geographical areas, furthering its regional strategy. An example is the Mondeo, a collaborative effort between Europe and North America launched in March 1993. North American versions of the car are the Ford Contour and Mercury Mystique, assembled in Kansas City and Cuautitlan, Mexico. The Mondeo is sold in 52 countries. The addition of the Contour and the Mystique raises the number of countries selling those particular models to 78, while the Ford Fiesta is sold in 42 world markets.

Europe provides significant market opportunity for Ford. The reduction of barriers and integration of the different country markets in Europe caused Ford to shift its strategy from multidomestic to regional. However, Ford's 2000 Plan forced Ford to integrate its European region more closely with the United States. The merging of the North American and European automotive divisions was the first step in that process.

ENTER JACQUES NASSER

Despite all of the reorganizing, by 1998 it was obvious that Ford 2000 was not working, especially in Europe. Profits were down, market share was slipping—Ford finally fell behind both Volkswagen and General Motors—and people complained about how Ford's products were old and tired and not well positioned in the market. In 1998, Jacques Nasser became CEO of Ford Motor Company and began to question the Ford 2000 strategy that had dominated Ford thinking over the previous few years. Price competition in Europe had forced down profits, and Ford found that its centralized strategy had pushed it too far away from the local markets. Nasser was convinced that Ford needed to reintroduce the market focus. The basic idea was to replace Ford 2000 with greater autonomy for brand units and regions, especially in Europe.

Nasser appointed a new head of European operations and created a luxury-car division called the Premier Auto Group, which was comprised of Jaguar, Volvo, Lincoln, and Aston Martin. The key was to increase sales of luxury cars, which have a much higher profit margin than other autos. Will the strategy work? Even when Nasser himself was head of Ford Europe, he couldn't make Ford Europe as profitable as Ford North America. Will his new strategies of decentralization and greater emphasis on the luxury division help turn around Ford Europe and enable it to weather the onslaught of the Japanese and Korean imports, as well as respond to competitive pressures from VW and GM?

INTRODUCTION

In some respects, the United States is the perfect example of economic integration—the largest economy in the world comprised of 50 states in the continental United States plus Alaska and Hawaii, a common currency, and perfect labor and capital mobility. However, it is just one country: What about the rest of the world? In Chapter 6, we discussed the efforts of the World Trade Organization to reduce tariff and nontariff barriers with the eventual goal of global free trade. But the WTO is moving slowly. Faster progress is occurring at the regional level where countries close together already engage in a significant amount of trade. Is this the more important movement? What does regional economic integration hope to accomplish, and where will it go in the new millennium?

In the mid- to late 1940s, countries decided that to help them emerge from the wreckage of World War II and promote economic growth and stability within their borders, they would have to assist—and get assistance from—nearby countries. This chapter discusses some of the important forms of economic cooperation, such as regional economic integration and commodity agreements. Regional economic integration is the political and economic agreements among countries that give preference to member countries to the agreement. For example, regional economic groups might reduce tariffs for member countries while keeping tariffs for nonmember countries. The lowest level of cooperation usually involves at least trade, although higher forms of regional economic integration go beyond trade. But trade is usually the cornerstone of any form of regional economic integration. Commodity agreements result in cooperation among producers of commodities, such as the oil-producing countries, or between producers and consumers of commodities, such as coffee and tin.

Why do you need to understand the nature of these agreements? Regional trading groups are an important influence on MNEs' strategies. They can define the size of the

Foreign-exchange clerk Sawako Iizuka points to the euro/yen rate as the European Union's single currency makes its debut in the Tokyo, Japan, money market on January 4, 1999. The European Union hopes the euro will unite its members' economies more closely, helping to create true regional economic integration.

regional market and the rules under which companies must operate. Companies in the initial stages of foreign expansion must be aware of the regional economic groups that encompass countries with good manufacturing locations or market opportunities. As companies expand internationally, they must change their organizational structure and operating strategies to take advantage of regional trading groups. As noted in the opening case, Ford changed from being a multidomestic to a regional company in Europe, then it centralized its operations worldwide, and more recently it decentralized back to Europe in order to be responsive to national differences. The development of European integration forced Ford to look at its operations more carefully so that it could operate successfully in the market.

As noted in Chapter 6, WTO members are required to grant the same favorable trade conditions to all WTO members. However, the WTO also allows a departure from this principle in the case of regional trade agreements. Nearly all of the WTO members have concluded regional trade agreements (RTAs) with other countries. As noted on the WTO's home page (www.wto.org/wto/develop/regional.htm), 107 RTAs were in existence as of the end of 1999. Thirty-eight of the RTAs were bilateral agreements, and 28 of those involved the European Union. We focus on the European Union (EU) and the North American Free Trade Agreement (NAFTA) because of the high level of integration in both areas and especially the size and degree of integration in the EU. That is not to minimize the importance of other groups to their member countries, but we will use the groups that follow to illustrate different types of regional integration. Internet links will be provided to those groups with home pages. The most important thing is to understand how these organizations and agreements affect company strategy.

REGIONAL ECONOMIC INTEGRATION

It's logical that most trade groups contain countries in the same area of the world. Neighboring countries tend to ally for several reasons:

- The distances that goods need to travel between such countries is short.
- Consumers' tastes are likely to be similar, and distribution channels can be easily established in adjacent countries.
- Neighboring countries may have a common history and interests, and may be more willing to coordinate their policies.[2]

Countries—even if they're not neighbors—will form trade alliances/groups/agreements if their political ideologies are similar. For example, Cuba, because of its communist political and economic philosophy, was a member of the former COMECON (the Council for Mutual Economic Assistance), an association of communist countries that was disbanded when the Soviet Union broke up.

There are four basic types of regional economic integration.

1. **Free trade area (FTA).** The goal of an FTA is to abolish all tariffs between member countries. Free trade agreements usually begin modestly by eliminating tariffs on goods that already have low tariffs, and there is usually an implementation period over which all tariffs are eliminated on all products. At the same time tariffs are being eliminated, the members of the FTA might explore other forms of cooperation, such as the reduction of nontariff barriers or trade in services and investment, but the focus is clearly on tariffs. In addition, each member country maintains its own external tariff against non-FTA countries.

2. **Customs union.** In addition to eliminating internal tariffs, member countries levy a common external tariff on goods being imported from nonmembers. For example, the North American Free Trade Agreement between Canada, the United States, and Mexico has eliminated tariffs on trade among the three countries, but each country maintains a separate tariff with the outside world. If a British company exports a product to the United States, it likely will enter the country at a different tariff rate than if the product were exported to Canada or Mexico because each NAFTA country can set its own external rate. But if a U.S. company were to export a product to the United Kingdom and France, two members of the European Union, which is also a customs union, the product would enter both countries at the same tariff rate. There would be no tariff advantage to the U.S. company to enter the EU by exporting to the United Kingdom versus France.

3. **Common market.** A common market, such as MERCOSUR, has all the elements of a customs union plus it allows free mobility of production factors such as labor and capital. This means that labor, for example, is free to work in any country in the common market without restriction. In the absence of the common market arrangement, workers would have to apply to immigration for a visa, and that might be difficult to come by.

4. **Complete economic integration.** Countries create even greater economic harmonization through the adoption of common economic policies. For example, the European Union has established a common currency complete with a common Central Bank. This level of cooperation creates a degree of political integration among member countries, which means they lose a bit of their sovereignty. No region has attained complete economic integration, although the European Union—which we'll read about shortly—comes the closest.

THE EFFECTS OF INTEGRATION

Regional economic integration can affect member countries in social, cultural, political, and economic ways. For example, prior to the NAFTA accord, Canada had a small but successful film industry. However, the reduction of trade barriers would have meant that U.S. films would have overrun the Canadian market. The provinces control film distribution in Canada, and one province—Quebec—requires that foreign, including U.S., films bear a Canadian government issue classification sticker before being sold or distributed in Canada. During the NAFTA negotiations, the Canadian government did not want to change these restrictions so that it could protect its film industry. The added regulatory restrictions by Quebec mean that fewer U.S. films are being distributed than would be the case in a free trade environment.

MNEs are especially concerned with the economic effects of integration. As we noted in Chapter 6, the imposition of tariff and nontariff barriers disrupts the free flow of goods, affecting resource allocation. Regional economic integration reduces or eliminates those barriers for member countries. It produces both **static effects** and **dynamic effects**. Static effects are the shifting of resources from inefficient to efficient companies as trade barriers fall. Dynamic effects are the overall growth in the market and the impact on a company of expanding production and achieving greater economies of scale. Static effects may develop when either of two conditions occurs.

- **Trade creation**—production shifts to more efficient producers for reasons of comparative advantage, allowing consumers access to more goods at a lower price than

Regional integration has social, cultural, political, and economic effects.

Static effects of integration— the shifting of resources from inefficient to efficient companies as trade barriers fall.

Dynamic effects of integration—the overall growth in the market and the impact on a company of expanding production and achieving greater economies of scale.

Trade creation—production shifts to more efficient producers for reasons of comparative advantage, allowing consumers access to more goods at a lower price than would have been possible without integration.

would have been possible without integration. Companies that are protected in their domestic markets face real problems when the barriers are eliminated and they attempt to compete with more efficient producers. The strategic implication is that companies that might not have been able to export to another country, even though they might be more efficient than producers in that country, are now able to export when the barriers come down. Thus there will be more demand for their products and the demand for the protected, less efficient products will fall.

Trade diversion—trade shifts to countries in the group at the expense of trade with countries not in the group.

- **Trade diversion**—trade shifts to countries in the group at the expense of trade with countries not in the group, even though the nonmember company might be more efficient in the absence of trade barriers.

For example, assume U.S. companies are importing the same product from Mexico and Taiwan. If the United States enters into an FTA with Mexico but not with Taiwan, some trade will be diverted from Taiwan to Mexico to take advantage of the elimination of tariffs between Mexico and the United States. This does not mean, however, that Mexican products are any better or cheaper (in the absence of integration) than the Taiwanese goods, but the lower tariff gives them a competitive edge in the market.

Dynamic effects of integration occur when trade barriers come down and the size of the market increases. For example, Argentina, a country of 35.7 million people, is a member of MERCOSUR, a common market encompassing Argentina, Brazil, Paraguay, and Uruguay. The size of that market is 207.7 million people. Argentinean companies could export to its neighbors in the absence of a trade agreement, but high tariffs would probably limit its ability to compete. When the trade barriers come down, however, the market size to the Argentinean company increases dramatically. Because of the larger size of the market, Argentinean companies can increase their production, which will result in lower costs per unit, a phenomenon we call economies of scale. Companies can produce more cheaply, which is good because they must become more efficient to survive.

Economies of scale—the cost per unit falls as the number of units produced rises; occurs in regional integration because of the growth in the market size.

Another important dynamic effect is the increase in efficiency due to increased competition. Many MNEs in Europe have attempted to grow through mergers and acquisitions to achieve the size necessary to compete in the larger market.

MAJOR REGIONAL TRADING GROUPS

There are two ways to look at different trading groups: by location and by type. There are major trading groups in every region of the world. It is impossible to cover every group in every region, so we will cover a few of the major groups. However, it is important to understand that each regional group fits into one of the types defined above: free trade area, customs union, common market, or economic integration, with most of them being an FTA or a customs union. A customs union is also a free trade area, and a common market is also a free trade area and customs union. Economic integration encompasses everything. The regional trading groups we will discuss are classified as follows:

Regional integration:
- **By location**—Europe, North America, Asia, Africa
- **By type**—free trade area, customs union, common market, economic integration
- **Offers location-specific advantages to foreign investors due to increased market size**

1. Free trade area—the European Free Trade Association (EFTA), the Central European Free Trade Agreement (CEFTA), the North American Free Trade Agreement (NAFTA), and the Association of South East Asian Nations (ASEAN)
2. Customs union—MERCOSUR

3. Common market—the Caribbean Community and Common Market, the Central American Common Market, the Andean Group

4. Economic integration—the European Union

Companies are interested in regional trading groups for their markets, sources of raw materials, and production locations. The larger and richer the new market, the more likely it is to attract the attention of the major investor countries and companies.

THE EUROPEAN UNION

The largest and most comprehensive of the regional economic groups is the European Union. It began as a customs union, but the formation of the Euro Parliament and the establishment of a common currency, the euro, make the EU the most ambitious of all the regional trade groups.

EUROPEAN EVOLUTION TO INTEGRATION

World War II left in its wake economic as well as human destruction throughout Europe. European political leaders realized that they needed to forge greater cooperation, but they struggled to determine what shape that cooperation should take. To help rebuild Europe, the U.S. Congress passed the Marshall Plan, a $13-billion aid package. This rebuilding established the 16-country Organization for European Economic Cooperation (OEEC). The OEEC carried out the Marshall Plan and also sought to improve currency stability, combine Europe's economic strengths, and improve its trade relations. However, the OEEC was not strong enough to provide the necessary economic growth. Europe needed further efforts at cooperation.

> The OEEC was the organization of European countries established to facilitate the implementation of the Marshall Plan after World War II.

Six key countries—Belgium, France, Germany, Italy, Luxembourg, and the Netherlands—came together in 1951 to establish the European Coal and Steel Community (ECSC). Shortly after the creation of ECSC, two more organizations were formed: the European Economic Community (EEC) and the European Atomic Energy Community (Euratom). As noted in Table 7.1, the EEC eventually emerged as the organization that would bring together Europe into the most powerful trading bloc in the world. Initially, the objectives of the EEC were the

> Early forms of European integration:
> • European Coal and Steel Community
> • European Economic Community
> • European Atomic Energy Community

- Elimination of customs duties between member states
- Establishment of an external common customs tariff
- Introduction of a common policy for agriculture and transport
- Creation of a European Social Fund
- Establishment of a European Investment Bank
- Development of closer relations between member states[3]

HISTORICAL OVERVIEW

The key milestones for the European Union are summarized in Table 7.1. When the doors to EEC opened on January 1, 1958, several institutions were in place to govern the affairs of the group. Immediately, the EEC set about to abolish internal tariffs so as to more closely integrate European markets and hopefully allow economic cooperation to help avoid further political conflict. The first round of tariff reductions began in

| TABLE 7.1 | **EUROPEAN UNION MILESTONES** |

From its inception in 1957, the EU has been moving toward complete economic integration. However, it is doubtful that its initial adherents ever dreamed that European cooperation would have achieved such integration as to move to a common currency.

1946	Winston Churchill calls for a United States of Europe.
1947	The Marshall Plan for the economic revival of a Europe devastated by war is announced.
1948	The Organization for European Economic Cooperation (OEEC) is created to coordinate the Marshall Plan.
1949	The North Atlantic Treaty is signed.
1951	The Six (Belgium, France, Germany, Italy, Luxembourg, Netherlands) sign the Treaty of Paris establishing the European Coal and Steel Community (ECSC).
1952	The ECSC Treaty enters into force.
1957	The Six sign the Treaties of Rome establishing the European Economic Community (EEC) and the European Atomic Energy Community (Euratom or EAEC). They become effective on January 1, 1958.
1958	The basis for the Common Agricultural Policy is established.
1959	The first steps are taken in the progressive abolition of customs duties and quotas within the EEC.
1960	The Stockholm Convention establishes the European Free Trade Association (EFTA) among seven European countries (Austria, Denmark, Norway, Portugal, Sweden, Switzerland, United Kingdom).
	The OEEC becomes the Organization for Economic Cooperation and Development (OECD).
1961	The first regulation on free movement of workers within the EEC comes into force.
1962	The Common Agricultural Policy is created.
1965	A Treaty merging the ECSC, EEC, and Euratom is signed. The treaty enters into force on July 1, 1967.
1966	Agreement reached on a value-added tax (VAT) system; a treaty merging the Executives of the European Communities comes into force; and the EEC changes name to European Community (EC).
1967	All remaining internal tariffs are eliminated and a common external tariff is imposed.
1972	The currency "snake" is established where the Six agree to limit currency fluctuations between their currencies to 2.25 percent.
1973	Denmark, Ireland, and the United Kingdom become members of the EC.
1974	The Council sets up a European Regional Development Fund (ERDF) and Regional Policy Committee.
1979	European Monetary System comes into effect; European Parliament is elected by universal suffrage for the first time.
1980	Greece becomes tenth member of the EC.
1985	Commission sends the Council a White Paper on completion of internal market by 1992.
1986	Spain and Portugal become the eleventh and twelfth members of the EC.
	Single European Act (SEA) is signed, improving decision-making procedures and increasing the role of the European Parliament; comes into effect on July 1, 1987.
1989	Collapse of the Berlin Wall; German Democratic Republic opens its borders.
1990	The first phase of European Monetary Union (EMU) comes into effect.
	Unification of Germany.
1992	European Union signed in Maastricht; adopted by member countries on November 1, 1993.
1993	The Single European Market comes into force (January 1, 1993).
	Council concludes agreement creating European Economic Area, effective January 1, 1994.
1994	European Monetary Institute comes into effect.
1995	Austria, Finland, Sweden become the thirteenth, fourteenth, and fifteenth members of the EU.
1998	An EU summit names the 11 countries that will join the European single currency.
1999	The euro, the single European currency, comes into effect (January 1, 1999).

Sources: http://europa.eu.int/abc/obj/chrono/en/; Ernst & Whinney, *Europe 1992: The Single Market,* p. 6; and HSBC, *European Union,* 3rd ed., Fourth Quarter 1998.

1959, and all internal tariffs were eliminated by 1967. At that time, a common external tariff was imposed, which moved the EEC from being an FTA to a customs union. By then, the name of the EEC had changed to the European Community (EC).

In 1962, shortly after the round of tariff reductions took place, the EEC established the Common Agricultural Policy, an essential program designed to stabilize food production in Europe and ensure a good living for European farmers. Through a series of subsidies—the largest expenditure in the community budget, reaching $45 billion in 1999—and other forms of protection, European farmers have been ensured of a good wage and the ability to compete in world markets. European consumers, although having access to agricultural products produced inside the market, pay dearly to support the agricultural industry through value-added taxes. Although employing only 4 percent of the labor force in Europe, the agricultural lobby is extremely powerful politically and is an important source of influence on European political and economic policy.

Several more countries joined the EC in the next two decades. Map 7.1 identifies the members of the European Union and other key European groups. Figure 7.1 provides a time line for changes in membership of the EEC and the European Free Trade Agreement (EFTA), another European attempt at integration that began in 1960 with just an FTA and later lost power and influence to the EEC. Two key events occurred in

Key EU milestones:

- **Elimination of internal tariffs**
- **Common external tariff**
- **Established common agricultural policy**
- **Expanded membership**
- **Established European Monetary System**

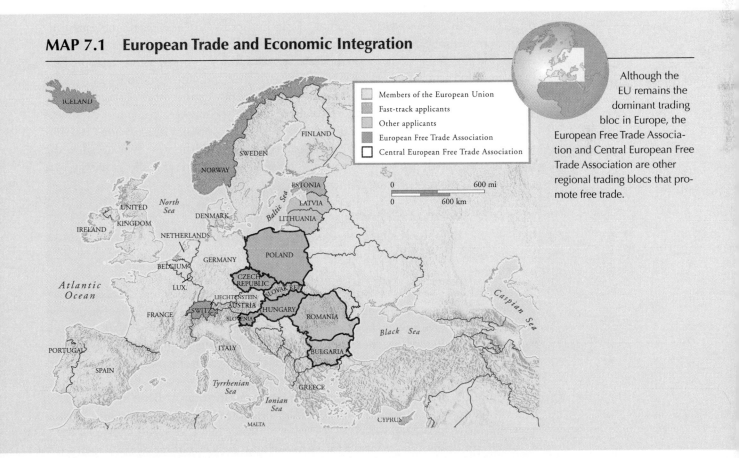

MAP 7.1 European Trade and Economic Integration

Legend:
- Members of the European Union
- Fast-track applicants
- Other applicants
- European Free Trade Association
- Central European Free Trade Association

Although the EU remains the dominant trading bloc in Europe, the European Free Trade Association and Central European Free Trade Association are other regional trading blocs that promote free trade.

FIGURE 7.1   A Time Line for EU Membership

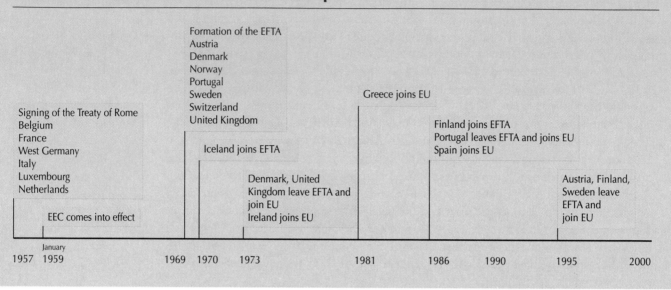

Formation of the EFTA
Austria
Denmark
Norway
Portugal
Sweden
Switzerland
United Kingdom

Greece joins EU

Signing of the Treaty of Rome
Belgium
France
West Germany
Italy
Luxembourg
Netherlands

Finland joins EFTA
Portugal leaves EFTA and joins EU
Spain joins EU

Iceland joins EFTA

Denmark, United
Kingdom leave EFTA and
join EU
Ireland joins EU

Austria, Finland,
Sweden leave
EFTA and
join EU

EEC comes into effect

| 1957 | January 1959 | 1969 | 1970 | 1973 | 1981 | 1986 | 1990 | 1995 | 2000 |

the close of the 1970s—the formation of the European Parliament and the establishment of the European Monetary System (EMS). The Euro Parliament, which is directly elected by the people, is an attempt to bring democracy into governing Europe. The European Monetary System was established to link individual national currencies together. Each country established a value for its currency against other currencies in the EC, and the member countries agreed to intervene in the markets to support those values. The goal was to stabilize exchange rates so that currency fluctuations did not replace tariffs as a way to discriminate against trade. Over the next two decades, the EMS went through periods of strength and weakness, but it eventually gave way to a new monetary order resulting in the euro.

THE EU'S ORGANIZATIONAL STRUCTURE

Initially, the European Union's organizational structure included the Commission, the Parliament, the Council of Ministers, and the Court of Justice. As noted on the EU's home page,

> They [the institutions of the EU] were created to give expression to an ever closer Union of European nations. As the Union's responsibilities have broadened, the institutions have grown larger and more numerous. In its first 20 years, the Commission would propose, the Parliament would advise, the Council of Ministers would decide and the Court of Justice would interpret. In the last 20 years, the Parliament has become directly-elected and acquired new powers, the European Court of Auditors has arrived on the scene, the European Investment Bank has emerged as a major source of finance for economic development, the Economic and Social Committee has demonstrated to the value of debate and cooperation between the economic and social partners and, most recently, the Committee of the Regions has been set up to advance regional interests and diversity.[4]

Treaties signed by member countries govern the operations of the different institutions of the EU. These treaties are subject to amendment as conditions change. In Chapter 3, we noted how important it is for MNE management to understand the political environment of every country where it operates. The same is true for the EU. To be successful in Europe, MNEs need to understand the governance of the EU, just as they need to understand the governance process of each of the individual European countries where they are investing or doing business. These institutions set parameters under which MNEs must operate, so management needs to understand the institutions and how they make decisions that could affect corporate strategy. Figure 7.2 provides a general structure of how the EU institutions work and fit together.

FIGURE 7.2   EU Organizational Structure

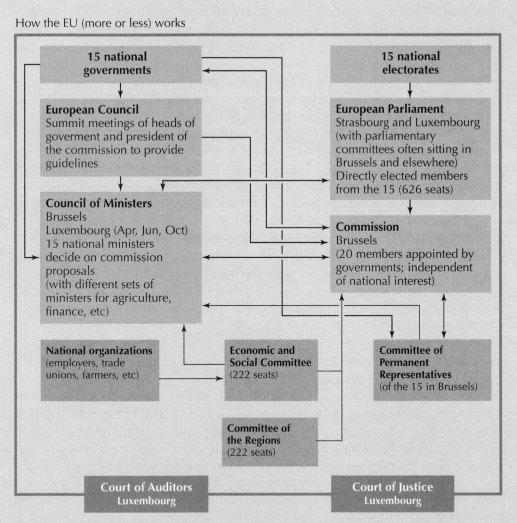

How the EU (more or less) works

The European Union has grown in structure since its inception when it was composed of only the Commission, the Parliament, the Council of Ministers, and the Court of Justice.

European Commission   At of the close of 1999, the Commission was composed of twenty people, two from France, Germany, Italy, Spain and the United Kingdom, and one from each of the other member states. These individuals tend to have held high positions in their respective national governments prior to joining the Commission, so they are well connected politically. However, they are required to act independently of instead of being advocates for their national governments. In addition, there are 15,000 staff working in different capacities. The Commission provides the EU's political leadership and direction. The original intent was for the Commission to act as a supranational government for Europe. There are three distinct functions of the Commission:

- Initiating proposals for legislation
- Guardian of the treaties
- Manager and executor of Union policies and of international trade relationships[5]

The Commission initiates proposals for legislation, is the guardian of the treaties, and is the manager and executor of Union policies and of international trade relationships.

The legislative process begins with a proposal from the Commission, which gathers input from various national constituencies and tries to determine what is in the best interest of the Community at large. The key is that legislation should take place in areas that are best dealt with by the Community rather than by individual states. This is known as the principle of subsidiarity—the EU should take action only when it will be more effective than if left to the individual states.[6] As guardian of the treaties, the Commission determines whether or not member states are correctly applying EU legislation. If the countries are not, the Commission may fine the countries or firms, subject to appeal by the Court of Justice. Finally, the Commission manages the annual budget of the EU, manages the EU, and negotiates trade agreements.

The 26 different Directorate-General (DG) offices carry out the work of the Commission. Some of the key DGs deal with trade relations with individual countries, regional trade groups such as NAFTA, and the WTO; competition inside the EU; monetary affairs; and foreign policy. More specifically, DG I is responsible for international trade policy, external political and economic relations with other regional trade groups such as NAFTA and APEC, and external relations in the area of nuclear energy. The work of DG I has a direct impact on companies exporting to or importing from the EU. Foreign companies need to be familiar with how trade policy is set and how their products will be viewed in the context of trade with the EU. In 1999, Pascal Lamy, a French socialist, was put in charge of DG I, which could be a concern to the United States given that the French are the most bitters foes of U.S. attempts to open agricultural markets in Europe.[7]

An example of how the Commission can affect corporate policy is in the area of parallel imports—where companies import products that are cheaper than the same local products. Companies such as Levi-Strauss can charge different prices for products in different countries in the EU, but sharp traders can spot the differences and buy goods at low prices in one country and sell them in another country where prices are higher. It used to be difficult to spot price differences because prices were in different currencies. Now that EU member states are using the euro, it is easier for traders to spot price differences. However, EU legislation outlaws parallel imports of cheap branded goods from outside of the EU. Due to complaints by consumer groups, parallel importers, and some retailers, the EU's single market commissioner is looking at the possibility of changing the law to allow parallel imports. Branded goods companies, such as

Levi-Strauss, are against changing the law, but powerful forces are in favor of changing the law. However, parallel goods are a small part of the overall consumption in Europe, so changing the law might not affect consumers that much.[8]

The Commission has always had a significant amount of power in the EU. However, in 1999, the Commission came under severe criticism, and its power was seriously curtailed. After serious allegations of fraud, mismanagement, and nepotism at the Commission, the entire 20-member Commission submitted mass resignations on March 16, 1999. The head of the Commission, Jacques Santer, was accused of allowing the Commission to become a "state within a state," meaning it was too powerful and autonomous.[9] However, many argue that the problems of the Commission may be good for the EU in the long run, because the power is now shifting to the Council, which more clearly represents the interests of the governments and is more likely to consider the interests of individuals in the EU. Initially, this was perceived as a weakness. The feeling was that national interests would get in the way of the work of the EU and that the Commission, acting in the interests of the EU as a whole rather than any specific government, would better advance the interests of the whole. However, the Commission became increasingly imperial and less democratic, so a move to shift power to the Council should bring democracy back into the decision making of the EU.[10]

> **The Commission has lost power vis-à-vis the Council of Ministers.**

European Council   The Council is also known as the Council of Ministers, which is composed of different ministers of the member countries. However, this doesn't mean that there are just 15 members of the Council of the EU (one for each member country at the end of 1999). There are more than 25 different Councils, such as Foreign Affairs, Economy and Finance, and Agriculture.[11] For example, the Agriculture Council of Ministers is comprised of the Ministers of Agriculture of all member countries. This specific Council whose members represent their member governments decides issues dealing with agriculture. In many respects, the Council is much more democratic than the Commission because its members are elected officials in their home countries. The Council of Ministers is presided over by a presidency, which rotates between the member states every six months.

> **The Council of Ministers is a collection of 25 different councils representing the different ministries in each country, such as the Ministers of Agriculture. They have the final say over legislation in conjunction with Parliament.**

The Council has a tremendous amount of authority because it can adopt Commission-proposed legislation, amend it, or ignore it. The Council has the final say in legislative matters in cooperation with Parliament. As the Parliament's role has strengthened in recent years, the Treaty on the EU provided for a codecision procedure where both the Council and Parliament must adopt a wide range of legislation.

The voting process in the Council is complex. There are three "pillars" of activity that must be decided by unanimity or a qualified majority. Instead of one country, one vote, the votes are allocated on the basis of population size. Germany, France, Italy, and the United Kingdom are allotted ten votes each; Spain, eight votes; Belgium, Greece, Netherlands, and Portugal, five votes each; Austria and Sweden, four votes each; Ireland, Denmark, and Finland, three votes each; and Luxembourg, two votes. Some legislation in Pillar One, such as legislation in areas relating to taxation, industry, culture, regional and social funds, must be passed by a unanimous vote. In other cases in Pillar One, such as agriculture, fisheries, internal market, environment, and transport, the Council decides by a qualified majority vote. All Commission proposals must be approved by at least 62 votes. In other cases, the qualified majority must be at least 62 votes from at least 10 member states. Most Pillar Two activities (Common Foreign and Security Policy) and Pillar Three activities (cooperation in the fields of Justice and Home Affairs) are decided by unanimity.[12]

At least twice a year, the heads of state and government of each member country meet as the European Council or European Summit. The President of the Commission is also a member of the European Council, and the President of the European Parliament is always invited to address the opening session. The European Council is important because it sets priorities, gives political direction, and resolves issues that the Council of Ministers cannot resolve. With the problems facing the Commission discussed above, the European Council and Council of Ministers have now taken control of the direction of the EU. "They are bolder and wiser than the European Commission, and they have a more direct democratic mandate."[13] The ascendancy of the European Council and Council of Ministers means that the efforts of the EU will have more influence and support by the individual countries, and this could hasten the integration process. Now the European Council will lead, the European Commission will be its servant and draftsman, and the European Parliament its sounding board.[14]

> **The European Council or European Summit is comprised of the heads of state and government of each member country.**

The European Parliament

The Parliament is comprised of 626 members elected every five years, and its membership is based on country population. It ranges from 99 members for Germany to only 6 from Luxembourg. The members are elected directly in each country, and they represent the extremes of the political spectrum and over 100 different political parties, although members are grouped into 8 different political groups or philosophies. The Parliament has become significantly stronger since its inception. Initially, the Parliament was simply an advisory body, but its responsibilities were widened through the Single European Act and Treaty of the European Union of 1993. The three major responsibilities of the Parliament are legislative power, control over the budget, and supervision of executive decisions. The Commission presents community legislation to the Parliament. Parliament must approve the legislation before submitting it to the Council for adoption. Parliament may approve legislation, amend it, or reject it outright. Parliament also approves the EU's budget each year and monitors spending.[15]

> **The three major responsibilities of the European Parliament are legislative power, control over the budget, and supervision of executive decisions.**

In the 1999 elections, Parliament ended up with a decidedly conservative complexion made up of several different coalitions of parties. However, no particular party or party group ended up with a majority, and decisions of Parliament must be passed with a majority vote, meaning that coalitions and compromises are essential for Parliament to be successful. The major conservative coalition, the European People's Party, had only 37 percent of the members of the 1999 Parliament. But it was the Parliament that issued a report on nepotism and incompetence in the Commission that forced the Commission to resign in 1999, so the Parliament is exhibiting more power than had been case in the early years of the EU.[16]

The European Court of Justice

The Court of Justice ensures consistent interpretation and application of EU treaties. Member states, Community institutions, or individuals and companies may bring cases to the Court. The Court of Justice is an appeals court for individuals, firms, and organizations fined by the Commission for infringing Treaty Law. There are 15 judges, one from each member state.[17] The reason why the

Court of Justice is relevant to MNCs is because it deals mostly with economic matters. It is hard to determine what the philosophy is of individual judges, because the Court does not release their opinions to ensure that national interests are not brought into the decision-making process. The Court is required to hear every case referred to it, even minor disputes over trade regulation and export issues. In recent cases, for example, "the Court of Justice has taken up a high-profile case involving aviation agreements between the U.S. and Europe; overturned a $3 billion subsidy the EU awarded to Air France; and accepted a case challenging the French government's ban on genetically modified corn. The Court also upheld the ban on exports of British beef as a result of disputes over mad-cow disease."[18]

The European Court of Justice ensures consistent interpretation and application of EU treaties.

Other EU Institutions   As noted, the institutions mentioned above are the key ones that govern the EU. However, there are others, such as the European Court of Auditors, the European Investment Bank, the Economic and Social Committee, the Committee of the Regions, the European Ombudsman, and the European Central Bank. More information on them can be found on the EU Web site, http://europa.eu.int/inst-en.htm. All play an important role supporting the other institutions described above.

THE SINGLE EUROPEAN MARKET

As Table 7.2 shows, in 1997 the EU membership had a population and GNP just behind NAFTA (Canada, the United States, and Mexico), making it a formidable economic bloc. However, the early part of the 1980s was a difficult time for the EU. From 1970 to 1975, the EC's GDP averaged 2.7 percent growth per year, but this figure dropped to approximately 1.4 percent annually from 1980 through 1985. In contrast, the United States recorded 2.2 percent and 2.5 percent growth rates for those periods, respectively, and Japan experienced rates of 7.6 percent and 3.8 percent, respectively.[19] It was evident the EU needed more than the elimination of tariffs to achieve economic growth. It needed to be one market. A variety of nontariff barriers was keeping it from being a true common market and from enjoying the benefits of expanded market size. As a result, the president of the Commission decided to eliminate the remaining barriers to a free market, such as customs posts, different certification procedures, rates of value-added tax, and excise duties.[20] Consequently, the EU issued a report in 1985 that identified 282 proposals that the EC needed to enact to complete an internal market. The target date for implementation of the proposals was December 31, 1992. The single market concept was developed and given the force of law by the Single European Act of 1987. Once the EU approved the proposals, called directives, they were turned over to the member states for passage into each country's national law.

Not all of the directives were expected to be put into effect by the end of 1992, and the Single Market is really an ongoing process. A survey of the European business community at the end of 1999 revealed that confidence in the single internal market remained high. However, the business community also revealed a number of obstacles to the single market. The most frequently cited obstacles were

The Single European Act was designed to eliminate the remaining nontariff barriers to trade in Europe. In spite of significant progress, there are still barriers to trade that need to be eliminated.

- Additional costs to render products or services compatible with national specifications
- Unusual testing, certification or approval procedures
- State aids favoring competitors

TABLE 7.2   COMPARATIVE DATA ON FIVE MAJOR TRADE GROUPS, 1997

	POPULATION (THOUSANDS)	GNP (MILLION US$)	PER CAPITA GNP (US$)
APEC	2,447,436	$16,918,386	$ 6,913
ASEAN	495,531	704,787	1,422
EU-15	374,225	8,565,466	22,889
EU Applicant-12	106,095	342,261	3,226
NAFTA	392,272	8,726,695	22,247
MERCOSUR	207,717	1,133,555	5,457

Source: World Bank, *World Bank Atlas 1999* (Washington, D.C.: The World Bank, 1999).

- Difficulties related to the VAT (value-added tax) system and VAT procedures
- Restrictions on market access; existence of exclusive networks[21]

THE TREATY OF MAASTRICHT

Not content with the economic integration envisaged in the Europe 1992 program, EC leaders met in Maastricht, the Netherlands, in December 1991 and approved the Treaty of Maastricht. This treaty, which took the EC to a higher level, had two goals: political union and monetary union.

The prospect of political union brought up a number of issues, such as a common European citizenship; joint foreign, defense, immigration, and policing policies; and common social policy concerning working conditions and employees' rights. In addition, the treaty strengthened Parliament significantly by giving it veto power over new national laws, as noted in the earlier section on the European Parliament.[22]

The Treaty of Maastricht was not easy to design because there are strong federalist tendencies in countries such as France and Germany and an abhorrence of centralized control from Brussels on the part of countries such as the United Kingdom and Denmark. Those opposing federalist tendencies included in the treaty the principle of **subsidiarity**, which implies that EU interference should occur only in areas of common concern and that most policies should be set at the national level. Further, not all countries accepted all points in the treaty.

The Euro   The most significant aspect of the Maastricht agreement was the decision to move to a common currency in Europe, with the new currency being called the euro. The roots to the system began in 1979, with the **European Monetary System (EMS)**. The EMS was set up to facilitate trade among members by minimizing exchange-rate fluctuations. A series of exchange relationships links the currencies of most members through a parity grid. The grid places each currency down the side and across the top of the grid. Then an exchange rate is established between each pair of currencies. For

The Treaty of Maastricht sought to foster political union and monetary union.

Subsidiarity implies that EU interference should occur only in areas of common concern and that most policies should be set at the national level.

example, the grid would contain an exchange rate between the German mark and the French franc, the Dutch guilder, the Italian lira, and so on. Then each country was obligated to maintain the exchange relationship between its currency and every other currency in the grid. Exchange rates could change by no more than 2.25 percent of their value. If there was pressure on a currency—for example, if the German mark were to rise against the lira—the governments of Germany and Italy would enter the foreign-exchange markets to support the value of their currencies within this 2.25 percent range by buying or selling their currencies to influence their prices.

In spite of the attempt of the EMS to reduce exchange-rate fluctuations, the EU decided at Maastricht that the next step was to replace each national currency with a single European currency. To do that, however, the countries had to converge their economies first. It is not possible to have 15 different monetary policies and one currency. So the member countries moved to converge their economies by

- Reducing inflation so that each country's inflation would be no more than 1.5 percentage points above the average of the three lowest inflation rates in Europe
- Reducing long-term interest rates so that each country's rate would be no more than two percentage points above the average of the three lowest
- Reducing the government's budget deficit to no more than 3 percent of GDP
- Reducing the stock of public debt so that it would not exceed 60 percent of GDP[23]

After a great deal of effort, 11 of the 15 countries in the EU were prepared to join monetary union on January 1, 1999. Those not participating in the new euro were Britain, Sweden, and Denmark (by their choice) and Greece (not ready).

The euro is being administered by the European Central Bank (ECB), which was established on July 1, 1998. The ECB is responsible for setting monetary policy and managing the exchange-rate system for all of Europe since January 1, 1999. The ECB is comprised of a six-person Executive Board that works with the governors of the Central Banks of the "in" countries to set monetary policy, and it is independent of all EU institutions and national governments. The ECB has a single-minded focus of controlling inflation, similar to the German central bank, so it will manage interest rates to keep inflation down. Initially, price stability was defined as 2 percent growth per year, and the ECB is not allowed to balance other objectives, such as unemployment, in setting its monetary policy.[24] Even though the ECB is establishing policy for the 11 countries, there are still differences in growth rates among member states, just as there are differences in growth from state to state in the United States. In 1999, for example, Portugal, Spain, Finland, and Ireland were growing at between 3.2 percent and 8.5 percent, compared with an average of only 1.9 percent in the rest of the euro area.[25]

In its first year of operation, the euro fluctuated in value between a high of $1.1827 per euro to a low of nearly $1.00 per euro. The euro will not show up as actual banknotes replacing individual national currencies until 2002, but companies are keeping books in euros, entering into euro loans, and pricing goods and services in euros as well as national currencies.

The move to the euro is affecting companies in a variety of ways. Banks had to update their electronic networks to handle all aspects of exchanging money, such as systems that trade global currencies, that buy and sell stocks, that transfer money between banks, that manage customer accounts, or that print out bank statements. Deutsche Bank estimated that the conversion process cost several hundred million dollars.[26] Other companies feel that the euro will increase price transparency (the ability to compare prices in different countries) and eliminate foreign-exchange costs and risks. Although some price differences are due to shipping costs and the like, there are still wide differences in Europe that will have to narrow now that everything is priced in euros. For example, the Ford Mondeo costs nearly 50 percent more in Germany than in Spain, and the difference between the cheapest and most expensive countries for some drug products can be as much as 300 percent. A survey of European corporate executives by KPMG revealed that 60 percent had significant price variations in the euro area. Of these, 64 percent expected the range to narrow over time.[27] Foreign-exchange costs should narrow as companies operate in only one currency in Europe, and foreign-exchange risks between member states will also disappear, although there will still be foreign-exchange risks between the euro and nonmember currencies, such as the U.S. dollar.

EU EXPANSION

The European Free Trade Association

- **Was established in 1960 as a free trade alternative to the EEC**
- **Has lost most of its members to the EU**

One of the EU's major challenges is that of expansion. The EU's first step in expansion was the creation of the European Economic Area (EAA) in 1991, which extended the customs union privileges of the EU to European Free Trade Association (EFTA) member countries. EFTA was established in 1960 as an alternative to the EEC, and it was simply a free trade agreement. This had special appeal to Switzerland, which was not interested in the more aggressive political integration that became part of the EEC. With the loss of Austria, Finland, and Sweden to the EU as full members in 1995, EFTA was reduced to only four countries: Norway, Iceland, Switzerland, and Liechtenstein. The EEA agreement with the EU allows the freedom of people, goods, services, and capital to Norway, Iceland, and Liechtenstein. Switzerland is the only EFTA member not included in the EEA, because its people voted in 1991 not to join. Because the EAA agreement is between only three countries and the EU, it is likely to dissolve if and when all countries become part of the EU.

In 1996, Turkey, with a population larger than any country in the EU except Germany, entered into a customs union agreement with the EU. Turkey is now a part of the single European market and has adopted the EU's trade legislation and common external tariff without becoming a complete member of the EU.[28] In addition, the EU has signed numerous free trade agreements with other countries around the world, making it the largest trading bloc in the world. This means that companies doing business in one EU country have access to a much larger market than anywhere else in the world.

The EU is set to expand to at least 12 more countries, mostly from Central and Eastern Europe.

The next level of expansion is likely to include the countries of Central and Eastern Europe, plus Malta and Cyprus. A number of European countries are interested in joining the EU as identified in Map 7.1. Some are expected to join soon, although there was no specific timetable for entry as of the end of 1999. But 12 countries had been admitted to application status by the end of 1999.

Prior to the end of the Soviet empire, the countries of the USSR and Central and Eastern Europe were linked together in a trading relationship known as the **Council for Mutual Economic Assistance (CMEA** or also known as **COMECON)**. However, the breakup of the Soviet Union and its allied countries in Eastern Europe dissolved the CMEA in June 1991. On July 1, 1992, the **Central European Free Trade Association (CEFTA)** went into effect, with the Czech Republic, Slovakia, Hungary, and Poland as members. CEFTA's goal was to establish a free-trade area by 2000 that has the EU's basic trade structure.[29] However, these countries are now interested in joining the EU and have been admitted to candidacy.

The admission of the 12 will not be easy. Most countries in Central and Eastern Europe are poor, have fledgling democracies, and depend greatly on agriculture—as much as 20 percent of GNP, compared with only 6 percent on average in the EU, straining the EU's financial resources. As noted in Table 7.2, these 12 have a significantly lower per capita GNP than the existing 15 members of the EU. Another problem of expansion is governance. Large members of the EU, such as France and Germany, fear that the addition of so many new countries would weaken their control and influence. But the addition of the 12 countries will certainly move the EU ahead of NAFTA in total population and GNP.

IMPLICATIONS OF THE EU ON CORPORATE STRATEGY

The EU is a tremendous market in terms of both population and income that companies cannot ignore. Merger and acquisition activity has really picked up in Europe. The market in Europe is still considered fragmented and inefficient compared with the United States, so most experts feel that mergers, takeovers and spin-offs will continue in Europe for years to come. U.S. companies are buying European companies to gain a market presence and get rid of competition. An example is Wal-Mart's acquisition of the German hypermarket chain, Wertkauf, in 1997, a second German chain, Spar Handels, in 1998, and Britain's third-largest food retailer, Asda Group, in 1999.[30]

European firms are also acquiring other European firms to improve their competitive advantage against U.S. companies and to expand their market presence. A good example is the purchase of Promodes Group, a French retailer, by Carrefour, another French retailer. That merger resulted in creating the number-one retailer in Europe.[31] Carrefour, in second place worldwide behind Wal-Mart, is still larger than Wal-Mart in foreign markets and is a formidable challenger to the number-one retailer in the world.

Although Europe is moving closer together through the euro and the Single Market program, it is still not as homogeneous as is the U.S. market. Differences in languages, cultures, and governments still splinter Europe, and the eventual addition of the 12 new countries will create even more divisions in the market. Thus companies need to develop a pan-European strategy without sacrificing different national strategies. Ford found this out as noted in the opening case. National differences still mean something, even though it is important to establish pan-European strategies in areas where it makes sense.

WHERE NEXT FOR THE EU?

The Economist identified five fundamental shifts that have occurred in the EU that will dramatically affect its future:

- The inversion of the Franco-German balance. France had always had political control of the EU and could take the high road as a result of World War II. However, Germany's confidence has returned with its reunification between East and West, and Germany is now the largest and richest country in Europe. Germany may be the only country that can lead Europe in the future.

- A sense that the EU should possess a capacity for collective military action separate or separable from NATO. This was confirmed in the Kosovo conflict where the United States took control of a European conflict.

- The introduction of the euro, discussed earlier in more detail.
- The weakening of the European Commission and the ascendancy of national governments in controlling the destiny of the EU.
- The planned enlargement of the EU to include at least 12 and possibly as many as 20 new members, most of them former communist countries in Central and Eastern Europe.[32]

These shifts in Europe are impacting and being affected by top priorities identified by Europeans themselves:

- Job creation
- Promoting peace
- Protecting the environment
- Reining in EU spending
- Protecting the food supply[33]

Many issues face the EU as we move into the new millennium, but there are many opportunities for companies to expand their markets and sources of supply as the EU grows and encompasses more of Europe.

NORTH AMERICAN FREE TRADE AGREEMENT (NAFTA)

The North American Free Trade Agreement

- **Was preceded by free trade agreements between the United States and Canada**
- **Includes Canada, the United States, and Mexico**
- **Went into effect on January 1, 1994**
- **Is a large trading bloc but includes countries of different size and wealth**

NAFTA rationale

- **U.S.-Canadian trade is the largest bilateral trade in the world**
- **The United States is Mexico's and Canada's largest trading partner**

NAFTA, which includes Canada, the United States, and Mexico, went into effect in 1994, but it originated with the Canada-U.S. Free Trade Agreement. The United States and Canada historically have had various forms of mutual economic cooperation. One is the Automotive Products Trade Agreement, effective in 1965, which provides for qualified duty-free trade in specified automotive products. In the early 1980s, the two countries discussed developing free trade in specific industries, such as steel and textiles. This discussion led to a broader discussion of free trade, and by 1987 negotiations were underway to open up trade even more. The negotiations resulted in the Canada-U.S. Free Trade Agreement (FTA), effective January 1, 1989. The FTA eliminated all tariffs on bilateral trade by January 1, 1998, although more than 85 percent of the bilateral trade was subject to tariffs of 5 percent or less even before the FTA took effect.

In February 1991, Mexico approached the United States to establish a free-trade agreement. The formal negotiations that began in June 1991 included Canada. The resulting North American Free Trade Agreement became effective on January 1, 1994.

NAFTA has a logical rationale, in terms of both geographic location and trading importance. Although Canadian-Mexican trade was not significant when the agreement was signed, U.S.-Mexican and U.S.-Canadian trade were. The two-way trading relationship between the United States and Canada is the largest in the world. As noted in Table 7.2, NAFTA is a powerful trading bloc with a combined population and total GNP greater than the 15-member EU but smaller than would be the case when the additional 12 join the EU. However, that also assumes that NAFTA stays the same size, and it could also add more countries in the future. Table 7.3 shows the breakdown of population, GNP, and per capita GNP for the three NAFTA members. What is significant, especially when compared with the EU, is the tremendous size of the U.S. economy in comparison to those of Canada and Mexico. In addition, Canada has a much richer economy than that of Mexico, even though its population is about one-third that of Mexico.

TABLE 7.3		COMPARATIVE NAFTA DATA		
		POPULATION (MILLIONS)	**GNP (BILLIONS US $)**	**GNP PER CAPITA (US $)**
NAFTA	Canada	30,287	$ 594,976	$19,640
	Mexico	94,349	348,627	3,700
	United States	267,636	7,783,092	29,080
		392,272	8,726,695	22,247

Source: World Bank, *World Bank Atlas 1999* (Washington, D.C.: The World Bank, 1999).

NAFTA covers the following areas:

- Market access—tariff and nontariff barriers, rules of origin, governmental procurement.
- Trade rules—safeguards, subsidies, countervailing and antidumping duties, health and safety standards.
- Services—provides for the same safeguards for trade in services (consulting, engineering, software, etc.) that exist for trade in goods.
- Investment—establishes investment rules governing minority interests, portfolio investment, real property and majority-owned or controlled investments from the NAFTA counties; in addition, NAFTA coverage extends to investments made by any company incorporated in a NAFTA country, regardless of country of origin.
- Intellectual property—all three countries pledge to provide adequate and effective protection and enforcement of intellectual property rights, while ensuring that enforcement measures do not themselves become barriers to legitimate trade.
- Dispute settlement—provides a dispute settlement process that will be followed instead of countries taking unilateral action against an offending party.[34]

> **NAFTA calls for the elimination of tariff and nontariff barriers, the harmonization of trade rules, and the liberalization of restrictions on services and foreign investment.**

Mexico made significant strides in tariff reduction after joining GATT in 1986. At that time, its tariffs averaged 100 percent. Since then, it has reduced tariffs dramatically. As a result of NAFTA, most tariffs on originating goods traded between Mexico and Canada were eliminated immediately or phased in over a ten-year period ending on December 31, 2003. In a few exceptions, the phaseout period will be completed by the end of 2008. Tariffs between the United States and Mexico were, in general, either eliminated immediately or over a five- or ten-year period ending on December 31, 2003. Although most tariffs will be eliminated in five or ten equal annual stages, there are some exceptions. In the first five years of NAFTA, Mexico trimmed its average tariff on U.S. goods from 10 percent to 2 percent, while U.S. tariffs on Mexican products dropped to less than 1 percent.[35]

> **Most tariffs will be eliminated by 2004, some by 2008.**

NAFTA provides the static and dynamic effects of economic integration discussed earlier in this chapter. For example, Canadian and U.S. consumers benefit from lower-cost agricultural products from Mexico, a static effect of economic liberalization. U.S. producers also benefit from the large and growing Mexican market, which has a huge appetite for U.S. products—a dynamic effect.

NAFTA is a good example of trade diversion; some U.S. trade with and investment in Asia has been diverted to Mexico.

In addition, NAFTA is a good example of trade diversion. Many U.S. and Canadian companies have established manufacturing facilities in Asia to take advantage of cheap labor. Now, U.S. and Canadian companies can establish manufacturing facilities in Mexico rather than in Asian countries to take advantage of relatively cheap labor. For example, IBM is making computer parts in Mexico that were formerly made in Singapore. In five years, IBM boosted exports from Mexico to the United States from $350 million to $2 billion. Had the subassemblies not been made in and exported from Mexico, they would have been made in Singapore and other Asian locations and exported to the United States. Gap Inc. and Liz Claiborne are increasingly buying garments from Mexican contractors, who can offer faster delivery than can Asian contractors.[36]

RULES OF ORIGIN AND REGIONAL VALUE CONTENT

Rules of origin—goods and services must originate in North America to get access to lower tariffs.

An important component of NAFTA is the concept of rules of origin and regional value content. Because NAFTA is a free trade agreement and not a customs union, each country sets its own tariffs to the rest of the world. That is why a product entering the United States from Canada must have a commercial or customs invoice that identifies the product's ultimate origin. Otherwise, an exporter from a third country would always ship the product to the NAFTA country with the lowest tariff and then reexport it to the other two countries duty-free. "Rules of origin ensure that only goods that have been the subject of substantial economic activity within the free trade area are eligible for the more liberal tariff conditions created by the NAFTA."[37]

According to local content rules, at least 50 percent of the net cost of most products must come from the NAFTA region. The exceptions are 55 percent for footwear, 62.5 percent for passenger automobiles and light trucks and the engines and transmissions for such vehicles, and 60 percent for other vehicles and automotive parts.[38] For example, a Ford car assembled in Mexico could use parts from Canada, the United States, and Mexico, and labor and other factors from Mexico. For the car to enter Canada and the United States according to the preferential NAFTA duty, at least 62.5 percent of its value must come from North America.

Local content

- The percentage of value that must be from North America for the product to be considered "North American" in terms of country of origin
- 50 percent for most products; 62.5 percent for most autos

SPECIAL PROVISIONS OF NAFTA

Additional NAFTA provisions

- Workers' rights
- The environment
- Dispute resolution mechanism

Most free trade agreements in the world are based solely on reducing tariffs. However, NAFTA is a very different free trade agreement. Due to strong objections to the agreement by labor unions and environmentalists, two side agreements covering those issues were included in NAFTA. When first debating NAFTA, opponents worried about the potential loss of jobs in Canada and the United States to Mexico as a result of Mexico's cheaper wages, poor working conditions, and lax environmental enforcement. NAFTA opponents thought companies would close down factories in the North and set them up in Mexico. As a result, the labor lobby in the United States forced the inclusion of labor standards, such as the right to unionize, and the environmental lobby pushed for an upgrade of environmental standards in Mexico and the strengthening of compliance. Labor rights and environmental issues are a constant source of concern to the NAFTA Commission, a cabinet-level body established with the responsibility of implementing the agreements and side agreements. The Commission supervises the work of all committees and working groups established under the Agreement. The

Commission is to meet at least once per year, work by consensus, and establish its own rules and procedures.[39]

From a labor standpoint, the NAFTA side agreement "sets forth the following general objectives: improving working conditions and living standards, promoting compliance with and effective enforcement of labor laws, promoting the Agreement's principles through cooperation and coordination, and promoting publication and exchange of information to enhance mutual understanding of Parties' laws, institutions and legal systems."[40]

From an environmental standpoint, the NAFTA side agreement, "include[s] the promotion of sustainable development, cooperation on the conservation, protection and enhancement of the environment, and the effective enforcement of and compliance with domestic environmental laws. The Agreement promotes transparency and public participation in the development and improvement of environmental laws and policies."[41] There is a strong positive correlation between pollution and economic growth, so it may be true that pollution could worsen in Mexico if NAFTA stimulates its economic growth. However, Mexican environmental standards are getting tougher and enforcement of those standards is improving. There is no evidence to support the idea that environmental standards and enforcement would lag behind as the economy grows. One could argue that NAFTA actually could force Mexico to strengthen its standards and enforcement. In addition, studies show that countries with low income levels cannot spend much money to clean up the environment, and that cleanup begins when income levels rise. Labor and environmental activists were emboldened with their success at disrupting the WTO meetings in Seattle, Washington, in November 1999, so they are expected to continue to press for improvements in labor rights and the environment in NAFTA countries.

Rather than rely on the World Trade Organization to settle disputes or to allow the U.S. government to act unilaterally on trade issues, NAFTA requires all three countries to negotiate as equals on trade disputes. The NAFTA Secretariat was established to administer the NAFTA dispute resolution processes.[42] The NAFTA Agreement encourages parties to resolve trade conflicts together without using the Secretariat, but if the Secretariat is used, procedures are followed that are similar to those in the WTO. The concern is that countries are ceding their sovereignty in trade issues to the Secretariat, but this is accepted in the spirit of NAFTA cooperation.

IMPACT OF NAFTA ON TRADE, INVESTMENT, AND JOBS

The test of any regional trading group is whether it creates trade and jobs. During the debates on NAFTA leading up to its ratification, U.S. proponents of NAFTA pointed out that reducing trade barriers in Mexico would result in an increase in exports to Mexico, resulting in the creation of U.S. and Canadian jobs. Because most trade between the United States and Canada was virtually duty-free, and because Mexico had easy access to U.S. and Canadian markets, many assumed that the major benefit would be the increase in exports to Mexico from both the United States and Canada.

Because Canadian and U.S. firms were investing in Mexico prior to NAFTA, many thought the agreement's improved investment rules would facilitate increased investment

TABLE 7.4		MERCHANDISE TRADE BETWEEN THE UNITED STATES AND CANADA AND BETWEEN THE UNITED STATES AND MEXICO								
	1993 AMOUNT	% OF TOTAL	1994 AMOUNT	1995 AMOUNT	1996 AMOUNT	1997 AMOUNT	1998 AMOUNT	% OF TOTAL	% GROWTH 1993–1998
Canada									
Exports to	101.2	22.2	114.8	127.6	135.2	152.1	156.8	23.4	54.9
Imports from	113.3	19.2	131.1	147.1	158.7	170.1	175.8	19.2	55.2
Mexico									
Exports to	41.5	9.1	50.7	46.2	56.8	71.1	78.4	11.7	88.9
Imports from	40.4	6.9	50.1	62.8	75.1	86.7	95.5	10.4	136.4
Total World									
Exports to	456.8		502.4	575.8	612.1	679.7	670.2		46.7
Imports from	589.4		668.6	749.6	803.3	876.4	917.2		55.6

Source: Christopher L. Bach, "U.S. International Transactions," *Survey of Current Business,* July 1999, pp. 94, 96.

Impact of NAFTA on trade

- **NAFTA members have become much more significant trading partners with each other**
- **Overall trade with NAFTA members has increased faster than trade with the rest of the world**
- **Exports to NAFTA members have increased, but imports have increased faster**

but would not result in a flood of investment capital into Mexico. Opponents, however, predicted the deindustrialization of Canada and the United States as firms moved to Mexico to take advantage of cheaper costs.

What has been the impact of NAFTA on trade and employment? The trade side is easy to measure. Table 7.4 illustrates the impact of NAFTA on U.S. merchandise trade with Canada and Mexico. Three things are evident from the table. First, U.S. exports to Canada and imports from Canada may not have changed as a percentage of total, but Mexico's share of the total increased from 1993 to 1998. In fact, Mexico replaced Japan as the second-largest market for U.S. exports, while remaining as the third most important supplier to the U.S. market after Canada and Japan. U.S. exports to Canada and Mexico rose from 31.3 percent of total exports in 1993 to 35.1 percent of total in 1998. Second, U.S. exports rose 46.7 percent from 1993 to 1998, but they rose faster to Canada (54.9 percent) and Mexico (88.9 percent). Although U.S. imports from Canada rose at the same rate as total imports (55.2 percent versus 55.6 percent), they rose much faster from Mexico (136.4 percent). Third, the Mexican peso crisis of 1994, which led to a steep recession in Mexico in 1995, resulted in a drop in U.S. exports to Mexico in 1995, but U.S. exports recovered in 1996 and were almost double their pre-NAFTA levels by 1998. Similarly, trade between Canada and Mexico increased during the same period. Mexican exports to Canada grew by 79 percent, and Canadian exports to Mexico grew by 37 percent, but they are marginal trading partners with each other.[43] The United States is a far more significant trading partner to Canada and Mexico than they are with each other.

The investment and employment pictures are far more complicated. One concern mentioned above is that investment in Mexico would rise dramatically due to lower wages and lax environmental standards in Mexico. Wages are significantly lower in Mexico than they are in the United States and Canada, as noted in Table 7.5. In fact,

TABLE 7.5   **HOURLY COMPENSATION COSTS FOR PRODUCTION WORKERS IN MANUFACTURING, IN U.S. DOLLARS**

Hourly compensation costs of manufacturing workers are significantly higher in the United States and Canada than in Mexico, where wages are also lower than in some of the newly industrialized countries in Asia.

COUNTRY	WAGE
Germany	$28.28
Japan	19.37
United States	18.24
Canada	16.55
Mexico	1.75
Hong Kong	5.42
Korea	7.22
Singapore	8.24
Taiwan	5.89

Source: United States Department of Labor, Bureau of Labor Statistics, "International Comparisons of Manufacturing Hourly Compensation Costs," 1997, http://stats.bls.gov/news.release/ichcc.t02.htm.

they are much lower than wages in many of the newly industrialized countries of Asia, which explains why companies like IBM are investing in Mexico instead of Asia for certain types of manufacturing. Foreign investment into Mexico has risen from $4 billion per year in 1993 to $10 billion per year in 1998.[44] However, only 2.6 percent of all U.S. foreign direct investment is in Mexico, compared with 10.6 percent in Canada. Mexico is only the twelfth most important location for U.S. foreign direct investment, and it is not even the most important location for U.S. FDI in the Americas—Brazil is more important. However, a lot of FDI is pouring into Mexico from other countries, like Germany and Japan, to take advantage of NAFTA.

It is virtually impossible to determine the employment impact of NAFTA because of the difficulty of trying to separate NAFTA from other factors. The U.S. Department of Commerce estimates that every $1 billion in U.S. exports translates into 14,000 U.S. jobs, so the increase in total U.S. exports to Canada and Mexico from 1993 to 1998 of $92.5 billion should translate into 1.3 million new U.S. jobs. But there was also an increase in imports. The U.S. trade deficit with Canada and Mexico rose from $11 billion in 1993 to $36.1 billion in 1998, an increase of 228 percent. Over the same period, the total U.S. trade deficit rose 86.3 percent, and NAFTA's portion of the total deficit rose from 8 percent in 1993 to 14.7 percent in 1998. But there is no way of knowing exactly how many jobs the imports have displaced or if the displaced workers have found other employment. However, U.S. trade with Mexico is still a relatively insignificant part of the total U.S. economy. The economy of Orange County, California, is greater than the economy of the entire country of Mexico, and U.S. trade with Mexico is less than 2 percent of the total U.S. GNP. Although some U.S. labor leaders point to

The impact of NAFTA on employment has been difficult to measure. More jobs have probably been created than lost to NAFTA, but there are too many confounding variables to measure the impact accurately.

possible NAFTA job losses of around 200,000—215,000 since 1993—the U.S. economy has added 16 million jobs since NAFTA was created, and total U.S. unemployment has been hovering at 4.5 percent, the lowest it has been in 40 years. In fact, the U.S. Government Accounting Office looked at the pros and cons of NAFTA on jobs and concluded that it is impossible to quantify the effect.[45]

However, that doesn't mean that NAFTA has benefited everyone equally. One of the major concerns in Mexico is that there are still significant disparities in income distribution. Since 1993, the gap has widened in Mexico between wages at local manufacturers and those at top export manufacturers, which are up to 67 percent higher.[46] Many Mexican companies are leapfrogging technology and establishing sophisticated operations that require workers with at least a high school education rather than employing unskilled, poorly educated workers. Workers at U.S. and Canadian companies that are put out of work by competition from Mexico may get jobs, but there is no guarantee that the jobs pay as much as their former jobs, especially if their former jobs were high-paying union positions.

NAFTA EXPANSION

U.S. political forces are holding up NAFTA expansion, but Canada and Mexico have developed NAFTA-like bilateral agreements with other countries, such as Chile.

When the United States began its discussions with Mexico and Canada, it perceived a future effort to pull together North, Central, and South America into an "Enterprise of the Americas." The idea was to have the United States enter into a series of bilateral trade relationships with Latin American countries that would result in a "hub and spokes" arrangement, with the United States as the hub and other countries at the other end of the free trade spokes. Eventually, these bilateral relationships would result in one huge multilateral relationship between all of the Americas—Canada and Mexico included. However, that has not taken place. U.S. protectionism has kept the United States from entering into other bilateral relationships, but that has not stopped Canada and Mexico. Both countries have entered into a free trade agreement with Chile, perceived to be the next country that could join NAFTA, and the agreements were modeled after NAFTA. In addition, Mexico entered into a free trade agreement with the European Union that would end all tariffs on bilateral trade by 2007 if the agreement is ratified in both countries. EU officials feel that the FTA is important for them, because their share of Mexican imports fell from 20 percent of the market in 1994 to only 5 percent in 1998.[47]

IMPLICATIONS OF NAFTA ON CORPORATE STRATEGY

Several predictions were made when NAFTA was signed. One prediction was that companies would look at NAFTA as one big regional market, allowing companies to rationalize production, products, financing, and the like. That has largely happened in a number of industries, especially automotive products and electronics, especially computers. Each country in NAFTA ships more automotive products, based on specialized production, to the other two countries than any other manufactured goods. Employment has increased in the auto industry in the United States since NAFTA, even as it has decreased in Mexico because of productivity.[48] Rationalization of automotive production has taken place for years in the United States and Canada, but Mexico is a recent entrant. Auto manufacturing has moved into Mexico from all over the world. Over 500,000 Mexicans make parts and assemble vehicles for all of the world's major auto producers. NAFTA's rules of origins requiring 62.5 percent regional content has forced European and Asian automakers to bring in parts suppliers and set up assembly operations in Mexico especially. In one case, a Canadian entrepreneur established a metal-stamping plant in Puebla, Mexico, to supply Volkswagen, the German auto manufacturer. The VW plant assembles the revitalized Beetle that is being supplied to the U.S. market.[49] DaimlerChrysler is producing 45,000 cars and 200,000 trucks in Mexico, of which between 80 and 90 percent are being exported to the United States and Canada. In 2000, DaimlerChrysler began producing a new model, the PT Cruiser, in Toluca, Mexico, for export to Canada, the United States, and Europe. It is using that one plant to manufacture that one model for the entire world.

> **NAFTA is causing MNEs to look at the region differently in terms of trade and investment.**

The examples above describe how production is intertwined among the member countries. However, some companies are simply leaving the United States and Canada and moving to Mexico. General Electric divisions even told their suppliers that they had better move to Mexico as a way to cut costs or risk being dropped as a GE supplier. GE has gone through the process of globalizing its production, reducing its U.S. domestic workforce by 50 percent since 1986 to 163,000 workers, while doubling its foreign employment to 130,000. GE employs 30,000 people in Mexico, and it has conducted seminars for suppliers on how to set up operations in Mexico, much to the chagrin of its U.S. workforce and union leaders.[50] The same can be said of apparel and furniture. However, NAFTA rules on apparel have caused the Mexican textile industry to bring jobs back from Asia, and U.S. textile companies are setting up operations in Mexico to supply both the Mexican and U.S. apparel markets. This is a good example of the concept of diversion being applied to investment—investment being diverted from Asia to NAFTA countries, especially Mexico.

Although low-end manufacturing is moving south, more sophisticated manufacturing and services are increasing in the United States as a result of NAFTA, especially in the Southeast. European, Asian, and U.S. companies are using the area along Interstate Highway 85 through the Southeast to supply the NAFTA market. Although an estimated 35,000 jobs were lost in the traditional industries in the Southeast due to NAFTA, an estimated 65,000 more sophisticated manufacturing and high-tech jobs were created. The problem is that not all of those who lost traditional jobs were placed in the more sophisticated jobs. This is a real education and training problem for the region.

A second prediction was that sophisticated U.S. companies would run Canadian and Mexican companies out of business once the markets opened up. That has not happened. In fact, U.S. companies along the border of Canada are finding that Canadian companies are generating more competition for them than low-wage Mexican companies. Also, many Mexican companies have restructured to compete with U.S. and Canadian companies. The lack of protection has resulted in much more competitive Mexican firms. NAFTA has forced companies from all three countries to reexamine their strategies and determine how best to operate in the market.

> **In general, U.S. companies have not run Canadian and Mexican companies out of business.**

A final prediction has to do with looking at Mexico as a consumer market rather than just a production location. Initially, the excitement over Mexico for U.S. and Canadian companies has been the low wage environment. However, as Mexican income continues to rise—which it must as more investment enters Mexico and more Mexican companies export production—demand will rise for foreign products. In so doing, the Canadian and U.S. trade deficits will fall, and the market will come more into balance.

> **Mexico is being looked at more as a market for U.S. and Canadian exports than just a location for low-cost production.**

But U.S. and Canadian companies need to make the transition to Mexico as a significant final consumer market.

REGIONAL ECONOMIC GROUPS IN LATIN AMERICA, ASIA, AND AFRICA

Other examples of regional integration can be found around the world, although the EU and NAFTA are the most successful, given the size of their respective economies and the degree of progress toward free trade. Economic integration in Latin America has changed over the years. Two of the original examples of regional economic integration in Latin America, the Latin American Free Trade Association (LAFTA) and the Caribbean Free Trade Association (CARIFTA), changed their names to the Latin American Integration Association (ALADI) and the Caribbean Community and Common Market (CARICOM). They also changed the focus of their activities. In spite of this evolution, the initial rationale for integration remains. The post–World War II strategy of import substitution to resolve balance-of-payments problems was doomed because of

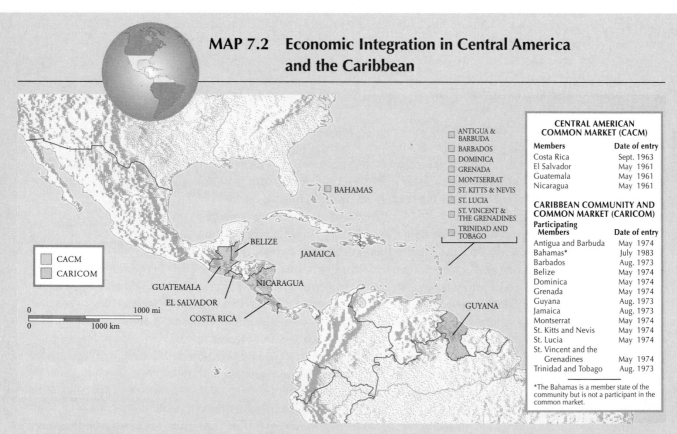

MAP 7.2   Economic Integration in Central America and the Caribbean

CACM
CARICOM

ANTIGUA & BARBUDA
BARBADOS
DOMINICA
GRENADA
MONTSERRAT
ST. KITTS & NEVIS
ST. LUCIA
ST. VINCENT & THE GRENADINES
TRINIDAD AND TOBAGO

BAHAMAS
BELIZE
JAMAICA
GUATEMALA   NICARAGUA
EL SALVADOR
COSTA RICA
GUYANA

CENTRAL AMERICAN COMMON MARKET (CACM)	
Members	**Date of entry**
Costa Rica	Sept. 1963
El Salvador	May 1961
Guatemala	May 1961
Nicaragua	May 1961

CARIBBEAN COMMUNITY AND COMMON MARKET (CARICOM)	
Participating Members	**Date of entry**
Antigua and Barbuda	May 1974
Bahamas*	July 1983
Barbados	Aug. 1973
Belize	May 1974
Dominica	May 1974
Grenada	May 1974
Guyana	Aug. 1973
Jamaica	Aug. 1973
Montserrat	May 1974
St. Kitts and Nevis	May 1974
St. Lucia	May 1974
St. Vincent and the Grenadines	May 1974
Trinidad and Tobago	Aug. 1973

*The Bahamas is a member state of the community but is not a participant in the common market.

Countries in Central America and the Caribbean have shifted their forms of integration from free trade areas to common markets: the Central American Common Market (CACM) and the Caribbean Community and Common Market (CARICOM).

Latin America's small national markets. Therefore, some form of economic cooperation was needed to enlarge the potential market size so that Latin American companies could achieve economies of scale and be more competitive worldwide.

Latin countries rely heavily on the United States as their major export market. However, the size and scale of cooperation within Latin American trading groups is increasing. Map 7.2 identifies the major trading groups in Central America—the Caribbean Community and Common Market (CARICOM) and the Central American Common Market (CACM). Map 7.3 identifies the major trading groups in South America.

The major trade group in South America is **MERCOSUR.** In 1991, Brazil, Argentina, Paraguay, and Uruguay established MERCOSUR as a subregional group of ALADI. MERCOSUR is significant because of its size: The four original members generate 80 percent of South America's GNP. In addition, MERCOSUR has signed free trade agreements with Bolivia and Chile and is negotiating with other countries to do the same. MERCOSUR is also trying to become a customs union, but as of the end of

MERCOSUR is a customs union between Brazil, Uruguay, Paraguay, and Argentina. It has been slow in developing a common external tariff, and economic problems of member countries have hampered progress.

MAP 7.3   Latin American Economic Integration

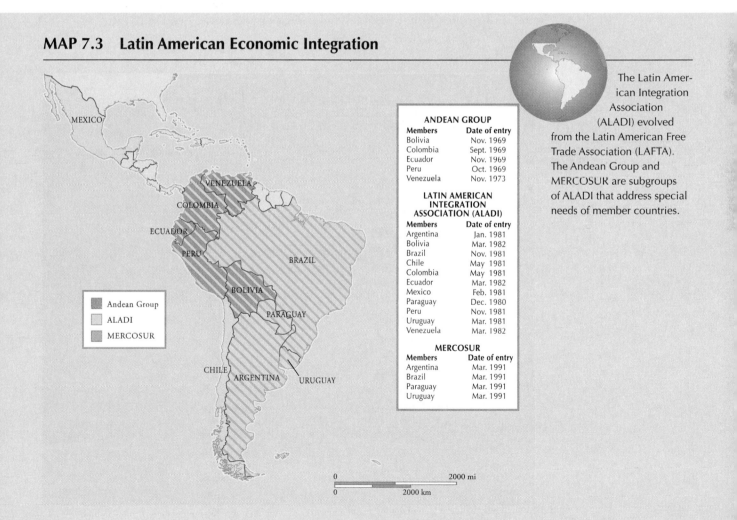

ANDEAN GROUP	
Members	Date of entry
Bolivia	Nov. 1969
Colombia	Sept. 1969
Ecuador	Nov. 1969
Peru	Oct. 1969
Venezuela	Nov. 1973

LATIN AMERICAN INTEGRATION ASSOCIATION (ALADI)	
Members	Date of entry
Argentina	Jan. 1981
Bolivia	Mar. 1982
Brazil	Nov. 1981
Chile	May 1981
Colombia	May 1981
Ecuador	Mar. 1982
Mexico	Feb. 1981
Paraguay	Dec. 1980
Peru	Nov. 1981
Uruguay	Mar. 1981
Venezuela	Mar. 1982

MERCOSUR	
Members	Date of entry
Argentina	Mar. 1991
Brazil	Mar. 1991
Paraguay	Mar. 1991
Uruguay	Mar. 1991

The Latin American Integration Association (ALADI) evolved from the Latin American Free Trade Association (LAFTA). The Andean Group and MERCOSUR are subgroups of ALADI that address special needs of member countries.

- Andean Group
- ALADI
- MERCOSUR

1999, that had not happened. In addition, the devaluation of the Brazilian real in early 1999 caused Brazilian exports to be more competitive than those of other member countries, threatening the stability of the alliance.[51]

Although the Andean Common Market (ANCOM) is not as significant economically as MERCOSUR, it is the second most important regional group in South America. As Map 7.3 shows, the **Andean Group** has been around since 1969. However, its focus has shifted from one of isolationism and statism (placing economic control in the hands of the state—the central government) to being open to foreign trade and investment.

Regional integration in Asia has not been as successful as the EU or NAFTA because most of the countries in the region have relied on the United States as major markets for their products. However, the Asian financial crisis of 1997–1998 demonstrated that weakness in one country resulted in contagion throughout the region. The **Association of South East Asian Nations** (ASEAN), organized in 1967, comprises Brunei, Cambodia, Indonesia, Laos, Malaysia, Myanmar, the Philippines, Singapore, Thailand, and Vietnam (see Map 7.4). It is promoting cooperation in many areas, including industry and trade. Member countries are protected in terms of tariff and nontariff barriers. Yet they hold promise for market and investment opportunities because of their large mar-

> **ASEAN is a relatively successful free trade area in Southeast Asia that relies more on the U.S. market for exports than on each other.**

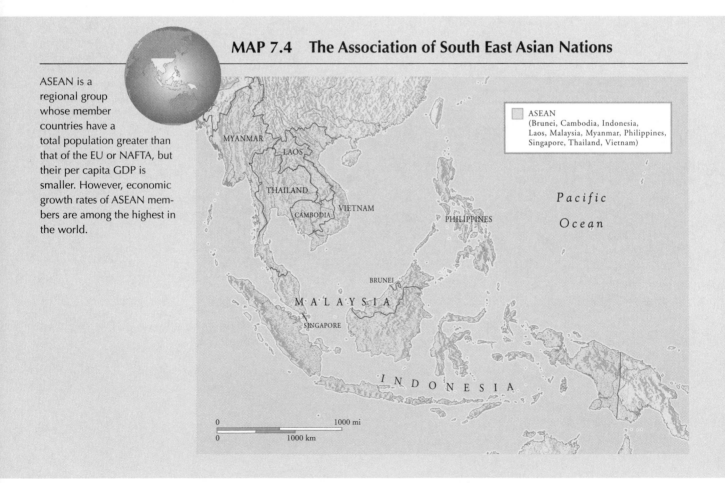

MAP 7.4   The Association of South East Asian Nations

ASEAN is a regional group whose member countries have a total population greater than that of the EU or NAFTA, but their per capita GDP is smaller. However, economic growth rates of ASEAN members are among the highest in the world.

ASEAN
(Brunei, Cambodia, Indonesia, Laos, Malaysia, Myanmar, Philippines, Singapore, Thailand, Vietnam)

MYANMAR
LAOS
THAILAND
CAMBODIA
VIETNAM
PHILIPPINES
Pacific Ocean
BRUNEI
MALAYSIA
SINGAPORE
INDONESIA

0   1000 mi
0   1000 km

ket size (495.5 million people). On January 1, 1993, ASEAN officially formed the **ASEAN Free Trade Area (AFTA)**. AFTA's goal is to cut tariffs on all intrazonal trade to a maximum of 5 percent by January 1, 2008. The weaker ASEAN countries would be allowed to phase in their tariff reductions over a longer period.

A significant event for ASEAN was the admission of Vietnam as a member in July 1995. Vietnam's membership added 72.5 million people, making it the second largest member of ASEAN after Indonesia and just above the Philippines. However, Vietnam's per capita income was only $190, making it the poorest country in the region. Cambodia, Laos, and Myanmar followed Vietnam as subsequent members of ASEAN. There are two major problems with AFTA/ASEAN. The first is that the Asian financial crisis resulted in a significant downturn in the economies of all member countries. The second is that the newer members—Cambodia, Laos, Myanmar, and Vietnam—have serious political problems. It is difficult to harmonize trade when the political climate is so unstable.

APEC, the **Asia Pacific Economic Cooperation** (http://www.apec.org), was formed in November 1989 to promote multilateral economic cooperation in trade and investment in the Pacific Rim.[52] It is comprised of 21 countries that border the Pacific Rim—both in Asia as well as the Americas. The members of APEC can be found in Table 7.2. Because APEC includes so many countries and is so spread out geographically, it is a largely ineffectual organization compared with the EU and NAFTA. APEC's major objectives are to

APEC is comprised of 21 countries that border the Pacific Rim; progress toward free trade is hampered by the size of APEC and the geographic distance between member countries.

- Resist protectionist pressures and maintain the momentum of trade liberalization
- Counter inward-looking regionalism elsewhere, such as in the EU and NAFTA
- Provide ways to deal with economic conflicts in the region[53]

Concern over the potential trade diversion of NAFTA was an important reason for the founding of APEC. By admitting NAFTA into APEC, Asian countries hoped to trade more with the United States. There was some feeling that the Clinton administration had lost a focus on Asia and that its influence and presence, especially compared to Japan, had slipped. In addition, several trade disputes occurred between the United States and several countries in Asia, notably Japan and China. It was hoped that the admission of the United States into APEC might facilitate a resolution of some of those problems.[54]

To accomplish its objectives, APEC leaders committed to achieve free and open trade in the region by 2010 for the industrial nations (which generate 85 percent of the regional trade) and by 2020 for the rest of the members.[55] Heads of state have met annually since their first meeting in the United States in 1993. Rather than rely on a complex bureaucracy to manage APEC, the host country of the annual meeting takes on the leadership responsibilities for that year.

At the time APEC was established, ASEAN was the dominant regional economic group in Asia. As a precondition to joining, ASEAN worked out an agreement that the presidency of APEC would alternate between an ASEAN and a non-ASEAN member of APEC.

APEC has the potential to become a significant economic bloc, especially because it generates such a large percentage of the world's output and merchandise trade. APEC is trying to establish "open regionalism," whereby individual member countries can determine whether to apply trade liberalization to non-APEC countries on an unconditional most favored nation basis or on a reciprocal, free trade agreement basis. The United States prefers the latter approach. The key will be whether or not the liberalization process continues at a good pace.[56] The problem with APEC is its size. A major reason why regional integration like the EU and NAFTA work is because of close geographic proximity and a unity of purpose. APEC has too many countries with diverse interests, and it was established as a counterforce to NAFTA. It is hard to maintain serious progress for something borne out of a defensive rather than an offensive strategy.

There are several African trade groups, but they rely more on their former colonial powers and other developed markets for trade than they do with each other.

Several African regional trade groups exist, and they are not necessarily mutually exclusive. The Ivory Coast, for example, is a member of several different organizations in Africa that promote political and economic development. Map 7.5 shows some of the major African groups. The problem is that African countries have been struggling to establish a political identity and are only recently adjusting to the freedom of South Africa. Civil war, corruption, and poor government infrastructures have hampered African countries and their ability to progress economically. Some African groups, such as the Organization for African Unity, have been preoccupied with political rather than trade issues. Most African countries rely on trade links with former colonial powers than with each other. African markets, with the notable exception of South Africa, are relatively small and undeveloped, making trade liberalization a relatively minor contributor to economic growth in the region.

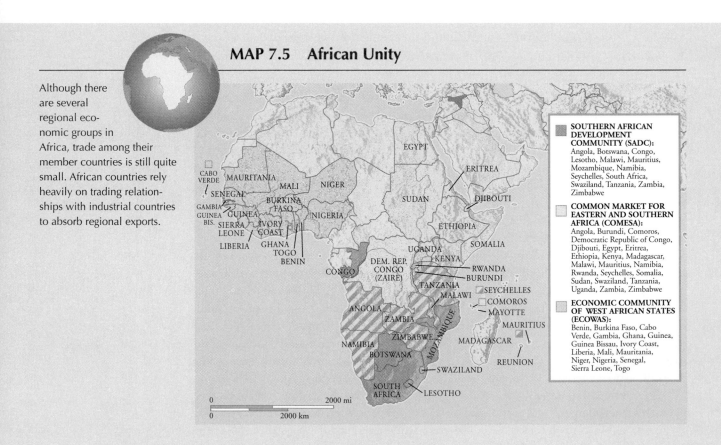

MAP 7.5   African Unity

Although there are several regional economic groups in Africa, trade among their member countries is still quite small. African countries rely heavily on trading relationships with industrial countries to absorb regional exports.

SOUTHERN AFRICAN DEVELOPMENT COMMUNITY (SADC): Angola, Botswana, Congo, Lesotho, Malawi, Mauritius, Mozambique, Namibia, Seychelles, South Africa, Swaziland, Tanzania, Zambia, Zimbabwe

COMMON MARKET FOR EASTERN AND SOUTHERN AFRICA (COMESA): Angola, Burundi, Comoros, Democratic Republic of Congo, Djibouti, Egypt, Eritrea, Ethiopia, Kenya, Madagascar, Malawi, Mauritius, Namibia, Rwanda, Seychelles, Somalia, Sudan, Swaziland, Tanzania, Uganda, Zambia, Zimbabwe

ECONOMIC COMMUNITY OF WEST AFRICAN STATES (ECOWAS): Benin, Burkina Faso, Cabo Verde, Gambia, Ghana, Guinea, Guinea Bissau, Ivory Coast, Liberia, Mali, Mauritania, Niger, Nigeria, Senegal, Sierra Leone, Togo

Looking to the Future
HOW MUCH TERRITORY WILL REGIONAL INTEGRATION COVER?

Will regional integration be the wave of the future, or will the World Trade Organization become the focus of global economic integration? The WTO's objective is to reduce barriers to trade in goods, services, and investment. Regional groups attempt to do that and more. Although the EU has introduced a common currency and is increasing the degree of cooperation in areas such as security and foreign policy, the WTO will never engage in those issues. Regional integration deals with the specific problems facing member countries, while the WTO needs to be concerned about all countries in the world. However, regional integration might actually help the WTO achieve its objectives in three major ways:

- Regionalism can lead to liberalization of issues not covered by the WTO.
- Regionalism, given that it typically involves fewer countries with more similar conditions and objectives, is more flexible.
- Regional deals lock in liberalization, especially in developing countries.

NAFTA and the EU are the key regional groups where significant integration is taking place. In the future, these groups will continue to develop stronger linkages, and then they will expand to include other countries. The key for NAFTA will be whether or not the U.S. Congress can avoid getting caught up in protectionist sentiment and allow expansion to take place. If it does not, Canada and Mexico will continue to engage in bilateral agreements with non-NAFTA countries in the region along the lines of the NAFTA agreement. The EU will continue to expand east until it meets Russia, and then its expansion will stop.

Regional integration in Africa will continue at a slow pace due to the existing political and economic problems there, but Asian integration, primarily in APEC, will pick up steam as the economies of East and Southeast Asia recover. However, the key to their growth will continue to be non-APEC members Japan and the United States.

COMMODITY AGREEMENTS

So far this chapter has focused on how countries cooperate to reduce trade barriers among themselves. However, producer and consumer countries of primary commodities have also come together to attempt to stabilize commodity prices and supply. Primary commodities, such as crude petroleum, natural gas, copper, tobacco, coffee, cocoa, tea, and sugar, are important because they account for 25 percent of world merchandise trade and about half of the export earnings of developing countries.[57] Primary commodities are extremely important to both consumers and producers. The economic slowdown precipitated by the Asian financial crisis in 1997 caused demand to fall for commodities, resulting in a fall in prices. The low commodity prices were a boon to consumer countries, because they helped companies to keep down costs and therefore prices. But, producer countries, especially developing countries, suffered because of low commodity revenues. This section deals with how

A commodity agreement is designed to stabilize the price and supply of a good; it takes the form of a producers' alliance or an international commodity control agreement.

countries use commodity agreements to stabilize the price and supply of selected commodities.

PRODUCERS' ALLIANCES AND ICCAS

Producers' alliances—exclusive membership agreements between producing and exporting countries, such as OPEC.

ICCAs—agreements between producing and consuming countries.

Commodity agreements are of two basic types: producers' alliances and international commodity control agreements (ICCAs). Producers' alliances are exclusive membership agreements between producing and exporting countries. Examples are the Organization of Petroleum Exporting Countries (OPEC) and the Union of Banana Exporting Countries. ICCAs are agreements between producing and consuming countries. Examples of ICCAs are the International Cocoa Organization (ICCO) and the International Sugar Organization. Membership of the 1993 ICCO Agreement, for example, comprises 41 countries, representing over 91 percent of world cocoa production and over 62 percent of world cocoa consumption.

Most developing countries traditionally have relied on the export of one or two commodities to supply the foreign currencies from industrial countries they need for economic development. This is especially true of the African developing countries. However, commodity prices are not stable. Both consumers and producers prefer a stabilized pricing system that allows for planning of future costs and earnings. Unfortunately, many short-term factors, such as weather conditions and business cycles, cause sudden changes in supply and demand resulting in price instability. In the face of strong market forces, countries try to counteract price instability through one of several different stabilization schemes:

- Stabilization of world commodity prices through the exercise of market power by a monopolistic producer or producer cartel or through international commodity agreements
- Stabilization of producer revenues through the use of risk-management instruments, such as commodities futures
- Stabilization of government revenues through precautionary savings funds
- Compensatory financing
- Stabilization of domestic producer and consumer prices through variable export taxes or tariffs, agricultural marketing boards, or domestic stockpiles and stabilization funds[58]

Buffer-stock system—a commodity agreement by which reserve stocks of the good are bought and sold to regulate the price; not very effective anymore.

One approach that was popular until the late 1980s was the buffer-stock system. A **buffer-stock system** is a partially managed commodity agreement that a central agency monitors. Free-market forces determine price within a certain range. If the price moves outside that range, the central agency buys or sells the commodity to support the price. Member countries provide funds that the buffer-stock manager can use to purchase the commodity. However, most international commodity agreements dropped their buffer-stock schemes in the late 1980s when it was determined that price shocks were relatively long lived and not much affected by buffer stocks.

Quota system—determines how producing and consuming countries divide total output and sales; used by OPEC.

Another approach is a **quota system**, where producing countries divide total output and sales to stabilize the price. For a quota system to work, participating countries must cooperate among themselves to prevent sharp fluctuations in supply. The quota system is most effective when a single country has a large share of world production or consumption because it is able to control supply much more easily. Two of the best examples of a quota system are wool, controlled by Australia, and diamonds, controlled by the DeBeers Company in South Africa. Because DeBeers controls most of the diamond mining in the world, it can control price by determining how many diamonds to release on the world market. Not all commodity agreements work well. Countries in producers' alliances tend to disagree on the quotas allotted to them.

The type of commodity also influences a commodity agreement's effectiveness. For some commodities, especially food, beverages, and agricultural raw materials, there are differences in substitutability. For example, tea can substitute for coffee, and sugar beets might substitute for cane sugar. This limits the ability of coffee and cane sugar producers to control price. However, not all commodities have a ready substitute, so those producers have more control over price.

THE ORGANIZATION OF PETROLEUM EXPORTING COUNTRIES (OPEC)

OPEC is an example of a producer cartel. It is a group of commodity-producing countries that have significant control over supply and that band together to control output and price. OPEC is part of a larger category of energy commodities, which also includes coal and natural gas. OPEC is not confined to the Middle East. The members are Algeria, Indonesia, Iran, Iraq, Kuwait, Libya, Nigeria, Qatar, Saudi Arabia, the United Arab Emirates, and Venezuela. OPEC controls prices by establishing production quotas on member countries. Saudi Arabia has historically performed the role of the dominant supplier in OPEC that can influence supply and price. Periodically, at least annually, OPEC oil ministers gather together to determine the quota for each country based on estimates of supply and demand.

Politics are also an important dimension to OPEC deliberations. OPEC member countries with large populations need large oil revenues to fund government programs. As a result, they are tempted to exceed their export quotas to generate more revenues. A major reason for the invasion of Kuwait by Iraq in 1990 was because Kuwait was producing more than its quota, which depressed world oil prices. Iraqi President Saddam Hussein blamed Kuwait for low world oil prices, which reduced the amount of revenue Iraq could earn with its oil exports. Thus he felt justified in invading Kuwait to gain control over its oil supplies so that he could increase his own oil revenues.

OPEC member countries produce about 40 percent of the world's crude oil and 14 percent of its natural gas. However, OPEC's oil exports represent about 60 percent of the oil traded internationally. Therefore, OPEC can have a strong influence on the oil market, especially if it decides to reduce or increase its level of production.[59] Sometimes OPEC policies work; sometimes they don't. In 1999, OPEC met and established strict production quotas to try to raise prices. It seemed to work so well that by the third quarter of the year, prices had nearly doubled. Several factors seemed key: Countries actually stuck to their quotas, the Asian economies were beginning to recover, and the U.S. economy was remaining strong. The last two factors led to strong demand at the same time production was being trimmed, causing prices to rise.[60]

Because commodities are the raw materials used in the production process, it is important for managers of companies that use commodities to understand the factors that influence their prices. During the Asia financial crisis, when commodity prices collapsed, commodity exporters suffered but commodity importers benefited from the lower commodity costs.

THE ENVIRONMENT

Pollution of the air, land, and sea clearly poses a threat to the future of the planet, and governments, companies, and individuals are concerned. Although many environmental problems are national in nature, they may have cross-national ramifications and require cross-national agreements. In addition, lax environmental rules and enforcement in one country could influence trade and investment flows as noted in the discussion on NAFTA. Some of these cross-national agreements are tied to regional groups, such as the EU and NAFTA. These agreements tend to have a strong influence because of the commitment of group members to environmental issues. One example is the concern over water along the U.S.-Mexico border and the impact of acid rain in waters along the U.S.-Canadian border. It would make sense for countries to tackle those issues on a regional basis.

However, these regional agreements still do not solve problems on a global basis, and the major source of influence for global environmental agreements is the United Nations. The United Nations is a political organization comprised of 185 countries (see www.un.org), and it is headquartered in New York City. The UN deals with a variety of political issues, such as security and world peace, but it also deals in humanitarian and economic issues. One of the key economic issues is that of the environment. In 1992, more than 100 heads of state met in Rio de Janeiro, Brazil, for the first international Earth Summit convened to address urgent problems of environmental protection and socioeconomic development. The assembled leaders signed the Convention on Climate Change and the Convention on Biological Diversity, endorsed the Rio Declaration and the Forest Principles, and adopted Agenda 21, a 300-page plan for achieving sustainable development in the twenty-first century.[61]

The Commission on Sustainable Development (CSD) was created to monitor and report on implementation of the Earth Summit agreements. A five-year review of Earth Summit was made in 1997 by the United Nations General Assembly meeting in special session. This special session of the UN General Assembly took stock of how well countries, international organizations, and sectors of civil society had responded to the challenge of the Earth Summit.[62]

Major types of environmental degradation are ozone depletion, air pollution, acid rain, water pollution, waste disposal, and deforestation. Ozone depletion results from the burning of fossil fuels and the emission of ozone-depleting chemicals, such as chlorofluorocarbons (CFCs). Ozone depletion may lead to global warming and the destruction of life as a result of excessive exposure to ultraviolet radiation. The Montreal Protocol on Substances that Deplete the Ozone Layer, a UN program, was originally signed in 1987 and amended in 1990, 1992, 1995 and 1997, and it calls for the phaseout of CFCs and other ozone-depleting chemicals by the year 2006.[63]

The UN also tackles environmental issues through the UN Environment Programme (UNEP), an agency of the Economic and Social Council. UNEP works on a variety of issues, including the management of chemicals, the transborder movements of

Many environmental problems require national solutions, but many cross national boundaries and need to be solved through treaties and agreements.

The United Nations is a 185-member-country organization that deals with many social, political, and environmental issues.

Ethical Dilemmas and Social Responsibility
THE SEATTLE WTO PROTEST SPOTLIGHTS
FREE TRADE'S EFFECTS ON
THE ENVIRONMENT

In November 1999, the WTO met in Seattle to set an agenda for the next round of trade talks. Everyone knew there would be protestors from all sides of the political spectrum representing labor, environmental, and other groups. However, nobody but the anarchists dreamed that the demonstrations would turn so violent. In the aftermath of the demonstrations, the question remains, "What is the relationship between free trade and the environment?" What responsibility do groups like the EU and NAFTA have to push for improvements in the environment as they liberalize trade and investment flows?

Prior to the Seattle meetings, the WTO had largely ignored environmental issues. Its mandate was to liberalize trade, not protect the environment. However, environmental issues are important to both the EU and NAFTA. In the early 1990s, Mexico complained to GATT that the United States was unfairly banning imports of tuna caught in nets that kill dolphins. GATT ruled against the United States, stating that discriminatory trade practices shouldn't be used to protect dolphins but that the United States should require Mexican canners to label their tuna as dolphin-safe tuna so that consumers could make a choice.

In some ways, this galvanized the environmental lobby to oppose trade agreements that did not consider the environment. Presidential candidate Bill Clinton argued against NAFTA in the 1992 elections, but he ended up supporting NAFTA as President by including a side agreement on the environment. Since then, environmental issues have been an important, though not highly effective, part of NAFTA. The WTO, and all regional trade agreements, has argued that free trade actually should help the environment. As trade increases, incomes rise, which results in a people that are both concerned about the environment and able to pay for cleaning it up. However, WTO also admits that increased trade can harm the environment. Instead of stopping trade, which extreme environmental groups advocate, WTO advocates increasing trade while dealing with the specific environmental issues. However, developing countries like Mexico are concerned that increased interest in environmental issues could just be an excuse for trade sanctions against them. Thus the developing countries are not as anxious to pursue environmental issues in trade agreements. Several environmental proposals that regional and global trading groups will have to consider are

- Eliminating environmentally damaging subsidies for farming, fishing, and fossil fuels
- Offering more scope for the labeling of eco-friendly products
- Assessing the environmental impact of the world trading system and of proposals for future liberalization
- Making agreements more transparent, accountable, and accessible to environmental NGOs—nongovernmental organizations[64]

hazardous wastes and their disposal, the protection of the marine environment from land-based activities, the Framework Convention on Climate Change (which is building on the Montreal Protocol), and the linkage of environmental and economic concerns. UNEP is important because of its global reach and its ability to marshal the resources of different agencies.

The problem with international environmental agreements is that countries differ significantly in how they deal with environmental issues. This problem is especially acute in developing countries, where some of the worst environmental damage occurs and laws tend to be the most lax. Some MNEs might be tempted to save costs by locating production facilities in countries in which environmental laws are weak. However, many MNEs are among the world's most environmentally responsible companies. They seek to reduce costs by redesigning manufacturing processes to use inputs more efficiently.

Environmental agreements force companies to act more responsibly in the countries where they are doing business. Initially, companies could perceive compliance as increasing the costs of doing business. However, the agreements put all companies on the same level, so environmental compliance should not disadvantage one company compared to another.

WEB CONNECTION

Check out our home page at www.prenhall.com/daniels for links to key resources for you in your study of international business.

SUMMARY

- Efforts at regional economic integration began to emerge after World War II as countries saw benefits of cooperation and larger market sizes. The major types of economic integration are the free trade area, the customs union, the common market, and complete economic integration.

- In its most limited form, economic integration allows countries to trade goods without tariff discrimination (a free trade area). In its most extensive form, all factors of production are allowed to move across borders, and some degree of social, political, and economic harmonization is undertaken (complete economic integration).

- The static effects of economic integration improve the efficiency of resource allocation and affect both produc-

tion and consumption. The dynamic effects are internal and external efficiencies that arise because of changes in market size.

- Once protection is eliminated among member countries, trade creation allows MNEs to specialize and trade based on comparative advantage.

- Trade diversion occurs when the supply of products shifts from countries that are not members of an economic bloc to those that are.

- Regional, as opposed to global, economic integration occurs because of the greater ease of promoting cooperation on a smaller scale.

- The European Union (EU) is an effective common market that has abolished most restrictions on factor mobility and is harmonizing national political, economic, and social policies. As of 1999, it was comprised of Austria, Belgium, Denmark, Finland, France, Germany, Greece, Ireland, Italy, Luxembourg, the Netherlands, Portugal, Spain, Sweden, and the United Kingdom.

- Some of the EU's major goals are to abolish intrazonal restrictions on the movement of goods, capital, services, and labor; to establish a common external tariff; to achieve a common agricultural policy; to harmonize tax and legal systems; to devise a uniform policy concerning antitrust; and to establish a common currency and common monetary policy.

- On January 1, 1999, the EU introduced a common currency, the euro, with banknotes due to be issued in 2002.

- The EU has several free trade agreements with countries and groups of countries, making it the world's largest and richest trading bloc. Twelve countries have been targeted for the next phase of expansion.

- The North American Free Trade Agreement (NAFTA) is designed to eliminate tariff barriers and liberalize investment opportunities and trade in services. Key provisions in NAFTA are labor and environmental agreements.

- There are key trade groups in other parts of the world, including Latin America, Asia, and Africa.

- Many developing countries rely on commodity exports to supply the hard currency they need for economic development. Instability in commodity prices has resulted in fluctuations in export earnings. Commodity agreements, using one of several stabilization schemes, seek to stabilize prices.

- Although many environmental issues can be solved at the national level, others require cross-national cooperation.

C A S E

CRYSTAL LAKE MANUFACTURING—A NAFTA DILEMMA[65]

At the close of 1999, Crystal Lake Manufacturing of Autaugaville, Alabama, was trying to decide if it could survive the NAFTA environment once tariffs are dropped on Mexican brooms shipped to the United States. In 1996, President Clinton announced that he would provide the industry "tariff relief on broom corn brooms for a period of three years that will provide time for the domestic industry to implement an adjustment plan that will facilitate its positive adjustment to import competition." Initially, the U.S. International Trade Commission had ruled that the industry should receive protection, but President Clinton refused to grant the industry relief until after the 1996 presidential elections. Then he reviewed the findings and decided to give the industry three years of tariff relief before exposing the industry to competition from Mexico and other developing countries in the region.

THE PRODUCT

The broom industry in the United States is composed of brooms that use natural fibers and brooms that use synthetic fibers. It is the natural-fibers part of the market and its relationship to U.S. trade agreements, especially the Caribbean Basin Initiative and NAFTA, that is at issue for Crystal Lake.

Broom-corn brooms are made of stiff fiber generated from broom corn, plus the handles, wire, and so on. The principal raw material for the brooms, known as broom corn, used to come primarily from the Midwest. However, midwestern farmers stopped growing broom corn in the 1970s, and the growing of broom corn gradually moved west and then south to Mexico to take advantage of cheaper labor rates. Virtually all of the broom corn U.S. producers use comes from Mexico.

Mexican broom-corn exporters supply the U.S. market primarily through two U.S. dealers. In addition to supplying the U.S. producers with broom corn, Mexican companies also supply broom corn to the broom industries in Honduras and Panama. U.S. producers of broom-corn brooms tend to use the two dealers to avoid currency risks, risks of price fluctuations, and inventory costs. In addition, the dealers can scour Mexico to find the best supplies, which tend to come from five different regions in Mexico.

The broom-corn broom production process is very labor intensive, using one of two different manufacturing processes. The first and most common in the United States is the "wire-bound" process, which involves the hand winding of tufts of broom corn by workers at individual workstations using a simple winding machine operated by a foot pedal. This is the process used at Crystal Lake Manufacturing, and it takes months, sometimes years, for a worker to master the wire-bound process. An experienced worker can produce 18 to 20 brooms over an 8-hour shift. Experience is key because broom makers are paid on a piece-rate basis. Approximately 25 percent of the cost of a broom using this method is the labor cost. Skilled workers get paid about $8.00 per hour in the United States, compared to significantly lower hourly wage rates in Mexico. In 1995, the average Mexican broom cost $1.92, compared with $3.00 to $3.40 per broom for U.S.-made brooms.

The second manufacturing process is the "nailed machine-made" process, in which the broom fibers are sewn together, usually by machine. This process is less labor intensive, but the machines are not cheap, costing about $150,000 each. It was estimated that only 16 percent of the broom-corn brooms manufactured in the United States in 1995 used this method, and 95 percent of them were made by four companies.

SUBSTITUTES

A major issue considered by the U.S. International Trade Commission (USITC) in making a ruling to President Clinton was whether all brooms—broom-corn brooms and synthetic brooms—should be lumped together as one product or should be considered as two products. It is clear that synthetic brooms are in direct competition to broom-corn brooms. Even though the products have different properties, they perform the same functions. The key is that some manufacturers such as Crystal Lake produce both types, even though other manufacturers specialize in broom-corn brooms. The significance is that diversified companies are not hurt by the fall in broom-corn broom sales if they can offset the losses with synthetic broom sales.

COMPETITORS

The competition in the broom industry is both domestic and foreign. The U.S. Cornbroom Task Force is composed of ten firms, one of which is Crystal Lake. Crystal Lake is one of three in the Task Force that markets a full range of cleaning supply products (broom-corn brooms, plastic brooms, mops, and cleaning brushes) on a national basis using its own brand name. It is hard to determine the exact size of the industry, although the USITC estimates that there are fewer than eighty producers in the United States. Most of the companies, like Crystal Lake, are family owned and relatively

small. For example, Warren Manufacturing in Arcola, Illinois, and American Broom Co. in Mattoon, Illinois, employ twenty and eighteen workers, respectively. Given the competitive pressures, companies were beginning to consolidate in order to be able to supply the big accounts that dominate the retail market. Many of the companies are in very small communities where the loss of jobs could have a real impact on the local economy. For example, Autaugaville, Alabama, has a population of 681 people, and Arcola, Illinois, which calls itself the Broom Capital of the World, has only 2,600 residents. One estimate put broom-corn broom employment at about 1,500 nationwide, generating sales of about $100 million annually in 1993, and another estimate put employment at 600 nationwide in 1996.

Foreign suppliers of broom-corn brooms to the U.S. market come principally from five countries: Mexico, Honduras, Colombia, Panama, and Hungary. Plastic brooms are sourced primarily from Brazil, Italy, and Venezuela, which accounted for more than 70 percent of the plastic broom imports in 1995.

THE BREAKING OF THE TARIFF WALLS

In 1992 and 1993 when NAFTA was being debated before passage, Crystal Lake management was clearly concerned about the potential impact of eliminating the 32-percent tariff on Mexican broom imports. It estimated that half the plant workers might lose their jobs as a result.

Table 7.6 provides data on shipments of corn brooms and plastic brooms by domestic and foreign producers for the five-year period ending in 1995. Foreign producers are broken into major supplier countries. Table 7.7 provides additional data on U.S. imports of corn brooms by source country for the five years ending in 1995. Finally, Table 7.8 provides information about U.S. production capacity, actual production, and capacity utilization of corn brooms for the five years ending in 1995.

INDUSTRY RESPONSE

In response to the rapid increase in corn broom imports into the United States, the U.S. Cornbroom Task Force, representing U.S. producers, filed petitions with the U.S. International Trade Commission to win protection from foreign competition. The Task Force filed petitions covered by two areas of U.S. trade law: section 302 of the North American Free Trade Agreement Implementation Act and section 202 of the Trade Act of 1974. Sections 302 and 202 set out tests for determining whether an industry is eligible for relief under the respective trade laws.

TABLE 7.6 Broom-Corn Brooms, Plastic Brooms, and All Brooms: U.S. Producers' Shipments, U.S. Imports, by Sources, and Apparent U.S. Consumption, 1991–1995 (dozens)

Item	1991	1992	1993	1994	1995
Broom-corn brooms:					
U.S. producers' shipments	1,132,125	1,087,100	1,097,977	1,071,269	951,989
U.S. imports from:					
Mexico	157,605	104,067	125,528	195,770	388,286
Panama	43,714	38,952	51,611	107,921	62,306
Honduras	30,174	71,289	70,927	66,817	45,914
Colombia	0	4,465	10,439	13,544	24,981
Hungary	28,920	26,880	43,980	34,208	9,000
All other	39,278	7,771	36,667	26,236	16,222
Total	299,692	253,423	337,151	444,496	546,709
Apparent consumption	1,431,817	1,340,523	1,435,128	1,515,765	1,498,698
Plastic brooms:					
U.S. producers' shipments	605,676	606,067	635,616	716,897	877,844
U.S. imports from:					
Italy	333,222	442,868	305,229	351,471	361,835
Brazil	198,179	546,509	488,956	436,439	340,264
Mexico	27,355	41,428	34,715	51,085	145,347
Venezuela	119,570	84,075	125,444	105,566	120,177
All other	99,284	239,426	205,175	159,167	180,457
Total	777,610	1,354,306	1,159,518	1,103,727	1,148,080
Apparent consumption	1,383,286	1,960,373	1,795,134	1,820,624	2,025,924
All brooms:					
U.S. producers' shipments	1,737,801	1,693,167	1,733,593	1,788,166	1,829,833
U.S. imports from:					
Mexico	184,960	145,494	158,242	246,855	533,633
Italy	336,050	442,868	305,229	351,471	362,435
Brazil	198,179	546,509	488,956	436,439	342,904
Venezuela	119,570	84,075	125,444	105,566	120,177
Panama	47,121	44,767	55,063	114,542	93,849
Honduras	30,174	77,179	76,642	81,508	51,682
Colombia	312	4,465	10,439	18,709	24,981
Hungary	34,920	29,880	43,980	34,625	9,000
All others	126,016	232,492	232,674	158,509	156,129
Total	1,077,301	1,607,729	1,496,670	1,548,223	1,694,789
Apparent consumption	2,815,102	3,300,896	3,230,263	3,336,389	3,524,622

Source: U.S. International Trade Commission (USITC). *Broom Corn Brooms: Investigations Nos. TA-201-65 and NAFTA 302-1,* Publication 2984 (Washington, D.C.: USITC, August 1996), pp. 11–14.

Under section 202, the Commission had to explain its decision in terms of three statutory criteria that must be present to reach a positive determination:

1. The subject article is being imported into the United States in increased quantities.
2. The domestic industry is seriously injured or threatened with serious injury.
3. Such increased imports are a substantial cause of the serious injury or threat of serious injury.

To qualify for the NAFTA provision in section 302, the Commission considers imports only from a NAFTA country and also must find that the increase in imports from a NAFTA country is a result of the reduction or elimination of a duty under NAFTA.

On July 26, 1996, the USITC Commissioners, in a split vote of 3–2, ruled as follows:

1. "broom-corn brooms are being imported into the United States in such increased quantities as to be a substantial cause of serious injury to the domestic industry producing an article like or directly competitive with the imported article; and
2. [pursuant to the NAFTA provisions] that imports of broom-corn brooms produced in Mexico account for a substantial share of total imports of such brooms and contribute importantly to the serious injury caused by imports; but find that imports of broom-corn brooms produced in Canada do not account for a substantial share of total imports and thus do not

TABLE 7.7 Broom-Corn Brooms: U.S. Imports for Consumption, by Sources, 1991–1995

Source	1991	1992	1993	1994	1995
			Quantity (*dozens*)		
U.S. imports from:					
Mexico	157,605	104,067	123,528	195,770	388,286
Panama	43,714	38,952	51,611	107,921	62,306
Honduras	30,174	71,289	70,927	66,817	45,914
Colombia	0	4,465	10,439	13,544	24,981
Hungary	28,920	26,880	43,980	34,208	9,000
All other	39,278	7,771	36,667	26,236	16,222
Total	299,692	253,423	337,151	444,496	546,709
			Value (*1,000 dollars*)		
U.S. imports from:					
Mexico	3,129	2,173	2,356	4,070	6,695
Panama	542	491	727	1,728	1,155
Honduras	404	1,073	1,663	1,652	1,216
Colombia	0	55	149	274	460
Hungary	232	200	329	197	62
All other	216	101	228	153	192
Total	4,523	4,094	5,452	8,073	9,780
			Unit Value (*dollars per dozen*)		
U.S. imports from:					
Mexico	$19.85	$20.88	$19,07	$20.79	$17.24
Panama	12.39	12.61	14.09	16.01	18.54
Honduras	13.38	15.05	23.45	24.72	26.49
Colombia	—	12.40	14.27	20.23	18.40
Hungary	8.04	7.45	7.48	5.77	6.87
All others	5.50	12.95	6.21	5.83	11.81
Total	15.09	16.15	16.17	18.16	17.89
			Ratio to U.S. Production (*percent based on quantity*)		
U.S. imports from:					
Mexico	14.0	9.5	11.3	18.4	40.9
Panama	3.9	3.7	4.7	10.2	6.6
Honduras	2.7	6.5	6.5	6.3	5.8
Colombia	—	0.4	1.0	1.3	2.6
Hungary	2.6	2.5	4.0	3.2	0.9
All other	3.5	0.7	3.3	2.5	1.7
Total	26.7	23.2	30.7	41.8	57.7

Source: U.S. International Trade Commission (USITC), *Broom Corn Brooms: Investigations Nos. TA-201-65 and NAFTA 302-1,* Publication 2984 (Washington, D.C.: USITC, August 1996), pp. 11–17.

contribute importantly to the serious injury caused by imports."

The Commission found that imports had increased at the expense of domestic production, especially after the NAFTA tariff reductions ensued in 1994. They found that companies were being hurt—operating income turned from a gain to a loss for a sample of U.S. producers between 1993 and 1994, and employment, hours worked, and total wages paid declined in 1995. In the case of NAFTA, the Commission

looked at all possible reasons why imports went up so significantly, but nothing emerged that was more important than or as important as the tariff reductions.

As a result of their findings, the Commission recommended to President Clinton that he impose a 32-percent tariff and give broom makers four years to adjust to the new competitive landscape before tariffs are removed for good. They also recommended that the duty-free treatment of brooms by the Caribbean Basin and Andean countries be suspended.

TABLE 7.8   **Broom-Corn Brooms: U.S. Capacity, Production, and Capacity Utilization, 1991–1995**

Item	1991	1992	1993	1994	1995
Capacity (dozens)	1,457,236	1,395,886	1,402,593	1,348,810	1,349,475
Production (dozens)	1,123,134	1,094,006	1,096,656	1,063,067	948,267
Capacity utilization (percent)	70.9	73.3	72.4	72.3	64.8

Compiled from data submitted in response to Commission questionnaires.

Capacity utilization calculated using data from those firms providing both capacity and production information.

Source: U.S. International Trade Commission (USITC), *Broom Corn Brooms: Investigations Nos. TA-201-65 and NAFTA 302-1,* Publication 2984 (Washington, D.C.: USITC, August 1996), pp. 11–18.

However, two commissioners disagreed. One of them, Commissioner Watson, argued the following against the broom-corn broom industry:

This is one of those cases where the parties disagree about nearly every issue. The petitioners argue that there is such a thing as a domestic broom-corn broom industry distinct from the broom industry generally. They also argue that industry is besieged and in danger of being swept onto the ash heap of history. They point to idled plants, increased unemployment, a loss of market share leading to lower production, and balance sheets heavily smudged by red ink. They claim that this perilous state was produced by a cascade of imports, particularly imports from Mexico.

Respondents disagree. They argue that the domestic broom-corn broom industry is but a part of a single broom industry. That industry, say respondents, is being whisked into the modern age by automation and the rapidly growing acceptance of plastic fiber as a substitute for broom corn. They bristle at the petitioners' complaints about competition and contend that what the domestic industry really needs are companies willing to try to mop up the profits to be had by investing in the equipment and training needed to increase productivity and lower the cost of production. The respondents accuse the petitioners of trying to sweep the success of such innovative American companies under the rug, and urge the Commission to peek beneath the petitioners' blanket charges to see an industry with an increasingly productive and well-paid workforce fully capable of standing upright against all competitors. The respondents acknowledge that imports of broom-corn brooms have increased, but contend that the increase is not nearly as important a

source of the broom-corn broom makers' woes as is the modernization of broom manufacturing. It is certainly not, they say, the result of NAFTA's knocking a small hole in the high tariff wall built against Mexican imports.

On September 6, 1996, President Clinton declined to impose an import tariff to protect U.S. broom makers under the provisions of NAFTA, despite a recommendation for one from the USITC. He directed the U.S. Trade Representative to seek a solution within 90 days of September 6, at which time he would look at the alternative solutions and make a determination. That took place on December 3 when he decided to provide the industry with tariff relief.

QUESTIONS

1. How have the Caribbean Basin Initiative and the NAFTA agreements affected the market share of the U.S. corn broom industry? Be sure to analyze the data to identify market share of different countries and trends over time.

2. Given the impact of import competition on the corn broom industry and the recommendation of the USITC, should President Clinton have allowed the industry to be shielded from competition through higher tariffs? Should the broom-corn broom industry be allowed to die in the United States? If not, what is the cost of protecting the industry?

3. If you were a worker at Crystal Lake Manufacturing, would you be in favor of NAFTA? Why or why not? If you were the purchasing agent for brooms for Wal-Mart, would you be in favor of NAFTA? Why or why not?

4. What are the different scenarios that Crystal Lake Manufacturing could face in the new millenium? What should be its strategies, given the different scenarios?

CHAPTER NOTES

1 The information in this case is from the following sources: http://ford.com; various issues of the Ford Motor Company's Annual Report; "Tough at the Top," *The Economist*, March 13, 1993, p. 76; Richard A. Melcher and John Templeman, "Ford of Europe: Slimmer, but Maybe Not Luckier," *Business Week*, January 18, 1993, pp. 44, 46; Timothy Aeppel, "Ford Reaches Fork in Road in Its European Operations," *Wall Street Journal*, October 6, 1992, p. 88; Richard A. Melcher, "Ford Is Ready to Roll in the New Europe," *Business Week*, December 12, 1988, p. 60; James B. Treece, Kathleen Kerwin, and Heidi Dawley, "Ford: Alex Trotman's Daring Strategy," *Business Week*, April 3, 1995, pp. 94–104; Diana T. Kurylko, "European Profits Are a Priority; New Focus World Car Is Crucial," *Automotive News*, September 14, 1998, p. 41; Paul Einstein, "Ford Europe Still Struggling," *Automotive Industries*, October 1, 1998, p. 30; David Sumner Smith, "Ford's Global Potential with Luxury Brands," *Marketing*, April 1, 1999, p. 18; Bradford Wernele, "Ford Blames Aging Products for European Sales Slide," *Automotive News*, April 26, 1999, p. 6; Fara Warner, "Does Ford of Europe's Chief Face Impossible Mission?" *Wall Street Journal*, June 18, 1999, p. B4; Kathleen Kerwin and Jack Ewing, "Nasser: Ford Be Nimble," *Business Week*, September 27, 1999, pp. 42–43; Kathleen Kerwin and Keith Naughton, "Remaking Ford," *Business Week*, October 11, 1999, pp. 134–142.

2 Bela Balassa, *The Theory of Economic Integration* (Homewood, IL: Irwin, 1961), p. 40.

3 "European Parliament Fact Sheets," http://www.europarl.eu.int/dg4/factsheets/en/1_1_1.htm (1999).

4 "Institutions of the European Union," http://europa.eu.int/inst-en.htm (1999).

5 "The European Commission," http://europa.eu.int/inst/en/com.htm#members (1999).

6 Ibid.

7 Brandon Mitchener and Geoff Winestock, "French Socialist Gets Trade Post at European Panel," *Wall Street Journal*, July 12, 1999, p. A14.

8 "Parallel Imports: Hardly the Full Monty," *The Economist*, February 27, 1999, p. 72.

9 David Thomas, Victorya Hong, and Joe Mapother, "EU Commissioners Quit En Masse, Putting Some Business in Limbo," *Business Week Online*, March 16, 1999 (http://www.businessweek.com/bwdaily/dnflash/mar1999/br90316a.htm).

10 "Europe's Future," *The Economist*, October 23, 1999, pp. 16–17.

11 "The Council of the European Union," http://europa.eu.int/inst/en/cl.htm#function (1999).

12 "The Council of the European Union," http://europa.eu.int/inst/en/cl.htm (1999).

13 "My Continent, Right or Wrong," in a Survey of Europe, *The Economist*, October 23, 1999, p. 4.

14 "City of Hypocrites," in a Survey of Europe, ibid.

15 "The European Parliament," http://europa.eu.int/inst/en/ep.htm#intro (1999).

16 "The European Parliament: Body Building," *The Economist*, July 24, 1999, pp. 46–47.

17 "The European Court of Justice," http://europa.eu.int/inst/en/cj.htm (1999).

18 Greg Steinmetz, "In Court of Justice, European Union Finds Mediator with Clout," *Wall Street Journal*, March 16, 1999, p. A1.

19 Ernst & Whinney, *Europe 1992: The Single Market*, September 1988, pp. 5–6.

20 HSCB, *European Union*, 1998, pp. 6–7.

21 "Update on the Single Market," http://europa.eu.int/comm/dg15/en/update/score/score5.htm (1999).

22 "The Maastricht Treaty: Where's the Beef?" *The Economist*, May 1, 1993, p. 54.

23 "From Here to EMU," *The Economist*, August 5, 1995, p. 72.

24 "Gambling on the Euro," *The Economist*, January 2, 1999, pp. 19–22.

25 "Converging by Diverging," *The Economist*, October 2, 1999, p. 84.

26 Edmund L. Andrews, "On Euro Weekend, Financial Institutions in Vast Reprogramming," *New York Times*, January 2, 1999 (Web version).

27 "Faster Forward," *The Economist*, November 28, 1998, p. 83.

28 John Barham and Caroline Southey, "Turkish-EU Customs Union Wins Backing from MEPs," *Financial Times*, December 14, 1995, p. 2.

29 Sandor Richter and Laszlo G. Toth, "After the Agreement on Free Trade Among Visegard Group Countries," *Russia and East European Finance and Trade*, July–August 1994, pp. 23–69.

30 Heidi Dawley, "Watch Out: Here Comes Wal-Mart," *Business Week*, June 28, 1999, p. 48.

31 Carol Matlack, Inka Resch, and Wendy Zellner, "En Garde, Wal-Mart," *Business Week*, September 13, 1999, p. 54.

32 "My Continent, Right or Wrong," p. 3.

33 Brandon Mitchener, "EU Citizens, Policy Makers Differ on Priorities for Future of Euro," *Wall Street Journal*, June 8, 1999 (Internet edition).

34 Linda M. Aguilar, "NAFTA: A Review of the Issues," *Economic Perspectives* (Federal Reserve Bank of Chicago, 1992), p. 14; "OAS Overview of the North American Free Trade Agreement," http://www.sice.oas.org/summary/nafta/naftatoc.stm, also on http://www.nafta.net.

35 Richard Lawrence, "NAFTA at 5: Happy Birthday?" *Journal of Commerce*, February 1, 1999.

36 Geri Smith and Elisabeth Malkin, "Mexican Makeover: NAFTA Creates the World's Newest Industrial Power," *Business Week*, December 21, 1998, pp. 50–52.

37 "OAS Overview of the North American Free Trade Agreement, Chapter Four: Rules of Origin," http://www.sice.oas.org/summary/nafta/naftatoc.stm.

38 Ibid.

39 "OAS Overview of the North American Free Trade Agreement, Chapter Twenty: Institutional Arrangements and Dispute Settlement Procedures," http://www.sice.oas.org/summary/nafta/nafta20.stm.

40 "Summary of the North American Agreement on Labor Cooperation," http://www.mac.doc.gov/nafta/3006.htm.

41 "Summary of the Agreement on Environmental Cooperation," http://www.mac.doc.gov/nafta/3005.htm.

42 "NAFTA Secretariat," http://www.nafta-sec-alena.org/english/index.htm.

43 Alejandro Ibarra-Yunez, "NAFTA After Five Years: The Economic and Regulatory Setting in Mexico," presented at annual meeting of the Academy of International Business, November 1999, Charleston, South Carolina.

44 Smith and Malkin, "Mexican Makeover," p. 51.

45 "Jesse vs. the Sour Grapes," *Wall Street Journal*, September 20, 1999, p. A28.

46 Smith and Malkin, "Mexican Makeover," p. 52.

47 Joel Millman, "EU and Mexico Reach Free-Trade Pact," *Wall Street Journal*, November 26, 1999, p. A9.

48 Sydney Weintraub, "A Politically Unpopular Success Story," *Los Angeles Times*, February 7, 1999.

49 Smith and Malkin, "Mexican Makeover," p. 51.

50 Aaron Bernstein, "Welch's March to the South," *Business Week*, December 6, 1999, pp. 74, 78.

51 "Mercosur's Malaise," *The Economist*, April 24, 1999, pp. 31–32.

52 *Europa World Year Book* (London, England: Europa Publications Limited, 1999) p. 114.

53 Fred Bergsten, "The Case for APEC," *The Economist*, January 6, 1996, p. 62.

54 Jane Khanna, "Asia-Pacific Economic Cooperation and Challenges for Political Leadership," *The Washington Quarterly*, Winter 1996. Available: NEXIS Library: GENERAL NEWS: NEWS: CURNWS.

55 Bergsten, "The Case for APEC."

56 http://www.apecsec.org.sg/apecnet.html.

57 Paul Cashin, Hong Liang, and C. John McDermott, "Do Commodity Price Shocks Last Too Long for Stabilization Schemes to Work?" *Finance & Development*, Vol. 36, No. 3, September 1999.

58 Ibid., p. 4.

59 "Frequently Asked Questions About OPEC," http://www.opec.org/faqs.htm#a15.

60 "Oil: The Latest Shock," *The Economist*, September 18, 1999, p. 70.

61 "Earth Summit+5," http://www.un.org/esa/earthsummit/ga97info.htm.

62 "Earth Summit+5," http://www.un.org/esa/earthsummit/.

63 "Ozone Treaties," http://www.unep.ch/ozone/home.htm

64 "Embracing Greenery," *The Economist,* October 9, 1999, pp. 89–90.

65 U.S. International Trade Commission (USITC), *Broom Corn Brooms: Investigations Nos. TA-201-65 and NAFTA 302-1*, Publication 2984 (Washington, D.C.: USITC, August 1996); "Sweeping Changes Are Being Feared," *Des Moines Register,* July 31, 1996, p. 10; Barnaby J. Feder, "Tiny Industry Fears NAFTA's Reach," *New York Times*, September 24, 1993, D1; "Report to the President on Investigation No. NAFTA-302-1 (Provisional Relief Phase): Broom Corn Brooms," http://www.usitc.gov/sec/I0513T1.htm; Paul Magnusson, "How Many Broom-Makers Does It Take to Kill a Trade Pact?" *Business Week*, July 20, 1992, pp. 29–30; Bill Mintz and Greg McDonald, "Free-Trade Agreement: For U.S. Firms, It's a Deal Likely to Cut Both Ways," *The Houston Chronicle,* August 13, 1992, p. A8; Paul Merrion and Sara Silver, "Broom Firms Still Bristling," *Crain's Chicago Business,* November 21, 1994, p. 15; Paul Merrion, "Trade Panel Deadlocks on Broom Makers' Appeal," *Crain's Chicago Business,* May 13, 1996, p. 45; Associated Press byline, "Tiny U.S. Broom Industry Could be Swept Away," *Los Angeles Times*, August 23, 1996, p. D7; and Doug Thompson, "Broom Firms Seeking Tariff Get Brush Off from Clinton," *Arkansas Democrat-Gazette*, September 6, 1996, p. 1D.

CHAPTER 8

Foreign Direct Investment

Who moves picks up, who stands still dries up. —ITALIAN PROVERB

OBJECTIVES

- To explain why investors and governments view direct investments differently than portfolio investments

- To demonstrate how companies acquire foreign direct investments

- To evaluate the relationship between foreign trade and international factor mobility, especially direct investment

- To classify companies' motivations for foreign direct investment

- To explain companies' advantages from foreign direct investments

- To show the major global patterns of foreign direct investment

Although there are more than 100 tire manufacturers worldwide, a few companies are accounting for a larger portion of global sales. This sales concentration has occurred because automobile manufacturers prefer to place large orders with a few tire suppliers for the original equipment market (OEM) and to offer replacement tires of the same brands wherever they sell cars. Moreover, the market has been demanding high-tech tires that provide better handling and more durability, which cost more to make than regular tires. Only those companies with high sales can effectively recoup the development costs. One major means of increasing sales has been for companies to acquire other companies. Map 8.1 shows the major acquisitions by the largest tire manufacturers.

Bridgestone Tire Company is the world's second largest company in terms of tire sales in 1999, up from fifth place in 1978. Until the mid-1980s the company geared all its sales efforts toward its home market in Japan, yet its foreign sales grew, mainly through indirect exports. Bridgestone's tires were part of the original equipment on exported Japanese automobiles, so they arrived in foreign markets in which the company made little or no export effort. Direct exports also grew as foreign consumers wanted Bridgestone replacements on the Japanese cars they had purchased. In the mid-1980s, Bridgestone's top management believed it was essential to strengthen this foreign growth, reasoning that it would be difficult to exceed the 50 percent market share Bridgestone already held in Japan.

But even earlier, in 1980, Bridgestone's president had announced that the company's first priority was to establish a manufacturing presence in the United States. Accordingly, it bought a truck-tire plant from Firestone in 1982. By 1987 one out of every ten new cars sold in the United States carried Bridgestone tires. Some dealers also carried Bridgestone tires as replacements. However, Bridgestone had a meager 2 percent of this larger replacement tire market. The company gradually became more confident in its ability to manage and control an automobile-tire manufacturing investment in the highly competitive U.S. market. Part of this confidence derived from its success in three areas: with foreign manufacturing facilities in four emeging economies, in Australia after buying out Uniroyal there, and with U.S. truck-tire manufacturing after 1982.

Then, in 1988, Bridgestone surprised analysts by buying Firestone's automobile-tire operations. This purchase gave Bridgestone five North American plants, which supplied about 40 percent of the tires for North American vehicles built by Ford and 21 percent of those built by GM, as well as plants in Portugal, Spain, France, Italy, Argentina, Brazil, and Venezuela.

But why should Bridgestone manufacture automobile tires in the United States? Why not continue exporting, because sales had grown by this means? Several factors could hurt Bridgestone's export activities to the United States. First were U.S. government-imposed restrictions on tire imports. Second were U.S. government restrictions against imports of Japanese automobiles, which would jeopardize the sale of original-equipment tires. The possibility of import restrictions already had led four major Japanese automakers to begin U.S. production, and all opted for U.S.-made tires once their plants were operating. Further, in late 1987, Germany's Continental Tire, which recently had bought General Tire, announced a joint venture in the United States with two Japanese companies, Toyo and Yokohama, aimed at gaining business from the Japanese automakers' U.S. plants. If this venture proved successful, even Bridgestone's sales in Japan might suffer if the automakers preferred to buy from one global supplier. Third,

MAP 8.1   Major Tire Producers and Their Recent Foreign Acquisitions

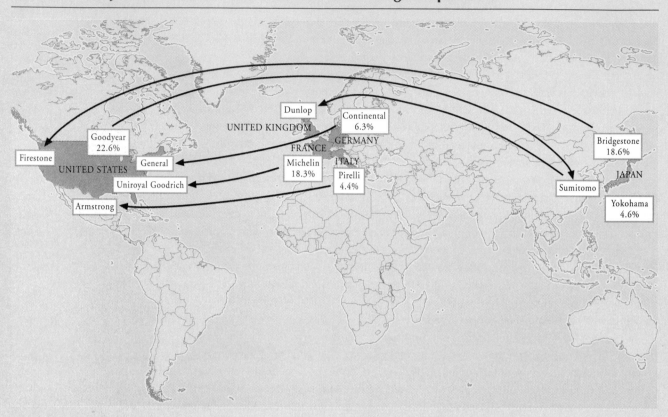

The percentages are the companies' global market share of tire sales. The arrows indicate the direction of recent acquisitions.

Source: Global market share figures come from "Sumitomo Rubber, Goodyear Union to Create Largest Tire Group," *Comline Daily News Transportation,* February 15, 1999; and Joseph B. White, "Goodyear, Sumitomo Rubber to Be Allies," *Wall Street Journal,* February 3, 1999, p. A3.

Bridgestone's exports also might suffer if Japanese costs rose more than U.S. costs. Most of Bridgestone's costs and its export prices were in yen. When the yen strengthened, U.S. importers had to pay more dollars to pay the yen prices. However, the strong 1988 yen meant that Bridgestone would pay less in yen for an investment in the United States. Finally, because of high transport costs for tires, which are bulky compared to their value, shipping them over large distances, except as part of vehicles' original equipment, is difficult and pricey.

But why buy Firestone rather than starting up a new automobile-tire facility? Because Firestone already had a significant U.S. market share, an acquisition would add less capacity to a glutted market than a start-up operation would. Bridgestone could sell most of its output to Firestone's existing customers. In fact, one of these, GM, awarded the investment as its supplier of the year in 1996 for its OEM sales to GM around the world. Another reason for acquiring Firestone was that Bridgestone had little experience in the United States, an environment very different from Japan's. The acquisition gave Bridgestone a U.S. management team that knew how to operate within the United States. ꙮ

INTRODUCTION

Recall from Chapter 1 that a foreign direct investment (FDI) is a company controlled through ownership by a foreign company or foreign individuals. FDI is important because production facilities abroad comprise a large and increasingly important part of international companies' activities and strategies. In fact, FDI is now more important than trade as a vehicle for international business.[2] Figure 8.1 shows its place in international business. No one explanation or theory encompasses all the reasons for such investment.[3]

The Bridgestone Tire case illustrates the numerous factors that influenced one Japanese company's decision to produce in a foreign country. Before deciding to invest in U.S. production facilities, Bridgestone faced a sequence of questions. Should it serve foreign markets? To sustain growth, Bridgestone had to either sell some new products or sell abroad—either of which would pose new risks.[4] Bridgestone chose to sell abroad because its managers believed its competitive advantage was more specific to producing tires than to knowing the Japanese market.

The Bridgestone Tire case also illustrates that companies can pursue different methods of acquiring FDI. Neither the motives nor the methods for acquiring such investment illustrated in the case are conclusive. This chapter further examines those various motives and methods.

Many companies must produce abroad if they are to sell abroad. The soft drink industry is a good example because transportation raises costs too high to make it profitable for soft-drink companies to sell in mass foreign markets by exporting. Here we see an ad for Coca-Cola in Malaysia, where the company has bottling operations.

FIGURE 8.1   The Place of FDI in International Business

FDI is a means by which international business is conducted.

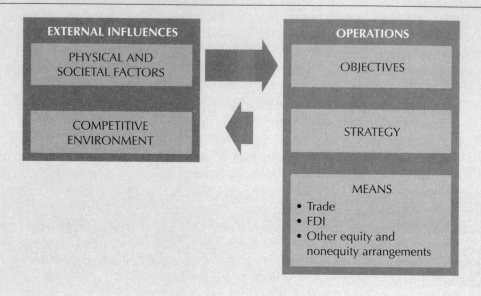

The growth of FDI has resulted in a heightened interest in three other questions:

1. What effect does FDI have on a country's economic, political, and social objectives?
2. What is, or should be, a company's locational pattern of foreign investment?
3. Should a company choose to operate abroad through some form other than direct investment, such as licensing?

In this chapter we teach you what FDI is, how it is done, and what its advantages are. This will prepare you for a more thorough treatment of the above questions in later chapters: question 1 in Chapter 11 ("The Impact of the Multinational Enterprise"), question 2 in Chapter 13 ("Country Evaluation and Selection"), and question 3 in Chapter 14 ("Collaborative Strategies").

THE MEANING OF FOREIGN DIRECT INVESTMENT

Companies want to control their foreign operations so that these operations will help achieve their global objectives. Governmental authorities worry that this control will lead to decisions contrary to their countries' best interests. The amount of ownership necessary for companies to control their foreign operations is not clear-cut.

THE CONCEPT OF CONTROL

You saw in Chapter 1 that for direct investment to take place, control must accompany the investment. Otherwise, it is a portfolio investment. If ownership is widely dispersed, then a small percentage of the holdings may be sufficient to establish control of managerial decision making. However, even a 100-percent share does not guarantee control. If a government dictates whom a foreign company can hire, what the company must sell at a specified price, and how the company must distribute its earnings, then control belongs to the government. Governments frequently do impose these decisions on foreign firms. But it is not only governments that may jeopardize the owners' control. If the company's owners do not regulate key resources the company needs, then those who control those resources may exert substantial influence on the company. Because direct investments can be difficult to define, governments have had to establish arbitrary ownership minimums. Usually, they stipulate that ownership of at least 10 or 25 percent of the voting stock in a foreign enterprise makes the investment direct.

THE CONCERN ABOUT CONTROL

Although defining direct investment is arbitrary, the concept is important. Both governments and companies are concerned with the issue of control.

Direct investment usually implies an ownership share of at least 10 or 25 percent.

Governmental Concern

Why should a government care whether an investment is controlled from abroad? Many critics of FDI worry that the host country's national interests will suffer somewhat if a multinational company makes decisions from afar on the basis of its own global or national objectives. For example, GM, a U.S. company, owns a 100-percent interest in Vauxhall Motors in the United Kingdom. Such control means that GM's corporate management in the United States can make decisions about personnel staffing, export prices, and the retention and payout of Vauxhall's profits. This level of control concerns the British public because decisions that directly affect the British economy can come from the United States.

When foreign investors control a company, decisions of national importance may be made abroad.

Investor Concern

Control is also important to foreign companies. They are reluctant to transfer vital resources—capital, patents, trademarks, and management know-how—to another organization that can make all its operating decisions independently. The company receiving these resources can use them to undermine the competitive position of the foreign company transferring them. This idea of denying rivals access to resources is called the **appropriability theory**.[5] For example, Bridgestone was hesitant to transfer either product technology, such as its SuperFiller radials, or process technology, such as its mold changeover methods, to other companies. Its management was well aware of how acquired technology can be used to competitive advantage. In fact, Bridgestone gained technology by manufacturing tires for Goodyear for many years in Japan under a licensing agreement. Goodyear terminated the agreement in 1997 because of Bridgestone's gains in competitive position.[6] In another case, Samsung Electronics from South Korea leapfrogged to become the world's largest memory-chip maker mostly by acquiring technology from other companies.[7]

Investors who control an organization
- **Are more willing to transfer technology and other competitive assets**
- **Usually use cheaper and faster means of transferring assets**

The control inherent in FDI may decrease a company's operating costs and increase its rate of technological transfer because:

1. The parent and subsidiary usually share a common corporate culture.
2. The company can use its own managers, who understand its objectives.
3. The company can avoid protracted negotiations with another company.
4. The company can avoid problems of enforcing an agreement.

This control through self-handling of operations (internal to the organization) is **internalization**.[8] For example, Intel found that transferring technology to independent motherboard manufacturers in Taiwan was too slow, so it moved into Taiwan with its own production facility.[9]

Despite the advantages of control, many circumstances exist in which assets are transferred to noncontrolled entities. For example, a company may transfer its trademarks and technology through licensing agreements. In addition, companies lack resources to control all aspects of their production, supplies, and sales, so they funnel the resources that they do have to those activities that are most important to their strategies and their performance.

METHODS AND RESOURCES FOR ACQUISITION

Direct investments usually, but not always, involve some capital movement.

Foreign direct investment is usually an international capital movement that crosses borders when the anticipated return (accounting for the risk factor and the cost of transfer) is higher overseas than at home. For example, Bridgestone transferred capital from Japan to the United States when it bought the shares of Firestone. Although most FDI requires some type of international capital movement, an investor may transfer many other types of assets. For example, Westin Hotels has transferred very little capital to foreign countries. Instead, it has transferred managers, cost control systems, and reservations capabilities in exchange for ownership in foreign hotels.

There are two other means of acquiring foreign investments that are not capital movements *per se*. First, a company may use funds it earns in a foreign country to establish an investment. For example, a company that exports merchandise but holds payment for those goods abroad can use settlement to acquire an investment. In this case, it has merely exchanged goods for equity. Although companies don't use this method extensively for initial investment, it is a major means of expanding abroad. A company may transfer assets abroad to establish a sales or production facility. If the earnings from the facility can increase the value of the foreign holdings, FDI has increased without a new international capital movement. Also, companies in different countries can trade equity. For example, Tabacalera in Spain acquired a share of Seita in France by giving Seita's owners stock in Tabacalera—a move that helped integrate the competitive strategies of the two tobacco companies.[10]

BUY-VERSUS-BUILD DECISION

There are two ways companies can invest in a foreign country. They can either acquire an interest in an existing operation or construct new facilities. A company must consider both alternatives carefully because both have advantages and disadvantages.

The advantages of acquiring an existing operation include
- **Adding no further capacity to the market**
- **Avoiding start-up problems**
- **Easier financing**

Reasons for Buying Whether a company makes a direct investment by acquisition or start-up depends, of course, on which companies are available for purchase. The large privatization programs occurring in many parts of the world have put hundreds of companies on the market, and MNEs have exploited this new opportunity to invest abroad. For example, much of the FDI in Central and Eastern European banking has come from privatization programs, such as Allied Irish's purchase of two Polish banks.[11] There are many reasons for seeking acquisitions. One is the difficulty of transferring some resource to a foreign operation or acquiring that resource locally for a new facility. Personnel is a resource that foreign companies find difficult to hire, especially if local unemployment is low. Instead of paying higher compensation than competitors do to entice employees away from their old jobs, a company can buy an existing company, which gives the buyer not only labor and management but also an existing organizational structure.

Through acquisitions, a company may also gain the goodwill and brand identification important to the marketing of mass consumer products, especially if the cost and risk of breaking in a new brand are high. Further, a company that depends substantially on local financing rather than on the transfer of capital may find it easier to gain access to local capital through an acquisition. Local capital suppliers may be more familiar with an ongoing operation than with the foreign enterprise. In addition, a foreign company may acquire an existing company through an exchange of stock, which circumvents home-country exchange controls.

In other ways, acquisitions may reduce costs and risks—and save time. A company may be able to buy facilities, particularly those of a poorly performing operation, for less than the cost of new construction. If an investor fears that a market does not justify added capacity, as in the Bridgestone case, acquisition enables it to avoid the risk of depressed prices and lower unit sales per producer that might occur if it adds one more producer to the market. Finally, by buying a company, an investor avoids inefficiencies during the start-up period and gets an immediate cash flow rather than tying up funds during construction.

Reasons for Building Although acquisitions offer advantages, a potential investor will not necessarily be able to realize them. Companies frequently make foreign investments where there is little or no competition, so finding a company to buy may be difficult. In addition, local governments may prevent acquisitions because they want more competitors in the market and fear market dominance by foreign enterprises. Even if acquisitions are available, they are less likely to succeed than start-up operations.[12] The acquired companies might have substantial problems. Personnel and labor relations may be both poor and difficult to change, ill will may have accrued to existing brands, or facilities may be inefficient and poorly located. Further, the managers in the acquiring and acquired companies may not work well together. For example Bridgestone found that the Firestone operations were less efficient than it had anticipated. On top of that, Firestone lost the GM account, and Bridgestone had to spend heavily to modernize Firestone plants in the United States and abroad before getting the account back. Finally, a foreign company may find local financing easier to obtain if it builds facilities, particularly if it plans to tap development banks for part of its financial requirements.

Companies may choose to build if
- **No desired company is available for acquisition**
- **Acquisition will carry over problems**
- **Acquisition is harder to finance**

THE RELATIONSHIP OF TRADE AND FACTOR MOBILITY

Whether a company first transfers capital or some other asset to acquire a foreign direct investment, the asset is a type of production factor. Eventually, the direct investment requires the movement of various types of production factors as investors infuse other resources into their operating facilities abroad. For example, Bridgestone acquired Firestone with a transfer of capital, but it has since transferred technology, trademarks, and managers to the Firestone operation as well. So now we will examine the relationship of trade theory to the movement of production factors.

TRADE THEORIES AND FACTOR MOBILITY

Both finished goods and production factors are partially mobile internationally.

We explained in Chapter 5 that trade often occurs because of differences in factor endowments among countries. But contrary to historical theories on trade, production factors themselves also may move internationally. Factor movement is an alternative to trade that may or may not be a more efficient allocation of resources. FDI is a major cause and means of factor movements. If trade could not occur and production factors could not move internationally, a country would have to either forgo consuming certain goods or produce them differently, which in either case would usually result in decreased worldwide output and higher prices. In some cases, however, the inability to use foreign production factors may stimulate efficient methods of substitution, such as the development of new materials as alternatives for traditional ones. For example, U.S. companies accelerated the production of synthetic rubber and rayon during World War II because wartime conditions made it impractical to move silk and natural rubber, not to mention silkworms and rubber plants.

SUBSTITUTION

There are pressures for the most abundant factors to move to an area of scarcity.

When the factor proportions vary widely among countries, pressures exist for the most abundant factors to move to countries with greater scarcity—where they can command a better return. In countries where labor is abundant compared to capital, laborers tend to be unemployed or poorly paid. If permitted, these workers will go to countries that have full employment and higher wages. Similarly, capital will tend to move away from countries in which it is abundant to those in which it is scarce. For example, Mexico gets capital from the United States, and the United States gets labor from Mexico.[13] If finished goods and production factors were both free to move internationally, the comparative costs of transferring goods and factors would determine the location of production. However, as is true of trade, there are restrictions on factor movements that make them only partially mobile internationally, such as U.S. immigration restrictions that limit the legal and illegal influx of Mexican workers, and Mexican ownership restrictions in the petroleum industry that limit U.S. capital investments into that industry.

A hypothetical example, shown in Figure 8.2, should illustrate the substitutability of trade and factor movements under different scenarios. Assume the following:

- The United States and Mexico have equally productive land available at the same cost for growing tomatoes.
- The cost of transporting tomatoes between the United States and Mexico is $0.75 per bushel.
- Workers from either country pick an average of two bushels per hour during a 30-day picking season.

The only differences in price between the two countries are due to variations in labor and capital cost. The labor rate is $20.00 per day, or $1.25 per bushel, in the United States and $4.00 per day, or $0.25 per bushel, in Mexico. The capital needed to buy

Ethical Dilemmas and Social Responsibility
CRITICS DEBATE THE ETHICS OF FDI AND EMPLOYMENT

Acme Boots announced it was moving out of the United States to gain tax advantages in Puerto Rico. The move stranded its U.S. employees, some of whom had 30 years of service with the company. Many critics of FDI argue that it is unethical for governments to lure companies away from existing locations by offering lucrative incentives—and for companies to move. Companies say that it is necessary because of home-country conditions over which they have no control, such as costs, taxes, market locations, and regulations. Do home-country governments have any ethical obligations—especially if their policies, such as environmental regulations or high taxes, burden domestic producers more than foreign ones? On the one hand, direct investment may lead to better global use of resources. On the other hand, it is the workers who suffer if they lose their jobs and cannot easily find new ones. For these employees, there is little solace in the economic gains that go to previously unemployed workers abroad or the lower consumer prices or higher corporate earnings resulting from the foreign production. Some people argue that the plight of these newly unemployed workers is no different from the results of technological change, such as when workers in clothespin factories lost their jobs with the invention of the electric clothes dryer. Other people argue that displacement from FDI is different because the workers cannot move abroad to take advantage of the new opportunities there and because their employers are responsible for the job losses. They argue that the company has an ethical obligation to give employees advance notice of the move and to provide training and help with job searches.

Proponents of FDI say that FDI will lead to global efficiencies and employ laborers from emerging economies who otherwise may not find work. Further, they say it will create a need for more highly paid managerial personnel at the company's home-country headquarters. Critics of FDI contend that this is unethical because the process creates economic distinctions between the "have" and "have-not" countries.

seeds, fertilizers, and equipment costs the equivalent of $0.30 per bushel in the United States and $0.50 per bushel in Mexico.

If neither tomatoes nor production factors can move between the two countries (see Figure 8.2[a]), the cost of tomatoes produced in Mexico for the Mexican market is $0.75 per bushel ($0.25 of labor plus $0.50 of capital), while those produced in the United States for the U.S. market cost $1.55 per bushel ($1.25 of labor plus $0.30 of capital). If the two countries eliminate trade restrictions on tomatoes between them (Figure 8.2[b]), the United States will import from Mexico because the Mexican cost

FIGURE 8.2   Comparative Costs of Tomatoes Based on Trade and Factor Mobility Between the United States and Mexico

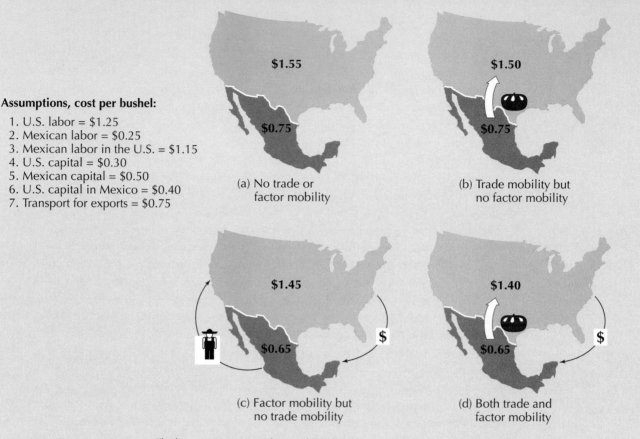

Assumptions, cost per bushel:

1. U.S. labor = $1.25
2. Mexican labor = $0.25
3. Mexican labor in the U.S. = $1.15
4. U.S. capital = $0.30
5. Mexican capital = $0.50
6. U.S. capital in Mexico = $0.40
7. Transport for exports = $0.75

$1.55

$0.75

(a) No trade or
   factor mobility

$1.50

$0.75

(b) Trade mobility but
   no factor mobility

$1.45

$0.65

$

(c) Factor mobility but
   no trade mobility

$1.40

$0.65

$

(d) Both trade and
   factor mobility

The lowest costs occur when trade and production factors are both mobile.

of $0.75 per bushel plus $0.75 for transporting the tomatoes to the United States will be $0.05 less than the $1.55 per bushel cost of growing them in the United States.

Consider another scenario in which neither country allows the importation of tomatoes but both allow certain movements of labor and capital (Figure 8.2[c]). Mexican workers can enter the United States on temporary work permits for an incremental travel and living expense of $14.40 per day per worker, or $0.90 per bushel. At the same time, U.S. companies will invest capital in Mexican tomato production, provided the capital earns more than it would earn in the United States—say, $0.40 per bushel, which is less than the Mexican going rate. In this scenario, Mexican production costs per bushel will be $0.65 ($0.25 of Mexican labor plus $0.40 of U.S. capital) and U.S. production costs will be $1.45 ($0.25 of Mexican labor plus $0.90 of travel and incremental costs plus $0.30 of U.S. capital). Each country would reduce its production costs—from $0.75 to $0.65 in Mexico and from $1.55 to $1.45 in the United States—by bringing in abundant production factors from abroad.

With free trade and the free movement of production factors (Figure 8.2[d]), Mexico will produce for both markets by importing capital from the United States. According to the above three assumptions, doing this will be cheaper than sending labor to the United States. In reality, neither production factors nor the finished goods they produce are completely free to move internationally. Slight increases or reductions in the extent of restrictions can greatly alter how and where goods may be produced most cheaply.

In the United States, for legal reasons, capital flows out more freely than labor flows in. The result is that U.S. companies make FDIs to produce goods that are then imported back into the United States. In fact, capital moves globally more easily than does labor because of differences in the costs of moving them. Moreover, technology, particularly in the form of more efficient machinery, generally is more mobile internationally than labor is. Differences in labor productivity and costs explain much of the movement of trade and direct investment. In other words, there is an incentive for companies to make FDIs when they can increase productivity by moving resources from one country to another.

COMPLEMENTARITY OF TRADE AND DIRECT INVESTMENT
In our tomato example for the United States and Mexico, we showed that factor movements may substitute for or stimulate trade. Even if the output from a foreign direct investment is sold locally rather than in export markets, world trade (exports) are stimulated by the FDI. About a third of world trade (exports) is among controlled entities, such as from parent to subsidiary, subsidiary to parent, and subsidiary to subsidiary of the same company. Many of the exports would not occur if overseas investments did not exist. One reason is that a company may export capital equipment as part of the value of its investment when building a facility abroad. It may have more confidence in this equipment than in equipment built locally, and it may want maximum worldwide uniformity. Another reason is that domestic operating units may export materials and components to their foreign facilities for use in a finished product. For example, Coca-Cola exports concentrate to its bottling facilities abroad. A foreign facility may produce part of the product line while serving as sales agent for exports of its parent's other products. Bridgestone, for example, continued to export its automobile tires from Japan for several years while using the sales force of its U.S. truck-tire manufacturing operations to handle those imports.

RELATIONSHIP OF FDI TO COMPANIES' OBJECTIVES
Foreign direct investment is a means of fulfilling any of the three major operating objectives we discussed in Chapter 1 that may influence companies to engage in international business:

1. To expand their sales
2. To acquire resources
3. To minimize risk

In addition, governments may own FDI or influence their home-based companies to establish FDI because of political motives.

However, companies can pursue operating modes other than FDI, such as exporting, importing from another company, or collaborating with another company to handle operations on its behalf. These modes are less risky than FDI because a company has

The lowest costs occur when trade and production factors are both mobile.

Factor mobility via direct investment often stimulates trade because of the need for
- **Components**
- **Complementary products**
- **Equipment for subsidiaries**

Businesses and governments are motivated to engage in FDI in order to
- **Expand sales**
- **Acquire resources**
- **Minimize competitive risk**
Governments may additionally be motivated by some desired political advantage.

| TABLE 8.1 | MOTIVATIONS FOR FDI AS AN ALTERNATIVE OR SUPPLEMENT TO TRADE |

These objectives usually outweigh the risks of FDI.

SALES EXPANSION OBJECTIVES	RESOURCE ACQUISITION OBJECTIVES	RISK MINIMIZATION OBJECTIVES	POLITICAL OBJECTIVES
Overcome high transport costs	Savings through vertical integration	Diversification of customer base (same motivations as for sales expansion objectives	Influence companies, usually through factors under resource acqui-sition objectives
Lack of domestic capacity	Savings through rationalized production	Diversification of supplier base (same motivations as for resource acquisition objectives)	
Low gains from scale economies	Gain access to cheaper or differ-ent resources and knowledge		
Trade restrictions	Need to lower costs as product matures	Following customers	
Barriers because of country-of-origin effects (nationalism, product image, delivery risk)	Gain governmental investment incentives	Preventing competitors' advantage	
Lower production costs abroad			

to neither expose an investment in a foreign country nor manage within an environment less familiar than at home. So why would a company risk operating in an environment less familiar than at home? Let's find out why, following Table 8.1's summary of the motivations for FDI.

FDI MOTIVATIONS TO ACHIEVE SALES EXPANSION

One reason managers will risk operating abroad is to expand sales. Below we discuss how transportation, trade restrictions, country-of-origin effects, and changes in comparative costs affect companies' sales.

TRANSPORTATION

Transportation raises costs so much that it becomes impractical to export some products.

When companies add the cost of transportation to production costs, some products become impractical to ship over great distances. Bridgestone's decision to invest in the United States was partly because the cost of transporting tires was too high. Many other products are impractical to ship great distances without a very large escalation in the price. A few of these products and their investing companies are newspapers (Thompson Newspapers, Canadian), margarine (Unilever, British-Dutch), dynamite (Nobel, Swedish), and soft drinks (PepsiCo, U.S.). For these companies, it is necessary to produce abroad if they are to sell abroad. When companies move abroad to produce basically the same products they produce at home, their direct investments are **horizontal expansions.**

Excess plant capacity

- **Usually leads to exporting rather than new direct investment**
- **May be competitive because of variable cost pricing**

Lack of Plant Capacity As long as a company has excess capacity at its plant(s), it may compete effectively in limited export markets despite high transport costs. This ability might occur if domestic sales cover fixed operating expenses, enabling the company to set foreign prices on the basis of variable rather than full (variable + fixed) costs. Such a pricing strategy may erode as foreign sales become more important or as output nears full plant capacity. Further, the company's average cost per unit decreases until it reaches full capacity. This helps explain why companies will export before establishing plants in more than one country. For example, Volkswagen placed its first plant to build the new Beetle at its facilities in Mexico, which served global markets. However, when demand pushed that plant toward capacity, Volkswagen announced it would build a second plant in Europe to serve the European market.[14]

This reluctance to expand total capacity while there is still substantial excess capacity is similar to the basis for a domestic-expansion decision. Internationally as well as domestically, growth is incremental. Most likely, a company will begin operations near the city in which its founders reside and will begin selling only locally. Eventually, sales may be expanded to a larger geographic market. As it reaches capacity, the company may build a second plant, warehouses, and sales offices in another part of the country to serve that region, save on transport costs, establish closer contact with customers and suppliers, and attain lower delivery costs. In fact, it may even acquire some of its customers or suppliers in order to reduce inventories and gain economies in distribution. Certain functions may be further scattered geographically, such as by locating financial offices near a financial center. As the product line evolves and expands, operations continue to disperse. In the pursuit of foreign business, not surprisingly, growing companies eventually find it necessary to acquire assets abroad, which are FDIs.

Scale Economies The manufacture of some products necessitates a high fixed capital cost for plant and equipment. For such products, especially if they are standardized or undifferentiated from competitors', the cost per unit drops significantly as output increases. Products such as ball bearings, alumina, and semiconductor wafers fall into this category. Companies can export large amounts of such products because the cost savings from scale economies overcome added transportation costs.

> In large-scale process technology, companies' exports reduce costs by spreading fixed costs over more units of output.

Companies that need to alter their products substantially for different foreign markets benefit less by scale economies. For these types of products, smaller plants to serve national rather than international markets will save transport costs. This need to alter products affects company production in two ways. Initially, it means an additional investment, which might spur management to locate facilities abroad. Next, it may mean that certain economies from large-scale production will be lost, which may shift the least-cost location from one country to another. The more the product has to be altered for the foreign market, the more likely it is that production will shift abroad. Electrolux, for example, a Swedish producer of major household appliances, first entered Asian markets by exporting to them. However, it was unable to gain more than minuscule sales with its line of appliances suitable for European and North American markets. So it launched a line of appliances aimed at these markets, including specially designed hoses to prevent rodents from chewing them, coatings on circuit boards to discourage ants, heavy zinc coatings to prevent rust, and electrical systems that are more tolerant of erratic electric supplies—all needs of the Asian market. Given the number of product alterations, there was little economy of scale to be gained by exporting. Instead, Electrolux shifted production to Asia to overcome transport costs.[15]

> In small-scale process technology, companies' country-by-country production reduces costs by minimizing transportation expenses.

If imports are highly
restricted, companies
- Often produce locally to
  serve the local market
- Are more likely to produce
  locally if market potential
  is high relative to scale
  economies

TRADE RESTRICTIONS

Governments restrict imports. Thus, companies may find they must produce in a foreign country if they are to sell there. For example, United Technologies, Schindler Holding, and Mitsubishi have made direct investments in Chinese elevator production because Chinese import restrictions prevent their serving that market by exporting to it.[16] Hyundai is increasing its FDI in India because of Indian import restrictions on automobile parts.[17] Governmental trade restrictions often favor big companies that can afford to commit large amounts of resources abroad, making foreign competitiveness more difficult for small companies that can afford only exportation as a means of serving foreign markets. When smaller companies have FDI—such as Amsco International, a producer of sterilization equipment, and Interlake, a manufacturer of fluid-handling products—they generally serve foreign markets from a handful of manufacturing bases rather than building plants in nearly all the places in which they have potential sales.[18]

Managers must view import barriers along with other factors, such as the market size of the country imposing the barriers. For example, import trade restrictions have been highly influential in enticing automobile producers to locate in Brazil because of its large market. Similar restrictions by Central American countries have been ineffective because of their small markets. However, Central American import barriers on products requiring lower amounts of capital investment for production and therefore smaller markets (for example, pharmaceuticals) have been highly effective at enticing direct investment.

Removing trade restrictions among a regional group of countries also may attract direct investment, possibly because the expanded market may justify scale economies. Or the removal of trade restrictions may result in trade diversion. In turn, companies may invest because of the trade diversion. For example, the Taiwanese textile industry could export clothing products into the United States as long as it faced the same duties as producers from other countries did. The reduction of duties through NAFTA offers tariff-saving advantages for Mexican production to serve the U.S. market that Taiwanese production does not have, so there has been some trade diversion from the more efficient output in Taiwan to less efficient output in Mexico. Many Taiwanese companies have reacted to NAFTA's passage by setting up factories in Mexico, and many U.S.-owned firms have shifted factories from Taiwan to Mexico.[19]

Consumers sometimes prefer
domestically produced goods
because of
- Nationalism
- A belief that these products are better
- A fear that foreign-made
  goods may not be delivered
  on time

COUNTRY-OF-ORIGIN EFFECTS

Government-imposed legal measures are not the only trade barriers to otherwise competitive goods. Consumer desires also may dictate limitations. Consumers may prefer to buy goods produced in their own country rather than another (perhaps because of nationalism). Or, they may believe that goods from a given country are superior, like German cars and French perfume, therefore preferring those countries' products. They may also fear that service and replacement parts for imported products will be difficult to obtain. In any of these cases, companies may find advantages in placing FDI where their output will have the best acceptance.

Nationalism   In many countries, companies have instituted promotional campaigns to persuade people to buy locally produced goods. For example, in the United States, some manufacturers have promoted "Made in the USA" to appeal to consumers of products that have been hit with import competition. A specific example is the campaign by the American Fiber, Textiles, and Apparel Coalitions to push "Crafted with Pride in the U.S.A."[20]

Product Image   Although products may be identical, consumers often view their quality differently on the basis of the country of origin.[21] There are examples of eventual image changes, such as the general improvement in the image of Japanese products that occurred concomitantly with the decline in image of U.S. products. However, it may take a long time and be very costly for a company to try to overcome image problems caused by manufacturing in a country that has a lower-status image for a particular product. Consequently, there may be advantages to producing in a country that has an existing high image.

Delivery Risk   Also, many consumers fear that service and replacement parts for foreign-made goods may be difficult to obtain from abroad. Industrial consumers often prefer to pay a higher price to a nearby producer in order to minimize the risk of nondelivery due to distance and strikes. For example, Hoechst Chemical of Germany located one of its dye factories in North Carolina because the textile industry in that region feared that delivery problems would plague German imports. Adding to this need to invest directly is the global rise in **just-in-time (JIT)** manufacturing systems, which decrease inventory costs by having components and parts delivered as needed. These systems favor nearby suppliers who can deliver quickly.

CHANGES IN COMPARATIVE COSTS

A company may export successfully because its home country has a cost advantage. The home-country cost advantage depends on the prices and productivity of the individual production factors, the size of the company's operations, the cost of transporting finished goods, and any regulations on how to produce. None of these conditions is static, so the least-cost location may change from one country to another. Recall that Bridgestone's decision to locate in the United States was based partly on a faster growth in Japanese costs (measured in dollars) than in U.S. costs, largely because of a rise in the value of the yen compared to the dollar.

> The least-cost production location changes because of inflation, regulations, transportation costs, and productivity.

Shifts in comparative production costs can be reasons for resource-seeking investments. A company may establish a direct investment to serve a foreign market but eventually export from that foreign market back to its home country. Production costs are discussed in the following section on resource-seeking investments.

FDI MOTIVATIONS TO ACQUIRE RESOURCES

A company may engage in international business to acquire goods or services from abroad. Of course, companies may obtain the goods and services from abroad by buying them from another company, but certain factors favor FDI to gain these resources. Let's examine some reasons for using FDI to acquire resources from abroad.

VERTICAL INTEGRATION

Vertical integration is a company's control of the different stages (sometimes collectively called a *value chain*) of making its product—from raw materials through production to its final distribution. As products and their marketing become more complicated,

> In international vertical integration, raw materials, production, and marketing are often located in different countries.

companies need to combine resources that are located in more than one country. Let's take steel as an example. If one country has the iron, a second has the coal, a third has the technology and capital for making steel products, and a fourth has the demand, there will be great interdependence among the four. The companies will need a tight relationship to ensure that production and marketing continue to flow. One way to help assure this flow is to gain a voice in the management of one or more of the foreign operations by investing in it. Most of the world's direct investment in petroleum may be explained by this concept of vertical integration. Because much of the petroleum supply is located in countries other than those with a heavy petroleum demand, the oil industry has become integrated vertically on an international basis.

Most vertical integration is supply oriented.

Advantages of vertical integration may accrue to a company through either market-oriented or supply-oriented investments in other countries. Of the two, there have been more examples in recent years of supply-oriented investments designed to obtain raw materials in other countries. This is because of the growing dependence on emerging economies for raw material supplies. Companies from industrial countries are more apt to have the resources necessary to invest in emerging economies than are companies from emerging economies to invest in industrial countries.

Companies may also gain certain economies through vertical integration. Because supply and/or markets are more assured, a company may be able to carry smaller inventories and spend less on promotion. By buying and selling within the family of companies, the foreign direct investor also has considerably greater flexibility in shifting funds, taxes, and profits among countries.

RATIONALIZED PRODUCTION

In rationalized production, different components or portions of a product line are made in different parts of the world. The advantages are
- **Factor-cost differences**
- **Long production runs**

Some companies produce different components or different portions of their product line in different parts of the world to take advantage of low labor costs, capital, and raw materials. This is **rationalized production**. For example, many Mexican plants are integrated with operations in the United States. Semifinished goods are exported from the United States to Mexico for the labor-intensive portion of the production, such as sewing car seats for GM or building TV cabinets for Panasonic.[22] As is the case with vertical integration, companies choose to own the production facilities in the different countries because of the need for a tight relationship to ensure a smooth production flow.

Many companies shrug off the possibility of rationalized production of parts. They fear work stoppages in many countries because of strikes or a change in import regulations in just one country. As an alternative to parts rationalization, a company can produce a complete product in a given country. However, only part of a company's product range is produced in that country. For example, a U.S. subsidiary in France may produce only product A, another subsidiary in Brazil only product B, and the home plant in the United States only product C. Each plant sells worldwide so that each can gain scale economies and take advantage of differences in input costs that may result in differences in total production cost. Each may get concessions to import because it can demonstrate that it can generate local jobs and incomes. For example, Mercedes-Benz has shifted some of its production to Brazil because of rising German costs.[23] Not only did the move reduce production costs, it also helped the company import other models into Brazil.

Another possible advantage of this type of rationalization is smoother earnings when exchange rates fluctuate.[24] Consider the value of the Japanese yen compared to the U.S. dollar. Honda produces some of its line in Japan and then exports this production to the United States. Honda also produces some of its line in the United States and then exports this production to Japan. If the yen strengthens, Honda may have to cut its profit margin to stay competitive on its exports to the United States. But this cut may be offset by a higher profit margin on the exports from the United States to Japan. Given the multiple origin of products' components and the production of different product models in different countries, it is becoming harder to determine the nationality of a product, as Figure 8.3 shows.

ACCESS TO PRODUCTION RESOURCES

The practice of seeking abroad some resource—labor, capital, technology, or information—not satisfactorily available in the home country closely resembles rationalized production, but is different in that a company goes abroad to gain some capability for its organization as a whole rather than for a specific product. Such companies as Digital Equipment have made investments in India to access Indian software talent.[25] Many non-U.S. companies have offices in New York City to gain better access to the U.S. capital market, or at least knowledge of what is happening within that market that can affect other worldwide capital occurrences. The search for knowledge as an FDI motive is widespread. For example, the French firm C.F.P. bought a share in Leonard Petroleum to learn U.S. marketing practices—and compete better against U.S. oil firms outside the United States. McGraw-Hill established an office in Europe to allow its personnel

A company may establish a presence in a country in order to improve its access to knowledge and other resources.

FIGURE 8.3

FDI, especially with vertical integration and rationalized production, obscures a product's nationality.

Source: By permission of Chip Bok and Creators Syndicate, Inc. Copyright © 1992.

there to uncover European technical developments by visiting universities, trade associations, and companies.

THE PRODUCT LIFE CYCLE THEORY

In Chapter 5, we explained the product life cycle (PLC) theory.[26] This theory shows how, for market and cost reasons, production often moves from one country to another as a product moves through its life cycle. During the introductory stage, production occurs in only one (usually industrial) country. During the growth stage, production moves to other industrial countries, and the original producer may decide to invest in production facilities in those foreign countries to earn profits there. In the mature stage, production shifts largely to emerging economies, and the same company may decide to control operations there as well.

GOVERNMENTAL INVESTMENT INCENTIVES

In addition to restricting imports, countries frequently encourage direct investment inflows by offering tax concessions or other subsidies. This subject is discussed in greater detail in Chapter 12, but briefly, such incentives affect the comparative cost of production among countries and entice companies to invest in a particular country to serve national or international markets. Many central and local governments offer direct-assistance incentives to attract FDI. For example, the Philippine government gave a six-year tax holiday, duty exemption on imports of machinery and equipment, and assistance in training personnel in order to entice Ford to build a car-assembly plant there.[27]

RISK MINIMIZATION OBJECTIVES

Companies may reduce risks by operating internationally, such as through sales diversification. Their choice of foreign direct investment as the means of reducing risk is due primarily to the same factors we have discussed for market expansion and resource acquisition motives. For example, Johnson Controls, a U.S. manufacturer of automobile parts and control systems for buildings, expanded into Europe largely to minimize its exposure to cyclical downturns in the United States.[28] Transportation costs, foreign import restrictions, and foreign consumer desires for product alterations may make FDI the preferred operating mode for sales diversification. Let's now examine some specific reasons to use FDI to minimize risk.

FOLLOWING CUSTOMERS

As we have said, many companies sell abroad indirectly. They sell products, components, or services domestically, which then become embodied in a product or service that their domestic customer exports. In the opening case, Bridgestone sold tires to Toyota and Honda, which in turn exported cars (including the tires) to foreign markets. In such cases, the indirect exporters commonly follow their customers when those customers make direct investments. Bridgestone decided to make automobile tires in the United States in order to continue selling to Honda and Toyota once those companies initiated U.S. production. More recently, it has followed those customers into markets in Thailand and Indonesia.[29] If it had failed to do so, such tire companies as Toyo and Yokohama could use their presence in the United States, Thailand,

---

The product life cycle theory explains why

- **New products are produced mainly in industrial countries**
- **Mature products are more likely to be produced in emerging economies**

Governmental incentives may shift the least-cost production location.

Companies can keep customers by following them abroad.

and Indonesia to undermine Bridgestone's connections with Honda and Toyota in Japan.

PREVENTING COMPETITORS' ADVANTAGE

Within *oligopolistic industries* (those with few sellers), several investors often establish facilities in a given country within a fairly short time of each other.[30] For example, between 1991 and 1995, eleven different automobile companies received licenses to make investments in Vietnam.[31] In many industries, most companies experience capacity-expansion cycles concurrently. Thus they would logically consider a foreign investment at approximately the same time. Externally, they might all be faced with changes in import restrictions or market conditions that indicate a move to direct investment to serve consumers in a given country. In spite of the prevalence of these motivators, many movements by oligopolists seem better explained by defensive motives.

In oligopolistic industries, competitors tend to make direct investments in a given country about the same time.

Much of the research in game theory shows that people often make decisions based on the "least-damaging alternative." Similarly, many companies ask, "Do I lose less by moving abroad or by staying at home?" Assume that some foreign market may be served effectively only by an investment in the market, but the market is large enough to support only one producer. To solve this problem, competitors could set up a joint operation and divide the profits among themselves, if antitrust laws permit this. If only one company establishes a direct investment, it will have an advantage over its competitors by garnering a larger market, spreading its R&D costs, and making a profit it can reinvest elsewhere. Once one company decides to produce in the market, competitors are prone to follow quickly rather than let that company gain advantages. The company's decision to invest depends not so much on the benefits it gains but rather on what it could lose by not entering the field. In most oligopolistic industries (such as automobiles, tires, and petroleum), this pattern helps explain the large number of producers compared to the size of the market in some countries. Along these same lines, sometimes a company will invest in a foreign competitor's home market to prevent that competitor from using the high profits it makes in that market to invest and compete elsewhere.[32]

POLITICAL MOTIVES

FDI sometimes depends on countries' political motives to reduce security risk. For example, the Chinese National Petroleum Corporation, a Chinese government-owned company, has been investing in Kazakhstan, Peru, the Sudan, and Venezuela so that China will be less dependent on foreign companies for its oil supplies.[33] The move may also help China hold down prices on production it receives. In the process of gaining control of resources, home countries also acquire much political control.

Governments give incentives to their companies to make direct investments in order to
- Gain supplies of strategic resources
- Develop spheres of influence

Control of resources is not necessarily the only political reason for direct investment. For example, during the early 1980s, the U.S. government instituted various incentives to increase the profitability of U.S. investment in Caribbean countries that were unfriendly to Cuba's Castro regime. The United States wanted to strengthen the economies of those friendly nations through the growth the FDI would bring and make it difficult for unfriendly leftist governments to gain control. But with the end of the Cold War, the U.S. ended investment incentives in the Caribbean region, and much investment was diverted to Mexico because of NAFTA.[34]

ADVANTAGES OF FOREIGN DIRECT INVESTMENT

Are companies profitable because they are multinational or multinational because they are profitable? Such a chicken-and-egg question has hounded direct investment theorists. On the one hand, evidence indicates that successful domestic companies (both large and small) are most likely to commit resources to FDI. On the other hand, ownership of FDI appears to make companies more successful domestically.[35] Let's take a look at companies' operating advantages before and after they become foreign direct investors.

MONOPOLY ADVANTAGES BEFORE DIRECT INVESTMENT

Most successful domestic companies, especially those with unique advantages, invest abroad.

Companies invest directly only if they think they hold some supremacy over similar companies in countries of interest. The advantage results from a foreign company's ownership of some resource—patents, product differentiation, management skills, access to markets—unavailable at the same price or terms to the local company. This edge is often called a **monopoly advantage**. Because of the increased cost of transferring resources abroad and the perceived greater risk of operating in a different environment, the company will not move unless it expects a higher return than it can get at home and unless it thinks it can outperform local firms.[36]

Companies from certain countries may enjoy a monopoly advantage if they can borrow capital at a lower interest rate than companies can from other countries. Prior to World War I, Great Britain was the largest source of direct investment because of the strength of the pound sterling and the resulting lower interest rates on borrowing sterling funds. From World War II until the mid-1980s, the strength of the U.S. dollar gave an advantage to U.S. firms. After that, this advantage shifted to Japanese companies, until the Japanese yen weakened in 1997.[37] More recently, capital markets have become so international that companies can more easily borrow abroad if interest rates are lower there.

A similar advantage is when the foreign company's currency has high buying power. During the two and a half decades following World War II, the U.S. dollar was very strong. By converting dollars to other currencies, U.S. companies could purchase more in foreign countries than they could in the United States. This advantage was an incentive for U.S. companies to make foreign investments. They could add production capacity more cheaply abroad than at home. Further, non-U.S. companies could not as easily make FDIs in the United States.

Currency values do not, however, provide a strong explanation for direct investment patterns. In the first half of the 1980s, U.S. companies did not significantly increase investment abroad, but foreign companies invested heavily in the United States despite the strong dollar. The major reasons were high expected returns in the United States because of a relatively strong U.S. economy and high U.S. interest rates. In the late 1980s and early 1990s, when the dollar was weak again, direct investment flowed both to and from the United States in record amounts.[38] The currency-strength scenario only partially explains direct investment flows.

ADVANTAGES AFTER DIRECT INVESTMENT

Direct investment makes companies more successful domestically.

To support the high costs necessary to maintain domestic competitiveness, companies frequently must sell on a global basis. To sell most efficiently, many companies establish direct investments abroad. The advantage accruing to more internationally oriented companies from spreading out some of the costs of product differentiation, R&D, and advertising is apparent compared to less internationally oriented companies. Among industry groups and groups of companies of similar size that spent comparable amounts on advertising and R&D, the more internationally oriented companies in almost every case earned more than the others.[39]

DIRECT INVESTMENT PATTERNS

Although foreign direct investment began centuries ago, its biggest growth has occurred since the middle of the twentieth century. Recent growth has resulted from several factors, particularly the more receptive attitude of governments to investment inflows, the process of privatization, and the growing interdependence of the world economy. By 1999, about 60,000 companies owned about 500,000 FDIs that produced a quarter of global output.[40] Let's now look at where FDI is owned and located and the industries in which it exists.

Looking to the Future
WILL FDI CONTINUE TO GROW WORLDWIDE?

In the near future, FDI should continue to grow more rapidly than international trade or gross domestic products. The reasons for this growth should remain as described in this chapter: the receptiveness of governments to investment flows, the process of privatization, and the growing interdependence of the world economy. Moreover, companies have more experience in manufacturing abroad, reducing their perceived risk in integrating global production. However, trade restrictions on products continue to diminish, making import substituting investment less important.

FDI in services may continue to grow in importance because of the difficulty of removing protectionist barriers on service trade, and because of the need of service providers (such as investment bankers, advertising agencies, and insurance companies) to react quickly to the overseas needs of their clients.

Western Europe, North America, and Japan should continue to be the major sources and recipients of FDI because of the wealth of the companies based there and the outlook for economic growth within those regions. NAFTA and the EU should further stimulate this FDI growth because of their large internal markets. Some former communist nations should receive much more attention now that regulatory changes permit some foreign ownership and as potential investors become more optimistic about risk and opportunities there. However, investors will be wary of those countries where corruption is rampant and where there is high political uncertainty to treatment of foreign direct investors. Among emerging economies, regulatory changes should be a factor. Such countries as Argentina, Brazil, and Mexico are privatizing many state companies and allowing levels of foreign investment that have until very recently been prohibited. These moves should stimulate those countries' receipt of FDI.

LOCATION OF OWNERSHIP

For worldwide FDI,

- **Almost all ownership is by companies from developed countries**
- **Emerging economy ownership is increasing**

The industrial countries account for a little over 90 percent of all direct investment outflows. This is understandable, because more companies from those countries are likely to have the capital, technology, and managerial skills needed to invest abroad.[41] Nevertheless, hundreds of firms from emerging economies have FDIs, although the holdings from individual emerging economy investors remain small compared to investments from industrial nations. For example, of the 100 companies that own the most FDI, only two of these are from emerging economies, Petróleos de Venezuela and Daewoo Corporation from South Korea.[42] Table 8.2 shows the top 10 foreign direct investors in terms of their foreign assets.

During much of the post–World War II period, the United States was the dominant investor. However, its share has been falling as the share from other industrial countries, especially the United Kingdom and Japan, has increased. Recently, FDI has been flowing more rapidly into the United States than from it. Much of this has been through

TABLE 8.2

THE WORLD'S TOP 10 FOREIGN DIRECT INVESTORS, RANKED BY FOREIGN ASSETS, 1997 (ASSETS AND SALES IN BILLIONS OF U.S. DOLLARS)*

The largest foreign direct investors are all from developed countries.

RANK	CORPORATION	COUNTRY	INDUSTRY	FOREIGN ASSETS	FOREIGN SALES	FOREIGN EMPLOYEES
1	General Electric	United States	Electronics	97.4	24.5	111,000
2	Ford Motor Company	United States	Automotive	72.5	48.0	174,105
3	Shell, Royal Dutch	Netherlands/United Kingdom	Petroleum	70.0	69.0	65,000
4	General Motors	United States	Automotive	—	51.0	—
5	Exxon Corporation	United States	Petroleum	54.6	104.8	—
6	Toyota	Japan	Automotive	41.8	50.4	—
7	IBM	United States	Computers	39.9	48.9	134,815
8	Volkswagen Group	Germany	Automotive	—	42.7	133,906
9	Nestlé SA	Switzerland	Food and beverages	31.6	47.6	219,442
10	Daimler-Benz	Germany	Automotive	—	50.4	—

*The threshold for FDI is 10 percent of equity, UNCTAD estimate.

Source: United Nations Conference on Trade and Development; *The World Investment Report, 1999* (Geneva: United Nations, 1999).

large foreign purchases of U.S. companies, such as British Petroleum's $61 billion acquisition of Amoco in 1998 and Vodaphone Group's (also from the United Kingdom) $58 billion acquisition of AirTouch in 1999.[43]

LOCATION OF INVESTMENT

The largest investors in the United States are the United Kingdom and Japan, accounting in 1998 for about 19 and 16 percent, respectively, of FDI there.[44] The largest locations of U.S.-owned FDI in 1998 were in the United Kingdom, Canada, and the Netherlands, which held 18, 11, and 8 percent of the value of U.S.-owned FDI. Figure 8.4 shows the direction of recent global FDI inflows and outflows.

The major recipients of FDI are developed countries, which received about 71 percent of the world's total in 1998, as shown in Figure 8.4. The small share going to emerging economies has caused concern about how those economies will meet their capital needs.

The interest in developed countries has come about for three main reasons:

1. More investments have been market seeking, and the markets are larger in developed countries.

Most FDI occurs in developed countries because they have the

- **Biggest markets**
- **Lowest perceived risk**
- **Least discrimination toward foreign companies**

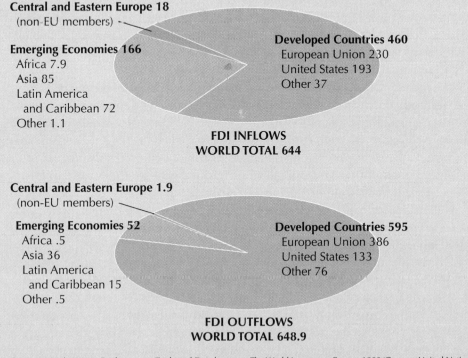

FIGURE 8.4   FDI Inflows and Outflows in Major World Regions, 1998 (in billions of U.S. dollars)

Central and Eastern Europe 18
(non-EU members)

Emerging Economies 166
Africa 7.9
Asia 85
Latin America
  and Caribbean 72
Other 1.1

Developed Countries 460
European Union 230
United States 193
Other 37

**FDI INFLOWS
WORLD TOTAL 644**

Central and Eastern Europe 1.9
(non-EU members)

Emerging Economies 52
Africa .5
Asia 36
Latin America
  and Caribbean 15
Other .5

Developed Countries 595
European Union 386
United States 133
Other 76

**FDI OUTFLOWS
WORLD TOTAL 648.9**

The developed countries are the largest owners and recipients of FDI.

Source: United Nations Conference on Trade and Development, *The World Investment Report, 1999* (Geneva: United Nations). The figures for inflows and outflows do not match because of estimation measurement discrepancies.

2. Political turmoil in many emerging economies has discouraged investors.

3. The industrial nations, through the Organization for Economic Cooperation and Development (OECD), are committed to liberalizing direct investment among their members.[45]

The OECD operates (with exceptions) under a principle that member countries should treat foreign-controlled companies no less favorably than domestic ones in such areas as taxes, access to local capital, and government procurement. The OECD member countries also have agreed on procedures through which direct investors can resolve situations that may result from conflicting laws between their home and host countries.

ECONOMIC SECTOR OF INVESTMENT

The highest recent growth in FDI has been in services.

Trends in the distribution of FDI generally conform to long-term economic changes in the home and host countries. Over time, the portion of FDI accounted for in the raw materials sector that includes mining, smelting, and petroleum has declined. The portion in manufacturing, especially resource-based production, grew steadily from the 1920s to the early 1970s but has since stabilized. In the 1980s and 1990s, FDI in the service sector (especially banking and finance) grew rapidly, as did FDI in technology-intensive manufacturing.

FDI IN COMPANIES' STRATEGIES

Direct investment is an integral means of carrying out global, multidomestic, and transnational strategies. Recall from Chapter 1 that multidomestic strategies differ from transnational and global strategies in that multidomestic strategies allow each foreign country operation to act somewhat independently. A transnational strategy allows each country to contribute ideas, resources, and direction so that the company's global operations are maximized. Global strategies integrate the company's operations, but most control and resources come from the headquarters' country.

Market-seeking direct investments—those that take place because companies must produce within the markets they serve (because of high costs of transportation or trade restrictions)—generally favor multidomestic strategies. Direct investments that are motivated by consumer or competitor moves are more likely to be global or transnational strategies. Resource-seeking investments to bring about vertical integration or rationalized production usually entail global or transnational strategies as well. Direct investment, because of its implied control, permits companies to make decisions to maximize global performance. When they depend instead on licensing or foreign production contracts, the interests of their partner companies may constrain their ability to implement global or transnational strategies.

Direct investments help to serve global efficiency by transferring resources to where they can be used more effectively. However, countries distort movements of resources by restricting the inward or outward flow of direct investments. Although these distortions are less important in motivating investments and their locations than political conditions and natural economic forces are, managers must consider them. To the extent that countries give preferential treatment to domestically headquartered or state-owned firms, the environment in which companies compete internationally is further complicated.

WEB CONNECTION

Check out our home page www.prenhall.com/daniels for links to key resources for you in your study of international business.

SUMMARY

- Direct investment is the control of a company in one country by a company based in another country. Because control is difficult to define, some arbitrary minimum share of voting stock owned is what defines direct investment.

- Countries are concerned about foreign control of companies within their borders because they fear their decisions will be contrary to national interests.

- Firms often prefer to control foreign production facilities because the transfer of certain assets to a noncontrolled entity might undermine their competitive position. They can also realize economies of buying and selling through a controlled entity.

- Although a direct investment abroad generally is acquired by transferring capital from one country to another, capital is not the only contribution or the only means of gaining equity. The investing company may supply technology, personnel, and markets in exchange for an interest in a foreign company.

- There are advantages and disadvantages to FDI by either acquisition or start-up.

- Production factors and finished goods are only partly mobile internationally. The cost and feasibility of transferring production factors rather than exporting finished goods internationally will determine which alternative is best for the company.

- Although FDI may be a substitute for trade, it also may stimulate trade through sales of components, equipment, and complementary products.

- Companies may undertake FDI to expand foreign markets or gain access to supplies of resources or finished products. Home governments may encourage such investment for political purposes.

- The price of some products increases too much if they are exported. Therefore, foreign production is often necessary to tap foreign markets because it skirts import barriers and reduces transportation costs.

- As long as companies have excess domestic capacity, they usually try to delay establishing foreign production because their average cost per unit of output goes down until they reach capacity.

- The extent to which scale economies lower production costs influences whether production is centralized in one or a few countries or dispersed among many countries.

- Governmental restrictions on imports often cause companies to undertake FDIs in the restricting country.

- Consumers may prefer to buy domestically produced products even though they are more expensive than foreign ones. They also may demand that foreign companies alter products to fit their needs. Both of these considerations can cause a company to establish foreign operations.

- FDI sometimes has chain effects: When one company makes an investment, some of its suppliers follow with investments of their own, followed by investments by their suppliers, and so on.

- Vertical integration controls the flow of goods from basic production to final consumption in an increasingly interdependent and complex world distribution system. It may lower operating costs and enable companies to transfer funds among countries.

- Rationalized production means producing different components or products in different countries to take advantage of factor costs.

- Within oligopolistic industries, companies often invest in a foreign country at about the same time. This occurs because they are responding to similar market conditions or because they wish to negate competitors' advantages in that market.

- The least-cost production location may shift over time, especially during a product's life cycle. It also may change because of governmental incentives that subsidize production.

- Monopolistic advantages help explain why companies are willing to take what they perceive as higher risks of operating abroad. Certain countries and currencies have had such advantages, which helps explain the dominance of companies from certain countries at certain times.

- FDI may enable MNEs to spread certain fixed costs more than domestic companies can. It also may enable them to gain access to needed resources, to prevent competitors from gaining control of needed resources, and to smooth sales and earnings on a year-to-year basis.

- Most FDI originates from and goes to developed countries. The fastest recent growth of FDI has been in the service sector.

C A S E
CRAN CHILE[46]

Cranberries are native to North America, their claim to fame being a spot at the first Thanksgiving dinner in 1621. The first commercial crop was handpicked in 1817. For most of the period following, almost all cranberry sales have been in the United States, and these sales have been heavily concentrated during the Thanksgiving season. Cranberries are so little known outside North America that there is no word for the fruit in most foreign languages.

The cranberry is a seasonal product. The vulnerability to seasonal demand became apparent to cranberry growers in 1959, when the U.S. Secretary of Agriculture warned a few days before Thanksgiving that a new pesticide sprayed on cranberries could be carcinogenic. Even though the warning proved unfounded, there was no market for the unsold berries. This spurred moves to try to increase cranberry sales during other times of the year.

Ocean Spray Cranberries, Inc. has done most of the work to build and diversify cranberry sales. Owned by more than 900 cranberry and grapefruit growers throughout the United States and Canada, its 1998 sales were nearly $1.5 billion, most notably from cranberry juice, which Ocean Spray created. In addition, Ocean Spray has worked with associations of cranberry growers to popularize recipes that will use cranberries year-round, such as cranberry chicken and cranberry-raisin pie. It has developed new products, such as Craisins—dried and sweetened cranberries that look something like red raisins. It has also worked with other companies to create products using cranberries—for example, with PepsiCo for a cranberry-raspberry lemonade, with Nabisco for a fat-free cranberry Fig Newton, and with Warner-Lambert for cranberry-flavored hard candy.

Although Ocean Spray has been the dominant force behind increased cranberry sales and has about two-thirds of the U.S. market, some other companies have also become major players. For example, Seagram's Tropicana unit has a cranberry-juice cocktail under its Twister label, and Quaker Oats uses cranberries in some of its Snapple drinks. Moreover, demand has jumped as a result of studies reporting that cranberries help combat urinary tract infections.

In addition to promoting new products using cranberries, Ocean Spray began marketing cranberry products abroad. These sales are being aided by grants from the U.S. Department of Agriculture's program to stimulate exports.

Continued growth in domestic and foreign sales is, of course, dependent on sufficient supplies of cranberries. A shortfall in supply prompted one man to grow cranberries himself. Warren Simmons developed the Pier 39 retail complex in San Francisco and founded the Tia Maria and Chevys Mexican Restaurant chains. In 1992 his Chevys restaurants ordered a large shipment of fresh cranberries from Ocean Spray to make cranberry margaritas, but Ocean Spray could not fill the order. Simmons investigated the shortage and concluded that supplies could not grow fast enough in North America to fulfill the growing demand. Although production was increasing, demand was growing even faster.

The conclusion that there will be inadequate future supplies of cranberries from North America is based on the following factors:

1. *Regulations* Cranberries grow in bogs, which alternatively can serve as wetlands that provide a habitat for plants and wildlife, control flooding, and serve as a nat-

ural filter for ground pollutants. As U.S. restrictions have become more stringent, it has become difficult and costly to add land for cultivation. For example, the application process for a three-acre expansion can cost as much as $100,000 in fees and take up to four years.

2. *Yields* Although research has been under way to increase yields, so far it has been difficult to maintain them at accustomed levels. (An average acre yields about 150 barrels per year, at 100 pounds per barrel.) Many bogs have become less fertile because of their many years of cultivation and because of decreases in the bumblebee population needed for pollination.

3. *Land costs* In some cranberry-growing regions, urbanization and land development have pushed land cost up so much that some areas are no longer profitable for

cranberry cultivation. Further, workers cannot afford nearby accommodations from their earnings. For example, in Richmond, British Columbia, known as the "Cranberry Capital of Canada," a one-acre plot of land now costs over a half million dollars.

Mr. Simmons sold his Chevys Mexican Restaurants in 1992 to PepsiCo and used the proceeds to invest in foreign cranberry production. He hired one of the few horticulturists specializing in cranberries to advise him on where and how to grow berries. He chose an isolated area near Valdivia, Chile, 450 miles south of Santiago, to establish his foreign direct investment, called Cran Chile. (See Map 8.2.) He chose this area because of its fertile soil, rain, and absence of environmental restrictions. By 1995, Simmons had invested about

MAP 8.2 Location of Cran Chile

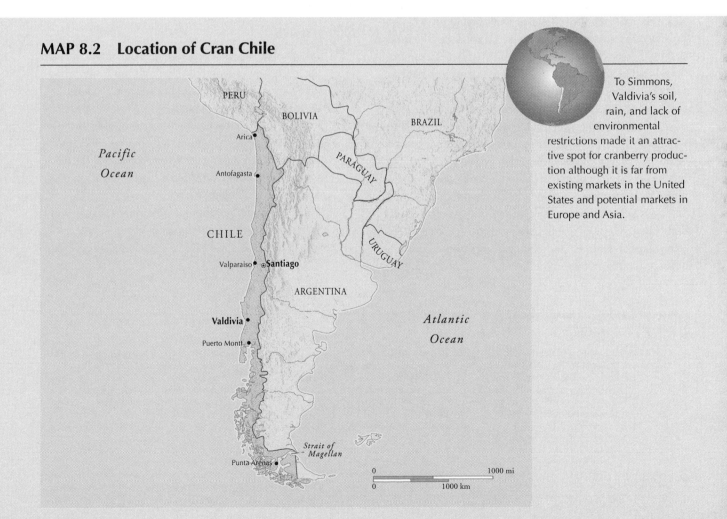

To Simmons, Valdivia's soil, rain, and lack of environmental restrictions made it an attractive spot for cranberry production although it is far from existing markets in the United States and potential markets in Europe and Asia.

$20 million to begin cultivating 700 acres with 250 employees. His plans are to plant 4,000 acres by the turn of the century, when his investment will have reached about $35 million. At that time, he estimates, Cran Chile will account for 10 percent of the world's cranberry land in cultivation.

One production problem Simmons faced was the great distance between Chile and cranberry processors in the United States. In 1995 Ocean Spray opened a new plant in Nevada with computerized warehouse processes, based on a just-in-time inventory system. This plant keeps an inventory of only three-week supplies, compared to customary five-week supplies. The company announced that eventually all its plants would operate that way. The JIT system will necessitate getting supplies to Ocean Spray very quickly once they are ordered—a difficult task from Chile.

Market conditions add another worry to Simmons's list. Simmons believed that he could sell to large cranberry processors (Ocean Spray, Quaker Oats, and Dole), who had projected increased sales in Asia and Europe. But the fruition of these sales may be difficult. Ocean Spray's CEO summarized the difficulty, saying, "We're introducing an unknown fruit in an unknown brand in a foreign market that's unknown to us." Ocean Spray's foreign expansion has already encountered some problems. For instance, it started selling juice in Britain in bottles, but had to change to small boxes because the British have small refrigerators. The introduction of cranberry juice in Japan was so disappointing that the company pulled out of the market temporarily. Not even Simmons expects sales to develop in Chile, where people don't like the taste of cranberries.

Finally, changes in environmental regulations could affect production either in the United States or in Chile. The vice president of Decas, the largest independent handler of cranberries in the United States, spoke out in an interview about the frustration of production going to Chile because of U.S. regulations. A representative of the U.S. Army Corps of Engineers, the agency responsible for administering the federal wetlands regulations, responded that no one who applied for a permit had been denied. But a permit approved in 1996 in Maine took five years to go through its hurdles. If regulations ease in the United States, there will be less need for U.S. companies to invest abroad. In the meantime, environmentalists have become more active in Chile. In fact, a $1 billion investment in a wood pulp plant was held up in 1996 until the company agreed not to dump waste into a river that ran into the wetlands.

In sum, Cran Chile represents a resource-seeking investment with a high risk but a potentially high return if production and marketing conditions go as Simmons anticipates.

QUESTIONS

1. What are the motivations and factors that influenced the foreign investment decision for Cran Chile? Compare these with those in the Bridgestone Tire case.

2. Do you see any ethical problems by investing where there are no environmental restrictions, such as those that make home-country investment more difficult? How might the differences in environmental restrictions between the United States and Chile affect the future of Cran Chile?

3. Relate Simmons's process of international expansion with companies' usual internationalization process (see Chapter 1).

CHAPTER NOTES

1 Data for the case were taken from Mike Tharp, "Bridgestone, Japan's Tire Giant, Now Seeking International Role," *New York Times*, November 21, 1980, p. D4; "Japan: Why a Tiremaker Wants a U.S. Base," *Business Week*, January 14, 1980, p. 40; Zachary Schiller and James B. Treece, "Bridgestone May Try an End Run around the Yen," *Business Week*, February 2, 1987, p. 31; Jonathan P. Hicks, "Decreasing Demand and Global Competition Propel Consolidation," *New York Times*, February 11, 1990, p. F8; Zachary Schiller and Roger Schreffler, "Why Tiremakers Are Still Spinning Their Wheels," *Business Week*, February 26,

1990, pp. 62–63; "When the Bridge Caught Fire," *Economist*, September 7, 1991, pp. 72–73; "Bridgestone/Firestone Is Named 1995 GM Supplier of the Year," *Business Wire*, May 15, 1996; "Bridgestone," *Jiji Press Ticker Service*, July 30, 1996; "World Tyre Industry," *Financial Times*, January 29, 1996, p. 12; Raju Narisetti and Gabriella Stern, "Goodyear Allies with a Japanese Tire Maker," *Wall Street Journal*, February 5, 1997, p. A3; "Bridgestone Buys Out Aircraft Tire Service Firm," *Jiji Press Ticker Service*, November 11, 1997; John Griffiths, "Consolidation Is Likely to Continue," *Financial Times*, September 16, 1999,

Auto Section, p. iv; Jennifer Scott Cimperman, "Race for Dominance," *The Plain Dealer*, August 15, 1999, p. 1D; and William Lewis and John Griffiths, "Goodyear Gets a Grip on Japanese Market," *Financial Times*, February 3, 1999, p. 20.

2 "Mergers Spur Foreign Direct Investment," *Journal of Commerce*, October 1, 1999, p. 5, giving 1998 data from the United Nations Conference on Trade and Development.

3 Some surveys of the considerable number of explanations may be found in Jean J. Boddewyn, "Foreign and Domestic Divestment and Investment Decisions," *Journal of Interna-*

tional Business Studies, Vol. XIV, No. 3, Winter 1983, pp. 23–35; A. L. Calvet, "A Synthesis of Foreign Direct Investment Theories and Theories of the Multinational Firm," *Journal of International Business Studies*, Spring–Summer 1981, pp. 43–60; John H. Dunning, "Toward an Eclectic Theory of International Production," *Journal of International Business Studies*, Spring–Summer 1980, pp.9–31; Robert Grosse, "The Theory of Foreign Direct Investment," *Essays in International Business*, No. 3, December 1981, pp. 1–51; M. Z. Rahman, "Maximisation of Global Interests: Ultimate Motivation for Foreign Investments by Transnational Corporations," *Management International Review*, Vol. 23, No. 4, 1983, pp. 4–13; Alan M. Rugman, "New Theories of the Multinational Enterprise: An Assessment of Internalization Theory," *Bulletin of Economic Research*, Vol. 38, No. 2, 1986, pp. 101–118; and T. A. Corley, "Progress in Multinational Studies at Reading and Elsewhere, 1981–86," Discussion Paper No. 120 (Reading, England: University of Reading International Investment and Business Studies, 1989).

4   For a discussion of the effect of growth change on growth alternatives, see Briance Mascarenhas, "Strategic Group Dynamics," *Academy of Management Journal*, Vol. 32, No. 2, June 1989, pp. 333–352.

5   Internalization theory, or holding a monopoly control over certain information or other proprietary assets, builds on earlier market-imperfections work by Ronald H. Coase, "The Nature of the Firm," *Economica*, Vol. 4, 1937, pp. 386–405. It has been noted by such writers as M. Casson, "The Theory of Foreign Direct Investment," Discussion Paper No. 50 (Reading, England: University of Reading International Investment and Business Studies, November 1980); and Stephen Magee, "Information and the MNC: An Appropriability Theory of Direct Foreign Investment," in *The New International Economic Order*, Jagdish N. Bhagwati, ed. (Cambridge, Mass.: MIT Press, 1977), pp. 317–340.

6   Claudia H. Deutsch, "Goodyear and Top Rival Cut Japan Tie," *New York Times*, February 6, 1997, p. C4.

7   Linsu Kim, "The Dynamics of Samsung's Technological Learning in Semiconductors," *California Management Review*, Spring 1997, pp. 86–100.

8   Alan M. Rugman, *Inside the Multinationals: The Economics of Internal Markets* (New York: Columbia University Press, 1981); David J. Teece, "Transactions Cost Economics and the Multinational Enterprise," Berkeley Business School International Business Working Paper Series, No. IB-3, 1985; and Peter W. Liesch and Gary A. Knight, "Information Internalization and Hurdle Rates in Small and Medium Enterprise Internationalization," *Journal of International Business Studies*, Vol. 30, No. 2, Second Quarter 1999, pp. 383–396.

9   Leslie Chang, "Intel Invades Taiwan Motherboard Turf," *Wall Street Journal*, October 31, 1995, p. A18.

10   "Spanish, French Tobacco Firms to Merge into Industry's Fourth-Biggest Company," *Wall Street Journal*, October 6, 1999, p. A18.

11   "Finance and Economics: Eastern Promise," *The Economist*, August 28, 1999, pp. 56–57.

12   Jiatao Li, "Foreign Entry and Survival: Effects of Strategic Choices on Performance in International Markets," *Strategic Management Journal*, Vol. 16, 1995, pp. 333–351.

13   Gordon Hanson and Antonio Spilimber, *Illegal Immigration, Border Enforcement, and Relative Wages: Evidence from Apprehensions at the U.S.-Mexico Border* (Cambridge, Mass.: NBER Working Paper No. 5592, 1996), shows the effect of wage differences on the movement of Mexican labor to the United States.

14   John Griffiths, "VW May Build Beetle in Europe to Meet Demand," *Financial Times*, November 11, 1998, p. 17.

15   Neal McGratt, "New Broom Sweeps into Asia," *Asian Business*, March 1996, p. 22.

16   Joseph Kahn, "Otis Elevator Plans Expansion in China to Defend Market Share," *Asian Wall Street Journal*, May 2, 1995, p. 3.

17   Mark Nicholson, "Hyundai's $1.1 bn Indian Unit to Make 200,000 Cars a Year," *Financial Times*, January 16, 1997, p. 4.

18   Stephen Baker, Kevin Kelly, Robert D. Hof, and William J. Holstein, "Mini-Nationals Are Making Maximum Impact," *Business Week*, September 6, 1993, pp. 66–69.

19   Diana Solis, "Mexico's Garment Industry Is Pivotal to Plans to Boost Economy Via Exports," *Wall Street Journal*, January 19, 1993, p. A8; and James P. Miller, "Zenith Is Shifting Taiwan Jobs to Mexico, Signaling Trend in Other Manufacturers," *Wall Street Journal*, November 12, 1991, p. A4.

20   Kenneth Dreyfack, "Draping Old Glory Around Just About Everything," *Business Week*, October 27, 1986, pp. 66–67; Sherri McLain and Brenda Sternquist, "Ethnocentric Consumers: Do They 'Buy American'?" *Journal of International Consumer Marketing*, Vol. 4, Nos. 1 and 2, 1992, pp. 39–58.

21   John S. Hulland, "The Effects of Country-of-Brand and Brand Name on Product Evaluation and Consideration: A Cross-Country Comparison," *Consumer Behavior in Asia: Issues and Market Practice*, 1999, pp. 23–39.

22   Stephen Baker, David Woodruff, and Bill Javetski, "Along the Border, Free Trade Is Becoming a Fact of Life," *Business Week*, June 18, 1990, pp. 41–42; and Lisa R. Van Wagner, "Putting Together the Pieces," *Export Today*, April 1992, pp. 10–11.

23   Peter Gumbel, "Mercedes-Benz Plans Brazilian Facility, Continuing Move from Costly Germany," *Wall Street Journal*, September 14, 1995, p. A5.

24   Sarkis Khoury, David Nickerson, and Venkataraman Sadanad, "Exchange Rate Uncertainty and Precommitment in Symmetric Duopoly: A New Theory of Multinational Production," *Recent Developments in International Banking and Finance*, Vols. IV and V, 1991; Jan Karl Karlsen and Michael H. Moffett, "On the Appropriateness of Economic or Strategic Exposure Management," Danish Summer Research Institute Paper, Copenhagen Business School, Copenhagen, Denmark, 1992.

25   Marcus Brauchli, "Bangladore Takes On Tasks a World Away," *Wall Street Journal*, January 6, 1993, p. A4.

26   Raymond Vernon, "International Investment and International Trade in the Product Cycle," *Quarterly Journal of Economics*, May 1966, pp. 191–207.

27   Jon Liden, "Ford Will Build Philippine Auto Plant After Receiving a Variety of Incentives," *Wall Street Journal*, April 10, 1998, p. A6.

28   Peter Marsh, "Going International Can Spread Risks," *Financial Times*, January 13, 1998, p. viii, referring to a study by Arthur D. Little and Technische Hochschule, "Best Practice in Globalising Manufacturing: A Survey of Selected European Companies," n.d.

29   "A Come-Back After Indy Wins," *Financial Times*, January 29, 1996, p. 14.

30   Edward B. Flowers, "Oligopolistic Reactions in European and Canadian Direct Investment in the United States," *Journal of International Business Studies*, Fall–Winter 1976, pp. 43–55; Frederick Knickerbocker, *Oligopolistic Reaction and Multinational Enterprise* (Cambridge, Mass.: Harvard University, Graduate School of Business, Division of Research, 1973). For opposing findings, see Lall and Siddharthan.

31   Reginald Chua, "Vietnam's Tiny Car Market Draws Crowd," *Wall Street Journal*, January 3, 1996, p. A4.

32   E. M. Graham, "Exchange of Threat Between Multinational Firms as an Infinitely Repeated Noncooperative Game," *The International Trade Journal*, Vol. IV, No. 3, pp. 259–277.

33   Tony Walker and Robert Corzine, "China to Pay $4.3 bn for Kazakh Oil Stake," *Financial Times*, June 5, 1997, p. 16.

34   Larry Rohter, "Impact of NAFTA Pounds Economics of the Caribbean," *New York Times*, January 30, 1997, p. 1A.

35   Mascarenhas, "Strategic Group Dynamics"; Yui Kimura, "Firm-Specific Strategic Advantages and Foreign Direct Investment Behavior of Firms: The Case of Japanese Semiconductor Firms" (Niigata, Japan: International Management Research Institute, International University of Japan, 1988).

36   Stephen H. Hymer, *A Study of Direct Foreign Investment* (Cambridge, Mass.: MIT Press, 1976); Alan M. Rugman, "Internationalization

as a General Theory of Foreign Direct Investment: A Re-Appraisal of the Literature," *Weltwirtschaftliches Archiv*, Band 116, Heft 2, 1980, pp. 365–379; and Yojin Jung, "Multinationality and Profitability," *Journal of Business Research*, Vol. 23, 1991, pp. 179–187.

37 Robert Z. Aliber, "A Theory of Direct Foreign Investment," in *The International Corporation*, Charles P. Kindleberger, ed. (Cambridge, Mass.: MIT Press, 1970), pp. 28–33; Robert Johnson, "Distance Deals," *Wall Street Journal*, February 24, 1988, p. 1; and Richard Waters, "Foreign Money for US Business Slows," *Financial Times*, June 11, 1998, p. 7.

38 Louis Uchitelle, "Overseas Spending by U.S. Companies Sets Record Pace," *New York Times*, May 20, 1988, p. 11; and "Investing Abroad Is Paying Off Big for U.S. Companies," *Business Week*, November 6, 1989, p. 34.

39 John D. Daniels and Jeffrey Bracker, "Profit Performance: Do Foreign Operations Make a Difference?" *Management International Review*, Vol. 29, No. 1, 1989, pp. 46–56.

40 UNCTAD Press Release, TAD/INF/2820, September 23, 1999.

41 United Nations Conference on Trade and Development, *World Investment Report,*

1995: Transnational Corporations and Competitiveness (Geneva: United Nations, 1995).

42 United Nations Conference on Trade and Development, *World Investment Report, 1999* (Geneva: United Nations, 1999).

43 "U.K. Firms Outrank U.S. in Investment for Foreign Firms," *Wall Street Journal*, January 18, 1999, p. A13.

44 Silvia E. Bargas and Rosaria Troia, "Direct Investment Positions for 1998: Country and Industry Detail," *Survey of Current Business*, Vol. 79, No. 7, July 1999, pp. 48–59.

45 Enery Quinones Lellouche, "How OECD Governments Co-Operate on Investment Issues," *OECD Observer*, June–July 1992, p. 10; and Marie-France Houde, "Foreign Direct Investment," *OECD Observer*, June–July 1992, pp. 9–13.

46 Data for the case were taken from Jennifer Wolcott, "Politics Corrals Bay State Bogs," *Christian Science Monitor*, October 15, 1992, pp. 14–15; Calvin Sims, "Taking Cranberries to Chile, Where They Are Really an Acquired Taste," *New York Times*, November 22, 1995, p. C13; Joseph Pereira, "Unknown Fruit Takes On Unfamiliar Market," *Wall Street Journal*, November 9, 1995, p. B1; Rod McFarlane,

"Abuzz Over Bees: Cranberry Growers Look to Export from New Zealand for Advice on Bumblebees," *La Cross Tribune*, July 3, 1995, p. A1; Adrian Seybert, "Corporate Welfare: Even Del's Took a Taste," *Providence Journal Bulletin*, June 18, 1995, p. F1; "Striking It Rich(mond)," *Equity*, Vol. 12, No. 9, October 1994, p. 50; Amy Vreeland, "Ocean Spray Names Successor to President and Chief Executive Officer," *PR Newswire*, June 19, 1995, p. 1; "Counting Widgets: County Firms Trim Costs Via Improved Control," *Plymouth County Business Review*, Vol. 14, No. 1, April 1995, p. 1; John Estrella, "Ocean Spray Enters Candy Industry," *Standard Times*, December 25, 1994, p. B1; John Estrella, "Ocean Spray Plans to Upgrade Plant," *Standard Times*, December 16, 1994, p. A7; William R. Long, "U.S. Businessman in Chile Works from the Ground Up," *Los Angeles Times*, February 11, 1994, p. A6; Mark Shanahan, "Proposed Cranberry Operation in Alfred Moving Slowly Through Tangle," *Portland Press Herald*, June 9, 1996, p. 1B; and Imogen Mark, "Chile Finds the Going Harder," *Financial Times*, August 16, 1996, p. 5.

PART THREE: THEORIES AND INSTITUTIONS: TRADE AND INVESTMENT
ROLLERBLADE, SEBAGO SHOES, AND NIVEA

BACKGROUND

This video looks at Rollerblade and Sebago Shoes, two U.S.-based companies, and NIVEA, a company based in Germany, each of which conducts business throughout the world. Products from all three companies share aspects of the international product life cycle, and all three companies face similar situations. For example, should they undertake foreign direct investment and build manufacturing facilities in other countries? Until now, each company has survived international competition by producing high-quality products. But now each company must decide on the future course of action it will take. The video discusses the international product life cycle and illustrates what that cycle means in terms of survival and success in the international environment. You will see how Sebago Shoes and Rollerblade have been successful outside the United States and how NIVEA has succeeded in the U.S. market. Furthermore, you will understand and appreciate how companies conduct business in an era of regional integration.

ROLLERBLADE, INC.

Rollerblade is a privately held company, based in Minnetonka, Minnesota, whose products are distributed worldwide. In 1980, it developed its skates as an off-season training tool for hockey players, and skiers quickly took up the skates. In 1986, the company redefined and expanded the in-line skate market to include fitness enthusiasts, recreation seekers, and cross-training athletes from numerous sports. Today, with an estimated 30 million participants, in-line skating has truly come into its own as a sport. Rollerblade, the pioneer of in-line skating, continues to lead the in-line skate industry. It has a majority market share, whereas none of the other 30-plus in-line skate companies have more than a 10 percent share.

SEBAGO SHOES

Shoe manufacturer Sebago Shoes was established in Portland, Maine, in 1946. From the very beginning, Sebago Shoes earned a reputation for its high quality, handmade shoes. As a small company, Sebago Shoes dealt primarily in the U.S. market, but soon started exporting its shoes to the world. Today, the company competes against traditional giants in the shoe industry from countries including Italy, France, Spain, and the Czech Republic. Retailers in 73 countries now carry Sebago Shoes.

NIVEA

In 1911, Oskar Toplowitz, the owner of Beiersdorf (the German company that manufactures NIVEA), started the development of a skin cream based on new ingredients. He named it NIVEA from the Latin word nivius, meaning "snow white." During the 1930s, the company increased its visibility by introducing products such as shaving cream, facial toner, and shampoo. During World War II, NIVEA's trademarks were taken over by companies from the countries against which Germany fought. Soon after the war ended, Beiersdorf set about buying back the trademark rights, a process finally completed in 1997. In the 1950s the NIVEA brand became increasingly well-known in many countries, and it soon grew into the umbrella brand for a wide range of skin care products. From the 1960s through 2000, NIVEA concentrated on getting its products into markets worldwide, and it succeeded handsomely.

QUESTIONS

As you watch the video, be prepared to answer the following questions:
1. What stage of the international product life cycle do you think Sebago's Docksiders are in? Answer the same question for Rollerblade's in-line skates and Nivea cream. What are their similarities and differences?
2. How could a company such as Rollerblade maintain its international market share?
3. What do you think has contributed to Sebago's, Rollerblade's, and Niveas's success in international business?
4. How could regional economic integration in Europe help a non-EU company such as Sebago Shoes?
5. Do you think any of the companies in this video should pursue foreign direct investment? If so, which companies? Which companies shouldn't pursue foreign direct investment and why?

World Financial Environment

CHAPTER 9

The Foreign-Exchange Market

All things are obedient to money. —ENGLISH PROVERB

OBJECTIVES

- ■ **To learn the fundamentals of foreign exchange**

- ■ **To identify the major characteristics of the foreign-exchange market and how governments control the flow of currencies across national borders**

- ■ **To understand why companies deal in foreign exchange**

- ■ **To describe how the foreign-exchange market works**

- ■ **To examine the different institutions that deal in foreign exchange**

One of the more daunting aspects of overseas travel for the business executive or the tourist is coping with currency. Recently, I traveled to Latin America (see Map 9.1) to visit alumni, interview candidates for our MBA program, and set up a foreign business excursion for graduate business students. I was in such a hurry to leave that I didn't even check the exchange rates in the *Wall Street Journal*—something I usually do. Even though the exchange rates in the *Journal* are the New York selling rates (my buying rates) for transactions of $1 million or more—and I didn't plan on exchanging $1 million—I could still have gotten a general idea of what to expect.

The first stop was Chile. I decided to carry a mixture of cash and traveler's checks, because on a trip to Brazil a few years earlier, I was attacked and nearly robbed in Rio de Janeiro. Traveler's checks provide security because they can be replaced. However, in that prior trip, the bank wouldn't cash traveler's checks at the Buenos Aires airport, so this time I came prepared for all possibilities. In addition, I like to use credit cards, as long as the local currency is stable. Credit card companies handle large volumes of currency daily, so they get favorable exchange rates.

When we cleared customs in Chile, the exchange rate was 350 pesos per dollar. I had no idea whether it was a good rate, so I waited to cash in until we arrived at the hotel. When we got to the hotel, I asked the woman at the front desk if she could cash $100 and she said she was out of pesos but would have some in 30 minutes. No big deal because we needed to unpack and rest before having lunch. After a nap, we headed down to the front desk to get some cash. But still the answer was, "Sorry. No pesos." She did suggest an exchange house two blocks away. So off we headed. After getting lost, we finally asked directions and found a Casa de Cambio (Exchange House) next to the metro (subway or underground). To our pleasant surprise, the exchange rate was 450 pesos per dollar, and there was no service charge. Usually when you convert currency at the airport, bank, or hotel, you have to pay a service charge on each transaction. We walked out of the Casa de Cambio with 45,000 pesos—10,000 more than if we had converted at the airport.

As we walked to lunch, I began to figure out how much things would cost. When I get foreign currency, I feel as if I'm spending Monopoly money—it just doesn't seem real for some reason. "Let's see, if I want to pay $10 for lunch, I should pay 4,500 pesos ($10 x 450 pesos, the exchange rate I got when I traded my dollars into pesos). That's easy. But what if lunch costs 7,800 pesos? How much is that? Never mind. It's more than $10 and less than $20 (between 4,500 and 9,000 pesos)." I said to myself that I might have to think about this some more.

After two wonderful days in Santiago, we checked out of the hotel—an experience in itself. Everyone was very pleasant but the system was a little slow. The clerk said, "Do you want to keep the charges on your American Express?" "Of course," I said. I figured AMEX could get a pretty good exchange rate for my room charge for two nights of 102,000 pesos. "That will be $255," he said. "Wait," I said. "What exchange rate are you using?" "400 pesos," he replied. "That's a horrible rate," I said. "I got 450 pesos down the street." "That is not possible, Señor. Maybe you misunderstood. Perhaps 405, or maybe 415, but not 450." "I know what exchange rate I got and it was 450," I replied. "That is a very good exchange rate, Señor." Yeah, right, I thought. Not only did I not get the AMEX rate, but the room cost me $127.50 per night! At my conversion rate of 450 pesos from the Casa de Cambio, I would have spent only $227 for two

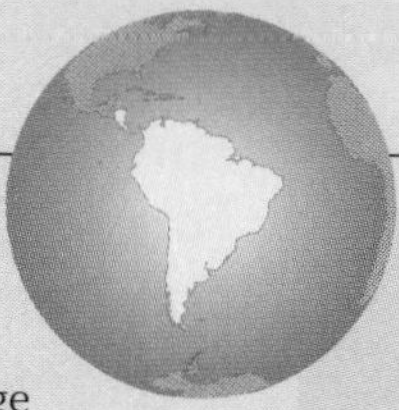

Tourists and business travelers hope for favorable exchange rates when traveling abroad.

MAP 9.1 A Trip Through South America's Exchange Rates

VENEZUELA

TRINIDAD & TOBAGO

GUYANA

SURINAME

FRENCH GUIANA

COLOMBIA

ECUADOR

PERU

BOLIVIA

PARAGUAY

SAO PAULO, BRAZIL
0.93 reals=U.S. $1.00

URUGUAY

SANTIAGO, CHILE
450 pesos=U.S. $1.00

BUENOS AIRES, ARGENTINA
1 peso=U.S. $1.00

```
0                    1000 mi
0             1000 km
```

nights (102,000 pesos/450 pesos), saving $28. It wasn't enough to cause an international incident, however, so I dropped it and thanked him for the lovely stay. I may be back, so I don't want him to remember an ugly American.

When I got to the Santiago airport, I decided to exchange Chilean pesos for Argentinean pesos, or "Argentino" for short but only dollars were available. This was confusing itself, because both Chile and Argentina used the term *peso* for their currency, even though the values are very different. I guess this is the same as the United States and Canada both using the term *dollar* for their currencies. Then I noticed that they were selling dollars for 410 pesos per dollar and buying for 430. Because I had bought at 450 at the Exchange House and sold at 430 at the airport, I made about $0.11 on every 1,000 pesos. It didn't amount to much—but if only I could have traded $1 million at that spread. . . .

When we arrived at the Buenos Aires airport a few hours later, I cashed some more money at the bank in the airport. This time the bank accepted traveler's checks and I converted $100 for 93.95 pesos, which was a little surprising because I had read that the exchange rate was $1 = 1 peso. To my surprise, the bank charged me 5 percent to cash the traveler's checks and another 1.05 percent service fee—a total of 6.05 pesos.

Because everything was expensive in Buenos Aires, I ran out of pesos fast, so I went to the American Express office the next day and it converted $100 for 99.8 pesos. Next time I'll ask before using traveler's checks. It can get confusing. At times I've sold traveler's checks at a better rate than cash, and other times not. When we left Buenos Aires, the exchange rate was the same for buying and selling—1:1. There was a $0.15 service charge, so it cost almost nothing to change currency—$100 to buy 99.8 pesos at American Express and $100 for selling 99.85 pesos (100 pesos less $0.15).

After a delay at the airport in Buenos Aires, we finally headed for São Paulo, Brazil. The currency market in Brazil has always been the haven of the black marketer. No one ever has a clue to the real value, and it varies with personal checks, traveler's checks, or cash. Every hotel and shop has its own rate, which requires astute shopping around.

The last time I had been in Brazil, the country was in the process of locking the currency onto the U.S. dollar to eliminate these price differences and stabilize its value, but it was still chaotic. Taxi drivers still preferred dollars, no matter what the exchange rate. Finally, the Brazilian government succeeded in stabilizing the currency in June 1994, and the Brazilian *real* (the name of the currency, pronounced *hey-all*) was fixed to the dollar (or pegged) about 1:1. When I arrived at the airport, I changed dollars into *reaeis* (pronounced *hey-ice*) at R$0.9300 = US $1.00. The bank asked no service charge, but it sold dollars (or bought R$) for R$0.99 = US $1.00. What a change from the historical value! The first time I went to Brazil, in 1964, the dollar was worth 1,200 cruzeiros, the name of the currency then. Since that time, the Brazilian currency has changed names seven times: cruzeiro (1942–1967), new cruzeiro (1967–1970), cruzeiro (1970–1986), cruzado (1986–1989), new cruzado (1989–1990), cruzeiro (again!) (1990–1993), cruzeiro real (1993–1994), and real (since 1994). Every change knocked three zeros off the currency. So, 1,200 cruzeiros became 1.2 new cruzeiros, and so on. At an exchange rate of 1:1, it was obviously easier to figure out how much everything cost in dollars. But everything was more expensive compared to U.S. costs. When the Brazilian government fixed the rate at 1:1, it made the real a little too strong, so the dollar lost much purchasing power there.

It can be confusing to travel overseas—whether on a business trip or for pleasure—and the more countries you go to in a single trip, the more confusing it gets. 〜

INTRODUCTION

In the previous part of the book, we discussed some key theories underlying international trade and investment. Now let's move to global financial markets and see how the foreign-exchange market works in international business.

To survive, both MNEs and small import and export companies must understand foreign exchange and exchange rates. In a business setting, there is a fundamental difference

At the Sydney Futures Exchange (above) the world currency market day is just beginning. Multinational enterprises (MNEs) seek futures contracts as a way to get foreign currency at favorable rates.

between making payment in the domestic market and making payment abroad. In a domestic transaction, companies use only one currency. In a foreign transaction, companies can use two or more currencies. For example, a U.S. company that exports skis to a French distributor will ask the French buyer to remit payment in dollars, unless the U.S. company has some specific use for French francs, such as paying a French supplier.

Assume you are a U.S. importer who has agreed to purchase a certain quantity of French perfume and to pay the French exporter 20,000 francs for it. Assuming you had the money, how would you go about paying? First, you would go to the international department of your local bank to buy 20,000 francs at the going market rate. Let's assume the franc/dollar exchange rate is 6.9969 francs per dollar. Your bank then would charge your account $2,858.41 (20,000/6.9969) plus the transaction costs and give you a special check payable in francs made out to the exporter. The exporter would deposit it in a French bank, which then would credit the exporter's account with 20,000 francs. So, the *foreign-exchange* transaction would be complete. **Foreign exchange** is money denominated in the currency of another nation or group of nations.[1] The market in which these transactions take place is the foreign-exchange market. Foreign exchange can be in the form of cash, funds available on credit and debit cards, traveler's checks, bank deposits, or other short-term claims.[2]

Foreign exchange—money denominated in the currency of another nation or group of nations

Exchange rate—the price of a currency

An **exchange rate** is the price of a currency. It is the number of units of one currency that buys one unit of another currency, and this number can change daily. For example, on April 24, 2000, one French franc could purchase U.S.$0.1429. Exchange rates make international price and cost comparisons possible.

The foreign-exchange market is made up of many different players. Some players buy and sell foreign exchange because they are exporters and importers of goods and services. Other players buy and sell foreign exchange because of foreign direct investments—both investing capital into and pulling dividends out of a country. Others are portfolio investors—they buy foreign stocks, bonds, and mutual funds hoping to sell them at a more profitable exchange rate later. These players have different objectives for buying and selling foreign currencies, and in the meantime they affect supply and demand for those currencies.

MAJOR CHARACTERISTICS OF THE FOREIGN-EXCHANGE MARKET

The foreign-exchange market has two major segments: the "over-the-counter" market (OTC) and the exchange-traded market. The OTC market is comprised of banks, both commercial banks like Bank of America and investment banks like Merrill Lynch, and other financial institutions, and is where most of the foreign-exchange activity takes place. The exchange-traded market is comprised of securities exchanges, such as the Chicago Mercantile Exchange and the Philadelphia Stock Exchange, where certain types of foreign-exchange instruments, such as exchange-traded futures and options, are traded. These markets will be discussed in more depth later in the chapter.

BRIEF DESCRIPTION OF FOREIGN-EXCHANGE INSTRUMENTS

Several different types of foreign-exchange instruments are traded in these markets, but the traditional foreign-exchange instruments that comprise the bulk of foreign-exchange trading are spot, outright forwards, and FX swaps. **Spot transactions** involve the exchange of currency the second day after the date on which the two foreign-exchange traders agree to the transaction. The rate at which the transaction is settled is the **spot rate. Outright forward** transactions involve the exchange of currency three or more days after the date on which the traders agree to the transaction. It is the single purchase or sale of a currency for future delivery. The rate at which the transaction is settled is the forward rate and is a contract rate between the two parties. The forward transaction will be settled at the forward rate no matter what the actual spot rate is at the time of settlement. In an **FX swap**, one currency is swapped for another on one date and then swapped back on a future date. Most often, the first leg of an FX swap is a spot transaction, with the second leg of the swap a future transaction. For example, assume that IBM receives a dividend in British pounds from its subsidiary in the United Kingdom but has no use for British pounds until it has to pay a British supplier in pounds in 30 days. It would rather have dollars now than hold on to the pounds for 30 days. IBM could enter into an FX swap where it sells the pounds for dollars to a trader in the spot market at the spot rate and agrees to buy pounds for dollars from the trader in 30 days at the forward rate. Although an FX swap is both a spot and a forward transaction, it is accounted for as a single transaction.

In addition to the traditional instruments, which were the only foreign-exchange instruments traded until the 1970s, there are *currency swaps, options and futures*.[3] Currency swaps are OTC instruments, options are traded both OTC and on exchanges, and futures are exchange-traded instruments. **Currency swaps** deal more with interest-bearing financial instruments (such as a bond), and they involve the exchange of principal and interest payments. **Options** are the right but not the obligation to trade foreign currency in the future. A **futures contract** is an agreement between two parties to buy or sell a particular currency at a particular price on a particular future date, as specified in a standardized contract to all participants in that currency futures exchange.

Foreign-exchange market
- **Over-the-counter (commercial and investment banks)**
- **Securities exchanges**

Traditional foreign-exchange instruments
- **Spot**
- **Outright forward**
- **FX swap**

The spot rate is the exchange rate quoted for transactions that require either immediate delivery or delivery within two days.

Outright forwards involve the exchange of currency beyond three days at a fixed exchange rate, known as the forward rate.

An FX swap is a simultaneous spot and forward transaction.

Three other key foreign-exchange instruments
- **Currency swaps**
- **Options**
- **Futures**

THE SIZE, COMPOSITION, AND LOCATION OF THE FOREIGN-EXCHANGE MARKET

Before we examine the market instruments in more detail, let's look at the size, composition, and geographic location of the market. Every three years, the Bank for International Settlements (http://www.bis.org), a Basel, Switzerland–based central banking institution that is owned and controlled by 45 national central banks, conducts a survey of foreign-exchange activity in the world. In the 1998 survey, it was estimated that $1.5 trillion in foreign exchange is traded every day.[4] This represents a growth of 26 percent in the three-year period since April 1995. Figure 9.1 illustrates the growth in foreign-exchange trading beginning with the 1989 survey. The $1.5 trillion daily turnover includes traditional foreign-exchange market activity only—spots, outright forwards, and FX swaps. Other over-the-counter (OTC) instruments added about $97 billion daily, and exchange-traded instruments added another $12 billion daily. Spot transactions have consistently fallen from 59 percent of traditional turnover in 1989 to 40 percent of total turnover in 1998.

The U.S. dollar is the most important currency in the foreign-exchange market because it comprises one side (buy or sell) of 87 percent of all foreign currency transactions worldwide, as Table 9.1 illustrates. This means that almost every foreign exchange transaction conducted on a daily basis has the dollar as one leg of the transaction. There are five major reasons why the dollar is so widely traded. It is

- An investment currency in many capital markets
- A reserve currency held by many central banks
- A transaction currency in many international commodity markets

Size of the foreign-exchange market
- **$1.5 trillion daily in traditional instruments**
- **$110 billion daily in other OTC and exchange-traded instruments**
- **Spot transactions are only 40 percent of total transactions**

FIGURE 9.1   Average Daily Volume in World Foreign-Exchange Markets, 1989–1998

The average daily volume of foreign-exchange transactions was $1.5 trillion worldwide in April 1998.

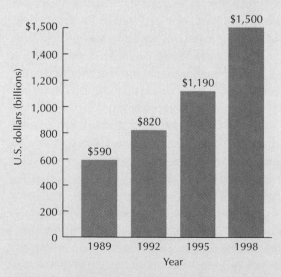

Source: Bank for International Settlements, *Central Bank Survey of Foreign Exchange and Derivatives Market Activity 1998* (Basel, Switzerland: BIS, May 1999), p. 2.

TABLE 9.1   **CURRENCY DISTRIBUTION OF GLOBAL FOREIGN EXCHANGE MARKET ACTIVITY**

	PERCENTAGE OF DAILY TURNOVER			
CURRENCY	APRIL 1989	APRIL 1992	APRIL 1995	APRIL 1998
U.S. dollar	90	82	83	87
Deutsche mark	27	40	37	30
Japanese yen	27	23	24	21
Pound sterling	15	14	10	11
Swiss franc	10	9	7	7
All others	31	32	39	44

Source: Bank for International Settlements, *Central Bank Survey of Foreign Exchange and Derivatives Market Activity 1998* (Basel, Switzerland: BIS, May 1999), Table B3, p. 9.

- An invoice currency in many contracts
- An intervention currency employed by monetary authorities in market operations to influence their own exchange rates[5]

Because of the ready availability of U.S. dollars worldwide, it is important as a vehicle for foreign-exchange transactions between two countries other than the United States. An example of how the dollar can be used as a vehicle currency for two other countries is when a Mexican company importing products from a Japanese exporter converts Mexican pesos into dollars and sends them to the Japanese exporter, who converts the dollars into yen. Thus the U.S. dollar is one leg on both sides of the transaction—in Mexico and in Japan. There may be a couple of reasons to go through dollars instead of directly from pesos to yen. The first reason is that the Japanese exporter might not have any need for pesos, whereas it can use dollars for a variety of reasons. The second reason is that the Mexican importer might have trouble getting yen at a good exchange rate if the Mexican banks are not carrying yen balances. However, the banks undoubtedly carry dollar balances, so the importer might have easy access to the dollars. Thus the dollar has become an important "vehicle" for international transactions, and it greatly simplifies life for a foreign bank because it won't have to carry balances in many different currencies.

Another way to consider foreign-currency trades is to look at the most frequently traded currency pairs. Seven of the top ten currency pairs involve the U.S. dollar, with the top two pairs being the U.S. dollar and the Deutsche mark (20.2 percent of total) and the U.S. dollar and Japanese yen (18.5 percent).[6] This reinforces the idea that the dollar is a vehicle currency for trading between other currencies, which is known as cross-trading.

These figures could all change with the introduction of the euro. In the first place, the sum of the global foreign-exchange market activity of euro countries is 52 percent of total, still behind the United States with 87 percent. But the euro could become a more important vehicle currency in the future, replacing the U.S. dollar in some cases, which could cause the dollar to lose market share. Time will tell.

The dollar is the most widely trade currency in the world

- **An investment currency in many capital markets**
- **A reserve currency held by many central banks**
- **A transaction currency in many international commodity markets**
- **An invoice currency in many contracts**
- **An intervention currency employed by monetary authorities in market operations to influence their own exchange rates**

The dollar is part of seven of the top ten currency pairs traded.
The dollar/Deutsche mark is number one.
The dollar/yen is number two.

The biggest market for foreign exchange is London, followed by New York and Tokyo.

Given that the dollar is clearly the most widely traded currency in the world, that would seem to indicate that the biggest market for foreign-exchange trading would be in the United States. But as Figure 9.2, on page 316, illustrates, the biggest market by far is in the United Kingdom. The four largest centers for foreign-exchange trading (the United Kingdom, the United States, Japan, and Singapore) account for 65 percent of total average daily turnover. The U.K. market is so dominant that more dollars are

MAP 9.2
International Time Zones and the Single World Market

The world's communication networks are now so good that we can talk of a single world market. It starts in a small way in New Zealand around 9:00 A.M., just in time to catch the tail end of the previous night's New York market. Two or three hours later, Tokyo opens, followed an hour later by Hong Kong and Manila and then half an hour later by Singapore. By now, with the Far East market in full swing, the focus moves to the Near and Middle East. Bombay opens two hours after Singapore, followed after an hour and a half by Abu Dhabi, and Athens an hour behind Jidda, and Beirut an hour behind still. By this stage, trading in the Far and Middle East is usually thin as dealers wait to see how Europe will trade. Paris and Frankfurt open an hour ahead of London, and by this time Tokyo is starting to close down, so the European market can judge the Japanese market. By lunchtime in London, New York is starting to open up, and as Europe closes down, positions can be passed westward. Midday in New York, trading

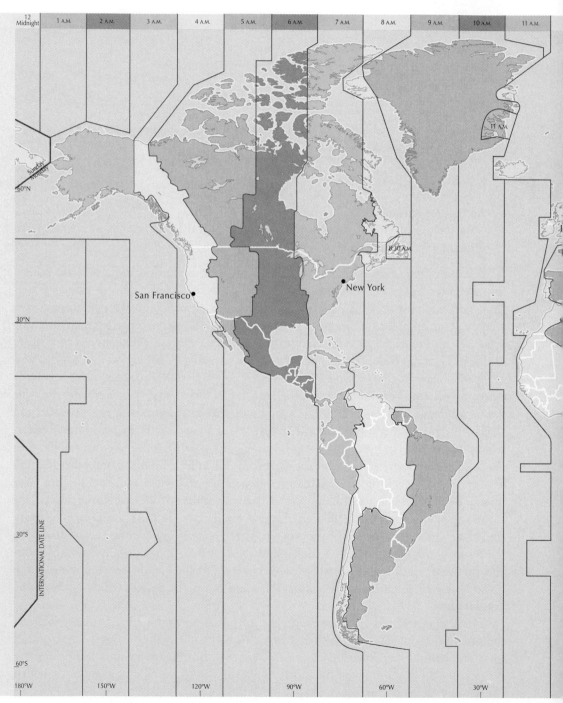

traded in London than in New York, and more Deutsche marks are traded in London than in Germany.[7] Why is London so important? There are two major reasons for London's prominence: (1) London, which is close to the major capital markets in Europe, is a strong international financial center where a large number of domestic and foreign financial institutions have operations; (2) London is positioned in a unique way because of the time zone. In Map 9.2, note that at noon in London, it is 7:00 A.M. in New York and

London is open when Tokyo closes and New York opens—it is centrally located in terms of time.

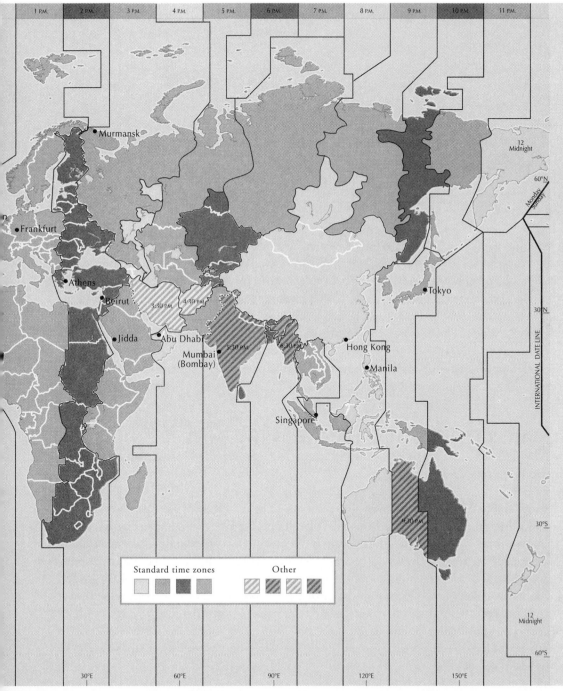

tends to be quiet because there is nowhere to pass a position to. The San Francisco market, three hours behind, is effectively a satellite of the New York market although very small positions can be passed on to New Zealand banks. (Note that in the former Soviet Union standard time zones are advanced an hour. Also note that some countries and territories have adopted half-hour time zones, as shown by hatched lines.)

Standard time zones   Other

Source: Adapted from Julian Walmsley, *The Foreign Exchange Handbook* (New York: John Wiley, 1983), pp. 7–8. Reprinted by permission of John Wiley & Sons, Inc. Some information taken from *The Cambridge Factfinders*, 3/e, edited by David Crystal (New York: Cambridge University Press, 1998), p. 440.

FIGURE 9.2   Geographical Distribution of Global Foreign-Exchange Market Activity, April 1998.

The largest volume of foreign-exchange transactions occurs in the United Kingdom (London) due to its central location.

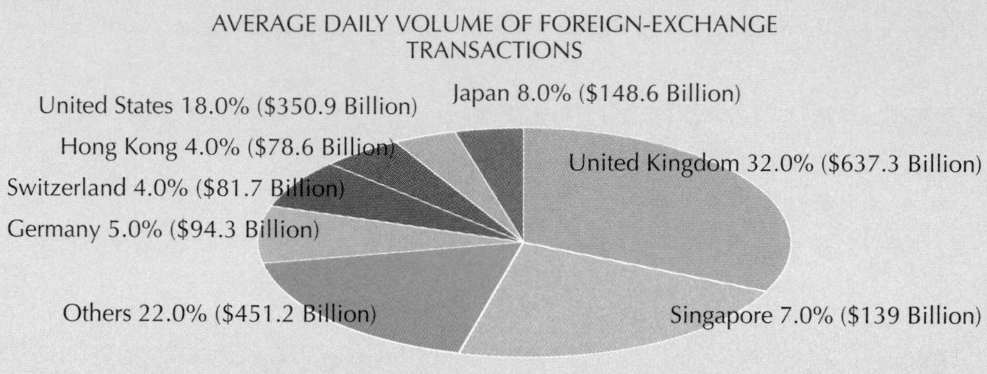

AVERAGE DAILY VOLUME OF FOREIGN-EXCHANGE TRANSACTIONS

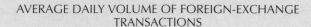

United States 18.0% ($350.9 Billion)

Japan 8.0% ($148.6 Billion)

Hong Kong 4.0% ($78.6 Billion)

Switzerland 4.0% ($81.7 Billion)

Germany 5.0% ($94.3 Billion)

United Kingdom 32.0% ($637.3 Billion)

Others 22.0% ($451.2 Billion)

Singapore 7.0% ($139 Billion)

Source: Bank for International Settlements, *Central Bank Survey of Foreign Exchange and Derivatives Market Activity 1998* (Basel, Switzerland: BIS, May 1999), p. 11.

evening in Asia. The London market opens toward the end of the trading day in Asia and is going strong as the New York foreign-exchange market opens up. London straddles both of the other major markets in the world. Figure 9.3 illustrates the volume of foreign-exchange trading on a daily basis and illustrates how market activity is concentrated on the time period when Asia and Europe are open or when Europe and the United States are open, even though the market is really open 24 hours a day. Currencies trade in greater volume during the business time of the markets, even though there is the opportunity for trades 24 hours a day. You can get a better price for currencies when the markets are active and liquid.

MAJOR FOREIGN-EXCHANGE INSTRUMENTS

Now let's examine in more detail the major foreign-exchange instruments: spot, forward, options, and futures.

THE SPOT MARKET

Most foreign-currency transactions take place between foreign-exchange traders, so the traders, who work for foreign-exchange brokerage houses or commercial banks, quote the rates. The traders always quote a **bid** (buy) and **offer** (sell) rate. The bid is the price at which the trader is willing to buy foreign currency, and the offer is the price at which the trader is willing to sell foreign currency. In the spot market, the **spread** is the difference between the bid and offer rates and is the trader's profit margin. The rate a trader quotes for the British pound might be $1.5975/85. This means the trader is willing to buy pounds at $1.5975 each and sell them for $1.5985. Obviously, a trader wants to buy low and sell high.

Key foreign-exchange terms

- **Bid**—the rate at which traders buy foreign exchange
- **Offer**—the rate at which traders sell foreign exchange
- **Spread**—the difference between bid and offer rates; the profit margin for the trader
- **American terms**—the number of dollars per unit of foreign currency
- **European terms**—the number of units of foreign currency per dollar

FIGURE 9.3   The Circadian Rhythms of the FX Market

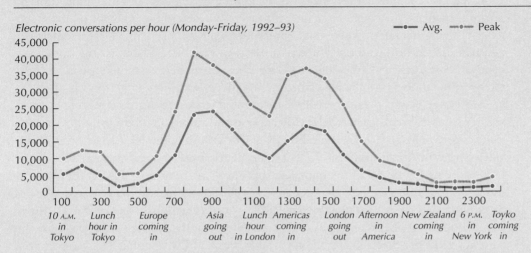

Electronic conversations per hour (Monday-Friday, 1992–93)   ●— Avg.   ●— Peak

| | Market activity heightens when Europe and Asia are open and when Europe and the United States are open. |

Note: Time (0100–2400 hours, Greenwich Mean Time)

Source: Reuters.

In this example, the trader quotes the foreign currency as the number of U.S. dollars for one unit of that currency. This method of quoting exchange rates is called the **direct quote**, also known in the foreign-exchange industry as "**American terms.**" It represents a quote from the point of view of someone in the United States. The other convention for quoting foreign exchange is "**European terms,**" which means a direct quote from the perspective of someone from Europe. From a U.S. point of view, this means the number of units of the foreign currency per U.S. dollar. This is also sometimes called the **indirect quote** in the United States, although *American terms* and *European terms* are the most accurate ways to describe the quotes.

Until 1978, exchange rates were quoted in European terms in Europe and American terms in the United States. But the United States decided to switch over to European terms to be consistent with the rest of the world. In European terms, exchange rates are quoted as the number of units of the foreign currency per U.S. dollar. The dollar is considered the **base currency**, also known as the quoted, underlying, or fixed currency, and the other currency is the **terms currency**. The terms currency is the numerator, and the base currency is the denominator. Thus for an exchange rate of ¥105/$ (indirect or European terms), the yen is the numerator (terms currency), and the dollar is the denominator (quoted or base currency). Now most currencies are quoted in European terms in the United States, with the exception of a few currencies, such as the Canadian dollar and British pound, which are always quoted direct, or the number of U.S. dollars per Canadian dollar or British pound.[8]

When traders quote currencies to their customers, they always quote the base currency first, followed by the terms currency. A quote for "dollar/yen" means that the dollar is the base currency and the yen is the terms currency. If you know the dollar/yen quote, you can divide that rate into 1 to get the yen/dollar quote. In other words, the exchange rate in American terms is the reciprocal or inverse of the exchange rate in European terms.

In a dollar-yen quote, the dollar is the denominator and the yen is the numerator. By tracking changes in the exchange rate, managers can determine whether the base currency is strengthening or weakening. For example, on January 15, 2000, the dollar-yen rate was ¥105/$1.00, and on January 16, the rate was ¥107/$1.00. As the numerator rises, the base currency—the dollar—is strengthening or getting more expensive. If the rate were to fall to ¥100, the base currency would be weakening or getting cheaper.

Most large newspapers, especially those devoted to business or those having business sections, quote exchange rates daily. Because most currencies constantly fluctuate in value, many managers check the values daily. For example, the *Wall Street Journal* provides quotes in American terms (U.S. $ equivalent) and European terms (currency per U.S. $) in Table 9.2. All of the quotes, except those noted as 30-, 90-, or 180-day forward, are spot quotes. The spot rates are the selling rates for interbank transactions of $1 million and more. Interbank transactions are transactions between banks. Retail transactions, those between banks and companies or individuals, provide fewer foreign currency units per dollar than interbank transactions. If I were going on a business trip, I could check the *Wall Street Journal* to get an idea of the exchange rate in my destination country, just as I did in the opening case, but I would get fewer units of the foreign currency for my dollars than is quoted in the *Journal*. There are also a number of good Internet sources for exchange-rate quotes.[9]

Cross rate—the relationship between two nondollar currencies.

A final definition that applies to the spot market is the **cross rate**. This is the exchange rate between non-U.S. dollar currencies. As an example, let's use the quotes for the Swiss franc and German mark in European terms Table 9.2 and figure the cross rate with the franc as the terms currency and the mark as the base currency. In Table 9.2, the spot rates for these currencies are 1.6763 francs per U.S. dollar and 2.0862 marks per U.S. dollar. The cross rate is calculated as follows

$$\frac{1.6763 \text{ francs}}{2.0862 \text{ marks}} = 0.80352 \text{ francs per mark}$$

This means 1 mark equals 0.80352 francs.

The *Wall Street Journal* also publishes a cross-rate table along with the dollar-exchange rates. Table 9.3 identifies the cross rates for several key currencies. The rows are treated as the terms currency and the columns as the base currency. For example, starting in the Japan row and going to the dollar column, we find that the exchange rate is ¥105.79/$1.00. The yen is the terms currency and the dollar is the base currency. Let's use the Swiss franc and the German mark (or Deutsche mark) as another example. Starting in the Swiss franc row and going across it to the German mark column (D-mark or Deutsche mark), we find that the cross rate is 0.80352 francs per mark, with the franc as the terms currency and the mark as the base currency. German and Swiss managers keep track of the cross rate because they trade extensively with each other, and any shift in the cross rate could cause a change in the price of goods. For example, assume a German exporter sells a product worth 100 marks to a Swiss importer for 80.35 francs (100 × .8035). If the cross rate changes to 0.900 francs per mark, the base currency (the mark) would be strengthening against the terms currency (the franc). Now the German exporter would have to determine what to do about the export price of the product. If the exporter were to change the price, the Swiss importer would have

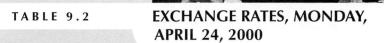

TABLE 9.2	EXCHANGE RATES, MONDAY, APRIL 24, 2000

Because most currencies constantly fluctuate in value, many managers check values daily. This table is from the Wall Street Journal.

	U.S. $ EQUIV.		CURRENCY PER U.S. $	
COUNTRY	MON	FRI	MON	FRI
Argentina (Peso)	1.0002	1.0009	.9998	.9991
Australia (Dollar)	.5952	.5927	1.6800	1.6871
Austria (Schilling)	.06813	.06817	14.678	14.669
Bahrain (Dinar)	2.6525	2.6525	.3770	.3770
Belgium (Franc)	.0232	.0233	43.0292	43.0040
Brazil (Real)	.5579	.5626	1.7925	1.7775
Britain (Pound)	1.5779	1.5780	.6338	.6337
1-month forward	1.5780	1.5781	.6337	.6337
3-months forward	1.5784	1.5785	.6336	.6335
6-months forward	1.5795	1.5796	.6331	.6331
Canada (Dollar)	.6771	.6780	1.4769	1.4750
1-month forward	.6776	.6784	1.4759	1.4740
3-months forward	.6785	.6793	1.4739	1.4720
6-months forward	.6799	.6808	1.4709	1.4689
Chile (Peso)	.001953	.001960	512.15	510.25
China (Renminbi)	.1208	.1208	8.2786	8.2785
Colombia (Peso)	.0005035	.0005016	1986.00	1993.50
Czech. Rep. (Koruna)				
Commercial rate	.02588	.02583	38.636	38.711
Denmark (Krone)	.1263	.1258	7.9183	7.9466
Ecuador (Sucre)				
Floating rate	.00004000	.00004000	24999.50	24999.50
Finland (Markka)	.1577	.1578	6.3421	6.3384
France (Franc)	.1429	.1430	6.9969	6.9928
1-month forward	.1432	.1433	6.9837	6.9796
3-months forward	.1438	.1438	6.9559	6.9519
6-months forward	.1446	.1447	6.9140	6.9108
Germany (Mark)	.4793	.4796	2.0862	2.0850
1-month forward	.4802	.4805	2.0823	2.0811
3-months forward	.4822	.4824	2.0740	2.0728
6-months forward	.4851	.4853	2.0615	2.0605
Greece (Drachma)	.002794	.002797	357.92	357.55
Hong Kong (Dollar)	.1284	.1284	7.7888	7.7885
Hungary (Forint)	.003635	.003634	275.07	275.20
India (Rupee)	.02291	.02292	43.650	43.625
Indonesia (Rupiah)	.0001268	.0001256	7885.00	7965.00
Ireland (Punt)	1.1903	1.1910	.8401	.8396
Israel (Shekel)	.2478	.2475	4.0350	4.0410
Italy (Lira)	.0004842	.0004845	2065.35	2064.14
Japan (Yen)	.009453	.009448	105.79	105.84
1-month forward	.009500	.009496	105.26	105.31
3-months forward	.009602	.009596	104.15	104.21
6-months forward	.009760	.009755	102.46	102.51

(Continued)

TABLE 9.2 (cont.)

COUNTRY	U.S. $ EQUIV.		CURRENCY PER U.S. $	
	MON	FRI	MON	FRI
Jordan (Dinar)	1.4085	1.4075	.7100	.7105
Kuwait (Dinar)	3.2584	3.2595	.3069	.3068
Lebanon (Pound)	.0006634	.0006634	1507.50	1507.50
Malaysia (Ringgit)	.2632	.2632	3.8000	3.8000
Malta (Lira)	2.3288	2.3299	.4294	4.292
Mexico (Peso)				
Floating rate	.1060	.1063	9.4370	9.4050
Netherland (Guilder)	.4254	.4257	2.3506	2.3492
New Zealand (Dollar)	.4956	.4941	2.0178	2.0239
Norway (Krone)	.1153	.1153	8.6693	8.6739
Pakistan (Rupee)	.01927	.01927	51.890	51.900
Peru (new Sol)	.2876	.2882	3.4770	3.4695
Philippines (Peso)	.02421	.02423	41.300	41.275
Poland (Zloty) (d)	.2330	.2330	4.2925	4.2925
Portugal (Escudo)	.004676	.004679	213.85	213.72
Russia (Ruble) (a)	.03501	.03500	28.565	28.575
Saudi Arabia (Riyal)	.2666	.2666	3.7509	3.7506
Singapore (Dollar)	.5875	.5889	1.7020	1.6980
Slovak Rep. (Koruna)	.02258	.02259	44.289	44.263
South Africa (Rand)	.1485	.1484	6.7340	6.7400
South Korea (Won)	.0009019	.0009022	1108.75	1108.45
Spain (Peseta)	.005634	.005638	177.48	177.37
Sweden (Krona)	.1137	.1139	8.7977	8.7821
Switzerland (Franc)	.5966	.5969	1.6763	1.6753
1-month forward	.5982	.5986	1.6717	1.6707
3-months forward	.6015	.6019	1.6624	1.6614
6-months forward	.6065	.6070	1.6487	1.6475
Taiwan (Dollar)	.03276	.03276	30.525	30.525
Thailand (Baht)	.02633	.02636	37.975	37.935
Turkey (Lira)	.00000166	.00000166	600750.00	601130.00
United Arab (Dirham)	.2723	.2723	3.6730	3.6729
Uruguay (New Peso)				
Financial	.08412	.08426	11.888	11.868
Venezuela (Bolivar)	.001486	.001488	673.00	672.25
SDR	1.3362	1.3349	.7484	.7491
Euro	.9375	.9381	1.0667	1.0660

Special Drawing Rights (SDR) are based on exchange rates for the U.S., German, British, French, and Japanese currencies.
Source: International Monetary Fund.
European Currency Unit (ECU) is based on a basket of community currencies.
a-Russian Central Bank rate. Trading band lowered on 8/17/98. b-Government rate. d-Floating rate; trading band suspended on 4/11/00.

Source: Exchange Rates, April 24, 2000. Republished with the permission of Dow Jones & Co., Inc. from *The Wall Street Journal,* Central Edition. Permission conveyed through Copyright Clearance Center, Inc.

TABLE 9.3 **KEY CURRENCY CROSS RATES, LATE NEW YORK TRADING, APRIL 24, 2000**

Many managers also examine currency cross rates, which are the exchange rates between non-U.S. dollar currencies.

	DOLLAR	EURO	POUND	SFRANC	GUILDER	PESO	YEN	LIRA	D-MARK	FFRANC	CDNDLR
Canada	1.4769	1.3846	2.3304	0.8810	.62831	.15650	.01396	.00072	.70794	.21106	....
France	6.9969	6.5596	11.040	4.1740	2.9766	.74143	.06614	.00339	3.3539	....	4.7376
Germany	2.0862	1.9558	3.2918	1.2445	.88752	.22107	.01972	.0010	....	.28816	1.4136
Italy	2065.4	1936.3	3258.9	1232.8	878.65	218.86	19.523	....	990.00	295.18	1398.4
Japan	105.79	99.18	166.93	63.109	45.906	11.210	....	.95122	50.709	15.120	71.630
Mexico	9.4370	8.8472	24.891	5.6297	4.0147	....	.08921	.00457	4.5235	1.3487	6.3897
Netherlands	2.3506	2.2037	3.7090	1.4923	....	.24986	.62222	.90114	1.1267	.33595	1.5916
Switzerland	1.6763	1.5715	2.6450	....	.71314	.17763	.01535	.00081	.80352	.23958	1.1350
U.K.	.63380	.5941	....	.3781 .26961	.06716	.00599	.06031	.30378	.09058	.42911	
Euro	1.06670	....	1.6831	.63632	.45378	.11383	.01008	.00052	.51130	.15245	.72223
U.S.	....	.9375	1.5779	.59635	.42542	.10597	.00945	.00048	.47934	.14292	.67709

Source: Republished with permission of Dow Jones & Company, from *The Wall Street Journal,* April 25, 2000, p. C17. Permission conveyed through Copyright Clearance Center, Inc.

to decide if it still makes sense to source from Germany. If the exporter keeps the price to the importer at 100 marks, the Swiss importer would have to come up with 90 francs (100 × .90) to buy the product. But the exporter could lower the price to 89.28 marks so that the product would still cost the Swiss importer 80.35 francs (89.28 × .90). However, if the exporter keeps the price at 100 marks, the importer would have two options.

1. Increase the price to consumers to reflect the higher cost of the product and keep the profit margin the same as before.
2. Keep the price the same and end up with a smaller profit margin due to the product's higher cost.

If the product were especially price sensitive, neither the exporter nor the importer would want to see the consumer price rise in Switzerland.

THE FORWARD MARKET

As noted earlier, the spot market is for foreign-exchange transactions that occur within two business days but in some transactions a seller extends credit to the buyer for a period that is longer than two days. For example, a Japanese exporter of consumer electronics might sell television sets to a U.S. importer with immediate delivery but payment due in 30 days. The U.S. importer is obligated to pay in yen in 30 days and may enter into a contract with a currency trader to deliver the yen at a *forward* rate—the rate quoted today for future delivery.

In addition to the spot rates for each currency, Table 9.2 shows the forward rates for the British pound, Canadian dollar, French franc, German mark, Japanese yen, and

Swiss franc. These are the most widely traded currencies in the forward market. Many currencies do not have a forward market due to the small size and volume of transactions in that currency.

The forward rate is the rate quoted for transactions that call for delivery after two business days.

A discount exists when the forward rate is less than the spot rate.

A premium exists when the forward rate exceeds the spot rate.

Building on what we said earlier, the difference between the spot and forward rates is either the **forward discount** or the **forward premium**. An easy way to understand the difference between the forward rate and the spot rate is to use currency quotes in American terms. If the forward rate for a foreign currency is less than the spot rate, the foreign currency is selling at a forward discount. If the forward rate is greater than the spot rate, the foreign currency is selling at a forward premium. As an example, let's take a look at the difference between the spot and forward rates for 90-day contracts for British pounds and Japanese yen. Table 9.2 gives the spot and forward quotes in both American and European terms, but we will use the quotes in American terms for this example. The spread, or difference between the spot and forward rate, is given in terms of points. As shown in Table 9.4, the spread in British pounds is only 5 points. The convention in the foreign-exchange market is to go out to the fourth decimal point when quoting most currencies, including the British pound, so 5 points is the difference between the spot and forward rates to the fourth decimal point. Because the forward rate is greater than the spot rate, the pound is at a premium in the 90-day forward market. The spread in Japanese yen is only 149 points; because the forward rate is greater than the spot rate, the yen is at a premium in the 90-day forward market. Notice that the Japanese yen points are quoted to the sixth decimal point. Again, the determination of whether or not the points are quoted on the fourth or the sixth or some other decimal point is whatever the convention is in the market. In Table 9.2, several currencies are quoted at a price other than the fourth decimal point. These forward quotes are valid for both outright forwards and FX swaps as discussed earlier in the chapter.

OPTIONS

An option is the right but not the obligation to trade a foreign currency at a specific exchange rate.

An **option** is the right but not the obligation to buy or sell a foreign currency within a certain time period or on a specific date at a specific exchange rate. An option can be purchased OTC from a commercial or investment bank, or it can be purchased on an exchange, such as the Philadelphia Stock Exchange. For example, assume a company purchases an OTC option to buy Japanese yen at 105 yen per dollar (0.00952 dollars per yen). The writer of the option, the commercial or investment bank in this case, will

TABLE 9.4	DIRECT QUOTES FOR CANADIAN DOLLARS AND JAPANESE YEN	
RATE	BRITISH POUND	JAPANESE YEN
Forward (90-day)	1.5784	.009602
Spot	1.5779	.009453
Points	+.0005	+.000149

charge the company a fee for writing the option. The more likely the option is to bene-fit the company, the higher the fee. The rate of 105 yen is called the strike price for the option. The fee or cost of the option is called the premium. On the date when the option is set to expire, the company can look at the spot rate and compare it with the strike price to see which is the better exchange rate. If the spot rate were 115 yen per dollar (0.00870 dollars per yen), it would not exercise the option because buying yen at the spot rate would cost less than buying them at the option rate. However, if the spot rate at that time were 100 yen per dollar (0.01 dollars per yen), the company would exercise the option because buying at the option rate would cost less than buying at the spot rate. The option provides the company flexibility, because it can walk away from the option if the strike price is not a good price. In the case of a forward contract, the cost is usually cheaper than for an option, but the company cannot walk away from the contract. So, a forward contract is cheaper but less flexible than an option.

FUTURES

A foreign currency **future** resembles a forward contract in that it specifies an exchange rate sometime in advance of the actual exchange of currency. However, a future is traded on an exchange not OTC. Instead of working with a banker, companies work with exchange brokers when purchasing futures contracts. A forward contract is tailored to the amount and time frame that the company needs, whereas a futures contract is for a specific amount and specific maturity date. The futures contract is less valuable to a company than a forward contract. However, it may be useful to speculators and small companies that do not have a good enough relationship with a bank to enter into a forward contract or that need a contract for an amount that is too small for the forward market. The differences between the forward contract, which is traded OTC, and exchange-based contracts, such as futures and options, is summarized in Table 9.5.

A futures contract specifies in advance the exchange rate to be used, but it is not as flexible as a forward contract.

FOREIGN-EXCHANGE CONVERTIBILITY

A key aspect of exchanging one currency for another is its convertibility. Fully convert-ible currencies are those that the government allows both residents and nonresidents to purchase in unlimited amounts. **Hard currencies**, such as the U.S. dollar and Japanese yen, are currencies that are fully convertible. They also are relatively stable in value or tend to be strong in comparison with other currencies. In addition, they are desirable assets to hold. Currencies that are not fully convertible are often called **soft currencies**, or **weak currencies**. They tend to be the currencies of developing countries, also known as exotic currencies, a concept that will be discussed later in the chapter.

Residents and nonresidents of a country can exchange a convertible currency for other currencies.

A hard currency is a currency that is usually fully convert-ible and strong or relatively stable in value in comparison with other currencies.

Most countries today have nonresident, or external, convertibility, meaning that for-eigners can convert their currency into the local currency and can convert back into their currency as well. For example, travelers to Zimbabwe can convert U.S. dollars (USD) into Zimbabwe dollars (ZWD) and convert ZWD back into USD when they leave. However, they have to show receipts of all conversions into ZWD inside the country to make sure that all transactions took place on the official market. Whatever the travelers converted in the official market was the maximum they would have been allowed to convert back into USD when they left. In addition, they have to declare elec-tronics products, such as cameras and stereos, upon entering the country and then prove they had them upon leaving. The government was afraid they would sell the products in

TABLE 9.5	**COMPARISON OF MARKET FEATURES FOR EXCHANGE-BASED AND OTC OPTIONS IN FOREIGN MARKETS**	
	EXCHANGE BASED (OPTIONS AND FUTURES)	**OTC (FORWARD CONTRACTS)**
Contract specifications	Standardized and customized	Customized
Regulation	Securities and Exchange Commission (SEC)	Self-regulated
Type of market	Open outcry, auction market	Dealer market
Counterparty to every transaction	"AAA"-rated Options Clearing Corporation (OCC)	Bank on the contra-side
Transparency/Visible prices	Yes	No
Margin required for short positions**	Yes	No[†]
Orders anonymously represented in the market	Yes	No
Required to mark positions daily	Yes	No[†]
Audit trail	Complete sequential and second-by-second audit trail of each transaction	No
Participants	Public customers, as well as corporate and institutional users	Corporate and institutional users

*Counterparty means the person on the other side of the transaction. For example, if IBM enters into an option on the PHLX, the counterparty to the contract would be a registered broker. If it enters into an OTC option with Citibank, the counterparty would be the bank.

**A margin is a percentage of the contract value that the company, IBM, for example, would have to pay to enter into the contract. At the end of the day, the exchange marks the value of the option to the new market price. If the value has gone up, the margin requirement also rises. That is not required in the OTC market.

[†]Not a requirement, but available.

Source: From Philadelphia Stock Exchange. Reprinted by permission.

the black market and then try to convert the proceeds into dollars and take them out of the country. Some countries limit nonresident convertibility.

To conserve scarce foreign exchange, some governments impose exchange restrictions on companies or individuals who want to exchange money. The devices they use include import licensing, multiple exchange rates, import deposit requirements, and quantity controls.

Governmental licenses fix the exchange rate by requiring all recipients, exporters, and others who receive foreign currency to sell it to its central bank at the official buying rate. Then the central bank rations the foreign currency it acquires by selling it at fixed rates to those needing to make payment abroad for essential goods. An importer may purchase foreign exchange only if that importer has obtained an import license for the goods in question.

Another way governments control foreign-exchange convertibility is to establish more than one exchange rate. This restrictive measure is called a **multiple exchange-rate system.** The government determines which kinds of transactions are to be conducted at which exchange rates. Countries with multiple exchange rates often have a very high exchange rate (takes more units of the local currency to buy dollars) for lux-

> **Licensing occurs when a government requires that all foreign-exchange transactions be regulated and controlled by it.**

> **In a multiple exchange-rate system, a government sets different exchange rates for different types of transactions.**

Ethical Dilemmas and Social Responsibility
THE NEED FOR CHECKS AND BALANCES

There are plenty of opportunities for a trader to make money illegally. One of the most publicized events in the derivatives markets in recent years involved 28-year-old Nicholas Leeson and 233-year-old Barings PLC. Leeson, a trader for Barings PLC, went to Singapore in the early 1990s to help resolve some problems Barings was having. Within a year, he was promoted to chief trader. The problem was that he was responsible for trading securities and booking the settlements, which meant that there were no checks and balances on his trading actions, opening the door to possible fraud. When two different people are assigned to trade securities and book settlements, the person booking the settlements can confirm independently whether or not the trades were accurate and legitimate. In 1994, Leeson bought stock index futures on the assumption that the Tokyo stock market would rise. Unfortunately, the market fell, and Leeson had to come up with cash to cover the margin call on the futures contract. A margin is a deposit made as security for a financial transaction otherwise financed on credit. When the price of an instrument changes and the margin rises, the exchange "calls" the increased margin from the other party, in this case Leeson.[10] However, Leeson soon ran out of cash from Barings, so he had to come up with more cash. One approach he used was to write options contracts and use the premium he collected on the contracts to cover his margin call. Unfortunately, he was using Barings's funds to cover positions he was taking for himself, not for clients, and he also forged documents to cover his transactions. As the Tokyo stock market continued to plunge, Leeson fell farther and farther behind and eventually fled the country, later to be caught and returned to Singapore for trial. Barings estimated that Leeson generated losses in excess of $1 billion, which put Barings into bankruptcy. Eventually, the Dutch bank ING purchased Barings. Leeson's activities in the derivatives market were illegal and a violation of solid internal controls.

Finally, Leeson went to prison in Singapore (where he was treated for colon cancer as well). On July 3, 1999, Leeson was released from prison, and he returned to his native Britain. Did he learn his lesson? He has apologized but has not provided all of the significant details on the actions that bankrupted Barings. However, he is now on the lecture trail, earning $100,000 a lecture.[11]

ury goods and financial flows, such as dividends. Then they have a lower exchange rate for other trade transactions, such as imports of essential commodities and semimanufactured goods.

Another form of foreign-exchange convertibility control is the **advance import deposit.** In this case, the government tightens the issue of import licenses and requires importers to make a deposit with the central bank, often for as long as one year and

> Some governments require an import deposit; that is, a deposit prior to the release of foreign exchange.

interest-free, covering the full price of manufactured goods they would purchase from abroad.

With quantity controls, the government limits the amount of foreign currency that can be used in a specific transaction.

Governments also may limit the amount of exchange through quantity controls, which often apply to tourism. A quantity control limits the amount of currency that a local resident can purchase from the bank for foreign travel. The government sets a policy on how much money a tourist is allowed to take overseas, and the individual is allowed to convert only that amount of money.

In the past, these currency controls have significantly added to the cost of doing business internationally and resulted in the overall reduction of trade. However, the liberalization of trade in recent years has eliminated a lot of these controls to the point that they are found to be a minor impediment to trade.[12]

HOW COMPANIES USE FOREIGN EXCHANGE

Commercial banks buy and sell foreign exchange, collect and pay money in transactions with foreign buyers and sellers, and lend money in foreign currency.

Most foreign-exchange transactions stem from the international departments of commercial banks, which perform three essential financial functions: They buy and sell foreign exchange, they collect and pay money in transactions with foreign buyers and sellers, and they lend money in foreign currency. In performing collections, the bank serves as a vehicle for payments between its domestic and foreign customers. Lending usually takes place in the currency of the bank's headquarters, but the bank might be able to provide loans in a foreign currency if it has a branch in that country.

Commercial banks buy and sell foreign currency for many purposes. For one, travelers going abroad or returning from a foreign country will want to purchase or sell back its foreign currency. Also, residents of one country wanting to invest abroad need to purchase foreign currency from a commercial bank. Further, suppose a Canadian exporter receives payment from a U.S. importer in U.S. dollars and wants to use the dollars to buy raw materials in Norway. The bank in this case simultaneously serves as a collector and acts as a dealer in a foreign-exchange transaction.

Companies need foreign exchange to settle imports and exports denominated in a foreign currency.

There are a number of reasons why companies use the foreign-exchange market. The most obvious is for import and export transactions. For example, a U.S. company importing products from an overseas supplier might have to convert U.S. dollars into a foreign currency to pay that supplier. In addition, company personnel traveling abroad need to deal in foreign exchange to pay for their local expenses.

Companies also use the foreign-exchange market for financial transactions, such as those in FDI. Say a U.S. company decided to establish a manufacturing plant in Mexico. It would have to convert dollars into pesos to make the investment. After the Mexican subsidiary generated a profit, it would have to convert pesos to dollars to send a dividend back to the U.S. parent.

Arbitrage is the buying and selling of foreign currencies at a profit due to price discrepancies.

Interest arbitrage involves investing in interest-bearing instruments in foreign exchange in an effort to earn a profit due to interest-rate differentials.

Sometimes companies—but mostly traders and investors—deal in foreign exchange solely for profit. One type of profit-seeking activity is **arbitrage**, which is the purchase of foreign currency on one market for immediate resale on another market (in a different country) to profit from a price discrepancy. For example, a trader might sell U.S. dollars for Swiss francs in the United States, then Swiss francs for German marks in Switzerland, and then the German marks for U.S. dollars back in the United States, the goal being to end up with more dollars. Assume the trader converts 100 dollars into 150 Swiss francs when the exchange rate is 1.5 francs per dollar. The

Speculators take positions in foreign-exchange markets with the major objective of earning a profit.

trader then converts the 150 francs into 225 German marks at an exchange rate of 1.5 marks per franc and finally converts the marks into 125 dollars at an exchange rate of 1.8 marks per dollar. In this case, arbitrage yields $125 from the initial sale of $100.

Interest arbitrage is the investing in debt instruments, such as bonds, in different countries. For example, a trader might invest $1,000 in the United States for 90 days or convert $1,000 into British pounds, invest the money in the United Kingdom for 90 days, and then convert the pounds back into dollars. The investor would try to pick the alternative that would be the highest yielding at the end of 90 days.

Investors can also use foreign-exchange transactions to speculate for profit or to protect against risk. **Speculation** is the buying or selling of a commodity, in this case foreign currency, that has both an element of risk and the chance of great profit. For example, an investor could buy German marks in anticipation of the mark's strengthening against other currencies. If it strengthens, the investor earns a profit; if it weakens, the investor incurs a loss. Speculators are important in the foreign-exchange market because they spot trends and try to take advantage of them. They can create demand for a currency by purchasing it in the market, or they can create a supply of the currency by selling it in the market.

> Speculators take a position on a currency and hope that the currency moves in such a way as to make them money.

As protection against risk, foreign-exchange transactions can hedge against a potential loss due to an exchange-rate change. For example, a U.S. parent company expecting a dividend in British pounds in 90 days could enter into a forward contract to hedge the dividend flow. It could go to the bank and agree to deliver pounds for dollars in 90 days at the forward rate. That way it would know exactly how much cash it is going to receive no matter what happens to the spot rate in 90 days. Foreign-exchange instruments such as outright forwards, FX swaps, options, and futures are used to hedge risks.

THE FOREIGN-EXCHANGE TRADING PROCESS

When a company sells goods or services to a foreign customer and receives foreign currency, it needs to convert the foreign currency into the domestic currency. When importing, the company needs to convert domestic to foreign currency to pay the foreign supplier. This conversion takes place between the company and its bank, and most of these transactions take place in the OTC market. Originally, the commercial banks are the ones that provided foreign-exchange services for their customers. Eventually, some of these commercial banks in New York and other U.S. money centers, like Chicago and San Francisco, began to look at foreign-exchange trading as a major business activity instead of just a service. They became intermediaries for smaller banks by establishing correspondent relationships with them. They also became major dealers in foreign exchange. On the left side of Figure 9.4 is a U.S. company that needs to sell marks for dollars. This could arise from a customer paying in marks or a German subsidiary sending a dividend to the U.S. company in marks. On the right side of the figure is a U.S. company that needs to buy marks with dollars. This could arise from having to pay marks to a German supplier. However, there are other markets and institutions where foreign exchange is traded. Most of the foreign-exchange activity takes place in the traditional instruments of spot, outright forward, and FX swaps, and commercial banks and investment banks or other financial institutions basically trade these instruments. However, companies could also deal with an exchange, such as the

> Companies work through their local banks to settle foreign-exchange balances, but they also use investment banks and exchanges.

FIGURE 9.4　Structure of Foreign-Exchange Markets

A company interested in exchanging currency can work with a commercial or investment bank in the OTC market or a broker on a securities exchange. Banks deal with each other in the inter-bank market, primarily through foreign-exchange brokers.

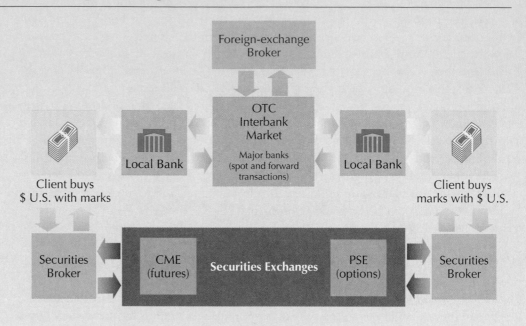

Philadelphia Stock Exchange to buy or sell an option contract, and the Chicago Mercantile Exchange to deal in foreign-currency futures.

The BIS estimates that there are about 2,000 dealer institutions worldwide that make up the foreign-exchange market. Of these, about 100 to 200 are market-making banks, which means that they are willing to quote bid and offer rates to anyone in the currency or currencies in which they deal. Of this group, only a select few are major players, and they will be identified and discussed below in the section on commercial and investment banks.

An estimated 63 percent of the foreign-exchange trades took place among reporting dealers in 1998.

Dealers can trade foreign exchange

- **Directly with other dealers (73 percent of the market in the U.K., the largest market in the world)**
- **Through voice brokers (11 percent in U.K.)**
- **Through electronic brokerage systems (16 percent in U.K.)**

As noted earlier, most of the foreign-exchange trades take place in the OTC market where most of the dealers operate. These dealers operate more in the interbank market with dealers of other banks than they do with corporate clients. The BIS estimated in 1998 that 63 percent of the foreign-exchange trades took place among reporting dealers. Fifty-nine percent of the business between dealers takes place across national borders, whereas 68 percent of the dealers' business with nonfinancial customers takes place in the domestic market.[13]

When a company needs foreign exchange, it typically goes to its commercial bank for help. If that bank is a large market-maker, the company can get its foreign exchange fairly easily. However, if the company is located in a small market using a local bank, where does the bank get its foreign exchange? Figure 9.5 illustrates how foreign-exchange dealers at the banks trade foreign exchange. A bank, dealing either on its own account or for a client, can trade foreign exchange with another bank directly or through a broker. In the broker market, it can use a voice broker or an electronic brokerage system. In both the U.S. and U.K. markets, direct dealing is by far the most

FIGURE 9.5   Foreign-Exchange Transactions

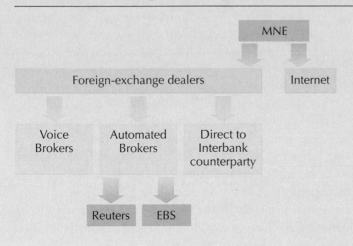

Companies get access to foreign exchange through dealers or the Internet. Dealers trade directly to an interbank counterparty or through voice brokers or automated brokers.

widely used method of trading currency (76 percent and 73 percent). As recently as 1980, only 50 percent of the foreign-exchange trading was conducted directly between bank dealers, with the remaining 50 percent by voice brokers. In 1998, voice brokers generated 10.3 percent of the foreign-exchange trades in the U.S. market and 11 percent in the U.K. market. Electronic brokerage systems (EBS) account for 13.7 percent of the U.S. market and 16 percent of the U.K. market, and this move from voice to electronic brokers steadily increased in the decade of the 1990s.[14]

A foreign-exchange broker is an intermediary who matches the best bid and offer quotes of interbank traders. There are a number of brokerage houses around the world, such as the Martin Brokers Group in London, owned by Trio Holdings, Exco, Tullett & Tokyo Forex International, and Intercapital Group. These brokers have traditionally dealt in the market by voice, linking up interbank traders. According to the BIS survey, there were 9 brokers in the United States in 1998, including the 2 major electronic brokerage systems, down from 17 in 1995.[15]

The use of brokers depends on a number of factors, such as the location of the market and the size and nature of the foreign-exchange transactions. Voice brokers are especially important for large foreign-exchange transactions. Brokers have filled an important role because of their ability to establish networks with a wide variety of banks, allowing banks to buy or sell currency from other banks faster than if they had to try to contact all the different potential banks themselves. However, the voice broker market has been rapidly giving way to electronic brokerage systems.

Historically, most trades took place by telephone. A dealer in one bank would call a dealer in another bank and execute a trade. If it did not have access to enough banks to get the currency it needed, it could operate through a broker. The move from voice to electronic brokerage systems was initiated by Reuters and then followed by other systems. The Reuters' system, known as Reuters' Dealing 2000-2, is the largest and most significant electronic brokerage system in the world. However, it is being challenged by

EBS (Electronic Brokering System), a partnership of 13 major market-making banks, including Citibank, set up to counter Reuters' domination of the foreign-exchange trading market. EBS is used by over 800 banks with 2,500 workstations that transact in excess of $90 billion in foreign exchange daily.[16] In addition, other banks are attempting to establish proprietary electronic brokerage networks to compete with Reuters and EBS. However, those two are the largest and most significant networks in the world.

A bank gets access to the automated system by purchasing the service from Reuters or EBS—or both—by paying a monthly fee and receiving a link through telephone lines to the bank's computers. Then the bank can use the automated system to trade currency. The automated system is efficient, because it lists bid and sell quotes, allowing the bank to trade immediately. For large transactions, many dealers prefer the familiarity of a trusted voice broker to find a buyer or seller. Electronic dealers are efficient but too impersonal for the large transactions. Most electronic trades average in the $1 million to $2 million range, although occasionally a trade of $10 million to $20 million will show up. Electronic brokerage systems deal primarily in the spot market, dominated mostly by U.S. dollar/Deutsche mark and U.S. dollar/yen trades. Many voice brokers are leaving the spot market and focusing more on derivatives, such as forwards and options.[17]

Internet trades of currency are becoming increasingly popular and are competing with dealers.

A current trend in currency trading is the establishment of Internet currency trading. Although it is relatively new, there is a possibility that corporations and institutions will shift more of their trade from dealers to the Internet, possibly getting better foreign-exchange quotes than they could get from the dealers. Several banks, including Chase Manhattan, have already set up Internet trading for relatively simple transactions, and Chase estimated that about 5 percent of its trades in 1999 were conducted via the Internet. As banks solve security issues associated with Internet trading, activity should pick up.[18]

COMMERCIAL AND INVESTMENT BANKS

It used to be that only the big money center banks could deal directly in foreign exchange. Regional banks had to rely on the money center banks to execute trades on behalf of their clients. The emergence of electronic trading has changed that, however. Now even the regional banks can hook up to Reuters and EBS and deal directly in the interbank market or through brokers. In spite of this, the greatest volume of foreign-exchange activity takes place with the big banks.

The top banks in the interbank market in foreign exchange are so ranked because of their ability to
- **Trade in specific market locations**
- **Engage in major currencies and cross-trades**
- **Deal in specific currencies**
- **Handle derivatives (forwards, options, futures, swaps)**
- **Conduct key market research**

There is more to servicing customers in the foreign-exchange market than size alone. Each year, *Euromoney* magazine surveys banks and corporations to identify their customers' favorite banks and the leading traders in the interbank market. The criteria for selecting the top foreign-exchange traders include

- Ranking of banks by corporations and other banks in specific locations, such as London, Zurich, and New York
- Capability to handle major currencies, such as the U.S. dollar and German mark
- Capability to handle major cross-trades; for example, those between the Deutsche mark and pound or the Deutsche mark and yen
- Capability to handle specific currencies
- Capability to handle derivatives (forwards, swaps, and options)
- Capability to engage in research

Other factors often mentioned are price, quote speed, credit rating, liquidity, back office/settlement, strategic advice, trade recommendations, out of hours service/night desk, systems technology, innovation, and risk appraisal.[19]

For this reason, large companies may use several banks to deal in foreign exchange by selecting those that specialize in specific geographic areas, instruments, or currencies. For example, AT&T uses Citibank for its broad geographic spread and wide coverage of different currencies, but it also uses Deutsche Bank for German marks, Swiss Bank Corp for Swiss francs, NatWest Bank for British pounds, and Goldman Sachs for derivatives.

Table 9.6 identifies the top banks in the world in terms of foreign exchange trading. They are the key players in the OTC market and include both commercial banks (such as Citibank and Chase Manhattan Bank) and investment banks (such as Warburg Dillon Read—the London-based investment banking division of Union Bank of Switzerland and Swiss Bank Corporation—and Goldman Sachs). Whether one is looking at overall market share of foreign-exchange trading, the ranking of best banks in specific locations, best banks in trading of specific currency pairs, or best dealers, these top 10 banks are usually at or near the top in every category.

One area that allows banks to develop niches is that of **exotic currencies**. An exotic is a currency from a developing country, such as the Russian ruble, the Malaysian ringgit, and the Mexican peso. Exotics are difficult for corporations to work with because the volume of activity in those currencies is pretty small, so the costs of dealing with those currencies are relatively high. It is hard to get a good price, and the bid/ask spread is usually higher than would be the case for a widely traded currency like the Japanese yen. In addition, local regulations governing the use of exotic currencies change daily,

An exotic currency is a currency of a developing country and is often unstable, weak, and unpredictable.

TABLE 9.6

TOP OTC COMMERCIAL AND INVESTMENT BANKS IN FOREIGN-EXCHANGE TRADES

BANK	ESTIMATED MARKET SHARE %	BEST IN LONDON	BEST IN NEW YORK	BEST IN TRADING EURO/DOLLAR	BEST IN TRADING $/YEN
1. Citibank/Salomon Smith Barney	7.75	1	1	2	1
2. Deutsche Bank	7.12	3	2	1	3
3. Chase Manhattan Bank	7.09	2	3	3	2
4. Warburg Dillon Read	6.44	6=	5=	7	6
5. Goldman Sachs	4.86		10		
6. Bank of America	4.39	6=	4	6	4
7. JP Morgan	4.00	10=			
8. HSBC	3.75	4	7	5	5
9. ABN Amro	3.37			4	
10. Merrill Lynch	3.27		5=	9	8

Source: "Life After Execution," *Euromoney*, May 1999, pp. 92, 94.

= means bank tied for that place (example 6= means bank tied for 6th place)

realignments of exchange rates are common, and the volume of activity in the currencies can be subject to wide swings.[20] Banks such as Citibank help their clients with exotics by cutting through the regulations on buying and selling, dealing with difficult exchange-rate systems, working with exchange controls on investments, and getting information on potential changes in rates. The banks also help their clients manage positions and move funds. We discuss the specific financial instruments they use, such as bills of exchange and letters of credit, in Chapter 17.

In addition to the OTC market, there are a number of exchanges where foreign-exchange instruments, mostly options and futures, are traded. Two of the best-known exchanges are the Chicago Mercantile Exchange and the Philadelphia Stock Exchange.

THE CHICAGO MERCANTILE EXCHANGE

The Chicago Mercantile Exchange (CME) is a not-for-profit corporation owned by its 2,725 members who have bought seats on the Exchange. As noted on its home page (http://www.cme.com), the CME is

> an international marketplace enabling institutions and businesses to manage their financial risks and allocate their assets. On its trading floors, buyers and sellers meet to trade futures contracts and options on futures through the process of open outcry. In selected contracts, trading continues virtually around the clock on the GLOBEX®2 electronic trading system. The Merc's diverse product line consists of futures and options on futures within four general categories: agricultural commodities, foreign currencies, interest rates and stock indexes.

The International Monetary Market (IMM) deals primarily in futures contracts for the British pound, the Canadian dollar, the German mark, the Swiss franc, the Japanese yen, and the Australian dollar.

The CME opened the International Monetary Market (IMM) in 1972 to deal primarily in futures contracts for the British pound, the Canadian dollar, the German mark, the Swiss franc, the Japanese yen, and the Australian dollar. As of the end of 1999, the IMM offered futures and futures options contracts (contracts that are options on futures contracts rather than options on foreign exchange per se) in the Deutsche mark, the Japanese yen, the Mexican peso, the Australian dollar, the British pound, the Canadian dollar, the French franc, the Swiss franc, the Brazilian real, the South African rand, the New Zealand dollar, and the Russian ruble. The IMM's contracts are for specific amounts and have a specific maturity date. For example, the IMM sets a futures contract in Japanese yen at 12.5 million yen. If a manager wanted to buy futures for 100 million yen, she would have to buy eight yen contracts from a broker. The contract sizes for other currencies are found on the CME home page or in the newspaper.

Even though these futures contracts have fixed maturity dates, they have a ready market. Futures contracts at the CME tend to be for small amounts compared to transactions in the interbank market. Further, the Commodity Futures Trading Commission, a U.S. government agency, limits how much the futures prices may vary each day, whereas there are no such restrictions in the banking market.

The CME has been losing business to both the Philadelphia Stock Exchange and the over-the-counter market because those markets have more creative, tailored financial offerings. As a result, the CME is struggling to find its niche in the currency markets. Its major users are speculators and currency investors. For example, wealthy individuals might invest their money in a foreign currency fund that invests in currencies, and those fund managers use the futures market as a way to hedge their investments and earn a return for their clients. In addition, smaller companies that lack the lines of credit needed to trade in the interbank market use the CME.[21]

THE PHILADELPHIA STOCK EXCHANGE

The Philadelphia Stock Exchange (PHLX) is the only exchange in the United States that trades foreign-currency options. The CME trades options on futures contracts rather than on spot contracts. Each option on the PHLX is for a specific amount of currency. For example, each British pound option is for 31,250 pounds. The PHLX offers standardized options and customized options. The PHLX lists eight-dollar-based and two cross-rate standardized currency option contracts, which settle in the actual physical currency. The dollar-based contracts are in Australian dollars, British pounds, Canadian dollars, Deutsche marks, euros, French francs, Japanese yen, and Swiss francs. In addition, cross-rate options are offered in Deutsche marks/yen and British pounds/Deutsche marks. Standardized currency option contracts are very specific about size and maturity dates.

Customized options are also written to allow a little more flexibility than is the case with the standardized options. The flexibility, however, comes with a higher cost. Customized

> The Philadelphia Stock Exchange (PHLX) is the only exchange in the United States that trades foreign-currency options.

Looking to the Future
EXCHANGE MARKETS IN THE NEW MILLENNIUM

Significant strides have been made and will continue to be made in the development of foreign-exchange markets. The speed at which transactions are processed and information is transmitted globally will certainly lead to greater efficiencies and more opportunities for foreign-exchange trading. The impact on companies is that costs of trading foreign exchange should come down, and companies should have faster access to more currencies.

In addition, exchange restrictions that hamper the free flow of goods and services should diminish as governments gain greater control over their economies and as they liberalize currency markets. Capital controls still impact foreign investment, but they will continue to become less of a factor for trade in goods and services.

The introduction of the euro should allow cross-border transactions in Europe to progress more smoothly. In 1999, foreign-exchange transactions had already begun to level off. As the euro solidifies its position in Europe, it will reduce exchange-rate volatility and should result in the euro taking some of the pressure off of the dollar to be the only major vehicle currency in the world.

Finally, technological developments may not cause the foreign-exchange broker to disappear entirely, but they will certainly cause foreign-exchange trades to be executed more quickly and cheaply. The growth of Internet trades in currency will take away some of the market share of dealers and allow more entrants into the foreign-exchange market.

options are available in the same currencies as the standardized options, plus options in the Mexican peso, the Italian lira, and the Spanish peseta.

The PHLX has been growing faster than the CME. Much of the growth has come from MNEs. Although options cost more than futures, big companies prefer them to futures (the CME instrument) because of their greater flexibility and convenience. We will provide some examples in Chapter 20 of how companies use options to hedge against foreign-exchange risks. However, the exchange-traded instruments are still very small compared with the OTC trades.

WEB CONNECTION

Check out our home page www.prenhall.com/daniels for links to key resources for you in your study of international business.

SUMMARY

- A major distinction between domestic and international transactions for goods and services is that one currency is used for domestic transactions but more than one currency is used for international transactions.

- Foreign exchange is money denominated in the currency of another nation or group of nations. The exchange rate is the price of a currency.

- The foreign-exchange market is divided into the "over-the-counter" market (OTC) and the exchange-traded market.

- The traditional foreign-exchange market is comprised of the spot, forward, and FX swap markets.

- Spot transactions involve the exchange of currency the second day after the date on which the two traders agree to the transaction.

- Outright forward transactions involve the exchange of currency three or more days after the date on which the traders agree to the transaction. An FX swap is a simultaneous spot and forward transaction.

- Other key foreign-exchange instruments are currency swaps, options, and futures.

- Currency swaps and options are traded OTC, but exchanges (like the Chicago Mercantile Exchange and the Philadelphia Stock Exchange) trade futures and options.

- Approximately $1.5 trillion in foreign exchange is traded every day. The dollar is the most widely traded currency in the world (on one side of 87 percent of all transactions), and London is the main foreign-exchange market in the world.

- Foreign-exchange traders quote bid (buy) and offer (sell) rates on foreign exchange. If the quote is in American terms, the trader quotes the foreign currency as the number of dollars and cents per unit of the foreign currency. If the quote is in European terms, the trader quotes the dollar in terms of the number of units of the foreign currency. The numerator is called the "terms currency," and the denominator is called the "base currency."

- A cross rate is the exchange rate between two nondollar currencies.

- A convertible currency is one companies can freely trade for other currencies. Some countries' currencies are partially convertible in that residents are not allowed to convert them into other currencies but nonresidents are.

- If the foreign currency in a forward contract is expected to strengthen in the future (the dollar equivalent of the foreign currency is higher in the forward market than in the spot market), the currency is selling at a premium. If the opposite is true, it is selling at a discount.

- An option is the right but not the obligation to trade foreign currency in the future. Options can be traded OTC or on an exchange.

- A future is an exchange-traded instrument that guarantees a future price for trading foreign exchange, but the contracts are for a specific amount and specific maturity date.

- Companies use foreign-exchange to settle imports and exports of goods and services, for foreign investments, and to earn money through arbitrage or speculation.

- Companies work with foreign exchange dealers to trade currency. Dealers also work with each other. Dealers can trade currency through voice brokers, electronic brokerage services, or directly with other bank dealers. Internet trades of foreign exchange are becoming more significant.

- The major institutions that trade foreign exchange are the large commercial and investment banks and securities exchanges. Commercial and investment banks deal in a variety of different currencies all over the world. The Chicago Mercantile Exchange specializes in futures contracts, and the Philadelphia Stock Exchange specializes in options.

C A S E

THE JAPANESE YEN[22]

At the ushering in of the new millennium, Nissan Motor Company of Japan was in deep trouble. Nissan had suffered losses in seven of the previous eight years, and it was saddled with 1999 losses of $264 million and debt of $13 billion. It was in such bad shape that it accepted a $5 billion injection of cash from Renault, the French automaker, in May 1999 in exchange for a 36.8 percent stake by Renault in Nissan. It also accepted as its new chief operating officer, Carlos Ghosn, the Brazilian-born executive of Renault who has had significant experience internationally and is one of the key people who turned around Renault.

Top management at Nissan was trying to forecast the yen/U.S. dollar exchange rate to plan its pricing and production strategies for the U.S. market. It wondered, should Nissan lower prices and pick up market share, hold prices and earn more profits, keep producing autos and trucks in the United States, or move its production to Mexico, Southeast Asia, or back to Japan?

Appreciating Nissan's dilemma requires a historical perspective on the yen and its value against the dollar (see Map 9.3 and Figure 9.6). In the post–World War II years, the yen was extremely weak against the dollar, which helped give rise to the export strength of Japan. The government controlled access to foreign exchange, favoring companies and industries that it wanted to succeed. The foreign-exchange market was anything but a free and open market. Licenses were required to gain access to foreign exchange. However, that began to change as the Japanese economy recovered from the war and Japanese export-based companies became global leaders in their industries. In the early 1980s, the dollar was strong against the yen and nearly every other currency in the world. In the fall of 1985, however, the dollar began to fall and the yen began to rise. From a high of ¥251.10 to the dollar at the end of 1984 to ¥200.50 to the dollar by the end of 1985, and the yen kept rising against the dollar. By the fall of 1986, the yen was trading at ¥150 per dollar. The Japanese coined this strengthening of the yen *endaka*, which literally translates "high yen." *Endaka* resulted in serious problems for Japanese exporters and potential pain for the entire Japanese economy, which was so dependent on international trade. However, one upside to *endaka* was that imports were all cheaper, and Japan relied heavily on imports of virtually all commodities. Thus its input costs fell, even as it found its export prices rising.

The strong yen was due primarily to a strong Japanese economy, large trade surpluses with the rest of the world, especially the United States, and the largest foreign-exchange reserves in the world. In addition, Japan had low unemployment, low interest rates, and low inflation. But cracks began to show in the Japanese economy. In late 1989, the stock market began to decline and inflationary pressures grew. In early 1990, there was open debate between the Ministry of Finance and the Bank of Tokyo over what the interest-rate policy should be. That debate drove the stock market down even further and shook investors' confidence in the Japanese government's ability to manage the economy and, therefore, the exchange rate.

Japan had once enjoyed the world's largest current-account surplus (that is, an excess of exports over imports), but since 1987 that surplus fell by one-third because of a

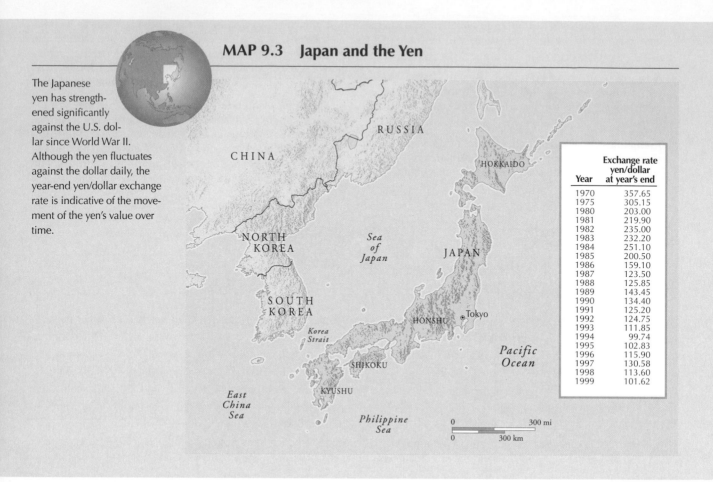

MAP 9.3   Japan and the Yen

The Japanese yen has strengthened significantly against the U.S. dollar since World War II. Although the yen fluctuates against the dollar daily, the year-end yen/dollar exchange rate is indicative of the movement of the yen's value over time.

Year	Exchange rate yen/dollar at year's end
1970	357.65
1975	305.15
1980	203.00
1981	219.90
1982	235.00
1983	232.20
1984	251.10
1985	200.50
1986	159.10
1987	123.50
1988	125.85
1989	143.45
1990	134.40
1991	125.20
1992	124.75
1993	111.85
1994	99.74
1995	102.83
1996	115.90
1997	130.58
1998	113.60
1999	101.62

huge outflow of Japanese capital. Prices on Japanese assets, especially land and buildings, had risen dramatically, and Japanese investors found they could get a better yield on their money outside Japan.

As inflation fears began to rise in Japan, the governor of the Bank of Japan raised interest rates in December 1989. The furor that ensued caused him to delay any further increases, however. Given that interest rates in the United States also were high at the time as a result of inflationary concerns, the demand for yen fell and the demand for dollars rose, increasing the price of the dollar in terms of yen. The Japanese government couldn't find a quick fix. In the first three months of 1990, the Bank of Japan used 17 percent of its foreign-exchange reserves to sell dollars for yen, hoping to prop up the yen. The United States pitched in by selling dollars for yen, but it didn't want to push the dollar down too much lest it undermine its own battle against inflation. Both Japan and the United States tried to convince the govern-

ments of Germany, the United Kingdom, and other countries to support the effort, but the U.S. government wanted those countries to sell their own currencies not U.S. dollars. Currency traders and speculators, however, believed that interest-rate policies, not intervention, were the key.

By late summer 1990, many analysts were predicting that the yen exchange rate would be ¥160 to the dollar by the end of the year. However, the U.S. economy began to weaken, and, as the U.S. government tried to avoid a recession, interest rates came down. The Persian Gulf War momentarily strengthened the dollar against the yen, but economic fundamentals prevailed. As Japanese interest rates rose and U.S. interest rates fell, the demand for the dollar fell, and so did the price. By the end of 1990, the yen exchange rate was hovering at ¥130 per dollar, after experiencing a high of 124.33 in the previous 12 months and a low of 159.79.

Relative calm reigned in 1991 and 1992 in terms of the yen/dollar exchange rate. In 1991, the rate shifted gradually

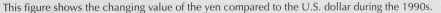

FIGURE 9.6 Japanese Yen per Dollar, Monthly Exchange Rate

This figure shows the changing value of the yen compared to the U.S. dollar during the 1990s.

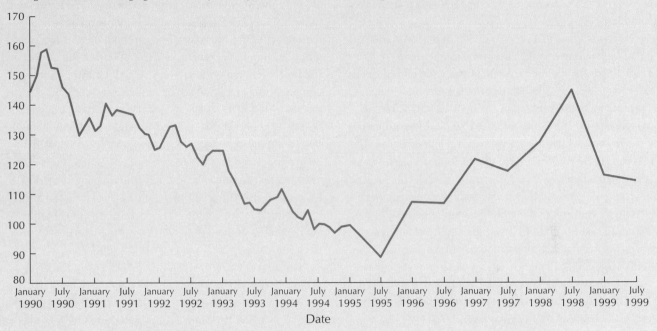

Source: Bloomberg Financial Markets and Commodities News: Online: Currency.

from ¥141 per dollar at the end of the first quarter to ¥125.2 per dollar by the end of the fourth quarter. As noted in Figure 9.6, the dollar continued its gradual descent against the yen.

In early 1993, the yen/dollar relationship began to change. The major catalyst was the G-7 meeting in February 1993, with an agenda expected to include a forced appreciation of the yen. On February 24, however, U.S. Treasury Secretary Lloyd Bentsen stated there would be no announcement on a policy at the end of the meeting, meaning that the governments couldn't agree on a new policy, and this sparked a massive sell-off of the dollar against the yen. It was felt U.S. President Clinton was using a strong yen as one way to eliminate the huge trade deficit between the United States and Japan.

As the yen continued to rise, Nissan found itself in a difficult position. The U.S. price of a Nissan auto sometimes rose three or four times a year during 1993–1995. However, many companies could not raise prices as fast as the yen was rising, so they were still losing profitability. At one point, U.S. autos enjoyed a $2,500 cost advantage over Nissan and

other Japanese autos, and the Japanese began to lose market share. The relatively cheap dollar also meant that U.S. automakers gained some advantage in third-country markets, such as Germany and France. As a result, Nissan had to commit to build more autos in the United States, rely more on U.S.-manufactured auto parts, and accept much lower profit margins. Further, Nissan had to improve its design and manufacturing operations in order to cut costs to offset some of the profit margin lost to the rising yen. The Automotive Business Practices Institute of Japan estimates that the Japanese cut 15 percent of their production costs between 1994 and 1996, compared with only 10 percent by the U.S. Big Three.

The second *endaka* hit in on April 18, 1995, when the yen hit ¥80.63. The impact on Japanese companies like Nissan was immense. Toyota announced that a one-point increase in the yen eliminated about $111 million in dollar-denominated profits. This occurred because many Japanese companies had operations in the United States that were generating profits in dollars, and these dollar profits were worth less yen as the dollar lost value against the surging yen. In addition, Japanese exporters were having trouble exporting products as the yen rose. Consumers were shifting demand to companies manufacturing products in a weaker currency environment. Companies scrambled to figure out ways to cut costs in order to be competitive in a strong yen environment.

However, the situation changed in mid-1995, and the dollar began to rise against the yen. From a low of ¥84.33 in 1995, the dollar climbed to over ¥110 by the end of 1996. With interest rates so low in Japan, investors were pulling their money out of yen and investing it in dollars. The Bank of Japan was keeping interest rates low in order to stimulate the economy, which had become mired in a recession. The relatively wide spread in rates was making Japanese assets very unattractive.

However, the falling yen was certainly beneficial to Nissan. Its earnings in the United States were being translated into higher yen, and it had the choice of keeping prices the same and earning more profits or lowering prices to pick up market share. In general, Japanese automakers raised their prices by an average of only $91 a vehicle in the first half of 1996, while U.S. automakers raised their car and family truck prices by an average of $226. However, many Japanese companies still feel that an exchange rate of ¥105 is a strong rate. As the dollar rate moves above ¥110, however, the psychology begins to change. Not only is Nissan having trouble trying to decide what to do, but so are U.S. auto companies. Even during the time when they had a solid foreign-exchange advantage over the Japanese, U.S. automakers were fighting hard to drive down costs to be more competitive. They had begun to commit resources to penetrate Japanese markets, but the strong dollar made such strategies difficult.

The yen/dollar exchange rate continued to fluctuate over the next few years. The Japanese economy collapsed in the mid-1990s under the weight of bad debts held by banks. Nissan's $13 billion in debt is an example of the same problem facing many Japanese companies. Banks held so much bad debt that they couldn't make new loans to companies that were doing well. Japanese banks began to consolidate through mergers as weak banks were forced to merge or go out of business. The Asian financial crisis of 1997–1998 was devastating to the Japanese economy, and the weak Japanese economy was not able to help Asia get out of its poor financial shape. The U.S. economy had to rescue Japan and the rest of Asia. As a result, the dollar rose against the yen in 1997 through early 1999. But then a new round of *endaka*

began in 1999. By the end of 1999, the yen was so strong against the dollar that Japanese companies were hurting, and the U.S. and Japanese governments were trying to figure out a way to support the dollar and strengthen the yen.

This could not have occurred at a worse time for Nissan. Many Japanese companies had already been announcing the impact of the strong yen on corporate profits. Toyota's group profit fell 16 percent for the first half of the 2000 fiscal year (ending on September 30, 1998; most Japanese companies have a fiscal year that ends on March 31) from the same period the previous year because of a strong yen. Mazda announced that its first six months were pretty good, despite the stronger yen, because of strong cost cutting. Sony announced that its group profit fell 25 percent from a year earlier because the strong yen hammered it. Honda announced that it was shrinking production in Japan and increasing it in the United States because of shifts in market demand and the difficulty of exporting in a strong yen environment.

Ghosn was trying to turn around Nissan, but the strong yen environment would make it increasingly difficult. He already announced in late 1999 that he was going to shut down 5 plants in Japan, cut 21,000 jobs, and cut back the number of suppliers that Nissan uses by 50 percent, and eliminate the time-honored Japanese practice of investing in suppliers. Nissan had its back to the wall, and Ghosn knew that he had to make Nissan successful or its failure might doom Renault as well. How will he succeed if the yen continues to remain strong against the dollar?

QUESTIONS

1. What are some of the major factors that have influenced the yen/dollar exchange rate in the past decade? Have different factors become more important at different times? If so, which ones?

2. What are the major options available to Nissan in a strong yen environment?

3. Assume that Nissan spends an average of ¥1.875 million to manufacture a car in Japan, plus $2,600 to market and distribute the car in the United States.
   a. Assuming the exchange rate at the end of each year since 1995, what would be the impact of the exchange rate on the dollar cost of the auto?
   b. If Nissan had wanted to sell the car at the end of 1999 for the same as it could have at the end of 1997, by how much would it have had to cut costs, given the exchange rates of the two years?

CHAPTER NOTES

1 Sam Y. Cross, *All About the Foreign Exchange Market in the United States* (New York: Federal Reserve Bank of New York, 1998), p. 9.

2 Ibid.

3 Ibid., p. 31.

4 Bank for International Settlements, *Central Bank Survey of Foreign Exchange and Derivatives Market Activity 1998* (Basel, Switzerland: BIS, May 1999), p. 2.

5 Cross, *All About the Foreign Exchange Market,* p. 19.

6 Bank for International Settlements, *Central Bank Survey*, p. 10.

7 Ibid., p. 12.

8 Cross, *All About the Foreign Exchange Market,* p. 33.

9 See "Currencies" page in "Market Prices" page of the *Financial Times*, http://www.ft.com/; see "Currencies" page in "Markets & Investing" page in CNN *Financial News*, http://www.cnnfn.com/markets/currencies/; see Web links for Chapter 9 on the home page for the textbook for more links.

10 More specifically, Leeson did not actually buy the contracts outright but paid a certain percentage of the value of the contract, known as the "margin." When the stock market fell, the index futures contract became riskier, and the broker who sold the contract required Leeson to increase the amount of the margin.

11 "The Collapse of Barings: A Fallen Star," *The Economist*, March 4, 1995, pp. 19–21; Glen Whitney, "ING Puts Itself on the Map by Acquiring Barings," *Wall Street Journal*, March 8, 1995, p. B4; John S. Bowdidge and Kurt E. Chaloupecky, "Nicholas Leeson and Barings Bank Have Vividly Taught Some Internal Control Issues," *American Business Review*, January 1997, pp. 71–77; "Trade in Barings Scandal Is Released from Prison," *Wall Street Journal*, July 6, 1999, p. A12; Ben Dolven, "Bearing Up," *Far Eastern Economic Review*, July 15, 1999, p. 47.

12 Natalia T. Tamirisa, "Exchange and Capital Controls as Barriers to Trade," *IMF Staff Papers*, Vol. 46, No. 1, March 1999, p. 69.

13 Bank for International Settlements, *Central Bank Survey*, p. 10.

14 Ibid., p. 15.

15 Ibid., p. 28.

16 EBS, "An Introduction," http://www.ebsp.com January 2000.

17 Stephanie Cook, "Will Brokers Go Broke?" *Euromoney*, May 1996, p. 90.

18 "Life After Execution," *Euromoney*, May 1999, p. 89.

19 "Treasures Put Their Views on Banks," *Euromoney*, May 1995 p. 65, and "Life After Execution," 90.

20 Euan Hagger, "Handle Exotics with Care," *Euromoney*, October 1992, p. 71.

21 Jeffrey Taylor, "Foreign Currency Trades Slow at Merc as Firms Back Away," *Wall Street Journal*, October 20, 1992, p. C1.

22 Most information for the case came from the following sources: "Economies on Currencies," *Euromoney*, May 1990, p. 145; "The Japanese Paradox," *The Economist*, April 7, 1990, p. 77; Fred R. Bleakley, "Japanese Firms Act to Lift U.S. Prices, Citing Dollar's Weakness Against Yen," *Wall Street Journal*, June 28, 1993, p. A2; "Bashed by the Mighty Yen," *The Economist*, June 5, 1993, p. 81; Louis Uchitelle, "No Quick Gain from Stronger Yen," *New York Times*, April 26, 1993, p. C1; Keith Bradsher, "Falling Yen Puts Car Makers in Japan in the Driver's Seat," *New York Times*, July 15, 1996, p. A1; Jim Mateja, "The Bottom Line; Car Companies Make Some Uncommon Price Moves for '97," *Chicago Tribune*, September 29, 1996, p. 21; Ronald E. Yates, "Dollar Gain a Threat to Exports to Japan; U.S. Goods Become More Expensive to Buy with Yen," *Chicago Tribune*, October 3, 1996, p. 1; Valerie Reitman, "The Japanese Formula: Nylon Seat Covers and a Falling Yen," *Wall Street Journal*, July 18, 1996, p. B1; Emily Thornton, "Will Japan Inc. Copy Nissan's New Model?" *Business Week*, November 1, 1999, p. 59; Emily Thornton, "Remaking Nissan," *Business Week*, November 15, 1999, pp. 70–74; "Yen's Strength Hurts Toyota Despite Net Rise," *Wall Street Journal*, November 19, 1999, p. A18; Norihiko Shibouzu, "Mazda Motor Posts a Profit for Half Year on Cut in Costs," *Wall Street Journal*, November 12, 1999, p. A15; Peter Landers, "Sony's Net Falls 25%, Underlining Strong Yen's Impact on Exports," *Wall Street Journal*, October 28, 1999, p. A21; and Robert L. Simison, "Honda Motor Co. Will Shrink in Japan While It Expands in North America," October 28, 1999, p. A21.

CHAPTER 10

The Determination
of Exchange Rates

A fair exchange brings no quarrel. —DANISH PROVERB

OBJECTIVES

- To describe the International Monetary Fund and its role in the determination of exchange rates

- To discuss the major exchange-rate arrangements countries use

- To identify the major determinants of exchange rates in the spot and forward markets

- To show how managers try to forecast exchange-rate movements using factors such as balance-of-payments statistics

- To explain how exchange-rate movements influence business decisions

China's currency is the renminbi (RMB), also known as the yuan. At the end of 1993, China announced it would adjust its exchange-rate system beginning January 1, 1994. After that date, rather than continuing to manage the system as a dual-track foreign-exchange system (we'll see what that is in a minute), it would allow the RMB to float according to market forces. Instead, however, the government locked the RMB onto the U.S. dollar and did all it could to keep the exchange rate fixed to the dollar. Six years later, as China moved into the twenty-first century, it was still trying to decide what to do with its currency. Should it devalue the currency and allow it to float according to market factors or keep its value locked onto the dollar at basically the same rate that had existed since the devaluation of 1994?

The concept of a managed exchange rate as represented by the dual-track system was part of the centrally planned economy under which China had operated for decades. The People's Bank of China (PBC) is the country's central bank. The State Administration of Exchange Control (SAEC), operating under the PBC's control, is responsible for implementing exchange-rate regulations and controlling foreign-exchange transactions in accord with state policy.

The dual-track system provided for two government-approved exchange rates: the official exchange rate and the swap-market rate. The SAEC set the official exchange rate for the renminbi based on China's balance of payments and the exchange rates of its major competitor countries, such as South Korea and Taiwan. When the SAEC first set the official rates in 1986, it set them at 3.72 RMB per dollar.

Primarily government-owned companies used the official exchange rate, mostly to purchase Foreign Exchange Certificates (FECs). FECs were a separate form of currency developed in 1980 for use by foreigners and foreign companies when paying for their expenses in China. However, the PBC decided to stop issuing FECs in 1994 and gradually withdraw them from circulation.

The other half of the dual-market system was the swap market, created in Shenzhen in 1985 for foreign and local businesses that had received official approval to exchange RMB and hard currency. The currency values in the swap market were based on supply and demand. By the end of 1993, there were around a hundred swap centers, one in most major cities in China, the largest in Shanghai. By the end of 1993, 80 percent of the hard-currency transactions in China were occurring in the swap market. At that time, the swap rate was 8.7 RMB per U.S. dollar, a significant discount from the official rate of 5.8 RMB per dollar. This created challenges for foreign MNEs, which had to keep their books at the official rate, even though the swap rate was a better indicator of the true value of the currency. In addition to the two government-approved markets—the official market and the swap market—a black market also existed. The black-market rate was at an even deeper discount than the swap market's.

As part of the move to the new exchange-rate system, the Chinese government closed the swap centers in early 1994. The swap center in Shanghai was replaced by the National Foreign Exchange Center, which is a national interbank center at which appointed banks can trade and settle foreign currencies. The remaining swap centers either became branches of the interbank system or economic information centers.

Even though China eliminated the dual exchange-rate system in 1994, there were still controls on both current and capital account transactions. After January 1994, companies in China could exchange renminbi into foreign currency to buy imports controlled by quotas if they had an import permit and an invoice. Foreign exchange for imports without quotas could be bought with just an import invoice. Foreign companies operated under different conditions than domestic companies. They could buy and sell renminbi as long as they maintained a balanced foreign-exchange account; that is, as long as earnings in foreign exchange from exports balanced off the demand for foreign exchange for imports. However, the government decided to devalue the RMB in 1994, taking its value from about 5.8 yuan per dollar to just over 8.2 yuan per dollar, which was about the same as the old swap rate. In 1996, the renminbi became fully convertible on a current account (trade in goods and services) but not a capital account (investment and income flows) basis. In addition, the government allows the RMB to trade in a very narrow range against the U.S. dollar. The Asian financial crisis of 1997 did not affect the value of the RMB, although many experts predicted that the Chinese had no choice but to devalue the RMB to remain competitive in global markets. China's economy went through tough times for the next two years, but the government was able to keep from devaluing the RMB. In the first half of 1999, China's trade surplus was only $8 billion, compared with a surplus of $22.5 billion the previous year, and foreign direct investment into China fell nearly 10 percent compared with the previous year, which slowed down the inflow of hard currency and put more pressure on the Chinese government to devalue the RMB. Even though foreign-exchange reserves were around $146 billion in mid-1999, the Chinese government was afraid that if it removed foreign-exchange controls, imports would surge and foreign-exchange reserves would fall drastically. China felt it needed to do more work on reforming the banking system and establishing better financial markets so that it could gain access to foreign capital. Others, however, were calling for lifting foreign currency controls so that the currency could respond better to supply and demand factors. Who would win?

INTRODUCTION

As we learned in Chapter 9, an exchange rate represents the number of units of one currency needed to acquire one unit of another currency. Although this definition seems simple, it is important that managers understand how governments set an exchange rate

At the start of the 1990s, before Iraq's invasion of Kuwait, one U.S. dollar bought three Iraqi dinars. At the decade's close, the dollar bought 1200 dinars. Most countries imposed trade sanctions on Iraq after the invasion. Iraq's difficulty of importing caused most of its domestic prices to soar. Iraq's difficulty in exporting oil, its major product, caused a glut in Iraqi supplies and gas prices that fell to 10 cents a gallon, the cheapest in the world. This photo shows Baghdad's heavy traffic, which is partially the result of the cheap gas prices.

and what causes the rate to change. Such understanding can help them anticipate exchange-rate changes and make decisions about business factors that are sensitive to those changes, such as the sourcing of raw materials and components, the placement of manufacturing and assembly, and the choice of final markets.

THE INTERNATIONAL MONETARY FUND

In 1944, toward the close of World War II, the major Allied governments met in Bretton Woods, New Hampshire, to determine what was needed to bring economic stability and growth to the postwar world. As a result of the meetings, the International Monetary Fund (IMF) came into official existence on December 27, 1945, and began financial operations on March 1, 1947.[2]

Twenty-nine countries initially signed the IMF agreement. There were 192 member countries at the end of 1999. The IMF's major objectives are

- To promote international monetary cooperation
- To facilitate the expansion and balanced growth of international trade
- To promote exchange-rate stability
- To establish a multilateral system of payments
- To make its resources available to its members experiencing balance-of-payments difficulties[3]

The Bretton Woods Agreement established a system of fixed exchange rates under which each IMF member country set a par value for its currency based on gold and the U.S. dollar. Because the dollar was valued at $35 per ounce of gold, the par value would be the same whether gold or the dollar were used as the basis for par value. This par value became a benchmark by which each country's currency was valued against other currencies. Currencies were allowed to vary within 1 percent of their par value (extended to 2.25 percent in December 1971), depending on supply and demand. Further moves from par value and formal changes in par value are possible with IMF approval. As we'll see later, par values were done away with when the IMF moved to greater exchange-rate flexibility.

Because of the U.S. dollar's strength during the 1940s and 1950s and its large reserves in monetary gold, currencies of IMF member countries were denominated in terms of gold and U.S. dollars. By 1947, the United States held 70 percent of the world's official gold reserves. Therefore, governments bought and sold dollars rather than gold. The understanding—though not set in stone—was that the United States would redeem dollars for gold. The dollar became the world benchmark for trading currency, and it has remained so, as noted in Chapter 9.

As a country joins the IMF, it contributes a certain sum of money, called a quota, relating to its national income, monetary reserves, trade balance, and other economic indicators. The quota is a pool of money that the IMF can draw on to lend to countries. It is the basis of how much a country can borrow from the IMF and the amount the country can receive from the IMF as the allocation of special assets called Special Drawing Rights (SDRs), which will be discussed shortly. Finally, the quota determines the voting rights of the individual members. At the end of 1999, the total quota held by the IMF was SDR 212 billion. The United States has the largest quota, comprising 17.6 percent of the total. The next four countries are Japan

The IMF was organized to promote exchange-rate stability and facilitate the international flow of currencies.

The Bretton Woods Agreement established a par value, or benchmark value, for each currency initially quoted in terms of gold and the U.S. dollar.

IMF quota—the sum of the total assessment to each country, which becomes a pool of money that the IMF can draw on to lend to other countries. It forms the basis for the voting power of each country—the higher its individual quota, the more votes it has.

(6.33 percent), Germany (6.19 percent), France (5.11 percent), and the United Kingdom (also 5.11 percent).[4] The Board of Governors, the IMF's highest authority, is composed of one representative from each member country. The number of votes a country has depends on the size of its quota. The Board of Governors is the final authority on key matters, but it leaves day-to-day authority to a 24-person Board of Executive Directors.[5]

IMF ASSISTANCE

In addition to identifying exchange-rate regimes, which we'll discuss in more depth later, the IMF provides a great deal of assistance to member countries. When Russia was facing severe economic challenges in the wake of the Asian financial crisis, the IMF stepped in to provide some financial assistance. In 1999, it notified the Russian government that it would approve a 17-month standby credit for Russia of $4.5 billion to support the government's 1999–2000 economic program. The funding would require quarterly reviews and the meeting of performance criteria and structural benchmarks, always a problem with Russia in the past. Russia had severe fiscal problems, partly because of a high degree of expenditures and partly because of its inability to collect taxes.[6] The IMF negotiates with a country to provide financial assistance if the country will agree to adopt certain policies to stabilize its economy. Often, as we saw in Chapter 4, these policies are not very popular.

The IMF lends money to countries to help ease balance-of-payments difficulties.

SPECIAL DRAWING RIGHTS (SDRs)

To help increase international reserves, the IMF created the **Special Drawing Right (SDR)** in 1969. The SDR is an international reserve asset created to supplement members' existing reserve assets (official holdings of gold, foreign exchange, and reserve positions in the IMF). SDRs serve as the IMF's unit of account and are used for IMF transactions and operations. By unit of account, we mean the unit in which the IMF keeps its records. For example, we noted above that the total quota the IMF holds is SDR 212 billion, which at current exchange rates near the end of 1999 was about $300 billion. The value of the SDR is based on the weighted average of five currencies. On January 1, 1981, the IMF began to use a simplified basket of five currencies for determining valuation. At the end of 1999, the U.S. dollar made up 39 percent of the value of the SDR; the euro (Germany), 21 percent; the Japanese yen, 18 percent; and the euro (France) and the British pound, 11 percent each. These weights were chosen because they broadly reflected the importance of the particular currency in international trade and payments. The value of the SDR can be found daily in key business publications, such as the *Wall Street Journal* and the *Financial Times* of London, as well as many online currency services. Unless the Executive Board decides otherwise, the weights of each currency in the valuation basket change every five years. The Board determined this rule in 1980. A new value was established in 1995 for the period 1996 to 2000, and the Board will decide whether or not to make a new determination in 2000 to become effective on January 1, 2001. One change to the basket in 1999 was that on January 1, 1999, the IMF replaced the currency amounts of the Deutsche mark (DM) and the French franc (FF) in the SDR valuation basket with equal amounts of the euro, based on the fixed conversion rates between the euro and the DM and the FF.

The SDR is
- **An international reserve asset given to each country to help increase its reserves**
- **The unit of account in which the IMF keeps its financial records**

Currencies making up the SDR basket are the U.S. dollar, the euro (previously the German mark and the French franc), the Japanese yen, and the British pound.

Although the SDR was intended to serve as a substitute for gold, it has not taken over the role of gold or the dollar as a primary reserve asset. In addition, several countries base the value of their currency on the value of the SDR.[7]

EVOLUTION TO FLOATING EXCHANGE RATE

The IMF's system was initially one of fixed exchange rates. Because the U.S. dollar was the cornerstone of the international monetary system, its value remained constant with respect to the value of gold. Other countries could change the value of their currency against gold and the dollar, but the value of the dollar remained fixed.

On August 15, 1971, President Richard Nixon announced that the United States would no longer trade dollars for gold until other industrial countries agreed to support a restructure of the international monetary system. The resulting Smithsonian Agreement of December 1971 had several important aspects.

- An 8-percent devaluation of the dollar (an official drop in the value of the dollar against gold)
- A revaluation of some other currencies (an official increase in the value of each currency against gold)
- A widening of exchange-rate flexibility (from 1 percent to 2.25 percent on either side of par value)

This effort did not last, however. World currency markets remained unsteady during 1972, and the dollar was devalued again by 10 percent in early 1973 (the year of the Arab oil embargo and the start of fast-rising oil prices and global inflation). Major currencies began to float against each other instead of relying on the Smithsonian Agreement.

Because the Bretton Woods Agreement was based on a system of fixed exchange rates and par values, the IMF had to change its rules to accommodate floating exchange rates. The Jamaica Agreement of 1976 amended the original rules to eliminate the concept of par values in order to permit greater exchange-rate flexibility. The move toward greater flexibility can occur on an individual-country basis as well as an overall system basis. Let's see how this works.

> **Exchange-rate flexibility was widened in 1971 from 1 percent to 2.25 percent from par value.**

> **The Jamaica Agreement of 1976 resulted in greater exchange-rate flexibility and eliminated the use of par values.**

EXCHANGE-RATE ARRANGEMENTS

The Jamaica Agreement formalized the break from fixed exchange rates. As part of this move, the IMF began to permit countries to select and maintain an exchange-rate arrangement of their choice, provided they communicate their decision to the IMF. The IMF has a surveillance program where it monitors the economic policies of countries that would affect those countries' exchange rates. It also consults annually with countries to see if they are acting openly and responsibly in their exchange-rate policies. Each year the countries notify the IMF of the exchange-rate arrangement they will use, and then the IMF uses the information provided by the country and evidence of how the country acts in the market to place each country in a specific category. There used to be three broad categories, but the IMF has now divided the countries into several categories, as Table 10.1 shows.

> **The IMF surveillance and consultation programs—designed to monitor exchange-rate policies of countries and to see if they are acting openly and responsibly in the exchange-rate policies**

FROM PEGGED TO FLOATING CURRENCIES

In the first three categories, countries lock the value of their currency onto another currency and allow the currency to vary by plus or minus 1 percent against that value. Several countries, especially those in the French franc zone in Africa, have basically adopted the franc as their currency, although the Franc zone countries have now

TABLE 10.1

EXCHANGE-RATE REGIMES, SECOND QUARTER 1999

Exchange rates can either be fixed or pegged to another currency under very narrow fluctuations (exchange arrangements with no separate legal tender, currency board arrangements, or other conventional fixed peg arrangements), pegged to something else with a wider band of fluctuation (pegged exchange rates within horizontal bands), and floating (crawling pegs, exchange rates within crawling bands, managed floating, or independently floating).

REGIMES	NUMBER OF COUNTRIES
Exchange arrangements with no separate legal tender	37
Currency board arrangements	8
Other conventional fixed peg arrangements	44
Pegged exchange rates within horizontal bands	8
Crawling pegs	6
Exchange rates within crawling bands	9
Managed floating with no pronounced path for exchange rate	25
Independently floating	48
Total	185

Exchange arrangements with no separate legal tender: The currency of another country circulates as the sole legal tender, or the member belongs to a monetary or currency union in which the members of the union share the same legal tender. An example would be the countries in the euro area.

Currency board arrangements: A monetary regime based on an implicit legislative commitment to exchange domestic currency for a specified foreign currency at a fixed exchange rate, combined with restrictions on the issuing authority to ensure the fulfillment of its legal obligation. Two examples would be Argentina and Hong Kong.

Other conventional peg arrangements: The country pegs its currency (formal or de facto) at a fixed rate to a major currency or a basket of currencies where the exchange rate fluctuates within a narrow margin of at most +/−1 percent around a central rate. For example, China pegs its currency to the U.S. dollar.

Pegged exchange rates within horizontal bands: The value of the currency is maintained within margins of fluctuation around a formal or de facto fixed peg that are wider than +/−1 percent around a central rate. Many countries that used to be considered managed floating are in this category because they basically peg their currency to something else. An example would be Denmark and Greece in the new Exchange Rate Mechanism in Europe, where they were not part of the euro in 1999 yet were still linking to the euro as much as possible but at a wider degree of flexibility.

Crawling pegs: The currency is adjusted periodically in small amounts at a fixed, preannounced rate or in response to changes in selective quantitative indicators. Costa Rica and Turkey are two examples.

Exchange rates within crawling bands: The currency is maintained within certain fluctuation margins around a central rate that is adjusted periodically at a fixed preannounced rate or in response to changes in selective quantitative indicators. Hungary, Poland, and Chile are three examples.

Managed floating with no preannounced path for the exchange rate: The monetary authority influences the movements of the exchange rate through active intervention in the foreign-exchange market without specifying, or precommitting to, a preannounced path for the exchange rate. The Czech Republic is an example.

Independent floating: The exchange rate is market determined, with any foreign-exchange intervention aimed at moderating the rate of change and preventing undue fluctuations in the exchange rate, rather than at establishing a level for it. Canada, the United States, and Mexico are three examples of countries in this category.

Source: International Monetary Fund, *International Financial Statistics*, November 1999, pp. 2–3.

switched to the euro. That same concept was being considered in Latin America, especially in Brazil and Argentina, and is called the dollarization of the economy. The idea would be to take all of their currency out of circulation and replace it with dollars. Basically, the U.S. Fed would make all monetary decisions instead of the governments of the local countries. Prices and wages would be established in dollars instead of the local currency, which would disappear. The concern is that this would result in a loss of sovereignty and could lead to severe economic problems if the United States decided to tighten monetary policy at the same time those countries needed to loosen policy to stimulate growth. However, this is the same problem facing the member countries in euro area.[8]

The next category contains only a few countries, and it is a slight variation from the first three categories. The countries in this pegged category simply have a wider band but are still locked onto something else, such as the euro for Denmark and Greece, two of the countries in this category.

The last four categories have some degree of floating exchange-rate arrangements, either managed float or free float. Many countries that used to be managed floating countries have been reclassified into the fixed peg regime because they are so tightly linked to some type of anchor, like the dollar. In addition, countries are changing their regime all of the time. Chile, for example, is listed in the IMF survey as a country that keeps its exchange rate within a crawling band, which means that the exchange rate is adjusted periodically at a fixed preannounced rate or in response to changes in selective quantitative indicators, which, for Chile, is inflation. But in late 1999, Chile suspended the trading bands, which it had established around the peso, and moved to a floating rate regime in an effort to stimulate export-led economic growth. Mexico did the same thing in 1994, and so did Brazil in early 1999.[9]

Map 10.1 identifies the countries that fit in each category listed in Table 10.1. Because a country's classification is subject to change constantly, it is important for managers to frequently consult the most recent issue of the IMF's *International Financial Statistics* for updates. In addition, it is necessary to supplement the International Financial Statistics tables with current events, as illustrated in the Chilean peso example above. It is important for MNEs to understand the exchange-rate arrangements for the currencies of countries in which they are doing business so that they can forecast trends more accurately. It is much easier to forecast a future exchange rate for a relatively stable currency that is pegged to the U.S. dollar, such as the Argentine peso, than for a currency that is freely floating, such as the Japanese yen.

BLACK MARKETS

Of the 185 IMF member countries, 88 have currencies that are reasonably flexible, 48 of which float independently. Many of the others control their currencies fairly rigidly. In many of these countries, a black market parallels the official market and is aligned more closely with the forces of supply and demand than is the official market. The less flexible a country's exchange-rate arrangement, the more there will be a thriving black market. A black market exists when people are willing to pay more for dollars than the official rate. As noted in the opening case, when China had an official exchange rate, the swap rate was significantly lower, indicating that the official rate was significantly overvalued. The movement to floating rates eliminates the need for a black market.

Broad IMF categories for exchange-rate regimes

- **Peg exchange rate to another currency or basket of currencies with only a maximum 1 percent fluctuation in value**
- **Peg exchange rate to another currency or basket of currencies with a maximum of $2\frac{1}{4}$ percent fluctuation in value**
- **Allow the currency to float in value against other currencies**

Countries may change the exchange-rate regime they use, so managers need to monitor country policies carefully.

A black market closely approximates a price based on supply and demand for a currency instead of a government-controlled price.

MAP 10.1
Exchange-Rate Arrangements as of June 30, 1999

Over half of the countries in the world have a floating exchange rate, although only one-quarter of the countries' currencies are independently floating like the U.S. dollar. Some countries have abandoned their currencies in favor of something else, such as the euro franc in many African countries, and others are considering adopting the dollar as their currency. See International Monetary Fund's Web site for more information about countries and their exchange rates. www.imf.org/external/country/index.htm.

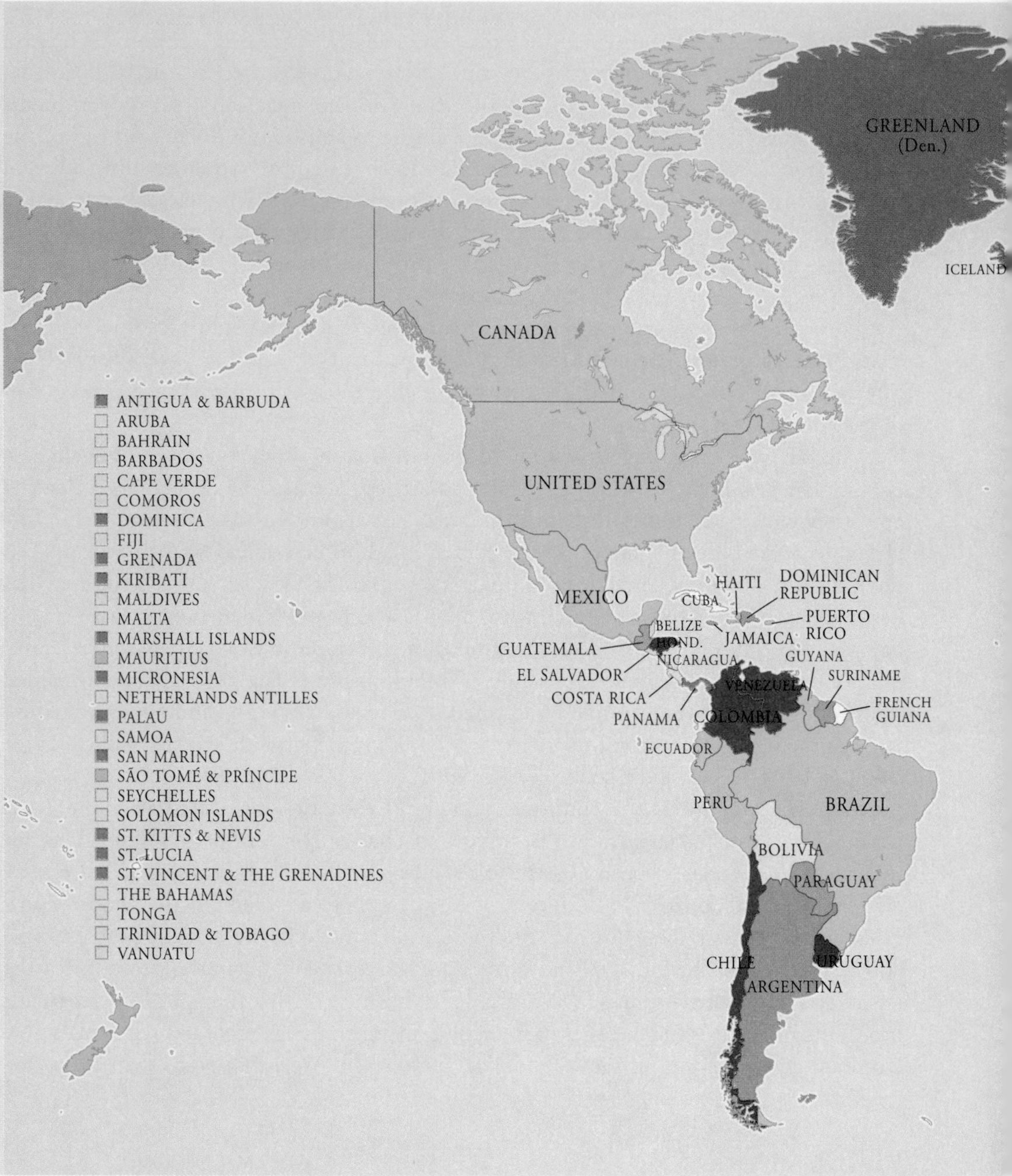

■ ANTIGUA & BARBUDA
□ ARUBA
□ BAHRAIN
□ BARBADOS
□ CAPE VERDE
□ COMOROS
■ DOMINICA
□ FIJI
■ GRENADA
■ KIRIBATI
□ MALDIVES
□ MALTA
■ MARSHALL ISLANDS
□ MAURITIUS
■ MICRONESIA
□ NETHERLANDS ANTILLES
■ PALAU
□ SAMOA
■ SAN MARINO
■ SÃO TOMÉ & PRÍNCIPE
□ SEYCHELLES
□ SOLOMON ISLANDS
■ ST. KITTS & NEVIS
■ ST. LUCIA
■ ST. VINCENT & THE GRENADINES
□ THE BAHAMAS
□ TONGA
□ TRINIDAD & TOBAGO
□ VANUATU

Source: Data from *International Financial Statistics* (Washington, D.C.: IMF, October 1999) p. 8.

THE ROLE OF CENTRAL BANKS

Central banks control policies that affect the value of currencies; the Federal Reserve Bank of New York is the central bank in the United States.

Each country has a central bank that is responsible for the policies affecting the value of its currency. The central bank in the United States is the Federal Reserve System (the Fed), a system of 12 regional banks. The New York Fed, representing the Federal Reserve System and the U.S. Treasury, is responsible for intervening in foreign-exchange markets to achieve dollar exchange-rate policy objectives and to counter disorderly conditions in foreign-exchange markets. It makes such transactions in close coordination

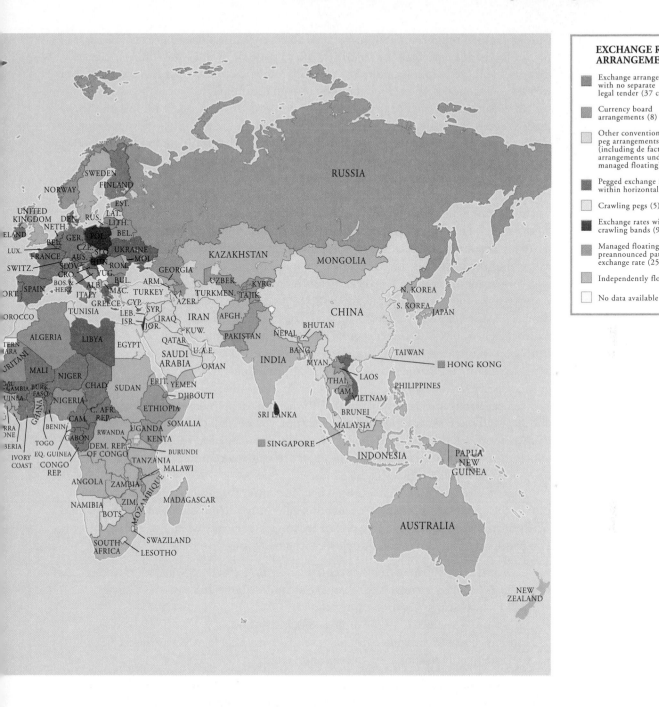

EXCHANGE RATE ARRANGEMENTS

- Exchange arrangements with no separate legal tender (37 countries)
- Currency board arrangements (8)
- Other conventional fixed peg arrangements (including de facto peg arrangements under managed floating) (44)
- Pegged exchange rates within horizontal bands (8)
- Crawling pegs (5)
- Exchange rates within crawling bands (9)
- Managed floating with no preannounced path for exchange rate (25)
- Independently floating (48)
- No data available

with the U.S. Treasury and Board of Governors of the Fed, and most often coordinates with the foreign-exchange operations of other central banks. The Fed will sell dollars for foreign currency if the goal is to counter upward pressure on the dollar. If the goal is to counter downward pressure, it will purchase dollars through the sale of foreign currency. Further, the Federal Reserve Bank of New York serves as fiscal agent in the United States for foreign central banks and official international financial organizations. It acts as the primary contact with other foreign central banks. The services it provides for these institutions include the receipt and payment of funds in U.S. dollars; purchase and sale of foreign exchange and Treasury securities; the custody of over $700 billion in currency, securities and gold bullion credited to over 200 foreign accounts, and the storage of over $75 billion in monetary gold for about 60 foreign central banks, governments, and official international agencies (approximately one-third of the world's known monetary gold reserves).[10] In the European Union, the European Central Bank now coordinates the activities of each member country's central bank to establish a common monetary policy in Europe, much as the Federal Reserve Bank does in the United States.

Central bank reserve assets are kept in three major forms: gold, foreign-exchange, and IMF-related assets. Foreign exchange was 80.5 percent of reserve assets worldwide in 1998.

Central bank reserve assets are kept in three major forms: gold, foreign-exchange reserves, and IMF-related assets. At the end of 1998, there were $1.4 trillion in reserves worldwide, of which 80.5 percent were in foreign exchange, followed by 13.8 percent in gold and 5.7 percent in IMF-related assets. The U.S. dollar was the most widely used currency as a reserve asset, with 60.3 percent of the total, up from 51.3 percent a decade earlier and the highest in 10 years. It was followed by the German mark at 12.1 percent and the Japanese yen at 5.1 percent.[11] However, the mix of reserve assets varies from country to country. For example, in 1998, 97 percent of China's reserves and 95.5 percent of Japan's reserves were in foreign exchange. However, only 57.8 percent of Germany's reserves and 41.1 percent of the United States' reserves were in foreign exchange. European countries tend to be more heavily weighted toward gold as a reserve asset than are other countries in the world, even though they have more foreign exchange than gold as reserve assets.

Central banks are concerned primarily with liquidity to ensure they have the cash and flexibility needed to protect their countries' currencies. The mix of currencies in a country's reserves is based on its major **intervention currencies**, that is, the currencies in which the country trades the most. The degree to which a central bank actively manages its reserves to earn a profit varies by country.

There are several ways that a central bank can intervene in currency markets. In the case of the U.S. Fed, this usually occurs through using foreign currencies to buy dollars when the dollar is weak, or selling dollars for foreign currency when the dollar is strong. Depending on the market conditions, a central bank may

Central banks intervene in currency markets by buying and selling currency to affect its price.

- Coordinate its action with other central banks or go it alone
- Enter the market aggressively to change attitudes about its views and policies
- Call for reassuring action to calm markets
- Intervene to reverse, resist, or support a market trend
- Announce or not announce its operations, be very visible or very discreet
- Operate openly or indirectly through brokers[12]

Governments vary in their intervention policies by country and by administration.

Government policies change over time, depending on the particular administration in office. In the first two and a half years of the first Clinton presidency, the U.S. Treasury intervened in the market by buying dollars on only 18 days, spending about $12.5 billion in the process. The Bush treasury/presidency, in 1989 alone, bought and sold dollars on 97 days and sold $19.5 billion.[13] The Bush administration intervened heavily because it was trying to keep the dollar in a rough trading range during a period when the dollar was rising against the mark and the yen. The Clinton administration chose to intervene more selectively to catch the market by surprise and get maximum

Ethical Dilemmas and Social Responsibility
BLACK MARKET ISSUES AREN'T BLACK AND WHITE

Trading currency on the black market presents an ethical dilemma. If a host-country government has instituted currency controls and foreign management can't get its company's cash out of the country, can it deal in the black market? By using the black market to convert local currency into U.S. dollars, for example, the company would be operating outside of the banking system and would not be able to send cash back to headquarters through normal banking channels. Also, in the local black market, one can obtain more local currency for hard currency but less hard currency for local currency than in the official market. Moreover, the existence of a local black market usually means that it is very difficult, if not impossible, to obtain hard currency there.

It is always tempting to trade hard currency for local currency on the black market. The problem is that countries have varying attitudes—both ethical and legal—toward the black market. For example, travelers to Mozambique in the late 1980s were warned by the government against dealing in the black market. Because of the civil war in that country and the virtual collapse of the economy following independence, hard currency was in high demand. To discourage black-market activity by foreigners and defend its economy, the government cracked down on illegal currency trades.

In Zimbabwe during the same period, the government permitted visitors to convert foreign currency to local currency at approved currency-exchange centers; any excess local currency could be converted back to foreign currency when the visitors left the country. However, the government emphatically warned visitors that they must prove that their transactions took place at the approved centers. Clearly, the government was discouraging currency trading on the black market.

In contrast, at that time, Brazilian airport officials would meet visitors at their planes and offer to trade in currency. The Brazilian government basically looked the other way with respect to black-market currency trading. The point is that it is important to be aware of the prevailing official attitude toward black-market dealings in order to avoid serious trouble.

Black-market currency trading provides a test of the legal justification for ethical behavior, first discussed in Chapter 3. If trading on the black market is illegal, and the government's objections are emphatic, as was the case in both Mozambique and Zimbabwe, companies should avoid dealing in that market under the assumption that the law will be enforced. However, the law might be more unevenly applied in other countries.

In 1999, China was trying to figure out what it needed to do to make its currency convertible on a capital account basis. The government had put controls into place to crack down on the illegal flow of hard currency. The reason for the controls is that during the Asian financial crisis, many individuals and companies were afraid that China would abandon its fixed exchange rate to the dollar and devalue the currency. So they engaged in a variety of fraudulent activities, including operating on the black market, to get money out of the country and into dollar accounts. The solution might be more controls, but in the long run, it will be in allowing the currency to float, eliminating the black market.

publicity out of the intervention. This less frequent, more subtle intervention proved more effective—and was more in line with the philosophy of the Federal Reserve Board, which was to intervene infrequently but with maximum impact.

In 1999, before the Chilean government announced that it would suspend its trading band on the peso and shift to a floating rate regime, it engaged in a hostile battle against peso sellers (speculators who were selling pesos for dollars) by raising interest rates. Governments around the world have used this strategy, often successfully. However, as was the case with Chile, it can also force an economy into recession as high lending rates make it impossible for companies to borrow money to expand growth and for consumers to finance credit purchases.[14]

In 1999, the Japanese yen began to strengthen dramatically against the U.S. dollar, which forced the Bank of Japan (Japan's central bank) to intervene in currency markets to drive down the yen against the dollar. The Japanese economy had finally begun to recover from its slow growth of the mid-1990s, and the Japanese government was afraid that a strong yen would slow down exports and choke off the recovery. In July 1999, the Bank of Japan (BOJ) tried to convince the U.S. Treasury to endorse its policy of intervention to weaken the yen, but Treasury was not interested, believing that sound economic policy rather than intervention would lead to an appropriate exchange-rate policy. However, the New York Fed flooded the market with yen that it holds for the Bank of Japan, so it helped the bank without using U.S. funds to do so.[15] On the first day of the trading year in 2000, the Bank of Japan intervened in the markets to keep the yen from rising to 100 yen per dollar. It was estimated that the Bank of Japan, following the orders of the Ministry of Finance in Japan, spent $70 billion to try to weaken the yen. As noted in Figure 10.1, however, it is very difficult, if not impossible, for intervention

FIGURE 10.1 Intervention and the Japanese Yen

The yen is depicted daily in late New York trading. This depiction is from the *Wall Street Journal*. The *Journal* gives the scale in terms of yen per dollar and inverts it to show the yen's strength. For example, the yen is stronger at 100 yen than at 130 yen per dollar. The size of the market and the volume of trading make it difficult for intervention to work effectively.

Source: Reprinted with permission of Dow Jones & Company, from Bill Spindle, "Japan Intervenes to Halt Dollar's Slide Toward 100 yen," *The Wall Street Journal,* January 5, 2000, p. A17. Permission conveyed through Copyright Clearance Center, Inc.

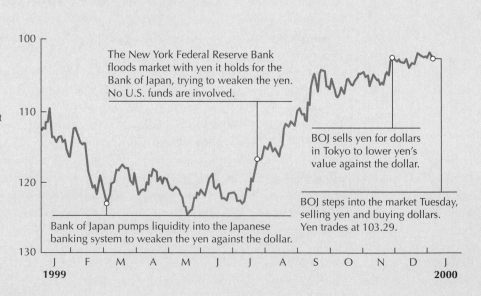

to have a lasting impact on the value of the currency. Intervention may temporarily halt a slide, but it cannot force the market to move in a direction that it doesn't want to, at least for the long run.

The Central Bank of Russia intervenes in the market in a different way. To control the use of foreign currency, the Central Bank requires exporters to deposit 75 percent of the hard-currency proceeds with the Central Bank, but when Russian president Vladimir Putin announced his economic policy, he said that he might go along with a Central Bank proposal to require exporters to deposit 100 percent of their proceeds with the Central Bank. This policy would help the Central Bank tighten its grip over foreign-exchange operations.[16]

Coordination of central bank intervention can take place on a bilateral or multilateral basis. The **Bank for International Settlements (BIS)** in Basel, Switzerland, links together the central banks in the world. The BIS was founded in 1930 and is owned and controlled by a group of central banks. The major objective of the BIS is to promote the cooperation of central banks to facilitate international financial stability. Although only 20 central banks are shareholders in the BIS—11 of which are the founding banks and are from the major industrial countries—the BIS has dealings with some 120 central banks worldwide.[17] The BIS acts as a central banker's bank. It gets involved in swaps and other currency transactions between the central banks in other countries. It also is a gathering place where central bankers can discuss monetary cooperation.[18]

> **The Bank for International Settlements in Basel, Switzerland, is owned by and promotes cooperation among central banks.**

THE DETERMINATION OF EXCHANGE RATES

One of the first steps in being able to forecast future values of a currency is to understand how exchange rates change in value. The exchange-rate regimes described earlier are either fixed or floating, with fixed rates varying in terms of how fixed they are, and floating rates varying in terms of how much they actually float. However, currencies change differently depending on whether they are in floating rate or fixed rate regimes.

FLOATING RATE REGIMES

Currencies that float freely respond to supply and demand conditions free from government intervention. This concept can be illustrated using a two-country model involving the United States and Japan. Figure 10.2 shows the equilibrium exchange rate in the market and then a movement to a new equilibrium level as the market changes. The demand for yen in this example is a function of U.S. demand for Japanese goods and services, such as automobiles, and yen-denominated financial assets, such as securities.

> **Demand for a country's currency is a function of the demand for that country's goods and services and financial assets.**

The supply of yen in this example is a function of Japanese demand for U.S. goods and services and dollar-denominated financial assets. Initially, the supply of and demand for yen in Figure 10.2 meet at the equilibrium exchange rate e_0 (for example, 0.009 dollars per yen, or 111 yen per dollar) and the quantity of yen Q_1.

Assume demand for U.S. goods and services by Japanese consumers drops because of, say, high U.S. inflation. This lessening demand would result in reduced supply of yen in the foreign-exchange market, causing the supply curve to shift to S'. Simultaneously, the increasing prices of U.S. goods might lead to an increase in demand for Japanese goods and services by U.S. consumers. This in turn would lead to an increase in demand for yen in the market, causing the demand curve to shift to D' and finally lead-

FIGURE 10.2   Equilibrium Exchange Rate

Comparatively high inflation in the United States compared with Japan raises the demand for yen but lowers the supply of yen, increasing the value of the yen in terms of U.S. dollars. If the Japanese government wants to keep the dollar/yen exchange rate at e_0, it needs to sell yen for dollars in order to increase the supply of yen in the market and therefore decrease the exchange rate.

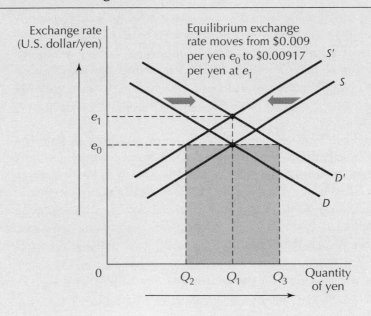

ing to an increase in the quantity of yen and an increase in the exchange rate. The new equilibrium exchange rate would be at e_1 (for example, 0.00917 dollars per yen, or 109 yen per dollar). From a dollar standpoint, the increased demand for Japanese goods would lead to an increase in supply of dollars as more consumers tried to trade their dollars for yen, and the reduced demand for U.S. goods would result in a drop in demand for dollars. This would cause a reduction in the dollar's value against the yen.

A government buys and sells its currency in the open market as a means of influencing the currency's price.

MANAGED FIXED RATE REGIME

In the preceding example, Japanese and U.S. authorities allowed changes in the exchange rates between their two currencies to occur for currencies to reach a new exchange-rate equilibrium. There can be times when one or both countries might not want exchange rates to change. Assume, for example, that the United States and Japan decide to manage their exchange rates. The U.S. government might not want its currency to weaken because its companies and consumers would have to pay more for Japanese products, which would lead to more inflationary pressure in the United States. Or the Japanese government might not want the yen to strengthen because it would mean unemployment in its export industries. But how can the governments keep the values from changing when the United States is earning too few yen? Somehow the difference between yen supply and demand must be neutralized.

In a managed fixed exchange-rate system, the New York Federal Reserve Bank would hold foreign-exchange reserves, which it would have built up through the years for this type of contingency. It could sell enough of its yen reserves (make up the difference

between Q_1 and Q_3 in Figure 10.2) at the fixed exchange rate to maintain that rate. Or the Japanese central bank might be willing to accept dollars so that U.S. consumers can continue to buy Japanese goods. These dollars would then become part of Japan's foreign-exchange reserves.

The fixed rate could continue as long as the United States had reserves or as long as the Japanese were willing to add dollars to their holdings. Sometimes, governments use fiscal or monetary policy, such as raising interest rates (like the Chileans did) to create a demand for their currency and keep the value from falling. Unless something changed the basic imbalance in the currency supply and demand, however, the New York Federal Reserve Bank would run out of yen and the Japanese central bank would stop accepting dollars because it would fear holding too many. At this point, it would be necessary to change the exchange rate so as to lessen the demand for yen.

If a country determines that intervention will not work, it must adjust its currency's value. If the currency is freely floating, the exchange rate will seek the correct level according to the laws of supply and demand. However, a currency that is pegged to another currency or to a basket of currencies usually is changed on a formal basis—in other words, through a devaluation or revaluation, depending on the direction of the change.

> Countries may be forced to revalue or devalue their currencies if economic policies and intervention don't work.

The above example used two currencies, the dollar and the yen. Many times, however, a number of countries intervene in currency markets, sometimes in a coordinated fashion. The G-7 comprises the finance ministers of seven key industrial countries: the United States, Canada, Japan, Germany, France, Italy, and the United Kingdom. Sometimes Russia is thrown in, resulting in the G-7+1. However, the G-7 is the most influential group of finance ministers in the world, and they meet periodically to discuss key economic issues, especially exchange rates. In 1999 and early 2000, the G-7 met several times to discuss the strengthening yen and whether or not coordinated action needed to be taken to push down the value of the yen. In early January, the yen weakened simply because the G-7 was scheduled to meet and propose intervention, even though it took no action.[19] In December 1999, a new group—the G-20—met for the first time. The G-20 is comprised of the G-7 plus Argentina, Australia, Brazil, China, India, Indonesia, Mexico, Russia, Saudi Arabia, South Africa, South Korea, and Turkey. The representatives of the European Union, including the European Central Bank, bring the tally to 20. This organization is considered important because it brings some developing countries into discussions previously held only by the industrial countries. The G-20 will be discussing a wide variety of issues, including appropriate exchange-rate policies for member countries.[20]

> The G-7 group of industrial countries meets often to discuss global economic issues, including exchange-rate values.
> The G-20 is an expansion of the G-7 to include some emerging economies.

AUTOMATIC FIXED RATE REGIME

As with the managed fixed exchange-rate system, assume that Japan and the United States agreed to maintain fixed exchange rates with each other by basing their domestic money supplies on the amount of reserves in their central banks and by denominating their currency values in terms of their reserve assets. Now suppose the United States has a shortage of yen. Under an automatic fixed exchange-rate system, the United States (hypothetically) would sell gold to get the needed yen. However, unlike with the managed system, there would be automatic adjustments to prevent the United States from

> Adjustment of exchange rates is based on changes in the domestic money supply rather than government intervention. Currency boards operate in this system.

running out of gold. As the United States sold off some of its gold, its money supply, which is tied to the amount of gold it holds, would fall. This would lead to higher interest rates and lower investment within the United States, followed by increased unemployment and lower prices. Meanwhile, the increase in gold in Japan would have the opposite effect. The higher U.S. interest rates and the decrease in U.S. prices compared to the Japanese rate and prices would cause an increase in the supply of yen in the United States as funds flowed in for investment and to purchase U.S. goods and services. This would result in a strengthening of the dollar and a weakening of the yen.

This system differs from the others in that the adjustment of exchange rates does not depend on government intervention but rather on changes in the domestic money supply. A change in exchange rate for a freely fluctuating currency is more a function of the supply and demand of the currency in the foreign-exchange market than in the domestic money market. So, although the law of supply and demand can determine exchange rates in an open market, many governments intervene in the market to influence exchange-rate movements. Although the automatic fixed exchange-rate system is possible, it is not as widely used as freely fluctuating currencies and managed fixed exchange-rate systems. However, currency boards, such as the ones operated by Argentina and Hong Kong, are examples of automatic fixed rate regimes, as would be dollarization.

PURCHASING-POWER PARITY

Purchasing-power parity (PPP) is a well-known theory that seeks to define relationships between currencies. In essence, it claims that a change in relative inflation (meaning a comparison of the countries' rates of inflation) between two countries must cause a change in exchange rates to keep the prices of goods in two countries fairly similar. According to the PPP theory, if, for example, Japanese inflation were 2 percent and U.S. inflation were 3.5 percent, the dollar would be expected to fall by the difference in inflation rates. Then the dollar would be worth fewer yen than before the adjustment, and the yen would be worth more dollars than before the adjustment.

> If the domestic inflation rate is lower than that in the foreign country, the domestic currency should be stronger than that of the foreign country.

International business managers can use the following formula to relate inflation to exchange-rate changes:

$$\frac{e_t - e_0}{e_0} = \frac{i_{h,t} - i_{f,t}}{1 + i_{f,t}}$$

where

e = the exchange rate quoted in terms of the number of units of the domestic (home) currency for one unit of the foreign currency (the direct rate)
i = the inflation rate
h indicates the home country (in these examples, the United States)
f indicates the foreign country (in these examples, Japan)
0 indicates the beginning of a period
t indicates the end of the period

The anticipated future exchange rate is given by

$$e_t = e_0 \left(\frac{1 + i_{h,t}}{1 + i_{f,t}} \right)$$

For example, assume the consumer price index (CPI) went from 100 to 103.5 in the United States and from 100 to 102 in Japan during a period when the exchange rate at the beginning of the period was 125 yen to the dollar, or 0.008 dollars per yen. The inflation rates are

$$i_{h,r} = \frac{103.5 - 100}{100} = 0.035$$

$$i_{f,t} = \frac{102 - 100}{100} = 0.02$$

Now the formula above gives

$$e_t = 0.008\left(\frac{1 + 0.035}{1 + 0.02}\right) = 0.00812$$

The exchange rate at the end of the period should be 0.00812 dollars per yen, or 123.15 yen per dollar. So the yen is worth more dollars, and the dollar is worth fewer yen when inflation is higher in the United States than in Japan.

An interesting illustration of the PPP theory for estimating exchange rates is the "Big Mac" index of currencies used by *The Economist* each year. Since 1986, *The Economist* has used the price of a Big Mac to estimate the exchange rate between the dollar and another currency (see Table 10.2). Because the Big Mac is sold in over 100 countries, it is easy to compare prices. PPP would suggest that the exchange should leave hamburgers costing the same in the United States as abroad. However, sometimes the Big Mac costs more, and sometimes less, demonstrating how far currencies are under- or overvalued against the dollar. Looking at Table 10.2, in 2000, a Big Mac cost an average of $2.51 in the United States and Baht55.0 in Thailand. Dividing the baht price of the Big Mac by the dollar price of the Big Mac yields a purchasing power parity exchange rate of Baht21.9 per dollar. However, the actual exchange rate was Baht38.0 per dollar, so that baht was undervalued against the dollar by 42 percent. Based on the actual exchange rate, a Big Mac costs only $1.45 in Thailand (Baht55/38), so Big Macs are a real bargain in Thailand compared within the United States. (Of course, transportation costs will eat up the difference.) European currencies outside of the euro zone were significantly overvalued against the dollar, whereas the euro zone currencies were only slightly overvalued. Most other currencies were undervalued against the dollar.[21]

There are supporters of the Big Mac index, also known as "McParity," but there also are detractors. Even though McParity may hold up in the long run, as some studies have shown, there are short-run problems that affect PPP:

- The theory of PPP falsely assumes that there are no barriers to trade and that transportation costs are zero.
- Prices of the Big Mac in different countries are distorted by taxes. European countries with high value-added taxes are more likely to have higher prices than countries with low taxes.
- The Big Mac is not just a basket of commodities; its price also includes nontraded costs such as rent, insurance, and so on.
- Profit margins vary by the strength of competition. The higher the competition, the lower the profit margin and therefore the price.[22]

TABLE 10.2   **THE HAMBURGER STANDARD**

	BIG MAC PRICES IN LOCAL CURRENCY	IN DOLLARS	IMPLIED PPP* OF THE DOLLAR	ACTUAL $ EXCHANGE RATE 30/03/99	UNDER (−)/OVER (+) VALUATION AGAINST THE DOLLAR, %
United States†	$2.51	2.51	—	—	—
Argentina	Peso2.50	2.50	1.00	1.00	0
Australia	A$2.59	1.54	1.03	1.68	−38
Brazil	Real2.95	1.65	1.18	1.79	−34
Britain	£1.90	3.00	1.32‡	1.58‡	+20
Canada	C$2.85	1.94	1.14	1.47	−23
Chile	Peso1.26	2.45	502	514	−2
China	Yuan9.90	1.20	3.94	8.28	−52
Czech Rep	Koruna54.37	1.39	21.7	39.1	−45
Denmark	Dkr24.75	3.08	9.86	8.04	+23
Euro area	Euro2.56	2.37	0.98§	0.93§	−5
France	Ffr18.50	2.62	7.37	7.07	+4
Germany	DM4.99	2.37	1.99	2.11	−6
Italy	Lire4,500	2.16	1,793	2,088	−14
Spain	Pta375	2.09	149	179	−17
Hong Kong	HK$10.2	1.31	4.06	7.79	−48
Hungary	Forint339	1.21	135	279	−52
Indonesia	Rupiah14,500	1.83	5,777	7,945	−27
Israel	Shekel14.5	3.58	5.78	4.05	+43
Japan	¥294	2.78	117	106	+11
Malaysia	M$4.52	1.19	1.80	3.80	−53
Mexico	Peso20.9	2.22	8.33	9.41	−11
New Zealand	NZ$3.40	1.69	1.35	2.01	−33
Poland	Zloty5.50	1.28	2.19	4.30	−49
Russia	Rouble39.5	1.39	15.7	28.5	−45
Singapore	S$3.20	1.88	1.27	1.70	−25
South Africa	Rand9.00	1.34	3.59	6.72	−47
South Korea	Won3,000	2.71	1,195	1,108	+8
Sweden	Skr24.0	2.71	9.56	8.84	+18
Switzerland	Sfr5.90	3.48	2.35	1.70	+39
Taiwan	NT$70.0	2.29	27.9	30.6	−9
Thailand	Baht55.0	1.45	21.9	38.0	−42

*Purchasing-power parity: local price divided by price in United States
†Average of New York, Chicago, San Francisco and Atlanta   ‡Dollars per pound   §Dollars per euro

Source: From *The Economist*, April 3, 1999. © 00 The Economist Newspaper Group, Inc. Reprinted with permission. Further reproduction prohibited.
   www.economist.com.

INTEREST RATES

Although inflation is the most important long-run influence on exchange rates, interest rates are also important. For example, an article on the foreign-exchange market in the *Wall Street Journal* noted the impact of interest rates on exchange rates.

> The dollar lost ground against the euro but ended higher against the yen as renewed prospects for higher interest rates in the euro zone supported the common currency against its major counterparts. A higher-than-expected demand for wage increases by a major German union sparked fears the European Central Bank will have to face increasing wage pressures from the dominant economy in the European Union. Germany's biggest union, IG Metall, demanded a 5.5% increase for the 3.4 million workers in Germany's metals and electronics industry this year. This is about four times the current rate of Germany's inflation, which has ranged between 1.2% and 1.5% in recent months. The aggressive wage demands ensure a tough collective-bargaining process. After an initial drop in tandem with the European bond market, the euro gradually gained ground on the dollar.[23]

To understand this phenomenon, we need to understand two key finance theories: the Fisher Effect and the International Fisher Effect. The first theory links inflation and interest rates, and the second links interest rates and exchange rates. The **Fisher Effect** is the theory that the nominal interest rate r in a country (the actual monetary interest rate earned on an investment) is determined by the real interest rate R (the nominal rate less inflation) and the inflation rate i as follows:

$$(1 + r) = (1 + R)(1 + i)$$

According to this theory, if the real interest rate is 5 percent, the U.S. inflation rate is 2.9 percent, and the Japanese inflation rate is 1.5 percent, then the nominal interest rates for the United States and Japan are computed as follows:

$$r_{US} = (1.05)(1.029) - 1 = 0.08045, \text{ or } 8.045 \text{ percent}$$

$$r_J = (1.05)(1.015) - 1 = 0.06575, \text{ or } 6.575 \text{ percent}$$

So the difference between U.S. and Japanese interest rates is a function of the difference between their inflation rates. If their inflation rates were the same (zero differential) but interest rates were 10 percent in the United States and 6.575 percent in Japan, investors would place their money in the United States, where they could get the higher real return.

The bridge from interest rates to exchange rates can be explained by the **International Fisher Effect (IFE)**, the theory that the interest-rate differential is an unbiased predictor of future changes in the spot exchange rate. For example, the IFE predicts that if nominal interest rates in the United States are higher than those in Japan, the dollar's value should fall in the future by that interest-rate differential, which would be an indication of a weakening, or depreciation, of the dollar. That is because the interest-rate differential is based on differences in inflation rates, as we discussed above. The previous discussion on purchasing-power parity also demonstrated that the country with the higher inflation should have the weaker currency. Thus the country with the higher interest rate (and the higher inflation) should have the weaker currency.

The nominal interest rate is the real interest rate plus inflation. Because the real interest rate should be the same in every country, the country with the higher interest rate should have higher inflation.

The IFE implies that the currency of the country with the lower interest rate will strengthen in the future.

Of course, these issues cover the long run, but anything can happen in the short run. During periods of general price stability, a country (such as Germany) that raises its interest rates is likely to attract capital and see its currency rise in value due to the increased demand. However, if the reason for the increase in interest rates is because inflation is higher than that of its major trading partners and the country's central bank is trying to reduce inflation, the currency will eventually weaken until inflation cools down.

Although the interest-rate differential is the critical factor for a few of the most widely traded currencies, the expectation of the future spot rate also is very important. Normally, a trader will automatically estimate the future spot rate using the interest-rate differential and then adjust it for other market conditions.

How do these theories relate to the euro example quoted in the *Wall Street Journal* above? If the European Central Bank had not raised interest rates, investors would have sold euros—especially euro Deutsche marks—for dollars where they could get a higher real return. Because the Central Bank announced that it was going to raise interest rates, investors wanted to keep their money in Europe, especially Germany.

OTHER FACTORS IN EXCHANGE-RATE DETERMINATION

Other key factors affecting exchange-rate movements are confidence and technical factors, such as the release of economic statistics.

Various other factors can cause exchange-rate changes. One factor not to be dismissed lightly is confidence. In times of turmoil, people prefer to hold currencies considered safe. For example, during the Kosovo crisis, money flowed into the United States because of concern over the safety of Western Europe if a true crisis were to occur in Yugoslavia and involve the Russians.

In addition to basic economic forces and confidence, exchange rates may be influenced by such technical factors as the release of national economic statistics, seasonal demands for a currency, and a slight strengthening of a currency following a prolonged weakness, or vice versa. In the fall of 1999, the dollar was weakening against the euro and the yen. In October 1999, the dollar fell because of the release of balance-of-trade statistics that showed the U.S. trade deficit was increasing.[24] On January 11, 2000, the dollar rose against the euro because of the announcement of the American Online/Time Warner merger.[25]

FORECASTING EXCHANGE-RATE MOVEMENTS

The preceding section looked at the effect of the law of supply and demand on exchange rates, showed how governments intervene to manage exchange-rate movements, and explained how inflation and interest rates can be important determinants of exchange rates. This section identifies factors that managers can monitor to get an idea of what will happen to exchange rates.

Managers need to be concerned with the timing, magnitude, and direction of an exchange-rate movement.

Because various factors influence exchange-rate movements, managers must be able to analyze those factors to formulate a general idea of the timing, magnitude, and direction of an exchange-rate movement. However, prediction is not a precise science, and many things can cause the best of predictions to differ significantly from reality.

FUNDAMENTAL AND TECHNICAL FORECASTING

Managers can forecast exchange rates by using either of two approaches: fundamental or technical. Fundamental forecasting uses trends in economic variables to predict future rates. The data can be plugged into an econometric model or evaluated on a more subjective basis. Technical forecasting uses past trends in exchange rates themselves to spot future trends in rates. Technical forecasters, or chartists, assume that if current exchange rates reflect all facts in the market, then under similar circumstances future rates will follow the same patterns.[26]

However, all forecasting is imprecise. A corporate treasurer who wants to forecast an exchange rate, say, the relationship between the British pound and the U.S. dollar, might use a variety of sources, both internal and external to the company. Many treasurers and bankers use outside forecasters to obtain input for their own forecasts. Forecasters need to provide ranges or point estimates with subjective probabilities based on available data and subjective interpretation. Biases that can skew forecasts include

- Overreaction to unexpected and dramatic news events
- Illusory correlation, that is, the tendency to see correlations or associations in data that are not statistically present but that are expected to occur on the basis of prior beliefs
- Focusing on a particular subset of information at the expense of the overall set of information
- Insufficient adjustment for subjective matters, such as market volatility
- Inability to learn from one's past mistakes, such as poor trading decisions
- Overconfidence in one's ability to forecast currencies accurately[27]

Good treasurers and bankers develop their own forecasts of what will happen to a particular currency and use fundamental or technical forecasts of outside forecasters to corroborate these. Doing this helps them determine whether they are considering important factors and whether they need to revise their forecasts in light of outside analysis. However, it is important to understand that no matter how carefully prepared a forecast is, it is still an educated guess. Forecasting includes predicting the timing, direction, and magnitude of an exchange-rate change. The timing is often a political decision, and not so easy to predict. Although the direction of a change probably can be predicted, the magnitude is difficult to forecast. Hitachi, the Japanese conglomerate, found this out in early 1999. Back in November 1998, Hitachi management estimated its fiscal year fourth quarter 1998 earnings (which ended on March 31, 1999, the typical close of the fiscal year for Japanese companies) based on a prediction of 125 yen to the dollar. This was accurate in terms of the direction but not the magnitude of the strengthening of the yen. It had based its profit forecasts and operating strategies on that rate, but the yen had actually averaged about 117.9 to the dollar from October to early February, hurting its ability to export as well as depressing the yen value of its overseas earnings. The Japanese government was not overly concerned about the rise of the yen, because it felt that Japanese companies could still be competitive at levels of 115 to 116 yen per dollar.[28] But as noted in Figure 10.1, the yen began to rise in mid-1999, going far beyond the safe level of 115 yen to the dollar.

It is hard to predict what will happen to currencies and to use those predictions to forecast profits and establish operating strategies. The problem with predicting the value of a freely floating currency like the yen is that you never know what could happen to its value. You might be tempted to think that a currency linked to the dollar, like the Argentine peso, would be much easier to predict. But as we approached the new millenium, companies operating in Argentina were faced with two scenarios: The peso would stay linked to the dollar and might even become dollarized, giving way to the dollar, or it

Fundamental forecasting uses trends in economic variables to predict future exchange rates.

Technical forecasting uses past trends in exchange-rate movements to spot future trends.

Looking to the Future
CHANGING TIMES WILL BRING GREATER EXCHANGE-RATE FLEXIBILITY

The international monetary system has undergone considerable change since the early 1970s when the dollar was devalued the first time. New countries have been born with the breakup of the Soviet empire, and with them have come new currencies. As they have gone through transition to a market economy, their currencies have adjusted as well. They will continue to change to a floating rate system as they get their economies under control.

It will be interesting to see what will happen to the currencies of Latin America. The future of the Argentine peso and the Brazilian real—the two big currencies of South America—is in doubt. They could either dollarize or freely float. It is possible to have something in between, but as the economies of the Americas continue to merge, their currencies will come closer together as well. A decade ago, it was unthinkable that a currency union could develop in North and South America. Nationalism and economic differences might preclude that from happening, but it is not as far-fetched now as it once was. Trading relationships and a strong desire by Latin American governments to get their economies under control lean more toward dollarization or at least some form of monetary union than ever before.

The euro will continue to succeed as a currency and will eventually take away market share from the dollar as a prime reserve asset. In addition, its influence will spread throughout Europe as noneuro zone countries adopt the euro or at least come into harmony with it. Increasing trade links throughout Europe will dictate closer alliance with the euro.

For Asia, there is no Asian currency that can compare with the dollar in the Americas and the euro in Europe. The yen is too specific to Japan, and the inability of the Japanese economy to reform and open up will keep the yen from wielding the same kind of influence as the dollar and the euro, even though the yen is one of the most widely traded currencies in the world. In fact, it is far more likely that the dollar will continue to be the benchmark in Asia as Asian economies rely heavily on the U.S. market for a lot of their exports.

The trend will continue to move toward greater flexibility in exchange-rate regimes. Even countries that lock onto the dollar will float against every other currency in the world as the dollar floats. Capital controls will continue to fall and currencies will move more freely from country to country. As the Chinese government gets more control over its political and economic situation, it will open up its currency even more and make it convertible for capital flows as well as goods flows.

might be turned loose to float freely like other currencies in Latin America. Which prediction is correct? How should a company position itself in these two different scenarios?

Key factors to monitor—the institutional setting, fundamental analysis, confidence factors, events, technical analysis

FACTORS TO MONITOR

For freely fluctuating currencies, the law of supply and demand determines market value. However, very few currencies in the world float freely without any government intervention. Most are managed to some extent, which implies that governments need to make political decisions about the value of their currencies. Assuming governments use a rational basis for managing these values (an assumption that may not always be realistic), managers can monitor the same factors the governments follow in order to try to predict values. These factors are

- The institutional setting
  - Does the currency float, or is it managed—and if so, is it pegged to another currency, basket, or other standard?
  - What are the intervention practices? Are they credible, sustainable?
- Fundamental analysis
  - Does the currency appear undervalued or overvalued in terms of PPP, balance of payments, foreign-exchange reserves, or other factors?
  - What is the cyclical situation in terms of employment, growth, savings, investment, and inflation?
  - What are the prospects for government monetary, fiscal, and debt policy?
- Confidence factors
  - What are market views and expectations with respect to the political environment, and the credibility of the government and central bank?
- Events
  - Are there national or international incidents in the news; possibility of crises or emergencies; governmental or other important meetings coming up (such as of the G-7, for example)?
- Technical analysis
  - What trends do the charts show? Are there signs of trend reversals?
  - At what rates do there appear to be important buy and sell orders? Are they balanced? Is the market overbought, oversold?
  - What are the thinking and expectations of other market players and analysts?[29]

BUSINESS IMPLICATIONS OF EXCHANGE-RATE CHANGES

Why do we need to bother with predicting exchange-rate changes? As illustrated in the Hitachi example, our operating strategies as well as translated overseas profits can be dramatically affected by exchange-rate changes. Hitachi estimated losses for the 1998 fiscal year to be $3.3 billion, largely because of exchange-rate changes. We will now look at how exchange-rate changes can affect companies' marketing, production, and financial decisions.

MARKETING DECISIONS

Marketing managers watch exchange rates because they can affect demand for a company's products at home and abroad. If Sony were selling its new Wega Trinitron XBR TV set for 325,000 yen, it would cost $2,500 in the United States when the exchange rate was 130 yen to the dollar. At a forecast rate of 120 yen, the TV would cost $2,708. As the yen continued to strengthen, Hitachi got more nervous. The Japanese government figured that Japanese companies could be competitive at 115 yen, which would

A strengthening of a country's currency value could create problems for exporters.

mean that the TV would cost $2,826, but as the yen actually approached 100 yen, the cost would rise to $3,250. At this point, would consumers be willing to pay $3,250 for a new TV set, or would they wait for the cost to come down? Should Sony pass on the new price to consumers or sell at the same price and absorb the difference in its profit margin? If the yen continues to strengthen beyond 100 yen, can it survive?

PRODUCTION DECISIONS

Companies might locate production in a weak currency country because
- **Initial investment there is relatively cheap**
- **Such a country is a good base for inexpensive exportation**

Exchange-rate changes also can affect production decisions. For example, a manufacturer in a country where wages and operating expenses are high might be tempted to locate production in a country with a currency that is rapidly losing value. The company's currency would buy lots of the weak currency, making the company's initial investment cheap. Further, goods manufactured in that country would be relatively cheap in world markets. For example, BMW made the decision to invest in production facilities in South Carolina because of the unfavorable exchange rate between the mark and the dollar. However, the company announced plans to use the facilities not only to serve the U.S. market but also to export to Europe and other markets.[30] The devaluation of the Mexican peso came shortly after the introduction of NAFTA, and companies had already begun to establish operations in Mexico to service North America, and the cheaper peso certainly helped their export strategies.

FINANCIAL DECISIONS

Exchange rates can influence the sourcing of financial resources, the cross-border remittance of funds, and the reporting of financial results.

Finally, exchange rates can affect financial decisions, primarily in the areas of sourcing of financial resources, remittance of funds across national borders, and reporting of financial results. In the first area, a company might be tempted to borrow money where interest rates are lowest. However, recall that interest-rate differentials often are compensated for in money markets through exchange-rate changes.

In deciding about cross-border financial flows, a company would want to convert local currency into its home-country currency when exchange rates are most favorable so that it can maximize its return. However, countries with weak currencies often have currency controls, making it difficult for MNEs to do so.

Finally, exchange-rate changes can influence the reporting of financial results. A simple example illustrates the impact exchange rates can have on income. If a U.S. company's Mexican subsidiary earns 1 million pesos when the exchange rate is 3.12 pesos per dollar, the dollar equivalent of its income is $320,513. If the peso depreciates to 8 pesos per dollar, the dollar equivalent of that income falls to $125,000. The opposite will occur if the local currency appreciates against that of the company's home country. This is the problem that Hitachi faced in the earlier example. The yen equivalent of Hitachi's dollar earnings in the United States continued to fall as the dollar fell against the yen.

It is important to learn about exchange rates and the forces that affect their change. Several years ago, a large U.S.-based telephone company was preparing a bid for a major telecommunications project in Turkey. The manager preparing the bid knew nothing about the Turkish lira, and he prepared his bid without consulting with the company's foreign-exchange specialists. He figured out the bid in dollars, then turned to the foreign-exchange table in the *Wall Street Journal* to see what rate he should use to convert the bid into lira. What he didn't realize was that the lira at that time was weakening against the dollar. By the time he received the bid, he had lost all of his profit to the change in the value of the lira against the dollar, and by the time he had finished the project, he had lost a lot of money. If he had talked to someone who knew anything about the lira, he could have forecast the future value and maybe entered into a hedging strategy to protect his receivable in lira. If managers don't understand how currency values are determined, they can make serious, costly mistakes.

WEB CONNECTION

Check out our home page www.prenhall.com/daniels for links to key resources for you in your study of international business.

SUMMARY

- The International Monetary Fund (IMF) was organized in 1945 to promote international monetary cooperation, to facilitate the expansion and balanced growth of international trade, to promote exchange-rate stability, to establish a multilateral system of payments, and to make its resources available to its members experiencing balance-of-payments difficulties.

- The Special Drawing Right (SDR) is a special asset the IMF created to increase international reserves.

- The exchange-rate arrangements of countries that are members of the IMF fall into three broad categories: pegged exchange rates, limited-flexibility arrangements, and more flexible arrangements, although the IMF breaks these groups down into several more categories.

- Many countries that strictly control and regulate the convertibility of their currency have a black market that maintains an exchange rate that is more indicative of supply and demand than is the official rate.

- Central banks are the key institutions in countries that intervene in foreign-exchange markets to influence currency values.

- The Bank for International Settlements (BIS) in Switzerland acts as a central banker's bank. It facilitates communication and transactions among the world's central banks.

- The demand for a country's currency is a function of the demand for its goods and services and the demand for financial assets denominated in its currency.

- A central bank intervenes in money markets by increasing a supply of its country's currency when it wants to push the value of the currency down and by stimulating demand for the currency when it wants its value to rise.

- Some factors that determine exchange rates are purchasing-power parity (relative rates of inflation), differences in real interest rates (nominal interest rates reduced by the amount of inflation), confidence in the government's ability to manage the political and economic environment, and certain technical factors that result from trading.

- Major factors that managers should monitor when trying to predict the timing, magnitude, and direction of an exchange-rate change include the institutional setting (what kind of exchange-rate system does the country use), fundamental analysis (what is going on in terms of the trade balance, foreign-exchange reserves, inflation, etc.), confidence factors (especially political factors), events (like meetings of the G-7 group of countries to discuss exchange rates), and technical analysis (trends in exchange-rate values).

- Exchange rates can affect business decisions in three major areas: marketing, production, and finance.

CASE

PIZZA HUT AND THE BRAZILIAN REAL[31]

In 1994, Pizza Hut celebrated the opening of its 10,000th restaurant worldwide by featuring the former Brazilian soccer star, Pele, kicking an autographed soccer ball through a ceremonial ribbon to open a store in São Paulo, Brazil. This event was viewed by people in twelve countries in Europe and the United States via an international satellite broadcast. Over the next six years, however, Pizza Hut came under increasing pressure in Brazil and was trying to decide if it should continue to operate there or pull out and invest in other countries.

Prior to October 7, 1997, Pizza Hut was part of the restaurants division of PepsiCo. However, poor operating performance forced PepsiCo to spin off its restaurant division into a new company in 1997, Tricon Global Restaurants, Inc. Tricon has four major divisions: Pizza Hut, Taco Bell, KFC, and Tricon Restaurants International. There are 29,000 Tricon restaurants around the world generating $10 billion in revenues and $20 billion in system-wide sales, making their total sales and revenues larger than those of McDonald's. Pizza Hut has more than 7,200 units in the United States and 3,000 units in more than 82 other countries. It operates through franchises (51.3 percent of total Pizza Hut sales and revenues), company-owned stores (25.9 percent), joint ventures (16.7 percent), and licenses (6.1 percent). However, Pizza Hut's five-year growth ending in 1998 was 0 percent, compared with 6 percent for Taco Bell and 4 percent for KFC.

What role will Brazil play in the growth of Pizza Hut worldwide? The three largest markets for Pizza Hut internationally are (1) the United Kingdom, (2) Canada, and (3) Australia. However, Pizza Hut's ten-year plan in the mid-1990s would put Brazil as the second or third largest market in the world by 2005. Brazil offers a number of location-specific advantages. First is its massive size. In 1998, Brazil was the fifth largest country in the world in GNP, but it ranked only 103rd in per capita income. It was also the seventh largest country in the world in land mass. Brazil is very urbanized, with São Paulo and Rio de Janeiro two of the largest cities in the world. The population is clustered in the major cities on the coast, so Brazil ranked only 175th in population in the world density, even lower than that of the United States.

From an economic standpoint, Brazil is a land of tremendous opportunity. Historically, Brazil's governments pursued an economic policy based on import substitution and the transition from agriculture to industry. Protective tariffs and import quotas were essential to stimulate domestic industry. State-owned enterprises were established in steel, oil, infrastructure, and other industries, and they received subsidized, long-term credit to expand.

When the military took over in 1964, power was centralized from the states and from congress to the executive branch of government. As the economy began to heat up during the late 1960s and early 1970s, inflation also began to rise, averaging about 20 percent per annum. The government tried traditional means of slowing down inflation, such as raising interest rates, but the large concentration of industrial power resulted in price inflexibility, the indexing of prices above costs, and the passing on of higher interest rates as an additional cost. Due to the protection, foreign trade remained a small percentage of GDP.

The first oil shock in 1973 created problems for Brazil, because in spite of its wealth of natural resources, Brazil relies on imported oil. Economic growth expanded the demand for oil, and the rise in prices worsened Brazil's trade balance. However, import controls gave the government some breathing room. In spite of this, the government was forced to borrow money from abroad, and about 50 percent of the foreign debt was tied to state-owned enterprises. Inflation during the latter 1970s increased to an annual rate of about 40 percent, and the private sector was beginning to show significant resentment to the favoritism shown to the state-owned enterprises. The second oil shock in 1979 was accompanied by rising interest rates on foreign debt, and Brazil went into more severe shock. The economy actually fell 2 percent in 1981, and Brazil was hit by recession, devaluation of the currency, rising real interest rates, real wage reductions, and a widening federal deficit.

The elected governments of 1985 and 1990 focused on foreign debt, inflation, and exchange-rate policies. Real per capita incomes actually fell 6 percent over the 1980s, and cumulative inflation during the 1980s reached 39,043,765 percent. Before he resigned from office in a corruption scandal in the early 1990s, President Collor had begun to tackle Brazil's serious economic problems, but he ran out of time. However, Fernando Henrique Cardoso instituted a new economic plan while he was finance minister that slowed down Brazil's inflation and stabilized the exchange rate. Prices that had been rising 30 to 50 percent per month suddenly slowed to single-digit figures, and Cardoso's popularity soared, allowing him to win the election in 1994 with 54 percent of the vote. However, Brazil continues to face serious economic and social problems. The state is still a dominant force in the economy, and privatization has been difficult. The vast gap between the rich and poor has widened in recent years, and there are problems with decent housing, clean water, and good sewage systems. However, trade restrictions have fallen, and Brazil is attracting a lot of foreign investment, both direct and portfolio.

Pizza Hut first entered Brazil in 1988 during a period of high inflation and economic instability through a franchisee who contacted Pizza Hut. At that time, Pizza Hut did not have a specific strategy for Brazil. In 1989, Pizza Hut opened a mall unit in São Paulo, and in 1991, it set up an office in Brazil dedicated to establishing a plan for Brazil. In addition to Pizza Hut, KFC was also operating in Brazil. However, the two restaurants were operating under different strategies. KFC expanded in Brazil through unit-by-unit franchising, whereas Pizza Hut expanded through corporate franchises. In a unit-by-unit franchise, an individual restaurant is franchised to a particular franchisee. In a corporate franchise, the corporate franchisee is given a whole territory, generally the same as a state boundary with the exception of São Paulo, and is not allowed to subfranchise (sell a franchise to someone else). The initial idea of using strong corporate franchises made sense to Pizza Hut, because it wanted franchisees with strong financial backing and experience in operating in an inflationary environment. However, the franchisees wield a great deal of power, hampering Pizza Hut's implementation of a Brazilian strategy.

Pizza Hut established targets for all franchisees in terms of how they must grow the business in order to maintain the franchise. Because of its size, São Paulo was divided up into five different franchises. One of Pizza Hut's original franchisees in São Paulo, United Food Companies (UFC), also became a supplier of cheese products to the franchisees, allowing UFC to move down the value chain and the other

franchisees to get access to cheese. Pizza Hut diversified to other suppliers, and imported cheese from abroad.

By 1993, UFC had established 35 stores in São Paulo, generating sales per store unit that were between 33 and 50 percent greater than at its U.S. counterparts. However, Brazil was also the only region in the world serviced solely by franchises—Pizza Hut had no equity interest in any of its stores. Management decided that it needed to own some stores in order to develop operating knowledge and expertise that it could share with its franchisees. The franchise value exists when the franchiser can make a valuable contribution to the franchisees, and Pizza Hut felt that it was lacking an important piece of operating knowledge. It was fairly easy to track the revenues and taxes of its franchisees, but it did not have a good understanding of the cost structure of the business. Therefore, Pizza Hut decided to buy UFC's 35 units in December 1993. Management soon found out that the restaurants were not very cost efficient, but they could get away with their inefficiencies due to the high prices they were charging.

In the first six months of Pizza Hut's operations, several problems arose. The first was management culture. Store managers had been operating relatively independently without any outside control, and now they had to adopt Pizza Hut's control process, not an easy thing to do. They rebelled against the outside control and did not appreciate having to manage differently and be held accountable for their actions. Second, staff at the stores was more numerous than Pizza Hut management realized. It was easy for the original franchisee to hide costs and employees during the initial negotiations, but Pizza Hut soon found out that it had hidden costs, and it could not go back to the original owners and complain.

The third major problem was inflation. Between 1964 and 1993 when Pizza Hut bought its first 35 units, the annual increase in the consumer price index in Brazil had been less than 20 percent only twice—in 1972 and 1973. In the 1990s, inflation had been out of control, 2,938 percent increase in 1990, 441 percent in 1991, 1,009 percent in 1992, and 2,148 percent in 1993. In early 1994, the CPI was rising at the rate of 1 percent a day. Then in June 1994, the government instituted the Real Plan, and inflation began to slow down. The new currency, the real, was pegged to the U.S. dollar, meaning that the government established a exchange rate between the real and dollar and would not allow the exchange rate to change as it had in the past. In addition, inflation dropped from an annual rate of 4,060 percent in the third quarter of 1994 to 33.4 percent by September 1995. The slowdown in inflation and implementation of the Real Plan affected business in many different ways. When the new currency came in and inflation slowed down, the stores took a big payroll hit. Although store managers had a fixed salary, they also received a bonus based on sales. Previously, the bonus was delayed 45 days, and the price increases allowed stores to cover the bonuses with cheaper money, and inflated sales were immediately invested so that the store could generate interest income. However, the inflationary benefit disappeared, effectively increasing bonuses by the lost inflation—as much as 45 percent in that period. The same problem hit purchases and mall leases. In the case of purchases, Pizza Hut used to collect sales immediately, because the stores operate on a cash and carry basis, and delay the payment of supplies, thereby allowing them to pay for supplies with inflated sales revenues. However, this benefit disappeared once inflation slowed down. Mall leases are based on 6 percent of sales and are typically delayed 30 to 45 days, thus allowing them to use inflated revenues to pay for the leases. However, the drop in inflation meant that mall lease payments basically went up 30 to 45 percent.

In addition, the slowdown in inflation made consumers more knowledgeable. When inflation was running wild, no one really knew how to compare prices. Prices were changing daily, and salaries were going up as well, so people did not have a good reference point. With the implementation of the Real Plan, however, people—as well as franchises—were able to compare prices and make more informed decisions. At approximately $19 to $20 for a medium pizza, many consumers wondered if Pizza Hut was worth the price, given the alternatives.

Beginning in 1995, Pizza Hut Brazil was faced with adapting to the new Brazilian operating environment. Because of the stabilization of prices and the exchange rate between the U.S. dollar and the Brazilian real, sales in Pizza Hut's São Paulo units dropped by nearly one-half from December 1994 to December 1995, even though the number of units increased. As people realized that the prices of Pizza Hut pizzas were high, store traffic fell. Although Pizza Hut's target increase in volume annually in Brazil was 19 percent, it was growing only 6 percent.

To stimulate sales, Pizza Hut tried two different strategies. PRI told the franchisees to reduce prices by 25 percent

to be more price competitive. McDonald's, the leading fast-food chain in Brazil, increased prices by 40 percent in January 1992 to catch up to inflation but later reduced them by 20 percent and advertised the drop as a vote of confidence in Brazil. The campaign was successful and helped McDonald's to grow. Many Pizza Hut units, however, dropped prices in the last week of November and first week of December 1995, and used the samba (a Brazilian dance of African origin) to announce the decision. However, the campaign failed. The press covered it as a desperation move to keep pace with McDonald's, and many felt that in adopting the samba, Pizza Hut adopted a strategy very inconsistent with the U.S. brand image that it had worked so hard to cultivate. One franchisee in Rio maintained that Pizza Hut would be better off putting more money into marketing than in dropping prices. Using that strategy, he was able to increase his volume, while those that dropped prices found that volume initially went up but then dropped back to the previous level.

In 1997, just as Tricon came into being, the bottom fell out of the Brazilian economy. The Asian financial crisis put serious pressure on the Brazilian real, which had already weathered the Mexican peso crisis in 1994 and 1995. Although the real is considered to be an independently floating currency, it actually uses inflation to target its value. Since the implementation of the Real Plan in June 1995, the real has depreciated against the dollar at a very steady and predictable rate as can be seen in Figure 10.3. When the Asian financial crisis hit in the fall of 1997, there was serious pressure against the real. Instead of devaluing the currency, the government decided to raise interest rates to over 40 percent. That saved the real, but it threw the Brazilian economy into a recession. As economic activity slowed down, sales at Pizza Hut plummeted. Then by mid-1998, the global economy seemed to be on the verge of recovery, and the Brazilian government was able to lower interest rates and get the economy moving again. However, that did not last long. In the summer of 1998, the Russian financial crisis, followed by a collapse in global capital markets, knocked the wind out of the sales of Brazilian recovery. Interest rates went up again, but the real was still in trouble. In January 1999, the real collapsed again. The final straw was the refusal of the governor of the state of Minas Gerais to pay off state debt to the federal government, which was a loss of confidence in the government's ability to control its debt. The governor of Minas Gerais, Itomar Franco, was the President of Brazil after Col-

FIGURE 10.3   The Brazilian Real

After the Brazilian government implemented the Real Plan in June 1995, the real depreciated steadily against the dollar.

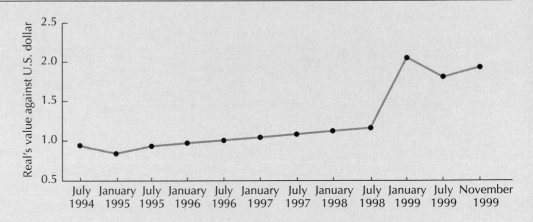

lor's impeachment and during the time when Cardoso established the Real Plan. Cardoso defeated Franco in the election, so the events of January 1999 were political payback.

As noted in Figure 10.3, however, the one-time devaluation of the real did not turn into a full-fledged drop in the currency. The government was able to gain control of the economy quickly, and the steady, predictable trend line of the real started up again. In the fall of 1999, inflation began to pick up in Brazil, but the Brazilian government ruled out an increase in interest rates, instead stating that it would be willing to intervene in currency markets to support the currency.

QUESTIONS

1. Do you think it makes sense for Pizza Hut to get out of Brazil, or should it try to weather the storm and stay in? Justify your position.

2. Where does the Brazilian real fit in the exchange-rate regimes in Table 10.1? What does that imply in terms of how you would predict future values of the real?

3. Discuss whether or not you think the Brazilian government should dollarize its economy and get rid of the real.

4. What are some of the ways that instability in the real might be affecting Pizza Hut's operations in Brazil?

CHAPTER NOTES

1 "China's Financial Fix," *The Economist*, July 10, 1993, pp. 69–70; James McGregor, "Reform in China Adds to Currency Woes," *Wall Street Journal*, June 2, 1993, p. A10; "China Needs Stable Currency Under Exchange Reform", *Agence France Paris*, January 31, 1994; and "China Reforms Its Foreign Exchange System," *Xinhua Foreign News Service*, December 28, 1993; Dusty Clayton, "Confusion in Wake of Move to Make Yuan Convertible," *South China Morning Post*, November 14, 1995, Business Section, p. 5; Seth Faison, "Fearing Deflation, Chinese Set Limits on New Factories," *New York Times*, August 19, 1999, p. A1; Dexter Roberts, "Is It Cold Enough for You?" *Business Week*, March 29, 1999, p. 39; James Kynge,

"Call to Widen Renminbi Band," *Financial Times*, November 3, 1999, p. 7; "China—Time Not Right for Renminbi Conversion," *China Daily*, November 2, 1999, p. 1.

2 "The IMF at a Glance," http://www.imf.org/external/np/exr/facts/glance.htm, September 5, 1999.

3 Ibid.

4 "IMF Quotas, Governors, and Voting Power," www.imf.org/eternal/np/sec/memdir/members.htm

5 Ibid.

6 www.imf.org/external/np/pr/1999/PR9935.htm.

7 See a current issue of *International Financial Statistics* for an example of a country that

uses the SDR as a basis for the value of its currency.

8 Guillermo A. Calvo and Carmen M. Reinhart, "Capital Flow Reversals, the Exchange Rate Debate, and Dollarization," *Finance & Development*, Vol. 36, No. 3, September 1999 (http://www.imf.org/external/pubs/ft/fandd/1999/09/calvo.htm); "No More Peso?" *The Economist*, January 23, 1999, p. 69; Steve H. Hanke, "How to Make the Dollar Argentina's Currency," *Wall Street Journal*, February 19, 1999, p. A19; Michael M. Phillips, "U.S. Officials Urge Cautious Approach to Dollarization by Foreign Countries," *Wall Street Journal*, April 23, 1999, p. A4.

9 Craig Torres, "Chile Suspends Trading Band on Its Peso," *Wall Street Journal*, September 7, 1999, p. A21.

10 "Welcome to the Federal Reserve Bank: International Operations," www.ny.frb.org/introduce, January 2000.

11 International Monetary Fund, *IMF Annual Report, 1999*, pp. 131–134.

12 Sam Y. Cross, *All About the Foreign Exchange Market in the United States* (New York: Federal Bank of New York, 1998), pp. 92–93.

13 David Wessel, "Intervention in Currency Shrinks Under Clinton," *Wall Street Journal*, September 14, 1995, p. C1.

14 Torres, "Chile Suspends Trading Band."

15 Michael M. Phillips and Peter Landers, "Japan Continues Solo Intervention to Hold Down Yen," *Wall Street Journal*, July 21, 1999, p. A15.

16 Jeanne Whalen, "Russia's Putin Tips Hand by Voicing Support of Lower Rates, More Foreign-Exchange Control," *Wall Street Journal*, January 7, 2000, p. A12.

17 "The Bank for International Settlements: Profile of an International Organisation," www.bis.org/about/index.htm, June 1999.

18 Michael R. Sesit, "For Now, Central Bankers Regain Reins," *Wall Street Journal*, August 4, 1993, p. C1.

19 Umberto Torresan, "Rate Outlook Aids Euro; Yen Is Hurt by G-7 Talk," *Wall Street Journal*, interactive ed., January 12, 2000.

20 David Wessel, "G-20 Talks Foster Dialogue, if Not Unity," *Wall Street Journal Europe*, interactive ed., December 17, 1999.

21 "Big MacCurrencies," *The Economist*, April 29, 2000, p. 75.

22 "McCurrencies: Where's The Beef?" *The Economist*, April 27, 1996. Quotes material contained in "For Here or to Go? Purchasing Power Parity and the Big Mac," Federal Reserve Bank of St. Louis, January 1996.

23 Torreson, "Rate Outlook Aids Euro."

24 Umberto Torreson, "Dollar Falls Against Yen, Euro on Rate Worries," *Wall Street Journal*, October 20, 1999, p. C17.

25 Umberto Torreson, "Huge U.S. Merger Provides Support as Dollar Strengthens Against the Euro," *Wall Street Journal*, January 11, 2000, p. C21.

26 "Forecasting Currencies: Technical or Fundamental?" *Business International Money Report*, October 15, 1990, pp. 401–402.

27 Andrew C. Pollock and Mary E. Wilkie, "Briefing," *Euromoney*, June 1991, pp. 123–124.

28 Stephanie Strom, "Hitachi Faults a Strong Yen for Its Losses," *New York Times*, electronic ed., February 5, 1999.

29 Cross, *All About the Foreign Exchange Market*, p. 114.

30 Oscar Suris, "BMW Expects U.S.-Made Cars to Have 80% Level of North American Content," *Wall Street Journal*, August 5, 1993, p. A2.

31 Various annual reports for PepsiCo and Tricon Global Restaurants Inc.; "Pepsi-Cola Wins Second Stadium Account," *Nation's Restaurant News*, August 28, 1995, p. 46; J. R. Whitaker, " Fast Food Francises Fight for Brazilian Aficionados," *Brandweek*, June 7, 1993, pp. 20–24; "Pele Kicks Open 10,000th Pizza Hut Restaurant," *Public Relations Journal*, May 1995, p. 16; "Pizza Hut Cooks in Brazil," *Advertising Age*, June 5, 1995, p. 4; interviews with Pizza Hut employees in Brazil; Peter Fritsch, "Brazil Denies Fresh Speculation on Devaluation," *Wall Street Journal*, December 2, 1998, p. A15; Peter Fritsch, "Brazil's Devaluation Reignites Global Fears of Spreading Malaise," *Wall Street Journal*, January 14, 1999, p. A1; "Real Firms on IMF Talks," *CNNfn*, Internet version, February 2, 1999; Ian Katz, "Brazil's Deepening Crisis," *Business Week Online*, March 22, 1999; Ian Katz, "Pulling Brazil Back from the Brink," *Business Week*, May 10, 1999, p. 50; Peter Fritsch, "Brazil Is Prepared to Support Local Currency," *Wall Street Journal*, November 22, 1999, p. A17.

VIDEO CASE

PART FOUR: INTERNATIONAL FINANCIAL SYSTEM
YAHOO! AND THE WORLD BANK

BACKGROUND

This video looks at Yahoo! Finance, a new system that people around the world can use for electronic commerce and investment transactions. The World Bank, an agency far larger than Yahoo!, is an international agency established in 1944, the same year as the International Monetary Fund (IMF). The World Bank provides loans for development to countries in need. The World Bank and the IMF together are major players in today's international monetary system.

The video illustrates the importance of the World Bank and the IMF in international financial markets and the role these two agencies play in the international monetary system. Futhermore, the video shows how the Bretton Woods Agreement of 1944 created a new era of international transactions.

YAHOO!

For information on this company, please refer to the video case for Part I, page 31.

THE WORLD BANK

The World Bank Group is made up of five organizations—the International Bank for Reconstruction and Development (IBRD), the International Development Association (IDA), the International Finance Corporation (IFC), the Multilateral Investment Guarantee Agency (MIGA), and the International Centre for the Settlement of Investment Disputes (ICSID). The term, World Bank, actually refers to only the IBRD and

the IDA. The World Bank is the world's largest provider of development assistance to developing countries and countries in transition, committing about $20 billion in new loans each year. Its main focus is to help people in developing countries raise their standard of living through finance for agriculture, schools, health programs, transportation, and other essential needs. The IBRD was established in July 1944 at the United Nations Monetary and Financial Conference in Bretton Woods, New Hampshire. The World Bank opened for business on June 25, 1946. In 1947 it gave its first loan of $250 million to France, to finance postwar construction. Today, the World Bank has a lending portfolio of $144 billion.

QUESTIONS

As you watch the video, be prepared to answer the following questions:

1. What contribution does Yahoo! make to the international financial markets?
2. What is the role of the World Bank in the global financial markets?
3. What was the significance of the 1944 Bretton Woods Agreement?
4. What is the role of the IMF in the world economy today?
5. What role do you think Yahoo! might play in the future of the world's financial markets?

The Dynamics of International
Business-Government Relationships

CHAPTER 11

Governmental Attitudes Toward Foreign Direct Investment

If a little money does not go out, great money will not come in.
—CHINESE PROVERB

OBJECTIVES

- **To examine the conflicting objectives of MNE stakeholders**
- **To discuss problems in evaluating MNE activities**
- **To evaluate the major economic impacts—balance of payments and growth—of MNEs on home and host countries**
- **To introduce the major criticisms about MNEs**
- **To provide an overview of the major political controversies surrounding MNE activities**

During the 1990s, China received more FDI than any other emerging economy. In spite of the amount and growth of FDI, however, China has not allowed investment to enter freely. Each investment proposal is examined separately by the Chinese Ministry of Foreign Trade and Economic Cooperation (MOFTEC) or by provincial-level authorities with jurisdiction over certain types of investments. These authorities decide whether the investment is in the best interests of China, and they may disallow an FDI entry or negotiate with the potential investor to try to improve the benefits for Chinese stakeholders. Before a proposal reaches MOFTEC, foreign companies typically have already participated in protracted negotiations (often over several years) with Chinese companies and provincial authorities. Map 11.1 shows the provinces of China.

That so much FDI has recently gone to China in spite of the arduous entry process is due to companies' strong motivations to operate in China. MNEs have long coveted China's potential as a market because of its large population. A Monsanto spokesman summed up this allure by stating, "You just can't look at a market that size and not believe that eventually a lot of goods are going to be sold there. One aspirin tablet a day to each of those guys, and that is a lot of aspirin." In addition to China's large population of about 1.3 billion people, its purchasing power has been increasing because of economic growth. This growth has translated into consumer spending, such as an increase in the percentage of Chinese households with color televisions and refrigerators. China is in the process of spending over a trillion dollars on infrastructure projects including dams, power plants, major highways and railroads, and subway systems. Projections are that the country will soon be the largest economy in the world as measured by purchasing-power parity.

Chinese governmental policies limit imports by a variety of means; thus foreign companies usually find FDI to be a more feasible means than exporting to serve the Chinese market. Further, when foreign companies bid on infrastructure projects, the winning bidder may be chosen because it offers to transfer technology to produce a high portion of the equipment within China. China has had a policy of promoting maximum self-sufficiency, primarily for political and cultural reasons. In addition, it promotes this self-sufficiency because its economy is potentially large enough to justify local production of almost any manufactured product.

Although market size is the main motivation for investing in China, companies have also been attracted to China because of its resources. For example, there have been substantial investments in the exploration and production of oil and coal. In addition, companies have looked at China as a source of inexpensive labor, particularly as unemployed labor supplies have decreased and as labor rates have increased in some other Asian economies (Singapore, Hong Kong, and Taiwan) that no longer can be considered cheap labor sources. For example, Winsor Industrial, which was Hong Kong's largest publicly traded textile company, began moving textile production out of Hong Kong in the 1980s and shifted manufacturing from its two remaining Hong Kong plants to China in 1995. Further, many companies in the electronics industry or suppliers to it, such as Motorola, Northern Telecom, Intel, and Samsung, have made FDI in China to serve both the Chinese and export markets.

Finally, many companies have been drawn to China because there are few, if any, countries with large market potentials in which they have not already established a strong presence. For example, GM is making a $2 billion investment in China because it sees the country as the world's last big growth market. Companies' earlier exclusion of China from investment plans was due primarily to China's effective prohibition of foreign investment from 1949 to 1979.

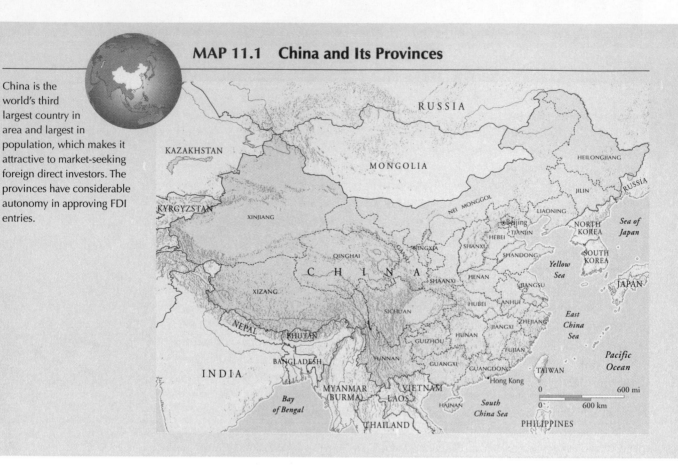

MAP 11.1 China and Its Provinces

China is the world's third largest country in area and largest in population, which makes it attractive to market-seeking foreign direct investors. The provinces have considerable autonomy in approving FDI entries.

These were the first 30 years of communist rule in China, during which time China also traded as little as possible with other countries. Although communist rule ushered in this economic isolationism, the isolationism was consistent with policies during much of Chinese history. China has historically feared that foreign contact will weaken it politically and pollute its culture. However, fearing that it had missed the industrial revolution, it approved the Law on Joint Ventures Using Chinese and Foreign Investment in 1979.

Concomitantly, China established special export zones (SEZs) in which it gave foreign companies incentives to invest, provided that all output was exported from China. The incentives were necessary because China's political environment was so uncertain that foreign companies were wary about making investments there. Foreign companies could establish joint ventures with Chinese companies to sell to the Chinese market. However, the government scrutinized proposals and approved them only if they served a top-level national priority for which China had to seek outside help. Chinese market-serving investments were generally made to improve an existing Chinese product or industry, rather than to create production of an entirely new product in China. For example, China approved a number of joint ventures in the petroleum industry, such as by Baker Marine and by Dresser Industries, because it considered future oil sales a high priority for earning foreign exchange. A proposal by Beatrice Foods succeeded because improvement in food preservation was a top governmental priority as China sought agricultural self-sufficiency.

Since that time, China has greatly increased its dependence on international business activities. Its trade (imports plus exports) as a percentage of GDP has risen and it has increased the number of SPZs. It now allows wholly foreign-owned ventures; however, these are rare because (1) foreign companies perceive that MOFTEC will view these more stringently and (2) foreign companies, rather than Chinese partners, must guide the proposal through the bureaucracy. Typically, investments are joint ventures, with the foreign partner owning 49 percent and the Chinese partner owning 51 percent. Further, China has become more active in seeking out foreign investment because Chinese companies may now look for joint venture partners on their own. Some contacts are even attempted on the Internet. For example, a recent notice read: "Shenyang Paraffin Wax Production project seeking foreign partner for the joint venture. The project has already spent about U.S. $31 million in infrastructure. An approximately U.S. $115 million of foreign investment is needed to complete the entire project. The return on the investment is forecasted at 22.24 percent." At the same time, Chinese authorities have increased efforts and become more adept at evaluating foreign companies' contributions to Chinese objectives.

International business managers' attitudes toward investing in China have had their ups and downs, primarily because of worrisome political conditions. The 1987 removal of the moderate Hu Yaobang as party chairman, the 1989 suppression of the prodemocracy movement, and ongoing threats against Taiwan have caused foreign investors to worry. However, the fact that Chinese governmental authorities have not taken measures against FDI during these political events has heightened investors' optimism. Moreover, potential investors have favorably viewed China's endorsement of a transition to a "socialist market economy" at the Fourteenth Communist Party Congress in 1992 and its subsequent permission for a few foreign firms to establish joint ventures in accounting, legal services, and insurance.

When considering production within China, a foreign company must first find a sponsoring Chinese organization that will approve its application to establish a representative office. The foreign company may then be assigned a Chinese company with which it negotiates. This same Chinese company may then negotiate with more than one foreign company to determine which will offer more in the arrangement. The following summarizes the steps needed for a joint venture approval.

1. Potential partners sign a letter of intent (not a binding contract) giving the broad outlines of a future contract.
2. The Chinese partner submits a proposal, including a preliminary feasibility study, to its immediate administrative superior, which is then passed on to provincial or national authorities, depending on the scale of the investment.
3. Once all the authorities in step 2 approve, the proposed investors must complete a feasibility study that includes the type and quantity of product, target market, sales projections, equipment, infrastructure and labor requirements, and projected foreign-exchange requirements.
4. The partners draft and sign a contract, while keeping authorities apprised of what their agreement will entail.
5. Agreements are presented to MOFTEC or local authorities for approval.
6. Within a month of approval (which stipulates a deadline for making the actual investment), the joint venture must register to obtain a business license. If deadlines are not met, the investor is liable for interest payments or compensation losses.

The same steps are necessary for a wholly owned investment; however, the foreign company must deal directly with all authorities, rather than having a proposed partner handle the arrangements.

Whether MOFTEC or regional authorities are in charge of approval depends on the priority for the particular type of investment. For example, operations that will sell all output in the export market can generally be approved at the provincial level. Further, MOFTEC prioritizes industries—those that it encourages, restricts, or prohibits. The higher the priority, the more likely that approval may be granted at the provincial level. The list of industries is quite detailed and specific. For example, the list approved in 1995 included industries within 18 categories. Those that would serve priority needs for which China clearly lacked up-to-date technology were in the encouraged category, such as water-saving irrigation equipment production and the manufacture of complete coal gasification equipment. Those that were either low-priority products or that Chinese companies already had special capabilities for were prohibited, such as the processing of teas and manufacture of blue and white porcelain. In between were restricted products, such as bicycle and sewing machine assembly and hotel operations. However, such priorities are subject to change. For example, the 1995 priorities put hotel investments lower than in the past. At times priorities and approval points have changed without publicity. In 1999, the Chinese government prohibited new investment that would add capacity or upgrade technology for 114 different products because of excess capacity in such areas as oil refining, steel, glass, and cement. This prohibition applied to both foreign and Chinese companies.

In essence, China has had a love-hate relationship with FDI. It would rather be independent of other countries, but it sees foreign companies' transfer of capital, technology, and management skills to its enterprises as a means of strengthening its independence. The Chinese are enthralled by foreign modern advancements, but they fear foreign cultural contamination. Two investment benefits have been most important to the Chinese: the transfer of technology within a high-priority industrial sector and the generation of exports. Exports earn foreign exchange to buy imports needed for development. The transfer of technology improves future export capa-

These oyster farmers at China's port of Xiamen stand on one of the busiest shipping lanes in the world—the South China Sea. China's eagerness to enter the global economy, as well as foreigners' eagerness to tap its huge markets and inexpensive labor, are fueling direct investment in the country—more than any other emerging economy in the 1990s.

bilities and helps Chinese companies become globally competitive without depending on partnerships with foreign companies. Such benefits to China do not always translate into achieving the foreign investors' objectives, which tend to be more operational, such as a return on investment or an increase in market share. The difference in perspective creates a challenge for managers initiating and continuing successful FDI in China. The country has enormous control over how MNEs operate within its borders.

INTRODUCTION

Multinational enterprises operate largely through foreign direct investment. Governmental policies encourage and restrict these operations. Figure 11.1 shows these relationships. The primary concern about FDI is that MNEs that make it are inadequately concerned about national societal interests because of their global bases of operations. Although not all MNEs are large, the sheer size of many of them concerns many countries. For example, the sales of GM, Exxon, and Mitsubishi exceed the GNP of such medium-size economies as Argentina, Indonesia, Poland, and South Africa.[2] Large MNEs such as these have considerable power in negotiating business arrangements with governments; outcomes are sometimes of greater consequence than are many treaties among countries. In fact, the executives of MNEs frequently deal directly with heads of state when negotiating the terms under which their companies may operate. Powerful pressure groups in both home and host countries have

The sheer size of MNEs is an issue.
- **Some have sales larger than many countries' GNPs.**
- **Some MNE executives deal directly with heads of state.**

FIGURE 11.1   Home- and Host-Country Influences on Companies' Use of FDI

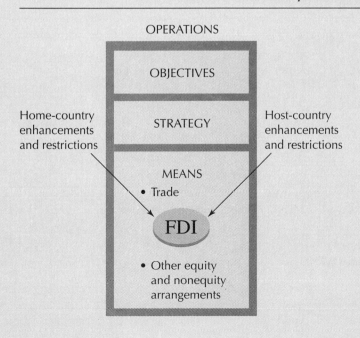

FDI is a major means for companies to conduct their international operations. Stakeholders influence how and whether companies operate through FDI.

Pressure groups push to restrict MNEs' activities at home and abroad.

pushed their governments to implement policies either restricting or enhancing MNEs' movements. These groups are sure to play an even greater role in international business. This chapter examines governmental attitudes toward FDI because of the major contentions regarding MNEs' practices. It also examines the main evidence supporting or refuting those contentions.

EVALUATING THE IMPACT OF FDI

The opening case illustrates the ambivalence of Chinese authorities toward FDI. In other countries as well, FDI's rapid growth has been controversial. As MNE managers and as national citizens, we need to understand the impact of FDI. Companies allocate resources among countries to optimize their performance; however, this allocation is constrained and altered by governmental perceptions of the impact of FDI. As managers, we must be aware of these perceptions and attempt at times to change them. As citizens, we need to argue for governmental policies that will enhance important national interests.

TRADE-OFFS AMONG CONSTITUENCIES

Firms must satisfy
- **Stockholders**
- **Employees**
- **Customers**
- **Society at large**

To survive, a company must satisfy different groups, which we call **stakeholders**. Stakeholders include stockholders, employees, customers, and society at large. In the short term, the aims of these groups conflict. Stockholders want additional sales and increased productivity, which result in higher profits and larger returns going to them. Employees want additional compensation. Customers want lower prices. Society at large would like to see increased corporate taxes or corporate involvement in social functions. In the long term, all of these aims must be achieved adequately or none will be attained at all because each stakeholder group is powerful enough to cause the company's demise.

Management must be aware of these various interests but serve them unevenly at any given period. At one time, gains may go to consumers; at another, to stockholders. Making necessary trade-offs is difficult enough in the domestic environment. However, abroad, where corporate managers are not so familiar with customs and power groups, the problem of choosing the best alternative is compounded—particularly if dominant interests differ among countries.

Management decisions made in one country have repercussions elsewhere.

The most cumbersome problem for companies in overseas relationships is not so much trying to serve conflicting interests within countries as handling cross-national controversies in a manner that will achieve global business objectives. Constituencies in any given country seek to fulfill their own, rather than global, objectives. For example, laborers in the United States have been little concerned about the number of global jobs their employers create. Instead, they have lobbied only for legislation to increase the number of jobs within the United States. Management's task, then, is complicated because decisions made in one country may have repercussions in another.

Among the many decisions MNE managers must make are those concerning:

- Locations of production, decision making, and R&D
- Methods of acquisition and operation
- Markets to be served
- Prices to charge
- Use of profits

In the opening case, for example, many Chinese authorities were concerned about such issues. Assume a U.S. investor has production facilities in both the United States and China. Which facility will export to New Zealand? This decision will determine where profits, taxes, employment, and capital flows will reside. Interests in either country, as well as in New Zealand, may claim that they should have jurisdiction over the sales.

TRADE-OFFS AMONG OBJECTIVES

An MNE's actions may affect a country's economic, social, and political objectives. In addition, a positive effect on one objective, such as full employment, may accompany a negative effect on another objective, such as domestic control over economic matters. In those instances, a country will struggle to rank its objectives. Naturally, it wants only benefits without costs, which is seldom possible to achieve. Nevertheless, much of the literature on MNEs attempts to isolate effects of their FDI on a single given objective. The country might be hoping the MNE can solve a given problem, such as its balance-of-payments deficit.

> **The effects of an MNE's activities may be simultaneously positive for one national objective and negative for another.**

In FDI, people sometimes erroneously assume that if one stakeholder gains, another must lose.[3] They also assume that if there are gains in one country, there must be losses in another country. Either may happen, but it is also possible that multiple stakeholders in more than one country will either gain or lose. No party would participate willingly in an FDI transaction in the belief that the FDI would harm its priorities. Controversies develop because things do not work out as anticipated, the precedence given to the objectives changes, and disagreements arise over the distribution of gains when it is acknowledged that different parties have benefited overall. The last problem is at the heart of most controversies. As described in the opening case, China has tried to encourage foreign investment while also securing more benefits from it by pushing for technology transfers that will improve its economy.

> **In an international transaction**
> - **Both parties may gain**
> - **Both parties may lose**
> - **One party may gain and the other lose**
> - **Even when both parties gain, they may disagree over the distribution of the benefits**

CAUSE-EFFECT RELATIONSHIPS

Just because two factors move in relation to each other does not mean they are connected. Yet opponents of FDI link MNEs to inequitable income and power distribution, environmental debasement, and societal deprivation, while proponents link them to higher tax revenues, employment, and exports. These linkages are particularly prone to arise when governments consider either restricting or encouraging FDI. Although the data presented by opponents or proponents of MNEs often are accurate and convincing, it is not certain what would have happened had MNEs not operated or not followed certain practices. Technological developments, competitors' actions, and governmental policies are just three of the variables that encumber cause-effect analysis.

> **Countries want a greater share of benefits from MNEs' activities.**

> **It is extremely hard to determine whether societal conditions are caused by MNEs' actions.**

INDIVIDUAL AND AGGREGATE EFFECTS

One astute observer has said, "Like animals in a zoo, multinationals (and their affiliates) come in various shapes and sizes, perform distinctive functions, behave differently, and make their individual impacts on the environment."[4] It is difficult to make general statements about MNEs' effects. Much of the literature on the subject, from the viewpoints of both proponents and opponents, takes isolated examples and presents them as typical. The examples chosen usually make interesting reading because of their spectacular or extreme nature, but it is dangerous for governments to make policies based on exceptions rather than the usual.

> **The philosophy and actions of each MNE are unique.**

Some countries have tried to evaluate MNEs and their activities individually. Although this might lead to greater fairness and better control, it is a cumbersome, time-consuming, and costly process. Therefore, many countries apply policies and control mechanisms to all MNEs. Although applying controls eliminates some of the bureaucracy, it carries with it the risk of throwing out some "good apples" along with the bad. Further, when examining foreign investments on either an individual or an aggregate basis, governments have been far from perfect in predicting future impacts.

POTENTIAL CONTRIBUTIONS OF MNEs

Although the sheer size of many MNEs makes them suspect to stakeholders, it also means they have assets that can contribute to a wide range of country objectives. MNEs control a large portion of the world's capital, which increases production. They account for most of the world's exports of goods and services, creating access to foreign exchange for a country's purchase of imports. They are the major producers and organizers of technology, which are increasingly important in determining national competitiveness and in solving environmental problems.[5] Figure 11.2 shows the major assets of MNEs that can satisfy stakeholders' objectives. Nevertheless, critics of MNEs argue that MNEs use these assets inadequately to satisfy these objectives.

ECONOMIC IMPACT OF THE MNE

MNEs may affect countries' balance-of-payments, growth, and employment objectives. Under different scenarios, these effects may be positive or negative for either host or home countries. Let's now see what these are.

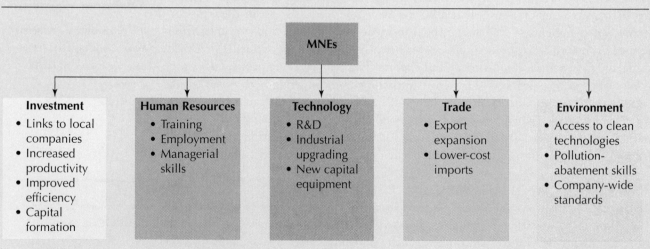

FIGURE 11.2   Resources and Possible Contributions of MNEs

MNEs can contribute directly to investment, human resources, technology, trade, and the environment, thus contributing to host-country objectives.

Source: Adapted from Transnational Corporations and Management Division, *World Investment Report 1992: Transnational Corporations: Engines of Growth, An Executive Summary* (New York: United Nations, 1992), p. 13. Reprinted by permission.

BALANCE-OF-PAYMENTS EFFECTS

Countries want capital inflows because they allow them to increase their imports. However, because FDI brings both capital inflows and outflows, countries worry that the balance-of-payments effect may be negative.

Place in the Economic System   Recall from the balance-of-payments discussion in Chapter 10 that if a country runs a trade deficit, it must compensate for that deficit by reducing its reserves or receiving an influx of capital. This influx of capital may be from unilateral transfers (such as foreign aid), from the receipt of credit, or from the receipt of foreign investment.[6] To put this another way, the more capital inflow a country receives, the more it can import and the more it can run a trade deficit. The ability to run a trade deficit is important for emerging economies because they have more goods and services available for their use than they produce themselves. The ability to use these additional resources helps them satisfy their growth objectives. FDI has recently been crucial because global foreign aid has stagnated and private investment flows have been accounting for a larger portion of the capital received by emerging economies.[7] China has recently been a large net receiver of FDI, and it has also been running a trade surplus. This capital accumulation has temporarily been going toward the buildup of Chinese reserves, which it holds largely in U.S. Treasury bills. This will enable China to run future trade deficits that will be necessary if it is to complete massive infrastructure projects.

Like China, other countries attempt to regulate trade and investment movements and the capital flows that parallel those movements. They do this through incentives, prohibitions, and other types of governmental intervention. A distinction about balance of payments is that gains are a zero sum—one country's trade or capital surplus is another's deficit. If both countries were looking only at a limited time period, then one country might justifiably be described as a winner at the expense of the other. In fact, a country may be willing to forgo short-term surpluses in favor of long-term ones, or vice versa. As countries regulate capital flows, they influence companies' decisions on whether to make FDIs. They also constrain companies' ability to move income from FDI to where they prefer to use it.

> One country's surplus is another's deficit, but long- and short-term economic goals differ.

Effect of Individual FDI   Two extreme hypothetical examples of FDI illustrate why countries need to evaluate each investment's effect on the balance of payments. In the first example, a foreign MNE makes an FDI by purchasing a Haitian-owned company through deposit of dollars in a Swiss bank for the former owners. The MNE makes no changes in management or operations, so profitability remains the same. However, dividends now go to the foreign owners rather than remaining in Haiti, so there is a drain on foreign exchange for Haiti and a subsequent inflow to another country. In the second example, a foreign MNE purchases unemployed resources (land, labor, materials, and equipment) in Haiti and converts them to the production of formerly imported goods. Because of rising demand, it reinvests all earnings in Haiti. The entire import substitution results in a gain in foreign exchange.

> The effect of an individual FDI may be positive or negative.

Most investments or nonequity arrangements (such as licensing or management contracts) fall somewhere between these two simplistic and extreme examples and are not evaluated so easily, particularly when policy makers attempt to apply regulations to aggregate investment movements. There are numerous measurement difficulties, but

> The formula to determine effects is simple, but the data to use must be estimated and are subject to assumptions.

economists are gradually developing guidelines that many governmental authorities use to evaluate companies' investment. Home and host governments follow these guidelines when determining whether to place outward and inward controls, respectively, on FDI. A basic equation for making an analysis is

$$B = (m - m_1) + (x - x_1) + (c - c_1)$$

where

$$B = \text{balance-of-payments effect}$$
$$m = \text{import displacement}$$
$$m_1 = \text{import stimulus}$$
$$x = \text{export stimulus}$$
$$x_1 = \text{export reduction}$$
$$c = \text{capital inflow for other than import and export payment}$$
$$c_1 = \text{capital outflow for other than import and export payment}$$

Although the equation is simple, the problem of choosing the proper values to assign to the variables is formidable. For instance, let's try to evaluate the effect of a Honda automobile plant in the United States, which would be an FDI by a Japanese MNE. To calculate the **net import change** $(m - m_1)$, we would need to know how much the United States would import in the absence of the plant. Clearly, the amount that Honda produces and sells in the United States is only an indication of what the United States would be importing because the selling price, product characteristics, and quality of those automobiles may differ from what otherwise would be imported. Moreover, some of the sales may have been at the expense of other automobile plants in the United States. The value of m_1 should include equipment, components, and materials brought in for manufacturing the product locally. For example, Honda buys many parts from suppliers who import them. The value of m_1 also should include estimates of import increases due to upward movements in national income caused by the capital inflow. For instance, if U.S. national income is assumed to rise $2 million as a result of the investment, the recipients of that income will spend some portion on imports, which is known as the **marginal propensity to import**. If this proportion is calculated to be 10 percent, imports should rise by $200,000.

The **net export effect** is export stimulus minus export reduction $(x - x_1)$. It is particularly controversial because conclusions vary widely depending on what evaluators assume. For the Honda example, we can argue that a U.S. plant merely substitutes for Japanese exports and production. By this assumption, there is no net export effect for the United States. For Japan, there is a negative net export effect because of Honda's export reduction. However, MNEs argue that their moves abroad are (largely) defensive. Under this assumption, Honda picks up business that would otherwise go to other automobile producers in the United States. Thus, Honda's export reduction from Japan is only its export replacement (loss) *caused* by moving a production plant to the United States—not the amount Honda would have lost anyway because of U.S. governmental trade restrictions or shifts in cost advantages because of a strong yen relative to the dollar. MNEs have argued further that their investments stimulate home-country exports of complementary products that can be sold in host countries through their foreign-owned facilities. Again, we must make assumptions about the amount of these exports that could have materialized had the subsidiaries not been established.

The **net capital flow** $(c - c_1)$ is the easiest figure to calculate because of controls at most central banks. The problem with using a given year for evaluation purposes is the time lag between an MNE's outward flow of investment funds and the inward flow of remitted earnings from the investment. So what appears at a given time to be a favorable or unfavorable capital flow may in fact prove over a longer period to be the opposite because companies plan eventually to take out more capital than they originally invest abroad. For example, the time it would take Honda to recoup the capital outflow is affected by its need to reinvest funds in the United States, its ability to borrow locally, and its perception of the future dollar/yen exchange rate. Given the number of variables, the capital flows will vary widely among companies and projects. A further complication arises because MNEs may transfer funds in disguised forms, such as through transactions between parent and subsidiary operations at arbitrary rather than market prices, misstating the real returns on the investments.

Although the equation presented earlier is useful for broadly evaluating the balance-of-payments effects of MNEs' investments, MNE stakeholders should use it with caution. As mentioned earlier, there are data problems. An investment movement might have some indirect effects on a country's balance of payments that are not readily quantifiable. For example, an investor might bring new technological or managerial efficiencies that other companies may copy. What these other companies do may affect the host country's economic efficiency and the ability of those companies to export.

Aggregate Assumptions and Responses Fairly widespread consensus exists that MNEs' investments are initially favorable to the host country and unfavorable to the home country but that the situation reverses after some time. This occurs because nearly all investors plan eventually to remit to the parent company more than they send abroad. If the net value of the FDI continues to grow through retained earnings, dividend payments for a given year ultimately may exceed the total capital transfers required for the initial investment. The time period before reversal may vary substantially, and there is much disagreement as to the aggregate time span required.

From the standpoint of home countries, restrictions on capital outflow improve short-term capital availability, but restrictions on capital outflows reduce future earnings inflows from foreign investments. Host country restrictions may erode confidence in the economy because companies fear they cannot move their funds where they want them. This fear reduces capital inflows and increases capital flight through loopholes in the regulations. The 1998 Chinese outward capital controls had these effects.[8] Consequently, the restrictions are useful only in buying the time needed to institute other means for solving balance-of-payments difficulties.

Governments also have sought to attract inflows of long-term capital as a means of developing production that will either displace imports or generate exports. The problem for governments, then, is how to benefit from foreign capital while minimizing the long-term adverse effects on their balance of payments. Many host countries have approached this problem by valuing new FDI only on the basis of contributions of freely convertible currencies, industrial equipment, and other physical assets—not contributions of goodwill, technology, patents, trademarks, and other intangibles. This valuation is then tied into regulations on the maximum repatriation of earnings, such as a percentage of the FDI valuation. The maximum is stated as a percentage of the investment's value. By holding down the stated value, the

The balance-of-payments effects of FDI usually are

- **Positive for the host country and negative for the home country initially**
- **Positive for the home country and negative for the host country later**

Home and host countries make policies to try to improve short- or long-term effects:

- **Home countries establish outflow restrictions.**
- **Host countries impose repatriation restrictions, asset-valuation controls, and conversion to debt as opposed to equity.**

host-country government can minimize eventual repatriation of earnings. In this respect, governments often exert strict control over the prices of equipment brought in, especially when the investor is also the equipment supplier, so that the investment value is not overstated. For example, China appraises equipment brought in by foreign investors and sometimes lowers the value that MNEs place on the equipment. Governments also often require part of the capital contribution to be in the form of loans. Whereas dividends from earnings on equity are capital outflows that continue indefinitely, interest payments on loans are capital outflows that continue only until the loans mature and are repaid.

GROWTH AND EMPLOYMENT EFFECTS

Growth and employment effects are not a zero-sum game because MNEs may use resources that were unemployed or underemployed.

Unlike balance-of-payments effects, the effects of MNEs on growth and employment are not necessarily a zero-sum game (gains equal losses) among countries. Classical economists assumed production factors were at full employment; consequently, a movement of any of these factors abroad would result in an increase in output abroad and a decrease at home. Even if this assumption were true, the gains in the host country might be greater or less than the losses in the home country.

The argument that both the home and the host countries may gain from FDI assumes that resources are not necessarily fully employed and that capital and technology cannot be easily transferred from use in one industry to another. For example, a brewer such as Anheuser-Busch may be producing at maximum capacity for its domestic market and be limited in developing export sales because of high transportation costs. It may not easily move into other product lines or readily use its financial resources to effect domestic productivity increases. By establishing a foreign production facility, the company may be able to develop foreign sales without decreasing resource employment in the United States. In fact, it may hire additional domestic personnel to manage the international operations and receive dividends and royalties from the foreign use of its capital and technology, further increasing domestic income.

Although stakeholders in both home and host countries may gain from FDI, some stakeholders argue that they are economic losers. Let's examine their arguments.

Home-country labor claims that jobs are exported through FDI.

Home-Country Losses   The United States is the home country for the largest amounts of foreign licensing and direct investment. Therefore, its policies understandably invite criticism. One of these critics is organized labor, which argues that foreign production often displaces what would otherwise be U.S. production.[9] Figure 11.3 shows this criticism humorously. Critics also cite many examples of highly advanced technology that has been at least partially developed through governmental contracts and then transferred abroad. In fact, some U.S. MNEs are moving their most advanced technologies abroad and are even, in some cases, producing abroad before they do so in the United States. An example is Boeing's transfer of aerospace technology to China to produce aircraft parts. According to critics, if Boeing did not transfer the technology, China would purchase the products in the United States, increasing U.S. employment and output. These critics further argue that the technology transfer will speed the process of China's seizing control of future global aircraft sales. However, others argue that China might have bought aircraft from Airbus Industrie or developed the technology itself had Boeing not made the sale.[10]

FIGURE 11.3

"Great. You move to Mexico, and we all end up working at McDonald's."

Home-country stakeholders fear losses from outward flows of FDI.

Another question is whether outsourcing production causes wages to decline in the home country. On the one hand, there is anecdotal evidence that it does. For example, computer programmers in the United States make three to six times the monthly salary of programmers in India. Companies such as Texas Instruments now receive work done in India by private satellite link. So the possibility of moving more work to India has caused a recent drag on the real wages of U.S. programmers.[11] On the other hand, there is evidence that moves by companies to lower-wage countries increase the overall home-country demand and wages for skilled labor. This increase is because the cost savings from producing abroad increase demand for the products because MNEs can sell them at a low price. Nike uses overseas labor to make its shoes, which lowers their price and increases demand. Nike then needs more managerial personnel in the United States.[12]

Host-Country Gains Most observers agree that an inflow of investment from MNEs can initiate greater local development through the employment of unused labor and other resources. A company will want to move resources such as capital and technology abroad when the potential return is high—especially in an area where they are in short supply.

The mere existence of resources in a country is no guarantee they will contribute to output. MNEs may enable idle resources to be used. Oil production, for instance, requires not only the presence of underground oil deposits but also the knowledge of how to find them and the capital equipment to bring the oil to the surface. Production

Host countries may gain through

- More optimal use of production factors
- Use of unemployed resources
- Upgrading of resource quality

is useless without markets and transportation facilities, which an international investor may be able to supply, especially in its home-country market.

Most observers also agree that an inflow of investment from MNEs can initiate an upgrading of resources by educating local personnel to use equipment, technology, and modern production methods. Even such seemingly minor programs as those promoting on-the-job safety may result in a reduction of lost worker time and machine downtime. This occurred after the U.S. company Renbco acquired Doe Run Peru, a metallurgical complex.[13] The transference of work skills increases efficiency, thereby freeing time for other activities. Further, additional competition may force existing companies to become more efficient. This happened with European retailers after Wal-Mart entered the European market and with Japanese retailers after Toys R Us, Tower Records, and Gap entered the Japanese market.[14]

Host-Country Losses   Some critics have claimed that there are examples of MNEs making investments that domestic companies otherwise would have undertaken. The result may be the displacement of local entrepreneurs and entrepreneurial drive. Or they may bid up prices by competing with local companies for labor and other resources, such as when local companies in northern Indiana in the United States complained about Toyota's hiring its best workers by paying them higher wages, although of course the workers did not complain.[15] Such critics argue, for example, that MNEs can raise funds in different countries because they have operations in those countries and are well known by banks, institutional investors, and individuals there. Local companies, especially those operating only domestically in an emerging economy, do not have these options. Thus, MNEs can tap cheaper capital and reduce their capital cost relative to that of local companies. They can then pay to attract the best personnel or entice customers from competitors through greater promotional efforts. However, evidence for these arguments is inconclusive. MNEs frequently pay higher salaries and spend more on promotion than local companies do, but it is uncertain whether these differences result from external advantages or represent the added costs of attracting workers and customers when entering new markets. Added compensation and promotion costs may negate any external cost advantages obtained from access to cheaper foreign capital. Additionally, in many instances, the local competition can also raise funds in other countries.

Critics also contend that FDI destroys local entrepreneurial drive, which has an important effect on development. Because the expectation of success is necessary to drive entrepreneurial activity, the collapse of small cottage industries in the face of MNEs' consolidation efforts may make the local population feel incapable of competing. There is substantial anecdotal evidence to support this contention. But there is also substantial anecdotal evidence to refute it. The presence of MNEs may sometimes increase the number of local companies in host-country markets because MNEs serve as role models that local talent can emulate. Moreover, an MNE often buys many services, goods, and supplies locally and may stimulate local entrepreneurship. For example, automobile producers typically add less than half the value of an automobile at the factory, buying the remaining parts, subassemblies, and modules from suppliers, some of whom are local companies.[16] In China, FDI has contributed to Chinese companies' acquisition of financial resources, which has helped them become viable suppliers.[17] In fact, true entrepreneurs will find areas in which to compete.

Host countries may lose if investments by MNEs
- **Replace local companies**
- **Take the best resources**
- **Destroy local entrepreneurship**
- **Decrease local R&D undertakings**

There is evidence that local R&D can enhance a country's competitive capability.[18] However, a country needs a fairly high technological base if its R&D is to result in product leadership. So governments seek technology from MNEs to build their bases and then seek local R&D to build on those bases. At this point, there is considerable evidence that the dependence on FDI will keep host countries from developing viable R&D. For example, Japan, Korea, and Taiwan have been much more restrictive on FDI inflows than have Hong Kong, Malaysia, Singapore, and Thailand. The former countries spend much more on R&D as a percentage of gross domestic product than do the latter ones. The purpose of China's preference for FDI to enter in the form of joint ventures with Chinese companies is to make the transition from dependence on foreign technology. MNEs enter joint ventures with Chinese companies that have a base of product experience allowing them to absorb incoming technology easily. These joint ventures are contracted for a specific period of time. China's expectation is that its companies will build on the technology they absorb through independent and indigenous R&D of their own in the future. However, a country that limits foreign companies' ownership may discourage those companies from transferring their technologies there.[19]

Another argument is that investors learn abroad. By observing foreign competitive conditions closely, they may gain access to technology abroad that they may copy in their home countries. Such early access may prevent original developers from exploiting their technologies as fully. It may also prevent the originating country from reaping as much economic benefit from the development. For example, foreign investment, especially from Japan, has increased rapidly in high-tech industries in California's Silicon Valley. This foreign investment may allow non-U.S. companies to develop competitive capacities in their home countries that are based on U.S. scientific and technical investments.[20] However, Japanese companies in the Silicon Valley also spend heavily on R&D there, and their results spill over to U.S. companies in the area.[21]

Critics also say that MNEs absorb local capital, either by borrowing locally or by receiving investment incentives.[22] This restricts funds available to local companies. Subsidiaries have borrowed heavily in local markets and have exploited investment incentives. But does this mean that local companies lack funding sources? The answer is unclear. For MNEs to have a noticeable effect on capital availability in a country, the amount of funds diverted to those investors would have to be larger than is probably the case. Further, few MNEs acquire all resources locally; the additional resources brought in usually yield a gain for the host economy. Some host countries prohibit the entry of MNEs believed to harm local companies. Some countries restrict local borrowing by MNEs and provide incentives for them to locate in depressed areas in which resources are idle rather than scarce.

Of particular concern to many countries is the foreign purchase of local firms. The employment effects continue to be debated because of assumptions about what would have happened had the acquisition not taken place, particularly when the local company that is not doing well is downsized. It is impossible to say for certain whether there was more or less employment because of the acquisition. There is simply no way of knowing what would have happened had direct investment not entered a country.[23]

General Conclusions Not all MNE activities will have the same effect on growth in either the home or the host country; nor are the effects of MNEs' activities easily determined. Although there are dangers in attempting to categorize, the following

FDI is more likely to generate growth

- When the product or process is highly differentiated
- When the foreign investors have access to scarce resources
- In the more advanced emerging economies

generalizations are helpful in understanding the circumstances under which foreign investment is most likely to have a positive impact on the host country:

1. *Emerging economies and developed countries.* Emerging economies are less likely than developed countries to have domestic firms capable of undertaking investments similar to those in which foreign investors from developed countries engage. Foreign investment in emerging economies is therefore less likely to be simply a substitute for domestic investment; it yields more growth than if it were located in developed countries.

2. *Degree of product sophistication.* When the foreign investor seeks to produce highly differentiated products or to introduce process technologies, local companies are less likely to undertake similar production on their own. The differentiation may derive from product style, quality, or brand name as well as from technology.

3. *Access to resources.* A foreign investor that has access to resources local companies cannot easily acquire is more likely to generate growth than merely to substitute for what local companies would otherwise do. Some of these resources are capital, management skills, and access to external markets.

4. *Degree of development of the emerging economy.* Foreign investors are more likely to transfer technology and serve as role models for growth in the more economically advanced of the emerging economies because they have more of a base to absorb new technology efficiently.

POLITICAL AND LEGAL IMPACT OF THE MNE

Countries are concerned that MNEs are

- **Foreign-policy instruments of their home-country government**
- **Independent of any government**
- **Pawns of their host-country government**

Because many MNEs are big and powerful, there is much concern that they will politically undermine the sovereignty of nation-states. The foremost concern is that an MNE will be a foreign policy instrument of its home-country government.[24] Most large MNEs have the majority of their sales and assets in their home countries and few foreigners on their executive boards.[25] Because the home countries of most MNEs are industrial countries, it is understandable that this concern is taken most seriously in emerging economies. But it is not restricted to them.

Critics of MNEs raise two other sovereignty issues. One is that the MNE may become independent of both the home and the host countries, making it difficult for either country to take actions considered in its best interests. The second issue is that the MNE might become so dependent on foreign operations that the host country can use it as a foreign-policy instrument against its home country or another country.

EXTRATERRITORIALITY

Extraterritoriality occurs when governments apply their laws to their domestic companies' foreign operations.

Recall that extraterritoriality is when governments apply their laws to their domestic companies' foreign operations. Host countries generally abhor any weakening of their sovereignty over local business practices. MNEs fear that home-country and host-country laws will conflict, because settlement inevitably must be between government offices, with companies caught in the middle. Laws need not be in complete conflict for extraterritoriality to come into play. Those home-country laws requiring companies to remit earnings or pay taxes at home on foreign earnings certainly have affected companies' foreign expansion and local governments' control over such expansion. Although extraterritoriality may result from legal differences between any two countries, and often does, the United States has been criticized the most for attempting to control U.S. companies abroad. So we will discuss primarily U.S. companies here.

Trade Restrictions   The primary focus of criticism has been the U.S. government's attempt to apply its Trading with the Enemy Act to foreign subsidiaries of U.S. companies to keep them from selling to certain unfriendly countries. A series of presidential orders has at times prevented some foreign subsidiaries from making sales to such countries as Libya, Nicaragua, South Africa, and Vietnam, even though the orders violated the laws of some of the countries in which the subsidiaries were operating, such as France and Canada, which require that the sales be made. The Cuban embargo has been a particularly thorny issue between Canada and the United States. Throughout most of the 1980s, the United States permitted foreign subsidiaries of U.S. companies to sell to Cuba, but the Cuban Democracy Act of 1992 changed that. The Act drew foreign criticism, especially in Canada, which led to discussions there on whether FDI from the United States should be limited and whether the Canada-U.S. free trade agreement should be reconsidered. Canada was not alone in its concern. Recall the case on U.S.-Cuban trade in Chapter 6. The U.S. government also restricted subsidiaries of U.S. companies from participating in the Arab boycott of Israel (now ignored by most Arab countries), even though the boycott was a foreign-policy instrument of the countries in which the subsidiaries resided. A distinguishing feature of the Arab boycott of Israel was its provision for a secondary boycott, meaning that a company doing business with Israel was denied the ability to do business with certain Arab countries. More recently, the United States has considered secondary boycotts against companies doing oil and gas business in Iran or Libya, a move that would be very unpopular among European governments and oil and gas companies.[26]

Antitrust Laws   A second focus of criticism has been the U.S. government's antitrust actions. The United States has acted against domestic firms' foreign investments when there has been concern about possible harm to U.S. consumers.[27] At various times, the U.S. government has

- Delayed U.S. companies from acquiring facilities in foreign countries—for example, Gillette's purchase of Braun in Germany was held up because Braun made electric shavers and the acquisition would reduce the number of competitors in the shaving market.
- Prevented U.S. companies from acquiring facilities in the United States that were owned by a company they were taking over abroad—for example, Gillette's purchase of a division of Sweden's Stora Kopparbergs Bergslags could not include that division's subsidiary, U.S. Wilkinson Sword, because it would increase Gillette's share of the razor blade market.
- Forced U.S. companies to sell their interests in foreign operations—for example, Alcoa's spin-off of Alcan because Alcan could then compete against Alcoa.
- Restricted entry of goods produced by foreign combines in which U.S. companies participated—for example, Swiss watches and parts.
- Pressured foreign companies to allow U.S. firms to make foreign sales using technology acquired from them—for example, the British company Pilkington licensed float-glass technology (used to make slate glass) to U.S. companies with the stipula-

tion that they could sell the output only in the United States, but then permitted U.S. companies to use the technology abroad after the U.S. Department of Justice brought suit against its U.S. subsidiary.[28]

The actions these companies were restrained from taking were legal in the countries in which they would have occurred.

One cumbersome problem for U.S. companies has been the U.S. Justice Department's ambiguity regarding their relationships to other companies abroad. This ambiguity has been partially mitigated by the publication of foreign merger guidelines, including case situations illustrating how antitrust enforcement principles would apply. Relationships that might be subject to challenge include participation in cartels to set prices or production quotas, granting of exclusive distributorships abroad, and formation of joint R&D or manufacturing operations in foreign countries. The United States also has signed a number of bilateral treaties with other industrialized countries that call for mutual consultation on restrictive business practices.

KEY SECTOR CONTROL

Closely related to the extraterritoriality issue is the fear that if foreign ownership dominates key industries, then decisions made outside of the country may have extremely adverse effects on the local economy or may exert an influence on politics in the host country. This issue raises two questions: Are the important decisions actually made outside the host countries? If so, are these decisions any different from those that would be made by local companies?

MNEs' home-country headquarters often decide on what, where, and how their foreign subsidiaries will produce and sell. These decisions might cause different rates of expansion in different countries and possible plant closings with subsequent employment disruption in some of them. Further, by withholding resources or allowing strikes, the MNE also may affect other local industries adversely.

Some observers argue that governments generally have more control over companies headquartered in their countries than over foreign companies' subsidiaries. Even MNEs with substantial operations abroad may have primary loyalty to their home countries. This loyalty arises because most MNEs have a majority of their assets, sales, employees, managers, and stockholders in their home countries. They depend on their home countries for most of their R&D and other innovations that enable them to compete globally. Their home-country governments have access to their global financial records and can tax them on their global earnings, which host-country governments cannot do. Further, MNEs can ask their home-country government for assistance in resolving conflicts of interest but cannot expect a foreign government to intercede on their behalf with the home-country government.[29] Given these factors, it is not surprising that during conflicts companies tend to favor their home country's objectives over a host country's.

What if an international company served as an instrument of foreign policy for its home-country government? What if it were powerful enough to disrupt or influence politics in a foreign country? These are serious concerns for host countries. The former fear is a carryover from colonial periods, when such companies as Levant and the British East India Company often acted as a political arm of their home-country government. The fear has resurfaced in the case of Japanese investment in the United States. Critics have pointed out that the Japanese government and Japanese companies lobby strongly to affect U.S. government policy, such as to prevent new import restrictions on Japanese goods. A country that is very dependent on foreign investment may be pressured to take actions that are unpopular locally. For example, the U.S. government pressured Mexico to eliminate political dissidence in Chiapas to improve investor confidence, which meant keeping a tight lid on the politics of protest in an area of rural poor.[30]

Aside from establishing policies that generally restrict the entry of foreign investment, countries have selectively prevented foreign domination of so-called **key industries**, which affect a large segment of the economy or population by virtue of their size or influence. Different countries view key industries differently. For example, NAFTA specifies that foreign investors from the three member countries generally are to be treated no less favorably than domestic investors are. But, because of different conceptions of what is "key," foreign ownership has been limited by Canada in cultural industries, by the United States in the airline and communications industries, and by Mexico in the energy and rail industries.[31] In other cases, governments have required MNEs to manage local subsidiaries with local personnel to ensure that the industries can survive, if necessary, without foreign domination. In the United States, the President can halt any foreign investment that endangers national security, and although national security is not defined in the enabling legislation, enforcement has been extended to include economic security. In a few cases, governments have supported the development of competitive local companies to ward off foreign domination. These include consortia of computer manufacturers (such as ICL in the United Kingdom; Telefunken and Nixdorf in Germany; and Siemens, CII, and Philips in Germany and the Netherlands) and consortia of aircraft producers (such as Messerschmitt-Boelkow-Blohm in Germany, British Aerospace in the United Kingdom, Aeritalia in Italy, and Construcciones Aeronauticas in Spain).

Should host countries be concerned that foreign government-owned enterprises make direct investments within their borders? Although any MNE may in time of conflict favor home-country interests, the government-owned enterprise may be more prone to do so and do so more quickly. Government officials in the home country may be able to influence such a company more readily. Thomson Electronics, for example, a French state-owned MNE, announced it would close down its U.S. assembly operation in 1998 and move it to Mexico to save money. Such cost-saving tactics were less possible in France because of the French government's interest in keeping jobs within the country.

MNE INDEPENDENCE

The discussion so far has centered on the fear that home-country governments unduly influence MNEs. Many observers also fear that these companies can, by playing one country against another, avoid coming under almost any unfavorable restriction. For instance, if they do not like the wage rates, union laws, fair employment requirements, or pollution and safety codes in one country, they can move elsewhere or at least threaten to do so. In addition, they can develop structures to minimize their payment of taxes anywhere.

MNEs can play one country against another but are reluctant to abandon fixed resources.

This ability to play one country against another, especially if the countries are within a regional trade agreement, is more likely to be evident when an MNE is negotiating initial permission to operate in a country. For example, Thailand and the Philippines, both members of ASEAN, vied with investment incentives to attract a GM car plant, whose output would be sold throughout the region.[32] (Similarly, foreign companies sometimes play one state against another when entering the United States.) However, the fact that companies, once operating, are generally reluctant to abandon fixed assets in one country to move abroad indicates that MNEs are limited in getting countries and states to compete in terms for them. Further, the country from which a company moves can usually restrict importation of the goods it produces abroad.

HOST-COUNTRY CAPTIVES

Critics have alleged that MNEs may become so dependent on foreign operations that they begin attempting to influence their home-country government to adopt policies favorable to the foreign countries, even when those policies may not be in the best interests of the home country. Such assertions are difficult to support because there is always disagreement on what policy actually will be in a country's "best interests." However, there certainly are many examples of lobbying efforts by MNEs seeking the adoption of policies that are more palatable to the foreign countries where they are doing business. For instance, many MNEs have lobbied against possible U.S. trade sanctions against China because they fear that Chinese retaliation will hurt them.[33]

BRIBERY

Payments to government officials have been widespread and have been intended to

- **Secure business from competitors**
- **Facilitate services**
- **Ensure safety of employees and facilities**

No discussion of the impact of MNEs would be complete without mentioning payments to government officials. Investigations of U.S. MNEs in the 1970s and of Italian companies in the 1990s, along with much anecdotal information from various years, indicate that the practice has been widespread. MNEs as well as local companies have made payments to officials in industrial countries as well as in emerging economies.

The situation is complicated by the cross-national differences in the rules governing payments. For example, the United States prohibits corporate payments to political parties, but most other countries do not. Also, even if two countries have similar laws on payments, one may enforce them and the other may not. The Berlin-based Transparency International assists citizens in setting up national chapters to try to fight local bribery, and it compiles an international corruption index calculated from surveys of the opinions of businesspeople and journalists. It ranked 99 countries in 1999 in terms of perception of countries' incidence of taking bribes. Table 11.1 shows this ranking.

A motive for bribery is to secure government contracts that otherwise might not be forthcoming at all or to obtain them at the expense of competitors. For example, Foote, Cone & Belding Communications made payments to the Italian Health Ministry to obtain a contract for an AIDS awareness ad campaign.[34] Another motive for bribery is to facilitate governmental services that companies are entitled to receive but that officials otherwise might delay, such as product registrations, construction permits, and import clearances. Other reported payments have been to reduce tax liabil-

TABLE 11.1 **INTERNATIONAL CORRUPTION: A SURVEY OF BUSINESS PERCEPTIONS**

RANK	COUNTRY	1999 CPI SCORE	RANK	COUNTRY	1999 CPI SCORE	RANK	COUNTRY	1999 CPI SCORE
1	Denmark	10.0	35	Tunisia	5.0	67	Romania	3.3
2	Finland	9.8	36	Greece	4.9	68	Guatemala	3.2
3	New Zealand	9.4	37	Mauritius	4.9	69	Thailand	3.2
4	Sweden	9.4	38	Italy	4.7	70	Nicaragua	3.1
5	Canada	9.2	39	Czech Republic	4.6	71	Argentina	3.0
6	Iceland	9.2				72	Colombia	2.9
7	Singapore	9.1	40	Peru	4.5	73	India	2.9
8	Netherlands	9.0	41	Jordan	4.4	74	Croatia	2.7
9	Norway	8.9	42	Uruguay	4.4	75	Ivory Coast	2.6
10	Switzerland	8.9	43	Mongolia	4.3	76	Moldova	2.6
11	Luxembourg	8.8	44	Poland	4.2	77	Ukraine	2.6
12	Australia	8.7	45	Brazil	4.1	78	Venezuela	2.6
13	United Kingdom	8.6	46	Malawi	4.1	79	Vietnam	2.6
			47	Morocco	4.1	80	Armenia	2.5
14	Germany	8.0	48	Zimbabwe	4.1	81	Bolivia	2.5
15	Hong Kong	7.7	49	El Salvador	3.9	82	Ecuador	2.4
16	Ireland	7.7	50	Jamaica	3.8	83	Russia	2.4
17	Austria	7.6	51	Lithuania	3.8	84	Albania	2.3
18	USA	7.5	52	South Korea	3.8	85	Georgia	2.3
19.	Chile	6.9	53	Slovak Republic	3.7	86	Kazakhstan	2.3
20	Israel	6.8				87	Kyrgyz Republic	2.2
21	Portugal	6.7	54	Philippines	3.6			
22	France	6.6	55	Turkey	3.6	88	Pakistan	2.2
23	Spain	6.6	56	Mozambique	3.5	89	Uganda	2.2
24	Botswana	6.1	57	Zambia	3.5	90	Kenya	2.0
25	Japan	6.0	58	Belarus	3.4	91	Paraguay	2.0
26	Slovenia	6.0	59	China	3.4	92	Yugoslavia	2.0
27	Estonia	5.7	60	Latvia	3.4	93	Tanzania	1.9
28	Taiwan	5.6	61	Mexico	3.4	94	Honduras	1.8
29	Belgium	5.3	62	Senegal	3.4	95	Uzbekistan	1.8
30	Namibia	5.3	63	Bulgaria	3.3	96	Azerbaijan	1.7
31	Hungary	5.2	64	Egypt	3.3	97	Indonesia	1.7
32	Costa Rica	5.1	65	Ghana	3.3	98	Nigeria	1.6
33	Malaysia	5.1	66	Macedonia	3.3	99	Cameroon	1.5
34	South Africa	5.0						

1999 CPI Notes

1999 CPI Score-relates to perceptions of the degree of corruption as seen by business people, risk analysts and the general public, and ranges between 10 (highly clean) and 0 (highly corrupt).

Source: From *Financial Times,* July 26, 1996, p. 3 using data from the Transparency Corruption Perception Index, 1996. Reprinted with permission of FT Pictures/Graphics.

ities, to keep a competitor from operating in a specific country (by General Tire in Morocco), and to gain governmental approval for price increases (by a group of rubber companies in Mexico). Some companies have made payments because of extortion. For example, Mobil made payments to forestall the closing of its Italian refinery, and Boise Cascade, IBM, and Gillette made payments to protect the safety of their employees.

Most reported payments have been in cash, but in some cases they have included products made by the company, such as ITT's gift of a color TV set to a Belgian official. Some payments have been made directly to governmental officials by the companies; most, however, have been made via intermediaries and by diverse methods. For example, the relative of a person having influence over a purchasing decision sometimes has been put on the payroll as a consultant. In other cases, the person having influence has been paid as a middleman at a fee exceeding normal commissions. Another common practice has been to overcharge a government agency and rebate the overcharge to an individual, usually in a foreign country.

Bribery scandals have replaced chiefs of state in Honduras, Italy, and Japan. Officials have been jailed in a number of countries, including Pakistan, Iran, and Venezuela, for accepting bribes. Officials in a number of companies have resigned, been fined, or gone to jail.

In 1977, the United States passed the Foreign Corrupt Practices Act (FCPA), which makes certain payments to foreign officials illegal. One of the seeming inconsistencies in the act is that payments to officials to expedite their compliance with the law are legal, but payments to other officials who are not directly responsible for carrying out the law are not. For example, a large payment to a customs official to clear legally permissible merchandise is legal, but even a small payment to a government minister to influence the customs official is illegal. The FCPA allows the former payment because governmental officials in many countries delay compliance of laws indefinitely until they do receive payments, even though such payments may be illegal in those countries.

Many critics of the FCPA have contended that U.S. firms lose business because firms from other countries not only have been permitted to make bribery payments but also have been able to take the expenses as a tax deduction. The CIA monitors bribery payments by non-U.S. companies so that the United States may put diplomatic pressure on foreign governments to stop the practices. The U.S. government has also pushed other countries to adopt legislation similar to the FCPA. However, the view that the FCPA has caused U.S. companies to engage less in bribes than their foreign competitors is questionable. In 1999, Transparency International ranked for the first time the perception of 19 leading exporting countries in terms of the degree their companies pay bribes in emerging economies. Figure 11.4 shows that U.S. companies fall in the middle of this ranking. Critics of the FCPA also argue that anticorruption laws might be seen as meddling in other countries' affairs.[35] However, Organization for Economic Cooperation and Development (OECD) countries agreed not to allow tax deductions for overseas bribes as of 1997. The Organization of American States has also adopted a Convention Against Corruption, which calls for criminalizing bribery and extraditing offenders.[36]

The U.S. legislation on bribery is controversial because

- **Some payments to expedite compliance with law are legal, but others are not**
- **Extraterritoriality issues emerge**
- **Business may be lost**

Ethical Dilemmas and Social Responsibility
ARE SOME BRIBES JUSTIFIABLE?

Although companies have been criticized for bribing foreign officials, attempts to stop the bribes, such as through FCPA, have been criticized. One such criticism is that businesses can't make payments but governments can. For example, the U.S. government frequently gives aid as a bribe, with the understanding that the host country will grant political concessions in return. Further, governments use high-level official visits and lobby aggressively for their home-based companies to help them gain foreign business. For example, the U.S. government has sometimes paid for ministry heads to visit the United States when a U.S. company is bidding on a contract, and has given scholarships to family members of officials that can provide business to U.S. companies.[37] A second criticism is that some bribes are allowed, but others are not. Further, some argue that judging the morality of bribery should be weighed against interfering with a custom that may be legally and culturally acceptable in some countries, which bribery is. In addition, it is sometimes argued that unethical "means" are justified to arrive at a desirable "end." For example, IBM and other U.S. companies claimed that the FCPA caused them to lose a contract for air traffic control systems in Mexico. They also alleged that their inability to make payments to Mexican authorities led Mexico to install inferior technology.[38] It is debatable whether such an "end" would justify a bribe. Relatedly, most MNE's executives believe that bribes to government officials in emerging economies are necessary to gain orders because most of their government officials are poorly paid and are immune from prosecution when accepting bribes.[39]

Given the illegality of U.S. companies paying government officials abroad to get business, U.S. companies have devised legal means to ingratiate themselves with those officials. For example, the insurance company Chubb has set up an insurance program at a Chinese university and has put as board members some of the same officials who will decide the fate of Chubb's license application. Many companies, such as Hewlett-Packard in China, pay journalists to attend their news conferences, presumably so they will write favorably about the companies. So many companies pay for foreign officials to visit their plants in the United States, while simultaneously enjoying tourist attractions, that a spokesperson for the industry-funded U.S.-China Business Council said, "You'd think Disney World was a training site."[40]

Finally, although there are pressures to prevent foreign companies from making payments to political parties, some companies argue that avoiding politics would be socially irresponsible. For example, Glaxo Wellcome, a British investor in the United States, donated to U.S. political action committees during the 1996 U.S. election—when such contributions became a political issue. Glaxo Wellcome's position was that it had 9,000 U.S. employees, paid U.S. taxes, and had a substantial effect on the U.S. economy. It made donations to ensure that policies would be in the best interest of its U.S. operations and employees.[41]

FIGURE 11.4   Likelihood of Paying Bribes Abroad by Nationality of Companies

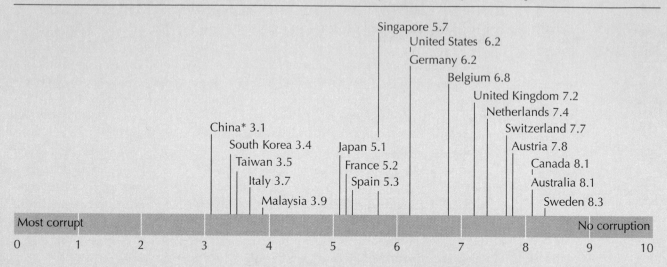

Transparency International used Gallup International to collect opinions of local executives, bankers, accountants, lawyers, and chambers of commerce in 14 emerging economies. The scales are 1 to 10. Higher scores indicate a lower incidence of paying bribes.

Source: *Toronto Sun*, October 27, 1999, p. 2, reporting data from Transparency International. Reprinted by permission.

DIFFERENCES IN NATIONAL ATTITUDES TOWARD MNEs

In theory, host countries may take completely restrictive or laissez-faire positions toward MNEs. In actuality, their policies fluctuate over time but are seldom completely restrictive or completely laissez-faire. Currently, countries such as Bhutan and Cuba are close to the restrictive end, and countries such as the United States and the Netherlands are near the laissez-faire end of the continuum. However, countries between these extremes have policies with varying degrees of restrictions as they attempt to attract investment and receive the most benefit from it.

The concern of home- and host-country stakeholders about companies' international operations increases with their international commitments. For example, home-country stakeholders are generally unconcerned when a company begins to export, but they are concerned when the company begins producing abroad because of fear that jobs and growth are being transferred. Likewise, host-country stakeholders give much more attention to foreign companies that are wholly owned direct investors than those who share ownership locally or those that are merely exporting into their market. This greater attention occurs because the company now employs local personnel, and with full ownership, the company may be able to pursue global or home-country objectives at the expense of local ones. Therefore, the need for companies to justify their operations grows in tandem with their increased international commitment.

Looking to the Future
WILL FDI BE WELCOME AS THE TWENTY-FIRST CENTURY PROGRESSES?

Governments will keep trying to garner a larger share of the benefits from the activities of MNEs. In the short term, most countries will probably welcome FDI. Debt problems limit the ability of emerging economies to access sufficient capital, except through investment inflows. Trade-deficit problems are likely to make the United States take a positive stance toward receiving FDI. The EU probably will welcome investment inflows to attain the growth its unification seeks. However, in the longer term, FDI may be less welcome. Historically, the attitudes toward FDI have tended to vary, leaning toward more restrictions when economies are thriving. Yet, it is possible that if rapid growth does not occur in some emerging economies after they receive substantial FDI, they may learn to regard as models such countries as Japan and South Korea, which have grown rapidly without much FDI.

Where MNEs are controlled will continue to be an issue. Some MNEs (such as Nestlé, SKF, ABB, ICI, Corn Products International, Coca-Cola, and Heinz) now have so many nationalities represented in their top management ranks, it is difficult to accuse them of favoring home-country interests. However, their internationalization leaves them open to the criticism of acting in their own, rather than national, interests. But some MNEs (including Sandoz, Michelin, Matsushita, and United Technologies) have few shares held outside their home countries and practically no foreigners in high-level corporate positions.[42]

Countries tend to be more concerned about large companies than small ones because of their greater potential impact on national economic and political objectives. But not all companies operating internationally are large. Smaller companies generally have smaller foreign investments and must do less to justify their entry and operations. Because they are assumed to have less impact on host societies, countries often treat their entries differently. Further, many governments of emerging economies prefer the entry of smaller companies because they may be more willing to yield to host-country wishes, increase competition because of their numbers, and supply smaller-scale technology more suited to emerging economy needs.[43]

The perception of a company's operations in one country may have an effect on the perception of stakeholders in other countries as well. For example, a company's confrontation with labor, tax authorities, or environmental pressure groups in one country may cause similar stakeholders in another country to be wary of the company's behavior. Further, as communications have become more rapid, negative publicity about company practices has become more extensive. As a company expands to more countries, the possibility of negative perceptions about its impact increases.

The relationship between MNEs and societies has generated so many allegations and controversies that it is impossible to examine all of them in this chapter. A number of them deal not so much with whether international business should take place but rather with certain practices. In these cases, the targets are specific operational areas of management that we will examine later in this book.

WEB CONNECTION

Check out our home page www.prenhall.com/daniels for links to key resources for you in your study of international business.

SUMMARY

- Management must understand the need to compromise and satisfy the conflicting interests of stockholders, employees, customers, and society at large. For managers of MNEs, the problem is more complex because the strengths of these competing groups vary among countries.

- The economic and political effects of MNEs are difficult to evaluate because of conflicting influences on different countries' objectives, intervening variables that obscure cause-effect relationships, and differences among MNEs' practices. Countries are interested not only in their absolute gains or losses but also in their performance compared to other countries.

- Because a balance-of-payments surplus in one country must result in a deficit elsewhere, MNEs' trade and investment transactions have been scrutinized closely for their effects. However, countries often are willing to accept short-term deficits to achieve a long-term surplus or other economic gains.

- Managers and government officials can calculate how FDI will affect a country's balance of payments, but so many assumptions underlie such calculations that there is room for disagreement. FDI projects differ so much that governments cannot easily make effective policies that apply to large groups of investors.

- Governments regulate FDI to improve their balance-of-payments positions by restricting capital flows, requiring partial local ownership of FDI, limiting local borrowing by foreign investors, and stipulating that a part of capital inflows must be in the form of loans rather than equity.

- The growth and employment effects of MNEs do not necessarily benefit one country at the expense of another. Many of these effects come from the employment of resources with or without the MNEs' activities.

- MNEs may contribute to growth and employment by using idle resources, using resources more efficiently, and upgrading resource quality.

- The factors affecting countries' growth and employment include the location in which MNEs operate, product sophistication, competitiveness of local companies, government policies, and degree of product differentiation.

- Political concerns about MNEs are that they could be a foreign-policy instrument of home-country or host-country governments or that they may avoid the control of any government.

- Extraterritoriality is the application of home-country laws to the operations of companies abroad. It sometimes leads to conflicts between home and host countries and may put an MNE in the untenable position of having to violate the laws of one country or the other.

- Countries most fear foreign control of key sectors in their economies because decisions made abroad may disrupt local economic and political stability. The foreign investors then may have enough power to affect local sovereignty adversely. So governments often restrict foreign ownership in key sectors of their economies.

- Some countries are more open to FDI than others. Moreover, countries' attitudes toward FDI change.

CASE

FDI IN SOUTH AFRICA[44]

In its 1999 annual report, South Africa's Reserve Bank said that "foreign direct investment inflows will be a prerequisite for faster economic growth and development." This report came five years after the end of apartheid, the system of minority white rule that lasted about forty years and prevented South African blacks from sharing equally in the political, economic, and social affairs of the country. The United Nations and other international organizations denounced apartheid. Most countries pressured to eliminate apartheid by imposing trade embargoes and investment restrictions on South Africa and by excluding its sports teams from international competition. At the same time, antiapartheid protests within South Africa crippled the economy at times. South Africa ended apartheid and held democratic elections in 1994. South Africans overwhelmingly elected Nelson Mandela as president, who was a member of the previously outlawed African National Congress (ANC) party and who had spent many years in jail because of his antiapartheid efforts.

Most business managers within and outside South Africa predicted that the 1994 changeover would lead to political instability and an unfavorable governmental attitude toward business. They reasoned that newly elected politicians would seek revenge against whites who had persecuted them and against businesses that some politicians had criticized as being allies of the old regime. However, the political changeover went smoothly, as did the 1998 election of another ANC presidential candidate, Thabo Mbeki. The ANC attitude toward business, especially toward foreign companies, has been favorable. At the time of the political changeover, the new political leaders predicted a flood of incoming foreign investment. They reasoned that foreign businesses would welcome South African opportunities because external sanctions and internal political protests would end. They reasoned that companies that left South Africa during apartheid would quickly return. (For example, 235 of 360 U.S. foreign direct investors left between 1986 and 1991.) However, FDI merely trickled into South Africa between 1994 and 1999. The South African head of Mercedes-Benz summed up the consequence of these two wrong predictions by saying, "What South Africa needs is for the politi-

cal miracle of the last five years to be matched by an economic miracle."

Why does the South African government want FDI? Jobs are the main reason. Estimates on 1999 South African unemployment ranged from 24 to 37 percent. Growth is another reason. South Africa's domestic savings and investment rates are too low to generate sufficient economic growth, particularly because the population rate has been growing at over 2 percent per year. A third reason is that foreign investment in state-owned companies can improve their products and services. For example, South Africa privatized a portion of Telkom, its national telephone company, by selling interests to Ameritech and Telekom Malaysia because service had become so bad that the number of customers was shrinking. Finally, competition from foreign investment can stimulate improvements in South African companies, the government's rationale for opening the banking sector to foreign investors in 1997.

South Africa has about 43 million people, a well-developed infrastructure, a sophisticated financial services sector, a GDP per capita of over $3,000 per year, mineral wealth, and good access to a market of over 100 million people in southern Africa. (Map 11.2 shows South Africa's location.) Yet, investors have been favoring locations elsewhere, such as in China and parts of Latin America. So, why hasn't more FDI gone into South Africa since apartheid? The answer lies in a combination of economic, risk, operational, incentive, and image problems.

Let's first look at economic problems. Investors go where they see large markets and market growth. But the downturn of Asian economies in the mid-1990s hit South Africa's economy hard because the country depended on Asian markets for export sales. World commodity prices on which South Africa depended heavily for export earnings also turned down. For example, the price of gold fell from $388 per ounce in 1996 to $289 per ounce in 1998, a 25-percent decline. Civil unrest and slow economic growth in much of southern Africa, such as in Angola, further hurt South Africa's export sales. Export problems caused declining earnings in South African export industries, and, in turn, stymied South

MAP 11.2   South Africa and Its Location

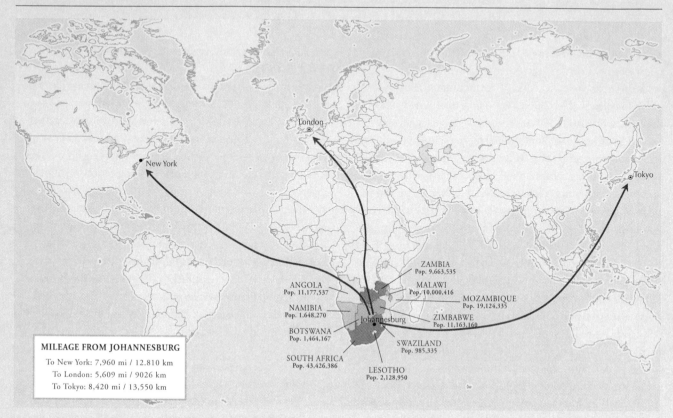

MILEAGE FROM JOHANNESBURG

To New York: 7,960 mi / 12.810 km
To London: 5,609 mi / 9026 km
To Tokyo: 8,420 mi / 13,550 km

ZAMBIA
Pop. 9,663,535

ANGOLA
Pop. 11,177,537

MALAWI
Pop. 10,000,416

MOZAMBIQUE
Pop. 19,124,335

NAMIBIA
Pop. 1,648,270

ZIMBABWE
Pop. 11,163,160

Johannesburg

BOTSWANA
Pop. 1,464,167

SWAZILAND
Pop. 985,335

SOUTH AFRICA
Pop. 43,426,386

LESOTHO
Pop. 2,128,950

London

New York

Tokyo

South Africa's location is advantageous for serving the high-population market of southern Africa. However, the distance figures indicate that South Africa is far from the markets of industrial countries.

African growth. The economic outlook influenced South African companies to make more FDI abroad in the 1991 to 1998 period than non–South African companies made in South Africa.

In terms of political risk, South Africa has enjoyed good political stability, but its crime rate is one of the highest in the world. This creates costs for companies. For example, the head of Wika Instruments, a U.S.-based electronics firm, has had many break-ins and has had to invest heavily in electric fences and security. Potential investors worry about such costs. Security for management transferred to South Africa is another problem. The head of the South African operation of Korean conglomerate Daewoo was shot dead in his car in an apparent bungled hijacking. The World Economic Forum ranks countries by asking international business managers their opinions on a variety of competitive factors. Of the 59 countries they ranked in 1999, South Africa was the lowest on protection provided by local police.

In 1996, the South African government initiated a tax holiday program for companies making new foreign direct investments in South Africa. However, three years later the government abruptly rescinded the program and replaced it with a low tax rate that applied to domestic as well as foreign investors. The rapid change in policy created uncertainty among foreign companies that were considering investments in South Africa. Further, some companies felt the change kept South Africa from being as attractive. For example, a General Motors vice president said, "Governments all over the world are offering competitive tax incentives. South Africa cannot afford not to do the same."

Foreign companies complain about many South African operational problems. They complain of government officials' request for bribes when they bid on government contracts. They complain about the difficulty and bureaucratic cost of complying with the government's affirmative action program to employ and advance more blacks and women. They complain about the shortage of skills, particularly because many educated South Africans are emigrating to other countries. For example, Xerox, which left South Africa in 1989 and returned in 1997, considers the dearth of qualified staff to be its biggest problem. It has set up a training program for technical and sales staff and has adopted a school in the predominately black township of Thembisa.

These problems have created image problems with foreign investors. Further, South Africa is so distant from industrial countries that potential investors either don't think of opportunities there, or they have misconceptions about it. South African officials surveyed corporate executives from around the world and concluded that one U.S. executive's response, "We still see South Africa as one big game reserve," typified its problem of attracting foreign investment. Abroad, people have the popular notion that South Africa's economy is dominated by mining, which now accounts for only about 8 percent of GDP. Abroad, people think that most of the world's diamonds come from South Africa, even though South Africa is only the world's fifth largest producer. The government of South Africa is convinced it needs to do a better job of marketing itself to potential investors.

In 1999 the South African government initiated an ambitious and unusual plan to attract more FDI. It will give $5 billion in defense contracts to foreign companies. These companies will have to provide state-of-the-art weapons and equipment, *and* they must develop new investments in South Africa. If a defense contractor lacks expertise in an industry

South Africa wants to attract, say, to build and operate a steel mill, it can recruit a partner that does. The government quickly negotiated deals for nearly $17 billion in development projects in such areas as automotive components, telecommunications, chemicals, and high-quality textiles. In addition, the government has a procurement policy that requires foreign suppliers to offset a portion of their sales with South African investments that will create jobs. There is a formula of required offset based on the salaries and wages the FDI pays in South Africa. Payments to previously disadvantaged workers count double.

Not everyone in South Africa agrees that the government should be attracting FDI. Many argue that much recent investment has been buyouts of South African companies that contribute little new economic benefit. Others criticize the use of defense contracts as leverage. They argue that South Africa has no outside military threats and perhaps needs no military at all. South Africa's Anglican archbishop said, "This would have been a good opportunity to do things differently and concentrate on the internal threats to democracy: threats from poverty, from joblessness, from lack of education, from crimes, from AIDS. The list goes on and on."

QUESTIONS

1. What are the costs and benefits to South Africa of having more foreign direct investment?
2. If South Africa is to receive more foreign direct investment, how should it prioritize policies to attract it?
3. Assume you represent a non–South African company and are considering foreign expansion. What factors would you consider when comparing South Africa with other countries where you might locate?
4. Discuss South Africa's "guns-for-FDI" program from the standpoint of benefits and problems for South Africa and for companies participating.

CHAPTER NOTES

1   The quotation is from Jonathan Kwitny, "U.S. Concerns Export Mainland-Bound Goods as Embargo Loosens," *Wall Street Journal*, March 11, 1971, p. 1. Other data were taken from Ian Johnson, "China Makes Cutbacks in Industrial Investment," *Wall Street Journal*, February 4, 1999, p. A17; Leslie Chang and Ian Johnson, "Foreign Investment in China Falls; Beijing's Policies May Be the Cause," *Wall Street Journal*, August 20, 1999, p. A9; Colm Foy and Angus Madison, "China: A World Economic Leader?" *Observer*, No. 215, January 1999, pp. 39–42; Lionel Barber, "Foreign Investment: A Palpable Shift in Sentiment," *Financial Times*, October 1, 1999, p. iii; Paulus Chan, "Doing Business in China: Trade, Legal and Cultural Considerations," *Nonwovens Industry*, February 1996; "China Investment Opportunities," www.aloha.com/ ~uci/chinainv/500.htm; Robert F. Dodds, Jr., "Offsets in Chinese Government Procurement: The Partially Open Door," *Law and Policy in International Business*, Vol. 26, No. 4, June 22, 1995, p. 1119; Aimin Yan and Barbara Gray, "Bargaining Power, Management Control, and Performance in United States–China Joint Ventures: A Comparative Case Study,"

Academy of Management Journal, Vol. 37, December 1994, p. 1478; Stanely Lubman, "What Dispute? Conflicts Between Chinese and Foreign Partners in Joint Ventures," *China Business Review*, Vol. 22, No. 3, May 1995, p. 46; "Guangzhou Evaluates Foreign Investment," *Xinhua News Agency*, February 17, 1995; Gregory E. Osland and Tamer S. Cavusgil, "Performance Issues in U.S.-China Joint Ventures," *California Management Review*, January 1996, p. 106; Nicholas Reynolds, "End of an Era Flagged as Garment Giant Crosses the Border," *South China Morning Post*, May 29, 1995, business section p. 3.

2 For many comparative statistics, see "GM: A Global Colossus That Is Richer Than Most Nations," *New York Times*, July 26, 1998, sec. 4, p. 4.

3 Jean J. Boddewyn and Thomas L. Brewer, "International-Business Political Behavior: New Theoretical Directions," *Academy of Management Review*, Vol. 19, 1994, pp. 119–143.

4 John H. Dunning, "The Future of Multinational Enterprise," *Lloyds Bank Review*, July 1974, p. 16.

5 *World Investment Report 1999: Foreign Direct Investment and the Challenge of Development* (Geneva: UNCTAD, 1999).

6 See also Paul Krugman, "A Country Is Not a Company," *Harvard Business Review*, January–February 1996, pp. 40–51.

7 John Plender, "Taming Wild Money," *Financial Times*, October 20, 1998, p. 17.

8 International Monetary Fund, *International Capital Markets: Developments, Prospects and Policy Issues* (Washington, D.C.: IMF, 1995); James Kynge, "China Orders Companies to Repatriate Dollar Holdings," *Financial Times*, September 30, 1998, p. 1.

9 Peter Wilamoski and Sarah Tinkler, "The Trade Balance Effects of U.S. Foreign Direct Investment in Mexico," *Atlantic Economic Journal*, Vol. 27, No. 1, March 1999, pp. 24–37.

10 Jeff Cole, Marcus W. Brauchli, and Craig S. Smith, "Orient Express," *Wall Street Journal*, October 13, 1995, p. A1; Craig Smith and David P. Hamilton, "Price of Entry into China Rises Sharply," *Wall Street Journal*, December 19, 1995, p. A12.

11 Keith Bradsher, "Skilled Workers Watch Their Jobs Migrate Overseas," *New York Times*, August 28, 1995, p. A1, quoting opinions of Jagdish Bhagwati.

12 Robert Feenstra and Gordon Hanson, "Foreign Investment, Outsourcing, and Relative Wages," Working Paper No. 5121 (Cambridge, MA: National Bureau of Economic Research, 1995). See also Fred R. Bleakley, "U.S. Firms Shift More Office Jobs Abroad," *Wall Street Journal*, April 22, 1996, p. A2.

13 Sally Bowen, "Developing a Refined Atmosphere," *Financial Times*, April 19, 1999, p. 12.

14 Ernest Beck and Emily Nelson, "Differences of Style," *Wall Street Journal*, October 6, 1999, p. A1; and Peter Montagnon and Michiyo Nakamoto, "Tokyo Gives Blessing to Foreign Takeovers," *Financial Times*, June 17, 1998, p. 6. However, evidence is inconclusive on the extent that local companies benefit from efficiencies that foreign companies bring in. See Brian J. Aitken and Ann E. Harrison, "Do Domestic Firms Benefit from Direct Foreign Investment? Evidence from Venezuela," *American Economic Review*, Vol. 89, No. 3, June 1999, pp. 605–618.

15 Timothy Aeppel, "Scaling the Ladder," *Wall Street Journal*, April 6, 1999, p. A1.

16 "The Road Ahead," *Financial Times*, August 26, 1996, p. 16.

17 Haishun Sun, "Macroeconomic Impact of DFI in China: 1979–96," *The World Economy*, Vol. 21, No. 5, July 1998, pp. 675–694.

18 Sanjaya Lall, *Changing Perceptions of Direct Foreign Investment in Development*, CIMBDA discussion paper No. E19 (Antwerp: University of Antwerp, 1995).

19 Theodore H. Moran, *Foreign Direct Investment and Development: The New Policy Agenda for Developing Countries and Economies in Transition* (Washington, D.C.: Institute for International Economics, 1998).

20 David J. Teece, "Foreign Investment and Technological Development in Silicon Valley," *California Management Review*, Vol. 34, No. 2, Winter 1992, pp. 88–106.

21 Manuel G. Serapio and Donald H. Dalton, "Globalization of Industrial R&D: An Examination of Foreign Direct Investments in R&D in the United States," *Research Policy*, No. 28, 1999, pp. 303–316.

22 Martin Feldstein, "Outbound FDI Increases National Income," *NBER Digest*, August 1994, p. 4.

23 Barry P. Bosworth and Susan M. Collins, "Capital Flows to Developing Economies: Implications for Saving and Investment," *Brookings Papers on Economic Activity* (Washington, D.C.: 1999), pp. 143–164.

24 Alan M. Rugman and Alain Verbeke, "Multinational Enterprises and Public Policy," *Journal of International Business Studies*, Vol. 29, No. 1, 1998, pp. 115–136; and David A. Lake, "Global Governance: A Relational Contracting Approach," in Aseem Prakash and Jeffrey A. Hart, eds., *Globalization and Governance* (London: Routledge, 1999), pp. 31–53.

25 Winfried Ruigrok, "Why Nationality Is Still Important," *Financial Times*, January 5, 1996, p. 8, referring to 1993 data from Winfried Ruigrok and Rob van Tulder, *The Logic of International Restructuring* (London: Routledge, 1995).

26 Afshin Molavi, "Senate Targets Libya Investors," *Financial Times*, December 22, 1995, p. 5; Robert S. Greenberger and Laurie Lande,

"Europeans Are Irked by Senate Move to Punish Foreign Investments in Libya," *Wall Street Journal*, December 22, 1995, p. A4; "Iran Scorns U.S. Plan to Step Up Sanctions," *Financial Times*, December 6, 1995, p. 7; Afshin Molavi and Bruce Clark, "Clinton Ready to Tighten Iran Stranglehold," *Financial Times*, November 17, 1995, p. 4.

27 Eduardo Lachica, "U.S. Decides to Enforce Antitrust Laws Against Collusion by Foreign Concerns," *Wall Street Journal*, April 7, 1992, p. C9.

28 These are but a few of the types of antitrust actions. See J. Townsend, "Extraterritorial Antitrust Revisited—Half a Century of Change," paper presented at the Academy of International Business, San Francisco, December 1983; "U.S. Seeks to Block Gillette's Purchase of Wilkinson Assets," *Wall Street Journal*, January 11, 1990, p. B6; and "U.S. Wins Accord with British on Glass Factories," *Wall Street Journal*, May 27, 1994, p. A12.

29 Yao-Su Hu, "Global or Stateless Corporations Are National Firms with International Operations," *California Management Review*, Vol. 34, No. 2, Winter 1992, pp. 107–126.

30 Richard Falk, "Toward Obsolescence: Sovereignty in the Era of Globalization," *Harvard International Review*, Summer 1995, pp. 34–35.

31 "What Is NAFTA?" *Wall Street Journal*, September 15, 1993, p. A16.

32 Edward Luce and Ted Bardacke, "Thailand and Philippines Compete for $1bn Car Plant," *Financial Times*, December 5, 1995, p. 1.

33 Richard Waters, "U.S. Big Business Fears Sanctions," *Financial Times*, May 16, 1996, p. 4.

34 Maureen Kline, "Three U.S.-Related Companies Dragged into Italian Investigation," *Wall Street Journal*, June 25, 1993, p. A7.

35 Robert S. Greenberger, "Foreigners Use Bribes to Beat U.S. Rivals in Many Deals, New Report Concludes," *Wall Street Journal*, October 12, 1995, p. 3; Robert Keatley, "U.S. Campaign Against Bribery Faces Resistance from Foreign Governments," *Wall Street Journal*, February 4, 1994, p. A6.

36 Nancy Dunne, "Kantor Calls for Bribery Action," *Financial Times*, July 26, 1996, p. 3.

37 Dana Milbank and Marcus W. Brauchli, "Greasing Wheels," *Wall Street Journal*, September 29, 1995, p. A1.

38 "Mexico Asks IBM for Proof of Alleged Bribe Request," *Wall Street Journal*, February 8, 1993. For the means-versus-end discussion, see Kent Hodgson, "Adapting Ethical Decisions to a Global Marketplace," *Management Review*, May 1992, pp. 53–57.

39 Nancy Dunne, "Bribery 'Helps Win Contracts in Developing World,'" *Financial Times*, January 21, 2000, p. 6, referring to a Gallup Poll survey of almost 800 executives.

40 Ibid.

41 Marcus W. Brauchli, Matthew Rose, and Jonathan Friedland, "Foreign Donors: We Have a Stake in America, Too," *Wall Street Journal,* October 31, 1996, p. A19.

42 William J. Holstein, Stanley Reed, Jonathan Kapstein, Todd Vogel, and Joseph Weber, "The Stateless Corporation," *Business Week,* May 14, 1990, p. 103.

43 Shujaat Islam, "Producing Prosperity: Multinationals in the Developing World," *Harvard International Review,* Spring 1993, pp. 42–44.

44 Victor Mallet, "Crisis Weathered Successfully: South Africa," *Financial Times,* September 24, 1999, world economy and finance section, p. 30; Carolyn Southey, "Investors Seek More Incentives," *Financial Times,* March 23, 1999, survey section, p. 1; Jon Jeter, "South Africa's Image Problem Deters Investors," *Washington Post,* October 17, 1999, p. A21; Ben Laurance, "South Africa: Down but Not Out," *The Observer,* February 14, 1999, p. 4; "Foreign Banks Move In," *The Banker,* Vol. 147, No. 858, August 1997, pp. 50–52; "Governor Goes for Gradualism," *The Banker,* Vol. 147, No. 858, August 1997, pp. 54–56; Jon Jeter, "South Africa Uses Arms Sales to Aid Economy," *Washington Post,* September 26, 1999, p. A25; Bernard Simon, "Shopping with Precision: Defense Offset," *Financial Times,* March 23, 1999, p. 4; Victor Mallet, "Battle to Keep Investment Flowing," March 23, 1999, survey edition, p. 1; Adrienne Roberts, "Overseas Interest Hard to Pin Down," *Financial Times,* September 20, 1999, survey edition, p. 4; and "Business: VeldCom," *Economist,* Vol. 347, No. 8068, May 16, 1998, p. 64.

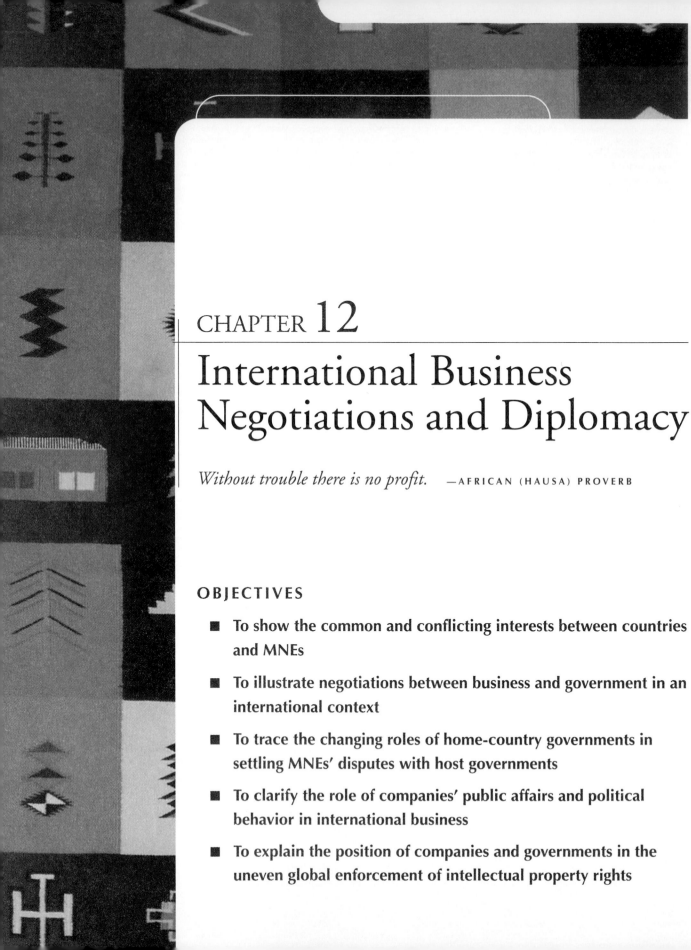

CHAPTER 12

International Business Negotiations and Diplomacy

Without trouble there is no profit. —AFRICAN (HAUSA) PROVERB

OBJECTIVES

■ To show the common and conflicting interests between countries and MNEs

■ To illustrate negotiations between business and government in an international context

■ To trace the changing roles of home-country governments in settling MNEs' disputes with host governments

■ To clarify the role of companies' public affairs and political behavior in international business

■ To explain the position of companies and governments in the uneven global enforcement of intellectual property rights

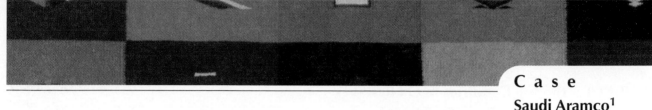

The companies holding the largest oil reserves in the world are all state owned. The biggest of these companies is Saudi Aramco. It ranks first in sales and reserves and third in refining. When there is concern over oil supply, Saudi Aramco can wield considerable clout. It has been able to influence other oil producers in OPEC to cut supplies and raise prices. However, when global oil supply greatly exceeds demand, petroleum producers without integrated refining and marketing operations are basically price takers. Recent disagreements within OPEC, along with increased production elsewhere, have prompted Saudi Aramco to secure sales through international vertical integration. At the same time, the company has been able to promise future energy supplies in exchange for permission to gain ownership on acceptable terms in foreign refining and marketing.

Because the Saudi Arabian government owns Saudi Aramco, it is difficult to separate company policies from those of the government–particularly since CEO Ali Naimi was appointed the country's oil minister in 1995. Further, many of Saudi Aramco's foreign deals are with state-owned oil companies, bringing into play the governmental interests of other countries. Reviewing some events that preceded and followed Aramco's first oil output in 1939 will help you understand changing Saudi-U.S. governmental relationships, private oil companies' positions in Saudi Arabia, and Saudi Aramco's strategy.

U.S. policy toward U.S. oil companies historically has fostered safeguarding sufficient and cheap oil supplies for U.S. needs and strengthening the U.S. political position in strategic areas worldwide. At least as far back as 1920, the United States realized that for the long term its own oil reserves were insufficient. In the short term, however, worldwide oil could not be sold as rapidly as it was being produced, and U.S. oil companies moved into a position to serve both U.S. and Middle Eastern interests. (The Middle East accounts for about two-thirds of the world's oil reserves. Map 12.1 shows that the world's top five countries in terms of proven oil reserves are all in the Middle East.) In the 1920s and 1930s, the U.S. government wanted U.S. oil companies to gain concessions in the Middle East to help ensure a long-term U.S. supply— and to weaken the positions of the British and the French. The U.S. companies were welcomed in the Middle East because they offered a degree of access to the U.S. market that would otherwise be impossible.

The first two U.S. companies to participate in Saudi Arabian oil production were Socal (Standard Oil of California) and Texaco, which formed a joint venture and negotiated large concessions in the 1930s. They built Saudi Arabia's first schools and compiled its first historical records. The U.S. government had no representatives there at that time, so the two companies conducted some quasi-official diplomacy that continued throughout World War II. They organized construction of a pipeline to the Mediterranean in 1945. In 1948, Exxon and Mobil joined Socal and Texaco in what became Aramco. Mobil owned 10 percent, and each of the others held a 30-percent interest.

These four companies, along with three others (Gulf, Shell, and BP), were known as the Seven Sisters. Before the 1970s, they collectively controlled such a large share of the world's oil from multiple sources that they were nearly invulnerable to the actions of any single country. The Cold War put a premium on maintaining cordial relations with strategic countries, and when Saudi Arabia's King Ibn-Saud demanded substantial revenue increases from Aramco, the U.S. government became directly involved in the negotiations. In 1951, the Saudi government

MAP 12.1 The Top Countries in Oil Reserves

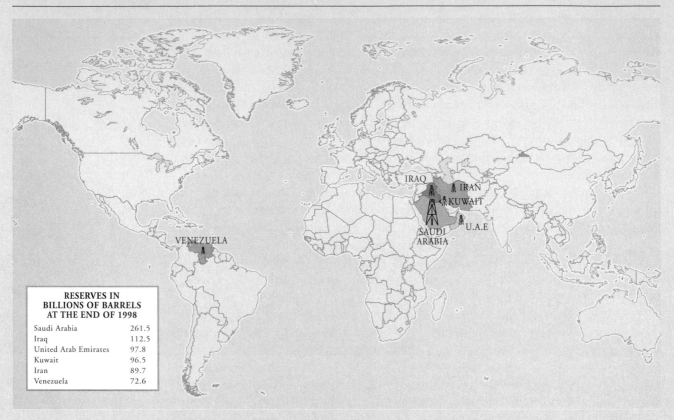

RESERVES IN BILLIONS OF BARRELS AT THE END OF 1998	
Saudi Arabia	261.5
Iraq	112.5
United Arab Emirates	97.8
Kuwait	96.5
Iran	89.7
Venezuela	72.6

About two-thirds of the world's known oil reserves are in the Middle East. The top five countries in terms of reserves are also in the Middle East.

Source: Bhushran Bahree, "Royal Dutch/Shell Group to Invest $800 Million in Iran," *Wall Street Journal*, November 16, 1999, p. 21, reporting data from BP Amoco Statistical Review.

allowed the oil companies to maintain their ownership in exchange for their payment of 50 percent of profits as taxes to Saudi Arabia. The U.S. government allowed the companies to deduct those taxes from their U.S. tax bills, placing the revenue increase to Saudi Arabia entirely at the expense of the U.S. Treasury.

In 1952, Saudi Arabia learned from Iran's experience what might happen if demands on Aramco were pushed further. Iran expelled Shah Reza Pahlavi and nationalized (took owner-ship of) British oil holdings. All major oil companies boycotted Iranian oil and brought its gov-ernment to the brink of economic collapse. With CIA support, the shah returned, and a new oil company replaced the nationalized holdings. The Seven Sisters shared 95-percent ownership of this new Iranian oil company.

When the Seven Sisters gained 95 percent of the Iranian oil holdings, the other 5 percent went to smaller, independent U.S. companies that previously had depended on the Seven Sis-ters for supplies. This marked the beginning of greater competition among distributors. It also meant producing countries could make agreements with the independents to gain a greater portion of the spoils. Yet as late as 1960, the producing countries were still unable to prevent the major oil companies from unilaterally repealing concessions by reducing the price they paid for oil. This price decrease, which reduced host government revenues, led to a meeting in Caracas of representatives from five oil-producing countries (Iran, Iraq, Kuwait, Saudi Arabia, and Venezuela) and the formation of the Organization of Petroleum Exporting Countries (OPEC). OPEC's purposes were to prevent oil companies from lowering the prices they paid them, to gain a greater share of oil revenues, and to move toward domestic rather than foreign ownership of the assets. At the time, however, OPEC lacked the power to achieve its goals.

Three new trends during the 1960s weakened the Seven Sisters and strengthened Saudi Arabia's position in Aramco.

1. More oil companies emerged and gained concessions in countries previously not among the major suppliers, such as Occidental in Libya, ENI in the former Soviet Union, and CFP in Algeria. These smaller companies lacked the Seven Sisters' diversification of supplies and were less able to move to other supply sources if a host country tried to change the terms of an agreement unilaterally.

2. Because of rapid expansion among industrial countries, oil demand grew faster than supply—the earlier oil glut was shrinking rapidly. No longer could even the Seven Sisters afford to boycott major supplier countries as they had earlier boycotted Iran.

3. The threat of military intervention to protect oil investors was lessening. The United States' failure to support the unsuccessful efforts of the British, French, and Israelis in preventing the Egyptian takeover of the Suez Canal in 1956 demonstrated that the major Western powers were unlikely to unify their efforts. The Soviet Union's growing strength meant there was a greater risk of a major war resulting from such intervention. The United States also was increasing its military involvement in an unpopular war in Vietnam in the 1960s and so was less able or inclined to lend military support to U.S. oil companies in the Middle East.

In 1970, Muammar al-Gaddafi of Libya demanded increased prices from Occidental. Because Occidental was almost completely dependent on Libya for its crude oil supply, the company relented. Gaddafi then did likewise to other oil companies and gained concessions from them as well. Other countries noted Libya's success, and they used OPEC to bolster their positions when dealing with the oil companies. OPEC's Teheran Agreement of 1971 boosted oil prices, but it was the 1973 embargo that proved they had sufficient power to back up their demands. OPEC then had 11 members and controlled about 93 percent of the world's oil exports.

As the largest OPEC oil-producing country, Saudi Arabia was able to use its strengths in several ways. Between 1972 and 1980, it bought out the Aramco partners, changed the name to Saudi Aramco, and increased the number of customers for its crude from the original four Aramco partners, even as the small companies built market share.

How did the former owners (Exxon, Texaco, Socal, and Mobil) fare in Saudi Arabia after the Saudi government bought them out? Initially, they helped manage the Saudi oil industry by making contributions that the Saudis could not gain easily from other sources, such as training Saudis and attracting qualified personnel from abroad, as well as managing the Saudi operation efficiently. As Saudi Aramco expanded, the four continued these efforts through lucrative contract arrangements. For example, Mobil became a joint venture partner with the

Saudi government in a refinery and a petrochemical complex. Mobil and others marketed crude oil exports when sales were not made directly to a foreign government, an important factor in the late 1980s when there was a glut due to new supplies (for example, from Mexico) and decreased demand. Further, the four oil companies provided valuable technical assistance in finding and extracting oil.

After the Saudi government took complete ownership of Aramco, it began to replace foreign management with Saudi management until Saudis held all top positions. It also gradually decreased its dependence on the four former U.S. owners. Its ability to do so was the result of several factors.

1. The number of oil companies worldwide grew, giving the Saudis more choice in where to contract services and sell crude oil.
2. Engineering giants, such as Bechtel and Fluor, have increasingly been competing to sell management and engineering services once available only from the oil companies.
3. The international boycott of Iraqi oil after Iraq invaded Kuwait left some countries seeking new supplies. Saudi Aramco could sell directly to those countries and decrease its dependence on private oil companies to serve as intermediaries.
4. Global market growth was shifting toward east and south Asia where there were government-owned companies to whom Saudi Aramco could sell.

Meanwhile, Saudi Aramco grew less confident about OPEC's ability to stabilize world oil supplies and prices. The problem of rising production by non-OPEC members was worsened by the reluctance of some OPEC countries (particularly Venezuela and Nigeria) to cut back production or keep to agreed-upon quotas.

Saudi Aramco has come to view international vertical integration as the best way to ensure a market for Saudi crude. Its first movement was to enter into a joint venture with Texaco in 1988, buying a 50-percent interest in Texaco's refining assets and marketing system in 23 U.S. states. This was followed by a joint venture in South Korea with Ssangyong in 1991. In 1994 it took a 40-percent stake in Petron, the largest refiner and distributor in the Philippines. Two years later, Saudi Aramco acquired a 45-percent interest in Petrogal, Portugal's largest company and owner of three refineries, and Galp, Portugal's largest chain of gasoline stations. It acquired "a large minority share" in the Italian company Erg, which owned 3 refineries and 2,200 fuel stations in Italy. It bought a half share in the Greek Vardinoyannis oil group and announced two joint ventures in India, one with Hindustan Petroleum Oil and one with the Indian Oil Corporation. In 1998, it formed a joint venture with Shell and Texaco that created the largest refiner and marketer of petroleum products in the United States.

Clearly, Saudi Aramco's position has evolved substantially as a result of changing supply-demand, competitive, and political conditions. Recently, the company has come closer to the stated strategy of its CEO, Abdallah S. Jum'ah: "to develop a global presence in the refining and retail sectors."

The operating terms of international companies

- Are influenced by governments of home and host countries
- Shift as priorities shift and as strengths of parties change

INTRODUCTION

Chapter 11 discussed how home and host countries evaluate MNEs. But evaluation is only part of the story. After that comes negotiation, and that's where business-government relationships become difficult. Governments may refuse companies original or

FIGURE 12.1   Business-Government Negotiations in International Operations

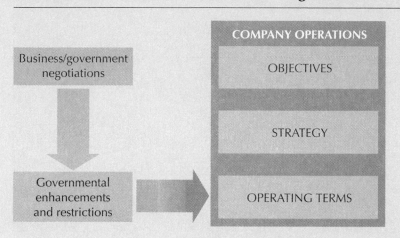

Negotiations between businesses and governments influence governmental enhancements and restrictions that determine companies' operating terms.

continued operating permission. At the same time, companies will not operate unless their terms of business are favorable. But countries and companies do come to agreements that, although not usually ideal for either party, are sufficient for an evolving relationship. The business negotiations and diplomacy between companies and governments determine the terms of international business operations. Figure 12.1 shows the relationships.

GOVERNMENTAL VERSUS COMPANY STRENGTH IN NEGOTIATIONS

As the Saudi Aramco case illustrates, both home- and host-country policies greatly influence the terms under which companies operate abroad. These strengths depend on such factors as competitive changes, the resources the parties have at their disposal, validation by public opinion, and joint efforts with other parties. However, companies have different viewpoints on how much they can influence their operating terms. Governments also have different viewpoints on how much power they can exert over international companies.

HIERARCHICAL VIEW OF GOVERNMENTAL AUTHORITY

Governments have regulations affecting international business. In a hierarchical view of governmental authority, companies accept regulations as "givens," in which case they comply with, circumvent, or avoid operating because of the regulations. Companies will comply when the regulations don't unduly constrain their desired mode of operations, when benefits are sufficiently attractive in spite of regulations, and when they cannot practically alter the regulations to their benefit. Companies will circumvent regulations they find unacceptable through loopholes, legal or illegal. For example, a firm's ability to control a foreign subsidiary in spite of a country's requirement for shared ownership might be possible if the company makes a side agreement with a local partner not to

An ongoing controversy is the effect of companies' international expansion on host countries and regions. Here we see the Carajas Mining Project in the Para state of Brazil. It brings needed jobs and economic development to people in one of the poorest areas of the world, but the cost is potential, irreparable damage to areas that are important to the world's ecology.

vote its shares of stock. Avoidance is simply the reverse of compliance as a company decides not to operate in a given locale because of its regulations.[2]

BARGAINING VIEW

MNEs and host countries have mutually useful assets.

As discussed in Chapter 11, the host country and the MNE may each control assets that are useful to the other. **Bargaining school theory** holds that the negotiated terms for a foreign investor's operations depend on how much the investor and host country need each other's assets.[3] If either a company or a country has assets that the other strongly desires and if there are few (or no) alternatives for acquiring them, negotiated concessions may be very one-sided. For example, the Saudi Aramco case illustrated that when a few large companies dominated the extraction, processing, shipment, and final sale of an oversupply of oil, emerging economies with petroleum deposits could do little but accept the terms they were offered because they lacked alternatives for exploiting their oil. If a government refused the terms, a company could easily find another country that would accept a similar proposal. As the supply of oil diminished and petroleum-producing countries found alternatives, the terms gradually favored producing countries.

But such shifts in needs have not always favored countries. For example, because of slow economic growth, in 1999 several oil-exporting countries sought to attract more FDI in their oil industries.[4] There are vast differences in bargaining strength among countries, among industries, and among companies.

Alternative sources for acquiring resources affect company and country bargaining strengths.

The bargaining relationship between companies and governments depends very much on whether the parties see agreements as zero-sum (one party's gain equals the other party's loss) or positive-sum (both parties have net benefits) gains. In the former, relationships may conflict because the parties think they lose by making any concessions. In the latter, the relationship may be seen as a partnership of cooperation and interdependence.[5]

Country Bargaining Strength   Generally, companies prefer to establish investments in highly developed countries because those countries offer large markets and a high degree of political stability. Countries such as the United States, Canada, and Germany are large recipients of foreign investment. Because they are such attractive countries to invest in, they make few concessions to MNEs. In all of these countries, however, regional areas vie for investments by offering incentives. For example, several U.S. states vied for a Mitsubishi polysilicon plant, and Alabama gave Mitsubishi a tax credit, $40 million in infrastructure, and training aids to get the investment.[6] If incentives are used, they are most appealing when they fit closely with companies' corporate strategies and when companies believe that the government has the credibility to fulfill its promises.[7]

The biggest bargaining strengths for countries are
- **Large markets**
- **Political stability**

Company Bargaining Strength   Some industries have traditionally enjoyed better bargaining positions than others. Foreign ownership in such areas as agriculture and extractive industries is not very welcome in many countries because of historical foreign domination of these sectors and the belief that the land and subsoil are public resources. Without a strong welcome, foreign companies in these industries lack strong bargaining positions.

Company bargaining assets include
- **Technology**
- **Marketing expertise**
- **Ability to export output**
- **Local product diversity**

The bargain struck between the foreign investor and the host country also depends on the number of companies offering similar resources. For example, GM and Ford competed for rights to build sedans in China, and GM and Daewoo competed to acquire a state-owned company in Poland.[8] Host countries could, therefore, play off one competitor against the other. Foreign investors are more likely to have a strong bargaining position in foreign operations when they have few competitors and when they control certain types of assets. These assets include:[9]

- *Technology.* For example, governments have allowed IBM 100-percent ownership of operations in a number of countries because of the local need for its unique technology. However, they have refused other companies the same ownership. The French government also approved IBM's minority stake in state-owned Groupe Bull because of the company's specialized technology.[10]
- *Marketing expertise.* For example, Coca-Cola apparently has been able to gain local consumer allies who believe its differentiated products are superior.
- *Ability to export output from the foreign investment, especially when exports go to other entities controlled by the parent company.* These investments earn foreign exchange for the country that might otherwise not be forthcoming. Recall from the China case in Chapter 11 that exporters are more welcomed than are companies seeking only to sell within China.
- *Product diversity.* Governments will allow more foreign ownership when a company provides greater product diversity, probably because a variety of products can save foreign exchange through import substitution. In the past, if a company offered to invest a large amount of capital, it did not usually affect its bargaining power. At least two factors played a role here:
  1. A large investment may be examined much more closely than a small one because of the potential impact (positive or negative) it might have on the economy. That is, the host country wants the benefits of the capital inflow but is leery of being so dependent on foreign ownership.
  2. The host-country government may be more likely to borrow funds externally to invest in large enterprises.

However, if a company has the ability to contribute large amounts of capital, this may improve its future bargaining strengths. Many emerging economies have encountered debt-servicing problems since the mid-1980s, so they must depend more on FDI for their future capital needs. Governments may not want to commit resources to negotiating with companies that are too small to make a substantial impact on their economies. So companies with small proposals may not be approved because they never reach the point of even being seriously considered.

JOINT COMPANY ACTIVITIES

To counter too high a dependence on foreign companies, countries have encouraged their own manufacturers to consolidate. They have given governmental assistance for R&D and preference to their own companies in awarding governmental contracts. The most notable effort has been the development of Airbus Industrie, a consortium in Europe to compete against Boeing in aircraft production. Other European cross-national efforts have occurred in such fields as consumer appliances, medical electronics, telecommunications, and television. For example, the Eureka program includes about 7,000 companies from 33 countries (30 of which are European) to develop a wide range of technologies.[11]

Two or more companies from different countries sometimes invest jointly abroad, not so much to strengthen the initial negotiating terms as to improve their positions in later negotiations. By investing a smaller amount in a given locality, each company can invest in more countries, reducing the impact of loss in one. Further, in conflicts, a host government may be more hesitant to deal simultaneously with more than one home government.

HOME-COUNTRY NEEDS

The interplay between an MNE's needs and those of the host country is not the only bargaining factor in negotiations. The home-country government seldom takes a neutral position in the relationship. Like the host-country government, the home-country government is interested in achieving certain economic objectives, such as increased tax revenues and full employment. It may give incentives to or place constraints on the foreign expansion of home-based companies in order to gain what it sees as its due share of the rewards from their transactions. Recall from the Saudi Aramco case that the U.S. government gave oil companies tax concessions so they could exploit foreign opportunities. However, the home or host government's influence on MNEs is tempered by the political interests and relations of the two governments.

When economic and political stakes are high, companies' home governments often help them sell. For example, when Turkey announced that it would place a large order for tanks, the governments of France, Germany, the United States, and Ukraine all dealt directly with the Turkish government to help secure the sales.[12]

OTHER EXTERNAL PRESSURES ON NEGOTIATION OUTCOMES

The complementary nature of the assets that MNEs and countries control would seem, at first, to dictate a mutual interest in doing business. Although there are pressures to find mutual interests, there are also constraints, particularly on governmental decision makers. Pressure may come from local companies with which the foreign investor is presently or potentially competing, from political opponents who seize the "external" issue as a means of turning voters against present political leadership, or from critics who reason that more benefits may accrue to the country if the government takes a strong stance against an MNE's proposal. Home-country governments may respond to their local pressure groups in ways that affect relationships with other governments, causing unexpected repercussions for MNEs. For example, yielding to pressure from its garment industry, the United Kingdom limited imports of Indonesian T-shirts, and the Indonesian government retaliated by denying the construction of a British-owned chemical project.[13] Companies also may face pressures from stockholders, workers, consumers, governmental officials, suppliers, and non-governmental organizations (NGOs) concerned with their own interests. These pressures may result in a relationship between company and host country quite different from what either expected. Managers and government officials should understand the types and strengths of these external groups because they affect the extent to which either side may be able to give in on issues.

NEGOTIATIONS IN INTERNATIONAL BUSINESS

Negotiations are a means by which a company may initiate, carry on, or terminate operations in a foreign country. At one time, negotiations were prevalent only for direct investments. However, today they play a part in other operating arrangements, such as licensing agreements, debt repayment, and large-scale export sales. The negotiation process often leads to multitiered bargaining: An MNE may need to reach an agreement with a local company to purchase an interest in it, sell technology or products to it, or loan money to it. That agreement must sometimes be presented to a host-country agency that may approve, disapprove, or propose entirely new terms. The MNE may need to negotiate with its home government to transfer technology or borrow funds. The home and host governments may negotiate loans, investment guarantees, and overall economic and political relationships. Figure 12.2 shows these multiple relationships. Even when some of these parties do not directly take part in the negotiations, the participants may take their needs into consideration.

> **Terms for operations are often decided in interrelated negotiations.**

BARGAINING PROCESS

Comprehensive bargaining among companies and governments may begin long before they agree (if they ever agree) on MNEs' terms of operations. Behavioral factors in addition to economic ones affect the agreement terms. They may renegotiate these terms later.

Acceptance Zones Before taking part in overseas negotiations, a manager probably has some experience with a domestic bargaining process similar to that in the foreign sphere. For example, collective bargaining with labor as well as agreements to acquire or merge facilities with another company usually start with an array of proposals, just like negotiations with foreign organizations. The proposals undoubtedly include provisions that one side or the other is willing either to give up entirely or to compromise on. These provisions are used as bargaining tokens, permitting each side to claim that it is reluctantly giving in on some point in exchange for compromise on another point. They also serve as face-saving devices, allowing either side to report to interested parties that

> **In the bargaining process, agreement occurs only if there are overlapping acceptance zones.**

FIGURE 12.2   Interrelated Negotiations

Interrelated negotiations may be necessary to reach agreement for foreign operating terms.

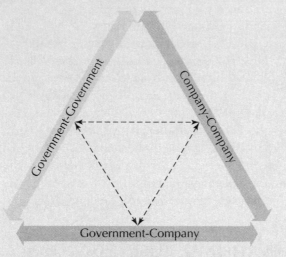

Source: From John M. Stopford and Susan Strange, *Rival States, Rival Firms*, 1991, Cambridge University Press. Reprinted with permission.

it managed to extract concessions. On some points, however, it is unlikely that any compromise can be reached.

As in domestic negotiations, the outcome of foreign negotiations will depend partly on other recent negotiations or events, which serve as models. Abroad, what has transpired recently either between other companies and a host-country government or between similar types of companies or the same company in similar countries may serve as a common reference. Negotiations are unlikely to stray too far from that established precedent.

Finally, there are zones of acceptance and nonacceptance for the proposals presented. If the acceptance zones overlap, an agreement is possible. If zones have no overlap, positive negotiations are not possible. For example, if GM insisted on 51-percent ownership of an Indian facility but would accept up to 100 percent and the Indian government or partner insisted on 51-percent local ownership but would accept up to 75 percent, there would be no overlap of acceptance zones in which to negotiate. However, if Ford insisted on a "significant" interest in an Indian facility (say, 25 percent) but would take as much as it could get and the Indian government or partner required 51-percent local ownership and wanted to maximize it, there would be a wide zone acceptable to both parties—for instance, 25 to 49 percent for Ford's ownership. (See Figure 12.3.) The final agreement would depend on each party's negotiating ability and strengths and on the other concessions that each made in the process. Because each side could only speculate on how far the other was willing to go, the exact amount of ownership allowed might fall anywhere within the overlapping acceptance zones.

Range of Provisions   The major difference between domestic and foreign negotiations is a matter of degree. International negotiations may take much longer and may include provisions unheard of in the home country, such as a negotiated tax

FIGURE 12.3   Acceptance Zones in Negotiating

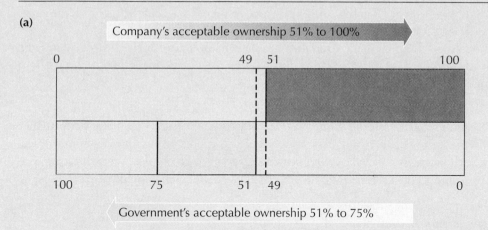

(a)

Company's acceptable ownership 51% to 100%

Government's acceptable ownership 51% to 75%

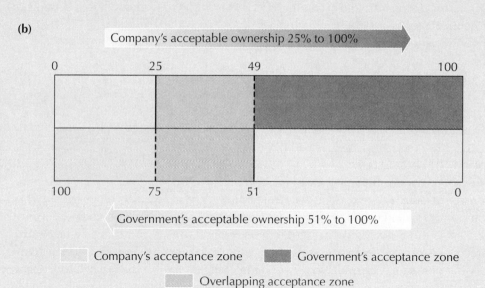

(b)

Company's acceptable ownership 25% to 100%

Government's acceptable ownership 51% to 100%

▢ Company's acceptance zone   ▢ Government's acceptance zone

▢ Overlapping acceptance zone

The lined section on the top bars reading from left to right is the company's acceptance zone, and the lined section on the bottom bars from right to left is the government's. In (a), there is no overlap, but in (b) the overlap is substantial. Although this figure illustrates ownership, the same technique may be used for other points of negotiation.

rate. Further, governments vary in their attitudes toward foreign investors, so their negotiating agendas also vary.

Most countries offer investment incentives to attract MNEs. Direct incentives that countries have offered foreign investors include tax holidays, employee training, R&D grants, accelerated depreciation, low-interest loans, loan guarantees, subsidized energy and transportation, exemption of import duties, and the construction of rail spurs and roads. Countries also provide indirect incentives, such as a trained labor force and labor laws that prevent work disruptions.

When managers negotiate to gain concessions from a foreign government, they should understand some problems the concessions might bring.

- Companies may face more domestic labor problems because of claims that they are exporting jobs to gain access to cheap labor.
- The foreign facility may be accused of dumping because of the subsidies given by the host government. For this reason, Toyota refused to accept British governmental assistance for fear other EU countries would not as readily allow its sales.
- It may be more difficult to evaluate management performance in the subsidized operation because much of the profits may be due to the incentives, rather than to management performance.
- There is always a risk that promises will be broken.

Negotiations are seldom a one-way street. Companies agree to many performance requirements aimed at helping host countries reach economic and noneconomic objectives, such as a favorable balance of payments, growth, high employment, and local control over important decisions. These performance requirements include

- Foreign-exchange deposits to cover the cost of imports and foreign-exchange payments on loans and dividends
- Limits on payments to the parent for services it provides to its host-country subsidiary
- Requirements to create a certain number of jobs or amount of exports
- Provisions to reduce the amount of equity held in subsidiaries
- Maximum prices on goods sold
- Obligatory levels of local input into products manufactured
- Limits on the use of expatriate personnel and on old or reconditioned equipment
- Control of prices on goods the MNE imports or exports to the host-country subsidiary
- Demands to enter into joint ventures

RENEGOTIATIONS

Agreements evolve after operations begin; the company position is usually, but not always, stronger before entry.

For early foreign investments in emerging economies, it was common for companies to obtain concessions on fixed terms for long periods or to expect that the original terms would not change. (These early investments were largely in the commodity and utility sectors.) But those days are gone. Not only may the terms of operations be bargained before any operations begin, the same terms may be rebargained anytime during start-up or after operations are underway. For example, three U.S. MNEs reached agreement with the state of Maharastra to build a $2.8 billion power plant (the largest foreign investment in India), in which Enron would own 80 percent and Bechtel Enterprises and General Electric would each own 10 percent. After investing $300 million, the government halted further work, but agreed to renegotiate the agreement. The companies lost about $250,000 per day during the renegotiations. Finally, they agreed to use more Indian naphtha (a fuel) rather than Qataran natural gas to generate electricity, allow the state of Maharastra to own 30 percent of the facility, reduce Enron's ownership to 50 percent, and reduce the price of power by 22.2 percent.[14]

Generally, a company's best bargaining position exists before it makes an investment in a foreign country. Once a company transfers capital and technology abroad and trains local nationals to direct operations, the parent company is needed much less than before. Further, the company now has assets that are not easily moved to more favorable locales. The result is that the host country may be in a better position to extract additional concessions from the company. This erosion of the MNEs' bargaining strength as countries gain assets from them is known as the **theory of the obsolescing bargain**. However, a company that is responsive to the local economy's changing needs and desires can maintain or even improve its bargaining position by offering additional resources the host country needs. One tactic is to promise to bring in (or withhold) the latest technology developed abroad. Another tactic is to use plant expansion or export markets as bargaining weapons. In addition, a company and country may exchange benefits, such as a company's ceding part of its ownership to local interests in exchange for guarantees on remission of its earnings.[15] A host government also may restrain from pushing too hard on companies once they are operating for fear this will make the country less attractive to other companies with which the government would like to do business.

BEHAVIORAL CHARACTERISTICS AFFECTING NEGOTIATIONS

In international negotiations, misunderstandings are a strong possibility because of cultural differences as well as possible language differences. Further, the background and expertise of government officials may be quite distinct from those of businesspeople. Their superiors may also evaluate them on very different criteria.

Misunderstandings may result from differences in
- **Nationalities**
- **Languages**
- **Professions**

Cultural Factors   In the 1930s, the humorist Will Rogers quipped, "America has never lost a war and never won a conference." Many people agree with this assessment of U.S. performance in business negotiations abroad. But companies from other countries have problems as well. Much of the problem stems from cultural differences that lead to misunderstandings and mistrust across the conference table. Although this discussion cannot list all the possible cultural differences, the following points based on the cultural framework in Chapter 2 indicate areas of possible misunderstanding.[16]

Some cultural differences among negotiators are evident:
- **Some negotiators are decision makers; some are not**
- **Some take a pragmatic view; others take a holistic view**
- **Some expressions do not translate well**

- Individual negotiators from some countries are more likely to have the power to make decisions than are their counterparts from some other countries in part because of differences between individualist and collectivist societies. Negotiators who have the power to make decisions may lose confidence when those counterparts must reach a group decision or keep checking with their head office.
- Negotiators from low-context cultures want to get to the heart of the matter quickly. Negotiators from high-context cultures want to spend time developing rapport and trust before addressing business details.
- Negotiators from pragmatist cultures attempt to separate the issues into small categories (getting closure on items in a linear fashion), while negotiators from idealistic cultures view negotiations more holistically.
- Negotiators from cultures with high trust are less prone to want to cover every possible contingency in a contract than are negotiators from cultures with low trust.
- Negotiators from monochronic cultures will want to give their undivided attention to one issue at a time. However, negotiators from polychronic cultures feel uncomfortable if they do not simultaneously take care of other business affairs.
- Negotiators from cultures that place a high importance on punctuality and schedules are more prone to set deadlines and then make concessions at the last minute to meet the schedules than are negotiators from cultures that place less importance on punctuality and schedules. Further, they may underestimate the importance their

counterparts place on the negotiations if their counterparts arrive late and don't stick to schedules.

The importance of cultural factors may change during renegotiations because the parties already know each other. If the relationship was amicable in the original negotiations, that quality is likely to be carried over. However, if the past relationship has been hostile, the renegotiations may be suffused by even more suspicion and obstruction than existed during the original process.

Language Factors   It may be difficult for negotiators to find words to express their exact meaning in another language, which may result in occasional pauses while translators resort to dictionaries. The pauses cause negotiations to take longer than if they were among people from the same country. Moreover, if negotiations stop while an interpreter translates, the process takes even longer. Negotiators find facial expressions difficult to judge because of cultural differences and the time lag caused by translation. Because English is widely understood worldwide, people with a different native language may understand quite well most of what is said in English, allowing them to eavesdrop on confidential comments and form responses while remarks are being translated into their language.

Cultural factors influence whether interpreters are acceptable. For example, Saudi managers generally prefer to negotiate in English, even if their English is not very good. When negotiators do use interpreters, each side should have its own. Good interpreters brief their teams on cultural factors affecting the negotiation process. But even with interpreters, negotiators cannot be certain that their statements are fully understood, especially if they use slang or attempt humor that is culture specific. Take as an example the experience of a U.S. politician who spoke through an interpreter in China.

> With typical American forthrightness, [the politician] said, "I'm going to tell you where I'm coming from." The interpreter said, "He'll now give you the name of his home town." Then he said, "I'm going to lay all my cards on the table." The interpreter said, "He'll play cards now." Then, making a joke, he said, "I'm not a member of any organized political party; I'm a Democrat." The interpreter said, "I think he just made a joke. Please laugh." The audience laughed and the politician knew he had their rapt attention.[17]

Negotiations may be based on
- **One's own culture**
- **The counterpart's culture**
- **Some hybrid of cultures**

Culturally Responsive Strategies[18]   The fact that managers' counterparts in negotiations come from countries with different cultures does not necessarily mean they will behave according to their culture's norm.[19] First, a counterpart may be an exception to the country's norm. Second, a counterpart may know the other's culture and be adaptive to it. So managers should determine at the start whether they will adjust to their counterparts, allow their counterparts to adjust to them, or follow some form of hybrid adjustment.

Figure 12.4 shows five strategic responses you might have if you were an international business manager in negotiations. The choice is highly dependent on how well you and your counterpart understand each other's culture. At one extreme, if you try to get your counterpart to adapt to you (Response 1), you need to convey that it is because of expediency rather than through lack of appreciation for the other's culture. For example, when ITT conducted merger talks with CGE of France, it did so in English and

FIGURE 12.4   Culturally Responsive Strategies and Their Feasibility

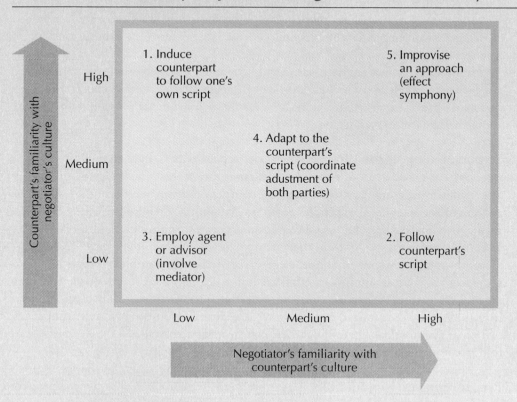

At each level of familiarity, a negotiator can consider feasible the strategies designated at that level and any lower level.

along ITT's style because the speed and success of starting operations were dependent on U.S. law and investment firms. At the other extreme, you may immerse yourself in your counterpart's culture, as in Response 2. For example, Coca-Cola sent personnel to Cambridge University to study the Chinese language and culture for a year before beginning a 10-year negotiation with a Chinese state-run organization. In Response 3, both you and your counterpart agree on go-betweens, middlemen, brokers, or other intermediaries to simplify negotiations because neither of you is familiar with the other's culture. Response 4 is a hybrid of approaches, such as having both parties speak in their own language or moving negotiations between the two countries. Finally, Response 5 is the conduct of negotiations different from what one might find in either culture. It might occur when parties have such global experience that they've lost most elements of their home cultures.

Professional Conflict   Governmental and business negotiators may start with mutual mistrust due to historic animosity or to differences in their professional status. The businesspeople may come armed with business and economic data that governmental officials don't fully understand, and the officials may counter with sovereignty

Business and governmental officials may mistrust each other and may not understand each other's objectives.

considerations that are nearly incomprehensible to the businesspeople. It may take considerable time before each side understands and appreciates the other's point of view. Even then, it is possible neither will attempt to develop a relationship designed for long-term objectives. Negotiators may see their rewards, such as new assignments, as dependent on immediate results and perhaps not expect to be around for longer-term problems.

Professional conflict has been particularly evident as many emerging economies have attempted to sell state-owned enterprises to foreign investors. The managers within these enterprises are suspicious of MNEs, fearful of foreign domination, and worried about their jobs after privatization.[20]

Negotiators should find some means to reinstitute future contacts.

Termination of Negotiations   When one or both parties want to end serious consideration of proposals, the method of cessation can be extremely important. It may affect the negotiators' positions with their superiors, who may wonder why their appointed negotiators have spent so much time and money without reaching an agreement. Also affected may be future transactions between the parties and their dealings with other organizations, both in that country and elsewhere in the world. Because termination is an admission of failure, negotiators are prone to publicly blame others to save face. Such accusations may complicate future dealings the country or the company may have with other parties. Fearing adverse consequences from termination, negotiators sometimes drag out the process until a proposal eventually dies unnoticed. Although termination is stressful, when it is necessary, the parties should attempt to find means that allow each to save face and that avoid publicity.

Role-playing can be used to anticipate others' approach, but it is hard to simulate stress situations.

Preparation for Negotiations   Role-playing is a valuable technique for projects requiring approval by a foreign government or agreement with a foreign company. By practicing their own roles and those of the counterpart negotiators—and by researching the country's culture and history to determine attitudes toward foreign companies—negotiators may be much better able to anticipate responses and plan their own actions.[21]

Role-playing presupposes that the company knows who will be negotiating for the other side. Commonly, MNEs use a team approach so that people with the necessary range of functional responsibilities take part in the decision making. It also is common to use people at different organizational levels at different points in the negotiations.

One factor not easily simulated is the stress of being away from family and coworkers for an extended period. Because of this factor, the location of negotiations may give one side or the other an advantage in bargaining. Negotiating in the "home field" gives managers an advantage because they can go home at night, eat familiar food, not have to explain travel expenses to superiors, and more easily take care of other business at the office. If managers must travel abroad for negotiations, they will likely be more alert if they arrive in time to be rested and adjust to any time changes.

HOME-COUNTRY INVOLVEMENT IN ASSET PROTECTION

Companies are concerned that foreign countries will appropriate their assets without their receiving adequate compensation for them. These assets include the value of their foreign direct investments as well as intangibles—patents, trademarks, and copyrights.

Ethical Dilemmas and Social Responsibility
THE ETHICS OF ACQUIRING INFORMATION AND INTANGIBLE ASSETS

There is a long tradition of governmental help for home-country companies engaged in international business. What constitutes an appropriate amount of governmental assistance is argued largely in economic terms, such as whether export financing programs constitute subsidies that warrant retaliation. But there also are ethical questions about such assistance.

Consider data collection and dissemination. The U.S. government collects and publishes much data on business conditions and competition in foreign countries. It then makes these data available at low cost. As long as the information is collected openly and is available at low cost to anyone (U.S. citizens as well as foreign citizens), there seems to be no ethical problem. However, there may be some point at which the method of collection, the type of information collected, or the restrictions on dissemination overstep ethical boundaries. For example, the French government expelled four U.S. diplomats because they reportedly sought to recruit French officials as industrial spies.[22] With the end of the Cold War, the U.S. Central Intelligence Agency (CIA) indicated that it was considering the collection and analysis of more business-economic data to share with U.S. companies.[23] The director of the CIA said, "We do not do industrial espionage." However, it does seek to find cases in which non-U.S. companies bribe foreign officials so that adverse publicity about the bribes might help U.S. companies get contracts. In so doing, the CIA has been caught in sticky situations. There have been allegations that the CIA eavesdropped on conversations between Japanese officials and car executives during U.S.-Japanese auto trade negotiations to obtain information that might help U.S. automakers' competitiveness.[24] With a yearly budget of about $30 billion and the latest technology for information gathering, the CIA might be able to gain more competitively useful information than companies or other government agencies could.

From an ethical standpoint, the following questions about information gathering in general might raise issues:

- Is it acquired by the CIA or another U.S. government agency?
- Is it collected openly or clandestinely?
- Is it in the public domain or proprietarily owned by companies?
- Is it made available to anyone or only U.S. companies?

Governmental spies are allegedly working with businesses from such countries as the United Kingdom, China, France, Israel, Japan, and South Korea.[25] The U.S. government justifies its spying as being competitive with what other governments are doing.

Another area of governmental assistance is in the protection of intangible assets, such as patents, trademarks, and copyrights. Although companies lose millions of dollars in revenues from unauthorized copying, many people argue that copying is justified in some circumstances because it gives poor people access to needed products. Take books, for example. Unauthorized copies of this book sell extensively in many emerging economies at a fraction of the price of those sold legitimately, especially in Asia. These sales give no revenues to either the legitimate publisher or the authors. Another industry in which the copying of products is rampant is pharmaceuticals. For example, Argentina is the world's ninth-largest market for pharmaceuticals, and local companies routinely copy and market medicines that MNEs have developed, such as antibiotics and cancer drugs.[26] They can sell these at a discounted price because they do not have to incur and recoup high development costs.

U.S. MNEs push the U.S. government to pressure foreign countries to stop the copying of both books and pharmaceuticals. If successful, MNEs will no longer lose sales. However, some consumers may be too poor to buy the legitimate version of the cut-rate copies. For example, many purchasers of copied books are students who buy texts that they could otherwise not afford because the price of a single textbook might equal the monthly income for a student's family. For them, the enactment and enforcement of strict copyright laws may mean a less adequate education. In the case of pharmaceuticals, the enactment and enforcement of strict patent laws may mean that some consumers could not afford life-saving medicines. The ethical challenge is to ensure that companies develop needed products and get paid adequately for them, while ensuring that poor people have access to them as well.

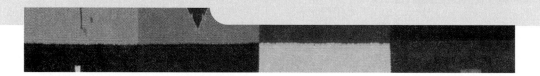

They push their home-country governments to deal directly with other governments to protect these assets.

HISTORICAL BACKGROUND OF HOME-COUNTRY PROTECTION

Historically, most foreign investment disputes concerned expropriation, particularly in emerging economies.[27] As late as the period between the two world wars, home countries ensured through military force and coercion that host governments would give foreign investors prompt, adequate, and effective compensation in cases of expropriation, a concept known as the **international standard of fair dealing**.[28] Host countries had little to say about this standard. In conferences attended by emerging economies at The Hague in 1930 and at Montevideo in 1933, participants established a treaty stating that "foreigners may not claim rights other or more extensive than nationals."[29] On the basis of this doctrine, Mexico used its own courts in 1938 to settle disputes arising from expropriation of foreign agricultural properties in 1915.[30] This same treaty formed the precedent for later settlements and, in the absence of specific treaties, still remains largely in effect.

The concept of home-country nonintervention by military force to protect investments has been strengthened by a series of UN resolutions and by the fact that most expropriations have been selective rather than general. That is, a country may have expropriated only some companies' assets—sometimes not even all of their assets. In these cases, intervention might lead to further takeovers and jeopardize payment settlements for the companies. As host countries' priorities have shifted toward attracting FDI, rather than expropriating it, there has been less concern about home-country intervention to protect investors. Instead, home governments have become more concerned that companies will receive equal legal treatment and will have their FDI approved fairly and expeditiously.[31]

Nevertheless, **dependencia theory** holds that emerging economies have practically no power as host countries when dealing with MNEs. Their assets are of little importance in bargaining. Further, MNEs can enlist the loyalties of their home governments and local elites to maintain their power. Although home-country governments today are not prone to use military intervention, they sometimes use other means to support MNEs, such as trade pressures, aid, and influence with international lending agencies. The dependencia theory is largely out of vogue today. However, some emerging economy leaders and political parties still hold those views,[32] and can sometimes effectively delay or prevent MNEs' investments.

THE USE OF BILATERAL AGREEMENTS

To improve foreign-investment climates for their MNEs, many industrial countries established bilateral treaties with other countries, often after long and difficult negotiations.[33] Although these agreements differ in detail, they generally provide home-country insurance to investors to cover losses from expropriation, political violence, governmental contract cancellation, and currency control, and to exporters for losses from nonpayment in a convertible currency. For example, the United States offers policies for small companies through the Small Business Administration and for companies in general through the Overseas Private Investment Corporation (OPIC) and Eximbank.[34] Coverage also is available through private insurers, international agencies such as the World Bank's Multilateral Investment Guarantee Agency, and some host-country governments. The home country, by approving an insurance contract, agrees to settle investors' losses on a government-to-government basis. For example, Chase Manhattan Bank acquired insurance from OPIC to invest in Venezuelan telecommunications projects.[35] If Chase Manhattan suffered losses as a result of political risk, OPIC would pay Chase Manhattan, and then the U.S. government would seek settlement from Venezuela. Other types of bilateral agreements include treaties of friendship, commerce, and navigation as well as prevention of double taxation.

Bilateral agreements improve climates for investments abroad.

MULTILATERAL AGREEMENTS AND SETTLEMENTS: FDI AND TRADE

When MNEs cannot reach agreement with organizations in a host country, they may agree to have a third party settle the dispute. The International Chamber of Commerce in Paris, the Swedish Chamber of Commerce, and specialized commodity associations in London frequently handle trade disputes. Because trade transactions are generally between private companies, these disputes do not generate the same hype as government-to-government or foreign-investment disputes. Government-to-government trade disputes are now largely the domain of the WTO, although allegations about unfair trade practices abroad are lodged with a company's home government, which in turn formally submits the allegations to the WTO.

A notable case of a multilateral settlement on foreign investment was between the United States and Iran. This case differed from many other attempted settlements because each country had large amounts of investments in the other's territory. When the two governments froze each other's assets because of political confrontations, Iran had substantially more invested in the United States than the United States had in Iran. The two countries agreed to appoint three arbitrators each to an international tribunal

Multilateral settlements of disputes may be handled by a neutral country or group of countries that are not involved.

at The Hague, and those six selected three more. Part of the assets the United States had held were set aside for the payment of arbitrated claims, and amounts have been relinquished as Iran has settled with U.S. investors on a case-by-case basis.[36]

The International Center for Settlement of Investment Disputes operates under the auspices of the World Bank and provides a formal organization to which parties can submit their disputes. Most bilateral investment treaties designate it as the arbitration center for disputes or indicate that its rules would be applicable in ad hoc arbitrations.[37] The World Bank also established the Multilateral Investment Guarantee Agency, which offers insurance against losses from expropriations, war, civil disturbances, currency convertibility, and breach of contract.

The WTO may become involved in selected aspects of investment issues and dispute settlement. Specifically, investment disputes can be linked to trade disputes, such as the prohibition of FDI that is necessary to export into a market. On a regional basis, NAFTA rules allow investors' claims to be submitted to a NAFTA tribunal.[38] The WTO has also discussed the possibility of a parallel program to settle investment disputes that are not related to trade. However, a core of emerging economies is opposed so far because of a belief that any agreement would compromise their ability to decide on development strategy and industrial policy.[39]

MULTINATIONAL AGREEMENTS: IPRs

International treaties and agreements help safeguard patents, trademarks, and copyrights.

The poet and essayist Ralph Waldo Emerson said, "If a man can write a better book, preach a better sermon, or make a better mousetrap than his neighbor, though he builds his house in the woods, the world will make a beaten path to his door." But if someone else gets hold of the design for the better book, sermon, or mousetrap, the number of people beating the way will be divided. Much of this chapter has centered on foreign direct investment. However, key areas of business-government and government-to-government conflicts in international business recently has been intellectual property rights (IPRs), or intangible assets.[40]

IPRs cover both industrial property, such as inventions and distinctive identifications of companies and products, and artistic property, such as books, recordings, films, and computer programs. Companies with substantial intangible assets want protection through enforceable patents, trademarks, and copyrights so that they may gain all the sales and profits because they created the property in the first place. They argue that the social benefit of protection is positive because otherwise there would be little incentive to develop new industrial and artistic property. Critics, however, argue that protection costs society dearly through high monopoly prices. Some countries use this argument to restrict the patenting of pharmaceuticals so that medicines are more affordable.

Countries differ substantially in their protection of IPRs, through laws and their enforcement. Generally, emerging economies offer less protection. Few of their companies create substantial intangible assets, thus they have nothing to gain if their governments protect IPRs vigorously. They can gain local production and low prices without making payments to companies in industrial countries. Even when two countries have similar levels of protection, their approaches differ. For example, U.S. patent applications are secret and are usually granted within two years. In contrast, Japanese applications are public and are granted in four to six years.[41] Because of different national approaches to IPRs, both companies and countries have stakes in any international agreement. The GATT agreement from the Uruguay Round (signed by most countries) provides for IPR reciprocity—a country must grant to foreigners the same property rights available to its own citizens.

Patents   The first major attempt to achieve cross-national cooperation in the protection of patents, trademarks, and other property rights was the Paris Convention, initiated in 1883 (and periodically revised since). This Convention gave rise to the International Bureau for the Protection of Industrial Property Rights (BIRPI). BIRPI grants reciprocity to foreigners whose countries are Convention members. A second major provision of the Paris Convention is that a registration in one country has a grace period of protection before a company registers it in other member countries. After registration, there is a transition period during which the patent holder has to use the patent within the market. If it fails to use it, then the country may grant rights to another company.[42]

The three most important contemporary cross-national patent agreements are the Patent Cooperation Treaty (PCT) of the World Intellectual Property Organization (WIPO), the European Patent Convention (EPC), and the European Economic Community (EEC) Patent Convention. The PCT and EPC allow companies to make a uniform patent search and application, which they can use to apply for patents in all signatory countries.

Patent-infringement battles are both costly and complex and may take years to settle. For example, Fonar, Inc., then a $15 million company, sued both General Electric and Hitachi for patent infringement of its medical technology. Hitachi settled for an undisclosed amount. General Electric had to pay over $100 million to Fonar after losing a court battle.[43] On the international level, the rapid development of technology and the varying patent rules and regulations in different countries make keeping up with patents difficult.[44] Companies usually change their patents from country to country to meet local needs, and patent infringement is often hard to prove. For example, a company in one country, where there is no patent protection on pharmaceuticals, could manufacture a drug patented by a company in the United States and sell it anywhere in the world. If the U.S. company were to bring suit, it would have to prove patent infringement. However, it would have difficulty getting the proof in the country where the alleged infringement occurred.

Trademarks   Companies may spend millions of dollars to develop brand names. If a trademark does not protect a brand name, then other companies may produce under the same brand name. For example, New Zealand growers began marketing what they called Chinese gooseberries as kiwifruit in the 1960s, but neglected to register a trademark. Now many companies from many countries can market "kiwifruit."[45]

Even if a brand name has a trademark, it may become generic in some countries because it takes on the name of a product rather than a brand. It then enters the public domain. "Swiss army knife" is actually a foreign trademark that has become a generic word in the United States. Because the Japanese have no name for vulcanized rubber, they call it "goodyear." Sometimes the issue of what is generic is decided in bilateral agreements. For example, the EU and the United States agreed that bourbon and Tennessee whiskey were names that only U.S. distillers could use, while Scotch whiskey, Irish whiskey, Cognac, Armagnac, Calvados, and Brandy de Jerez belong to regions of Europe.[46]

One development in cross-national cooperation for trademark protection is the Trademark Registration Treaty, commonly known as the Vienna Convention. According to the Vienna Convention, a company has three years after it registers a trademark internationally before it has to use it. Once the trademark has been registered internationally, each country in the treaty must accept it or provide grounds for refusal within fifteen months after its registration so that the company will have time to act before the

Looking to the Future
SOME NEW ROLES FOR DIPLOMACY IN THE NEW CENTURY

Probably the most significant factor influencing possible change in business-government diplomacy is the end of the Cold War, which pitted the communist and noncommunist blocs against each other for nearly half a century. During that period, governments tended to influence business activities because of political-military objectives, sometimes protecting their home-based companies to gain or maintain spheres of influence abroad and sometimes withholding support for fear it might lead an otherwise neutral country to support the other bloc. But political schisms are not yet a thing of the past, so managers must continue to contend with government-to-government animosities when planning international expansion strategies.

New alignments of countries based on economic factors may well replace some of the political-military rivalries of the recent past. For example, a new economic rivalry between Europe and North America may become as intense as the old political rivalry between the communist and noncommunist blocs. Companies may still have to satisfy national interests in their operations to the same degree as before. In the short term, it appears most countries will welcome foreign companies' operations or at least take a laissez-faire attitude toward them because of a belief that, on balance, they serve the countries' national economic interests. But there are likely to be many exceptions; for example, India and South Korea, which traditionally have not welcomed wholly owned foreign operations. Another exception centers on the privatization of state-owned enterprises, for which prospective buyers must negotiate on much more than the price.

Historically there have been broad swings in host-country attitudes toward private ownership, especially foreign ownership. The present welcoming of FDI could easily reverse, particularly if governments feel their own constituencies are not receiving a just share of global economic benefits. For example, Sri Lanka has passed legislation to allow the renationalization of privatized companies where new owners fail to manage them successfully.[47] Regardless of the direction national policies take, companies are likely to face ever more sophisticated governmental officials when they negotiate their operating terms abroad.

Government-to-government cooperation to deal with MNEs is apt to develop slowly, at least on a global scale. There are simply too many divergent interests among countries that tend to divide them on issues of economic development, product-specific interests, and regional viewpoints. One such issue is the protection of intangibles—it pits the interests of industrial countries, which create most of the products that can be patented, trademarked, or copyrighted, against the interests of many emerging economies, which do not want to pay for their use. Countries may collectively cease trade preferences for countries that do not protect IPRs.

three-year period is over. Between the time a company registers a trademark and the time it enters a foreign country, another company sometimes begins using the trademark in the foreign country. The first company using it can then delay or prevent entry of the original trademark holder. For example, in 1996 the Swedish home-furnishing chain Habitat wanted to enter the Italian market. However, a small company, Galliano Habitat, won a court order to prevent Habitat from using its trademark in Italy.[48]

Copyrights   Most large publishing and recording companies have extensive interests in foreign competitive markets. Without international copyright laws, a foreign producer could copy a book, software, CD, or tape and then distribute it at cut-rate prices in the country in which it was first produced. The Universal Copyright Convention (UCC) and the Berne Convention, the major cross-national agreements, honor the copyright laws of their signatory countries. In 1996, some 150 WIPO members agreed to extend copyright coverage to material on the Internet and other on-line services.[49]

Piracy   Not all countries are members of the various conventions to protect IPRs. Of those that are, some enforce the agreements haphazardly. Even if enforced, the penalties may be too small to deter violations. For example, a repeat trademark counterfeiter in the United Kingdom, whose profits were estimated at $5 million, received only a three-month jail sentence.[50] The terms *piracy* and *counterfeiting* describe this production without the consent of the company holding the patent, trademark, or copyright. Reports of lost sales due to piracy vary substantially, but all estimates are significant. For example, the International Anticounterfeiting Coalition estimates worldwide counterfeiting at $500 billion a year, or about 9 percent of the value of world trade.[51] The European Commission estimates that 5 to 7 percent of world trade is of pirated goods.[52]

> Not all countries offer effective protection to IPRs.

Piracy has occurred for several reasons.

- Cashing in on massive advertising by placing well-known trademarked labels on copies of products is tempting and has happened with almost every type of goods, from baseball caps to automobiles.[53] Fake labels even go on merchandise that the copied companies do not make.
- Technology allows copyrighted material such as tapes to be reproduced cheaply without loss of quality.[54]
- Some countries offer little protection for certain products. For example, when the drug company Pfizer introduced Feldene, an antiarthritic drug, to Argentina, five Argentine companies were already selling generic copies in the market.[55]
- Many people see nothing morally wrong in buying counterfeit goods. Indeed, the Software Publishers Association's executive director said, "It's ironic that people who would never think about stealing a candy bar from a drugstore seem to have no qualms about copying a $500 software package."[56]

What about gains or losses for consumers? Sometimes they get good-quality merchandise with a prestige label for a fraction of what the legitimate product would have cost. Some companies have even contracted counterfeiters to be legitimate suppliers. Sometimes consumers enjoy flaunting a fake product that is admittedly not of high quality and that fools no one as being genuine, such as a $15 counterfeit Rolex watch.[57] Often, however, shoddy or even dangerous merchandise is substituted for the original goods. For example, a hundred Nigerian children died from a counterfeit cough medicine.[58]

Various manufacturers' associations have sprung up around the world to deal with piracy. These associations propose greater border surveillance, stiffer penalties for dealing in counterfeit goods, and cessation of aid to countries that do not join and adhere to international agreements. The WTO has taken over the international property rights administration from WIPO, making enforcement more effective.[59] It allows countries to take trade sanctions against countries that do not protect intellectual property rights. Companies such as Microsoft are also successfully tracking down infringers and bringing cases against them,[60] but it is difficult to prove infringement when the violations are slight changes on trademarks or product models. Other companies identify their products through high technology, such as holographic images and magnetic or microchip tags—technology that has cost them millions of dollars.[61] Vuitton, a French luggage manufacturer, is using a withdrawal strategy. It used to sell through independent retailers, but it now sells registered and numbered goods only in company-owned retail outlets. Still other companies are warning the public of imitations and advising consumers on how to discern the genuine product.

COLLECTIVE ACTIONS TO DEAL WITH INTERNATIONAL COMPANIES

The preceding discussion dealt primarily with complaints by companies about the actions (or lack of actions) by governments to protect their assets, both tangible and intangible. But governments are also concerned with the actions of MNEs, and they have sought to deal collectively with them and to issue guidelines of expected behavior.

The League of Nations made the first widespread attempt to regulate international companies on a multilateral basis in 1929. Then, the attention was on foreign exploitation of the tropical commodities industry. However, the onset of the Great Depression squashed the effort. Since World War II, several attempts have been made to deal with the relationship between MNEs and governments. Among these were the International Trade Organization (ITO) of 1948, which never became operative, the attempts in 1951 by the UN Economic and Social Council (ECOSOC) to regulate antitrust, and the 1961 Code for Liberalization of Capital Movements established by the Organization for Economic Cooperation and Development (OECD). It appears that none of these attempts has had much effect on MNEs' operations because of the different interests of industrial and emerging economies.

In 1975, the United Nations created the Center on Transnational Corporations to address complaints from many emerging economies (the so-called Group of 77, which now comprises more than 100 such countries). The Center collects information on MNE activities, is a forum for publicizing common complaints, and has considered the adoption of several codes of conduct for MNE activities. The OECD, which is composed of industrial countries, approved its own code in 1976. The codes of both the Group of 77 and the OECD are necessarily vague to accommodate varying countries as well as groups within them.

Nongovernmental organizations (NGOs) and industry associations have also instituted a number of codes dealing with specific practices, such as infant formula sales and environmental practices, with specific areas of the world, such as employment practices in northern Mexico and Northern Ireland,[62] or with specific industries, such as the

---

Collective attitudes toward MNE activities

- **Are clarified by a number of organizations**
- **Are usually fairly vague**
- **Involve voluntary compliance**
- **May make it easier for countries to legislate**

International Council of Toy Makers' code to provide good working conditions and avoid the use of child labor.[63] The codes are also voluntary; adoption does not guarantee enforcement. However, they voice a collective attitude toward specific MNE practices that makes it easier for governments to pass restrictive legislation at the national level supporting public opinion.

In 1995, the United States issued a voluntary code for foreign operations of U.S. companies. The code calls for companies operating abroad to provide a safe workplace, recognize the rights of workers to organize, and not produce with either forced or child labor. The code also asks companies to report on their positive achievements in the workplace.[64]

CORPORATE CITIZENSHIP AND PUBLIC RELATIONS

Many companies strongly believe that by acting as good corporate citizens abroad, they will reduce local animosities and remove concerns that might affect their short- or long-term competitive ability. Figure 12.5 illustrates this belief humorously. Some companies have even published their own codes of conduct. These actions may not be sufficient, however, because employees, government officials, consumers, and other groups may not know or understand the positive effects of the company's international operations.

Because of conflicting pressures from different groups, someone can almost always accuse an MNE of bad behavior. For instance, if it offers higher wages, it may be accused of monopolistic practices and of stimulating inflation by attracting workers from competitors. If it pays only the going wage, it may be accused of exploiting workers. By understanding the power of competing groups it serves, the MNE could emphasize practices that benefit most of those groups. Within any given economy, there is usually a range of prices the market will pay, wages workers will want, and returns that companies make on investments. The MNE may, for example, offer wage rates or investment returns that are among those of the top group of companies in the country

Companies publicize good-citizenship activities, pointing out when
- **Business conduct satisfies social objectives**
- **Nonbusiness functions help society**

FIGURE 12.5 Improving Performance Through Socially Responsible Behavior

Doonesbury   BY GARRY TRUDEAU

Critics have staged protests against Nike's use of contractors in foreign countries who pay their employees low wages. The Doonesbury cartoon parodies the good performance that can result from such protests.

without being accused of disruptive practices, and still satisfy the market, workers, and stockholders.

The theologian Saint Augustine recounted in the fifth century that in his youth he used to pray, "Give me chastity and continence, but not yet." Like Saint Augustine, many companies try to put off public relations efforts as long as possible. Often a company's public relations efforts are defensive; that is, they are a reaction to public criticism. Once a company is on the defensive, however, these efforts may be too little, too late. The CEO of Levi-Strauss said, "In today's world, an exposé on working conditions on '60 Minutes' can undo years of effort to build brand loyalty." To head off possible criticism about its suppliers' labor practices, the company terminated contracts in China and Peru and worked with suppliers to alter their practices in Turkey and Bangladesh. Not only did Levi-Strauss prevent criticism, but the publicity about its changed policies brought the company goodwill.[65]

Companies should work to increase the number of supporters and dampen potential criticism. They can survey customers and workers to allay misconceptions and anticipate criticism, heading off more damaging accusations later. Many MNEs use advocacy publicity at home and abroad to win support for their international activities. Such publicity may take the form of newspaper and magazine ads, reports, and films showing the positive effects a company's activities have had on home- and host-country societies.

Although it may not always be possible to dispel criticism from abroad, the MNE can do several things to mitigate it. One may be as fundamental as having the parent company managers continue an existing policy. On the question of what to centralize and what to decentralize, there is much to be said for permitting local managers to determine policies concerning local customs and social matters. On such sensitive issues as employment and worker output, changes should be made only after consultation with stakeholders. Headquarters personnel also may serve a useful public relations function locally. They have higher status than local managers do and so may sometimes be better received by higher governmental authorities.

The MNE might increase the number of local proponents through
- **Ownership sharing**
- **Avoiding direct confrontation**
- **Local management**
- **Local R&D**

An MNE also may foster local participation designed both to reduce the image of foreignness and to develop local proponents whose personal objectives may be fulfilled by the company's continued operations. The parent company can assist the development of local suppliers, establish stock option plans, and gradually replace home-country personnel with local nationals. Carried to extremes, however, local participation can result in the host country's becoming less dependent on the foreign company. So the company's strategy might be to hold out some resources so that it remains needed. For instance, a home-country R&D laboratory could be in charge of new-product development, while the host-country R&D facility could handle adaptations for local market and production conditions.

Some companies have taken on additional social functions to build local support and enhance their performance.[66] For example, Dow Chemical financed a kindergarten in Chile, Citibank participated in a reforestation program in the Philippines, and McDonald's sponsored a telethon in Australia to raise funds for disabled children. Johnson & Johnson sends Kenyans abroad to study nursing, and Sony sends Chilean music students abroad to study. Merck gives away a drug that fights river blindness in Africa. Volvo awards an annual prize for the outstanding global innovation or discovery in the environmental field. GM publishes a public-interest report to highlight its efforts in a wide array of activities, such as environmental cleanup programs in Mexico and Eastern Europe, cancer research, AIDS education, and global celebration of Earth Day.[67]

Good corporate citizenship and its publicity may not be enough to guarantee business. If public opinion is against foreign private ownership in general, all foreign companies lose out. For a company doing business as a key firm in a key sector, criticisms may come simultaneously from so many directions that the company defense gradually loses strength. Even in these extreme cases, a company's public affairs department may identify the worst problem areas. If it does this in advance, the company may establish policies to prevent or minimize losses, including decreasing reinvestment, selling ownership to local governments or another company, and shifting into less visible local enterprises.

Occasionally, an MNE may need to be uncompromising in its dealings with a government, even when the adversarial positions become public. It may have a strong bargaining position, or it may perceive that compromises will weaken its position in other countries. Even in these instances, however, the MNE should attempt to keep the government from losing face because it may need future governmental support.

WEB CONNECTION

Check out our home page www.prenhall.com/daniels for links to key resources for you in your study of international business.

SUMMARY

- Although host countries and MNEs may hold resources that, if combined, could achieve objectives for both, conflict may cause one or both parties to withhold those resources, preventing the full functioning of international business activities.

- Both MNE managers and host-country governmental officials must respond to interest groups that may perceive different advantages or no advantage at all to the business-government relationship. Therefore, the relationship's final outcome may not be the one expected from a purely economic viewpoint.

- Negotiations are playing a more important role in determining the terms under which a company may operate in a foreign country. This negotiating process is similar to the domestic processes of company acquisition and collective bargaining. The major differences in the international

sphere are the much larger number of provisions, the general lack of a fixed time duration for an agreement, and cultural differences among negotiators.

- The terms under which an MNE may operate in a given country will depend on how much the company needs the country and vice versa. As needs evolve over time, new terms of operation might alter an MNE's bargaining strength.

- Generally, a company's best bargaining position is before it makes an investment. Once it commits resources to the foreign operation, the company may not be able to move elsewhere easily.

- Because international negotiations occur largely between parties whose cultures, educational backgrounds, and expectations differ, it is difficult for these negotiators to understand each other's sentiments and present convincing arguments. Role-playing offers negotiators a means of anticipating responses and planning an approach to the actual bargaining.

• Historically, developed countries used military intervention and coercion to ensure that the terms agreed on between their investors and host countries would be carried out. A series of international resolutions have replaced these methods for settling disputes. Recently, developed countries have used the promise of giving or withholding loans and aid and the threat of trade sanctions.

• Most countries have established bilateral treaties in which host countries agree to compensate investors for losses from expropriation, civil disturbances, and currency devaluation or control.

• Independent international organizations frequently arbitrate trade disputes. These organizations rarely settle investment disputes, however, because governments like to control what occurs within their borders.

• International agreements seek to protect important intangible property such as patents, trademarks, and copyrights. Because companies often spend millions of dollars to develop this property, worldwide protection is important to them.

• A big problem for companies has been the pirating of intangible assets in countries that have not signed international agreements or do not actively enforce their own laws on protection of IPRs.

• Companies use public relations to develop a good image, overcome a bad one, and create useful proponents for their positions.

C A S E

PEPSICO IN INDIA[68]

Despite PepsiCo's operations in nearly 150 countries and territories, its late chairman, D. Wayne Calloway, said, "We are still basically an American company with offshore interests. As the nineties progress, that's going to change. We'll be a truly global consumer products company." A key part of that strategy was the company's launching of an Indian snack-food and soft drink joint venture in 1990. At that time, the company announced plans to invest $1 billion in India during the 1990s. However, as we will see, it wasn't that easy.

THE GLOBAL COMPETITIVE SOFT DRINK MARKET

Two companies, Coca-Cola and PepsiCo, have dominated the global soft drink market. The United States has been the biggest market, with annual per capita consumption of about 32 cases. Analysts agree that this consumption figure is so large that almost all growth must come from building market share rather than getting people to increase consumption. The fierce competition between the two companies within the United States has resulted in industry returns on assets and sales that are less than half what they have been abroad. Within the United States the two companies are close rivals. But in terms of total global sales, Coca-Cola far outsells PepsiCo. Consequently, Coca-Cola has been much stronger

where profits are higher and where sales growth is expected to be much faster. For example, per capita soft drink consumption outside the United States is only about 14 percent of that in the United States, so there is much more room to grow abroad. Globally, players other than Coca-Cola and PepsiCo are small in comparison. However, some have large shares in specific country or regional markets—Cadbury Schweppes in the United Kingdom, for example.

In the soft drink industry, there is a tremendous advantage in being first into a market. Not only is brand loyalty built up fast and difficult to change, but the early entrants gain the best bottlers and distributors. Coca-Cola preceded PepsiCo into Western Europe, Latin America, and Japan, and PepsiCo has had an uphill battle building market share in those areas. PepsiCo, however, beat Coca-Cola into the former Soviet Union in 1974 and dominates that market.

Because of the first-in advantage, PepsiCo has pushed hard in recent years to enter markets in which Coca-Cola is not dominant. For example, PepsiCo entered Myanmar ahead of Coca-Cola in 1990. When the United States lifted its trade embargo with Vietnam in 1994, PepsiCo began soft drink production there within hours. The two companies compete in nearly all countries. Map 12.2 shows some recent battles between them.

MAP 12.2   Some PepsiCo Global Battles with Coca-Cola

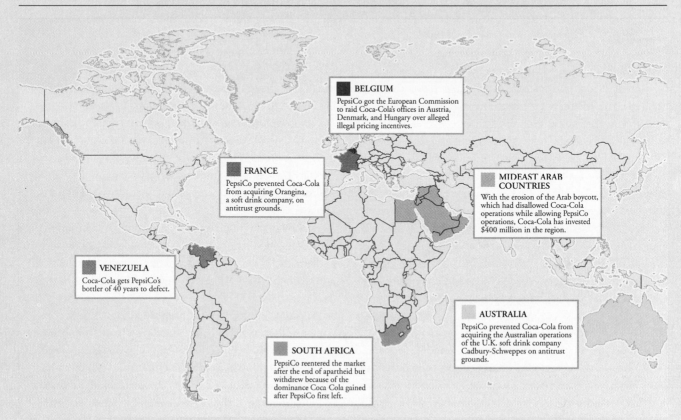

BELGIUM
PepsiCo got the European Commission to raid Coca-Cola's offices in Austria, Denmark, and Hungary over alleged illegal pricing incentives.

FRANCE
PepsiCo prevented Coca-Cola from acquiring Orangina, a soft drink company, on antitrust grounds.

MIDEAST ARAB COUNTRIES
With the erosion of the Arab boycott, which had disallowed Coca-Cola operations while allowing PepsiCo operations, Coca-Cola has invested $400 million in the region.

VENEZUELA
Coca-Cola gets PepsiCo's bottler of 40 years to defect.

AUSTRALIA
PepsiCo prevented Coca-Cola from acquiring the Australian operations of the U.K. soft drink company Cadbury-Schweppes on antitrust grounds.

SOUTH AFRICA
PepsiCo reentered the market after the end of apartheid but withdrew because of the dominance Coca Cola gained after PepsiCo first left.

PepsiCo and Coca-Cola compete in nearly every country. The map highlights some significant battles in the late 1990s.

INDIAN MARKET POTENTIAL

PepsiCo had been in the Indian market during the mid-1950s but pulled out because it wasn't profitable enough. Coca-Cola had operated in India since 1950 but left in 1977 because of disagreements with the Indian government. Coca-Cola's departure created an opportunity for PepsiCo, which did not begin its three years of formal negotiations with the Indian government until 1985. After Coca-Cola's departure, an Indian company, Parle Exports, became the dominant supplier in India with its soft drink, Thums Up. By 1988, Parle Exports had estimated annual sales of about $150 million, which made up between 60 percent and 70 percent of the market. It also was exporting a mango pulp drink, Maaza Mango, to various markets, including the United States.

The Indian market for soft drinks has been growing rapidly. When Coca-Cola departed, annual soft drink sales by all companies in India were a little over a half billion bottles a year. By 1990, they were about 3 billion bottles a year and were expected to quadruple during the 1990s. India's population growth was expected to make it surpass China as the world's most populated country. Its middle class is already much larger than China's. Moreover, many observers have predicted that India will become an economic giant with growing incomes supporting more sales. Another indication of market potential was that India's per capita consumption of soft drinks was estimated at only three bottles per year in 1989, compared to more than four times that per year in neighboring Pakistan, and forty times that in Latin America, also low-income areas.

INDIA'S ATTITUDE TOWARD FOREIGN INVESTMENT

India's attitude toward FDI was summed up by the president of the Associated Chambers of Commerce and Industry of India, who said, "Most of our people, in all political parties, have no concept of how the world is moving. My political friends think it's the seventeenth century and that every investment . . . is going to come into India and take over." His reference was to the long domination of India by the British, French, and Portuguese, who extracted great wealth from India without returning noticeable benefit to its economy.

Because of the political sensitivity, negotiations tended to be long and were usually public. India approved foreign investment on a case-by-case basis, with approval necessary at the highest government level. By the time PepsiCo began its negotiations, the maximum equity holding allowed for foreign investors was only 40 percent of an Indian enterprise. Further, foreign companies were required to develop exports to compensate for imported equipment and components and for dividend payments. There were many rules for investing in the country. For example, when PepsiCo began its negotiations, Gillette had just received approval on an investment. Gillette wanted to move into India because Indians buy more razor blades than in any other country. So the company spent seven years negotiating during two changes of government and finally agreed to settle for a 24-percent equity holding, to export 25 percent of its output, and not to use its name on its products. The name issue has been important to Indian authorities because they believe that a locally associated brand name provides greater continuity if the foreign investor leaves the market on its own or by government decree.

Coca-Cola and IBM both left India at about the same time because of the strict operating restrictions that arose after their initial entry. Coca-Cola objected to three governmental demands: that it reduce its equity holding from 100 to 40 percent, that it divulge its secret formula, and that it use dual trademarks so that Indian consumers would familiarize themselves with a local logo. Coca-Cola was particularly adamant about the latter two demands. It had always relied on the secret formula's mystique for its promotion, and it feared an expropriation once Indian consumers embraced the new trademark.

MNEs have also felt that Indian competitors influence government authorities to prevent foreign competition. Officially, the authorities tell the foreign company that its application has simply run into "political difficulties," but behind the scenes MNEs believe that Indian business leaders align themselves with Indian political leaders. For example, when the government gave Coca-Cola its directives in 1977, Ramesh Chauhan, the head of Parle Exports, was an ally of Prime Minister Moraji Desai.

THE NEGOTIATIONS

PepsiCo first negotiated a joint venture arrangement with two Indian companies it felt could ease the negotiation process. The joint venture was contingent on government approval to operate. One of the two companies was a division of Tata Industries, perhaps India's most powerful private company. The second was a government-owned company, Punjab Agro Industries, to signal that the public interest would be served in the venture.

Although the initial investment was only $15 million, PepsiCo needed approval at the cabinet level. There were 20 parliamentary debates, 15 committee reviews, and 5,000 articles in the press about the proposed investment over a three-year period.

PepsiCo and its partners proposed that the new company reside in the politically volatile state of Punjab, where they enlisted the support of Sikh (a religious group) leaders who lobbied publicly on their behalf. They claimed that Sikh terrorism might be subdued by providing jobs and help to Punjabi farmers. The partners estimated that the investment would create 25,000 jobs in the Punjab and another 25,000 elsewhere. They also pointed out that China and the former Soviet Union had allowed entry of foreign soft drink producers, so India was behind even socialist countries. They argued further that new technology and know-how would prevent some of the wastage of Punjabi fruits, which they estimated at 30 percent. Finally, they contended that little competition with foreign companies had kept prices and profit margins artificially high so that there was little incentive for local companies to grow and distribute widely. Competitive soft drink sales were limited primarily to the largest cities.

Opponents contended that foreign capital and imports should be restricted to those high-technology areas in which India lacked expertise, that the venture's proposed production of processed foods (such as potato chips, corn chips, fruit drinks, and sauces) wasn't needed, and that imported equipment would hurt India's balance of payments. Also, journalists reported that PepsiCo had a CIA connection aimed at undermining India's independence.

The agreement with the PepsiCo group, signed in 1988, included the following provisions:

1. The company would export five times the value of its imports, about $150 million over the first ten-year period of operations. (This would improve India's balance of payments.)
2. Soft drink sales would not exceed 25 percent of the joint venture's sales. (This would promote production of products with more nutrition than soft drinks.)
3. PepsiCo would limit its ownership to 39.9 percent. (This would vest more control in India.)
4. Seventy-five percent of concentrate would be exported. (This would improve India's balance of payments.)
5. The joint venture would establish an agricultural research center. (This would improve Indian agricultural technology.)
6. In soft drinks the company could sell Pepsi Era, 7-Up Era, and Miranda Era. (This would put an Indian brand name on soft drinks.)
7. The joint venture would set up fruit and vegetable processing plants. (This would help alleviate Indian agricultural shortages.)

AFTERMATH AND RENEGOTIATION

Once India approved PepsiCo's venture, Coca-Cola applied to reenter the Indian market through production within an export processing zone. Producing in this way would allow Coca-Cola to sell 25 percent of its output within India rather than in export markets. The proposal threatened PepsiCo because Indian consumers still remembered the Coca-Cola name. But after 16 months, India denied Coca-Cola's application, leading a company official to say that India "doesn't follow its own rules."

In late 1989, a new prime minister, V. P. Singh, took power in a minority government. As finance minister in the mid-1980s, he had promoted liberalizing FDI. However, after taking power, he almost immediately made conflicting statements about such investment. In early 1990, the PepsiCo venture began production of snack foods and announced that soft drink production would start up by summer. Prime Minister Singh announced the government would reexamine the PepsiCo agreement.

Several events ensued. Because of India's strict FDI regulations, the U.S. government, without public reference to PepsiCo, threatened to impose trade sanctions against India. Indian governmental officials and the joint venture's management then met secretly. Subsequently, PepsiCo agreed to place a new logo, Lehar, above the Pepsi insignia. It also lobbied publicly against trade sanctions against India. The U.S. government backed down. India's Minister of Food Processing Industries also announced tax breaks for food processors.

In 1991, P. V. Narasimha Rao was elected prime minister and launched broad economic changes, including a welcome attitude toward FDI. He established the Foreign Investment Promotion Board and changed ownership requirements to allow 51-percent foreign ownership of companies. The new policies gave confidence to foreign investors, and both IBM and Coca-Cola reentered the market. Coca-Cola announced its return in 1993 through a joint venture with Parle Exports and agreed to export three times the value of its imports. It also announced it would export plastic beverage cases to compensate for its imports of concentrate. Three years later, Indian authorities approved a $700 million expansion by Coca-Cola.

However, in 1995, political opponents of FDI garnered enough strength to harass PepsiCo. A group of 400 militant protestors smashed Pepsi bottles and burned Pepsi posters. PepsiCo's first Kentucky Fried Chicken (KFC) restaurant in Bangalore needed police protection because of threats. Then it closed temporarily because of allegations of using too much monosodium glutamate and because India's chicken industry diverts available land to meat instead of traditional food production. KFC's second restaurant in New Delhi closed for a month because government inspectors found two flies in its kitchen. Both PepsiCo's and Coca-Cola's sales were temporarily suspended because prices on bottles were smudged.

Because India is one of the few countries in which PepsiCo outsells Coca-Cola, the two companies have fought what many observers think is a "dirty war" for that market. For example, PepsiCo received approval from Indian authorities to use artificial sweeteners in carbonated drinks, and it introduced Diet Pepsi before Coca-Cola could launch Diet Coke. Then Coca-Cola brought an old law to the attention of Indian authorities, which required sugar in sweetened carbonated water. Authorities pulled Diet Pepsi from distribution until Indian courts could make a ruling. By the time the courts ruled in favor of PepsiCo, Coca-Cola was ready to introduce its own product. Both companies have used the United States as a staging ground for the Indian battle as well. For example, Coca-Cola sponsored the erection of a statue in Atlanta of Mahatma Gandhi to build goodwill in India. PepsiCo filed a suit in the United States accusing Coca-Cola of illegal and unethical business practices in

India, including attempts to raid PepsiCo's employees and interfere with contracts, customers, and consultants.

QUESTIONS

1. Evaluate the provisions to which PepsiCo agreed in 1988. Could the company have negotiated better terms?

2. In light of later events, should Coca-Cola have abandoned the Indian market in 1977?

3. From an Indian standpoint, evaluate the government's restrictions on FDI.

4. What behavioral factors might affect negotiations involving managers and government officials from the United States and India?

CHAPTER NOTES

1 Data for the case were taken from Louis Morano, "Multinationals and Nation-States: The Case of Aramco," *Orbis*, Summer, 1979, pp. 447–468; "Aramco Has Been the Bridge Between Two Nations," *The Oil Daily*, September 18, 1989, p. B19; Gerald F. Seib and Peter Waldman, "Best of Friends," *Wall Street Journal*, October 26, 1992, p. A1; "World Oil Industry: More Private Co.'s but State-Owned Co.'s Still Dominate," *Petroleum Times*, Vol. 16, No. 11, June 3, 1996, p. 8; Karen Matusic, "Saudi's Greek Refining Deal Extends Downstream Reach," *Reuter European Business Report*, March 14, 1996; Paul Mollet, "Aramco Man Gets Top Job," Petroleum *Economist*, Vol. 62, No. 9, September 1995, p. 36; Steven Swindells, "Saudi Oil Power Seen Growing in Europe," *Reuters Financial Service*, May 27, 1996; Richard J. Barnet and John Cavanaugh, *Global Dreams Imperil Corporations and the New World Order* (New York: Simon & Schuster, 1994); Joe Avancena, "Aramco Plans to Acquire Petrogal Shares," *Moneyclips*, August 31, 1996; Neil Fullick, "Asia and Gulf Increasing Ties Because of Crude Oil," *Reuter Asia-Pacific Business Report*, September 10, 1996; Mark Emond, "FTC Okays Biggest R&M Merger," *National Petroleum News*, February 1998, p. 13; Kjell Roland, "New Producers, Consumers, Issues Rapidly Changing Supply Picture," *Oil & Gas Journal*, March 2, 1998, pp. 103–107; and Anthony Cave Brown, *A History of Aramco and the Royal House of Saud* (Boston: Houghton Mifflin, 1999).

2 Jean J. Boddewyn and Thomas L. Brewer, "International-Business Political Behavior: New Theoretical Directions," *Academy of Management Review*, Vol. 19, No. 1, 1994, pp. 119–143.

3 J. Grieco, "Foreign Investment and Development: Theories and Evidence," in *Investing in Development: New Roles for Private Capital?* T. Moran, ed. (New Brunswick, NJ: Transaction Books, 1986); and D. Encarnation, *Dislodging Multinationals: India's Strategy in Comparative Perspective* (Ithaca, NY: Cornell University Press, 1989).

4 John Rossant, "Does Big Oil Have Saudi Arabia Over a Barrel?" *Business Week*, February 22, 1999, p. 35.

5 Boddewyn and Brewer, "International-Business Political Behavior."

6 Paul Kemezis, "Eastern States Diversify," *Chemical Week*, May 13, 1998, p. 41; and Paul Kemezis, "Eastern Gulf States Build Momentum," *Chemical Week*, May 15, 1996, p. 30.

7 Thomas P. Murtha and Stephanie Ann Lenway, "Country Capabilities and the Strategic State: How National Political Institutions Affect Multinational Corporations' Strategies," *Strategic Management Journal*, Vol. 15, 1994, pp. 113–129.

8 "GM Wins Biddings for China Auto Project," *Wall Street Journal*, October 24, 1995, p. A3; and Christopher Bobinski and Kevin Done, "Daewoo Overtakes GM in Race for Polish Carmaker," *Financial Times*, August 28, 1995, p. 2.

9 For a detailed discussion of these variables, see Sushil Vachani, "Enhancing the Obsolescing Bargain Theory: A Longitudinal Study of Foreign Ownership of U.S. and European Multinationals," *Journal of International Business Studies*, Vol. 26, No. 1, 1995, p. 159.

10 Laurence Hooper, "France Chooses IBM to Bolster Groupe Bull," *Wall Street Journal*, January 29, 1992, p. A3.

11 Caroline Mothe and Bertrand V. Quelin, "Creating New Resources Through European Contracts," *Technology Analysis and Strategic Management*, March 1999, pp. 31–43.

12 Edward Taylor, "As Turkey Plans Biggest Tank Order in Years, Firms from Four Nations Go to Battle for Job," *Wall Street Journal*, November 11, 1999, p. A19.

13 John M. Stopford, "The Impact of the Global Political Economy on Corporate Strategy" (Pittsburgh: Carnegie Mellon University, Carnegie Bosch Institute for Applied Studies in International Management, 1994), Working paper 94-7.

14 Miriam Jordan, "Enron of U.S. Settles Indian Power Dispute," *Wall Street Journal*, January 9,

1996, p. A10; Allen R. Myerson, "Tentative Pact Allows Enron to Continue Project in India," *New York Times*, November 22, 1995, p. C1; "The Mugging of Enron," *Euromoney*, October 1995, pp. 22–33; and "Enron to Drop Case Against India," *Wall Street Journal*, July 26, 1996, p. A8.

15 Vachani, "Enhancing the Obsolescing Bargain Theory."

16 Some differences for U.S. negotiators are noted in Toshyuki Arai, "Negotiating with Japanese Corporations," *Export Today*, November–December 1992, pp. 32–35; and David L. James, "Don't Think About Winning," *Across the Board*, April 1992, pp. 49–51.

17 James, "Don't Think About Winning."

18 For an elaboration of this subject, see Stephen E. Weiss, "Negotiations with 'Romans'—Part 1," *Sloan Management Review*, Vol. 35, No. 2, Winter 1994, pp. 51–61; and Stephen E. Weiss, "Negotiations with 'Romans'—Part 2," *Sloan Management Review*, Vol. 35, No. 3, Spring 1994, pp. 85–99.

19 Nancy J. Adler, Richard Brahm, and John L. Graham, "Strategy Implementation: A Comparison of Face-to-Face Negotiations in the People's Republic of China and the United States," *Strategic Management Journal*, Vol. 13, No. 6, September 1992, p. 463.

20 Brian Mertens, "The Push for Privatisation," *Asian Business*, June 1998, pp. 42–45.

21 Julian Gresser, "Breaking the Japanese Negotiating Code: What European and American Managers Must Do to Win," *European Management Journal*, Vol. 10, No. 3, September 1992, pp. 286–293.

22 Robert S. Greenberger, "Foreigners Use Bribes to Beat U.S. Rivals in Many Deals New Report Concludes," *Wall Street Journal*, October 12, 1995, p. 3.

23 Amy Borrus, "Why Pinstripes Don't Suit the Cloak-and-Dagger Crowd," *Business Week*, May 17, 1993, p. 39; and Jeff Cole, "Hughes Aircraft Cancels Paris Display After Warning of a French Spy Scheme," *Wall Street Journal*, April 26, 1993, p. A4.

24 William Dawkins, "Japan Angered by Claims of U.S. Spy at Car Talks," *Financial Times*, October 17, 1995, p. 1.

25 Robert Keatley, "CIA Finds a New Focus: Espionage and Bribery That Hurt U.S. Business," *Wall Street Journal*, January 15, 1994, p. A8.

26 Johnathan Friedland, "Bristol-Myers Aims to Boost Patent Laws as Argentine Unit Sells Pirate Drugs," *Wall Street Journal*, September 23, 1996, p. A16.

27 Thomas L. Brewer, "International Investment Dispute Settlement Procedures: The Evolving Regime for Foreign Direct Investment," *Law & Policy in International Business*, Vol. 26, No. 2, 1995, pp. 633–672.

28 George Schwarzenberger, "The Protection of British Property Abroad," *Current Legal Problems*, Vol. 5, 1952, pp. 295–299; Oliver J. Lissitzyn, *International Law Today and Tomorrow* (Dobbs Ferry, NY: Oceana Publications, 1965), p. 77; and Gillis Wetter, "Diplomatic Assistance to Private Investment," *University of Chicago Law Review*, Vol. 29, 1962, p. 275.

29 Ian Brownlie, *Principles of Public International Law* (Oxford, England: Oxford University Press, 1966), pp. 435–436.

30 Green H. Hackworth, *Digest of International Law* (Washington, D.C.: U.S. Government Printing Office, 1942), pp. 655–661.

31 Michael A. Geist, "Toward a General Agreement on the Regulation of Foreign Direct Investment," *Law & Policy in International Business*, Vol. 26, No. 3, Spring 1995, pp. 673–717.

32 For an extensive treatise on the theory, see Robert A. Packenham, *The Dependency Movement: Scholarship and Politics in Development Studies* (Cambridge, MA: Harvard University Press, 1992). For some different national views of its validity, see Ndiva Kofele-Kale, "The Political Economy of Foreign Direct Investment: A Framework for Analyzing Investment Laws and Regulations in Developing Countries," *Law & Policy in International Business*, Vol. 23, No. 2–3, 1992, pp. 619–671; Walter T. Molano, "Lessons for Latin America," *Christian Science Monitor*, December 8, 1995, p. 18; and Stanley K. Sheinbaum, "Very Recent History Has Absolved Socialism," *New Perspectives Quarterly*, Vol. 13, No. 1, January 1996.

33 Paul Jensen, "Political Risk Coverage Eases Entry into Perilous Markets," *Export Today*, November–December 1992, pp. 39–42; and Malcolm Richard Wilkey, "Introduction to Dispute Settlement in International Trade and Foreign Direct Investment," *Law & Policy in International Business*, Vol. 2, No. 2, 1995, pp. 613–631.

34 At this writing, the future to extend OPIC is in question. See Nancy Dunne, "House Clips Wings of U.S. Overseas Investment Agency," *Financial Times*, September 13, 1996, p. 6; and Nancy Dunne, "Record Year Lifts OPIC Hopes on Reauthorization," *Financial Times*, December 6, 1996, p. 19.

35 "OPIC Approves $1.6 bn in New Financing and Insurance," *International Trade Finance*, September 23, 1998, pp. 9–10.

36 Richard B. Lillich and Daniel B. McGraw, eds., *The Iran–United States Claims Tribunal: Its Contribution to the Law of State Responsibility* (Irvington-on-Hudson, NY: Transnational Publishers, 1998).

37 Brewer, "International Investment Dispute Settlement Procedures."

38 Ibid.

39 Frances Williams, "WTO Push for Investment Rules Pact," *Financial Times*, October 17, 1996, p. 4.

40 A good overview of the issues can be found in Keith E. Maskers, "Intellectual Property Rights and the Uruguay Round," *Economic Review: Federal Reserve Bank of Kansas City*, First Quarter 1993, pp. 11–26.

41 Eric Schine and Paul Magnusson, "Clay Jacobson Calls It Patently Unfair," *Business Week*, August 19, 1991, p. 48. Uruguay may also use the cognac label. See "Denominación 'Cognac' Solo Se Puede Usar En Dos Países," *El País* [Montevideo, Uruguay], June 25, 2000, p. 1.

42 Peggy E. Chaudhry and Michael G. Walsh, "Intellectual Property Rights," *Columbia Journal of World Business*, Vol. 30, No. 2, Summer 1995, pp. 80–92.

43 Jan N. Conlin and Ronald J. Schutz, "The Patent Files," *Chief Executive*, June 1998, pp. 44–47.

44 Thomas J. Maronick, "European Patent Laws and Decisions: Implications for Multinational Marketing Strategy," *International Marketing Review*, Vol. 5, No. 2, Summer 1988, pp. 20–30.

45 "Jeu Zespri," *Economist*, August 10, 1996, p. 48.

46 "EU and U.S. End Drink Dispute," *Wall Street Journal*, March 29, 1994, p. A10.

47 Amal Jayasinghe, "Sri Lanka May Reclaim Companies," *Financial Times*, August 8, 1996, p. 6; and David Owen, "Socialists 'Might Renationalize France Télécom,'" *Financial Times*, February 10, 1997, p. 3.

48 Andrew Hill, "Habitat's Move into Italy Challenged," *Financial Times*, May 8, 1996, p. 2.

49 Frances Williams, "Welcome for Updated Rules on Copyright," *Financial Times*, December 23, 1996, p. 3.

50 Alfred T. Checkett, "Can We Do More to Fight Counterfeiting?" *Security Management*, February 1999, pp. 129–130.

51 Robert Colvin, "Innovative Technologies Help Thwart Counterfeiting," *Modern Plastics*, July 1999, p. 57.

52 "Countering Counterfeiting," *Business Europe*, July 28, 1999, pp. 5–6.

53 "Car Knockoffs Spread in China," *Wall Street Journal*, November 20, 1995, p. A10; Andrea Adelson, "Retail Fact, Retail Fiction," *New York Times*, September 16, 1995; Joseph Kahn, "China's Consumers Profit by Ferreting Fake Brands," *Wall Street Journal*, January 4, 1996, p. B1.

54 Steven Erlanger, "Thailand, Where Pirated Tapes Are Everywhere and Profitable," *New York Times*, November 27, 1990, pp. B1–B2.

55 Michael G. Harvey and Ilkka A. Ronkainen, "International Counterfeiters: Marketing Success Without the Cost and the Risk," *Columbia Journal of World Business*, Vol. 20, No. 3, Fall 1985, p. 39.

56 Peter H. Lewis, "As Piracy Grows, the Software Industry Counterattacks," *New York Times*, November 8, 1992, p. 12F.

57 For specific descriptions see, David H. Freedman, "Faker's Paradise," *Forbes*, April 5, 1999, pp. 48–54.

58 "Fake Drugs," *Economist*, May 2, 1992, pp. 85–86.

59 Shenliang Deng, Pam Townsend, Maurice Robert, and Normand Quesnel, "A Guide to Intellectual Property Rights in Southeast Asia and China," *Business Horizons*, November–December 1996, pp. 43–51.

60 Stephen Baker and Inka Resch, "Piracy!" *Business Week*, July 26, 1999, p. 90.

61 Colvin, "Innovative Technologies Help Thwart Counterfeiting."

62 David M. Schilling and Ruth Rosenbaum, "Principles for Global Corporate Responsibility," *Business and Society Review*, Vol. 94, Summer 1995, pp. 55–56.

63 Robert Taylor, "Code of Conduct for Toy Makers," *Financial Times*, June 4, 1996, p. 4.

64 Robert S. Greenberger, "Clinton to Unveil Voluntary Business Code," *Asian Wall Street Journal*, March 27, 1995, p. 12.

65 Robert D. Haas, "Ethics in the Third World," *Across the Board*, May 1994, pp. 12–13.

66 Gary A. Weaver, Linda Klebe Trevino, and Philip L. Cochran, "Integrated and Decoupled Corporate Social Performance: Management Commitments, External Pressures, and Corporate Ethics Practices," *Academy of Management Journal*, Vol. 42, No. 5, 1999, pp. 539–552.

67 "1992 General Motors Public Interest Report"; Michael Schroeder and Jonathan Kapstein, "Charity Doesn't Begin at Home Anymore," *Business Week*, February 25, 1991, p. 91; Elyse Tanouye, "Merck's Drug Giveaway Hits Roadblocks," *Wall Street Journal*, September 23, 1992, p. B1; and Sony Annual Report 1995.

68 Data for the case were taken from Subrata N. Chakravarty, "How Pepsi Broke into India," *Forbes*, November 27, 1989, pp. 43–44; Lincoln Kaye, "Pepping Up the Punjab," *Far Eastern Economic Review*, October 27, 1988, pp. 77–78; Steven R. Weisman, "Pepsi Sets Off a Cola War in India," *New York Times*, March 21, 1988, p. 28; Anthony Spaeth, "India Beckons—and Frustrates," *Wall Street Journal*, September 22, 1989, pp. R23–R25; "A Passage to India," *Panorama*, February

1989, n.p.; Barbara Crossette, "After Long Fight, Pepsi Enters India," *New York Times,* May 24, 1990, p. C2; Michael J. McCarthy, "India Gives Final Approval to Pepsi's Plans," *Wall Street Journal,* May 24, 1990, p. A5; Anthony Spaeth and Ajai Singh, "India Rejects Coca-Cola's Bid to Sell Soft Drinks, Giving Pepsi an Advantage," *Wall Street Journal,* March 16, 1990, p. B5; "India Clears Venture, Includes Coke's Return," *New York Times,* June 24, 1993, p. C3; "Coke Returns to India," *Herald Times* [Bloomington, IN], p. B6; Joyce E. Davis and Ricardo Sookdeo, "Pepsi Opens a Second Front," *Fortune,* August 8, 1994,

pp. 71–76; Miriam Jordan, "Indian Nationalists Pick the Next Target," *Wall Street Journal,* August 8, 1995, p. A9; "KFC Outlet in India Reopens," *Wall Street Journal,* December 5, 1995, p. A12; John F. Burns, "India Effort vs. Foreign Business Upsets American Chain," *New York Times,* September 14, 1995, p. C6; "New Delhi Suspends Sales of Pepsi, Coke," *BC Cycle,* January 20, 1996; "PepsiCo Will Not Be Thrown Out of India," *Agence France Presse,* November 21, 1995; Narayan Madhavan, "Indian Leftists to Launch Campaign Against Pepsi," *Reuter Asia-Pacific Business Report,* October 15, 1995; Miriam Jordan,

"U.S. Ambassador to India Means Business," *Wall Street Journal,* July 31, 1996, p. A11; Amy Louise Kazmin, "Why New Delhi Is Picking on Pepsi," *Business Week,* May 18, 1998, p, 54; Nikhil Deogun and Jonathan Karp, "Pepsi Sues Coke Unit to Defend Indian Turf," *Wall Street Journal,* April 20, 1998, p. A12; Miriam Jordan, "Debut of Rival Diet Colas in India Leaves a Bitter Taste," *Wall Street Journal,* July 21, 1999, p. B1; Steven Shabad, "Coke vs. Pepsi—Again," *World Press Review,* July 1998, p. 26; and "Pepsi-Cola's International Focus Looks Sharp," *Beverage Industry,* May 1998, pp. 8–9.

PART FIVE: THE DYNAMICS OF INTERNATIONAL BUSINESS-GOVERNMENT RELATIONSHIPS
TEVA SPORTS SANDALS AND DECKERS OUTDOOR CORPORATION

While spending his college summers in the 1980s as a boatman working on the Colorado River, Mark Thatcher fell in love with a sport like white water rafting. Determined to avoid a 9-to-5 job, he soon saw an opportunity to fill the need for a well-made water sandal that would appeal to fellow boatmen and water sports enthusiasts. And so, the Teva sandal was born. Thatcher literally took his first samples on the road, working out of an old pickup truck to market them at outfitters along the rivers of Arizona, New Mexico, Utah, and Wyoming. National success came quickly, with international success not far behind.

Today there are over 60 different Teva styles, in categories like casual, precision sport, wilderness, and utility. With their patented strapping system, they are designed for men, women, and children, and the company markets them as comfortable and stylish yet hardy enough for outdoor uses such as kayaking and sailing.

Now based in Flagstaff, Arizona, Teva (the name means "nature" in Hebrew) is still a privately owned firm with which Thatcher is closely associated. It makes its products in Costa Rica, Mexico, China, the United States, and other countries under exclusive license to Deckers Outdoor Corporation. Teva sells its sandals through Deckers wholesale and distribution arm, at most sporting goods and specialty outdoor gear shops.

In 1996, Teva realized the great potential of the Internet in both building its brand and serving customer needs. Teva launched its own Web site through which it sells its sandals. Customers from all over the world can browse, check product information, or purchase products directly from the company. Making the full range of products available has been one of the biggest challenges the company has faced from its Internet presence. Not every retailer carries all Teva styles in all sizes, so the Web site has to go above and beyond traditional retail offerings.

Still a big factor in Teva's international success, however, is the international production and marketing savvy of Deckers, which has exclusive rights to manufacture, distribute, and sell Teva products. Deckers handles all the domestic and international negotiations, contracts, and agreements concerning new plant locations, raw materials purchasing, and sales to distributors at home and abroad. If Teva needs a new manufacturing plant overseas to increase capacity, Deckers will research sites, select a location, and negotiate all of the relevant government regulations, laws, restrictions, and customs until it can get all parties to agree. If Teva needs new sources of raw materials, Deckers investigates suppliers' ability to deliver high-quality materials on time and at reasonable cost, and negotiates the best possible contract for Teva. When wholesalers are ready to place their orders, Deckers assures them of receiving the styles and quantities they want, when they want them.

In all of these tasks, Deckers must work with a myriad of government regulations and cultural norms in each of the countries in which it operates. Language differences, exchange rate fluctuations, and even ethical issues can all come into play.

Sources: Scott Walters, "Taking the Trade Online," Arizona Daily Sun, Sept. 26, 1999; p. 19; "Mark Thatcher," The Pine (NAU alumni magazine), Winter 1999, p. 9, Teva Sports Sandals and Deckers Outdoor Corp.

QUESTIONS

1. If Deckers outsources its manufacturing to other companies overseas, what are some of the challenges it might face in ensuring that these companies adhere to high standards in their employment practices? Does Teva have any responsibility to Deckers' decisions on plant locations and labor practices, or is that Deckers' sole responsibility?

2. What are the major challenges Deckers is likely to face in interacting with different governments abroad? How can it develop the expertise it needs to be successful in widely different manufacturing environments overseas?

3. Should Teva continue to let Deckers take care of all of its global efforts? What are the pros and cons of letting Deckers do so much?

4. How can international firms acquire expertise in their dealings with the governments of foreign nations? Do you think Deckers faces any handicaps in building its international relationships, and if so, what are they and how can they be overcome?

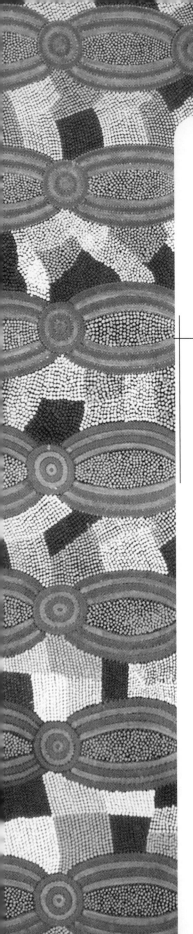

Operations: Overlaying Tactical Alternatives

CHAPTER 13

Country Evaluation and Selection

If the profits are great, the risks are great. —CHINESE PROVERB

OBJECTIVES

- To discuss company strategies for sequencing the penetration of countries and committing resources
- To explain how clues from the environmental climate can help managers limit geographic alternatives
- To examine the major variables a company should consider when deciding whether and where to expand abroad
- To overview methods and problems of collecting and comparing information internationally
- To describe some simplifying tools for determining a global geographic strategy
- To introduce how managers make final investment, reinvestment, and divestment decisions

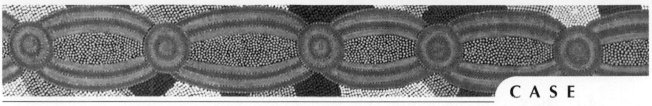

Blockbuster Video, with about 6,000 stores in 2000, is by far the world's biggest video rental chain. Most of Blockbuster's domestic (U.S.) growth occurred between 1987 and 1992, during which its number of stores increased from 238 to 2,989. This increase was partially the result of growth in the video rental market as more people tried out their new VCRs. Much of Blockbuster's growth came at the expense of thousands of mom-and-pop-type stores that stocked a small supply of tapes along with their other merchandise.

Blockbuster's primary growth strategy has been to attract customers by offering a big selection of tapes. It designed its stores to be very large to accommodate 7,000 to 13,000 tapes representing 5,000 to 8,500 different titles—much more than its competitors. By expanding rapidly, Blockbuster has been able to gain economies of scale to offset the more than $100 million it spends per year on advertising. It buys vast numbers of tapes, which gives it buying clout with the film studios that sell tapes.

To finance its growth in the United States, Blockbuster has relied on acquisitions in exchange for Blockbuster stock, has franchised about half of its stores rather than obtaining ownership, and has raised equity capital for company-owned stores.

Despite its impressive U.S. growth, by 1992 Blockbuster had acquired only a 13-percent share of the U.S. home video market. Although there was room to grow in the United States, the company announced plans to focus on expanding abroad during the 1990s.

The shift in market emphasis from domestic to foreign resulted for three reasons: the maturing of the U.S. market for sales of VCRs, the threat of competition from pay-per-view movies, and the growth in retail sales of videotapes for home use—the sell-through market—as opposed to rentals. Blockbuster was slow to enter the sell-through market, giving retailers such as Kmart a head start on gaining market share. Further, because film distributors typically sell rental tapes for about $65 and sell-through tapes for about $14 (legal restrictions prevent renting sell-through tapes), many more retailers can afford to compete against Blockbuster for tape sales than for tape rentals.

Given Blockbuster's need to expand abroad, it had to decide where abroad. Initially, Blockbuster's major foreign expansion was to the world's higher-income, industrial areas—Canada, Europe, and Japan. This was a logical move, because the market for video rentals is limited by the number of VCRs consumers own, a number that varies widely among countries (see Map 13.1). The future market depends on growth of the VCR market. Among countries with high incomes, the percentage of TV-owning households having VCRs varies substantially (for example, 68 percent for Germany versus 92 percent for the United Kingdom). Within emerging economies, many households with VCRs use them primarily to record television shows rather than to view rented videotapes because they lack sufficient income for rentals. Additional factors limit Blockbuster's market in emerging economies: Movie tickets usually cost less than videotape rentals, and competitors rent cheap and unauthorized videotapes, which are sometimes copied directly from television movie channels in the United States.

Blockbuster entered the British market in 1990 and by the end of 1991 had built 15 stores. All were company owned rather than franchises because franchising was not yet developed in the United Kingdom video store market. Also, with only 15 stores, Blockbuster could not justify large advertising outlays; such advertising is an incentive for investors to buy into franchises. To increase its presence in that country, Blockbuster in 1992 bought Cityvision, the United Kingdom's largest

MAP 13.1   Numbers of Homes with VCRs Worldwide

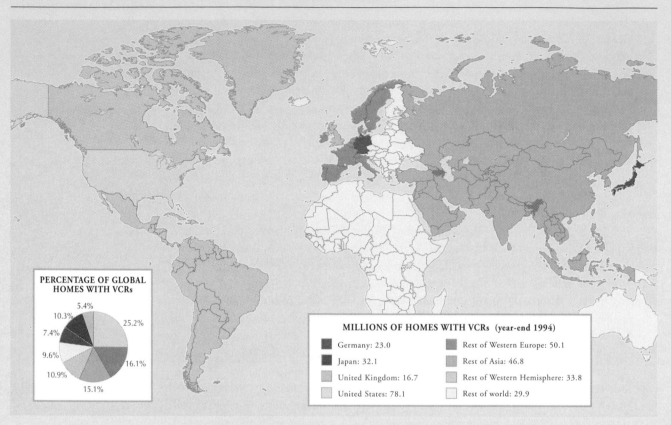

PERCENTAGE OF GLOBAL HOMES WITH VCRs

5.4%
10.3%
7.4%
9.6%
10.9%
15.1%
25.2%
16.1%

MILLIONS OF HOMES WITH VCRs (year-end 1994)

Germany: 23.0	Rest of Western Europe: 50.1
Japan: 32.1	Rest of Asia: 46.8
United Kingdom: 16.7	Rest of Western Hemisphere: 33.8
United States: 78.1	Rest of world: 29.9

Four countries—Germany, Japan, the United Kingdom, and the United States—have 48 percent of the world's homes with VCRs but only about 9 percent of the world's population.

Source: Data from *Screen Digest*, August 1995, pp. 177–180.

video store chain with 775 stores in the United Kingdom and 23 in Austria. Blockbuster initially operated the stores under Cityvision's name for its stores, Ritz. It later converted them to Blockbuster stores as a springboard for the company's expansion into France, Germany, and Italy via joint ventures.

In 1991, Blockbuster bought a chain of 25 Major Video stores in Canada for conversion into Blockbuster stores. This move brought the company economies of scale because much of the Canadian population lives within reception range of Blockbuster's advertisements on TV broadcasts from the United States. Blockbuster also set up franchise operations in Chile, Mexico, Australia, Spain, and Venezuela—mainly because people in those countries requested Blockbuster there. Blockbuster also established a franchise in Ireland, largely in response to a move into the U.S. market by Xtra-vision, Ireland's largest video chain. By 1990, Xtra-vision had 50 U.S. stores under the Videosmith and Video Library names.

In 1991, Blockbuster also decided to enter Japan. It opted on a 50/50 joint venture to gain know-how about the market from a knowledgeable Japanese partner, Fujita Shoten. (Fujita Shoten's chairman had established an earlier 50/50 joint venture with McDonald's, which now has about 800 restaurants in Japan. Fujita Shoten also has a stake in Toys 'R' Us Japan.) Block-buster planned to expand through franchising its outlets and expected to have a thousand Japanese stores by the year 2000. In deciding to move into Japan, company executives saw the following conditions that afforded opportunities for Blockbuster:

- There were no major video rental chains in Japan. The largest rental chain, the Culture Con-venience Club, had only small-scale outlets.
- There were only 1800 movie theaters in Japan, less than one-tenth the number in the United States. They were controlled by Japanese film studios that limited distribution of foreign films to about 100 theaters. Despite distribution problems, however, U.S. films had 60 percent of the Japanese film market.
- Existing video stores catered mainly to Japanese males under 25 years of age by renting tapes of pornographic and violent films. Blockbuster would target an older and more family-oriented market and would not offer adult videos.

Blockbuster's management reasoned that there was a big, unfulfilled demand for U.S. videos and that it could introduce these more rapidly into the Japanese market than Japanese competi-tors could (at the time, the wait for U.S. releases in Japan was about a year).

When Blockbuster entered Japan, it planned to earn 12 to 15 percent of its income from video game rentals, as it does in the United States. However, it was unable to meet this goal. Japanese law requires permission from the author of copyrighted material before anyone can sell or rent the material. Of the two giants in the video game industry, Sega Enterprises gave its permission but Nintendo refused.

Because space is so limited and expensive in Japan, Blockbuster had to reduce the size of its stores. However, redesigning the stores' interiors allowed them to carry about 8,000 titles and 10,000 tapes. Blockbuster allows each country's managers to decide which tapes to buy for their stores. All tape purchases are made locally through distributors representing film stu-dios. This arrangement is expedient because the local distributors can perform certain tasks more easily, such as providing for subtitles or dubbing, dealing with local censorship issues, converting films to the tape format (for example, VHS, Beta, or Secam) preferred in that coun-try, and acquiring local films to meet local demand. On this last point, Hollywood productions dominate markets worldwide; however, where there is a strong local film industry, such as in the United Kingdom and France, there is market demand for more tapes made from local films.

In 1995, Blockbuster announced a new emphasis on emerging economies in the Asia-Pacific region because of rapid economic growth in the area, which has led to more VCR own-ership. For example, the number of VCRs in China grew from 1.2 million in 1990 to 14.8 mil-lion in 1994. This emphasis was also because of Blockbuster's high-end growth in Japan, which indicated the company could be successful in Asia. Blockbuster opened its first store in Taiwan in 1997, expanded to 52 stores by 1998, and planned to have 220 stores by the year 2003. In 1999, Blockbuster bought KPS in Hong Kong. KPS had recently gone bankrupt, but until then had 38 outlets, the largest of any chain in Hong Kong.

Blockbuster has also used its foreign experience to help it grow in the United States. In 1992, the company acquired a 50-percent interest in the Virgin Retail Group, whose stores sell recorded music. This U.K. company owns megastores in the United Kingdom, France, Germany, Italy, Austria, the Netherlands, and Australia. Virgin manages the operations and plans for major expansion into the U.S. market. Its first store, in Los Angeles, was modeled after Virgin's megastores, which offer 200 listening booths, a stage for live performances, and specialty rooms so classical music lovers needn't mix with heavy metal fans. ༺༻

Companies gain opportunities and face risks in any country where they may operate. For example, McDonald's has found sales growth in France through its franchise operations. At the same time, because of its high visibility, it has been a target of protests by dissident groups. The photo shows a French McDonald's where farmers toppled Ronald McDonald by dumping apples to protest U.S. restrictions on French agricultural products. In another instance, Breton separatists bombed a McDonald's to bring worldwide attention to their desire for independence.

INTRODUCTION

Companies lack resources to take advantage of all international opportunities.

Companies seldom have enough resources to take advantage of all opportunities. Committing human, technical, and financial resources to one locale may mean forgoing projects in other areas. So managers must be choosy. They must know how to pick the best location for their business interests.

Figure 13.1 repeats the framework introduced in Chapter 1 and highlights that the choice of where to operate is a big part of carrying out a business strategy. The figure also shows that external factors influence country selection. A company should look to those countries with economic, political, cultural, and geographic conditions that mesh with its strengths. Managers might ask, "Where can we best leverage our already developed competencies?" and "Where can we go to best sustain, improve, or extend our competencies?" A company needs to determine the order of entry into potential countries and set the allocation of resources and rate of expansion among them.

Companies need to
- **Determine the order of country entry**
- **Set the rates of resource allocation among countries**

CHOOSING MARKETING AND PRODUCTION SITES, AND GEOGRAPHIC STRATEGY

In choosing geographic sites, a company must decide
- **Where to sell**
- **Where to produce**

Companies must determine where to market and where to produce. In so doing, managers will need to answer two basic questions: "Which markets should we serve?" and "Where should we place production to serve those markets?" The answers to these questions can be one and the same, particularly if transport costs or government regulations mean that local production is necessary for serving the chosen market. Many service industries, such as hotels, construction, and retailing, must locate facilities near their foreign customers, so decisions on market and production location are connected.[2] If a company develops a product that consumers find attractive, it must still find production cost advantages so that it can price the product favorably enough to sell it. These

FIGURE 13.1   Place of Location Decisions in International Business Operations

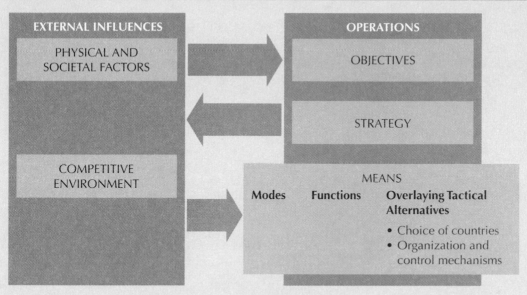

A company's choice of countries for its operations should be determined by the interaction of its objectives, competencies, and comparative environmental fit with conditions within different countries.

production cost advantages may come from abroad, allowing the company to sustain a long-term competitive edge.

Decisions on market and production locations may be highly interdependent for other reasons. A company may have excess production capacity already in place that will influence its ability to serve markets in different countries. Or it may find a given market very attractive but forgo sales there because it is unwilling to invest in needed production locations.

The process of determining an overall geographic strategy must be flexible because country conditions change. A plan must let a company both respond to new opportunities in different locations and withdraw from less profitable ones. Unfortunately, there is little agreement on a comprehensive theory or technique for choosing the best location, one that helps companies get the most out of their resources. Further, it is hard for companies to formulate strategies when they have to make assumptions about factors in the foreign environment, such as future costs and prices, competitors' reactions, and technology.

Nevertheless, managers can use several geographic strategies. A company may expand its international sales by marketing more of its existing product line, by adding products to its line, or by some combination of these two. Most companies begin by asking "Where can we sell more of our products?" instead of "What new product can we make to maximize sales in a given market?" In this chapter we assume that for the most part, the company has pursued the first question. In essence, a company needs to decide where to operate and what portion of operations to place within each location.

FIGURE 13.2   Flowchart for Choosing Where to Operate

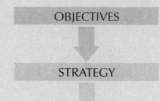

OBJECTIVES

STRATEGY

Overlaying Tactic: Choice of Countries

Choosing new locations

- Scan for alternatives
- Choose and weight variables
- Collect and analyze data for variables
- Use tools to compare variables and narrow alternatives

Allocating among locations

- Analyze effects of reinvestment versus harvesting in existing operating locations
- Appraise interdependence of locations on performance
- Examine needs for diversification versus concentration of foreign operations

Making final decisions

- Conduct detailed feasibility for new locations
- Estimate expected outcome for reinvestments
- Make location and allocation decisions based on company's financial decision-making tools

Figure 13.2 shows the major steps international business managers take in making these decisions. The following discussion examines these steps in depth.

SCAN FOR ALTERNATIVE LOCATIONS

Without scanning, a company may

- **Overlook opportunities**
- **Examine too many possibilities**

To compare countries, managers use scanning techniques based on broad variables that indicate opportunities and risks. That way, decision makers can perform a detailed analysis of a manageable number of geographic locations. Scanning is like weeding out—it is useful in that a company might otherwise consider too few or too many possibilities.

A company can easily overlook or disregard some promising options. Some locations may be skipped rather than rejected, simply because managers either never think of them or decide to go where "everyone else has gone." For example, the former vice chairman of Chrysler said, "The chief executive who gets asked repeatedly by the press and Wall Street analysts, 'Why are you so slow on your China strategy?' quickly gets the idea he's missing something and orders a China strategy. These 'forced' actions, taken because of 'peer pressure,' almost always result in disaster."[3] A company may lump certain locales within a region together and reject them before it sufficiently examines differences among them.

A detailed analysis of every alternative might result in maximized sales or a least-cost production location, but the cost of so many studies would erode profits. A company with 1,000 products that might locate in any of 150 countries would need 150,000 different studies. Plus, other alternatives must be considered as well, such as whether to export or to set up a foreign production unit. Companies should examine any conditions that would enhance the probability of making an investment before they perform a more detailed feasibility study.

CHOOSE AND WEIGHT VARIABLES

When scanning, managers will take the **environmental climate** into consideration. The environmental climate is the external conditions in a host country that could significantly affect the success or failure of a foreign business enterprise. It can determine whether a company will make a detailed study as well as the terms under which it will initiate a project. The environmental climate reveals both opportunities and risks.

OPPORTUNITIES

Managers make investment decisions after weighing opportunities against risks. Opportunities are determined by revenues less costs. From a broad scanning perspective, there are variables that indicate the amount of revenue, cost factors, and risk that might be forthcoming from one country to another.

The factors that have the most influence on the placement of marketing and production emphasis are market size, ease and compatibility of operations, costs, resource availability, and red tape. Some of these variables are more important for the market-location decision; others are more important for the production-location decision. Some variables affect both.

Market Size   Sales potential is probably the most important variable managers use in determining where and whether to make an investment.[4] The assumption, of course, is that sales will occur at a price above cost, so that where there are sales, there are profits.

In some cases, a company can obtain past and current sales figures on a country-to-country basis for the type of product it wants to sell. In many cases, however, such figures are unavailable, leaving managers to estimate current demand. Either way, management must make projections about what will happen to future sales.[5] One way is to base projections on a similar or complementary product for which sales figures are available, such as Blockbuster's projections of video rental potential based on VCR data. Often, data such as GNP, per capita income, growth rates, population, size of the middle class, and level of industrialization are also good indicators of market size and future sales.[6]

The triad market of North America, Japan, and Western Europe accounts for about half the world's total consumption and an even higher proportion of purchases of such products as computers, consumer electronics, and machine tools.[7] It is not surprising, then, that most MNEs expend a major part of their efforts on these areas. For example,

Expectation of a large market and sales growth is probably a potential location's major attraction.

Blockbuster's early foreign expansion was to the triad. However, the dominance of the triad is being challenged because of the growth in certain emerging economies.

Ease and Compatibility of Operations

Regardless of the industry, U.S. companies put more emphasis on Canada, the United Kingdom, and Mexico than would be indicated by those countries' economic size.[8] Managers prefer to go where they perceive it's easier to operate. For U.S. companies, Canada and Mexico rank high because of geographic proximity, which makes it easier and cheaper for the companies to control their foreign subsidiaries. Moreover, since the advent of NAFTA, U.S. companies encounter fewer border restrictions for their operations in Canada and Mexico than they do for most other locales. Also, at the early stages of international expansion, managers feel more comfortable doing business in their own language and in a similar legal system, which explains the appeal of Canada and the United Kingdom to U.S. companies. Language and cultural similarities may also keep operating costs and risks low because of greater ease in understanding employees and customers.[9] Finally, economic similarity influences where initial foreign operations will reside. Both Canada and the United Kingdom have high per capita incomes, similar to the United States.

After companies pare alternatives to a reasonable number, they must prepare much more detailed feasibility studies. These studies can be expensive. The more time and money companies invest in examining an alternative, the more likely they are to accept it regardless of its merits, a situation known as an *escalation of commitment*. A feasibility study should have clear-cut decision points at which managers can cut the commitment before it escalates.

Proposals for expansion may originate almost anywhere within a company, but top-level managers usually have the final say in whether they are approved. They should give precedence to those that fit the organization's motives, limitations, and policies because others are more apt to encounter problems. For example, Blockbuster failed in Germany because it could not duplicate the successful formula it uses elsewhere. In the United States, Blockbuster depends on evening, Sunday, and holiday rentals, when people decide at the last minute to fill their leisure time. But laws in Germany prevented Blockbuster from operating at these times. Further, Blockbuster creates a store environment in the United States that attracts the whole family. However, in Germany consumers prefer to see family entertainment in a movie house and seek pornographic films from video stores.[10]

Companies may limit consideration of proposals to locales that will permit them to operate with product types and plant sizes familiar to the managers. From a policy standpoint, management may find it useful to ensure its proposal group includes personnel with backgrounds in each functional area—marketing, finance, personnel, engineering, and production. From a policy standpoint, many companies further limit consideration of proposals to only those countries that permit them to own an acceptable percentage of operations and that allow sufficient remittance of profits.

Companies also consider local availability of resources in relation to their needs. Many foreign operations require local resources, a requirement that may severely restrict the feasibility of given locales. For example, the company may need to find local personnel who are knowledgeable enough about its type of technology. Or it may need to add local capital to what it is willing to bring in. If local equity markets are poorly devel-

---

Companies are highly attracted to countries that
- **Are located nearby**
- **Share the same language**
- **Have market conditions similar to those in their home countries**

Companies often pare proposals to those countries that
- **Offer size, technology, and other factors familiar to company personnel**
- **Allow an acceptable percentage of ownership**
- **Permit sufficient profits to be easily remitted**

oped and local borrowing is expensive, the company may consider locating in a different country.

Companies sometimes use a **lead country strategy**, which is introducing a product on a test basis in a small-country market that they consider representative of a region before investing to serve larger-country markets. For example, Colgate-Palmolive used this strategy for the successful launching of its Optims shampoo.[11] On the basis of a test market in Hong Kong, Colgate-Palmolive introduced Optims throughout Asia.

Costs and Resource Availability   So far, we have discussed market-seeking operations. However, companies also go abroad to secure resources that are either unavailable or expensive in their home countries. Often, a company considers making a product or component abroad for sale where it produces or for export into other markets. It must examine the costs of labor, raw material inputs, capital, utilities, real estate, taxes, and transfer costs in relation to productivity. Before collecting all this information in a final feasibility study, the company can narrow the alternative locations by examining a few key indicators.

Labor compensation is an important cost of manufacturing for most companies. However, capital intensity is growing in most industries, which reduces labor costs as a percentage of total costs and decreases the difference in production cost from one location to another.[12] At any rate, companies can examine current labor costs, trends in those costs, and unemployment rates to approximate cost differences among countries. Labor, however, is not a homogeneous commodity. If a country's labor force lacks the specific skill levels required, a company may have to train, redesign production, or add supervision—all of which are expensive. In the case of specialized units, such as an R&D lab, the existing availability of specific skills is almost essential.

When companies move into emerging economies because of labor-cost differences, their advantages may be short lived because:

- Competitors follow leaders into low-wage areas.
- There is little first-in advantage for this type of production migration.
- Foreign costs rise quickly because of pressure on wage or exchange rates.

As a result, some companies, especially those with rapidly evolving technologies, seek to locate production close to product-development activities. Doing this allows for a tight link between product and process technologies (for example, making smaller disk drives is as much a manufacturing problem as it is a technical one), a faster market entry with new products, and unique production technologies that cannot be easily copied by competitors.[13] These factors tend to push more of a company's production into industrial countries, in which most R&D occurs.

Increasingly, companies need to be near suppliers and customers in an area where the infrastructure will allow them to move supplies and finished products efficiently. Regional headquarters should reside near specialized private and public institutions such as banks, factoring firms, insurance groups, public accountants, freight forwarders, customs brokers, and consular offices, all of which handle international functions. If a company is looking for a production location that will serve sales in more than one country, the ease of moving goods in and out of the country is very important. The company may compare countries in terms of their port facilities and trade liberalization agreements with other countries.[14]

Costs—especially labor costs—are an important factor in companies' production-location decisions.

Corporate tax rates on income also affect location decisions by MNEs. Countries with a 1-percent lower tax rate attract up to three times more FDI from the United States. In addition, different tax rates among states affect location of FDI within the United States.[15] The difference in rates seems especially important within regional trading groups, in which companies can serve the entire region from any of several countries.

Companies should add any other important costs specific to their own operations into their analysis. If precise data are unavailable, they may use proxies on operating conditions. For example, if a country's infrastructure is well developed and components can be easily imported, operating costs are likely to be low. If the country already turns out competitive products containing inputs similar to those required for the production being considered, management can conclude that labor costs will be sufficiently low.

Companies should consider different ways to produce the same product.

The continual development of new production technologies makes cost comparisons among countries more difficult. As the number of ways in which the same product can be made increases, a company must compare the cost of producing with a large labor input in a low-wage country and that of producing with capital intensity in a high-wage country. For example, Volkswagen moved production of its Golf Syncro from Germany to Slovakia and switched from a highly automated, capital-intensive assembly line to a labor-intensive plant because the low Slovakian wages and high productivity cut costs from those in Germany.[16] A company might have to compare large-scale production to reduce fixed costs per unit by serving multicountry markets and multiple smaller-scale production units to reduce transport and inventory costs.[17]

Because of other considerations, a company may not necessarily opt for the least-cost production location.[18] For example, BMW calculated that Mexico would be the least-cost location for North American production. However, the company chose a U.S. location because it feared that a Mexican-made vehicle would lack the same luxury image.[19] The Japanese firm Sharp Manufacturing moved its microwave assembly from Malaysia to the United States to gain more dependable transportation facilities for European export sales.[20] However, in a sense, the companies' decisions were least cost. BMW did not have to incur high marketing expenses to convince U.S. consumers of Mexican quality, and Sharp could reduce inventories by using more dependable transportation links.

The degree of red tape is not directly measurable.

Red Tape   Companies frequently compare the degrees of red tape necessary to operate in given countries because red tape increases their operating costs. Red tape includes the difficulty of getting permission to operate, bringing in expatriate personnel, obtaining licenses to produce and sell certain goods, and satisfying government agencies on such matters as taxes, labor conditions, and environmental compliance. For example, Ukraine has thousands of government employees who have the power to block exports, ban sales, levy licensing fees, seize money from private bank accounts, and generally cause trouble for foreign businesses. They act not only in what they think is the national interest, but also to protect friends and state companies from competition and to receive bribes for favors.[21] The degree of red tape is not directly measurable, so companies commonly rate countries subjectively on this factor.

RISKS

Is a projected rate of return of 9 percent in Bolivia the same as a projected rate of 9 percent in France? Should a company calculate return on investment (ROI) on the entire earnings of a foreign subsidiary or just on the earnings that can be remitted to the parent? Does it make sense for a company to accept a low return in one country if doing so will help the company's competitive position elsewhere? Is it ever rational for a company to invest in a country that has an uncertain political and economic future? These are but a few of the unresolved questions that companies must consider when making international capital-investment decisions.

Risk and Uncertainty   Companies use a variety of financial techniques to compare potential projects, including discounted cash flow, economic value added, payback period, net present value, return on sales, return on assets employed, internal rate of return, accounting rate of return, and return on equity. The differences among these techniques is best explained in a finance course; however, the international implications of all of them are roughly the same. We will refer only to ROI as a means of explaining risk considerations in international business.

Given the same expected return, most decision makers prefer a more certain outcome to a less certain one. To calculate an estimated ROI, a company averages the various returns it deems possible for investments. Table 13.1 shows that two identical projected ROIs may have very different certainties of achievement as well as different probabilities. In the table, the certainty of a 10 percent projected ROI is higher for investment B than for investment A (40 percent versus 30 percent). Further, the probability of earning at least 10 percent is also higher for B (.40 + .30 = .70 or 70 percent) than for A (.30 + .20 + .15 = .65 or 65 percent). Experience shows that most, but not all, investors will choose alternative B over alternative A. In fact, as uncertainty increases, investors may require a higher estimated ROI.

Often, companies may reduce risk or uncertainty by insuring. However, insuring against nonconvertibility of funds or expropriation is apt to be costly. In the initial process of scanning to develop a manageable number of alternatives, the company should give some weight to the elements of risk and uncertainty. At the later and more detailed stage of the feasibility study, management should determine whether the degree

TABLE 13.1   **COMPARISON OF ROI CERTAINTY**

To determine the estimated return on investment (ROI), (1) multiply each ROI as a percentage by its probability to derive a weighted value and (2) add the weighted values. (The weighted value is probability × percentage.)

ROI AS PERCENTAGE	INVESTMENT A		INVESTMENT B	
	PROBABILITY	WEIGHTED VALUE	PROBABILITY	WEIGHTED VALUE
0	.15	0	0	0
5	.20	1.0	.30	1.5
10	.30	3.0	.40	4.0
15	.20	3.0	.30	4.5
20	.15	3.0	0	0.0
Estimated ROI		10.0%		10.0%

of risk is acceptable without incurring additional costs. If it is not, management needs to calculate an ROI that includes expenditures, such as for insurance, to increase the outcome certainty of the operation.

When a company operates abroad, it usually has higher uncertainty than at home because the foreign operations are in environments with which it is less familiar. As a company gains experience in operating in a particular country or in similar countries, it improves its assessments of consumer, competitor, and government actions—thereby reducing its uncertainty.[22] In fact, foreign companies have a lower survival rate than local companies for many years after they begin operations, a situation known as the **liability of foreignness**. However, those foreign companies that learn about their new environments and manage to overcome their early problems have survival rates comparable to those of local companies in later years.[23] The learning process also helps explain why companies often evaluate reinvestments or expanded investments within a country very differently than investments in a country where they lack experience. (We will discuss reinvestment decisions later in this chapter.)

Competitive Risk   A company's innovative advantage may be short lived. Even when it has a substantial competitive lead time, the time may vary among markets. One strategy for exploiting temporary innovative advantages is known as the **imitation lag**. To pursue this strategy, a company moves first to those countries most likely to adapt and catch up to the innovative advantage, and later to other countries.[24] Those countries apt to catch up more rapidly are the ones whose companies invest a great deal in technology and that offer little protection for the innovator's intellectual property rights. If the country also offers import protection, a local producer can, despite inefficiencies, gain a cost advantage over imported goods.

Companies also may develop strategies to find countries in which there is least likely to be significant competition. For example, Kao, Japan's top maker of toiletries and home-cleaning products, has concentrated its international expansion in Southeast Asia because that market has been growing and because U.S. and European competitors are less entrenched there.[25] Chrysler received approval for an assembly plant in Vietnam, thinking it would be one of only four automobile manufacturers in the market. However, it changed its mind about entering the Vietnamese market after learning that twelve companies had received approval. Chrysler's decision was based on a belief that there would be too much competition compared to the size of the market.[26]

However, companies may gain advantages in locating where competitors are. To begin with, the competitors may have performed the costly task of evaluating locations, so a follower may get a "free ride." Moreover, there are clusters of competitors in various locations—think of all the computer firms in California's Silicon Valley. These clusters attract multiple suppliers and personnel with specialized skills. They also attract buyers who want to compare potential suppliers but don't want to travel great distances between them. Companies operating in the cluster area may also gain better access to information about new developments because of coming in contact frequently with personnel from the other companies.[27]

Monetary Risk   If a company's expansion occurs through direct investment abroad, exchange rates on and access to the invested capital and earnings are key considerations. The concept of *liquidity preference* is a common theory that helps explain companies' capital budgeting decisions in general and can be applied to their international expansion decisions.

Liquidity preference is the theory that investors usually want some of their holdings to be in highly liquid assets, on which they are willing to take a lower return. Liquidity is needed in part to make near-term payments, such as paying out dividends; in part to cover unexpected contingencies, such as stockpiling materials if a strike threatens supply; and in part to be able to shift funds to even more profitable opportunities, such as purchasing materials at a discount during a temporary price depression.[28]

Sometimes companies want to sell all or part of their equity in a foreign facility so that the funds may be used for other types of expansion endeavors. However, the ability to find local buyers varies substantially among countries, depending largely on the existence of a local capital market. For example, the Mexican glass manufacturer Vitro decided to sell its U.S. subsidiary, Anchor Glass. The developed U.S. capital market facilitated the sale and transfer of funds to Mexico.[29]

Assuming a company does find a local purchaser for its foreign facility, chances are that it intends to use the funds in another country. If the funds are not convertible, the selling company will be forced to spend them in the host country. Of more pressing concern for most investors is the ability to convert earnings from operations abroad and the cost of doing so. For example, Vitro easily transferred the proceeds from the sale of Anchor to Mexico because the United States had no exchange controls. If the facility had been in a country with exchange controls, Vitro would have had more problems with the transfer. It is not surprising that investors may be willing to accept a lower projected ROI for projects in countries with strong currencies than for those in countries with weak currencies.

Present capital controls and recent exchange-rate stability are useful indicators of countries' monetary situation. Additionally, companies need to predict countries' likely future exchange rate deterioration and exchange controls. Some indicators of future problems are countries' negative trade balances, decreasing official reserves, high inflation, and governmental budget deficits.

Political Risk   In Chapter 2, we discussed the consequences of political risk and explained that it occurs because of changes in political leaders' opinions and policies, civil disorder, and animosity between the host and other countries—particularly with the company's home country. It may cause property takeovers, damage property, disrupt operations, and change the rules governing business. Managers use three approaches to predict political risk: analyzing past patterns, using expert opinion, and examining the social and economic conditions that might lead to such risk.

> **Political risk may come from wars and insurrections, takeover of property, and/or changes in rules.**

Companies cannot help but be influenced by past patterns of political risk. However, predicting the risk on that basis holds many dangers. Political situations may change rapidly for better or worse as far as foreign companies are concerned. For example, the perceived political risk of doing business in Vietnam improved rapidly during the early 1990s as its government sought foreign investment and trade.[30] However, Vietnam's historical record of violence, expropriations, and regulation of international business would indicate high political risk. In a broader sense, expropriation of property occurred frequently in the 1970s and early 1980s, but it has been negligible in recent years. Nevertheless, companies continue to worry sufficiently about takeovers so that many still seek insurance against them.

> **Management can make predictions based on past patterns.**

Substantial variations in political risk frequently exist within countries as well. Except in a few countries, government takeovers of companies have been highly selective. Similarly, unrest that leads to property damage and disruption of supplies or sales may not endanger the operations of all foreign companies. This may be because of the limited geographic focus of the unrest. For example, companies suffered no property damage or business disruption in Slovenia after the breakup of Yugoslavia; however, they did in other areas in the former Yugoslavia.

Asset takeover or property damage does not necessarily mean a full loss to investors. Governments have preceded most takeovers with a formal declaration of intent and have followed with legal processes to determine the foreign investor's compensation. Companies may examine past settlement patterns as an indicator of whether and how they may be compensated. In addition to the asset's book value, other factors may determine the adequacy of compensation. First, the compensation may earn a different return elsewhere. Second, other agreements (such as purchase and management contracts) may create additional benefits for the former investor. In analyzing political risk, managers should predict the likely loss if political problems occur.

Companies should
- **Examine views of governmental decision makers**
- **Get a cross-section of opinions**
- **Use expert analysts**

Companies may also rely on experts' opinions about a country's political situation, with the purpose of ascertaining how influential people may sway future political events affecting business. The first step is reading statements made by political leaders both in and out of office to determine their philosophies on business in general, foreign input to business, the means of effecting economic changes, and their feelings toward given foreign countries. Modern technology has improved access to press reports in foreign countries. On-line services include full-text reports from newspapers and television from major parts of the world, and reports are sometimes available within hours of the original publication or broadcast. However, published statements may appear too late for a company to react. The second step is for managers to visit the country and "listen." Embassy officials and foreign and local businesspeople are useful sources of opinions about the probability and direction of change. Journalists, academicians, middle-level local governmental authorities, and labor leaders usually reveal their own attitudes, which often reflect changing political conditions that may affect the business sector.

Companies may determine opinions more systematically by relying on analysts with experience in a country. These analysts might rate a country on specific political conditions that could lead to problems for foreign businesses, such as the fractionalization of political parties that could cause disruptive changes in government. A company also may rely on commercial risk-assessment services, such as those published by Business International, Economist Intelligence Unit, Euromoney, Political Risk Services, Bank of America World Information Services, Control Risks Information Services (CRIS), Institutional Investor, Moody's Investors Service, S. J. Rundt & Associates, Standard & Poor's Ratings Group, and Business Environment Risk Information (BERI).[31]

Political instability does not always affect all foreign businesses in a country.

Finally, companies may examine countries' social and economic conditions that could lead to political instability. However, there is no general consensus as to what constitutes dangerous instability or how such instability can be predicted. The lack of consensus is illustrated by the diverse reactions of companies to the same political situations. For example, in the late 1990s most MNEs shunned investing in Indonesia because of political uncertainty, but H. J. Heinz made a large investment there.[32] Further, different nationalities of companies may perceive risks to be different for

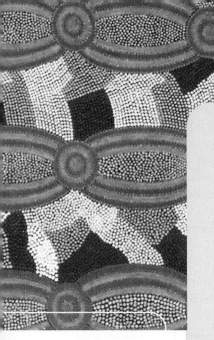

Ethical Dilemmas and Social Responsibility
GLOBAL ECONOMIC EFFICIENCY, NONECONOMIC OBJECTIVES, AND COMPANY COMPETITIVE VIABILITY: ARE THEY COMPATIBLE?

There are no ethical qualms when MNEs shift their emphasis among countries in response to stages in products' life cycles and changes in economic conditions. However, MNEs are frequently criticized when they shift emphasis in response to legal and political changes. Some have been criticized for promoting potentially dangerous products more heavily abroad when their domestic laws dampen domestic demand. For example, the U.S. government restricts advertising of tobacco products, and companies have countered with heavy cigarette promotion in emerging economies where markets are growing. At the end of the Cold War, U.S. defense spending decreased, and defense contractors turned more attention to foreign countries, many of which had either repressive regimes or conflicts that might escalate substantially. Relativists maintain it would be unethical to prohibit foreign sales because of changed domestic laws and political conditions. Normativists maintain it is unethical for a government to permit its companies from doing abroad what it prohibits them from doing domestically.

MNEs sometimes have been criticized for doing any business in countries with repressive regimes on the grounds that their presence strengthens those regimes. In fact, MNEs favor locations in which there is a nonbelligerent workforce, and such regimes often foster this characteristic; thus, FDI often increases when a dictatorship, especially a military one, is in power. Once again, relativist versus normativist viewpoints come into play.

MNEs have justified their foreign investments largely on the grounds that those investments promote global efficiencies through low-cost production and high sales. But they sometimes make moves into foreign markets to counteract what would otherwise be a competitor's advantage. For example, a company may enter a potential global competitor's home market simply to prevent the competitor from amassing sufficient capital to expand worldwide. Such a move can be justified on competitive grounds but perhaps not on global efficiency grounds. Is it ethical? Would it make any difference if the foreign investor made no profit in the other company's home country? What if such an action led to reduced worldwide competition?

Similarly, MNEs often respond to countries' trade restrictions by locating behind these tariff walls. In fact, they sometimes negotiate a monopoly position behind such walls in emerging economies. The MNEs argue that such moves are necessary because markets would otherwise be lost; however, it is hard to justify these moves on global efficiency grounds. This brings up the dilemma of whether countries should work toward regulating FDI with global efficiency as their objective or whether each country should continue to be allowed to serve its own interests by competing for FDI.

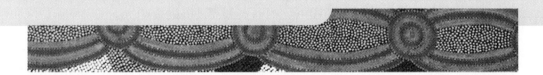

the same locales, generally because of differences in their familiarity with the locales.[33] Other uncertainties include the time lag between a political event and an investor's ability to react. However, similar symptoms of political instability may result in different consequences for business in different countries. At times, political parties may change rapidly with little effect on business; at other times, sweeping changes for business may occur without a change in government. Rather than political stability itself, the direction of change in government seems to be very important. But even if a company accurately predicts the direction of change in government that will affect business, it will still be uncertain as to the time lag between the change and its effect.

Frustration occurs when there is a difference between a country's level of aspirations and its level of welfare and expectations—the higher the difference, the higher the level of frustration. If there is a great deal of frustration in a country, groups may disrupt business by calling general strikes and destroying property and supply lines. They might also replace governmental leaders. Moreover, frustrated groups and political leaders might try to blame problems on foreigners by making threats against foreign governments and expropriating foreign properties or changing the rules for foreign-owned companies. But what is frustration? It is dissatisfaction from unfulfilled need. One cannot measure frustration directly. Nor can it be said that one country has higher frustration than another simply because it is poorer. People in the poorer country may either be aspiring for less, or they may expect their aspirations to be fulfilled with present political directions. Companies may examine growth in urbanization, literacy, televisions per capita, advertising expenditures, and labor unionization as indicators of growing aspirations. They may examine infant survival rates, caloric consumption, hospital beds per capita, piped water supply per capita, and income per capita as indicators of welfare. They may also examine trends in changes for the indicators of welfare to obtain indicators of expectations.

COLLECT AND ANALYZE DATA

Information is needed at all levels of control.

Companies undertake business research to reduce uncertainties in their decision process, expand or narrow the alternatives they consider, and assess the merits of their existing programs. Efforts to reduce uncertainties include attempts to answer such questions as these: "Can qualified personnel be hired?" "Will the economic and political climate allow for a reasonable certainty of operations?" Alternatives may be expanded by asking, "Where are possible new sources of funds or sales?" or they may be narrowed by querying, "Where among the alternatives would operating costs be lowest?" Evaluation and control are improved by assessing present and past performance: "Is the distributor servicing sufficient accounts?" "What is our market share?" Clearly, there are numerous details that, if a company ascertains them, can be useful in its objectives.

Companies should compare the cost of information with its value.

A company can seldom, if ever, gain all the information its managers would like. This is because of time constraints and the cost of collecting information. Managers should estimate the costs of data collection and compare them with the probable payoff from the data in terms of revenue gains or cost savings.

PROBLEMS WITH RESEARCH RESULTS AND DATA

The lack, obsolescence, and inaccuracy of data on many countries make much research difficult and expensive to undertake. Data discrepancies sometimes create uncertainties about location decisions. In most industrial countries, such as the United States, governments collect very detailed demographic and purchasing data, which are available cheaply to any company or individual. (But even in the United States, GNP figures are estimated to be understated by as much as 15 percent, and the 1990 census may have missed between 4 million and 6 million people.[34])

Using samples based on available information, a company can draw fairly accurate inferences concerning market-segment sizes and locations, at least within broad categories. In the United States, the fact that so many companies are publicly owned and are required to disclose much operating information enables a company to learn competitors' strengths and weaknesses. Further, companies may rely on a multitude of behavioral studies dealing with U.S. consumer preferences and experience. With this available information, a company can devise questionnaires or test-market with a selected sample so that responses should reflect the behavior of the larger target group to whom the company plans to sell. Contrast this situation to that in a country whose basic census, national income accounts, and foreign trade figures are suspect and where no data are collected on consumer expenditures. In many countries, business is conducted under a veil of secrecy, consumers' buying behavior is speculated on, market intermediaries are reluctant to answer questions, and expensive primary research may be required before meaningful samples and questions can be developed.

Twenty countries have agreed to standards for collecting and publishing 17 categories of data on the Internet. This agreement through the IMF came about because of a belief that the Mexican financial crisis of 1994 may have been averted had international financial authorities had better and more timely information about Mexico's trade, debt, and foreign-exchange reserves. It is expected that other countries will join the original 20 because of embarrassment from being left out of the group.[35]

Reasons for Inaccuracies　For the most part, incomplete or inaccurate published data result from the inability of many governments to collect the needed information. Poor countries may have such limited resources that other projects necessarily receive priority in the national budget. Why collect precise figures on the literacy rate, the leaders of a poor country might reason, when the same outlay can be used to build schools to improve that rate?

Education affects the competence of governmental officials to maintain and analyze accurate records. Economic factors also hamper record retrieval and analysis, because hand calculations may be used instead of costly electronic data-processing systems. The result may be information that is years old before it is made public. Finally, cultural factors affect responses. Mistrust of how the data will be used may lead respondents to answer incorrectly, particularly if questions probe financial details.

Of equal concern to the researcher is the publication of false or purposely misleading information designed to persuade businesspeople to follow a certain course of action. For example, the government of Indonesia inflated figures on its improving economic conditions and on the social welfare of its citizens so that investors and lenders would

Information inaccuracies result from
- **Inability to collect data**
- **Purposeful misleading**

Looking to the Future
WILL LOCATIONS AND LOCATION-MODELS CHANGE?

International geographic expansion is a two-tiered consideration: How much of a company's sales and production should be outside its home country? And how should outside sales and production be allocated among countries? As yet, no comprehensive model exists to answer these questions, and perhaps differences among companies and dynamic environmental conditions make such a model impractical. Meanwhile, companies are apt simply to place more emphasis on certain locales than on others as they see opportunities evolving. Typical of this tendency was a plan by Mattel to double its international sales in five years while decreasing the portion of domestic sales from 65 percent to 50 percent. Mattel also planned for most international sales increases to come from Europe and Japan.[36]

The need for companies to allocate among opportunities because of insufficient resources is liable to play an even more important role in the near future. The receptiveness of more countries to FDI and the global move toward privatization have combined to create more opportunities from which companies may choose. At the same time, companies may not have increased their resource bases concomitantly to enable them to take advantage of all these new opportunities.

Because data availability should continue to improve, global environmental scanning will assume greater importance. Companies will continue to need information because of global strategies of competitors and economic and political volatility. However, the information explosion will present new challenges as timely analysis may necessitate even greater reliance on tools that reduce the number of alternatives under consideration.

An intriguing future possibility is the near office-less headquarters for international companies. Technology may permit managers to work from anywhere as they e-mail and teleconference with their colleagues, customers, and suppliers elsewhere. Thus, managers could decide where they want to live and work from their homes anywhere in the world. The use of offices at home is already occurring for companies' domestic operations.[37] However, we are not convinced of this possibility. The same technology should enable managers to travel less, but business travel has soared along with advances in communications.

believe the country had a rosy future. The World Bank republished the figures, giving them more credence.[38] Even if governmental and private organizations do not purposely publish false statements, many may be so selective in the data they include that false impressions are created. Therefore, it is useful for managers to consider carefully the source of such material in light of possible motives or biases.

However, not all inaccuracies are due to governmental collection and dissemination procedures. A large proportion of the studies by academicians describing international business practices are based on broad generalizations that may be drawn from too few observations, on nonrepresentative samples, and on poorly designed questionnaires.

People's desire and ability to cover up data on themselves—such as unreported income to avoid taxes—may distort published figures substantially. In the United

States, illegal income from such activities as drug trade, theft, bribery, and prostitution is not included in GNP figures. Worldwide, income from organized crime is substantial, but it does not appear in national income accounts, or it appears in other economic sectors because of money laundering.[39]

Comparability Problems   Countries publish censuses, output figures, trade statistics, and base-year calculations for different time periods. So companies need to compare country figures by extrapolating from those different periods.

There also are numerous definitional differences among countries. For example, a category as seemingly basic as "family income" may include only the nuclear family—parents and children—in some countries, but may include the extended family—the nuclear family plus grandparents, uncles, and cousins—elsewhere. Similarly, some countries define literacy as some minimum level of formal schooling, others as attainment of certain specified standards, and still others as simply the ability to read and write one's name. Further, percentages may be published in terms of either adult population (with different ages used for adulthood) or total population. The definitions of accounting rules such as depreciation also differ, resulting in noncomparable net national product figures.

Countries vary in how they measure investment inflows. They might record the total value of the project (regardless of what portion may be locally owned or financed), the value of foreign capital invested, or the percentage of the project owned by foreign interests.

Figures on national income and per capita income are particularly difficult to compare because of differences in activities taking place outside the market economy, such as within the home, and therefore not showing up in income figures. The extent to which people in one country produce for their own consumption (for example, grow vegetables, bake bread, sew clothes, or cut hair) will distort comparisons with other countries where different portions of people buy these products and services.

Another comparability problem concerns exchange rates, which must be used to convert countries' financial data to some common currency. A 10-percent appreciation of the Japanese yen in relation to the U.S. dollar will result in a 10-percent increase in the per capita income of Japanese residents when figures are reported in dollars. Does this mean that the Japanese are suddenly 10 percent richer? Obviously not, because their yen income, which they use for about 85 percent of their purchases in the Japanese economy, is unchanged and buys no more. Even if changes in exchange rates are ignored, purchasing power and living standards are difficult to compare, because costs are so affected by climate and habit. Exchange rates, even when using purchasing-power parity (PPP) are a very imperfect means of comparing national data.

EXTERNAL SOURCES OF INFORMATION

Although we have indicated variables that may be useful for making locational decisions, it is impossible to include a comprehensive list of information sources. There are simply too many. A routine search on the Internet often yields thousands of sources, and Lexis/Nexis gives full-text citations from about 5,000 sources. The following discussion highlights the major types of information sources in terms of their completeness, reliability, and cost.

Problems in information comparability arise from
- **Differences in collection methods, definitions, and base years**
- **Distortions in currency conversions**

Specificity and cost of information vary by source.

Individualized Reports   Market research and business consulting companies will conduct studies for a fee in most countries. Naturally, the quality and the cost of these studies vary widely. They generally are the most costly information source because the individualized nature restricts proration among a number of companies. However, the fact that a company can specify what information it wants often makes the expense worthwhile.

Specialized Studies   Some research organizations prepare fairly specific studies that they sell to any interested company at costs much lower than for individualized studies. These specialized studies sometimes are printed as directories of companies that operate in a given locale, perhaps with financial or other information about the companies. They also may be about business in certain locales, forms of business, or specific products. They may combine any of these elements as well. For example, a study could deal with the market for imported auto parts in Germany.

Service Companies   Most companies that provide services to international clients—for example, banks, transportation agencies, and accounting firms—publish reports. These reports usually are geared toward either the conduct of business in a given area or some specific subject of general interest, such as tax or trademark legislation. Because the service firms intend to reach a wide market of companies, their reports usually lack the specificity a company may want for making a final decision. However, much of the data give useful background information. Some service firms also offer informal opinions about such things as the reputations of possible business associates and the names of people to contact in a company.

Governmental Agencies   Governments and their agencies are another source of information. Different countries' statistical reports vary in subject matter, quantity, and quality. When a government or governmental agency wants to stimulate foreign business activity, the amount and type of information it makes available may be substantial. For example, the U.S. Department of Commerce not only compiles such basic data as news about and regulations in individual foreign countries and product-location-specific information in the National Trade Data Bank but also will help set up appointments with businesspeople abroad.

International Organizations and Agencies   Numerous organizations and agencies are supported by more than one country. These include the United Nations (UN), the World Trade Organization (WTO), the International Monetary Fund (IMF), the Organization for Economic Cooperation and Development (OECD), and the European Union (EU). All of these organizations have large research staffs that compile basic statistics as well as prepare reports and recommendations concerning common trends and problems. Many of the international development banks even help finance investment-feasibility studies.

Trade Associations   Trade associations connected to various product lines collect, evaluate, and disseminate a wide variety of data dealing with technical and competitive factors in their industries. Many of these data are available in the trade journals published by such associations; others may or may not be available to nonmembers.

Information Service Companies   A number of companies have information-retrieval services that maintain databases from hundreds of different sources, including many of those already described. For a fee, or sometimes for free at public libraries, a company can obtain access to such computerized data and arrange for an immediate printout of studies of interest.

The Internet   Printed publications are quickly becoming archives that are older than information one may find on the Internet. This is because Internet changes appear immediately, whereas changes for periodicals must be printed, disseminated, cataloged, and shelved before they are available. The amount of materials available on the Internet and World Wide Web is expanding very rapidly; however, finding these materials is still somewhat haphazard because of cataloging methods. As with other sources, one must be concerned about the reliability of information from Internet sources.

INTERNAL GENERATION OF DATA

MNEs may have to conduct many studies abroad themselves. Sometimes the research process may consist of no more than observing keenly and asking many questions. Investigators can see what kind of merchandise is available, can see who is buying and where, and can uncover the hidden distribution points and competition. In some countries, for example, the competition for ready-made clothes may be from seam-stresses working in private homes rather than from retailers. The competition for vacuum cleaners may be from servants who clean with mops rather than from other electrical-appliance manufacturers. Surreptitiously sold contraband may compete with locally produced goods. Traditional analysis methods would not reveal such facts. In many countries, even bankers have to rely more on clients' reputations than on their financial statements. Shrewd questioning may yield very interesting results. But such questioning is not always feasible. For example, Bass thinks that women consume most of its Barbicon Malt with Lemon, which sells well in Saudi Arabia. But it cannot be sure because in that country it cannot hold focus groups to discuss products, rely on phone books for random surveys, stop strangers on the street, or knock on the door of someone's house.[40]

Often a company must be extremely imaginative, extremely observant, or both. For example, one soft drink manufacturer wanted to determine its Mexican market share relative to that of its competitors. Management could not make reliable estimates from the final points of distribution because sales were so widespread. So the company hit on two alternatives, both of which turned out to be feasible: The bottle cap manufacturer revealed how many caps it sold to each of its clients, and customs supplied data on each competitor's soft drink concentrate imports.

COUNTRY COMPARISON TOOLS

Once companies collect information on possible locations through scanning, they need to analyze the information. Two common tools for analysis are grids and matrices. However, once companies commit to locations, they need continual updates, which they commonly make through environmental scanning. We shall now discuss grids, matrices, and environmental scanning.

GRIDS

Grids are tools that
- **May depict acceptable or unacceptable conditions**
- **Rank countries by important variables**

A company may use a grid to compare countries on whatever factors it deems important. Table 13.2 is an example of a grid with information placed into three categories. The company may eliminate certain countries immediately from consideration because of characteristics it finds unacceptable. These factors are in the first category of variables, where country I is eliminated. The company assigns values and weights to other variables so that it ranks each country according to attributes it considers important. For example, the table graphically pinpoints country II as high return–low risk, country III as low return–low risk, country IV as high return–high risk, and country V as low return–high risk.

Both the variables and the weights will differ by product and company, depending on the company's internal situation and its objectives. The grid technique is useful even when a company does not compare countries because it can set a minimum score nec-

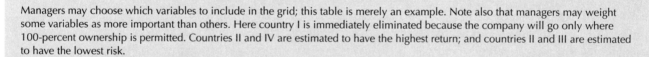

TABLE 13.2   **SIMPLIFIED GRID TO COMPARE COUNTRIES FOR MARKET PENETRATION**

Managers may choose which variables to include in the grid; this table is merely an example. Note also that managers may weight some variables as more important than others. Here country I is immediately eliminated because the company will go only where 100-percent ownership is permitted. Countries II and IV are estimated to have the highest return; and countries II and III are estimated to have the lowest risk.

VARIABLE	WEIGHT	I	COUNTRY II	III	IV	V
1. Acceptable (A), Unacceptable (U) factors						
a. Allows 100-percent ownership	—	U	A	A	A	A
b. Allows licensing to majority-owned subsidiary	—	A	A	A	A	A
2. Return (higher number = preferred rating)						
a. Size of investment needed	0–5	—	4	3	3	3
b. Direct costs	0–3	—	3	1	2	2
c. Tax rate	0–2	—	2	1	2	2
d. Market size, present	0–4	—	3	2	4	1
e. Market size, 3–10 years	0–3	—	2	1	3	1
f. Market share, immediate potential, 0–2 years	0–2	—	2	1	2	1
g. Market share, 3–10 years	0–2	—	2	1	2	0
Total			18	10	18	10
3. Risk (lower number = preferred rating)						
a. Market loss, 3–10 years (if no present penetration)	0–4	—	2	1	3	2
b. Exchange problems	0–3	—	0	0	3	3
c. Political-unrest potential	0–3	—	0	1	2	3
d. Business laws, present	0–4	—	1	0	4	3
e. Business laws, 3–10 years	0–2	—	0	1	2	2
Total			3	3	14	13

essary for either investing additional resources or committing further funds to a more detailed feasibility study. Grids do tend to get cumbersome, however, as the number of variables increases. Although they are useful in ranking countries, they often obscure interrelationships among countries.

MATRICES

Generally, managers use two matrices when comparing countries: opportunity-risk matrices and country attractiveness–company strength matrices.

Opportunity-Risk Matrix   To show more clearly the summary of data that can be illustrated on a grid, we can plot risk on one axis and opportunity on the other, a technique many companies use. Figure 13.3 is a simplified example that includes only six countries. The grid shows that the company has current operations in four of the countries (all except countries A and E). Of the two nonexploited countries, A has low risk but low opportunity and E has low risk and high opportunity. If resources are to be spent in a new area, E appears to be a better bet than A. Of the other four countries, there are large commitments in D and F, medium ones in C, and a small one in B. In the future time horizon being examined, it appears that F will have low risk and high opportunity. D's situation is expected to improve during the studied period, C's situation is deteriorating, and B's appears mixed (it will have better opportunity but more

With an opportunity-risk matrix, a company can
- **Decide on indicators and weight them**
- **Evaluate each country on the weighted indicators**
- **Plot to see relative placements**

FIGURE 13.3   Opportunity-Risk Matrix

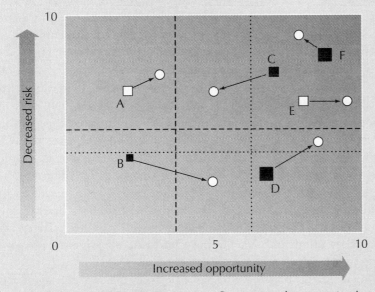

Countries above the horizontal dashed line have less risk and those to the right of the vertical dashed line have greater opportunity than the current world average. The dotted lines represent a projection of the world average for these variables in the future.

□ = No operations in the country
■ = Current operations (size of square represents size of company operations in the country)

○ = Future placement (such as five years from present)
- - - = World average rating, present
...... = World average rating, future

risk). Note that the world averages being used for comparison also shift during the period under consideration. The matrix is important as a reflection of the placement of a country in comparison to other countries.

But how are values plotted on such a matrix? The company must determine which factors are good indicators of its risk and opportunity and weight them to reflect their importance. For instance, on the risk axis a company might give 40 percent (0.4) of the weight to expropriation risk, 25 percent (0.25) to foreign-exchange controls, 20 percent (0.2) to civil disturbances and terrorism, and 15 percent (0.15) to exchange-rate change, for a total allocation of 100 percent. It would then rate each country on a scale of 1 to 10 for each variable (with 10 indicating the best score and 1 the worst) and multiply each variable by the weight it allocates to it. For instance, if the company gives country A a rating of 8 on the expropriation-risk variable, the 8 would be multiplied by 0.4 for a score of 3.2. The company would then sum all of country A's risk-variable scores to place it on the risk axis. The company would use a similar procedure to plot the location of country A on the opportunity axis. Once the scores are determined for each country, management can determine the average scores for all countries' risks and opportunities and divide the matrix into quadrants.

A key element of this kind of matrix, and one that is not always included in practice, is the projection of the future country location. Such a placement's usefulness is obvious if the projections are realistic. Therefore, it is helpful to have forecasters who are knowledgeable not only about the countries but also about forecasting methods.

The country attractiveness–company strength matrix highlights the fit of a company's product to the country.

Country Attractiveness–Company Strength Matrix

Another matrix highlights a company's specific product advantage on a country-by-country basis. Figure 13.4 illustrates this type of matrix for market expansion before countries are plotted. The company should attempt to concentrate its activities in the countries that appear in the top left corner of the matrix and to take as much equity as possible in investments there. In this position, country attractiveness is the highest, and the company has the best competitive capabilities to exploit the opportunities. In the top right corner, the country attractiveness is also high, but the company has a weak competitive strength for those markets, perhaps because it lacks the right product. If the cost is not too high, the company might attempt to gain greater domination in those markets by remedying its competitive weakness. Otherwise, it might consider either divestment (reducing its investment) or strengthening its position through joint venture operations with another company whose assets are complementary. A company might divest in countries in the bottom right corner or "harvest" by pulling out all possible cash it could generate while at the same time not replacing depreciated facilities. It could also license, thereby generating some income without the need to make investment outlays. In other areas, the company must analyze situations individually in order to decide which approach to take. These are marginal areas that require specific judgment.

Although this type of matrix may serve to guide decision making, managers must use it with caution. First, it is often difficult to separate the attractiveness of a country from a company's position. In other words, the country may seem attractive because of the company's fit with it. Second, some of the recommended actions take a defeatist attitude to a company's competitive position. There are simply many examples of companies that built competitive strength in markets that competitors had previously dominated or that built profitable positions without being the competitive leader. Third, a

FIGURE 13.4 Country Attractiveness–Company Strength Matrix

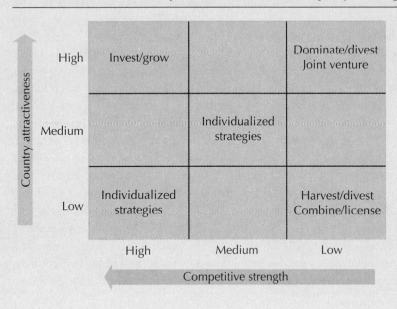

Although countries are not plotted on this matrix, those that would appear closest to the top left-hand corner are the most desirable for operations and those that would be closest to the bottom right-hand corner are the least desirable.

company may choose to stay in a market to prevent competitors from using their dominance there to fund expansion elsewhere.

ENVIRONMENTAL SCANNING

International companies rely on **environmental scanning**, which is the systematic assessment of external conditions that might affect their operations.[41] For example, a company might assess societal attitudes that could foreshadow legal changes. Most MNEs employ at least one executive to conduct environmental scanning continuously. The most sophisticated of these companies tie the scanning to the planning process and integrate information on a worldwide basis. Companies are most likely to seek economic and competitive information in their scanning process, and they depend heavily on managers based abroad to supply them with information.

ALLOCATING AMONG LOCATIONS

The scanning tools we have just discussed are useful for narrowing alternatives among countries. They are also useful in allocating operational emphasis among countries, but there are other factors companies need to consider. We shall now discuss three of these: reinvestment versus harvesting, the interdependence of locations, and diversification versus concentration.

REINVESTMENT VERSUS HARVESTING

A company usually makes new foreign investments by transferring capital abroad. If the investment is successful, the company will earn money that it may remit back to headquarters or reinvest to increase the value of the investment. Over time, most of the value

A company may have to make new commitments to maintain competitiveness abroad.

of a company's foreign investment comes from reinvestment. If the investment is unsuccessful or if its outlook is less favorable than possible investments in other countries, the company may consider harvesting the earnings to use elsewhere or even to discontinue the investment.

Reinvestment Decisions   Companies treat decisions to replace depreciated assets or add to the existing stock of capital from retained earnings in a foreign country somewhat differently from original investment decisions. Once committed to a given locale, a company may find it doesn't have the option of moving a substantial portion of the earnings elsewhere—to do so would endanger the continued successful operation of the given foreign facility. The failure to expand might result in a falling market share and a higher unit cost than that of competitors.

Aside from competitive factors, a company may need several years of almost total reinvestment and allocation of new funds to one area in order to meet its objectives. Over time, a company may use the earnings to expand the product line further, integrate production, or expand the market served from present output. Another reason a company treats reinvestment decisions differently is that once it has experienced personnel within a given country, it may believe they are the best judges of what is needed for that country, so headquarters managers may delegate certain investment decisions to them.

Companies must decide how to get out of operations if
- **They no longer fit the overall strategy**
- **There are better alternative opportunities**

Harvesting   Companies commonly reduce commitments in some countries because those countries have poorer performance prospects than do others, a process known as **harvesting** or **divesting**. For example, although Woolworth depended on its German stores for about a quarter of its operating profits, the company reasoned it should divest itself of more than 500 of those stores because of forecasted lower earnings in Germany, growth prospects in Latin America, and the need to expand its Foot Locker operations elsewhere in Western Europe.[42] First Boston moved its administration for the whole of Asia from Hong Kong to Singapore because it believed Hong Kong had greater political risk.[43] PepsiCo withdrew from Myanmar because of concern that Myanmar's poor human rights record would affect sales in other countries.[44] Chevron announced a $2 billion downsizing of its U.S. home operation to increase its business abroad.[45]

Managers are less likely to propose divestments than investments.

Some indications suggest that companies might benefit by planning divestments better and by developing divestment specialists. Companies have tended to wait too long before divesting, trying instead expensive means of improving performance. Local managers, who fear losing their positions if the company abandons an operation, propose additional capital expenditures. In fact, this question of who has something to gain or lose is a factor that sets decisions to invest apart from decisions to divest. Both types of decisions should be highly interrelated and geared to the company's strategic thrust. Ideas for investment projects typically originate with middle managers or with managers in foreign subsidiaries who are enthusiastic about collecting information to accompany a proposal as it moves upward in the organization. After all, the evaluation and employment of these people depend on growth. They have no such incentive to propose divestments. These proposals typically originate at the top of the organization after upper management has tried most remedies for saving the operation.[46]

Companies may divest by selling or closing facilities. They usually prefer selling because they receive some compensation. A company that considers divesting because of a country's political or economic situation may find few potential buyers except at very low prices. In such situations, the company may try to delay divestment, hoping the situation will improve. If it does, the firm that waits out the situation generally is in a better position to regain markets and profits than one that forsakes its operation. For example, many MNEs divested their South African operations during the late 1980s primarily because of internal political unrest caused by South Africa's policy of apartheid, trade embargoes by foreign investors' home-country governments, and consumer pressure from outside South Africa. As more companies attempted to divest, there were fewer buyers for facilities even at lower prices. By the early 1990s, the dissolution of apartheid laws brought a more positive outlook on South Africa's future. Companies that had remained (such as Hoechst, Crown Cork & Seal, and Johnson Matthey) could move faster to increase their South African business than could companies that had abandoned the market.[47] Some companies, such as Goodyear, bought back their old properties at a price well above what they had sold them for.[48]

A company cannot always simply abandon an investment either. Governments frequently require performance contracts, such as substantial severance packages to employees, that make a loss from divestment greater than the direct investment's net value. Further, many large MNEs fear adverse international publicity and difficulty in reentering a market if they do not sever relations with a foreign government on amicable terms. Occidental Petroleum and Email and Elders decided to take losses and leave the Chinese market, but the Chinese government made their departures slow and expensive.[49]

INTERDEPENDENCE OF LOCATIONS

The derivation of meaningful financial figures is not easy when foreign operations are concerned. Profit figures from individual operations may obscure the real impact those operations have on overall company activities. For example, if a U.S. company were to establish an assembly operation in Australia, the operation could either increase or decrease exports from the United States. Alternatively, the same company might build a plant in Malaysia to produce with cheaper labor; however, doing that would necessitate more coordination costs at headquarters.[50] Or perhaps by building a plant in Brazil to supply components to Volkswagen of Brazil, the company may increase the possibility of selling to Volkswagen in other countries. As a result of the Australian, Malaysian, or Brazilian project, management would have to make assumptions about the changed profits in the United States and elsewhere.

The preceding discussion assumes that although overall company returns are difficult to calculate, those for the operating subsidiary are fairly easily ascertained. However, this is not always the case. Much of the sales and purchases of foreign subsidiaries may be made from and to units of the same parent company. The prices the company charges on these transactions will affect the relative profitability of one unit compared to another. Further, a company may not set the net value of a foreign investment realistically, particularly if it bases part of the net value on exported capital equipment that is obsolete at home and useless except in the country where it is being shipped. By stating a high value, a government may permit the company to repatriate a larger portion of its earnings.

DIVERSIFICATION VERSUS CONCENTRATION

Ultimately, a company may gain a sizable presence and commitment in most countries, however there are different paths to that position. Although any move abroad means some geographic diversification, the term **diversification strategy** is when the company

---

Strategies for ultimately reaching a high level of commitment in many countries are

- **Diversification—go to many fast and then build up slowly in each**
- **Concentration—go to one or a few and build up fast before going to others**
- **A hybrid of the two**

moves rapidly into many foreign markets, gradually increasing its commitments within each. A company can do this, for example, through a liberal licensing policy to ensure sufficient resources for the initial widespread expansion. The company eventually will increase its involvement by taking on activities that it first contracted to other companies. At the other extreme, with a **concentration strategy**, the company will move to only one or a few foreign countries until it develops a very strong involvement and competitive position there. There are, of course, hybrids of these two strategies; for example, moving rapidly to most markets but increasing the commitment in only a few. The following subsections discuss major variables a company should consider when deciding which strategy to use.[51] (See Table 13.3.)

Growth Rate in Each Market   When the growth rate in each market is high, a company usually should concentrate on a few markets because it will cost a great deal to expand output sufficiently in each market. Further, costs per unit are typically lower for the market-share leader. Slower growth in each market may result in the company's having enough resources to build and maintain a market share in several different countries.

> Fast growth favors concentration because companies must use resources to maintain market share.

Sales Stability in Each Market   A company's earnings and sales may be smoothed because of operations in various parts of the world. This smoothing results from the leads and lags in the business cycles. In addition, a company whose assets and earnings base are in a variety of countries will be less affected by occurrences within a single one; for exam-

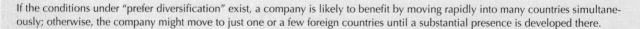

TABLE 13.3

PRODUCT AND MARKET FACTORS AFFECTING CHOICE BETWEEN DIVERSIFICATION AND CONCENTRATION STRATEGIES

If the conditions under "prefer diversification" exist, a company is likely to benefit by moving rapidly into many countries simultaneously; otherwise, the company might move to just one or a few foreign countries until a substantial presence is developed there.

PRODUCT OR MARKET FACTOR	PREFER DIVERSIFICATION IF:	PREFER CONCENTRATION IF:
1. Growth rate of each market	Low	High
2. Sales stability in each market	Low	High
3. Competitive lead time	Short	Long
4. Spillover effects	High	Low
5. Need for product adaptation	Low	High
6. Need for communication adaptation	Low	High
7. Economies of scale in distribution	Low	High
8. Program control requirements	Low	High
9. Extent of constraints	Low	High

Source: Igal Ayal and Jehiel Zif, "Marketing Expansion Strategies in Multinational Marketing," *Journal of Marketing*, Vol. 43, Spring 1979, p. 89. Reprinted by permission of the American Marketing Association.

ple, a strike or expropriation will affect earnings from only a small portion of total corporate assets. Further, currency appreciation in some countries may offset depreciation in others. Although diversification is usually of secondary importance as a motive for foreign expansion, it is nevertheless an added advantage from operating abroad.

The more stable that sales and profits are within a single market, the less advantage there is from a diversification strategy. Similarly, the more interrelated markets are, the less smoothing is achieved by selling in each.

Competitive Lead Time   The first company to enter a market often gains advantages in terms of brand recognition and because it can line up the best suppliers, distributors, and local partners. This is called **first-in advantage** and may be difficult for followers to counteract.[52] However, so many resources may be necessary to capitalize on the first-in advantage that companies may be unable to move quickly into many markets. Thus, sequential entry is more common than simultaneous entry into multiple markets. If a company determines that it has a long lead time before competitors are likely to be able to copy or supersede its advantages, then it may be able to follow a concentration strategy and still beat competitors into other markets.

The longer the lead time, the more likely the company is to use a concentration strategy.

Spillover Effects   **Spillover effects** are situations in which the marketing program in one country results in awareness of the product in other countries. They are advantageous because additional customers may be reached with little additional cost. This can happen if the product is advertised through media sent cross-nationally, such as Blockbuster's U.S. television ads that reached Canadians. When marketing programs reach many countries, such as by cable television or the Internet, a diversification strategy has advantages.

Need for Product, Communication, and Distribution Adaptation   Companies may have to alter products and their marketing to sell in foreign markets, a process that, because of cost, favors a concentration strategy. The adaptation cost may limit the resources the company has for expanding in many different markets. Further, if the adaptations are unique to each country, the company cannot easily spread the costs over sales in other countries to reduce total unit costs. For example, Ben & Jerry's took a concentration strategy by moving into the British market with as rapid an increase in distribution as possible so it could cover the high fixed costs of its local adaptations in ice cream production and advertising.[53]

Adaptation means additional costs for the company because it
- May not have the resources to spread to many markets
- Cannot readily gain economies of scale through expansion

Program Control Requirements   The more a company needs to control its operations in a foreign country, the more it should develop a concentration strategy. This is because the company will need to use more of its resources to maintain that control. Its need for more control could result for various reasons, including the fear that collaboration with a partner will create a competitor or the need for highly technical assistance for customers.

Diversification often implies external arrangements that may cause control to be lost.

Extent of Constraints   If a company is constrained by the resources it needs to expand internationally compared to the resources it can muster, it will likely follow a concentration strategy. For example, Ben & Jerry's first tried to enter the United Kingdom and

Constraints limit resources from going to many locations simultaneously.

Russian markets almost simultaneously but quickly dissolved its Russian operation. A company manager explained the decision by saying, "We simply don't have the people and resources. We're a small company. You tie up two or three senior managers and you have a measurable effect on the company's performance."[54]

MAKING FINAL COUNTRY SELECTIONS

So far we have examined comparative opportunities on a very broad basis. At some point, a company must perform a much more detailed analysis of specific projects and proposals in order to make allocation decisions. For new investments, companies need to make on-site visits and detailed estimates of all costs and expenses. They will need to evaluate whether they should enter the market alone or with a partner. For acquisitions, they will need to examine financial statements in detail. For expansion within countries where they are already operating, managers within those countries will most likely submit capital budget requests that include details of expected returns. As we indicated earlier, companies use a variety of financial criteria to evaluate foreign investments. In addition, they rely on qualitative analysis that includes such factors as expected competitive response and the fit of new activities with existing ones. If, for example, a company's large industrial customer decides to produce in a particular country, the company's decision may be one of "how to enter" rather than "whether to enter" that country as well.

> **Most companies examine proposals one at a time and accept them if they meet minimum-threshold criteria.**

Because companies have limited resources at their disposal, it might seem that they maintain a storehouse of foreign investment proposals that they may rank by some predetermined criteria. If this were so, management could simply start allocating resources to the top-ranked proposal and continue down the list until it could make no further investments. This is often not the case, however. Companies tend to evaluate investment proposals separately, and their decision is commonly known as a **go–no-go decision.** A positive decision usually means the project meets some minimum-threshold criteria. Of course, before a company makes a go–no-go decision, it has approved the project at various levels of increased detail.

Two major factors restricting companies from comparing investment opportunities are cost and time. Clearly, some companies cannot afford to conduct very many investigations simultaneously. If they are conducted simultaneously, they are apt to be in various stages of completion at a given time. For example, suppose a company completes its investigation for a possible project in Australia but is still researching projects in New Zealand, Japan, and Indonesia. Can the company afford to wait for the results from all the surveys before deciding on a location? Probably not. The time interval between completions probably would invalidate much of the earlier results and necessitate updating, added expense, and further delays. Another time-inhibiting problem is governmental regulations that require a decision within a given period. Also, other companies may impose time limits on partnership proposals.

During all of this evaluating and selecting, companies still have the pressure of satisfying stockholders and employees. Few companies can afford to let resources lie idle or be employed for a low rate of return during a waiting period. This applies not only to financial resources but also to such resources as technical competence, because the companies reduce their lead time over competitors when they make decisions.

WEB CONNECTION

Check out our home page www.prenhall.com/daniels for links to key resources for you in
your study of international business.

SUMMARY

- Because companies seldom have sufficient resources to
exploit all opportunities, two major considerations facing
managers are which markets to serve and where to locate
the production to serve those markets.

- Company decisions on market and production location
are highly interdependent because they often need to
serve markets from local production, because they want
to use existing production capacity, and because they
may be unwilling to invest in those production locations
necessary to serve a desired market.

- Scanning techniques aid managers in considering alternatives that might otherwise be overlooked. They also help
limit the final detailed feasibility studies to a manageable
number of those that appear most promising.

- The ranking of countries is useful for determining the
order of entry into potential markets and for setting the
allocation of resources and rate of expansion to different
markets.

- Because each company has unique competitive capabilities and objectives, the factors affecting the geographic
expansion pattern will be slightly different for each. Nevertheless, certain variables that have been shown to influence most companies are the relative size of country markets, the ease of operating in the specific countries, the
availability and cost of resources, and the perceived relative risk and uncertainty of operations in one country versus another.

- The amount, accuracy, and timeliness of published data
vary substantially among countries. Managers should be
particularly aware of different definitions of terms, different collection methods, and different base years for
reports, as well as misleading responses.

- Sources of published data on international business
include consulting firms, governmental agencies, international agencies, and organizations that serve international
businesses. The cost and specificity of these publications
vary widely.

- Some tools companies frequently use to compare opportunities in various countries are grids that rate country
projects according to a number of separate dimensions
and matrices on which companies may plot one attribute
on a vertical axis and another on the horizontal axis, such
as opportunity and risk or country attractiveness and
company strength.

- Because of the interdependence of operations in different
countries, it is difficult to derive meaningful financial figures to evaluate the effects or return from operations in a
single country.

- Once a feasibility study is complete, most companies
do not rank investment alternatives but rather set some
minimum-threshold criteria and either accept or reject a
foreign project based on those criteria. This type of decision results because multiple feasibility studies seldom
are finished simultaneously and there are pressures to act
quickly.

- Companies normally treat reinvestment decisions separately from new investment decisions because a reinvestment may be necessary to protect existing resources' viability and because there are people on location who can
better judge the worthiness of proposals.

- Using a similar amount of internal resources, a company
may choose initially to move rapidly into many foreign
markets with only a small commitment in each (a diversification strategy) or to pursue a strong involvement and

- commitment in one or a few locations (a concentration strategy).

- **The major variables a company should consider when deciding whether to diversify or concentrate are the growth rate and sales stability in each market, the expected lead time over competitors, the spillover affects, the degree of need for product and marketing adaptation**

in different countries, the need to maintain control of the expansion program, and the constraints the company faces.

- **Companies must develop locational strategies for new investments and devise means of deemphasizing certain areas and divesting if necessary.**

CASE

ROYAL DUTCH SHELL/NIGERIA[55]

In 1999, Royal Dutch/Shell (Shell) proposed an $8.5 billion integrated oil and natural gas investment in Nigeria over a five-year period, which would be the largest industrial investment ever made in Africa. The proposal called for 70 percent of the cost to come from private companies (mainly Shell) and the other 30 percent from the Nigerian government. Shell had three reasons for its proposal: Investment analysts had criticized its low return on capital compared to its competitors, and Nigeria offers low-cost petroleum extraction. Shell faced high political risk within its existing Nigerian facilities, and the company felt an additional Nigerian investment could win friends and lower risk in Nigeria. Shell had been criticized severely outside Nigeria for its Nigerian political activities and environmental policies, and the company reasoned the new investment could help dispel this criticism. Nevertheless, the two private companies that Shell proposed to share in the investment, France's Elf Aquitaine and Italy's Eni, both responded that it would take some time before they could even consider the proposal.

NIGERIAN SITUATION

Nigeria, a British colony until 1960, has a population of over 115 million, making it by far the most populous country in Africa. The country is organized into fairly autonomous states and the government has the challenge of trying to unite 250 different ethnic and linguistic groups. Ethnic conflict has at times been severe, especially in the 1966–1970 period when civil war broke out between the predominately Moslem Hausas and the predominately Christian Ibos, who seceded

unsuccessfully to form the Republic of Biafra. During that period, oil companies received demands for royalty payments on Biafran oil from the governments of both Nigeria and Biafra.

Nigeria has had a series of military coups, and military rule has existed more years than civilian rule since Nigeria gained its independence. In 1998, an elected civilian government replaced a Hausa-speaking military junta, which sought to quell, sometimes brutally, any moves by minority groups for more autonomy.

The Nigerian National Petroleum Corporation (NNPC), a government-owned company, is a joint venture partner in all Nigerian petroleum projects. Nigeria has more foreign direct investment than any other country in Africa.

SHELL IN NIGERIA

Shell has long considered political risk in its decision making. In the early 1970s, Shell's planners realized that technical tools for predicting where oil might be found had become quite sophisticated; however, they reasoned that they should not make exploration-location decisions based only on the likelihood of finding oil at a given cost. There were many political factors that could affect the security of their ownership and of getting oil to market. They developed rating schemes to examine the underlying conditions within and between countries that could affect the security of assets and the ability to export them to their markets. Shell hired political specialists to rate these conditions in a uniform manner so that company planners could plot on one axis the technical feasibility (opportunity) of securing oil and on the second axis the political risk of securing that oil. This tool served to help plan a portfolio of countries to serve as suppliers.

Shell also perfected scenario analysis to help understand conditions that might affect future global demands and supplies of petroleum and to prepare for different contingencies. One of the factors it noted was the size of a country's oil reserves did not necessarily correspond with the country's eagerness to sell the oil. For example, a country might wish to hold back supplies because it was already running a balance-of-payments surplus, because it could not absorb increased income efficiently into its economy, or because it expected future prices to exceed the present value of invest-

ing oil income. In this analysis, Nigeria has consistently shown up as a country willing to sell almost unlimited supplies, even though its reserves are not nearly as ample as countries such as Saudi Arabia, which is more prone to limit supplies.

However, Shell began selling in Nigeria in the late 1920s, before it developed its sophisticated tools to help deal with risk and uncertainty. In 1937, it formed a joint venture with British authorities that had exclusive rights to explore for oil. The joint venture found oil for the first time in 1956 in Ogoniland and later in other areas of Nigeria. Map 13.2 shows Nigeria and Ogoniland, the latter being a small 404-square-mile area of Nigeria at the

MAP 13.2 Nigeria and Ogoniland

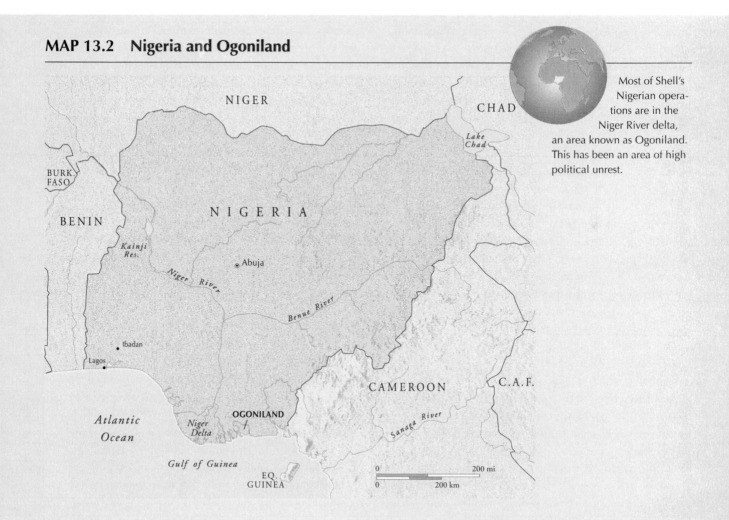

Most of Shell's Nigerian operations are in the Niger River delta, an area known as Ogoniland. This has been an area of high political unrest.

delta of the Niger River. Subsequently, this joint venture sold exploration rights to other oil companies; however, by 1999 Shell's operations still controlled about half of Nigeria's oil output. Although Shell procures oil in a large portfolio of countries, the Nigerian operations are significant, accounting for about 10 percent of the company's petroleum sources.

THE OGONI SITUATION

The Shell joint venture includes nearly one hundred oil wells, two refineries, and a fertilizer plant in Ogoniland. The Nigerian government's revenues from these operations have traditionally gone to the country's central government, and very little has been redistributed back to Ogoniland. Beginning in 1992, a group of Ogonis, led by the author Kenule Saro-Wiwa, formed the Movement for the Survival of Ogoni People (MOSOP). MOSOP began campaigning for political self-determination, a greater share of oil revenues, compensation for losses from Shell's activities, and restoration of the environment in Ogoniland. Some specific charges have been that Shell oil spills have despoiled farmlands and fishing areas, that oil flares have affected health, and that the laying of pipes destroyed freshly planted crops. Saro-Wiwa accused Shell of waging an ecological war against the Ogoni people to complete a genocide. MOSOP demonstrations have resulted in violence as the Nigerian army, using troops from other ethnic groups, have opened fire on crowds and attacked Ogoni villages. Ogonis began sabotaging Shell facilities, and the situation became so severe that Shell ceased operations in that part of Nigeria in early 1993. The Nigerian government arrested Saro-Wiwa and eight others for inciting and directing supporters to violence, held them in jail nearly a year, and then hanged them in 1995. Shortly before his arrest, Saro-Wiwa had said, "They are going to arrest us all and execute us. All for Shell."

Although Shell publicly opposed the executions and had written a letter to the Nigerian head of state requesting clemency for Saro-Wiwa, the company has been accused of not doing enough. A representative from Greenpeace, one of Shell's major critics, said, "Shell is the most powerful political actor on the Nigerian stage—both historically and currently. In Nigeria, the power doesn't come from the people, it comes from Shell. If Shell wanted to make a dif-

ference, they would." But the managing director of Shell's operation in Nigeria said, "We did not negotiate. We were not in a position to negotiate his release. We had no power to do so."

After the executions, Shell faced many, sometimes conflicting, pressures outside Nigeria. These included that it should divest all Nigerian operations, that it should not invest in new projects, that it should forgo trying to reopen operations in Ogoniland, and that it should pay all environmental and other costs in Ogoniland.

In 1997, Shell faced the first shareholder resolution presented to any company in the United Kingdom. The resolution called for more public accountability of the company's Nigerian operations. The shareholder group supporting the resolution included eighteen public and private pension funds, five religious institutions, and an academic fund. At about the same time, protesters marched in Washington to urge boycotting the purchase of Nigerian oil; the European Union froze $295 million in aid to Nigeria while considering an arms sales or full embargo on business with Nigeria; the World Bank announced it would not go forward with a $100 million investment in a gas plant in which Shell planned to participate; various organizations in South Africa called for Shell to divest its Nigerian operations; and pressures mounted in the United Kingdom for a consumer boycott of Shell.

AFTERMATH OF THE RESOLUTION

At Shell's 1998 annual meeting, groups that had criticized Shell a year earlier congratulated the company on its efforts to seek independent verification of the environmental and social impact of its global operations. However, attendees asked many questions about the Nigerian operation, indicating that Nigeria continues to be a problem for Shell. Shell's chairman said, "Nigeria is very difficult to solve . . . we'll be working on this for many years to come."

Meanwhile, two ethnic groups—the Ijaw and the Akassas—in addition to the Ogonis, have stepped up their complaints about the lack of economic benefits going to the people where oil fields are located. Shell has faced sabotage of its pipeline, work-stopping occupation of facilities by protestors, kidnapping of employees, and the hijacking of expensive equipment for ransom. The company even put some Ijaw youth on its payroll and asked them to stay at home and out of trouble.

Shell reasons that its proposal for massive expansion will demonstrate its support of a civilian democratic government, thus helping to lessen criticism of its earlier handling of the Ogoni problems. Next, the company believes the best way to get funds to the neglected regions is by increasing Nigerian oil revenues. Shell estimates that the proposal will bring an additional $20 billion to the government of Nigeria over a 25-year period. Finally, much of the investment will go toward natural gas production, thus solving the environmental problem from flaring. However, if the government does not address the development problems adequately, groups in the oil-producing areas will likely pressure the company to provide infrastructure and social services. Not only will this reduce profits, it will also put Shell into activities for which it lacks expertise.

QUESTIONS

1. What specific political risk problems does Shell face in Nigeria? What are the underlying reasons for these problems?
2. Given the high political risk in Nigeria, why doesn't Shell go somewhere else?
3. What actions can Shell take to quell criticism about its operations in Nigeria?
4. Should Shell go forward with its proposal for an $8.5 billion investment in Nigeria?

CHAPTER NOTES

1 We wish to acknowledge the cooperation of Mr. Joseph R. Baczko, president and chief operating officer of Blockbuster Entertainment Corporation, for granting information in an interview. Supplementary data were taken from Ken Stewart, "Turf Battle Looms in Emerald Isle; Blockbuster Opening Threatens Xtra-vision," *Billboard,* September 29, 1990, p. 49; Terry Ilott, "Blockbuster Clinches Cityvision Brit Vid Bid," *Variety,* January 27, 1992, p. 69; "Blockbuster Acquires 25 Stores in Canada," *Supermarket News,* Vol. 41, No. 27, July 1, 1991, p. 24; Steve McClure, "Blockbuster Hits Japan with Hopes for 1,000 Stores," *Billboard,* April 6, 1991, p. 89; Garth Alexander, "Blockbuster Bends Japan's Video Rules," *Variety,* Vol. 345, No. 2, October 21, 1991, p. 57; Terry Ilott, "Blockbuster's Bid Could Boost U.K. Vid Biz," *Variety,* Vol. 345, No. 8, December 2, 1991, p. 66; Leslie Helm, "Selling Hollywood in Japan," *Los Angeles Times,* September 21, 1992, p. D1; Richard Turner, "Disney Leads Shift From Rentals to Sales in Videocassettes," *Wall Street Journal,* December 24, 1991, p. A1; Helene Cooper, "Blockbuster Entertainment, U.K. Firm Plan a Chain of 'Megastores' in the U.S.," *Wall Street Journal,* November 17, 1992, p. B7; Gail DeGeorge, Jonathan B. Levine, and Robert Neff, "They Don't Call It Blockbuster for Nothing," *Business Week,* October 19, 1992, p. 113; Louise Lucas, "Blockbuster Poised to Buy Assets of KPS," *Financial Times,* November 27, 1998, p. 18; Khanh T. L. Tran, "Blockbuster Finds Success in Japan That Eluded the Chain in Germany," *Wall Street Journal,* August 19, 1998, p. A14;

Sam Andrews, "Blockbuster Video Moves Ahead with Buy of KPS," *Billboard,* Vol. 111, No. 3, January 16, 1999, p. 10; "Blockbuster in Taiwan, Tower in Thailand, and Radio City in the Philippines," *Billboard,* Vol. 111, No. 9, February 27, 1999 p. APQ4; and Martin Croft, "Fast Forward through Europe," *Marketing Week,* Vol. 22, No. 1, February 4, 1999, pp. 32–33.

2 Masaaki Kotabe, "Patterns and Technological Implications of Global Sourcing Strategies," *Journal of International Marketing,* Vol. 1, No. 1, 1993, pp. 26–43.

3 Bob Lutz, *GUTS: The Seven Laws of Business That Made Chrysler the World's Hottest Car Company* (New York: John Wiley, 1998).

4 John T. Harvey, "The Determinants of Direct Foreign Investment," *Journal of Post Keynesian Economics,* Vol. 12, No. 2, Winter 1989–1990, pp. 260–272.

5 Philip Parker, "Choosing Where to Go Global: How to Prioritise Markets," *Financial Times,* November 16, 1998, mastering marketing section, pp. 7–8.

6 For overall export indicators, see Robert T. Green and Ajay K. Kohli, "Export Market Identification: The Role of Economic Size and Socioeconomic Development," *Management International Review,* Vol. 31, No. 1, 1991, pp. 37–50.

7 Kenichi Ohmae, "Becoming a Triad Power: The New Global Corporation," *International Marketing Review,* Autumn 1986, pp. 36–49; and "Foreign Investment and the Triad," *Economist,* August 24, 1991, p. 57.

8 Irving B. Kravis and Robert E. Lipsey, "The Location of Overseas Production and Pro-

duction for Export by U.S. Multinational Firms," *Journal of International Economics,* Vol. 12, May 1982, pp. 201–223, found that U.S. companies, regardless of industry, tended to enter foreign markets by going first to Canada, and then to the United Kingdom and Mexico. Since then, aggregate foreign direct investment figures by U.S. companies indicate a continued emphasis on those three countries.

9 For problems of going where cultures are dissimilar, see Keith D. Brouthers, Lance Eliot Brouthers, and George Nakos, "Entering Central and Eastern Europe: Risks and Cultural Barriers," *Thunderbird International Business Review,* Vol. 40, No. 5, September–October 1998, pp. 485–504.

10 Tran, "Blockbuster Finds Success in Japan"; and Cecile Rohwedder, "Blockbuster Hits Eject Button as Stores in Germany See Video-Rental Sales Sag," *Wall Street Journal,* January 16, 1998, p. B9A.

11 Christopher Power, "Will It Sell in Podunk? Hard to Say," *Business Week,* August 10, 1992, pp. 46–47.

12 Alan David MacCormack, Lawerence James Newman III, and Donald B. Rosenfield, "The New Dynamics of Global Manufacturing Site Locations," *Sloan Management Review,* Summer 1994, pp. 69–79.

13 Andrew Bartmess and Keith Cerny, "Building Competitive Advantage Through a Global Network of Capabilities," *California Management Review,* Winter 1993, pp. 78–103.

14 Nagesh Kumar, "Multinational Enterprises, Regional Economic Integration, and Export-Platform Production in the Host Countries:

An Empirical Analysis for the U.S. and Japanese Corporations," *Weltwirtschaftliches Archive,* Vol. 134, No. 3, 1998, pp. 450–483.

15 James Hines, *Tax Policy and the Activities of Multinational Corporations,* Working Paper No. 5589 (Cambridge, MA: National Bureau of Economic Research, 1996).

16 "Volkswagen Switches Work to Low-Cost Unit in Slovakia," *Financial Times,* December 19, 1995, p. 4.

17 Mary Amiti, "Trade Liberalisation and the Location of Manufacturing Firms," *The World Economy,* Vol. 21, No. 7, September 1998, pp. 953–962.

18 Kasra Ferdows, "Making the Most of Foreign Factories," *Harvard Business Review,* March–April 1997, pp. 73–88.

19 Robert Keatley, "Luxury-Auto Makers Consider Mexico: Its Low-Cost Labor vs. Image Perception," *Wall Street Journal,* November 27, 1992, p. A4.

20 Karen E. Thuermer, "Selecting a New Location Is a Matter of Meeting Criteria," *Export Today,* April 1993, pp. 20–23.

21 Matthew Brzezinski, "Ukraine's Bureaucrats Stymie U.S. Firms," *Wall Street Journal,* November 4, 1996, p. A14.

22 Gabriel R. G. Benito and Geir Gripsrud, "The Internationalization Process Approach to the Location of Foreign Direct Investments: An Empirical Analysis," in Milford B. Green and Rod B. McNaughton, eds., *The Location of Foreign Direct Investment* (Aldershot, U.K.: Avebury, 1995), pp. 43–58.

23 Srilata Zaheer and Elaine Mosakowski, "The Dynamics of the Liability of Foreignness: A Global Study of Survival in Financial Services," Discussion Paper #213, Strategic Management Research Center, Carlson School of Management, University of Minnesota, St. Paul, Minnesota, May 1995.

24 Parker, "Choosing Where to Go Global."

25 Masayoshi Kanabayashi, "Japan's Top Soap Firm, Kao, Hopes to Clean Up Abroad," *Wall Street Journal,* December 17, 1992, p. B5.

26 Jeremy Grant, "Chrysler to Rethink Plans for Vietnam Plant," *Financial Times,* April 18, 1996, p. 5.

27 Michael E. Porter, "Clusters and the New Economics of Competition," *Harvard Business Review,* November–December 1998, pp. 77–90.

28 Liquidity preference is much like options theory, associated with the work of Robert C. Merton, Myron S. Scholes, and Fisher Black. For a good, terse coverage, see John Krainer, "The 1997 Nobel Prize in Economics," *FRBSF Economic Letter,* No. 98-05, February 13, 1998.

29 Leslie Crawford, "Vitro to Sell U.S. Glass Operations," *Financial Times,* August 16, 1996, p. 13.

30 Robert Greenberger, "Heading for Hanoi," *Wall Street Journal,* February 9, 1993, p. A1.

31 For a good discussion of the different services and their methods, see Llewellyn D. Howell and Brad Chaddick, "Model of Political Risk for Foreign Investment and Trade," *Columbia Journal of World Business,* Fall 1994, pp. 71–91; and William D. Coplin and Michael K. O'Leary, eds., *The Handbook of Country and Political Risk Analysis* (East Syracuse, NY: Political Risk Services, 1994).

32 Richard Borsuk, "Heinz of the U.S. to Invest in Indonesia; Move Shows Interest in Wake of Crisis," *Wall Street Journal,* February 12, 1999, p. A15.

33 Stewart Dalby, "Political Worries Hit Investors," *Financial Times,* December 18, 1995, p. 4, quoting data collected by the Control Risk Group.

34 Karen Pennar and Christopher Farrell, "Notes from the Underground Economy," *Business Week,* February 15, 1993, pp. 98–101; and Felicity Barringer, "Federal Survey Finds Census Missed 4 Million to 6 Million People," *New York Times,* April 19, 1991, p. A8.

35 Robert Chote, "Nations Rally to IMF's Statistics Standards," *Financial Times,* July 30, 1996, p. 4.

36 Lisa Bannon, "Mattel Plans to Double Sales Abroad," *Wall Street Journal,* February 11, 1998, p. A3.

37 Deborah Hargreaves, "'Virtual' Staff Make Themselves at Home in Offices of the Future," *Financial Times,* May 14, 1999, p. 8.

38 Marcus W. Brauchli, "Speak No Evil," *Wall Street Journal,* July 14, 1998, p. A1.

39 Vincent Boland, "Earnings from Organised Crime Reach $1,000bn," *Financial Times,* February 14, 1997, p. 1.

40 Tara Parker-Pope, "Nonalcoholic Beer Hits the Spot in Mideast," *Wall Street Journal,* December 6, 1995, p. B1.

41 Chun Wei Choo, "The Art of Scanning the Environment," *Bulletin of the American Society for Information Science,* February–March 1999, pp. 21–24.

42 Jeffrey A. Trachtenberg, "Woolworth Explores Sale of German Unit," *Wall Street Journal,* November 10, 1992, p. A16; and Richard Tomkins and Graham Bowley, "German Woolworth Stores to be Sold," *Financial Times,* September 23, 1998, p. 19.

43 "A Hub to Replace Hong Kong," *Euromoney,* February 1995, pp. 80–81.

44 Ted Bardacke, "PepsiCo Joins List of Groups Quitting Burma," *Financial Times,* January 28, 1997, p. 1.

45 Frederick Rose, "Chevron to Sell Nearly a Third of U.S. Refining," *Wall Street Journal,* September 28, 1993, p. A3.

46 Jean J. Boddewyn, "Foreign and Domestic Divestment and Investment Decisions: Like or Unlike?" *Journal of International Business Studies,* Vol. 14, No. 3, Winter 1983, p. 28.

47 Elizabeth Weiner and Mark Maremont, "Business Gets Ready to March Back to Pretoria," *Business Week,* February 25, 1991, p. 53.

48 Haig Simonian, "Goodyear Buys Back South Africa Business for $121m," *Financial Times,* November 19, 1996, p. 1.

49 Julia Leung, "For China's Foreign Investors, the Door Marked 'Exit' Can be a Tight Squeeze," *Wall Street Journal,* March 12, 1991, p. A14.

50 Bartmess and Cerny, "Building Competitive Advantage."

51 Igal Ayal and Jehiel Zif, "Market Expansion Strategies in Multinational Marketing," *Journal of Marketing,* Vol. 43, Spring 1979, pp. 84–94.

52 Briance Mascarenhas, "Order of Entry and Performance in International Markets," *Strategic Management Journal,* October 1992, pp. 499–510.

53 Diane Summers, "Chunky Monkey Invasion," *Financial Times,* August 11, 1994, p. 7.

54 Neela Banerjee, "Ben & Jerry's Is Discovering That It's No Joke to Sell Ice Cream to Russians," *Wall Street Journal,* September 9, 1995; and Betsy McKay, "Ben & Jerry's Post-Cold War Venture Ends in Russia with Ice Cream Melting," *Wall Street Journal,* February 7, 1997, p. A12.

55 Data for the case were taken from David Lascelles, Jurek Martin, and Paul Adams, "Shell 'Regrets' Execution but Continues Nigeria Strategy," *Financial Times,* November 11–12, 1995, p. 3; Paul Adams, Robert Corzine, William Lewis, and Roger Matthews, "Shell Facing New Onslaught over Nigeria," *Financial Times,* December 15, 1995, p. 3; Tony Hawkins and Simon Kuper, "Foreign Investors Are in No Hurry to Divest," *Financial Times,* November 14, 1995, p. 9; David Lascelles, "Shell under Pressure as EU Toughens Stance on Nigeria," *Financial Times,* November 14, 1995, p. 18; Richard Hudson and Matthew Rose, "Shell Is Pressured to Scrap Its Plans for New Plant in Nigeria Amid Protests," *Wall Street Journal,* November 14, 1995, p. A10; Simon Kuper and David Lascelles, "ANC Sanctions Threat to Shell over Nigeria," *Financial Times,* November 18–19, 1995, p. 1; Pierre Wack, "Scenarios: Uncharted

Waters Ahead," *Harvard Business Review,* September–October 1985, pp. 73–89; Steve Kretzmann, "Nigeria's 'Drilling Fields,'" *Multinational Monitor,* January–February 1995, pp. 8–11; Simon Kuper, "Shell 'Ignored' Warnings on Nigerian Pollution," *Financial Times,* May 14, 1996, p. 4; William Lewis, "Shell Faces UK First in Investors' Resolution on Ethics," *Financial Times,* February 24, 1997, p. 1; William Wallis and Robert Corzine, "An Unhappy History of Neglect," *Financial Times,*

February 23, 1999, Nigeria section, p. 5; William Wallis, "Ethnic Fighting Flares in Nigerian Oil Delta," *Financial Times,* June 2, 1999, p. 6; Robert Corzine, "Shell Puts Faith in Nigeria's Future," *Financial Times,* February 8, 1999, p. 6; Bhushan Bahree, "Shell Suggests a Joint Pursuit to Exploit Energy in Nigeria," *Wall Street Journal,* February 9, 1999, p. A19; Robert Corzine, "Shell Calms Fears on Environment," *Financial Times,* May 9–10, 1998,

p. 22; Robert Corzine, "Shell Plans $8.5 bn Project," *Financial Times,* February 8, 1999, p. 1; Robert Corzine and William Wallis, "Risk of More Disruption for Oil Companies," *Financial Times,* February 2, 1999; and John Bray, "Petroleum and Human Rights: The New Frontiers of Debate," *Oil & Gas Journal,* November 1, 1999, pp. 65–69. For up-to-date information on Shell's situation in Nigeria from the Internet, see www.shellnigeria.com/.

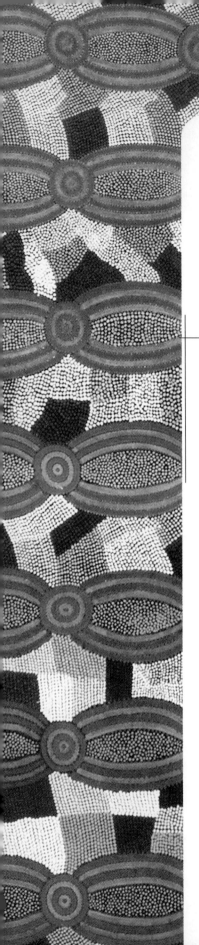

CHAPTER 14

Collaborative Strategies

When one party is willing, the match is half made.

—AMERICAN PROVERB

OBJECTIVES

- To explain the major motives that guide managers when choosing a collaborative arrangement for international business

- To define the major types of collaborative arrangements

- To describe what companies should consider when entering into arrangements with other companies

- To discuss what makes collaborative arrangements succeed or fail

- To discuss how companies can manage diverse collaborative arrangements

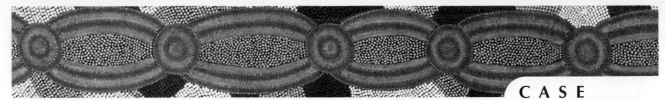

Mexican-based Grupo Industrial Alfa S.A. (GIASA)—or Alfa—announced two new joint ventures in 1999, one with DuPont to manufacture polyester fiber in Mexico and one with Ford to make aluminum cylinder heads in the Czech Republic for the automotive industry. Such announcements are typical for Alfa, one of Latin America's largest companies, because most of its business is through collaborative agreements, especially joint ventures with foreign companies.

From its founding in 1894 until 1974, Alfa's activities were part of a family enterprise in Monterrey controlled by the Garza and Sada families. During this time, foreign competition had only slightly affected the company. Its major lines of business—steel, beer, and banking—included products and services not easily imported into Mexico. There also were prohibitions against foreign ownership in all three industries. However, although the company was fairly immune from foreign competition, its outlook was for slow growth because of its product lines.

In 1973, the Mexican government sought to keep out foreign control of companies by enacting laws that restricted foreign equity in new and existing ventures. The Garza and Sada families saw these Mexicanization laws as a signal to diversify into growth industries that foreigners would find difficult to control. They reasoned they might be able to buy some subsidiaries from foreign companies that were unwilling to accept minority ownership. They also reasoned they were in a good position to share in collaborative arrangements with foreign companies that sought business activities in Mexico. Further, they felt that to capitalize on these possibilities, they should shed the family image. By extending ownership beyond the family, they could raise capital through selling additional shares. Moreover, good professional management could be attracted to the company once nonfamily members could advance into top positions.

In 1974, Alfa divided the enterprise into four companies—Alfa, Cydsa, Visa, and Vitro—and went public by issuing shares in each of them. At that time, the assets of the newly formed Alfa were estimated at $315 million, of which 75 percent was in steel. Alfa's management, with help from some top international consulting groups, agreed that diversification should be based on minimizing cyclical changes in earnings, entering growth industries, and using resources for which Mexico had advantages.

Among Alfa's first moves was the acquisition of the TV production facilities and brands of three U.S. companies: Philco, Magnavox, and Admiral. Through these acquisitions, Alfa captured 35 percent of Mexico's market for TV sets as well as the right to continue using the three trade names for sales in Mexico. By 1980, Alfa had assets of $1.9 billion, 157 subsidiaries, and 49,000 employees. Two events other than the Mexicanization laws external to Alfa contributed to its growth: the discovery of huge oil and natural gas reserves and private-enterprise government incentives for industry, including nearly free energy. Suddenly foreign companies were rushing to find ways of expanding their business in Mexico. Most expansion had to include Mexican partners. Alfa was large, had good profits, and possessed management that had a good reputation. It was in an excellent position to acquire the foreign resources it wanted. In fact, its biggest problem was in how to choose among the many opportunities. (Map 14.1 shows some of the alliances Alfa made with foreign companies.)

Alfa established numerous Mexican companies in which it owned a majority interest, with a foreign partner holding a minority interest. The foreign partners came from many countries, including Japan (Hitachi, electric motors; Yamaha, motorcycles), Canada (International Nickel, nonferrous metal exploration), the Netherlands (AKZO, artificial fibers), and Germany (BASF,

MAP 14.1   Alfa's International Collaborative Arrangements

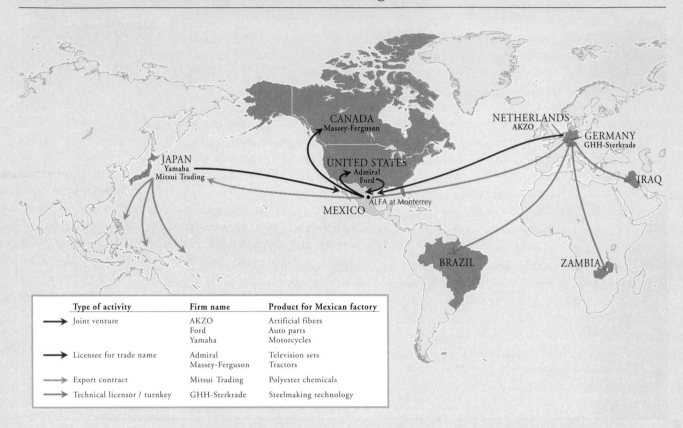

Type of activity	Firm name	Product for Mexican factory
→ Joint venture	AKZO Ford Yamaha	Artificial fibers Auto parts Motorcycles
→ Licensee for trade name	Admiral Massey-Ferguson	Television sets Tractors
→ Export contract	Mitsui Trading	Polyester chemicals
→ Technical licensor / turnkey	GHH-Sterkrade	Steelmaking technology

This map shows only a sampling of Alfa's collaborative arrangements for sales and production within and outside Mexico. In the cases of export contracts and technical license/turnkey collaborations, Mitsui Trading and GHH-Sterkrade conduct international business with Alfa's products and technologies outside Japan and Germany, respectively.

petrochemicals). For two U.S. companies—Ford and DuPont—the joint venture operations meant substantial departures from usual policies. Ford's 25-percent interest in a Mexican plant making aluminum cylinder heads for the U.S. and Canadian automobile markets was the first minority interest the company had ever taken in a joint venture. DuPont had taken minority interests before, accepting 49 percent to Alfa's 51 percent in a Mexican synthetic fibers joint venture; however, it had always managed the ventures. In this case, Alfa managed the venture because its policy was to import technology but maintain management control.

In many of these joint venture operations, the Mexican output has used the foreign partner's trademark, which helps the products gain Mexican consumer acceptance. For this reason, when Alfa bought 100 percent of Massey-Ferguson's tractor operation in Mexico in 1979, it paid the Canadian company a royalty fee to use the Massey-Ferguson trade name. In the aluminum cylinder head joint venture, Ford was attracted not by a captive Mexican market, but rather by the lower costs of producing components to serve the U.S. and Canadian markets. In addition to cheap energy, Mexico offered an abundance of cheap labor and no taxes on rein-vested earnings. Alfa itself also became interested in export markets: It established a sales arrangement under which Japan's Mitsui Trading Company would handle exports of Alfa's poly-ester chemicals abroad.

Alfa developed direct reduction steel production, bypassing the high capital costs of blast furnaces. To transfer this patented technology to new plants in other countries would have required substantial on-site personnel and construction assistance. Alfa lacked both personnel that could be spared and foreign construction experience, so it transferred the technology to four foreign engineering companies: GHH-Sterkrade (Germany), Kawasaki Heavy Industries (Japan), and Pullman Swindell and Dravo (both from the United States). Those companies have in turn acted as agents on behalf of Alfa and constructed steel plants in such countries as Brazil, Indonesia, Iran, Iraq, Venezuela, and Zambia. Alfa continues to receive fees for the use of the technology in foreign mills. The engineering companies receive fees for building the plants, in what are known as turnkey projects.

In the late 1970s, Alfa borrowed heavily from foreign banks to expand. In the 1980s, all this expansion came to a grinding halt. First oil prices plummeted, causing Mexico to devalue the peso. Alfa lost so much money between 1980 and 1985 that it had to shut down 40 of its plants and reduce the number of its employees by almost 19,000. Meanwhile, many foreign companies that had made agreements with Alfa in the 1970s found that their expected Mexi-can expansion (via joint ventures with Alfa) had been put on hold. Alfa simply lacked the resources to carry out so many agreements with so many different foreign companies.

By 1987, foreign banks had converted part of Alfa's debt into a 27-percent stake in the company rather than have Alfa default. By 1989, Mexico's economy and Alfa's financial stand-ing had turned around to such an extent that Alfa was able to buy back the foreign banks' own-ership, an event hailed in the Mexican press as the "Mexicanization" of Alfa. Once again, Alfa embarked on expansion through alliances with foreign companies. Alfa also learned from its earlier dollar-debt problems and it survived the 1994 Mexican devaluation of the peso. Although Mexico has lifted many restrictions on foreign ownership—especially to investors from Canada and the United States with the ratification of NAFTA—many foreign companies still prefer collaborative arrangements with Mexican companies because of the Mexican bureaucracy. Foreign companies continue to seek out partnerships with Alfa because it has proven capable at dealing with this bureaucracy and because it can manage multiple collabo-rative arrangements simultaneously and efficiently. ❧

INTRODUCTION

Figure 14.1 shows that companies must choose an international operating mode to ful-fill their objectives and carry out their strategies. Many of the modes from which they may choose involve collaboration with other companies. In addition, a company may produce at home or abroad. In Chapter 8 we explained the reasons for producing abroad rather than exporting, and we discussed why (appropriability and internalization theories) companies would want to control foreign production through direct invest-ment. Nevertheless, companies frequently handle much of their international opera-tions through collaborative forms that lessen their control. Figure 14.2 shows the types of collaborative modes (highlighted in blue). The truly experienced MNE with a fully global orientation usually uses most of the operational modes available, selecting them

Airlines increasingly collaborate with each other to gain global economies and market advantages. They frequently combine routes, terminal services, and frequent-flyer programs. Here we see airlines from Malaysia, Saudi Arabia, Singapore, the United Kingdom, and Australia.

according to specific product or foreign operating characteristics. Further, those modes may be combined. For example, KFC has a joint venture with Mitsubishi in Japan, which, in turn, franchises outlets within Japan. When collaboration is of strategic importance (having a large impact on total performance) to one or more of the companies, it is known as a *strategic alliance*. In reality, the term *strategic alliance* often describes a wide variety of collaborations, whether or not they are of real strategic importance.

FIGURE 14.1   Collaborative Arrangements as International Business Operating Modes

Companies must handle international business operations on their own or collaborate with other companies. Their choice is influenced externally by physical and societal factors and by their competitive environment. Their choice is also influenced by their objectives and strategies.

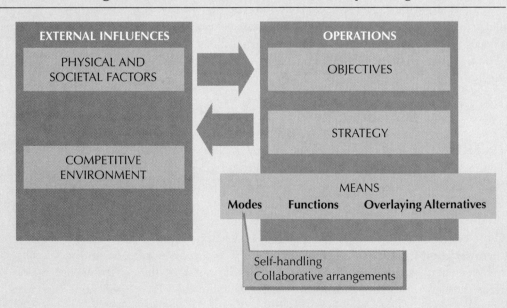

FIGURE 14.2   Alternative Operating Modes for Foreign Market Expansion

PRODUCTION OWNERSHIP	PRODUCTION LOCATION	
	Home country	Foreign country
Equity arrangements	a. Exporting	a. Wholly owned operations b. Partially owned with remainder widely held c. Joint ventures d. Equity alliances
Nonequity arrangements		a. Licensing b. Franchising c. Management contracts d. Turnkey operations

A company may use more than one operating mode within the same location. Those shaded in blue are collaborative arrangements. Note that exporting is the only mode for market expansion where production is in the home country.

Collaborations provide different opportunities and problems than do trade or wholly owned direct investment.

The Alfa case shows that companies can use several types of collaborative strategies to exploit international opportunities. Alfa established joint ventures with foreign companies, engaged in acquiring and selling process and product technology through licensing and turnkey contracts, and paid for the use of trademarks through licensing agreements.

This chapter discusses the motives for and types of collaborative arrangements, as well as the problems and methods of managing these arrangements.

MOTIVES FOR COLLABORATIVE ARRANGEMENTS

The same reasons why companies establish collaborative arrangements for domestic operations carry over to their international operations as well. For example, a company such as McDonald's that franchises most of its operations in the United States also franchises most of its operations in foreign countries—for the same reasons, which we'll discuss in the next section. Companies also establish collaborative arrangements abroad for different reasons than they collaborate domestically. For example, in the opening case, DuPont established a joint venture with Alfa because Mexican laws prohibited its gaining 100-percent ownership. Figure 14.3 shows both the general and internationally specific reasons for collaborative arrangements. This figure also refers back to the four objectives of international business introduced in Chapter 1.

Keep in mind that each organization participating in a collaborative agreement has its own primary objective for operating internationally and its own motive for collaborating. For example, Ford sought resource acquisition and Alfa sought diversification

FIGURE 14.3   Relationship of Strategic Alliances to Companies' International Objectives

OBJECTIVES OF INTERNATIONAL BUSINESS
- Sales expansion
- Resource acquisition
- Diversification
- Competitive risk minimization

MOTIVES FOR COLLABORATIVE ARRANGEMENTS
General
- Spread and reduce costs
- Specialize in competencies
- Avoid competition
- Secure vertical and horizontal links
- Gain market knowledge

MOTIVES FOR COLLABORATIVE ARRANGEMENTS
Specific to International Business
- Gain location-specific assets
- Overcome legal constraints
- Diversify geographically
- Minimize exposure in risky environments

Collaborative arrangements may serve companies' goals, regardless of whether they operate internationally. In addition, there are gains from collaborative arrangements that are specific to companies' international operations.

through its aluminum cylinder head joint venture. Ford's motivation for collaboration was mainly to overcome legal constraints, while Alfa's was to gain competence in an additional product (securing horizontal links).

MOTIVES FOR COLLABORATIVE ARRANGEMENTS: GENERAL

In this section, we'll explain the reasons that companies collaborate with other companies in either domestic or foreign operations: to spread and reduce costs, to allow them to specialize in their competencies, to avoid competition, to secure vertical and horizontal links, and to gain market knowledge.

Spread and Reduce Costs   To produce or sell abroad, a company must incur certain fixed costs. At a small volume of business, it may be cheaper for it to contract the work to a specialist rather than handle it internally. A specialist can spread the fixed costs to more than one company. If business increases enough, the contracting company then may be able to handle the business more cheaply itself. Companies should periodically reappraise the question of internal versus external handling of their operations.

A company may have excess production or sales capacity that it can use to produce or sell for another company. The company handling the production or sales may lower its average costs by covering its fixed costs more fully. Likewise, the company contracting out its production or sales (outsourcing) will not have to incur fixed costs that may have to be charged to a small amount of production or sales. Using this capacity also

---

Sometimes it is cheaper to get another company to handle work, especially
- *At small volume*
- *When the other company has excess capacity*

may reduce start-up time for the outsourcing company, providing earlier cash flow. Further, the contracted company may have environment-specific knowledge, such as how to deal with regulations and labor, that would be expensive for the contracting company to gain on its own. Also, contracting companies may lack the resources to "go it alone. " By pooling their efforts, they may be able to undertake activities that otherwise would be beyond their means. This is especially important for small companies.[2] But it is important for large companies when the cost of development and/or investment is very high. For example, Disney estimates that the development cost of its Hong Kong theme park will be over $3 billion, an amount that strains the capabilities of even a company as large as Disney. So the Hong Kong government will share ownership and costs.[3]

Cooperative ventures may, however, increase operating costs. Negotiating with another company and transferring technology to it can be expensive. Also, maintaining relationships with other companies costs money.

Specialize in Competencies   The **resource-based view of the firm** holds that each company has a unique combination of competencies. A company may seek to improve its performance by concentrating on those activities that best fit its competencies, depending on other firms to supply it with products, services, or support activities for which it has lesser competency. Large, diversified companies are constantly realigning their product lines to focus on their major strengths. This realigning may leave them with products, assets, or technologies that they do not wish to exploit themselves but that may be profitably transferred to other companies. For example, Caterpillar, Coca-Cola, and Philip Morris do not think their competencies lie in the clothing business, so they have licensed their logos to other companies to put them on clothing.[4] However, a licensing or other collaborative arrangement has a limited time frame, which may allow a company to exploit a particular product, asset, or technology itself if at a later date if its core competencies change.

> Licensing can yield a return on a product that does not fit the company's strategic priority based on its best competencies.

Avoid Competition   Sometimes markets are not large enough to hold many competitors. Companies may then band together so as not to compete. For example, AT&T and GTE originally announced separate Mexican joint ventures to compete against Telmex, the Mexican telecommunications monopoly, once the Mexican government allowed competition. They merged their two joint ventures (one involving Alfa) so that they would more likely survive.[5] Companies also may combine certain resources to combat larger and more powerful competitors. For example, Daimler-Benz, China's state-run Aviation Industry General, and Samsung Aerospace formed a consortium to develop a new passenger aircraft so they could better compete against larger aircraft manufacturers such as Boeing and Airbus.[6] Or companies may simply collude to raise everyone's profits. Only a few countries, mainly English-speaking ones, make and enforce laws against collusion.[7]

Another example of avoiding competition involves the major aluminum producers, which have developed swap contracts that allow them to save transport costs. These companies are all vertically integrated, but not in each country in which they operate. Alcan has smeltering, manufacturing, and sales in Canada, but only manufacturing and sales in France. Pechiney has smeltering, manufacturing, and sales in France, but only manufacturing and sales in Canada. Alcan might give Pechiney smeltered output in Canada in exchange for the same amount of smeltered output delivered to Alcan in France. Thus the companies continue to compete for sales in each market without having to be as vertically integrated in each. Similarly, Ford's European plants make cars for Mazda to sell in Europe, and Mazda's Japanese factories make vehicles for Ford to sell in Japan.[8]

Secure Vertical and Horizontal Links   There are potential cost savings and supply assurances from vertical integration. However, companies may lack the competence or resources necessary to own and manage the full value chain of activities. For example, recall the Saudi Aramco case in Chapter 12. Saudi Aramco has abundant oil reserves but lacks final distribution skills so it has established collaborative arrangements in countries that assure markets for its petroleum.

Horizontal links may provide finished products or components. For finished products, there may be economies of scope in distribution, such as by having a full line of products to sell, thereby increasing the sales per fixed cost of a visit to potential customers. For example, Duracell, the biggest maker of consumer batteries, and Gillette, the biggest maker of razor blades, combine their sales forces in many parts of the world to gain economies of scope.[9] There may also be a better smoothing of earnings through diversification into products with sales fluctuations at different times. The opening case showed how Alfa has used collaborative arrangements to diversify into a broader range of products.

One of the fastest growth areas for collaborative arrangements has been in industries with projects too large for any single company to handle—for example, new aircraft and communications systems. From such an arrangement's inception, different companies (sometimes from different countries) agree to take on the high cost and high risk of developmental work for different components needed in the final product. Then a lead company buys the components from the companies that did parts of the developmental work.

Gain Market Knowledge   Many companies pursue collaborative arrangements to learn about a partner's technology, operating methods, or home market so that their own competencies will broaden or deepen, making them more competitive in the future. Recall Chapter 11's case on FDI in China that Chinese governmental authorities allow foreign companies to tap the Chinese market in exchange for their transference of technology. Sometimes each partner can learn from the other, a motive driving joint ventures between U.S. and European wine makers, such as the Opus One Winery owned by Robert Mondavi from the United States and Baron Philippe de Rothschild from France.[10]

MOTIVES FOR COLLABORATIVE ARRANGEMENTS: INTERNATIONAL

In this section, we'll continue discussing the reasons why companies enter into collaborative arrangements, covering those reasons that apply only to international operations. Specifically, these reasons are to gain location-specific assets, overcome legal constraints, diversify geographically, and minimize exposure in risky environments.

Gain Location-Specific Assets   Cultural, political, competitive, and economic differences among countries create barriers for companies that want to operate abroad. When they feel ill-equipped to handle these differences, they may seek collaboration with local companies who will help manage local operations. For example, in the opening case, AT&T's decision to team with Alfa was undoubtedly due in part to Alfa's greater ability to deal with Mexican political authorities, who are important in assuring efficient operations.

In other countries, foreign companies may team with local companies to gain operational assets. For example, most foreign companies in Japan need to collaborate with Japanese companies who can help in securing distribution and a competent workforce—two assets that are difficult for foreign companies to gain on their own there. Access to distribution was the primary reason that Merck entered a joint venture with Chugai in Japan for the development and marketing of over-the-counter drugs.[11]

Overcome Legal Constraints As the Alfa case showed, Mexican law required foreign companies to share ownership with Mexicans. Some of the foreign companies we discussed, such as Ford, may have preferred to wholly own the Mexican operation but were not legally permitted to do so. Other legal factors may influence the company's choice. These include differences in tax rates and in the maximum funds it can remit to its home country.

Collaboration can be a means of protecting an asset. Many countries provide little de facto protection for intellectual property rights such as trademarks, patents, and copyrights unless authorities are prodded consistently. To prevent pirating of these proprietary assets, companies sometimes have made collaborative agreements with local companies, which then monitor that no one else uses the asset locally. Also, some countries provide protection only if the internationally registered asset is exploited locally within a specified period. If a company does not use the asset within the country during that specified period, then whatever entity first does so gains the right to it.

Diversify Geographically By operating in a variety of countries (geographic diversification), a company can smooth its sales and earnings because business cycles occur at different times within the different countries. Collaborative arrangements offer a faster initial means of entering multiple markets. Moreover, if product conditions favor a diversification rather than a concentration strategy (recall the discussion in Chapter 13), there are more compelling reasons to establish foreign collaborative arrangements. However, these arrangements will be less appealing for companies whose activities are already widely extended or those that have ample resources for such extension.

Minimize Exposure in Risky Environments Companies worry that political or economic changes will affect the safety of assets and their earnings in their foreign operations. One way to minimize loss from foreign political occurrences is to minimize the base of assets located abroad—or share them. A government may be less willing to move against a shared operation for fear of encountering opposition from more than one company, especially if they are from different countries and can potentially elicit support from their home governments. Another way to spread risk is to place operations in a number of different countries. This strategy reduces the chance that all foreign assets will encounter adversity at the same time.

TYPES OF COLLABORATIVE ARRANGEMENTS

The forms of foreign operations differ in the amount of resources a company commits to foreign operations and the proportion of the resources located at home rather than abroad. Licensing, for example, may result in a lower additional capital commitment than a foreign joint venture will.

Legal factors may be
- **Direct prohibitions against certain operating forms**
- **Indirect (for example, regulations affecting profitability)**

Collaboration hinders nonassociated companies from pirating the asset.

The higher the risk managers perceive in a foreign market, the greater their desire to form collaborative arrangements in that market.

Collaborative arrangements allow for greater spreading of assets among countries.

The type of collaborative arrangement managers choose may necessitate trade-offs among objectives.

Companies have a wider choice of operating form when there is less likelihood of competition.

Throughout this discussion, keep in mind that there are trade-offs. For example, a decision to take no ownership in foreign production, such as through licensing it to a foreign company, may reduce exposure to political risk. However, learning about that environment will be slow, delaying (perhaps permanently) your reaping the full profits from producing and selling your product abroad.

Keep in mind also that when a company has a desired, unique, difficult-to-duplicate resource, it is in a good position to choose the operating form it would most like to use. The preferred form may be exporting, selling from a wholly owned direct investment, or participating in a collaborative arrangement. However, when it lacks this bargaining strength, it faces the possibility of competition. It may have to settle on a form that is lower on its priority list; otherwise, a competitor may preempt the market.

A further constraint facing managers is finding a desirable collaboration partner. For example, if the collaboration includes a transfer of technology, it may be impossible to find a local company familiar enough with the technology. In effect, there are costs associated with transferring technology to another entity. Usually it is cheaper to transfer within the existing corporate family, such as from parent to subsidiary, than to transfer to another company. The cost difference is especially important when the technology is complex because a subsidiary's personnel are more likely to be familiar with approaches the parent uses.

SOME CONSIDERATIONS IN COLLABORATIVE ARRANGEMENTS

We have just discussed reasons for companies' entering collaborative arrangements. Before explaining the types of arrangements, we shall discuss two variables that influence managers' choice of one type of arrangement over another: their desire for control over foreign operations and their companies' prior foreign expansion.

Internal handling of foreign operations usually means more control and no sharing of profits.

Control The more a company depends on collaborative arrangements, the more likely it is to lose control over decisions, including those regarding quality, new product directions, and where to expand output. This is because each collaborative partner has a say in these decisions, and the global performance of each may be improved differently. External arrangements also imply the sharing of revenues, a serious consideration for undertakings with high potential profits because a company may want to keep them all for itself. Such arrangements also risk allowing information to pass more rapidly to potential competitors. The loss of control over flexibility, revenues, and competition is an important variable guiding a company's selection of forms of foreign operation.

Prior Expansion of the Company When a company already has operations (especially wholly owned ones) in place in a foreign country, some of the advantages of contracting with another company to handle production or sales are no longer as prevalent. The company knows how to operate within the foreign country and may have excess capacity it can use for new production or sales. However, much depends on whether the existing foreign operation is in a line of business or performs a function that is closely related to the product, service, or activity being transferred abroad. When there is similarity, as with production of a new type of office equipment when the company already produces office equipment, it is likely that the new production will be handled inter-

Ethical Dilemmas and Social Responsibility
WHEN WHAT'S RIGHT FOR ONE PARTNER ISN'T RIGHT FOR THE OTHER PARTNER

One potential ethical problem arising from collaborative arrangements is a company's skirting of unethical practices by having a partner handle them. A second problem is that a company might treat its partner unethically.

How should a company deal with foreign partners whose practices on pollution, labor relations, and bribery are very different from those in its home country? On the one hand, the company might take an arm's length approach and simply transact business on the basis of quality, delivery time, and price—leaving the supplier or licensee to operate the way it is accustomed to. On the other hand, it may try to interfere with those practices.[12] Increasingly, nongovernmental organizations (NGOs) criticize companies for what their suppliers do, or even the suppliers of their suppliers. This creates a dilemma. If a company does try to influence these practices, such as by including operating provisions in its contracts, it may still be very difficult and costly to monitor compliance with the provisions.

All partners put resources into collaborative arrangements. The question is whether any partner should take resources from the operation that are not specified in the agreement. For example, one partner in a joint venture may transfer a scientist to the operation who, in addition to working on the venture's R&D, learns about breakthroughs that would be useful to that partner. Would it be ethical to pass this information along? Or a highly qualified manager may be hired by a joint venture. After the manager gains experience, would it be ethical for one of the partners in the venture to hire him or her away? Would the ethical issues be any different if one partner felt it was contributing more than the other compared to its income from the venture?

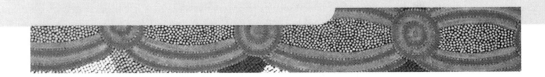

nally. In highly diversified companies or where operations are limited (such as when subsidiaries produce components only for the parent), the existing foreign facility may be handling goods or functions so dissimilar to what is being planned that it is easier to deal with an experienced external company.

LICENSING

Under a licensing agreement, a company (the licensor) grants rights to intangible property to another company (the licensee) to use in a specified geographic area for a specified period. In exchange, the licensee ordinarily pays a royalty to the licensor. The rights may be exclusive (the licensor can give rights to no other company) or nonexclusive

MNEs want returns from their intangible assets.

(it can give away rights). The U.S. Internal Revenue Service classifies intangible property into five categories.

1. Patents, inventions, formulas, processes, designs, patterns
2. Copyrights for literary, musical, or artistic compositions
3. Trademarks, trade names, brand names
4. Franchises, licenses, contracts
5. Methods, programs, procedures, systems

Usually, the licensor is obliged to furnish technical information and assistance, and the licensee is obliged to exploit the rights effectively and to pay compensation to the licensor.

Major Motives for Licensing   Frequently, a new product or process may affect only part of a company's total output and then only for a limited time. The sales volume may not be large enough to warrant establishing overseas manufacturing and sales facilities. A company that is already operating abroad may be able to produce and sell at a lower cost and with a shorter start-up time, thus preventing competitors from entering the market. For the licensor, the risk of operating facilities and holding inventories lessens. The licensee may find that the cost of the arrangement is less than if it developed the new product or process on its own.

For industries in which technological changes are frequent and affect many products, companies in various countries often exchange technology rather than compete with each other on every product in every market. Such an arrangement is known as **cross-licensing**. For example, DBStar from the United States and Transtar from France entered a technology-sharing, cross-licensing agreement for computer data storage whereby DBStar will sell to the North American market and Transtar will sell to the European market.[13]

Another consideration of licensing concerns whether a company has enough resources to exploit all markets, a particular concern for small companies. But large ones also may be constrained. The United Kingdom's largest retailer, Marks & Spencer, for example, has insufficient resources to establish its own facilities everywhere that might support its St. Michael brand. For some of the larger markets, such as France and Canada, Marks & Spencer has subsidiaries. For some smaller markets, such as Norway and Portugal, it uses licensing arrangements.[14]

Payment   The amount and type of payment for licensing arrangements vary. Each contract tends to be negotiated on its own merits. Figure 14.4 shows the major factors that determine the payment amount. In the upper left-hand box, agreement-specific factors underlie negotiated clauses that may affect the value to the licensee. For example, the value will be greater if potential sales are high. The upper right-hand box in the figure lists environment-specific factors that may affect the license's value. For example, the licensee might pay a low amount if its government sets upper limits on payment or if other companies are vying to sell similar technology. Because neither the licensor nor the licensee can be sure of the price the other is willing to accept, the bottom of the figure illustrates how the bargaining range is based on their expectations.

Some emerging economies set price controls on what licensees can pay or insist that licensees be permitted to export licensed goods. Their reasoning is that selling only to

FIGURE 14.4 Determinants of Compensation for International Licensing of Technology

AGREEMENT-SPECIFIC FACTORS

Affecting the Technology Value
- Market restrictions (including exports)
- Exclusivity of the license
- Limits on production size
- Product quality requirements
- Grantback provisions
- Tie-in provisions
- Duration of the agreement
- Age of the technology
- Duration of the patent
- Other constraints on the use of technology

ENVIRONMENT-SPECIFIC FACTORS

Affecting the Technology Value
- Government (of both licensor's and licensee's countries) regulation of licensing
- Level of competition in the licensee's product market
- Level of competition among alternative suppliers of similar technology
- Political and business risks in the licensee's country
- Product and industry norms
- Technology-absorbing capacity of the licensee's country

LICENSOR'S OFFER PRICE

Upper limit: Smaller of
1. Estimate of licensee's additional profits from use of technology
   or
2. Estimate of licensee's cost of obtaining same or similar technology from alternative sources

Lower limit:
Estimate of direct transfer costs, opportunity costs, and R&D costs

Zero price

Bargaining Range

LICENSEE'S BID PRICE

Upper limit: Smallest of
1. Estimate of additional profits from use of technology
   or
2. Estimate of costs of developing same or similar technology
   or
3. Estimate of costs of obtaining same or similar technology from best alternative source

Lower limit:
Estimate of licensor's direct transfer costs

The upper left-hand box lists factors in the licensing agreement that can affect the technology's value to the licensee. The upper right-hand box gives factors external to the negotiations that can affect pricing. The bottom portion shows how the bargaining range derives from the licensor's and the licensee's estimates of profits and costs.

the local market results in small-scale production that spreads fixed costs inadequately and raises consumer prices. Licensors have countered that if licensees export, they should pay higher royalties because the companies could not sell exclusive rights to parties in other countries. MNEs also have argued that the development of process technologies for small-scale production in countries with small markets is often too costly but is done when economically feasible.

Companies commonly negotiate a "front-end" payment to cover transfer costs and then follow with another set of fees based on actual or projected use. Licensors do this because it usually takes more than simply transferring publications and reports to move technology abroad. The move requires engineering, consultation, and adaptation. The licensee usually bears the transfer costs so that the licensor is motivated to assure a smooth adaptation. Of course, the license of some assets, such as copyrights, have much lower transfer costs.

Technology may be old or new, obsolete or still in use at home, when a company licenses it. For example, Crown Cork and Seal held onto its manufacturing technology for cans until it developed a new one. Then it licensed the older technology to companies in emerging economies. Many other companies transfer technology at an early or even a developmental stage so that products hit different markets simultaneously. This simultaneous market entry is important when selling to the same industrial customers in different countries and when global advertising campaigns can be effective. For example, an alliance between AT&T and Eo licenses "personal communicator" technology to Matsushita so that the product will be available in Japan at about the same time AT&T sells it in the United States.[15] On the one hand, new technology may be worth more to a licensee because it may have a longer useful life. On the other hand, newer technology, particularly that in the development phase, may be worth less because of its uncertain market value.

Sales to Controlled Entities   Although we think of licensing agreements as being collaborative arrangements among unassociated companies, most licenses are given to companies owned in whole or part by the licensor.[16] A license may be necessary to transfer technology abroad because operations in a foreign country, even if 100-percent owned by the parent, usually are subsidiaries, which are separate companies from a legal standpoint. When a company owns less than 100 percent, a separate licensing arrangement may be a means of compensating the licensor for contributions beyond the mere investment in capital and managerial resources.

FRANCHISING

Franchising includes providing an intangible asset (usually a trademark) and continually infusing necessary assets.

Franchising is a specialized form of licensing in which the franchisor not only sells an independent franchisee the use of the intangible property (usually a trademark) essential to the franchisee's business but also operationally assists the business on a continuing basis, such as through sales promotion and training. In many cases, the franchisor provides supplies. For example, Domino's Pizza grants to franchisees the goodwill of the Domino's name and support services to get started, such as store and equipment layout information and a manager training program. As part of the continual relationship, it offers economies and standardization through central purchasing, such as centrally purchasing mozzarella cheese in New Zealand to use worldwide.[17] In a sense, a franchisor and a franchisee act almost like a vertically integrated company because the parties are interdependent and each produces part of the product or service that ultimately reaches the consumer.

Franchising is said to have originated when King John of England granted tax-collecting franchises. In the eighteenth century, German brewers franchised beer halls as distributors.[18] Today, franchising is most associated with the United States, and more than half of U.S. franchisors have foreign operations.[19] The fastest growth businesses of U.S. foreign franchising have been food and business services because the U.S. market for these businesses is fairly mature. U.S. companies can find more growth abroad than at home.

Not all franchising is by U.S. companies. Foreign-owned franchise operations are growing rapidly in the United States. Pronuptia, a French bridal wear franchisor, and food franchisors such as Wimpy's and Bake 'N' Take from the United Kingdom and Wienerwald from Germany have been among some of the earliest and most successful. There also have been many foreign acquisitions of franchisors based in the United States. Burger King, Hardees, Holiday Inn, Howard Johnson's, Baskin-Robbins, Meineke Discount Mufflers, and Great American Cookie are U.S. franchisors that non-U.S. companies have acquired.

Organization of Franchising   A franchisor most often penetrates a foreign country by setting up a master franchise and giving that organization (usually a local one) the rights to open outlets on its own or develop subfranchisees in the country or region. Subfranchisees pay royalties to the master franchisee, which then remits some predetermined percentage to the franchisor. McDonald's handles its Japanese operations this way.

In some cases, franchisors enter foreign markets by franchising directly with individual franchisees. However, if the franchisor is not well known to many local people, it may find it difficult to convince them to make investments. People are usually willing to make investments in known franchises because the name is a guarantee of quality that can attract customers. It therefore is common for lesser-known franchisors to enter foreign markets with some company-owned outlets that serve as a showcase to attract franchisees.

Operational Modifications   Securing good locations for franchises can be a major problem. Finding suppliers can add difficulties and expense. For example, McDonald's had to build a plant to make hamburger buns in the United Kingdom, and it had to help farmers develop potato production in Thailand. Another concern for foreign franchise expansion has been governmental or legal restrictions that make it difficult to gain satisfactory operating permission.

Many franchise failures abroad result from the franchisor's not developing enough domestic penetration first. Franchisors need to develop sufficient cash and management depth before considering foreign expansion. However, even a franchisor that is well established domestically may have difficulty in attaining foreign penetration, as evidenced by problems of Burger King in the United Kingdom, Wendy's in Australia, and Long John Silver's in Japan.[20] A dilemma for successful domestic franchisors is that their success comes from three factors: product and service standardization, high identification through promotion, and effective cost controls. When entering many foreign countries, franchisors may encounter difficulties in transferring these success factors. At

Many types of products and many countries participate in franchising.

Franchisors face a dilemma
- *The more standardization, the less acceptance in the foreign country*
- *The more adjustment to the foreign country, the less the franchisor is needed*

the same time, the more adjustments made to the host country's different conditions, the less a franchisor has to offer a potential franchisee. U.S. franchisors' success in Japan is mostly due to that country's enthusiastic assimilation of Western products. Companies such as McDonald's have been able to copy their U.S. outlets almost exactly. Yet such U.S. food franchisors as Dunkin' Donuts and Perkits Yogurt fared poorly in the United Kingdom because it was too difficult to change certain British eating habits. However, if the franchisors had offered menus more acceptable to the British, they would have offered little that was different to a prospective franchisee. Even in countries in which franchises have succeeded, some operating adjustments usually are necessary. For example, KFC had to redesign its equipment and stores in Japan to save space because of higher rents. To cater to Japanese tastes, it eliminated mashed potatoes and put less sugar in its cole slaw. Pizza Hut alters its toppings by country, and in Saudi Arabia it must have two dining rooms—one for single men and one for families (single women are not allowed to go out without their families). McDonald's changed the pronunciation of its name in Japan to "MaKudonaldo" and substituted *Donald* for *Ronald McDonald* because of pronunciation difficulties.[21]

MANAGEMENT CONTRACTS

Management contracts are used primarily when the foreign company can manage better than the owners.

One of the most important assets a company may have at its disposal is management talent, which it can transfer internationally, primarily to its own foreign investments. Management contracts are means by which a company may transfer such talent—by using part of its management personnel to assist a foreign company for a specified period for a fee. The company may gain income with little capital outlay. Contracts usually cover three to five years, and fixed fees or fees based on volume rather than profits are most common.

A company usually pursues management contracts when it believes that a foreign company can manage its existing or new operation more efficiently than it can. For example, the British Airport Authority (BAA) has contracts to manage airports in Naples (Italy) and Melbourne (Australia) because it had developed successful airport management skills.[22]

With management contracts, the host country gets the assistance it wants without needing foreign direct investment. In turn, the management company receives income without having to make a capital outlay. A management contract may also allow the supplier to gain foreign experience, increasing its capacity to internationalize. For example, Ansett Transport Industries of Australia developed contracts to operate Air Vanuatu for the government of Vanuatu (island country east of Australia). These contracts led to other management contracts in the South Pacific, which in turn led to Ansett holding equity interests in Transcorp Airways (Hong Kong), Air New Zealand, Air Norway, Ladeco (Chile), and America West (United States).[23]

TURNKEY OPERATIONS

Turnkey operations are
- **Most commonly performed by construction companies**
- **Often performed for a governmental agency**

Turnkey operations are a type of collaborative arrangement in which one company contracts another to build complete, ready-to-operate facilities. Companies building turnkey operations are frequently industrial-equipment manufacturers and construction companies. They also may be consulting firms and manufacturers that decide an investment on their own behalf in the country is infeasible.

The customer for a turnkey operation is often a governmental agency. Many companies have chosen to perform design and construction duties, particularly where there are restrictions on foreign ownership. Recently, most large projects have been in those emerging economies that are moving rapidly toward infrastructure development and industrialization.

One characteristic that sets the turnkey business apart from most other international business operations is the size of the contracts. Most contracts are for hundreds of millions of dollars, and many are for billions, which means that only a few very large companies—such as Bechtel, Fluor, and Kellogg Rust—account for most of the international market. Smaller firms often serve as subcontractors for primary turnkey suppliers. However, large companies are vulnerable to economic downturns when governments cancel big contracts. For example, Fluor took heavy losses when oil prices fell and oil exporters suspended construction expansion.[24]

The nature of these contracts places importance on hiring executives with top-level contacts abroad, as well as on ceremony and building goodwill, such as opening a facility on a country's independence day or getting a head of state to inaugurate a facility. For example, the Swedish-Swiss company ABB and Brazil's Companhia Brasileira de Projectos e Obras formed a joint venture to construct a turnkey dam for the government of Malaysia. They timed the signing of the $5.2 billion contract so that the Malaysian premier could be present for the ceremony.[25] Although public relations is important to gaining turnkey contracts, other factors—such as price, export financing, managerial and technological quality, experience, and reputation—are necessary to sell contracts of such magnitude.

Payment for a turnkey operation usually occurs in stages as a project develops. Commonly, 10 to 25 percent comprises the down payment, with another 50 to 65 percent paid as the contract progresses, and the remainder paid once the facility is operating in accordance with the contract. Because of the long time frame between conception and completion, the company performing turnkey operations can encounter currency fluctuations and should cover itself through escalation clauses or cost-plus contracts. Because the final payment is usually made only if the facility is operating satisfactorily, it is important to specify in a contract what constitutes "satisfactorily." For this reason, many companies insist on performing a feasibility study as part of the turnkey contract so they don't build something that, although desired by a local government, may be too large or inefficient. Inefficiency could create legal problems, such as determining who caused it, that hold up final payment.

Many turnkey contracts are for construction in remote areas, necessitating massive housing construction and importation of personnel. Projects may involve building an entire infrastructure under the most adverse conditions. So turnkey operators must have expertise in hiring workers willing to work in remote areas for extended periods, and in transporting and using supplies under very adverse conditions.

If a company holds a monopoly on certain assets or resources, such as the latest refining technology, other companies will find it difficult to compete to secure a turnkey contract. As the production process becomes known, however, the number of competitors for such contracts increases. U.S. companies have moved largely toward projects involving high technology, while companies from such countries as India, Korea, and Turkey can compete better for conventional projects for which low labor costs are important.[26]

Joint ventures may have various combinations of ownership.

JOINT VENTURES

A type of ownership sharing popular among international companies is the joint venture, in which more than one organization owns a company. Recall from the opening case that Alfa participates in numerous joint ventures. Although companies usually form a joint venture to achieve particular objectives, it may continue to operate indefinitely as the objective is redefined. Joint ventures are sometimes thought of as 50/50 companies, but often more than two organizations participate in the ownership. Further, one organization frequently controls more than 50 percent of the venture. The type of legal organization may be a partnership, a corporation, or some other form permitted in the country of operation. When more than two organizations participate, the joint venture is sometimes called a **consortium**.

Almost every conceivable combination of partners may exist in a joint venture, including

- Two companies from the same country joining together in a foreign market, such as Exxon and Mobil in Russia
- A foreign company joining with a local company, such as Sears Roebuck and Simpsons in Canada
- Companies from two or more countries establishing a joint venture in a third country, such as that of Diamond Shamrock (U.S.) and Sol Petroleo (Argentina) in Bolivia
- A private company and a local government forming a joint venture (sometimes called a mixed venture), such as that of Philips (Dutch) with the Indonesian government
- A private company joining a government-owned company in a third country, such as BP Amoco (private British-U.S.) and Eni (government-owned Italian) in Egypt

The more companies in the joint venture, the more complex the management of the arrangement will be. For example, when the Australian government privatized Hazelwood Power Station, a British company (National Power), an Australian company (the Commonwealth Bank Group), and two U.S. companies (PacifiCorp and Destec Energy) bought the electric utility company. This involved four companies in the decision making.[27] Figure 14.5 shows that as a company increases the number of partners and decreases the amount of equity it owns in a foreign operation, its ability to control that operation decreases.

Certain types of companies favor joint ventures more than others do. Companies that like joint ventures are usually new at foreign operations or have decentralized domestic decision making. Because these companies are used to extending control downward in their organizations, it is easier for them to do the same thing internationally. There is also evidence that the incidence of entering into joint ventures varies by host country. Companies are more prone to form joint ventures in countries where the cultural characteristic of trust is high, because their host-country companies erect fewer barriers with foreign companies.[28]

Equity alliances help solidify collaboration.

EQUITY ALLIANCES

An **equity alliance** is a collaborative arrangement in which at least one of the collaborating companies takes an ownership position (almost always minority) in the other(s). In some cases, each party takes an ownership, such as by buying part of each other's shares

FIGURE 14.5 Control Complexity Related to Collaborative Strategy

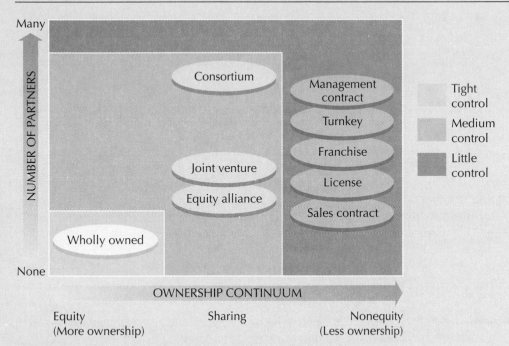

NUMBER OF PARTNERS

Many

Consortium

Joint venture

Equity alliance

Wholly owned

None

Management contract

Turnkey

Franchise

License

Sales contract

Tight control

Medium control

Little control

OWNERSHIP CONTINUUM

Equity
(More ownership)

Sharing

Nonequity
(Less ownership)

The more equity and the fewer partners, the more easily a company can usually control its foreign operations. Note that the nonequity arrangements may take one or many partners.

Source: The figure was adapted from *European Management Journal*, Vol. 12, No. 1, Shaker Zahra and Galal Elhagrasey, "Strategic Management of International Joint Ventures," March 1994, pp. 83–93, with permission from Elsevier Science.

or by swapping some shares with each other. The purpose of the equity ownership is to solidify a collaborating contract, such as a supplier-buyer contract, so that it is more difficult to break—particularly if the ownership is large enough to secure a board membership for the investing company. The airline industry epitomizes the use of equity alliances. We will discuss the airline industry in the ending case of this chapter.

PROBLEMS OF COLLABORATIVE ARRANGEMENTS

Although collaborative arrangements have many advantages, some companies avoid them. Many arrangements develop problems that lead partners to renegotiate their relationships. Partners might renegotiate responsibilities, ownership, or management structure.[29] In spite of new relationships, many agreements break down or are not renewed at the end of an initial contract period. For example, in the case of joint ventures, about half break up because one or all partners become dissatisfied with the venture. In about three-quarters of breakups, one partner buys out the other's interest so that the operation continues as a wholly owned foreign subsidiary.[30] In other breakups, companies agree to dissolve the arrangement or they restructure their alliance.

Figure 14.6 shows that joint venture divorce (and divorce from other collaborative arrangements) can be planned or unplanned, friendly or unfriendly, mutual or

About half of joint ventures break down, primarily because partners
- **View the joint ventures' importance differently**
- **Have different objectives for the joint ventures**
- **Disagree on control issues or fail to provide sufficient direction**
- **Perceive they contribute more than their counterparts do**
- **Have incompatible operating cultures**

FIGURE 14.6 Alternative Dissolution of Joint Ventures

DIVORCE SCENARIOS	EXAMPLES	OUTCOMES	EXAMPLES
Planned	General Motors (U.S.) and Toyota (Japan)	Termination by Acquisition	Daewoo Motors (South Korea) and General Motors (U.S.)
vs. Unplanned	AT&T (U.S.) and Olivetti (Italy)	Termination by Dissolution	Meiji Milk (Japan) and Borden (U.S.)
Friendly	Vitro (Mexico) and Corning (U.S.)	Termination by Reorganization/ Restructuring of the Alliance	Matsushita Electric Industries Co. (Japan) and Solbourne Computer (U.S.)
vs. Unfriendly	Coors Brewing Co. (U.S.) and Molson Breweries (Canada)		
Both agree	Ralston Purina (U.S.) and Taiyo Fishery (Japan)		
vs. One Partner Refuses to Agree	Sover S.P.A. (Italy) and Suzhou Spectacles No. 1 Factory (China)		

There is considerable variation in both the way that joint ventures dissolve and the outcome of the operation after the dissolution. Any of the scenarios might have any of the outcomes.

Source: Adapted from Manuel G. Serapio, Jr., and Wayne F. Cascio, "End Games in International Alliances," *Academy of Management Executive,* May 1996, p. 67.

nonmutual. The major strains on collaborative arrangements are due to five factors: the importance to the partners, differing objectives, control problems, comparative contributions and appropriations, and differences in culture.[31] In spite of our focus on these problems, we do not mean to imply that there are no success stories. There are. For example, the joint venture between Xerox (U.S.) and Rank (U.K.) has performed well for a long period of time, and it even has a joint venture itself in Japan with Fuji Photo, which has also performed well.[32]

COLLABORATION'S IMPORTANCE TO PARTNERS

One partner may give more management attention to a collaborative arrangement than the other does. If things go wrong, the active partner blames the less active partner for its lack of attention, and the less active partner blames the more active partner for making poor decisions. The difference in attention may be due to the different sizes of partners. For example, if the joint venture is between a large and a small company, the venture comprises a larger portion of operations for the small company than for the large one, so the small company may take more interest in the venture. However, when companies are required to share ownership because of legal restrictions, such as in China, they may prefer partnering with companies smaller than themselves because they can more easily manage the operation.[32]

DIFFERING OBJECTIVES

Although companies enter into collaborative arrangements because they have complementary capabilities, their objectives may evolve differently over time. For instance, one partner may want to reinvest earnings for growth and the other may want to receive dividends. One partner may want to expand the product line and sales territory, and the other may see this as competition with its wholly owned operations. A partner may wish to sell or buy from the venture, and the other partner may disagree with the prices.

CONTROL PROBLEMS

By sharing the assets with another company, one company may lose some control on the extent or quality of the assets' use. For example, Oleg Cassini, Inc., gave an exclusive license to Jovan, the Beecham Group's (U.K.) U.S. subsidiary, to promote and extend sales of various Cassini fragrances, cosmetics, and beauty aids worldwide. Jovan subsequently introduced Diane Von Furstenberg products instead and denied Cassini the right to license the Cassini name to other companies. Cassini sued. The case was settled when Jovan agreed to market the Cassini products. However, its sales of the products through discount stores won Cassini an award in a later suit for image injury.[34]

Some companies have well-known trademarked names that they license abroad for the production of some products that they have never produced or had expertise with. For example, Pierre Cardin licenses its label to more than 800 licensees in 93 countries. These licensees put the label on hundreds of products, from clothing to sheets and clocks to deodorants. Monitoring and maintaining control of so much diversity is difficult. Two U.S. companies, Saks Fifth Avenue and Eagle Shirtmakers, dropped sales of Pierre Cardin–labeled products because the lack of quality control on some licensees' products adversely affected the image of others.[35]

In collaborative arrangements, even though control is ceded to one of the partners, both may be held responsible for problems. For example, in KFC's joint venture in China, the financial reporting to Chinese authorities was the Chinese partner's responsibility. However, China held both partners liable for tax evasion as a result of underreporting income.[36] Moreover, in joint ventures and management contracts, there are gray areas as to who controls employees. For example, in Holiday Inn's 10-year management contract in Tibet, it couldn't give incentives to or discipline its staff. Consequently, there was little it could do when waiters and waitresses took their lunch breaks at the same time guests were showing up for lunch.[37]

When no single company has control of a collaborative arrangement, the operation may lack direction. Studies support this concern. They show that when two or more partners attempt to share in an operation's management, failure is much more likely than when one partner dominates.[38] However, the dominating partner must consider the other company's interests. For this reason, studies also show that joint ventures with an even split in ownership are likely to succeed because the financial ownership ensures that management will consider both partners' interests.[39]

PARTNERS' CONTRIBUTIONS AND APPROPRIATIONS

One partner's capability of contributing technology, capital, or some other asset may diminish compared to its partner's capability over time. For example, in P&G's joint venture with Phuong Dong Soap & Detergent in Vietnam, P&G wanted to expand, but Phuong had neither the funds to expand nor the willingness to allow P&G to gain a larger ownership.[40] The weak link may cause a drag on the collaborative arrangement, resulting in dissention between the partners. Further, one partner may be suspicious that the other is taking more from the operation (particularly knowledge-based assets) than it is. In almost all collaborative arrangements, there is a danger that one partner will use the other partner's contributed assets, enabling it to become a competitor. (Probably the only exception would be turnkey projects to build infrastructure.) In fact, there are many examples of companies "going it alone" after they no longer needed their partner, particularly if the purpose of the collaboration is to gain knowledge. For example, Coca-Cola learned all it needed to know from its distributorship partner, Pripps Ringes, in Norway and Sweden, and then set up its own distributorship operations there.[41] It is difficult for companies that compete head-on within their core businesses in some markets to cooperate fully for the same core business in another market. In the case of joint ventures, both are apt to see substantial gains when each partner offers market expansion and technology to the other. For example, Toshiba offered Motorola access to the Japanese market, and Motorola gave Toshiba access to the U.S. market for technologies that were complementary rather than competitive.[42]

DIFFERENCES IN CULTURE

Companies differ by nationality in how they evaluate the success of their operations. For example, U.S. companies tend to evaluate performance on the basis of profit, market share, and specific financial benefits. Japanese companies tend to evaluate primarily on how an operation helps build its strategic position, particularly by improving its skills. European companies rely more on a balance between profitability and achieving social objectives.[43] These differences can mean that one partner is satisfied while the other is not. Anheuser-Busch attributed its joint venture breakup with Modelo (Mexican) to the fact that Modelo was run like a family business and was reluctant to share control.[44] Moreover, some companies don't like to collaborate with companies of very different cultures. For example, British companies would least like to partner with Japanese companies, primarily because of language difficulties.[45] In spite of these potential problems, joint ventures from culturally distant countries survive at least as well as those between partners from similar cultures.[46]

In addition to national culture, differences in corporate cultures may also create problems within joint ventures. For example, one company may be accustomed to promoting managers from within the organization, while the other opens its searches to outsiders. One may use a participatory management style, and the other an authoritarian style. One may be entrepreneurial and the other risk averse. For this reason many companies will develop joint ventures only after they have had long-term positive experiences with the other company through distributorship, licensing, or other contractual arrangements. Compatibility of corporate cultures also is important in cementing relationships.[47]

Looking to the Future
WHY INNOVATION BREEDS COLLABORATION

More than 40 years ago, John Kenneth Galbraith wrote that the era of cheap invention was over and, "because development is costly, it follows that it can be carried out only by a firm that has the resources associated with considerable size."[48] The statement seems prophetic in terms of the estimated billions of investment dollars needed to bring a new commercial aircraft to market, eliminate death from AIDS, and commercialize the transmission and manipulation of information with photonics. Moreover, markets must be truly global if high development costs are to be recouped. The sums companies need for developing and marketing these new inventions are out of reach of most companies acting alone. Of course, companies might become ever larger through internal growth or through mergers and acquisition. Although we have seen some examples of such growth, governments have nevertheless placed limits because of antitrust concern. Further, companies realize the cost of integrating a merged or acquired company can be very high.[49] Therefore, collaborative arrangements will likely become even more important in the future. They are likely to involve both horizontal and vertical linkages among companies from many industries in many countries.

Although some product developments require huge sums, most are much more modest. Nevertheless, companies lack all the product- and market-specific resources to go it alone everywhere in the world, especially if national differences dictate operating changes on a country-to-country basis. These situations present opportunities for alliances that employ complementary resources from different companies.

Collaborative arrangements will bring both opportunities and problems as companies move simultaneously to new countries and to contractual arrangements with new companies. For example, collaborations must overcome differences in a number of areas:

- Country cultures that may cause partners to obtain and evaluate information differently
- National differences in governmental policies, institutions, and industry structures that constrain companies from operating as they would prefer
- Corporate cultures that influence ideologies and values underlying company practices that strain relationships among companies
- Different strategic directions resulting from partners' interests that cause companies to disagree on objectives and contributions
- Different management styles and organizational structures that cause partners to interact ineffectively[50]

The more partners there are in an alliance, the more strained the decision-making and control processes will be.

MANAGING FOREIGN ARRANGEMENTS

If collaboration can better achieve the company's strategic objectives than "going it alone" can, the company should give little consideration to taking on duties itself. However, as the arrangement evolves, partners will need to reassess certain decisions. For example, a company's resource base may change compared to that of other companies, making collaboration either more or less advantageous. Further, the external environment changes. Perhaps a certain location becomes economically risky, or its host government forbids foreign ownership in areas the arrangement would like to do future business. Because of these changes, a company needs continually to reexamine the fit between collaboration and its strategy. We shall now discuss how companies change their operating forms, how they may find and negotiate with potential partners, and how they need to assess performance of collaborative arrangements.

DYNAMICS OF COLLABORATIVE ARRANGEMENTS

The evolution to a different operating mode may
- **Be the result of experience**
- **Necessitate costly termination fees**
- **Create organizational tensions**

In Chapter 1, we discussed how companies typically move from external to internal handling of foreign operations and how they deepen their mode of commitment over time.[51] However, the cost of switching from one form to another—for example, from licensing to wholly owned facilities—may be very high because of having to gain expertise from and possibly pay termination fees to another company.[52]

Collaboration with a local company provides the opportunity to learn from the local partner, enabling the company confidently to make a deeper commitment. At the same time, the learning in one market may enable a company to enter another market at a higher level of commitment. However, the ability to carry over learning from one market to another is enhanced by cultural similarity among markets.[53]

Tension may develop internally as a company's international operations change and grow. For example, moving from exporting to foreign production may reduce the size of a domestic product division. Various profit centers all may perceive they have rights to the sales in a country the company is about to penetrate. Legal, technical, and marketing personnel may have entirely different perspectives on contracts. Under these circumstances, a team approach to evaluating decisions and performance may work. A company also must develop means of evaluating performance by separating those things that are controllable and noncontrollable by personnel in different profit centers.

FINDING COMPATIBLE PARTNERS

A company can seek out a partner for its foreign operations or it can react to a proposal from another company to collaborate with it. In either case, it is necessary to evaluate the potential partner not only for the resources it can supply but also for its motivation and willingness to work with the other company. A company can identify potential partners by monitoring journals and technical conferences. Partners can also be found through social activities. After a company makes contact and builds rapport with managers of one local firm, those managers may offer introductions to managers in other firms.[54] A company can increase its own visibility by participating in trade fairs, distributing brochures, and nurturing contacts in the locale of potential collaboration—increasing the probability that companies will be considered a partner by other companies. The proven ability to handle similar types of collaboration is a key professional qualification. For example, Alfa's track record has made it a candidate for collaboration to companies entering the Mexican market. Because Alfa has this track record, a partner may be able to depend more on trust rather than expensive control mechanisms to ensure that its interests will not be usurped. Once into a collaboration, partners may also be able to build partner trust through their actions in the collaborative arrangement.[55] But every company has to start somewhere. Without a proven track record, a company may have to negotiate harder with and make more concessions to a partner.

NEGOTIATING PROCESS

In addition to the points discussed in Chapter 12 about cross-national negotiations, some technology transfer considerations are unique to collaborative arrangements. The value of many technologies would diminish if they were widely used or understood. Contracts historically have included provisions that the recipient will not divulge this information. In addition, some sellers have held onto the ownership and production of specific components so that recipients will not have the full knowledge of the product or the capability to produce an exact copy of it. Many times, a company wants to sell techniques it has not yet used commercially. A buyer is reluctant to buy what it has not seen, but a seller that shows the process to the potential buyer risks divulging the process technology. It has become common to set up preagreements that protect all parties.

Another controversial area of negotiation is the secrecy surrounding arrangements' financial terms. In some countries, for example, governmental agencies must approve licensing contracts. Sometimes these authorities consult their counterparts in other countries regarding similar agreements to improve their negotiating position with MNEs. Many MNEs object to this procedure because they believe that contract terms between two companies are proprietary information with competitive importance and that market conditions usually dictate the need for very different terms in different countries.

In technology agreements
- *Seller does not want to give information without assurance of payment*
- *Buyer does not want to pay without evaluating information*

CONTRACTUAL PROVISIONS

By transferring assets to a joint venture or intangible property rights to another company in a licensing agreement, a company undoubtedly loses some control over the asset or intangible property. A host of potential problems attend this lack of control and should be settled in the original agreement. Provisions should outline

Transferring rights to an asset can create control problems, such as poor product quality.

- Terminating the agreement if the parties do not adhere to the directives
- Methods of testing for quality
- Geographical limitations on the asset's use
- Which company will manage which parts of the operation outlined to the agreement
- What each company's future commitments will be
- How each company will buy from, sell to, or use intangible assets that come from the collaborative arrangement

Contracts should be spelled out in detail, but if courts must rule on disagreements both parties are apt to lose something in the settlement. A good example occurred with McDonald's in France. The company franchised stores to Raymond Dayan at less than its normal fee because of doubts the French would ever take to fast-food restaurants. Dayan, with the help of McDonald's, found very good Paris locations for 14 stores, which he opened over several years and operated successfully. However, under the franchise agreement McDonald's had the right to revoke the agreement if the company found the stores fell short of its cleanliness standards. McDonald's canceled the agreement on these grounds. A court case resulted, and Dayan claimed that McDonald's action was simply a ruse to make him pay McDonald's usual licensing fee. He lost out on continued use of the McDonald's trademark, but McDonald's lost something, too. Dayan immediately replaced his McDonald's stores with his own trademark—O'Keefe's Hamburgers—and he had the clientele, the know-how, and the best locations in Paris. He later sold these stores to the French firm Quick, the largest fast-food chain in France, which now operates them under the Quick logo.[56]

Many other possible conflicts can develop between companies. Contract termination and formal settlement of disputes are costly and cumbersome. If possible, it is much better for parties to settle disagreements on a personal basis. The ability to develop a rapport with the management of another company is an important consideration in choosing a partner.

PERFORMANCE ASSESSMENT

When collaborating with another company, managers must

- **Continue to monitor performance**
- **Assess whether to take over operations**

Management also should estimate potential sales, determine whether the arrangement is meeting quality standards, and assess servicing requirements to check whether the other company is doing an adequate job. Mutual goals should be set so that both parties understand what is expected, and the expectations should be spelled out in the contract.

In addition to the continual assessment of the partner's performance in collaborative arrangements, a company also needs to assess periodically whether the type of collaboration should change. For example, a joint venture may replace a licensing agreement. In some cases, even though a partner is doing what is expected, a company may assess that collaboration is no longer in its best interest. For instance, the company may decide that it wants a wholly owned FDI so that it has greater freedom.

WEB CONNECTION

Check out our home page www.prenhall.com/daniels for links to key resources for you in your study of international business.

SUMMARY

- Some advantages of collaborative arrangements, whether a company is operating domestically or internationally, are to spread and reduce costs, allow a company to specialize in its primary competencies, avoid certain competition, secure vertical and horizontal links, and learn from other companies.

- Some motivations for collaborative arrangements that are specific to international operations are to gain location-specific assets, overcome legal constraints, diversify among countries, and minimize exposure in risky environments.

- The forms of foreign operations differ in how much resources a company commits and the proportion of resources committed at home rather than abroad. Collaborative arrangements reduce a company's commitment.

- Although the type of collaborative arrangement a company chooses should match its strategic objectives, the choice often will mean a trade-off among objectives.

- Licensing is granting another company the use of some rights, such as patents, copyrights, or trademarks, usually for a fee. It is a means of establishing foreign production and reaching foreign markets that may minimize capital outlays, prevent the free use of assets by other companies, allow the receipt of assets from other companies in return, and allow for income in some markets in which exportation or investment is not feasible.

- Franchising differs from licensing in that granting the use of intangible property (usually a trademark) is an essential asset for the franchisee's business and the franchisor assists in the operation of the business on a continuing basis.

- Management contracts are a means of securing income by managing a foreign operation while providing little capital outlay. This sometimes helps the supplier to gain foreign experience, increasing its capacity to internationalize.

- Turnkey projects are contracts for construction of another company's operating facilities. These projects have been large and diverse, necessitating specialized skills and abilities to deal with top-level government authorities.

- Joint ventures are a special type of collaborative arrangement in which two or more organizations have equity in the venture. There are various combinations of owners, including local governments and private companies and two or more companies from the same or different countries.

- Equity alliances occur when a company takes an equity position in the company with which it has a collaborative arrangement so as to solidify the collaborating contract.

- A common motive for jointly owned operations is to take advantage of complementary resources that companies have at their disposal.

- Problems occur in collaborative arrangements because partners place different levels of importance on and have different objectives for the venture, find a shared ownership arrangement difficult to control, worry that their partner is putting in too little or taking out too much from the operation, and misunderstand each other because of their different country or company cultures.

- Contracting for the outside management of a company's foreign business does not negate management's responsibility to ensure company resources are working. Management constantly needs to assess the other company's work.

- Companies may use different types of collaborative arrangements for their foreign operations in different countries or for different products. As diversity increases, coordinating and managing the foreign operations becomes more complex.

CASE

INTERNATIONAL AIRLINE ALLIANCES[57]

Map 14.2 shows the world's twenty-five largest airlines and the countries where they have their headquarters. Most of the world's major airlines are in or have announced they will join one of five alliances whereby they combine routes, sales, airline terminal services, and frequent-flier programs. For example, by year-end 1999, Air Canada, Air New Zealand, All Nippon Airways, Ansett Australia, Austrian Airlines, Lufthansa, Mexicana, Scandinavian Airlines System

MAP 14.2 The Top 25 Passenger Airline Companies

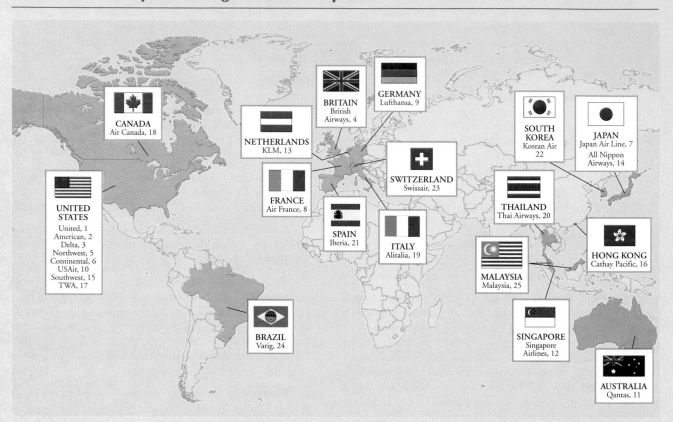

CANADA
Air Canada, 18

BRITAIN
British
Airways, 4

GERMANY
Lufthansa, 9

SOUTH KOREA
Korean Air
22

JAPAN
Japan Air Line, 7
All Nippon
Airways, 14

NETHERLANDS
KLM, 13

UNITED STATES
United, 1
American, 2
Delta, 3
Northwest, 5
Continental, 6
USAir, 10
Southwest, 15
TWA, 17

FRANCE
Air France, 8

SWITZERLAND
Swissair, 23

THAILAND
Thai Airways, 20

SPAIN
Iberia, 21

ITALY
Alitalia, 19

HONG KONG
Cathay Pacific, 16

MALAYSIA
Malaysia, 25

BRAZIL
Varig, 24

SINGAPORE
Singapore
Airlines, 12

AUSTRALIA
Qantas, 11

Note the preponderance of airlines in Europe and the United States. The rankings are based on revenue passenger kilometers flown (the number of paid passengers multiplied by the distance that each paid passenger flies). Airlines are sometimes measured, instead, by operating revenue, operating profit, net profit, passengers flown, and fleet size. These measures result in different rankings.

Source: *World Transport Magazine* supplied the information based on 1998 operations.

(SAS), Singapore Airlines, Thai Airlines, United Airlines, and Varig were either in the Star Alliance or had announced plans to join it.

In addition, many airlines hold ownership in other airlines. For example, KLM from the Netherlands has partial ownership of Northwest Airlines in the United States and Alitalia in Italy. Singapore Airlines bought 49 percent of Virgin Airlines in the United Kingdom in 1999.

These alliances have blurred the competitive distinctions among the major international carriers. However, the airline industry is unique in that its need to form collaborative arrangements has been important almost from the start of

international air travel because of regulatory, cost, and competitive factors.

REGULATORY FACTORS

Countries have always seen airlines as key industries in which they want domestic service that is controlled by domestically owned companies. For example, the United States grants U.S.-based airlines the right to carry all passengers between domestic points, and it limits foreign ownership in U.S.-based airlines to 25 percent of voting stock and 49 percent of total equity. Many countries have ensured national control through whole or partial government ownership of airlines. Examples are Iberia, KLM, Lufthansa, and Thai Airways. Many government-owned airlines are monopolies within their domestic markets, and many of these lose money but then receive government subsidies. Governments can further protect their airlines by regulating

- Which foreign carriers have landing rights
- Which airports and aircraft the carriers can use
- Frequency of flights
- Whether foreign carriers can fly beyond the country—for instance, the Japanese government restricted United from flying from the United States to Japan and then beyond to Australia
- Overflight privileges
- Fares they can charge

Countries agree on the restrictions and rights through treaties, usually to give equal treatment to each country's carriers. The International Air Transport Association (IATA) comprises nearly all the world's airlines. Given the extent of governmental ownership of airlines, governments comprise much of the membership. Today, IATA is mainly concerned with global safety standards. However, at times it has restricted competition on routes by requiring uniform fares, meal service, and baggage allowances.

Five factors influence governments' protection of their airlines:

1. Countries believe they can save money by maintaining small air forces and relying on domestic airlines in times of unusual air transport needs. For example, the U.S. government used U.S. commercial carriers to help carry troops to Somalia in 1992.

2. In aviation's early days, airlines were heavily subsidized to carry mail overseas, and governments wanted to support their own fledgling companies rather than foreign ones. This consideration has shifted somewhat because mail subsidies no longer are very important internationally. For example, revenues from mail account for less than 0.5 percent of revenues for U.S. airlines.

3. Public opinion favors spending "at home," especially for government-paid travel. The public sees the maintenance of national airlines and the requirement that government employees fly on those airlines as foreign-exchange savings. (For example, when a U.S. resident uses a foreign airline internationally—say, Air France from New York to Paris—this is a service import for the United States.)

4. Airlines are a source of national pride, and aircraft (sporting their national flags) symbolize a country's sovereignty and technical competence. This national identification has been especially important for emerging economies, whose airlines once were largely foreign owned. For example, the former PanAm controlled airlines in Brazil, Colombia, Mexico, Panama, and Venezuela. As soon as countries were technically and financially capable, they developed national airlines and prohibited foreign ownership.

5. Countries have worried about protecting their airspace for security reasons. This is less of a concern today because foreign carriers routinely overfly a country's territory to reach inland gateways, such as British Air's flights between London and Denver. Further, overflight treaties are quite common, even among unfriendly nations. For example, Cubana overflies the United States en route to Canada, and American Airlines overflies Cuba en route to South America.

National attitudes and regulations not only give rise to separate national airlines but also limit airlines' expansion internationally. With few exceptions, airlines cannot fly on lucrative domestic routes in foreign countries. For example, Lufthansa cannot compete on the New York–Los Angeles route because the U.S. government allows only U.S. airlines on that route. Airlines also cannot easily control a flight network abroad that will feed passengers into their international flights. For example, Air France has no U.S. domestic flights to feed passengers into Chicago for connections to Paris, but American has scores of such flights. However, Air France has a monopoly on air travel within France. Further, airlines usually cannot service pairs of foreign countries. United cannot fly between Brazil and Portugal because the Brazilian and Portuguese governments give landing rights only to Brazilian and Portuguese airlines. To avoid these restrictions, airlines must ally themselves with carriers from other countries.

Airlines have sought cooperative agreements to complement their route structures and capabilities. Privatization has been a recent impetus to forming alliances. For example, privatized airlines, such as British Airways and Air Canada, can no longer look to their governments for support. Instead, they must find new means to be competitive internationally. Similarly, privatization in Eastern Europe and Latin America has enabled foreign carriers to take stakes in countries' airlines in those regions. Further, deregulation of airlines in the United

States and the European Union have forced airlines to find new means to compete.

COST FACTORS

Certain airlines have always dominated certain international airports. They have amassed critical capabilities in those airports, such as baggage handlers and baggage handling equipment. Sharing these capabilities with other airlines may spread costs. For example, KLM has long handled passenger check-in, baggage loading, and maintenance for a number of other airlines in Amsterdam. Other contracts commonly cover the use of airport gates, ground equipment such as generators, and commissary services. Airlines also sometimes sublease aircraft to each other. When traffic on a route is low, airlines sometimes make market agreements to fly on alternate days. Or they may agree to share service in the same aircraft, which then has a dual flight designation.

The high cost of maintenance and reservations systems has led to recent joint ventures. Swissair, Lufthansa, and Guiness Peat Aviation are partners in a maintenance center in Ireland. United, British Airways, USAirways, Swissair, Alitalia, and Air Canada share ownership in Covia, which operates and delivers the Apollo reservation system. United, USAirways British Air, Alitalia, Swissair, KLM, Olympic, Austrian Airlines, AerLingus, Sabena, and TAP Air Portugal founded another reservation system, Galileo.

COMPETITIVE FACTORS

A number of airlines have established marketing agreements to complement their route structures. For example, Continental handles SAS's operations in its Newark facilities, and a high portion of SAS traffic from Newark to Scandinavia comes from Continental's connections. Continental also contracted SAS to help improve its in-flight service. The joint use of facilities within alliances may be the wave of the future because it is nearly impossible to add gates at the largest airports and existing airlines own all the gates.

A problem with these marketing agreements is that the connections from one airline to another show up as separate route codes in reservations systems. These come up last on the screens of travel agents, and the agents tend to recommend the first scheduled flights they see. Further, when passengers see that they must change airlines, they worry about making those connections across great distances within ever-

larger airline terminals. This worry factor puts connections between two different airlines at a disadvantage to connections on the same airline. When KLM bought an interest in Northwest, the two airlines were able to secure the same route codes on their connecting flights. Northwest's ticket counters show KLM's logo as well. The alliance gives Northwest service to about 80 European cities. They have come as close as possible to a merger without actually making one.

MANAGEMENT OF ALLIANCES

A problem in the proliferation of alliances is that relationships are intertwined among so many airlines, it's difficult to determine whether companies are competing, cooperating, or colluding. Management may find it increasingly hard to be cooperative, say, in joint maintenance agreements while trying to compete directly on some routes.

Government restrictions to prevent full mergers among airlines from different countries may be a blessing in some ways because corporate and national cultures may be difficult to mesh. For example, pilots at Air Canada are unionized, but those at Continental are not. Analysts conclude that the problems of combining unions after PanAm's acquisition of National was a major contribution to PanAm's eventual demise.

Other things simply may not mesh well in alliances. In the now defunct USAirways–British Airways agreement, British Airways was strong in connections from London to Europe and Asia. But USAirways's strength was at New York's LaGuardia Airport, which is purely domestic—most connecting passengers had to change airports. When Northwest and KLM allied, it was expected that KLM would help Northwest improve its service; however, the organizations could not work well in that effort because of entrenched Northwest employees who would not cooperate.

QUESTIONS

1. Discuss a question raised by the manager of route strategy of American Airlines: Why should an airline not be able to establish service anywhere in the world simply by demonstrating that it can and will comply with the local labor and business laws of the host country?

2. The president of Japan Air Lines has claimed that U.S. airlines are dumping air services on routes between the United States and Europe, meaning they are sell-

ing below their costs because of the money they are losing. Should governments set prices so that carriers make money on routes?

3. What will be the consequences if a few large airlines or networks come to dominate global air service?

4. Some airlines, such as Southwest and Alaska Air, have survived as niche players without going international or developing alliances with international airlines. Can they continue this strategy?

CHAPTER NOTES

1 Data for the case were taken from James Flanigan, "The Strategy," *Forbes*, October 29, 1979, pp. 42–52; "Dravo Agrees to Market Type of Plant for Grupo," *Wall Street Journal*, September 23, 1980, p. 38; "Mexico: Exporting a Cheaper Way of Making Steel," *Business Week*, June 11, 1979, p. 53; Keith Bradsher, "Back from the Brink, Mexico's Giant Alfa Slims Down for Hard Times," *International Management*, Vol. 41, No. 9, September 1986, pp. 65–66; Matt Moffett, "Monterrey Sides with Mexican President," *Wall Street Journal*, May 22, 1989, p. A8; Stephen Baker, "Mexico's Giants March North," *Business Week*, November 13, 1989, pp. 63–64; Daniel Dombey, "Increased Overseas Sales Fuel Advances at Alfa and Desc," *Financial Times*, August 1, 1995, p. 15; Paul B. Carrol, "Garza Sadas Build an Unrivaled Latin Empire," *Wall Street Journal*, December 11, 1995, p. A9; "Energy/Mining: Joint U.S.-Mexico Power Plant Opened," *Mexico Business Monthly*, Vol. 6, No. 7, August 1996; Leslie Crawford and Daniel Dombey, "Merger Plan Hits Mexico Telecom's Monopoly," *Financial Times*, April 24, 1996, p. 1; "Grupo Alfa, BASF Mexico to Expand Petrochemical Plants," *Mexico Trade and Law Reporter*, Vol. 5, No. 9, September 1, 1995; Leslie Crawford and Daniel Dombey, "Mexico Gives Way to Nationalistic Pressure: A Change of Foreign Ownership Rules Threatens the Country's Privatisation Process," *Financial Times*, April 2, 1996, p. 27; "Top 100 Latin American Companies by Market Capitalisation," *Financial Times*, January 24, 1997; Adolfo Garza, "North Star," *Business Mexico*, October 1998, pp. 42–46; "Mexican Companies Seek to Expand Global Presence," *University of New Mexico Economic News & Analysis on Mexico*, October 6, 1999; McAllister Isaacs III, "Power of Two Provides Push for Polyster," *Textile World*, August 1999, p. 28; Henry Tricks, Andrea Mandel-Campbell, and Richard Lapper, "Alfa Moves to Branch Out," *Financial Times*, September 1, 1999, p. 17; and Quentin Reed, "Nemak Plans Czech Plant," *Financial Times*, November 26, 1999, p. 14.

2 Michael Selz, "Networks Help Small Companies Think and Act Big," *Wall Street Journal*, November 12, 1992, p. B2; and Joel Bleeke and David Ernst, "Sleeping with the Enemy," *Harvard International Review*, Summer 1993, pp. 12–14.

3 Bruce Orwall, "Disney's Hong Kong Deal Is Valued at Over $3 Billion," *Wall Street Journal*, September 15, 1999, p. B8.

4 John Wilman, "Coca-Cola Aims to Put Fizz into Fashion," *Financial Times*, January 2, 1999, p. 1.

5 Crawford and Dombey, "Merger Plan Hits Mexico Telecom's Monopoly."

6 Jeff Cole, "Europeans Gain on Boeing for a Partnership in Asia," *Wall Street Journal*, May 8, 1995, p. 2.

7 Philip Parker, "How Do Companies Collude?" *Financial Times*, September 28, 1998, mastering marketing section, pp. 10–11.

8 Paul Ingrassia, "Ford Nears Pact to Make Cars in Europe for Mazda in a Buy-Sell Arrangement," *Wall Street Journal*, October 28, 1991, p. A3.

9 Peter Marsh, "Profile Duracell," *Financial Times*, May 10, 1999, p. 27.

10 Jason Wilson, "Best of Both Worlds," *Continental*, April 1999, pp. 49–51.

11 "Merck and Chugai Form OTC Venture," *Financial Times*, September 19, 1996, p. 17.

12 Philip Rosenzweig, "How Should Multinationals Set Global Workplace Standards?" *Financial Times*, March 27, 1998, mastering global business section, pp. 11 12.

13 "DBStar and Transtar Sign U.S.-European Cross-Licensing Agreement," *Business Wire*, August 26, 1996.

14 Jacques Horovitz and Nirmalya Kumar, "Strategies for Retail Globalisation," *Financial Times*, March 18, 1998, reaching the global customer section, pp. 5–6.

15 Louise Kehoe, "AT&T Alliances Open New Market," *Financial Times*, November 17, 1992, p. 19.

16 John A. Sondheimer and Sylvia E. Bargas, "U.S. International Sales and Purchases of Private Services," *Survey of Current Business*, September 1994, p. 114.

17 Pierre Dussauge, "Domino's Pizza International, Inc.," Case #398-048-1 (Jouy-en-Josas, France: H.E.C., 1998).

18 John F. Preble, "Global Expansion: The Case of U.S. Fast-Food Franchisors," *Journal of Global Marketing*, Vol. 6, Nos. 1–2, 1992, p. 186, citing D. Ayling, "Franchising in the U.K.," *The Quarterly Review of Marketing*, Summer 1988, pp. 19–24.

19 John K. Ryans, Jr., Sherry Lotz, and Robert Krampf, "Do Master Franchisors Drive Global Franchising?" *International Marketing*, Vol. 8, No. 2, 1999, p. 33.

20 Lawrence S. Welch, "Developments in International Franchising," *Journal of Global Marketing*, Vol. 6, Nos. 1–2, 1992, p. 81–96.

21 Peng S. Chan and Robert T. Justis, "Franchise Management in East Asia," *Academy of Management Executive*, Vol. 4, No. 2, 1990, pp. 75–85. For other changes by McDonald's in Europe, see Heather Ogilvie, "Welcome to McEurope: An Interview with Tom Allin, President of McDonald's Development Co.," *Journal of European Business*, Vol. 2, No. 67, July–August 1991, pp. 5–12.

22 Bertrand Benoit, "BAA Wins License to Run Chinese Airports," *Financial Times*, August 30, 1999, p. 13.

23 Lawrence S. Welch and Anubis Pacifico, "Management Contracts: A Role in Internationalisation?" *International Marketing Review*, Vol. 7, No. 4, 1990, pp. 64–74.

24 David J. Jefferson, "Biggest Builder, Fluor, Sees Kuwaiti Contracts as a Mixed Blessing," *Wall Street Journal*, April 18, 1991, p. A1.

25 "Signing of ABB Deal for Malaysia's Bakun Dam on September 30," *Agence France Presse*, September 21, 1996; and "Malaysia Signs Dam Contract," *Financial Times*, October 3, 1996, p. 7.

26 Joan Gray, "International Construction," *Financial Times*, April 12, 1985, pp. 13–17; and Erdener Kaynak, "Internationalization of Turkish Construction Companies," *Columbia Journal of World Business*, Winter 1992, pp. 61–75.

27 Benjamin A. Holden and Nicholas Bray, "British, Australian and Two American Firms to Purchase Utility in Australia," *Wall Street Journal*, August 5, 1996, p. A4.

28 Scott Shane, "The Effect of National Culture on the Choice Between Licensing and Direct Foreign Investment," *Strategic Management Journal*, Vol. 15, 1994, pp. 627–642.

29 Linda Longfellow Blodgett, "Factors in the Instability of International Joint Ventures: An Event History Analysis," *Strategic Management Journal*, Vol. 13, No. 6, September 1992, pp. 475–481.

30 Joel Bleeke and David Ernst, "The Way to Win in Cross-Border Alliances," *Harvard Business Review*, November–December 1991, pp. 127–135.

31 There are many different ways of classifying the problems. Two useful ways are found in Manuel G. Serapio, Jr., and Wayne F. Cascio, "End Games in International Alliances," *Academy of Management Executive*, Vol. 10, No. 1, 1996, pp. 62–73; and Joel Bleeke and David Ernst, "Is Your Strategic Alliance Really a Sale?" *Harvard Business Review*, January–February 1995, pp. 97–105.

32 David Hamilton, "United It Stands," *Wall Street Journal*, September 26, 1996, p. R19.

33 Gregory E. Osland and S. Tamer Cavusgil, "Performance Issues in U.S.-China Joint Ventures," *California Management Review*, Vol. 38, No. 2, Winter 1996, pp. 106–130.

34 "Oleg Cassini Inc. Sues Firm Over Licensing," *Wall Street Journal*, March 28, 1984, p. 5; and "Cassini Awarded $16 Million in Fragrance Line Squabble," *Wall Street Journal*, June 2, 1988, p. 28.

35 William H. Meyers, "Maxim's Name is the Game," *New York Times Magazine*, May 3, 1987, pp. 33–35.

36 Marcus W. Brauchli, "PepsiCo's KFC Venture in China Is Fined for Allegedly False Financial Reporting," *Wall Street Journal*, July 27, 1994, p. A10.

37 Nicholas D. Kristof, "A Not-So-Grand Hotel: A Tibet Horror Story," *New York Times*, September 25, 1990, p. A4.

38 J. Peter Killing, "How to Make a Global Joint Venture Work," *Harvard Business Review*, Vol. 60, No. 3, May–June 1982, pp. 120–127.

39 Bleeke and Ernst, "The Way to Win in Cross-Border Alliances."

40 Samantha Marshall, "P&G Squabbles with Vietnamese Partner," *Wall Street Journal*, February 27, 1998, p. A14.

41 Greg McIvor, "Coca-Cola Ends Link with Nordic Producers," *Financial Times*, June 20, 1996, p. 15. For factors that appear to influence the ability of foreign companies to gain knowledge about local operating conditions, see Andrew C. Inkpen and Paul Beamish, "Knowledge, Bargaining Power, and the Instability of International Joint Ventures," *Academy of Management Review*, Vol. 22, No. 1, 1997, pp. 177–202. For evidence on the buyout and dissolution of joint ventures after one party learns from the other, see Jean-Francois Hennart, Thomas Roehl, and Dixie S. Zietlow, "'Trojan Horse' or 'Workhorse'? The Evolution of U.S.-Japanese Joint Ventures in the United States," *Strategic Management Journal*, Vol. 20, 1999, pp. 15–29. For information on the competition between collaborators, see Tarun Khanna, Ranjay Gulati, and Nitin Nohria, "The Dynamics of Learning Alliances: Competition, Cooperation, and Relative Scope," *Strategic Management Journal*, Vol. 19, March 1998, pp. 193–210.

42 Yumiko Ono, "Borden's Messy Split with Firm in Japan Points Up Perils of Partnerships There," *Wall Street Journal*, February 21, 1991, p. B1; and Henry W. Lane and Paul W. Beamish, "Cross-Cultural Cooperative Behavior in Joint Ventures in LDCs," *Management International Review*, Vol. 30, special issue, 1990, pp. 87–102.

43 Bleeke and Ernst, "The Way to Win in Cross-Border Alliances."

44 Leslie Crawford, "Anheuser's Cross-Border Marriage on the Rocks," *Financial Times*, March 18, 1998, p. 16.

45 Sue Cartwright and Cary Cooper, "Why Suitors Should Consider Culture," *Financial Times*, September 1, 1995, p. 6.

46 Seung Ho Park and Gerardo R. Ungson, "The Effect of National Culture, Organizational Complementarity, and Economic Motivation on Joint Venture Dissolution," *Academy of Management Journal*, Vol. 40, No, 2, 1997, pp. 279–307. Harry G. Barkema, Oded Shenkar, Freek Vermeulen, and John H. J. Bell, "Working Abroad, Working with Others: How Firms Learn to Operate International Joint Ventures," *Academy of Management Journal*, Vol. 40, No. 2, 1997, pp. 426–442, found survival differences only for differences in uncertainty avoidance.

47 Bleeke and Ernst, "The Ways to Win in Cross-Border Alliances"; John D. Daniels and Sharon L. Magill, "The Utilization of International Joint Ventures by United States Firms in High Technology Industries," *Journal of High Technology Management Research*, Vol. 2, No. 1, 1991, pp. 113–131.

48 John Kenneth Galbraith, *American Capitalism* (Boston: Houghton Mifflin, 1952), pp. 91–92.

49 Jeffrey Reuer, "Collaborative Strategy: The Logic of Alliances," *Financial Times*, October 4, 1999, mastering strategy section, pp. 12–13.

50 These are adapted from Arvind Parkhe, "Interfirm Diversity, Organizational Learning, and Longevity in Global Strategic Alliances," *Journal of International Business Studies*, Vol. 22, No. 4, Fourth Quarter 1991, pp. 579–601.

51 See also, Seev Hirsch and Avi Meshulach, "Toward a Unified Theory of Internationalization," Working Paper 10-91 (Copenhagen: Institute of International Economics and Management, 1991).

52 Bent Petersen and Torben Pedersen, "Research on the Entry Mode Choice of the Firm: How Close to a Normative Theory?" Working Paper 20-92 (Copenhagen: Institute of International Economics and Management, 1992).

53 Harry G. Barkema, John H. J. Bell, and Johannes M. Pennings, "Foreign Entry, Cultural Barriers, and Learning," *Strategic Management Journal*, Vol. 17, 1996, pp. 151–166.

54 Anne Smith and Marie-Claude Reney, "The Mating Dance: A Case Study of Local Partnering Processes in Developing Countries," *European Management Journal*, Vol. 15, No. 2, 1997, pp. 174–182.

55 Sanjiv Kumar and Anju Seth, "The Design of Coordination and Control Mechanisms for Managing Joint Venture-Parent Relationships," *Strategic Management Journal*, Vol. 19, 1998, pp. 579–599; T. K. Das and Bing-Sheng Teng, "Between Trust and Control: Developing Confidence in Partner Cooperation in Alliances," *Academy of Management Journal*, Vol. 23, No. 3, July 1998, pp. 491–512; and Arvind Parkhe, "Building Trust in International Alliances," *Journal of World Business*, Vol. 33, No. 4, 1998, pp. 417–437.

56 "Judge Revokes License of Paris McDonald's," *International Herald Tribune* [Zurich], September 12, 1982, p. 14; Steven Greenhouse, "McDonald's Tries Paris, Again," *New York Times*, June 12, 1988, p. 1F; and Andrew Jack, "McDonald's Makes Fast-Food Inroads on the French Palate," *Financial Times*, February 21, 1996, p. 14.

57 Data for the case were taken from Andrea Rothman, "U.S. to World: Airline Deals Hinge on Open Skies," *Business Week*, January 11, 1992, p. 46; Andrea Rothman, Seth Payne, and Paula Dwyer, "One World, One Giant Airline Market?" *Business Week*, October 5, 1992, p. 56; "All Aboard," *The Economist*, February 29, 1992, p. 78; "Wings Across the Water," *The Economist*, July 25, 1992, p. 62; Agis Salpukas, "Europe's Small Airlines Shelter under Bigger Wings," *New York Times*, November 8, 1992, p. E4; "Code Breakers," *The Economist*, November 21, 1992, pp. 78–79; Bridget O'Brian and Laurie McGinley,

"Mixing of U.S., Foreign Carriers Alters Market," *Wall Street Journal*, December 21, 1992, p. B1; Bill Poling, "United, American Spar with USAir, BA over Proposed Deal," *Travel Weekly*, November 12, 1992, p. 49; Joan M. Feldman, "The Dilemma of 'Open Skies,'" *The New York Times Magazine*, April 2, 1989, p. 31; Philippe Gugler, "Strategic Alliances in Services: Some Theoretical Issues and the Case of Air-Transport Services," paper prepared for the Danish Summer Research Institute (DSRI), Denmark, August 1992; Martin Tolchin, "Shift Urged on Foreign Stakes in Airlines," *New York Times*, January 9, 1993, p. 17; Agis Salpukas, "The Big Foreign Push to Buy into U.S. Airlines," *New York Times*, October 11, 1992, p. F11; Robert Crandell, "When Less Really Means More," *Financial Times*, September 17, 1996, p. 17; Emma Tucker, "Commission to Approve Lufthansa-SAS Venture," *Financial Times*, January 16, 1996, p. 3; Scott McCartney, Diane Brady, Susan Carey, and Asra Q. Nomani, "U.S. Airlines' Prospects Are Grim on Expanding Access to Asian Skies," *Wall Street Journal*, September 25, 1996, p. A1; Michael Skapinker, "Austrian Air Switches Allegiance to Star Alliance," *Financial Times*, September 22, 1999, p. 9; Edward Alden and Michael Skapinker, "United Airlines-Lufthansa Join Battle for Air Canada," *Financial Times*, October 20, 1999, p. 1; Michael Skapinker, "Continental Chairman Calls for Creation of Third Air Alliance," *Financial Times*, October 5, 1998, p. 20; Michael Skapinker, "Passengers Not Convinced," *Financial Times*, November 19, 1998, business of travel section, p. iii; Michael Skapinker, "Boarding Business Class Now," *Financial Times*, July 9, 1998, p. 13; J. A. Donoghue, "Network Is Everything," *Air Transport World*, Vol. 36, No. 8, August 1999, p. 9; Leonard Hill, "Global Challenger," *Air Transport World*, Vol. 36, No. 12, pp. 52–54; Robert Gribben, "City," *The Daily Telegraph* [London], December 21, 1999, p. 29; Michael A. Taverna and John D. Morrocco, "Airlines Play Catch-Up in Partnership Game," *Aviation Week and Space Technology*, Vol. 150, No. 12, March 22, 1999, p. 70; and Leonard Hill, "80 Years Young," *Air Transport World*, Vol. 36, No. 10, October 1999, pp. 44–47.

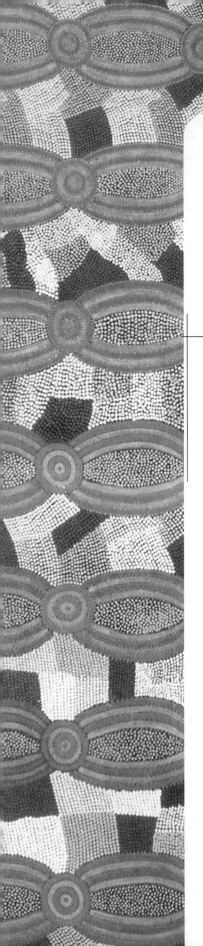

CHAPTER 15

Control Strategies

Form your plans before sunrise. —INDIAN-TAMIL PROVERB

OBJECTIVES

- To explain the special challenges of controlling foreign operations

- To describe organizational structures for international operations

- To show the advantages and disadvantages of decision making at headquarters and at foreign subsidiary locations

- To highlight both the importance of and the methods for global planning, reporting, and evaluating

- To give an overview of some specific control considerations affecting MNEs, such as the handling of acquisitions and the shifts in strategies to fulfill international objectives

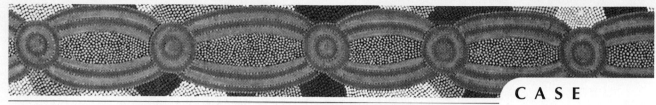

The United Nations ranks Nestlé as the most international of the world's 100 largest manufacturers. The Swiss-based company was international from the start—it began with a 1905 merger between an American and German company. Today, about 98 percent of Nestlé's sales are outside Switzerland, and about half of top management at the Vevey headquarters is non-Swiss. An Austrian, a German, a Frenchman, an Italian, a Swiss, and an American have held Nestlé's CEO position.

Map 15.1 shows Nestlé's factories by country and percentages of sales by region and product. In 1998, sales from factories in 78 countries totaled 117.3 billion Swiss francs. With such a wide geographic spread of operations, Nestlé still maintains clear-cut policies on which decisions will be made at headquarters in Switzerland and which will be made in host countries, as well as the roles corporate and host-country managers will play.

A major responsibility of Nestlé's corporate management is to give the company strategic direction. To do this, it decides in which geographic areas and to which products it plans to allocate efforts. For example, in the 1980s, Nestlé became less dependent on chocolate and emerging economy markets by placing more emphasis on culinary products and on the North American market. In the 1990s, it placed more emphasis on emerging economies, especially China. Throughout most of its history, Nestlé has concentrated on manufacturing, marketing, and wholesale distribution and has avoided vertical expansion into plantations or retail food sales. To maintain this control, its corporate management handles all acquisition decisions as well as those regarding which products it will research at its headquarters in Switzerland. This decision making is handled through product groups, such as the chocolate and confectionery products group. Headquarters expects each country's operations to provide a positive cash flow to the parent. In fact, Nestlé tries to move almost all cash to Switzerland, where a specialized staff decides in which currencies it will be held and to what countries it will be transferred.

Headquarters also researches conditions affecting commodities and mandates amounts and prices for purchases of supplies. For example, headquarters might require that all overseas companies contract for a supply of green coffee for, say, three to six months at some maximum price. The company is heavily dependent on introducing new products that may take several years to become profitable, so it must ensure that the more established products remain sufficiently profitable to generate needed funds. If a new product does not become profitable within a reasonable time, such as its failed mineral water product in Brazil, or if it has run its cycle of profitability, such as Libby's vegetable-canning operations, or if its development potential seems low, such as Beech-Nut's baby food, management in Switzerland decides to divest the business. Other divestments occur because certain activities of acquired companies do not fit the corporate development strategy. For example, Nestlé spun off a printing and packaging business that was part of the acquired Buitoni-Perugina company.

The budget that originates from each country is the main means to ensure that each country carries its share within the corporation. Managers in each country prepare budgets annually, revise them quarterly, and submit them to corporate headquarters for approval. Actual performance reports go to Switzerland monthly, where they are compared with the budget and the previous year's performance. The head of the country operations must explain any deviations satisfactorily or corporate management will intervene, such as by replacing that individual. Corporate headquarters also serves as a source of information. The successes, failures, and

MAP 15.1
Nestlé's Factories, Sales, and Products

Nestlé has sales in virtually every country of the world and has factories in 78 countries. The numbers in parentheses indicate the number of factories within each of the 78 countries. The two pie charts show the percentage of sales in 1998 by geographic area and by product divisions.

Source: www.nestle.com, 1999.

general experiences of product programs in one country are passed on to managers in others. For example, headquarters disseminated information on the success of a white chocolate bar in New Zealand and on a line of Lean Cuisine frozen food in the United States in this way.

Despite the centralized directives described above, Nestlé's country and product managers have a great deal of discretion in certain matters, especially marketing. Most product research is centralized so that duplication of efforts is minimized. When headquarters develops a new product, corporate management offers it to the country managers and may urge initial trials. However, it does not force them to launch a new product if they do not find it acceptable. If country managers introduce the product, they are fairly free to adapt it as long as corporate management does not find the changes harmful. For example, one of Nestlé's best-selling products, Nescafé instant coffee, is blended and colored slightly differently from country to country.

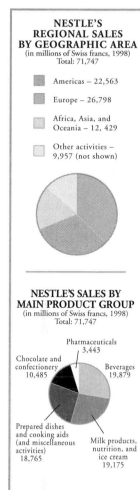

**NESTLE'S
REGIONAL SALES
BY GEOGRAPHIC AREA**
(in millions of Swiss francs, 1998)
Total: 71,747

Americas – 22,563

Europe – 26,798

Africa, Asia, and
Oceania – 12, 429

Other activities –
9,957 (not shown)

**NESTLE'S SALES BY
MAIN PRODUCT GROUP**
(in millions of Swiss francs, 1998)
Total: 71,747

Pharmaceuticals
3,443

Chocolate and
confectionery
10,485

Beverages
19,879

Prepared dishes
and cooking aids
(and miscellaneous
activities)
18,765

Milk products,
nutrition, and
ice cream
19,175

To control its international business, Nestlé relies heavily on budgets and reports—as well as on information-gathering visits to foreign operations. The company has several policies to bring corporate and subsidiary management closer together. One policy is to alternate people between jobs in the field and jobs at headquarters. For example, the CEO of Nestlé USA spends one week of each month at Vevey. Another policy is to schedule meetings and training programs to bring large groups of managers together. Still another policy is to ensure that corporate headquarters management can converse with subsidiary management in French, English, German, and Spanish. (The executive board conducts business in English.) Further, the compensation system and management style seeks to limit turnover among employees.

Although Nestlé's control mechanisms are clearly defined, they change as the company and its competitive environment change. During the 1980s, the company decentralized—largely because of the management philosophy of its new managing director, who reduced the corporate staff, pushed more authority down to the operating level, and replaced 25-page monthly reports with a 1-page reporting form. At one time the company sought to balance functional, geographic, and product viewpoints by establishing company units in charge of each headquarters. This meant that the heads of three units had to agree on a decision—sometimes a slow process. To slim down the corporate staff and speed decision making, Nestlé replaced this structure with a board of general managers that primarily represents the zones into which Nestlé divides the world.

Many company actions require new decisions on where to place control. Nestlé prefers to gain first-in advantages in markets; however, when this is not possible, Nestlé's policy is to expand largely through acquisition of existing companies. Nestlé's acquisitions have blurred the established lines of responsibility. Because acquired companies are unlikely to have the exact product and geographic operations to fit Nestlé's structure, Nestlé must accommodate these operations. For example, Nestlé acquired Libby, McNeill & Libby, a U.S. company with substantial international operations, including a subsidiary in the United Kingdom. Nestlé had to iron out not only how Libby would relate to Nestlé's existing U.S. operations but also whether the U.K. subsidiary should continue to report to Libby or report to Nestlé's European operations instead. There was a gradual transition by which the subsidiary eventually reported to the European operations. In another case, Nestlé's acquisition of Stouffer Foods put it into hotel ownership for the first time. Because Stouffer had been highly profitable and because corporate management at Nestlé's Swiss headquarters lacked hotel experience, initially many more decisions than usual were made at the subsidiary level.

Control questions facing all companies:

- **Where should decision-making power reside?**
- **How should foreign operations report to headquarters?**
- **How can the company ensure that it meets its global objectives?**

INTRODUCTION

The Nestlé case illustrates concerns all international companies share: where decision-making power resides, how foreign operations should report to headquarters, and how to ensure the company meets its global objectives. Behind each of these concerns is a

Thanks to the technological revolution, members of organizations in different parts of the world may now communicate easily, enhancing international coordination and control. This photo shows BP Amoco chief executive Sir John Brown speaking from London on a video screen in New York, to announce the takeover of the Atlantic Richfield Company (ARCO). At the far right is BP Amoco deputy chief executive Rodney Chase. At the table is ARCO chief financial officer Maria Knowles.

more fundamental one—that of control. Figure 15.1 shows that control is necessary to achieve international objectives. It is much more than just the ownership of sufficient voting shares to direct company policies. **Control** is management's planning, implementation, evaluation, and correction of performance to ensure that the organization meets its objectives. Top management's toughest challenge is to balance the company's global needs with its need to adapt to country-level differences.

Control keeps a company's direction or strategy on track. For example, Nestlé managers know that, although cost and innovation are important, the company's major competitive advantage lies in the marketing of differentiated consumer products. As such, its subsidiary managers concentrate on marketing—such as branding, advertising, and distribution—rather than on acquiring capital or spending heavily on R&D. Nestlé managers also have a clear-cut understanding of competitive entry strategies. They look to acquire first-in advantages or companies with an established brand and significant market share. Headquarters managers allocate resources to emphasize those product and geographic markets in which it prefers to grow more rapidly. It would be almost inconceivable for a manager, in say Peru, to launch a new product in Peru or build a plant in Bolivia (Nestlé has no manufacturing in Bolivia) without considerable scrutiny and approval from corporate management in Switzerland. Further, Nestlé allows its country-level managers to adjust to specific environmental and competitive conditions in their countries of operation. At the same time, the subsidiaries share information, fixed costs from new product development, and spillover advantages, which make it easier for Nestlé to sell to international distributors such as Carrefour and Wal-Mart. In contrast, Prudential Securities' operations in Australia, Hong Kong,

FIGURE 15.1 Control in International Business

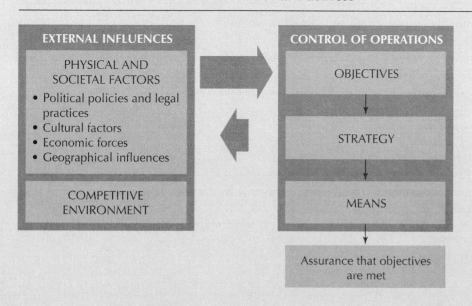

Control is the assurance that the company's objectives are met. The process involves setting objectives, a strategy to achieve them, and the means to carry out the strategy.

Japan, and Singapore became so independent that they moved in different directions. The result was the company's inability to gain advantages from its multinational status, such as exchanging useful information.[2]

Control is also needed so that individuals cannot make decisions that endanger the entire company. For example, Barings, a British investment bank, collapsed in 1995 after a 28-year-old futures trader in Singapore lost about $1.3 billion through speculative and fraudulent trading. Subsequent investigations showed that neither headquarters nor external auditors sufficiently understood the trader's complex dealings, and there was no clear-cut point at headquarters to control the amount of risk he could take.[3]

Several factors make control more difficult internationally than it is domestically.

Foreign control is usually more difficult than domestic control because of

- **Distance—it takes more time and expense to communicate**
- **Diversity—country differences make it hard to compare operations**
- **Uncontrollables—there are more dissimilar outside stockholders and governmental influences**
- **Degree of certainty—there often are rapid changes in the environment and data problems**

1. *Distance*. In spite of the growth in e-mail and fax transmissions, many communications are still best handled by face-to-face or voice-to-voice contact. The geographic distance (especially when operations span multiple time zones) and cultural disparity separating countries increase the time, expense, and possibility of error in cross-national communications.
2. *Diversity*. This book has emphasized the need for an MNE to adjust to each country in which it operates. When market size, type of competition, nature of the product, labor cost, currency, and a host of other factors differentiate operations among countries, the task of evaluating performance or setting standards to correct or improve business functions is extremely complicated.
3. *Uncontrollables*. Evaluating employees' and subsidiaries' performance is of little use in maintaining control unless there is some means of taking corrective action. Effective corrective action may be minimal because many foreign operations must contend with the dictates of outside stockholders in the foreign company, whose objectives may differ somewhat from those of the parent, and with government regulations over which the company has no short-term influence. Further, most companies handle their international operations through foreign subsidiaries, which are separate legal entities even when the parent has a 100-percent ownership. (This chapter will deal primarily with the subsidiary form but explain other forms near the end.)
4. *Degree of certainty*. Control implies setting goals and developing plans to meet those goals. Economic and industry data are much less complete and accurate for some countries than for others. Further, political and economic conditions are subject to rapid change in some locales. These factors impede planning, especially long-range planning.

Although these factors make control more difficult in the international context, managers still try to ensure that foreign operations comply with overall corporate goals and philosophies. This chapter discusses five aspects of the international control process:

1. Planning
2. Organizational structure
3. Location of decision making

4. Control mechanisms
5. Special situations

PLANNING

Planning is an essential element of managerial control. A company must adapt its resources and objectives to different and changing international markets and this takes planning. Because planning has been both implicitly and explicitly discussed already, this section presents an overview of the process.

THE PLANNING LOOP

As Figure 15.2 shows, planning must mesh a company's objectives and capabilities with its internal and external environments. It must also involve continuing reassessment—thus the concept of a loop back to early steps in the planning process. The first step (A) is to develop a long-range **strategic intent**, an objective that will hold the organization together over a long period while it builds global competitive viability.[4] Although few companies start with such an intent, most develop one as they progress toward significant international positions. Some, such as Honda and Canon, developed strategic intents to become major global competitors while they were still small domestic companies. The strategic intent may encompass whether and where a company wants to be a leader, such as dominating its domestic market, dominating a regional or global market, or attaining profit results without being the market leader.[5] The strategic intent may also set priorities. For example, Johnson & Johnson states that its responsibilities are to customers, suppliers and employees, the community and environment, and shareholders—in that order.[6]

The next planning step (B) is to analyze internal resources, along with environmental factors in the home country. These resources and factors affect and constrain each company differently and sometimes each product differently for the same company. Basically, the most successful companies internationally are those that find the right fit between what they need and what they are good at.[7] For example, a small company inexperienced in foreign operations may lack financial and human resources, even though it may have unique product capabilities. Unlike a larger counterpart, it may have to collaborate with another company, perhaps by licensing foreign production rather than owning facilities abroad. But it still will need to control its foreign operations through a contract with the licensee that stipulates sales targets, product characteristics, and so on.

Only by making an internal analysis (step B) can a company set the overall rationale for its international activities (step C). Managers must examine these activities in conjunction with the means of competing, such as by keeping prices low or differentiating through brand recognition. For instance, a company competing largely on price and faced with rising domestic costs may pursue one of several means for cost reduction, such as locating production where costs are lower or expanding exports to spread fixed costs.

Because each country in which the company is operating or contemplating operating is unique, managers must do a local analysis (step D) before examining the final

In planning, companies must mesh objectives with internal and external constraints and set means to implement, monitor, and correct.

FIGURE 15.2   International Planning Process

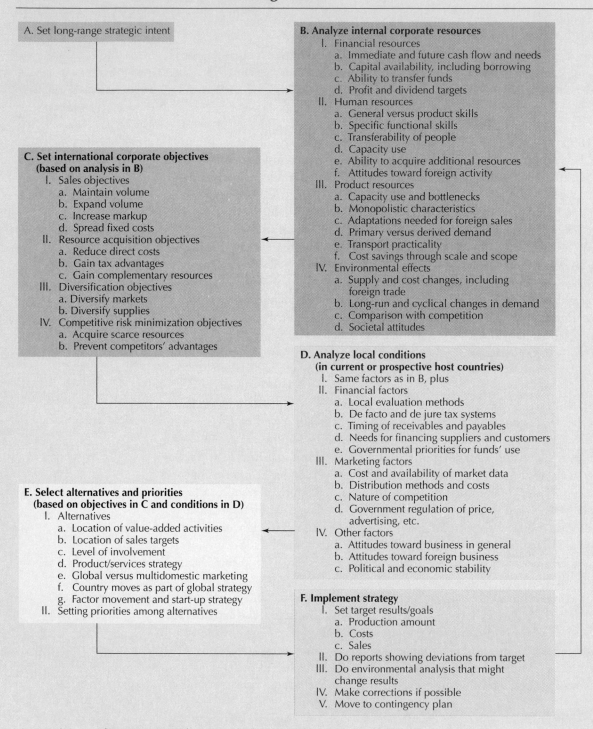

A. Set long-range strategic intent

B. Analyze internal corporate resources
- I. Financial resources
  - a. Immediate and future cash flow and needs
  - b. Capital availability, including borrowing
  - c. Ability to transfer funds
  - d. Profit and dividend targets
- II. Human resources
  - a. General versus product skills
  - b. Specific functional skills
  - c. Transferability of people
  - d. Capacity use
  - e. Ability to acquire additional resources
  - f. Attitudes toward foreign activity
- III. Product resources
  - a. Capacity use and bottlenecks
  - b. Monopolistic characteristics
  - c. Adaptations needed for foreign sales
  - d. Primary versus derived demand
  - e. Transport practicality
  - f. Cost savings through scale and scope
- IV. Environmental effects
  - a. Supply and cost changes, including foreign trade
  - b. Long-run and cyclical changes in demand
  - c. Comparison with competition
  - d. Societal attitudes

C. Set international corporate objectives (based on analysis in B)
- I. Sales objectives
  - a. Maintain volume
  - b. Expand volume
  - c. Increase markup
  - d. Spread fixed costs
- II. Resource acquisition objectives
  - a. Reduce direct costs
  - b. Gain tax advantages
  - c. Gain complementary resources
- III. Diversification objectives
  - a. Diversify markets
  - b. Diversify supplies
- IV. Competitive risk minimization objectives
  - a. Acquire scarce resources
  - b. Prevent competitors' advantages

D. Analyze local conditions (in current or prospective host countries)
- I. Same factors as in B, plus
- II. Financial factors
  - a. Local evaluation methods
  - b. De facto and de jure tax systems
  - c. Timing of receivables and payables
  - d. Needs for financing suppliers and customers
  - e. Governmental priorities for funds' use
- III. Marketing factors
  - a. Cost and availability of market data
  - b. Distribution methods and costs
  - c. Nature of competition
  - d. Government regulation of price, advertising, etc.
- IV. Other factors
  - a. Attitudes toward business in general
  - b. Attitudes toward foreign business
  - c. Political and economic stability

E. Select alternatives and priorities (based on objectives in C and conditions in D)
- I. Alternatives
  - a. Location of value-added activities
  - b. Location of sales targets
  - c. Level of involvement
  - d. Product/services strategy
  - e. Global versus multidomestic marketing
  - f. Country moves as part of global strategy
  - g. Factor movement and start-up strategy
- II. Setting priorities among alternatives

F. Implement strategy
- I. Set target results/goals
  - a. Production amount
  - b. Costs
  - c. Sales
- II. Do reports showing deviations from target
- III. Do environmental analysis that might change results
- IV. Make corrections if possible
- V. Move to contingency plan

The initial step in planning is setting the company's long-range strategic intent, followed by a loop from Step F to Step B in which short- and medium-term steps are taken to achieve the intent.

alternatives (step E). For instance, changes in local stability and market growth undoubtedly influenced Nestlé's decision to increase emphasis on emerging economies.

The selection among the alternatives in step E determines the extent to which a company follows a global, transnational, or multidomestic strategy. These alternatives include

- Location of value-added functions—the choice of where to locate each of the functions that comprise the entire value-added chain, from research to production to after-sales servicing.
- Location of sales targets—the allocation of sales among countries and the level of activity in each, particularly in terms of market share.
- Level of involvement—the choice of operating through wholly owned facilities, partially owned facilities, or contract arrangements and whether the choice varies among countries.
- Product/services strategy—the extent to which a worldwide business offers the same or different products in different countries.
- Marketing—the extent to which a company uses the same brand names, advertising, and other marketing elements in different countries.
- Competitive moves—the extent to which a company makes competitive moves in individual countries as part of a global competitive strategy.
- Factor movement and start-up strategy—whether production factors are acquired locally or brought in by the company and whether the operation begins through an acquisition or start-up.[8]

Managers must rank alternatives so they can easily add or delete strategies (step F) as resource availability changes. A parent company may, for example, plan to remit dividends from one of its foreign subsidiaries back to itself. However, this may become impossible if a government puts foreign-exchange controls into effect. Management must then decide among its alternatives, such as borrowing more at home, remitting more from other subsidiaries, or forgoing domestic expansion or dividends. Without priorities, the company may have to make hurried decisions to accomplish its objectives even partially.

Finally, management should set specific objectives for each subsidiary, along with ways to measure both deviations from the plan and conditions that may cause such deviations. Through timely evaluation, the company can take corrective actions. There must be a constant loop from step F to step B in Figure 15.1 to ensure the company is making timely decisions.[9] We'll discuss evaluation methods later in this chapter.

We must make a distinction between operating plans and strategic plans. Strategic plans are longer term and similar to step A. They outline major commitments, such as what businesses the company will be in and where, and are less subject to reevaluation. Operating plans formulate short-term objectives and the means to carry them out. Although input for a strategic plan may come from all parts of the organization, only upper-level management can plan changes in international policies because they can see all the company's worldwide activities.

UNCERTAINTY AND PLANNING

The more uncertainty there is, the harder it is to plan. It is generally agreed that conditions in the international sphere are more uncertain than those in the domestic sphere because international operations are complex. International managers have to monitor many subsidiaries—many with different products—in different foreign markets.

A company's international operations have more complexity and uncertainty than its domestic ones.

ORGANIZATIONAL STRUCTURE

No matter how good a plan is, it will achieve little unless there is an appropriate means of implementing it. International companies try to set up organizational structures (the formal patterns of their lines of communication and responsibilities) that group individuals and operational units in strategic ways. The structure depends on many factors, including

- Degree of multidomestic, global, and transnational policies employed
- Location and type of foreign facilities
- Impact of international operations on total corporate performance

The form, method, and location of operational units at home and abroad will affect taxes, expenses—and control. Consequently, organizational structure has an important effect on the fulfillment of corporate objectives. We shall now examine the major structures of companies' international operations.

SEPARATE VERSUS INTEGRATED INTERNATIONAL STRUCTURES

All of a company's foreign subsidiaries may report to the same department or division of headquarters because that department or division is responsible for all the company's international business. This is an international division structure. But different subsidiaries may report to different departments or divisions of headquarters because responsibility is split at headquarters by function (such as production and marketing), by product lines (such as consumer products and industrial products), or by geographic area (such as Asia and Europe). These are functional, product, and geographic structures, respectively. Figure 15.3 shows simplified organizational structures of international businesses. Most companies basically use one of these structures. Note that no structure is without drawbacks.

An international division
- **Creates a critical mass of international expertise**
- **May have problems getting resources from domestic divisions**

International Division Structure   Grouping international business activities into their own division—Figure 15.3(a)—puts internationally specialized personnel together to handle such diverse matters as export documentation, foreign-exchange transactions, and relations with foreign governments. This prevents duplication of these activities in more than one place in the organization. It also creates a large enough critical mass so that personnel within the division can wield power within the organization to push for international expansion. However, an international division might have to depend on the domestic divisions for products to sell, personnel, technology, and other resources. Because domestic division managers are usually evaluated on the basis of performance within the domestic divisions for which they are responsible, they may withhold their best resources from the international division to improve their own performances. Given the separation between domestic and foreign operations, this structure is probably best suited for multidomestic strategies, where there is little integration and standardization between domestic and foreign operations.[10]

Although international division structure is not popular among European MNEs, it is popular among U.S. MNEs. One apparent reason for this difference is that U.S. companies depend much more on the domestic market than do European companies.

FIGURE 15.3   **Placement of International Activities within the Organizational Structures for International Businesses**

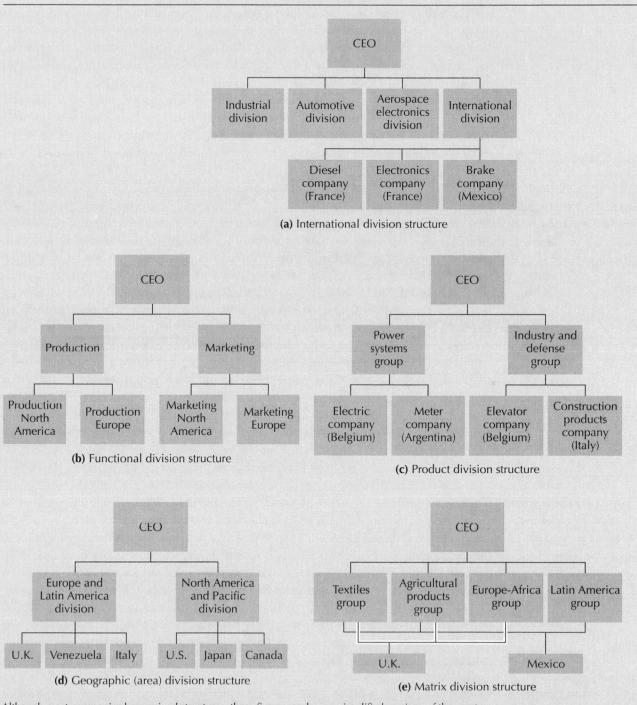

(a) International division structure

(b) Functional division structure

(c) Product division structure

(d) Geographic (area) division structure

(e) Matrix division structure

Although most companies have mixed structures, these five examples are simplified versions of the most common organizational structures for international businesses.

Functional divisions are popular among companies with narrow product lines.

Functional Division Structure   Parts (b), (c), and (d) in Figure 15.3 show organizational structures that integrate international operations. Functional divisions, like those shown in Figure 15.3(b), group personnel organizationally so that marketing people report to other marketing people, finance to other finance people, and so on. Functional divisions are popular among companies with a narrow range of products, particularly if the production and marketing methods are undifferentiated among them. However, as they add new and different products this structure becomes cumbersome. For example, in a company such as Westinghouse (which produces more than 8,000 different products in such diverse areas as real estate finance, nuclear fuel, television production, electronics systems, and soft drink bottling), it is hard to imagine that a head of production could understand how to produce all these products. But many oil and mineral extraction companies, such as Exxon, use this structure, which is ideal when products and production methods are basically undifferentiated among countries.

Product divisions are popular among international companies with diverse products.

Product Division Structure   Product divisions, as Figure 15.3(c) illustrates, are particularly popular among companies that make a variety of diverse products, especially those that have become diverse through acquisitions, such as Westinghouse. Because these divisions may have little in common, they may be highly independent of each other. As is true for the functional structure, the product division structure is well-suited for a global strategy because both the foreign and domestic operations for a given product report to the same manager, who can find synergies between the two, such as by sharing information on the successes and failures of each. Most likely, there will be duplicated functions and international activities among the product divisions. Moreover, there is no formal means by which one product division can learn from another's international experience. Finally, different subsidiaries from different product divisions within the same foreign country will report to different groups at headquarters. For example, Figure 15.3(c) illustrates that the Belgian electric and elevator subsidiaries report to different headquarters divisions. So synergy could be lost within countries if different subsidiaries don't communicate with each other or to a common manager. For example, at one time in Westinghouse, one subsidiary was borrowing funds locally at an exorbitant rate, while another in the same country had excess cash.

Geographic divisions are popular when foreign operations are large and are not dominated by a single country or region.

Geographic (Area) Division Structure   Companies use geographic divisions, as in Figure 15.3(d), if they have large foreign operations that are not dominated by a single country or area (including the home country). This structure is more common to European MNEs, such as Nestlé, than to U.S. MNEs, which tend to be dominated by the strong domestic market. Recall that Nestlé can use this structure because no one region dominates its operations. The structure is useful when maximum economies in production can be gained on a regional rather than a global basis because of market size or the production technologies for the industry. A drawback is possible costly duplication of work among areas. For example, Ford abandoned its geographic structure in favor of a product division structure because of costly design duplication between Europe and North America.[11]

A matrix organization gives functional, product, and geographic groups a common focus.

Matrix Division Structure   Because of the problems inherent in either integrating or separating foreign operations, many companies, such as Tenneco Automotive, are moving toward matrix organizations, illustrated in Figure 15.3(e). In this organizational structure, a subsidiary reports to more than one group (functional, product, or geographic). This structure is based on the theory that because each group shares responsibility over foreign operations, the groups will become more interdependent, exchange information, and exchange resources with each other.[12] For example, product-group managers must compete among themselves to ensure that R&D personnel responsible to a functional group, such as production, also develop technologies for product groups. These product-group managers also must compete to ensure that geographic-group managers emphasize their lines sufficiently. Not only do product groups compete; functional and geographic groups also must compete among themselves to obtain resources held by others in the matrix. For example, as Figure 15.3(e) shows, the amount of resources for development of textile products in Mexico depends partly on the competition between the Europe-Africa group and the Latin America group and partly on the competition between the textiles group and the agricultural products group for resources.

A matrix organization does have drawbacks. One drawback concerns how groups compete for scarce resources and to enact their preferred operating methods. When lower-level managers fail to agree, upper management must decide which operating method to follow and how to allocate the resources, which takes time. Further, for whatever reasons, upper management may favor a specific executive or group. As others in the organization see this occurring, they may perceive that the locus of power lies with a certain individual or group. Consequently, other group managers may think that pushing their own group's unique needs is futile, thus eliminating the multiple viewpoints that a matrix is supposed to bring. Or a superior may neglect control of subordinates because of assuming wrongly that someone else is overseeing them. In Figure 15.3(e), for example, managers in the Latin America group might not pay close attention to day-to-day Mexican textile operations because they assume that managers in the textile division are doing this. Meanwhile, managers in the textile division may wrongly assume that managers in the Latin America group are overseeing the textile operation in Mexico closely. The false assumption that someone else was handling the responsibility was a factor in the loss of control and the demise of Barings.[13] For these reasons, some companies that adopted dual-reporting systems have gone back to conventional structures with clear lines of responsibility, including Dow Chemical, Digital Equipment, and Citibank.[14]

DYNAMIC NATURE OF STRUCTURES

A company's structure can evolve as its business evolves. When a company is only exporting, an export department attached to a product or functional division may suffice. (In most companies, departments are within divisions.) But if international operations continue to grow—say the company starts overseas production in addition to exporting—an export department may no longer be sufficient. Perhaps an international division replaces the department, or perhaps each product division takes on worldwide responsibility for its own products. Or, if the international division becomes very large, the company may split it into geographic divisions.

MIXED NATURE OF STRUCTURES

Because of growth dynamics, companies seldom, if ever, have all their activities corresponding to the simplified organizational structures described here; most have a mixed structure. For example, a recent acquisition might report to headquarters until it can be consolidated efficiently within existing divisions. Or circumstances regarding a particular country, product, or function might necessitate that it be handled separately, apart from the overall structure. Some operations may be wholly owned, thus enabling a denser network of communications to develop than in others where there is only partial or no ownership of the foreign operations. Further, the overall structure gives an incomplete picture of divisions in the organization. For example, PepsiCo is organized by product lines—soft drinks and snacks—which would seem to imply that each product line is integrated globally. However, each line has its own international division, which separates it from domestic operations.[15]

EVOLVING STRUCTURES

As companies grow in size, product lines, and dependence on foreign operations, control becomes more complex. New structures continue to evolve to deal with this complexity.

Because of the increase in alliances among companies, control increasingly must come from negotiation and persuasion rather than from authority of superiors over subordinates.

Network Organizations

No company is fully independent. Each is a customer of and a supplier to other companies. Such interdependence is known as a **network alliance**. Each company must decide what products, functions, and geographic areas it will own and handle itself and what it will outsource to others. A company can control what it handles itself with clear superior-subordinate relationships, known as hierarchies. However, when it depends on another company—say, as an essential supplier—which is superior and which is subordinate is not clear. Therefore, the location of control in a network alliance is ambiguous and is known as a **heterarchy**.[16] Likewise, when a company shares ownership with another, such as in a joint venture, there is usually a heterarchical relationship. Corning is a good example of a heterarchy because half of its earnings come from alliances, particularly joint ventures. Corning management cannot dictate what its alliance partners must do. Instead, it serves as a broker, conflict negotiator, and facilitator for them.[17]

Many Japanese companies are linked similarly in *keiretsus*, networks in which each company owns a small percentage of other companies in the network. There are long-term strong personal relationships among high-level managers in the different companies, and the same directors often serve on more than one board. Sometimes *keiretsus* are vertical, such as that between Toyota and its parts suppliers. Sometimes they are horizontal.[18] For example, the Mitsubishi *keiretsu* consists of core companies in which no single company dominates. The businesses are extremely diverse, including mining, real estate, credit cards, and tuna canning. Typically, the core companies within a keiretsu buy and sell with each other only if it makes business sense. In Mitsubishi's case, it is hard to understand why a real estate company would need to do business with, or invest in, a tuna canning company. However, managers can exchange information that is useful to more than one company, underwrite each other's financing, and gain more clout when lobbying for governmental legislation. Strong, long-term personal relationships among managers in the companies build common interests that do not depend on formal controls.[19] Nevertheless, this cushioning from stand-alone competition may retard a company's attainment of optimum efficiency.[20]

Operations in noncore competencies may become separate companies.

Spin-Off Organizations

Companies sometimes develop new products or services that do not fit easily within existing competencies. To bring the new product or service to its potential, the parent company may create—"spin off"—a separate company in which the parent will retain some, but not necessarily all, ownership. At the same time, the spin-off permits the parent to concentrate on new learning and to use its resources elsewhere. Such U.S. companies as Johnson & Johnson, Raychem, and Thermo Electron have spun off companies that subsequently have operated almost independently. The spin-off is different from simply having a product division because each company must stand on its own and satisfy its own group of stockholders. Each company gains because it can specialize in its competencies and need not await higher approval before implementing its decisions. However, evidence is mixed on whether companies perform better or worse from spin-offs.[21] Japanese companies have historically used spin-offs, the most notable example being Todota Automated Loomworks' spin-off of newly developed automobile competencies that became Toyota Motors.[22]

Lead Subsidiary Organizations   The major competency for designing, producing, and selling a product does not necessarily lie in the company's home country. As a result, some companies have moved the headquarters of certain divisions to foreign countries. For instance, AT&T moved its corded telephone division from the United States to France, Siemens moved its air-traffic management division from Germany to the United Kingdom, Hyundai shifted its personal computer division from Korea to the United States, and the Finnish company Nokia built its capabilities for a telecommunications product in the United Kingdom. Although these divisional headquarters are still accountable to corporate headquarters, other global operations, including those in the home country, must report to them.[23]

Some divisions may be headquartered in a foreign country.

LOCATION OF DECISION MAKING

You might think that organizational structures tell us who makes decisions in a company, but that is not always the case. The higher the managerial level at which managers make decisions, the more they are centralized; the lower the level, the more they are decentralized. Whether decision making should be centralized or decentralized depends on whether we're talking about the company as a whole or some part of it, such as a particular subsidiary. For purposes of this discussion, decisions made at the foreign-subsidiary level are considered decentralized, while those made above the foreign-subsidiary level are considered centralized.

The location of decision making may vary within the same company over time as well as by product, function, and country. In addition, actual decision making is seldom as one-sided as it may appear. A manager who has decision-making authority may consult other managers before exercising that authority. Putting these exceptions aside, this section discusses why companies would place decision control at either the corporate or the subsidiary level. We usually associate centralized decision making with a global strategy, decentralized decision making with a multidomestic strategy, and a combination of the two with a transnational strategy. The reason for choosing one over the other is partly a function of companies' attitudes. For example, an ethnocentric attitude would influence a company to develop competencies, such as knowledge and technology, in its home country and control how they are transferred aboard. A polycentric attitude would cause the company to delegate decisions to foreign subsidiaries because headquarters personnel believe only people on the spot know best what to do. A geocentric

Centralization implies higher-level decision making, usually above the country level.

attitude would permit more openness to capabilities either at home or abroad and be conducive to a transnational strategy.

Some conditions favor the location of decisions in one place or the other. Basically, companies should choose the location based on a combination of three trade-offs:

- Balancing pressures for global integration versus pressures for local responsiveness
- Balancing the capabilities of headquarters versus subsidiary personnel
- Balancing the expediency versus the quality of decisions

PRESSURES FOR GLOBAL INTEGRATION VERSUS LOCAL RESPONSIVENESS

The higher the pressure for global integration, the greater the need to centralize decision making. The higher the pressure for responsiveness to local conditions, the greater the need to decentralize decision making. We shall now discuss the reasons for pressures one way or the other.

Decisions on moving goods or other resources internationally are more likely to be made centrally.

Resource Transference A company may want to move its resources—capital, personnel, or technology—from its facilities in one country to its facilities in another. For example, it may decide to move capital from one country to another where the projected return is higher, hurting the performance in one country but improving its global or overall performance. Decisions about these moves usually occur centrally because making them requires information from all operating units. Such information is often available only at headquarters. Otherwise, every unit would have to disseminate reports to every other unit, and there would be no clear-cut way to determine whether and how a resource from one locale would be used elsewhere. Further, a subsidiary will likely favor its own projects and performance, the major factor that influenced Royal Dutch/Shell to centralize financial control of U.S. operations that were once handled autonomously by its subsidiary, Shell Oil, in the United States.[24] Similarly, if the company needs to export output from its operations in one country to its operations in another country (for example, with vertical integration or when interdependent components make up the company's final product), centralized control may help assure this flow. However, if a subsidiary is not part of a company's integrated operation—for example, because it operates in a highly protected market—there is little need for centralized control. But the subsidiary's strategies and importance to global operations may shift.[25]

Another centralized decision in resource transference may concern jurisdiction over exports. For example, if a company has manufacturing facilities in the United States and Germany, which facility will export to South Africa? By answering that question centrally, the company may avoid price competition among the subsidiaries and take into consideration production costs, transportation costs, tax rates, foreign-exchange controls, and where there is excess production capacity.

Global standardization usually reduces costs, but some revenue may be lost in the process.

Standardization Worldwide uniformity of an MNE's products, purchases, methods, and policies may reduce its global costs substantially, even if some costs increase for a particular subsidiary. Such standardization is highly unlikely if each subsidiary makes its own decisions. For example, if an MNE standardizes machinery in its production process, it may see savings from quantity discounts on purchases, consolidation of

mechanics' training, maintenance of manuals, and carrying of spare parts inventories. The company may realize economies, not only through scale of production, but also in such activities as advertising, R&D, and the purchase of group insurance. Product uniformity gives a company greater flexibility in filling orders when supply problems arise because of strikes, disasters, or sudden increases in demand. Production can simply expand in one country to meet shortages elsewhere. However, the downside of standardization is that revenue losses may exceed the gains from cost savings; for example, because some subsidiaries end up with products that do not quite fit demand. Of course, some products are more suitable to global standardization than are others. GE's jet engines require no local adaptation, whereas Nestlé's food products do. The food industry usually does not need to integrate operations across countries because transportation costs offset savings from scale economies. At the same time, it has a high need to adapt to local conditions because tastes, competitors, and distributors differ at the local level. Figure 15.4 shows engines in the top left quadrant (more suitable for centralized control) and food products in the bottom right quadrant (more suitable for decentralized control.)

The more different the foreign environment is from the home environment, the more delegation occurs.

Systematic Dealings With Stakeholders Increasingly, the people with whom a company must deal—government officials, employees, suppliers, consumers, and the general public—are aware of what that company does in other countries of operation. Concessions the company grants to stakeholders in one country may then be demanded

FIGURE 15.4 Environmental Influences and Control of MNEs

Strong

Forces for global integration and centralized control

Centralized Control, Undifferentiated by Country
- Construction and mining machinery
- Nonferrous metals
- Industrial chemicals
- Scientific measuring instruments
- Engines

Control to Fit Different Country Needs with Overlaid Control of Integration by Parent Company
- Drugs and pharmaceuticals
- Photographic equipment
- Computers
- Automobiles

Ad Hoc Variation of Control
- Metals (other than nonferrous)
- Machinery
- Paper
- Textiles
- Printing and publishing

Control to Fit Differing Needs of Each Subsidiary
- Beverages
- Food
- Rubber
- Household appliances
- Tobacco

Weak Forces for local responsiveness and decentralized control **Strong**

Note how control of these industries (and mechanisms to implement control) are influenced by the strengths of forces that favor local responsiveness and forces that favor global integration.

Source: Adapted from Figures 2 and 5 and discussion in Sumantra Ghoshal and Nitin Nohria, "Horses for Courses: Organizational forms for Multinational Corporations," *Sloan Management Review,* Winter 1993, pp. 23–36.

in other countries. The company may face a dilemma if it can't afford the same concessions in another country. Suppose that, for public relations purposes, company management in Finland decided to give preferential prices to the Finnish government and to establish a profit-sharing plan for employees. Profits in Finland allowed the company to give such concessions. If government officials and employees in, say, Norway—where profits aren't quite as high—ask for similar treatment, the result may be even less profits if the company complies or poor public relations if it does not.

Even pricing and product decisions in one country can affect demand in other countries. With the growing mobility of consumers, especially industrial consumers, a good or bad experience with a product in one country may eventually affect sales elsewhere. This is especially true if industrial consumers themselves want uniformity in their end products. If prices differ substantially among countries, consumers may even find that they can import more cheaply than they can buy locally. Centralized decision making is necessary to ensure that operations in different countries operate toward achieving global objectives.

Global competition also may cause a company to make decisions in one country to improve performance elsewhere. For example, if a supplier gives price concessions to an automaker in Brazil, that supplier may more easily gain business in other countries in which the automaker manufactures because the automaker may prefer to deal with the same supplier worldwide. Usually such dealings with potential global customers or competitors need centralized decision making because headquarters personnel are the only ones with information on all the countries where the company operates, such as information on what a global competitor is doing in one country that may have an impact elsewhere. However, in some cases the subsidiary may be the best place to make decisions about the customer or competitor. For example, IBM's top management feared that its eroding Japanese market share would spill into other markets because Japanese competitors would have resources and confidence to fight IBM elsewhere. IBM gave its Japanese subsidiary decision-making power. The subsidiary increased its manufacturing capacity substantially, and it developed new products specific to the Japanese market.[26]

Transnational strategies imply

- **A hybrid of multidomestic and global strategies**
- **Gaining knowledge and capabilities from anywhere in the organization**
- **Information flows up and down, horizontal and vertical**

Transnational Strategy Chapter 1 defined the transnational company as a company whose strategy takes advantage of the benefits of both a global and a multidomestic strategy.[27] The upper right quadrant of Figure 15.4 illustrates industries that are ideal candidates for a transnational strategy because they have both a need for global integration and a need for local responsiveness. For example, the pharmaceutical industry has a strong need for integration because it depends on the sale of undifferentiated products for which scale of production is important to cover the high cost of product development. Pharmaceutical companies also face most of the same competitors everywhere they sell. Nevertheless, companies need high local responsiveness because different governmental authorities must approve each product in each country where they sell, and because sales and distribution differ substantially from place to place.

MNEs are attempting to weaken decision-making partitions so that more and better information flows within the organization. In so doing, headquarters can better use subsidiaries' unique knowledge, and subsidiaries can better understand headquarters' global needs and pertinent conditions in other subsidiaries. In fact, if headquarters ignores sub-

sidiaries' viewpoints, the company suffers. For example, Procter & Gamble (P&G) at one time allowed its country subsidiaries in Europe nearly total autonomy in adapting technology, products, and marketing approaches. To capture Europe-wide scale economies, P&G put one office in charge of formulating strategy for all of Europe, but it ignored the subsidiaries' local knowledge, underestimated their strengths, and discouraged their managers. P&G has since moved to greater standardization; however, teams representing the subsidiary operations now help drive the standardization process. Companies have established various practices to improve the flow of information. For example, ABB has a sophisticated information retrieval system that disseminates information about and to the approximately 1,300 entities in its federation of companies. In addition, it brings together as many as 5,000 managers of all levels in meetings.[28] At 3M's European operations the company has given incentives for country subsidiaries to work together on key accounts.[29] Ford is linking its design groups in North America and Europe through videoconferencing and computer networks in the development of new automobile designs.[30]

As subsidiaries have become more interdependent, for example, because of rationalized or vertically integrated production or because of dealing with common competitors and customers, there has been a tendency for managers to initiate informal contact with their peers in the other subsidiaries. Such companies as Digital have established cross-cultural teams to tackle issues common to different country operations. These teams generally are composed of people chosen because of their skills and expertise, rather than position, and are made up of equals, rather than a superior with subordinates. The ability to reach consensus is dependent on the groups' enthusiasm and peer pressure within the groups, rather than formal procedures. The advantage is the generation of more and perhaps better ideas. The disadvantages are the time it takes to decide on the cross-unit issues and the increased potential for conflict.[31]

Ad Hoc Strategy   The bottom left corner of Figure 15.4 shows industries that gain little from global integration, and also have little need to adapt to local conditions. Companies with these characteristics may either centralize or decentralize, depending, for example, on such factors as the experience and competency of the personnel at headquarters compared to subsidiaries, which we shall discuss next. At the same time, the companies may mix control by function, such as decentralizing marketing while centralizing finance.

CAPABILITIES OF HEADQUARTERS VERSUS SUBSIDIARY PERSONNEL

Upper management's perception of the competence of corporate versus local managers will influence the location of decision making. There are differences in capabilities between headquarters and local management. Decentralization may seem called for when the local management team is large rather than lean, local managers have worked a long time with the company, and local managers have developed successful track records. However, the subsidiary's capability may increase or decrease over time, and this change may be caused by subsidiary managers' initiatives.[32]

Although some decisions are better left to corporate management, doing so may cause morale problems among local managers who perceive their responsibility has been taken away. When local managers are prevented from acting in the best interest of their

The more confidence there is in foreign managers, the more delegation occurs.

own operation, they tend to think, "I could have done better, but corporate management would not let me." If local managers cannot participate in developing global strategies, they may lack the positive attitude to work hard to implement global strategic decisions.[33] These managers also may not gain the experience needed to advance within the company.

By giving groups of local managers autonomy in certain areas, an MNE may be able to attract a higher caliber of personnel who might not want to work in its home country. For example, European scientists working at Pfizer's small U.K. laboratory have been responsible for many of Pfizer's discoveries.[34] There are many ways in which subsidiaries can have autonomy over certain activities, such as developing a specific product or technology or conducting certain market testing.

Centralization may hurt local managers because they
- **Cannot perform as well**
- **Do not acquire training through increased responsibility**

DECISION EXPEDIENCY AND QUALITY

A poor decision may be better than a good one that comes too late. However, a poor decision with major consequences should usually be avoided if possible. The following discussion highlights these points.

Cost and Expediency   Although corporate management may be more experienced in advising or making certain decisions, the time and expense in centralization may not always justify the better advice. For example, corporate managers may need to visit a foreign subsidiary to see conditions firsthand before rendering their better judgment. But many decisions cannot wait. Bringing in corporate personnel may not be warranted unless the decision has large ramifications on the company.

Companies must consider how long it takes to get help from headquarters in relation to how rapidly a decision must be made.

Importance of the Decision   Any discussion of location of decision making must consider the importance of the particular decisions. Sometimes a company asks, "How much can we lose through a bad decision?" The greater the potential loss and the more important the issue, the higher in the organization the level of control usually is. In the case of marketing decisions, for example, local autonomy is not nearly as prevalent for product design as for advertising, pricing, and distribution. Product design generally necessitates a considerably larger capital outlay than the other functions do; consequently, the potential loss from a wrong decision is higher. Further, advertising, pricing, and distribution decisions may be more easily reversed if an error in judgment occurs. Rather than telling local managers what decisions they can make, the company can set limits on expenditure amount, allowing local autonomy for small outlays and requiring corporate approval on larger ones.

More important decisions are made at higher organization levels.

CONTROL IN THE INTERNATIONALIZATION PROCESS

There are various factors that influence how much control a company needs at different stages of internationalization. We discuss those factors below.

LEVEL OF IMPORTANCE

The more important the specific foreign operations are to total corporate performance, the higher the corporate level to which those units should report. The organizational structure or reporting system therefore should change over time to parallel the company's increased involvement in foreign activities.

The more important the foreign operations, the higher in the organizational structure they report.

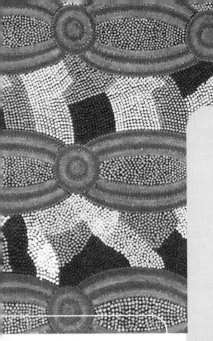

Ethical Dilemmas and Social Responsibility
WHEN PUSH COMES TO SHOVE, JUST WHO'S IN CONTROL?

A corporate policy on ethics requires a control system to ensure compliance, which should be compatible with managerial reward systems. The essential problem is that when managers are prodded to improve their performance, they may violate the ethical policy, unless they are not held responsible for performance that suffers through pursuit of the policy. Emerging economies are concerned about control that moves management and technical functions to the home country, leaving the menial and low-skilled jobs in the emerging economies. Critics recall colonial eras in which people from the colonies were forbidden responsible positions and were dependent on the colonial powers, which controlled their destinies.[35] These critics have been particularly concerned that almost all R&D takes place in industrial countries, which presents dilemmas for MNEs. There are some potent arguments for centralizing most R&D in home countries. These include the availability of many people to work directly for the company, the proximity to private research organizations and universities doing related work, and the general advantages of centralized authority in reducing duplication of efforts. Companies may partially address this concern by allowing subsidiaries in emerging economies to do adaptive R&D. However, MNEs with considerable R&D outside their home country seldom allow the foreign operations complete autonomy.[36] Corporate management may allocate budgets, approve plans, and offer suggestions. Therefore, because of centralized R&D, emerging economies may be continually at the mercy of interests in industrial countries.

Although emerging economies complain that MNEs control practices from abroad, they nevertheless want them to prevent dire effects locally. For example, Union Carbide delegated almost all decision making and day-to-day control to managing its joint venture in Bhopal, India; however, the Indian government blamed the parent company for the deaths that resulted from a chemical leak. Although an Indian government agency was responsible for making safety inspections at the facility, it was widely known that the agency was inadequately staffed. This brought up ethical questions (as well as legal ones) concerning responsibility. The Indian government, which owned 49.1 percent of the joint venture, denied responsibility because of its lack of a controlling interest and its delegation of management to Union Carbide. Union Carbide, in turn, initially claimed that responsibility rested in the joint venture. The ethical question is whether headquarters should be responsible for actions taken at the subsidiary level and whether minority stockholders should be responsible for what majority stockholders do.

At one end of the spectrum is the company that merely exports temporary surpluses through an intermediary who takes title and handles all the export details. This entire operation is apt to be so insignificant to total corporate performance that top-level management is concerned very little with it. In this case, the foreign activities should be handled at a low level in the corporate hierarchy. Anyone in the organization who knows enough about inventories and has time to discern whether orders can be filled could handle the operation.

At the other end of the spectrum is the company that has passed through intermediate stages and now owns and manages foreign manufacturing and sales facilities. Every functional and advisory group within the company undoubtedly will be involved in the facilities' establishment and direction. Because sales, investments, and profits of the foreign operations are now a more significant part of the corporate total, people very high in the corporate hierarchy are involved.

CHANGES IN COMPETENCIES

The larger the total foreign operations, the more likely that headquarters has specialized staff with international expertise. The larger the operations in a given country, the more likely that country unit has specialized staff.

Small companies, especially those that are fairly new to international operations, may have little if any staff in foreign countries. Further, because they typically have narrow product lines and lean structures, they are able to get key headquarters players in different functions to work closely, both together and with foreign customers or suppliers. For example, such headquarters involvement helped CISCO, when it was a small U.S. manufacturer of networking gear, to gain contracts with Japan's Nippon Telegraph & Telephone, and helped Pall, a small U.S.-based maker of filters, to develop extensive offshore manufacturing.[37] However, as a company's operations grow abroad, it develops a foreign management group that is capable of operating more independently of headquarters in the overseas markets. Simultaneously, corporate managers may no longer be able to deal effectively with international business operations because the company has entered so many different foreign markets; thus foreign operations tend to become more decentralized. This creates a dilemma. The subsidiary in this situation has its own capabilities, but its importance to total global performance because of its size may dictate a greater need for headquarters to intervene.[38] But as foreign operations continue to grow, people with foreign experience move into headquarters positions, and headquarters can afford staff specialists to deal with the company's multiple international operations. At that point, recentralization becomes feasible. Nevertheless, if a specific foreign country operation is very large, such as Nestlé's U.S. subsidiary, then it can afford its own specialized personnel.

CHANGES IN OPERATING FORMS

As the operating form evolves, so must the organizational structure.

The use of multiple operating forms, such as exporting, licensing, and joint venture, and the move from one to another may create the need to change areas of responsibility in the organization. Or it may mean that departments in the organization are not equally involved with all forms. For example, the legal department may have little day-to-day responsibility regarding exports but a great deal for licensing to the countries in which the exports are sold. Organizational mechanisms, such as joint committees and the planned sharing of information, are useful to ensure activities complement each other. It also is useful for the company to plan organizational change so as to minimize obstacles when responsibilities shift from one group to another.

A further consideration is how important the nonequity operation is to the company's overall operations. For example, if a company contracts with only one supplier for an essential component, the contract is likely to be controlled more closely and from higher in the organization than would contracts that are of less strategic importance.

CONTROL MECHANISMS

So far, we have discussed how companies group their operations for the purpose of communications and control and what companies should consider when deciding where control should be located. We shall now move to the subject of the mechanisms they can use to help ensure that control is implemented.

CORPORATE CULTURE

Every company has certain common values its employees share. These constitute its **corporate culture** and form a control mechanism that is implicit and helps enforce the company's explicit bureaucratic control mechanisms. For example, without setting explicit rules, managers may conform to company tradition in terms of how they dress, how late they work, whether they socialize with other managers, and whether they go to others in the company for advice. MNEs have more difficulty relying on a corporate culture for control because managers from different countries may have different norms and little or no exposure to the values prevalent at corporate headquarters. The incompatibility of organizational cultures is a detriment to the acceptance of knowledge, which MNEs need to transfer from operations in one country to operations in another to gain competitive advantage.[39] To try to overcome this problem, many companies encourage a worldwide corporate culture by promoting closer contact among managers from different countries. The aim is to convey a shared understanding of global goals and norms for reaching those goals, along with the transference of "best practices" from one country to another.[40] Frequent transfers of managers among operations in different countries help develop increased knowledge of and commitment to a common set of values and objectives; fewer procedures, less hierarchical communication, and less surveillance are needed. For example, Nestlé moves management trainees around Europe so that they learn to react like Europeans rather than like any specific nationality. Matsushita brings foreign employees to Japan, partly to train them in the company culture but primarily to get Japanese employees to evolve toward a more global culture.[41]

The degree of control corporate headquarters imposes on the selection of top managers for foreign subsidiaries may dictate to a great extent how much formal control over the subsidiaries' operations the corporate personnel feel is necessary. Using home-country nationals in subsidiaries' management or even having headquarters set the standards for local managers' selection and training may be perceived by local managers as a means of ensuring primary loyalty to the corporate culture rather than the subsidiary culture. Corporate culture may be effective even if the operations are only partially owned or when the parent requires long-range planning assistance from the subsidiaries.

> People trained at headquarters are more likely to think like headquarters personnel.

COORDINATING METHODS

Rather than changing overall structure, many companies are finding mechanisms to pull product, function, and area together.

Because each type of organizational structure has advantages and disadvantages, companies in recent years have developed mechanisms to pull together some of the diverse functional, geographic (including international), and product perspectives without abandoning their existing structures. Some of these mechanisms are

- Developing teams with members from different countries for planning to build scenarios on how the future may evolve[42]
- Strengthening corporate staffs (adding or creating groups of advisory personnel) so that headquarters and subsidiary managers with line responsibilities (decision-making authority) must listen to different viewpoints—whether or not they take the advice
- Using more management rotation, such as between domestic and international positions, to break down parochial views
- Keeping international and domestic personnel in closer proximity to each other, such as by placing the international division in the same building or city as the product divisions
- Establishing liaisons among subsidiaries within the same country so that different product groups can get combined action on a given issue
- Developing teams from different countries to work on special projects of cross-national importance, so that they share viewpoints
- Placing foreign personnel on the board of directors and top-level committees to bring foreign viewpoints into top-level decisions
- Giving all divisions and subsidiaries credit for business resulting from cooperative efforts so that they are encouraged to view activities broadly
- Basing reward systems partially on global results so that managers are committed to global as well as local performance

Companies also use staff departments (for example, legal or personnel) to centralize activities common to more than one subsidiary. For instance, at Heinz all the geographic divisions use one expatriate-transfer-and-compensation policy, to minimize duplicated effort.

REPORTS

Reports must be timely in order to allow managers to respond to their information.

Reports are another control mechanism. Headquarters needs timely reports to allocate resources, correct plans, and reward personnel. Decisions on how to use capital, personnel, and technology are almost continuous so reports must be frequent, accurate, and up-to-date to assure meeting the MNE's objectives. Headquarters uses reports to evaluate the performance of subsidiary personnel so as to reward and motivate them. These personnel adhere to reports and try to perform well on what is in them so that they receive more rewards. They also seek feedback so that they know how well they are performing and can alter their performance accordingly.[43]

Written reports are more important in an international setting than in a domestic one because subsidiaries' managers have much less personal contact with managers above them. Corporate managers miss out on much of the informal communication that could tell them about the performance of the foreign operations. The following discussion highlights the content and evaluation of reports headquarters would use to control international operations.

Types of Reports   Most MNEs use reports for foreign operations that resemble those they use domestically. There are several reasons for this.

1. If the reports have been effective domestically, management often believes they also will be effective internationally.
2. There are economies from carrying over the same types of reports. The need to establish new types of reporting mechanisms is eliminated, and corporate management is already familiar with the system.
3. Reports with similar formats presumably allow management to better compare one operation with another.

MNEs use reports to identify deviations from plans that could indicate problem areas. The focus of the reports may be to monitor short-term performance or longer-term indicators that match the organization's strategy. Usually, the emphasis is on evaluating the subsidiary rather than the subsidiary manager, although the subsidiary's profitability is an important ingredient in the managerial evaluation.

Reports are intended first to evaluate operating units and second to evaluate management in those units.

Visits to Subsidiaries   Not all information exchange occurs through formalized written reports. Within many MNEs, certain members of the corporate staff spend much time visiting subsidiaries. Although this attention may alleviate misunderstandings, there are some "rules" to conducting visits properly. On the one hand, if corporate personnel visit the tropical subsidiaries only when there are blizzards at home, the personnel abroad may perceive the trips as mere boondoggles. On the other hand, if a subsidiary's managers offer too many social activities and not enough analysis of operations, corporate personnel may consider the trip a waste of time. Further, if visitors arrive only when the corporate level is upset about foreign operations, local managers may always be overly defensive. Nevertheless, visits can serve to control foreign operations by collecting information and offering advice and directives.

Management Performance Evaluation   MNEs should evaluate subsidiary managers separately from their subsidiary's performance so as not to penalize or reward them for conditions beyond their control. For example, in Chapter 13 we discussed how headquarters allocates the capital budget to its foreign subsidiaries. Such budgeting decisions take into account the outlook for operations in countries, which may be outside a subsidiary manager's control. For example, a company may decide not to expand further in a country because of its slow growth and risky economic and political environment and still reward that country's managers for doing a good job under adverse conditions.

Companies should evaluate managers on things they can control, but there is disagreement concerning what is within their control.

However, what is within a subsidiary manager's control varies from company to company because of decision-making authority differences, and from subsidiary to subsidiary because of local conditions. Take currency gains or losses. Who is responsible depends on whether working capital management decisions occur at headquarters or at the subsidiary level, and whether there are instruments such as forward markets in a particular country that allow for hedging against currency value changes.

Another uncontrollable area is when headquarters managers make decisions that will optimize the entire company's performance, perhaps at the expense of a particular

Looking to the Future
CONTROL/NO CONTROL—THE CONSTANT
BALANCING ACT

Technological factors and government-to-government agreements are favoring more global integration and standardization. But the legal, cultural, economic, and political differences in norms among countries are not about to be eliminated. Therefore, the balancing act to satisfy the needs for global integration and national responsiveness will continue. Companies will continue to experiment with mechanisms to handle these opposing forces. These mechanisms will be further complicated by ever-changing individual and operating unit capabilities.

As overseas sales and profits as a percentage of total sales and profits increase, headquarters is likely to pay more attention to foreign operations. Similarly, there will be pressures to centralize control to deal with the growing number of global competitors and the more homogenized needs of global consumers. However, managers in foreign subsidiaries may see the erosion of their autonomy over marketing, production, and financial decisions. To keep those managers motivated, the company may need to give them opportunities to work at corporate headquarters and in cross-national management teams so that they share in global responsibilities and understand the need for headquarters control. But with such cross-national fertilization comes the risk of clashes between cultural traditions. For example, in work teams at Ericsson Telecom, Swedes and Americans quickly became frustrated with each other over cultural norms the two groups had developed as children. The Swedes had grown up learning that silence is golden and a good job will be recognized. The Americans had learned early that class participation would improve their grades and they needed to promote themselves. The Americans viewed the Swedes as overly detached; the Swedes viewed the Americans as overly aggressive.[44] The lesson is that the human side of the organization may keep companies from developing global practices as rapidly as top headquarters' management would like.

On the other hand, MNEs might push decentralization because of their size. A number of them already have sales larger than many countries' GDPs. To manage such large organizations may require even greater decentralization and more horizontal communication among subsidiaries in different countries that are mutually dependent on parts, products, and resources. This mutual dependence among subsidiaries may in turn require new heterarchical relationships within the organizational structure.

Companies must evaluate results in comparison to budgets.

subsidiary. In addition, the normal profit-center records may well obscure the importance the subsidiary has within the total corporate entity.

One way to overcome the problems of evaluating performance is to look at a budget agreed upon by headquarters and subsidiary managers. Doing this can help the MNE differentiate between a subsidiary's worth and its management's performance. The budget should cover the goals for each subsidiary that will help the MNE achieve an overall objective.

Cost and Accounting Comparability   Different costs among subsidiaries may prevent a meaningful comparison of their operating performance. For example, the ratio of labor to sales for a subsidiary in one country may be much higher than that for a subsidiary in another country, even though unit production costs may not differ substantially. So management must ensure that it is comparing relevant costs. Chapter 19 will show that different accounting practices also can create reporting and accountability problems. Most MNEs keep one set of books that are consistent with home-country principles and another to meet local reporting requirements. Clearly, headquarters needs to use considerable discretion in interpreting the data it uses to evaluate and change subsidiary performance.

It is hard to compare countries using standard operating ratios.

Evaluative Measurements   Headquarters should evaluate subsidiaries and their managers on a number of indicators rather than relying too heavily on one. Financial criteria tend to dominate the evaluation of foreign operations and their managers. Although many different criteria are important, the most important for evaluating both the operation and its management are budget compared with profit and budget compared with sales value, because these immediately affect consolidated corporate figures. Many nonfinancial criteria are also important, such as market-share increase, quality control, and managers' relationship with host governments.

A system that relies on a combination of measurements is more reliable than one that doesn't.

Information Systems   This discussion has centered on information headquarters management needs to evaluate the performance of subsidiaries and their management. Although this information is crucial, corporate management requires additional data to plan, take action, and share to improve performance.[45] This might include

Management should reevaluate information needs periodically to keep costs down and should ensure that information is being used effectively.

- Information generated for centralized coordination, such as subsidiary cash balances and needs so that headquarters can move funds effectively
- Information on external conditions, such as analyses of local political and economic conditions, so that headquarters can plan where to expand and constrict operations
- Information for feedback from parent to subsidiaries, such as R&D breakthroughs, so that subsidiaries can compete more effectively
- Information that subsidiaries can share so that they can learn from each other and be motivated to perform as well as other subsidiaries
- Information for external reporting needs, such as to stakeholders and tax authorities

Companies face three problems in acquiring information: the cost of information compared to its value, redundant information, and information that is irrelevant. For example, much of the information that is useful to a subsidiary, such as whom to contact to clear items at customs, is irrelevant to headquarters and should not be transmitted. To cope, companies should periodically reevaluate the information sources they use.

With expanding global telecommunications and computer links—especially the World Wide Web and e-mail—managers throughout the world can share information quicker and easier than ever before. On the one hand, this technology may permit more centralization, because corporate management can more easily examine the global conditions and performance. On the other hand, managers in foreign locations may become more autonomous because they have more information at their disposal.

Information centers may permit a choice between centralization or decentralization.

CONTROL IN SPECIAL SITUATIONS

Acquisitions, shared ownership, and changes in strategies create control problems. We shall now discuss each of these.

ACQUISITIONS

An acquired company usually does not achieve a complete fit with the existing organization.

A policy of expansion through acquisition can create some specific control problems. For Nestlé, some of its U.S. acquisitions resulted in overlapping geographic responsibilities and markets as well as new lines of business with which corporate management had no experience. Another control problem is that the acquiring company's criteria for evaluating performance may be different from that of the acquired company's accustomed performance criteria. For example, U.S. executives tend to focus more on profitability than on market potential, whereas the opposite is true in Korean companies.[46] When a U.S. company acquires a Korean company, it must communicate and implement new performance standards. Still another problem is that existing management in an acquired firm is probably accustomed to considerable autonomy.

Attempts to centralize certain decision making or change operating methods may result in distrust, apprehension, and resistance to change on the part of the acquired company. Moreover, resistance may come not only from the personnel but also from governmental authorities wanting to protect their domestic economies. These authorities may use a variety of means to ensure that decision making remains vested within the country.

SHARED OWNERSHIP

Shared ownership usually makes control harder than with wholly owned operations, but there are mechanisms that can work.

Ownership sharing limits the flexibility of corporate decision making. For example, Nestlé shares ownership with Coca-Cola in a joint venture for the production and sale of canned coffee and tea drinks, and Nestlé has less autonomy for this operation than for those it owns wholly because Coca-Cola has an equal voice in decision making. Nevertheless, there are administrative mechanisms to gain control even with a minority equity interest. These mechanisms include spreading the remaining ownership among many shareholders, contract stipulations that board decisions require more than a majority (giving veto power to minority stockholders), dividing equity into voting and nonvoting stock, and side agreements on who will control decision making. A company can also maintain control over some asset the subsidiary needs, such as a patent, a brand name, or a raw material. In fact, maintaining control is a motive for having separate licensing or franchising agreements or management contracts with a foreign subsidiary.

When a joint venture is with a competitor, control issues transcend the joint venture itself. Employees in the partner's organization may have been conditioned over the years to conspire against the other. It becomes difficult to get them to cooperate for the success of the joint venture.[47]

CHANGES IN STRATEGIES

Most recent changes in strategies have involved movements from multidomestic to transnational or global operations. But regardless of the type of change, there will be a need for new reporting relationships, changes in the type of information collected, and a need for new performance appraisal systems.[48] For example, when Citibank moved from a multidomestic to a regional strategy within Europe, it needed to introduce interdependence among operations and collect results not only on a country-by-country basis, but also by product and customer.[49] In addition to the practical problems of changing systems, there are human resource problems as well.

It is difficult to remove control from operations when managers are accustomed to much autonomy. Within Europe, for example, many U.S. companies owned very independent operations for decades in the United Kingdom, France, and Germany. These companies often have faced difficult obstacles when integrating these operations because the country managers perceive that integration brings personal and operating disadvantages. Managers who fear losses through a changed strategy continue to guard their autonomy and functional specialties and maintain existing allegiances.

THE ROLE OF LEGAL STRUCTURES IN CONTROL STRATEGIES

When operating abroad, companies may choose among legal forms that affect their decision making, taxes, maintenance of secrecy, and legal liability. Most choose a subsidiary form for which there are further legal alternatives that vary by country.

BRANCH AND SUBSIDIARY STRUCTURES

When establishing a foreign operation, a company often must decide between making that operation a branch or a subsidiary. A foreign branch is a foreign operation not legally separate from the parent company. Branch operations are possible only if the parent holds 100-percent ownership. A subsidiary, however, is an FDI that is legally a separate company, even if the parent owns all of the voting stock. The parent controls a subsidiary through its voting stock and through the control mechanisms we have discussed. Because a subsidiary is legally separate from its parent, legal authorities in each country generally limit liability to the subsidiary's assets. Creditors or winners of legal suits against the subsidiary do not usually have access to the parent's other resources. This concept of limited liability is a major factor in the choice of the subsidiary form; otherwise, claims against a company for its actions in one country could be settled by courts in another.

Because subsidiaries are separate companies, a question arises concerning which decisions the parent may be allowed to make. Generally, this does not present a problem because there have been few limiting situations. However, court cases in several countries, such as France and the United States, have ruled that companies were conspiring to prevent competition when the parent dictated which markets its subsidiary could serve. Another factor of control is public disclosure. Generally, the greater the control the owner has, the greater the secrecy it can maintain. In this respect, branches are usually subject to less public disclosure because they are covered by tight corporate restrictions.

From these examples, it should be clear that there are control advantages to either the branch or the subsidiary form. Each form also has different tax advantages and implications and may have different initiation and operating costs as well as abilities to raise capital. A company must consider its objectives for control, liability, secrecy, and taxes when deciding whether to use a branch or subsidiary to operate abroad.

There are tax and liability differences for branches and subsidiaries.

TYPES OF SUBSIDIARIES AND HOW THEY AFFECT CONTROL STRATEGIES

Each legal form has different operating restrictions.

A company establishing a subsidiary in a foreign country can usually choose from a number of alternative legal forms. There are too many forms to list here; however, some distinctions between them are worth mentioning so that you understand there are many considerations. In addition to differences in liability, forms vary in terms of

- Ability of the parent to sell its ownership
- Number of stockholders required to establish the subsidiary
- Percentage of foreigners who can serve on the board of directors
- Amount of required public disclosure
- Whether equity may be acquired by noncapital contributions, such as goodwill
- Types of businesses (products) that are eligible
- Minimum capital required for establishing the subsidiary

Before making a decision on a legal operating form, an MNE should analyze all of these differences in terms of its corporate objectives.

WEB CONNECTION

Check out our home page www.prenhall.com/daniels for links to key resources for you in your study of international business.

SUMMARY

- Control of MNEs is difficult because of the geographic and cultural distances separating countries, the need to operate differently among countries, the large number of uncontrollables abroad, and the high uncertainty resulting from rapid change in the international environment and problems in gathering reliable data in many places.

- Good planning should include the establishment of a long-range strategic intent, analysis of internal corporate resources, setting of international objectives, analysis of local conditions abroad, selection of alternatives and priorities, and implementation of a strategy.

- As a company expands internationally, the corporate structure must include a means by which foreign operations report. The more important the foreign operations, the higher up in the hierarchy they should report.

- Whether a company separates or integrates international operations, it usually needs to develop some control mechanism/structure to prevent costly duplication of efforts, to ensure that headquarters managers do not withhold the best resources from the international operations, and to include insights from anywhere in the organization that can benefit performance.

- The level at which decisions are made should depend on the competence of each level's managers, the expediency needs weighed against decision quality, and the effects the decisions will have on the company's global and national performance.

- Even though worldwide uniformity of policies and centralization of decision making may not be best for a particular foreign subsidiary, overall company gains may be more than enough to overcome the individual country losses. When top management prevents subsidiaries' managers from doing their best job, however, there may be a negative effect on employee morale.

- Transnational strategies attempt to use competencies from everywhere in the MNE's worldwide organization.

- Many critics in emerging economies argue that centralization of decision making in MNEs continues emerging economies' historical dependency on industrial countries. These critics are pressuring for increased decentralization of decision making.

- The corporate culture is an implicit control mechanism. It is more difficult to establish and maintain in MNEs because values differ among countries, but bringing managers together enhances the common culture.

- Timely reports are essential for control so that corporate/headquarters management can allocate resources properly, correct plans, and evaluate and reward personnel.

- Many MNEs use international reporting systems similar to their domestic ones because home-country management is familiar with them and because uniformity makes it easier to compare different operations.

- Generally, MNEs evaluate their subsidiaries and their subsidiary managers separately. However, MNEs may use some of the same criteria, including financial and nonfinancial performance, for both.

- Special control problems arise for acquired operations, operations that have historical autonomy, and operations that are not wholly owned. The legal status of foreign operations may also raise control problems.

CASE

GE'S TUNGSRAM ACQUISITION*

General Electric (GE), headquartered in the United States, is the world's largest public company in terms of market capitalization (number of shares times share price). It is made up of 10 major business divisions, one of which is GE Lighting (GEL), with annual sales of about $3.5 billion in 1999. Figure 15.5 shows that GEL accounts for about $750 million, or about 5 percent, of GE's profits. Competitors Philips Lighting, a unit of the Dutch-based Philips, and Osram, a subsidiary of the German-based Siemens, have sales about equal to those of GEL, so the three companies collectively control about 75 percent of the world's lighting market.

Since the late 1980s, GEL has included global expansion as part of its fundamental strategy because of comparative market growth expectations, antitrust inhibitions to its U.S. growth, and U.S. lighting acquisitions by Philips (Westinghouse) and Osram (Sylvania). The most important of GEL's global expansions was its acquisition of the Hungarian firm, Tungsram, that country's largest manufacturing company. From a control standpoint, GEL needs to improve Tungsram's performance and to build a global operating strategy that will encompass Tungsram and other foreign operations. To meet these challenges, GEL has relied on corporate reorganiza-

tion, restructuring of operations (including R&D), infusion of GE's corporate culture, and implementation of a standardized reporting system.

TUNGSRAM

Founded in 1896, Tungsram is the world's third oldest of the major lighting companies, after only GE and Philips. The company has developed important lighting source innovations and has traditionally sold most of its production outside of Hungary. Its market position eroded during the closing era of communist rule in Hungary; nevertheless, by the late 1980s, it still ranked fifth among Europe's light source manufacturers and held about 7 percent of the European market share.

In 1987, the Hungarian government hired the consulting company Arthur D. Little (ADL) to assess and advise on Tungsram. ADL concluded that Tungsram's cost levels were too high and its exploitation of marketing opportunities too low. Further, it was investing only 1 to 2 percent of sales as compared with 4 to 6 percent for competitors, who were also spending a higher share of sales on R&D. Nevertheless, ADL concluded that Tungsram could be turned around with

*This case has been condensed by John D. Daniels and is included with the authors' permission. The original case by Professors Paul Marer and Vincent Mabert, both from the Kelley School of Business at Indiana University, was published as "GE Acquires and Restructures Tungsram: The First Six Years (1990–1995)," in *OECD, Trends and Policies in Privatisation*, Vol. III, No. 1 (Paris: OECD, 1996), pp. 149–185. They revised the case in 1999 as "GE's Acquisition of Hungary's Tungsram."

FIGURE 15.5   1999 Forecast of GE Profits by Product Divisions

Although GE's lighting division is its second smallest division in terms of profits, analysts expected it to earn about $750 million in 1999.

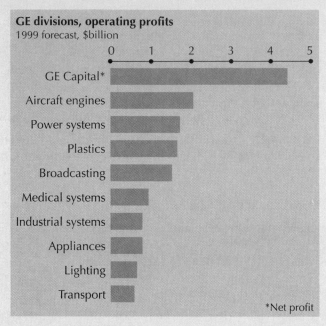

GE divisions, operating profits
1999 forecast, $billion

GE Capital*
Aircraft engines
Power systems
Plastics
Broadcasting
Medical systems
Industrial systems
Appliances
Lighting
Transport

*Net profit

Source: From "The House that Jack Built," *The Economist*, September 18, 1999. © 00 The Economist Newspaper Group, Inc. Reprinted with permission. Further reproduction prohibited. www.economist.com.

restructuring help from a foreign investor who could provide capital, production technology, and management know-how. Between 1990 and 1999, GE invested about $950 million in Tungsram and, in the process, gained nearly 100 percent of its shares.

CORPORATE REORGANIZATION

During the early 1990s, GEL made other foreign acquisitions, such as Thorn in the United Kingdom and Luma in Sweden. GEL managed these acquisitions on a multidomestic basis, meaning it allowed them to operate quite autonomously. GEL believed each country's operations differed significantly in terms of R&D, production capability, product structure, and market characteristics. However, in 1992, GE decided to move rapidly toward more control at either the regional or global level. GE reasoned that more centralization, regionally or globally, would facilitate the transfer of experience from one subsidiary to another, especially through the standardization of operations, functions, and products. In addition, GE wanted to gain a common image within and among its different product groups so that

it could introduce new products more effectively into foreign markets. GEL established a European headquarters in London (GEL-London), and Tungsram lost much of the autonomy it had enjoyed until then.

GEL-London decided (1) to introduce GE brand lightbulbs as a high-priced quality brand into Europe by using the yellow and blue GE logo, which was well known and carried a quality image in the United States, and (2) to continue selling under the Tungsram name, but to position Tungsram as a low-priced (value for money) brand to be promoted less than the GE brand. Although GEL-London felt the positioning of Tungsram at the low end of the market was consistent with the quality image of former Eastern bloc products, this has been a sensitive issue among Hungarians, who are proud of Tungsram's century-old tradition, scientific achievements, global reach, and name recognition in Europe. During the second half of the 1990s, Tungsram's sales were about 10 percent in Central and Eastern Europe, 40 percent in Western Europe, 15 to 20 percent in the United States (under both the Tungsram and GE labels), and 30 to 35 percent elsewhere.

RESTRUCTURING

Once the Hungarian government decided to privatize Tungsram and to allow foreign investors to bid on ownership, GE had to move fast. A closer audit after acquisition showed that many costly changes were necessary to make Tungsram competitive. For example, Tungsram's labor productivity was low due to overstaffing, bureaucratic administrative structures, and insufficient automation; thus GE reduced the labor force from nearly 20,000 in early 1990 to about 9,500 in 1993, mainly through early retirement, job relocation, voluntary separation, and a hiring freeze. The production facilities could not maintain the quality standards demanded in Western markets. Thus GE upgraded the telecommunication system, acquired personal computers and software, refurbished buildings, bought new equipment, and spent to improve on health, safety, and environmental standards. It increased capital outlays to about 10 percent of sales. It also wrote off obsolete inventories and uncollectible Soviet debts and eliminated some noncore businesses.

GEL's acquisitions resulted in R&D operations scattered among different countries. With the move away from multidomestic practices, GEL consolidated its European R&D in Hungary so that about half of its professional R&D resides in Hungary and about half in the United States. A team representing all of GE's major business units makes decisions on GE's R&D priorities. Once GEL gains approval from this team for its projects, it appoints a program manager for each project. The program manager chooses team members from a large "talent pool" located in different countries and made up of functional specialists, such as marketing and accounting personnel, as well as scientists and engineers. Task-oriented teams form and disband as needs change. The teams inform the entire talent pool of planned programs and projects. GEL encourages individuals to volunteer as team members but the selection is up to the program manager. The company demotes individuals who, over a period of time, do not serve as team members and sways them to leave the company. GEL rewards not only technical competence but also initiative, business sense, and the ability and willingness to work constructively with others.

CULTURE AS CONTROL

GE has long had a strong corporate culture, which helps unify behavior among its personnel. This culture is partially based on U.S. cultural norms, such as pride and optimism, and partially on the styles and practices of GE's top man-

agers, such as the use of massive layoffs and quick sale of underperforming businesses.

During 1990–1991, GEL proceeded cautiously with changing the inherited corporate culture at Tungsram. One reason was GE's unfavorable experiences in France after its 1988 acquisition of a medical equipment manufacturer. GE had tried quickly to integrate the manufacturer into its U.S. division and to impose its corporate culture on the French facility. The experiment met strong resistance and prompted unfavorable publicity. However, in 1992, following the appointment of a new CEO at Tungsram, GEL decided to introduce the GE corporate culture at Tungsram more decisively and quickly. The new CEO was an American with much experience in managing GE subsidiaries abroad; thus GEL expected his managerial style and practices to reflect GE headquarters' norm. Further, GE translated a 95-page manual, *Integrity: The Spirit and Letter of our Commitment,* into Hungarian and required all Tungsram employees (as it does in the United States) to pledge observance of its contents. The manual prescribes behavior to try to eliminate corruption, instructs that one must deal fairly with coworkers (regardless of nationality, gender, or creed), and requires absolute fairness in dealing with competitors and suppliers.

Many aspects of GE's culture are almost opposite to those that existed at Tungsram. For example, the norm in the United States is to be inner directed—believing that it is up to each individual to succeed and that outside constraints can be overcome if only one tries hard enough. However, the norm in Hungary (perhaps brought about by long periods of foreign domination when there was no self-determination) is to be outer directed—believing that uncontrollable outside forces, rather than the will of the individual, are decisive in determining outcomes. In addition, GE's use of layoffs and sell-offs to improve performance contrasts sharply with the experience at Tungsram, where there is a history of paternalism. For example, from the start many Tungsram employees lived in company housing and vacationed at company resorts. Their children attended company schools. During evenings and weekends employees and their families rooted for Tungsram sport teams. The best way to get a job at Tungsram was to be recommended by a current employee; however, once employed, satisfactory work performance led to lifetime job security. Moreover, even the manual contradicted Hungarian norms. Because of foreign rule, Hungarians learned to survive by pretending to accept foreign mandates, which they circumvented while avoiding direct confrontation. For example, under communist rule—during which there was no legal certainty, standards were not absolute, and power was exercised arbitrarily—people became masters of finding back-door approaches to solving problems. Personal relationships and reciprocal favors were much more important than formal rules. Thus GE has tried to enforce a universal code in a culture that believes in ethical relativism.

On the one hand, GE is quite satisfied with what it has accomplished in the transfer of its corporate culture to Hungary. Tungsram's CEO said that GE is not seeking a complete eradication of cultural differences, but is working toward a degree of homogeneity that is like "a pea soup, not a stew." Several aspects of GE's efforts to bind together the separate national and corporate cultures have been those common to many multinationals, such as extensive training in language and business skills and the rotation of employees among geographic locations. On the other hand, the leader of the labor union at Tungsram said, "GE's [corporate] strategy is to make everyone insecure. The owner assesses us from the United States, where the structure of the economy and industrial relations are different. GE tries to employ here overseas methods, which causes conflict." Further, a *Financial Times* article said, "By comparison with some multinationals, which try to cultivate a reputation for cultural sensitivity, GE risks being accused of arrogance in its approach. . . . Those employees who find [this] difficult tend to leave."

CONTROL BY REPORTS

When Hungary had central planning, the government set costs and prices. It also owned companies, which faced no domestic competition and could not go bankrupt. The purpose of companies' reporting systems was to check plan fulfillment, not to control costs or improve profits. Under GE, all units must prepare standard reports on just about all aspects of costs and operations. Everyone faces a great deal of pressure to improve on previous performance. Benchmarking—comparing performance indicators at one plant with those achieved by other plants that manufacture similar products, or with industry standards—has become an important tool of management control.

Improvement, then, has become the key word at Tungsram. Reducing labor, inventory, and scrap costs are critical to profitability. Initially, GE compared Tungsram's performance against its U.S. counterparts within the GE lighting division, concentrating on scrap rate, material content, and labor costs. But this was difficult because of different operat-

ing methods. GE invested to make Tungsram technically equivalent to facilities in the United States. GEL also implemented enterprise resource planning (ERP) modules, which standardize business practices everywhere. For example, under ERP, GEL's order processing is uniform throughout the company. So the way an order is entered in the records, how it is fulfilled, and how it is billed is the same anywhere in the company, whether the customer is in the United Kingdom or in Saudi Arabia. Standardization of equipment and business practices eases GE's ability to compare performance through benchmarking. Apparently, the standardization, benchmarking, and reporting are helping to improve performance inasmuch as Tungsram has reduced its scrap rate, material content, and labor costs.

However, making Tungsram as good as other GE units is not GE's ultimate aim. GE compares its managers and its operations against the best in the industry. If they are not leaders, GE gets rid of them. To help make them better, GE partners with other companies to share information on practices. For example, its partnering with Motorola helped implement a quality control program called Six Sigma. Its partnering with DHL led to better approaches to control the inbound and outbound flow of materials. Concomitantly, GE sets goals for its Tungsram subsidiary, which put pressure on managers to improve. The reporting system measures performance against stated goals.

QUESTIONS

1. Define national and corporate cultures. How did GE's and Tungsram's cultures differ? How did GE attempt to use its culture as a control mechanism in Hungary and elsewhere?

2. What were the pros and cons of changing GEL's European operations from multidomestic to regional or global? Would such a change work the same for all of GE's product divisions?

3. Suppose as a Hungarian you are one of the following: (a) the manager of one of Tungsram's plants in Hungary; (b) a blue-collar worker employed at a Tungsram plant; (c) a former white-collar Tungsram worker laid off after 23 years of service; or (d) a government official specializing in economic issues. What would be your thoughts on the sale of Tungsram to GE?

4. In what ways does GE attempt to gain synergy among its operations in different countries and among its different businesses?

CHAPTER NOTES

1 Data for the case were taken from Graham Turner, "Inside Europe's Giant Companies: Nestlé Finds a Better Formula," *Long Range Planning*, Vol. 19, No. 3, June 1986, pp. 12–19; Mark Alpert and Aimety Dunlap Smith, "Nestlé Shows How to Gobble Markets," *Fortune*, January 16, 1989, pp. 74–78; Zachary Schiller and Lois Therrien, "Nestlé's Crunch in the U.S.," *Business Week*, December 24, 1990, pp. 24–25; John Templeman, Stewart Toy, and Dave Lindorff, "Nestlé: A Giant in a Hurry," *Business Week*, March 22, 1993, pp. 50–54; Sid Astbury, "Food Maker Applies Lessons Learned from Japan," *Asian Business*, Vol. 29, No. 6, June 1993, p. 12; Greg Steinmetz and Tara Parker-Pope, "All Over the Map," *Wall Street Journal*, September 26, 1996, p. R4; Barry B. Burr, "Limits for Business and Government," *Pensions and Investments*, October 17, 1994, p. 10; Helmut Maucher, *Leadership in Action* (New York: McGraw-Hill, 1994); various company reports; William Hall, "Nestlé Plans to Cut Costs Further," *Financial Times*, May 6, 1999, p. 20; "Nestlé Sticks to Strategy of Broad Categories of Brands," *Wall Street Journal*, September 24, 1999, p. B5; and www.nestle.com.

2 Ahn Mi-young, Sid Astbury, David Hulme, Ian Jarrett, and Jonathan Sikes, "Why HQ Should Relax Its Grip," *Asian Business*, Vol. 30, No. 6, June 1994, pp. 46–48.

3 John Gapper and Nicholas Denton, "The Barings Report," *Financial Times*, October 18, 1995, p. 8; Sara Calian, "Rogue Trader Says Deceiving Barings Wasn't Difficult, 'Star' Status Helped," *Wall Street Journal*, February 13, 1996, p. A10; and Paul Stonham, "Whatever Happened at Barings? Part One: The Lure of Derivatives and Collapse," *European Management Journal*, Vol. 14, No. 2, April 1996, pp. 167–175.

4 Gary Hamel and C. K. Prahalad, "Strategic Intent," *Harvard Business Review*, May–June 1989, pp. 63–76.

5 Christopher Carr, "Global, National and Resource-Based Strategies: An Examination of Strategic Choice and Performance in the Vehicle Components Industry," *Strategic Management Journal*, Vol. 14, 1993, pp. 551–568.

6 "Dusting the Opposition," *The Economist*, Vol. 335, No. 7912, April 29, 1995, p. 71.

7 Ian Turner, "Management International Organizations: Lessons from the Field," *European Management Journal*, Vol. 12, No. 4, December 1994, pp. 417–431.

8 Part of the explanation is adapted from George S. Yip, *Total Global Strategy: Managing for Worldwide Competitive Advantage* (Upper Saddle River, NJ: Prentice Hall, 1992).

9 For two discussions of the importance of implementation and the need to revise plans, see William G. Egelhoff, "Great Strategy or Great Strategy Implementation—Two Ways of Competing in Global Markets," *Sloan Management Review*, Winter 1993, pp. 37–50; and Lawrence Hrebeniak, "Implementing Global Strategies," *European Management Journal*, December 1992, pp. 392–403.

10 G. S. Yip, P. M. Loewe, and M. Y. Yoshino, "How to Take Your Company to the Global Market," *Columbia Journal of World Business*, Winter 1988, pp. 37–48.

11 Oscar Suris, "Ford to Further Revamp Global Auto Operations," *Wall Street Journal*, October 11, 1996, p. A3.

12 John W. Hunt, "Is Matrix Management a Recipe for Chaos?" *Financial Times*, January 12, 1998, p. 10.

13 Gapper and Denton, "The Barings Report."

14 "The Discreet Charm of the Multicultural Multinational," *Economist*, July 30, 1994, pp. 57–58.

15 Robert Frank, "Excitement Brews in Beverage Industry as Enrico's Rise at PepsiCo Stirs Market," *Wall Street Journal*, February 26, 1996, p. B8.

16 Ian D. Turner, "Strategy and Organization," *Management Update: Supplement to the Journal of General Management*, Summer 1989, pp. 1–8; and Gunnar Hedlund, "The Hypermodern MNC—A Hetarchy?" *Human Resource Management*, Spring 1986, pp. 9–35.

17 James R. Houghton, "A Chairman Reflects: The Age of the Hierarchy Is Over," *New York Times*, September 24, 1989, p. C2.

18 Vertical versus horizontal *keiretsus* are discussed in Kosaku Yoshida, "New Economic Principles in America—Competition and Cooperation," *Columbia Journal of World Business*, Winter 1992, pp. 31–44.

19 Michael L. Gerlach, "The Japanese Corporate Network: A Blockmodel Analysis," *Administrative Science Quarterly*, March 1992, pp. 105–139.

20 Brian Bremner and Emily Thornton, "Fall of a Keiretsu," *Business Week*, March 15, 1999, p. 34; and Greg Hundley and Carol K. Jacobson, "The Effects of the Keiretsu on the Export Performance of Japanese: Help or Hindrance?" *Strategic Management Journal*, Vol. 19, 1998, pp. 927–937.

21 Tony Jackson, "Breaking Up Is Hard to Do," *Financial Times*, March 19, 1999, p. 21.

22 Kiyohiko Ito and Elizabeth L. Rose, "The Genealogical Structure of Japanese Firms: Parent-Subsidiary Relationships," *Strategic Management Journal*, Vol. 15, 1994, pp. 35–51; and Michael Scott Morton, "Emerging Organizational Forms: Work and Organization in the 21st Century," *European Management Journal*, Vol. 13, No. 4, December 1995, pp. 339–345.

23 Joann S. Lublin, "Firms Ship Unit Headquarters Abroad," *Wall Street Journal*, December 9, 1992, p. B1; Pervez Ghauri, "New Structures in MNCs Based in Small Countries: A Network Approach," *European Management Journal*, Vol. 10, No. 3, September 1992, pp. 357–364; and Karl Moore, "How Subsidiaries Can Be More Than Bit Players," *Financial Times*, February 20, 1998, Mastering Global Business section, pp. 14–15.

24 Robert Corzine and Hillary Durgin, "Shell Oil Stripped of Independence Over Investment," *Financial Times*, March 12, 1999, p. 15.

25 James H. Taggart, "Strategy Shifts in MNC Subsidiaries," *Strategic Management Journal*, Vol. 19, 1998, pp. 663–681; and Nagesh Kumar, "Multinational Enterprises, Regional Economic Integration, and Export-Platform Production in the Host Countries: An Empirical Analysis for the US and Japanese Corporations," *Weltwirtschaftliches Archiv*, Vol. 134, No. 3, 1998, pp. 450–483.

26 Edward E. Lucente, "Managing a Global Enterprise" (Pittsburgh: Carnegie Bosch Institute for Applied Studies in International Management, 1993), Working paper 94-2.

27 For a detailed examination of the characteristics of a transnational strategy, see Christopher A. Bartlett and Sumantra Ghoshal, *Managing Across Borders* (Boston: Harvard Business School Press, 1989).

28 Christopher A. Bartlett and Sumantra Ghoshal, "Beyond the M-Form: Toward a Managerial Theory of the Firm," *Strategic Management Journal*, Vol. 14, 1993, pp. 23–46.

29 Mary Ackenhusen, Daniel Muzyka, and Neil Churchill, "Restructuring 3M for an Integrated Europe: Implementing the Change," *European Management Journal*, Vol. 14, No. 2, 1996, pp. 151–159.

30 "Ford's Reorganization," *Economist*, January 7, 1995, pp. 52–53.

31 James McCalman, "Lateral Hierarchy: The Case of Cross-Cultural Management Teams," *European Management Journal*, Vol. 14, No. 5, 1996, pp. 509–517.

32 Julian Birkinshaw and Neil Hood, "Multinational Subsidiary Evolution: Capability and Charter Change in Foreign-Owned Subsidiary Companies," *Academy of Management Review*, Vol. 23, No. 4, 1998, pp. 773–795; and Julian Birkinshaw, Neil Hood, and Stefan Jonsson, "Building Firm-Specific Advantage in Multinational Corporations: The Role of Subsidiary Initiative," *Strategic Management Journal*, Vol. 19, March 1998, pp. 221–241.

33 W. Chan Kim and Renée A. Mauborgne, "Making Global Strategies Work," *Sloan Management Review*, Spring 1993, pp. 11–28.

34 Stephen D. Moore, "Pfizer's English Site Is Research Boon, Developing Some of Firm's

Major Drugs," *Wall Street Journal*, September 6, 1996, p. B8.

35 Peter Smith Ring, Stefanie Ann Lenway, and Michelle Govekar, "Management of the Political Imperative in International Business," *Strategic Management Journal*, Vol. 11, 1990, pp. 141–151.

36 Robert Nobel and Julian Birkinshaw, "Innovation in Multinational Corporations: Control and Communication Patterns in International R&D Operations," *Strategic Management Journal*, Vol. 19, 1998, pp. 479–496.

37 Stephen Baker, Kevin Kelly, Robert D. Hof, and William J. Holstein, "Mini-Nationals Are Making Maximum Impact," *Business Week*, September 6, 1993, pp. 66–69.

38 Nitin Nohria and Sumantra Ghoshal, "Differentiated Fit and Shared Values: Alternatives for Managing Headquarters-Subsidiary Relations," *Strategic Management Journal*, Vol. 15, July 1994, pp. 491–502.

39 Tatiana Kostova, "Transnational Transfer of Strategic Organizational Practices: A Contextual Perspective," *Academy of Management Review*, Vol. 24, No. 2, 1999, pp. 308–324.

40 Nohria and Ghoshal, "Differentiated Fit and Shared Values"; and Anne-Wil K. Harzing, *Managing the Multinationals* (Cheltenham, U.K.: Edward Elgar, 1999).

41 Templeman et al., "Nestlé: A Giant in a Hurry"; and "The Glamour of Gaijins," *Economist*, September 21, 1991, p. 80.

42 Daniel Erasmus, "A Common Language for Strategy," *Financial Times*, April 5, 1999, Mastering Information Management section, pp. 7–8.

43 Anil K. Gupta, Vijay Govindarajan, and Ayesha Malhotra, "Feedback-Seeking Behavior Within Multinational Corporations," *Strategic Management Journal*, Vol. 20, 1999, pp. 205–222.

44 Michael Maccoby, *Sweden at the Edge: Lessons for American and Swedish Managers* (Philadelphia: University of Pennsylvania Press, 1991).

45 For a good discussion of information flows in MNEs, see Anil K. Gupta and Vijay Govindarajan, "Knowledge Flows Within Multinational

Corporations," *Strategic Management Journal*, Vol. 21, No. 4, April 2000, pp. 473–496.

46 Michael A. Hitt, Beverly B. Tyler, Camilla Hardee, and Daewoo Park, "Understanding Strategic Intent in the Global Marketplace," *Academy of Management Executive*, Vol. 9, No. 2, 1995, pp. 12–19.

47 For a discussion of the difficulties of bringing competitors together, see John Hunt, *Structural and Organizational Changes in Global Firms* (Pittsburgh: Carnegie Bosch Institute for Applied Studies in International Management, 1993), Working paper 94-4.

48 Mahmoud Ezzamel, Simon Lilley, and Hugh Willmott, "The 'New Organization' and the 'New Managerial Work,'" *European Management Journal*, Vol. 12, No. 4, 1994, pp. 454–461.

49 Thomas W. Malnight, "The Transition from Decentralized to Network-Based MNC Structures: An Evolutionary Perspective," *Journal of International Business Studies*, Vol. 27, No. 1, First Quarter 1996, pp. 43–65.

PART SIX: OPERATIONS:
OVERLAYING TACTICAL ALTERNATIVES
MTV EUROPE

BACKGROUND

This video focuses on a variety of international business management issues. At one time, MTV faced the strategic challenge of how to penetrate overseas markets. One of the first questions it faced was whether it would be better to go after developed or developing countries. The company decided to look first to developed countries, specifically in Europe. Having chosen this market, the company had to select from three plans of attack—(a) go after all of Europe with a pan-European strategy, (b) create regional channels, or (c) regionalize certain aspects of the channels. MTV selected the third option, customizing its services not only for each specific country but also for specific localities within each country. Ultimately, MTV Europe successfully penetrated the European market by following company president Peter Einstein's lead in listening to viewers' preferences from the various European countries.

The video looks at the strategic approach MTV Europe took in penetrating the European market and at the way it adapted its operations to European consumer preferences by country and region.

MTV EUROPE

For additional information on this company, please refer to the video case for Part Two, page 155.

QUESTIONS

As you watch the video, be prepared to answer the following questions:

1. How would you describe MTV Europe's international efforts? How did the company screen potential markets in Europe?

2. Consider again the three options MTV faced—(a) to go after all Europe, (b) to create regional channels, or (c) to regionalize parts of the channels. Why did MTV choose the third option? Would you have chosen the same one? Why or why not?

3. Why did MTV decide to penetrate markets in developed countries?

4. "Be there, giving them what they want, in whatever form." What do these words mean in terms of international business? In terms of MTV's strategic approach?

Operations: Managing Business Functions Internationally

CHAPTER **16**

Marketing

May both seller and buyer see the benefit. —TURKISH PROVERB

OBJECTIVES

- To introduce techniques for assessing market sizes for given countries

- To describe a range of product policies and the circumstances in which they are appropriate

- To contrast practices of standardized versus differentiated marketing programs for each country in which sales are made

- To emphasize how environmental differences complicate the management of marketing worldwide

- To discuss the major international considerations within the marketing mix: product, pricing, promotion, branding, and distribution

Avon, which commenced operations in 1886, is now one of the world's largest manufacturers and marketers of beauty and related products. About 62 percent of its sales are in cosmetics, fragrances, and toiletries, with the rest in gift and decorative items, apparel, and fashion jewelry and accessories. The company is headquartered in the United States, but about 65 percent of its sales, 59 percent of its assets, and 75 percent of its employees are outside the country. It has direct investments in 50 countries and sells in another 84 through licensing, franchising, and distributor arrangements. Map 16.1 shows the location of Avon's direct investments and its breakdown of sales by region.

Avon moved into the Canadian market in 1914. Its next foreign market entry was 40 years later—into Venezuela. Since then, Avon has accelerated its international expansion, and its growth in foreign sales now exceeds its growth in U.S. sales. Avon's emphasis on foreign operations is due to a slowed U.S. growth potential. First, there is little or no usage gap (untapped market) in the United States for cosmetics, fragrances, and toiletries. Even if there were, only about 5 percent of the world's women live in the United States and Canada. Second, Avon's U.S. sales rely on independent salespersons (almost always women working part time and known as "Avon ladies" or "Avon representatives") who make direct sales to households by demonstrating products and giving beauty advice. They then place sales orders with Avon and deliver orders to the customers once they receive them. But as more U.S. women have entered the workforce full time, they have become less receptive to door-to-door salespersons, have less time to spend on makeup demonstrations, want to receive their purchases immediately, and are less willing to work as Avon ladies.

Concomitantly, many foreign markets have been ideal for Avon's growth. For example, the lack of developed infrastructure in the rural areas of such countries as Brazil, China, and the Philippines deters women from leaving their homes to shop for cosmetics. But in these countries, Avon ladies reach consumers in some of the most remote areas, such as by canoe in the Amazon region of Brazil. (Avon has more active representatives in Brazil than Brazil has members in its armed forces.) In transitional economies—such as Hungary, Poland, the Czech Republic, and Slovakia—Avon's market entry has coincided with pent-up demand from the period of centrally planned economic policies. In rapid-growth economies, such as Chile and Malaysia, Avon taps a growing middle-class market that can afford its products. In all of the aforementioned countries, there are ample labor supplies of potential Avon ladies.

Product lines vary by country, primarily because they are geared to the needs of specific markets. For example, Avon sells a skin cream, Sol & Cor, only in the Brazilian market. The cream provides a combination of moisturizer, sunscreen, and insect repellent. The company also sells creams in parts of Asia to lighten the complexion, but the desire for skin lightening is too small elsewhere to justify marketing efforts.

When Avon develops new products for a given country, it disseminates the information to its facilities elsewhere. For example, Avon-Japan developed emulsion technologies to produce lotions and creams with lighter textures and higher hydration levels, and many Avon operations in other countries now use the process. Avon also has a Far East office in Hong Kong that sources goods from 9 countries and issues about 2,000 supplier contracts for about 600 new products per year. The office finds sources of products for country groups, tests and handles quality assurance, and designs and develops new products. For example, the office buys gift items for the U.S. market and lingerie for European markets.

MAP 16.1 Avon's Foreign Direct Investment and Breakdown of Sales by Region

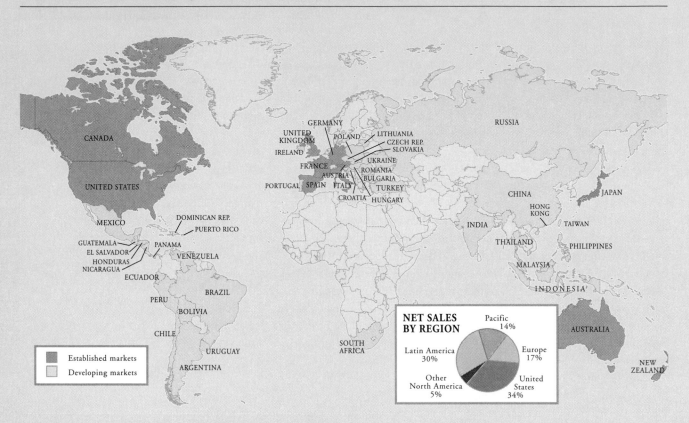

Most of Avon's sales are international. This map shows all the countries (50 in all) in which Avon has foreign direct investments. Those countries in the developing markets category are where Avon expects most future growth to occur.

Source: Avon 1995 and 1999 Annual Reports.

In addition to developing products for specific markets, Avon emphasizes standardized products using global brands that appeal to women of many nationalities. One of these is a family of skin-protection products using the Anew brand. The first to use alpha hydroxy acid, these products have become the market leader in virtually every country in which Avon sells them. Some other global brands are Rare Gold and Far Away fragrances. Through standardized products and brands, Avon creates a uniform global quality image while saving costs from uniform ingredients and packaging. Global branding also helps inform consumers that the company is international. This helps sales in countries such as Thailand, where consumers prefer to buy products made by foreign companies.

Although Avon prominently displays its name on most of its products worldwide, most of its brand names differ among countries. The company prints instructions in local languages, but may or may not put the brand names in that language. It often uses English or French brand names because consumers consider the United States and France as high-quality suppliers for beauty products. For example, Avon sells skin care products called Rosa Mosqueta (in Spanish),

Revival (in English), and Renaissage (in French) in Chile, Argentina, and Japan, respectively. In each case, the Avon logo appears prominently on the products' containers as well.

Each country operation sets its own prices to reflect local market conditions and strategic objectives. The prices are subject to change for each sales campaign. Avon runs a new campaign with different special offers every two weeks in the United States and every three weeks abroad. The shortness of campaigns is helpful for adjusting prices in highly inflationary economies.

Avon's promotion is primarily through brochures that Avon ladies deliver to potential customers during each campaign. The company prints about 600 million brochures in 15 languages, dwarfing the circulation of any magazine or commercial publication. Additionally, Avon relies on both print and television advertising.

The basic aim of Avon's campaign is the same throughout the world—to promote its products and image, increase the number of customers served, and recruit new representatives. However, the specific needs and execution of the promotion differ among markets. For example, in 1996 Avon's ads in the United States and Canada used the theme "Just Another Avon Lady" to show that women in all walks of life use Avon. In Germany, the ads sought to change Avon's image of being old-fashioned. In Japan, where more than 2,000 cosmetic companies compete and Avon is not a leading competitor, the company sought consumer awareness of its name. In the Philippines, Avon used a top entertainer and fashion model to counter similar ads by Revlon and Max Factor.

Avon seeks to develop a global image of being a company that supports women and their needs. It sponsored "The Olympic Women" exhibit at the Atlanta Olympics, where many women competed under the sponsorship of various Avon subsidiaries. Avon publicizes how being an Avon lady heightens the role of women. For example, its publicity has shown how civil war in El Salvador caused casualties and disabled men, leaving women with little education to head households; however, by being Avon ladies, they can earn income while continuing their duties at home. The company also gives annual Women of Enterprise Awards to leading women entrepreneurs. Avon's activities have generated further favorable publicity in media reports, such as a 20-page article in *Veja*, a weekly Brazilian magazine. Perhaps Avon's biggest social responsibility project is its work internationally in fighting breast cancer. Avon ladies disseminate information about breast cancer along with their promotion brochures and sell pins to raise money for local needs.

Avon basically duplicates its distribution method in foreign countries, which means it sells to independent representatives who have taken orders from customers they have visited. However, it varies aspects of its distribution among countries. To begin with, not all of Avon's distribution abroad is door-to-door. In Russia, during decades of communist rule, women became wary of knocks on the door—a discomfort that persists—so representatives sell at work or through personal networks. Such selling is similar in India because women associate door-to-door transactions with old-newspaper and old-clothes buyers. In parts of Brazil, many upscale customers are cloistered in apartments that are virtually inaccessible to salespeople because of security entrances. Avon-Brazil advertises on television and offers an 800 number to reach that clientele. In response to the 1998 Chinese law prohibiting house-to-house sales, Avon opened retail stores in China.

A drawback of direct selling is that customers cannot obtain a product whenever they want it. They must wait until a representative visits them to place an order and then wait again to receive it. In response to this drawback, Avon-Malaysia opened a retail outlet called a beauty boutique, where customers can buy Avon products and receive as much personal attention as when they buy at home. Moreover, representatives can go to the boutique to obtain products immediately, rather than waiting for Avon to fill their orders. The concept proved so successful that Avon opened additional beauty boutiques in Malaysia and duplicated the concept in Chile.

In an interesting departure from the Malaysian experience, Avon-Argentina opened a "Beauty Center" in an upscale suburb of Buenos Aires. In addition to selling products, as in Malaysia, this center provides customers with a wide variety of services, such as hairstyling and manicures. The center also serves to build an upscale image among customers who would normally shop at retail outlets and buy imported products. Avon now follows this same approach in Mexico and Venezuela.

In some countries, particularly emerging economies, getting merchandise to consumers in rural areas is a major challenge. Mail systems are unreliable, and personal delivery to representatives is expensive. Because of this problem, Avon-Philippines pioneered a system of branch selling. Instead of delivering orders to the homes of district managers, who in turn would arrange delivery to representatives as in the United States, Avon-Philippines has established franchise centers that stock merchandise. Franchise managers visit the centers and pick up merchandise for the representatives in their district. This saves the representatives from making arduous treks, sometimes two hours by bus. The centers have experimented with more retail-like services such as wide aisles, shopping carts, and scanners at checkout so that the franchise managers can fill and pay for their orders quickly. Avon has since adopted the franchise center concept in other countries, such as Indonesia.

In the preceding discussion, Avon transferred successful practices in one country to other countries. To encourage the transfer of know-how, Avon brings marketing personnel from different countries together to share what they call "best practices." They also promote competi-

The Internet is connnecting producers and consumers globally. The photo on the left shows a hammock weaver in a remote region of Guyana called Rupununi. Until recently, the weavers from the Wapishana and Macushi tribes would have had to use an unreliable postal service if they were promoting their hammocks abroad. But the weavers sent one of their members to Georgetown, the capital of Guyana, to learn about the Internet. On the right, you see her answering inquiries to the Web page she set up. So far, Internet sales have been good.

tion among countries, such as contests for best brochure cover and best color cosmetics advertisement.

Avon anticipates that international operations will account for the bulk of its growth in the foreseeable future. Although Avon's foreign expansion has been aggressive, its products are still not available to more than half the world's women. Avon classifies the countries in which it sells as either developing markets or established markets. It expects most of its future growth to be in the former.

INTRODUCTION

The Avon case points out that similar marketing principles are at work in domestic and foreign markets. However, environmental differences often cause managers to apply these principles differently abroad.

This chapter begins our discussions of international operating functions. Figure 16.1 shows the place of functions in international business. Specifically, we will examine how managers analyze market potential in different countries and apply international product, pricing, promotion, branding, and distribution strategies—the marketing mix—to

Domestic and international marketing principles are the same, but managers often

- **Overlook foreign environmental differences**
- **Interpret foreign information incorrectly**

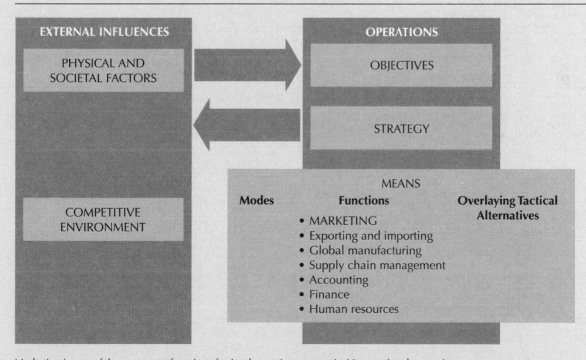

FIGURE 16.1 Marketing in International Business

Marketing is one of the necessary functions for implementing companies' international strategies.

those countries. We will also discuss whether companies should follow globally integrated or nationally responsive marketing strategies.

MARKET SIZE ANALYSIS

Chapter 13 explained the importance of market potential in determining a company's allocation of efforts among different countries, discussed some common variables used as broad indicators for comparing countries' market potentials, and briefly introduced types of sources and problems for collecting information on international markets. Once companies decide to enter markets, they must then analyze data to determine their market potential in each country and their marketing mix to meet the potential. This section covers some techniques that estimate the potential size of markets, as well as gap analysis—a tool to help managers decide what part of the marketing mix to emphasize most.

TOTAL MARKET POTENTIAL

Companies find income and population to be the most important determinants of a country's market size.

To determine potential demand, managers first estimate the possible sales of the category of products for all companies and then estimate its own market-share potential. For the most part, companies use the same techniques to determine market size in foreign countries that they use domestically. Therefore, we will concentrate on those techniques and nuances that apply specifically to international markets.

Domestically or internationally, the major indicators for potential sales of most products are present income and population, plus the growth in each. Managers may examine countries at different average income levels because, as incomes change, product demand may change. For example, Korean demand for apparel, cosmetics, and automobiles has grown with increased per capita income—a trend that closely parallels the experience of industrial countries in earlier years.[2] In fact, companies have expanded heavily into high-growth Asian markets in recent years. They expect the demand for their products—such as automobiles, videotape rentals, and washing machines—will increase as those economies develop in a pattern similar to the growth that occurred earlier in industrial countries. Management may collect data on the consumption or number of a given product in countries with different per capita incomes and then project sales or numbers of the given product at different income levels by plotting a path through which average demand changes as incomes change (see Figure 16.2). In other words, a company can estimate that a country's per capita consumption of a product will move along the trend line as its per capita income increases. By multiplying the country's expected per capita consumption by its population, a company can estimate the potential demand.

Companies must consider variables other than income and population when estimating potential demand for their products in different countries.

Companies have found reasonably good fits for many products by using this tool. However, so many variables other than per capita income affect demand that the analysis breaks down for some products in some countries. The main reasons are:

- *Obsolescence and leapfrogging of products.* Consumers in emerging economies do not necessarily follow the same patterns as those in higher-income countries.[3] In many emerging economies, consumers have leapfrogged the use of traditional telephones by jumping from having no telephones to using cellular phones exclusively.

FIGURE 16.2   Per Capita Televisions and Per Capita Income at PPP

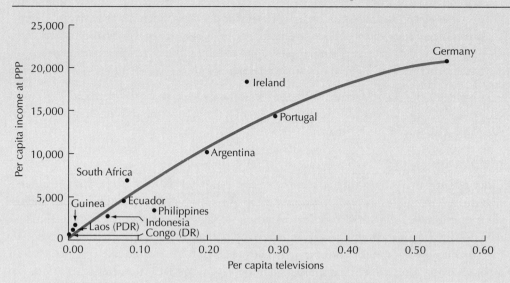

As per capita incomes rise as measured by purchasing-power parity (PPP), people acquire more televisions. A company may estimate that the number of televisions will move along the trend line.

Source: Income and population figures are from *World Development Report 1999/2000* (Washington, D.C.: World Bank, 1999). Television figures are from *World Factbook, 1998* (Washington, D.C.: Central Intelligence Agency, American Statistics Index, 1999).

- *Costs*. If costs of essential products are high, consumers may spend more than what one would expect based on per capita income. The expenditures on food in Japan are higher than would be predicted by either population or income level because food is expensive and work habits promote eating out. However, if costs are high for a nonnecessity, expenditures will likely be lower. For example, Norwegians spend less than one might expect on fresh fruit because the costs are high.
- *Income elasticity*. A common tool to predict total market potential is to divide the percentage of change in product demand by the percentage of change in income in a given country. The more that demand increases, the more elastic is the demand in response to income change. Income elasticity varies by product and by income level. Demand for necessities, such as food, is usually less elastic than is demand for discretionary products, such as automobiles. Because a large portion of people in emerging economies are poor, a change in income level affects food consumption there much more than it would in a higher-income country.
- *Substitution*. Consumers in a given country may have products or services that substitute more conveniently in some countries than in others for the products that companies would like to sell. For example, there are fewer automobiles in Hong Kong than one would expect based on income and population because the crowded conditions make the efficient mass transit system a desirable alternative to automobiles.
- *Income inequality*. Where income inequality is high, the per capita income figures are usually low because many people have little income. This masks the fact that there are middle- and upper-income people who have substantial income to spend.

In Brazil and India, for example, the sale of luxury products is higher than one would expect by looking at per capita income figures. Reebok successfully sells luxury footwear in India.[4]

- *Cultural factors and taste.* Countries with similar per capita incomes may have different preferences for products and services because of values or tastes. For example, Denmark and Switzerland have very similar per capita incomes, but per capita consumption of frozen food is much higher in Denmark because of Danes' penchant for convenience.

Given all the above factors, managers cannot project potential demand perfectly. However, by considering all the factors that may influence the sale of their products, they can make workable estimates.

GAP ANALYSIS

Once a company is operating in a country and estimates that country's market potential, it must calculate how well it is doing there. A useful tool in this respect is **gap analysis**, a method for estimating a company's potential sales by identifying market segments it is not serving adequately.[5] When sales are lower than the estimated market potential for a given type of product, the company has potential for increased sales. Figure 16.3 is a bar showing four types of gaps: usage, competitive, product line, and distribution. To construct such a bar, a company first needs to estimate the potential demand for all competitors in the country for a relevant period, say for the next year or the next five years. This figure is the height of the bar. Second, a company needs to estimate current

---

The difference between total market potential and companies' sales is due to gaps:

- **Usage**—less product sold by all competitors than potential
- **Product line**—company lacks some product variations
- **Distribution**—company misses geographic or intensity coverage
- **Competitive**—competitors' sales not explained by product line and distribution gaps

---

FIGURE 16.3   Gap Analysis

Gap analysis is a tool to help managers estimate why sales are less than the potential. The top of the bar represents total sales potential for a given period. Point *A* is the total of sales for all companies. The difference between *A* and the top of the bar is a usage gap. From the bottom of the usage gap bar to *B* are competitors' current sales. The company loses to competitors who distribute where the company does not, have product variations the company lacks, or are doing a better job of marketing. The bar sizes vary overall and by country because gap sizes vary.

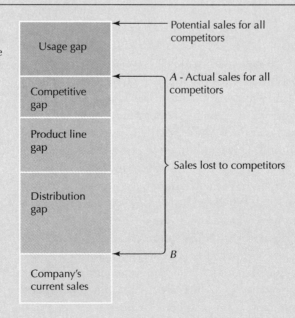

sales by all competitors, which is point *A*. The space between point *A* and the top of the bar is a usage gap, meaning that this is the growth potential for all competitors in the market for the relevant period. Third, a company needs to plot its own current sales of the product, point *B*. Finally, the company divides the difference between point *A* and point *B* into three types of gaps based on its estimate of sales lost to competitors. The distribution gap represents sales lost to competitors who distribute where the company does not. The product line gap represents sales lost to competitors who have product variations the company does not have. The competitive gap is the remaining unexplained sales lost to competitors who may have a better image or lower prices.

Companies may have different-size gaps in different markets. The large Swiss chocolate companies Nestlé, Jacobs Suchard, Lindt & Sprüngle, and Barry Callebaut, have altered their marketing programs among countries because of their different gaps.[6] In some markets, they have found substantial usage gaps; that is, less chocolate is being consumed than would be expected on the basis of population and income levels. Industry specialists estimate that in many countries more than 80 percent of the population has never tasted a chocolate bar. They project that if more people in those countries could be persuaded to try chocolate bars, the companies' sales should increase with the market increase. This assumption has led the two companies to promote sales in those areas for chocolate in general.

The U.S. market shows another type of usage gap. Nearly everyone in this market has tried most chocolate products, but per capita consumption has fallen because of growing concern about weight. To increase chocolate consumption in general, Nestlé for a short time promoted chocolate as an energy source for the sports minded. Note, however, that building general consumption is most useful to the market leader. Nestlé, with U.S. chocolate sales below those of Mars and Hershey, actually benefited its competitors during the short-lived campaign.

The Swiss chocolate companies also have found that they have product line gaps in some hot climates in the market for sweetened products. By developing new products, such as chocolate products that melt less easily, they may be able to garner a larger share of that market. Lindt & Sprüngle bought Ghirardelli to bolster its product line in high-priced chocolates. In some markets, such as Japan, they have not yet achieved sufficient distribution to reach their sales potentials. Nestlé formed a joint venture with a Japanese cake and candy maker, Fujiya, to make Kit Kat bars and increase distribution.

Finally, there are competitive gaps—sales by competitors that cannot be explained by differences between one's own product line and distribution and those of the competitors. That is, competitors are making additional sales because of their prices, advertising campaigns, goodwill, or any of a host of other factors. In such markets as the United Kingdom, where per capita consumption is nearly as high as in Switzerland, companies believe that most of the potential market demand is being fulfilled and that any increase in sales would have to come at the expense of competitors.

PRODUCT POLICY

Most marketing texts categorize companies' product policies, although there is some variation in the categories they use. The treatment of these policies tends to be domestically focused. This section highlights the international application of five common product policies.

PRODUCTION ORIENTATION

With production orientation, companies focus primarily on production—either efficiency or high quality—with little emphasis on marketing. There is little analysis of consumer needs; rather, companies assume customers want lower prices or higher quality. Although this approach has largely gone out of vogue, it is used internationally for certain cases.

- Commodity sales, especially those for which there is little need or possibility of product differentiation by country
- Passive exports, particularly those that serve to reduce surpluses within the domestic market
- Foreign-market segments or niches that may resemble the market at which the product is aimed initially

Price is the most important factor in selling many commodities.

Companies sell many raw materials and agricultural commodities, such as sugar and tin, primarily on the basis of price because there is universal demand for the undifferentiated product. However, even for commodity sales, companies have realized that marketing efforts may yield positive international sales results. For example, the promotion of the Chiquita brand on bananas has helped increase global supermarket distribution in a glutted market. In addition, oil producers, such as Petroven and Aramco, have bought branded gasoline-distribution operations abroad to help them sell an otherwise undifferentiated product. Commodity producers also put efforts into business-to-business marketing by providing innovative financing and assuring timely, high-quality supplies.

Passive sales occur when
- **Advertising spills over**
- **Foreign buyers seek new products**

Many companies begin exporting very passively. Sometimes, for unknown reasons, they receive orders or requests for product information from abroad. Potential customers and distributors learn of foreign products through reports in scientific and trade journals, advertising that spills across borders, buying trips, and observations of products that others have brought into the country. At this point, companies adapt their products very little, if at all, to foreign consumers' preferences. This practice suffices for many companies that view foreign sales as an appendage to domestic sales. This type of company frequently exports only if it has excess inventory for the domestic market. In fact, fixed costs are sometimes covered from domestic sales so that lower prices are offered on exports as a means of liquidating inventories without disrupting the domestic market.

The unaltered domestic product may have appeal abroad.

A company may develop a product aimed at achieving a large share of its domestic market and then find there are market segments abroad willing to buy that product. Sometimes the product may have universal appeal, such as French champagne. Other times, a company may target a mass market at home as well as niche markets in foreign locations; one example is U.S. bourbon producers that sell to niche markets worldwide. A company is also using a production orientation if it sells to countries that have only a small market potential regardless of whether changes are geared to unique consumer needs. Particularly in small emerging economies, MNEs may make few changes because the market size does not justify the expense to them and because competitors are apt to be other MNEs that do not make product alterations. Companies may not even adjust the voltage requirements and plugs of electrical products to local standards, leaving the job of conversion to local purchasers instead.

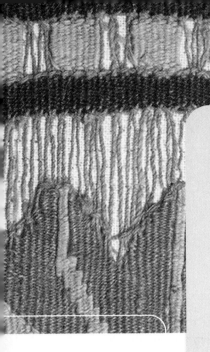

Ethical Dilemmas and Social Responsibility
WHAT PRODUCTS SHOULD COMPANIES MARKET INTERNATIONALLY?

Critics complain that MNEs pay too little attention to the needs of emerging economies. For example, they chide pharmaceutical companies for spending less on antimalarial research than on research for diseases more prevalent in industrial countries, even though malaria results in more fatalities.[7] At the same time, they complain that MNEs sell DDT in emerging economies, even though DDT is needed to kill malaria-carrying mosquitoes.[8] They criticize so-called superfluous products and luxury goods for shifting spending away from necessities and contributing to the enhancement of elitist class distinctions. They also question making soft drinks available to consumers who lack funds for pharmaceuticals. Soft drink companies have responded that consumers should make their own choices, that introducing sanitary bottling operations has aided other industries (including pharmaceuticals), and that attempts to add vitamins or nutrition to tasty food has failed in the marketplace.[9] Nevertheless, critics question whether this is sufficient justification. Even if products reach only affluent customers, companies may be criticized. For example, Benetton has been taken to task for opening hard-currency-only shops for tourists in Cuba and North Korea because the shops are an affront to the local population who are economically and legally prohibited from buying the merchandise.[10]

Critics have also complained that MNEs promote products to people who do not understand the products' negative consequences. The most famous case involved infant formula sales in emerging economies, where infant mortality increased when bottle-feeding supplanted breast-feeding. Because of low incomes and poor education, mothers frequently overdiluted formula and gave it to their babies in unhygienic conditions. Critics argued that promoting formula increased bottle-feeding. Infant formula manufacturers claimed that other factors increased bottle-feeding—specifically, more working mothers and fewer products and services being made in the home. The promotion, they argued, persuaded people to give up their "home brews" in favor of the most nutritious breast milk substitute available. Regardless, the World Health Organization passed a voluntary code to restrict formula promotion in developing countries. Critics hit Nestlé hardest because it had the largest share of infant formula sales in emerging economies and because its name-identified products facilitated the organization of a boycott. The company ceased advertising that could discourage breast-feeding, limited free formula supplies at hospitals, and banned personal gifts to health officials.[11] Despite these events, few governments have prohibited infant formula sales or promotion. In the absence of regulations (for infant formula and other products), how far companies should go to protect consumers is unclear. The controversy has been compounded by the transmission of HIV virus through breast milk, a particular problem in Africa where many women are HIV/AIDS infected.[12]

Is it unethical for a company to give in to the pressure groups that organize a boycott? A French company, Roussel Uclaf, developed the abortion pill RU486, now called mifepristone. A German company, Hoechst, then acquired Roussel Uclaf. Hoechst, fearful of adverse publicity, initially forbade the sale of mifepristone except in the three countries (the United Kingdom, France, and Switzerland) where Roussel Uclaf had already begun selling it. The

French health ministry has insisted that the product remain on sale because it is "the moral property of women." Yet U.S. anti-abortion activists took out full-page newspaper advertisements urging U.S. consumers not to use Allegra, a Hoechst antihayfever treatment, because Hoechst continued to sell mifepristone outside the United States.[13] Thus, Hoechst faced ethical criticism whether it marketed the abortion pill in the United States or not. Subsequently, it donated its U.S. patent rights to the Population Council, a nonprofit research organization.[14]

SALES ORIENTATION

Internationally, sales orientation means a company tries to sell abroad what it can sell domestically on the assumption that consumers are sufficiently similar globally. A company may make this assumption because the distance between it and its foreign markets makes information about the foreign markets difficult to obtain. However, the more distant a market, the less international marketers should assume about it.[15] This orientation differs from the production orientation because of its active rather than passive approach to promoting sales. However, there is much anecdotal evidence of foreign product failures because of assumptions that product acceptance will be the same as at home or that heavy sales efforts abroad can overcome negative foreign attitudes toward the product. Yet there also are successful examples of transferring products abroad with little or no research on what foreign consumers want, particularly when sales target teenagers and industrial markets.[16]

The greatest ability for a company with a sales orientation to sell the same product in multiple countries occurs when consumer characteristics are similar and when there is a great deal of spillover in product information, such as between the United States and Canada. A company may first develop the product for its home market. It may develop a new product to launch almost simultaneously in multiple countries, as Gillette did with its Mach 3 razor.[17] Or it may develop the product abroad and introduce it later to its home market, as Mars did with Whiskas, a cat food.

A company may develop a product with an appeal in more than one country
- **Because of spillover in product information from its home country**
- **Through a simultaneous multicountry launch**
- **By developing the product abroad**

CUSTOMER ORIENTATION

A customer orientation takes geographic areas as given.

In a company that operates according to sales orientation, management usually is guided by answers to questions such as: Should the company send some exports abroad? Where can the company sell more of product X? That is, the product is held constant and the sales location is varied. In contrast, a customer orientation asks: What can the company sell in country A? In this case, the country is held constant and the product is varied.

Sometimes a company wants to penetrate markets in a given country because of the country's size, growth potential, proximity to home operations, currency or political stability, or any of a host of other reasons. In the extreme of this approach, a company would move to products completely unrelated to its existing product lines. Though an uncommon strategy, some companies have adopted it. For example, Chilena de Fosforos, a Chilean match producer, wanted to tap the Japanese market because of Japanese growth and size, competition within the Chilean market, and the promotional appeal of being able to say "We supply Japan." However, because the company was not price competitive in Japan for matches, it began making chopsticks—a product that would use its poplar forest resources and wood-processing capabilities. Chilena de Fosforos successfully entered the Japanese market with chopsticks.[18]

As with a production orientation, a company using a customer orientation may do so passively. Increasingly, purchasing agents are setting product specifications and then seeking out contracts for the foreign manufacture of components or finished products. For example, the Hong Kong company S. T. King makes clothing to the specifications of companies such as Calvin Klein. In responding to foreign-product requests, a company may make a product that differs markedly from what it sells domestically. In such cases, the supplier depends on the buyer to determine what final customers want. The supplier is primarily concerned with pricing and delivering what it is selling abroad.

STRATEGIC MARKETING ORIENTATION

Most companies committed to continual rather than sporadic foreign sales adopt a strategy that combines production, sales, and customer orientations. Companies that don't make changes to accommodate the needs of foreign markets may lose too many sales, especially if aggressive competitors are willing to make desired adaptations. Yet expertise concerning a type of product may be important, and companies want the products they sell abroad to be compatible with their expertise and with their means of dealing with competitors. Companies therefore tend to make product variations abroad without deviating very far from their experience. For example, breweries such as Heineken, Stroh, Bass, and Lion, when faced with restrictions against alcoholic beverages in Saudi Arabia, have turned to sales of nonalcoholic beer (marketed as malt rather than beer).[19] Products such as computers or even coffee or tea would probably be too far from managers' areas of expertise.

The most common strategy is product changes as adaptations, done by degree.

An attitude of reacting to consumers' product preferences does not necessarily mean that a company must forgo the economics of standardization. A company may well do market research in a number of countries to develop a product for a global market segment, as Avon did in developing skin-protection products. Instead of merely trying to sell a domestic product abroad, the company designs a product to fit some global market segment. Global products tend to be possible for many industrial products because purchasers want uniformity.

SOCIETAL MARKETING ORIENTATION

Companies with societal marketing orientations realize that successful international marketing requires serious consideration of potential environmental, health, social, and work-related problems that may arise when selling or making their products abroad.[20] Such groups as consumer associations, political parties, and labor unions are becoming more globally aware—and vocal. Companies must increasingly consider not only how a product is purchased but also how it is disposed of and how it might be changed to be more socially desirable. For example, about one-third of the world's population—or approximately 2 billion people—have no electricity in their homes. The biggest problem is the high cost of constructing major power plants. However, two environmental concerns are that there will be inadequate future supplies of fossil fuels and that too much pollution will be created by burning fossil fuels to generate electricity. These concerns have led to high expenditures on solar research, which have yielded marketable products aimed at the needs of electricity shortages in emerging economies. These products include small-scale solar panels to provide electricity to homes in Brazil, to herders' tents in Tibet, and to mobile refrigeration units atop camels in the desert of Somalia.[21]

REASONS FOR PRODUCT ALTERATION

Now that we have discussed companies' product orientations, we shall examine the legal, cultural, and economic reasons for companies to alter their products to fit the needs of customers in different countries.

Legal factors are usually related to safety or health protection.

Legal Reasons   Explicit legal requirements are the most obvious reason for altering products for foreign markets. The exact requirements vary widely by country but are usually meant to protect consumers. Pharmaceuticals and foods are particularly subject to regulations concerning purity, testing, and labeling. Automobiles sold in the United States must conform to safety and pollution standards not found in many other countries.

Companies produce to the requirements of their domestic market, but these requirements may be different in foreign countries. For example, Dormont Manufacturing (a U.S. company) makes hoses that hook up deep-fat fryers and the like to gas outlets. Although the hoses have gone through rigorous U.S. and Canadian approval processes, Dormont faces country-by-country differences in Europe. Italy requires that metal tubes be extendable and have no covering, while the United Kingdom prohibits extendibility and requires a rubber coating.[22] The EU has been trying to harmonize standards on a host of products.

When foreign legal requirements are less stringent than domestic ones, a company may not be legally compelled to alter its products for foreign sale. However, the company will have to weigh such decisions as whether following high domestic standards abroad will raise prices and whether domestic or foreign ill will may result. Some companies have met home-country criticism for selling abroad—especially in emerging economies—such products as toys, automobiles, contraceptives, and pharmaceuticals that did not meet home-country safety or quality standards.

One of the more cumbersome product alterations for companies is adjusting to different laws on packaging that protect the environment. Some countries prohibit certain types of containers, such as Denmark's ban on aluminum cans. Other countries restrict the volume of packaging materials to save resources and decrease trash; exporters of Scotch whiskey to Germany must remove the bottles from the cardboard boxes. There also are differences in national requirements as to whether containers must be reusable and whether companies use packaging materials that must be recycled, incinerated, or composted.[23]

A recurring issue is the need to arrive at international product standards and eliminate some of the wasteful product requirements for alterations among countries. Although countries have reached agreement on some products (sprocket dimensions on movie film, technical standards on mobile phones, bar codes to identify products), other products (railroad gauges, power supplies, and electrical socket shapes) continue to vary.[24] In reality, there is both consumer and economic resistance to standardization, such as U.S. consumers' reluctance to adapt the metric system. Economically, a complete changeover would be more costly than simply educating people and relabeling. Containers would have to be redesigned and production retooled so that sizes would be in even numbers. (Would football have first down with 9.144 meters to go?) Even for new products or those still under development, such as video-CDs, companies and countries are slow to reach agreement because they want to protect the investments they've already made.[25] At best, international standards will come very slowly.

Marketing managers must also watch for the indirect legal requirements that may affect product content or demand. In some countries, companies cannot easily import certain raw materials or components, forcing them to construct an end product with local substitutes that may alter the final result substantially. Legal requirements such as high taxes on heavy automobiles also shift companies' sales to smaller models, thus indirectly altering demand for tire sales and grades of gasoline.

Cultural Reasons   Consumer buying behavior is complex. Marketing managers find it difficult to determine in advance whether consumers in foreign markets will accept new or different products. For example, Rubbermaid has found that most Americans like housewares in neutral blues or almond colors, but the Dutch want them in white and Southern Europeans want them in red. Americans prefer open-top wastebaskets, and Europeans want them with tight lids.[26] To be competitive, Rubbermaid must alter colors and covers by market. Tyson Foods capitalizes on taste differences by selling white meat from chicken in the United States and dark meat from chicken in Mexico at premium prices.[27]

> Examination of cultural differences may pinpoint possible problem areas.

Economic Reasons   If foreign consumers lack sufficient income, they may not be able to buy the product the MNE sells domestically. The company therefore may have to design a cheaper model. Mattel has been unable to sell enough Holiday Barbie dolls in some foreign countries because prices are too high, so it is developing lower-priced dolls for those markets.[28] Where consumers buy personal items in small quantities, such as one aspirin, one piece of chewing gum, or one cigarette, the company usually needs new types of packaging.

> Personal incomes and infrastructures affect product demand.

Even if a market segment has sufficient income to purchase the same product the company sells at home, differences in infrastructure may require product alterations. Emerging economies generally have poorer infrastructures, and companies may gain advantages by selling products that will withstand rough terrain and utility outages. The Japanese infrastructure for automobiles reflects crowded conditions and high land prices. Some U.S. automobile models are too wide to fit into elevators that carry cars to upper floors to be parked, and they cannot make narrow turns on back streets. On the Explorer, which does fit the Japanese infrastructure, Ford nevertheless had to install retractable side-view mirrors to help the vehicle fit into tight spaces.[29]

ALTERATION COSTS

Some product alterations are cheap to make yet have an important influence on demand. One such area is packaging, which is a common alteration exporters make. For example, in Panama, Aunt Jemima Pancake Mix and Ritz Crackers sell in cans rather

> Some alterations cost less than others.

than boxes because of the high humidity—a low-cost change with a high potential pay-off. Before making a decision, marketing managers should always compare the cost of an alteration with the cost of lost sales from no alterations.

One cost-saving strategy a company can use to compromise between uniformity and diversity is to standardize a great deal while altering some end characteristics. Whirlpool puts the same basic compressor, casing, evaporator, and sealant system in its refrigerators for all countries, but changes such features as doors and shelves for different countries.[30] Heinz has found that many nationalities do not like a sweet ketchup, as is preferred in the United States, so it keeps its base recipe the same but adds spices, curry, or hot pepper, depending on the market.[31]

EXTENT AND MIX OF THE PRODUCT LINE

Narrowing the product line allows for concentration of efforts.

Most companies produce multiple products. It is doubtful that all of these products could generate sufficient sales in a given foreign market to justify the cost of penetrating that market. Even if they could, a company might offer only a portion of its product line, perhaps as an entry strategy. For example, Whirlpool entered the South Korean refrigerator market by targeting only the top 2 percent of incomes with its highest-priced models in only half the colors available elsewhere. This strategy saves on translation of product pamphlets, inventory, and promotional costs. If successful, the company may consider moving to other target segments with an expanded product line.[32]

In reaching product line decisions, marketing managers should consider the possible effects on sales and the cost of having one product as opposed to a family of products. Sometimes a company finds it must produce and sell some less lucrative products if it is to sell the more popular ones, such as sherry glasses to match crystal wine and water glasses. Or a company may be forced into a few short production runs in order to gain the mass market on other products. A company that must set up some foreign production to sell in the foreign market may be able to produce locally those products in its line that have longer production runs and import the other products needed to help sell the local production.

Broadening the product line may gain distribution economies.

If the foreign market is small compared to the domestic market, selling costs per unit may be high because of the fixed costs associated with selling. In such a case, the company can broaden the product line to be handled, either by grouping sales of several manufacturers or by developing new products for the local market that the same sales-person can handle. For example, Avon sells products in some countries that it does not handle in the United States to increase the average order per household, such as Crayola products in Brazil, Disney products in Mexico, and the *Reader's Digest* in Canada, Brazil, Australia, France, and New Zealand.

PRODUCT LIFE-CYCLE CONSIDERATIONS

Product life cycles may differ by country in
• Time of introduction
• Shape of curve

There may be differences among countries in either the shape or the length of a product's life cycle. A product facing declining sales in one country may have growing or sustained sales in another. For example, cars are a mature product in Western Europe, the United States, and Japan. They are in the late growth stage in South Korea and in the early growth stage in India. In Europe, automobile companies emphasize lifestyle appeals to sell cars with speed and accessories. In India, they emphasize fuel consumption, price, and cost.[33]

PRICING

Within the marketing mix, companies place much importance on price. A price must be low enough to gain sales, but high enough to guarantee the flow of funds required to carry on other activities, such as R&D, production, and distribution. The proper price will not only assure short-term profits but also give the company the resources necessary to achieve long-term competitive viability. Pricing is more complex internationally than domestically because of the following factors:

- Different degrees of governmental intervention
- Greater diversity of markets
- Price escalation for exports
- Changing values of currencies
- Differences in fixed versus variable pricing practices
- Retailers' strength with suppliers

Let's examine each of these factors.

GOVERNMENTAL INTERVENTION

Every country has laws that affect the prices of goods at the consumer level. A governmental price control may set either maximum or minimum prices. Controls against lowering prices usually prevent companies from eliminating competitors in order to gain monopoly positions. An example of this type of control is in Germany, which prohibits giveaways and discounts through coupon and boxtop specials unless these remain a consistent policy of the company throughout the years. Germany also permits retailers to have sales only twice a year, once in the summer and once in the winter.[34] A company accustomed to relying on such devices to increase its sales at home must develop new methods in Germany. Many countries set maximum prices for numerous products, which can lower companies' profits. As an example, Venezuelan price controls hit P&G and some of its suppliers hard. Although P&G was willing to wait it out while negotiating with governmental authorities, its suppliers could not afford to sell it the phosphates it needed to make detergents. P&G had to suspend operations until Venezuela lifted its price controls on phosphates.[35] Price controls may also cause companies to lower the quality of a product. Sometimes companies change the brand name to reintroduce the higher-quality product later.

The WTO permits countries to establish restrictions against any import that comes in at a price below that charged to consumers in the exporting country. Although countries may not establish restrictions, the possibility that they will makes it more difficult for companies to differentiate markets through pricing. A company might want to export at a lower price than that charged at home for several reasons. One reason might be to test sales in the foreign market. For example, a company may find it cannot export to a given country because tariffs or transportation costs make the price to foreign consumers prohibitively high. Yet its preliminary calculations show that by establishing foreign production, it may be able to reduce the price to the foreign consumer substantially. Before committing resources to produce overseas, the company may want to test the market by exporting so as to sell the product at the price it would charge if it produced locally. A company may be able to complete this test marketing before companies in the importing country can persuade their government to restrict imports. Nestlé

Governmental price controls may

- **Set minimum or maximum prices**
- **Prohibit certain competitive pricing practices**

tested the U.K. market in this way by exporting for a year from Canada to see if enough of a market would develop to justify completing a frozen-food plant to make Lean Cuisine products.[36] Shipping such dishes as spaghetti bolognese in refrigerated ships and paying customs duties made the costs of the exported products much higher than their U.K. selling prices. However, the cost of this test was small compared to the value of the information gained and the amount of Nestlé's eventual commitment.

A company may also charge different prices in different countries because of competitive and demand factors. It may feel that prices can be kept high in the domestic market by restricting supply to that market. Excess production then can be sold abroad at a lower price, as long as that price covers variable costs and contributes to overhead.

GREATER MARKET DIVERSITY

Although there are numerous ways a company can segment the domestic market and charge different prices in each segment, country-to-country variations create even more natural segments. For example, companies can sell few sea urchins or tuna eyeballs in the United States at any price, but they can export them to Japan, where they are delicacies.[37] Levi's manages to sell jeans in Europe for more than twice the U.S. price.[38] In some countries, a company may have many competitors and thus little discretion in setting its prices. In other countries, it may have a near monopoly due either to the stage in the product life cycle or to government-granted manufacturing rights not held by competitors. In near-monopoly markets, a company may exercise considerable pricing discretion, using any of the following:

- A skimming strategy—charging a high price for a new product by aiming first at consumers willing to pay the price, and then progressively lowering the price
- A penetration strategy—introducing a product at a low price to induce a maximum number of consumers to try it
- A cost-plus strategy—pricing at a desired margin over cost

Country-of-origin stereotypes also limit pricing possibilities. For example, exporters in emerging economies often must compete primarily through low prices because of negative perceptions about their products' quality. But there are dangers in lowering prices in response to adverse stereotypes because a lower price may reduce the product image even further.

Diversity in buying on credit affects sales. Credit buying increases costs, which consumers in some countries are more willing to pay than are consumers in other countries. For example, the Japanese are more reluctant than Americans to rely on consumer credit. Thus, in Japan it is less possible than in the United States to use credit payments as a means of inducing the sale of goods. The tax treatment of interest payments also affects whether consumers will pay in cash or by credit.

PRICE ESCALATION IN EXPORTING

Another reason pricing is complex internationally is price escalation. If standard markups occur within distribution channels, lengthening the channels or adding expenses somewhere within the system will further increase the price to the consumer. For example, assume the markup is 50 percent and the product costs $1.00 to produce. The price to the consumer would be $1.50. However, if production costs were to increase to $1.20,

FIGURE 16.4 Price Escalation in Exporting if Companies Use Cost-Plus Pricing

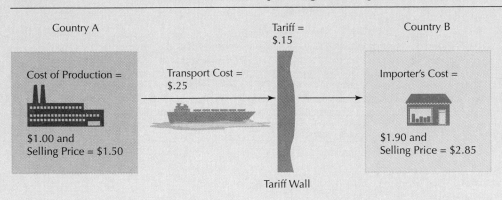

Country A

Cost of Production =

$1.00 and
Selling Price = $1.50

Transport Cost =
$.25

Tariff =
$.15

Tariff Wall

Country B

Importer's Cost =

$1.90 and
Selling Price = $2.85

If both the producer/exporter and the importer/distributor charge 50 percent more than their costs, the added $.40 of transport and tariff costs actually increase the price to consumers in country B to $1.35 more than in country A because of markups. This may prevent the product from selling competitively.

the 50-percent markup would make the price $1.80, not $1.70 as might be expected. Figure 16.4 shows price escalation in export sales, which occurs for two reasons:

1. Channels of distribution usually span greater distances and so exporters need to contract with organizations that know how to sell in foreign markets.
2. Tariffs are an additional cost that may be passed on to consumers.

There are two main implications of price escalation. Seemingly exportable products may turn out to be noncompetitive abroad if companies use cost-plus pricing—which many do.[39] To become competitive in exporting, a company may have to sell its product to intermediaries at a lower price to lessen the amount of escalation. It should determine what price will maximize profits.

CURRENCY VALUE AND PRICE CHANGES

For companies accustomed to operating with one (relatively) stable currency, pricing in highly volatile currencies can be extremely troublesome. Marketing managers should make pricing decisions to assure the company of enough funds to replenish its inventory and still make a profit. Otherwise, it may be making a "paper profit" while liquidating itself—that is, what shows on paper as a profit may result from the company's failure to adjust for inflation while the merchandise is in stock. The company must consider not only inflation's effect on prices but also the possibility its income taxes will be based on the paper profits rather than on real profits. Table 16.1 illustrates a pricing plan to make a target profit (after taxes) of 30 percent on the cost of replacing inventory when the company collects from its sale (replacement cost). The company that does not use a similar plan may soon lack sufficient funds to operate because of receiving too little to have enough merchandise to sell later. The longer the company waits to receive payment for its merchandise, the more important it becomes for it to use a graduated pricing model. For example, Peruvian inflation in the late 1980s forced P&G to raise its detergent prices 20 to 30 percent every 2 weeks. P&G also eliminated its 60-day free credit to retailers and began charging interest on 15- to 30-day payments.[40]

Pricing decisions must consider replacement costs.

TABLE 16.1 **EFFECT OF TAX AND INFLATION ON PRICING**

For the sake of simplicity, this example assumes a company waits a year before it gets paid for its inventory—either because the inventory is stocked before it is sold or because purchasers take time to pay. If the payment cycle is shorter, the company would need to adjust the inflation rate.

The pricing structure for payment one year after acquiring inventory is calculated as follows: Replacement cost is cost plus inflation until collection, or $1,000 + 0.36(1,000) = 1,360$; income after taxes is profit goal times replacement cost, or $0.30(1,360) = 408$. Income after taxes is 60 percent of taxable income; thus taxable income may be calculated as $408 \div 0.6$, or 680; tax is $0.4(680) = 272$; sales price is original cost (1,000) plus taxable income (680); markup on replacement is sales price (1,680) less replacement cost (1,360), or 320.

Assume: Cost at beginning is 1,000
36% inflation
40% tax rate
30% profit goal on replacement cost after taxes

IF SOLD AND COLLECTED AS SOON AS INVENTORY IS ACQUIRED		IF SOLD AND COLLECTED A YEAR AFTER INVENTORY IS ACQUIRED	
Cost	1,000	Replacement cost	1,360
Markup	500	Markup on replacement	320
Sales price	1,500	Sales price	1,680
— Cost	1,000	— Original cost	1,000
Taxable income	500	Taxable income	680
Tax @ 40%	200	Tax @ 40%	272
Income after taxes	300	Income after taxes	408

Two other pricing problems occur because of inflationary conditions:

1. The receipt of funds in a foreign currency that, when converted, buy less of the company's own currency than had been expected

2. The frequent readjustment of prices necessary to compensate for continual cost increases

In the first case, the company sometimes (depending on competitive factors and governmental regulations) can specify in sales contracts an equivalency in some hard currency. For example, a U.S. manufacturer's sale of equipment to a company in Uruguay may specify that payment be made in dollars or in pesos at an equivalent price, in terms of dollars, at the time payment is made. In the second case, frequent price increases make it more difficult for the company to quote prices in letters or catalogs. Perpetual price rises may even hamper what the company would otherwise prefer for distribution. For example, price increases in vending machine sales are frequently difficult to effect because of the attendant need to change machines and to come up with coins or tokens that correspond to the desired percentage increase in price.

Currency-value changes also affect pricing decisions for any product that has potential foreign competition. For example, when the U.S. dollar is strong, companies can sell non–U.S.-made goods more cheaply in the U.S. market because their price in dollars decreases. In such a situation, U.S. producers may have to accept a lower profit margin to be competitive. When the dollar is weak, however, foreign producers may have to adjust their margins downward.

When companies sell similar goods in multiple countries, price differences among them must not exceed by much the cost of bringing the goods in from a lower-priced country, or spillover in buying will occur. Ice cream manufacturers can vary their prices by a large percentage from country to country because the transportation costs compared to the product's price render large-scale movements across borders impractical. However, if the transportation costs compared to the product's price are low, consumers can feasibly buy abroad and import when prices vary substantially from country to country. For example, about 20 percent of South Korea's car imports enter the country through overseas purchases. Unofficial distributors sell them at prices below those of official distributors in South Korea.[41] The handling of goods through unofficial distributors, the **gray market**, can undermine the longer-term viability of the distributorship system, cause a company's plants in different countries to compete with each other, and make it harder for companies to spot counterfeit goods. Companies may try to keep prices fairly close among countries to prevent such movements. The gray market is illegal in many countries, but companies have to monitor compliance and can find enforcement difficult.[42]

FIXED VERSUS VARIABLE PRICING

MNEs often negotiate export prices, particularly to foreign distributors. Small companies, especially those from emerging economies, frequently give price concessions too quickly, limiting their ability to negotiate on a range of marketing factors that affect their costs:

- Discounts for quantity or repeat orders
- Deadlines that increase production or transportation costs
- Credit and payment terms
- Service
- Supply of promotional materials
- Training of sales personnel or customers[43]

Table 16.2 shows ways in which an exporter may deal more effectively in price negotiations.

The extent to which manufacturers can or must set prices at the retail level varies substantially by country. For instance, Indian law requires that bottlers print prices on soft drink containers.[44] There is also substantial variation in whether, where, and for what products consumers bargain in order to settle on an agreed price. For instance, in the United States consumers commonly bargain for automobiles, real estate, and large orders of industrial supplies, but not for grocery items. In contrast, consumers in Guatemala bargain for food in traditional markets while normally accepting fixed prices for automobiles. Bargaining is much more prevalent in purchases from street vendors in India than in Singapore, whereas bargaining in high-priced specialty stores is more frequent in Singapore than in India. Clearly, laws and customs limit companies' abilities to price as they choose.

There are country-to-country differences in
- **Whether manufacturers set prices**
- **Whether prices are fixed or bargained in stores**
- **Where bargaining occurs**
- **How sale prices can be used**

TABLE 16.2   **PREPARATIONS FOR PRICE DISCUSSIONS**

The suggested approach for exporters is to delay a pricing commitment while discussing a whole package of other commitments.

IMPORTER'S REACTION TO PRICE OFFER	EXPORTER'S POSSIBLE RESPONSE
1. The initial price quoted is too high; a substantial drop is required.	Ask the buyer what is meant by too high; ask on what basis the drop is called for; stress product quality and benefits before discussing price.
2. Better offers have been received from other exporters.	Ask for more details on such offers; find out how serious such offers are; convince the buyer that the exporter has a better offer.
3. A counteroffer is required; a price discount is expected.	Avoid making a better offer without asking for something in return, but without jeopardizing loss of interest; when asking for something in return, make a specific suggestion, such as "If I give you a 5% price discount, would you arrange for surface transport including storage costs?"
4. The price $_____ is my last offer (the importer specifies a lower price).	Avoid accepting such an offer immediately; find out the quantities; determine if there will be repeat orders; ascertain who will pay for storage, publicity, after-sales service, and so on.
5. The product is acceptable, but the price is too high.	Agree to discuss details of the costing; promote product benefits, reliability as a regular supplier, timely delivery, unique designs, and so on.
6. The initial price quoted is acceptable.	Find out why the importer is so interested in the offer; recalculate the costing; check competition; contact other potential buyers to get more details on market conditions; review the pricing strategy; accept a trial order only.

Source: Claude Celich, "Negotiating Strategies: The Question of Price," *International Trade Forum*, April–June 1991, p. 12. Reprinted with permission.

RETAILERS' STRENGTH WITH SUPPLIERS
Dominant retailers with clout can get suppliers to offer them lower prices, in turn enabling them to compete on being the lowest cost retailer. But, they have this clout only where they have the dominance. For example, Wal-Mart, Marks & Spencer, and Carrefour have such clout in their domestic U.S., U.K., and French markets, respectively. However, they have been hard-pressed to gain the same advantage when entering the other's dominant market.

PROMOTION
Promotion is the presentation of messages intended to help sell a product or service. The types and direction of messages and the method of presentation may be extremely diverse, depending on the company, product, and country of operation.

THE PUSH-PULL MIX
Promotion may be categorized as push, which uses direct selling techniques, or pull, which relies on mass media. An example of push is Avon's door-to-door selling of cosmetics; an example of pull is magazine advertisements for a brand of cigarettes. Most companies use combinations of both marketing strategies. For each product in each country, a company must determine its total promotional budget as well as the mix of the budget between push and pull.

Several factors help determine the mix of push and pull among countries

- Type of distribution system
- Cost and availability of media to reach target markets
- Consumer attitudes toward sources of information
- Price of the product compared to incomes

Generally, the more tightly controlled the distribution system, the more likely a company is to emphasize a push strategy because it requires a greater effort to get distributors to handle a product. This is true, for example, in Belgium, where distributors are small and highly fragmented, forcing companies to concentrate on making their goods available. Also affecting the push-pull mix is the amount of contact between salespeople and consumers. In a self-service situation, in which there are no salespersons to whom customers can turn for opinions on products, it is more important for the company to use a pull strategy by advertising through mass media or at the point of purchase.

Because of diverse national environments, promotional problems are extremely varied. For example, in rural India over half the population is illiterate, and only one-third of households have television sets. Colgate-Palmolive reaches this audience to sell toothpaste with half-hour infomercials from video vans that travel through the countryside.[45] In many countries, government regulations pose an even greater barrier. For example, Scandinavian television has long refused to accept commercials. Another effect on the promotional mix is the direct or indirect tax many countries place on advertising.

Finally, the amount of consumer involvement in making a purchase decision varies by country because of income levels. When a product's price compared to consumer income is high, consumers usually will want more time and information before making a decision. Information is best conveyed in a personal selling situation, which fosters two-way communication. In emerging economies, MNEs usually have to use push strategies for mass consumer products because incomes are low compared to price.

STANDARDIZATION OF ADVERTISING PROGRAMS

The savings from using the same advertising programs as much as possible, such as on a global basis or among countries with shared consumer attributes, are not as great as those from product standardization. Nevertheless, they can be significant.

In addition to reducing costs, advertising standardization may improve the quality of advertising at the local level (because local agencies may lack expertise), prevent internationally mobile consumers from being confused by different images, and speed the entry of products into different countries. For example, Coca-Cola's "I'd like to buy the world a Coke" ads showing people singing in 12 languages was a truly standardized campaign that reached 3.8 billion viewers in 131 countries.[46] Standardized advertising usually means a program that is *similar* from market to market rather than one that is *identical* in each. For example, Coca-Cola's print ads for the United States and France used the same concept of "refreshment" and showed young people who had been playing sports. In the United States, the slogan was "Coke is it!" and the ad showed a baseball player in action. In France, the slogan was "Un Coca-Cola pour un sourire" ("A Coca-Cola for a smile") and the ad showed soccer players. Some of the problems that hinder complete standardization of advertising relate to translation, legality, and message needs.

Push is more likely when
- **Self-service is not predominant**
- **Advertising is restricted**
- **Product price is a high portion of income**

Advantages of standardized advertising include
- **Some cost savings**
- **Better quality at local level**
- **Rapid entry to different countries**

Standardization usually implies using the same advertising agency globally. However, companies may differentiate campaigns among countries even if they use the same agency everywhere. By using the same agency, companies such as IBM, Colgate, and Tambrands have found that they can take good ideas in one market and quickly introduce them into other markets because they need not worry about legal and ethical problems from having one agency copy what another has done. However, some companies, such as Blockbuster and Procter & Gamble, prefer to use more than one agency to keep the agencies in a state of perpetual competition and to cover one agency's weak spots by drawing on the ideas of another agency.[47]

Translation When media reach audiences in multiple countries, such as MTV programs aired throughout most of Europe, ads in those media cannot be translated because viewers watch the same transmission. However, when a company is going to sell in a country with a different language, translation is usually necessary. For example, Wal-Mart encountered considerable ill will when it sent circulars to Quebec in English only instead of in French or a combination of the two languages.[48] In contrast, to market its motorcycles abroad, Harley-Davidson published its magazines in foreign languages and staged beer-and-band rallies.[49] The most audible problem in commercial translation is dubbing, because words on an added sound track never quite correspond to lip movements. Marketing managers can avoid dubbing problems by creating commercials in which actors do not speak, along with a voice or print overlay in the appropriate language. Pillsbury does this in India, where its Doughboy ads are in six languages.[50] Marketing managers may use voice and print overlays for ads in different countries with the same language to accommodate different spellings and accents.[51]

On the surface, translating a message would seem to be easy. However, some messages, particularly plays on words, simply don't translate—even between countries that have the same language. The number of ludicrous but costly mistakes companies have made attest to translation difficulties. Sometimes what is an acceptable word or direct translation in one place is obscene, misleading, or meaningless in another. For example, the Milk Board's ad "Got milk?" comes out as "Are you lactating?" in Spanish.[52] Another problem is in choosing the language when a country has more than one. For example, in Haiti, a company might use Creole to reach the general population but French to reach the upper class.[53]

Legality What is legal advertising in one country may be illegal elsewhere. The differences result mainly from varying national views on consumer protection, competitive protection, promotion of civil rights, standards of morality, and nationalism. In terms of consumer protection, policies differ on the amount of deception permitted, what can be advertised to children, whether companies must list warnings on products of possible harmful effects, and the extent to which they must list ingredients. The United Kingdom and the United States allow direct comparisons with competitive brands (such as Pepsi versus Coca-Cola), while the Philippines prohibits them. Only a few countries regulate sexism in advertising. However, an interesting twist on sexism is South Korea's ban on advertising cigarettes to women. This ban has led Philip Morris to aim its Virginia Slims at men in Korea, even though it targets the same brand toward women in the United States.[54]

Looking to the Future
WILL THE "HAVES" AND THE "HAVE-NOTS" MEET THE "HAVE-SOMES"?

Most projections are that disparities between the "haves" and "have-nots" will grow in the fore-seeable future, both within and among countries. Globally, the affluent segment will have more purchasing power and will not likely forgo buying because of antimaterialistic sentiments. As people's discretionary income increases, what are now luxury products become more common-place (partly because it takes fewer hours of work to purchase them),[55] and seemingly dissimilar products and services (such as cars, travel, jewelry, and furniture) compete with each other for the same discretionary spending. Because of better communications and rising educational lev-els of the haves, they will want more choices. However, these choices may not fall primarily along national lines. Rather, companies will identify consumer niches that cut across country lines.

At the other extreme, because of growing numbers of poor people with little disposable income, companies will have opportunities to develop low-cost standardized products to fit the needs of the have-nots. Thus, companies will have conflicting opportunities—to develop luxury to serve the haves and to cut costs to serve the have-nots.

Despite the growing proportions of haves and have-nots, demographers project the actual numbers of people moving out of poverty levels and into middle-income levels will increase. This is largely because of population and income growth in many emerging economies, espe-cially in Asia. Such a shift will likely mean that companies' sales growth in emerging economies will mainly be for products that are mature in industrial countries, such as telephones and household appliances. Further, with increased access to the Internet, customers will be able to purchase goods from anywhere in the world. In the process, companies will find it more difficult to charge different prices in different countries. But they will more effectively be able to cut out middlemen in the distribution of their products.

What products and services are likely to enjoy the major growth markets? It is probable that data generation and storage will continue to be a major growth area during the next few decades. It also is probable that among the market-growth leaders will be companies making breakthroughs in process technologies to improve productivity, such as lasers, optics, and robot-ics, and those making breakthroughs in energy conservation, such as solar photovoltaics, fuel cells, and coal conversion.

Some governments restrict the advertising of some products (such as contraceptives and feminine hygiene products) because they feel they are in bad taste. Elsewhere, gov-ernments restrict ads that might prompt children to misbehave or people to break laws (such as advertising automobile speeds that exceed the speed limit) and those that show barely clad women. New Zealand banned a Nike ad in which a rugby team tackles the coach, as well as a Chanel ad in which the model said to her male lover before kissing him, "I hate you. I hate you so much I think I'm going to die from it darling." In both cases, the ads were deemed to threaten violence.[56]

Message Needs   An advertising theme may not be appropriate everywhere because of national differences in how well consumers know the product and how they perceive it, who will make the purchasing decision, and what appeals are most important. Recall from the discussions of gap analysis and product life cycles how product-knowledge conditions vary. For example, American Express's U.S. campaign "Do You Know Me?" is aimed at gaining market share from other credit cards. However, in some markets the company first needed to build credit-card usage. Because Japanese consumers perceive that their products are of good quality, advertisers within Japan concentrate more on image than on messages emphasizing quality.[57]

Whether purchasing decisions for specific products are made by the husband, wife, or jointly varies among countries. So marketing managers not only need to place ads where the right decision makers will see them, they must also use messages that may appeal differently to men and women.[58] The importance of different appeals may be affected by differences in economic or cultural factors. For example, a theme for selling Green Giant frozen vegetables in the United States is convenience, which didn't work in Japan because Japanese mothers take pride in the amount of time they take to prepare a meal. Instead, Green Giant used an appeal that the frozen vegetables allow the opportunity to prepare the families' favorite foods more often. Green Giant also advertises canned corn according to the main way it is eaten in different countries—as a hot side dish in the United States, a pizza topping in the United Kingdom, a cold addition to salads in France, an after-school treat in Japan, and a topping for ice cream in South Korea.[59]

BRANDING

A **brand** is an identifying mark for products or services. When a company registers a brand legally, it is a trademark. A brand gives a product or service instant recognition and may save promotional costs. MNEs must make four major branding decisions:

1. Brand versus no brand
2. Manufacturer's brand versus private brand
3. One brand versus multiple brands
4. Worldwide brand versus local brands

The international environment substantially affects only the last of these.

Some companies, such as Coca-Cola, have opted to use the same brand and logo globally. Other companies, such as Nestlé, associate many of their products under the same family of brands, such as the Nestea and Nescafé brands, in order to share these brands in their goodwill. Nevertheless, there are a number of problems in trying to use uniform brands internationally.

LANGUAGE FACTORS

One problem is that brand names may carry a different association in another language. For example, GM thought its Nova model could easily be called the same in Latin America, because the name means "star" in Spanish. However, people started pronouncing it "no va," which is Spanish for "it does not go." Coca-Cola tries to use global branding wherever possible but discovered that the word *diet* in Diet Coke had a connotation of illness in Germany and Italy. The brand is called Coca-Cola Light outside the United States.

Unilever has successfully translated the brand name for its fabric softener, while leaving its brand symbol, a baby bear, intact on the packaging. The U.S. name *Snuggle* is

Kuschelweich in Germany, *Cajoline* in France, *Coccolino* in Italy, and *Mimosin* in Spain. But *Snuggle* did not quite convey the same meaning in English-speaking Australia, where Unilever uses *Huggy.*

Pronunciation presents other problems, because a foreign language may lack some of the sounds of a brand name or the pronunciation of the name may have a different meaning than the original. For example, McDonald's uses Donald McDonald in Japan because the Japanese have difficulty pronouncing the letter *R.* Marcel Bich dropped the *H* from his name when branding Bic pens because of the fear of mispronunciation in English. Perrier's popular French soft drink, Pschitt, has an unappetizing meaning when pronounced in English.

Different alphabets present still other problems. For example, consumers judge English brand names by whether the name sounds appealing, while brand names in Mandarin and Cantonese need to have visual appeal as well because the Mandarin and Cantonese alphabets are pictograms. Such companies as Coca-Cola, Mercedes-Benz, and Boeing have taken great pains to assure not only that the translation of their names is pronounced roughly the same as in English but also that the brand name is meaningful. For example, Coca-Cola is pronounced *Ke-kou-ke-le* in Mandarin and means tasty and happy. Further, companies have sought names that are considered lucky in China, such as a name with eight strokes in it and displayed in red rather than blue.[60]

BRAND ACQUISITIONS

Much international expansion takes place through acquisition of companies in foreign countries that already have branded products. For example, when Avon acquired Justine in South Africa, it kept the Justine name because the brand was well known and respected. When Maytag, virtually unknown by consumers in China, formed a joint venture with the Chinese washing machine company Rongshida, it used the brand name Rongshida Maytag to take advantage of the better known brand.[61] Sunbeam has continued to use acquired brand names in Italy (Rowenta, Oster, Cadillac, Aircap, and Stewart) because they are well known and enjoy goodwill. However, Sunbeam has found that stretching the promotional budget over so many brands means that promotions are not as effective as they might be given that less is spent on any one brand to build significant positive recognition.[62]

COUNTRY-OF-ORIGIN IMAGES

Companies should consider whether to create a local or a foreign image for their products. The products of some countries, particularly developed countries, tend to have a higher-quality image than do those from other countries.[63] There are also image differences concerning specific products from specific countries. For example, the French company BSN-Gervais Dannone brews Kroenenbourg, a large-selling bottled beer in Europe, and the company's director general frankly admits that the Kroenenbourg brand "sounds German."[64] Also, Czechs associate locally made products with poor quality, so P&G has added German words to the labels of detergents it makes in the Czech Republic.[65]

Images of products are affected by where they are made.

But images can change. Consider that for many years various Korean companies sold abroad under private labels or under contract with well-known companies. Some of these Korean companies, such as Samsung, now emphasize their own trade names and the quality of Korean products.

In an innovative effort to create a British ice cream flavor along the lines of its American Cherry Garcia, Ben & Jerry's ran a contest for the best name and flavor. Cool Britannia won out over such entrants as Minty Python, Grape Expectations, Choc Ness Monster, and The Rolling Scones.[66]

GENERIC AND NEAR-GENERIC NAMES

If a brand name is used for a class of product, the company may lose the trademark.

Companies want their product names to become household words, but not so much that competitors can use trademarked brand names to describe their similar products. In the United States, the brand names Xerox and Kleenex are nearly synonymous with copiers and paper tissues, but have nevertheless remained proprietary brands. Some other names that were once proprietary, such as cellophane, linoleum, and Cornish hens, have become *generic*—available for anyone to use.

In this context, companies sometimes face substantial differences among countries that may either stimulate or frustrate their sales. For example, aspirin and Swiss army knives are proprietary names in Europe but generic in the United States, a situation that impairs European export sales of those products to the United States because U.S. companies can produce aspirin and Swiss army knives.

DISTRIBUTION

A company may accurately assess market potential, design goods or services for that market, price them appropriately, and promote them to probable consumers. However, it will have little likelihood of reaching its sales potential if it doesn't make the goods or services conveniently available to customers. Companies need to place their goods where people want to buy them. For example, does a man prefer to buy shampoo in a grocery store, barber shop, drugstore, or some other type of outlet?

Distribution is the course—physical path or legal title—that goods take between production and consumption. In international marketing, a company must decide on the method of distribution among countries as well as the method within the country where final sale occurs.

A company may enter a market gradually by limiting geographic coverage.

Companies may limit early distribution in given foreign countries by attempting to sell regionally before moving nationally. Many products and markets lend themselves to this sort of gradual development. In many cases, geographic barriers divide countries into very distinct markets; for example, Colombia is divided by mountain ranges and Australia by a desert. In other countries, such as Zimbabwe and Bolivia, very little wealth or few potential sales may lie outside the large metropolitan areas. In still others, advertising and distribution may be handled effectively on a regional basis. For example, most multinational consumer goods companies have moved into China one region at a time.[67]

We have already discussed operating forms for foreign-market penetration. In Chapter 17, we shall discuss distribution channels to move goods among countries and how the title to goods gets transferred. This section does not review these aspects of distribution; it discusses distributional differences and conditions within foreign countries that an international marketer should understand.

DIFFICULTY OF STANDARDIZATION

Distribution reflects different country environments:
- **It may vary substantially among countries.**
- **It is difficult to change.**

Within the marketing mix, MNEs find distribution one of the most difficult functions to standardize internationally, for several reasons. Each country has its own distribution system, which an MNE finds difficult to modify because it is entwined with the country's cultural, economic, and legal environments. Nevertheless, many retailers are successfully moving internationally.

Some of the factors that influence how goods will be distributed in a given country are citizens' attitudes toward owning their own store, the cost of paying retail workers, labor legislation differentially affecting chain stores and individually owned stores, legislation restricting the operating hours and size of stores, the trust that owners have in their employees, the efficacy of the postal system, and the financial ability to carry large inventories. For example, Hong Kong supermarkets, compared to those in the United States, carry a higher proportion of fresh goods, are smaller, sell smaller quantities per customer, and are located more closely to each other (see Table 16.3). This means that companies selling canned, boxed, or frozen foods will encounter less per capita demand in Hong Kong than in the United States. They would also have to make smaller deliveries because of store sizes and would have a harder time fighting for shelf space.

A few other examples should illustrate how distribution norms differ. Finland has few stores per capita because general-line retailers predominate there, while Italian distribution has a fragmented retail and wholesale structure. In the Netherlands, buyers' cooperatives deal directly with manufacturers. Japan has cash-and-carry wholesalers for retailers that do not need financing or delivery services. In Germany, mail-order sales are very important; not so in Italy, however, because of the country's unreliable postal system.[68] China has banned door-to-door sales, hurting companies such as Avon and Amway.[69]

How do these differences affect companies' marketing activities? One soft drink company, for example, has targeted most of its European sales through grocery stores. However, the method for getting its soft drinks to those stores varies. In the United Kingdom, one national distributor has been able to gain sufficient coverage and shelf

TABLE 16.3

SOCIOCULTURAL ELEMENTS OF SUPERMARKET TECHNOLOGY IN THE UNITED STATES AND HONG KONG

Different conditions (columns 2 and 3) with respect to sociocultural elements (column 1) have caused supermarkets in Hong Kong to sell a high proportion of fresh foods, to handle customers more frequently, to sell in low quantities, and to be located closer to competitors.

SOCIOCULTURAL ELEMENTS	UNITED STATES	HONG KONG
Dietary habits	Like meats	Like seafood and meats
	Used to frozen foods	Used to fresh foods
Shopping patterns	Objective to save time	Objective to preserve freshness of food
	Infrequent	
		More frequent
Living conditions	Better conditions	Conditions not as good
	Spacious	Crowded
Size of refrigerator	Bigger	Smaller
Availability of car	More available	Less available
Population density	Less dense	Very dense
Urbanization	Low	High

Source: From "Development of Supermarket Technology: The Incomplete Transfer Phenomenon" by Sukching Ho and Ho-fuk Lau, *International Marketing Review*, Spring 1988, p. 27. Reprinted with permission.

space so that the soft drink company can concentrate on other aspects of its marketing mix. In France, a single distributor has been able to get good coverage in the larger supermarkets but not in the smaller ones; consequently, the soft drink company has been exploring how to get secondary distribution without upsetting its relationship with the primary distributor. In Norway, regional distributors predominate, so the soft drink company has found it difficult to effect national promotion campaigns. In Belgium, the company could find no acceptable distributor, so it has had to assume that function itself.

CHOOSING DISTRIBUTORS AND CHANNELS

We will now compare why companies self-handle their distribution or contract other companies to do it for them, and discuss how they should choose outside distributors.

Distribution may be handled internally
- **When volume is high**
- **When there is a need to deal directly with the customer due to the nature of the product**
- **When the customer is global**
- **To gain a competitive advantage**

Internal Handling   When sales volume is low, it is usually more economical for a company to handle distribution by contracting with an external distributor. By doing so, however, it may lose a certain amount of control. Managers should reassess periodically whether sales have grown to the point that they can handle distribution internally.

Circumstances conducive to the internal handling of distribution include not only high sales volume but also

- When a product has the characteristic of high price, high technology, or the need for complex after-sales servicing (such as aircraft), the producer probably will have to deal directly with the buyer. The producer may simultaneously use a distributor within the foreign country that will serve to identify sales leads.
- When the company deals with global customers, especially in business-to-business sales—such as an auto-parts manufacturer that sells original equipment to the same automakers in multiple countries—such sales may go directly from the producer to the global customer.
- When the company views its main competitive advantage to be its distribution methods, such as some food franchisors, it eventually may franchise abroad but maintain its own distribution outlet to serve as a "flagship." Amway, Avon, and Tupperware are examples of companies that have successfully transferred their house-to-house distribution methods from the United States to their operations abroad. Matsushita, which sells in Japan largely within its 20,000 corner shops containing only its products, is establishing a network of 3,000 retail outlets in China. Dell Computer has successfully handled its own mail-order sales in Europe.[70]

Some evaluation criteria for distributors include their
- **Financial capability**
- **Connections with customers**
- **Fit with a company's product**
- **Other resources**

Distributor Qualifications   A company usually can choose from a number of potential distributors. Common criteria for selecting a distributor include

- Its financial strength
- Its good connections
- Extent of its other business commitments
- Current status of its personnel, facilities, and equipment[71]

The distributor's financial strength is important because of the potential long-term relationship between company and distributor and because of the assurance that money will be available for such things as maintaining sufficient inventory. Good connections are particularly important if sales must be directed to certain types of buyers, such as governmental procurement agencies. The amount of other business commitments can indicate whether the distributor has time for the company's product and whether it currently handles competitive or complementary products.[72] Finally, the current status of the distributor's personnel, facilities, and equipment indicates not only its ability to deal with the product but also how quickly start-up can occur.

Spare Parts and Repair   Consumers are reluctant to buy products that may require spare parts and service in the future unless they feel assured these will be readily available in good quality and at reasonable prices. The more complex and expensive the product, the more important after-sales servicing is. When after-sales servicing is important, companies may need to invest in service centers for groups of distributors that serve as intermediaries between producers and consumers. Earnings from sales of parts and after-sales service sometimes may match that of the original product.

Spare parts and service are important for sales.

Gaining Distribution   Companies must evaluate potential distributors, but distributors must choose which companies and products to represent and emphasize. Both wholesalers and retailers have limited storage facilities, display space, money to pay for inventories, and transportation and personnel to move and sell merchandise, so they try to carry only those products that have the greatest profit potential.

In many cases, distributors are tied into exclusive arrangements with manufacturers that prevent new competitive entries. For example, there are about 25,000 Japanese outlets that sell only Shiseido's cosmetics, 13,000 that sell only Toshiba products, and 11,000 that sell only Hitachi products.[73] A company that is new to a country and wants to introduce products that some competitors are already selling may find it impossible to find distributors to handle its brands. Even established companies sometimes find it hard to gain distribution for their new products, although they have the dual advantage of being known and of being able to offer existing profitable lines only if distributors accept the new unproven products.

A company wanting to use existing distribution channels may need to analyze competitive conditions carefully to offer effective incentives for those distributors to handle the product. It may need to identify problems distributors have to gain their loyalty by offering assistance. For example, Coca-Cola has held seminars for mom-and-pop stores abroad on how to operate more efficiently and compete with larger distributors.[74] Companies alternatively may offer other incentives such as higher profit margins, after-sales servicing, and promotional support—any of which may be offered on either a permanent or introductory basis. The type of incentive should also depend on the comparative costs within each market. In the final analysis, however, incentives will be of little help unless the distributors believe a company's products are viable. The company must sell the distributors on its products as well as on itself as a reliable company.

Distributors choose what they will handle. Companies
• May need to give incentives
• May use successful products as bait for new ones
• Must convince distributors that product and company are viable

HIDDEN COSTS IN FOREIGN DISTRIBUTION

When companies consider launching products in foreign markets, they must determine what final consumer prices will be to estimate sales potential. Because of different national distribution systems, the cost of getting products to consumers varies widely from one country to another. Five factors that often contribute to cost differences in distribution are infrastructure conditions, the number of levels in the distribution system, retail inefficiencies, size and operating-hours restrictions, and inventory stock-outs.

In many countries, the roads and warehousing facilities are so poor that getting goods to consumers quickly, at a low cost, and with minimum damage or loss en route is problematic. For example in Nigeria, Nestlé has had to build small warehouses across the country instead of depending on a central warehouse one would normally expect based on the country's area. Roads are in such poor condition that travel is slow and trucks are prone to breakdowns. Further, because of crime, Nestlé uses armed guards on its trucks and allows them to travel only during daylight hours.[75]

Differences in infrastructure create additional operating adjustments. For example, Domino's Pizza, which depends on call-in orders and quick deliveries for its competitive advantage, faces a different situation in Iceland because most people don't own phones. It has contracted with local establishments, such as drive-in movie theaters, so that drivers can borrow cellular phones from them to call Domino's. In Japan, it has had to install large wall maps and ask detailed questions of callers (which takes time) because houses are not numbered sequentially.[76] Many countries have multitiered wholesalers that sell to each other before the product reaches the retail level. For example, national wholesalers sell to regional ones, who sell to local ones, and so on. This sometimes occurs because wholesalers are too small to cover more than a small geographic area. Japan typifies such a market: There are, on average, 2.21 wholesale steps between producer and retailer in Japan, compared with 1.0 in the United States and 0.73 in France. Because each intermediary adds a markup, product prices are driven up. However, such overall figures obscure differences by product. For example, fresh food passes through much longer and complex channels than such products as electronic goods.[77]

In some countries, particularly emerging economies, low labor costs and a basic distrust by owners of all but family members result in retail practices that raise consumer prices. This distrust is evident in companies' preference for counter service rather than self-service. In the former, customers wait to be served and shown merchandise. A customer who decides to purchase something gets an invoice to take to a cashier's line to pay. Once the invoice is stamped as paid, the customer must go to another line to pick up the merchandise after presenting the stamped invoice. Some companies have counter service for purchases as small as a pencil. The additional personnel add to retailing costs, and the added time people must be in the store means fewer people can be served in the given space. In contrast, most retailers in some (mainly industrialized) countries have equipment that improves the efficiency of handling customers and reports, such as electronic scanners, cash registers linked to inventory control records, and machines connecting purchases to credit-card companies.

Many countries, such as France, Germany, and Japan, have laws to protect small retailers. These effectively limit the number of large retail establishments and the efficiencies they bring to sales.[78] Many countries also limit operating hours as a means of protecting employees from having to work late at night or on weekends. At the same time, the limit keeps retailers from covering the fixed cost of their space over more hours, so these costs are passed on to consumers. In Sweden, 7-Eleven stores cannot use longer opening hours as a competitive advantage because Swedish law prohibits sales of a full range of goods between midnight and 6 A.M.[79] Where retailers are small, as is true of most grocers in Spain, there is little space to store inventory. Wholesalers must incur the cost of making small deliveries to many more establishments and sometimes may have to visit each retailer more frequently because of stock outages.

THE INTERNET AND ELECTRONIC COMMERCE

Estimates vary widely on the current and future number of worldwide on-line households and the electronic commerce generated through on-line sales. Nevertheless, they all indicate substantial growth.[80] Figure 16.5 shows one estimate of growth of Internet-connected computers. As electronic commerce increases, customers worldwide can quickly compare prices from different distributors, which should drive prices down.

Electronic commerce offers companies an opportunity to promote their products globally. It also permits suppliers to deal more quickly with their customers. For example, Lee Hung Fat Garment Factory of Hong Kong supplies apparel to about 60 companies in Europe and now flashes picture samples of merchandise to them over the Web. Customers, such as Kingfisher of the United Kingdom, can tinker with the samples and transmit new versions back to Hong Kong so that Lee Hung Fat produces exactly what the distributors want.[81]

Global Internet sales are not without problems. Many households, especially in emerging economies, lack access to Internet connections.[82] Therefore, if a company wants to reach mass global markets, it will need to supplement its Internet sales with sales using other means of promotion and distribution. A company also needs to set up and promote its Internet sales, which can be very expensive. Royal Bank of Canada is spending about $75 million up front to promote Internet sales in the United States.[83]

A company cannot easily differentiate its marketing program for each country where it operates. The same Web advertisements and prices reach customers everywhere, even though different appeals and prices for different countries might yield more sales and profits. If the company makes international sales over the Internet, it must deliver what

The growth in on-line households creates new distributional opportunities and challenges in selling globally over the Internet.

FIGURE 16.5   Growth of the Global On-line Population

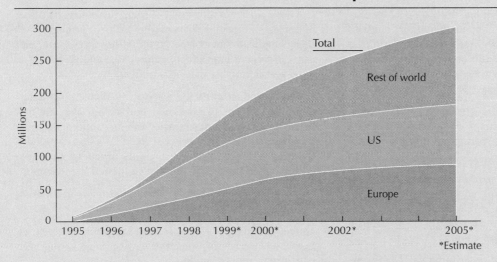

Although the on-line (Internet) population is growing rapidly, a very small percentage of the world's population is expected to be on-line by 2005. The percentage is especially small in emerging economies. This figure shows the worldwide growth—and projected growth—of Internet-connected computers from 1995 to 2005.

Source: Paul Taylor, "How the Internet Will Reshape Worldwide. Business Activity," *Financial Times*, April 7, 1999, information technology section, p. 1. Reprinted by permission.

it sells expeditiously. This may necessitate placing warehouses and service facilities abroad, which the company may or may not own and manage itself.[84]

Finally, the company's Internet ads and prices must comply with the laws of each country where the company makes sales. This is a challenge because a company's Web page reaches Internet users everywhere. For example, Land's End, a U.S. merchandiser, has long depended on its unconditional lifetime guarantee to help sell its merchandise. But German law prohibits such a guarantee on the grounds that it is a gimmick hidden in the sales price. Land's End may have to exclude Germany from its Internet sales.[85] Clearly, although the Internet creates new opportunities for companies to sell internationally, it also creates new challenges for them.

WEB CONNECTION

Check out our home page www.prenhall.com/daniels for links to key resources for you in your study of international business.

SUMMARY

- Although the principles for selling abroad are the same as those for selling domestically, the international businessperson must deal with a less familiar environment, which may change rapidly.

- Tools for assessing foreign demand for products include estimates based on what has happened in other countries and studies of historical trends. Some problems with the results from these tools include country differences in product obsolescence, product costs, income elasticities, product substitution, income inequality, and cultural factors and tastes.

- Gap analysis is a tool that helps companies determine why they have not met their market potentials for given countries.

- A standardized approach to marketing means maximum uniformity in products and programs among the countries in which sales occur. Although this approach minimizes expenses, most companies make changes to fit country needs in order to increase sales volume.

- A variety of legal and other environmental conditions may call for altering products in order to capture foreign demand. In addition to determining when to alter products, companies also must decide how many and which products to sell abroad.

- Because of different demand characteristics, a product may be in a growth stage in one country and in a mature, or declining, stage in another. Companies can usually exert more control over pricing during the growth stage.

- Government regulations may directly or indirectly affect the prices companies charge. International pricing is further complicated because of fluctuations in currency values, differences in product preferences, and variations in fixed versus variable pricing practices.

- For each product in each country, a company must determine not only its promotional budget but also the mix between push and pull strategies and promotions. The relationship between push and pull should depend on the distribution system, cost and availability of media, consumer attitudes, and the product's price compared to incomes.

- Major problems for standardizing advertising in different countries are translation, legality, and message needs.

- Global branding is hampered by language differences, expansion by acquisition, nationality images, and laws concerning generic names.

- Distribution channels vary substantially among countries. The differences may affect not only the relative costs of operating but also the ease of making initial sales.

C A S E

DENTAL NEWS AND HOTRESPONSE*

In 1987, John Schwartz, an American living in Hong Kong, founded the family-owned *Dental News*, a quarterly magazine circulating to people interested in dental equipment, supplies, and technical developments. Medi Media Pacific, a Hong Kong–based company specializing in medical publications, bought *Dental News* from the Schwartz family in 1993. Havas, a French multimedia company, acquired Medi Media Pacific in 1999. Both Medi Media and Havas have contracted Logan Media International to handle all print activity from its headquarters in McMinnville, Oregon (USA). The Schwartz family owns Logan Media International, which is headed by Allen Logan Schwartz, the son of *Dental News*'s founder. Allen, collaborating closely with his brother, John Schwartz, also conceived and developed Hotresponse under another company, Dissemination Inc., which their father had recently established to exploit market synergies between print and the Internet. Hotresponse is an on-line service that connects magazine subscribers with magazine advertisers. The first client for Hotresponse was *Dental News* in 1998. Since then, Dissemination Inc. has obtained other Hotresponse clients, such as *Esquire Magazine, Maxim, Outside,* and Penton Publishers.

Initially, *Dental News* circulated only to Asia-Pacific countries until its founders envisioned expansion into other emerging markets. In the early 1990s, Charles Buckwalter, president of Conexion International in Miami, Florida (USA), a publishing service for international markets, contacted *Dental News* about publishing *Dental News* for Latin America. *Dental News* put him in touch with Logan Media International, which contracted Conexion to help publish Latin American *Dental News* editions. Logan Media and Conexion launched a Spanish edition (*América Latina Noticias Dentales*) in 1994 and a Portuguese edition (*Brasil Dental News*) in 1995. Subsequently, *Dental News* has introduced a fourth edition for Russia and the Commonwealth of Independent States (CIS)—countries that were once part of the USSR.

Dental News is free to subscribers. Therefore, the magazine must sell enough advertising to pay publication and distribution costs. Companies will advertise where they believe enough potential customers will see their ads and where they have evidence that the ads generate substantial interest in their

products. *Dental News* targets nontriad markets (those outside Western Europe, Japan, and English-speaking North America). The *Dental News* management is convinced and has persuaded advertisers that potential dental product customers (such as dentists, public health officials, lab technicians, dental hygienists, and dental school professors) are inundated with product information in the triad countries. But, potential customers elsewhere have too little access to information and would like more. Still, companies will advertise in *Dental News* only if *Dental News* has a subscription base large enough to reach enough potential dental product customers.

Dental News elicits subscriptions from exhibition booths it places at dental trade shows and dental conferences held all over the world. The largest of the conferences is the annual meeting of the Fédération Dentaire Internationale (FDI). *Dental News* arranges for its magazine to be placed in registration packets at these dental conferences. In exchange, *Dental News* provides advertising for upcoming meetings and lists these meetings in the calendar that appears in each of its magazine issues. For instance, the October–December 1999 Asia-Pacific issue gave information about upcoming meetings in Hawaii (USA), Malaysia, China, New Zealand, India, Hong Kong, Sri Lanka, Thailand, Singapore, and Japan. Increasingly, word of mouth is important in adding new circulation as existing subscribers tell their colleagues about the publication.

Yet, *Dental News* is concerned that the subscription base does not become too large. Otherwise, the cost of publishing and distributing would exceed advertising revenues. Raising advertising prices to compensate for added distribution might not be feasible. Although the magazines are free, subscribers must renew their subscriptions once a year so that *Dental News* knows that subscribers are alive, interested in the magazine, and receive publications at correct addresses. By the year 2000, *Dental News*'s Asia-Pacific and Spanish-Latin American circulations were a little over 50,000 each. The edition for Brazil had about 25,000 subscribers and the one for Russia and the CIS about 15,000.

The format for the four editions is identical. The articles are in English on the left-hand side of the pages and in

*We appreciate the time and efforts of Charles Buckwalter and Allen Logan Schwartz, who provided data for the case preparation.

Mandarin, Spanish, Portuguese, or Russian on the right-hand side. The content is the same except for advertisements and calendars of coming events. In terms of the calendars, all four editions include information on the world meetings, but each edition includes information only on those national and regional meetings that will take place within its circulation area. In terms of advertisements, one edition may have ads that another edition doesn't have because companies may advertise in one, two, three, or all four regions, depending on where they want to distribute. However, *Dental News* gives companies discounts for advertising in multiple editions. Further, the language of ads may vary by edition. Most companies place their advertisements in Spanish for *América Latina Noticias Dentales* and in Portuguese for *Brasil Dental News.* However, they put them in English for *Asia-Pacific Dental News* because that edition reaches so many different language groups.

Dental News sells ads through seven contractors who have responsibility for different parts of the world. For example, Japan Advertising Communications sells advertising in Japan, and a salesperson in Clark, South Dakota (USA), sells advertising in Europe. Once a company signs a contract to advertise, it sends materials to *Dental News* in Hong Kong, where that office prepares page films that it ships to printers in each region. For example, the office sends page films to Carvajal in Cali, Colombia, which prints the Spanish edition. Map 16.2 shows the flow from sales to advertiser, to compiler, to printer for an advertiser in Germany. Each magazine's content is primarily advertisements.

The magazine also includes articles of product profiles (usually from information supplied by advertisers), reprints from dental newsletters, and speeches from conferences. The Hong Kong office edits articles in English and sends the edited versions to translators in Beijing, Mexico City, Sao Paulo, and Moscow for translation into Mandarin, Spanish, Portuguese, and Russian. The translators return them to Hong Kong, where the office prepares page films that it also sends to regional printers. Once the regional edition is printed, it must be distributed to subscribers. For example, after Carvajal prints the Spanish language edition, it ships the magazines to each country where there are subscribers. Once they reach each country, Carvajal arranges for them to be mailed or delivered by courier, depending on the reliability of the mail service. Map 16.2 shows the distribution from the printer in Colombia to a subscriber in Chile. But this is not the end of the flow.

Dental News provides another service to bring advertisers and subscribers together. Each edition contains a response card for readers to tear out, complete, and send to their *Dental News* regional office. Respondents complete the cards by entering codes for those advertisers from whom they want more information, and they check off categories of demographic information, such as whether they have a private practice or work in a clinic. Let's say a subscriber in Santiago, Chile, wants more information from several advertisers. He or she can complete one card to request information from multiple advertisers, such as from Franz Sachs in Germany, NSK Nakanishi in Japan, Sultan Chemists in the United States, Bien-Air in Switzerland, Dentalwerk in Austria, and BJM Laboratories in Israel. This is much easier for the subscriber than writing separately to each of the companies. The subscriber mails the preaddressed card to *Dental News's* office in Mexico City where a staff collates and forwards responses for each advertiser. The Mexico City office typically gets 6,000 to 8,000 company requests per issue of *América Latina Noticias Dentales.* Once the advertiser, say Franz Sachs in Germany, receives the information from Mexico City, it can then respond directly to the interested subscribers or indirectly through distributors in the subscribers' areas. Map 16.2 also shows the flow of this process. A problem with the system is that subscribers may have to wait more than two months between the time of requesting information and the time they receive it from advertisers.

In 1998, *Dental News* began using the services of Hotresponse in addition to the response card system. Basically, Hotresponse provides *Dental News* a Web page (www.read-errespnse.com) for subscribers. When subscribers register on the Web page for the first time, they must provide Hotresponse with their name, contact information, and demographic details. Interestingly, subscribers have been more willing to provide complete demographic details through the Web response than through the card response. When subscribers register, Hotresponse gives them a password for future log-ons. Thereafter, when they log on, they can access advertisers' brochures directly, find out the names and addresses of distributors, and e-mail the manufacturers directly. What takes weeks or months in the card response system takes only a few seconds electronically.

When subscribers log on, the Hotresponse office in Oregon records what product information they access, along with the name, location, and demographic profile of subscribers. Once a week, Hotresponse merges the accesses for

MAP 16.2   *Dental News:* Connecting Advertisers to Subscribers Internationally

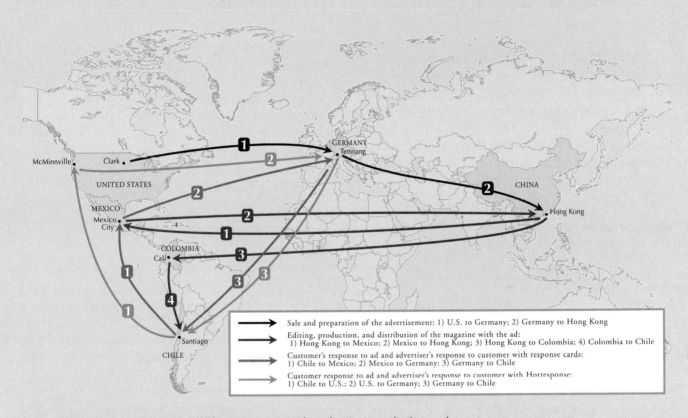

Legend:

➤ Sale and preparation of the advertisement: 1) U.S. to Germany; 2) Germany to Hong Kong

➤ Editing, production, and distribution of the magazine with the ad:
   1) Hong Kong to Mexico; 2) Mexico to Hong Kong; 3) Hong Kong to Colombia; 4) Colombia to Chile

➤ Customer's response to ad and advertiser's response to customer with response cards:
   1) Chile to Mexico; 2) Mexico to Germany; 3) Germany to Chile

➤ Customer response to ad and advertiser's response to customer with Hotresponse:
   1) Chile to U.S.; 2) U.S. to Germany; 3) Germany to Chile

Supplying dental products is international so companies need to advertise in media that reach target customers in many countries. *Dental News* has four editions that go to four different regions of emerging markets, and its production, advertising, and subscriptions are all international. This map shows what happens when *Dental News* sells an ad to a supplier in Germany for its edition going to Spanish-speaking Latin America to which a potential customer in Chile responds. The black arrow shows the international flow of selling and preparing advertisements for the publication. The red arrow shows the international flow of editing the magazine's content, preparing page sheets, printing, and distributing. The purple arrow shows the customer's and advertiser's responses through response cards. The green arrow shows the customer's and advertiser's responses by using the Web connection from Hotresponse, which takes minutes, whereas the response card may take more than two months.

each advertiser with the demographic profiles of the subscribers. It places the data in an Excel spreadsheet, prepares a summary demographic profile of people accessing each advertiser's information, and forwards reports via e-mail to all the advertisers. By the beginning of 2000, subscribers to *América Latina Noticias Dentales* were accessing between 1,500 and 2,000 advertisers per issue of *Dental News*. At the same time, card responses did not decrease. *Dental News*

estimates that there are about 150,000 dentists in Spanish-speaking Latin America, but it does not know how many of these are on-line.

If subscribers use the *Dental News* Web page to connect directly to manufacturers via e-mail, they may even place orders directly. Some companies forward the orders to their warehouses and distributors to fill. Others fill orders directly. Three developments have enhanced this latter option: (1) The rise in credit-card usage allows purchasers to buy without having to go to a bank to request foreign exchange to transfer to sellers; (2) intermediaries will now consolidate shipments from various suppliers, send the orders, and arrange for customs' clearance on arrival; and (3) governments have lowered trade restrictions, which allows orders to more easily enter countries.

What is the advantage of contacting an advertiser through the *Dental News* Web page rather than directly through the advertiser's Web page? Subscribers can log on just once to access information from multiple advertisers. Advertisers can receive information on who is accessing their information and pass sales leads to their salespeople and distributors. They can use the demographic profiles to help prepare future promotions.

QUESTIONS

1. Why do you believe *Dental News* continues to receive card responses, even though people can respond on the Web through Hotresponse?

2. As more people come on-line, will there be a need to print the editions of *Dental News?* Why or why not?

3. As more people come on-line, do you believe dental product companies will sell more directly, rather than going through distributors? Do you think this may vary by type of dental product and by company? If so, why?

4. Within the marketing mix (product, price, promotion, branding, and distribution), which are most important when *Dental News* tries to sell advertising to companies producing dental products?

CHAPTER NOTES

1 Avon Annual Report for 1995; "Acquisition of Upscale Direct Seller Opens Doors for Avon in South Africa," *Outlook*, May–June 1996, p. 4; "Big Hit in Small Markets," *Outlook*, January–February 1996, p. 6; "A Steady Stream of Suitors, *Outlook*, January–February 1996, p. 14; Paulette Thomas, "U.S. Cosmetics Makers Market American Look to World Women," *Asian Wall Street Journal*, May 8, 1995, p. 20; "Boutiques of Beauty," *Outlook*, November–December 1995, pp. 11–13; "The Fundamentals in the Asia Pacific Region," *Outlook*, September–October 1995, p. 4; "Thai Journalists Take a Global Look at Avon," *Outlook*, September–October 1995, p. 5; "Reaching More Women Every Year," *Outlook*, September–October 1995, p. 7; "Branching Out in the Philippines," *Outlook*, September–October 1995, pp. 10–13; "Resource in the East," *Outlook*, September–October 1995, p. 14; "The Changing Face of Avon," *Outlook*, July–August 1996, pp. 14–20; "Argentina Center Pampers Women," *Outlook*, September–October 1996, p. 7; "Avon Emerges in Russia," *Outlook*, September–October 1996, pp. 10–15; Rasul Bailay, "Avon Tries Twist on Sales Technique for Push into India," *Wall Street Journal*, July 2, 1996, p. B8; "Brazil Bounces Back," *Outlook*, March–April 1995, pp. 8–13; James Brooke, "In the Amazon, Guess Who's Calling?" *New York Times*, July 7, 1995, p. A4; and Veronica Byrd and Wendy Zellner, "The Avon Lady of the Amazon," *Business Week*, October 24, 1994, p. 93.

2 Michael Schuman, "U.S. Companies Crack South Korean Market," *Wall Street Journal*, September 11, 1996, p. A14.

3 David J. Arnold and John A. Quelch, "New Strategies in Emerging Markets," *Sloan Management Review*, Fall 1998, pp. 7–20.

4 Mark Nicholson, "Doing Business in India," *Financial Times*, August 18, 1998, p. 10.

5 J. A. Weber, "Comparing Growth Opportunities in the International Marketplace," *Management International Review*, No. 1, 1979, pp. 47–54.

6 "Chocolate Makers in Switzerland Try to Melt Resistance," *Wall Street Journal*, January 5, 1981, p. 14; William Hall, "Swiss Chocolate Groups Aim to Keep Outlook Sweet," *Financial Times*, April 11–12, 1998, p. 23; and William Hall, "Wraps Come Off Chocolate's Best-Kept Secret," *Financial Times*, June 5, 1998, p. 20.

7 "Limited Imagination," *The Economist*, September 28, 1996, pp. 80–85.

8 Lorraine Mooney, "A DDT Ban Would Be Deadly," *Wall Street Journal*, September 2, 1999, p. A14.

9 Mark Turner, "Feasting on Famine Food," *Financial Times*, November 24, 1998, p. 6.

10 "Benetton Opens a Havana Boutique Aimed at Tourists; Exile Groups Protest," *Wall Street Journal*, January 26, 1993, p. A10.

11 "Cause for Concern; With Nestlé in the Spotlight Again over Its Advertising Tactics," *Marketing Week*, February 11, 1999, pp. 28–31.

12 Michael Waldholz, "Sparks Fly at AIDS Meeting Over Breast-Feeding," *Wall Street Journal*, July 12, 2000, p. B2.

13 Andrew Jack, Bruce Clark, and Daniel Green, "Boycott Forces Hoechst to Drop Abortion Pill," *Financial Times*, April 9, 1997, p. 1.

14 Annette Fuentes, *In These Times*, March 21, 1999, p. 10.

15 Sigurd Villads Troye and Van R. Wood, "A Conceptual Perspective of International Marketing: Meeting the Educational Challenges of the 1990s and Beyond," *1989 International Management Symposium* (Monterey, CA: Monterey Institute of International Studies, 1989), pp. 84–95.

16 Shawn Tally, "Teens: The Most Global Market of All," *Fortune*, May 16, 1994, pp. 90–97.

17 Erica Zlomislic, "Gillette Invests Heavily in Mach 3 R&D; Prepares $300-Million Ad Blitzkrieg," *Strategy*, April 27, 1998, p. 1.

18 Matt Moffett, "Learning to Adapt to a Tough Market, Chilean Firms Pry Open Door to Japan," *Wall Street Journal*, June 7, 1994, p. A10.

19 Tara Parker-Pope, "Nonalcoholic Beer Hits the Spot in Mideast," *Wall Street Journal*, December 6, 1995, p. B1.

20 Troye and Wood, "A Conceptual Perspective of International Marketing."

21 Julie Edelson Halpert, "Harnessing the Sun and Selling It Abroad," *New York Times*, June 5, 1996, p. C1; Caspar Henderson, "The Solar Revival," *Financial Times*, July 3, 1996, p. 8; and Jenny Gregory, *Financing Mechanisms for Renewable Energy Systems: A Guide for Development Workers* (London: IT Publications, 1996).

22 Timothy Aeppel, "Europe's 'Unity' Undoes a U.S. Exporter," *Wall Street Journal*, April 1, 1996, p. B1.

23 "Abolishing Litter," *The Economist*, August 22, 1992, pp. 59–60; and Philippe Bruno and Bernd Graf, "The New EC Environmental Framework for Packaging," *Export Today*, March 1993, pp. 17–23.

24 See *Financial Times*, October 13, 1995, for special section on international standards.

25 "Discjockeying," *The Economist*, January 28, 1995, p. 60; and Michiyo Nakamoto and Alice Rawsthorn, "Electronics Rivals End Battle Over Format of Video Discs," *Financial Times*, September 16–17, 1995, p. 1

26 Raju Narisetti, "Can Rubbermaid Crack Foreign Markets?" *Wall Street Journal*, June 6, 1996, p. B1.

27 Joel Millman, "Illegal U.S. Chickens Pour into Mexico," *Wall Street Journal*, June 24, 1998, p. A15.

28 Lisa Bannon, "Mattel Plans to Double Sales Abroad," *Wall Street Journal*, February 11, 1998, p. A3.

29 Andrew Pollack, "Gulliver's Japanese Travels," *New York Times*, July 7, 1995, p. 17.

30 Peter Marsh and Nikki Tait, "Whirlpool's Platform for Growth," *Financial Times*, March 26, 1998, p. 8.

31 Gabriella Stern, "Heinz Aims to Export Taste for Ketchup," *Wall Street Journal*, November 20, 1992, p. B1.

32 Michael Schuman, "U.S. Companies Crack South Korean Market," *Wall Street Journal*, September 11, 1996, p. A14.

33 Arvind Sahay, "Finding the Right International Mix," *Financial Times*, November 16, 1998, mastering marketing section, pp. 2–3.

34 Daniel Benjamin, "Germany Considers Legalizing the Ancient Art of Haggling," *Wall Street Journal*, July 19, 1994, p. B1.

35 Alicia Swasy, "Foreign Formula," *Wall Street Journal*, June 15, 1990, p. A7; and "Venezuela Sets Price Controls," *Wall Street Journal*, January 11, 1994, p. A10.

36 Mark Alpert and Aimety Dunlap Smith, "Nestlé Shows How to Gobble Markets," *Fortune*, Vol. 119, January 16, 1989, p. 76.

37 Andrea C. Rutherford, "Sea Urchin Industry Is Threatened by Its Own Growth," *Wall Street Journal*, July 11, 1992, p. B2; and "Japanese Snap Up Eye of Tuna," *Wall Street Journal*, April 7, 1994, p. A10.

38 Nina Munk, "The Levi Straddle," *Forbes*, January 17, 1994, pp. 44–45.

39 Matthew B. Myers, "The Pricing of Export Products: Why Aren't Managers Satisfied with the Results?" *Journal of World Business*, Vol. 32, No. 3, 1997, pp. 277–289.

40 Swasy, "Foreign Formula."

41 Robin Bulman, "Auto Dealerships in Korea See Red over Gray Market," *Journal of Commerce*, September 5, 1996, p. 1A.

42 John Willman, "Levi's Threatens Legal Action on 'Grey' Imports," *Financial Times*, October 1, 1998, p. 12; and John Griffiths, "Non-Franchised Dealers," *Financial Times*, December 3, 1998, auto section, p. v.

43 Claude Cellich, "Negotiating Strategies: The Question of Price," *International Trade Forum*, April–June 1991, pp. 10–13.

44 "New Delhi Suspends Sale of Pepsi, Coke," *BC Cycle*, January 20, 1996.

45 Miriam Jordan, "In Rural India, Video Vans Sell Toothpaste and Shampoo," *Wall Street Journal*, January 10, 1996, p. B1.

46 Kevin Goldman, "Prof. Levitt Stands by Global-Ad Theory," *Wall Street Journal*, October 13, 1992, p. B7.

47 "A Passion for Variety," *The Economist*, November 30, 1996, pp. 68–71.

48 "Wal-Mart Again Runs into Language Law Trouble," *Wall Street Journal*, June 14, 1994, p. A4.

49 Kevin Kelly and Karen Lowry Miller, "The Rumble Heard Round the World: Harleys," *Business Week*, May 24, 1993, pp. 58–60.

50 Miriam Jordan, "Pillsbury Presses Flour Power in India," *Wall Street Journal*, May 5, 1999, p. B1.

51 Harold M. Spielman, "Local Partnerships: The Strategic Asset in Multicultural Research," *Journal of Advertising Research*, Vol. 35, No. 1, January–February 1995.

52 Rick Wartzman, "Read Their Lips," *Wall Street Journal*, June 3, 1999, p. A1.

53 Michael Christie, "Marketing Overseas: When Translating Isn't Enough," *Export Today*, March 1995, pp. 16–17.

54 Namjo Cho, "Korean Men Take a Drag on Virginia Slims," *Wall Street Journal*, January 14, 1997, p. B10.

55 Michael Cox, "The Low Cost of Living," *Wall Street Journal*, April 9, 1998, p. A22.

56 Sally D. Goll, "New Zealand Bans Reebok, Other Ads It Deems Politically Incorrect for TV," *Wall Street Journal*, July 25, 1995, p. A12.

57 "The Enigma of Japanese Advertising," *The Economist*, August 14, 1993, pp. 59–60.

58 John B. Ford, Michael S. LaTour, and Tony L. Henthorne, "Perceptions of Marital Roles in Purchase Decision Processes: A Cross-Cultural Study," *Journal of the Academy of Marketing Science*, Spring 1995, pp. 120–131.

59 Tara Parker-Pope, "Custom-Made," *Wall Street Journal*, September 26, 1996, p. R22.

60 Bernd H. Schmitt, "Language and Visual Imagery: Issues of Corporate Identity in East Asia," *Columbia Journal of World Business*, Winter 1995, pp. 28 36.

61 Darlene M. Liao, "Outfitting Chinese Households," *The China Business Review*, November–December 1998, pp. 32–34.

62 Myron M. Miller, "Sunbeam in Italy: One Success and One Failure," *International Marketing Review*, Vol. 7, No. 1, 1990, pp. 68–73.

63 John S. Hulland, "The Effects of Country-of-Brand and Brand Name on Product Evaluation and Consideration: A Cross Country Comparison," in T. S. Chan, ed., *Consumer Behavior in Asia: Issues and Marketing Practice* (New York: Haworth Press, 1999), pp. 23–39.

64 William H. Flanagan, "Big Battle Is Brewing as French Beer Aims to Topple Heineken," *Wall Street Journal*, February 22, 1980, p. 16.

65 E. S. Browning, "Eastern Europe Poses Obstacles for Ads," *Wall Street Journal*, July 30, 1992, p. B6.

66 Tara Parker-Pope, "Minty Python and Cream Victoria? Ice Creams Leave Some Groaning," *Wall Street Journal*, July 3, 1996, p. B1.

67 Sally D. Goll, "Few Retailers in China Carry Modern Goods," *Asian Wall Street Journal*, April 11, 1995, p. A1.

68 Cecilie Rohwedder, "U.S. Firms Go After Europeans," *Wall Street Journal*, January 6, 1998, p. A15.

69 Craig S. Smith and Ian Johnson, "China, Worried About Direct Marketers' Growth, Bans Practice," *Wall Street Journal*, April 22,1998, p. A16.

70 Michiyo Nakamoto, "Matsushita Plans Network of 3,000 Shops Across China," *Financial Times*, September 29, 1995, p. 1; Patrick Oster and Igor Reichlin, "Breaking into European Markets by Breaking the Rules," *Business Week*, January 20, 1992, pp. 88–89; Jack G. Kaikati, "Don't Crack the Japanese Distribution System—Just Circumvent It," *Columbia Journal of World Business*, Summer 1993, pp. 35–45; Tony Jackson, "Tupperware Decides It's Time to Party on Its Own," *Financial Times*, December 5, 1995, p. 20; Paulette Thomas, "U.S. Cosmetics Makers Market American Look to World's Women," *Asian Wall Street Journal*, May 5, 1995, p.10.

71 For aspects of contractual considerations see Kojo Yelpaala, "Strategy and Planning in Global Product Distribution—Beyond the Distribution Contract," *Law & Policy in International Business*, Vol. 25, 1994, pp. 839–944.

72 See for example, "The International Supplier Selection: The Relevance of Import Dependence," *Journal of Global Marketing*, Vol. 9, No. 3, 1996, pp. 23–45.

73 "Taking Aim," *The Economist*, April 24, 1993, p. 74; and John Fahy and Fuyuki Taguchi, "Reassessing the Japanese Distribution System," *Sloan Management Review*, Winter 1995, pp. 49–61.

74 Bert Rosenbloom, "Motivating Your International Channel Partners," *Business Horizons*, Vol. 33, No. 2, March–April 1990, pp. 53–57.

75 Greg Steinmetz and Tara Parker-Pope, "All Over the Map," *Wall Street Journal*, September 26, 1996, p. R4.

76 Parker-Pope, "Custom-Made."

77 Fahy and Taguchi, "Reassessing the Japanese Distribution System."

78 Andrew Jack, "Carrefours Up Sharply but Hits at Government," *Financial Times*, February 29, 1996, p. 14; Bob Davis, Peter Gumbel, and David P. Hamilton, "Red-Tape Traumas," *Wall Street Journal*, December 14, 1995, p. A1; John Griffiths, "Too Many Car Dealers in Europe," *Financial Times*, October 22, 1996, p. 2; and "A Matter of Convenience," *The Economist*, January 25, 1997, pp. 60–62.

79 Hugh Carnegy, "Swedish 7-Eleven Stores Lose Some of Their Convenience," *Financial Times*, March 29, 1996, p. 1.

80 Paul Taylor, "How the Internet Will Reshape Worldwide Business Activity," *Financial Times*, April 7, 1999, information technology section, p. 1; and Jonathan Reynolds, "Reaching the Virtual Customer," *Financial Times*, March 18, 1998, mastering global business section, pp. 12–13.

81 Karen Witcher, "Family Garment Business in Hong Kong Uses Internet to Gain Access to Global Customer Pool," *Wall Street Journal*, November 24, 1999, p. B15.

82 Priscilla Awde, "The Internet in Developing Countries," *Financial Times*, November 24, 1999, Section 2, p. 1.

83 Larry M. Greenberg, "Canada Banks Try Web to Win U.S. Customers," *Wall Street Journal*, October 28, 1999, p. A18.

84 Scott Thurm, "Getting the Goods," *Wall Street Journal*, November 22, 1999, p. R39.

85 Brandon Mitchener, "Border Crossings," *Wall Street Journal*, November 22, 1999, p. R41.

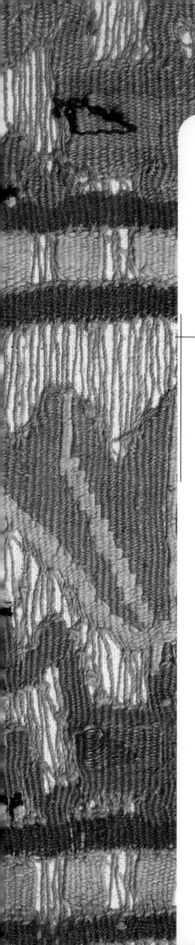

CHAPTER 17

Export and Import Strategies

There may be trade and none able to do it.   —CHINESE PROVERB

OBJECTIVES

- To identify the key elements of export and import strategies

- To compare direct and indirect selling of exports

- To discuss the role of several types of trading companies in exporting

- To show how freight forwarders help exporters with the movement of goods

- To identify the methods of receiving payment for exports and the financing of receivables

- To discuss the role of countertrade in international business

It is not always easy to engage in trade, especially for small companies. The top U.S. exporters generate about 30 percent of U.S. merchandise exports, and their shipments are bigger on average than are the shipments of smaller exporters. However, most of the U.S. companies engaged in export activity are small, as is Grieve Corporation (only 125 employees) of Round Lake, Illinois, near Chicago.

Grieve Corporation manufactures laboratory and industrial ovens, furnaces, and heat processing systems for the U.S. market only. Before Grieve Corporation got involved in exporting, it experienced problems when one of its customers would move its manufacturing facilities overseas. Initially, Grieve Corporation would continue to supply that customer with furnaces, but eventually this market would begin to erode as the customer would source locally. The company had not considered exports proactively for three main reasons:

1. *The nature of its product.* Industrial ovens and furnaces are rather large and bulky and also relatively expensive. Top management assumed the product's size would make shipping costs so high that Grieve would price itself out of the market. For example, one overseas shipment of a fully automated conveyorized system to the Philippines entailed shipping costs of $40,999.

2. *Doubts about its success abroad.* Grieve is a small business, and top management assumed it could not be successful internationally. Managers were so busy doing all that needed to be done in the domestic market with a relatively thin management structure that they just didn't have time to think strategically about the international market.

3. *Concern about competition.* More seasoned exporters from Germany, Japan, and the United Kingdom offered relatively fierce competition. Even within the United States, the company had strong competition from local producers in markets outside the Chicago area.

However, Grieve realized that something had to be done. Not only was it losing customers overseas to local suppliers, it was beginning to experience competition from abroad. Top management realized it needed to combat the competition or lose the market entirely. In addition, Grieve Corporation had to make shipments to both California and Connecticut, its number-one and number-two markets, and it had to contend with location competition and high transportation costs, so it decided that the international market might not be so bad. Patrick J. Calabrese, Grieve's president, attended a one-day seminar featuring the U.S. ambassadors to the ASEAN countries to determine whether or not it made sense to enter the Asian market. He left that seminar convinced there might be strong market opportunities in one of the world's fastest-growing regions. However, he was not familiar with the market, and the company had no sales offices or representatives in the ASEAN countries. He also was concerned about the British, German, and Japanese competition already entrenched in that market.

Grieve's marketing staff decided to sample potential interest in Asia by advertising in trade publications circulating in Southeast Asia, such as the *Asian Industrial Reporter*, the *Asian Literature Showcase*, and the *World Industrial Reporter*. To learn more about the market, Calabrese worked with a representative from the International Trade Administration of the Chicago Export Assistance Center. This office helped him plan a trip to Asia by arranging for interpreters at each stop on his itinerary and by arranging meetings with U.S. embassy personnel. His trip was intended primarily to determine market potential and identify possible agents. Calabrese had received inquiries from some distributors that were familiar with Grieve's product line but he had not pursued them. However, Calabrese's staff had begun filing correspondence by country rather than by company name, so it was relatively easy to locate potential distributors and customers along with the leads provided by Commerce. In addition to these distributors, Calabrese used the U.S. Department of Commerce's Agent/Distributor Search to identify several other possible distributors. The trip was a big success for Grieve. Interviews were held with 28 potential agents over 28 days, and exclusive agents were signed up in each country.

Calabrese quickly learned that he had to cut shipping costs. So Grieve redesigned its packaging to be more compact. In addition, it began shopping among freight forwarders to find the best rates, which varied depending on the forwarder's experience and its relationship with a particular steamship company.

Calabrese also learned how important it was for him to visit potential customers in Asia personally rather than relying on a sales manager. He said:

> The one thing that I found is that almost to an individual [Asian customers] are very keen on a personal association. If I were to give anybody advice, I would never send a second-level individual. Never send a marketing manager or sales manager; I would send a top manager. If your company isn't too large to prohibit it, I would send the president or chairman. On the other end, you are talking to the owner of a small distributor or the president of a small manufacturing company and you've got to meet them on an equal level. My limited experience is they are very cognizant of this; in other words, they are pretty much attuned to a president talking to a president. They also like to feel secure that they are dealing with someone who can make decisions.
>
> Another thing I found is that potential customers want to feel that you are financially secure and that you have sufficient funding to continue to work with them for a period of years, because it takes some time and some money on our end to get these people going.
>
> Follow-up is incredibly important. I heard all kinds of stories about American businessmen who would come over and spend a day and talk to potential customers and leave catalogues. Then the first time the potential customers would send a fax asking for information, they didn't hear from them for two weeks, and that just turns them right off.

Although Grieve faces high transport costs and significant competition from foreign companies as it works to penetrate foreign markets, top management is optimistic. The company has a good product. As Calabrese pointed out, "Our strength is that we are selling engineered products, using our forty-five years of expertise to build something for them." Through his experiences in Southeast Asia, Calabrese learned some valuable lessons about exporting successfully:

1. Know your product well. Many people who go to Asia from the United States know very little about their own product. In some cases, potential agents who have studied company brochures know more about the product than the company representative.
2. Learn about the competition in the foreign market and the potential sale for your products.
3. Advertise in the local market before going there to determine the interest level and to build contacts.
4. Work hard. Too many foreign visitors want to spend a lot of time playing golf or seeing the sights.
5. Build a strong response base back home. Most foreigners complain about poor factory backup, lengthy delays in getting correspondence answered, and delays in getting quotations.
6. Arrange for your own transportation and don't rely on the potential representative to solve your problems for you. That shows a lack of understanding of the local environment.
7. Provide someone at the home office who can be the principal contact for the representative. People need someone who will answer questions and provide assistance.

8. Learn the customs and business etiquette of the countries you visit. Once again, the U.S. Department of Commerce can provide assistance in this area.

9. Have the authority to make decisions and commit the company. If you are going to meet with the top person in the representative organization, be responsible yourself.

Calabrese obviously learned a great deal from his initial foray overseas. Once he gained experience in Asian markets, he expanded his export activity to other countries. This new way of doing business has created some challenges, but it also has helped Grieve be more successful and profitable.

INTRODUCTION

As the Grieve case demonstrates, successful exporting is a complex process. Once a company has identified the good or service it wants to sell, it must explore market opportunities, a process that entails a significant amount of market research. Next, it must develop a production or service development strategy, prepare the goods or services for market, determine the best means for transporting the goods or services to the market, sell the goods or services, and receive payment. All of these steps require careful planning and preparation. Without a separate export staff, a company must rely on specialists to move goods and services from one country to another, agents or distributors to sell the goods or services, and banks to collect payment.

As noted in Chapter 14, companies can have many strategies when entering foreign markets. In this chapter we will focus primarily on the export strategy (see Figure 17.1), drawing from strategic concepts discussed in Chapter 14. This chapter flows logically from Chapter 16 on marketing, because much of what we will discuss deals with elements in the marketing mix, especially channels of distribution.

As noted in Chapter 1, exporting is sending goods and services from one country to another, and importing is bringing goods and services into one country from another. Exports result in the receipt of money or claims on money, and imports result in the

Morocco's economy and distribution are typical of most emerging economies. Most people have little income to spend, but imports constitute a substantial portion of their expenditures. People largely buy in small individually owned shops. Here we see a Moroccan market in Marrakesh, where customers can find Moroccan goods as well as goods from all over the world.

FIGURE 17.1   Exporting & Importing in International Business

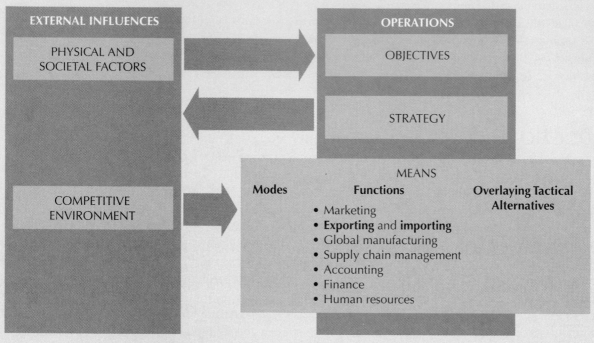

Exporting and importing are necessary functions for implementing companies' international strategies.

payment of money or claims on money. Typically, we focus on the export and import of goods, but services are becoming increasingly important in the global economy. The United States is the largest exporter of services in the world, and services trade worldwide were about $1.1 trillion in 1998, 22 percent of total world trade. For the remainder of the chapter, we will discuss export and import strategies, third-party intermediaries used to facilitate exports and imports, trade financing, and countertrade.

EXPORT STRATEGY

Entry mode depends on ownership advantages of the company, location advantages of the market, and internalization advantages of integrating transactions within the company.

A company's choice of entry mode to a foreign market depends on different factors, such as the ownership advantages of the company, location advantages of the market, and internalization advantages of integrating transactions within the company.[2] Ownership advantages are specific assets, international experience, and the ability to develop differentiated products. For example, Boeing capitalizes on its ownership advantage through the development of sophisticated aircraft; doing the same would be difficult for a new entrant to the market. Location advantages of the market are a combination of market potential (its size and growth potential) and investment risk. Internalization advantages are the benefits of holding on to specific assets or skills within the company and integrating them into its activities rather than licensing or selling them. For example, Grieve Corporation could have explored licensing its technology to manufacturers in Southeast Asia but preferred to maintain control over its technology and serve Southeast Asia through exports from its own U.S. plants.

In general, companies that have low levels of ownership advantages either do not enter foreign markets or use low-risk entry modes such as exporting. Exporting requires a lower level of investment than other modes, such as FDI, but it also offers a lower risk–return on sales. Exporting allows significant management operational control but does not provide as much marketing control, because the exporter is farther from the final consumer and often must deal with independent distributors abroad that control many of the marketing functions.[3]

However, the choice of exporting as an entry mode is not just a function of these ownership, location, and internalization advantages. It also must fit the company's overall strategy. Companies consider these questions before deciding to export.

- What does the company want to gain from exporting?
- Is exporting consistent with other company goals?
- What demands will exporting place on its key resources—management and personnel, production capacity, and financing—and how will these demands be met?
- Are the expected benefits worth the costs, or would company resources be better used for developing new domestic business?[4]

These are strategic questions that must take into account global concentration, synergies, and strategic motivations. Global concentration means that many global industries have only a few major players, and a company's strategy for penetrating a particular market might depend on the competition. If the competition is servicing markets through exporting, the company might be able to do okay with the same strategy. However, if the competition is servicing the local market through foreign direct investment, the company might not be as successful in the future if it only exports to the market. Global synergies arise when the company can share its expertise in areas such as R&D, marketing, and manufacturing with its operations abroad. Global strategic motivations are the reasons why a company might want to enter a market. For example, it might export to or invest in a market in a specific country as a means of combating a competitor in that market, not just because of specific market or profit potential.[5]

Exporting occurs for several good reasons. Companies can export goods and services to related companies such as branches and subsidiaries, or it can export to independent customers. Sometimes companies export final goods to its related companies overseas who then sell the goods to consumers. Other times, companies export semifinished goods that are used by its related companies in the manufacturing process. In many cases, however, the sale is to an outsider, and the exporter may sell directly to the buyer or indirectly through an intermediary.

CHARACTERISTICS OF EXPORTERS

Research conducted on the characteristics of exporters has resulted in two basic conclusions:

1. The *probability* of being an exporter increases with company size, as defined by revenues.

Companies that have lower levels of ownership advantages either do not enter foreign markets or use low-risk strategies such as exporting.

Strategic considerations affect the choice of exporting as an entry mode.

The probability of a company's being an exporter increases with the size of the company.

Export intensity is not positively correlated with company size.

2. Export *intensity*, the percentage of total revenues coming from exports, is not positively correlated with company size. The greater the percentage of exports to total revenues, the greater the intensity.

The first conclusion is based on the idea that small companies can grow in the domestic market without having to export, but large companies must export if they are to increase sales.[6] The exceptions are small high-tech or highly specialized companies that operate in market niches with a global demand and small companies that sell expensive capital equipment. In a study of Canadian companies, the two conclusions above were confirmed, but the author found that firm size was not the most important factor in determining the propensity to export, number of countries served, and export intensity. Factors such as the risk profile of management and industry factors were as important as size. In other words, managers who were more likely to take a risk were also more likely to engage in exporting, and companies were more likely to engage in exporting if they were operating in industries where the leading companies were exporters.[7]

The largest companies are the biggest exporters, but small companies are expanding their export capability.

The largest companies, such as General Electric, Boeing, and General Motors, are still the biggest exporters. But small companies are expanding their export capability. A survey of 10,000 small businesses in the United States found that 36 percent of the companies derived 5 percent or more of revenues from sales abroad, up from 27 percent in 1992.[8]

Grieve is a perfect example illustrating these concepts. Although considered a small company in terms of total sales, its export revenues are significant and are the key to its survival. It must export to maintain its market share abroad and its competitive position in the United States.

WHY COMPANIES EXPORT

Exporting
- **Expands sales**
- **Achieves economies of scale in production**
- **Is less risky than FDI**
- **Allows the company to diversify sales locations**

Companies export primarily to increase sales revenues. This is true for service companies as well as manufacturers. Many of the former, such as accountants, advertisers, lawyers, and consultants, export their services to meet the needs of clients working abroad. Grieve exported products to clients that had moved abroad. Companies that are capital and research intensive, such as biotechnology and pharmaceutical companies, must export to spread their R&D expenditures over a larger sales volume. R&D expenditures for those industries are so high as a percentage of sales that the companies have to increase revenues worldwide to be able to support the R&D efforts. Export sales can be a means of alleviating excess capacity in the domestic market. In addition, some companies export rather than invest abroad because of the perceived high risk of operating in foreign environments. Finally, many companies export to a variety of markets as a diversification strategy. For example, Grieve developed markets in Southeast Asia to expand its sales base and diversify its markets from strictly U.S. sales. Because economic growth is not the same in every market, export diversification can allow a company to take advantage of strong growth in one market to offset weak growth in another.

STAGES OF EXPORT DEVELOPMENT

Many companies begin exporting by accident rather than by design. Consequently, they tend to encounter a number of unforeseen problems. They also may never get a chance to see how important exports can be. For these reasons, developing a good export strategy is important. As Figure 17.2 shows, export development has three broad phases.[9]

FIGURE 17.2 Phases of Export Development

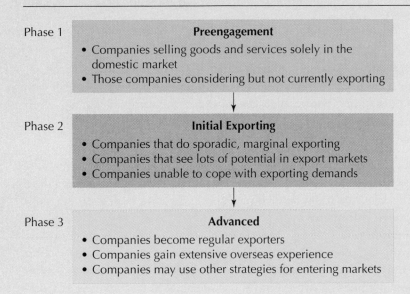

Phase 1

Preengagement
- Companies selling goods and services solely in the domestic market
- Those companies considering but not currently exporting

Phase 2

Initial Exporting
- Companies that do sporadic, marginal exporting
- Companies that see lots of potential in export markets
- Companies unable to cope with exporting demands

Phase 3

Advanced
- Companies become regular exporters
- Companies gain extensive overseas experience
- Companies may use other strategies for entering markets

As companies gain greater expertise and experience in exporting, they diversify their markets to countries that are farther away or have business environments that differ from that of their home country.

These phases have little to do with company size but rather on degree of export development—both large and small companies can be at any stage. In fact, more new companies are exporting sooner in their own life cycle because there is a new generation of entrepreneurs and managers with a keen awareness of international business. In addition, the ability to generate sales on the Internet is one reason why companies are exporting faster. As a company establishes a home page, Internet surfers from all over the world can have instant access to the company's product line and even initiate sales directly.

As companies move from initial to advanced exporting, they tend to export to more countries and expect exports as a percentage of total sales to grow.

POTENTIAL PITFALLS OF EXPORTING

To understand the elements in an export strategy, let's first identify the major problems that exporters often face. Aside from problems that are common to international business in general and not unique to exporting, such as language and other cultural factors, the following are mistakes companies new to exporting most frequently make.

1. Failure to obtain qualified export counseling and to develop a master international marketing plan before starting an export business
2. Insufficient commitment by top management to overcome the initial difficulties and financial requirements of exporting
3. Insufficient care in selecting overseas agents or distributors
4. Chasing orders from around the world instead of establishing a base of profitable operations and orderly growth
5. Neglecting export business when the domestic market booms
6. Failure to treat international distributors on an equal basis with their domestic counterparts
7. Unwillingness to modify products to meet other countries' regulations or cultural preferences

8. Failure to print service, sales, and warranty messages in locally understood languages
9. Failure to consider use of an export management company or other marketing intermediary when the company does not have the personnel to handle specialized export functions[10]

DESIGNING AN EXPORT STRATEGY

Designing an export strategy can help managers avoid making the costly mistakes mentioned above. Figure 17.3 shows an international business transaction chain, which we'll discuss in the remainder of the chapter. A successful export (and import) strategy must take each element of the transaction chain into consideration.

To establish a successful export strategy, management must

In designing an export strategy, managers must
- **Assess export potential**
- **Get expert counseling**
- **Select market or markets**
- **Formulate and implement an export strategy**

1. *Assess the company's export potential by examining its opportunities and resources.* First of all, the company needs to determine if there is a market for its goods and services. Next it needs to make sure it has enough production capacity to deliver the goods or services to foreign customers.

2. *Obtain expert counseling on exporting.* Most governments provide assistance for their domestic companies, although the extent of commitment varies by country. For U.S. companies, the best place to start is with the nearest Export Assistance Center of the International Trade Administration (ITA) of the U.S. Department of Commerce. Such assistance is invaluable in helping an exporter get started. In the Grieve case, for example, Calabrese used a lot of information provided by the U.S. government to learn about Asian markets. Other government agencies also assist exporters. As a company's export plan increases in scope, it probably will want to secure specialized assistance from banks, lawyers, freight forwarders, export management companies, export trading companies, and others.

3. *Select a market or markets.* This key part of the export strategy may be done passively or actively. In the former, the company learns of markets by responding to requests from abroad that result from trade shows, advertisements, or articles in trade publications. Grieve's Calabrese took a more active approach by selecting Southeast Asia as an area for export development as a result of a seminar he attended featuring the U.S. ambassadors to the ASEAN countries. A company also can determine the markets to which products like its own are currently being exported. For example, in the U.S. setting, U.S. Census Trade Statistics identifies the markets for different classifications of exports, and the National Trade Data Bank (NTDB) provides specific industry reports for different countries. The NTDB is updated monthly, so potential exporters can get the most recent studies. Similar forms of assistance are found in other countries.

4. *Formulate and implement an export strategy.* In this step, a company considers its export objectives (immediate and long term), specific tactics it will use, a schedule of activities and deadlines to achieve its objectives, and the allocation of resources to accomplish the different activities. Then it implements the strategy by getting the goods and services to foreign consumers.

A detailed export business plan is an essential element in implementing an effective export strategy. Table 17.1 provides a sample of such a plan. The development of the plan depends on the nature of the company. For a small or medium-size company, the

FIGURE 17.3   International Business Transaction Chain

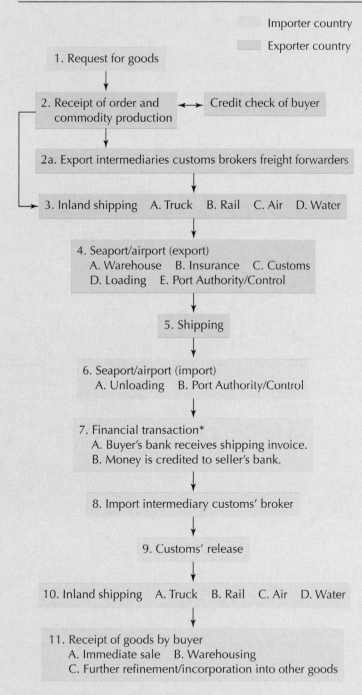

In between negotiating a sale and delivering/receiving the goods and services, both the exporter and the importer need to consider a variety of shipping and financial issues.

Importer country
Exporter country

1. Request for goods

2. Receipt of order and commodity production ⟷ Credit check of buyer

2a. Export intermediaries customs brokers freight forwarders

3. Inland shipping   A. Truck   B. Rail   C. Air   D. Water

4. Seaport/airport (export)
   A. Warehouse   B. Insurance   C. Customs
   D. Loading   E. Port Authority/Control

5. Shipping

6. Seaport/airport (import)
   A. Unloading   B. Port Authority/Control

7. Financial transaction*
   A. Buyer's bank receives shipping invoice.
   B. Money is credited to seller's bank.

8. Import intermediary customs' broker

9. Customs' release

10. Inland shipping   A. Truck   B. Rail   C. Air   D. Water

11. Receipt of goods by buyer
    A. Immediate sale   B. Warehousing
    C. Further refinement/incorporation into other goods

*Financial transactions occur at every stage of this process.

Source: Export America, Vol. 1, November 1999, p. 17.

TABLE 17.1 AN EXPORT BUSINESS PLAN

A detailed export business plan is an essential element in implementing an effective export strategy. The plan must consider company resources, identify specific markets, and establish specific plans for dealing with marketing, legal, manufacturing, personnel, and financial elements. Finally, it must include a schedule for implementing the plan.

I. Executive summary
   A. Key elements of the plan
   B. Description of business and target markets
   C. Brief description of management team
   D. Summary of financial projections

II. Business history
   A. History of company
   B. Products-services offered and their unique advantages
   C. Domestic-market experience
   D. Foreign-market experience
   E. Production facilities
   F. Personnel—international experience and expertise
   G. Industry structure, competition

III. Market research
   A. Target countries
      1. Primary
      2. Secondary
      3. Tertiary
   B. Market conditions in target countries
      1. Existing demand
      2. Competition
      3. Strengths and weaknesses of the economy—barriers to entry, etc.

IV. Marketing decisions
   A. Distribution strategies
      1. Indirect exporting
      2. Direct exporting
      3. Documentation
      4. Direct investment, strategic alliances
   B. Pricing strategy
   C. Promotion strategy

V. Legal decisions
   A. Agent/distributor agreements
   B. Patent, trademark, copyright protection
   C. Export/import regulations
   D. ISO 9000
   E. Dispute resolution

VI. Manufacturing and operations
   A. Location of production facilities for exports
   B. Capacity of existing facilities
   C. Plans for expansion
   D. Product modification necessary to adapt to local environment

VII. Personnel strategies
   A. Personnel needed to manage exports
   B. Experience and expertise of existing personnel
   C. Training needs of existing personnel
   D. Hiring needs in the short term and long term

VIII. Financial decisions
   A. Pro forma financial statements and projected cash flows assuming export activity
   B. Identification of key assumptions
   C. Current sources of funding—private and bank funding
   D. Financial needs and future sources of funding
   E. Tax consequences of export activity
   F. Potential risk and sources of protection

IX. Implementation schedule

plan usually gets the attention of the top levels of management, as was the case with Grieve Corporation. Larger companies might establish a separate export department to deal with the export of all products. Research has shown that commitment precedes success in exporting, and the development of an export department is one indicator of commitment by top management.[11] In Chapter 15, we discussed several different organizational forms that MNEs might adopt, so the export function might be allocated to an international division, the different lines of business, or the regional-national organizations. But whether the company is large or small, or whether the export function is centralized into an export department or diffused into different product or regional organizations, it is important to follow the steps outlined in Table 17.1 so that an effective strategy is carried out.

IMPORT STRATEGY

So far we've talked mostly about exporters and exporting. Importing is the bringing of goods and services into a country and results in the importer paying money to the exporter in the foreign country. Traditional goods imports are fairly easy to understand. When Nissan North America brings the new Infinity XVL sedan from Nissan Japan to the U.S. market, it creates an import. In addition to merchandise imports, such as the Infinity XVL sedan, there are a variety of service imports. SAP software, from the German software company of the same name, is a service (even though it comes in a package, software *is* considered a service). Foreign banks such as Deutsche Bank that provide financial services to U.S. customers also create service imports.

There are two basic types of imports: those that provide industrial and consumer goods and services to individuals and companies that are not related to the foreign exporter and those that provide intermediate goods and services to companies that are part of the firm's global supply chain. Why import in the first place? Companies import goods and services because they can be supplied to the domestic market at a cheaper price and better quality than competing goods manufactured in the domestic market. In the case of the Infinity XVL sedan, Nissan manufactures some of its product line in the United States, but some of its product line is manufactured in Japan and exported to the United States. The Infinity XVL fits in the latter category. As we will see in Chapter 18, there are strategic reasons to manufacture some products in one location and others in another location. Specialization of production and export to markets around the world is more efficient than manufacturing every product in every market. Nike buys shoes manufactured in several Asian countries, including Korea, Taiwan, China, Thailand, Indonesia, and Vietnam because of the cheaper cost. It would be impossible to manufacture the same product in an industrial country and be able to sell it at a reasonable price because of the relatively high labor costs. Finally, companies import products that are not available in the local market. For example, North America imports bananas from tropical climates because the climate of North America is not suitable for growing bananas. Were it not for imports, nobody in North American could consume fresh bananas.

There is not as much research done on import strategies as is the case for export strategies. However, there are three broad types of importers:

1. Those that are looking for any product around the world that they can import. They might specialize in certain types of products—such as sports equipment or household items—but they are simply scanning the globe and looking for any product that will generate positive cash flow for them.
2. Those that are looking at foreign sourcing to get their products at the cheapest price. A small Utah-based company called For Every Body (www.foreverybody. com) started out selling a variety of bath and body products. Soon, however, it began to branch out into decorative products for homes, so it identified manufacturers in China that could supply it with specific products for its stores.
3. Those that use foreign sourcing as part of their global supply chain. This strategy will be discussed in Chapter 18.

The import process is illustrated in Figure 17.3, and it basically mirrors the export process. In fact, the export business plan in Table 17.1 could easily be adapted to an import business plan. Managers need to research potential markets, both in terms of the

---

Two basic types of imports

- **Industrial and consumer goods to independent individuals and companies**
- **Intermediate goods and services that are part of the firm's global supply chain**

Three broad types of importers

- **Looking for any product around the world to import and sell**
- **Looking for foreign sourcing to get their products at the cheapest price**
- **Using foreign sourcing as part of their global supply chain**

countries themselves and the suppliers. Then they need to determine the legal ramifications of importing the products, both in terms of the products themselves and the countries from which they come. Managers also need to deal with third-party intermediaries such as freight forwarders and customs agents, and they need to arrange financing for the purchase.

Importing requires a certain degree of expertise in dealing with institutions and documentation, which a company may not have. Consequently, a company may elect to work through an **import broker**. The import broker obtains various governmental permissions and other clearances before forwarding necessary paperwork to the carrier that is to deliver the goods to the importer. Import brokers in the United States are certified as such by the U.S. Customs Service to perform the functions necessary to bring products into the country.

An import broker is an intermediary who helps an importer clear customs.

THE ROLE OF CUSTOMS AGENCIES

When importing goods into any country, a company must be totally familiar with the customs operations of the importing country. In this context, "customs" are the country's import and export procedures and restrictions, not its cultural aspects. The primary duties of the U.S. Customs Service (www.customs.ustreas.gov) are the assessment and collection of all duties, taxes, and fees on imported merchandise, the enforcement of customs and related laws, and the administration of certain navigation laws and treaties. As a major enforcement organization, it also deals with smuggling operations.[12]

Customs agencies assess and collect duties and ensure import regulations are adhered to.

An importer needs to know the way to clear goods, the duties to pay, and the special laws that exist regarding the importation of products. On the procedural side, when merchandise reaches the port of entry, the importer must file documents with customs officials, who assign a tentative value and tariff classification to the merchandise. The U.S. government has over 10,000 tariff classifications, and approximately 60 percent of them are subject to interpretation; that is, a particular product could fit more than one classification. It is almost an art form for companies to figure out the tariff classification that will give them the lowest possible tariff. Then customs officials examine the goods to determine whether there are any restrictions on their importation. If there are restrictions, the goods may be rejected and not allowed to enter the country. If the goods are allowed to enter, the importer pays the duty and the goods are released. The amount of the duty depends on the product's country of origin, the type of product, and other factors.

A broker or other import consultant can help an importer minimize import duties by

Ways a customs broker can help
- **Value products to help them qualify for more favorable duty treatment**
- **Qualify for duty refunds through drawback provisions**
- **Defer duties by using bonded warehouses and foreign trade zones**
- **Limit liability by properly marking an import's country of origin**

- *Valuing products in such a way that they qualify for more favorable duty treatment.* Different product categories have different duties. For example, finished goods typically have a higher duty than do parts and components.
- *Qualifying for duty refunds through drawback provisions.* Some exporters use in their manufacturing process imported parts and components on which they paid a duty. In the United States, the drawback provision allows domestic exporters to apply for a 99-percent refund of the duty paid on the imported goods, as long as they become part of the exporter's product.
- *Deferring duties by using bonded warehouses and foreign trade zones.* Companies do not have to pay duties on imports stored in bonded warehouses and foreign trade zones until the goods are removed for sale or used in a manufacturing process.

Drawback provisions allow U.S. exporters to apply for a refund of 99 percent of the duty paid on imported components, provided they are used in the manufacture of goods that are exported.

- *Limiting liability by properly marking an import's country of origin.* Because governments assess duties on imports based in part on the country of origin, a mistake in marking the country of origin could result in a higher import duty. For example, in the United States, if a product or its container is not properly marked when it enters the country, the product could be assigned a marking duty equal to 10 percent of the customs value. This would be in addition to the normal tariff.[13]

DOCUMENTATION

When a shipment arrives at a port, the importer must file specific documents with the port director in order to *take title* to the shipment. (Take title means the importer receives the products without purchasing them—without laying out any money.) These documents are of two different types: those that determine whether customs will release the shipment and those that contain information for duty assessment and statistical purposes. The specific documents customs require vary by country but include an entry manifest, a commercial invoice, and a packing list. For example, the exporter's commercial invoice contains information such as the port of entry to which the merchandise is destined, information on the importer and exporter, a detailed description of the merchandise including its purchase price, the currency used for the sale, and the country of origin.

Importers must submit to customs documents that determine whether the shipment is released and what duties are assessed.

THIRD-PARTY INTERMEDIARIES

As noted in Figure 17.3, both exporters and importers use a variety of third-party intermediaries—companies that facilitate the trade of goods but that are not related to either the exporter or the importer. A company that either exports or is planning to export must decide whether its internal staff will handle certain essential activities or if it will contract other companies. Regardless, the following functions must occur:

Third-party intermediaries—companies that facilitate the trade of goods but that are not related to either the exporter or the importer

1. Stimulate sales, obtain orders, and do market research
2. Make credit investigations and perform payment-collection activities
3. Handle foreign traffic and shipping
4. Act as support for the company's overall sales, distribution, and advertising staff

Handling these functions internally can be costly and can require expertise a company doesn't have. Most companies initially use external specialists and intermediary organizations to assume some or all of these functions, although a company later may develop in-house capabilities to perform them. Specialists are useful for such duties as preparing export documents, preparing customs documents in the importing country, and identifying the best means of transportation. Most companies can benefit at some time from using an intermediary organization. Some of these act as agents on behalf of the exporter, and some take title to the goods and sell them abroad. Others perform certain specialized aspects of the export process. For example, a freight forwarder is responsible for moving the products from domestic to foreign markets.

Companies use external specialists for exporting before developing internal capabilities.

Exporting may be either direct or indirect. Direct exports are goods and services sold to an independent party outside of the exporter's home country. Indirect exports are sold to an intermediary in the domestic market who then sells the goods in the export market. Services are more likely to be sold in a direct basis, but goods are exported both directly and indirectly.

Direct exports—goods and services are sold to an independent party outside of the exporter's home country

Indirect exports—goods and services are sold to an intermediary in the domestic market who then sells the goods in the export market

DIRECT SELLING

Direct selling involves sales representatives, agents, distributors, or retailers.

Exporters undertake direct selling to give them greater control over the marketing function and to earn higher profits. **Direct selling** is when an exporter sells through sales representatives, to distributors, to foreign retailers, or to final end users. A **sales representative** sells products in foreign markets on a commission basis, without taking title to the goods. The sales representative may have exclusive rights to sell in a particular geographic area or may have to compete with other sales representatives that represent the firm. It is more common for sales representatives to have exclusive rights to a territory. For example, Grieve's sales representatives operated on an exclusive basis in their respective markets.

A sales representative usually operates on a commission basis.

A **distributor** in a foreign country is a merchant who purchases the products from the manufacturer and sells them at a profit. Distributors usually carry a stock of inventory and service the product. They also usually deal with retailers rather than end users in the market.

A distributor is a merchant who purchases the products from the manufacturer and sells them at a profit.

Companies should consider the following points about each potential foreign sales representative or distributor:

- The size and capabilities of its sales force
- Its sales record
- An analysis of its territory
- Its current product mix
- Its facilities and equipment
- Its marketing policies
- Its customer profile
- The principles it represents and the importance of the inquiring company to its overall business
- Its promotional strategies[14]

A company that has sufficient financial and managerial resources and decides to export directly rather than working through an intermediary must set up a solid organization. This organization may take any number of forms ranging from a separate international division, to a separate international company, to full integration of international and domestic activities. Whatever the form, there commonly is an international sales force separate from the domestic sales force because of the different types of expertise required in dealing in foreign markets.

Exporters can also sell directly to foreign retailers. Usually, these products are limited to consumer lines, but the growth of large retail chains around the world has facilitated the export of products to the large chains, which gives the exporter instant coverage to a wide area. Exporters can also sell directly to end users. This can be done through catalogs or at trade shows, or the sales can be in response to foreign buyers getting a hold of company brochures or responding to advertisements in trade publications.

DIRECT EXPORTING THROUGH THE INTERNET AND ELECTRONIC COMMERCE

Internet marketing allows all companies—both large and small—to engage in direct marketing quickly, easily, and cheaply.

Electronic commerce is an important way for companies to export their products to end users. It is especially important for SMEs (small and medium-size enterprises) that can't afford to establish an elaborate sales network internationally. E-commerce is easy to

Ethical Dilemmas and Social Responsibility
IS DEMAND ALWAYS JUST CAUSE TO EXPORT?

There are several ethical issues in exporting. Two of them are the exportation of hazardous substances and whether or not to sell sensitive technology to countries that could be or are enemies to the exporter's domestic country. Concerning the exportation of hazardous substances, especially pesticides and chemicals, most people feel that exporting companies should accept the ethical norms of a host country. However, regulations concerning pesticides are more lax in many developing countries than they are in industrial countries. So exporting pesticides or harmful chemicals that are illegal in a company's home country but not in the host country raises an ethical dilemma. There is a major argument over the concept of prior informed consent (PIC), which would require each exporter of a banned or restricted chemical to obtain through its home-country government the express consent of the importing country to receive the banned or restricted substance. Countries favoring the PIC concept argue that many developing countries are not adequately informed of the danger of certain chemicals and therefore need the assistance of industrial countries. Those against PIC argue that this principle infringes on the national sovereignty of importing countries and replaces their ethical norms with those of the exporting country.[15]

Second, governments often control the export of so-called sensitive technology to certain countries, but there are a number of companies that try to bypass the controls and sell the technology to whomever will buy it. Before the Iron Curtain fell in 1989, Toshiba shipped to the former Soviet Union sensitive technology that could be used in submarine warfare. The company transshipped products through different ports in order to disguise the sale and shield itself from prosecution. However, this illegal activity was eventually uncovered. Another example of the exportation of sensitive technology involves the arming of Saddam Hussein prior to the Persian Gulf War. A British company was found guilty of exporting a large gun, disguised as industrial pipes, that could be used as an offensive weapon. The company lied about the nature of the export but eventually was found out. In addition, German companies were guilty of selling to Libya chemicals that could be used in chemical warfare. In these cases, documents were falsified to keep the authorities from finding out the transactions' true nature.

Sometimes shippers lie to freight forwarders about the nature of their products. One freight forwarder was working with a company that was shipping large drums to Sweden by air. The forwarder asked the shipper if the drums contained hazardous materials, and the shipper said no. In fact, unfortunately, the drums contained a very toxic material. This substance leaked through the drum and ate through the bottom of a 747 just as it was landing in Sweden.

start, it provides faster and cheaper delivery of information, it provides quick feedback on new products, it helps to improve customer service, it is available to a global audience, it helps to level the field of competition, it can be a strategic tool to access different markets, it's cheaper than a phone call, and it helps establish electronic data interchange (EDI) with both suppliers and customers.[16]

Through Internet exporting, companies can establish home pages in different languages to target different audiences. In the case of industrial products, they can install software to track hits to their home page and then send sales reps to potential customers or have local distributors contact them. In the case of consumer products, companies such as J. Crew can sell their products directly to consumers all over the world. Internet marketing is a direct form of marketing that is exploding in importance.

INDIRECT SELLING

In **indirect selling**, the exporter sells goods directly to or through an independent domestic intermediary in the exporter's home country that exports the products to foreign markets. The major types of indirect intermediaries are the **export management company (EMC)**; the **export trading company (ETC)**; export agents, merchants, or remarketers; and piggyback marketers. EMCs and ETCs sometimes act as agents operating on a commission and sometimes take title to the merchandise. The terms *EMC* and *ETC* are sometimes used interchangeably, especially for the smaller intermediaries. The larger intermediaries, however, are almost always referred to as export trading companies or simply trading companies because they typically deal with both exports and imports. We will discuss both types of intermediaries.

EXPORT MANAGEMENT COMPANIES

An EMC acts as the export arm of a manufacturer.

An EMC usually acts as the export arm of a manufacturer—although it also can deal in imports—and often uses the manufacturer's own letterhead in communicating with foreign sales representatives and distributors. The EMC primarily obtains orders for its clients' products through the selection of appropriate markets, distribution channels, and promotion campaigns. It collects, analyzes, and furnishes credit information and advice regarding foreign accounts and payment terms. The EMC also may take care of export documents, arrange transportation (including the consolidation of shipments among multiple clients to reduce costs), set up patent and trademark protection in foreign countries, and assist in establishing alternative forms of doing business, such as licensing or joint ventures.[17]

EMCs operate on a contractual basis, usually as an agent of the exporter.

EMCs operate on a contractual basis and provide exclusive representation in a well-defined foreign territory. The contract specifies pricing, credit and financial policies, promotional services, and basis for payment. An EMC might operate on a commission basis for sales (unless it takes title to the merchandise) and a retainer for other services. EMCs usually concentrate on complementary and noncompetitive products so that they can present a more complete product line to a limited number of foreign importers.

Most EMCs are small, entrepreneurial ventures that specialize by product, function, or market area.

In the United States, most EMCs are small, entrepreneurial ventures that tend to specialize by product, function, or market area. Although EMCs perform an important function for companies that need their expertise, a manufacturer that uses an EMC may lose control over foreign sales because they are passing off that responsibility to an inde-

Looking to the Future
HOW WILL TECHNOLOGY AFFECT EXPORTING?

Exporting continues to differ among countries in terms of its importance in generating GDP and, therefore, jobs. When the global economy is growing and barriers come down, exports tend to increase. When the world is in an economic slowdown, nontariff barriers to trade combine with low demand to slow the rate of export growth. Predictions of export activity are directly tied to predictions of economic growth. Future economic growth is tied to efforts to reduce trade barriers. Examples of these efforts are the EU and NAFTA. When barriers to trade rise, exporters from large countries such as the United States pull back their exporting efforts and focus on domestic markets.

Advances in transportation and communications will continue to facilitate export growth and make it easier for companies to reach international markets. One example of advances in communication is electronic data interchange, the electronic movement of information. As freight forwarders continue to automate, they become more able to transmit documents electronically, which will reduce border delays in getting goods to market. Also, advances in communications will allow shippers to track shipments more accurately so that they can predict when the shipments will arrive in port to be claimed by the importer.

An area in which companies probably will receive little relief in the next few years is governmental assistance, especially in the financial area. Most industrial countries have serious federal budget deficits, a result of economic slowdown and reduced tax receipts, and so have been forced to privatize and cut governmental services. One of those areas affected will be exports. In the United States, cutbacks in funding to the Department of Commerce, the SBA, and the Ex-Im Bank have made it more difficult for exporters to get assistance, especially access to loan guarantees. Predictions say this situation will not improve soon; pressure will continue on the small exporter to penetrate markets alone.

One of the major developments in the future is going to be the use of the Internet for companies to engage in direct exporting. E-commerce will bring producers and consumers from all over the world in ways and at a level never before seen. Small and medium-size companies that cannot afford to have a large export staff will be able to generate Internet sales relatively easily and cheaply. This will be one of the major developments in exporting and importing.

pendent party. If the EMC does not actively promote the product, the company will not generate many exports. The manufacturer needs to balance the desire for control with the cost of performing the export functions directly.[18]

Rizzo Company of Scottsdale, Arizona, is an example of an EMC that takes title to products. The company purchases manufactured goods and sells them worldwide. In many respects, Rizzo Company is another domestic customer for the manufacturer. It takes title to the goods and demands a two-year exclusive agreement to export the goods, promising in return not to represent competing products in the assigned foreign market. Then Rizzo takes all of the risk and earns the return in export markets.

Last Concepts of Phoenix, Arizona, is an EMC that does not take title to the products as does Rizzo. Last Concepts locates foreign customers for a manufacturer, negotiates prices, ensures that the goods meet requirements for warranties and labeling, assists in getting export licenses, arranges the services of freight forwarders, and manages the letter of credit process with the customer's bank. In return, Last Concepts charges a fee or commission for its services.[19]

EXPORT TRADING COMPANIES

ETCs resemble EMCs, and the terms are often used interchangeably. ETCs operate more on the basis of demand than of supply. ETCs are like independent distributors that match up buyers and sellers. ETCs find out what foreign customers want and then identify different domestic suppliers for the products. Rather than representing a manufacturer, an ETC looks for as many manufacturers as it can find to supply overseas customers. Because ETCs could control the foreign distribution of products and collaborate with producers of competing products, they could be open to antitrust allegations.

In 1982, the U.S. government enacted the Export Trading Company Act, which removed some of the antitrust obstacles to the creation of ETCs in the United States. It was hoped that ETCs would lead to greater exports of U.S. goods and services. The legislation allows banks to make equity investments in commercial ventures that qualify as ETCs, something that would not be possible in absence of the legislation. The Federal Reserve Board must approve these applications before the bank can start export operations. Many of the banks concentrate on customers in their geographical market and in parts of the world in which they already have a good banking network. ETCs are important to banks, because banks provide the financial side of the export business, so being able to invest in an ETC gives the banks access to more of the business than just the financing side.

NON-U.S. TRADING COMPANIES

As Table 17.2 notes, there are 19 trading companies in the Fortune Global 500 companies ranked according to revenues. These 19 companies ranked third in total revenues of the industries included in the Global 500 survey. Two things are interesting about Table 17.2. One is that there are no U.S. trading companies on the list. In fact, only four countries are represented: Japan (11 companies), South Korea (3 companies), Germany (3 companies), and China (2 companies). The second interesting point is that several of the trading companies suffered losses in 1998. In fact, the trading companies group ranked fourth in total profits, even though it was third in revenues. In the United States, there is a large number of small trading companies, while the trading companies from other countries are among the biggest companies in their respective countries and in the world. Of the top 10 largest companies in the world in terms of revenues, 3 are Japanese trading companies.[20] Let's see why Japan dominates the trading company industry.

The *sogo shosha*, the Japanese equivalent word for trading company, can trace its roots back to the late nineteenth century, when Japan embarked on an aggressive modernization process. At that time, the trading companies were called *zaibatsu*—large, family-owned businesses composed of financial and manufacturing companies usually held together by a large holding company. These companies were very powerful, so U.S. General Douglas MacArthur (sent to Japan to institute New Deal reforms after WWII) broke them up and made many of their activities illegal. However, the families and relationships did not go away, so the *zaibatsu* reformed into the *keiretsu* organizations,

---

ETCs are like EMCs, but they tend to operate on the basis of demand rather than of supply. They identify suppliers to fill orders in overseas markets.

ETCs in the United States are exempt from antitrust provisions to allow them to collaborate with other companies to penetrate foreign markets.

The largest trading companies in the world are from Japan, South Korea, Germany, and China, not the United States.

Japanese trading companies are known as *sogo shoshas*; they are the trading arms of the large *keiretsus*—Japanese business groups that are networks of manufacturing, service, and financial companies.

TABLE 17.2		TOP GLOBAL TRADING COMPANIES, 1998				
RANK	COMPANY	COUNTRY	1998 REVENUE ($ MILLIONS)	1998 PROFITS ($ MILLIONS)	PROFIT % OF REVENUE	RANK
1	Mitsui	Japan	109,373	233	0	7
2	Itochu	Japan	108,749	(267)	(0)	15
3	Mitsubishi	Japan	107,184	244	0	6
4	Marubeni	Japan	93,569	(921)	(1)	17
5	Sumitomo	Japan	89,021	(102)	(0)	14
6	Nissho Iwai	Japan	67,742	(771)	(1)	18
7	Veba Group	Germany	43,407	1,330	3	1
8	Tomen	Japan	30,935	22	0	8
9	Samsung	South Korea	28,839	13	0	11
10	Viag	Germany	27,922	661	2	2
11	Nichimen	Japan	25,476	(170)	(1)	16
12	Hyundai	South Korea	24,373	6	0	12
13	Kanematsu	Japan	17,199	(325)	(2)	19
14	Sinochem	China	13,793	68	0	5
15	Toyota Tsusho	Japan	13,519	7	0	10
16	LG International	South Korea	13,388	9	0	9
17	Cofco	China	12,402	93	1	4
18	Metallgesellschaft	Germany	11,991	151	1	3
19	Kawasho	Japan	9,179	(7)	(0)	13

Source: From *Fortune,* 8/2/99, p. F-21. © 1999 TIME, INC. Reprinted by permission.

meeting the letter of the law even if they didn't exactly meet the spirit of the law. However, there was greater concern after World War II about the reconstruction of Japan than of eliminating all vestiges of the past, so the *keiretsus* linking financial, manufacturing, and trading companies started up again.

When these trading companies were first organized after World War II, their primary functions became handling paperwork for import and export transactions, financing imports and exports, and providing transportation and storage services. However, their operations expanded significantly beyond exporting to include investing in production and processing facilities, establishing fully integrated sales systems for certain products, expanding marketing activities, and developing large bases for the integrated processing of raw materials.[21]

An example of the type of activities that the Japanese trading companies pursue is the joint purchase by Itochu Corporation and Arco of the western U.S. coal operations of Coastal States Energy Company. Although Itochu holds a 35-percent equity interest in the coal operations, located primarily in Utah (U.S.), it uses its marketing expertise in Japan and elsewhere in the Pacific Rim to sell the coal.[22] Just as the Japanese trading companies are part of the larger corporate relationships known as *keiretsu*, Korean trading companies are part of the large Korean business groups called *chaebol*. Although the Korean trading companies modeled themselves after their Japanese counterparts, there are some differences. The *sogo shoshas* are loosely linked to the rest of the *keiretsu*, while the companies in the *chaebol* are tightly linked to each other, with a high degree of intercompany transactions with each other and with the trading companies. The *sogo shoshas* are not only more loosely linked to their *keiretsus* but also more professionally managed, with the *chaebol* still very dependent on family patriarchs. The Japanese trading companies are big in commodities and are heavily involved in triangular trading. For example, a Japanese company may sell Latin American commodities to the United States, whereas the Korean companies derive about 70 percent of their revenues from Korean exports.[23] However, the *chaebol* are trying hard to challenge the *sogo shoshas* in the trading company market.

PIGGYBACK EXPORTS

Sometimes an exporter can use another exporter as an intermediary. For example, a company may agree to supply products to a foreign distributor even though it does not produce the entire range of products. Then it might look for other manufacturers to fill the gaps in the product line. In this way, the second manufacturer becomes an exporter indirectly by using the first exporter's distribution channels.

FOREIGN FREIGHT FORWARDERS

To assist in the transport of goods from one country to another, companies usually employ the services of a **freight forwarder**, known as the travel agents of cargo. A freight forwarder is an agent for the exporter in moving cargo to an overseas destination.[24] The freight forwarder is used for both imports and exports, because one company's exports is another company's imports. Even export management companies and other types of trading companies often use the specialized services of foreign freight forwarders.

The foreign freight forwarder is the largest export intermediary in terms of value and weight of products managed. However, the services it offers are more limited than those of an EMC. Once an exporter makes a foreign sale, it hires the freight forwarder to obtain the best routing and means of transportation based on space availability, speed, and cost. The freight forwarder will get the products from the manufacturing facility to the air or ocean terminal and then overseas. The forwarder secures space on planes or ships and necessary storage prior to shipment, reviews the letter of credit, obtains export licenses, and prepares necessary shipping documents. It also may advise on packing and labeling, purchase transportation insurance, repack shipments damaged en route, and warehouse products, which saves the exporter the capital investment of warehousing. However, the freight forwarder does not take title to the goods or act as a sales representative in a foreign market. It simply deals with the preparation and transportation of goods.

The freight forwarder usually charges the exporter a percentage of the shipment value, plus a minimum charge dependent on the number of services provided. The forwarder also receives a brokerage fee from the carrier. Despite these costs, using a freight forwarder is usually less costly for an exporter than providing the service internally, because most companies, especially the SMEs, find it difficult to set up a full-time

Chaebol—Korean business groups that are similar to *keiretsu* and also contain a trading company as part of the group

Piggyback exports are products exported by a company through another manufacturer's channels of distribution.

A foreign freight forwarder is an export or import specialist dealing in the movement of goods from producer to consumer.

The typical freight forwarder is the largest export intermediary in terms of value and weight handled.

department to deal with freight issues and keep up with shipping regulations. The forwarder also can get exporters shipping space more easily (because of its close relationship with carriers) and consolidate shipments to obtain lower rates.

Freight forwarders, especially the smaller ones, sometimes specialize in mode used—such as surface freight, ocean freight, and airfreight—and geographical area served. Increasingly, however, the freight forwarders handle many modes—truck, rail, and airfreight, for example.[25] The movement of goods across different modes from origin to destination is known as **intermodal transportation**.

Ocean freight is the cheapest way to move merchandise, but it also is the slowest. Even though it still dominates global trade, its position is eroding somewhat. Ocean freight rates are based on space first, and weight second. Rate schedules also differ depending on the ports and the direction the goods travel. For example, different rates apply to shipments from the United States to Germany and to shipments from Germany to the United States. Forwarders help manufacturers get the best contract and help prepare the products for export. Exporters can load merchandise in a container for shipment overseas, or they can rely on a freight forwarder to consolidate their shipment with others. As mentioned in the opening case, Grieve's president believes in getting quotes from different freight forwarders when booking space on cargo ships. Even large companies compare rates. The person who handles the export of Shell Oil Company's nonhazardous lubricating oils and greases negotiates rates with the steamship lines himself, but if the forwarders' steamship line rates are lower, he will use them instead.[26]

Three trends favor the airfreight business over ocean freight: more frequent shipments, lighter-weight shipments, and higher-value shipments. The trend toward global manufacturing, as we will discuss in Chapter 18, and shrinking product cycles has created a boom in airfreight traffic. Airfreight is much more effective in accomplishing these objectives than is ocean freight. Higher-value shipments are more likely to use airfreight as long as they are not too bulky, because the exporter wants to get the product in the hands of the importer as soon as possible and collect on the sale. In most cases the exporter cannot get paid for the sale until delivery.

DOCUMENTATION

Freight forwarders also can help exporters fill out exporting documents. One of these documents is an **export license**. Each country determines whether domestic products or products transshipped through its borders can be exported to certain countries. In the United States, an exporter needs to check with the U.S. Department of Commerce to determine if its products can be shipped under a general license or if they must be exported under an individually validated license (IVL). For example, exports of certain high-tech products might be restricted for national security reasons, so an exporter must apply for an IVL to determine whether the exportation is permitted.

Of the many documents that must be completed, some of the most important (excluding financial documents, which we discuss in the next section) follow:

- A *pro forma invoice* is an invoice, like a letter of intent, from the exporter to the importer outlining the selling terms, price, and delivery if the goods are actually shipped. If the importer likes the terms and conditions, it will send a purchase order and arrange for payment. At that point, the exporter can issue a commercial invoice.

Different transportation modes—surface freight (truck and rail), ocean freight, airfreight

Intermodal transportation—the movement across different modes from origin to destination

Factors favoring airfreight over ocean freight: more frequent shipments, lighter-weight shipments, higher-value shipments

An export license allows products to be shipped to specific countries.

Key export documents are pro forma invoice, commercial invoice, bill of lading, consular invoice, certificate of origin, shipper's export declaration, and export packing list.

- A *commercial invoice* is a bill for the goods from the buyer to the seller. It contains a description of the goods, the address of buyer and seller, and delivery and payment terms. Many governments use this form to assess duties.

- A *bill of lading* is a receipt for goods delivered to the common carrier for transportation, a contract for the services rendered by the carrier, and a document of title.

- A *consular invoice* sometimes is required by countries as a means of monitoring imports. Governments can use the consular invoice to monitor prices of imports and to generate revenue for the embassies that issue the consular invoice.

- A *certificate of origin* indicates where the products originate and usually is validated by an external source, such as the chamber of commerce. It helps countries determine the specific tariff schedule for imports.

- A *shipper's export declaration* is used by the exporter's government to monitor exports and to compile trade statistics.

- An *export packing list* itemizes the material in each individual package, indicates the type of package, and is attached to the outside of the package. The shipper or freight forwarder, and sometimes customs officials, use the packing list to determine the nature of the cargo and whether the correct cargo is being shipped.

EXPORT FINANCING

Financial issues related to exporting:
- **Product price**
- **Method of payment**
- **Financing of receivables**
- **Insurance**

From the exporter's point of view, there are four major issues that relate to the financial aspects of exporting: the price of the product, the method of payment, the financing of receivables, and insurance.

PRODUCT PRICE

Export pricing is influenced by
- **Exchange rates**
- **Transportation costs**
- **Duties**
- **Multiple channels**
- **Insurance costs**
- **Banking costs**

Product pricing of exports entails many of the same factors that managers consider in pricing their products for domestic markets. But, as we saw in Chapter 16, there also are differences, such as taking exchange rates into consideration. If the exporter bills in its own home-country currency, the importer absorbs the foreign-exchange risk and must decide whether to pass on any possible exchange-rate differences to the consumer. If the exporter bills in the currency of the importer's country, the foreign-exchange risk falls on the exporter. Another difference between domestic and export pricing is that export prices tend to escalate from transportation costs, duties, multiple wholesale channels in the importing countries, cost of insurance, and banking costs.

Finally, the export's price may depend on dumping laws in the importing country. Recall from Chapter 6 that dumping is the sale of exports below cost or below what they sell for in the domestic market. In 1993, when the Japanese yen rose significantly against the U.S. dollar, U.S. automakers sought dumping sanctions from the U.S. government if Japanese automakers didn't increase their prices to reflect the increased import costs. An exporter must be aware of the dumping laws in each foreign market and the degree to which these laws are enforced.

METHOD OF PAYMENT

The flow of money across national borders is complex and requires the use of special documents. Exporters and importers must deal in foreign exchange, and the transfer of funds from one bank to another across national borders can be complicated and take time.

In descending order in terms of security to the exporter, the basic methods of payment for exports are

- Cash in advance
- Letter of credit
- Draft or bill of exchange
- Open account
- Other payment mechanisms, such as consignment sales or countertrade

Methods of payments are
- **Cash in advance**
- **Letter of credit**
- **Draft or bill of exchange**
- **Open account**
- **Consignment**
- **Countertrade**

When an individual or a company pays a bill in a domestic setting, it typically uses a check. This is also known as a *draft* or a *bill of exchange*. A draft is an instrument in which one party (the drawer) directs another party (the drawee) to make a payment. The drawee can either be a company like the importer or a bank. In the latter case, the draft would be considered a bank draft. Documentary drafts and documentary letters of credit are often used to protect both the buyer and the seller. They require that payment be made based on the presentation of documents conveying the title. If the exporter requests payment to be made immediately, the draft is called a *sight draft*. If the payment is to be made later, for example, 30 days after delivery, the instrument is called a *time draft*. A time draft is more flexible to the importer and more risky to the exporter because the longer the exporter has to wait for the money, the more likely something could go wrong and the importer not be able to pay. In addition, if the exporter is assuming the foreign-exchange risk, the risk increases as the time increases. A time draft drawn on a bank and bearing the bank's promise to pay at a future date is known as a *banker's acceptance*. Banks assist in establishing and collecting a draft and usually charge the exporter a modest fee that ranges from about one-eighth to one-quarter percent of the value of the draft, with a minimum of $35 to $75 and a maximum of $150 to $200.

Documentary draft—an instrument instructing the importer to pay the exporter if certain documents are presented

Sight draft—payments must be made immediately
    Time draft—payment is to be made at a future date

With a bill of exchange, it is always possible the importer will not be able to make payment to the exporter at the agreed-upon time. A **letter of credit (L/C)**, however, obligates the buyer's bank in the importing country to honor a draft presented to it, provided the draft is accompanied by the prescribed documents. However, the exporter still needs to be sure that the bank's credit is valid as well. The letter of credit can be a forgery, issued by a "nonexistent bank." The exporter, even with the added security of the bank, still needs to rely on the importer's credit because of possible discrepancies that could arise in the transaction. A letter of credit does not eliminate foreign-exchange risk if the sale is denominated in a currency other than that of the exporter's country. However, a letter of credit denominated in the exporter's currency means the exporter incurs no risk of loss as a result of possible exchange-rate fluctuations. As with a draft, a letter of credit may be issued at sight or time. Even in the case of a letter of credit drawn with a sight draft, it may take two or three days for the cash to clear, so the exporter's collecting bank might be able to extend immediate credit to the exporter. In addition, the exporter might try to discount the letter of credit (sell it to someone else at less than face value) to get instant access to cash.

A letter of credit obligates the buyer's bank to pay the exporter.

When an exporter requires a letter of credit, the importer is responsible for arranging for it at the importer's bank. Figure 17.4 explains the relationships among the parties to a letter of credit. A letter of credit can be revocable or irrevocable. A revocable letter of credit is one that can be changed by any of the parties. However, both exporter and importer may prefer an irrevocable letter of credit (see Figure 17.5), which is a letter that cannot be canceled or changed in any way without the consent of all parties to the transaction. With

A revocable letter of credit may be changed by any of the parties to the agreement.
    An irrevocable letter of credit requires all parties to agree to a change in the documents.

FIGURE 17.4   Letter-of-Credit Relationships

A letter of credit guarantees the exporter that the importer's bank will pay for the imports. The credit relationship exists between the importer and the importer's bank (the opening bank). A confirmed letter of credit has an added guarantee from the exporter's bank: If the importer's bank defaults, the exporter's bank must pay.

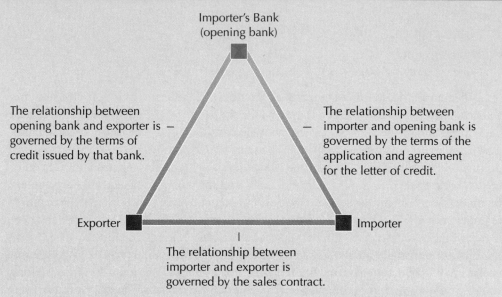

Importer's Bank
(opening bank)

The relationship between opening bank and exporter is — governed by the terms of credit issued by that bank.

The relationship between importer and opening bank is — governed by the terms of the application and agreement for the letter of credit.

Exporter   Importer

The relationship between importer and exporter is governed by the sales contract.

Source: Adapted from *Export and Import Financing Procedures* (Chicago: The First National Bank of Chicago), p. 22.

this type of L/C, the importer's bank is obligated to pay and is willing to accept any drafts (bills of exchange) at sight, meaning these drafts will be paid as soon as the correct documents are presented to the bank. As noted above, an L/C can also be issued at time. The exporter must adhere precisely to all the conditions on the letter of credit—such as the method of transportation and the description of the merchandise— otherwise, the letter of credit will not be paid without approval of all parties to an elimination of the discrepancies. The L/C in Figure 17.5 is a hard-copy typed L/C, but First Security Bank and many other banks are now issuing L/Cs electronically. They can establish an L/C system template on the customer's system that allows them to submit the L/C to the bank, and the bank can then transfer the L/C electronically to the overseas supplier—which is faster than filling out a paper copy, taking it to the bank, and mailing it to the overseas supplier.

A confirmed irrevocable letter of credit adds an obligation to pay for the exporter's bank.

A letter of credit transaction may include a confirming bank in addition to the parties mentioned above. With a **confirmed letter of credit**, the exporter has the guarantee of an additional bank, sometimes in the exporter's home country, sometimes in a third country. It rarely happens that the exporter establishes the confirming relationship. Usually, the opening bank seeks the confirmation of the L/C with a bank with whom they already have a credit relationship. If this letter of credit is irrevocable, none of the conditions can be changed unless all four parties to it agree in advance.

Open account—the exporter bills the importer but does not require formal payment documents; usually for members of the same corporate group

An exporter occasionally may sell on **open account**. This means the necessary shipping documents are mailed to the importer before any payment from or definite obligation on the part of the buyer. Releasing goods in this manner is somewhat unusual because the exporter risks default by the buyer. An exporter ordinarily sells under such conditions only if it has successfully conducted business with the importer for an

FIGURE 17.5   An Irrevocable Export Letter of Credit

IRREVOCABLE DOCUMENTARY CREDIT

ISSUED IN SALT LAKE CITY, UTAH ON <u>1 AUG 2000</u>

BENEFICIARY
XYZ COMPANY
HONG KONG

APPLICANT
ABC COMPANY
123 ANY STREET
ANY TOWN, UT 99999

ADVISING BANK
FIRST SECURITY TRADE SERVICES LTD.
NEW HENRY HOUSE, 3RD FLOOR
10 ICE HOUSE STREET CENTRAL
HONG KONG

TRANSSHIPMENTS PERMITTED
PARTIAL SHIPMENTS PERMITTED

AMOUNT
USD $257,000.00
TWO HUNDRED FIFTY SEVEN THOUSAND
AND 00/100 UNITED STATES DOLLARS

DATE AND PLACE OF EXPIRY
31 DEC 2000, HONG KONG

WE HEREBY ISSUE OUR IRREVOCABLE DOCUMENTARY CREDIT

CREDIT AVAILABLE WITH <u>ANY BANK</u> BY <u>NEGOTIATION</u> OF DRAFT AT <u>30 DAYS B/L DATE</u> DRAWN ON <u>FIRST SECURITY BANK OF UTAH, N.A.</u> FOR 100 PERCENT OF INVOICE AMOUNT.

SHIPMENT FROM: <u>HONG KONG</u>   SHIPMENT TO: <u>U.S. WEST COAST PORT</u>

NO LATER THAN: <u>01 DEC 2000</u> COVERING SHIPMENT OF <u>GENERAL MERCHANDISE</u> FOB <u>HONG KONG</u>
WHEN ACCOMPANIED BY THE FOLLOWING DOCUMENTS:

- 2 SIGNED COMMERCIAL INVOICES IN ORIGINAL AND 1 COPY
- 2 PACKING LISTS IN ORIGINAL
- 1 CERTIFICATE OF ORIGIN IN ORIGINAL
- FULL SET PLUS 1 COPY OF CLEAN ON BOARD OCEAN B/L'S MARKED FREIGHT COLLECT

CONSIGNED TO: ABC COMPANY
1234 SOUTHWEST LANE
SALT LAKE CITY, UT 84111

NOTIFY: FORWARDING COMPANY, INC.
AMELIA EARHART DRIVE
SALT LAKE CITY, UT 84101

SPECIAL CONDITIONS:
- DOCUMENTS MUST BE PRESENTED TO PAYING/NEGOTIATING BANK WITHIN 21 DAYS AFTER THE DATE OF SHIPMENT HOWEVER WITHIN VALIDITY OF LETTER OF CREDIT.
- DOCUMENTS MUST BE PRESENTED IN ONE MAIL.
- INSURANCE COVERED BY BUYER.
ALL CHARGES EXCEPT THE OPENING BANK'S CHARGES ARE FOR THE ACCOUNT OF THE BENEFICIARY.

NOTE THAT WE WILL ASSESS A DISCREPANCY FEE OF USD40.00 ON EACH PRESENTATION OF DOCUMENTS CONTAINING DISCREPANCIES.

REIMBURSEMENT INSTRUCTIONS:
VIA REGISTERED MAIL TO:
FIRST SECURITY BANK OF UTAH, N.A.
INTERNATIONAL DEPARTMENT
41 EAST 100 SOUTH
P.O. BOX 30004
SALT LAKE CITY, UT 84130

CONFIRMATION INSTRUCTIONS:
WITHOUT ADDING YOUR CONFIRMATION.

WE HEREBY ENGAGE WITH DRAWERS, ENDORSERS, AND BONA FIDE HOLDERS THAT DRAFTS DRAWN AND NEGOTIATED IN CONFORMITY WITH THE TERMS OF THIS CREDIT WILL BE DULY HONORED ON PRESENTATION AND THAT DRAFTS ACCEPTED WITHIN THE TERMS OF THIS CREDIT WILL BE DULY HONORED AT MATURITY. EACH DRAFT MUST BE ENDORSED ON THE REVERSE THEREOF BY THE NEGOTIATING BANK. THE AMOUNT OF EACH DRAFT MUST BE ENDORSED ON THE REVERSE OF THIS CREDIT BY THE NEGOTIATING BANK.

THE NUMBER OF THE CREDIT AND THE NAME OF OUR BANK MUST BE QUOTED ON ALL DRAFTS REQUIRED. IF THE CREDIT IS AVAILABLE BY NEGOTIATION, THE AMOUNT OF EACH DRAWING MUST BE ENTERED ON THE REVERSE OF THIS CREDIT BY THE NEGOTIATING BANK.

THIS CREDIT IS SUBJECT TO THE UNIFORM CUSTOMS AND PRACTICE FOR DOCUMENTARY CREDITS, 1993 REVISION, INTERNATIONAL CHAMBER OF COMMERCE, PUBLICATION NO. 500.

_____
AUTHORIZED SIGNATURE(S)

First Security Bank - Financial Services Division - 41 East 100 South - Salt Lake City, Utah 84111
Telephone (801) 246-5334 - SWIFT Address: FSBUUS55

A letter of credit is a precisely worded document whose terms must be adhered to in order for the exporter to receive payment.

extended time. This is generally the arrangement when the importer and exporter are members of the same corporate group.

FINANCING RECEIVABLES

The increased distances and time of exporting can create cash flow problems for the exporter. This is especially true if the exporter extends payment through a time draft.

Because exporting is risky, banks often are unwilling to provide funding for it. This is a major problem for small exporters that do not have the working capital to sustain themselves between production and payment. These companies complain that banks will not fund small needs for working capital arising from exporting but provide funding readily to domestic clients that are greater credit risks. Small exporters need to find a way to access funds or guarantee their export revenues so that banks will lend them working capital.

Exporters can get financing from banks and through factoring or forfaiting.

However, there are many other funding sources that exporters can access, both public and private.[27] Exporters can get access to funds through **factoring** and **forfaiting**. Factoring is the discounting of a foreign account receivable. Basically the factoring company is a finance provider in situations where a bank may be hesitant to lend money to the exporter. The exporter turns over its export receivables, sometimes for a small administrative fee, over to the factor. In return, the factor gives the exporter about 80 to 85 percent of value of the receivables up front and then collects the debt itself, paying the balance to the exporter after collecting the debt.[28] Pinnacle Display, a British startup printer company, accessed funds this way. When Pinnacle first started, it desperately needed working capital, but the banks wouldn't lend it any money, even though it had a lot of firm orders from reputable clients. A factoring company bought Pinnacle's high-end receivables (those from the best customers) and advanced it some funds to help it out of its desperate situation. It worked out fine, and Pinnacle Display has been growing strongly ever since.[29]

Factoring—the discounting of a foreign account receivable

Forfaiting is similar to factoring. Typically, a forfaiter buys from an exporter the debt due from its customer, usually in the form of a promissory note or bill of exchange. A bank in the importer's country usually guarantees these instruments. This allows the exporter to get paid immediately and is usually a cheaper form of payment for the importer than if it had to borrow from a bank or get credit extended to it by the exporter. An example of forfaiting involves International Remote Imaging Systems (IRIS), a U.S.-based manufacturer of medical equipment. The company sold $750,000 of equipment to medical labs in Turkey. However IRIS needed to extend credit to the importer for two years because of the order's size. To receive payment sooner, IRIS found a Turkish bank willing to guarantee the note receivable from the Turkish importer and then sold the receivable to a forfaiter—allowing it to get paid right away.

Forfaiting—similar to factoring but usually for longer time periods and with a guarantee from a bank in the importer's country

In addition, exporters can apply for guarantees from government agencies in order to get banks to loan them money while waiting for receivables, such as the Small Business Association (www.sba.gov) and the Export-Import Bank of the United States. The Ex-Im Bank is an independent federal agency that supports the export of U.S. goods and services through loan guarantees and insurance programs. Ex-Im Bank offers four programs: working capital guarantees, export credit insurance, guarantees of commercial loans to foreign buyers, and direct loans to foreign buyers.[30] The Bank does not compete with commercial lenders, but assumes the risks they cannot accept. It always must have a reasonable assurance of repayment. The programs are open for companies of all sizes, and enhancements have been made in some programs to support environ-

Government agencies, such as the Export-Import Bank in the United States, can provide direct loans to exporters or guarantee foreign receivables so that exporters can get bank financing of receivables

mental goods and services. However, the Ex-Im Bank has favored the large exporters, such as Boeing, even though it tries to help out the little exporter.

Ex-Im Bank's working capital guarantees cover 90 percent of the principal and interest on commercial loans to creditworthy small and medium-size companies. With the guarantees, lenders can provide funds on a single project or revolving credit basis. Export credit insurance policies protect against both political and commercial risks of a foreign buyer defaulting on payment. The insurance helps exporters finance receivables more easily by assigning the policy's proceeds to the lender. Guarantees of commercial loans to foreign buyers of U.S. goods or services cover 100 percent of principal and interest against political and commercial risks of nonpayment. Direct loans can also be made to foreign buyers of U.S. goods.[31]

INSURANCE

There are two kinds of insurance that are used most often in exports. The first kind of insurance covers the transportation of products. Damaging weather conditions, rough handling by carriers, and other hazards to cargo make insurance an important protection for exporters.[32] The terms of sale determine whether the exporter or the importer is responsible for the insurance, and that should affect the cost of the export. Marine cargo insurance and air carrier insurance should be purchased to protect against damage or loss.

The second type of insurance covers political, commercial, and foreign-exchange risk. Some private sector insurance companies will cover these types of risks for established exporters with a proven track record, but government agencies tend to be the most important insurer for these risks. In the United States, for example, the Ex-Im Bank offers commercial and political risk insurance. Political risks include war and expropriation. Commercial risks arise from buyer default and insolvency. Insurance premiums are based on the risk of the transaction, including the country where the risk has been incurred.

Two types of export insurance
- **Insurance on transportation risks, such as weather, rough handling by carriers**
- **Political, commercial, and foreign-exchange risk that might keep the exporter from collecting from the importer**

COUNTERTRADE

Sometimes countries have so much difficulty generating enough foreign exchange to pay for imports that they need to devise creative ways to get the products they want. Both companies and governments often must find creative ways of settling payment, such as trading goods for goods as part of the transaction. **Countertrade** is any one of several different arrangements by which goods and services are traded for each other. Countertrade can be divided into two basic types: barter, based on clearing arrangements used to avoid money-based exchange; and buybacks, offsets, and counterpurchase, which are used to impose reciprocal commitments.[33] Countertrade has also been called a hostage exchange, as opposed to a contract exchange, because it creates artificial bonds and dependencies specific to transactions.[34]

It is difficult to know how big the countertrade market is. Estimates in the past have ranged from 20 to 40 percent of total exports, but that figure is difficult to verify. Anecdotal evidence shows that countertrade increased in Asia as a result of the Asian financial crisis of 1997. Shortly after the onset of the crisis, the government of Thailand required that at least 50 percent of the value of government purchase contracts from foreign companies with a value of more than Baht 300 million ($7.5 million) must be met by counterpurchases from Thailand.[35] There are several types of countertrade, but the three most common are barter, buybacks, and offset.

Countertrade is when goods and services are traded for each other.

Two types of countertrade—to avoid money-based exchange and to impose reciprocal commitments

BARTER

Barter, the oldest form of countertrade, is a transaction in which goods are traded for goods of equal value without any flow of cash. In 1997, for example, a Swiss bank arranged for the sale of an Airbus aircraft to a country of the former Soviet Union in a deal that was met with payments in crude oil.[36] This is a lot better than a deal several years ago between McDonnell-Douglas and the former Yugoslavia where McDonnell-Douglas received as payment a large variety of consumer products ranging from canned ham and jam to peas. There are barter firms that act as an intermediary between the exporter and importer, often taking title to the goods received by the exporter for a price or selling the goods for a fee and a percentage of the sales value.

Buybacks are products the exporter receives as payment that are related to or originate from the original export. An example would be where a company exports capital equipment for a country's mining operation and receives as payment minerals to sell on world markets. A specific example—PepsiCo provided Pepsi syrup to state-owned bottling plants in Russia and received Stolichnya vodka, which it marketed in the West.

OFFSET TRADE

Another type of countertrade, called **offset trade**, is becoming increasingly important. Offset trade is when an exporter sells products for cash and then helps the importer find opportunities to earn hard currency. Offsets are most often used for big-ticket items, such as military sales. Offset arrangements are usually one of two types.

- Direct offsets include any business that relates directly to the export. Generally, the exporter seeks contractors in the importer's country to joint venture or coproduce certain parts if applicable. For example, an aircraft exporter could partner with a company in the importer's country to manufacture components that would be used in the manufacture of the aircraft.
- Indirect offsets include all business unrelated to the export. Generally the exporter is asked by the importer's government to buy a country's goods or invest in an unrelated business.[37] Some of the most common direct offset practices in military sales include coproduction, licensed production, subcontractor production, overseas investment, and technology transfer. Examples of indirect offsets might include assisting in the export of unrelated products from the host country or generating tourist revenues for the host country.

McDonnell-Douglas and the sale of F-18A fighter aircraft to Canada provides an example of offset trade. This sale was to net McDonnell-Douglas nearly $3 billion, a significant amount of money for one transaction. Over the eight-year period specified for delivery dates, Canada would average imports from McDonnell-Douglas of several hundred million dollars per year. Given the weakness of the Canadian dollar compared to the U.S. dollar at the time of the sale, this significant increase in imports concerned the Canadian government. Consequently, the negotiations for the sale of the aircraft included not only the technical capabilities of the F-18As and their cost but also the offset agreement in the form of industrial benefits that McDonnell-Douglas could promise the Canadian government. The Canadian offset agreement covered fifteen years with a three-year grace period. The total offset program commitment of $2.9 billion covered the following three areas: aerospace and electronics, advanced technology, and diversified activities. The aerospace and electronics area, the most important of the three,

FIGURE 17.6 An Offset Transaction

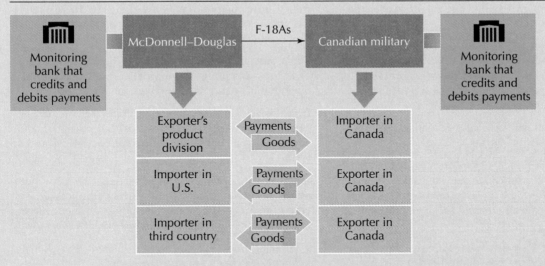

In this form of countertrade, the exporter is required to find ways for the importing country to earn foreign exchange to pay for the exports.

Source: From Pompiliu Verzariu, *Countertrade, Barter, Offsets*, © 1985, New York: McGraw-Hill. Reprinted by permission of The McGraw-Hill Companies.

included designated production, coproduction, technology transfer, and joint R&D. The diversified activities portion of the offset agreement included investment and technology development, export development, and tourism development.

Figure 17.6 shows how a complex transaction such as the F-18A sale to Canada might be structured. As noted in the figure, the transaction involves the primary exporter, the importing government, and other secondary exporters and importers.

Whether companies get into the complexities of offset trade depends mainly on the demand for their products, whether they have alternative sources of supply, and the extent of foreign-exchange problems in the buying country. In any case, offset trade results primarily from foreign-exchange shortages and is a good example of how companies and governments can compensate for such a shortage through creative business transactions.

WEB CONNECTION

Check out our home page www.prenhall.com/daniels for links to key resources for you in your study of international business.

SUMMARY

- The probability of a company's becoming an exporter increases with company size, but the extent of exporting does not directly correlate with size.

- Companies new to exporting (and also some experienced exporters) often make many mistakes. One way to avoid mistakes is to develop a comprehensive export strategy that includes an analysis of the company's resources as well as its market opportunities.

- Companies export to increase sales revenues, use excess capacity, and diversify markets.

- As a company establishes its export business plan, it must assess export potential, obtain expert counseling, select a country or countries where it will focus their exports, formulate its strategy, and determine how to get its goods to market.

- Importers need to be concerned with strategic issues (why import rather than buy domestically) and procedural issues (what are the steps that need to be followed to get goods into the country).

- Customs agencies assess and collect duties, as well as ensure that import regulations are adhered to.

- Exporters may deal directly with agents or distributors in a foreign country or indirectly through export management companies or other types of trading companies. Internet marketing is a new form of direct exporting that is allowing many small and medium-size companies to access export markets as never before.

- Trading companies can perform many of the functions for which manufacturers lack the expertise. In addition, exporters can use the services of other specialists, such as freight forwarders, to facilitate exporting. These specialists can help an exporter with the complex documentation that accompanies exports.

- There are four major issues in the financial aspects of exporting—the price of the product, the method of payment, the financing of receivables, and insurance.

- Export prices are a function of domestic pricing pressures, the impact of exchange rates, and price escalation due to longer channels of distribution, tariffs, and so forth.

- In descending order in terms of security, the basic methods of payment for exports are cash in advance, letter of credit, draft, open account, and other payment mechanisms such as consignment sales or countertrade.

- A letter of credit is a financial document that obligates the importer's bank to pay the exporter.

- Governmental agencies in some countries, such as the Ex-Im Bank in the United States, provide assistance in terms of direct loans to importers, bank guarantees to fund exporters' working capital needs, and insurance against commercial and political risk.

- Countertrade is any one of several different arrangements by which goods and services are traded for each other, on either a bilateral or a multilateral basis. Barter means trading goods for goods. Offsets are agreements by which the exporter helps the importer earn foreign exchange or the transfer of technology or production to the importing country.

CASE

SUNSET FLOWERS OF NEW ZEALAND, LTD.[38]

After 18 months of residing in the United States, John Robertson, a New Zealander, glances frequently at a map of the United States on his wall, wondering when he will get the time and resources to travel into the various metropolitan areas of the central, southern, and eastern states. Through such travel, he believes, he can gain an improved appreciation of the characteristics of the markets for fresh-cut flowers, an item that he began importing into the United States from New Zealand during his summer "vacation" from school.

In August, Robertson and his family left New Zealand for Seattle so he could study for his MBA degree at the University of Washington. A month earlier, he had resigned from his job and leased their house and small farm. On completion of the degree, the Robertsons intended to return to New Zealand, where John would seek employment in a senior management position with a company involved in exporting.

New Zealand is a country the size of Oregon with a population of nearly 4 million in 1998. The relatively small size of its population base coupled with its distance from world markets (see Map 17.1) inhibits its ability to establish an industrial base competitive with those of the world's leading industrial countries. Therefore, New Zealand depends heavily on world trade, importing fuel and manufacturing products and gaining most of its foreign exchange through exports of agricultural produce. Its f.o.b. exports average around 22 percent of its GDP, compared with the U.S. figure of 12 percent (*f.o.b.* stands for "free on board," which includes the cost of the product to the city of export but excludes international shipping costs). To hold its place in the world economy, New Zealand lobbies hard to remove the restrictions imposed on imported agricultural products by the EU, Japan, and the United States. Along with this campaign, efforts are being made to diversify into horticultural products such as fresh flowers and fruit.

Immediately prior to leaving New Zealand, Robertson had worked for almost four years as the financial manager of a company involved in growing, wholesaling, and exporting live ornamental trees and shrubs. To sell its products on world markets, the company used agents, including two based in the United States, one in Japan, and one in Europe. The agents were paid retainers and typically provided services for several exporters. The experience gained from working for this company provided Robertson with a background in the procedures necessary for exporting. It also gave him insight into the problems that exporters face when trying to compete in foreign markets, where control over representation is hindered by distance and lack of knowledge of business procedures.

It was while working for this company that Robertson was introduced to cut-flower products. The Robertsons raised enough money to purchase a farm and then became acquainted with their neighbors, the Pratts, who were first-class horticulturists. The Pratts had developed a new variety of the Leucadendron plant that yielded a beautiful, red leaf-like flower, which the Robertsons and Pratts felt they could export successfully.

During their first year of production, the Robertsons and Pratts formed a new entrepreneurial venture. They exported their yield through an established export company whose principal line of business was exporting fresh fruit and vegetables. The company had a large market share of this business and also had assumed a significant share of the exports of cut flowers from New Zealand. The New Zealand cut-flower export industry was small and, with the exception of

trade in orchids, immature. Export companies provided the many part-time cut-flower growers with the marketing infrastructure that they themselves were unable to put together.

As the harvesting season progressed, the returns paid to the venture by the exporter declined until they reached a point at which production levels of 10,000 stems or fewer became only marginally profitable. Gary Pratt and John Robertson met with the exporter to discuss the trends. The exporter explained that price was a function of volume and that the lower prices resulted from the increased volumes of cut flowers being placed on world markets. Export market returns were substantiated by documentation.

Pratt and Robertson were not convinced by the explanation. However, they knew little about world markets for fresh-cut flowers, and they could only speculate as to the reasons for the price movements. As there were no other established cut-flower export companies to turn to, the only way to research the matter seemed to be to do so themselves. Robertson's going to the United States for his MBA studies presented the opportunity to carry out some research there.

During his first semester of school, Robertson had little time to do research. At the end of the winter quarter, when he picked up a sample cart of Leucadendron flowers consigned by Pratt to him at Sea-Tac Airport, his ideas on how to approach the market were not yet defined. He took the flowers home and, on inspection, found that they had kept well in transit and their quality was good.

In the six days remaining before school began again, Robertson decided to concentrate on researching the production and shipping costs associated with the product, production forecasts, import procedures, the basic structure of the U.S. cut-flower industry, and market reaction to the Leucadendron.

When he had picked up the samples from the airport, Robertson was told by airline officials that if he were going to undertake imports of invoice value greater than $250, he would have to engage the services of a customs broker. Presuming such brokers to be the experts on import procedures, he made an appointment with one. The broker was most helpful. Imported cut flowers had to be inspected by the U.S. Department of Agriculture (USDA) on arrival. Once given clearance, duty was assessed at the rate of 8 percent on f.o.b. value. The broker would arrange for these clearances through the USDA and the U.S. Customs Service. The broker would charge a fee for such services. Robertson learned that this fee is fixed for shipments regardless of size but varies among brokers; the broker with whom the meeting was held

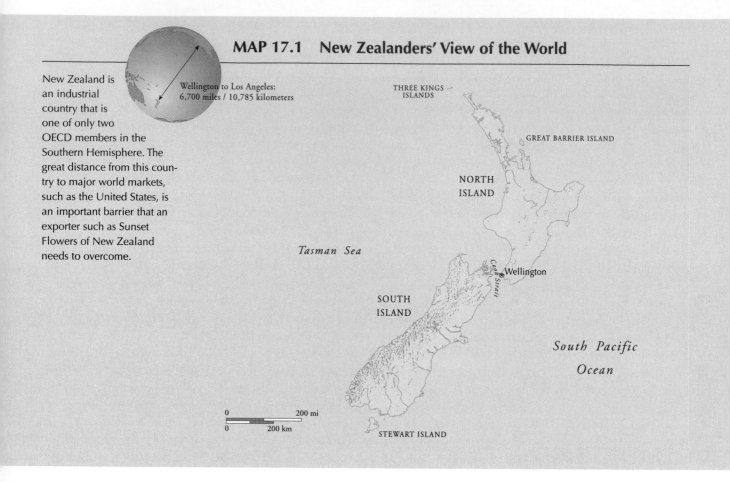

MAP 17.1   New Zealanders' View of the World

New Zealand is an industrial country that is one of only two OECD members in the Southern Hemisphere. The great distance from this country to major world markets, such as the United States, is an important barrier that an exporter such as Sunset Flowers of New Zealand needs to overcome.

Wellington to Los Angeles: 6,700 miles / 10,785 kilometers

THREE KINGS ISLANDS

GREAT BARRIER ISLAND

NORTH ISLAND

Tasman Sea

Cook Strait

Wellington

SOUTH ISLAND

South Pacific Ocean

0   200 mi
0   200 km

STEWART ISLAND

---

charged $50 per shipment. The broker also volunteered to arrange for freight forwarding companies to handle transportation to foreign markets.

As Robertson prepared his market strategy, he consulted numerous U.S. publications that helped him get a feel for the U.S. market. In addition, he asked Pratt to mail him a copy of a market-research publication funded by the New Zealand Export-Import Corporation that included research on the U.S. flower market. From that publication, he learned that the major agricultural exports from New Zealand in order of importance were kiwi fruit, apples, berryfruit, processed kiwi fruit, flowers and plants, squash, frozen vegetables, and onions. So he knew that there were experienced cut-flower exporters and third-party intermediaries in New Zealand and that the world market for cut flowers was used to seeing New Zealand products. Robertson finally contacted a Seattle wholesaler who was willing to place a large order for flowers, provided he was given exclusive rights to distribute the flowers in Washington State. Robertson was pleased with the reaction

from the wholesaler but wondered if he had made the approach with insufficient preparation. Had he underpriced the product? Was the wholesaler's credit sound? Were exclusive rights typically given in this industry, and should he have conceded them? Was the reaction one that is normal when a new product is shown to a market? Would repeat orders be placed? In addition to these market-related issues, there were administrative and organizational issues to consider. What should be his role in the marketing chain? Should he act as an agent taking a commission or buy from Pratt and resell the product? What form of organization should he establish?

Robertson also checked out some Web sites on cut flowers and noticed that several companies had great Web sites on cut flowers whereby they had pictures of the products and used the site to generate sales. One company, called proflowers.com, advertised that it could ship directly from the grower to the customer and that it could ship cut flowers all over the world. Robertson wondered if that might be one way to get access to the market.

QUESTIONS

1. Using Table 17.1, develop an import-marketing plan that Robertson could use.
2. What were the key intermediaries that Robertson used? Should he try to develop the expertise of those intermediaries so that he doesn't have to pay them for their services? Why or why not?
3. What are the pros and cons of using a Web page to sell the Leucadendron flowers? What should Robertson put on his Web page?

CHAPTER NOTES

1 "Exporting Pays Off," *Business America*, May 17, 1993, p. 19; and interview with Mr. Patrick J. Calabrese, president of Grieve Corporation.

2 John H. Dunning, "The Eclectic Paradigm of International Production: Some Empirical Tests," *Journal of International Business Studies*, Vol. 19, Spring 1988, pp. 1–31.

3 Sanjeev Agarwal and Sridhar N. Ramaswami, "Choice of Foreign Market Entry Mode: Impact of Ownership, Location and Internalization Factors," *Journal of International Business Studies*, Vol. 23, No. 1, First Quarter 1992, pp. 2–5.

4 U.S. Department of Commerce, *A Basic Guide to Exporting, 1998* (U.S. Department of Commerce and Unz & Co., Inc., November 1997), p. 3.

5 W. Chan Kim and Peter Hwang, "Global Strategy and Multinationals' Entry Mode Choice," *Journal of International Business Studies*, Vol. 23, No. 1, First Quarter 1992, pp. 32–35.

6 Andrea Bonaccorsi, "On the Relationship Between Firm Size and Export Intensity," *Journal of International Business Studies*, Vol. 23, No. 4, Fourth Quarter 1992, p. 606.

7 Jonathan L. Calof, "The Relationship Between Firm Size and Export Behavior Revisited," *Journal of International Business Studies*, Vol. 25, No. 2, Second Quarter 1994, pp. 367–387.

8 Paul Magnusson, "The Split-Up That's Slanting the Trade Deficit," *Business Week*, June 7, 1999, p. 38.

9 Leonidas C. Leonidous and Constantine S. Katsikeas, "The Export Development Process: An Integrative Review of Empirical Models," *Journal of International Business Studies*, Vol. 27, No. 3, Third Quarter 1996, pp. 524–525.

10 "Most Common Mistakes of New-to-Export Ventures," *Business America*, April 16, 1984, p. 9.

11 Paul Beamish, Lambros Karavis, Anthony Goerzen, and Christopher Lane, "The Relationship Between Organizational Structure and Export Performance," *Management International Review*, Vol. 39, First Quarter 1999, p. 51.

12 See the home page of U.S. Customs for an organizational chart and of specific responsibilities; "Mission Statement, Organizational Chart," www.customs.ustreas.gov/about/about.htm.

13 Ibid.; and U.S. Department of the Treasury, U.S. Customs Service, *Importing into the United States* (Washington, D.C.: U.S. Government Printing Office, September 1991), p. 41.

14 U.S. Department of Commerce, *A Basic Guide to Exporting, 1998*, pp. 19–25.

15 Tom L. Beauchamp and Norman E. Bowie, *Ethical Theory and Business*, 4th ed. (Upper Saddle River, NJ: Prentice Hall, 1993), pp. 514–515.

16 A. J. Campbell, "Ten Reasons Why Your Business Should Use Electronic Commerce," *Business America*, May 1998, pp. 12–14.

17 U.S. Department of Commerce, *A Basic Guide to Exporting, 1998*, p. 20; Philip MacDonald, *Practical Exporting and Importing*, 2nd ed. (New York: Ronald Press, 1959), pp. 30–40.

18 "Basic Question: To Export Yourself or to Hire Someone to Do It for You?" *Business America*, April 27, 1987, pp. 14–17.

19 Frank G. Long, "Compare Before Choosing Export Management Firm," *Arizona Business Gazette*, January 18, 1996, p. 10.

20 Jeremy Kahn, "The Fortune Global 500: The World's Largest Corporations," *Fortune*, August 2, 1999, pp. F1–F23.

21 "Arco, Itochu Units to Purchase Coastal's Utah Coal Operations," *PR Newswire*, October 24, 1996. Available in LEXIS/NEXIS NEWS: CURNWS.

22 Ibid.

23 Assif Shameen, "Playing Korea's Recovery: The Trading Companies May Be One Way to Do It," *Asiaweek*, September 20, 1996, p. 66. Available in LEXIS/NEXIS NEWS: CURNWS.

24 U.S. Department of Commerce, *A Basic Guide to Exporting, 1998*, p. 63.

25 Helen Richardson, "Freight Forwarder Basics: Contract Negotiation," *Transportation & Distribution*, May 1996. Available in LEXIS/NEXIS NEWS: CURNWS.

26 Ibid.

27 See "Obtaining Financing," in *Tradeport*, www.tradeport.org/ts/financing/index.html, January 2000.

28 Steve Marsh, "Factoring for the Millenium," *Credit Management*, December 1999, pp. 34–35.

29 Ibid.

30 www.exim.org

31 www.eximbank.gov.

32 U.S. Department of Commerce, *A Basic Guide to Exporting, 1998*, p. 66.

33 J-F. Hennart, "Some Empirical Dimensions of Countertrade," *Journal of International Business Studies*, Vol. 21, 1990, pp. 243–270.

34 Chong Ju Choi, Soo Hee Lee, and Jai Boem Kim, "A Note on Countertrade: Contractual Uncertainty and Transaction Governance in Emerging Economies," *Journal of International Business Studies*, Vol. 30, No. 1, First Quarter 1999, p. 196.

35 Jonathon Bell, "Plane Trading," *Airfinance Journal*, June 1998, pp. 34–36.

36 Ibid.

37 American Countertrade Association, "Forms of Countertrade," www.countertrade.org/index.html.

38 Adapted from Harry R. Knudson, "Sunset Flowers of New Zealand, Ltd.," *Journal of Management Case Studies*, Vol. 1, No. 4, Winter 1985. Reprinted with permission.

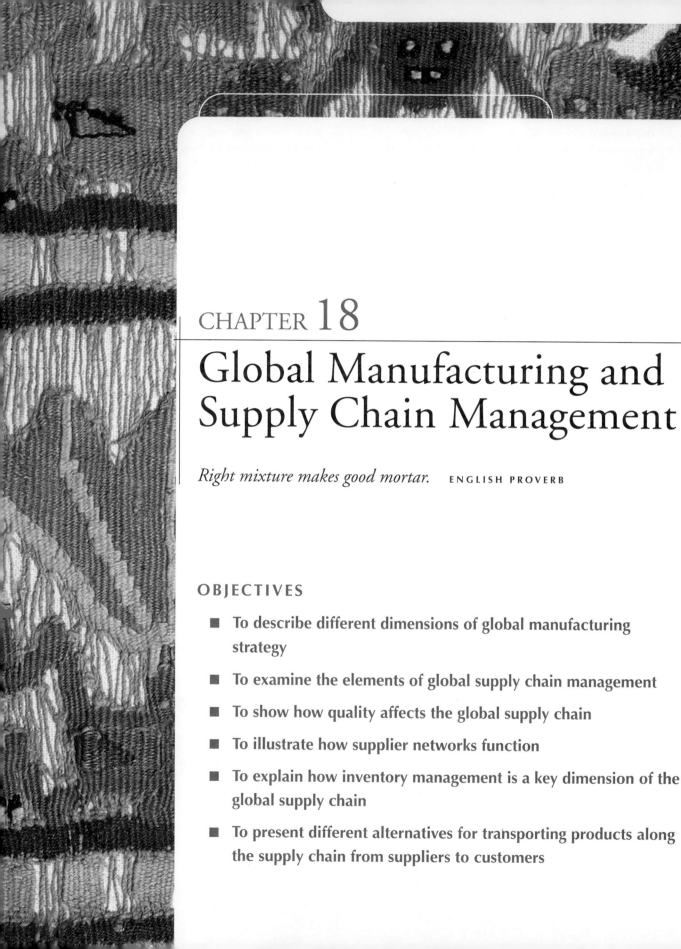

CHAPTER 18

Global Manufacturing and Supply Chain Management

Right mixture makes good mortar. ENGLISH PROVERB

OBJECTIVES

- To describe different dimensions of global manufacturing strategy

- To examine the elements of global supply chain management

- To show how quality affects the global supply chain

- To illustrate how supplier networks function

- To explain how inventory management is a key dimension of the global supply chain

- To present different alternatives for transporting products along the supply chain from suppliers to customers

Samsonite Corporation is a U.S.-based company that manufactures and distributes luggage all over the world. In fiscal year 1999, Samsonite, which is listed on NASDAQ, generated $697.4 billion in revenues but incurred a loss equal to $6.79 per share. Although Samsonite began in 1910 in Denver, Colorado, it took many years for it to become a global company. In 1963, Samsonite set up its first European operation in the Netherlands and later began production in Belgium. Shortly thereafter, it erected a joint venture plant in Mexico to service the growing but highly protected Mexican market. By the end of the 1960s, Samsonite was manufacturing luggage in Spain and Japan as well. In addition to its manufacturing operations, Samsonite was selling luggage worldwide through a variety of distributors.

In the 1970s, business began to take off in Europe. In 1974, Samsonite developed its first real European product, called the Prestige Attaché, and business began to expand in Italy, causing it to rival Germany as Samsonite's biggest market in Europe. Although the U.S. market began to turn to softside luggage in the 1980s, the European market still demanded hardside luggage, so Samsonite developed a new hardside suitcase for Europe called the Oyster case. Then softside luggage began to increase in importance, although Europe was still considered a hardside market. In the 1980s, Samsonite opened a new plant in France to manufacture the Prestige Attaché and other key products.

With the fall of the Iron Curtain in the early 1990s, Samsonite purchased a Hungarian luggage manufacturer and began to expand throughout Eastern Europe. During this same time period, Samsonite established several joint venture companies through Asia, including China, to extend its reach there.

To establish products of high quality, Samsonite embarked on two different programs. The first is an internal program where Samsonite conducts a drop test, a tumble test, a wheel test, and a handle test to determine if its products are strong enough and of sufficient quality for customers. The second program is two different, independent quality assurance tests. The first is the European-based ISO 9002 certification to demonstrate how companies implement quality in their operations. The second is the GS Mark, which is the number-one government-regulated third-party product test market of Germany.

The GS Mark, *Gepruefte Sicherheit* (translated "Tested for Safety"), is designed to help companies comply with European product liability laws as well as other areas of quality and safety. To enhance quality, Samsonite introduced state-of-the art CAD-CAM machinery in its plants. Samsonite also introduced a manufacturing technique whereby autonomous cells of about a dozen employees assembled a product from start to finish.

As noted in Map 18.1, Samsonite had six company-owned production facilities and one joint venture production facility in Europe in 2000. In addition, it has subsidiaries, joint ventures, distributors, and agents set up to service the European market. Although Samsonite initially serviced the European markets through exports, the transportation costs were high, and the demand for luggage soared in Europe, so Samsonite decided to begin production in Belgium in 1965. In the early years, Samsonite had a decentralized supply chain as illustrated in Figure 18.1, whereby it operated through different wholesale layers before it finally got the product to the retailers. As Samsonite's business grew, management decided to centralize its supply chain so that products were manufactured and shipped to a central European warehouse, which then directly supplied retailers upon request (see Figure 18.2). This centralized structure

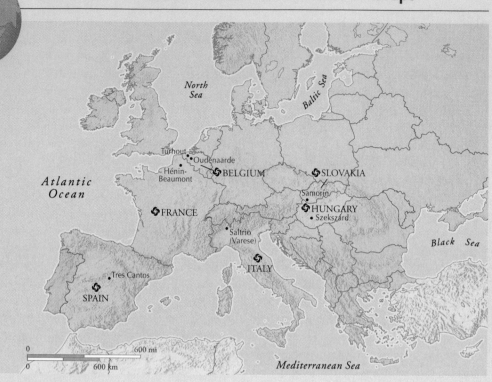

MAP 18.1   Samsonite's Production Facilities in Europe

Samsonite has six company-owned production facilities and one joint venture production facility in Europe where it manufactures products sold throughout Europe. Each European country of operations is labeled here with Samsonite's corporate logo.

was put into place to eliminate the need to rely on wholesalers. Samsonite had to worry about transporting manufactured products to the warehouse, storing them, and transporting them to the retailers in the different European markets. Samsonite invested heavily in information technology to link the retailers to the warehouse and thereby manage its European distribution system more effectively. Retailers would place an order with a salesperson or the local Samsonite office in their area, and the order would be transmitted to the warehouse and shipping company by modem.

As noted earlier, Samsonite sold two basic types of suitcases: hardside and softside. Most of the R&D was initially done in the United States, but the need to develop products for the European market caused the company to establish R&D facilities in Europe. Samsonite invested heavily in R&D and the manufacture of specialized machinery to help keep a competitive edge. To facilitate the transportation and storage of suitcases, Samsonite located its production facilities close to the centralized warehouse. Softside luggage is less complex technologically, and Samsonite purchased Oda, the Belgium softside luggage company to enter that market. Then it licensed its technology to other European companies. By the mid-1990s, 48 percent of Samsonite's sales came from hardside luggage, 22 percent from softside, and 30 percent from attaché cases and travel bags, some of which were hardside and some softside.

As Samsonite expanded throughout the world, it continued to manufacture its own products and license production to other manufacturers. Then Samsonite entered into subcontract arrangements in Asia and Eastern Europe. In Europe, the subcontractors provide final goods as

FIGURE 18.1   Samsonite's Decentralized Supply Chain (1965–1974)

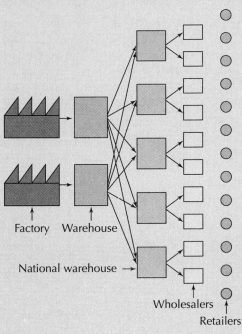

Factory   Warehouse

National warehouse →

Wholesalers

Retailers

In the early years of market penetration in Europe, Samsonite shipped luggage from its factories in Europe to factory warehouses, then to national warehouses. From there, luggage was shipped to wholesalers, who sold to retailers. This cumbersome distribution system lengthened the time it took to get product to retailers and increased the cost.

Source: F. DeBeule and D. Van Den Bulcke, "The International Supply Chain Management of Samsonite Europe," Discussion Paper 1998/E/34, Centre for International Management and Development, University of Antwerp, p. 13.

FIGURE 18.2   Samsonite's Centralized Supply Chain (1975–mid-1980s)

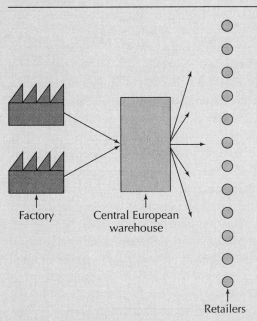

Factory   Central European warehouse

Retailers

Samsonite decided to supply the European market by shipping products directly from the factory to a centralized European warehouse and from there to the retailers upon request.

Source: F. DeBeule and D. Van Den Bulcke, "The International Supply Chain Management of Samsonite Europe," Discussion Paper No. 1998/E/34, Centre for International Management and Development, University of Antwerp, p. 14.

FIGURE 18.3   Samsonite's Global Supply Chain (1996–)

As Samsonite expanded production throughout Europe, it had to deal with subcontractors as well as their own factories. Its success in Europe was due to its ability to manage the supply chain from supplier to factory to warehouse to consumer.

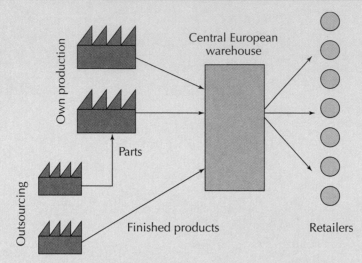

Source: F. DeBeule and D. Van Der Bulcke, "The International Supply Chain Management of Samsonite Europe," Discussion Paper No. 1998/E/34. Centre for International Management and Development, University of Antwerp, p. 21.

well as subassemblies used in Samsonite factories. Figure 18.3 illustrates Samsonite's coordination of outsourced parts and finished goods, along with its own production.

Samsonite is a good example of the challenges a firm faces in determining how best to manage the supply chain from supplier to consumer. The greater the geographic spread of the company, the more challenging the management of the supply chain becomes.

INTRODUCTION

The Samsonite case illustrates a number of dimensions of the supply chain networks that link suppliers with manufacturers and customers. The objective of this chapter is to examine these different networks and how a company can manage the links most effectively to reach customers. As Figure 18.4 shows, Global Manufacturing and Supply chain management is important in companies international business strategies. We will start by discussing global manufacturing strategy and then move to supply chain management issues. In terms of global supply chain management, we will look at supplier networks, inventory management, and transportation networks.

Supply chain—the coordination of materials, information, and funds from the initial raw material supplier to the ultimate customer

A company's **supply chain** encompasses the coordination of materials, information, and funds from the initial raw material supplier to the ultimate customer.[2] It is the management of the value-added process from the suppliers' supplier to the customers' customer.[3]

Figure 18.5 illustrates the concept of a global supply chain. Suppliers can be part of the manufacturer's organizational structure, as would be the case in a vertically integrated company, or they can be independent of the company. The direct suppliers also have their networks. In a global context, the suppliers can be located in the country

A big part of international business is getting goods where they need to go, and getting them there affordably, safely, and on time. MNEs ship many of their goods internationally by container. Singapore's container port is one of the world's largest.

where the manufacturing or assembly takes place, or they can be located in one country and shipped to the country of manufacture or assembly. The output of the suppliers can be shipped directly to the factory or to an intermediate storage point. The output of the manufacturing process can be shipped directly to the customers or to a warehouse network as was the case with Samsonite. The output can be sold directly to the end consumer or to a distributor, wholesaler, or retailer who then sells the output to the final consumer. As was the case in the supplier network, the output can be sold domestically or internationally.

An important dimension of the supply chain is **logistics**, also sometimes called **materials management**. According to the U.S.-based Council of Logistics Management, "logistics is that part of the supply chain process that plans, implements, and controls the efficient, effective flow and storage of goods, services, and related information from the point of origin to the point of consumption in order to meet customers' requirements."[4] The difference between supply chain management and materials management is one of degree. Materials management, or logistics, focuses much more on the transportation and storage of materials and final goods, whereas supply chain management extends beyond that to include the management of supplier and customer relations.

The companies that we will study in this chapter are considered to be part of a global network that links together designers, suppliers, subcontractors, manufacturers, and

Logistics (materials management)—that part of the supply chain process that plans, implements, and controls the efficient, effective flow and storage of goods, services, and related information from the point of origin to the point of consumption, to meet customers' requirements

FIGURE 18.4   Global Manufacturing and Supply Chain Management in International Business

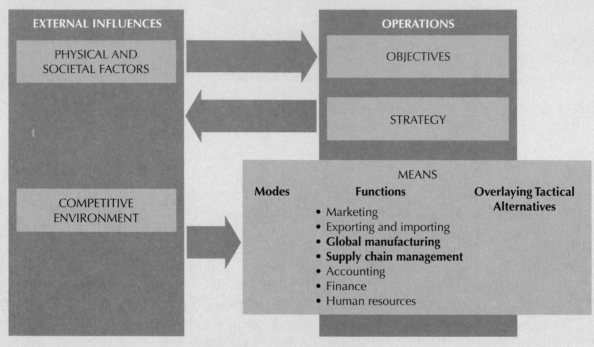

Both global manufacturing and global supply chain management are necessary functions for implementing companies' international strategies

FIGURE 18.5   The Global Supply Chain

The global supply chain links the suppliers' supplier with the customers' customer, accounting for every step of the process between the raw material and the final consumer of the good or service.

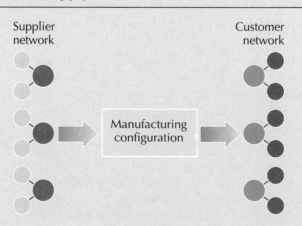

customers. The supply chain network is quite broad, and the coordination of the network takes place through interactions between firms in the networks.[5]

GLOBAL MANUFACTURING STRATEGIES

In the opening case, Samsonite initially exported to Europe, but it eventually set up Samsonite-Europe and established manufacturing facilities in different countries. Samsonite invested in Europe because of the location-specific advantages of the European market (big demand). It entered through foreign direct investment because it wanted to take advantage of the firm-specific assets that it possessed (an excellent product line and a solid manufacturing process) and internalize those advantages rather than sell them to an outside manufacturer.[6] Although Samsonite entered into some licensing agreements and subcontracted some manufacturing, the majority of its production, especially of its high-end hardside luggage, was kept under control of the company's network.

Although Samsonite engaged in its own manufacturing for the most part, it also subcontracted manufacturing to other firms. The latter strategy, known as virtual manufacturing, is followed by a number of companies. Nike, for example, does not own any manufacturing facilities, but it subcontracts manufacturing to other companies. So Nike is basically a design and marketing company. Mattel does not own manufacturing facilities in China to manufacture Barbie dolls, but it subcontracts the manufacturing to a Hong Kong–based company that has investments in China. The toys in McDonald's Happy Meals or Burger King meals are also subcontracted to a Hong Kong–based manufacturer that produces the toys in China. These are all examples of virtual manufacturing.

The success of a global manufacturing strategy depends on four key factors: compatibility, configuration, coordination, and control.[7]

> **Virtual manufacturing—subcontracting the manufacturing process to another firm**

MANUFACTURING COMPATIBILITY

Compatibility in this context is the degree of consistency between the foreign investment decision and the company's competitive strategy. Direct manufacturing made sense in Samsonite's case but not in Nike's case. Company strategies that managers must consider are

- Efficiency/cost—reduction of manufacturing costs
- Dependability—degree of trust in a company's products and its delivery and price promises
- Quality—performance reliability, service quality, speed of delivery, and maintenance quality of the product(s)
- Flexibility—ability of the production process to make different kinds of products and to adjust the volume of output
- Innovation—ability to develop new products and ideas[8]

> **Compatibility—the degree of consistency between FDI decisions and a company's competitive strategy**

> **Key company strategies:**
> - **Efficiency/cost**
> - **Dependability**
> - **Quality**
> - **Flexibility**
> - **Innovation**

Cost-minimization strategies and the drive for global efficiencies force MNEs to establish economies of scale in manufacturing, often by producing in areas with low-cost labor. This is one of the major reasons why many MNEs established manufacturing facilities in Asia, Mexico, and Eastern Europe. This type of foreign direct investment is known as offshore manufacturing, but clearly any manufacturing that takes place outside

> **Cost-minimization strategies—economies of scale, low-cost labor areas**

Offshore manufacturing—any investment that takes place in a country different from the home country

Maquiladora—an offshore manufacturing facility along the border between the United States and Mexico that can take advantage of low labor costs, special tariff provisions, and close supply chains across the border

of a company's home country is considered "offshore." Offshore manufacturing escalated sharply in the 1960s and 1970s in the electronics industry as one company after another set up production facilities in the Far East, mostly in Taiwan and Singapore. Those locations were attractive because of low labor costs, availability of cheap materials and components, and proximity to markets. Even the athletic shoe market left the United States for Taiwan and Korea. As wages rose in Korea, however, manufacturing began to shift to other low-cost countries—China, Indonesia, Malaysia, Thailand, and Vietnam.

An important type of offshore manufacturing for U.S. companies is Mexico's *maquiladora* operations, also known as *maquilas*. Under the Mexican *maquiladora* concept, U.S. companies ship components from the United States to Mexican border facilities duty-free and assemble the final products using Mexican workers. The U.S. companies then import the final products into the United States. U.S. duties are levied on the imports only to the extent of the value added in Mexico. However, the tariff provisions between the United States and Mexico do not allow *maquiladora* output to be sold in Mexico. The benefits of establishing a *maquila* are especially attractive to companies for which 30 percent or more of the product cost is labor. The NAFTA agreement will eventually eliminate the tariff advantages of *maquilas* because tariffs on all products will eventually be eliminated, but the *maquilas* are close to the border and therefore close to the distribution and warehousing facilities of the U.S. companies.

But the need for responsiveness or *flexibility* because of differences in national markets may result in regional manufacturing to service local markets. As a company's competitive strategies change, so do its manufacturing strategies. In addition, MNEs may adopt different strategies for different product lines, depending on the competitive priorities of those products.

MANUFACTURING CONFIGURATION

Manufacturing configuration
• Centralized manufacturing in one country
• Manufacturing facilities in specific regions to service those regions
• Multidomestic—facilities in each country

Next, the company's managers need to determine the configuration of manufacturing facilities. There are three basic configurations MNEs consider as they establish a global manufacturing strategy. The first is to have centralized manufacturing and offer a selection of standard, lower-priced products to different markets. That is basically a manufacture and export strategy. It is common for new-to-export companies to use this strategy, typically through their home-country manufacturing facilities. The second configuration is the use of regional manufacturing facilities to serve customers within a specific region. That is what Samsonite did initially in Europe with its production facilities in Belgium. Third, market expansion in individual countries, especially when the demand in those countries becomes significant, might argue for a multidomestic approach in which companies manufacture products close to their customers, using country-specific manufacturing facilities to meet local needs.[9] Although Samsonite did not manufacture in every country where it sold its products, it divided its broad European regional strategy into smaller areas, setting up seven factories to manufacture products for the European market. Unless the company has manufacturing facilities in every country where it is doing business, it must combine exporting with manufacturing. In reality, MNEs choose a combination of these approaches depending on their product strategies.

Some companies specialize manufacturing according to product or process.

Often, countries will also specialize in the production of parts or final goods, a process described in Chapter 8 as rationalization. When Samsonite opened a new factory in Hénin-Beaumont, France, in the 1980s, it manufactured the Prestige Attaché case and the Beauty case, which allowed it to stop production of those products in Oudenaarde, Belgium, so that it could focus on the new Oyster product line there. That allowed Samsonite to specialize in the manufacture of certain products in certain plants. It then exported its production to the centralized European warehouse for distribution to retailers all over Europe.

COORDINATION AND CONTROL

Coordination and control fit well together. Coordinating is the linking or integration of activities into a unified system.[10] The activities include everything along the global supply chain from purchasing to warehousing to shipment. It is hard to coordinate supplier relations and logistics activities if those issues are not considered when the manufacturing configuration is set up. Samsonite took configuration and coordination into account when it sets up its second manufacturing facility in Europe. As demand increased in Europe and new product lines were added, Samsonite knew that it needed to open up a second plant. However, it wanted to maintain the central European warehouse concept, so it identified a location that would allow it to coordinate transportation and storage relatively easily and quickly. Once the company determines the manufacturing configuration that it will use, it must adopt a control system to ensure that company strategies are carried out. One aspect of control structure is the organizational structure, and Samsonite established a European headquarters in Oudenaarde, Belgium, to coordinate all of its activities in Europe.

PLANT LOCATION STRATEGIES

Once MNEs determine that they will engage in FDI to supply foreign markets, they need to determine which countries to invest in and where in the specific countries. Samsonite selected Oudenaarde for its first manufacturing site in Europe because of its central location to major markets in Germany and France and because of incentives offered by the Belgium government. It selected its site in Hénin-Beaumont because of its close proximity to Oudenaarde and to Samsonite's central European warehouse. Selecting the number of plants and their locations depends on factors such as transportation costs, duties, the need to be close to the market, foreign-exchange risk, economies of scale in the production process, technological requirements of the manufacturing process, government incentives, proximity to shipping routes, climate, proximity to competitors and suppliers, and national image.[11]

An example of the location decision was the selection of Thailand by General Motors as the site of its first major plant in Southeast Asia. GM picked Thailand over the Philippines because "there are more auto suppliers, the labor climate is better, the economic growth is faster and the utilities are more dependable than the Philippines." It also picked Thailand because of "its proximity to other growing Asian markets, such as Vietnam."[12] Of course, this decision was made just prior to the Asian financial crisis, so GM's plans were delayed for a short period, but the decision was correct, and GM will be successful in Asia as the economy recovers. This reemphasizes the importance of establishing regional plants to service specific foreign markets. Because of transportation costs, localization demands, tariffs, and manufacturing costs, it does not make sense for GM to service the entire world through one huge manufacturing facility in the United States.

LAYOUT PLANNING STRATEGIES

Plant layout—decisions about the physical arrangement of economic activity centers within a manufacturing facility

Layout planning involves decisions about the physical arrangement of economic activity centers within a manufacturing facility.[13] Economic activity centers are where the different production tasks are performed. Remember that Samsonite introduced a manufacturing technique where autonomous cells of about a dozen employees assembled a product from start to finish. The plant layout strategy that Samsonite established determined how to configure these cells in the manufacturing facility. You might assume that each foreign manufacturing unit in the same company would manufacture products the same way and that the same products are manufactured the same way all over the world. But the manufacturing process is not that simple. Take automobiles, for example. If you were to tour a Toyota facility in Japan and one in Thailand, you would notice striking differences in how the auto is assembled. In Japan, the auto assembly plant is highly automated, while in Thailand, it is labor intensive. Similarly, Volkswagen's German manufacturing is highly automated while its manufacturing in Brazil is labor intensive.

The cost of land can affect plant layout by forcing the layout up (lots of floors) instead of out (lots of land).

Another factor that can affect the design of a plant is the cost of land. Swire Coca-Cola, a Hong Kong–based company, has bottling facilities in many locations, including Salt Lake City, Utah, and New Territories, Hong Kong. The Salt Lake facility is similar to many high-volume plants in the United States, with all operations taking place on one level and the product moving continuously from start to finish. In other words, the production process can take up some land—be expansive—because the cost of land is low. In Hong Kong, where land is expensive, the assembly plant is a high-rise building where the process moves from one floor to the next. The general concepts in layout planning strategy are the same all over the world, but how the plants are configured may depend a great deal on unique factors in each foreign location.

GLOBAL SUPPLY CHAIN MANAGEMENT

Earlier in the chapter, we defined global supply chain management and provided a simplified view of a global supply chain in Figure 18.5. A comprehensive supply chain strategy should include the following elements: (1) customer service requirements, (2) plant and distribution center network design, (3) inventory management, (4) outsourcing and third-party logistics relationships, (5) key customer and supplier relationships, (6) business processes, (7) information systems, (8) organizational design and training requirements, (9) performance metrics, and (10) performance goals.[14] In this section, we will discuss information systems as a key part of the global supply chain management system. In the remainder of the chapter, we will discuss total quality management, inventory management, and two key networks: supplier networks and transportation networks. Global supply chain management integrates these networks beyond the firm itself to improve customer satisfaction levels and enhance profitability.

A key to making the global supply chain work is a good information system.

The key to making a global information system work is information. As noted earlier in the chapter, Samsonite invested heavily in information technology that allowed it to speed up the delivery time to retailers. Information could be transmitted to the warehouse directly by the retailer or through a salesperson, which triggered an order to ship immediately. Many companies use electronic data interchange (EDI) to link suppliers and manufacturers, especially in food manufacturing and car making where suppliers replenish in high volumes. In a global context, EDI has been used to link exporters with

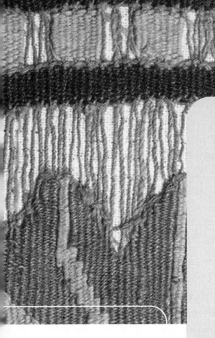

Ethical Dilemmas and Social Responsibility
WHAT SUPPLIER RELATIONS APPROACH YIELDS THE BEST RESULTS?

A utilitarian view of ethical conduct argues that the worth of actions or practices is determined by their consequences. That is, an action or practice is right if it leads to the best possible balance of good consequences and bad consequences for all parties affected.[15] How does that concept work in the case of supplier relations? When an MNE such as Toyota develops close relationships with its suppliers, both parties become exposed to risk. In working with a supplier, Toyota requires a full understanding of that supplier's manufacturing capabilities and financial position. This requirement is difficult for non-Japanese companies because they are not used to providing such detailed information to customers. Toyota takes a hard-line approach to improving quality and driving down costs, but in turn it provides its suppliers with a stable business relationship. It shares development information with a supplier's competitors but not in such a way as to damage its relationship with the supplier. Even though it is in Toyota's self-interest to keep costs as low as possible in order to maximize its competitiveness within the industry, the company also upholds its ethical obligation to treat its suppliers fairly. As long as Toyota maintains a stable business relationship with suppliers and helps them become more competitive as manufacturers, its actions result in a positive utilitarian outcome.

In contrast, some of GM's supplier relations in the past have been far less positive. When GM requires suppliers to enter into contractual agreements and then tears up the contracts and forces the suppliers to renegotiate, it is acting in its own self-interest and to the suppliers' detriment. Given the negative impact on the suppliers, one could argue that GM's actions do not constitute positive ethical conduct according to the utilitarian view. Following the departure of its head of purchasing to Volkswagen, GM was forced to look at its past actions to determine if that is the way it wanted to act in the future. As Toyota increases its production in the United States to take advantage of currency differences and market opportunities, it will form more relationships with U.S. auto parts manufacturers—providing a basis for comparison with the tactics of U.S. automakers. In the face of this competition, U.S. automakers may find that they have to adjust their supplier relations or lose some suppliers to Toyota. As companies continue to outsource and deal with suppliers from different countries and cultures, they will have to adjust to different attitudes toward supplier relations.

customs to facilitate quick processing of customs forms, speeding up the delivery of products across borders. However, EDI has some drawbacks. It is relatively limited and inflexible. It provides basic information but does not adapt easily to rapidly changing market conditions, a necessary condition in the global marketplace. It is relatively expensive to implement, so many small and medium-size companies find it difficult to afford. Also, it is based on proprietary rather than widely accepted standards, so systems tend only to be able to link together suppliers and their customers. In addition, it focuses more on the business-to-business value chain and does not deal effectively with end-use customers.[16]

The next wave of technology affecting the global supply chain was the implementation of packaged information technology packages known as enterprise resource planning (ERP). Companies such as the German software giant SAP, Oracle, Baan, and PeopleSoft introduced software to integrate everything in the back office of the firm—the part of the business that dealt with the firm itself but not the customer (known as the front office). ERP is essential for bringing together the information inside the firm, but its inability to tie in to the customer and take advantage of e-commerce has been a problem.

The next technological wave linking together the parts of the global supply chain is e-commerce. As an example, Dell Computer Corporation has a factory in Ireland that supplies custom-built PCs all over Europe. Customers can transmit orders to Dell via call centers or Dell's Web site. The company relays the demand for components to its suppliers. Trucks deliver the components to the factory and haul off the completed computers within a few hours. Dell has established an **extranet** for its suppliers—a linkage to Dell's information system via the Internet—so that they can organize production and delivery of parts to Dell when they need it. Dell uses the Internet to plug its suppliers into its customer database so that it can keep track of changes in demand. It also uses the Internet to plug customers into the ordering process and allows them to track the progress of their order from the factory to their doorstep.[17]

Most experts agree that the Internet will revolutionize communications across all levels of the global supply chain, but it will occur at different speeds in different areas. In a survey of 500 managers of large global companies, more than half of the European and North American firms had implemented corporate **intranets**—the use of the Internet to link together parts of the firm. However, only about 40 percent of the firms had customer extranets, and only about 20 to 25 percent had supplier extranets. In other words, the use of the Internet for e-commerce (the sale of products to end-use customers) was ahead of the use of the Internet for external e-business (the use of the Internet for suppliers and other external users except for customers).[18] The real attraction of the Internet in global supply chain management is that it not only helps to automate and speed up internal processes in a company through the intranet but also spreads efficiency gains to the business systems of its customers and suppliers. Companies will be able to design Web pages to drive demand, which will drive production via the extended value chain.[19] The challenge in global supply chain management is that some networks can be managed through the Internet, but others—especially in emerging markets—cannot because of the lack of technology. The use of the Internet varies by location and by industry. North America is at least five years ahead of some countries in Europe, especially southern Europe. Industries such as computing and electronics, aerospace and defense, and motor vehicles are blasting ahead, while industrial equipment, food and agriculture, heavy industries, and consumer goods are lagging behind.[20] It is no coincidence that the leaders in e-commerce are those who have invested significant amounts of money over the years to information technology—notably in the defense and motor vehicles industries.

QUALITY

An important aspect of all levels of the global supply chain is total quality management. **Quality** is defined as meeting or exceeding the expectations of the customer. More specifically, it is the conformance to specifications, value, fitness for use, support (provided by the company), and psychological impressions (image).[21] For example, no one wants to buy computer software that has a lot of bugs. However, the need to get software to market quickly may mean getting the product to market as soon as possible and correcting errors later. In the airline industry, service is a key. Some airlines, such as Singapore Air, have developed a worldwide reputation for excellence in service. That is a distinct competitive advantage in attracting the business traveler especially.

Quality, or lack thereof, can have serious ramifications for a company. In the summer of 1999, Coca-Cola ran into serious problems in Europe because of a breakdown in quality controls. In July, Coca-Cola recalled 180,000 plastic bottles of water after discovering traces of nonhazardous coliform bacteria in the drink. Apparently, the contamination occurred at a bottling plant in southwest Poland because plant personnel failed to clean the bottling line every 48 hours as required. That came on the heels of other health problems in Belgium, France, and Portugal.[22]

Quality can mean zero defects, an idea perfected by Japanese manufacturers who refuse to tolerate defects of any kind. Before the strong emphasis on zero defects, U.S. companies operated according to the premise of **acceptable quality level (AQL)**. This premise allowed an acceptable level of bad quality. It held that unacceptable products would be dealt with through repair facilities and service warranties. This type of manufacturing/operating environment required buffer inventories, rework stations, and expediting. The goal was to push through products as fast as possible and then deal with the mistakes later. However, it is increasingly evident that AQL is inferior to zero defects, and global companies that take quality more seriously will beat the competition.[23]

TOTAL QUALITY MANAGEMENT

The Japanese approach to quality is **total quality management (TQM)**. TQM is a process that stresses three principles: customer satisfaction, employee involvement, and continuous improvements in quality.[24] The goal of TQM is to eliminate all defects. TQM often focuses on benchmarking world-class standards, product and service design, process design, and purchasing.[25]

The center of the entire process, however, is customer satisfaction, which to achieve may raise production costs. The difference between AQL and TQM centers on the attitude toward quality. In AQL, quality is a characteristic of a product that meets or exceeds engineering standards. In TQM, quality means that a product is "so good that the customer wouldn't think of buying from anyone else."

TQM is a process of continuous improvement at every level of the organization—from the mail room to the board room. It implies that the company is doing everything it can to achieve quality at all stages of the process, from customer demands, to product design, to engineering. For example if management accounting systems are focused strictly on cost, they will preclude measures that could lead to higher quality. The key is to understand the company's overall strategy. TQM does not use any specific production philosophy or require the use of other techniques such as a just-in-time system for inventory delivery. TQM is a proactive strategy. Although benchmarking—determining

Quality—meeting or exceeding the expectations of a customer

Zero defects—the refusal to tolerate defects of any kind

Acceptable quality level—there is a tolerable level of defects, and defects can be corrected through repair and service warranties

TQM (total quality management)—a process whose goal is to eliminate all defects

the best processes used by the best companies—is an important part of TQM, using the best practices of other companies is not intended to be a goal. TQM means that a company will try to be better than the best.

Executives who have adopted the zero-defects philosophy of TQM claim that long-run production costs decrease as defects decrease. The continuous improvement process is also known as *kaizen*, which means identifying problems and enlisting employees at all levels of the organization to help eliminate the problems. The key is to make continuous improvement a part of the daily work of every employee. TQM in a global setting is challenging because of cultural and environmental differences. In 1987, Samsonite entered into a cooperation agreement with a Hungarian luggage manufacturer to produce and supply low-end softside luggage for Samsonite, but it did not produce good enough products due to the lack of advanced technology and the low quality of its products. Samsonite was forced to invest heavily in the Hungarian partner to get it up to world-class standards. Eventually, its efforts were successful.

QUALITY STANDARDS

There are three different levels of quality standards: a general level, an industry-specific level, and a company level. The first level is a general standard, such as the Deming Award, which is presented to firms demonstrating excellence in quality, and the Malcolm Baldridge National Quality Award, which is presented annually to companies that demonstrate quality strategies and achievements. However, even more important than awards is certification of quality. As part of the effort to establish the single European market, the EU, through the International Standards Organization in Geneva, established the ISO 9000 certification, which became effective in 1987. ISO 9000 is a set of five universal standards for a Quality Assurance system that is accepted around the world. About 90 countries have adopted ISO 9000 as national standards. The standards apply uniformly to companies in any industry and of any size. ISO 9000 is intended to promote the idea of quality at every level of an organization. Initially, it was designed to harmonize technical norms within the EU. Now it is an important part of business operations throughout Europe and has been adopted in over 70 countries worldwide, including the United States.

Basically, under ISO 9000, companies must document how workers perform every function that affects quality and install mechanisms to ensure that they follow through on the documented routine. ISO 9000 certification entails a complex analysis of management systems and procedures, not just of quality-control standards. Rather than judging the quality of a particular product, ISO 9000 evaluates the management of the manufacturing process according to standards it has created in 20 domains, from purchasing to design to training. A company that wants to be ISO certified must fill out a report and then be certified by a team of independent auditors.[26] The process can be expensive and time-consuming. Each site of a company must be separately certified. The certification of one site cannot cover the entire company. Although ISO certification is becoming an important consideration for companies expecting to do business in the EU, it is not the solution to all quality issues as noted in Figure 18.6. However, ISO certification of suppliers will help them to get more business, especially with European companies. When companies, especially European companies, are choosing among different suppliers, it would be very beneficial for the supplier to have ISO certification.

Kaizen—the Japanese process of continuous improvement, the cornerstone of TQM

Levels of quality standards
- **General level—ISO 9000, Malcolm Baldridge National Quality Award**
- **Industry-specific level**
- **Company level**

ISO 9000—a European set of quality standards intended to promote quality at every level of an organization

FIGURE 18.6   ISO 9000 Certification: An Important Edge?

Source: DILBERT reprinted by permission of United Feature Syndicate, Inc.

ISO 9001 is the most comprehensive and detailed standard in the series of ISO standards. It is used when the company has to assure conformance to customers for specific requirements for design, development, production, installation, and servicing. ISO 9002 is directed to sites not dealing with design and after-market service and therefore is intended to assure conformance to specific requirements for production and installation. Samsonite notes in its corporate profile that several of its suitcases have been given ISO 9002 certification. That probably means that some but not all of its facilities have passed ISO 9002 inspections. ISO 9003 focuses on final inspection of products or services and testing.

The ISO guidelines provide interpretation of the standards for particular industries: The ISO 9004 Quality Management System describes the philosophy behind the standards by providing guidelines for developing and implementing a quality system. It describes the primary elements of a quality system: product and service requirements, organization and control, customer satisfaction, customer–product responsibility, and system guidance. ISO 9004-2 does all the above but focuses on the service industry. ISO 9004-3 describes what a software company must account for in connection with development, supply, and maintenance in order to comply with a standard (usually 9001).

U.S. companies that operate in Europe are becoming ISO certified to maintain access to the European market. When DuPont lost a major European contract to an ISO-certified European company, it decided to become certified. By doing so, not only was DuPont able to position itself better in the European market, it also benefited from the experience of going through ISO certification and focusing on quality in the organization. Some European companies are so fanatical about ISO certification that they will not do business with a supplier that is certified if its suppliers are not also ISO certified. They want to be sure that quality flows back to every level of the supply chain.

In addition to the general standards described above, there are industry-specific standards for quality, especially for suppliers to follow. In addition, individual companies set their own standards for suppliers to meet if they are going to continue to supply them. Samsonite's concerns in Eastern Europe and its subsequent work with Eastern European

Non-European companies operating in Europe need to become ISO certified in order to maintain access to that market.

suppliers to meet its quality requirements are an example of how companies set their own standards and work with suppliers.

SUPPLIER NETWORKS

Sourcing—the process of a firm having inputs supplied to it from outside suppliers (both domestic and foreign) for the production process.

Global sourcing and production strategies can be better understood by looking at Figure 18.7. **Sourcing** is the firm's process of having inputs (raw materials and parts) supplied to it for the production process. Figure 18.7 illustrates the basic operating environment choices (the home country or any foreign country) by stage in the production process (sourcing of raw materials and parts and the manufacture and assembly of final products). Global sourcing is the first step in the process of materials management, also called logistics, which includes sourcing, inventory management, and transportation between suppliers, manufacturers, and customers.

For example, Ford assembles cars in Hermosillo, Mexico, and ships them into the United States for end-use consumers. The cars are designed by Mazda, a Japanese company, and use some Japanese parts. Ford can purchase parts manufactured in Japan and ship them to the United States for final assembly and sale in the U.S. market, or it can have Japanese- and U.S.-made parts shipped to Mexico for final assembly and sale in the United States and Mexico. For Mexican assembly, some of the parts come from the United States, some from Japan, and a small percentage from Mexico. When Ford decided to manufacture the Escort in Europe, it used the global sourcing of parts from plants in 15 different countries for final assembly in the United Kingdom and Germany, as Figure 18.8 illustrates.

Companies can manufacture parts internally or purchase them from external manufacturers.

Companies can manufacture parts internally or purchase them from external (unrelated) manufacturers. Samsonite manufactured most of the parts that went into its luggage, but it sourced some of its parts from unrelated suppliers—such as wheels for suitcases from Czech suppliers. As mentioned earlier, Samsonite sourced semifinished

FIGURE 18.7 Global Sourcing and Production Strategy

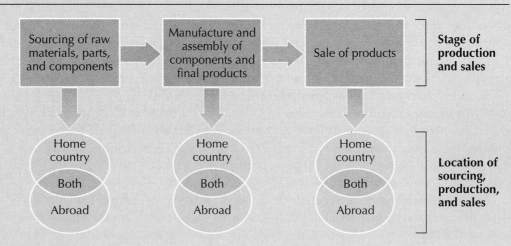

Companies have many possibilities for sourcing raw materials, parts, and components, and assembling them into final goods to serve worldwide markets. For example, a U.S. company could source components in the United States, assemble them in Mexico, and export the final product back to the United States or to other countries. To be global a company must choose "abroad" at least once.

softside parts from East European subcontractors to use in its own factories. Companies can also assemble their own products internally or subcontract to external companies, as noted earlier in the examples of Nike, Mattel, and McDonald's Happy Meals toys. Manufacture of parts and final assembly may take place in the company's home country, the country in which it is trying to sell the product, or a third country.[27]

Sourcing in the home country enables companies to avoid numerous problems, including those connected with language differences, long distances and lengthy supply lines, exchange-rate fluctuations, wars and insurrections, strikes, politics, tariffs, and complex transportation channels. However, for many companies domestic sources may be unavailable or more expensive than foreign sources. In Japan, foreign procurement is

> **Using domestic sources for raw materials and components allows a company to avoid problems with language differences, distance, currency, political problems, tariffs, and other problems.**

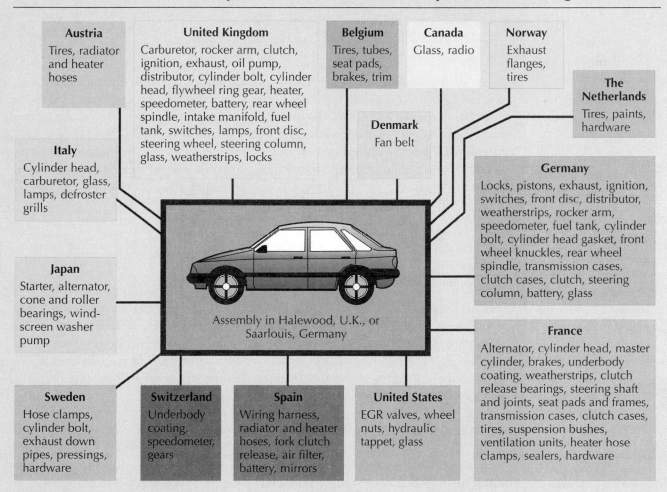

FIGURE 18.8   The Global Component Network for Ford's European Manufacturing of the Escort

Austria
Tires, radiator and heater hoses

United Kingdom
Carburetor, rocker arm, clutch, ignition, exhaust, oil pump, distributor, cylinder bolt, cylinder head, flywheel ring gear, heater, speedometer, battery, rear wheel spindle, intake manifold, fuel tank, switches, lamps, front disc, steering wheel, steering column, glass, weatherstrips, locks

Belgium
Tires, tubes, seat pads, brakes, trim

Canada
Glass, radio

Norway
Exhaust flanges, tires

The Netherlands
Tires, paints, hardware

Denmark
Fan belt

Italy
Cylinder head, carburetor, glass, lamps, defroster grills

Germany
Locks, pistons, exhaust, ignition, switches, front disc, distributor, weatherstrips, rocker arm, speedometer, fuel tank, cylinder bolt, cylinder head gasket, front wheel knuckles, rear wheel spindle, transmission cases, clutch cases, clutch, steering column, battery, glass

Japan
Starter, alternator, cone and roller bearings, windscreen washer pump

Assembly in Halewood, U.K., or Saarlouis, Germany

France
Alternator, cylinder head, master cylinder, brakes, underbody coating, weatherstrips, clutch release bearings, steering shaft and joints, seat pads and frames, transmission cases, clutch cases, tires, suspension bushes, ventilation units, heater hose clamps, sealers, hardware

Sweden
Hose clamps, cylinder bolt, exhaust down pipes, pressings, hardware

Switzerland
Underbody coating, speedometer, gears

Spain
Wiring harness, radiator and heater hoses, fork clutch release, air filter, battery, mirrors

United States
EGR valves, wheel nuts, hydraulic tappet, glass

Ford assembles Escorts in only two facilities in Europe, but parts and components used in the automobiles come from all over the world.

Source: World Development Report (New York: Oxford University Press, 1987), p. 39.

critical, because nearly all of that country's uranium, bauxite, nickel, crude oil, iron ore, copper, coking coal and approximately 30 percent of its agricultural products are imported. Japanese trading companies came into being expressly to acquire the raw materials necessary to fuel Japan's manufacturing.

Companies pursue global sourcing strategies for a number of reasons:

Companies outsource abroad to lower costs and improve quality, among other reasons.

1. To reduce costs—due to less expensive labor, less restrictive work rules, and lower land and facilities costs
2. To improve quality
3. To increase exposure to worldwide technology
4. To improve delivery of supplies
5. To strengthen the reliability of supply by supplementing domestic with foreign suppliers
6. To gain access to materials available only abroad, possibly because of technical specifications or product capabilities
7. To establish a presence in a foreign market
8. To satisfy offset requirements (as discussed in Chapter 17)
9. To react to competitors' offshore sourcing practices[28]

In some ways global sourcing is more expensive than domestic sourcing. For example, transportation and communications are more expensive, and companies may have to pay brokers and agent fees. Given the longer length of supply lines, it often takes more time to get components from abroad, and lead times are less certain. This increases the inventory carrying costs and makes it more difficult to get parts to the production site in a timely manner. If imported components come in with errors and need to be reworked, the cost per unit will rise, and some components may have to be shipped back to the supplier.

Three major configurations of outsourcing have emerged:

Major outsourcing configurations
• **Vertical integration**
• **Arm's-length purchases from outside suppliers**
• **Japanese** *keiretsu* **relationships with suppliers**

1. Vertical integration
2. Arm's-length purchases from outside suppliers
3. Japanese *keiretsu* relationships with suppliers

Vertical integration is where the company owns the entire supplier network or at least a significant part of it. It may have to purchase raw materials from outside suppliers, but the company produces the most expensive parts. Arm's-length purchases is the same as outsourcing. The Japanese *keiretsus*, as discussed in Chapter 15, are a group of independent companies that work together to manage the flow of goods and services along the entire value-added chain.[29]

MAKE OR BUY DECISION

MNE managers struggle with deciding which production activities to perform internally and which are best to subcontract to independent companies, also sometimes called **outsourcing**. That is the make or buy decision. In the latter case, they also need to decide whether the activities should be carried on in the home market or abroad.

Outsourcing—purchasing inputs from outside suppliers not related to the company

In deciding whether to make or buy, MNEs could focus on those parts that are critical to the product and that they are distinctively good at making. They could outsource parts when suppliers have a distinct comparative advantage, such as greater scale, lower-cost structure, or stronger performance incentives. They also could use outsourcing as an implied threat to underperforming employees that if they don't improve, the companies will move their business elsewhere.[30]

In determining whether to make or buy, the MNE needs to determine the design and manufacturing capabilities of potential suppliers compared to its own capabilities. If the supplier has a clear advantage, management needs to decide what it would cost to catch up to the best suppliers and whether it would make sense to do so.

SUPPLIER RELATIONS

When Honda was designing the Accord, it sent engineers to 33 key subcontractors in Japan and 28 in the United States, which together make parts that represent 60 to 70 percent of the car's value. The purpose of the visits was to reduce manufacturing costs by obtaining suggestions on parts designs. As a result of supplier inputs and other efforts at cost control, Honda was able to reduce the cost of components and not increase the price of the new model.[31]

If an MNE decides it must outsource rather than integrate vertically, it must determine how to work with suppliers. Toyota pioneered the Toyota Production System to work with unrelated suppliers. Toyota sends a team of manufacturing experts to each of its key suppliers to observe how the supplier organizes its factory and makes its parts. Then the team advises on how to cut costs and boost quality. For example, Toyota approached Bumper Works, a small 100-person factory in Illinois, and asked its management to design and manufacture a bumper that would meet Toyota's rigid specifications. After demonstrating that it could satisfy Toyota, Bumper Works became the sole supplier for that company's U.S. facilities. However, Toyota expected annual price reductions, higher-quality bumpers, and on-time deliveries. Toyota helped Bumper Works determine how to change the dies in its metal-stamping process so that it could provide the flexibility that Toyota required for different types of bumpers.

It is also common for Toyota to identify two suppliers for each part and have the suppliers compete aggressively with each other. The supplier that performs the best gets the most business. However, both suppliers know that they will have an ongoing relationship with Toyota and will not be dumped easily.[32]

This is a good example of the close relationships that Japanese companies develop with their suppliers. It is very different from the arm's-length relationship that U.S. companies tend to have with their suppliers. Further, Toyota has been able to reduce the number of supplier relationships it develops, which allows it to focus on a few key suppliers, promising to give them a lot of business if they perform up to Toyota standards. For example, for its British operations, Toyota relies on about 150 parts suppliers, compared with the 500 to 1000 suppliers typical for other European automakers.[33]

THE PURCHASING FUNCTION

The purchasing agent is the link between the company's outsourcing decision and its supplier relationships. Just as companies go through stages of globalization, so does the purchasing agent's scope of responsibilities. Typically, purchasing goes through four phases before becoming "global":

1. Domestic purchasing only
2. Foreign buying based on need
3. Foreign buying as part of procurement strategy
4. Integration of global procurement strategy[34]

Make or buy—outsource or supply parts from internal production

If MNEs outsource instead of source parts from internal production, they need to determine the degree of involvement with suppliers.

Global progression in the purchasing function
- *Domestic purchasing only*
- *Foreign buying based on need*
- *Foreign buying as part of a procurement strategy*
- *Integration of global procurement strategy*

Phase 4 occurs when the company realizes the benefits from integration and coordination of purchasing on a global basis and is most applicable to the MNE as opposed to, say, the exporter. When purchasing becomes this global, MNEs often face the centralization/decentralization dilemma. Should they allow each subsidiary to make all purchasing decisions, or should they centralize all or some of the purchasing decisions? The primary benefits of decentralization include increased production facility control over purchases, better responsiveness to facility needs, and more effective use of local suppliers. The primary benefits of centralization are increased leverage with suppliers, getting better prices, eliminating administrative duplication, allowing purchasers to develop specialized knowledge in purchasing techniques, reducing the number of orders processed, and enabling purchasing to build solid supplier relationships.[35]

Companies pursue five major sourcing strategies as they move into phases 3 and 4 in the preceding list (foreign buying as part of procurement strategy and integration of global procurement strategy):

Sourcing strategies in the global context
- **Assign domestic buyers for foreign purchasing**
- **Use foreign subsidiaries or business agents**
- **Establish international purchasing offices**
- **Assign foreign purchasing to one division**
- **Integrate and coordinate worldwide sourcing**

1. Assign domestic buyer(s) for international purchasing
2. Use foreign subsidiaries or business agents
3. Establish international purchasing offices
4. Assign the responsibility for global sourcing to a specific business unit or units
5. Integrate and coordinate worldwide sourcing[36]

These strategies move from the simple to the more complex, similar to the concept illustrated in Figure 1.7 on the usual patterns of internationalization. Companies start by using a domestic buyer and progress all the way to integrating and coordinating worldwide sourcing into the company's purchasing decisions so that there is no difference between domestic and foreign sources.

Figure 18.9 summarizes some of the key concepts in the preceding discussion in terms of selecting the best supplier to use. The key is for managers to select the best supplier, establish a solid relationship, and continually evaluate the supplier's performance to ensure the best price, quality, and on-time delivery possible.

Today, many of the supplier alliances are strategic in nature and entail more than just the purchasing of inputs. Previously, relationships between buyer and supplier were characterized by low commitment, limited information sharing, and contractual agreements. Now relationships are *alliances* in which buyer and seller provide more information about order quantities and timing, upcoming design changes, long-range plans, and so on.[37]

INVENTORY MANAGEMENT

Distance, time, and uncertainty in foreign environments cause foreign sourcing to complicate inventory management.

Whether a company decides to source parts from inside or outside the company or from domestic of foreign sources, it needs to manage the flow and storage of inventory. This is true of raw materials and parts sourced from suppliers, work in process and finished goods inventory inside the manufacturing plant, and finished goods stored at a distribution center, such as the centralized European warehouse for Samsonite.

If the company sources parts from a variety of suppliers from around the world, distance, time, and the uncertainty of the international political and economic environment can make it difficult for managers to determine correct reorder points for the

FIGURE 18.9 Assessing the Organization's Global Sourcing Needs and Strategy

STEPS IN GLOBAL SOURCING PROCESS	QUESTIONS ANSWERED AT EACH STEP
Evaluate operating and competitive environments.	Is global sourcing a valuable competitive option? Can global sourcing help us better meet customers' real needs?
Define scope of international purchasing effort.	How intensive and extensive does the global sourcing effort need to be? • What items should we global source? • What structure and infrastructure are needed? • What skills will our purchasers need? • Does a cost/benefit analysis support the selected scope?
Identify and evaluate potential suppliers worldwide.	Who are the best suppliers for each item? Where are they located worldwide? Can they provide world-class support to our global operations? What is their total order performance? • Total cost • Delivery • Quality • Innovation • Responsiveness
Determine appropriate nature of buyer-supplier relationship.	Given our needs, the supplier's location and capabilities, and the channel's logistical challenges, what type of buyer-supplier relationship should we establish?
Request/evaluate proposals from suppliers.	Are the proposals truly comparable at the total ownership level? Who is the best supplier in the short term? Long term?
Select "best" supplier, establish contract terms and conditions, and build desired relationship.	Is future negotiation needed? Are roles and responsibilities clearly understood? Are performance expectations clearly stated and understood? How are resources, risks, and rewards going to be shared?
Continual reevaluation of implementation status, requirements, and capabilities.	Is the buyer-supplier relationship fully established? Effective? Is the selected supplier performing at world-class standards? Based on changes in our own operations, our competitive requirements, and our customers' needs, does this relationship still make sense?

Source: Stanley E. Fawcett, "The Globalization of the Supply Environment," *The Supply Environment,* Vol. 2 (Tempe, AZ: NAPM, 2000). Reprinted by permission.

manufacturing process. For example, if a manufacturer in a country with a weakening currency regularly imports inventory from a country with a strong currency, management may want to stockpile inventory in anticipation of a devaluation, despite large carrying costs and the risk of damage or pilferage. This was true in Brazil in late 1998 when the fear of devaluation was pretty high. Companies that had stockpiled foreign-sourced parts prior to the devaluation of January 1999 were better off than companies that carried lean inventories. After the devaluation, it would have been more expensive in Brazilian real terms to purchase foreign inventory. Another reason for stockpiling inventory is the perceived risk that political chaos or legislation will slow down imports. Rapidly changing international events can ruin a smoothly running inventory-control system.

JUST-IN-TIME SYSTEMS

JIT—sourcing raw materials and parts just as they are needed in the manufacturing process

In Chapter 8, we briefly mentioned just-in-time inventory systems as a reason why companies might hesitate sourcing parts from foreign suppliers. "JIT systems focus on reducing inefficiency and unproductive time in the production process to improve continuously the process and the quality of the product or service."[38] The JIT system gets raw materials, parts, and components to the buyer "just in time" for use, sparing companies the cost of storing large inventories. That is what Dell hoped to accomplish in its Irish plant by having parts delivered just as they were to enter the production process and then go out the door to the consumers as soon as the computers were built. However, the use of JIT means that parts must have few defects and must arrive on time. That is why companies need to develop solid supplier relationships to ensure good quality and delivery times if JIT is to work.

It is hard to combine foreign sourcing and JIT production without having safety stocks of inventory on hand, which defeats the concept of JIT.

Foreign sourcing can create big risks for companies that use JIT, because interruptions in the supply line can cause havoc. JIT implies that inventories must be small, but foreign sourcing almost always requires large inventories to counteract the risk of interruption in supply. Companies such as Toyota that have set up manufacturing and assembly facilities overseas to service local markets have practically forced their domestic parts suppliers to move overseas as well to allow Toyota to continue with JIT manufacturing. That is why so many Japanese parts suppliers, such as Denso, a major Toyota supplier, have moved to the United States and Mexico to be near their major customers.

A company's inventory management strategy—especially in terms of stock sizes and whether or not JIT will be used—determines frequency of needed shipments. The less frequent the delivery, the more likely the need to store inventory somewhere. Because JIT requires delivery just as the inventory is to be used, some concession must be made for inventory arriving from foreign suppliers. Sometimes that means adjusting the arrival time to a few days before use rather than a few hours. Kawasaki, U.S.A. carries a minimum of three days' inventory on parts coming from Japan, with an average inventory of five days.[39]

Quality of inventory is important, because inventory with significant amounts of defects will create problems with JIT. If the buyer has to purchase more because of expected defects, there will be not only wasted inventory but also higher carrying costs. Nike contracts out the manufacture of shoes to China, but it also has a Nike team on hand at the factories in China to ensure high-quality manufacturing. The geographic distance between buyer and supplier, language differences, and cultural differences can increase the time it takes to educate suppliers on how to supply products of high quality.[40]

JIT typically implies sole sourcing for specific parts in order to get the supplier to commit to the stringent delivery and quality requirements inherent in JIT. However, if the only supplier is a foreign supplier, it would be too risky to permit just one supplier. That means cultivating multiple suppliers, at least one of which may be a foreign supplier. The problem is that using multiple suppliers may preclude the buyer from getting volume pricing from the supplier. One strategy is that buyers may use a sole supplier for all but critical inputs. Then it is best to cultivate solid secondary suppliers.[41]

Looking to the Future
TO BE GLOBAL, SUPPLY CHAIN LINKS MUST BE STRONG

In establishing manufacturing facilities to serve worldwide markets, MNEs started with large home-market plants and exported to foreign markets. As the importance of those markets increased, companies needed to establish manufacturing facilities abroad, almost in a multidomestic approach. Now, however, they are finding that they need much stronger control over manufacturing operations worldwide in order to take advantage of market differences and to drive down costs.

Improvements in communications technology will continue to facilitate the flow of information worldwide. The increasing use of the Internet to establish extranet connections with suppliers and customers will give companies significant flexibility in establishing relationships and should improve quality, delivery time, and responsiveness to consumer demands. Companies will have available a wider array of suppliers to choose from, and suppliers can be more responsive to consumer demands by getting the right inventory to the production system at the right time. As Andy Grove, the chairman of Intel said, "In five years' time, all companies will be Internet companies, or they won't be companies at all."[42]

As companies examine their core competencies, they will have to decide if they want to be in the manufacturing business as Samsonite is or if they want to outsource their manufacturing as Nike does. Whichever strategy they adopt, they will certainly have to develop a stronger global supply chain management system.

FOREIGN TRADE ZONES

In recent years, **foreign trade zones (FTZs)** have become more popular as an intermediate step in the process between import and final use. FTZs are areas in which domestic and imported merchandise can be stored, inspected, and manufactured free from formal customs procedures until the goods leave the zones. The zones are intended to encourage companies to locate in the country by allowing them to defer duties, pay fewer duties, or avoid certain duties completely. Sometimes inventory is stored in an FTZ until it needs to be used for domestic manufacture. As noted above, one of the problems with JIT is the length of the supply line when relying on global sourcing, possibly causing either the buyer or the supplier to stockpile inventory somewhere until it is needed in the manufacturing process. One place to stockpile inventory is in a warehouse in an FTZ.

FTZs can be general-purpose zones or subzones. A general-purpose zone usually is established near a port of entry, such as a shipping port, a border crossing, or an airport, and usually consists of a distribution facility or an industrial park. A subzone usually is physically separate from a general-purpose zone but is under the same administrative structure. Since 1982, the major growth in FTZs has been in subzones rather than general-purpose zones because companies have sought to defer duties on parts that are foreign sourced until they need to be used in the production process. For example, the major growth in subzones in the United States has been in the automobile industry,

> Foreign trade zones—special locations for storing domestic and imported inventory and avoiding paying duties until the inventory is used in production or sold

especially in the Midwest. Subzone activity is spreading to other industries, especially shipbuilding, pharmaceuticals, and home appliances, and becoming more heavily oriented to manufacturing and assembly than was originally envisioned.

FTZs are used worldwide. In Japan, they are being established for the benefit of foreign companies exporting products to that country. Japanese zones serve as warehousing and repackaging facilities at which companies can display consumer goods for demonstration to Japanese buyers.[43]

In the United States, FTZs have been used primarily as a means of providing greater flexibility as to when and how customs duties are paid. However, their use in the export business has been expanding. The exports for which these FTZs are used fall into one of the following categories:

- Foreign goods transshipped through U.S. zones to third countries
- Foreign goods processed in U.S. zones, then transshipped abroad
- Foreign goods processed or assembled in U.S. zones with some domestic materials and parts, then reexported
- Goods produced wholly of foreign content in U.S. zones and then exported
- Domestic goods moved into a U.S. zone to achieve export status prior to their actual exportation[44]

An example of how an FTZ can be used occurs at a subzone in Texas, where a Coastal Corporation subsidiary refines imported oil. If the subsidiary exports the refined oil products, it pays no duty at all. If it sells the products domestically, it saves over $250,000 a year in interest on duties postponed until the products leave the zone.[45]

Kawasaki, U.S.A. established an assembly operation in an FTZ using parts from Japan. By becoming an FTZ, Kawasaki bypassed U.S. Customs and had the parts delivered directly to its assembly operations. In addition, Kawasaki did not have to pay duties on the inventory until the final goods left the zone. Not only did Kawasaki speed up delivery of parts by five days, but it also improved its cash flow.

TRANSPORTATION NETWORKS

Transportation links together suppliers, companies, and customers.

For a firm, the transportation of goods in an international context is extremely complicated in terms of documentation, choice of carrier (air or ocean), and the decision on whether to establish its own transportation department or outsource to a third-party intermediary. Transportation is one of the key elements of a logistics system. The key is to link together suppliers and manufacturers and manufacturers and final consumers. Along the way, the company has to determine what its warehouse configuration will be. For example, McDonald's provides food items to its franchises around the world. It has warehouses in different countries to service different geographic areas. In the Samsonite case, there was no discussion of the issues surrounding transportation and warehousing from suppliers to Samsonite's factories, but the movement of goods from factories to retailers was an important issue.

Third-party intermediaries, such as Emery, DHL, Fedex, and UPS, are crucial in storing and transporting goods.

Third-party intermediaries are an important dimension to transportation networks. For example, Emery Worldwide is a division of CNF Transportation Inc., a company that specializes in transportation and logistics solutions for companies. It is a $2.5 bil-

lion integrated carrier providing global air and ocean freight transportation, logistics management, customs brokerage, and expedited services to manufacturing, industrial, retail, and government customers. Based in Redwood City, California, Emery provides service to 229 countries through a network of more than 600 service centers and agent locations around the world. One of Emery's customers is Iomega, the Roy, Utah, company that manufactures the Zip drive, a personal storage solution that can help people manage information. Iomega entered into an agreement with Emery to use Emery's warehouse facilities in Singapore to store inventory and supply finished product to customers all over Asia. Iomega designs the products in its Utah facilities and subcontracts parts to be made by suppliers all over Asia. Some parts are supplied by more than one suppler. Emery handles the shipment of parts from the suppliers to its distribution center in Singapore. One section of the distribution center is dedicated to Iomega products. In the section is an assembly line where Iomega personnel, most of whom are brought into Singapore from Sri Lanka as guest workers, can engage in "pick-n-pack," an assembly operation where they pick parts off a conveyer belt and pack them for customers. Then the final goods are packaged and stored by Emery until they are sent to the Changi Airport Airfreight Centre for shipment to customers in Asia. In this example, you can see all of the elements of the transportation networks that are so essential in international logistics.

Singapore has one of the largest container ports in the world. Most goods are transported internationally by container. Goods can be loaded into containers and sent to ports by rail or truck. Then they can be sent overseas by airfreight or ocean freight. The transportation company, like Emery, can try to fill up a container just with the company's products, or it can combine the products with those of another company to share container space.

The logistics management that companies like Emery engage in is very detail oriented, requiring the ability to gather, track, and process large quantities of information. To be effective, logistics companies need to implement key technologies, including communications technologies, satellite tracking systems, bar-coding applications, and automated materials handling systems.[46] Emery employs all these technologies at its Singapore facilities to help companies like Iomega ship their goods worldwide.

WEB CONNECTION

Check out our home page www.prenhall.com/daniels for links to key resources for you in your study of international business.

SUMMARY

- A company's supply chain encompasses the coordination of materials, information, and funds from the initial raw material supplier to the ultimate customer.

- Suppliers can be related to or independent from the manufacturer. Suppliers can be domestic or foreign.

- Logistics, or materials management, is that part of the supply chain process that plans, implements, and controls the efficient, effective flow and storage of goods, services, and related information from the point of origin to the point of consumption in order to meet customers' requirements.

- Companies can manufacture products or enter into virtual manufacturing through subcontracting to other manufacturers.

- The success of a global manufacturing strategy depends on compatibility, configuration, coordination, and control.

- Cost-minimization strategies and the drive for global efficiencies often force MNEs offshore to low-cost manufacturing areas, especially in Asia and Eastern Europe.

- Three broad categories of manufacturing configuration are one centralized facility, regional facilities, and multidomestic facilities.

- A major challenge for MNEs is selecting the number of plants and their locations for servicing customers worldwide.

- Layout planning involves decisions about the physical arrangement of economic activity within a manufacturing facility.

- The key to making a global supply chain system work is information. Companies are rapidly turning to the Internet as a way to link suppliers with manufacturing and eventually with end-use customers.

- Quality is defined as meeting or exceeding the expectations of customers.

- Total quality management is a process that stresses customer satisfaction, employee involvement, and continuous improvements in quality.

- Quality standards can be general (ISO 9000), industry specific, and company specific.

- Global sourcing is the process of a firm having raw materials and parts supplied to it from domestic and foreign sources.

- Domestic sourcing allows the company to avoid problems related to language, culture, currency, tariffs, and so forth.

- Foreign sourcing allows the company to reduce costs and improve quality, among other things.

- Under the make or buy decision, companies have to decide if they will make their own parts or buy them from an independent company.

- Companies go through different purchasing phases as they become more committed to global sourcing.

- When a company sources parts from suppliers around the world, distance, time, and the uncertainty of the international political and economic environment can make it difficult for managers to manage inventory flows accurately.

- Just-in-time focuses on reducing inefficiency and unproductive time in the production process to improve continuously the process and quality of the product or service.

- The transportation system links together suppliers with manufacturers and manufacturers with customers.

CASE

DENSO CORPORATION AND GLOBAL SUPPLIER RELATIONS[47]

In 1999, DENSO Corporation, the Japanese auto parts supplier formerly known as NIPPONDENSO, was struggling to determine what strategy it should pursue to succeed and move forward into the twenty-first century. Should it continue to be tightly linked to Toyota as its major parts supplier? Or, given that it makes products other than auto parts, should it become less dependent on the automotive industry in general and Toyota in particular? And, because the demand for its product varies so much from customer to customer, DENSO also wondered how it could better manage its production and inventory levels.

BACKGROUND ON DENSO

DENSO is the third-largest auto parts supplier in the world, just behind Delphi of the United States and Bosch of Germany. Prior to 1949, it was a part of Toyota, but then it spun off into a separate company, even though Toyota still retains 24.63 percent of DENSO's issued stock. Thus DENSO is part of the Toyota *keiretsu* that includes companies in automotive parts, steel, precision machinery, automatic looms, textiles, household wares, office and housing units, and other products. As Map 18.2 shows, DENSO's world headquarters and most of its domestic manufacturing facilities are in Aichi prefecture on the east coast of Japan and close to Toyota City, the headquarters for Toyota Corporation. Toyota's domestic manufacturing plants are also located in Aichi prefecture, so there is a close proximity between DENSO and Toyota plants.

As illustrated in Figure 18.10, only 8.2 percent of DENSO's 1999 revenues were in nonautomotive products,

mostly in telecommunications and environmental systems. The wireless technology that DENSO developed for cars is being used to bring out new forms of mobile communication for individuals, a highly competitive market. In terms of environmental systems, DENSO manufactures water purifiers, spot heaters, and biodegradation garbage disposals. However, its real strength is the automotive parts industry.

Although DENSO is a major supplier to Toyota, it supplies parts to all companies manufacturing automobiles in Japan. In addition, it is the most global of the Japanese auto parts companies. DENSO generated 37.2 percent of its fiscal 1999 revenues from overseas sales. DENSO has 12 domestic plants, 74 international companies (of which 55 are production facilities), and employs over 81,000 workers. Map 18.3 shows that DENSO has production facilities in every world region except Africa and Russia. DENSO initially expanded overseas to supply Toyota's overseas plants, but now it

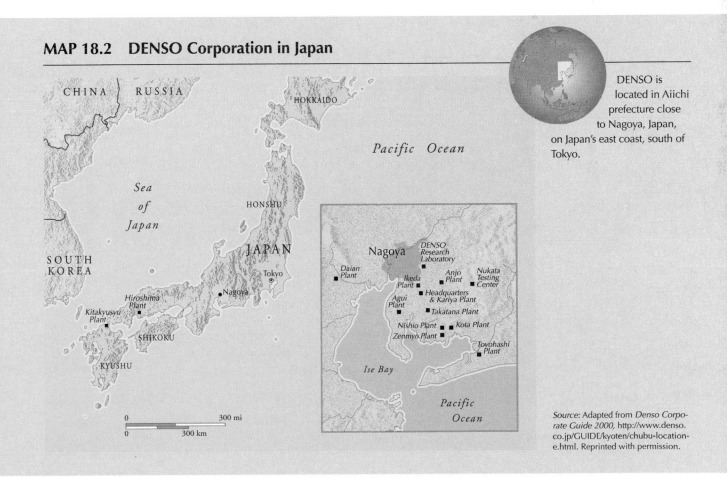

MAP 18.2 DENSO Corporation in Japan

DENSO is located in Aiichi prefecture close to Nagoya, Japan, on Japan's east coast, south of Tokyo.

Source: Adapted from *Denso Corporate Guide 2000,* http://www.denso.co.jp/GUIDE/kyoten/chubu-location-e.html. Reprinted with permission.

FIGURE 18.10   DENSO Sales Breakdown, FY 1999

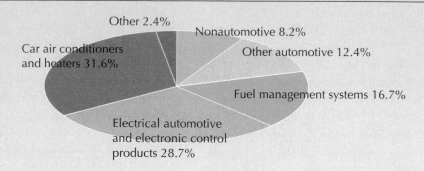

MAP 18.3   DENSO's Global Network

With production facilities in almost every world region, DENSO is Japan's most global auto parts company.

supplies other auto companies overseas as well. Toyota has 41 production companies in 25 countries in every region of the world.

QUALITY STANDARDS AND MANUFACTURING PRACTICES OF DENSO

DENSO has to meet tough quality standards. First, it needs to satisfy Toyota's rigid quality standards by using TQM and striving for zero defects. Second, it complies with both ISO 9001 and QS9000 certification so that it can qualify as a supplier for auto manufacturers in Europe and North America. QS9000 is a quality standard specifically for the auto industry. Chrysler, Ford, and General Motors established QS9000 in 1994 to provide requirements and measurables (events that can be quantified and specific measures that can be used to describe those events) for the automotive industry. QS9000 is derived from ISO 9001, but it is more specific to the auto industry. Under the guidelines, suppliers must adapt their quality systems to meet the expectations of the automakers. QS9000 is required for any supplier of Ford, General Motors, and Chrysler (now DaimlerChrysler).

DENSO separates its production facilities into a parts manufacturing area, a subassembly area, and a final assembly area. It uses a flexible and automated assembly line with significant robotics. The Takatana Plant of DENSO assembles instrument panels for its customers. DENSO has created a "green belt" around the plant, perhaps so workers can look at trees, not factories. It also has invested heavily in an information system for production control, even though it traditionally has used and is currently using a kanban sytem. The kanban system is a JIT system pioneered by Toyota. *Kanban* literally means "card" or "visible record" in Japanese. The kanban cards are used to control the flow of production through a factory. For example, Toyota uses kanban in the assembly of a Lexus at its Tsutsumi assembly plant just south of Toyota City, and DENSO supplies automatic air conditioners to the plant on a JIT basis. In the kanban system used by Toyota, DENSO ships air conditioners to the Tsutsumi plant just before they need to go into production. They are kept in a bin that has a card attached to it identifying the number of air conditioners in the bin. When the assembly process begins, a production-order card signifies that a bin of air conditioners needs to be moved to the assembly line. When the bin is emptied, it is moved to a storage area and replaced with a full bin. The kanban card is removed from the empty bin and used to order a replacement from DENSO. DENSO ships parts to Toyota approximately 8 to 10 times a day, 24 hours a day. In order to service Toyota, DENSO keeps roughly a 5-day inventory of some parts.

The same process used by Toyota is also used by DENSO to manufacture the air conditioner. An air conditioner requires an electronic control unit, a cabin air temperature sensor, an ambient air temperature sensor, a solar radiation sensor, a coolant temperature sensor, an evaporator sensor, a compressor with magnetic clutch, a heater core, a condensor, expansion valves, and so on. DENSO manufactures some of these parts, and outside suppliers manufacture others. In 1999, DENSO's assembly plant for its instrument clusters (speedometer, etc.) was running on one eight-hour shift, which was at about 80 percent capacity. However, its parts production was running two shifts.

DENSO had pretty good labor relations, because its labor union is a company union. However, DENSO management still maintained that salary negotiations are pretty tough. Workers are hired for life and paid a salary, which is based on a mixture of age, expertise, and performance. There is a relatively small wage gap among DENSO employees. Employee performance is evaluated every six months, with a bonus paid every six months.

DENSO'S FUTURE

In assessing DENSO's strengths and weaknesses, management feels that its production and production training are very strong. However, it needs to further improve its R&D if it is going to continue to move forward into the future. The key is to continue to develop new products, both inside and outside of the auto industry, if it is going to continue to generate revenues. DENSO still engages in lifetime employment, and it feels that this employment system helps it to improve continuously.

Domestic demand in Japan has been relatively flat during the mid- to latter half of the 1990s, which has made it difficult for DENSO to keep generating growth in revenues. Because it is dependent on the auto industry, its fortunes rise and fall with those of Toyota and its other key customers. It is making a big push to sell to DaimlerChrysler, because it is the fifth-largest auto company in the world, just behind GM, Ford, Toyota, and the VW Group. Approximately 40 percent of DENSO's sales come from overseas operations. DENSO's plants in the United States and Mexico service the U.S. market. As a whole, DENSO is still growing, but demand varies for different divisions. The electronics division, for example, is growing, so DENSO management has been shifting employment to that division. Because of lifetime employment, DENSO does not want to lay off workers, so it finds new product lines where it can shift workers. Then it retrains them for the job. Each of its plants has an education facility on site. Usually, however, DENSO's employees stay in one division until they retire.

A major challenge DENSO faces is that Toyota is still based on a kanban system, even though the rest of the industry is moving away from kanban. Toyota uses forecasts, which can help DENSO plan its production, but the final production cycle is based on kanban. Mitsubishi and Honda, however, request products based on a forecast of demand and do not use kanban. Their final orders are placed three days in advance, and they have much more fluctuation in demand than does Toyota. Toyota tries to schedule a relatively flat production schedule, meaning that there is not a great deal of fluctuation in its demand, whereas the demand from Mitsubishi and Honda fluctuates a great deal. Even though DENSO supplies all major auto companies in Japan, it relies on Toyota for 50 percent of its revenues. It needs to figure out how to diversify its revenue base more without losing Toyota's business.

An alternative to kanban is MRP—material requirements planning. MRP is a computerized information system that addresses complex inventory situations like DENSO's (manufacturing parts for its own use as well as for several different auto companies). MRP calculates the demand for parts from the production schedules of the companies that use the parts. DENSO's dilemma is that some of its customers forecast demand, but Toyota uses kanban and requires delivery of parts when it empties its bins. DENSO is hoping that it can establish a good MRP or similar computer-based information system to solve the complexity of producing so many parts for so many different companies.

QUESTIONS

1. How has DENSO's relationship with Toyota affected its international strategy?
2. What types of quality programs has DENSO adopted, and how do you think they will affect DENSO's future as a global supplier?
3. Why does it make a difference whether DENSO uses kanban or MRP?
4. What challenges will DENSO face as it diversifies its customers and its product lines?
5. What do you notice in the layout of the Takatana Plant that demonstrates DENSO's commitment to its employees?

CHAPTER NOTES

1 F. De Beule and D. Van Den Bulcke, "The International Supply Chain Management of Samsonite Europe," Discussion Paper No. 1998/E/34, Centre for International Management and Development, University of Antwerp; "Samsonite History," www.samsonite.com; "Company Briefing Book," Wall Street Journal, interactive ed, January 27, 2000; and "Tüv Essen," http://tuvessen.com/certification.

2 Deloitte & Touche, "Energing the Supply Chain," The Review, January 17, 2000, p. 1.

3 Stanley Fawcett, "Supply Chain Management: Competing Through Integration," in Ethical Theory and Business by Tom L. Beauchamp and Norman E. Bowie (Upper Saddle River, NJ: Prentice Hall, 1993), p. 514.

4 "Council of Logistics Management," http://clm1.org.

5 Homin Chen and Tain-Jy Chen, "Network Linkages and Location Choice in Foreign Direct Investment," Journal of International

Business Studies, Vol. 29, No. 3, Third Quarter 1998, p. 447.

6 For a discuss of firm-specific advantages, location-specific advantages, and internalization, see the following: John H. Dunning, International Production and the Multinational Enterprise (London: Allen & Unwin, 1981); Peter Buckley & Mark Casson, The Future of the Multinational Enterprise (London: Macmillan Press, 1976); and Peter Caves, "International Corporations: The Industrial Economics of Foreign Investment," Economica, Vol. 56, 1971, pp. 279–293.

7 Stanley E. Fawcett and Anthony S. Roath, "The Viability of Mexican Production Sharing: Assessing the Four Cs of Strategic Fit," Urbana, Vol. 3, No. 1, 1996, p. 29.

8 S. C. Wheelwright, "Reflecting Corporate Strategy in Manufacturing Decisions," Business Horizons, Vol. 21, February 1978; S. C. Wheelwright, "Manufacturing Strategy: Defining the Missing Link, Strategic Manage-

ment Journal, Vol. 5, 1984, pp. 77–91; Frank DuBois, Brian Toyne, and Michael D. Oliff, "International Manufacturing Strategies of U.S. Multinationals: A Conceptual Framework Based on a Four-Industry Study," Journal of International Business Studies, Vol. 24, No. 2, Second Quarter 1993, pp. 313–314; Robert H. Hayes, Steven C. Wheelwright, and Kim B. Clark, Dynamic Manufacturing (New York: Free Press, 1988), pp. 10–11.

9 Michael E. McGrath and Richard W. Hoole, "Manufacturing's New Economies of Scale," Harvard Business Review, May–June 1992, p. 94.

10 Fawcett and Roath, "The Viability of Mexican Production Sharing," p. 29.

11 Paul M. Swamidass, "A Comparison of the Plant Location Strategies of Foreign and Domestic Manufacturers in the U.S.," Journal of International Business Studies, Second Quarter 1990, p. 302.

12 Gabriella Stern, "GM Is Expected to Pick Thailand as Site for First Major Plant in Southeast Asia," *Wall Street Journal*, May 16, 1996, p. A2.

13 Lee J. Krajewski and Larry P. Ritzman, *Operations Management: Strategy and Analysis*, 4th ed. (Reading, MA: Addison-Wesley, 1996), p. 398.

14 Deloitte Counseling, "Energizing the Supply Chain: Trends and Issues in Supply Chain Management," 2000. Available online at www.dc.com.

15 Tom L. Beauchamp and Norman E. Bowie, *Ethical Theory and Business*, 4th ed. (Upper Saddle River, NJ: Prentice Hall), pp. 21–22.

16 "You'll Never Walk Alone," in "Business and the Internet: A Survey," *The Economist*, June 26, 1999, p. 11–12.

17 Ibid., p. 11.

18 "The Net Imperative," in "Business and the Internet: A Survey," p. 6.

19 "You'll Never Walk Alone," p. 17.

20 Ibid., pp. 17, 20.

21 Krajewski and Ritzman, *Operations Management*, pp. 141–142.

22 Nikhil Deogun and Elizabeth Williamson, "Coke Reports New Quality Breakdown, Recalls Products in Poland," *Wall Street Journal*, July 6, 1999, p. A4.

23 Hayes, Wheelwright, and Clark, *Dynamic Manufacturing*, p.17.

24 Krajewski and Ritzman, *Operations Management*, p. 140.

25 Ibid., p. 156.

26 Jonathan B. Levine, "Want EC Business? You Have Two Choices," *Business Week*, October 19, 1992, p. 58.

27 Masaaki Kotabe and Glen S. Omura, "Sourcing Strategies of European and Japanese Multinationals: A Comparison," *Journal of International Business Studies*, Spring 1989, pp. 120–122.

28 Robert M. Monczka and Robert J. Trent, "Global Sourcing: A Development Approach," *International Journal of Purchasing and Materials Management*, Spring 1991, p. 3.

29 Russell Johnston and Paul R. Lawrence, "Beyond Vertical Integration—The Rise of the Value-Adding Partnership," *Harvard Business Review*, July–August 1988, p. 98.

30 John McMillan, "Managing Suppliers: Incentive Systems in Japanese and U.S. Industry," *California Management Review*, Summer 1990, p. 38.

31 Karen Lowry Miller, Larry Armstrong, and David Woodruff, "A Car Is Born," *Business Week*, September 13, 1993, p. 68

32 Joseph B. White, "Japanese Auto Makers Help Parts Suppliers Become More Efficient," *Wall Street Journal*, September 10, 1991, p. 1.

33 Ibid.

34 Monczka and Trent, "Global Sourcing," pp. 4–5.

35 Stanley E. Fawcett, "The Globalization of the Supply Environment." *The Supply Environment*, Vol 2 (Tempe, AZ: NAPM, 2000).

36 Robert M. Monczka and Robert J. Trent, "Worldwide Sourcing: Assessment and Execution," *International Journal of Purchasing and Materials Management*, Fall 1992, pp. 17–18.

37 F. Ian Stuart and David McCutcheon, "Problem Sources in Establishing Strategic Supplier Alliances," *International Journal of Purchasing and Materials Management*, Winter 1995, p. 4.

38 Krajewski and Ritzman, *Operations Management*, p. 732.

39 Shawnee K. Vickery, "International Sourcing: Implications for Just-in-Time Manufacturing," *Production and Inventory Management Journal*, Third Quarter 1989, p. 67.

40 Ibid., p. 69.

41 Ibid., p. 70.

42 "The Net Imperative," p. 1.

43 "World Becomes Smaller as Japan, Central Europe Catch Zone Fever," *The Journal of Commerce and Commercial*, October 1991, p. 6B.

44 John J. DaPonte, Jr., "Foreign-Trade Zones and Exports," *American Export Bulletin*, April 1978.

45 Ken Slocum, "Foreign-Trade Zones Aid Many Companies but Stir Up Criticism," *Wall Street Journal*, September 30, 1987, p. 1.

46 Fawcett, "The Globalization of the Supply Environment," p. 11.

47 Company reports from Toyota and Denso; interviews with Denso management.

CHAPTER **19**

Multinational Accounting and Tax Functions

Even between parents and children, money matters make strangers.
—JAPANESE PROVERB

OBJECTIVES

- **To examine the major factors influencing the development of accounting practices in different countries and the worldwide harmonization of accounting principles**

- **To explain how companies account for foreign-currency transactions and translate foreign-currency financial statements**

- **To describe the impact of accounting methods on the evaluation of foreign operations**

- **To investigate the U.S. taxation of foreign-source income**

- **To examine some of the major non-U.S. tax practices and to show how international tax treaties can alleviate some of the impact of double taxation**

On March 7, 1998, Daimler-Benz and Chrysler shocked the global automotive industry by announcing the largest merger in automotive history, creating the fifth-largest auto company in the world with annual revenues around $130 billion. This merger of German and U.S. companies brought together two organizations that had not only different products and cultures, but very different accounting traditions as well. The new company, DaimlerChrysler, had to determine which currency and accounting standards it would use to report its results to investors all over the world.

DIFFERENT ACCOUNTING TRADITIONS

Historically, German companies tend to be much more conservative than U.S. companies in reporting earnings and information in general. Company law is the predominant influence on accounting in Germany. The legal system in Germany is highly codified and prescriptive, because it is based on the Roman law system rather than the Anglo-Saxon common law favored in the United States and United Kingdom. The tax laws strongly influence the extent to which annual accounts form the basis for tax accounts. Any allowance or deduction claimed for tax purposes must be charged in the annual accounts.

The accounting tradition in Germany gives preference to the information needs of creditors and tax authorities. There is a very conservative approach to valuation in Germany, with strict application to historical cost accounting, which means valuing assets at their original acquisition cost. German companies also rely more on banks as a source of funding than on equity capital markets. Consistent with the emphasis on creditor interests, there is a much more prudent interpretation of historical cost accounting principles than usually occurs in the United States. To protect creditors, the law requires German corporations to create a legal reserve. Depreciation rates are determined by the tax rules, and accelerated methods are common.

Provisions for future losses or expenses are an important aspect of accounting in Germany. These provisions show up in reserves on the balance sheet of German companies. Traditionally, German companies use these provisions to smooth their earnings rather than have wide swings in earnings from year to year as would be more likely in the United States. In good years, managers add to their reserves under the assumption that good times won't last forever, and in bad years, these provisions will be used to supplement lower earnings. The undervaluation of assets and overstatement of expenses and liabilities gives rise to hidden reserves that allow German companies to retain cash in the business to protect creditors. If expenses are abnormally high, profits are low, which means that the company can't pay dividends or taxes. That helps management trap cash in the business, which is also preferable to creditors. Managers report financial information annually, rather than quarterly, as in the United States, and footnote disclosures tend not to be extensive, leading to the charge that German financial statements are not transparent.

U.S. accounting standards are oriented to the stock market, which means they are much more transparent than would be the case in Germany. In addition, U.S. standards focus on earnings, while German accounting focuses more on asset valuations on the balance sheet. U.S. accounting standards are much less conservative than German standards, and an independent body sets them, whereas German standards are included in the law.

DAIMLER-BENZ'S INITIAL DECISION TO LIST IN NEW YORK

In 1993, Daimler-Benz management decided to depart from German reporting in order to list shares known as American Depositary Receipts (ADRs) on the New York Stock Exchange. An ADR, sometimes called an American Depositary Share, represents an actual share of stock (or some multiple of a share of stock) held by a custodial bank in the United States. Thus the ADRs are traded rather than the actual shares of stock. At the time, no German company was listing in the United States because of stiff reporting requirements. The U.S. Securities and Exchange Commission requires all foreign companies who want to list shares on a U.S. exchange either to adopt U.S. accounting standards or to reconcile their home-company net income and share-holder's equity to U.S. generally accepted accounting principles (GAAP). In addition, they have to provide basically the same amount of disclosure as do U.S. companies.

Although German sentiment was running high against capitulating to the SEC, Daimler-Benz needed access to the U.S. stock market, so it decided to reconcile its financial statements to U.S. GAAP and list on the exchange. It still used German GAAP for German reporting, but it reconciled its consolidated statements to U.S. GAAP.

When Daimler-Benz announced on March 25, 1993, that it was nearing an agreement with the SEC on the nature of its financial reporting for U.S. listing, it declared DM4 billion ($2.45 billion) in hidden reserves as an extraordinary profit on its 1992 balance sheet. These hidden reserves emerged partly as a result of applying uniform valuation methods throughout the company. Previously the company had used different accounting methods for different subsidiaries, so there was no uniformity in accounting. Since 1992, however, Daimler-Benz decided to provide results on a uniform basis.

To prepare its financial statements for the listing, the German, U.S., and U.K. offices of KPMG, a global public accounting firm, worked with Daimler-Benz to determine how results would be presented within the SEC's Form 20-F (the filing required for foreign companies listing in the United States). In addition to KPMG, other global service firms played an important role. Citibank was the depositary bank for the ADR, and Deutsche Bank Capital Corporation of New York and Goldman, Sachs & Company acted as investment bank advisers. The U.S.-based international law firm of Skadden, Arps, Slate, Meagher & Flom advised Daimler-Benz on matters relating to the registration and listing of the shares.

Since 1993, Daimler-Benz gradually adopted U.S. GAAP for its consolidated reporting. Initially, it simply identified areas of reporting not covered by German GAAP and used U.S. GAAP for those areas. Because it was reconciling to U.S. GAAP anyway, it was easier to adopt as much U.S. GAAP as it could. Finally, Daimler-Benz simply adopted U.S. GAAP, as noted in the Summary of Accounting Policies in its 1997 annual report, the last annual report before the merger. Although Daimler-Benz was using U.S. GAAP for its financial statements, it was still providing them in German marks, not U.S. dollars.

THE MERGER

On November 17, 1998, DaimlerChrysler stock began trading on stock exchanges worldwide under the symbol DCX. It was the first company in the world to introduce a "global share," which is a registered share on 21 stock exchanges worldwide. The global shares took the place of the ADRs that Daimler-Benz had been trading. In the notes to the 1998 consolidated financial statements, management states that the DaimlerChrysler financial statements are prepared according to U.S. GAAP with a few exceptions. Also, the statements are presented in the euro, instead of the Deutsche mark or the dollar—the first company to do so. Prior years' earnings in Deutsche marks and dollars had to be restated in terms of euros for comparative purposes. The estimated cost of converting to euros for financial reporting as well as for invoicing was 120 U.S. dollars.

The company that audited the 1998 financial statements, KPMG Deutsche Treuhand-Gesellschaft, stated that it audited the statements in accordance with German and U.S. generally accepted auditing standards and that it did so in accordance with U.S. GAAP. Some of the items in the financial statements were prepared according to GAAP established by the European Community and by the International Accounting Standards Committee, but the SEC permitted DaimlerChrysler to do that.

The income statement and balance sheet of DaimlerChrysler are found in Tables 19.1 and 19.2, respectively. The income statement is similar to what you would find for a U.S. company, but the balance sheet is different. Although the financial statements are presented in euro, there is a column for the U.S. dollar equivalent of the income statement and balance sheet accounts. U.S. companies tend to present their balance sheet in terms of decreasing liquidity. That means that the most liquid assets, such as cash, receivables, and inventory, are presented first, followed by the least liquid assets, such as intangible assets and property, plant, and equipment. As noted in Table 19.2, DaimlerChrysler presents its balance sheet from least liquid to most liquid assets, just the opposite of a U.S. company.

It was not easy to bring together the accounting systems of two different companies from two different countries. DaimlerChrysler management first had to determine which accounting standards it would use (U.S. GAAP) and which currency would be its reporting currency (euro). Then it had to deal with different hardware, software, and reporting formats. It has done so successfully. Now the world waits to see if the strategic issues can be resolved just as easily—so that the DaimlerChrysler merger can succeed in the marketplace.

Several small countries have developed international business income by establishing regulations that allow companies and individuals to pay low taxes, operate with few restrictions, and maintain secrecy over their bank accounts. Basically, companies or individuals register trust companies (companies that establish their legal headquarters) in these locales and put funds in banks located within the same country. These countries are known as bank haven or tax haven countries. The photo shows one of the many banks in Liechtenstein that depends on foreign deposits. Liechtenstein has almost three trust companies for each of its citizens.

TABLE 19.1   **DAIMLER-CHRYSLER CONSOLIDATED STATEMENTS OF INCOME**

(IN MILLIONS, EXCEPT PER SHARE AMOUNTS)	NOTE	CONSOLIDATED YEAR ENDED DECEMBER 31,				FINANCIAL SERVICES YEAR ENDED DECEMBER 31,		
		1998 (NOTE 1) $	1998 €	1997 €	1996 €	1998 €	1997 €	1996 €
Revenues	30	154,615	131,782	117,572	101,415	7,908	6,545	5,548
Cost of sales	5	(121,692)	(103,721)	(92,953)	(78,995)	(6,157)	(5,075)	(4,347)
Gross margin		32,923	28,061	24,619	22,420	1,751	1,470	1,201
Selling, administrative and other expenses	5	(19,041)	(16,229)	(15,621)	(13,902)	(921)	(760)	(652)
Research and development		(5,833)	(4,971)	(4,408)	(4,081)	—	—	—
Other income	6	1,425	1,215	957	848	106	82	58
Merger costs	1	(803)	(685)	—	—	—	—	—
Income before financial income and income taxes		8,671	7,391	5,547	5,285	936	792	607
Financial income, net	7	896	763	633	408	23	4	—
Income before income taxes and extraordinary item		9,567	8,154	6,180	5,693	959	796	607
Tax benefit relating to a special distribution				1,487[1]				
Income taxes				(1,005)[2]				
Total income taxes	8	(3,607)	(3,075)	482	(1,547)	(361)	(307)	(234)
Minority interest		(153)	(130)	(115)	23	(2)	(1)	(2)
Income before extraordinary item		5,807	4,949	6,547	4,169	596	488	371
Extraordinary item: loss on early extinguishment of debt, net of taxes	9	(151)	(129)	—	(147)	—	—	—
Net income		5,656	4,820	6,547[3]	4,022	596	488	371
Earnings per share	31							
Basic earnings per share								
Income before extraordinary item		6.05	5.16	6.90	4.24	—	—	—
Extraordinary item		(0.16)	(0.13)	—	(0.15)	—	—	—
Net income		5.89	5.03	6.90[3]	4.09	—	—	—
Diluted earnings per share								
Income before extraordinary item		5.91	5.04	6.78	4.20	—	—	—
Extraordinary item		(0.16)	(0.13)	—	(0.15)	—	—	—
Net income		5.75	4.91	6.78[3]	4.05	—	—	—

[1] Reflects the tax benefit relating to a special distribution (see Note 20).
[2] Includes nonrecurring tax benefits of € 1,003 relating to the decrease in valuation allowance as of December 31, 1997, applied to the domestic operations that file a combined tax return.
[3] Excluding nonrecurring tax benefits, 1997 net income would have been € 4,057 and basic and diluted earnings per share would have been € 4.28 and € 4.21, respectively.
The accompanying notes are an integral part of these Consolidated Financial Statements.
All balances have been restarted from Deutsche Marks into Euros using the exchange rate as of January 1, 1999.
Source: Courtesy of DaimlerChrysler Corporation.

TABLE 19.2   **DAIMLER CHRYSLER BALANCE SHEET**

(IN MILLIONS)	NOTE	1998 (NOTE 1) $	CONSOLIDATED AT DECEMBER 31, 1998 €	CONSOLIDATED AT DECEMBER 31, 1997 €	FINANCIAL SERVICES AT DECEMBER 31, 1998 €	FINANCIAL SERVICES AT DECEMBER 31, 1997 €
Assets						
Intangible assets	10	3,004	2,561	2,422	104	51
Property, plant and equipment, net	10	34,649	29,532	28,558	53	39
Investments and long-term financial assets	16	3,344	2,851	2,397	632	631
Equipment on operating leases, net	11	17,203	14,662	11,092	12,001	9,571
Fixed assets		58,200	49,606	44,469	12,790	10,292
Inventories	12	13,840	11,796	10,897	654	505
Trade receivables	13	8,922	7,605	7,265	654	761
Receivables from financial services	14	31,054	26,468	21,717	26,460	21,658
Other receivables	15	12,642	10,775	11,376[1]	5,936	6,214
Securities	16	14,267	12,160	10,180	597	418
Cash and cash equivalents	17	7,731	6,589	6,809	681	702
Current assets		88,456	75,393	68,244	34,982	30,258
Deferred taxes	8	5,885	5,016	5,688	17	14
Prepaid expenses	19	7,197	6,134	6,430	133	71
Total assets (thereof short-term 1998: € 57,953; 1997: € 54,370)		159,738	136,149	124,831	47,922	40,635
Liabilities and stockholders' equity						
Capital stock		3,005	2,561	2,391		
Additional paid-in capital		8,534	7,274	2,958		
Retained earnings		24,091	20,533	21,892[1]		
Accumulated other comprehensive income		(1)	(1)	1,143		
Treasury stock		—	—	(424)		
Preferred stock		—	—			
Stockholders' equity	20	35,629	30,367	27,960	4,639	4,379
Minority interests		810	691	782	17	28
Accrued liabilities	22	40,629	34,629	35,787	412	508
Financial liabilities	23	47,436	40,430	34,375	36,810	31,381
Trade liabilities	24	15,074	12,848	12,026	242	90
Other liabilities	25	10,851	9,249	7,912	2,366	1,610
Liabilities		73,361	62,527	54,313	39,418	33,081
Deferred taxes	8	4,886	4,165	2,502	2,665	2,366
Deferred income	26	4,423	3,770	3,487	771	273
Total liabilities (thereof short-term 1998: € 58,181; 1997: € 50,918)		124,109	105,782	96,871	43,283	36,256
Total liabilities and stockholders' equity		159,738	136,149	124,831	47,922	40,635

[1]Includes a tax receivable/tax benefit of approximately € 1.49 billion relating to the special distribution (see Note 20).
The accompanying notes are an integral part of these Consolidated Financial Statements.
All balances have been restated from Deutsche Marks into Euros using the exchange rate as of January 1, 1999.
Source: Courtesy of DaimlerChrysler Corporation.

INTRODUCTION

The accountant is essential in providing information to financial decision makers.

International business managers cannot make good decisions without adequate and timely information about accounting and taxation (Figure 19.1). Although accounting and information systems specialists provide such information, managers must also understand which data they need and the problems specialists face in gathering it from around the world. The accounting and finance functions of any MNE are closely related. Each relies on the other in fulfilling its own responsibilities.

The financial manager of any company, domestic or international, is responsible for procuring and managing the company's financial resources. This individual is usually one of the members of the top management team of a company. For example, Manfred Gentz comes to the 17-member Board of Management of DaimlerChrysler from the Daimler-Benz side, and he is the head of Finance and Controlling, a position he is to hold until 2003. Gregory B. Maffei was the chief financial officer (CFO) for Microsoft in 1999, and he was also senior vice president, Finance and Administration, serving as one of only 15 executive officers of the firm.[2] The controller or chief accountant of Microsoft would report to Mr. Maffei. The CFO relies on the accountant to provide the right information. Doug Ivester, chairman of the Board of Directors and chief executive officer of Coca-Cola until he was succeeded by Douglas Daft in 2000, came from an accounting background. He was hired from the public accounting firm of Ernst &

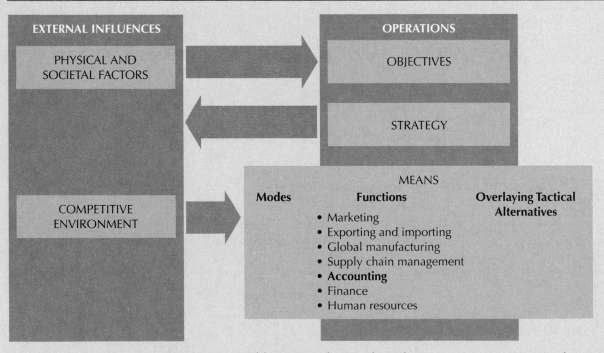

FIGURE 19.1   Accounting in International Business

Accounting is one of the necessary functions for implementing companies' international strategies.

Young (then Ernst & Whinney), where he was the managing partner of the Coca-Cola audit. After serving as chief financial officer, he moved into top management and was responsible for developing and implementing many of Coca-Cola's key strategies.

The actual and potential flow of assets across national boundaries complicates the finance and accounting functions. The MNE must learn to cope with differing inflation rates, exchange-rate changes, currency controls, expropriation risks, customs duties, tax rates and methods of determining taxable income, knowledge backgrounds of local accounting personnel, and local as well as home-country reporting requirements.

A company's controllership (accounting) function collects and analyzes data for internal and external users. The traditional role of the controller is:

> Management accounting [the role of the controller] is the process of identification, measurement, accumulation, analysis, preparation, interpretation, and communication of financial information used by management to plan, evaluate, and control within an organization and to assure appropriate use of accountability for its resources. Management accounting also comprises the preparation of financial reports for nonmanagement groups such as shareholders, auditors, regulatory agencies, and tax authorities.[3]

However, the role of the corporate controller has expanded beyond the traditional roles of management accounting (see Figure 19.2). Today's controller is engaged in

The controller of an international company must be concerned about different currencies and accounting systems.

FIGURE 19.2

The role of the corporate controller has expanded beyond the traditional roles of management accounting.

Source: From *The Wall Street Journal*—Permission, Cartoon Features Syndicate.

other activities in the international arena, such as evaluating potential acquisitions abroad, disposing of a subsidiary or a division, managing cash flow, seeking new sources of financing, hedging currency and interest rate risks, tax planning, and helping in the planning of corporate strategy.[4] Today's accountant must have a much broader perspective of business in general, and international business in particular for the purposes of this book, than was the case even as recently as a decade ago.

As Chapter 15 noted, foreign managers and subsidiaries are usually evaluated based on data from the controller's office. The controller generates reports for internal consideration, local governmental needs, creditors, employees, stockholders, and prospective investors. The controller handles the impact of many different currencies and inflation rates on the statements and should be familiar with different countries' accounting systems.

This chapter discusses some key accounting and tax issues facing companies that do business abroad. Initially, we will examine how accounting differs around the world and how global capital markets are forcing countries to consider harmonizing their accounting and reporting standards. Then we will examine some unique issues facing MNEs, such as accounting for foreign-currency transactions, translating foreign-currency financial statements, reporting on foreign operations to shareholders and potential investors, and dealing with tax issues. Although the focus will be on problems of MNEs, many of these issues affect any company doing business overseas, even a small importer or exporter. Foreign-currency transactions, such as denominating a sale or purchase in a foreign currency, must be accounted for in dollars, and this is true of both large and small firms. In addition, even small companies have to figure out how to tax the earnings on foreign revenues.

FACTORS INFLUENCING THE DEVELOPMENT OF ACCOUNTING AROUND THE WORLD

Both the form and the substance of financial statements are different in different countries.

One problem that an MNE such as DaimlerChrysler faces is that accounting standards and practices vary around the world. Financial statements in different countries even look different from each other. To illustrate that, let's compare the balance sheet of DaimlerChrysler from Table 19.2 with those of companies from two other countries. Table 19.3 contains the balance sheet for Intel, the U.S.-based microcomputer components company, and Table 19.4 contains the balance sheet for Marks & Spencer, the U.K.-based retail company. The balance sheets for DaimlerChrysler and Intel are in the format of

$$\text{assets} = \text{liabilities} + \text{shareholders' equity}$$

The major difference between DaimlerChrysler and Intel is the order of liquidity. DaimlerChrysler starts with the least liquid assets and goes to the most liquid assets, whereas Intel starts with the most liquid assets and moves to the least liquid.

The balance sheet for Marks & Spencer is in the analytical format of

$$\text{fixed assets} + \text{current assets} - \text{current liabilities} - \text{noncurrent liabilities} = \text{capital and reserves}$$

TABLE 19.3   INTEL CORPORATION BALANCE SHEET

DECEMBER 26, 1998, AND DECEMBER 27, 1997,
(in millions—except per share amounts)

	1998	1997
Assets		
Current assets:		
Cash and cash equivalents	$ 2,038	$ 4,102
Short-term investments	5,272	5,630
Trading assets	316	195
Accounts receivable, net of allowance for doubtful accounts of $62 ($65 in 1997)	3,527	3,438
Inventories	1,582	1,697
Deferred tax assets	618	676
Other current assets	122	129
Total current assets	**13,475**	**15,867**
Property, plant and equipment:		
Land and buildings	6,297	5,113
Machinery and equipment	13,149	10,577
Construction in progress	1,622	2,437
	21,068	18,127
Less accumulated depreciation	9,459	7,461
Property, plant and equipment, net	**11,609**	**10,666**
Long-term investments	**5,365**	**1,839**
Other assets	**1,022**	**508**
Total assets	**$31,471**	**$28,880**
Liabilities and stockholders' equity		
Current liabilities:		
Short-term debt	$ 159	$ 212
Long-term debt redeemable within one year	—	110
Accounts payable	1,244	1,407
Accrued compensation and benefits	1,285	1,268
Deferred income on shipments to distributors	606	516
Accrued advertising	458	500
Other accrued liabilities	1,094	842
Income taxes payable	958	1,165
Total current liabilities	**5,804**	**6,020**
Long-term debt	**702**	**448**
Deferred tax liabilities	**1,387**	**1,076**
Put warrants	**201**	**2,041**
Commitments and contingencies		
Stockholders' equity:		
Preferred Stock, $.001 par value, 50 shares authorized; none issued	—	—
Common Stock, $.001 par value, 4,500 shares authorized; 3,315 issued and outstanding (3,256 in 1997) and capital in excess of par value	4,822	3,311
Retained earnings	17,952	15,926
Accumulated other comprehensive income	603	58
Total stockholders' equity	**23,377**	**19,295**
Total liabilities and stockholders' equity	**$31,471**	**$28,880**

Source: The Consolidated Balance Sheet reprinted from the 1998 Annual Report of Intel Corporation is courtesy of Intel Corporation, copyright © 1999, all rights reserved.

Some terms are different, such as inventories under the current assets section of Intel's report and stocks for Marks & Spencer, and receivables and payables or liabilities for Intel and DaimlerChrysler and debtors and creditors for Marks & Spencer. In addition, Intel presents only a set of consolidated financial statements, while Marks & Spencer presents both company (meaning parent company) and group (consolidated) financial

TABLE 19.4   **MARKS & SPENCER BALANCE SHEET**

MARCH 31, 1998	NOTES	THE GROUP 1998 £m	THE GROUP 1997 £m	THE COMPANY 1998 £m	THE COMPANY 1997 £m
Fixed assets					
Tangible assets:					
Land and buildings		**3,523.4**	3,056.7	**3,202.3**	2,736.6
Fixtures, fittings and equipment		**528.9**	500.1	**389.5**	364.5
Assets in the course of construction		**123.4**	53.1	**54.3**	26.5
	11	**4,175.7**	3,609.9	**3,646.1**	3,127.6
Investments	12	**69.7**	36.6	**361.6**	371.6
		4,245.4	3,646.5	**4,007.7**	3,499.2
Current assets					
Stocks		**500.2**	445.1	**361.9**	310.6
Debtors:					
Receivable within one year	13	**948.9**	819.2	**1,366.1**	1,456.4
Receivable after more than one year	13	**1,096.4**	906.6	**175.8**	167.4
Investments	14	**242.3**	361.8	—	—
Cash at bank and in hand	15,16	**614.9**	671.5	**86.9**	87.8
		3,402.7	3,204.2	**1,990.7**	2,022.2
Current liabilities					
Creditors: amounts falling due within one year	17	**2,345.0**	1,775.1	**1,287.1**	1,124.0
Net current assets		**1,057.7**	1,429.1	**703.6**	898.2
Total assets less current liabilities		**5,303.1**	5,075.6	**4,711.3**	4,397.4
Creditors: amounts falling due after more than one year	18	**187.2**	495.8	—	150.0
Provisions for liabilities and charges	20	**31.0**	31.8	**27.9**	27.9
Net assets		**5,084.9**	4,548.0	**4,683.4**	4,219.5
Capital and reserves					
Called up share capital	25	**715.6**	709.2	**715.6**	709.2
Share premium account		**325.7**	259.8	**325.7**	259.8
Revaluation reserve		**506.1**	456.3	**509.7**	461.9
Profit and loss account		**3,518.4**	3,104.0	**3,132.4**	2,788.6
Shareholders' funds (all equity)	26	**5,065.8**	4,529.3	**4,683.4**	4,219.5
Minority interests (all equity)		**19.1**	18.7	—	—
Total capital employed		**5,084.9**	4,548.0	**4,683.4**	4,219.5

Source: From Marks & Spencer Balance Sheet, 31 March 1998. Reprinted by permission.

statements. Some observers argue that differences in format are a minor matter, a problem of form rather than substance. In fact, however, the substance also differs, in that companies can measure assets and determine income differently in different countries. This concept was illustrated in the case of Daimler-Benz when it reported different income numbers in 1992 under German GAAP and U.S. GAAP. In 1994, Daimler-Benz reported net income of DM895 million in accordance with the German commercial code, but it reported a net loss of DM1,052 million under U.S. GAAP, a difference of DM1,947 million, approximately $1.2 million.

ACCOUNTING OBJECTIVES

Accounting is defined as

> a service activity whose function is to provide quantitative information, primarily financial in nature, about economic entities that is intended to be useful in making economic decisions—in making reasoned choices among alternative courses of action.[5]

It is important for the accounting process to identify, record, and interpret economic events. Every country needs to determine what objectives of the accounting system it has put into place.

According to the **Financial Accounting Standards Board (FASB)**, the private sector body that establishes accounting standards in the United States, financial reporting, the external reporting of accounting information, should provide information for the purposes of

- Investment and credit decisions
- Assessment of cash flow prospects
- Evaluation of enterprise resources, claims to those resources, and changes in them[6]

To establish objectives, managers have to determine who are the major users of financial information. The **International Accounting Standards Committee (IASC)**, composed of professional accounting organizations from 104 countries, identifies the following key users:

- Investors
- Employees
- Lenders
- Suppliers and other trade creditors
- Customers
- Governments and their agencies
- Public[7]

It is important to identify users, because a focus on different users might result in different financial information being reported. For example, Germany's major users have historically been creditors, so accounting has focused more on the balance sheet, which contains a description of the company's assets. In the United States, however, the major users are investors, so accounting has focused more on the income statement. Investors see the income statement as an indication of the future success of the company, which affects the company's stock and its flow of dividends. There is no consensus on whether there should be a uniform set of accounting standards and practices for all classes of

Sidebar notes:

Accounting provides information for decision making.

The Financial Accounting Standards Board (FASB) sets accounting standards in the United States.

The IASC is an international private sector organization that sets accounting standards.

Critical users of accounting information are investors, employees, lenders, suppliers and other trade creditors, customers, governments and their agencies, and the public.

Equity markets are an important source of influence on accounting in the United States and the United Kingdom. Banks are influential in Germany and Switzerland, and taxation is a major influence in Japan and France.

users worldwide, or even for one class of users, but the general movement seems to be toward investors.

In Figure 19.3, we identify some of the forces leading to the development of accounting practices internationally. Although all the factors shown in the figure are significant, their importance varies by country. For example, investors are an influence in the United States and the United Kingdom, but creditors—primarily banks—are more of an influence in Germany and Switzerland.

Taxation has a big influence on accounting standards and practices in Japan and France, but it is less important in the United States. Certain international factors also have weight, such as former colonial influence and foreign investment. For example, most countries that are current or former members of the British Commonwealth have accounting systems similar to the United Kingdom's, former French colonies use the French model, and so forth. Thus companies from those countries use the standards and practices similar to companies from other countries in the same group. These differences in accounting influences have resulted in differences in accounting standards and

FIGURE 19.3 Environmental Influences on Accounting Practices

Other external users
1. Creditors
2. Institutional investors
3. Noninstitutional investors
4. Securities exchange

Enterprise users
1. Management
2. Employees
3. Supervisory councils
4. Board of directors

Nature of the enterprise
1. Form of business organization
2. Operating characteristics

Accounting profession
1. Nature and extent of profession
2. Professional associations
3. Auditing

Characteristics of the local environment
1. Rate of economic growth
2. Inflation rate
3. Public versus private ownership and control of the economy
4. Cultural attitudes

International influences
1. Colonial history
2. Foreign investors
3. International committees
4. Regional cooperation
5. Regional capital markets

Development of accounting objectives, standards, and practices

Academic influences
1. Educational infrastructure
2. Basic and applied research
3. Academic associations

Government
1. User and tax planners
2. Regulators

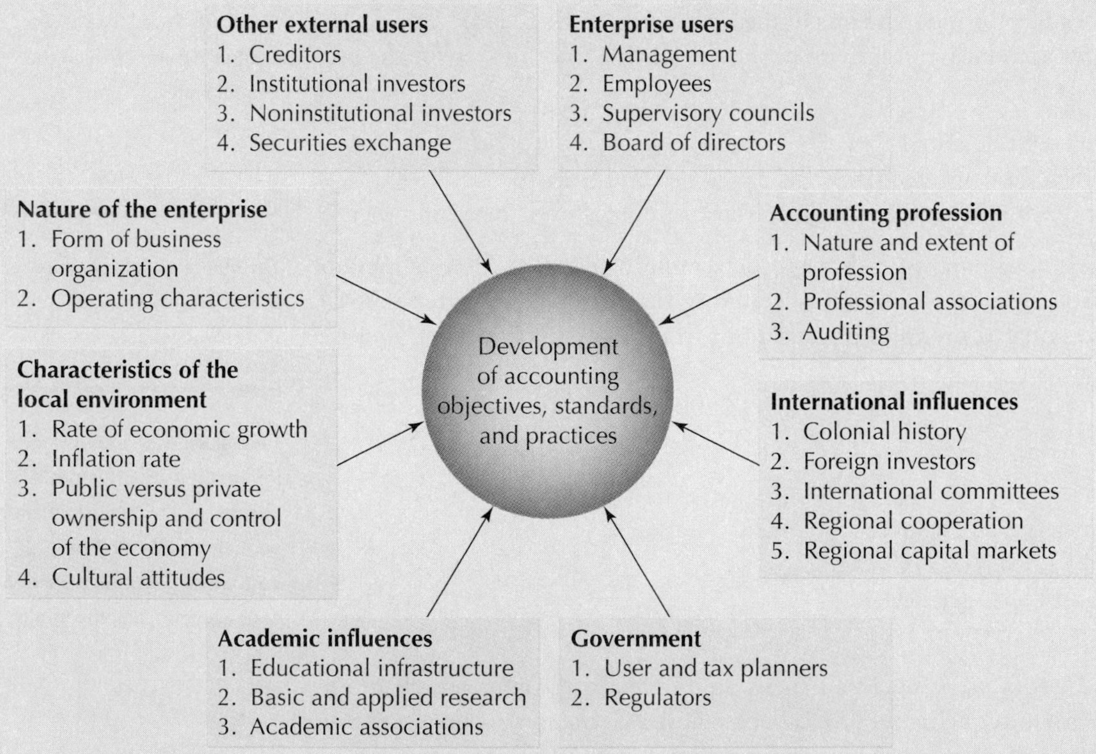

The importance of any of these environmental influences on accounting practices varies by country.

Source: Reprinted from *The International Journal of Accounting*, Fall 1975, by Lee H. Radebaugh, "Environmental Factors Influencing the Development of Accounting Objectives, Standard and Practices—The Peruvian Case, p. 41, with permission from Elsevier Science.

practices. As we saw in the opening case, the differences complicate things for MNEs, because they need to prepare and understand reports generated according to local **generally accepted accounting principles (GAAP)** as well as prepare financial statements consistent with the GAAP in the home country. Each country may have its own GAAP, which are the accounting standards recognized by the profession as being required in the preparation of financial statements by external users.

> Generally accepted accounting principles (GAAP) are those established in each country that must be followed by companies in generating their financial statements.

CULTURAL DIFFERENCES IN ACCOUNTING

A major source of influence on accounting standards and practices is culture. Of special interest to international investors are the differences in measurement and disclosure practices among countries—measurement meaning how companies value assets, including inventory and fixed assets; disclosure meaning how and what information companies provide in their annual and interim reports for external users of financial data.

Figure 19.4 depicts the accounting practices of various groupings of countries within a matrix of the cultural values of secrecy-transparency and optimism-conservatism. With respect to accounting, secrecy and transparency indicate the degree to which companies disclose information to the public. Countries such as Germany, Switzerland, and Japan tend to have less disclosure (illustrating the cultural value of secrecy) than

> Culture influences measurement and disclosure practices.
> Measurement—how to value assets
> Disclosure—the presentation of information and discussion of results

FIGURE 19.4 Cultural Differences in Measurement and Disclosure for Accounting Systems

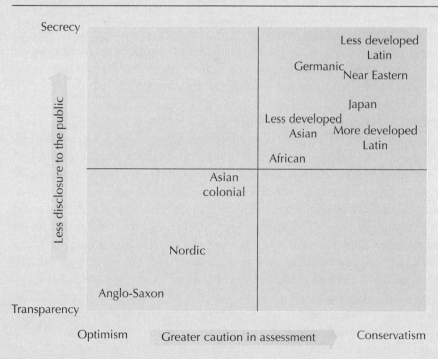

> Anglo-Saxon countries (such as the United Kingdom and the United States) have accounting systems that tend to be transparent and optimistic. Systems in Germanic countries, for example, tend to be secretive and conservative.

Source: From Lee H. Radebaugh and Sidney J. Gray, *International Accounting and Multinational Enterprises,* 4th ed. (New York: John Wiley & Sons, 1997). Reprinted by permission of John Wiley & Sons, Inc.

do the United States and the United Kingdom—Anglo-Saxon countries—which are more transparent or open with respect to disclosure. This is illustrated by the more extensive footnote disclosures in reports of the Anglo-Saxon countries than is the case elsewhere.

Optimism and conservatism (in an accounting, not a political, sense) are the degree of caution companies exhibit in valuing assets and recognizing income—an illustration of the measurement issues mentioned above. Countries more conservative from an accounting point of view tend to understate assets and income, while optimistic countries tend to be more liberal in their recognition of income. As noted earlier in the chapter, banks primarily fund German companies, and banks are concerned with liquidity. So German companies tend to be very conservative in recording profits—which keeps them from paying taxes and declaring dividends—while piling up cash reserves to service their bank debt. In contrast, U.S. companies want to show earnings power to impress and attract investors. British companies tend to be more optimistic in earnings recognition than are U.S. companies, but U.S. companies are much more optimistic than continental European and Japanese companies. The Asian financial crisis demonstrated that most Asian countries still fit squarely in the upper-right quadrant of measurement and disclosure. In particular, companies from Korea and Southeast Asia were guilty of a lack of transparency, which made it difficult for banks and investors to know where to lend and invest their money. They often put their money in Asian companies on the basis of relationships and reputation instead of good financial information. One of the reforms the IMF strongly recommended was for Asian countries to improve transparency in financial reporting of their companies so that the capital markets could operate more efficiently.

In spite of the differences shown in Figure 19.4, there is clear evidence that countries in the upper-right quadrant, especially the Germanic and Latin European countries, are moving toward more optimism and transparency due to the influence of capital markets, which require disclosures more in line with the Anglo-Saxon model.

CLASSIFICATION OF ACCOUNTING SYSTEMS

Although accounting standards and practices differ significantly worldwide, we can still group systems used in various countries according to common characteristics. Figure 19.5 illustrates one approach to classifying accounting systems. It does not attempt to classify all countries but simply illustrates the concept using several developed Western countries.

The authors used the concept of natural science to classify countries. As you move from left to right, you move from the general to the specific. Macro-uniform systems are shaped more by governmental influence than are micro-based systems. The major accounting influences on countries that fit into the macro-uniform category are a strong legal system, especially a codified legal system rather than a common law system, and tax law. These systems also tend to be more conservative and secretive about disclosure. Japan and Germany are legal-based systems, and Spain and France are tax-based systems. The former and current centrally planned economies would also fit in the macro category. However, China is trying to adopt international accounting standards that are more in line with capital markets, thus being more micro than macro in orientation.

Micro-based systems include features that support pragmatic business practice and have evolved from the British system. The United States is an example of a country that

---

Secrecy and transparency refer to the degree to which corporations disclose information to the public.

Optimism and conservatism refer to the degree of caution companies display in valuing assets and recognizing income.

British companies are optimistic when recognizing income, and U.S. companies are slightly less optimistic. Japanese companies are even less optimistic than U.S. ones.

Macro-uniform accounting systems are shaped more by governmental influence, whereas micro-based systems rely on pragmatic business practice.

FIGURE 19.5   Classification of Accounting Systems of Developed Western Countries

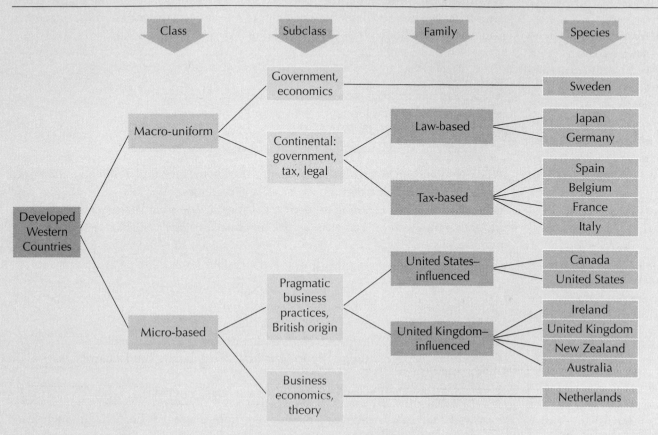

Accounting systems can be macro-uniform or micro-based depending on how important governmental influence is.

Source: From C. W. Nobes, "A Judgmental International Classification of Financial Reporting Practices," *Journal of Business Finance and Accounting,* Spring 1983, p. 7. Reprinted by permission of Blackwell Publishers.

fits in the micro category. It exhibits more optimism and transparency than countries in the macro category, and it also relies less on legal and tax requirements than do Germany, France, and Japan. The focus tends to be more on capital markets and less on banks and tax authorities. Other countries that closely model the United States are Mexico and Canada, two members of NAFTA. The British model is also a micro-based model, but it relies even less on legal and tax influences than does the United States. Current and former members of the British Commonwealth, such as the Bahamas, Australia, and New Zealand, also fit into this category.

The bottom line is that MNEs need to adjust to different accounting systems around the world, making the accounting function more complex and costly to perform. The financial statements of a company include not only the statements themselves but also the accompanying footnotes. In Tables 19.1 to 19.4, we provided only a few of the financial statements. Companies that list on stock exchanges usually provide an income statement, a balance sheet, a statement of stockholder's equity, and a cash flow statement. In addition, they provide extensive footnotes, depending on the country where they list. The financial statements of one country differ from those in another country in six major ways:

- Language
- Currency
- Type of statements (income statement, balance sheet, etc.)
- Financial statement format
- Extent of footnote disclosures
- Underlying GAAP on which the financial statements are based

A company wishing to provide financial information for investors throughout the world needs to deal with all six issues. As far as language goes, English tends to be the first choice of companies choosing to raise capital abroad, but other languages do appear. In its 1998 annual report, DaimlerChrysler lists the languages available for the following publications:

- Annual report (German, English)
- Form 20-F (English—this is a report specifically for foreign companies registering with the Securities and Exchange Commission)
- DaimlerChrysler Services (*debis*) Annual Report (German, English)
- DaimlerChrysler Aerospace (*Dasa*) Annual Report (German, English)
- DaimlerChrysler Interim Reports for first, second, and third quarters (German, English, and French)
- DaimlerChrysler Environmental Report (German, English)[8]

Intel and Marks & Spencer also provide their information in English, although Intel uses American English and Marks & Spencer uses British English. Many companies also provide a significant amount of information on their home pages on the Internet in different languages. Managers can just click on the desired language button, and all the information is provided in that language. For example, Erickson, the Swedish telecommunications company, has a home page full of information for people all over the world. The company's link www.ericsson.com.br gives financial information, as well as general information, in Portuguese.

A second issue in classifying systems is currency. As we saw in DaimlerChrysler's case, the financial statements are provided in euro, although the 1998 figures are provided in dollars in the English version of the annual report. Intel's financial statements are in U.S. dollars, and Marks & Spencer's reports are in British pounds. Not only does Ericsson provide its balance sheet and income statement in Portuguese to Brazilian readers, but it also provides the information in reals, Brazil's currency.

As noted earlier, a company can issue several major financial statements. Most countries require the balance sheet and income statement. Not all require a statement of cash flows, but it is becoming more common. Foreign corporations that want to list their securities on the New York Stock Exchange must provide a statement of cash flows because that is required for U.S. companies as well.

Financial statement format is not a big issue, but it can be confusing for a manager to read a balance sheet prepared in an analytical format, as is the case with Marks & Spencer, when the manager is used to seeing it in the balance format, as is the case with Intel. A major area of difference is the use of footnotes. Footnote disclosures in the United States tend to be the most comprehensive in the world. For example, U.S. companies go into great detail describing the way certain information is determined as well as the detail behind the numbers. Greater transparency is synonymous with more extensive footnote disclosures.

Finally, the most problematic area is that of differences in underlying GAAP. A major hurdle in raising capital in different countries is dealing with widely varying accounting and disclosure requirements. Some countries care more about those differences than others. In Germany and the Netherlands, for example, the principle of mutual recognition applies. That means that a foreign registrant that wants to list and have its securities traded on the Frankfurt or Amsterdam stock exchange need only provide information prepared according to the GAAP of the home country. However, other exchanges, like the New York Stock Exchange and NASDAQ, require foreign registrants either to reconcile their home-country financial statements with the local GAAP or to provide new financial statements prepared in accordance with local GAAP. In the United States, this information is provided in a document called Form 20-F, which companies must file with the SEC. That is what Daimler-Benz did before it adopted U.S. GAAP for its financial statements registered in the United States.

Major approaches to dealing with accounting and reporting differences:
- **Mutual recognition**
- **Reconciliation to local GAAP**
- **Recast financial statements in terms of local GAAP**

HARMONIZATION OF DIFFERENCES IN ACCOUNTING STANDARDS

Despite the many differences in accounting standards and practices, a number of forces are leading to harmonization, such as

- A movement to provide information compatible with the needs of investors
- The global integration of capital markets, which means that investors have easier and faster access to investment opportunities around the world and therefore need financial information that is more comparable
- The need of MNEs to raise capital outside of their home-country capital markets while generating as few different financial statements as possible
- Regional political and economic harmonization, such as the efforts of the EU, which affects accounting as well as trade and investment issues
- Pressure from MNEs for more uniform standards to allow greater ease and reduced costs in general reporting in each country

Major forces leading to harmonization:
- **Investor orientation**
- **Global integration of capital markets**
- **MNEs' need for foreign capital**
- **Regional political and economic harmonization**
- **MNEs' desire to reduce accounting and reporting costs**

Spurred by these developments, some countries and organizations are working to harmonize accounting standards on a regional as well as an international level. Regionally, the most ambitious effort is taking place in the EU. The European Commission is empowered to set directives, which are orders to member countries to bring their laws into line with EU requirements within a certain transition period. The EU's initial accounting directives identified the type and format of financial statements that European companies have to use, the measurement bases on which they should prepare

The EU is harmonizing accounting to promote the free flow of capital.

Other countries in Europe, including those of Eastern Europe and the former Soviet Union, are following the lead of the EU.

financial statements, and the importance of consolidated financial statements. It also required auditors to ensure that financial statements reflect a true and fair view of the operations of the company being audited instead of just adhering to the national laws of the different countries. The EU's influence is spreading beyond its members. Other countries in Europe, both Eastern and Western, are in the process of adopting EU accounting directives in preparation for becoming members.

The EU's directives have improved the comparability of financial statements, but member countries can still interpret the directives differently. So EU companies listing outside their home countries must still provide two sets of financial statements—the home-country statements and reconciliation. To enhance the harmonization process, the EU has decided to support the harmonization efforts of the International Accounting Standards Committee (IASC). The reason for choosing the IASC is that the EU can influence standards because it is represented on the IASC, and it also avoids funding and developing a competing standards-setting body.[9]

The IASC comprises professional accounting bodies and is attempting to harmonize accounting standards.

The IASC, organized in 1973 by the professional accounting bodies of Australia, Canada, France, Germany, Japan, Mexico, the Netherlands, the United Kingdom and Ireland, and the United States, has worked toward harmonizing accounting standards. The IASC comprises 143 professional accounting organizations representing 104 countries and 2 million accountants. Its business is conducted by the IASC Board, which comprises representatives of accountancy bodies in 13 countries (or combinations of countries) and 3 organizations with an interest in financial reporting.[10] Map 19.1 identifies IASC member countries and organizations. In addition to the member countries, there are 4 observers (the European Union, the Financial Accounting Standards Board of the United States, the International Organization of Securities Commissions [IOSCO], and China) who participate in the decision-making process but who do not vote.

Initially, the IASC wanted to develop standards that would have rapid and broad acceptance, focusing mostly on improved disclosure. However, it became obvious that the major stock exchanges of the world would never accept such loose standards for companies that wanted to list on the exchanges. There were too few standards and too many alternatives permitted for the standards that had been issued. In addition, there was no enforcement mechanism other than the best efforts of the member organizations to ensure that the standards would be adhered to in the individual countries.

IOSCO wants the IASC to develop a core set of accounting standards that securities regulators can have confidence in.

The turning point in the significance of IASC standards came in 1995 when IOSCO announced publicly that it would endorse IASC standards if the IASC developed a set of core standards acceptable to IOSCO. IOSCO is significant because it is comprised of the stock market regulators of most of the stock markets in the world, including the SEC in the United States. Once IASC completed its work, IOSCO would permit foreign companies to list on their exchanges using IASC standards without having to reconcile to local GAAP. At the beginning of 2000, IASC had nearly completed its work, but it was not clear if it would be successful.

The major challenge to the supremacy of IASC GAAP is the United States. Because the U.S. stock market is the largest stock market in the world, hosting about half of the world's stock market capitalization (the number of shares of stock traded times the market price of the shares), U.S. accounting standards dominate. For IASC standards to have universal acceptance, the U.S. SEC will have to accept the standards, and it is not clear that it ever will. There are still too many differences between IASC GAAP and

MAP 19.1 Membership of the International Accounting Standards Committee

The IASC membership consists of 143 accountancy bodies from 104 countries. The members from the United States are the American Institute of Certified Public Accountants, the Institute of Management of Accountants, the National Association of State Boards of Accountancy, and the Institute of Internal Auditors. The IASC board is made up of representatives of accountancy bodies from 13 countries, the Nordic Federation of Public Accountants, and up to 4 other organizations with an interest in financial reporting.

See <http://www.ifac.org/MemberBodies.html> for list of member countries of IASC (Same as membership of International Federation of Accounts—IFAC)

U.S. GAAP.[11] In addition, European companies that wanted to list on the London Stock Exchange, the largest exchange in Europe and the one most likely to host foreign listings, could adopt international accounting standards (IASs) for their listings, and that was the major reason companies adopted IASs. However, the London Stock Exchange now allows mutual recognition for members of the EU, so their companies no longer have to adopt IASs to list on the London Stock Exchange. It is not yet clear which standards will dominate on a worldwide basis, those of the IASC or those of the United States.

Each year, a survey is commissioned by the *Financial Times* of London to identify compliance with IASC GAAP. It looks at country as well as company adoption. The 1999 survey shows that there is increasing convergence among national standards and

IASs and increasing use of IASs as national standards. However, there is a wide variance in terms of how countries adopt IASs. Some companies adopt all of the standards; others say that they are in substantial compliance but adopt only some of the standards.[12] Very few U.S. companies make reference to IASs. U.S. software giant Microsoft used to state in its annual report that it complied with IASs, but it stopped doing so in 1998 with no explanation. If the world eventually adopts IASs, U.S. companies will be able to use them for domestic listings as well, but that may not happen for a few years, if ever.

TRANSACTIONS IN FOREIGN CURRENCIES

In addition to eliminating or minimizing foreign-exchange risk, a company must concern itself with the proper recording and subsequent accounting of assets, liabilities, revenues, and expenses that are measured or denominated in foreign currencies. These transactions can result from the purchase and sale of goods and services as well as the borrowing and lending of foreign currency.

RECORDING OF TRANSACTIONS

Any time an importer has to pay for equipment or merchandise in a foreign currency, it must trade its own currency for that of the exporter to make the payment. Assume Sundance Ski Lodge, a U.S. company, buys skis from a French supplier for 28,000 francs when the exchange rate is 0.1500 dollars per franc. Sundance records the following in its books:

Purchases	4,200	
Accounts payable		4,200
FF28,000 @ $0.1500		

If Sundance pays immediately, there is no problem. But what happens if the exporter extends 30-days' credit to Sundance? The original entry would be the same as above, but during the next 30 days, anything could happen. If the rate changed to 0.1600 dollar per franc by the time the payment was due, Sundance would record a final settlement as

Accounts payable	4,200	
Gain on foreign exchange	280	
Cash		4,480

The merchandise stays at the original value of $4,200, but there is a difference between the dollar value of the account payable to the exporter ($4,200) and the actual number of dollars that the importer must come up with to purchase the French francs to pay the exporter ($4,480). The difference between the two accounts ($280) is the gain on foreign exchange and is always recognized as income.

The company that denominates the sale or purchase in the foreign currency (the importer in the above case) must recognize the gains and losses arising from foreign-currency transactions at the end of each accounting period, usually monthly. In the example above, assume the end of the month has arrived and Sundance still has not paid the French exporter. The skis continue to be valued at $4,200, but the payable has to be updated to the new exchange rate of $0.1600 per franc. The journal entry would be

Accounts payable	280	
Gain on foreign exchange		280

Foreign-currency receivables and payables give rise to gains and losses whenever the exchange rate changes.

Transaction gains and losses must be included in the income statement in the accounting period in which they arise.

The liability now would be worth $4,480. If settlement were to be made at the end of the next month and the exchange rate were to remain the same, the final entry would be

Accounts payable	4,480	
Cash		4,480

If the U.S. company were an exporter and anticipated receiving foreign currency, the corresponding entries (using the same information as in the example above) would be

Accounts receivable	4,200	
Sales		4,200
Cash	4,480	
Gain on foreign exchange		280
Accounts receivable		4,200

In this case, a loss results because the company received less cash than if it had collected its money immediately.

CORRECT PROCEDURES FOR U.S. COMPANIES

The procedures that U.S. companies must follow to account for foreign-currency transactions are found in Financial Accounting Standards Board (FASB) Statement No. 52, "Foreign Currency Translation." Statement No. 52 requires companies to record the initial transaction at the spot exchange rate in effect on the transaction date and record receivables and payables at subsequent balance sheet dates at the spot exchange rate on those dates. Any foreign-exchange gains and losses that arise from carrying receivables or payables during a period in which the exchange rate changes are taken directly to the income statement.[13]

Procedures vary in other countries, however. Some countries recognize transaction losses but not gains in their income statements. That means that a loss reduces income and a gain increases income. Other countries allow a loss that occurs from a major devaluation to adjust the value of the underlying asset rather than be taken directly to income. The IASC pretty much follows the procedure required in the United States, but it allows a company to write up (increase) the value of an asset by the amount of foreign-exchange loss resulting from a one-time devaluation of the currency. That increase would then be written off over the useful life of the asset as a higher depreciation charge rather than be taken directly to the income statement as a one-time loss. As an example, assume that a company from South Korea purchases from a German supplier a large piece of equipment used in manufacturing textiles and has to pay the supplier in German marks. Shortly after purchasing the equipment but before payment is made, the Korean won devalues against the Deutsche mark by 10 percent. According to the IASC standard, the Korean company could increase the value of the asset by 10 percent and write off that increase as a higher depreciation expense over the life of the asset. As more countries move to a freely floating exchange-rate system, as discussed in Chapter 10, there are fewer examples of major devaluations occurring. However, countries that have a soft peg to another currency (meaning that they peg the value of their currency to something else, such as the U.S. dollar, but allow changes to occurs against the dollar) could still experience a devaluation of their currency.

The FASB requires that U.S. companies report foreign-currency transactions at the original spot exchange rate and subsequent gains and losses on foreign-currency receivables or payables be put on the income statement.

TRANSLATION OF FOREIGN-CURRENCY FINANCIAL STATEMENTS

Translation—the process of restating foreign-currency financial statements

Consolidation—the process of combining the financial statements of a parent and its subsidiaries into one set of financial statements

Even though U.S.-based MNEs receive reports originally developed in a variety of different currencies, they eventually must end up with one set of financial statements in U.S. dollars to help management and investors understand their worldwide activities in a common currency. The process of restating foreign-currency financial statements into U.S. dollars is **translation**. The combination of all of these translated financial statements into one is **consolidation**, as illustrated in the financial statements of Daimler-Chrysler, Intel, and Marks & Spencer.

Translation in the United States is a two-step process:

1. Companies recast foreign-currency financial statements into statements consistent with U.S. GAAP. This occurs because a U.S. company with a subsidiary in Brazil must keep the books and records in Brazil according to Brazilian GAAP. For consolidation purposes, however, the resulting financial statements have to be issued according to U.S. GAAP in format as well as content. As an example of content, Brazil might require that inventories be valued a certain way. For the U.S. consolidated financial statements, however, inventories must be valued according to U.S., not Brazilian, standards.
2. Companies translate all foreign-currency amounts into U.S. dollars.

FASB Statement No. 52 describes how companies must translate their foreign-currency financial statements into dollars. All U.S. companies, as well as foreign companies that list on a U.S. exchange, must use Statement No. 52.

TRANSLATION METHODS

The functional currency is the currency of the primary economic environment in which the entity operates.

Statement No. 52 allows companies to use either of two methods when translating foreign-currency financial statements into dollars: the current-rate method or the temporal method. The method the company chooses depends on the **functional currency** of the foreign operation, which is the currency of the primary economic environment in which that entity operates. For example, one of Coca-Cola's largest operations outside the United States is in Japan. The primary economic environment of the Japanese subsidiary is Japan, and the functional currency is the Japanese yen. The FASB identifies several factors that can help management determine the functional currency. Among the major factors are cash flows, sales prices, sales market data, expenses, financing, and intercompany transactions. For example, if the cash flows and expenses are primarily in the foreign operation's currency, that is the functional currency. If they are in the parent's currency, that is the functional currency.

The current-rate method applies when the local currency is the functional currency.

If the functional currency is that of the local operating environment, the company must use the **current-rate method**. The current-rate method provides that companies translate all assets and liabilities at the current exchange rate, which is the spot exchange rate on the balance sheet date. All income statement items are translated at the average exchange rate, and owners' equity is translated at the rates in effect when the company issued capital stock and accumulated retained earnings.

The temporal method applies when the parent's reporting currency is the functional currency.

If the functional currency is the parent's currency, the MNE must use the temporal method. The **temporal method** provides that only monetary assets (cash, marketable

Looking to the Future

WHAT WILL BECOME THE COCA-COLA OF ACCOUNTING STANDARDS?

There are two parts to this chapter—accounting and taxation. From an accounting standpoint, the key question is "What will become the Coca-Cola of accounting standards—U.S. GAAP or IASC GAAP?" In other words, which will have the most recognized brand name in accounting standards? IASC GAAP has a lot going for it. It is being set by most of the major countries in the world, so it is the product of a great deal of negotiation, compromise, and broad-based input. It is appealing to the Europeans, because they have a lot of influence in the development of its standards. Plus it has the backing of the EU Commission. It is also modeled after the capital-markets orientation of the United Kingdom and the United States.

However, IASC GAAP also has some shortcomings. It lacks an effective enforcement mechanism; it deals with a narrow, although important, range of issues; and it has been criticized for having developed standards that have too many alternatives and that are too much a product of compromise rather than principle.

U.S. GAAP's major criticism is that it is set only by the United States—why should the United States be able to dictate accounting standards for the rest of the world? That is a valid criticism, but the major vote in favor of U.S. GAAP is that half of the world's stock market capitalization is located in the United States and that companies that want access to U.S. capital must play by U.S. rules. Accounting standards are set with the stock market in mind, and that is what is now driving much of the growth in capital worldwide. It is doubtful that the U.S. SEC will ever let foreign companies list on U.S. exchanges using IASC GAAP, because then all U.S. companies that list on U.S. exchanges will sue to be allowed to use IASC GAAP as well, because it is much easier to implement. The SEC is not excited about tinkering with the best stock market in the world by allowing a watering down of accounting standards. However, that doesn't mean that the U.S. standard-setting process will become more inward looking. Quite the opposite. In the future, U.S. accounting standards will become even more international as the FASB cooperates with standard setters from around the world, including the IASC, to establish new accounting standards. More likely than not, the SEC will allow certain IASC standards to be used for foreign companies, as it has already done with cash flow statements and consolidation accounting, while reserving the right to keep U.S. GAAP for the majority of the reporting. As IASC GAAP moves closer to U.S. GAAP, some of the concerns may disappear.

It is hard to predict what will happen in taxation, because tax policy is subject to the whim of governments. Certainly tax differences among countries in the EU will narrow in the years to come. Harmonization should take place in the determination of taxable income and in the tax rates themselves. MNEs will need to be more creative in their tax planning worldwide as they seek to minimize their tax liabilities.

securities, and receivables) and liabilities are translated at the current exchange rate. The company translates inventory and property, plant, and equipment at the historical exchange rates, the exchange rates in effect when the assets were acquired. In general, the company translates most income statement accounts at the average exchange rate, but it translates cost of goods sold and depreciation expenses at the appropriate historical exchange rates.

Companies can choose the translation method—current rate or temporal rate—that is most appropriate for a particular foreign subsidiary, so they don't have to use one or the other for all subsidiaries. DaimlerChrysler, with manufacturing and sales offices all over the world, uses the current rate for some and temporal for others. Some of its most important functional currencies are the Brazilian real, French franc, British pound, Italian lira, Japanese yen, Spanish peseta, and U.S. dollar. Of course, the German mark is the key functional currency for DaimlerChrysler. Coca-Cola operates in 200 countries and uses 50 different functional currencies. This is typical of most MNEs.

Figure 19.6 summarizes the selection of translation method, depending on the choice of functional currency. As in the preceding explanation, if the functional currency is the currency of the country where the foreign subsidiary is located, the current-rate method applies. If the functional currency is the reporting currency of the parent company, the temporal method applies.

Tables 19.5 and 19.6 show a balance sheet and income statement developed under both approaches in order to compare the differences in translation methodologies. Some of the key assumptions are

$1.5000	Historical exchange rate when fixed assets were acquired and capital stock was issued
$1.6980	Current exchange rate on December 31, 1999
$1.5617	Average exchange rate during 1999
$1.5606	Exchange rate during which ending inventory was acquired
$1.5600	Historical exchange rate for cost of goods sold

FIGURE 19.6   Selection of Translation Method

According to FASB Statement No. 52, management can choose either the current-rate method or the temporal method to translate the financial statements of a foreign subsidiary or branch from the foreign currency to the parent currency (the U.S. dollar for a U.S. firm). The choice of translation method depends on the choice of functional currency.

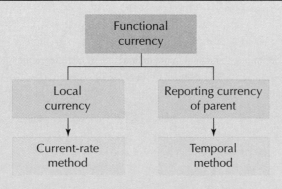

TABLE 19.5   **BALANCE SHEET, DECEMBER 31, 1999**

	POUNDS	TEMPORAL METHOD		CURRENT-RATE METHOD	
		RATE	DOLLARS	RATE	DOLLARS
Cash	20,000	1.6980	33,960	1.6980	33,960
Accounts receivable	40,000	1.6980	67,920	1.6980	67,920
Inventories	40,000	1.5606	62,424	1.6980	67,920
Fixed assets	100,000	1.5000	150,000	1.6980	169,800
Accumulated dep.	(20,000)	1.5000	(30,000)	1.6980	(33,960)
Total	180,000		284,304		305,640
Accounts payable	30,000	1.6980	50,940	1.6980	50,940
Long-term debt	44,000	1.6980	74,712	1.6980	74,712
Capital stock	60,000	1.5000	90,000	1.5000	90,000
Retained earnings	46,000	*	68,652	*	77,481
Accum. trans. adj.					12,507
Total	180,000		284,304		305,640

*Retained earnings is the sum of all income earned in prior years and translated into dollars and this year's income. There is no single exchange rate used to translate retained earnings into dollars.

Also, the beginning balance in retained earnings for both methods is assumed to be $40,000. The British pound was rising in value (strengthening) between the time when the capital stock was issued ($1.500) and the end of the year ($1.6980), so the balance sheet reflects a positive accumulated translation adjustment under the current-rate method. This is consistent with the idea that assets were gaining value in a strong currency.

TABLE 19.6   **INCOME STATEMENT, 1999**

	POUNDS	TEMPORAL METHOD		CURRENT-RATE METHOD	
		RATE	DOLLARS	RATE	DOLLARS
Sales	230,000	1.5617	359,191	1.5617	359,191
Expenses					
CGS	(110,000)	1.5600	(171,600)	1.5617	(171,787)
Depreciation	(10,000)	1.5000	(15,000)	1.5617	(15,617)
Other	(80,000)	1.5617	(124,936)	1.5617	(124,936)
Taxes	(6,000)	1.5617	(9,370)	1.5617	(9,370)
	24,000		38,285		37,481
Transl. gain (Loss)			(9,633)		
Net income	24,000		28,652		37,481

DISCLOSURE OF FOREIGN-EXCHANGE GAINS AND LOSSES

A major difference between the two translation methods is in the recognition of foreign-exchange gains and losses. Under the current-rate method, the gain or loss is called an accumulated translation adjustment and is taken directly to the balance sheet as a separate line item in owners' equity. Under the temporal method, the gain or loss is taken directly to the income statement and thus affects earnings per share.

ENVIRONMENTAL REPORTS

Earlier in the chapter, we discussed the major financial statements companies must present for listing on stock exchanges in the United States and elsewhere. One report that is not required but is often presented by companies is an environmental report. Typically the environmental report is separate from the annual report and is not part of the financial statements or footnotes. However, DaimlerChrysler devotes a page in its annual report to environmental issues. Although it provides a general statement on its environmental programs, it does not provide a significant amount of quantitative information. It does mention that recycled materials represent 14 percent of total plastics in its new S-Class automobile compared to 6.5 percent in the predecessor model.[14]

The SKF Group, headquartered in Sweden, is one of the world's leading producers of rolling bearings and bearing steel. It is a huge company with over 45,400 employees and 80 manufacturing sites around the world. Table 19.7 illustrates some of the information in SKF's environmental report, including raw material and energy usage and extent of recycling.

Although there are no mandatory environmental disclosure requirements like there are financial reporting requirements, DaimlerChrysler refers to the certification of its production facilities in Germany and Austria according to the European Eco Audit Ordinance, and SKF included a compliance statement by Lloyd's Register Quality Assurance Limited. Lloyd's audited SKF's sites and the health, safety, and environmental information in the SKF Environmental Report. However, environmental reporting varies a lot from company to company and country to country, especially because it is voluntary information.

TAXATION

Tax planning is crucial for any business because taxes can profoundly affect profitability and cash flow. This is especially true in international business. As complex as domestic taxation seems, it is simple compared to the intricacies of international taxation. The international tax specialist must be familiar with both the home country's tax policy on foreign operations and the tax laws of each country in which the international company operates.

Taxation has a strong impact on several choices:

- Location of the initial investment
- Choice of operating form, such as export or import, licensing agreement, overseas investment
- Legal form of the new enterprise, such as branch or subsidiary

TABLE 19.7

KEY ENVIRONMENTAL PERFORMANCE DATA FOR SKF GROUP

The SKF Group is a Swedish company that manufactures rolling bearings, bearing steel, and industrial precision components at around 80 manufacturing sites throughout the world. It provides a separate environmental report to show what it is doing to comply with environmental standards.

PARAMETER COUNTRY MAIN PRODUCT	UNITS	KATRINEHOLM SWEDEN HOUSINGS	SCHWEINFURT GERMANY BEARINGS	HOFORS SWEDEN STEEL	ELGIN U.S. SEALS	NILAI MALAYSIA BEARINGS	SAINT CYR FRANCE BEARINGS	PINEROLO ITALY BEARING BALLS	LEVERKUSEN GERMANY SEALS
Raw material-metal	Tons	13,250	26,318	317,000	4,080	19,830	34,000	14,800	1,800
Turning chips	Tons	11,750	10,018	3,850	0	1,122	4,800	0	15
	% recycled	100	100	100	N/A	100	100	N/A	100
Other metal scrap	Tons	0	5,320	89,000	690	125	5,600	631	1,225
	% recycled	N/A	100	100	100	100	100	100	100
Grinding swarf	Tons	100	3,016	750	0	297	1,000	4,162	0
	% recycled	0	100	82	N/A	50	25	0	N/A
Used oil	m³	20	698	66	54	225	330	148	4
	% recycled	100	100	100	100	100	18	100	100
Paper and carton	Tons	10	371	48	138	189	130	6	140
	% recycled	100	100	100	100	50	100	50	100
Water	1000 m³	59	876	6,500	57	75	140	185	40
Heating energy	GWh	11	96	25	0	0	0	0	9
Electric energy	GWh	50.7	113	370	17.8	27	65	34	13
Fuel oil	m³	18.4	319	8,900	0	1	900	0	0
Natural gas	1 000 Nm³	0	2,094	0	25	0	2,731	1,200	1,800
Coal	Tons	0	0	8,800	0	0	0	0	0
LPG	Tons	187	82	10,300	35	60	3	0	0
Alcohols	m³	11.4	249	1	4	275	0	0	7
Naphtha	Tons	6.8	260	17	7	0	230	0	4
Chlorinated solvents	Tons	0	0	0	0	0	0	0	0
Other solvents	Tons	16.8	0	31	9	66	0	62	26
Cutting oil	m³	33.3	570	99	0	91	400	436	9
Lubricating oil	m³	12.5	175	103	17	25	40	188	10
Grease	Tons	1.2	11	68	3	29	140	1	0.1
Synthetic rubber	Ions	0	0	0	2,308	12	12	0	600
Other hydrocarbons	Tons	47.9	450	291	10	59	270	0	3
PCB on site	Yes/No	No	No	No	No	No	No	No	No
Freons	Kg	1	0	0	100	0	0	0	0

N/A = not applicable

Source: From SKF Environmental Report, 1999. Reprinted by permission.

- Method of financing, such as internal or external sourcing and debt or equity
- Method of setting transfer prices

This section examines taxation for the company with international operations, using U.S. tax policy because of the nature and extent of U.S. FDI. However, as any country finds domestic companies generating more and more foreign-source income, it must decide on the principles of accounting for that income. Principles of taxation that U.S.-based MNEs face at home and abroad are, or could be, applicable to companies domiciled in other countries.

EXPORTS OF GOODS AND SERVICES

Many manufacturers find it easier and more profitable to sell expertise, such as patents or management services, than to export goods or invest abroad. Generally, payment comes from royalties and fees, and the foreign government usually taxes this payment. Because the parent makes the sale of services, the sale also must be included in the parent's taxable income.

To gain tax advantages from exporting, a U.S. company can set up a **foreign sales corporation (FSC)** according to strict IRS guidelines. To qualify as an FSC, a company must be engaged in the exporting of either merchandise or services, such as engineering or architectural services. Also substantial economic activity must occur outside the United States. An FSC cannot be a mailbox company in Switzerland that simply passes documents from the United States to the importing country. It must

- Maintain a foreign office
- Operate under foreign management
- Keep a permanent set of books at the foreign office
- Conduct foreign economic processes (such as selling activities)
- Be a foreign corporation[15]

If a foreign corporation qualifies as an FSC, a portion of its income is exempt from U.S. corporate income tax. Also, any dividends that the FSC gives to its parent company are exempt up to 15 percent of export earnings from U.S. income taxation as long as the income is foreign trade income.

It is estimated that some 6,000 corporations are taking advantage of FSC provisions, resulting in tax breaks worth billions of dollars. Boeing Company, the biggest user of the FSC, saved $130 million in U.S. income taxes in 1998, which was 12 percent of its entire earnings that year.[16] In 1999, the World Trade Organization, at the request of the European Union, investigated the 14-year-old FSC provision and ruled that it was an illegal export subsidy. Although some see the WTO ruling as a political response by the EU to rulings that favor the United States in trade issues with Europe—a makeup call in basketball terminology—the U.S. government will need to appeal the ruling and determine whether or not the FSC will be allowed to stand in the future.

FOREIGN BRANCH

A foreign branch is an extension of the parent company rather than an enterprise incorporated in a foreign country. Any income the branch generates is taxable immediately to the parent, whether or not cash is remitted by the branch to the parent as a distribution

---

An exporter can use an FSC to shelter some of its income from taxation.

The FSC must be engaged in substantial business activity.

Foreign branch income (or loss) is directly included in the parent's taxable income.

of earnings. However, if the branch suffers a loss, the parent is allowed to deduct that loss from its taxable income, reducing its overall tax liability.

FOREIGN SUBSIDIARY

While a branch is a legal extension of a parent company, a foreign corporation is an independent legal entity set up in a country (incorporated) according to the laws of incorporation of that country. When an MNE purchases a foreign corporation or sets up a new corporation in a foreign country, that corporation is called a subsidiary of the parent. Income that is earned by the subsidiary is either reinvested in the subsidiary or remitted as a dividend to the parent company. Subsidiary income is either taxable to the parent or tax deferred; that is, not taxed until it is remitted as a dividend to the parent. Which tax status applies depends on whether the foreign subsidiary is a controlled foreign corporation—CFC (a technical term in the U.S. tax code)—and whether the income is active or passive.

> Tax deferral means that income is not taxed until it is remitted to the parent company as a dividend.

A **controlled foreign corporation (CFC)** from the standpoint of the U.S. tax code is any foreign corporation of which more than 50 percent of its voting stock is held by "U.S. shareholders." A U.S. shareholder is any U.S. person or company that holds 10 percent or more of the CFC's voting stock. Any foreign subsidiary of an MNE would automatically be considered a CFC from the standpoint of the tax code. However, a joint venture company abroad that is partly owned by the U.S.-based MNE and partly by local investors might not be a CFC if the U.S. MNE does not own more than 50 percent of the stock of the joint venture company. Table 19.8 shows how this might work. Foreign corporation A is a CFC because it is a wholly owned subsidiary of a U.S. parent company (U.S. person V). Foreign corporation B also is a CFC because U.S. persons V, W, and X each own 10 percent or more of the voting stock, which means they qualify as U.S. shareholders and their combined voting stock is more than 50 percent of the total. This situation might exist if three U.S. companies partner together with a foreign partner to establish a joint venture overseas. Such collaborative arrangements are not uncommon, especially in telecommunications and high-tech industries. Foreign corporation C is not a CFC because, even though U.S. persons V and W qualify as U.S. shareholders, their combined stock ownership is only 40 percent. U.S. persons X and Y do not qualify as U.S. shareholders because their individual ownership shares are only 8 percent each.

> In a CFC, U.S. shareholders hold more than 50 percent of the voting stock.

If a foreign subsidiary qualifies as a CFC, the U.S. tax law requires the U.S. investor to classify the foreign-source income as active income or Subpart F (or passive) income. **Active income** is derived from the direct conduct of a trade or business, such as from sales of products manufactured in the foreign country. **Subpart F income**, or passive income, which is specifically defined in Subpart F of the U.S. Internal Revenue Code, comes from sources other than those connected with the direct conduct of a trade or business. Subpart F income includes

> Active income is that derived from the direct conduct of a trade or business. Passive income usually is derived from operations in a tax-haven country.

- *Holding company income*—primarily dividends, interest, rents, royalties, and gains on sale of stocks
- *Sales income*—from foreign sales corporations that are separately incorporated from their manufacturing operations, and the product is manufactured outside of and sold for use outside of the CFC's country of incorporation and the CFC has not performed significant operations on the product

| TABLE 19.8 | DETERMINATION OF CONTROLLED FOREIGN CORPORATIONS | | |

A controlled foreign corporation must have U.S. shareholders holding more than 50 percent of the voting shares.

| | PERCENTAGES OF THE VOTING STOCK | | |
SHAREHOLDER	FOREIGN CORPORATION A	FOREIGN CORPORATION B	FOREIGN CORPORATION C
U.S. person V	100%	45%	30%
U.S. person W		10	10
U.S. person X		20	8
U.S. person Y			8
Foreign person Z		25	44
Total	100%	100%	100%

- *Service income*—from the performance of technical, managerial, or similar services for a company in the same corporate family as the CFC and outside the country in which the CFC resides

A tax-haven country is one with low taxes or no taxes on foreign-source income.

Subpart F income usually derives from the activities of subsidiaries in tax-haven countries such as the Bahamas, the Netherlands Antilles, Panama, and Switzerland. The U.S. government treats any country whose income tax is lower than that of the United States as a tax-haven country. The tax-haven subsidiary may act as an investment company, a sales agent or distributor, an agent for the parent in licensing agreements, or a holding company of stock in other foreign subsidiaries, which are called grandchild, or second-tier, subsidiaries. This is illustrated in Figure 19.7. In the role of holding company, its purpose is to concentrate cash from the parent's foreign operations into the low-tax country and to use the cash for global expansion.

Figure 19.8 illustrates how the tax status of a subsidiary's income is determined. All non-CFC income—active and Subpart F—earned by the foreign corporation is deferred until remitted as a dividend to the U.S. shareholder (the parent company in this example). In contrast, a CFC's active income is tax deferred to the parent, but its Subpart F income is taxable immediately to the parent as soon as the CFC earns it. If a foreign branch earns the income, it is immediately taxable to the parent company, whether it is active or Subpart F. There is an exception, however. If the foreign-source income is the lower of $1 million or 5 percent of the CFC's gross income, none of it is treated as Subpart F income. At the other extreme, if the foreign-source income is more than 70 percent of total gross income, all the corporation's gross income for the tax year is treated as Subpart F income. Also, foreign-source income subject to high foreign taxes is not considered Subpart F income if the foreign tax rate is more than 90 percent of the maximum U.S. corporate income tax rate. Assuming a corporate tax rate of 35 percent in the United States, that means that a parent would not have to consider any income as

FIGURE 19.7   A Tax-Haven Subsidiary as a Holding Company

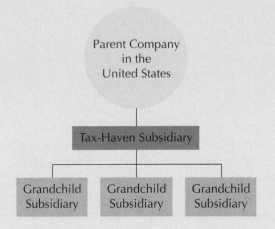

A parent company can shelter income from U.S. income taxation by using a tax-haven subsidiary located in a low-tax country.

Subpart F income that is earned in a country with a corporate tax rate greater than 31.5 percent (90% × 35%).[17]

TRANSFER PRICES

A major tax challenge as well as an impediment to performance evaluation is the extensive use of transfer pricing in international operations. A **transfer price** is a price on goods and services sold by one member of a corporate family to another, such as from a

A transfer price is a price on goods and services one member of a corporate family sells to another.

FIGURE 19.8   Tax Status of Active and Subpart F Income from Foreign Subsidiaries of U.S. Companies

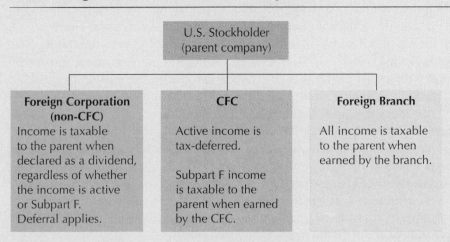

Different rules regarding the tax status and deferrability of income are in effect for non-CFCs, CFCs, and foreign branches.

parent to its subsidiary in a foreign country. Because the price is between related entities, it is not necessarily an **arm's-length price**; that is, a price between two companies that do not have an ownership interest in each other. The assumption is that an arm's-length price is more likely than a transfer price to reflect the market accurately.

Companies establish arbitrary transfer prices primarily because of differences in taxation between countries. For example, if the corporate tax rate is higher in the parent company's country than in the subsidiary's country, the parent could set a low transfer price on products it sells the subsidiary in order to keep taxable profits low in its country and high in the subsidiary's country. The parent also could set a high transfer price on products sold to it by the subsidiary.

Arbitrary transfer pricing affects performance evaluation.

Companies also may set arbitrary transfer prices for competitive reasons or because of restrictions on currency flows. In the former case, if the parent ships products or materials at a low transfer price to the subsidiary, the subsidiary would be able to sell the products to local consumers for less. In the latter case, if the subsidiary's country has currency controls on dividend flows, the parent could get more hard currency out of the country by shipping in products at a high transfer price or by receiving products at a low transfer price. Because prices can be manipulated for reasons other than market conditions, arbitrary transfer pricing makes evaluating subsidiary and management performance difficult. In addition, the tax authorities of a country (such as the Internal Revenue Service in the United States) can audit the transactions of an MNE to determine whether the prices were made on an arm's-length basis. If not, they can assess a penalty and collect back taxes from the company.

TAX CREDIT

Every country has a sovereign right to levy taxes on all income generated within its borders. However, MNEs run into a problem when they earn income that is taxed in the country where the income is earned and where it might also be taxed in the parent country as well. This could result in double taxation.

The IRS allows a tax credit for corporate income tax U.S. companies pay to another country. A tax credit is a dollar-for-dollar reduction of tax liability and must coincide with the recognition of income.

In U.S. tax law, a U.S. MNE gets a credit for income taxes paid to a foreign government. For example, when a U.S. parent recognizes foreign-source income (such as a dividend from a foreign subsidiary) in its taxable income, it must pay U.S. tax on that income. However, the U.S. Internal Revenue Service allows the parent company to reduce its tax liability by the amount of foreign income tax already paid. However, it is limited by the amount it would have had to pay in the United States on that income. For example, assume that U.S. MNE A earns $100,000 of foreign-source income on which it paid $40,000 (40 percent tax rate) on that income. If that income is considered taxable in the United States, A would have to pay $35,000 in income taxes (35 percent tax rate). In the absence of a tax credit, A would have paid a total of $75,000 in income tax on the $100,000 of income, a 75 percent tax rate. However, the IRS allows A to reduce its U.S. tax liability by a maximum of $35,000—what it would have paid in the United States if the income had been earned there. If A's subsidiary had paid $20,000 in foreign income tax (a 20 percent tax rate), it would have been able to claim the entire $20,000 as a credit because it was less than the U.S. liability of $35,000. A will pay a total of $35,000 in corporate income tax on its foreign source income—$20,000 to the foreign government and $15,000 to the U.S. government.

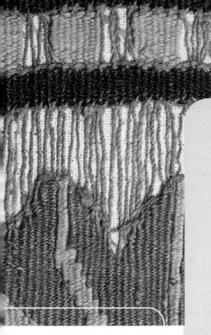

Ethical Dilemmas and Social Responsibility
IN TRANSFER PRICING, "LEGAL" DOESN'T ALWAYS MEAN "ETHICAL"

Arbitrary transfer pricing can create legal and ethical problems. In the United States and many other countries, companies are expected to establish transfer prices on an arm's-length basis. Doing this ensures that companies pay taxes on profits based on market decisions. However, when companies manipulate profits to minimize global tax payments and maximize cash flows, they may be breaking the law. Laws in this regard are much more rigid in Canada, France, Germany, the United Kingdom, and the United States. The U.S. government, for example, requires that companies use an arm's-length price on intracompany transactions between the United States and foreign countries; otherwise, the IRS will allocate profits between the two taxing jurisdictions. Sometimes foreign companies underinvoice shipments to the United States to minimize customs payments. The U.S. Customs Service can fine them, and force them to correct the invoice and pay the proper duty.

Some countries, such as Italy, Japan, and Korea, are less interested in rigid transfer-pricing policies. Others, such as Ireland, Puerto Rico, and a few other tax-haven countries, have no transfer-pricing policies. So an MNE needs to determine whether it is ethical to transfer profits to low-tax countries through arbitrary transfer-pricing policies. By shifting profits to a low-tax country, the MNE is not harming tax collection in that country, but it is harming tax collection in the country from which the profits are shifted. In trying to maximize cash flows, management of an MNE is likely to assume that "legal" means "ethical." If there are no legal requirements for transfer-pricing policies in a particular country, management is likely to assume that the absence of law implies permission to pursue the company's self-interest.

In some cases, an MNE might take advantage of transfer-pricing policies to transfer cash out of weak-currency developing countries. If a developing country has currency controls and does not allow cash to be shipped out in the form of dividends, a company might be tempted to charge a high transfer price on a product shipped to the country as a way of getting cash out. Doing this also results in lower taxable income in the developing countries and lower tax payments, which create a problem for developing countries that desperately need hard currency. Such behavior by MNEs could be construed as unethical. Further, if a country has laws that establish the need for market-based transfer prices, the actions could be construed as illegal. It is doubtful that an MNE's home country would encourage the use of market-based transfer prices, because a high price on exports to developing countries would result in greater taxable income in the home country.

TAXATION OF U.S. CITIZENS ABROAD

In Chapter 21, we discuss the compensation packages that companies offer employees to transfer abroad. For a variety of factors, those packages tend to be much higher than their packages in the home country. However, there is a tax effect to higher income, and companies have to make sure that employees are not made worse off by accepting an overseas assignment. Governments, however, treat overseas compensation in a variety of ways. Some try to tax expatriate (citizens working abroad) income, while others seem less concerned. They tax income earned in their national borders but not income earned abroad.

The U.S. policy of taxing such foreign income has changed significantly throughout history. The more lenient the tax treatment, the easier it is to send employees abroad. Under current law U.S. expatriates are allowed to exclude up to $74,000 and a qualified housing allowance of their foreign-source income from U.S. taxation. The housing allowance is the difference between the actual housing expenses of the taxpayer and a base housing amount determined by the U.S. government. The allowance can be significant—expatriates in high-cost areas such as Tokyo and Hong Kong might have to pay between $5,000 and $10,000 per month in housing. The exclusion is limited to the lesser of $74,000 (in 1999) or foreign-earned income less the housing cost amount exclusion.[18]

An expatriate might receive a significant amount of income that both foreign and U.S. authorities could tax. Income taxes paid to foreign governments can be credits or deductions, similar to the way in which corporate taxes are treated. However, companies sending expatriates abroad generally must make up the difference between what the expatriate would have paid in taxes in the United States and what must be paid because of the foreign assignment. The difference in tax liability is usually a result of the higher compensation earned by the expatriate as a result of allowances for housing, hardship, cost of living, and so forth. That tax-equalization practice can be quite expensive for the company.

> **U.S. citizens working abroad can exclude $74,000 of their income from U.S. taxation and can claim a housing exclusion for housing expenses in excess of a base amount determined by the IRS.**

NON-U.S. TAX PRACTICES

Differences in tax practices around the world often cause problems for MNEs. Lack of familiarity with laws and customs can create confusion. In some countries, tax laws are loosely enforced. In others, taxes generally may be negotiated between the tax collector and the taxpayer, if they are ever paid at all.

Variations among countries in GAAP can lead to differences in the determination of taxable income. This in turn may affect the cash flow required to settle tax obligations. For example, in France companies can depreciate assets faster than would be the case in the United States, which means that they can write off their value against income, thus lowering taxable income. In Sweden, companies can reduce the value of inventories, which increases their cost of goods sold and lowers taxable income.

Taxation of corporate income is accomplished through one of two approaches in most countries: the separate entity approach, also known as the classical approach, or the integrated system approach. In the **separate entity approach**, which the United States uses, each separate unit—company or individual—is taxed when it earns income. For example, a corporation is taxed on its earnings, and stockholders are taxed on the distribution of earnings (dividends). The result is double taxation.

> **Problems with different countries' tax practices arise from**
> • **Lack of familiarity with laws**
> • **Loose enforcement**

> **In the separate entity approach, governments tax each taxable entity when it earns income.**

Most other industrial countries use an **integrated system** to eliminate double taxation. The British give a dividend credit to shareholders to shelter them from double taxation. That means that when shareholders report the dividends in their taxable income, they also get a credit for taxes paid on that income by the company that issued the dividend. That keeps the shareholder from paying tax on the dividend because the company had already paid a tax on it. In Germany, a split-rate system means that two different tax rates are levied on corporate earnings. Because shareholders have to pay tax on dividends, the corporation pays a low tax on income that is distributed as a dividend and a higher tax on income that is retained in the business and not distributed as a dividend. In addition, the shareholder gets a credit for taxes paid by the corporation on that dividend.

> An integrated system tries to avoid double taxation of corporate income through split tax rates or tax credits.

Countries also have unique systems for taxing the earnings of the foreign subsidiaries of their domestic companies. Some, such as France, use a territorial approach and tax only domestic-source income. Others, such as Germany and the United Kingdom, use a global approach, taxing the profits of foreign branches and the dividends received from foreign subsidiaries. The United States is the only country to tax unremitted earnings in the form of Subpart F income.

VALUE-ADDED TAX

A **value-added tax (VAT)** has been around since 1967 in most Western European countries and is used in other countries as well. A VAT is computed by applying a VAT tax rate on total sales. However, any company that purchased materials or other inputs into its manufacturing process from companies that might have already paid a VAT on their sales, needs to pay the tax only on the difference between its sales and inputs that have already been taxed. As the name implies, VAT means that each independent company is taxed only on the value it adds at each stage in the production process. For a company that is fully integrated vertically, the tax rate applies to its net sales because it owned everything from raw materials to finished product.

> With a value-added tax, each company pays tax only on the value it adds to the product.

The VAT rates vary significantly among European countries, despite efforts by the EU toward harmonization among its members. However, the EU is narrowing differences in rates for like categories of goods. The VAT does not apply to exports, because the tax is rebated (or returned) to the exporter and is not included in the final price to the consumer. This practice results in an effective stimulus for exports. In addition, it is considered by U.S. tax officials and MNEs to be a subsidy to European exports, because the export price can be lower than the domestic price of goods by the amount of the VAT.

TAX TREATIES: THE ELIMINATION OF DOUBLE TAXATION

The primary purpose of tax treaties is to prevent international double taxation or to provide remedies when it occurs. The United States has active tax treaties with more than forty-eight countries. The general pattern between two treaty countries is to grant reciprocal reductions on dividend withholding and to exempt royalties and sometimes interest payments from any withholding tax.

The United States has a withholding tax of 30 percent for owners (individuals and corporations) of U.S. securities that are issued in countries with which it has no tax treaty. However, interest on portfolio obligations and on bank deposits is normally exempted from withholding. When a tax treaty is in effect, the U.S. rate on dividends

> The purpose of tax treaties is to prevent double taxation or to provide remedies when it occurs.

generally is reduced to 15 percent and the tax on interest and royalties is either eliminated or reduced to a very low level.

An example is a protocol to the 1980 tax treaty between the United States and Canada. It took effect on January 1, 1996, and

1. Reduces the withholding rate on dividends paid to a corporation owning 10 percent or more of the voting stock of the payer to 6 percent for payments in 1996, and 5 percent thereafter
2. Reduces the withholding rate on interest to 10 percent
3 Reduces the tax resulting from the imposition of both U.S. estate tax and Canadian income tax on transfers at death[19]

Several treaties and protocols were signed between the United States and foreign countries with an effective date of January 1, 1996, and they were very similar. In those treaties involving the reduction of withholding rates on dividends, the rate was typically 5 percent, although the rate for Portugal was 15 percent in some cases, 10 percent in others.

PLANNING THE TAX FUNCTION

Companies should set up
- Branches in early years to recognize losses
- Subsidiaries in later years to shield profits

Because taxes affect both profits and cash flow, they are a consideration in MNEs' investment decision process. If a U.S. MNE decides to generate revenues through exports, it can set up an FSC to reduce its tax bill—assuming that the FSC survives the WTO process or that the United States can come up with something else if the FSC has to be eliminated. When a U.S. parent company decides to set up operations in a foreign country, it can do so through a branch or a foreign subsidiary. If the parent expects the foreign operations to show a loss for the initial years of operation, it should begin with a branch, because the parent can deduct branch losses against its current year's income. As the operation becomes profitable, the status is better upgraded to subsidiary status. If tax deferral applies to the subsidiary's income, then the income of the subsidiary will not be taxed until it declares a dividend. In addition, it makes sense for the MNE.

Debt and equity financing both have tax ramifications.

Tied in with the initial investment decision as well as with continuing operations is the financing decision. Both debt and equity financing affect taxation. If loans from the parent finance foreign operations, the repayment of principal is not taxable, but the interest income to the parent is taxable. Also, the interest that the subsidiary pays is generally a business expense for that entity, which reduces taxable income in the foreign country. Dividends are taxable to the parent and are not a deductible business expense for the subsidiary. One reason why international finance subsidiaries are set up outside the United States is to escape withholding tax requirements.

An MNE aiming to maximize its cash flow worldwide should concentrate profits in tax-haven or low-tax countries. This can be accomplished by carefully selecting a low-tax country for the initial investment, setting up companies in tax-haven countries to receive dividends, and carrying out judicious transfer pricing. For example, because of its low-tax status and membership in the EU, Ireland can be both a manufacturing center to supply the EU with goods and a tax-haven country. The Subpart F income provisions require complicated tax planning, but opportunities still exist. Tax law is very complex, and a company needs the counsel of an experienced tax specialist.

SUMMARY

- The MNE must learn to cope with differing inflation rates, exchange-rate changes, currency controls, expropriation risks, customs duties, tax rates and methods of determining taxable income, levels of sophistication of local accounting personnel, and local as well as home-country reporting requirements.

- A company's accounting or controllership function is responsible for collecting and analyzing data for internal and external users.

- Major users of financial information are investors, employees, lenders, suppliers and other trade creditors, customers, governments and their agencies, and the public.

- Some of the major factors that influence the development of accounting standards and practices are finance and capital markets, taxation, legal systems, inflation, former colonial influence, and culture.

- Culture can have a strong influence on the accounting dimensions of measurement and disclosure. The cultural values of secrecy and transparency refer to the degree of disclosure of information. The cultural values of optimism and conservatism refer to the valuation of assets and the recognition of income. Conservatism results in the undervaluation of both assets and income.

- Financial statements differ in terms of language, currency, type of statements (income statement, balance sheet, etc.), financial statement format, extent of footnote disclosures, and the underlying GAAP on which the financial statements are based.

- Stock exchanges may permit mutual recognition or require reconciliation to local GAAP.

- The major forces for harmonization of accounting standards and practices are global investors and global capital markets.

- The EU is engaged in the most effective regional effort to harmonize accounting standards.

- The IASC is a global organization of public accountants from different countries that is trying to harmonize accounting standards and is the major competition with U.S. GAAP to become the standard for financial reporting worldwide.

- When transactions denominated in a foreign currency are translated into dollars, all accounts are recorded initially at the exchange rate in effect at the time of the transaction. At each subsequent balance sheet date, recorded dollar balances representing amounts owed by or to the company that are denominated in a foreign currency are adjusted to reflect the current rate.

- The translation of financial statements means measuring and expressing in the parent currency and in conformity with parent country's GAAP the assets, liabilities, revenues, and expenses that are measured or denominated in a foreign currency.

- According to FASB Statement No. 52, the financial statements of foreign companies are translated into dollars by using the current-rate or temporal method. According to the current-rate method, all balance sheet accounts (except owners' equity) are translated into dollars at the current exchange rate in effect on the balance sheet date. All income statement accounts are translated at the average exchange rate in effect during the period.

- Companies enter foreign-exchange gains and losses arising from foreign-currency transactions on the income statement during the period in which they occur. Companies enter gains and losses arising from translating financial statements by the current-rate method as a separate component of owners' equity. Companies enter gains and losses arising from translating according to the temporal method directly on the income statement.

- International tax planning has a strong impact on the choice of location for the initial investment, the legal form of the new enterprise, the method of financing, and the method of setting transfer prices.

- Tax deferral means that the income a subsidiary incorporated outside the home country earns is taxed only when it is remitted to the parent as a dividend, not when it is earned.

- A controlled foreign corporation (CFC) must declare its Subpart F income as taxable to the parent in the year it is earned, whether or not it is remitted as a dividend.

- A transfer price is a price on goods and services sold by one member of a corporate family to another and is thus subject to be set in an arbitrary rather than arms'-length fashion.

- Transfer prices can be set to take advantage of differences in tax rates in different countries, for competitive reasons, or to avoid restrictions on currency flows.

- A tax credit allows a parent company to reduce its tax liability by the direct amount its subsidiary pays a foreign government on income that must also be taxed by the parent company's government.

- Countries' policies vary as to what is taxable income and how they assess taxes. The United States taxes each separate unit (the separate entity approach), while most other industrial countries use an integrated system that minimizes or eliminates double taxation.

- The purpose of tax treaties is to prevent international double taxation or to provide remedies when it occurs.

CASE

COCA-COLA AND ITS GLOBAL CHALLENGES[20]

A Coke is a Coke is a Coke no matter where on the planet you drink it. But a Coke Light can be a Diet Coke and a Mellow Yellow can be a Lychee Mello. Fanta is a dozen different things—Peach in Botswana, passion fruit (what else?) in France, and flower-flavored in Japan (huh?). Other countries have their own flavors—only Italy can pour a Beverly (and some travelers who've tried it are just fine with that).

That little quote lifted from Coca-Cola's home page on the Internet (www.cocacola.com) describes the global dimension of the U.S.-based company—one of the top brands in the world. However, Coca-Cola, for all its success around the world, entered the twenty-first century with some serious problems. After years of annual increases in earnings of at least 15 percent, 1998 was a very bad year. In the fourth quarter, earnings fell 27 percent from their level in the fourth quarter of 1997. For the year, operating income fell 1 percent compared with 1997, and operating revenues were $18.813 billion dollars, compared with $18.868 billion in 1997. In 1998, revenues were basically flat again. Earnings per share fell from $1.64 in 1997 to $1.42 in 1998, and return on capital fell from 39.5 percent to 30.2 percent. Finally, Coca-Cola's 1999 third-quarter net income fell 11 percent over the third quarter in 1998, which marked the company's fifth consecutive quarter of declining profits. What has caused these problems, and what is the impact on Coca-Cola's financial disclosures to investors all over the world?

From 1886, when Atlanta pharmacist J. S. Pemberton mixed up his first batch of Coca-Cola, to 1998, Coca-Cola's worldwide revenues vaulted from $50 to more than $18 billion a year. Prior to 1995, Coca-Cola operated three divisions: soft drinks international, soft drinks U.S., and foods. In 1995, however, Coca-Cola changed its organizational structure by combining the U.S. and international soft drinks businesses and forming five regional groups each headed by a group president: North America (United States and Canada), Africa, Greater Europe, Latin America, and Middle and Far East. There is also a corporate segment in addition to the geographic segments listed above.

Coca-Cola is basically a beverages company and is the world's largest manufacturer, marketer, and distributor of soft drink concentrates and syrups, both of which it sells to bottling and canning operations. It also manufactures fountain/postmix soft drink syrups, which it sells to fountain wholesalers and some fountain retailers. Further, Coca-Cola has substantial equity investments in numerous soft drink bottling and canning operations, and it owns and operates sizable bottling and canning operations outside the United States. However, Coca-Cola's current strategy is to spin off its bottling and canning operations into independent companies and to have the largest of those companies become anchor companies in different parts of the world. In 1986, Coca-Cola purchased several poorly performing U.S. bottlers and combined them with its own network, forming a new company called Coca-Cola Enterprises (CCE). Coca-Cola then took CCE public but retained a 49-percent stake. Coca-Cola then sold many of its foreign bottlers to CCE and used CCE to acquire other bottlers worldwide. In 1998, Coca-Cola's anchor bottlers produced and distributed approximately 43 percent of Coke's total worldwide unit case volume. Because Coca-Cola will retain varying percentages of ownership in these bottling operations, it generates revenues from selling concentrate to as well as from earning dividends from them. In its foods division, Coca-Cola processes and markets citrus and other juice and juice-drink products, primarily orange juice. It is the world's largest marketer of packaged citrus products.

The company averages a 47-percent worldwide market share in flavored carbonated soft drinks. Its market share is 42 percent in the United States and about 50 percent internationally. In terms of total sales, Coca-Cola has four of the world's top five carbonated soft drinks: Coca-Cola and Coca-Cola Classic (number 1), Diet Coca-Cola and Coca-Cola Light (number 3), Fanta (number 4), and Sprite (number 5). Coca-Cola is the worldwide market leader in the three largest carbonated soft drink segments: cola (61 percent of the world market), orange (32 percent), and lemon-lime (36 percent).

As Figure 19.9 shows, Coca-Cola's North American revenues and profits are 37 percent and 27 percent of total revenues and profits, respectively. North America is Coca-Cola's largest market in terms of revenues, but Greater Europe and the Middle and Far East combined are greater. It is interesting to note that Greater Europe and the Middle and Far East are more profitable as a percentage of total than their revenues as a percentage of total and are each about the same as North America in terms of operating income.

Foreign exchange is a major issue for Coca-Cola, given its international scope. Balance sheets and income statements for all of the countries in which it operates must be translated into U.S. dollars so that they can be combined with Coca-Cola's domestic dollar results. By operating in over 200 countries and 50 functional currencies, Coca-Cola is directly impacted by exchange-rate changes. As we see in Figure 19.9, 73 percent of Coke's profits are generated outside of North America, and most of the key countries in which Coke did business in 1998 had weak currencies. That meant that foreign earnings were translated at a lower amount (they were worth fewer dollars as the foreign currencies fell against the dollar), and foreign assets were worth less as well.

In the mid-1980s, Coca-Cola's management saw that international operations were increasing significantly and that the nature of its business had changed since it wrote its last accounting manual. The company needed a comprehensive, easy-reference accounting manual to help it maintain strong financial controls over its operations. Management also felt it would help headquarters acquire reliable information about units all over the world and help local subsidiaries operate at peak efficiency. In addition, Robert Goizueta, CEO at the time, became concerned about the poor financial information he was getting. He also noticed that the company, in effect, was going downhill because it was investing equity capital at 16 percent but earning only 8 to 10 percent on some of its investments. He decided to evaluate the company's performance by type of business worldwide. Across the top of his financial chart, he identified Coca-Cola's lines of business. Down the side, he listed key financial measures: margins, cash flow reliability, capital requirements, and the like.

FIGURE 19.9 Coca-Cola's Revenues and Profits by Geographical Area

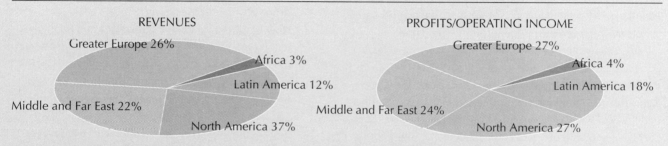

Coca-Cola generates 63 percent of its revenues and 73 percent of its profits outside North America. Greater Europe is the largest foreign market in revenues and profits, although the Middle and Far East markets are a close second.

But to make the concept work, Goizueta needed reliable information. A team consisting of a project manager and three senior accountants worked for eight months to develop the new accounting manual. The team set up a universal chart of accounts so that each account in the balance sheet and income statement would be consistent for all Coca-Cola subsidiaries around the world. Based on the chart of accounts, the team wrote definitions of each account and developed policies and procedures governing the use of each and the flow of information into the financial statements. Then the team wrote a section describing how to translate financial statements in local currencies to U.S. dollars. The team gave drafts of the report to audit, legal, and tax managers for their comments, and other field accounting managers gave their input before a final policy took effect. Accounting policy began to have a significant impact on Coke's overall business strategy.

During Goizueta's tenure as CEO, Coca-Cola shares rose 3,500 percent. But then tragedy struck. In October 1997, Goizueta died of cancer, and Doug Ivester, a former accountant, took his place. In 1997, Coca-Cola posted an 18 percent rise in profits. However, the strong growth in profits—and Doug Ivester—did not last for long. In August 1998, the Russian ruble devalued amid financial crisis in Russia, and Coke's operations collapsed. With capacity running at less than 50 percent, Coca-Cola's revenues fell, and their dollar equivalent after being translated from rubles to dollars fell even more. Continued weakness in the global economy, in Asia and Latin America as well as Russia, really hurt Coca-Cola. Coke's global expansion, earlier labeled a strength to Coke because of its diversification into different markets, became a millstone around Coke's neck. In January 1999, Coke reported a 14 percent drop in 1998 profits. Consumers in developing countries all over the world were turning to cheaper local products, and Coke was forced to drop prices to pick up market share. However, the drop in prices translated into lower revenues. As foreign currencies weakened, the revenues were translated into even lower dollar revenues and profits.

In 1999, Ivester announced that Coca-Cola was going to purchase the beverages division of Cadbury-Schweppes, which includes Schweppes beverages, Canada Dry, and Dr. Pepper. But Ivester ran into trouble with antitrust regulators in Europe, and the deal was blocked. By the time the purchase was completed, Coke was shut out of Europe in terms of Schweppes products, and the acquisition was only half as large as originally announced. In fact, European regulators were so furious

at Coca-Cola management and how they treated the process that they are starting to look into a variety of allegations being brought against Coca-Cola, especially by PepsiCo. Then in June 1999, a series of incidents occurred in Belgium, France, and Poland where schoolchildren and others complained of getting sick after drinking Coke products. Many feel that Ivester was slow in responding to the complaints and that Coca-Cola handled the entire process poorly. Even though nobody became seriously ill, Coke's reputation in Europe dropped like a rock. In November 1999, France rejected a bid by Coca-Cola to purchase Orangina over concerns that Coke was becoming too dominant in the soft drink market. In December 1999, Ivester retired from his position after being CEO for only two years, and Doug Daft, former head of the Middle and Far East Group and the Africa Group, replaced him. The change will be effective in April 2000. Daft, a native Australian, has had significant experience abroad for Coca-Cola, having spent 30 years running Coke operations in the Middle and Far East, and he comes from a strong marketing and management background. He appointed as his second in command and president and chief operating officer, Jack Stahl, a 20-year veteran of Coca-Cola who has worked as chief financial officer and head of Coke's North American group since 1994. In October 1999, he was given responsibility for all of the Americas as well as Coke's juice unit, Minute Maid Company. Daft and Stahl and their new team have quite a challenge ahead of them to return Coke to the glamour days of Goizueta's reign.

QUESTIONS

1. Based on this short description of the forces affecting Coca-Cola's success, what are some of the things that need to happen for Coke to improve?

2. Daft and Stahl come to Coca-Cola's top leadership with very different backgrounds. What do you think they each bring to the table to help Coke return to a strong position in the future?

3. How has the strong dollar affected Coke's financial statements? In 1999, the dollar rose for the first seven months of the year and then began to fall the last five months of the year. At year-end, the dollar was about where it was at the beginning of the year. How might that affect Coca-Cola's earnings?

4. Besides the foreign-exchange problem, what do you see as some of the key accounting issues facing Coca-Cola?

CHAPTER NOTES

1 Timothy Aeppel, "Daimler Says Mercedes Has Operating Loss," *Wall Street Journal*, May 7, 1993, p. A11; Timothy Aeppel, "Daimler-Benz Discloses Hidden Reserves of $2.45 Billion, Seeks Big Board Listing," *Wall Street Journal*, March 25, 1993, p. A10; "Daimler Plays Ball," *The Economist*, March 27, 1993, p. 76; Herbert Fromme, "Daimler Drives into Trouble," *World Accounting Report*, May 1993, pp. 2–3; Christopher Parkes, "Daimler to Make New York Debut in October," *Financial Times*, July 28, 1993, p. 23; Lee H. Radebaugh and S. J. Gray, *International Accounting and Multinational Enterprises*, 4th ed. (New York: John Wiley & Sons, Inc., 1997), pp. 91–93, 386–390; Anita Raghavan and Christi Harlan, "Daimler-Benz's Listing Is Likely to Draw More Foreign Firms to the U.S. Market," *Wall Street Journal*, March 31, 1993, p. A4; and various issues of *Daimler-Benz Annual Report* and *DaimlerChrysler Annual Report*.

2 "Directors and Officers," *Microsoft Annual Report 1999*, p. 45.

3 "Statement on Management Accounting No. 1A," Institute of Management Accountants, 1981, as quoted in Paul J. Wendell, *Corporate Controller's Manual* (New York: Warham, Gorham & Lamont, 1998), pp. A1–3.

4 Ibid.

5 "Basic Concepts and Accounting Principles Underlying Financial Statements of Business Enterprises," *Statement of the Accounting Principles Board No. 4* (New York: American Insti-

tute of Certified Public Accountants, 1970), paragraph 40.

6 Financial Accounting Standards Board, Statement of Financial Accounting Concepts No. 1, "Objectives of Financial Reporting by Business Enterprises" (Stamford, CT: FASB, 1979), paragraphs 34–54.

7 International Accounting Standards Committee, *International Accounting Standards 1998* (London: IASC, 1998), paragraph 9, pp. 36–37.

8 *DaimlerChrysler Annual Report 1998*, p. 120.

9 "EU Puts Weight Behind IASC," *IASC Insight*, March 1996, pp. 1, 3.

10 www.iasc.org.uk.

11 Elizabeth MacDonald, "The Outlook," *The Wall Street Journal*, interactive ed., October 18, 1999.

12 David Cairnes, *FT International Accounting Standards Survey 1999* (London: Financial Times Business, 1999).

13 Financial Accounting Standards Board, Statement of Financial Accounting Standards No. 52, "Foreign Currency Translation" (Stamford, CT: FASB, December 1981), pp. 6–7.

14 *DaimlerChrysler Annual Report 1998*, p. 53.

15 William H. Hoffman, William A. Raabe, James E. Smith and David M. Maloney, *West Federal Taxation: Corporations, Partnerships, Estates, and Trusts*, 2000 ed. (Cincinnati: South-Western, 2000), Section 9, p. 33.

16 Paul Magnusson, "U.S. Exporters Get the Word: Guilty," *Business Week*, August 16, 1999, p. 42.

17 Hoffman et al., *West Federal Taxation*, Chapter 9, p. 30.

18 Ibid., Chapter 9, pp. 25–27.

19 "U.S. Tax Treaty Developments," *Deloitte & Touche Review*, February 5, 1996, p. 5.

20 Sources for the case were various issues of the annual report of the Coca-Cola Company; Timothy K. Smith and Laura Landro, "Profoundly Changed, Coca-Cola Co. Strives to Keep on Bubbling," *Wall Street Journal*, April 24, 1986, p. 1; Andrew L. Nodar, "Coca-Cola Writes an Accounting Procedures Manual," *Management Accounting*, October 1986, pp. 52–53; "Assessing Brands: Broad, Deep, Long and Heavy," *The Economist*, November 16, 1996, pp. 72, 75; Dean Foust, "Man on the Spot," *Business Week*, May 3, 1999, pp. 142–151; "Going for Coke," *The Economist*, August 14, 1999, p. 51; Betsy McKay, "Coke's Sales Overseas Should Rise from Scaled-Down Cadbury Deal," *Wall Street Journal*, August 2, 1999, p. A4; "Coke Shuffles Global Management, but Ivester Mum on Successor," *Wall Street Journal*, interactive ed., October 29, 1999; Betsy McKay and Nikhil Deogun, "After Short Tenure, Ivester Quits as the Chairman of Coca-Cola," *Wall Street Journal*, interactive ed., December 7, 1999; Betsy McKay, Street Seeks Real Thing on Coke Outlook," *Wall Street Journal*, January 17, 2000, p. C1; Betsy McKay, "New Coke Chairman Heeds Advice, Chooses Stahl as Second-in-Command," *Wall Street Journal*, interactive ed., January 19, 2000.

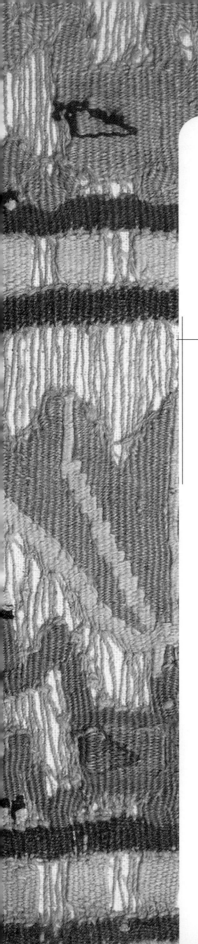

CHAPTER 20

The Multinational Finance Function

To have money is a good thing; to have a say over the money is even better.

—YIDDISH PROVERB

OBJECTIVES

- To describe the multinational finance function and how it fits in the MNE's organizational structure

- To show how companies can acquire outside funds for normal operations and expansion

- To discuss the major internal sources of funds available to the MNE and show how these funds are managed globally

- To explain how companies protect against the major financial risks of inflation and exchange-rate movements

- To highlight some of the financial aspects of the investment decision

Wilfred Corrigan formed LSI Logic Corporation, a world leader in the design, production, and sale of advanced custom semiconductors, in November 1980 in Malpitas, California. Corrigan was able to use his track record as the former chairman and president of Fairchild Camera & Instrument Corporation to convince some U.S. venture capitalists to invest nearly $7 million in the new venture. By the end of 1998, LSI Logic had generated $1.49 billion in sales, a 15.5 percent increase over the previous year, and Corrigan was still the chairman and CEO.

LSI Logic, which began with only 4 employees, grew to 6,420 employees worldwide by the end of 1998. Corrigan's solution of two key issues—the nature of the product and the initial infusion of cash—provided a solid foundation for growth. He next had to decide how LSI Logic should service its customers worldwide and how and where it would raise capital to keep expanding.

From his experience at Fairchild, Corrigan knew that a producer of microchips had to think globally in terms of the location of production and target markets. He quickly decided that to be successful, he needed to concentrate on three key geographic areas—Asia, Europe, and the United States. He called this his "global triad strategy," defining the triad more specifically as Japan, Western Europe, and North America (see Map 20.1). His key organizational strategy was to incorporate companies in the producing and consuming countries that would be jointly owned by LSI Logic and local investors, with LSI Logic holding the controlling interest. Although LSI Logic opened its first offices in Europe and Asia in only the early 1980s, Europe and Asia generated nearly 25 percent of LSI Logic's business by 1990 and 32 percent by 1998.

Once Corrigan got operations under way, he began to look for more cash. LSI Logic turned to Europe in search of venture capital, which it found in a European investing community hungry for U.S. high-tech stock. The company subsequently was able to raise $10 million, mostly—but not exclusively—in the United Kingdom. At this point, LSI Logic was growing rapidly. When Corrigan took the company public in the United States it raised over $162 million, an average of $21 a share.

Despite the European and U.S. successes, Corrigan still had not been able to raise capital in Japan. However, he learned that the Japanese brokerage house Nomura Securities had purchased large blocks of LSI stock for its clients in Japan. Encouraged by this information, Corrigan traveled to Japan to meet with Nomura officials and to try to decide what LSI Logic's next move should be. As a result of the visit, Corrigan decided to establish a Japanese subsidiary of LSI Logic (called LSI Logic Corporation K.K.), of which the parent company owned 70 percent and 25 Japanese investors together owned 30 percent. The new investment was just right for LSI Logic—it gained access not only to the Japanese consumer market but also to the Japanese capital market. As a Japanese company, LSI Logic Corporation K.K. could establish lines of credit with Japanese banks and did so at only 6 percent, compared with 9 percent in the United States at the time.

When business in Japan was under way, Corrigan once more turned his attentions to Europe. He planned to set up a new European company and needed to decide on its structure. The company could be set up as a European company, or it could be set up as a branch of the U.S. parent that would use U.S. capital and be totally controlled and protected by the parent. Corrigan decided on the former. Corrigan was convinced that by setting up a European

MAP 20.1   Triad Strategy for LSI Logic Corporation—Revenues, 1998

LSI Logic's global business and financing strategy focuses on three of the world's largest markets: Japan, Western Europe, and North America. In 1990, Europe and Asia generated nearly 25 percent of LSI Logic's revenues. That percentage rose to 32 percent by the end of 1998, as this map shows. Europe and Asia will continue to be increasingly important to LSI Logic, especially as the Japanese market strengthens.

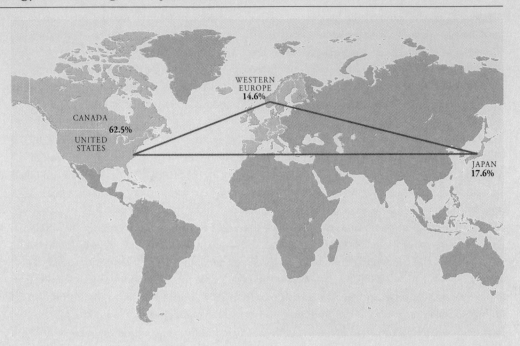

company, he would be able to get more money by selling shares at a higher price than would be possible by issuing more stock in the United States. He reasoned that Europeans would be hungry for new high-tech stock and would be willing to pay a higher price than would Americans, who already held a lot of LSI Logic stock. The parent company retained an 82-percent ownership share in the new company and sold the rest in a private offering to European investors, one of which was the venture capital arm of five German banks.

In 1985 and again in 1987, Corrigan returned to European capital markets. Both times LSI Logic floated a bond issue, a financial instrument issued by the company in order to borrow money for the public on a long-term basis (more than one year). Swiss Bank Corp put the first issue of $23 million together. Morgan Stanley and Prudential-Bache Capital Funding floated the second, a bond issue with securities convertible into common stock. LSI Logic was attracted to the Eurobond market, the market for U.S. bonds issued in Europe, for two main reasons: a decent price (lower interest rates than were being offered in the United States) and a quicker time frame.

In its 1998 annual report, LSI Logic identified two critical areas of international finance: global borrowings in foreign currencies and foreign-exchange risk management. In terms of the former, management noted that it had entered into credit arrangement with the Dutch bank, ABN AMRO, which allowed it to borrow funds on an adjustable rate basis, meaning that interest rates on the loan adjusted to the market rate every six months. One of the major loans on the credit facility was a Japanese yen loan by LSI Logic, the parent, and another was a Japanese yen loan by its Japanese subsidiary. From the standpoint of foreign-exchange risk, LSI Logic bought materials and sold products in foreign currencies, especially the Japanese yen, so it was heavily exposed to a possible change in exchange rates. However, it entered into a number of different hedging transactions and stated in its annual report that a 10-percent swing of the dollar against the yen or the euro would not have a material affect on earnings. 🝏

INTRODUCTION

Why do you need to understand capital markets, cash management, and financial risk? Having a good product idea is not sufficient for success. MNEs need to get access to capital markets in different countries in order to finance expansion. Indeed, finance is integral to firms' international strategies, as Figure 20.1 shows. The small company involved only tangentially in international business may be concerned primarily about the foreign-exchange function of its commercial bank and not global capital markets. It may use the bank to buy and sell foreign exchange and hedge foreign-exchange risk, but it probably doesn't think about borrowing money or issuing stock on foreign capital markets. However, the MNE investing and operating abroad usually is concerned about access to capital in local markets as well as in large global markets. LSI Logic's access of capital in Japan and Europe illustrates that point. This chapter examines external sources of funds available to companies operating abroad and internal sources of funds that arise from intercompany links. It also examines global cash management, risk-management strategies, and international dimensions of the capital investment decision.

To expand, MNEs raise capital in different countries by borrowing and issuing stock. They sometimes list their stock on exchanges in more than one country. The photo shows the New York Stock Exchange (NYSE), which is the world's largest in terms of the volume of trade conducted. MNEs from many countries list on the NYSE, and citizens of many countries buy shares on this exchange.

FIGURE 20.1   **Finance in International Business**

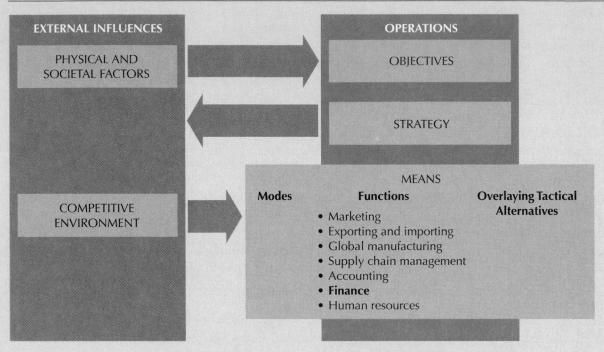

Finance is one of the necessary functions for implementing companies' international strategies.

The corporate finance function acquires and allocates financial resources among the company's activities and projects. Four key functions are

- **Capital structure**
- **Capital budgeting**
- **Long-term financing**
- **Working capital management**

THE FINANCE AND TREASURY FUNCTIONS IN THE INTERNATIONALIZATION PROCESS

One of the most important people on the management team, crucial to a company's success, is the vice president of finance, also known as the chief financial officer (CFO). The functions of the CFO are often divided into the controllership and treasury functions. The CFO's controller responsibilities were discussed in Chapter 19. This chapter focuses on the CFO's most important global treasury responsibilities. Figure 20.2 illustrates how the CFO's responsibilities fit into the organizational structure of the firm and how global finance fits into the treasury function. The vice president of finance, also known as the chief financial officer (CFO), reports directly to the president and chief operating officer of the company, who reports to the chairman and chief executive officer, who reports to the board of directors.

The finance function in the firm focuses on cash flows. The management activities related to cash flows can be divided into four major areas:

- Capital structure—determining the proper mix of debt and equity
- Capital budgeting—analyzing investment opportunities
- Long-term financing—selection, issuance, and management of long-term debt and equity capital, including location (in the company's home country or elsewhere) and currency (the company's home currency or a foreign currency)

FIGURE 20.2   Location of Treasury Function in the Corporate Organizational Structure

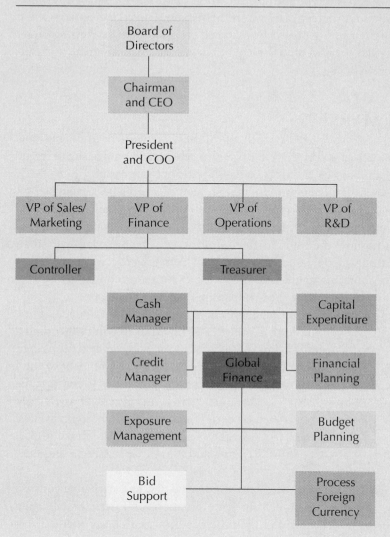

The treasury function falls under the responsibility of the chief financial officer, and it comprises domestic and foreign responsibilities. The global finance function within treasury is a resource to all of the strategic business units of a company.

- Working capital management—proper management of the company's currency assets and liabilities (cash, receivables, marketable securities, inventory, trade receivables, short-term bank debt)[2]

The CFO acquires financial resources and allocates them among the company's activities and projects. Acquiring resources (financing) means generating funds either internally (within the company) or from sources external to the company at the lowest possible cost. When LSI Logic needed funds to expand, it issued stock and borrowed money in the U.S. market, but it also did both of these activities in Europe and Japan. Allocating resources (investing) means increasing stockholders' wealth through the allocation of funds to different projects and investment opportunities.[3]

Country-specific factors are a more important determinant of capital structure than is any other factor.

The CFO's job is more complex in a global environment than in the domestic setting because of forces such as foreign-exchange risk, currency flows and restrictions, different tax rates and laws pertaining to the determination of taxable income, and regulations on access to capital in different markets. In the remainder of the chapter, we will examine the following six areas: global debt markets, global equity markets, offshore financial centers, internal sources of funds, foreign-exchange risk management, and capital budgeting in a global context.

GLOBAL DEBT MARKETS

The CFO must determine the degree to which a firm funds the growth of the business by debt, which is known as leverage. The degree to which companies use leverage instead of equity capital—known as stocks or shares—varies from country to country. Country-specific factors are a more important determinant of a company's capital structure than is any other factor because companies tend to follow the financing trends in their own country and their particular industry within their country. Japanese companies are more likely to follow the capital structure of other Japanese companies than they are of U.S. or European companies, for example. Leveraging is often perceived as the most cost-effective route to capitalization, because the interest companies pay on debt is a tax-deductible expense, while the dividends paid to investors are not.

However, leveraging may not be the best approach in all countries for two major reasons. First, excessive reliance on long-term debt increases financial risk and so requires a higher return for investors. Second, foreign subsidiaries of an MNE may have limited access to local capital markets, making it difficult for the MNE to rely on debt to fund asset acquisition.[4] In a study of foreign subsidiaries of U.S. MNEs, it was found that the debt/asset of those studied averaged 0.54, which means that 54 percent of assets were funded by debt and 46 percent were funded by equity. The debt/asset ratio on average for companies in a few countries was as follows: the Netherlands (0.32), Brazil (0.37), Australia (0.49), Mexico (0.51), Canada (0.52), England (0.64), Japan (0.65), and Germany (0.69).[5]

In addition, different tax rates, dividend remission policies, and exchange controls may cause a company to rely more on debt in some situations and more on equity in others. It is important to understand that the different debt and equity markets discussed in this chapter have different levels of importance for companies worldwide.

One of the major causes of the Asian financial crisis was that Asian companies relied too much on debt to fund their growth, especially bank debt. The lack of development of bond and equity markets forced companies to rely on bank debt for growth. Many of the Asian banks borrowed dollars from international banks and lent the money to local companies in local currencies, not dollars. When the Asian currencies fell against the dollar, many of the banks could not service their loans and went into bankruptcy. Some of the Asian companies that borrowed dollars directly from foreign banks couldn't generate enough local currency to pay off the debt, and they were brought close to bankruptcy. As a result, many have been forced to exchange debt for equity, thereby losing some of their control or selling themselves outright to foreign investors who could pay off their dollar debt.[6]

An MNE that needs to raise capital through debt markets has a number of options. The local domestic debt market is the first source that a company will tap. This means Japan for Japanese companies, but it could also mean Japan for the Japanese subsidiary of a U.S. company. Toyota lists several types of long-term debt in its annual report. It issued ¥200 billion (about $1.6 billion) bonds maturing at two different times, but it also issued U.S. dollar bonds as well.[7] LSI Logic floated a Eurobond issue in European capital markets and also borrowed Japanese yen to fund operations in Japan and Deutsche marks in Germany to fund operations there. So, companies can tap international banks for local currency borrowings or Eurodollar borrowings, as well as the longer-term bond markets.

> Companies can use local and international debt markets to raise funds.

Sometimes, the subsidiaries of foreign companies can obtain credit easier than local companies can because of their access to hard currency. They can enter into **back-to-back loans** during periods when interest rates are high or credit is frozen. A back-to-back loan is one made between a company in country A with a subsidiary in country B and a bank in country B with a branch in country A. For example, the Italian subsidiary of a U.S. food company gained access to Italian loans when its U.S. parent provided dollars to the U.S. branch of an Italian bank. Under that condition, the Italian bank lent money to the Italian subsidiary of the U.S. parent.[8]

> In a back-to-back loan, the parent company in country A deposits cash in the local branch of a bank from country B, and the bank from country B loans funds to the parent's subsidiary in country B.

EUROCURRENCIES

The Eurocurrency market is an important source of debt financing for the MNEs to compliment what they can find in their domestic market. A **Eurocurrency** is any currency that is banked outside of its country of origin. Currencies banked inside of their country of origin are also known as onshore, and currencies banked outside of their country of origin are also known as offshore. In essence, the Eurocurrency market is an offshore market. The Eurocurrency market started with the deposit of U.S. dollars in London banks, and it was called the Eurodollar market. As other currencies entered the offshore market, the broader *eurocurrency* name is used for the market. Given the introduction of the euro as the new currency in Europe, the term *Eurocurrency* is confusing, but the Eurocurrency market predates the euro, and the confusion will probably not go away. Eurocurrencies could be dollars or yen in London, euro in the Bahamas, or British pounds in New York. Eurodollars, which constitute a fairly consistent 65 to 80 percent of the Eurocurrency market, are dollars banked outside of the United States. Dollars held by foreigners on deposit in the United States are not Eurodollars, but dollars held at branches of U.S. or other banks outside of the United States are. Smaller Eurocurrency market segments exist for Japanese yen (Euroyen), German marks (Euromarks), and other currencies, such as British pounds (Eurosterling), French francs, and Swiss francs. However, the new euro will become an increasingly important player in the market in the future as it replaces other currencies in Europe. Will an offshore euro be called a Euroeuro? It will be interesting to see what the market determines.

> A Eurocurrency is any currency banked outside of its country of origin.

The major sources of Eurocurrencies are

- Foreign governments or individuals who want to hold dollars outside of the United States
- Multinational corporations that have cash in excess of current needs

> Major sources of Eurocurrencies
> - Foreign governments or individuals
> - MNEs
> - Foreign banks
> - Countries with large balance-of-payments surpluses

- European banks with foreign currency in excess of current needs
- Countries such as Germany, Japan, and Taiwan that have large balance-of-trade surpluses held as reserves.

The demand for Eurocurrencies comes from sovereign governments, supranational agencies such as the World Bank, companies, and individuals. Eurocurrencies exist partly for the convenience and security of the user and partly because of cheaper lending rates for the borrower and better yield for the lender.

The Eurocurrency market is a wholesale (companies and other institutions) rather than a retail market (individuals), so transactions are very large. Public borrowers such as governments, central banks, and public sector corporations are the major players. MNEs are involved in the Eurodollar market; however, nearly four-fifths of the Eurodollar market is in the interbank market.

> **A Eurocredit is a type of loan that matures in one to five years.**
>
> **Syndication occurs when several banks pool resources to make a large loan in order to spread the risk.**

The Eurocurrency market is both short- and medium term. Short-term borrowing has maturities of less than one year. Anything over one year is considered a **Eurocredit**, which may be a loan, line of credit, or other form of medium- and long-term credit, including **syndication**, in which several banks pool resources to extend credit to a borrower.

A major attraction of the Eurocurrency market is the difference in interest rates compared with those in domestic markets. Because of the large transactions and the lack of controls and their attendant costs, Eurocurrency deposits tend to yield more than domestic deposits do, and loans tend to be cheaper than they are in domestic markets. Traditionally, loans are made at a certain percentage above the **London Inter-Bank Offered Rate** (**LIBOR**), which is the deposit rate that applies to interbank loans within London. The LIBOR rates quoted on January 20, 2000, were

> **LIBOR is the interest rate that banks charge each other on Eurocurrency loans.**

> 5.8100% one month; 6.0400 percent three months; 6.2200 percent six months; 6.6500 percent one year. British Banker's Association average of interbank offered rates for dollar deposits in the London market based on quotations at 16 major banks.[9]

At the same time, the prime rate in the United States was 8.50 percent, based on the best rate on corporate loans posted by 75 percent of the nation's 30 largest banks. In addition, prime rates were listed as 6.50 percent for Canada, 3.00 percent for Germany, 3.375 percent for Switzerland, 5.75 percent for Britain, and 1.375 percent for Japan. However, the *Wall Street Journal* noted that it is very difficult to compare prime rates and the LIBOR rate because lending practices vary so much from country to country.

How much above LIBOR the interest rate charged to a borrower is depends on the creditworthiness of the customer and must be large enough to cover expenses and build reserves against possible losses. The Eurocurrency market's unique characteristics mean that the borrowing rate usually is less than it would be in the domestic market. Most loans are variable rate, and the rate-fixing period generally is six months, although it may be one or three months. Another unique characteristic of the Eurocurrency market is that it is completely unregulated. No single country or agency, not even the Bank for International Settlements, regulates Eurocurrency transactions.

INTERNATIONAL BONDS: FOREIGN, EURO, AND GLOBAL

Many countries have active bond markets available to domestic and foreign investors. Japan is one such country. The earlier long-term debt example of Toyota involves bonds issued in Japan. One bond issue for ¥50 billion matures (must be paid back) in 2018 at

Ethical Dilemmas and Social Responsibility
WHAT'S WRONG WITH BANKING IN A TAX-HAVEN COUNTRY?

Cash flow management gives rise to numerous ethical dilemmas. Many critics question the practice of setting up subsidiaries in tax-haven countries such as the Cayman Islands to take advantage of lower tax rates and the secrecy there. MNEs have been known to transfer money illegally into tax-haven countries to pay bribes. This practice became common knowledge in the United States when President Nixon ran for reelection in the early 1970s, and it was later found out that his reelection committee had obtained illegal campaign contributions and kept the money in offshore bank accounts so that they wouldn't be discovered.

The secrecy possible in tax-haven countries makes them natural locations in which to hide cash. However, not all use of tax havens is illegal. Although the governments of high-tax countries may criticize domestic companies that shelter income in tax-haven countries, those companies may simply be taking advantage of differences in tax rates and not necessarily acting unethically.

In 1996, John M. Mathewson, a U.S. citizen who operated Guardian Bank & Trust Ltd. on the Cayman Islands, was arrested on money laundering and tax fraud. In the subsequent years, he has provided information to U.S. government authorities that has resulted in several convictions and ongoing investigations. He provided information to U.S. federal agents on over 1,000 individuals and their shell companies (companies set up on paper but with no real business behind them). His initial charge was that he was laundering money from a U.S. ring that sold illegal cable-TV converter boxes.

The Cayman Islands is an interesting place, because it has over $500 billion in banking deposits, making it the world's fifth-largest banking center. Mr. Mathewson charged that the Cayman Islands government was assisting in massive tax evasion schemes and that over 95 percent of the deposits in the Cayman Islands were made by U.S. citizens trying to avoid taxes, a charge the Cayman government and banking authorities dispute. However, it is clear from the investigations into Mr. Mathewson's clients, which were still going on in January 2000, that everyone from criminals to doctors to businessmen and even to a golf pro were using phony accounts to hide taxable earnings from the IRS.

an interest rate of 3 percent, and another bond issue for ¥150 billion matures in 2008 at an interest rate of 2 percent. Even though the domestic bond market dominates total bond issues, with the U.S. market offering the best opportunities, the international bond market still fills an important niche in financing. One of the reasons why the U.S. bond (and stock) markets in the United States are so influential is because the companies of continental Europe and Japan still rely disproportionately on banks for finance—on average about 75 percent of corporate funding. That varies across Europe from 70 percent in Germany and France to 80 percent in Spain but much lower in Britain. The euro may change that as Europe moves to one large liquid market under a single currency, but that remains to be seen.[10]

The international bond market can be divided into foreign bonds, Eurobonds, and global bonds. **Foreign bonds** are sold outside of the borrower's country but are denominated in the currency of the country of issue. For example, a French company floating a bond issue in Swiss francs in Switzerland would be selling a foreign bond. Foreign bonds typically make up about 18 percent of the international bond market. They also have creative names, such as Yankee bond (issued in the United States), Samurai bond (issued in Japan), and Bulldog bond (issued in England).

A **Eurobond** is usually underwritten (placed in the market for the borrower) by a syndicate of banks from different countries and sold in countries other than the one in whose currency the bond is denominated. A bond issue floated by a U.S. company in dollars in London, Luxembourg, and Switzerland is a Eurobond. Eurobonds make up approximately 75 percent of the international bond market.

The **global bond**, introduced by the World Bank in 1989, is a combination of a domestic bond and a Eurobond in that it must be registered in each national market according to that market's registration requirements. It also is issued simultaneously in several markets, usually those in Asia, Europe, and North America. Global bonds are a small but growing segment of the international bond market.

The international bond market is an attractive place to borrow money. For one thing, it allows a company to diversify its funding sources from the local banks and bond market and in maturities that might not be available in the domestic markets. In addition, the international bond markets tend to be less expensive than local bond markets. However, not all companies are interested in global bonds or Eurobonds. Before the Asian financial crisis, Asian companies relied on their domestic banks more because of the ready availability of cheap loans. In addition, the companies and banks tended to develop a cozier relationship than might be the case with Western companies and banks.[11] However, the Asian financial crisis demonstrated the fundamental flaws in this strategy as banks went bankrupt and companies couldn't generate enough funds to pay back the loans.

Although the Eurobond market is centered in Europe, it has no national boundaries. Unlike most conventional bonds, Eurobonds are sold simultaneously in several financial centers through multinational underwriting syndicates and are purchased by an international investing public that extends far beyond the confines of the countries of issue.

U.S. companies first issued Eurobonds in 1963 as a means of avoiding U.S. tax and disclosure regulations. They are typically issued in denominations of $5,000 or $10,000, pay interest annually, are held in bearer form, and are traded over the counter (OTC), most frequently in London.[12] Any investor who holds a bearer bond is entitled to receive the principal and interest payments. In contrast, for a registered bond, which is more typical in the United States, the investor is required to be registered as the bond's owner in order to receive payments. An OTC bond is traded with or through an investment bank rather than on a securities exchange, such as the London Stock Exchange.

An example of a non–U.S. dollar Eurobond issue is found in the 1998 annual report of Marks & Spencer, the British retail company. In 1993, Marks & Spencer issued a

---

Foreign bonds are sold outside of the country of the borrower but in the currency of the country of issue.

Eurobonds are sold in countries other than the one in whose currency the bond is denominated.

A global bond is registered in different national markets according to the registration requirements of each market.

Eurobonds are typically issued in denominations of $5,000 or $10,000, pay interest annually, are held in bearer form, and are traded over the counter.

£150 million Eurobond at 7 3/8 percent fixed rate maturing in five years. Marks & Spencer then entered into an interest rate swap with another company where it agreed to exchange its fixed rate obligation with a floating rate obligation.[13] An investment bank would have facilitated the swap. Marks & Spencer probably got a reasonably good Eurobond fixed interest rate because it is a British company and was issuing the bond in Eurosterling. The counterparty (the other company in the swap agreement) might have wanted a fixed rate obligation in sterling initially but couldn't get it for whatever reason, so it had to settle for a floating rate obligation. As interest rates in Britain began to come down, it made sense for Marks & Spencer to enter into the swap to lower its overall interest charge. In a floating rate bond, the interest rate changes every six months, so as interest rates come down, the holder of the floating rate bond would end up paying lower interest to the bondholders. The holder of the floating rate bond might have wanted to trade to a fixed rate bond to eliminate the uncertainty of future interest rates and lock in an interest rate that was attractive to it.

The top five investment banks in the world that deal in the Eurobond market are Deutsche Bank (Germany), Morgan Stanley Dean Witter (U.S.), Warburg Dillon Read (Switzerland), ABN Amro (the Netherlands), and Merrill Lynch (U.S.).[14] The ranking varies a little depending on the specific currency being issued, but these are the top banks.

Occasionally, Eurobonds may provide currency options, which enable the creditor to demand repayment in one of several currencies, reducing the exchange risk inherent in single-currency foreign bonds. More frequently, however, both interest and principal on Eurobonds are payable to the creditor in U.S. dollars. It is also possible to issue a Eurobond in one currency, say the U.S. dollar, and then swap the obligation to another currency, similar to the interest-rate swap just described. For example, a U.S. company with a subsidiary in Britain would generate lots of British pounds through normal operations, and it could use the pounds to pay off a British pound bond. If the U.S. company had issued Eurobonds in dollars in London, it could enter into a swap agreement through an investment bank to exchange its future dollar obligations with a British pound obligation and use the pound revenues to pay off the swapped obligation.

> Some Eurobonds have currency options, which allow the creditor to demand repayment in one of several currencies.

EQUITY SECURITIES AND THE EUROEQUITY MARKET

Another source of financing is equity securities, where an investor takes an ownership position in return for shares of stock in the company and the promises of capital gains—an appreciation in the value of the stock—and maybe dividends. One way a company can get access to capital is through a private placement with a venture capitalist. In this case, a wealthy venture capitalist (or perhaps a venture capital firm investing money of one or several wealthy individuals) will invest money in a new venture in exchange for stock. LSI Logic used venture capital when it initially expanded into Europe. However, venture capital in Europe is only beginning to explode. The money available for investment in European Internet and high-tech start-ups in Europe is estimated at about $10 billion, one-third of what is available in the United States. However, many U.S. venture capital firms are setting up operations in Europe to identify new investment opportunities. In 1998, over half of the private placements in Europe were for buyouts, and only 10.2 percent were used for new start-ups. But that is beginning to change as Internet companies are beginning to catch on in Europe.[15] Another source of demand

> Many companies around the world are using private placements to raise equity capital because it is easier and cheaper.

for private placements is the corporate restructuring market in Europe. In recent years, European mergers have primarily taken place between firms in the same country, but now mergers are crossing national borders. Cross-European mergers have increased the demand for cash, and private placements have helped to fill that demand.[16]

In addition to private placements, companies can access the equity-capital market, more commonly known as the stock market. Companies can raise new capital by listing their stocks (also known as shares) on a stock exchange, and they can list on their home-country exchange or on a foreign exchange. The growth in globalization has forced companies to look at equity markets as an alternative to debt markets and banks as a source of funds. As in Map 20.2 notes, the 10 largest stock markets in the world in terms of **market capitalization** (the total number of shares of stock listed times the market price per share) are in the developed countries. Hong Kong and Singapore do not

> **Stock markets are another source of equity capital.**

> **The three largest stock markets in the world are in the United States, Japan, and London.**

MAP 20.2　Market Capitalization, 1998 (in billions of U.S. dollars)

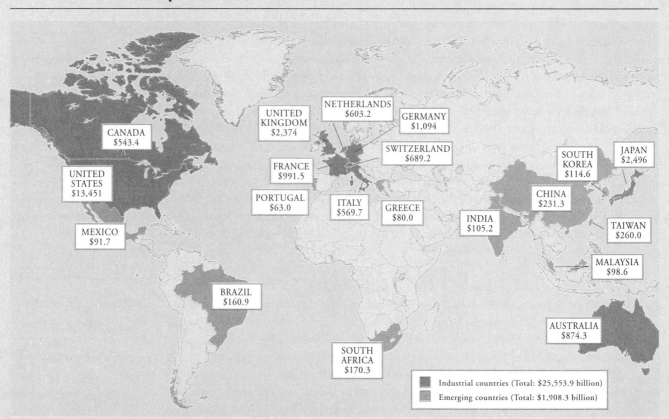

Stock markets in the developed countries far surpass those in emerging countries in terms of market capitalization (a measure of the size of a stock market: total number of shares listed, times the price per share). Forty-nine percent of the world's market capitalization is in the U.S. market, which is comprised of the New York Stock Exchange, the American Stock Exchange, and the NASDAQ Stock Exchange. The map illustrates the top 10 industrial markets and the top 10 emerging markets. Totals include all markets worldwide, not just the industrial and emerging countries shown on the map.

Source: International Finance Corporation, *Emerging Stock Markets Factbook 1999* (Washington, D.C.: IFC, 1999), p. 24.

show up on the map, because they are developed instead of emerging markets, but Portugal and Greece, two members of the EU, are emerging markets.

It has been interesting to track the development of the emerging stock markets, as Figure 20.3 shows. The emerging markets grew steadily as a percentage of total stock market capitalization until the end of 1994. They dipped a little bit as a percentage of total in 1995 but recovered in 1998 to 11.1 percent of total. By the end of 1997, however, the Asian financial crisis had clobbered the emerging stock markets, and they plunged to only 9.4 percent of total. Total stock market capitalization in the emerging markets actually fell in 1997 and 1998, and the money investors wanted to put into the stock market moved to the developed markets, especially the United States, which climbed from 33.5 percent of total in 1994 to 49 percent of total in 1998.

From 1993 to 1998, the total world market capitalization nearly doubled, which meant that companies could raise good money by issuing stock. Some of the explosion in market activity was the result of privatizations taking place in emerging markets, and some was general economic growth in the world. Yet the stock market was clearly becoming a more significant force in raising new capital for expansion and to facilitate mergers and acquisitions.

Another significant event in the past decade is the creation of the **Euroequity market**, the market for shares sold outside the boundaries of the issuing company's home country. Prior to 1980, few companies thought of offering stock outside the national boundaries of their headquarters country. Since then, hundreds of companies worldwide have issued stock simultaneously in two or more countries in order to attract more capital from a wider variety of shareholders.

In some cases, companies list on only one foreign exchange. It is expensive to list on foreign exchanges and so companies often list on one big one, such as the New York Stock Exchange or the London Stock Exchange. However, some companies list

The Euroequity market is the market for shares sold outside the boundaries of the issuing company's home country.

FIGURE 20.3   Growth of Emerging Stock Markets

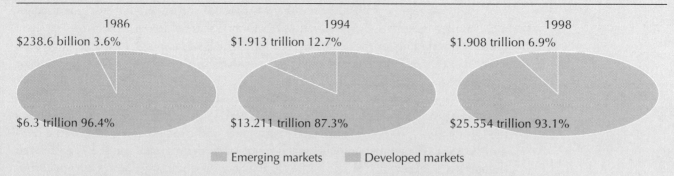

The market capitalization of emerging stock markets rose from 3.6 percent of the world's total in 1986 to 12.7 percent in 1994, and back to 6.9 percent in 1998. The Asian financial crisis devastated emerging stock markets, and they only started to recover in 1999.

Source: International Finance Corporation, *Emerging Stock Markets Factbook 1999* (Washington, D.C.: IFC, 1999), pp. 16–17.

on different exchanges, especially if they have foreign investments in several countries and are trying to raise capital in those countries. For example, when DaimlerChrysler merged and issued global shares around the world, it did so on 21 different markets in 8 different countries: Germany, the United States, Austria, Canada, France, Britain, Japan, and Switzerland. However, the U.S. and German markets were the most important ones. The U.S. market is important for U.S. and foreign companies looking for equity capital and is popular for Euroequity issues partly because of the market size and the speed with which offerings are completed. The large pension funds in the United States can buy big blocks of stock at low transaction costs. Pension fund managers regard foreign stocks as a good form of portfolio diversification.

The New York Stock Exchange identifies four major reasons why a foreign company should list on the NYSE (and these reasons could apply to U.S. companies trying to determine the benefits of listing on a foreign exchange):

- NYSE provides opportunities to develop a broad shareholder constituency in the United States through exposure to the widest possible range of individual and institutional investors.
- NYSE facilitates U.S. mergers and acquisitions through the use of an NYSE-listed security as acquisition currency.
- NYSE increases the visibility of a company, its products and services, and the trading of its shares in the United States.
- NYSE supports a company's incentive program for its U.S. employees by providing a liquid market in the United States for its shares.[17]

An ADR is a negotiable certificate issued by a U.S. bank and representing shares of stock of a foreign corporation.

There are 379 foreign companies listing on the New York Stock Exchange, more than triple the number of companies that listed in 1993. The countries with the most companies listing on the NYSE are Canada (69), the United Kingdom (46), Mexico (28), Chile (23), and Brazil (21). By May 1999, 866 foreign companies were listed on one of the three big U.S. exchanges, with more listed on NASDAQ (418) than on the NYSE (385).

The most popular way for a Euroequity to get a listing in the United States is to issue an **American Depositary Receipt (ADR)**. ADRs are traded like shares of stock, with each one representing some number of shares of the underlying stock. For example, Daimler-Benz initially issued ten ADRs for one share of its stock, because one share of stock was trading for the equivalent of $467, which was too high for the U.S. market. Eventually, Daimler-Benz reduced its price per share so that it could issue one ADR for one share.

The United States is not the only market for Euroequities. There are also Global Depositary Receipts and European Depositary Receipts, but the U.S. market dominates the DR market. However, a much larger percentage of the total shares traded on the London Stock Exchange belongs to foreign companies than is true for the NYSE, even though the total trading volume in the United States is quite large. Many foreign corporations try to raise capital in the United States, but they don't want to list on an exchange because they don't want to comply with the onerous reporting requirements of the Securities and Exchange Commission. However, those that do get access to 49 percent of the world's market capitalization, which is a significant advantage to a U.S. listing.

The global share offering by DaimlerChrysler is the first of its kind in the world, although Celanese AG, another German firm, followed it in 1998. The desire by DaimlerChrysler to diversify its investor base has not worked out the way it had hoped. By the end of 1999, 80 percent of DaimlerChrysler's share trading had migrated to Frankfurt, and the percentage of Americans holding DaimlerChrysler shares had fallen from 44 percent to 25 percent of the total. Although DaimlerChrysler is incorporated in Germany, two-thirds of its profits are from the United States, but it is having a hard time attracting back U.S. investors, especially institutional investors.

In spite of the troubles of DaimlerChrysler, it is still important for MNEs to list their securities on foreign exchanges as mentioned above in the NYSE example. As MNEs generate more of their revenues outside of their home country, it is easier to attract investors from the countries where they are operating. As global stock markets continue to grow, especially in the emerging markets, it will be even easier for companies to raise equity capital outside of their home markets.

Although Daimler-Benz ADRs had traded on the Frankfurt and New York exchanges at the same price, that is not true for all ADRs. For example, Taiwan Semiconductor shares were worth 70 percent more in New York than they were in Taiwan in January 2000. Also, the ADRs of Infosys, an Indian software contractor, traded at nearly two-and-a-half times their value in India. At the same time, ADRs for Singapore, Japanese, and British companies were trading at the same value as in their home market. There are a couple of reasons why that is the case. The latter countries are relatively open to the outside world, so traders spotting price differences in two markets can buy or sell securities until the price difference disappears. However, Taiwan and India have regulated markets where foreigners are allowed to own only a certain percentage of the shares and where currency controls make it difficult to buy and sell assets. In addition, the ADRs represent only a small percentage of the companies' shares. As the Asian markets are beginning to recover, the demand for high-tech stocks is pushing up the prices for ADRs. As markets open up, these price differences should eventually disappear.[18]

There are a number of movements to improve stock market activity around the world. In Europe, the Frankfurt Exchange and London Stock Exchange announced an alliance to improve trades of German and British shares in each other's markets, but that has not been very successful. In fact, its has been said that the alliance is dead in all but name.[19] However, the major innovation in share trading around the world is Internet trading. U.S. electronic trading companies such as E*Trade and Charles Schwab & Company are now doing business in Europe and competing with local e-trade companies. Some of the large investment banks, such as J. P. Morgan, Morgan Stanley Dean Witter, and Warburg Dillon Read, have joined together to strengthen Tradepoint, a British-based electronic exchange. More than 20 European fund managers, led by Merrill Lynch Mercury Asset Management and Barclays Global Investors, are building their own electronic network, called E-Crossnet, which will help reduce broker's role and the cost of making trades. A NASDAQ-type exchange called Easdaq has been established in Brussels and is concentrating on high-tech European stocks. The whole world of e-trade could provide strong competition to stock exchanges in European as well as developing countries, just as it is beginning to put pressure on the major exchanges in the United States.[20]

> A global share offering, such as the one issued by Daimler-Chrysler, is the simultaneous offering of actual shares on different exchanges.

> A major source of competition to the stock exchanges will be electronic trading of stocks through companies such as E*Trade.

OFFSHORE FINANCIAL CENTERS

Offshore financial centers are cities or countries that engage in a variety of financial transactions and that provide significant tax advantages to companies and individuals who do business there. Usually, the financial transactions are conducted in currencies other than the currency of the country and are thus the centers for the Eurocurrency market. Generally, the markets in these centers are regulated differently, and usually more flexibly, than domestic markets. These centers provide an alternative, (usually) cheaper source of funding for MNEs so that they don't have to rely strictly on their own national markets. Offshore financial centers have one or more of the following characteristics.

- Large foreign-currency (Eurocurrency) market for deposits and loans (that in London, for example)
- Market that is a large net supplier of funds to the world financial markets (that in Switzerland, for example)
- Market that is an intermediary or pass-through for international loan funds (those in the Bahamas and the Cayman Islands, for example)
- Economic and political stability
- Efficient and experienced financial community
- Good communications and supportive services
- Official regulatory climate favorable to the financial industry, in the sense that it protects investors without unduly restricting financial institutions[21]

These centers are either operational centers, with extensive banking activities involving short-term financial transactions, or booking centers, where little actual banking activity takes place but where transactions are recorded to take advantage of secrecy and low (or no) tax rates. In the latter case, individuals may deposit money offshore to hide it from their home-country tax authorities, either because the money was earned illegally—such as in drug trade—or because the individual or company does not want to pay tax. London is an example of an operational center; the Cayman Islands is an example of a booking center. Although there are many offshore financial centers, the most important are Bahrain (for the Middle East), Brussels, the Caribbean (servicing mainly Canadian and U.S. banks), Dublin, Hong Kong, London, New York, Singapore, and Switzerland. London is a crucial center because it offers a variety of financial services in both debt and equity transactions and has a large domestic market as well as serving the offshore market. The Caribbean centers (primarily the Bahamas, the Cayman Islands, and the Netherlands Antilles) are essentially offshore locations for New York banks. Switzerland has been a primary source of funds for decades, offering stability, integrity, discretion, and low costs. Singapore has been the center for the Eurodollar market in Asia (sometimes called the Asiadollar market) since 1968, thanks to its strategic geographic location, its strong worldwide telecommunications links, and governmental regulations that have facilitated the flow of funds. Hong Kong is critical because of its unique status with respect to China and the United Kingdom and its geographic proximity to the rest of the Pacific Rim. Bahrain, an island country in the Persian Gulf, is the financial center of petrodollars (dollars generated from the sale of oil) in the Middle East.

Offshore financial centers are good locations for establishing finance subsidiaries that can raise capital for the parent company or its other subsidiaries. They allow the finance subsidiaries to take advantage of lower borrowing costs and tax rates.

INTERNAL SOURCES OF FUNDS

Although the term *funds* usually means "cash," it is used in a much broader sense in business and generally refers to working capital; that is, the difference between current assets and current liabilities. A company that wants to expand operations or needs additional capital can look not only to the debt and equity markets but also to sources within itself. For an MNE, the complexity of internal sources is magnified because of the number of its subsidiaries and the diverse environments in which they operate. Figure 20.4 shows a parent company that has two foreign subsidiaries. The parent, as well as the two subsidiaries, may be increasing funds through normal operations. These funds may be used on a company-wide basis, perhaps through loans. The parent can loan funds directly to one subsidiary or guarantee an outside loan to the other. Equity capital from the parent is another source of funds for the subsidiary.

Funds also can go from subsidiary to parent. The subsidiary could declare a dividend to the parent as a return on capital or could loan cash directly to the parent. If the subsidiary declared a dividend to the parent, the parent could lend the funds back to the subsidiary. The dividend would not be tax deductible to the subsidiary, but it would be included as income to the parent, and the parent would have to pay tax on the dividend. If the subsidiary loaned money to the parent, the interest paid by the parent would be tax deductible to the parent and would be taxable income to the subsidiary.

Intercompany financial links become extremely important as MNEs increase in size and complexity. Goods as well as loans can travel between subsidiaries, giving rise to receivables and payables. Companies can move money between and among related entities by paying quickly (leading payments) or can accumulate funds by deferring payment (lagging payments). They also can adjust the size of the payment by arbitrarily raising or lowering the price of intercompany transactions in comparison with the market price, a transfer pricing strategy.

Thus cash comes from debt and equity markets both domestically and overseas and from internal sources. In addition, companies can generate cash from normal operations,

Funds are working capital, or current assets minus current liabilities.

Sources of internal funds:
- **Loans**
- **Dividends**
- **Intercompany receivables and payables**
- **Investments through equity capital**

FIGURE 20.4 Internal Sources of Working Capital for MNEs

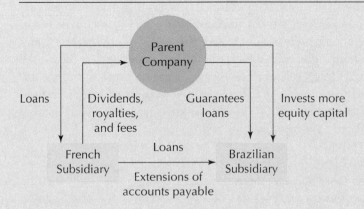

There are many ways in which MNEs can use internal cash flow to fund worldwide operations.

from selling cars if you are DaimlerChrysler or selling semiconductors if you are LSI Logic. The problems of managing cash globally are complex. International cash management is complicated by differing inflation rates, changes in exchange rates, and governmental restrictions on the flow of funds. To understand how companies can utilize their internal sources of funds more effectively in a global setting, we need to discuss global cash management and the multilateral netting of funds.

GLOBAL CASH MANAGEMENT

Effective cash management is a chief concern of the CFO, who must answer the following three questions to ensure effective cash management:

1. What are the local and corporate system needs for cash?
2. How can the cash be withdrawn from subsidiaries and centralized?
3. Once the cash has been centralized, what should be done with it?

Cash budgets and forecasts are essential in assessing a company's cash needs.

The cash manager, who reports to the treasurer as illustrated in Figure 20.1, must collect and pay cash in its normal operational cycle and then must deal with financial institutions, such as commercial and investment banks, in generating and investing cash. Before the cash manager remits any cash into the MNE's control center, whether at regional or headquarters level, she must first assess local cash needs through cash budgets and forecasts. Because the cash forecast projects the excess cash that will be available, the cash manager will know how much cash can be invested for short-term profits.

Dividends are a good source of intercompany transfers, but governments often restrict their free movement.

Once local cash needs are met, the cash manager must decide whether to allow the local manager to invest any excess cash or to have it remitted to a central cash pool. If the cash is centralized, the manager must find a way of making the transfer. A cash dividend is the easiest way to distribute cash, but governmental restrictions may interfere. For example, foreign-exchange controls may prevent the company from remitting as large a dividend as it would like. Cash also can be remitted through royalties, management fees, and repayment of principal and interest on loans.

Many developing countries with large foreign debt, such as Brazil, have made transferring money abroad difficult for companies operating within them because they want to curtail the outflow of foreign exchange. For example, one U.S. company with large operations in Brazil used dividends, loan repayments, and sales commissions to transfer funds out of Brazil. The Brazilian operation was treated as a manufacturing facility, and all export sales were made by a sales subsidiary of the U.S. parent. When the manufacturing facility was established in Brazil, it was financed primarily through debt rather than equity. The parent could get more cash out of Brazil by paying off principal and interest than it could by paying a dividend, which was subject to large taxes. When the Brazilian manufacturer made foreign sales, he could pay a commission to the sales company in the United States, which allowed him to transmit more funds abroad. However, the Brazilian government constantly tried to lower the amount of the commission, while the parent company tried to increase it.

Multilateral netting enables companies to reduce the amount of cash flow and move cash more quickly and efficiently.

MULTILATERAL NETTING

An important cash-management strategy is netting cash flows internationally. Netting means a company establishes one center to handle all internal cash, funds, and financial transactions. For example, an MNE with operations in four European countries could

FIGURE 20.5   Multilateral Cash Flows

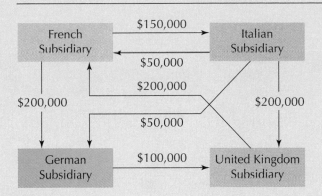

Multilateral cash flows in the absence of netting require each subsidiary to settle intercompany obligations.

have several different intercompany cash transfers resulting from loans, the sale of goods, licensing agreements, and the like. In Figure 20.5 for example, there are seven different transfers among the four subsidiaries. Table 20.1 identifies the total receivables, payables, and net position for each subsidiary. Rather than have each subsidiary settle its accounts independently with subsidiaries in other countries, many MNEs are establishing cash-management centers in one city (such as Brussels) to coordinate cash flows among subsidiaries from several countries. Figure 20.6 illustrates that each subsidiary in a net payable position (where its payments out exceed its receivables in) transfers funds to the central clearing account. The clearing account's manager then transfers funds to the accounts of the net receiver subsidiaries. In this example only four transfers need to take place. The clearing account manager receives transactions information and computes the net position of each subsidiary at least monthly. Then the manager orchestrates the settlement process. The transfers take place in the payer's currency, and the foreign-exchange conversion takes place centrally.

TABLE 20.1   NET POSITIONS OF SUBSIDIARIES IN FOUR COUNTRIES (IN DOLLARS)

Net positions show total receivables less total payables

SUBSIDIARY	TOTAL RECEIVABLES	TOTAL PAYABLES	NET POSITION
French	250,000	350,000	(100,000)
German	250,000	100,000	150,000
Italian	150,000	300,000	(150,000)
U.K.	300,000	200,000	100,000

FIGURE 20.6   Multilateral Netting

Multilateral netting allows subsidiaries to transfer net intercompany flows to a cash center, or clearing account, which disburses cash to net receivers.

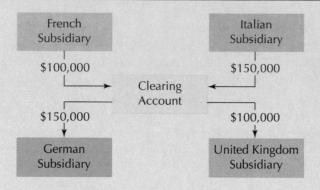

The advantages of establishing their clearing accounts and mechanisms for transferring funds across national boundaries include

- Optimizing the use of excess cash
- Reducing interest expenses and maximizing interest yields
- Reducing costly foreign exchange, swap transactions, and intercompany transfers
- Minimizing administrative paperwork
- Centralizing and speeding information for tighter control and improved decision making.[22]

The multilateral netting process has several advantages over having each foreign operation of an MNE handle payments independently:

- Savings in foreign-exchange conversion costs, because the central manager can effect large exchanges
- Savings of transfer charges and commissions, again due to the large size and smaller number of transactions
- Quicker access to the funds

Even though there are significant benefits to netting activities, not every MNE uses netting techniques. One reason is that for netting to work, companies need to establish custom software that not only does the netting at a central location where the MNE nets cash flows but also allows subsidiaries to link to the netting center to upload receivables and payables data automatically. Netting also becomes more economically feasible the more subsidiaries and currencies involved.

FOREIGN-EXCHANGE RISK MANAGEMENT

Major financial risks arise from exchange-rate changes.

As illustrated above, global cash-management strategy focuses on the flow of money for specific operating objectives. Another important objective of an MNE's financial strategy is to protect against the foreign-exchange risks of investing abroad. The strategies that it adopts to do this may mean the internal movement of funds as well as the use of one or more of the foreign-exchange instruments described in Chapter 9, such as options and forward contracts.

If all exchange rates were fixed in relation to one another, there would be no foreign-exchange risk. However, rates are not fixed, and currency values change frequently. Instead of infrequent one-way changes, currencies fluctuate often and both up and down. A change in the exchange rate can result in three different exposures for a company: translation exposure, transaction exposure, and economic exposure.

Three types of foreign-exchange exposure—translation, transaction, economic or operational

TRANSLATION EXPOSURE

Foreign-currency financial statements are translated into the reporting currency of the parent company (assumed to be U.S. dollars for U.S. companies) so that they can be combined with financial statements of other companies in the corporate group to form the consolidated financial statements. Exposed accounts—those translated at the balance sheet rate or current exchange rate—either gain or lose value in dollars when the exchange rate changes. For example, assume a subsidiary of a U.S. company operates in Mexico and has 900,000 pesos in a bank account there. If the Mexican peso were to depreciate in relation to the dollar from 7.9 pesos per dollar to 8.5 pesos per dollar, the subsidiary's bank account would drop in value from $113,924 (900,000/7.9) to $105,882 (900,000/8.5) as a result of the depreciation. However, the subsidiary still has pesos in the bank account; it's just that the dollar equivalent of the pesos has fallen, resulting in a loss.

The combined effect of the exchange-rate change on all assets and liabilities is either a net gain or loss. However, the gain or loss does not represent an actual cash flow effect because the cash, in the example above, is only translated into dollars, not converted into dollars. The problem is that reported earnings can either rise or fall against the dollar because of the translation effect, and this can affect earnings per share and stock prices. A good example is Coca-Cola. In 1998 when most foreign currencies were falling against the dollar, Coca-Cola management announced in its annual report that earnings would have been higher if the dollar had not been so strong. When Coca-Cola translated its foreign earnings into dollars, they were lower than they would have been if the dollar had remained at the same level as the previous year.

Translation exposure arises because, as the exchange rate changes, the dollar value of the exposed asset or liability changes.

TRANSACTION EXPOSURE

Denominating a transaction in a foreign currency represents foreign-exchange risk because the company has accounts receivable or payable in foreign currency that must be settled eventually. For example, assume a U.S. exporter delivers merchandise to a British importer at a total price of $500,000 when the exchange rate is 1.5000 dollars per pound, or £333,333 ($500,000/1.5000). If the exporter were to receive payment in dollars, there would be no immediate impact on the exporter if the dollar/pound exchange rate changed. If payment were to be received in pounds, however, the exporter might incur a foreign-exchange gain or loss. For example, with the exchange rate at 1.5000 dollars per pound, the sale would be carried on the exporter's books at $500,000, but the underlying value in which the sale is denominated would be £333,333. If the rate moved to 1.4000 dollars per pound by the time the receivable was collected, the exporter would receive 333,333 pounds, but that payment would be worth $466,666 (the 333,333 × 1.4000), a loss of $33,334. This would be an actual cash flow loss to the exporter.

Transaction exposure arises because the receivable or payable changes in value as the exchange rate changes.

ECONOMIC EXPOSURE

Economic exposure, also known as operating exposure, is the potential for change in expected cash flows. Economic exposure arises from the pricing of products, the sourcing and cost of inputs, and the location of investments. Pricing strategies have both an immediate and a long-term impact on cash flows. For example, the inventory sold to the British importer probably was sold to final users before the exchange rate changed, but future sales would be affected by the rate change. Assume the exporter sold its most recent shipment of $500,000 at an exchange rate of 1.5000 dollars per pound for a cost to the importer of 333,333 pounds. If the British pound were to weaken to 1.4000 dollars per pound, the exporter would have two choices. The first choice is to continue to sell the product to the British importer for $500,000, which would now cost the importer 357,143 pounds. At the higher price, the importer might lose market share if consumers were not willing to pay the higher price. Or the importer could absorb the cost increase in its profit margin and continue to sell the product for a total of 333,333 pounds. The exporter's second choice is to sell the inventory to the importer for fewer dollars so that the pound equivalent is still 333,333 pounds. At the new exchange rate of 1.4000, the sale price would have to be $466,666. The exporter would end up with lower revenues and thus a lower profit margin. Exporters and importers must always determine the impact of a price change on volume. This example illustrates the impact of an exchange-rate change on any cash flows. If a U.S. parent were to receive a dividend, royalty, or management fee in foreign currency, a drop in the foreign currency would result in weaker dollars when the foreign currency amount is converted into dollars.

EXPOSURE-MANAGEMENT STRATEGY

To protect assets adequately against risks from translation, transaction, and economic exposure of exchange-rate fluctuations, management must

- Define and measure exposure
- Organize and implement a reporting system that monitors exposure and exchange-rate movements
- Adopt a policy assigning responsibility for minimizing—or *hedging*—exposure
- Formulate strategies for hedging exposure

Defining and Measuring Exposure   Most MNEs will see all three types of exposure: translation, transaction, and economic. To develop a viable hedging strategy, an MNE must forecast the degree of exposure in each major currency in which it operates. Because the types of exposure differ, the actual exposure by currency must be kept track of separately. For example, the translation exposure in Brazilian reals should be kept track of separately from the transaction exposure because the transaction exposure will result in an actual cash flow, while the translation exposure may not. Thus the company generates one report on translation exposure and another on transaction exposure. The company may adopt different hedging strategies for the different types of exposure.

A key aspect of measuring exposure is forecasting exchange rates. Estimating exchange rates is similar to fortune-telling: Approaches range from gut feelings to sophisticated economic models, each having varying degrees of success. Whatever the approach, a company should estimate and use ranges within which it expects a currency

Looking to the Future
CAPITAL MARKETS AND
THE INFORMATION EXPLOSION

It is difficult to forecast trends in global capital markets because of rapid economic changes worldwide. As world trade increases and global interdependence rises, the velocity of financial transactions also must increase. Financial markets will continue to be dominated by the world's largest—New York, Tokyo, and London. However, action increasingly will take place in the emerging nations within Eastern Europe, Latin America, and Southeast Asia as those markets recover from the Asian financial crisis that hit in 1997 and the Russian crisis that hit in 1998 and affected Brazil in 1999. As fund managers continue to diversify their portfolios to include securities of emerging countries and as investment advisers continue to recommend that their clients diversify their portfolios away from domestic to global funds, the interest in emerging-country markets will continue to rise. This will clearly benefit investors through high returns and also will help the emerging nations in capital formation. However, a key consideration for the future is the impact of e-trades on securities trading. As electronic trading increases in Europe, share trading will be affected greatly in Europe.

Two events will significantly influence the cash-management and hedging strategies of MNEs in the future: the information and technology explosion, and the growing number and sophistication of hedging instruments (financial derivatives such as options and forwards). The information explosion will continue to enable companies to get information more quickly and cheaply. In addition, electronic data interchange (EDI) will allow them to transfer information and money instantaneously worldwide. Companies will significantly reduce paper flow and increase the speed of delivery of information and funds, enabling them to manage cash and to use intercompany resources much more effectively than before. Consequently, companies will reduce not only the cost of producing information but also interest and other borrowing costs.

to vary over the forecasting period. Some companies develop in-house capabilities to monitor exchange rates, using economists who also try to obtain a consensus of exchange-rate movements from the banks with whom they deal. Their concern is to forecast the direction, magnitude, and timing of an exchange-rate change. Other companies contract out this work.

A Reporting System   Once the company has decided how to define and measure exposure and estimate future exchange rates, it must create a reporting system that will assist in protecting it against risk. To achieve this, substantial participation from foreign operations must be combined with effective central control. Foreign input is important to ensure that the information it uses in forecasting is effective. Because exchange rates move frequently, the company must obtain input from those who are attuned to the foreign country's economy. Central control of exposure protects resources more efficiently than letting each subsidiary and branch manage its own exposure. Each organizational unit may be able to define its own exposure, but the

The reporting system should use both central control and input from foreign operations.

company also has an overall exposure. AT&T, for example, requires its strategic business units (SBUs) to coordinate foreign-currency transactions with corporate treasury so that its foreign-exchange hedging unit can undertake the most cost-effective hedging strategy possible. To set hedging policies on a separate-entity basis might not take into account the fact that exposures of several entities (that is, branches, subsidiaries, affiliates, and so on) could offset one another. For example, one SBU of AT&T might have an exposed asset position in yen, and another might have an exposed liability position in yen. Without central control, both SBUs might incur hedging costs to protect their exposed positions. However, AT&T's central foreign-exchange unit in corporate treasury could offset the exposed asset position with the exposed liability position and not have to incur hedging costs.

Management of an MNE should devise a uniform reporting system for all of its subsidiaries. The report should identify the exposed accounts the company wants to monitor, the amount of exposure by currency of each account, and the different time periods under consideration. Exposure should be separated into translation, transaction, and economic components, with the transaction exposure identified by cash inflows and outflows over time.

The time periods on the report depend on the company. Companies can identify their exposure positions for different periods into the future, such as thirty, sixty, and ninety days; six, nine, and twelve months; or two, three, and four years. The reason for the longer time frame is that operating commitments, such as plant construction and production runs, are fairly long term.[23]

Once each basic reporting unit has identified its exposure, the data should be sent to the next organizational level for preliminary consolidation. That level may be a regional headquarters (for Latin America or Europe, for example) or a product division, depending on the company's organizational structure. The preliminary consolidation enables the region or division to determine exposure by account and by currency for each time period. The resulting reports should be routine, periodic, and standardized to ensure comparability and timeliness in formulating strategies. Final reporting should be at the corporate level, where top management can see the amount of foreign-exchange exposure. Specific hedging strategies can be taken at any level, but each level of management must be aware of the size of the exposure and the potential impact on the company.

A Centralized Policy   It is important for management to decide at what level hedging strategies will be determined and implemented. Several hedging strategies will be discussed in the next section. To achieve maximum effectiveness in hedging, top management should determine hedging policy. Having an overview of corporate exposure and the cost and feasibility of different strategies at different levels in the company, the corporate treasurer should be able to design and implement a cost-effective program for exposure management. However, the company may have to decentralize some exposure management decisions so it can react quickly to a more rapidly changing international monetary environment. However, such decentralization should stay within a well-defined policy established at the corporate level. Some companies run their hedging operations more as profit centers and nurture in-house trading desks. Those working at the trading desks actually buy and sell foreign exchange in the market rather than having the trader at a commercial bank effect the trades for the company. Most MNEs, however, are traditional and conservative in their approach, preferring to cover exposure (enter into a hedging strategy that minimizes losses due to exposed positions) rather than to extract huge profits or risk huge losses.

Formulating Hedging Strategies   Once a company has identified its level of exposure and determined which exposure is critical, it can hedge its position by adopting numerous strategies, each with cost/benefit implications as well as operational implications. The safest position is a balanced position in which exposed assets equal exposed liabilities.

LSI Logic notes in its annual report that it uses operational and financial strategies to reduce exposure. Operational strategies involve adjusting the flow of money and resources in normal operations in order to reduce foreign-exchange risk. First, management must determine the working capital needs of a subsidiary. Then it needs to adjust the flows of receivables, payables, and inventory. Although it may be wise to collect receivables as fast as possible in a country in which the local currency is expected to depreciate, the company must consider the competitive implications of doing so. If it tries to collect receivables too fast and does not give the buyer proper time to make payment, the buyer may go to another seller who is willing to offer better credit terms.

The use of debt to balance exposure is an interesting strategy. Many companies "borrow locally," especially in weak-currency countries, because that helps them to avoid foreign-exchange risk from borrowing in a foreign currency. Companies in Asian countries that borrowed dollars found themselves in serious trouble when the local currencies devalued against the dollar, because they couldn't generate enough local currency revenues to pay off the higher debt. If they had borrowed in local currency, they would not have had the same problem. One problem with this strategy is that interest rates in weak-currency countries tend to be high, so there must be a trade-off between the cost of borrowing and the potential loss from exchange-rate variations. Protecting against loss from transaction exposure becomes complex. In dealing with foreign customers, it is always safest for the company to denominate the transaction in its own currency because it won't have any foreign-exchange exposure. The risk shifts to the foreign customer who has to come up with your currency. Or, it could denominate purchases in a weaker currency and sales in a stronger currency. If forced to make purchases in a strong currency and sales in a weak currency, it could resort to contractual measures such as forward contracts or options or try to balance its inflows and outflows through astute sales and purchasing strategies.

Another operational strategy, leads and lags, protects cash flows among related entities, such as a parent and subsidiaries. A **lead strategy** means collecting foreign-currency receivables before they are due when the foreign currency is expected to weaken or paying foreign-currency payables before they are due when the foreign currency is expected to strengthen. With a **lag strategy**, a company delays collection of foreign-currency receivables if that currency is expected to strengthen or delays payables when the currency is expected to weaken. In other words, a company usually leads into and lags out of a hard currency and leads out of and lags into a weak currency.

There are two problems with a lead and lag strategy. First, it may not be useful for the movement of large blocks of funds. If there are infrequent decisions over small amounts of money, it is easy to manage the system, but as the number, frequency, and

---

Hedging strategies can be operational or contractual.

Operational strategies include
• **Using local debt to balance local assets**
• **Taking advantage of leads and lags for intercompany payments**

A lead strategy means collecting or paying early.
A lag strategy means collecting or paying late.

size of transactions increase, it becomes difficult to manage. Second, leads and lags are often subject to governmental control, and it may be difficult to get permission to move currency.

Sometimes an operational strategy means shifting assets overseas to take advantage of currency changes. When the yen strengthened against the U.S. dollar, for example, Toyota shifted more of its manufacturing into the United States to take advantage of the cheaper dollar. As long as the yen was strong, it was difficult to export from Japan to the United States, so the companies could service U.S. demand through production in the United States.

In addition to the operational strategies just mentioned, a company may hedge exposure through contractual arrangements, using derivatives such as forward contracts and options. The most common hedge is a forward contract. For example, assume a U.S. exporter sells goods to a British manufacturer for £1 million, with payment due in 90 days. The spot exchange rate is 1.5000 dollars per pound, and the forward rate is 1.4500 dollars per pound. At the time of the sale, it is recorded on the exporter's books at $1.5 million, and a corresponding receivable is set up for the same amount. However, the exporter is concerned about the exchange risk. The exporter can enter into a forward contract, which will guarantee that the receivables convert into dollars at a rate of 1.4500 dollars per pound, no matter what the actual future exchange rate is. This move will yield $1.45 million. Even though the company gets $50,000 less than it could have at the initial spot rate, it has eliminated any risk for the future. Or the exporter could wait until it collects the receivable in 90 days and gamble on a better rate in the spot market. If the actual rate at that time is 1.4700 dollars per pound, the exporter will receive $1.47 million, which is not as good as the initial receivable of $1.5 million but is better than the forward yield of $1.45 million. But if the dollar strengthens to 1.4000 dollars per pound, the exporter would be much better off with the forward contract.

A foreign-currency option is more flexible than a forward contract because it gives its purchaser the right, but not the obligation, to buy or sell a certain amount of foreign currency at a set exchange rate within a specified amount of time. For example, assume a U.S. exporter decides to sell merchandise to a British manufacturer for £1 million when the exchange rate is $1.5000 per pound. At the same time, the exporter goes to Goldman Sachs, its investment banker, and enters into an option to deliver pounds for dollars at an exchange rate of $1.5000 per pound at an option cost of $25,000. When the exporter receives the £1 million from the manufacturer, it must decide whether to exercise the option. If the exchange rate is above $1.5000, it will not exercise the option, because it can get a better yield by converting pounds at the market rate. The only thing lost is the $25,000 cost of the option, which is like insurance. However, if the exchange rate is below $1.5000, say $1.4500, the exporter will exercise the option and trade pounds at the rate of $1.5000. The proceeds will be $1.5 million less the option cost of $25,000.

A good example of how companies use operational and financial hedging strategies is Coca-Cola. Because approximately 74 percent of Coke's operating income in 1998 came from outside of the United States, foreign-currency changes can have a major impact on reported earnings. Coke manages its foreign-currency exposures on a consolidated basis, which allows it to net certain exposures from different operations around the world and allows it to take advantage of natural offsets, whereby British pound

---

Forward contracts can establish a fixed exchange rate for future transactions.

Currency options can assure access to foreign currency at a fixed exchange rate for a specific period of time.

receivables offset British pound payables, for example. It also uses derivative financial instruments to further reduce its net exposure to currency fluctuations. Coke enters into forward-exchange contracts and purchases currency options in several currencies, most notably the European currencies and Japanese yen, to hedge firm sales commitments. It also purchases currency options to hedge certain anticipated sales.[24]

THE CAPITAL BUDGETING DECISION IN AN INTERNATIONAL CONTEXT

The last international dimension of the treasury function that we will discuss in the chapter is the capital budgeting decision whereby the MNE needs to determine which projects and countries will receive its capital investment funds. The parent company must compare the net present value or internal rate of return of a potential foreign project with that of its other projects and that of others available in the host country to determine the best place to invest its resources. The technique used to compare different projects is capital budgeting. Several aspects of capital budgeting are unique to foreign project assessment.

> The parent company needs to compare the net present value or internal rate of return of a foreign project with that of its other projects and with that of others available in the host country.

- Parent cash flows must be distinguished from project cash flows. Parent cash flows refer to cash flows from the project back to the parent in the parent's currency. Project cash flows refer to the cash flows in local currency from the sale of goods and services.
- Remittance of funds to the parent, such as dividends, interest on loans, and payment of intracompany receivables and payables, is affected by differing tax systems, legal and political constraints on the movement of funds, local business norms, and differences in how financial markets and institutions function.
- Differing rates of inflation must be anticipated by both the parent and subsidiary because of their importance in causing changes in competitive position and in cash flows over time.
- The parent must consider the possibility of unanticipated exchange-rate changes because of their direct effects on the value of cash flows, as well as their indirect effects on the foreign subsidiary 's competitive position.
- Parent company must evaluate political risk in a target market because political events can drastically reduce the value or availability of expected cash flows.
- Terminal value (the value of the project at the end of the budgeting period) is difficult to estimate because potential purchasers from host, home, or third countries— or from the private or public sector—may have widely divergent perspectives on the value of the project. The terminal value is critical in determining the total cash flows from the project. The total cash outlay for the project is partially offset by the terminal value—the amount of cash the parent company can get from the subsidiary or project if it sells it eventually.[25]

Because of all the forces listed above, it is very difficult to estimate future cash flows, both to the subsidiary and to the parent company. There are two ways to deal with the variations in future cash flows. One is to determine several different scenarios and then determine the net present value or internal rate of return (IRR) of the project. The other is to adjust the hurdle rate, which is the minimum rate of return that the project must achieve in order for it to receive capital. The adjustment is usually made by increasing the hurdle rate above its minimal level.

Once the budget is complete, the MNE must examine both the return in local currency and the return to the parent in dollars from cash flows to the parent. Examining the return in local currency will give management a chance to compare the project with other investment alternatives in the country. However, cash flows to the parent are important, because it is from these cash flows that dividends are paid to shareholders. If the MNE cannot generate sufficient return to the parent in the parent's currency, it will eventually fall behind in its ability to pay shareholders and pay off corporate debt.

WEB CONNECTION

Check out our home page www.prenhall.com/daniels for links to key resources for you in your study of international business.

SUMMARY

- The corporate finance function deals with the acquisition of financial resources and their allocation among the company's present and potential activities and projects.

- CFOs need to be concerned with the international dimensions of the company's capital structure, capital budgeting decisions, long-term financing, and working capital management.

- Country-specific factors are the most important determination of a company's capital structure.

- Two major sources of funds external to the MNEs normal operations are debt markets and equity markets.

- A Eurocurrency is any currency banked outside of its country of origin, but primarily dollars banked outside the United States.

- A foreign bond is one sold outside the country of the borrower but denominated in the currency of the country of issue. A Eurobond is a bond issue sold in a currency other than that of the country of issue. A global bond is one issued simultaneously in North America, Asia, and Europe according to the listing requirements of each market.

- The three largest stock markets in the world are in New York, Tokyo, and London, with the U.S. markets controlling nearly half of the world's stock market capitalization.

- The stock markets in emerging countries in Asia, Eastern Europe, and Latin America were among the world's most dynamic until the Asian financial crisis hit in 1997, but they are beginning to recover at the start of the new millennium.

- Euroequities are shares listed on stock exchanges in countries other than the home country of the issuing company. Most foreign companies that list on the U.S. stock exchanges do so through American Depositary Receipts, which are financial documents that represent a share or part of a share of stock in the foreign company. ADRs are easier to trade on the U.S. exchanges than are foreign shares.

- Offshore financial centers such as Bahrain, the Caribbean, Hong Kong, London, New York, Singapore, and Switzerland deal in large amounts of foreign currency and enable companies to take advantage of favorable tax rates.

- The major sources of internal funds for an MNE are dividends, royalties, management fees, loans from parent to subsidiaries and vice versa, purchases and sales of inventory, and equity flows from parent to subsidiaries.

- Global cash management is complicated by differing inflation rates, changes in exchange rates, and governmental restrictions on the flow of funds. A sound cash-management system for an MNE requires timely reports from affiliates worldwide.

- Management must protect corporate assets from losses due to exchange-rate changes. Exchange rates can influence the dollar equivalent of foreign-currency financial statements, the amount of cash that can be earned from foreign-currency transactions, and a company's production and marketing decisions.

- Foreign-exchange risk management involves defining and measuring exposure, setting up a good monitoring and reporting system, adopting a policy to assign responsibility for exposure management, and formulating strategies for hedging exposure.

- Companies can enter into operational or financial strategies for hedging exposures. Operational strategies include balancing exposed assets with exposed liabilities, using leads and lags in cash flows, and balancing revenues in one currency with expenses in the same currency. Financial strategies involve using forward contracts, options, or other financial instruments to hedge an exposed position.

- When deciding to invest abroad, MNE management must evaluate the cash flows from the local operation as well as the cash flows from the project to the parent. The former allows management to determine how the project stacks up with other opportunities in the foreign country, and the latter allows management to compare projects from different countries.

CASE

3M AND ITS FOREIGN-EXCHANGE RISK-MANAGEMENT STRATEGY[26]

At the end of 1999, Janet Yeomans, vice president and treasurer of 3M (Minnesota Mining and Manufacturing Co.), had experienced an interesting year in terms of swings in the value of the U.S. dollar against other major world currencies. When the Asian financial crisis hit in 1997, the dollar had been enjoying a period of strength, which continued throughout 1997 and most of 1998. After rising against the yen by 70 percent in just three years, the dollar fell by 15 percent in just a day and a half in early October 1998. It also fell against other major currencies by an average of around 11 percent. At the beginning of 1999, the dollar strengthened somewhat. But it dipped back down again at the beginning of the third quarter and then rose and fell during the rest of the year until the end of 1999, where it ended up at the same level as at the beginning of the year. By early 2000, the dollar was near parity with the euro, but it was weakening slightly against the yen. Where would the dollar head over the next few years and what does its fluctuation in value mean to 3M?

The impact of a fluctuating dollar is no trivial issue for 3M. 3M is a U.S.-based MNE that generates 51.9 percent of its revenues from outside of the United States, as shown in Table 20.2. It operates three major product divisions: industrial and consumer products; transportation, safety and specialty materials; and health care materials, with the first seg-ment generating nearly 50 percent of 3M's revenues and more than half of its products. Three of 3M's most famous brands are Scotch Tape, Scotchgard, and Post-its.

As noted in Table 20.2, Europe and the Middle East generate 25.6 percent of 3M's revenues, with Asia/Pacific back at 15.8 percent and Latin America, Africa, and Canada at 10.2 percent. In spite of 3M's heavy exposure overseas, it was generating a disproportionately greater amount of operating income from domestic operations—58.1 percent compared with revenues of only 48.1 percent. Europe and the Middle East, while generating nearly twice the revenues as the Asia/Pacific segment, had about the same amount of operating income in 1998.

3M's major organizational thrust is by product group, with each group having worldwide responsibility. In 1998, the profits of the industrial and consumer markets division of 3M fell by 6.3 percent after four consecutive years of strong growth. Two major contributing factors were the strong U.S. dollar and the Asian economic crisis. The same was true for the transportation, safety, and specialty material markets where sales fell 1.8 percent from 1997, with two contributing factors being the stronger U.S. dollar and the Asian economic crisis. The one division that experienced growth in 1998 was the health care markets division, which saw sales

TABLE 20.2   **GEOGRAPHIC AREAS, MINNESOTA MINING AND MANUFACTURING COMPANY, 1996–1998**

3M derives 48.1 percent of its revenues and 58.1 percent of its profits from the United States. Operations in Asia/Pacific were significantly more profitable than would be expected in 1998, given the level of their revenues. However, restructuring charges reduced operating income in 1998, so it is a little difficult to compare segment revenues and operating income accurately.

(MILLIONS)		UNITED STATES	EUROPE AND MIDDLE EAST	ASIA PACIFIC	LATIN AMERICA, AFRICAN, AND CANADA	ELIMINATIONS AND OTHER	TOTAL COMPANY
Net sales to customers	1998	$7,231 (48.1%)	$3,850 (25.6%)	$2,375 (15.8%)	$1,539 (10.2%)	$ 26	$15,021
	1997	7,242	3,640	2,632	1,530	26	15,070
	1996	6,655	3,620	2,577	1,359	25	14,236
Operating income	1998	$1,185 (58.1%)	$ 516 (25.3%)	$ 503 (24.7%)	$ 349 (17.1%)	$(514)*	$ 2,039
	1997	1,290	431	611	360	(17)	2,675
	1996	1,125	463	617	304	(18)	2,491
Property, plant and equipment—net	1998	$3,376	$1,107	$ 709	$ 374	$—	$ 5,566
	1997	3,133	1,013	532	356	—	5,034
	1996	2,842	1,099	598	305	—	4,844

*Operating income for 1998 includes a $493 million restructuring change.
Source: From 3M Annual Report, 1998. Reprinted by permission.

rising by 2.4 percent in U.S. dollars. Interestingly, 3M noted that sales rose 5 percent in local currencies, even though they rose less in dollars.

In addition to the product line orientation, 3M has an international division headed by Executive Vice President Ronald Baukol. 3M's sales in 1998 were basically the same as in 1997, but the stronger U.S. dollar reduced sales by 6 percent. In addition, unit sales were not very strong. After experiencing double-digit growth in unit sales for four consecutive years, unit sales grew by only 4 percent in 1998. Slower economic growth in Japan and Latin America really slowed down in 1998, and volume actually declined in Asia outside of Japan. However, 3M had a good year in Europe in terms of revenues, even though its profits were not that strong. Overall, profits from overseas operations were down 2.8 percent in 1998, and changes in exchange rates reduced operating income by 17 percent. However, some of this impact was offset by price increases, cost controls, and productivity gains. Overall, 3M sells products in 200 countries with offices in 60 countries, which means that a lot of its

sales are exports from the United States or foreign manufacturing locations.

3M must translate its foreign-currency financial statements into dollars, and it explains that process in the section on accounting policies in the annual report:

> Local currencies generally are considered the functional currencies outside the United States, except in countries treated as highly inflationary. Assets and liabilities for operations in local-currency environments are translated at year-end exchange rates. Income and expense items are translated at average rates of exchange prevailing during the year. Cumulative translation adjustments are recorded as a component of stockholders' equity.

One impact of this strategy can be found by examining the statement of shareholders' equity in Table 20.3. Note that 3M had to reduce shareholders' equity in both 1996 and 1997 because of the strong dollar, whereas it showed a slight translation gain in 1998.

| **TABLE 20.3** | **CONSOLIDATED STATEMENT OF CHANGES IN STOCKHOLDERS' EQUITY AND COMPREHENSIVE INCOME** |

Foreign currency translation adjustments negatively impacted stockholders' income in 1996 and 1997 (as evident by the balance lines in this statement), but had a small positive impact in 1998, probably due to weakness in the dollar toward the end of the year.

(DOLLARS IN MILLIONS, EXCEPT PER-SHARE AMOUNTS)	TOTAL	COMMON STOCK AND CAPITAL IN EXCESS OF PAR	RETAINED EARNINGS	TREASURY STOCK	UNEARNED COMPEN-SATION ESOP	ACCUMULATED OTHER COMPRE-HENSIVE INCOME
Balance at December 31, 1995	$6,884	$296	$9,164	$(2,053)	$(437)	$ (86)
Net income	1,526		1,526			
Cumulative translation—net	(76)					(76)
Fair value adjustments	(1)					(1)
Total comprehensive income	1,449					
Dividends paid ($1.92 per share)	(803)		(803)			
Special dividend of Imation Corp. common stock	(1,008)		(1,008)			
Amortization of unearned compensation	25				25	
Reacquired stock (7.6 million shares)	(532)			(532)		
Issuances pursuant to stock option and benefit plans (5.7 million shares)	269		(123)	392		
Balance at December 31, 1996	$6,284	$296	$8,756	$(2,193)	$(412)	$(163)
Net income	2,121		2,121			
Cumulative translation—net	(369)					(369)
Fair value adjustments	(7)					(7)
Total comprehensive income	1,745					
Dividends paid ($2.12 per share)	(876)		(876)			
Amortization of unearned compensation	33				33	
Reacquired stock (18.7 million shares)	(1,693)			(1,693)		
Issuances pursuant to stock option and benefit plans (6.6 million shares)	433		(153)	586		
Balance at December 31, 1997	$5,926	$296	$9,848	$(3,300)	$(379)	$(539)
Net income	1,175		1,175			
Cumulative translation—net	29					29
Fair value adjustments	2					2
Total comprehensive income	1,206					
Dividends paid ($2.20 per share)	(887)		(887)			
Amortization of unearned compensation	29				29	
Reacquired stock (7.4 million shares)	(618)			(618)		
Issuances pursuant to stock option and benefit plans (4.6 million shares)	280		(156)	436		
Balance at December 31, 1998	$5,936	$296	$9,980	$(3,482)	$(350)	$(508)

Source: From 3M: Consolidated Statement of Changes in Stockholders' Equity and Comprehensive Income. Reprinted by permission.

Given the size of 3M's foreign operations and the impact on consolidated revenues and earnings from currency changes, should 3M actively hedge its exposure? A real debate was brewing among MNEs in 1998 about the wisdom of hedging foreign-exchange risks in the financial markets through forward contracts, options, and swaps. In mid-1998, 3M announced that currency fluctuations had cost the company $330 million in profits and $1.8 billion in revenues in the previous 3 years. In spite of that and the fact that analysts and investors were furious with 3M management, Yeomans maintained that 3M preferred to focus on operational strategies to hedge exposures instead of spending money on forwards, swaps, and options. Coca-Cola uses financial hedge instruments, but it still expected earnings to fall by 10 percent in 1998 due to currency problems. Coca-Cola is much larger than 3M and generates 74 percent of its operating income outside of the United States, so it takes currency exposure seriously. IBM does not hedge its foreign operations, because it generates costs in local currency to match its revenues, using an operational hedge. However, a strong dollar would still reduce the dollar equivalent of IBM's overseas earnings. Eastman Kodak used to aggressively hedge foreign currency exposures. In fact, its foreign-exchange operations used to be a profit center, but that ended in 1993 when the CEO determined that the costs of hedging exceeded the benefits. Now, Kodak hedges only a few specific contracts.

What does 3M do? Although Janet Yeomans is responsible for foreign-currency operations as part of her treasury role, a financial risk-management committee, composed of senior management, provides oversight for risk management and derivative activities. The committee determines 3M's financial risk policies and objectives, and provides guide-lines for using derivatives. The committee also establishes procedures for control and valuation, risk analysis, counterparty credit approval, and ongoing monitoring and reporting. Although we have discussed the other issues in the chapter, we need to define counterparty risk. Counterparty credit risk implies that the counterparty (such as the investment bank that writes an options contract or a commerical bank that enters into a forward contract) could possibly default on its end of the deal. Counterparty credit risk involves determining whether or not the counterparty is sufficiently strong to stand behind the derivatives that it issues.

Even though 3M has a policy of using operating hedges instead of financial hedges for its overseas operations, it still uses financial instruments to hedge intercompany transactions and specific cash flows. However, it does not hedge the possibility that the dollar equivalent of local currency revenues might fall.

QUESTIONS

1. Given how 3M translates its foreign-currency financial statements into dollars, how could a rising dollar affect 3M's revenues, operating income, and shareholders' equity?

2. How can 3M hedge its foreign-exchange exposure?

3. Is 3M right in avoiding financial hedges? Why or why not?

4. What is your opinion of 3M's strategy for managing foreign-exchange risk? Should risk management be centralized, or should it be decentralized?

5. Assuming it should be decentralized, should it be the responsibility of the business divisions (such as industrial and consumer products division) or the international division?

CHAPTER NOTES

1 LSI Logic, *Annual Report, 1998*; Ken Siegmann, "An American Tale of Semi-Success: How American Chip Companies Regained Lead," *San Francisco Chronicle*, December 20, 1993, p. B1; Udayan Gupta, "Raising Money the New-Fangled Way," in "Global Finance & Investing: A Special Report," *Wall Street Journal*, September 18, 1987, p. 14D; several articles from *Wall Street Journal*, interactive edition on LSI Logic's company background, financial overview, and company news, January 21, 2000.

2 David K. Eiteman, Arthur I. Stonehill, and Michael H. Moffett, *Multinational Business Finance*, 8th ed. (Reading, MA: Addison-Wesley, 1998), p. 3.

3 Alan C. Shapiro, *Modern Corporate Finance* (New York: Macmillan, 1988), p. 1.

4 "Theory versus the Real World," *Finance & Treasury*, April 26, 1993, p. 1.

5 Ibid., p. 2.

6 "Henry Sender, "Financial Musical Chairs," *Far Eastern Economic Review*, July 29, 1999, pp. 30–36.

7 "Long-Term Debt," *Toyota Annual Report 1998*, p. 42.

8 "Italy," in *Financing Foreign Operations* (New York: Business International Corporation, June 1990), p. 13.

9 "Money Rates," *Wall Street Journal*, January 21, 2000, p. C6.

10 "Europe's American Dream," *The Economist*, November 21, 1998, p. 71.

11 "An Offer They Can Refuse," *Euromoney*, February 1995, p. 76.

12 Anant Sundaram, "International Financial Markets," in *Handbook of Modern Finance*, Dennis E. Logue, ed. (New York: Warren, Gorham, Lamont, 1994), pp. F3–4.

13 "Analysis of Borrowings," footnote 19, *Marks & Spencer Annual Report and Financial Statements 1998*, p. 63.

14 "EMU Shuffles the Rankings," *Euromoney*, May 1999, p. 106.

15 "Europe's Start-up Stampede," *The Economist*, January 15, 2000, p. 63.

16 "Private Equity Stirs Up the Pot," *Euroweek*, October 1999, pp. 27–34.

17 "Non-U.S. Listed Companies," www.nyse.com/international/international.html.

18 "American Depositary Receipts: Over the Odds," *The Economist*, January 15, 2000, p. 77.

19 "The Quick and the Dead," *The Economist*, September 18, 1999, p. 84.

20 Stanley Reed, "Bourse Busters," *Business Week*, August 16, 1999, pp. 52–53.

21 "How the Heavyweights Shape Up," *Euromoney*, May 1990, p. 56.

22 Henri Waszkowski, "New Cash Pooling Systems Cut Transaction Fees, Optimize Use of Excess Cash," *Corporate Cashflow Magazine*, December 1995. Available NEXIS LIBRARY:GENERAL:NEWS:CURNSW.

23 Helmut Hagemann, "Anticipate Your Long-Term Foreign Exchange Risks," *Harvard Business Review*, March–April 1977, p. 82.

24 "Financial Risk Management," *Coca-Cola Annual Report 1998*.

25 Eiteman et al., *Multinational Business Finance*, pp. 584–585.

26 *3M Annual Report, 1998*; Peter Coy, De'Ann Weimer, and Amy Barrett, "Perils of the Hedge Highwire," *Business Week*, October 26, 1998, pp. 74–77.

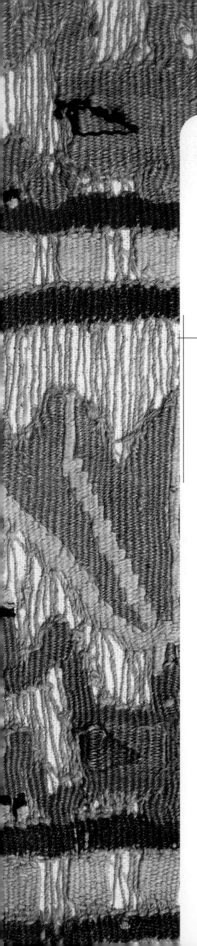

CHAPTER 21

Human Resource Management

If the leader is good, the followers will be good. —PHILIPPINE PROVERB

OBJECTIVES

- To illustrate the importance of human resources in international business relations
- To explain the unique qualifications of international managers
- To evaluate issues that arise when companies transfer managers abroad
- To examine companies' alternatives for recruitment, selection, compensation, and development of international managers
- To discuss how national labor markets can affect companies' optimum methods of production
- To describe country differences in labor policies and practices
- To highlight international pressures on MNEs' relations with labor worldwide
- To examine the effect of international operations on collective bargaining

Dow Chemical is a U.S.-based company with over half its revenues abroad. About three-quarters of its top management committee are managers who either were non–U.S. born or have had considerable foreign experience.

This placement of foreign-born and/or internationally experienced persons in Dow's leadership might suggest the process of internationalization. For example, Peter Drucker, a leading management authority, stated that a truly multinational company "demands of its management people that they think and act as international businessmen [businesswomen] in a world in which national passions are as strong as ever." A company whose top management includes people from various countries and with varied country experiences presumably is less likely to place the interests of one country above those of others and supposedly will have a more worldwide outlook. Whether this is true is debatable. However, the experience of working abroad under some very different environmental conditions is very useful for grasping some problems that are not as prevalent in a purely domestic context.

To make international operations an integral part of the company's total commitment, Dow had to gain a dedication to international business from a broad spectrum of managers. The company estimates that it took about 20 years to bring this about. Until 1954, only about 6 percent of Dow's business was abroad, and of that, over 80 percent was from its one foreign subsidiary in Canada. The attitude in the late 1950s was expressed by a company historian:

> As for the overseas operations, a majority of the veterans regarded them as a sideline. The foreign market was all right as a place for getting rid of surplus products, but the only truly promising market was in the United States. They questioned the idea of the company becoming too deeply involved in countries whose politics, language, culture, monetary controls, and ways of doing business were strange to them.

Some of Dow's younger managers did not share this ethnocentric attitude, but Dow needed to take dramatic steps to convert the majority of managers to an international outlook. One method the company's president employed in 1958 was to give international responsibilities to people who were widely perceived to be destined for top-level positions in the company. Dow appointed C. B. Branch, manager of Dow's fastest-growing department, to be head of foreign operations. It assigned Herbert "Ted" Dow Doan, a 31-year-old member of the board of directors, to visit Europe on a fact-finding mission. (Ted Doan's father and grandfather both had been Dow presidents.) Both Branch and Doan quickly went on to become presidents of Dow. Thus the company's managers readily grasped the importance of international operations.

In addition to providing international exposure to headquarters' top-level managers, companies need to attract and retain high-quality personnel (largely local people) within each country where they operate. To do this, Dow gives people from all over the world the same opportunity to reach top management levels. A company's local human resources needs also change as corporate strategies evolve. For instance, Dow hired many more non–U.S. scientists and technicians in the 1980s when it strengthened its R&D in Europe and Asia.

Companies also must transfer people to foreign locations when qualified local managers are not readily available. When Dow sends managers to foreign operations, what qualifications should they have? Robert Lundeen, a former Dow chairman who had served twelve years as president of the Pacific division and three years as president of the Latin American division, gave some indication of his philosophy. After speaking about the obvious technical needs, he said, "When I worked in Asia, I observed that many Americans seemed to delight in their insularity, and that attitude hurts the ability . . . do business in foreign countries."

For many years, Dow had difficulty in convincing people to take foreign assignments because of bad experience in repatriating them to acceptable positions. Dow has reacted to this problem by

- Sending some of its best people abroad so that "everybody will want them when they come back"
- Assigning higher-level supervisors to serve as "godfathers" by looking after the transferred employees' home-career interests
- Providing each transferee with a written guarantee of a job at the same or higher level on return from the foreign assignment

Because some managers have difficulty adjusting to foreign locations, Dow briefs all prospective transferees on company transfer policies, as well as information about the country where they will be assigned, compiled by personnel in the host country. Dow follows this with a meeting between transferees and their spouses and recently repatriated employees and their spouses to explain the emotional issues involved in the move's early stages. Couples are also given the option of attending a two-week language and orientation program.   ෨෯

INTRODUCTION

The Dow case highlights one company's efforts to deal with international human resources, which are more comprehensive than in most MNEs.[2] In addition, Dow invests heavily in developing its global intellectual assets, which include human capital (the knowledge that each individual has and generates) and organizational capital (the

When companies operate abroad, their human resource managers must find the right people to work in and manage the foreign facilities. Many companies, especially U.S. companies, have assembly plants in Mexico, called *maquiladoras* (like the one pictured), which take advantage of lower Mexican labor costs than in countries where they sell the production. These companies must adhere to Mexican labor laws and labor characteristics. The plants are one of Mexico's main sources of export revenues.

knowledge that has been captured/institutionalized within the structure, processes, and culture of the organization).[3]

Most international companies agree on the importance of having qualified personnel to achieve foreign growth and operational objectives. For instance, at a roundtable discussion of chief executives on how the world is changing and what, if anything, management can do to keep change under control, the chairman of Unilever said, "The single most important issue for us has been, and will continue to be, organization and people."[4] Figure 21.1 shows the importance of international human resources in international business.

The need for highly qualified people is crucial. Any company must determine its human resource needs, hire people to meet those needs, motivate them to perform well, and upgrade their skills so that they can move to more demanding tasks. Several factors make international human resource management different from domestic management:

- *Different labor markets.* Each country has a different mix of available workers and a different mix of labor costs. MNEs may gain advantages by accessing these various human resource capabilities. For example, GM's Mexican upholstery operation employs low-cost production workers, and IBM's Swiss R&D facility hires skilled physicists. Whether companies seek resources or markets abroad, they may produce the same product differently in different countries; for example, substituting hand labor for machines because of diverse labor markets.

FIGURE 21.1 Human Resources in International Business

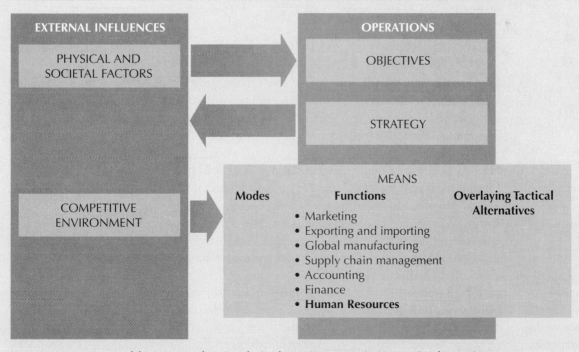

Human resources is one of the necessary functions for implementing companies' international strategies.

- *International worker mobility problems.* There are legal, economic, physical, and cultural barriers to overcome when moving workers to a foreign country. Yet MNEs benefit from moving people, especially when there are shortages of people with needed skills in a particular country. In such situations, companies often must develop special recruitment, training, compensation, and transfer practices.
- *National management styles and practices.* Employees' attitudes toward different management styles vary from country to country, and so do prevalent management practices and labor-management relations. These differences may strain relations between headquarters and subsidiary personnel or make a manager less effective when working abroad than when working at home. At the same time, the experience of working with different national practices offers companies some opportunities for transferring successful practices from one country to another.
- *National orientations.* Although a company's goals may include attaining global efficiencies and competitiveness, its personnel (both labor and management) may emphasize national rather than global interests. Certain human resource practices can alleviate national orientations.
- *Strategy and control.* Companies find that some country operations are more important for global corporate success than others. Further, country operations differ in cross-national integration, dependence on headquarters for resources, and need for national responsiveness. These differences may change over time. Management qualifications and styles need to parallel the needs of these different operations so that overall global strategy may more likely be achieved.

This chapter emphasizes these points by first discussing implications for managerial personnel and then examining labor personnel issues.

MANAGEMENT QUALIFICATIONS AND CHARACTERISTICS

The first place to start in our discussion of international human resource management is to examine relationships between headquarters and subsidiaries, national variations in managerial styles, and management qualifications and characteristics for headquarters and subsidiaries.

HEADQUARTERS-SUBSIDIARY RELATIONSHIP

Headquarters and subsidiary management must consider country and global needs.

International staffing is two-tiered. First, subsidiaries need people who can manage well locally. Second, headquarters needs people who can effectively coordinate and control worldwide and regional operations. These two staffing needs are closely related, because headquarters managers usually choose and evaluate subsidiary managers. Both must be sufficiently aware of and willing to accept trade-offs between global integration and national responsiveness.

Headquarters-subsidiary relationships are affected by
- **Company philosophy (ethnocentric or polycentric)**
- **Benefits of independence or interdependence**

These trade-offs are complex and depend on the company's philosophy (for example, polycentric or ethnocentric) and countries' operational benefits from independence compared to interdependence. There is much less need to impose standard human resource practices—such as hiring qualifications and training programs—or a corporate culture abroad when a company has a multidomestic strategy than when it has a global or transnational strategy.[5] Regardless of where the company lies between these extremes, it may face dilemmas because the technology, policy, and managerial style it has developed in one place may be only partly applicable elsewhere. International managers, at headquarters and in subsidiaries, must be equipped to know when to introduce and when not to introduce practices to a country.

Headquarters and subsidiary managers must communicate well to ensure that they understand each other. Because of distance that impairs travel for face-to-face meetings and different time zones that complicate voice-to-voice transmissions, much of the communication between headquarters and subsidiaries is written and sent by e-mail, faxes, and letters. But these written communications are not perfect substitutes for face-to-face and voice-to-voice communications that allow immediate questions and clarifications when managers are unsure they understand exactly what others mean. Nevertheless, Dow Chemical has been able to reduce the number of international trips by bringing groups together electronically.[6]

Communication difficulties are further compounded when managers' native languages differ. Corporate communications, directives, and manuals may be translated, which takes time and expense. If they are not, the content may be understood perfectly abroad, but the comprehension time may be longer because people read more slowly in a second language. Likewise, communication problems may force a manager working abroad to work harder to do the same quality work as home-country counterparts. Although headquarters managers often overlook these inherent inefficiencies, they hold subsidiary management responsible. Cultural differences color the intents and perceptions of what is communicated. Managers may assume erroneously that foreigners will react the same way as their compatriots to decision making and leadership styles—a particular problem with team projects that include various nationalities. The problem is magnified in cooperative arrangements when business activities include not just different nationalities but also different companies.[7]

Communication between headquarters and subsidiary management is eased somewhat by English becoming the international language of business. Managers cannot learn all the languages in every country in which their companies operate. So business between, say, Italy and Saudi Arabia may be conducted in English. Even some MNEs from non-English-speaking countries have adopted English as their official language.[8] A working knowledge of the subsidiary country's language nevertheless can help headquarters managers gain acceptance by subsidiary personnel as well as a better grasp of what is happening in the foreign country.

MATCHING STYLE TO OPERATIONS

Where there is a need for cross-border integration, whether between headquarters and subsidiaries or among subsidiaries, feeling-type managers (those concerned with how their decisions will affect others, particularly others' feelings) are apt to be more effective than thinking-type managers (those concerned with processing information analytically and impersonally). The reason is that the collaborative nature of integration requires a high level of cooperation. Cooperation is enhanced by understanding and considering the feelings of people who can expedite or retard the integration.[9]

Similarly, when MNEs follow a multidomestic strategy, there is little need or possibility to transfer human resource competencies from one unit to another. The operation in Singapore might work independently to develop human resource practices that deal effectively with labor shortages and high worker mobility without transferring information on such practices to units of the company in other countries. In a global strategy,

International communications are complex and more likely to be misunderstood than domestic ones are.

the company would attempt to transfer its home-country policies and practices to its foreign units because it feels that such policies are generalizable outside the parent country. In a transnational strategy, the company would attempt to transfer the best policies and practices, regardless of where they originate.[10]

There is also a need to manage in a style that subordinates will accept. Recall from Chapter 2 that there are different national norms in terms of employee preference, such as between authoritarian and participatory styles of leadership and individualism versus collectivism in the workplace. Although any country has successful managers whose styles vary, there is substantial anecdotal evidence of a better chance of success when managerial actions are congruent with subordinates' preferences and expectations.[11] Thus, managers may improve their performance by conforming to the preferred management styles of the people with whom they are working.

QUALIFICATIONS SPECIFIC TO HEADQUARTERS AND SUBSIDIARIES

So far, we have emphasized managerial qualifications for the relationship between headquarters and subsidiaries. In addition, headquarters managers who are responsible for international operations have duties different from their domestic counterparts. Similarly, foreign subsidiary managers have responsibilities that are generally different from home-country managers at similar organizational levels. We shall now discuss these.

Corporate managers abroad
- **Deal at top levels in many countries**
- **Experience the rigors of foreign travel**
- **Face difficulties if they have risen entirely through domestic divisions**

Headquarters Management   Headquarters managers who are responsible for international business must interact frequently with high-level authorities in foreign countries to negotiate investments, sell technology, evaluate new market opportunities, assess monetary conditions, and so on. Their tasks are even more difficult than those of subsidiary managers because they must be away from home for extended and indefinite periods. Their international trips are stressful before, during, and after they travel.[12] Before, they must make arrangements while trying to complete all pending work and to spend more quality time with their families. During their trip, they eat, sleep, and move in unfamiliar places while seeking the confidence and rapport of people in many different foreign countries. After they return, they face the work that has piled up in their absence, the preparation of expense reports, and the guilt from being away from the family. Further, they may suffer jet lag, a condition in which one's biological clock tells the body the wrong time to sleep, eat, and feel alert or drowsy; this clock can adjust by only one or two hours a day.[13] But frequent moves between time zones may also have long-term adverse physical and mental affects, such as slower and less accurate reactions.[14] Figure 21.2 depicts these managers' jet lag problems. Even if headquarters personnel are not faced with the rigors of foreign travel, they may be ill at ease with the foreign aspects of their responsibilities if their rise to the corporate level has been entirely through work in domestic divisions.

Headquarters personnel traveling abroad can also face problems of isolation, particularly in their personal lives. They are apt to miss family celebrations of their home country's holidays.[15] International trips are apt to be longer and farther away than domestic ones, making it difficult to return home on weekends. As one international executive commented wryly:

> Often you won't be able to plan in advance when you are leaving on business or when you will return. Being present at birthdays, school plays, anniversaries, family reunions, and other events may become the exception instead of the rule. While

FIGURE 21.2

"*I've never actually met him—as soon as he's over the jet lag, it's time for another trip in search of overseas markets.*"

Source: From *Punch Magazine*. Reprinted by permission.

The travel required to oversee international operations is stressful.

you're away, mortgage payments will probably be due, the MasterCard bill will arrive, the furnace will fail, your child will get chicken pox, the IRS will schedule a full audit, the family car will be totaled, and your spouse will sue for divorce.[16]

In summary, it takes a special type of individual to adjust to so much travel and so many different environments. Moreover, the individual also needs a special family to accept the absences and recovery period from travel fatigue.

Subsidiary Management Although foreign subsidiaries usually are much smaller than their parents, their top managers often have to perform top-level management duties. This may mean having responsibility for a wide variety of business functions and spending time on external relations with the community, government, and general public. Managers with comparable profit or cost responsibility in the home country may be performing middle-management tasks there and lack the breadth of experience necessary for a top management position in a foreign subsidiary. A subsidiary manager also must be able to work independently because the subsidiary lacks many staff functions, such as market research, to reduce the costs of duplication. At headquarters, a manager can get advice from specialists by walking to the next office or floor or making a few telephone calls. The subsidiary manager, however, ends up relying much more heavily on his or her personal judgment.

Top managers in subsidiaries usually have broader duties than do managers of similar-sized home-country operations.

INTERNATIONAL MANAGERIAL TRANSFERS

Managers are either **locals**, citizens of the countries in which they are working, or **expatriates**, noncitizens. Expatriates are either **home-country nationals**, citizens of the country in which the company is headquartered, or **third-country nationals**, citizens of nei-

International managers are isolated and have less access to staff specialists.

ther the country in which they are working nor the headquarters country. Locals or expatriates may be employed in the company's home country or in its foreign operations. Most managerial positions in both headquarters and foreign subsidiaries are filled by locals rather than expatriates. The one exception is for project management in some emerging economies, such as Saudi Arabia, where there is an acute shortage of qualified local candidates. Nevertheless, expatriates play an important role in companies' international business. We shall now discuss the reasons companies staff with locals and expatriates, as well as companies' human resource practices for expatriates.

REASONS FOR STAFFING WITH LOCALS

Foreign managerial slots are difficult to fill because

- **Many people don't want to move**
- **There are legal impediments to using expatriates**

Many people enjoy the excitement of living and working abroad, but many others do not want to work in a foreign country, particularly if they perceive an assignment will be long term or permanent. However, some nationalities (Americans, Australians, British, and Dutch) are more willing to accept foreign assignments than are others (French, Germans, Italians, Spanish, and Swiss).[17] The most common reason managers reject a foreign assignment is their perception that the assignment will have a negative effect on their family's lifestyle because of unacceptable living conditions, inadequate educational opportunities for their children, and the inability to be near aged parents. Career considerations are also important, because the foreign assignment may take the manager outside the corporate mainstream for advancement and because the spouse can rarely get a permit to work in a comparable job abroad.[18] If the couple are not married, the "significant other" may not even be able to get permission to live in the foreign location. There is a distinction between a foreign assignment of fixed duration and one that is open-ended. Many more people can cope with a position abroad if they know that they will return home after a specific time period.

Managers view fixed-term and open-ended assignments differently.

There are also legal impediments to staff with expatriates, such as licensing requirements that prevent companies from using expatriate accountants and lawyers. In many cases, companies have established offices to employ people who cannot or will not work where a company would prefer. For example, they have established R&D labs and regional staff offices when personnel refused to move to the country where global headquarters is located.

Local managers may help sales and morale.

The greater the need for local adaptations, the more advantageous it is for companies to use local managers, because they presumably understand local conditions better than expatriates would.[19] The need to adapt may arise because of unique environmental conditions, barriers to imports, or the existence of strong local competitors or large local customers.

When the host country feels animosity toward foreign-controlled operations, local managers may be perceived locally as "better citizens" because they presumably put local interests ahead of the company's global objectives. This local image may play a role in employee morale as well, because many subsidiary employees prefer to work for someone from their own country.[20]

If a company gives most top jobs only to expatriates, it may find difficulty in attracting and keeping good locals. The possibility of advancement provides an incentive to local employees to perform well; without this incentive, they may seek employment elsewhere.

Finally, a reason for staffing with locals is that they usually cost less. Companies must pay moving expenses for expatriates as well as salary adjustments for their move to foreign countries. The National Foreign Trade Council, an association of multinational companies, estimates that U.S. firms typically spend $600,000 to $1 million for

Ethical Dilemmas and Social Responsibility
WHAT ARE FAIR LABOR PRACTICES ANYWAY?

Critics have argued that MNEs have too often established capital-intensive rather than labor-intensive production methods, which do not contribute fully to increasing employment in emerging economies. Ethical dilemmas arise whether or not a labor-saving production method is more economical. For example, in India, machine-made textiles are less expensive to produce than hand-woven ones are. However, hand-woven textiles employ millions of people in India, and their production represents a strong cultural value of self-reliance. As the country's production of machine-made textiles has increased (some by MNEs), the number of unemployed weavers and reports of starvation deaths among them have increased. On the one hand, critics have argued that the hand-loom industry should be subsidized and that on ethical grounds, companies should not establish production that will cause unemployment. On the other hand, other critics argue that the perpetuation of inefficient production merely condemns workers and their descendants to lifetimes of drudgery.

The evidence is mixed on whether MNEs alter production to minimize costs. There are undoubtedly engineering biases toward duplicating facilities built to save labor in industrialized countries. Management control systems also may heavily emphasize output per person, which is more relevant to production needs in industrialized countries. Further, many governmental authorities in emerging economies want showcase plants as symbols of modernization. However, case studies point to substantial alterations by MNEs, such as using human labor instead of mechanized loading equipment, because of local costs and availabilities.

But when labor is substituted for capital, the productivity of the labor is low, so wages are low. Some companies, nevertheless, have been heavily criticized for their labor rates compared to the price of their end products and what they pay celebrities to advertise them. For example, although Nike has worked to assure its contract manufacturers curtail sweatshop conditions, critics still complain because Nike's suppliers in emerging economies pay workers only a few dollars a day, while Nike sells some of its shoes for over $100 and pays sports figures, such as André Agassi, millions of dollars to advertise them.[21] Companies have been further criticized for having merchandise produced in so-called "sweatshops." However, there is disagreement among companies, unions, and human rights groups who have tried to develop a voluntary code of conduct for the apparel industry on what constitutes a sweatshop. For example, some contend that it is sufficient for companies to pay the local minimum or prevailing wage, but others argue for paying wages high enough to meet some standard of needs. Some contend that employees should be required to work no more than 48 hours per week, and others argue for a 60-hour-per-week standard.[22] Some companies have addressed these criticisms by establishing codes of conduct and by monitoring worker conditions in foreign factories that serve as suppliers. However, they have found it difficult to effect changes in the foreign factories and even more difficult to quell criticism of their practices.[23]

MNEs also are criticized for exploiting women in many emerging economies, where they have had less formal education than men have, have been trained since childhood in tasks requiring manual dexterity, and are willing to accept lower wages than men will. Their qualifications are thus ideal for certain labor-intensive activities. Without the constraints of sex discrimination legislation, companies advertise openly that they want female workers. Governments even encourage the practice. For example, Malaysia has advertised "the manual dexterity of the Oriental female" within its investment-promotion programs. But the ethical issue is broader. As women have been enticed into the workplace in emerging economies, sometimes living in company-provided dormitories, critics argue that social costs have increased because of resultant instability within the family unit and increase in unemployment among the traditional male heads of households. Companies argue that these practices make more jobs and income available and that the employment gives women more independence from their traditional subservient roles.

As another example, some critics contend that the hiring of children by MNEs in emerging economies is unethical because the practice denies children access to the education needed for their future development. The International Labor Organization (ILO) estimates that there are 250 million children between ages 5 and 14 in emerging economies who are working. About half of these work fulltime.[24]

But what if the choice isn't between working and education? For many of the poor children in these countries, there is no opportunity for education, whether or not they work. Without the opportunity for work, many may join the legions of abandoned street children, such as those in Guatemala City who sniff glue to kill hunger pains and steal just enough to subsist. Relatedly, Bangladesh criticized a proposed U.S. law that would restrict the importation of child-made products, arguing that such a law could force thousands of children into begging or prostitution. The ILO agrees that the threat of trade sanctions might endanger rather than protect children. Nevertheless, some private groups, such as Fifa, the world soccer's governing body, have adopted codes of not using or selling merchandise made by child labor.[25] UNICEF acknowledges the need for children to work in poverty situations, but has called for the elimination of child labor that is hazardous or exploitative.

a three-year assignment abroad for each expatriate.[26] Most human resource managers are pressured to control the cost of expatriate assignments, and the majority of these are responding by hiring more locals.[27]

REASONS FOR USING EXPATRIATES

Although expatriate managers comprise a minority of total managers within MNEs, companies employ expatriates because of their competence to fill positions, their need to gain foreign experience, and their ability to control operations according to headquarters' preferences.

The most qualified person may be an expatriate.

Companies use expatriate managers when they cannot find qualified local candidates. This is partly determined by a country's level of development. Expatriates constitute a much smaller portion of subsidiary managers in industrial than in developing countries. This also is determined by the need to transfer technologies abroad. When a company transfers new products or production methods, especially in start-up operations, it usually needs to transfer personnel to or from subsidiaries until the operation is running smoothly.

MNEs transfer people so that they may understand the overall corporate system. In companies with specialized activities only in certain countries (such as extraction separated from manufacturing or basic R&D separated from applied R&D), long-term foreign assignments may be the only means of developing a manager's breadth. When there are cross-national mergers, such as Daimler-Benz and Chrysler to form Daimler-Chrysler, international transfers between the two companies are important so that the newly merged company does not continue to operate like two separate companies.[28] These assignments also enhance a manager's ability to work in a variety of social systems and are therefore valuable training tools for ultimate corporate responsibility, involving both domestic and foreign operations. However, as valuable as the foreign assignment may be for learning, companies have been slow at rewarding people who have international experience with top-level corporate positions. For example, few CEOs at the largest U.S. companies have worked outside the United States, and few large U.S. companies have foreigners either as board members or in high corporate positions. (Dow therefore represents a small minority of companies.) Yet perhaps the situation is changing. Many CEOs now assert that international experience and mixing of nationalities at the top will be more important in the future.

> **Multicountry experience gives upward-moving managers new perspectives.**

MNEs use home-country expatriates to control foreign operations because they are used to doing things the headquarters way. They transfer foreign nationals for stints at headquarters so that they too can learn the headquarters way. By transferring many home- and host-country nationals, a company can begin to develop a new hybrid corporate culture that understands both global integration and national responsiveness. In fact, there is evidence of a new cadre of expatriates who neither carry their home-country values everywhere they go, nor go native. Instead, they are developing a global management culture.[29]

> **People transferred from headquarters are more likely to know corporate policies.**
>
> **People transferred to headquarters learn the headquarters way.**

The type of ownership of foreign operations influences how companies use expatriates for control. For example, expatriates transferred abroad to a joint venture may be in an ambiguous situation, not knowing for sure whether they represent and should report to both partners or just the partner that transferred them. Nevertheless, many companies with local partners insist on using their own personnel for positions in which they fear local personnel will make decisions in their own, rather than the joint venture's, best interest. For example, foreign partners commonly transfer expatriates to their Chinese joint ventures to ensure that money is spent only on business-related items.[30]

HOME-COUNTRY VERSUS THIRD-COUNTRY NATIONALS

Most companies' advances in technology, product, and operating procedures originate in their home countries, and they transfer them to their foreign operations later. Because they use expatriates to infuse new methods, personnel with recent home-country experience (usually home-country nationals) are apt to have the desired qualifications.

However, third-country nationals sometimes might have more compatible technical and personal adaptive qualifications than do home-country expatriates. For example, a U.S. company used U.S. personnel to design and manage a Peruvian plant until local managers could be trained. Years later, the company decided to manufacture in Mexico using a plant that more closely resembled the Peruvian operations than its U.S. operations

> **Third-country nationals may know more about**
> - **Language**
> - **Operating adjustments**

in terms of size, product qualities, and factor inputs. The company used its Spanish-speaking Peruvian managers effectively to plan and start up the Mexican facility because they knew the technical needs and could easily adapt to living in Mexico. When companies establish lead operations abroad, such as headquarters for a product division or a country operation that is larger than that in the home country, third-country nationals are more likely to have the competencies needed for the foreign assignments.

SOME INDIVIDUAL CONSIDERATIONS FOR TRANSFERS

We have discussed the importance of nationality when deciding whom to transfer to foreign assignments. But whom among the home-country nationals or among the foreign nationals should the company transfer? We shall now discuss individual attributes that companies consider.

Technical competence factors are a necessary attribute.

Technical Competence   Unless a foreign assignment is clearly intended for training an expatriate, local employees will resent someone coming in from a foreign country (usually at higher compensation) who they feel is no more qualified than they are. Corporate decision makers, expatriate managers, and local managers concur that technical competence, usually indicated by past domestic or foreign job performance, is the largest determinant of success in foreign assignments.[31] The expatriate must know the technical necessities of the position and, if necessary, how to adapt to foreign variations, such as scaled-down plants and equipment, varying standards of productivity, lack of efficient infrastructure and internal distribution, nonavailability of credit, and restrictions on available communications media. Because of the need for technical competence, managers usually have several years' work experience before a company offers them a foreign assignment.

Adaptiveness   Although some companies rely only on technical competence to select expatriates, three types of adaptive characteristics are important for an expatriate's success when entering a new culture:

1. Those needed for self-maintenance, such as being self-confident and able to reduce stress
2. Those related to the development of satisfactory relationships with host nationals, such as flexibility and tolerance
3. Cognitive skills that help one to perceive correctly what is occurring within the host society[32]

An expatriate who lacks any of these may be unable to function effectively. Unfortunately, companies cannot always assess these adaptability characteristics accurately. If the expatriate cannot adapt, he or she may leave the foreign assignment, either by choice or by company decision.

Recent surveys indicate that less than 10 percent of expatriates fail to complete their assignments abroad—a much lower rate than had been found in earlier studies and one that is no higher than in domestic assignments.[33] Nevertheless, because the relocation cost for expatriates is high, the cost of the turnover is high as well.[34] In addition, the company incurs a high cost in lost performance if the expatriate is ineffective because of not adapting well. We have discussed how some managers decline expatriate positions because of their negative perceptions about the effect of the assignment on their families' lifestyle. For some of those managers who do accept positions, this perception becomes a reality.

A reason for failure in a foreign assignment is the family's inability to adjust.[35] A move means new living and shopping habits, new school systems, and unfamiliar business practices. In addition, close friends and relatives—the personal support system—are left behind. However, some individuals do enjoy and adapt easily to a foreign way of life; MNEs should use them if possible. Some companies even maintain a core international group of employees who are the only ones assigned abroad. Other employees can do a number of things to help themselves adjust to foreign locations, including learning the language and associating with support groups abroad, such as religious groups and expatriate associations. They can seek information from people who have worked in the locale and who have positive rather than negative memories of it.

> **Family adaptation is important.**

Local Acceptance   Expatriates may encounter some acceptance problems regardless of who they are. It usually takes time for managers to gain recognition of their authority, and expatriates may not be there long enough to achieve this. Local employees may feel that the best jobs go to overpaid foreigners, especially because companies sometimes send managers abroad to reward or find a place for them, rather than for what they can contribute effectively.[36] Expatriates may have to make unpopular decisions to meet global objectives. Or local management may have had experiences with expatriates who made short-term decisions and then left before dealing with the longer-term implications. If negative stereotypes are added to these attitudes, the expatriate may find it very difficult to succeed. Certain individuals may encounter insurmountable problems when dealing as an expatriate with employees, suppliers, and customers; for example, a Jewish manager in Libya, a very young manager in Japan, or a female manager in Saudi Arabia. The U.S. Civil Rights Act extends the nondiscrimination provisions of civil rights law to cover U.S. citizens' employment abroad, except where foreign law prohibits the employment of a certain class of individual. Because most discrimination problems abroad are cultural rather than legal, companies face challenges in handling the requirements of this act.[37]

> **Expatriates may meet with local prejudice.**

But do companies overreact to these acceptance problems? Consider stereotypes of women: They should not give orders to men, they are temperamental, their place is in the home, clients will not accept them, employees will not take them seriously, they don't have the stamina to work in harsh areas, they will not be given work permits, they don't want to upset their husbands' careers. Partly because of these stereotypes, MNEs have given very few expatriate positions to women, especially to foreign women in the companies' home countries. Yet women have succeeded as expatriates in such male-dominated places as India, Japan, and Thailand because they were seen in the workplace first as foreigners and then as women. This should not imply that the successful women confronted no problems. They have faced discrimination outside the workplace, such as in banks and immigration offices, and have encountered sexist remarks that, although deemed totally inoffensive locally, would be unacceptable elsewhere. They have used such coping devices as giving off the "right signals" through attire and demeanor, have adapted communication styles that would not seem abrasive, and have simply accepted that cultural norms are different.[38] Suggestions for companies to improve the acceptability of women as expatriates may be applied to other groups as well. These include selecting well-qualified women who could command more authority, giving a clear title and job position, disseminating in advance information about the person's high qualifications, placing expatriate women in locations where there are already some local women in management positions who might serve as mentors, and establishing longer than normal assignments to develop role models for acceptance.[39]

Securing a Successful Foreign Assignment   Although the preceding discussion highlights difficulties with foreign assignments, most expatriate assignments are successful. Indeed, many students seem more concerned about getting foreign assignments than avoiding them. In reality, the chances of being offered a foreign assignment soon after graduation are small. Companies generally want people to prove themselves domestically before transferring them abroad; therefore, demonstrating a good work record is probably the major prerequisite to becoming an expatriate. Once this prerequisite is met, an employee may gain an edge over other candidates by additionally demonstrating a knowledge of the language and environment of a foreign assignment. Of course, an individual who simply wants the experience of living and working abroad may take off to a foreign country and work at temporary jobs—with or without governmental work permits—to earn enough to survive. Thousands of young people do this to help them find what they want career-wise, and the experience helps them become valuable employees later on.[40]

POSTEXPATRIATE SITUATIONS

Coming home can require adaptation in many areas, including
- Financial
- Job
- Social

About 12 percent of returning expatriates leave their companies within one year of repatriation.[41] Problems with repatriation arise in three general areas: personal finances, readjustment to home-country corporate structure, and readjustment to life at home. Companies give expatriates many financial benefits to encourage them to accept a foreign assignment. While abroad, they may live in the best neighborhoods, send their children to the best private schools, employ domestic help, socialize with the upper class, and still save more money than before the move. But they lose this lifestyle on their return home. Returning expatriates often find that many of their peers were promoted above them while they were abroad, that they now have less autonomy in the job, that they are "little fish in a big pond," and that they now have less in common with their friends than before the foreign assignments. Some human resource practices for smoothing reentry include providing expatriates with ample advance notice of when they will return, maximum information about their new jobs, placement in jobs that will build on their foreign experiences, housing assistance, and a reorientation program, as well as requiring frequent visits to headquarters and using a formal headquarters mentor to look after their interests while they are abroad.[42]

The significance of an overseas assignment to one's career may be positive, neutral, or negative, depending on individual differences, the company's commitment to foreign operations, and the communication links between headquarters and expatriate personnel.

For companies with a very high commitment to global operations such as Dow Chemical, multicountry experience may be as essential as multifunctional and multiproduct experience in reaching upper-echelon organizational levels. Nevertheless, some companies with a high international commitment so separate foreign and domestic operations that they function almost as two companies. If the domestic business dominates, there may be not only little interchange of personnel between domestic and foreign operations but also little advancement of personnel with international experience to top-level positions.

In any case, very few people reach the top rungs of large companies anyway, with or without foreign work experience. Some companies, particularly those with international divisions, depend heavily on a cadre of specialists who may either rotate between foreign locations and international headquarters assignments or spend most of their careers abroad. Although not reaching the top management levels of the parent, they can reach plateaus above most domestic managers in terms of compensation and responsibility. Many people just have a penchant for international living. For example, after stints in Singapore and London, a Morgan Stanley expatriate in India said, "I still don't want to go back to the U.S. It's a big world—lots of things to see."[43]

In some companies, foreign assignments carry a high career risk, regardless of corporate executives' statements to the contrary. This risk may arise for two reasons. First, there may be little provision to fit someone into the domestic or headquarters organization on repatriation. An office simply does not stay vacant while one is abroad for several years; a repatriated employee cannot easily bump a replacement. Holding a position available while an employee is abroad is particularly difficult when the foreign assignment is of indefinite length. Such open-ended assignments are a significant portion of the total. At Hewlett-Packard, such assignments constitute 25 percent of foreign transfers.[44] Second, some "out of sight, out of mind" issues may occur. A General Dynamics executive said he would never have known about domestic openings if a friend had not kept him apprised of the organization's promotional pipeline.[45]

When repatriated employees have career problems, it becomes more difficult to convince other people to take foreign assignments. Very few companies follow Dow Chemical's example and make written guarantees that repatriated employees will come back to jobs at least as good as those they left. (However, companies do not guarantee future positions to their domestic managers either.) Some companies simply explain the career risk and compensate employees so highly that they are enticed to become expatriates. Other companies integrate foreign assignments into career planning and are developing mentor programs to look after the expatriates' domestic interests.[46]

Foreign nationals who are transferred to headquarters sometimes confront a different problem. If the assignment is a promotion from a manager's subsidiary post rather than part of a planned rotation, then the move to headquarters may be permanent. For example, the Brazilian head of a Brazilian subsidiary may have performed so well that the MNE wants to give that manager multicountry responsibility at the corporate offices in New York or Frankfurt. Because the manager would not be able to return to Brazil without taking a demotion, he or she might refuse the transfer.

EXPATRIATE COMPENSATION

If a U.S. company transfers its British finance manager, who is making $70,000 per year, to Italy, where the going rate is $80,000 per year, what should the manager's salary be? Or if the Italian financial manager is transferred to the United Kingdom, what pay should the company offer? Should it compensate in dollars, pounds, or lira? Whose holidays should apply? Which set of fringe benefits should apply? These are but a few of the

MNEs must pay enough to entice people to move but must not overpay.

many questions a company must solve when it moves people abroad. The most oft-mentioned problem by MNEs in developing an international workforce is in dealing with differing pay levels, benefits, and perks.[47] On the one hand, the company must keep costs down; on the other, it must maintain high employee morale.

The amount and type of compensation necessary to entice a person to move to another country vary widely by person and locale. Company practices also vary widely in terms of compensation for differences. Companies with very few expatriate employees may work out a foreign compensation package on an individual basis. As international activities grow, however, it becomes too cumbersome to handle each transfer in this way. As long as consistency is sought in transfer policy, some people inevitably will receive more than would be necessary to entice them to go abroad. Overall, the package may multiply the compensation cost in comparison with what the expatriate had been making domestically. Table 21.1 illustrates a typical package.

Living is more expensive abroad because

- **Habits change slowly**
- **People don't know how and where to buy**

Cost of Living　Most expatriates encounter cost-of-living increases, primarily because their accustomed way of living is expensive to duplicate in a new environment. Habits are difficult to change. For example, Westerners pay dearly in some parts of Asia to rent

TABLE 21.1	**TYPICAL FIRST-YEAR COST FOR A U.S. EXPATRIATE (MARRIED, TWO CHILDREN) IN TOKYO, JAPAN**

An expatriate's cost to the company may be several times what it would be for the same employee in his or her home country.

Direct compensation costs	
Base salary	$100,000
Foreign-service premium	15,000
Goods and services differential	73,600
Less: U.S. housing norm*	(15,400)
U.S. hypothetical taxes	(17,200)
Company-paid costs	
Schooling (two children)	15,000
Annual home leave	4,800
Housing*	150,000
Japanese income taxes†	84,000
Transfer/moving costs	38,000
Total company costs	$447,800

*Assumes company rents housing in its name and provides to expatriate. If company pays housing allowance instead, Japanese income taxes (and total costs) will be about $65,000 higher.
†Note that Japanese income taxes will increase each year as some company reimbursements, most notably for taxes, become taxable.
Source: Organization Resources Counselors, Inc.

accommodations with Western bathrooms and kitchens. Knowledge of the local country is a second consideration. Expatriates may obtain food and housing at higher than the local rate because they don't know the language well, where to buy, or how to bargain for reductions. Housing costs also vary substantially because of crowded conditions that raise land prices as well as shortages of domiciles that are acceptable to expatriates.

Most companies raise salaries (sometimes called a "goods-and-services differential") to account for higher foreign-country costs. After the expatriate returns home, the company removes the differential. A few companies reduce the cost-of-living differential over time, reasoning that as expatriates become better assimilated, they should be able to adjust more to local purchasing habits; for example, by buying vegetables from a native market instead of using imported packaged goods. When moves are to areas with a lower cost of living, few companies reduce an employee's pay because doing so might adversely affect the employee's morale. Expatriates may then receive a windfall.

Companies compare their expatriate compensation packages with other companies, often with information from consulting firms, such as Towers Perrin, that specialize in international compensation.[48] In addition, they rely on estimates of cost-of-living differences, even if the estimates are imperfect. They commonly use such sources as the U.S. State Department's cost-of-living index published yearly in *Labor Developments Abroad*, the *U.N. Monthly Bulletin of Statistics*, and surveys by the *Financial Times*, *P-E International*, *Business International*, and the International Monetary Fund's *Staff Papers*. In using any of these sources, companies must determine which items are included in order to adjust omitted ones separately. Some items commonly omitted are housing, schooling, and taxes. Differences in inflation and exchange rates may quickly render surveys and indexes obsolete, so companies need to make cost-of-living adjustments frequently.

The ultimate objective of cost-of-living adjustments is to ensure that expatriates' after-tax income will not suffer as a result of a foreign assignment. Because taxes are usually assessed on the adjustments companies make to the base salaries, companies have to adjust even further upward if the foreign tax rate is higher than the home country's.

MNEs use various cost-of-living indexes and
- **Increase compensation when foreign cost is higher**
- **Do not decrease compensation when foreign cost is lower**
- **Remove the differential when the manager is repatriated**

Foreign-Service Premiums and Hardship Allowances

There are bound to be things expatriates will have to do without when living abroad, ranging from nuisance to hardship. Consequently, companies frequently give expatriates foreign-service premiums just for being posted in a foreign location. This practice appears to be dropping off, however, especially in so-called world capitals in which companies assume there is little deprivation and difficulty to get people to transfer.[49] Further, the hardships from foreign assignments are decreasing as advances in transportation and communication enable expatriates to keep in closer contact with people in their home countries, as the openness of economies allows them to buy familiar products and services, and as the general level of housing, schooling, and medical services increasingly meet expatriates' needs.

But few would deny that living conditions in certain locales still present particularly severe hardships, such as harsh climatic or health conditions, or political unrest that places the expatriate and family in danger. For instance, expatriate personnel in such MNEs as Goodyear, Eastman Kodak, and Sanyo have been targeted for kidnapping and armed assault. Figure 21.3 shows attacks against U.S. citizens and U.S. facilities abroad from 1995 to 1999. Companies have had to not only rethink their hardship allowances but also purchase ransom insurance, provide training programs on safety for expatriates

Employees may encounter living problems for which the company gives extra compensation.

FIGURE 21.3   Attacks on U.S. Citizens, 1999

The attacks include those on tourists and government employees but indicate the widespread nature of violence that expatriates can encounter.

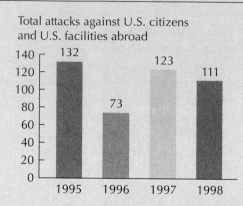

Total attacks against U.S. citizens and U.S. facilities abroad

1995	132
1996	73
1997	123
1998	111

Over the four-year period where the attacks occurred

Latin America	318
Europe	50
Africa	15
Western Europe	13
Middle East	12
Near East/South Asia	8
Eurasia	7
Asia	7
East Asia and Pacific	5
North America	4

Source: From *USA TODAY*, September 21, 1999. Copyright 2000, USA TODAY. Reprinted with permission.

and families, pay for home alarm systems and security guards, and spend management time in considering their legal liability for handling employee safety issues. Yet even where conditions are less severe, expatriates may encounter living conditions that are substandard (or better) than what they had at home. Thus, companies need to alter expatriate compensation by country. It may make sense, for example, for companies to offer the expatriates a different set of perks in London than in Tokyo.[50]

Finally, hardship may occur because of potential changes in total family income and status. In the home country, all members of the family may be able to work. About a quarter of companies provide spouses of expatriates with job-search assistance, often through networks with other companies.[51] For example, Eastman Kodak tries to find employment for spouses; when it can't, it pays for a partial loss in income.[52] However, governments seldom grant people other than the transferred employee permission to work in a foreign country. So the spouse (or live-in companion) of an expatriate may have to either give up well-paying and satisfying employment or be separated from the partner for long periods. Some companies increase the expatriate's compensation, and about one-third of large U.S. companies assist couples with commuter marriages.

MNEs may have to provide more fringe benefits to employees in remote areas.

Remote Areas   Many large-scale international projects are in areas so remote that companies would get few people to transfer there if they did not create an environment more like that at home or make other special arrangements. For example, Lockheed Aircraft set up its own color TV broadcasting station in Saudi Arabia for its expatriates there. Also, INCO built schools, hospitals, churches, supermarkets, a golf course, a yacht club, a motel, and a restaurant for its expatriates in Indonesia.

Expatriates in remote areas often are handled very differently from employees elsewhere. To attract the large number of people necessary for construction and start-up, MNEs usually will offer fixed-term contract assignments at high salaries and hire most people from outside the company. Some people are attracted to these assignments and are willing to undergo difficult living conditions because they can save money at a rate that would be impossible to achieve at home.

FIGURE 21.4 Variance in CEO Pay Packages Among Countries

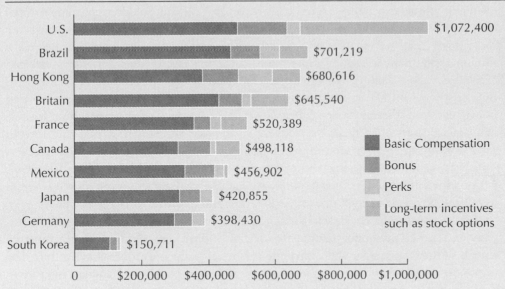

The average annual pay package of the chief executive of an industrial company with annual revenues of $250 million to $500 million in 10 countries. Figures are from April 1998 and are not weighted to compensate for different costs of living or levels of taxation.

Basic Compensation

Bonus

Perks

Long-term incentives such as stock options

U.S. $1,072,400
Brazil $701,219
Hong Kong $680,616
Britain $645,540
France $520,389
Canada $498,118
Mexico $456,902
Japan $420,855
Germany $398,430
South Korea $150,711

Source: *New York Times*, January 17, 1999. Reprinted by permission of NYT Pictures.

Complications of Nationality Differences As companies employ expatriates from both home and third countries, compensation issues have become very complex. There is no consensus among companies on how to deal with most of these. For example, salaries for similar jobs vary substantially among countries, as do the relationships of salaries within the corporate hierarchy. Figure 21.4 shows the disparity of annual pay packages by company nationality. The method of payment also varies substantially. Long-term incentives, such as options on restricted stock, are popular in the United States but not in Germany. However, German managers often receive compensation that U.S. managers do not, such as housing allowances and partial payment of salary outside Germany, neither of which is taxable. However, there is nearly a consensus to maintain expatriates on their home-country retirement systems because of the complexities of standardization and the need to protect people in the locales in which they are most apt to retire.

MANAGEMENT RECRUITMENT AND SELECTION

Some companies have personnel record systems at headquarters that include data on home- and foreign-country nationals. These data include not only the usual technical and demographic data but also—if the company is international—information on such adaptive capabilities as foreign-language qualifications, willingness to accept foreign assignments, and results of company-administered tests. However, a company may encounter problems in bringing foreign managers into the system; if the company owns less than 100 percent of the foreign facility, the other stockholders may complain. To the extent that companies have records, they can compare employees to gauge which ones may be best suited for positions with international responsibility.

Foreign personnel are not easily encompassed in information inventories because foreign operations may not be wholly owned.

Companies that know more about their employees' technical capabilities than about their adaptive ones must focus on measuring adaptability for foreign-transfer purposes. For example, people who have successfully adjusted to domestic transfers or have previous international experience are more likely to adapt abroad. In addition, some companies use a variety of personality testing mechanisms as assessment aids. Companies are increasingly including spouses and children in tests and extensive interviews because a foreign assignment is usually more stressful for the family than for the transferred employee.[53] For example, the expatriate employees generally receive an advancement, but the spouses must start at the bottom in developing new social relations and learning how to carry out the day-to-day management of the home. The separation from friends, family, and career often make the nonworking spouses very lonely so that they turn to their working spouses for more companionship. But the working spouses may have less time because of their new jobs. This may lead to marital stress, which in turn affects work performance. Interviewers thus look not only at likely adaptiveness but also at whether marriages are strong enough to weather the stress and not hurt work performance.

One way a company can staff foreign operations is to buy an existing foreign company and use its personnel. Companies may also form joint ventures with companies abroad so that the partner will contribute personnel to the operation as well as hire new personnel. In Japan, where the labor market is tight and people are reluctant to move to new companies, foreign firms use Japanese partners extensively. However, if a company's partner handles staffing arrangements, the employees may see their primary allegiance to that partner rather than to the foreign investor.

Acquisitions and joint ventures secure staff but the staff may be
- **Inefficient**
- **Hard to control**

INTERNATIONAL DEVELOPMENT OF MANAGERS

To carry out global operations, companies need people with a variety of specialized skills. Therefore, programs to develop managers internationally must be tailored to some extent to specific individuals and situations.[54] In addition, there are three developmental needs:

1. Top executives must have a global mind-set that is free of national prejudices. They must also know the global environment so they can exert the leadership necessary to attain a global mission.
2. Managers with direct international responsibility must be able to effect a proper balance in well-being between corporate and national operations.
3. Managers without direct international responsibility must understand the importance of international competition on the company's well being.

Managers may gain the above attitudes and knowledge before they join the company.

There is an increase in international studies in universities.

To help meet these developmental needs, business schools are increasing their international offerings and requirements, but there is no consensus as to what students should learn to help prepare them for international responsibilities. Two approaches are (1) to convey specific knowledge about foreign environments and international operating adjustments and (2) to train in interpersonal awareness and adaptability. The former may tend to remove some of the fear and aggression that are aroused when dealing with the unknown. However, the understanding of a difference does not necessarily imply a willingness to adapt to it, particularly to a cultural difference. The Peace Corps uses sensitivity training, which is designed to develop attitudinal flexibility. Although either approach generally helps a person adjust better than those who lack training, there appears to be no significant difference in the effectiveness of the two approaches.[55]

Companies continue the international development of employees after they employ them. They also train employees because many employees feel ill-equipped to handle worldwide responsibilities as they move up in their organizations. To counter this, a company can train those people who are about to take a foreign assignment, such as through language and orientation programs. Or it could include international business components in external or internal programs for employees that may or may not work abroad. Examples of internal programs are those at PepsiCo International and Raychem, which bring foreign nationals to U.S. divisions for periods of six months to a year; IBM's regional training centers, in which managers from several countries are gathered for specific topics; P&G's training on globalization issues; and GE's, Motorola's, and Honda of America's programs to teach foreign languages and cultural sensitivity.

The most common predeparture training is an informational briefing. Topics covered typically include cultural differences, job design, compensation, housing, climate, education, health conditions, home sales, taxes, transport of goods, job openings after repatriation, and salary distribution. Companies sometimes follow predeparture training with cultural training about six months after expatriates arrive in a foreign country so that they may relate better to issues covered.

While working in foreign countries, managers are challenged to break down nationalistic barriers that impair the companies' development of global corporate cultures and achievement of integrated global strategies. To balance a company's global and national needs, managers must be neither too ethnocentric nor too polycentric. So MNEs are challenged to develop managers who are committed to the subsidiary at which they work and to the parent company's global well-being. However, companies rarely find such a dual allegiance.

Figure 21.5 shows four types of expatriate managers: *free agent, heart at home, going native,* and *dual citizen.*[56] There are two types of free agent. The first includes people who put their careers above either the parent company or the foreign operation where they are working. They often are highly effective, but they will move with little warning from one company to another in foreign assignments, may serve their own short-term interests at the expense of the company's long-term ones, and do not want to return to their home country. The second type of free agent includes people whose careers have plateaued at home and who take a foreign assignment only for the paycheck. The heart at home type is overly ethnocentric and is usually eager to be repatriated. When the company wants strong headquarters control, this type of person may be very effective. The going native type learns and accepts the local way of doing business and wants to stay in the foreign location and be left alone by headquarters. This type of person may be very appropriate for situations in which the company follows multidomestic practices. The dual citizen type has a clear understanding of global needs, why he or she is needed at the foreign subsidiary, and local realities that may necessitate national responsiveness. This person usually finds mechanisms by which to work out differences between headquarters and subsidiary and is overall the most effective type of expatriate manager.

Postemployment training may include

- **Environment-specific information**
- **Adaptiveness training**
- **Training by an unaffiliated company abroad**

FIGURE 21.5   Allegiance of Expatriate Managers

The "dual citizen" type of manager is most effective at balancing global and local needs. However, each of the other types can be very effective for specific types of foreign operations.

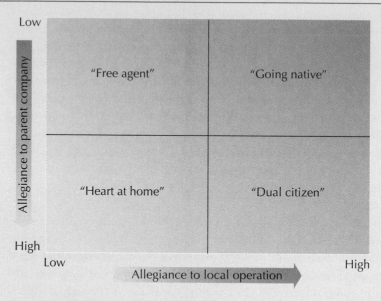

To counterbalance a heart at home, the company may send younger managers abroad and do everything possible to facilitate cultural adjustment. To counterbalance going native, the company may send people abroad who have strong ties to the company, limit their time away from headquarters, keep in close contact with them (perhaps through a mentor program), and provide them with assistance in repatriation. In either situation, the company should handle the international transfer so that the expatriate understands why he or she is being sent to the post, how the performance will be measured, the objectives of the parent company and local unit, and the location of control. These suggestions also may be applied to other than expatriate employees. For example, local managers in foreign subsidiaries may be less apt to be a heart at home if they have closer contact with headquarters and see their own future as tied more to global than to local interests.

How much managers need to be developed internationally depends on the importance of international operations to the company. Dow Chemical is an MNE already highly dependent on and committed to international operations. Its international human resource needs are more extensive than those of a company that merely exports or imports a small portion of its output or supplies. Such a company's primary need is for personnel that are technically trained or knowledgeable about trade documentation, foreign-exchange risk, and political-economic conditions that may affect trade flows. An MNE such as Dow shares this need but also needs a multinational workforce and managers who can integrate this workforce effectively.

LABOR-MARKET DIFFERENCES

As a company moves to foreign production, it must consider how to staff, motivate, and compensate its foreign workforce. The norms in these human resource activities vary substantially from one country to another. Thus, there is some danger in a company's attempting to duplicate organizational structures and job descriptions abroad, particularly in emerging economies. Labor-saving devices that are economically justifiable at home, where wage rates are high, may be more costly than labor-intensive types of production in a country with high unemployment rates and low wages. Using labor-intensive methods also may ingratiate the company with governmental officials, who must cope with the host country's unemployment. Because of differences in labor skills and attitudes, the company also may find it advantageous to simplify tasks and use equipment that would be considered obsolete in a more advanced economy.

MNEs may shift labor or capital intensities if costs differ in foreign labor markets.

INTERNATIONAL LABOR MOBILITY

There is pressure for people to emigrate from countries with high unemployment and low wages (usually emerging economies) to countries with labor shortages and high wages. This is tempered by countries' legal entry restrictions to minimize the economic and social problems of absorbing large numbers of immigrants. Because of these restrictions, companies depend less today on imported labor than in earlier generations, despite the presence of sizable numbers of legal and illegal workers in industrial countries.[57]

Companies have an incentive to hire immigrant workers because they often will work for a fraction of what domestic workers with comparable skills will demand. This is especially true of illegal immigrants who cannot afford to return to their own countries. It is also true within the European Union, where workers may move legally from one country to another in response to wage rate differences. For example, construction workers from other EU countries (mainly Britain, Ireland, and Portugal) work in Germany at considerably less than the wage for German labor.[58] In other cases, companies have sought specialists from abroad. Shared Resources, a small U.S.-based computer system company, recruits employees in India to work on three-year contracts in Columbus, Ohio.[59] Not surprisingly, critics have complained that companies are unethical by hiring foreign employees at less cost than domestic ones.[60]

Migrant workers in many countries have permission to stay for only short periods, such as three to six months for New Zealand's workers from Fiji and Tonga. In many other cases, workers leave their families behind in the hope of returning home after saving enough money while working in the foreign country. This creates workforce uncertainty for employers. In the late 1980s, the United States experienced a net loss of Korean scientists and engineers. Another uncertainty is the extent to which government authorities will restrict the number of foreign workers because of pressures from domestic laborers to protect their job opportunities and from groups prejudiced against foreigners.

The influx and use of foreign workers create additional workplace problems. For example, in parts of Western Europe, companies relegate certain nationality groups to less complex jobs because their language makes training them difficult. A result has been the development of homogeneous ethnic work groups at cross-purposes with other groups in the organization, as well as the emergence of "go-betweens" who can communicate with management and labor.

There is pressure for labor to move from high-unemployment and low-wage areas to places of perceived opportunities.

Companies are less certain of labor supply when they depend on foreign laborers because

- **Countries become restrictive**
- **Workers return home**
- **Turnover necessitates more training**

LABOR COMPENSATION DIFFERENCES

Companies can sometimes gain competitive advantages by establishing production facilities where they can pay labor less than their competitors pay. We shall now examine national differences in the amount and method of paying workers, along with the dynamics of comparative labor costs.

REASONS FOR COUNTRY DIFFERENCES IN LABOR COMPENSATION

The amount of compensation companies pay depends on workers' contributions to the business, supply of and demand for particular skills ("going wage") in the area, cost of living, government legislation, and collective-bargaining ability. Companies' methods of payment (salaries, wages, commissions, bonuses, and fringe benefits) depend on customs, feelings of security, taxes, and governmental requirements. Both the amount and method of payment are affected by a country's culture. For example, within a highly individualistic society such as the United States, there is a preference for compensation based on proportional contribution—the result being a heavy reliance on bonuses and a high disparity in incomes within the organization. In a more collectivist society, such as China, there is a preference for more egalitarian allocations, regardless of contributions.[61] In an economy where people have a high need to avoid risk, there is a preference for job and income protections over income.[62]

MNEs usually pay slightly better than their local counterparts in lower-wage countries, although they still pay less than what they do in higher-wage countries. They pay more because of their management philosophies and structures. An MNE's typical management philosophy, particularly in contrast to that of a local, family-run company, is often to attract high-level workers by offering higher relative wages. In addition, its product and process technologies may allow it to compensate employees more than local companies do. Further, when a company first comes into a country, experienced workers may demand higher compensation because they have doubts about whether the new operation will succeed.

MNEs may need to pay more than local companies to entice workers from existing jobs.

DIFFERING COSTS OF BENEFITS

Fringe benefits differ radically from one country to another. Direct-compensation figures therefore do not accurately reflect the amount a company must pay for a given job in a given country. The types of benefits that are either customary or have been required also vary widely. In Japan, for example, large companies commonly give workers such benefits as family allowances, housing loans and subsidies, lunches, children's education, and subsidized vacations; thus, fringe benefits make up a much higher portion of total compensation in Japan than in the United States. Moreover, in many countries, companies commonly give end-of-the-year bonuses, housing allowances, long vacations, profit sharing, and payment supplements based on the number of children the worker has.

Fringe benefits vary substantially among countries.

In many countries, firing or laying off an employee may be either impossible or very expensive, resulting in unexpectedly higher costs for a company accustomed to the economies of manipulating its employment size. In the United States, for example, companies expect to lay off workers when demand falls seasonally or cyclically. In many countries, however, a company has no legal recourse except to fire workers, and then perhaps only if it is closing down its operations, at which time it must pay high sever-

In many countries, it is impossible or expensive to lay off workers.

ance compensation.[63] To curtail operations in such countries, a company must come to an agreement with its unions and the government on such issues as extended benefits and the retraining and relocation of workers. At the same time, unemployment benefits are low in the United States compared with those in Western Europe, so there is more incentive for unemployed U.S. workers to find new jobs.[64]

Too often, companies compare compensation expenses on a per-worker basis, which may bear little relationship to the total employment expenditure. Workers' abilities and motivations vary widely; consequently, it is the output associated with labor cost that is important. Seemingly cheap labor actually may raise the total compensation expenditure because of the need for more supervision, added training expenses, and adjustments in the method of production. For example, Quality Coils, a small U.S. company, moved some operations to Mexico because hourly wages were only about one-third of what it paid in Connecticut. However, the company later returned to Connecticut because of high absenteeism and low productivity in Mexico.[65] Further, if labor turnover is high, there is a continual need to retrain a workforce.[66]

Differences among countries in amount and type of compensation change. Salaries and wages (as well as other expenditures) may rise more rapidly in one locale than in another. Therefore, the competitiveness of operations in different countries may shift. For example, in the 1980s, Korean workers made hundreds of thousands of shoes for Nike and Reebok; however, as Korean labor costs grew, most of these jobs shifted to China and Indonesia.[67] But the process of comparing costs is complex. An example will illustrate shifting capabilities. Assume U.S. productivity per worker in manufacturing increased by 2.8 percent (or 1.028 of what it was before), and hourly compensation rates went up by 10.2 percent (or 1.102) of what they were before. The result was a unit labor-cost increase of 7.2 percent (1.102 divided by 1.028). Meanwhile, in the United Kingdom, productivity increased by 5.9 percent (or 1.059 of what it was before) and hourly compensation rates by 16.2 percent (or 1.162 of what they were before), amounting to a unit labor-cost increase of 9.7 percent (1.162 divided by 1.059). This meant that labor costs adjusted to productivity were rising more rapidly in the United Kingdom than in the United States in terms of local currencies. But if the pound depreciated substantially in relation to the dollar, the labor cost measured in dollars could actually have become more favorable in the United Kingdom than in the United States.

Relative costs change, so MNEs must consider
- **Productivity change**
- **Labor-rate change**
- **Conversion of labor rate to competitor's currency**

COMPARATIVE LABOR RELATIONS

In each country in which an MNE operates, it must deal with a group of workers whose approach will be affected by the sociopolitical environment of the country. The environment affects whether they join labor unions, how they bargain, and what they want from companies.

SOCIOPOLITICAL ENVIRONMENT

There are striking international differences in how labor and management view each other. When there is little mobility between the two groups (children of laborers become laborers, and children of managers become managers), a marked class difference exists, and companies may face considerable labor strife. Labor may perceive itself in a class struggle, even though it may have been closing wage gaps for some time. In such

Overall attitude in a country affects how labor and management view each other and how labor will try to improve its lot.

countries as Brazil, Switzerland, and the United States, labor demands are largely met through an adversarial process between the directly affected management and labor. Unions in the United States negligibly influence members' vote in political elections. In contrast, labor groups in many countries vote the way their labor leaders instruct them, so their demands are met primarily through national legislation rather than collective bargaining with management. Such mechanisms as strikes or slowdowns to effect changes also may be national in scope. In this situation, a company's production or ability to distribute its product may be much more dependent on the way labor perceives conditions in the whole country, rather than how it perceives conditions in the company where it works.

The use of mediation by an impartial party is mandatory in Israel and voluntary in the United States and the United Kingdom. Among countries that have mediation practices, attitudes toward it are diverse; for example, there is much less enthusiasm for it in India than in the United States. Not all differences are settled either through changes in legislation or through collective bargaining. Other means are the labor court and the government-chosen arbitrator. For example, in Austria wages in many industries are arbitrated semiannually.

Union membership as a portion of the total workforce has been falling in most countries. This is illustrated in Figure 21.6. There are several reasons for this decline:

- *Increase in white-collar workers as a percentage of total workers.* White-collar workers see themselves more as managers than as laborers.
- *Increase in service employment in relation to manufacturing employment.* There is more variation in service assignments than in manufacturing, so workers believe their own situations are different from their coworkers'.
- *Rising portion of women in the workforce.* Traditionally, women have been less prone to join unions.
- *Rising portion of part-time and temporary workers.* Workers don't see themselves in the job long enough for a union to help them much.
- *Trend toward smaller average plant size.* Workers don't see themselves so separate from managers.
- *Decline in the belief in collectivism among younger workers.* Few of today's younger workers have been economically deprived, so they do not look to collective solutions.[68]

In spite of the overall decrease in union membership, the unions in Sweden have maintained their strength because they have forged cooperative relationships with large companies (such as ABB, Electrolux, and Volvo) to improve corporate competitiveness and to share in the rewards from the results.

UNION STRUCTURE

Union structure can be
- **National or local**
- **Industry or company**
- **One or several for the same company**

Companies in a given country may deal with one or several unions. A union itself may represent workers in many industries, in many companies within the same industry, or in only one company. If it represents only one company, the union may represent all plants or just one plant. Although there are diversities within countries, one type of relationship is most prevalent within most countries. For example, unions in the United States tend to be national, representing certain types of workers (for example, airline pilots, coal miners, truck drivers, or university professors). Thus a company may deal with several different national unions. Each collective-bargaining process

FIGURE 21.6 Trade Union Decline in Industrialized Countries

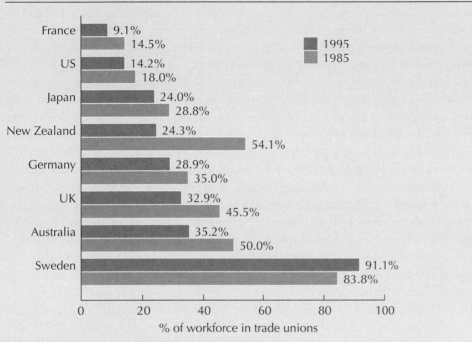

Various factors have influenced the decline of trade union membership in industrialized countries.

% of workforce in trade unions

Source: From "Collective Responsibility," by Robert Taylor from *Financial Times*, September 13, 1999. Reprinted by permission.

usually is characterized by a single company on one side rather than an association of different companies that deals with one of the unions representing a certain type of worker in all the companies' plants. In Japan, one union typically represents all workers in a given company and has only very loose affiliations with unions in other companies. This allegedly explains why Japanese unions are less militant than those in most other industrialized countries: They seldom strike, and when they do, they may stop working for only a short period of time or may continue working while wearing symbolic armbands. Because of the workers' closer affiliation with the company, Japanese union leaders are hesitant to risk hurting the company's ability to compete in world markets. In Sweden, bargaining tends to be highly centralized in that employers from numerous companies in different industries deal together with a federation of trade unions. In Germany, employers from associations of companies in the same industries bargain jointly with union federations, although there has been a recent tendency for companies and their workers to use legal loopholes to negotiate separate agreements.[69]

PROTECTION FROM CLOSURES AND REDUNDANCY

In response to proposed layoffs, shifts in production location, and cessation of operations, workers in many countries have actually taken over plants and continued to produce until they ran out of raw materials and components. The process has sometimes been peaceful and sometimes violent. The results of these efforts have sometimes prevented the plant's closing and other times not.

Workers' takeover of plants has been done to publicize their plight.

That workers will go so far to try to prevent a plant from closing indicates how important this issue is in some countries, particularly those in Western Europe where prenotification has been negotiated or legislated almost everywhere. Workers want prenotification so that they have time to try to counter companies' decisions and, if unsuccessful, to adjust better to their changed situations. The Western European situation contrasts with that in Canada and the United States, where few contracts require employers to give more than a week's notice of closure.

The lifetime-employment custom in Japan offers some contrasts to labor practices in North America and Western Europe. Some Japanese employees, usually skilled male workers in large companies, enjoy lifetime employment. In turn, these employees voluntarily switch companies less frequently than do their counterparts in North America and Europe. Other Japanese workers are temporaries. The number of temporaries is large, constituting about 40 percent of the workforce even in a large company such as Toyota. In addition, there are many part-time workers. When business takes a downturn or when labor-saving techniques are introduced, Japanese companies keep the lifetime employees on the payroll by releasing the temporary workers, reducing the variable bonuses of lifetime employees, and transferring workers to other product divisions.[70]

There is some evidence, although inconclusive, that this system has enabled Japanese companies to introduce automated systems more effectively than companies elsewhere can because lifetime employees have little concern about job security. It also has helped Japanese companies to spend heavily on training because the lifetime employees have a strong moral commitment to stay with their employers. The temporary workers have tolerated the system because of the labor shortage that has existed during recent decades in Japan and because many are women who, because of culture, are disinclined to engage in adversarial behavior.

CODETERMINATION

Particularly in Northern Europe, labor participates in the management of companies, a process known as **codetermination**. Most commonly, labor is represented on the board of directors, either with or without veto power.

Despite some voluntary moves toward codetermination, most existing examples have been mandated by legislation, such as that in Germany.[71] These moves have been dictated by employee pressures because of the employees' belief that they have risks and stakes in the organization just as stockholders do. Although there are some early examples of workers deterring investment outflows, acquisitions, and plant closures, codetermination apparently has had little effect on companies' international business decisions or the speed with which companies reach those decisions. One reason for this minimal effect is that workers are so divided in terms of what they want that it is hard for their representatives to take strong stances on issues.

TEAM EFFORTS

In some countries, companies emphasize work teams to foster group cohesiveness and involve workers in multiple rather than a limited number of tasks. It is common for companies to compensate employees partly on group output so that their peers will exert pressure to reduce absenteeism and increase work efforts. Involving workers in multiple tasks by rotating their jobs within work groups reduces boredom and develops replacement skills that are useful when someone is absent. Companies have also instituted practices that allow workers' groups to control their own quality and repair their own equipment. Although the team efforts have worked well in some places, such as Sweden, they don't work everywhere. Levi-Strauss introduced the team concept to its U.S. factories with poor results because its workers wanted to be paid on an individual incentive system.[72] But companies have adapted the team concept to particular national cultures. For example, in Japanese quality circles, small groups of workers concentrate on very focused problems. GE tried transferring this concept to work groups in the United States, but workers found it too constricting. Now GE has large group meetings on nonfocused issues, where workers may suggest costly and broad company changes. GE's management accepts most of the suggestions and recognizes individual contributions.[73]

INTERNATIONAL PRESSURES ON NATIONAL PRACTICES

The International Labor Organization (ILO) dates back to 1919. Its premise is that the failure of any country to adopt humane labor conditions is an obstacle to other countries that want to improve their conditions. Several associations of unions from different countries also support similar ideals. These associations include various international trade secretariats representing workers in specific industries; for example, the International Confederation of Free Trade Unions (ICFTU), the World Federation of Trade Unions (WFTU), and the World Confederation of Labour (WCL). Through these organizations' activities and the general enhancement of communications globally, people increasingly are aware of differences in labor conditions among countries. Among the newsworthy reports have been legal proscriptions against collective bargaining in Malaysia, wages below minimum standards in Indonesia, and the use of forced labor in Burma.[74] The ILO has also brought attention to the prevalence of child labor in emerging economies. Once it makes such conditions known, pressures for changes through economic and political sanctions from abroad follow.

> **The ILO monitors labor conditions worldwide.**

Another area influencing MNE labor practices has been codes of conduct on industrial relations issued by the OECD and the ILO. Another is the Social Charter, a nonbinding statement of intent by EU heads of government. Although the codes and charter are voluntary, they may signal future transnational regulations of MNE activities. Trade unions have been anxious to get clarifications of the guidelines and make them legally enforceable because the contents are so vague that there is room for many interpretations.

MULTINATIONAL OWNERSHIP AND COLLECTIVE BARGAINING[75]

An unresolved debate is whether companies weaken labor, especially collective bargaining, by having multinational operations. We shall now examine this issue along with labor union responses to companies' multinationality.

MNE ADVANTAGES

Critics argue that MNES weaken labor because they are able to hold out longer before settling a strike, can easily move to another country where labor conditions are more favorable to them, and are so big and complex that unions cannot determine whether they can afford to meet their demands. Let's now examine these arguments.

Product and Resource Flows   If an MNE can divert output from its facilities in different countries and sell it to the consumers in the country where a strike is occurring, it has little pressure to settle a strike because it continues to receive revenues. Moreover, because each country may comprise only a small percentage of an MNE's total worldwide sales, profits, and cash flows, a strike in one country may affect an MNE's global performance only minimally. So, once again, the MNE has little pressure to settle. By simply holding out longer, it may have an advantage over labor in collective bargaining that a domestic company does not have.

However, the MNE can continue to supply customers in the struck country only if it has excess capacity and produces an identical product in more than one country. Even if these two conditions are present, the MNE would still confront the transport and tariff costs that led it to establish multiple production facilities in the first place. If the MNE partially owns the struck operation, partners or even minority stockholders may balk at sustaining a lengthy work stoppage. Further, if the idle facilities normally produce components needed for integrated production elsewhere, then a strike may have far-reaching effects. For example, because of a strike at one GM facility in the United States, GM's Mexican plants could not get parts needed for assembly operations. However, because of Mexican laws against layoffs, GM had to maintain its Mexican workers on the payroll, thus adding pressure on GM to reach an agreement.[76] In summary, there appear to be advantages of international diversification for collective bargaining, but only in limited circumstances.

Production Switching   Companies sometimes threaten to move production to other countries to reduce labor costs. This pressures unions to demand less so their jobs are more secure. For example, Daimler-Benz's German workers agreed to accept lower wages after the company procured agreements from French, Czech, and British labor to work for less than autoworkers in Germany.[77]

Although sometimes production shifts would seem more plausible when a company has facilities in more than one country, at other times they would seem more plausible when facilities in different countries are owned by different companies. For example, suppose a Canadian company competes with Korean imports from a Korean company. If Canadian workers demand and get substantial wage increases that result in higher product prices, the Korean competitor will likely seize the opportunity to build Canadian market share at the expense of the Canadian company and its workers. But suppose the Korean company also owns the facility in Canada. The Korean management would have to weigh the cost-saving advantages of moving its production from Canada to Korea against the losses it would incur in Canada by discarding its facilities there.

Size and Complexity of MNEs   Observers often say it is difficult for labor unions to deal with MNEs because of the complexities in the location of decision making and the difficulties in interpreting financial data. It often is assumed that when the real decision makers are far removed from the bargaining location, at home-country headquarters, for example, arbitrarily stringent management decisions will result. Conceivably, the opposite might happen, particularly if the demands abroad seem low in comparison with those being made at home. In reality, labor relations usually are delegated to subsidiary management.

Labor may be at a disadvantage in MNE negotiations because the

- *Country bargaining unit is only a small part of MNE activities*
- *MNE may continue serving customers with foreign production or resources*

MNE limitations come from capacity, legal restrictions, shared ownership, integrated production, and differentiated products.

MNEs may threaten workers with the prospect of moving production abroad.

Labor claims it is disadvantaged in dealing with MNEs because

- *Decision making is far away*
- *It is hard to get full data on MNEs' global operations*

Unions examine MNEs' financial data to determine MNEs' ability to meet labor demands. Interpreting these data is complex because of disparities among managerial, tax, and disclosure requirements in home and host countries. Labor has been particularly leery of the possibility that MNEs will use artificial transfer prices (recall the discussion in Chapter 19) to give the appearance that a given subsidiary cannot meet labor demands. However, these concerns place an overreliance on a company's ability to pay rather than on the seemingly more important going-wage rates in the industry and geographic area. Although MNEs may have more complex data, at least one set of financial statements must satisfy local authorities. This set should be no more difficult to interpret than that of a purely local company. In terms of transfer pricing, it is very doubtful that MNEs set artificial levels to aid in collective bargaining situations. If they understate profits in one country, they would have to overstate them elsewhere. This would give them a disadvantage in collective bargaining, where profits are overstated. Moreover, any decision to set artificial transfer prices would also have to consider income taxes, tariffs, and opinions of minority stockholders.

LABOR INITIATIVES

We shall now examine the initiatives that unions can take to counter the power of MNEs. Internationally, they can share information, assist bargaining units in other countries, and deal simultaneously with the MNEs. Nationally, they can pressure for laws that restrict MNEs.

Information Sharing The most common international cooperation among unions is exchanging information, which helps them refute company claims as well as cite precedents from other countries on bargaining issues. International confederations of unions, trade secretariats composed of unions in a single industry or a complex of related industries, and company councils that include representatives from an MNE's plants around the world all participate in the information exchange. European work councils (EWCs) represent a company's employees throughout the European Union. Through an EWC, a company informs and consults with employees on such issues as its corporate strategies so that they do not face global changes unexpectedly, leaving them with little time to react.[78]

> Labor might strengthen its position relative to MNEs through cross-national cooperation.

Assistance to Foreign Bargaining Units Labor groups in one country may support their counterparts in other countries by refusing to work overtime to supply a market normally served by striking workers' production, sending financial aid to workers in other countries, and disrupting work in their own countries. For example, French workers pledged to disrupt work at Pechiney in support of striking workers in the company's U.S. facilities.[79] However, this type of support is still extremely rare.

Simultaneous Actions There have been a few examples of simultaneous negotiations and strikes. But labor's cooperation across borders is a problem because of national differences in union structures and what workers want. The percentage of workers in unions is much higher in some countries than others; for example, it is much higher in Germany than in neighboring France. Many organized workers in France and Portugal belong to communist unions that do not get along with unions representing the bulk of

Looking to the Future
WHICH COUNTRIES WILL HAVE THE JOBS OF THE FUTURE?

As capital and technology continue to become more mobile among countries and companies, human resource development should account increasingly for competitive differences. Consequently, companies' access to and retention of ever more qualified personnel should become more important. This will be a challenge because companies will have more difficulty retaining the highly skilled, highly valued workers in the future.[80]

Demographers are nearly unanimous in projecting that populations will grow much faster in emerging economies (China being an exception) than in industrial countries, at least up to the year 2030. At the same time, in industrial countries the number of retirees as a percentage of the population will grow as people live longer and retire earlier. People will also need to be educated for more years to get the so-called "better jobs." Overall, these industrial-country trends indicate that there will be fewer people to do the productive work within society. Industrial countries may adjust in any of several ways or combinations of them, and each way has a number of social and economic consequences to which MNEs must adapt.

One adjustment might be for industrial countries to encourage emigration from emerging economies, which do not generate enough jobs for their potential workers. In Canada, the United States, and parts of Western Europe, there has been a fairly long-term entry of foreign workers, both legally and illegally, from emerging economies. This entry generates assimilation costs within industrial countries and a brain drain from emerging economies if highly qualified people leave. Further, in economic downturns, unemployed industrial-country citizens will likely blame foreign workers for their plight. Under this scenario, companies will have to spend more time on paperwork for work permits and develop means of incorporating different nationalities into their workforces.

Another potential adjustment in industrial countries is a continued push toward adopting robotics and other labor-saving equipment. Although this may help solve some of the employee shortages in industrial countries, companies will need workers with higher work-skill levels. In fact, less educated members of the workforce may be either unemployable or forced to take lesser-paying jobs in the service sector. Gaps between haves and have-nots thus may widen within industrial countries as well as between those countries and emerging economies. In this scenario, have-nots may pressure governments to pressure companies to shift technological development away from labor-saving priorities.

A third possible adjustment is the acceleration of industry migration to emerging economies to tap ample supplies of labor. At the same time, emerging economies may devise ways to reverse their brain drains, thus shifting even more production away from industrial countries. For example, India is already attempting to do this for the approximately 15 million overseas Indians, many of whom are highly educated and skilled.[81] India is doing this primarily by offering investment incentives and high-interest bank accounts for educated overseas Indians to return. Under this scenario, more low-skilled jobs will go to emerging economies, and industrial-country governments will face a dilemma of what to do with marginal workers.

workers elsewhere in Europe. In addition, both wage rates and workers' preferences differ widely.[82] For instance, Spanish workers are more willing to work on weekends than are German workers. Further, there undoubtedly has been a growing nationalism among workers as their fear of foreign competition has grown.

National Approaches Unions' initiatives to counter MNEs' power have been primarily on a national basis. There is little worker enthusiasm to support workers in another country, because workers tend to view each other as competitors. Even when labor in one country helps labor in another, it may have its own interests in mind. For example, a union representing U.S. tomato pickers helped its Mexican counterpart to win a stronger contract—thus dissuading the Campbell Soup Company from moving operations to Mexico.[83] Even in Canada and the United States, which have long shared a common union membership, there has been a move among Canadian workers to form unions independent of those in the United States. One Canadian organizer summed up much of the attitude by saying, "An American union is not going to fight to protect Canadian jobs at the expense of American jobs." The logic is that international unions will adopt policies favoring the bulk of their membership, which in any joint Canadian-U.S. relationship is bound to be American.

National legislation in some countries has provided for worker representation on boards of directors, regulated the entry of foreign workers, and limited imports and foreign investment outflows. It is probable that most future initiatives will be at the national rather than international level.

WEB CONNECTION

Check out our home page www.prenhall.com/daniels for links to key resources for you in your study of international business.

SUMMARY

- The tasks of international managers differ from those of purely domestic managers in several ways, including needing to know how to adapt home-country practices to foreign locales and being more likely to deal with high-level governmental officials.

- The top-level managers of foreign subsidiaries normally perform much broader duties than do domestic managers with similar cost or profit responsibilities. They must cope with communications problems between corporate headquarters and the subsidiaries, usually with less staff assistance.

- MNEs employ more local than expatriate managers because the locals understand regional operating conditions and may focus more on long-term operations and goals. Doing so also demonstrates that opportunities are available for local citizens, shows consideration for local interests, avoids the red tape of cross-national transfers, and usually is cheaper.

- MNEs transfer people abroad to infuse technical competence and home-country business practices, to control foreign operations, and to develop managers.

- MNEs that transfer personnel abroad should consider how well the people will be accepted, how to treat them when the foreign assignment is over, and how well they will adapt.

- When transferred abroad, an expatriate's compensation usually is increased because of hardship and differences in cost of living.

- Companies frequently acquire personnel abroad by buying existing companies. They also may go into business with local companies, which then assume most staffing responsibilities.

- Two major international training functions are to build a global awareness among managers in general and to equip managers to handle the specific situations entailed in a foreign assignment.

- When setting up a new operation in a foreign country, a company may use existing facilities as guides for determining labor needs. However, it should adjust to compensate for different labor skills, costs, and availabilities.

- When companies depend on an imported labor supply, they encounter special stability, supervision, and training problems.

- Because of national variations in fringe benefits, direct-compensation figures do not accurately reflect the amount a company must pay for a given job. In addition, job-security benefits (no layoffs, severance pay, etc.) add substantially to compensation costs.

- Although per-worker comparisons are useful indicators of labor-cost differences, it is the output associated with total costs that is relevant for international competitiveness. These costs may shift over time, thus changing international competitive positions.

- A country's sociopolitical environment will determine to a great extent the type of relationship between labor and management and affect the number, representation, and organization of unions.

- Codetermination is a type of labor participation in a company's management and usually is intended to cultivate a cooperative rather than an adversarial environment.

- International organizations pressure companies to follow internationally accepted labor practices wherever they operate, regardless of whether the practices conflict with the norms and laws of the host countries.

- MNEs are often blamed for weakening the position of labor in the collective-bargaining process because of those companies' international diversification, threats to export jobs, and complex structures and reporting mechanisms.

- International cooperation among labor groups to confront MNEs is minimal. Labor groups' initiatives include information exchanges, simultaneous negotiations or strikes, and refusals to work overtime to supply the market in a struck country.

CASE

OFFICE EQUIPMENT COMPANY (OEC)[1]

In 2000, the managing director (a U.S. national) of the Office Equipment Company (OEC) in Medellín, Colombia (see Map 21.1), announced suddenly that he would leave within one month. The company had to find a replacement. OEC manufactures a wide variety of small office equipment (such as copying machines, recording machines, mail scales, and paper shredders) in eight different countries and distributes and sells products worldwide. It has no manufacturing facilities in Colombia but has been selling and servicing there since the early 1980s. OEC first tried selling in Colombia through independent importers but quickly became convinced that to make sufficient sales it needed to have its own staff there. Despite Colombia's political tur-moil, which at times has bordered on being a full-scale civil war, OEC's operation there (with about 100 employees) has enjoyed good and improving sales and profitability.

OEC is constructing its first factory in Colombia, scheduled to begin operations in early 2002. This factory will import components for personal computer printers and assemble them locally. Colombia offers an abundant supply of cheap labor, and the assembly operation will employ about 150 people. By assembling locally, OEC expects to ward off trade restrictions on other office equipment it imports for sale within Colombia. This plant's construction is being supervised by a U.S. technical team, and a U.S. expatriate will direct the production. This director will report to

MAP 21.1 Colombia

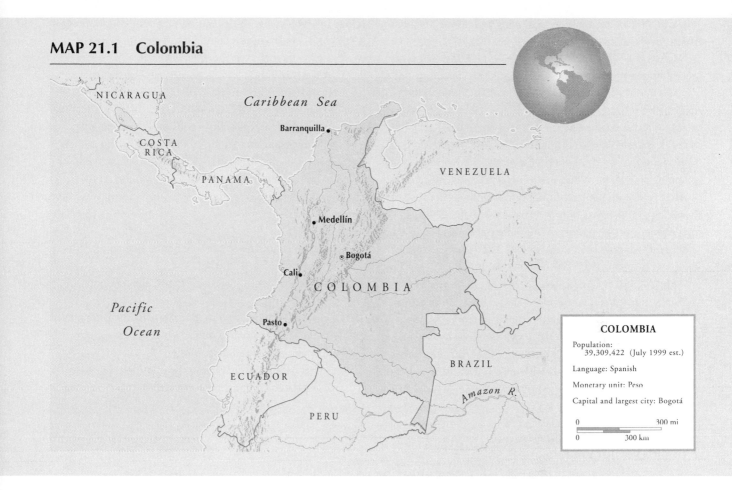

NICARAGUA

Caribbean Sea

Barranquilla

COSTA
RICA

PANAMA

VENEZUELA

Medellín

• Bogotá

Cali

COLOMBIA

*Pacific
Ocean*

Pasto

BRAZIL

ECUADOR

Amazon R.

PERU

COLOMBIA

Population:
39,309,422 (July 1999 est.)

Language: Spanish

Monetary unit: Peso

Capital and largest city: Bogotá

0 — 300 mi
0 — 300 km

OEC's U.S. headquarters on all production and quality-control matters but will report to the managing director in Colombia on all other matters, such as accounting, finance, and labor relations.

OEC, by policy, will replace the exiting managing director with an internal candidate. The company employs a combination of home-, host-, and third-country nationals in top positions in foreign countries, and managers commonly rotate among foreign and U.S. locations. In fact, it has been increasingly evident to OEC that international experience is an important factor in deciding who will be appointed to top corporate positions. The sales and service facility in Colombia reports to a Latin American regional office in the United States. A committee at this office, charged with selecting the new managing director, quickly narrowed its choice to five candidates.

TOM ZIMMERMAN A thirty-year OEC veteran, Zimmerman is well versed in all the technical and sales aspects required in the job. He has never worked abroad for OEC but has visited various of the company's foreign facilities as part of sales teams. His superiors consider him competent. He will retire in about four and a half years. Neither he nor his wife speaks Spanish. Their children are grown and living with their own children in the United States. Zimmerman currently is in charge of an operation that is about the size of that in Colombia after the new factory begins operating. However, Zimmerman's present position will become redundant because the operation he heads is being merged with another.

BRETT HARRISON Harrison, 40, has spent fifteen years at OEC. His superiors consider him highly competent and capable of moving into upper-level management within the next few years. He has never been based abroad but has worked for the last three years in the Latin American regional office and frequently travels to Latin America. Both he and his wife speak Spanish adequately, and their two children, ages 14 and 15, are just beginning to study the language.

His wife holds a responsible marketing position with a pharmaceuticals company.

CAROLYN MOYER   Moyer joined OEC twelve years ago after getting her MBA from a prestigious university. At 37, she has already moved between staff and line positions of growing responsibility. For two years, she was second in command of a product group that was about the size of the newly expanded one in Colombia. Her performance in that post was considered excellent. Currently, she works on a planning staff team. When she joined OEC, she indicated her interest in eventual international responsibilities because of her undergraduate major in international affairs. She has recently expressed interest in international duties because of a belief it will help her advancement. She speaks Spanish well and is unmarried.

FRANCISCO CABRERA   Cabrera, 35, currently is an assistant managing director in the larger Mexican operation, which produces and sells for the Mexican market. A Mexican citizen, he has worked for OEC in Mexico for all his twelve years with the company. He holds an MBA from a Mexican university and is considered to be a likely candidate to head the Mexican operation when the present managing director

retires in seven years. He is married with four children (ages 2 to 7) and speaks English adequately. His wife does not work outside the home or speak English.

JUAN MORENO   At 27, Moreno is assistant to the present managing director in Colombia. He has held that position since joining OEC upon his U.S. college graduation four years ago. Unmarried, he is considered competent, especially in employee relations, but lacking in experience. He had been successful in increasing OEC's sales, in part because he is well connected with local families who can afford to buy new office equipment for their businesses.

QUESTIONS

1. Which candidate should the committee choose for the assignment, and why?
2. What problems might each candidate encounter in the position?
3. How might OEC go about minimizing the problems that each candidate would have in managing the Colombian operations?
4. What factors would need to be considered in each candidate's compensation package?

CHAPTER NOTES

1 The data for the case were taken from Edwin McDowell, "Making It in America: The Foreign-Born Executive," *New York Times*, June 1, 1980, Section 3, p. 11; Don Whitehead, *The Dow Story* (New York: McGraw-Hill, 1968); Paul L. Blocklyn, "Developing the International Executive," *Personnel*, Vol. 66, March 1989, pp. 44–47; "Globesmanship," *Across the Board*, Vol. 27, Nos. 1, 2, January–February 1990, pp. 24–34; "Popoff on Challenges for Dow and for the Industry," *Chemical Week*, May 18, 1994, pp. 26–28; Susan J. Sinsworth, "Issues Management Is Central to Frank Popoff's Globalization Strategy," *Chemical Engineering News*, Vol. 72, No. 21, May 23, 1994, pp. 25–29; Gordon Petrash, "Dow's Journey to a Knowledge Value Management Culture," *European Management Journal*, Vol. 14, No. 4, August 1996, pp. 365–373; and Vijay Govindarajan and Anil Gupta, "Success Is All in the Mindset," *Financial Times*, February 27, 1998, mastering global business section, p. 2.

2 Gary R. Oddou and Mark E. Mendenhall, "Succession Planning for the 21st Century: How Well Are We Grooming Our Future Business Leaders?" *Business Horizons*, January–February 1991, pp. 26–34.

3 Gordon Petrash, "Dow's Journey to a Knowledge Value Management Culture," *European Management Journal*, Vol. 14, No. 4, August 1996, pp. 365–373.

4 "Globesmanship," *Across the Board*, Vol. 27, Nos. 1, 2, January–February 1990, p. 26, quoting Michael Angus.

5 John M. Hannon, Ing-Chung Huang, and Bih-Shiaw Jaw, "International Human Resource Strategy and Its Determinants: The Case of Subsidiaries in Taiwan," *Journal of International Business Studies*, Vol. 26, No. 3, Third Quarter 1995, pp. 531–554.

6 Matt Hamblen, "NetMeeting Cuts Dow Travel Expenses," *Computerworld*, Vol. 32, No. 10, March 9, 1998, p. 20.

7 Wayne E. Cascio and Manuel G. Serapio, Jr., "Human Resources Systems in an International Alliance: The Undoing of a Done Deal?" *Organizational Dynamics*, Winter 1991, pp. 63–75; and Heinz-Dieter Meyer, "The Cultural Gap in Long-Term International Work Groups: A German-American Case Study," *European Management Journal*, Vol. 11, No. 1, March 1993, pp. 93–101.

8 David A. Weeks, *Recruiting and Selecting International Managers*, Report No. 998 (New York: The Conference Board, 1992).

9 Kendall Roth, "Managing International Interdependence: CEO Characteristics in a Resource-Based Framework," *Academy of Management Journal*, Vol. 38, No. 1, 1995, pp. 200–231.

10 Sully Taylor, Schon Beechler, and Nancy Napier, "Toward An Integrative Model of Strategic International Resource Management," *Academy of Management Review*, Vol. 21, No. 4, 1996, pp. 959–985, discusses these in the context of multidomestic and a combination of global and transnational strategies.

11 See, for example, Terri A. Scandura, Mary Ann Von Glinow, and Kevin B. Lowe, "When East Meets West: Leadership 'Best Practices' in the United States and the Middle East," *Advances in Global Leadership*, Vol. 1, 1999, pp. 233–246.

12 Ricahrd S. DeFrank, Robert Konopaske, and John M. Ivancevich, "Executive Travel Stress: Perils of the Road Warrior," *Academy of Management Executive*, vol. 14, no. 2, May 2000, pp. 58–71.

13 For a good discussion of the adjustment problem, see Joann S. Lublin, "More Toasts, Less Sleep: The Globe-Trotting CEO," *Wall Street Journal*, November 19, 1998, p. B1.

14 Raj Persaud, "Too Much Jetlag Can Damage Your Mind," *Business Traveler,* May 2000, p. 21.

15 Jonathan Kaufman, "On the Road Again," *Wall Street Journal,* November 19, 1996, p. A1.

16 David C. Waring, "Doing Business Overseas," *Cornell Enterprise,* Fall–Winter 1988, p. 29.

17 Robert Taylor, "Companies Cut Back Overseas Transfer Benefits," *Financial Times,* July 18, 1996, p. 1, reporting a survey by Monks Partnership, an independent remuneration adviser.

18 Weeks, *Recruiting and Selecting International Managers.*

19 For a good example of IBM in Korea, see Edward E. Lucente, *Managing a Global Enterprise,* Working Paper No. 94-2 (Pittsburgh: Carnegie Bosch Institute for Applied Studies in International Management, 1993).

20 Peter Coy and Neil Gross, "When the Going Gets Tough, Yanks Get Yanked," *Business Week,* April 26, 1993, p. 30.

21 "Workers Foot the Bill: Nike," *South China Sunday Morning Post,* March 5, 1995, agenda section, p. 1; and "Politically Incorrect," *Industry Week,* November 1, 1999, p. 23.

22 Steven Greenhouse, "Voluntary Rules on Apparel Proving Elusive," *New York Times,* February 1, 1997, p. 1.

23 Joseph Perreira, "Reebok Finds Ills at Indonesian Factories," *Wall Street Journal,* October 18, 1999, p. A3; and Lisa Bannon, "Mattel's Asian Plants Will Address Problems," *Wall Street Journal,* November 18, 1999, p. B15.

24 Robert Taylor, "ILO Seeks Ban on Worst Child Labor Abuse," *Financial Times,* June 8, 1999, p. 6.

25 "Child Labour Code Agreed," *Financial Times,* September 5, 1996, p. 4.

26 Kirsten Downey Grimsley, "Working Matters: Job Relocation Gets Derailed," *Los Angeles Times,* November 1, 1999, Southern California Living section, p. 1.

27 Valerie Frazee, "Relo Administrators Believe Expats Are Overpaid," *Business and Management Practices,* Vol. 3, No. 4, July 1998, p. 4, quoting a survey by Runzheimer International of 103 international relocation administrators from U.S.-based companies showing that 72 percent feel pressure to cut the costs, and 52 percent are responding by hiring locals.

28 Jeffrey Ball, "DaimlerChrysler's Transfer Woes," *Wall Street Journal,* August 24, 1999, p. B1.

29 "The Elusive Euro-Manager," *The Economist,* November 7, 1992, p. 83; and Barry Newman, "Expat Archipelago," *Wall Street Journal,* December 12, 1995, p. A1.

30 Ingmar Bjorkman and Annette Schaap, "Outsiders in the Middle Kingdom: Expatriate Managers in Chinese–Western Joint Ventures," *European Management Journal,* Vol. 12, No. 2, 1994, pp. 147–153.

31 Martine Gertsen, "Intercultural Competence and Expatriates," Working Paper No. 1, 1990,

Copenhagen School of Economics and Business Administration, Institute of International Economics and Management.

32 J. Stewart Black and Mark Mendenhall, "Cross-Cultural Training Effectiveness: A Review and a Theoretical Framework for Future Research," *Academy of Management Review,* Vol. 15, No. 1, January 1990, p. 117.

33 John D. Daniels and Gary Insch, "Why Are Early Departure Rates from Foreign Assignments Lower than Historically Reported?" *Multinational Business Review,* Vol. VI, No. 1, Spring 1998, pp. 13–23.

34 Jack Anderson, "The Survey's In: Although Costly, Good Expatriate Executives Are Sound Investments," *International Herald Tribune,* September 3–4, 1994, p. 15, referring to a study by the Confederation of Business and Industry and Ernst & Young of 600 MNEs; and Meg G. Birdseye and Jon S. Hill, "Individual, Organizational/Work and Environmental Influences on Expatriate Turnover Tendencies: An Empirical Study," *Journal of International Business Studies,* Vol. 26, No. 4, Fourth Quarter 1995, pp. 787–813.

35 Karen Dawn Stuart, "Teens Play a Role in Moves Overseas," *Personnel Journal,* March 1992, pp. 72–78. PHH Relocation estimated that for 1995, the top three locations for U.S. transfers were Mexico, Chile, and Belgium in "At Home Abroad," *Wall Street Journal,* February 2, 1996. A survey by Windham International of 138 companies indicated that the expected biggest relocations for 1996 would be China, India, and Mexico in "China Blues," *Wall Street Journal,* March 19, 1996, p. A1.

36 J. Stewart Black and Hal B. Gregersen, "The Right Way to Manage Expats," *Harvard Business Review,* March–April 1999, pp. 52–61.

37 Patricia Feltes, Robert K. Robinson, and Ross L. Fink, "American Female Expatriates and the Civil Rights Act of 1991: Balancing Legal and Business Interests," *Business Horizons,* March–April 1993, pp. 82–86.

38 R. I. Westwood and S. M. Leung, "The Female Expatriate Manager Experience," *International Studies of Management & Organization,* Vol. 24, No. 3, 1994, pp. 64–85; and Sully Taylor and Nancy Napier, "Working in Japan: Lessons from Women Expatriates," *Sloan Management Review,* Spring 1996, pp. 76–84.

39 Paula M. Caligiuri and Wayne F. Cascio, "Can We Send Her There? Maximizing the Success of Western Women in Global Assignments," *Journal of World Business,* Vol. 33, No. 4, 1998, pp. 394–416.

40 Kerr Inkson, Judith Pringle, Michael B. Arthur, and Sean Barry, "Expatriate Assignment Versus Overseas Experience: Contrasting Models of International Human Resource Development," *Journal of World Business,* Vol. 32, No. 4, 1997, pp. 351–368.

41 Windham International and National Foreign Trade Council, *Global Relocation Trend: 1994 Survey Report,* November 1994.

42 Jodi Zurawski, "Plan for Expatriates: 'Welcome Home' Before They Say 'Bon Voyage,'" *Human Resources Professional,* Summer 1992, pp. 42–44; and Linda K. Stroh, Hal B. Gregersen, and J. Stewart Black, "Closing the Gap: Expectations Versus Reality Among Repatriates," *Journal of World Business,* Vol. 33, No. 2, 1998, pp. 111–124.

43 Newman, "Export Archipelago."

44 Amanda Bennett, "What's an Expatriate?" *Wall Street Journal,* April 21, 1993, p. R5.

45 Claudia H. Deutsch, "Getting the Brightest to Go Abroad," *New York Times,* June 17, 1990, p. C1.

46 Ibid. Most indications are that these involve a minority of companies; however, Weeks, *Recruiting and Selecting International Managers,* found the inclusion of international experience in succession plans of 61 percent of large companies.

47 Bennett, "What's an Expatriate?" referring to a study by Organizational Resources Counselors involving 45 companies.

48 Robert Taylor, "Recruitment: World of Difference in Human Resources," *Financial Times,* January 7, 2000, p. 11.

49 Ibid.; and Judith Rehak, "Overseas Fat Cats Face Tough Order. Slim Down," *International Herald Tribune,* May 11–12, 1996, p. 17.

50 George T. Milkovich and George T. Bloom, "Rethinking International Compensation," *Compensation and Benefits Review,* January 1998, pp. 15–23.

51 Geoffrey W. Latta, "Expatriate Policy and Practice: A Ten-Year Comparison of Trends," *Compensation and Benefits Review,* Vol. 31, No. 4, July–August 1999, pp. 35–39, quoting studies by Organization Resources Counselors.

52 Alison Maitland, "A Hard Balancing Act: Management of Dual Careers," *Financial Times,* May 10, 1999, management section, p. 11.

53 Diane E. Lewis, "Families Make, Break Overseas Moves," *Boston Globe,* October 4, 1998, p. 5D.

54 Christopher A. Bartlett and Sumantra Ghoshal, "What Is a Global Manager?" *Harvard Business Review,* September–October 1992, pp. 124–132.

55 P. Christopher Earley, "Intercultural Training for Managers: A Comparison of Documentary and Interpersonal Methods," *Academy of Management Journal,* Vol. 30, No. 4, December 1987, pp. 685–698.

56 J. Stewart Black and Hal B. Gregersen, "Serving Two Masters: Managing the Dual Allegiance of Expatriate Employees," *Sloan Management Review,* Summer 1992, pp. 61–71, covers the typologies of expatriates.

57 Vincent Cable, "The Diminished Nation-State: A Study In the Loss of Economic Power," *Daedalus,* Vol. 124, No. 2, 1995, pp. 22–53.

58 "Foreign Workers in Germany," *The Economist*, April 22, 1995, pp. 67–68.

59 Timothy Aeppel, "A Passage to India Eases a Worker Scarcity in Ohio," *Wall Street Journal*, October 5, 1999, p. B1.

60 Aviva Geva, "Moral Problems of Employing Foreign Workers," *Business Ethics Quarterly*, Vol. 9, No. 3, July 1999, pp. 381–403.

61 Chao C. Chen, "New Trends in Rewards Allocation Preferences: A Sino-U.S. Comparison," *Academy of Management Journal*, Vol. 38, No. 2, 1995, pp. 408–428.

62 Paul S. Hempel, "Designing Multinational Benefits Programs: The Role of National Culture," *Journal of World Business*, Vol. 33, No. 3, 1998, pp. 277–294.

63 "In Europe, Cash Eases the Pain of Getting Fired," *Business Week*, March 16, 1992, p. 26; and Greg Steinmetz, "Americans, Too, Run Afoul of Rigorous German Rules," *Wall Street Journal*, February 2, 1996, p. A6.

64 Roy B. Helfgott, "Labor Market Models in Europe and America and Unhappiness with Both," *Business Horizons*, Vol. 39, No. 2, March–April 1996, pp. 77–84.

65 Bob Davis, "Illusory Bargain," *Wall Street Journal*, September 15, 1993, p. A11.

66 "Asia's Costly Labour Problems," *The Economist*, September 21, 1996, p. 62.

67 Steve Glain, "Korea Is Overthrown as Sneaker Champ," *Wall Street Journal*, October 7, 1993, p. A12.

68 Robert Taylor, "Challenge Facing Endangered Species," *Financial Times*, August 14, 1995, p. 10; and "Adapt or Die," *The Economist*, July 1, 1995, p. 54.

69 Frances Bairstow, "The Trend Toward Centralized Bargaining—A Patchwork Quilt of International Diversity" Colombia Journal of World Business, Spring 1985, pp. 75–83.

70 Eamonn Fingleton, *Blindside: Why Japan Is Still on Track to Overtake the U.S. by the Year 2000* (New York: Houghton Mifflin, 1995).

71 John T. Addison, "Nonunion Representation in Germany," *Journal of Labor Research*, Vol. 20, No. 1, Winter 1999, pp. 73–91.

72 Ralph T. King, Jr., "Jeans Therapy," *Wall Street Journal*, May 20, 1998, p. A1.

73 Amal Kumar Naj, "Shifting Gears," *Wall Street Journal*, May 5, 1993, p. A1.

74 Francis Williams, "ILO Boycott Urged over Burma 'Slavery,'" *Financial Times*, June 16, 1999, p. 8.

75 Unless otherwise noted, information in this section is taken largely from the following treatises: Gerald B. J. Bomers and Richard B. Peterson, "Multinational Corporations and the Industrial Relations: The Case of West Germany and the Netherlands," *British Journal of Industrial Relations*, March 1977, pp. 45–62; Duane A. Kujawa, "Collective Bargaining and Labor Relations in Multinational Enterprise: A U.S. Policy Perspective," paper presented at New York University Conference on Economic Issues of Multinational Firms, November 1976; Duane Kujawa, "U.S. Manufacturing Investment in the Developing Countries: American Labour's Concerns and the Enterprise Environment in the Decade Ahead," *British Journal of Industrial Relations*, Vol. 19, No. 1, March 1981, pp. 38–48; and Roy B. Helfgott, "American Unions and Multinational Enterprises: A Case of Misplaced Emphasis," *Columbia Journal of World Business*, Vol. 18, No. 2, Summer 1983, pp. 81–86.

76 Neil Templin, "GM Strike Hits Mexican Output as Talks on Settlement Resume," *Wall Street Journal*, March 20, 1996, p. A3.

77 Steinmetz, "Americans, Too, Run Afoul of Rigorous German Rules."

78 D. Van Den Bulcke, *The European Works Council: A New Challenge for Multinational Enterprises* (Antwerp: University of Antwerp Centre for International Management and Development Discussion Paper No. 1996/E/26, 1996); and Robert Taylor, "Unions to Join Works Council at Philip Morris," *Financial Times*, January 30, 1996, p. 1.

79 David Moberg, "Like Business, Unions Must Go Global," *New York Times*, December 19, 1993, p. F13.

80 For a good discussion of the changing power of employees, see Frank P. Doyle, "The Changing Workplace: People Power: The Global Human Resource Challenge for the 1990s," *Columbia Journal of World Business*, Vol. 25, Nos. 1, 2, Spring–Summer 1990, pp. 36–45.

81 James Kynge, "India Seeks to Reverse Its Brain Drain," *Financial Times*, June 27, 1996, p. 4.

82 Steven E. Gross and Per L. Winterup, "Global Pay? Maybe Not Yet," *Compensation and Benefits Review*, Vol. 30, No. 4, July 1999, pp. 25–34.

83 Moberg, "Like Business, Unions Must Go Global."

PART SEVEN: OPERATIONS: MANAGING BUSINESS FUNCTIONS INTERNATIONALLY
McDONALD'S

Every day McDonald's serves more than 43 million people in 119 countries around the world. That adds up to more than *15 billion* customer visits a year.

From modest beginnings as a simple hamburger chain that opened in Illinois in 1954, McDonald's has grown to consist of 27,000 restaurants around the world. Almost 1,800 new stores were added in 1999, about 90 percent of them outside the United States. The company has opened its 3,000th restaurant in Japan, its 1,000th in Germany, and its 1,000th in the United Kingdom. McDonald's accounts for nearly half of all of the globally branded fast-food restaurants outside the United States, but achieves nearly two-thirds of the total sales in its industry. Management attributes this huge market share to the power of its brand.

The company has earned nearly 18 percent annual total return to shareholders over the past 10 years, with a free cash flow of more than $1.1 billion in 1999. That represents a 29 percent increase over 1998. In all market segments, at home and abroad, sales for 1999 increased in constant currencies (a measure that excludes the effect of foreign currency translation on reported results, except for hyperinflationary economies such as Russia, whose functional currency is the U.S. dollar). The annual increases in sales in constant currencies were 12 percent in Europe, 6 percent in Asia and the Pacific, and 15 percent in Latin America. U.S. sales increased 5 percent for the year. Consolidated operating income was over $3 billion, an increase of 10 percent in constant currencies.

Weak foreign currencies negatively affected translated sales and revenues from abroad. Revenues in Latin America were adversely affected by the currency devaluation in Brazil and by difficult economic conditions in several markets, whose severity the firm had underestimated. This was partially offset by a positive translation affect of the strong

Japanese yen. Under McDonald's affiliate structure in Japan, the company records a royalty in revenue based on a percentage of Japan's sales. Even though overall revenues were positively affected by the impact of the strong yen on Japan's revenues, the impact of the strong yen was even greater on sales. This is so because all of Japan's sales are included in systemwide sales, whereas Japanese revenues included in total revenues is a much smaller number. In all, foreign currency translation negatively affected combined operating margins (those of both company-operated and franchised restaurants) by $108 million, or 3 percent for the year.

McDonald's also added three new brands in 1999—Donatos Pizza and Boston Market, both in the United States, and Aroma Café in the United Kingdom.

McDonald's has always been a franchising company and remains committed to franchising as its primary way of doing business both at home and abroad. About 80 percent of its restaurants worldwide are franchisee owned and operated.

QUESTIONS

As you watch the video, be prepared to answer the following questions:

1. What are the special accounting problems an international firm like McDonald's encounters when it operates abroad? How does McDonald's deal with some of these?

2. How does a company like McDonald's benefit from having operations in so many different parts of the world?

3. Do you think the idea of a single currency like the euro offers an advantage or a disadvantage to an international firm? Why?

4. How does taxation affect the international business of a firm like McDonald's?

Glossary

Absolute advantage: A theory first presented by Adam Smith, which holds that because certain countries can produce some goods more efficiently than other countries can, they should specialize in and export those things they can produce more efficiently and trade for other things they need.

Acceptable quality level: A concept of quality control whereby managers are willing to accept a certain level of production defects, which are dealt with through repair facilities and service centers.

Accounting: The process of identifying, recording, and interpreting economic events.

Acquired advantage: A form of trade advantage due to technology rather than the availability of natural resources, climate, etc.

Acquired group memberships: Affiliations not determined by birth, such as religions, political affiliations, and professional and other associations.

Acquisition: The purchase of one company by another company.

Active income: Income of a CFC that is derived from the active conduct of a trade or business, as specified by the U.S. Internal Revenue Code.

Ad valorem duty: A duty (tariff) assessed as a percentage of the value of the item.

ADR: *See* American Depositary Receipt.

Advance import deposit: A deposit prior to the release of foreign exchange, required by some governments.

AFTA: *See* ASEAN Free Trade Area.

ALADI: *See* Latin American Integration Association.

American Depositary Receipt (ADR): A negotiable certificate issued by a U.S. bank in the United States to represent the underlying shares of a foreign corporation's stock held in trust at a custodian bank in the foreign country.

American system: *See* U.S. terms.

Andean Group (ANCOM): A South American form of economic integration involving Bolivia, Colombia, Ecuador, Peru, and Venezuela.

APEC: *See* Asia Pacific Economic Cooperation.

Appropriability theory: The theory that companies will favor foreign direct investment over such non-equity operating forms as licensing arrangements so that potential competitors will be less likely to gain access to proprietary information.

Arbitrage: The process of buying and selling foreign currency at a profit resulting from price discrepancies between or among markets.

Area division: *See* Geographic division.

Arm's-length price: A price between two companies that do not have an ownership interest in each other.

Ascribed group memberships: Affiliations determined by birth, such as those based on gender, family, age, caste, and ethnic, racial, or national origin.

ASEAN: *See* Association of South East Asian Nations.

ASEAN Free Trade Area (AFTA): A free-trade area formed by the ASEAN countries on January 1, 1993, with the goal of cutting tariffs on all intrazonal trade to a maximum of 5 percent by January 1, 2008.

Asia Pacific Economic Cooperation (APEC): A cooperation formed by twenty-one countries that border the Pacific Rim to promote multilateral economic cooperation in trade and investment in the Pacific Rim.

Association of South East Asian Nations (ASEAN): A free-trade area involving the Asian countries of Brunei, Indonesia, Malaysia, the Philippines, Singapore, and Thailand.

Back-to-back loan: A loan that involves a company in Country A with a subsidiary in Country B, and a bank in Country B with a branch in Country A.

Balance of payments: Statement that summarizes all economic transactions between a country and the rest of the world during a given period of time.

Balance-of-payments deficit: An imbalance of some specific component within the balance of payments, such as merchandise trade or current account, that implies that a country is importing more than it exports.

Balance-of-payments surplus: An imbalance in the balance of payments that exists when a country exports more than it imports.

Balance of trade: The value of a country's exports less the value of its imports ("trade" can be defined as merchandise trade, services, unilateral transfers, or a combination of these).

Balance on goods and services: The value of a country's exports of merchandise trade and services minus imports.

Bank for International Settlements (BIS): A bank in Basel, Switzerland that facilitates transactions among central banks, effectively the central banks' central bank.

Bargaining school theory: A theory holding that the negotiated terms for foreign investors depend on how much investors and host countries need each other's assets.

Barter: The exchange of goods for goods instead of for money.

Base currency: The currency whose value is implicitly 1 when a quote is made between two currencies; for example, if the cruzeiro is trading at 2962.5 cruzeiros per dollar, the dollar is the base currency and the cruzeiro is the quoted currency.

Basic balance: The net current account plus long-term capital within a country's balance of payments.

Bid (buy): The amount a trader is willing to pay for foreign exchange.

Bill of exchange: *See* Commercial bill of exchange.

Bill of lading: A document that is issued to a shipper by a carrier, listing the goods received for shipment.

BIRPI: *See* International Bureau for the Protection of Industrial Property Rights.

BIS: *See* Bank for International Settlements.

Black market: The foreign-exchange market that lies outside the official market.

Body language: The way people move their bodies, gesture, position themselves, etc., to convey meaning to others.

Bonded warehouse: A building or part of a building used for the storage of imported merchandise under supervision of the U.S. Customs Service and for the purpose of deferring payment of customs duties.

Booking center: An offshore financial center whose main function is to act as an accounting center in order to minimize the payment of taxes.

Branch (foreign): A foreign operation of a company that is not a separate entity from the parent that owns it.

Brand: A particular good identified with a company by means of name, logo, or other method, usually protected with a trademark registration.

Bretton Woods Agreement: An agreement among IMF countries to promote exchange-rate stability and to facilitate the international flow of currencies.

Broker (in foreign exchange): Specialists who facilitate transactions in the interbank market.

Buffer-stock system: A partially managed system that utilizes stocks of commodities to regulate their prices.

Bundesbank: The German central bank.

Buy local legislation: Laws that are intended to favor the purchase of domestically sourced goods or services over imported ones, even though the imports may be a better buy.

Buybacks: Counterdeliveries related to, or originating from, an original export.

CACM: *See* Central American Common Market.

Canada-U.S. Free Trade Agreement: An agreement, enacted in 1989, establishing a free-trade area involving the United States and Canada.

Capital account: A measure of transactions involving previously existing rather than currently produced assets.

Capital market: The market for stocks and long-term debt instruments.

Capitalism: An economic system characterized by private ownership, pricing, production, and distribution of goods.

Caribbean Community and Common Market (CARICOM): A customs union in the Caribbean region.

CARICOM: *See* Caribbean Community and Common Market.

Caste: A social class separated from others by heredity.

CEFTA: *See* Central European Free Trade Association.

Central American Common Market (CACM): A customs union in Central America.

Central bank: A governmental "bank for banks," customarily responsible for a country's monetary policy.

Central European Free Trade Association (CEFTA): An association which went into effect on July 1, 1992, with an initial membership of the Czech Republic, Slovakia, Hungary, and Poland, and whose goal was to establish a free trade area that includes the basic trade structure of the EU by the year 2000.

Centralization: The situation in which decision making is done at the home office rather than the country level.

Centrally planned economy (CPE): *See* Command economy.

Certificate of origin: A shipping document that determines the origin of products and is usually validated by an external source, such as a chamber of commerce; it helps countries determine the specific tariff schedule for imports.

CFC: *See* Controlled foreign corporation.

Chaebol: Korean business groups that are similar to *keiretsu* and also contain a trading company as part of the group.

Chicago Mercantile Exchange: The largest commodity exchange in the world, dealing primarily in agricultural products, U.S. treasury bills, coins, and some metals.

CIA: The Central Intelligence Agency, a U.S. governmental agency charged with gathering intelligence information abroad.

Civil law system: A legal system based on a very detailed set of laws that are organized into a code; countries with a civil law system, also called a codified legal system, include Germany, France, and Japan.

Civil liberties: The freedom to develop one's own views and attitudes.

COCOM: *See* Coordinating Committee on Multilateral Exports.

Code of conduct: A set of principles guiding the actions of MNEs in their contacts with societies.

Codetermination: A process by which both labor and management participate in the management of a company.

Codified legal system: *See* Civil law system.

Collaborative arrangement: A formal, long-term contractual agreement among companies.

COMECON: *See* Council for Mutual Economic Assistance.

Command economy: An economic system in which resources are allocated and controlled by government decision.

Commercial bill of exchange: An instrument of payment in international business that instructs the importer to forward payment to the exporter.

Commercial invoice: A bill for goods from the buyer to the seller.

Commission on Transnational Corporations: A United Nations agency that deals with multinational enterprises.

Commodities: Basic raw materials or agricultural products.

Commodity agreement: A form of economic cooperation designed to stabilize and raise the price of a commodity.

Common law system: A legal system based on tradition, precedent, and custom and usage, in which the courts interpret the law based on those conventions; found in the United Kingdom and former British colonies.

Common market: A form of regional economic integration in which countries abolish internal tariffs, use a common external tariff, and abolish restrictions on factor mobility.

Communism: A form of totalitarianism initially theorized by Karl Marx in which the political and economic systems are virtually inseparable.

Communitarian paradigm: The government defines needs and priorities and partners with business in a major way.

Comparable access: A protectionist argument that companies and industries should have the same access to foreign markets as foreign industries and companies have to their markets.

Comparative advantage: The theory that there may still be global efficiency gains from trade if a country specializes in those products that it can produce more efficiently than other products.

Compound duty: A tax placed on goods traded internationally, based on value plus units.

Concentration strategy: A strategy by which an international company builds up operations quickly in one or a few countries before going to another.

Confirmed letter of credit: A letter of credit to which a bank in the exporter's country adds its guarantee of payment.

Conservatism: A characteristic of accounting systems that implies that companies are hesitant to disclose high profits or profits that are consistent with their actual operating results; more common in Germanic countries.

Consolidation: An accounting process in which financial statements of related entities, such as a parent and its subsidiaries, are combined to yield a unified set of financial statements; in the process, transactions among the related enterprises are eliminated so that the statements reflect transactions with outside parties.

Consortium: The joining together of several entities, such as companies or governments, in order to strengthen the possibility of achieving some objective.

Consular invoice: A document that covers all the usual details of the commercial invoice and packing list, prepared in the language of the foreign country for which the goods are destined, on special forms obtainable from the consulate or authorized commercial printers.

Consumer-directed market economy: An economy in which there is minimal government participation while growth is promoted through the mobility of production factors, including high labor turnover.

Consumer price index: A measure of the cost of typical wage-earner purchases of goods and services expressed as a percentage of the cost of these same goods and services in some base period.

Consumer sovereignty: The freedom of consumers to influence production through the choices they make.

Continental terms: *See* European terms.

Control: The planning, implementation, evaluation, and correction of performance to ensure that organizational objectives are achieved.

Controlled foreign corporation (CFC): A foreign corporation of which more than 50 percent of the voting stock is owned by U.S. shareholders (taxable entities that own at least 10 percent of the voting stock of the corporation).

Convertibility: The ability to exchange one currency for another currency without restrictions.

Coordination: Linking or integrating activities into a unified system.

Copyright: The right to reproduce, publish, and sell literary, musical, or artistic works.

Corporate culture: The common values shared by employees in a corporation, which form a control mechanism that is implicit and helps enforce other explicit control mechanisms.

Correspondent (bank): A bank in which funds are kept by another, usually foreign, bank to facilitate check clearing and other business relationships.

Cost-of-living adjustment: An increase in compensation given to an expatriate employee when foreign living costs are more expensive than those in the home country.

Council for Mutual Economic Assistance (CMEA or COME-CON): A regional form of economic integration that involved essentially those communist countries considered to be within the Soviet bloc; terminated in 1991.

Council of Ministers: One of the five major institutions of the EU; composed of one member from each country in the EU and entrusted with making major policy decisions.

Countertrade: A reciprocal flow of goods or services valued and settled in monetary terms.

Country analysis: A process of examining the economic strategy of a nation state, taking a holistic approach to understanding how a country, and in particular its government, has behaved, is behaving, and may behave.

Country-similarity theory: The theory that a producer, having developed a new product in response to observed market conditions in the home market, will turn to markets that are most similar to those at home.

Country size theory: The theory that larger countries are generally more self-sufficient than smaller countries.

Court of Justice: One of the five major institutions of the EU; composed of one member from each country in the EU and serves as a supreme appeals court for EU law.

CPE (centrally planned economy): *See* Command economy.

Creolization: The process by which elements of an outside culture are introduced.

Cross-licensing: The exchange of technology by different companies.

Cross rate: An exchange rate between two currencies used in the spot market and computed from the exchange rate of each currency in relation to the U.S. dollar.

Cultural imperialism: Change by imposition.

Cultural relativism: The belief that behavior has meaning and can be judged only in its specific cultural context.

Culture: The specific learned norms of a society, based on attitudes, values, and beliefs.

Culture shock: A generalized trauma one experiences in a new and different culture because of having to learn and cope with a vast array of new cues and expectations.

Currency swaps: The exchange of principal and interest payments.

Current-account balance: Exports minus imports of goods, services, and unilateral transfers.

Current-rate method: A method of translating foreign-currency financial statements that is used when the functional currency is that of the local operating environment.

Customs duties: Taxes imposed on imported goods.

Customs union: A form of regional economic integration that eliminates tariffs among member nations and establishes common external tariffs.

Customs valuation: The value of goods on which customs authorities charge tariffs.

Debt-service ratio: The ratio of interest payments plus principal amortization to exports.

Decentralization: The situation in which decisions tend to be made at lower levels in a company or at the country-operating level rather than at headquarters.

Deferral: The postponing of taxation of foreign-source income until it is remitted to the parent company.

Demand conditions: Includes three dimensions: the composition of home demand (or the nature of buyer needs), the size and pattern of growth of home demand, and the internationalization of demand.

Democracy: A political system that relies on citizens' participation in the decision-making process.

Dependencia theory: The theory holding that LDCs have practically no power when dealing with MNEs as host countries.

Dependency: A state in which a country is too dependent on the sale of one primary commodity and/or too dependent on one country as a customer and supplier.

Derivative: A foreign-exchange instrument such as an option or futures contract that derives its value from some underlying financial instrument.

Derivatives market: Market in which forward contracts, futures, options, and swaps are traded in order to hedge or protect foreign-exchange transactions.

Devaluation: A formal reduction in the value of a currency in relation to another currency; the foreign-currency equivalent of the devalued currency falls.

Developed country: High-income country.

Developing country: A poor country, also known as an emerging country.

Direct foreign investment: *See* Foreign direct investment.

Direct identification drawback: A provision that allows U.S. firms to use imported components in the manufacturing process without having to include the duty paid on the imported goods in costs and sales prices.

Direct investment: *See* Foreign direct investment.

Direct quote: A quote expressed in terms of the number of units of the domestic currency given for one unit of a foreign currency.

Direct selling: A sale of goods by an exporter directly to distributors or final consumers rather than to trading companies or other intermediaries in order to achieve greater control over the marketing function and to earn higher profits.

Directive: A proposed form of legislation in the EU.

Disclosure: The presentation of information and discussion of results.

Discount (in foreign exchange): A situation in which the forward rate for a foreign currency is less than the spot rate, assuming that the domestic currency is quoted on a direct basis.

Distribution: The course—physical path or legal title—that goods take between production and consumption.

Distributor: A merchant in a foreign country that purchases products from the manufacturer and sells them at a profit.

Diversification: A process of becoming less dependent on one or a few customers or suppliers.

Diversification strategy: A strategy by which an international company produces or sells in many countries to avoid relying on one particular market.

Divestment: Reduction in the amount of investment.

Documentary draft: An instrument instructing the importer to pay the exporter if certain documents are presented.

Drawback: A provision allowing U.S. exporters to apply for refunds of 99 percent of the duty paid on imported components, provided they are used in the manufacture of goods that are exported.

Dumping: The underpricing of exports, usually below cost or below the home-country price.

Duty: A governmental tax (tariff) levied on goods shipped internationally.

Dynamic effects of integration: The overall growth in the market and the impact on a company of expanding production and achieving greater economies of scale.

E-commerce: The use of the Internet to join together suppliers with companies and companies with customers.

Economic Community of West African States (ECOWAS): A form of economic integration among certain countries in West Africa.

Economic exposure: The foreign-exchange risk that international businesses face in the pricing of products, the source and cost of inputs, and the location of investments.

Economic integration: The abolition of economic discrimination between national economies, such as within the EU.

Economic system: The system concerned with the allocation of scarce resources.

Economics: A social science concerned chiefly with the description and analysis of the production, distribution, and consumption of goods and services.

Economies of scale: The lowering of cost per unit as output increases because of allocation of fixed costs over more units produced.

ECOWAS: *See* Economic Community of West African States.

ECU: *See* European Currency Unit.

EEC: *See* European Economic Community.

EEC Patent Convention: An important cross-national patent convention that involves the members of the EU.

Effective tariff: The real tariff on the manufactured portion of developing countries' exports, which is higher than indicated by the published rates because the ad valorem tariff is based on the total value of the products, which includes raw materials that would have had duty-free entry.

EFTA: *See* European Free Trade Association.

Elastic (product demand): A condition in which sales are likely to increase or decrease by a percentage that is more than the percentage change in income.

Electronic data interchange (EDI): The electronic movement of money and information via computers and telecommunications equipment.

Embargo: A specific type of quota that prohibits all trade.

EMC: *See* Export management company.

Emerging country: Low- and middle-income country; also known as developing country.

EMS: *See* European Monetary System.

Enterprise resource planning (ERP): Software that can link information flows from different parts of a business and from different geographic areas.

Entrepôt: A country that is an import/export intermediary; for example, Hong Kong is an entrepôt for trade between China and the rest of the world.

Environmental climate: The external conditions in host countries that could significantly affect the success of a foreign business enterprise.

Environmental scanning: The systematic assessment of external conditions that might affect a company's operations.

EPC: *See* European Patent Convention.

Equity alliance: A situation in which a cooperating company takes an equity position (almost always a minority) in the company with which it has a collaborative arrangement.

ERP: *See* Enterprise resource planning.

Essential-industry argument: The argument holding that certain domestic industries need protection for national security purposes.

ETC: *See* Export trading company.

Ethnocentrism: A belief that one's own group is superior to others; also used to describe a company's belief that what worked at home should work abroad.

Eurobond: A bond sold in a country other than the one in whose currency it is denominated.

Eurocredit: A loan, line of credit, or other form of medium- or long-term credit on the Eurocurrency market that has a maturity of more than one year.

Eurocurrency: Any currency that is banked outside of its country of origin.

Eurocurrency market: An international wholesale market that deals in Eurocurrencies.

Eurodollars: Dollars banked outside of the United States.

Euroequity market: The market for shares sold outside the boundaries of the issuing company's home country.

European Commission: One of the five major institutions of the EU; composed of a president, six vice presidents, and ten other members whose allegiance is to the EU and serving as an executive branch for the EU.

European Community (EC): The predecessor of the European Union.

European Council: One of the five major institutions of the European Union; made up of the heads of state of each of the EU members.

European Currency Unit (ECU): A unit of account based on a currency basket composed of the currencies of the members of the EU.

European Economic Community (EEC): The predecessor of the European Community.

European Free Trade Association (EFTA): A free-trade area among a group of European countries that are not members of the EU.

European Monetary System (EMS): A cooperative foreign-exchange agreement involving most of the members of the EU and designed to promote exchange-rate stability within the EU.

European Parliament: One of the five major institutions of the EU; its representatives are elected directly in each member country.

European Patent Convention (EPC): A European agreement allowing companies to make a uniform patent search and application, which is then passed on to all signatory countries.

European terms: The practice of using the indirect quote for exchange rates.

European Union (EU): A form of regional economic integration among countries in Europe that involves a free-trade area, a customs union, and the free mobility of factors of production that is working toward political and economic union.

Exchange rate: The price of one currency in terms of another currency.

Eximbank: *See* Export-Import Bank.

Exotic currencies: The currencies of developing countries; also called *exotics.*

Expatriates: Noncitizens of the country in which they are working.

Experience curve: The relationship of production-cost reductions to increases in output.

Export-Import Bank (Eximbank): A U.S. federal agency specializing in foreign lending to support exports.

Export-led development: An industrialization policy emphasizing industries that will have export capabilities.

Export license: A document that grants government permission to ship certain products to a specific country.

Export management company (EMC): A company that buys merchandise from manufacturers for international distribution or sometimes acts as an agent for manufacturers.

Export packing list: A shipping document that itemizes the material in each individual package and indicates the type of package.

Export tariff: A tax on goods leaving a country.

Export trading company (ETC): A form of trading company sanctioned by U.S. law to become involved in international commerce as independent distributors to match up foreign buyers with domestic sellers.

Exports: Goods or services leaving a country.

Exposure: A situation in which a foreign-exchange account is subject to a gain or loss if the exchange rate changes.

Exposure draft: The first draft of an accounting standard, which is open to comment by parties other than the IASC.

Expropriation: The taking over of ownership of private property by a country's government.

Externalities: External economic costs related to a business activity.

Extranet: The use of the Internet to link a company with outsiders.

Extraterritoriality: The extension by a government of the application of its laws to foreign operations of companies.

Factor conditions: Inputs to the production process, such as human, physical, knowledge, and capital resources and infrastructure.

Factor mobility: The free movement of factors of production, such as labor and capital, across national borders.

Factor-proportions theory: The theory that differences in a country's proportionate holdings of factors of production (land, labor, and capital) explain differences in the costs of the factors and that export advantages lie in the production of goods that use the most abundant factors.

Factoring: The discounting of a foreign account receivable.

FASB: *See* Financial Accounting Standards Board.

Fatalism: A belief that events are fixed in advance and human beings are powerless to change them.

Favorable balance of trade: An indication that a country is exporting more than it imports.

FCPA: *See* Foreign Corrupt Practices Act.

FDI: *See* Foreign direct investment.

Fees: Payments for the performance of certain activities abroad.

Financial Accounting Standards Board (FASB): The private-sector organization that sets financial accounting standards in the United States.

FIRA: *See* Foreign Investment Review Act.

First-in advantage: Any benefit gained in terms of brand recognition and lining up of the best suppliers, distributors, and local partners because of entering a market before competitors do.

First-mover advantage: A cost-reduction advantage due to economies of scale attained through moving into a foreign market ahead of competitors.

Fisher Effect: The theory about the relationship between inflation and interest rates; for example, if the nominal interest rate in one country is lower than that in another, the first country's inflation should be lower so that the real interest rates will be equal.

Fixed price: A method of pricing in which bargaining does not take place.

Floating currency: A currency whose value responds to the supply of and demand for that currency.

Floating exchange rate: An exchange rate determined by the laws of supply and demand and with minimal governmental interference.

Foreign bond: A bond sold outside of the borrower's country but denominated in the currency of the country of issue.

Foreign Corrupt Practices Act (FCPA): A law that criminalizes certain types of payments by U.S. companies, such as bribes to foreign governmental officials.

Foreign direct investment (FDI): An investment that gives the investor a controlling interest in a foreign company.

Foreign exchange: Checks and other instruments for making payments in another country's currency.

Foreign-exchange control: A requirement that an importer of a product must apply to governmental authorities for permission to buy foreign currency to pay for the product.

Foreign freight forwarder: A company that facilitates the movement of goods from one country to another.

Foreign investment: Direct or portfolio ownership of assets in another country.

Foreign Investment Review Act (FIRA): A Canadian law intended to limit foreign control of that country's economy.

Foreign sales corporation (FSC): A special type of corporation established by U.S. tax law that can be used by a U.S. exporter to shelter some of its income from taxation.

Foreign trade zone (FTZ): A government-designated area in which goods can be stored, inspected, or manufactured without being subject to formal customs procedures until they leave the zone.

Forfaiting: Similar to factoring but usually for longer time periods and with a guarantee from a bank in the importer's country.

Forward contract: A contract between a company or individual and a bank to deliver foreign currency at a specific exchange rate on a future date.

Forward discount: *See* Discount.

Forward premium: *See* Premium.

Forward rate: A contractually established exchange rate between a foreign-exchange trader and the trader's client for delivery of foreign currency on a specific date.

Franchising: A specialized form of licensing in which one party (the franchisor) sells to an independent party (the franchisee) the use of a trademark that is an essential asset for the franchisee's business and also gives continual assistance in the operation of the business.

Free-trade area (FTA): A form of regional economic integration in which internal tariffs are abolished, but member countries set their own external tariffs.

Freight forwarder: *See* Foreign freight forwarder.

Fringe benefit: Any employee benefit other than salary, wages, and cash bonuses.

FSC: *See* Foreign sales corporation.

FTZ: *See* Foreign trade zone.

Functional currency: The currency of the primary economic environment in which an entity operates.

Functional division: An organizational structure in which each function in foreign countries (e.g., marketing or production) reports separately to a counterpart functional group at headquarters.

Futures contract: A foreign-exchange instrument that specifies an exchange rate, an amount of currency, and a maturity date in advance of the exchange of the currency.

FX swap: A simultaneous spot and forward transaction.

G-7 countries: *See* Group of 7.

GAAP: *See* Generally accepted accounting principles.

Gap analysis: A tool used to discover why a company's sales of a given product are less than the market potential in a country; the reason may be a usage, competitive, product line, or distribution gap.

GATT: *See* General Agreement on Tariffs and Trade.

General Agreement on Tariffs and Trade (GATT): A multilateral arrangement aimed at reducing barriers to trade, both tariff and nontariff ones; at the signing of the Uruguay round, the GATT was designated to become the World Trade Organization (WTO).

Generalized System of Preferences (GSP): Preferential import restrictions extended by industrial countries to developing countries.

Generally accepted accounting principles (GAAP): The accounting standards accepted by the accounting profession in each country as required for the preparation of financial statements for external users.

Generic: Any of a class of products, rather than the brand of a particular company.

Geocentric: Operations based on an informed knowledge of both home and host country needs.

Geographic division: An organizational structure in which a company's operations are separated for reporting purposes into regional areas.

Geography: A science dealing with the earth and its life, especially with the description of land, sea, air, and the distribution of plant and animal life.

Global bond: A combination of domestic bond and Eurobond that is issued simultaneously in several markets and must be registered in each national market according to that market's registration requirements.

Global company: A company that integrates operations located in different countries.

Global sourcing: The acquisition on a worldwide basis of raw materials, parts, and subassemblies for the manufacturing process.

Globally integrated company: *See* Global company.

Go–no-go decision: A decision, such as on foreign investments, that is based on minimum-threshold criteria and does not compare different opportunities.

Grandchild subsidiary: An operation that is under a tax-haven subsidiary; also called a second-tier subsidiary.

Grantback provisions: Stipulations requiring that licensees provide licensors with the use of improvements made on the technology originally licensed.

Gray market: The handling of goods through unofficial distributors.

Gross domestic product (GDP): The total of all economic activity in a country, regardless of who owns the productive assets.

Gross national product (GNP): The total of incomes earned by residents of a country, regardless of where the productive assets are located.

Group of 7 (G-7): A group of developed countries that periodically meets to make economic decisions; this group consists of Canada, France, Germany, Italy, Japan, the United Kingdom, and the United States.

GSP: *See* Generalized System of Preferences.

Hard currency: A currency that is freely traded without many restrictions and for which there is usually strong external demand; often called a freely convertible currency.

Hardship allowance: A supplement to compensate expatriates for working in dangerous or adverse conditions.

Harvesting: Reduction in the amount of investment; also known as divestment.

Hedge: To attempt to protect foreign-currency holdings against an adverse movement of an exchange rate.

Heterarchy: An organizational structure in which management of an alliance of companies is shared by so-called equals rather than being set up in a superior-subordinate relationship.

Hierarchy of needs: A well-known motivation theory stating that there is a hierarchy of needs and that people must fulfill the lower-order needs sufficiently before they will be motivated by the higher-order ones.

High-context culture: A culture in which most people consider that peripheral and hearsay information are necessary for decision making because they bear on the context of the situation.

High-need achiever: One who will work very hard to achieve material or career success, sometimes to the detriment of social relationships or spiritual achievements.

High-value activities: Activities that either produce high profits or are done by high-salaried employees such as managers.

Historically planned economy (HPE): The World Bank's term for Second-World countries in transition to market economies.

History: A branch of knowledge that records and explains past events.

Home country: The country in which an international company is headquartered.

Home-country nationals: Expatriate employees who are citizens of the country in which the company is headquartered.

Horizontal expansion: Any foreign direct investment by which a company produces the same product it produces at home.

Host country: Any foreign country in which an international company operates.

HPE: *See* Historically planned economy.

Hyperinflation: A rapid increase (at least 1 percent per day) in general price levels for a sustained period of time.

IASC: *See* International Accounting Standards Committee.

Idealism: Trying to determine principles before settling small issues.

Ideology: The systematic and integrated body of constructs, theories, and aims that constitute a society.

IFE: *See* International Fisher Effect.

ILO: *See* International Labor Organization.

IMF: *See* International Monetary Fund.

Imitation lag: A strategy for exploiting temporary monopoly advantages by moving first to those countries most likely to develop local production.

Import broker: An individual who obtains various governmental permissions and other clearances before forwarding necessary paperwork to the carrier that will deliver the goods from the dock to the importer.

Import deposit requirement: Governmental requirement of a deposit prior to the release of foreign exchange.

Import licensing: A method of governmental control of the exchange rate whereby all recipients, exporters, and others who receive foreign exchange are required to sell to the central bank at the official buying rate.

Import substitution: An industrialization policy whereby new industrial development emphasizes products that would otherwise be imported.

Import tariff: A tax placed on goods entering a country.

Imports: Goods or services entering a country.

In-bond industry: Any industry that is allowed to import components free of duty, provided that the components will be re-exported after processing.

Independence: An extreme situation in which a country would not rely on other countries at all.

Indigenization: The process of introducing elements of an outside culture.

Indirect quote: An exchange rate given in terms of the number of units of the foreign currency for one unit of the domestic currency.

Indirect selling: A sale of goods by an exporter through another domestic company as an intermediary.

Individualistic paradigm: Minimal government intervention in the economy.

Individually validated license (IVL): A special export license under which certain restricted products need to be shipped.

Industrial country: High-income country; also known as developed country.

Industrialization argument: A rationale for protectionism that argues that the development of industrial output should come about even though domestic prices may not become competitive on the world market.

Inelastic (product demand): A condition in which sales are likely to increase or decrease by a percentage that is less than the percentage change in income.

Infant-industry argument: The position that holds that an emerging industry should be guaranteed a large share of the domestic market until it becomes efficient enough to compete against imports.

Inflation: A condition where prices are going up.

Infrastructure: The underlying foundation of a society, such as roads, schools, and so forth, that allows it to function effectively.

Input-output table: A tool used widely in national economic planning to show the resources utilized by different industries for a given output as well as the interdependence of economic sectors.

Intangible property: *See* Intellectual property rights.

Integrated system: A system for taxation of corporate income aimed at preventing double taxation through the use of split rates or tax credits.

Intellectual property rights: Ownership rights to intangible assets, such as patents, trademarks, copyrights, and know-how.

Interbank market: The market for foreign-exchange transactions among commercial banks.

Interbank transactions: Foreign-exchange transactions that take place between commercial banks.

Interdependence: The existence of mutually necessary economic relations among countries.

Interest arbitrage: Investing in debt instruments in different countries and earning a profit due to interest-rate and exchange-rate differentials.

Interest rate differential: An indicator of future changes in the spot exchange rate.

Intermodal transportation: The movement across different modes from origin to destination.

Internalization: Control through self-handling of foreign operations, primarily because it is less expensive to deal within the same corporate family than to contract with an external organization.

International Accounting Standards Committee (IASC): The international private-sector organization that sets financial accounting standards for worldwide use.

International Bureau for the Protection of Industrial Property Rights (BIRPI): A multilateral agreement to protect patents, trademarks, and other property rights.

International business: All business transactions involving private companies or governments of two or more countries.

International division: An organizational structure in which virtually all foreign operations are handled within the same division.

International Fisher Effect (IFE): The theory that the relationship between interest rates and exchange rates implies that the currency of the country with the lower interest rate will strengthen in the future.

International Labor Organization (ILO): A multilateral organization promoting the adoption of humane labor conditions.

International Monetary Fund (IMF): A multigovernmental association organized in 1945 to promote exchange-rate stability and to facilitate the international flow of currencies.

International Monetary Market (IMM): A specialized market located in Chicago and dealing in select foreign-currency futures.

International Organization of Securities Commissions (IOSCO): An international organization of securities regulators that wants the IASC to establish more comprehensive accounting standards.

International standard of fair dealing: The concept that investors should receive prompt, adequate, and effective compensation in cases of expropriation.

International Trade Administration (ITA): A branch of the U.S. Department of Commerce offering a variety of services to U.S. exporting companies.

Intervention currencies: The currencies in which a particular country trades the most.

Intranet: The use of the Internet to link together the different divisions and functions inside a company.

Intrazonal trade: Trade among countries that are part of a trade agreement, such as the EU.

Investment Canada: A Canadian act whose intent is to persuade foreign companies to invest in Canada.

Invisibles: *See* Services.

IOSCO: *See* International Organization of Securities Commissions.

Irrevocable letter of credit: A letter of credit that cannot be canceled or changed without the consent of all parties involved.

Islamic law: A system of theocratic law based on the religious teachings of Islam; also called Muslim law.

ISO 9000: A quality standard developed by the International Standards Organization in Geneva that requires companies to document their commitment to quality at all levels of the organization.

IVL: *See* Individually validated license.

Jamaica Agreement: A 1976 agreement among countries that permitted greater flexibility of exchange rates, basically formalizing the break from fixed exchange rates.

JIT: *See* Just-in-time manufacturing.

Joint venture: A direct investment of which two or more companies share the ownership.

Just-in-time (JIT) manufacturing: A system that decreases inventory costs by having components and parts delivered as they are needed in production.

Kaizen: The Japanese process of continuous improvement, the cornerstone of TQM.

Keiretsu: A corporate relationship linking certain Japanese companies, usually involving a noncontrolling interest in each other, strong high-level personal relationships among managers in the different companies, and interlocking directorships.

Key industry: Any industry that might affect a very large segment of a country's economy or population by virtue of its size or influence on other sectors.

Labor market: The mix of available workers and labor costs available to companies.

Labor union: An association of workers intended to promote and protect the welfare, interests, and rights of its members, primarily by collective bargaining.

LAFTA: *See* Latin American Free Trade Association.

Lag strategy: An operational strategy that involves delaying collection of foreign-currency receivables if the currency is expected to strengthen or delaying payment of foreign-currency payables when the currency is expected to weaken; the opposite of a lead strategy.

Laissez-faire: The concept of minimal governmental intervention in a society's economic activity.

Latin American Free Trade Association (LAFTA): A free-trade area formed by Mexico and the South American countries in 1960; it was replaced by ALADI in 1980.

Latin American Integration Association (ALADI): A form of regional economic integration involving most of the Latin American countries.

Law: A binding custom or practice of a community.

Lead country strategy: A strategy of introducing a product on a test basis in a small-country market that is considered representative of a region before investing to serve larger-country markets.

Lead strategy: An operational strategy that involves collecting foreign-currency receivables early when the currency is expected to weaken or paying foreign-currency payables early when the currency is expected to strengthen; the opposite of a lag strategy.

Lead subsidiary organization: A foreign subsidiary that has global responsibility (serves as corporate headquarters) for one of a company's products or functions.

Learning curve: A concept used to support the infant industry argument for protection; it assumes that costs will decrease as workers and managers gain more experience.

Letter of credit: A precise document by which the importer's bank extends credit to the importer and agrees to pay the exporter.

Liability of foreignness: Foreign companies' lower survival rate than local companies for many years after they begin operations.

LIBOR: *See* London Inter-Bank Offered Rate.

License: Formal or legal permission to do some specified action; a governmental method of fixing the exchange rate by requiring all recipients, exporters, and others that receive foreign exchange to sell it to the central bank at the official buying rate.

Licensing agreement: Agreement whereby one company gives rights to another for the use, usually for a fee, of such assets as trademarks, patents, copyrights, or other know-how.

Licensing arrangement: A procedure that requires potential importers or exporters to secure permission from governmental authorities before they conduct trade transactions.

Lifetime employment: The Japanese custom that workers are effectively guaranteed employment with the company for their working lifetime and that workers seldom leave for employment opportunities with other companies.

LIFFE: *See* London International Financial Futures Exchange.

Liquidity preference: A theory that helps explain capital budgeting and, when applied to international operations, means that investors are willing to take less return in order to be able to shift the resources to alternative uses.

Lobbyist: An individual who participates in advancing or otherwise securing passage of legislation by influencing public officials before and during the legislation process.

Local content: Costs incurred within a given country, usually as a percentage of total costs.

Locally responsive company: Synonym for *multidomestic company.*

Locals: Citizens of the country in which they are working.

Logistics: That part of the supply chain process that plans, implements, and controls the efficient, effective flow and storage of goods, services, and related information from the point of origin to the point of consumption, to meet customers' requirements; sometimes called materials management.

London Inter-Bank Offered Rate (LIBOR): The interest rate for large interbank loans of Eurocurrencies.

London International Financial Futures Exchange (LIFFE): An exchange dealing in futures contracts for several major currencies.

London Stock Exchange (LSE): A stock exchange located in London and dealing in Euroequities.

Low-context culture: A culture in which most people consider relevant only information that they receive firsthand and that bears very directly on the decision they need to make.

Maastricht (Treaty of): The treaty approved in December 1991 that was designed to bring the EU to a higher level of integration and is divided into Economic and Monetary Union (EMU) and political union.

Macro political risk: Negative political actions affecting a broad spectrum of foreign investors.

Management contract: An arrangement whereby one company provides management personnel to perform general or specialized management functions to another company for a fee.

Manufacturing interchange: A process by which various plants produce a range of components and exchange them so that all plants assemble the finished product for the local market.

Maquiladora: An industrial operation developed by the Mexican and U.S. governments in which U.S.-sourced components are shipped to Mexico duty-free, assembled into final products, and re-exported to the United States.

Marginal propensity to import: The tendency to purchase imports with incremental income.

Market capitalization: A common measure of the size of a stock market, which is computed by multiplying the total number of shares of stock listed on the exchange by the market price per share.

Market economy: An economic system in which resources are allocated and controlled by consumers who "vote" by buying goods.

Market environment: The environment that involves the interactions between households (or individuals) and companies to allocate resources, free from governmental ownership or control.

Market socialism: The state owns significant resources, but allocation comes from the market price mechanism.

Materials management: *See* Logistics.

Matrix: A method of plotting data on a set of vertical and horizontal axes, in order to compare countries in terms of risk and opportunity.

Matrix division structure: An organizational structure in which foreign units report (by product, function, or area) to more than one group, each of which shares responsibility over the foreign unit.

Measurement: How to value assets.

Mentor: A person at headquarters who looks after the interests of an expatriate employee.

Mercantilism: An economic philosophy based on the beliefs that a country's wealth is dependent on its holdings of treasure, usually in the form of gold, and that countries should export more than they import in order to increase wealth.

Merchandise exports: Goods sent out of a country.

Merchandise imports: Goods brought into a country.

Merchandise trade balance: The part of a country's current account that measures the trade deficit or surplus; its balance is the net of merchandise imports and exports.

MERCOSUR: A major subregional group established by Argentina, Brazil, Paraguay, and Uruguay, which spun off from ALADI in 1991 with the goal of setting up a customs union and common market.

MFA: *See* Multifibre Arrangement.

MFN: *See* Most-favored-nation clause.

Micro political risk: Negative political actions aimed at specific, rather than most, foreign investors.

Middle East: The countries on the Arabian peninsula plus those bordering the eastern end of the Mediterranean; sometimes also including other adjacent countries, particularly Jordan, Iraq, Iran, and Kuwait.

Ministry of International Trade and Industry (MITI): The Japanese governmental agency responsible for coordinating overall business direction and helping individual companies take advantage of global business opportunities.

Mission: What the company will seek to do and become over the long term.

Mission statement: A long-range strategic intent.

Mixed economy: An economic system characterized by some mixture of market and command economies and public and private ownership.

Mixed venture: A special type of joint venture in which a government is in partnership with a private company.

MNE: *See* Multinational enterprise.

Monochronic culture: A culture in which most people prefer to deal with situations sequentially (especially those involving other people), such as finishing with one customer before dealing with another.

Monopoly advantage: The perceived supremacy of foreign investors in relation to local companies, which is necessary to overcome the perceived greater risk of operating in a different environment.

Most-favored-nation (MFN): A GATT requirement that a trade concession that is given to one country must be given to all other countries.

Multidomestic company: A company with international operations that allows operations in one country to be relatively independent of those in other countries.

Multilateral agreement: An agreement involving more than two governments.

Multilateral Investment Guarantee Agency (MIGA): A member of the World Bank Group that encourages equity investment and other direct investment flows to developing countries by offering investors a variety of different services.

Multinational corporation (MNC): A synonym for *multinational enterprise.*

Multinational enterprise (MNE): A company that has an integrated global philosophy encompassing both domestic and overseas operations; sometimes used synonymously with multinational corporation or transnational corporation.

Multiple exchange-rate system: A means of foreign-exchange control whereby the government sets different exchange rates for different transactions.

Muslim law: *See* Islamic law.

National responsiveness: Readiness to implement operating adjustments in foreign countries in order to reach a satisfactory level of performance.

Nationalism: The feeling of pride and/or ethnocentrism focused on an individual's home country or nation.

Nationalization: The transfer of ownership to the state.

Natural advantage: Climatic conditions, access to certain natural resources, or availability of labor, which gives a country an advantage in producing some product.

Need hierarchy: *See* Hierarchy of needs.

Neomercantilism: The approach of countries that apparently try to run favorable balances of trade in an attempt to achieve some social or political objective.

Net capital flow: Capital inflow minus capital outflow, for other than import and export payment.

Net export effect: Export stimulus minus export reduction.

Net import change: Import displacement minus import stimulus.

Netting: The transfer of funds from subsidiaries in a net payable position to a central clearing account and from there to the accounts of the net receiver subsidiaries.

Network alliance: Interdependence of countries; each company is a customer of and a supplier to other companies.

Network organization: A situation in which a group of companies is interrelated, and in which the management of the interrelation is shared among so-called equals.

Newly industrializing country (NIC): A Third-World country in which the cultural and economic climate has led to a rapid rate of industrialization and growth since the 1960s.

Nonmarket economy: *See* Command economy.

Nonmarket environment: Public institutions (such as government, governmental agencies, and government-owned businesses) and nonpublic institutions (such as environmental and other special-interest groups).

Nonpublic institutions: Special-interest groups, such as environmentalists.

Nonresident convertibility: The ability of a nonresident of a country to convert deposits in a bank to the currency of any other country; also known as external convertibility.

Nontariff barriers: Barriers to imports that are not tariffs; examples include administrative controls, "Buy America" policies, and so forth.

Normal quote: Synonym for *direct quote.*

North American Free Trade Agreement (NAFTA): A free-trade agreement involving the United States, Canada, and Mexico that went into effect on January 1, 1994 and will be phased in over a period of fifteen years.

OAU: *See* Organization of African Unity.

Objectives: Specific performance targets to fulfill a company's mission.

Obsolescing bargain (theory of): The premises that a company's bargaining strength with a host government diminishes after the company transfers assets to the host country.

OECD: *See* Organization for Economic Cooperation and Development.

OEEC: *See* Organization for European Economic Cooperation.

Offer rate: The amount for which a foreign-exchange trader is willing to sell a currency.

Official reserves: A country's holdings of monetary gold, Special Drawing Rights, and internationally acceptable currencies.

Offset: A form of barter transaction in which an export is paid for with other merchandise.

Offset trade: A form of countertrade in which an exporter sells goods for cash but then helps businesses in the importing country find opportunities to earn hard currency.

Offshore financial centers: Cities or countries that provide large amounts of funds in currencies other than their own and are used as locations in which to raise and accumulate cash.

Offshore manufacturing: Manufacturing outside the borders of a particular country.

Oligopoly: An industry in which there are few producers or sellers.

OPEC: *See* Organization of Petroleum Exporting Countries.

Open account: Conditions of sale under which the exporter extends credit directly to the importer.

Operational centers: Offshore financial centers that perform specific functions, such as the sale and servicing of goods.

OPIC: *See* Overseas Private Investment Corporation.

Opinion leader: One whose acceptance of some concept is apt to be emulated by others.

Optimism: A characteristic of an accounting system that implies that companies are more liberal in recognition of income.

Optimum-tariff theory: The argument that a foreign producer will lower its prices if an import tax is placed on its products.

Option: A foreign-exchange instrument that gives the purchaser the right, but not the obligation, to buy or sell a certain amount of foreign currency at a set exchange rate within a specified amount of time.

Organization of African Unity (OAU): An organization of African nations that is more concerned with political than economic objectives.

Organization for Economic Cooperation and Development (OECD): A multilateral organization of industrialized and semi-industrialized countries that helps formulate social and economic policies.

Organization for European Economic Cooperation (OEEC): A sixteen-nation organization established in 1948 to facilitate the utilization of aid from the Marshall Plan; it evolved into the EU and EFTA.

Organization of Petroleum Exporting Countries (OPEC): A producers' alliance among twelve petroleum-exporting countries that attempt to agree on oil production and pricing policies.

Organizational structure: The reporting relationships within an organization.

Outright forward: A forward contract that is not connected to a spot transaction.

Outsourcing: The use by a domestic company of foreign suppliers for components or finished products.

Overseas Private Investment Corporation (OPIC): A U.S. government agency that provides insurance for companies involved in international business.

Over-the-counter (OTC) market: Trading in stocks, usually of smaller companies, that are not listed on one of the stock exchanges; also refers to how government and corporate bonds are traded, through dealers who quote bids and offers to buy and sell "over the counter."

Par value: The benchmark value of a currency, originally quoted in terms of gold or the U.S. dollar and now quoted in terms of Special Drawing Rights.

Parliamentary system: A form of government that involves the election of representatives to form the executive branch.

Passive income: Income from investments in tax-haven countries or sales and services income that involves buyers and sellers in other than the tax-haven country, where either the buyer or the seller must be part of the same organizational structure as the corporation that earns the income; also known as Subpart F income.

Patent: A right granted by a sovereign power or state for the protection of an invention or discovery against infringement.

Patent cooperation treaty: A multilateral agreement to protect patents.

Peg: To fix a currency's exchange rate to some benchmark, such as another currency.

Penetration strategy: A strategy of introducing a product at a low price to induce a maximum number of consumers to try it.

Philadelphia Stock Exchange (PSE): A specialized market dealing in select foreign-currency options.

Piggyback exporting: Use by an exporter of another exporter as an intermediary.

Piracy: The unauthorized use of property rights that are protected by patents, trademarks, or copyrights.

Planning: The meshing of objectives with internal and external constraints in order to set means to implement, monitor, and correct operations.

Plant layout: Decisions about the physical arrangement of economic activity centers within a manufacturing facility.

PLC: *See* Product life cycle theory.

Pluralistic societies: Societies in which different ideologies are held by various segments rather than one ideology being adhered to by all.

Political freedom: The right to participate freely in the political process.

Political ideology: The body of constructs (complex ideas), theories, and aims that constitute a sociopolitical program.

Political risk: Potential changes in political conditions that may cause a company's operating positions to deteriorate.

Political science: A discipline that helps explain the patterns of governments and their actions.

Political system: The system designed to integrate a society into a viable, functioning unit.

Polycentrism: Characteristic of an individual or organization that feels that differences in a foreign country, real and imaginary, great and small, need to be accounted for in management decisions.

Polychronic culture: A culture in which most people are more comfortable dealing simultaneously with all the situations facing them.

Porter diamond: A diagram showing four conditions— demand, factor endowments, related and supporting industries, and firm strategy, structure, and rivalry—that usually must all be favorable for an industry in a country to develop and sustain a global competitive advantage.

Portfolio investment: An investment in the form of either debt or equity that does not give the investor a controlling interest.

Positive-sum gain: A situation in which the sums of gains and losses, if added together among participants, is positive, especially if all parties gain from a relationship.

Power distance: A measurement of preference for consultative or autocratic styles of management.

PPP: *See* Purchasing-power parity.

Pragmatism: Settling small issues before deciding on principles.

Premium (in foreign exchange): The difference between the spot and forward exchange rates in the forward market; a foreign currency sells at a premium when the forward rate exceeds the spot rate and when the domestic currency is quoted on a direct basis.

Pressure group: A group that tries to influence legislation or practices to foster its objectives.

Price escalation: The process by which the lengthening of distribution channels increases a product's price by more than the direct added costs, such as transportation, insurance, and tariffs.

Prior informed consent (PIC): The concept of requiring each exporter of a banned or restricted chemical to obtain, through the home-country government, the expressed consent of the importing country to receive the banned or restricted substance.

Privatization: Selling of government-owned assets to private individuals or companies.

Product division: An organizational structure in which different foreign operations report to different product groups at headquarters.

Product life cycle (PLC) theory: The theory that certain kinds of products go through a cycle consisting of four stages (introduction, growth, maturity, and decline) and that the location of production will shift internationally depending on the stage of the cycle.

Production switching: The movement of production from one country to another in response to changes in cost.

Promotion: The process of presenting messages intended to help sell a product or service.

Protectionism: Governmental restrictions on imports and occasionally on exports that frequently give direct or indirect subsidies to industries to enable them to compete with foreign production either at home or abroad.

Protestant ethic: A theory that there is more economic growth when work is viewed as a means of salvation and when people prefer to transform productivity gains into additional output rather than into additional leisure.

Pull: A promotion strategy that sells consumers before they reach the point of purchase, usually by relying on mass media.

Purchasing power: What a sum of money actually can buy.

Purchasing-power parity (PPP): A theory that explains exchange-rate changes as being based on differences in price levels in different countries.

Push: A promotion strategy that involves direct selling techniques.

Quality: Meeting or exceeding the expectations of a customer.

Quantity controls: Government limitations on the amount of foreign currency that can be used for specific purposes.

Quota: A limit on the quantitative amount of a product allowed to be imported into or exported out of a country in a year.

Quota system: A commodity agreement whereby producing and/or consuming countries divide total output and sales in order to stabilize the price of a particular product.

Quoted currency: The currency whose value is not 1 when an exchange rate is quoted by relating one currency to another.

Rationalization: *See* Rationalized production.

Rationalized production: The specialization of production by product or process in different parts of the world to take advantage of varying costs of labor, capital, and raw materials.

Reciprocal quote: The reciprocal of the direct quote; also known as the *indirect quote.*

Regression: A statistical method showing relationships among variables.

Reinvestment: The use of retained earnings to replace depreciated assets or to add to the existing stock of capital.

Relationship enterprises: Networks of strategic alliances among big companies, spanning different industries and countries.

Renegotiation: A process by which international companies and governments decide on a change in terms for operations.

Repatriation: An expatriate's return to his or her home country.

Representative democracy: A type of government in which individual citizens elect representatives to make decisions governing the society.

Resource-based view of the firm: A perspective that holds that each company has a unique combination of competencies.

Return on investment (ROI): The amount of profit, sometimes measured before and sometimes after the payment of taxes, divided by the amount of investment.

Revaluation: A formal change in an exchange rate by which the foreign-currency value of the reference currency rises, resulting in a strengthening of the reference currency.

Reverse culture shock: The encountering of culture shock when returning to one's own country because of having accepted what was encountered abroad.

Revocable letter of credit: A letter of credit that can be changed by any of the parties involved.

Rio Declaration: The result of the Rio Earth Summit, which sets out fundamental principles of environmentally responsive behavior.

Rio Earth Summit: A meeting held in Rio de Janeiro in June 1992 that brought together people from around the world to discuss major environmental issues.

ROI: *See* Return on investment.

Rounds: Conferences held by GATT to establish multilateral agreements to liberalize trade.

Royalties: Payments for the use of intangible assets abroad.

SADC: *See* Southern African Development Community.

SADCC: *See* Southern African Development Co-ordination Conference.

Sales representative (foreign): A representative that usually operates either exclusively or nonexclusively within an assigned market and on a commission basis, without assuming risk or responsibility.

Sales response function: The amount of sales created at different levels of marketing expenditures.

SDR: *See* Special Drawing Right.

Second-tier subsidiaries: Subsidiaries that report to a tax-haven subsidiary.

Secondary boycott: The boycotting of a company that does business with a company being boycotted.

Secrecy: A characteristic of an accounting system that implies that companies do not disclose much information about accounting practices; more common in Germanic countries.

Secular totalitarianism: A dictatorship not affiliated with any religious group or system of beliefs.

Securities and Exchange Commission (SEC): A U.S. government agency that regulates securities brokers, dealers, and markets.

Separate entity approach: A system for taxation of corporate income in which each unit is taxed when it receives income, with the result being double taxation.

Service exports: International received earnings other than those derived from the exporting of tangible goods.

Service imports: International paid earnings other than those derived from the importing of tangible goods.

Services: International earnings other than those on goods sent to another country; also referred to as invisibles.

Services account: The part of a country's current account that measures travel and transportation, tourism, and fees and royalties.

Settlement: The actual payment of currency in a foreign-exchange transaction.

Shipper's export declaration: A shipping document that controls exports and is used to compile trade statistics.

Sight draft: A commercial bill of exchange that requires payment to be made as soon as it is presented to the party obligated to pay.

Silent language: The wide variety of cues other than formal language by which messages can be sent.

Single European Act: A 1987 act of the EU (then the EC) allowing all proposals except those relating to taxation, workers' rights, and immigration to be adopted by a weighted majority of member countries.

Smithsonian Agreement: A 1971 agreement among countries that resulted in the devaluation of the U.S. dollar, revaluation of other world currencies, a widening of exchange-rate flexibility, and a commitment on the part of all participating countries to reduce trade restrictions; superseded by the Jamaica Agreement of 1976.

Society: A broad grouping of people having common traditions, institutions, and collective activities and interests; the term *nation-state* is often used in international business to denote a society.

Soft budget: A financial condition in which an enterprise's excess of expenditures over earnings is compensated for by some other institution, typically a government or a state-controlled financial institution.

Soft currency: *See* Weak currency.

Sogo shosha: Japanese trading companies that import and export merchandise.

Sourcing strategy: The strategy that a company pursues in purchasing materials, components, and final products; sourcing can be from domestic and foreign locations and from inside and outside the company.

Southern African Development Community (SADC): An organization endeavoring to counter the economic influence of South Africa in the region by focusing on economic objectives, such as regional cooperation in attracting investment.

Sovereignty: Freedom from external control, especially when applied to a body politic.

Special Drawing Right (SDR): A unit of account issued to countries by the International Monetary Fund to expand their official reserves bases.

Specific duty: A duty (tariff) assessed on a per-unit basis.

Speculation: The buying or selling of foreign currency with the pros-pect of great risk and high return.

Speculator: A person who takes positions in foreign exchange with the objective of earning a profit.

Spillover effects: Situations in which the marketing program in one country results in awareness of the product in other countries.

Spin-off organization: A company now operating almost independently of the parent because its activities do not fit easily with the parent's existing competencies.

Spot market: The market in which an asset is traded for immediate delivery, as opposed to a market for forward or future deliveries.

Spot rate: An exchange rate quoted for immediate delivery of foreign currency, usually within two business days.

Spread: In the forward market, the difference between the spot rate and the forward rate; in the spot market, the difference between the bid (buy) and offer (sell) rates quoted by a foreign-exchange trader.

Stakeholders: The collection of groups, including stockholders, employees, customers, and society at large, that a company must satisfy to survive.

State capitalism: A condition where some developed countries, such as Japan and Korea, have intervened in the economy to direct the allocation and control of resources.

Static effects of integration: The shifting of resources from inefficient to efficient companies as trade barriers fall.

Stereotype: A standardized and oversimplified mental picture of a group.

Strategic alliance: An agreement between companies that is of strategic importance to one or both companies' competitive viability.

Strategic intent: An objective that gives an organization cohesion over the long term while it builds global competitive viability.

Strategic plan: A long-term plan involving major commitments.

Strategy: The means companies select to achieve their objectives.

Subpart F income: Income of a CFC that comes from sources other than those connected with the active conduct of a trade or business, such as holding company income.

Subsidiarity: A principle that implies that EU interference should take place only in areas of common concern and that most policies should be set at the national level.

Subsidiary: A foreign operation that is legally separate from the parent company, even if wholly owned by it.

Subsidies: Direct or indirect financial assistance from governments to companies, making them more competitive.

Substitution drawbacks: A provision allowing domestic merchandise to be substituted for merchandise that is imported for eventual export, thus allowing the U.S. firm to exclude the duty paid on the merchandise in costs and in sales prices.

Supply chain: The coordination of materials, information, and funds from the initial raw material supplier to the ultimate customer.

Swap: A simultaneous spot and forward foreign-exchange transaction.

Syndication: Cooperation by a lead bank and several other banks to make a large loan to a public or private organization.

Tariff: A governmental tax levied on goods, usually imports, shipped internationally; the most common type of trade control.

Tax credit: A dollar-for-dollar reduction of tax liability that must coincide with the recognition of income.

Tax deferral: Income is not taxed until it is remitted to the parent company as a dividend.

Tax treaty: A treaty between two countries that generally results in the reciprocal reduction on dividend withholding taxes and the exemption of taxes or royalties and sometimes interest payments.

Tax-haven countries: Countries with low income taxes or no taxes on foreign-source income.

Tax-haven subsidiary: A subsidiary of a company established in a tax-haven country for the purpose of minimizing income tax.

Technology: The means employed to produce goods or services.

Technology absorbing capacity: The ability of the recipient to work effectively with technology, particularly in relation to the need for training and equity in the recipient in order to effect a transfer.

Temporal method: A method of translating foreign-currency financial statements used when the functional currency is that of the parent company.

Terms currency: Exchange rates are quoted as the number of units of the terms currency per base currency.

Terms of trade: The quantity of imports that can be bought by a given quantity of a country's exports.

Theocratic law system: A legal system based on religious precepts.

Theocratic totalitarianism: A dictatorship led by a religious group.

Theory of country size: The theory which holds that countries with large land areas are more apt to have varied climates and natural resources, and therefore, generally are more nearly self-sufficient than smaller countries.

Theory of obsolescing bargain: The erosion of bargaining strength from a group as countries gain assets from them.

Third-country nationals: Expatriate employees who are neither citizens of the country in which they are working nor citizens of the country where the company is headquartered.

Tie-in provisions: Stipulations in licensing that require the licensee to purchase or sell products from/to the licensor.

Time draft: A commercial bill of exchange calling for payment to be made at some time after delivery.

Time series: A statistical method of illustrating a pattern over time, such as in demand for a particular product.

TNC: *See* Transnational company.

Tort: A civil wrong independent of a contract.

Total quality management (TQM): The process that a company uses to achieve quality, where the goal is elimination of all defects.

Totalitarianism: A political system characterized by the absence of widespread participation in decision making.

TQM: *See* Total quality management.

Trade creation: Production shifts to more efficient producers for reasons of comparative advantage, allowing consumers access to more goods at a lower price than would have been possible without integration.

Trade diversion: A situation in which exports shift to a less efficient producing country because of preferential trade barriers.

Trade Related Aspects of Intellectual Property Rights (TRIPS): A provision from the Uruguay round of trade negotiations requiring countries to agree to enforce procedures under their national laws to protect intellectual property rights.

Trademark: A name or logo distinguishing a company or product.

Transaction exposure: Foreign-exchange risk arising because a company has outstanding accounts receivable or accounts payable that are denominated in a foreign currency.

Transfer price: A price charged for goods or services between entities that are related to each other through stock ownership, such as between a parent and its subsidiaries or between subsidiaries owned by the same parent.

Transit tariff: A tax placed on goods passing through a country.

Translation: The restatement of foreign-currency financial statements into U.S. dollars.

Translation exposure: Foreign-exchange risk that occurs because the parent company must translate foreign-currency financial statements into the reporting currency of the parent company.

Transnational: (1) An organization in which different capabilities and contributions among different country-operations are shared and integrated; (2) multinational enterprise; (3) company owned and managed by nationals from different countries.

Transnational company (TNC): A company owned and managed by nationals in different countries; also may be synonymous with multinational enterprise.

Transparency: A characteristic of an accounting system that implies that companies disclose a great deal of information about accounting practices; more common in Anglo-Saxon countries (United States, United Kingdom).

Triad strategy: A strategy proposing that an MNE should have a presence in Europe, the United States, and Asia (especially Japan).

TRIPS: *See* Trade Related Aspects of Intellectual Property Rights.

Turnkey operation: An operating facility that is constructed under contract and transferred to the owner when the facility is ready to begin operations.

Underemployed: Those people who are working at less than their capacity.

Unfavorable balance of trade: An indication of a trade deficit—that is, imports are greater than exports.

Unilateral transfer: A transfer of currency from one country to another for which no goods or services are received; an example is foreign aid to a country devastated by earthquake or flood.

Unit of account: A benchmark on which to base the value of payments.

United Nations (UN): An international organization of countries formed in 1945 to promote world peace and security.

United Nations Conference on Trade and Development (UNCTAD): A UN body that has been especially active in dealing with the relationships between developing and industrialized countries with respect to trade.

Universal Copyright Convention: A multilateral agreement to protect copyrights.

Unrequited transfer: *See* Unilateral transfer.

U.S.-Canada Free Trade Agreement: *See* Canada-U.S. Free Trade Agreement.

U.S. shareholder: For U.S. tax purposes, a person or company owning at least 10 percent of the voting stock of a foreign subsidiary.

U.S. terms: The practice of using the direct quote for exchange rates.

Value-added tax (VAT): A tax that is a percentage of the value added to a product at each stage of the business process.

Value chain: The collective activities that occur as a product moves from raw materials through production to final distribution.

Variable price: A method of pricing in which buyers and sellers negotiate the price.

VAT: *See* Value-added tax.

VER: *See* Voluntary export restrictions.

Vertical integration: The control of the different stages as a product moves from raw materials through production to final distribution.

Virtual manufacturing: Subcontracting the manufacturing process to another firm.

Visible exports: *See* Merchandise exports.

Visible imports: *See* Merchandise imports.

Voluntary export restraint (VER): A negotiated limitation of exports between an importing and an exporting country.

Weak currency: A currency that is not fully convertible.

West African Economic Community: A regional economic group involving Benin, Burkina Faso, Côte d'Ivoire, Mali, Mauritania, Niger, and Senegal.

Western hemisphere: Literally the earth's area between the zero and 180th meridian, but usually indicates the continents of the Americas and adjacent islands, excluding Greenland.

WIPO: *See* World Intellectual Property Organization.

World Bank: A multilateral lending institution that provides investment capital to countries.

World Intellectual Property Organization (WIPO): A multilateral agreement to protect patents.

World Trade Organization (WTO): A voluntary organization through which groups of countries negotiate trading agreements and which has authority to oversee trade disputes among countries.

WTO: See World Trade Organization.

Zaibatsu: Large, family-owned Japanese businesses that existed before World War II and consisted of a series of financial and manufacturing companies usually held together by a large holding company.

Zero defects: The elimination of defects, which results in the reduction of manufacturing costs and an increase in consumer satisfaction.

Zero-sum game: A situation in which one party's gain equals another party's loss.

Photo Credits

Company Index and Trademarks

Name Index

Subject Index